The Handbook of Historical Economics

Edited by

Alberto Bisin

Giovanni Federico

ELSEVIER

ACADEMIC PRESS

An imprint of Elsevier

Academic Press is an imprint of Elsevier
125 London Wall, London EC2Y 5AS, United Kingdom
525 B Street, Suite 1650, San Diego, CA 92101, United States
50 Hampshire Street, 5th Floor, Cambridge, MA 02139, United States
The Boulevard, Langford Lane, Kidlington, Oxford OX5 1GB, United Kingdom

Notices

Knowledge and best practice in this field are constantly changing. As new research and experience broaden our
understanding, changes in research methods, professional practices, or medical treatment may become necessary.

Practitioners and researchers must always rely on their own experience and knowledge in evaluating and using any
information, methods, compounds, or experiments described herein. In using such information or methods they should be
mindful of their own safety and the safety of others, including parties for whom they have a professional responsibility.

To the fullest extent of the law, neither the Publisher nor the authors, contributors, or editors, assume any liability for any
injury and/or damage to persons or property as a matter of products liability, negligence or otherwise, or from any use or
operation of any methods, products, instructions, or ideas contained in the material herein.

Library of Congress Cataloging-in-Publication Data
A catalog record for this book is available from the Library of Congress

British Library Cataloguing-in-Publication Data
A catalogue record for this book is available from the British Library

ISBN: 978-0-12-815874-6

For information on all Academic Press publications
visit our website at https://www.elsevier.com/books-and-journals

Publisher: Brian Romer
Editorial Project Manager: Liz Heijkoop
Production Project Manager: Punithavathy Govindaradjane
Designer: Matthew Limbert

Typeset by VTeX

Contents

PART 3 TOPICS

List of contributors

Daron Acemoglu
Massachusetts Institute of Technology, Cambridge, MA, United States

Robert C. Allen
Faculty of Social Science, New York University Abu Dhabi, Abu Dhabi, United Arab Emirates

Quamrul H. Ashraf
Department of Economics, Williams College, Williamstown, MA, United States

Sascha O. Becker
Monash University, Melbourne, Victoria, Australia
University of Warwick, Coventry, United Kingdom
CAGE, Coventry, United Kingdom
CEPR, London, United Kingdom
CESifo, Munich, Germany
IZA, Bonn, Germany
ROA, Maastricht, Netherlands
ifo Institute, Munich, Germany

Alberto Bisin
Department of Economics, New York University, New York, NY, United States
NBER, Cambridge, MA, United States
CEPR, London, United Kingdom

Samuel Bowles
Sante Fe Institute, Santa Fe, NM, United States

Stephen Broadberry
Nuffield College, Oxford, United Kingdom

Davide Cantoni
Ludwig-Maximilians-Universität Munich, Munich, Germany
CEPR, London, United Kingdom
CESifo, Munich, Germany

Jung-Kyoo Choi
Kyungpook National University, Daegu, Republic of Korea

Martina Cioni
Department of Economics and Statistics, University of Siena, Siena, Italy

Gregory Clark

Department of Economics, University of California, Davis, CA, United States

Department of Economic History, LSE, London, United Kingdom

CEPR, London, United Kingdom

Georgy Egorov

Northwestern University–Kellogg School of Management, Evanston, IL, United States

NBER, Cambridge, MA, United States

Giovanni Federico

Division of Social Sciences, NYUAD, Abu Dhabi, United Arab Emirates

CEPR, London, United Kingdom

Ewout Frankema

Wageningen University, Wageningen, The Netherlands

Oded Galor

Department of Economics, Brown University, Providence, RI, United States

Paola Giuliano

UCLA, Los Angeles, CA, United States

NBER, Cambridge, MA, United States

CEPR, London, United Kingdom

IZA, Bonn, Germany

Jeremy Greenwood

University of Pennsylvania, Philadelphia, PA, United States

Nezih Guner

CEMFI, Madrid, Spain

George J. Hall

Brandeis University, Waltham, MA, United States

Gary D. Hansen

UCLA, Los Angeles, CA, United States

NBER, Cambridge, MA, United States

Sung-Ha Hwang

Korean Advanced Institute of Science and Technology (KAIST), Seoul, Republic of Korea

Marc Klemp

Department of Economics, University of Copenhagen, Copenhagen K, Denmark

Karen A. Kopecky

Federal Reserve Bank of Atlanta, Atlanta, GA, United States

David K. Levine
Department of Economics, RSCAS European University, San Domenico di Fiesole, Italy
Department of Economics, WUSTL, St. Louis, MO, United States

Sara Lowes
UC San Diego, La Jolla, CA, United States
NBER, Cambridge, MA, United States
Canadian Institute for Advanced Research (CIFAR), Toronto, ON, Canada

Matt Malis
Wilf Family Department of Politics, New York University, New York, NY, United States

Robert A. Margo
Boston University, Boston, MA, United States

Andrea Matranga
Chapman University, Orange, CA, United States

Salvatore Modica
Department of Economics, Business and Statistics (SEAS), Università di Palermo, Palermo, Italy

Joel Mokyr
Departments of Economics and History, Northwestern University, Evanston, IL, United States
Berglas School of Economics, Tel Aviv University, Tel Aviv, Israel

Eric Monnet
Paris School of Economics, Paris, France

Andrea Moro
Department of Economics, Vanderbilt University, Nashville, TN, United States

Suresh Naidu
Columbia University, New York, NY, United States
NBER, Cambridge, MA, United States

Nathan Nunn
Harvard University, Cambridge, MA, United States
Canadian Institute for Advanced Research (CIFAR), Toronto, ON, Canada

Lee E. Ohanian
UCLA, Los Angeles, CA, United States
NBER, Cambridge, MA, United States

Fatih Ozturk
UCLA, Los Angeles, CA, United States

Luigi Pascali
Pompeu Fabra University, Barcelona, Spain

Torsten Persson
IIES, Stockholm University, Stockholm, Sweden
CEPR, London, United Kingdom
CESIfo, Munich, Germany
LSE, London, United Kingdom
NBER, Cambridge, MA, United States

Pablo Querubin
Wilf Family Department of Politics, New York University, New York, NY, United States

Jared Rubin
Chapman University, Orange, CA, United States

Thomas J. Sargent
New York University, New York, NY, United States

Shanker Satyanath
Wilf Family Department of Politics, New York University, New York, NY, United States

Konstantin Sonin
University of Chicago, Chicago, IL, United States

David Stasavage
New York University, New York, NY, United States

Guido Tabellini
Department of Economics and IGIER, Università Bocconi, Milan, Italy
CEPR, London, United Kingdom
CESIfo, Munich, Germany

Felipe Valencia Caicedo
Vancouver School of Economics, University of British Columbia, Vancouver, BC, Canada
CEPR, London, United Kingdom
IZA, Bonn, Germany

Michelangelo Vasta
Department of Economics and Statistics, University of Siena, Siena, Italy
CEPR, London, United Kingdom

François R. Velde
Federal Reserve Bank of Chicago, Chicago, IL, United States

Thierry Verdier
Paris School of Economics, Paris, France
Ecole des Ponts-Paris Tech, Champs-sur-Marne, France
PUC-Rio, Rio de Janeiro, Brazil
CEPR, London, United Kingdom

Hans-Joachim Voth
University of Zurich, UBS International Center of Economics in Society, Zurich, Switzerland
CEPR, London, United Kingdom

Ludger Woessmann
University of Munich, Munich, Germany
ifo Institute, Munich, Germany
CESifo, Munich, Germany
IZA, Bonn, Germany
CAGE, Coventry, United Kingdom

Noam Yuchtman
LSE, London, United Kingdom
CEPR, London, United Kingdom
CESifo, Munich, Germany

Merger or acquisition? An introduction to *The Handbook of Historical Economics*

1 Historical Economics

Economists have always looked at history for insights. Adam Smith used historical evidence so extensively in the Wealth of Nations that "on top of being the founder of modern economic thinking, [he] could also be regarded as one of the first modern economic historians" [Manioudis and Milonakis (2020)]. However, the study of economic history became an established academic field only about a century later and for most of the 20th century it remained an historical discipline.

Historical Economics was born arguably in the 1960s, with the so-called Cliometric revolution; Margo (2021). We think of Cliometrics as an *acquisition* of economics by history in the sense that historians trained in economics started to use formal economic reasoning and statistical testing to tackle big issues, such as the efficiency of slavery (Conrad and Meyer, 1958; Fogel and Engerman, 1974); or the contribution of railways to American economic growth; Fogel (1964). In the following decades, Historical Economics spread quickly in the United States and more slowly in Europe; Cioni et al. (2021). Now, arguably, a second revolution is unfolding, as the field is attracting the renewed interest of economists, in turn *acquiring* history. It is generally difficult to identify the origins of a change of paradigm in a field, but in this case we should certainly cite the early contributions of Douglas North (North and Thomas (1973)) and Avner Greif (Greif, 1989, 1993) on institutions, as an inspirational trait d'union with the pathbreaking empirical approach in e.g., La Porta et al. (1998) and Acemoglu et al. (2001).[1]

The most evident novelty in Historical Economics at this turn, the sense in which we think of this as an *acquisition* of history by economics, lies in the radical shift in the research questions: the Cliometricians studied the economic past for the sake of its knowledge, while most recently Historical Economists often search in the past the answer to questions about current economic conditions. This general research agenda, which is referred to as *Persistence Studies*, has flourished recently, tackling on issues ranging from the effects of the colonial forced labor in Peru (Dell, 2010) to those of location of portage sites (transshipment between different means of transportation) on urban geography of the United States (Li et al., 2012). At the same time modern work in Historical economics is also characterized by resorting to state-of-the-art econometrics to identify causal relationships and by a more explicit relationship between empirical analysis and theoretical models. The essence of the new wave is well represented by the work of Daron Acemoglu, James Robinson, and co-authors on the role of institutions in economic growth. On the one hand, their pioneering study in the field, Acemoglu et al. (2001), aims at identifying the causal effects of a past historical event (the different types of colonial institutions) on a current outcome (GDP per capita in 1995). The Instrumental variable approach they

---

[1] Robert Townsend's book on general equilibrium modeling of the economy of an English manor (Townsend, 1993) can also be considered an early gem in Historical Economics, though it arguably had less of an impact in the development of the field.

adopt, and the clever choice of the instrument (settlers' mortality), have been wildly popular in later work in Historical economics.[2] On the other hand, their work on institutions has been supported by a conspicuous effort in developing theoretical models about institutional change - surveyed in (Acemoglu et al., 2021) - which also has spurred a lot of work in the discipline.

Finally, one other perhaps less prominent but nevertheless essential feature of important aspect of recent work in Historical Economics is the expansion of the boundaries of the discipline beyond economic themes as traditionally intended.[3] Historical Economists have dealt with political science issues such as the effect of compulsoring voting on political participation (Bechtel et al., 2016), the determinants of the rise to power of Nazi party in Germany (Adena et al., 2015; Satyanath et al., 2017; Voigtländer and Voth, 2014) and of the Fascist party in Italy (Acemoglu et al., 2020), or the effects of American bombings in Vietnam (Dell and Querubin, 2018).[4]

In the meanwhile, scholars have continued to pursue the more traditional post-Cliometric research agenda. First and foremost, they have greatly enhanced our knowledge of past economies but they have also gained new insights tackling "traditional questions" in history by exploiting suitable advances in economics, econometrics, and computing power. For instance, Becker and Woessmann (2009) have given a new interpretation to the Weber thesis about the positive consequences of the Reformation on economic growth of Prussia. He argued that the Protestant ethic fostered development, while Becker and Woessman show that the Reformation increased human capital because Protestants were asked to read the Bible by themselves instead of relying on the clergy's interpretation.[5]

In short, Historical Economics is a lively broad field of study with a glorious past and an exciting and challenging future. This Handbook tries to present the current frontier and to serve as a guide for future research on the field. We aim at offering a balanced view of the field, with its peculiarities, its scientific achievements, but also its shortcomings. In the end, the specific comparative advantages of history and economics which in our opinion the chapters distill and identify provide a forceful argument in favor of a *merger* between the disciplines along these lines.

The first three chapters (Part 1 of the Handbook) outline the evolution of the discipline as sketched out in this Introduction (Margo, 2021; Cioni et al., 2021; Nunn, 2021). Part 2 deals with Sources, Methods, and Models of Historical Economics. A few of the chapters collected here illustrate and discuss the data sources researchers are developing and using in the field, including e.g., the new uses of traditional sources, such as censuses and maps (Giuliano and Matranga, 2021), archeological (Matranga

---

[2] The turn of Historical Economics towards causal analysis is consistent with the recent empirical turn in economics and is largely prevalent in the recent work, even if formal dynamical models are used as well (Nunn, 2020).

[3] This is also consistent with a trend in economics - which is at times accused of an "imperialist attitude" towards social sciences in general.

[4] Some years ago, some of these Persistent Studies have been collected in a book evocatively titled *The long economic and political shadow of history*, Michalopoulos and Papaioannou (2017).

[5] Other interesting examples of new takes on traditional questions include: Alesina et al. (2013) who confirm Ester Boserup's thesis regarding the origins of gender role differences in different forms of agriculture practiced traditionally (specifically, shifting and plough cultivation); Juhász (2018) who finds strong evidence for the classic hypothesis that industry protection reduces technological adoption by studying the effects on the development of the French cotton industry of the differential effectiveness of Napoleon's continental blockade on the North and the South of France; Squicciarini and Voigtländer (2015) who document a strong relationship between economic growth and endowment of high end human capital in early 19th century France (measured with the subscriptions to the Encyclopedie), as predicted by traditional growth theory in economics (Barro et al., 1995; Acemoglu, 2012).

and Pascali, 2021) and anthropological data (Lowes, 2021). Other chapters in Part 2 focus on the use in Historical Economics of statistical and econometric methods for causal analysis developed in economics (Valencia Caicedo, 2021; Cantoni and Yuchtman, 2021; Voth, 2021; Bisin and Moro, 2021; Hansen et al., 2021; Monnet and Velde, 2021). These chapters highlight the variety of methods successfully exploited in the field, from causal inference (Regression discontinuity, Instrumental Variable analysis, Natural Historical Experiments, ...) to formal structural methods. Part 2 contains also a series of chapters on the theoretical analysis of institutional change. As we already noticed and will discuss later in this Introduction, institutions have been at the core of Historical Economics and much empirical work has been devoted to this issue. But the study of institutions in historical analysis is very complex - how are they defined, how they change, how they are measured - and it requires analytical frameworks of reference which theoretical work is attempting to provide. Five chapters in this section of the book (Acemoglu et al., 2021; Bowles et al., 2021; Levine and Modica, 2021; Persson and Tabellini, 2021; Bisin and Verdier, 2021) provide a careful and comprehensive survey of the different approaches and results. Part 3 of the Handbook contains a selection of results of Historical Economics. Of course it would have been impossible to cover all (or even most) results in the field. More modestly, the chapters in Part 3 aim at giving a flavor of the recent work in Historical Economics. It contains, in the tradition of the Handbook series, several surveys of some major field of research: the development of commodity markets (Federico, 2021), the economic history of Africa (Frankema, 2021), the economic history of religion (Becker et al., 2021), and the consequences of foreign intervention after WWII (Malis et al., 2021). It also includes four interpretative essays, which build on the authors' previous work (Ashraf et al., 2021; Broadberry, 2021; Clark, 2021; Mokyr, 2021) and a few case studies of new research work (Hall and Sargent, 2021; Stasavage, 2021; Greenwood et al., 2021). We have selected these latter not only for the historical relevance of the topics (respectively, the historical origins of the state, the funding of wars in United States history, the socio-economic effects of the diffusion of contraceptive technology); but also as examples of the range of methodologies used in Historical Economics - from the statistical and econometric analysis of historical series (Hall and Sargent, 2021) and spatial cross-sections (Stasavage, 2021) to the calibration of a dynamic structural model (Greenwood et al., 2021).

2 Sources, methods, models, topics

In this section we turn to a brief discussion of the chapters in the Handbook, to provide the reader with a more detailed roadmap of the various contributions it collects.

2.1 Part 1: The evolution of the discipline

Margo (2021) outlines the origins and the development of Historical Economics from an institutional point of view, stressing the consequences for the profession. The Cliometric revolution was a reaction to the decline in standing of economic history after the mathematization of economics. Cliometricians tried to stave off this decline by adopting the approach and the methods of economics. They wanted to maintain the 'economic history' as a subfield of economics, as labor or development economics, as such they taught it in most undergraduate and graduate programs in economics. Their success was only temporary, and in the 1980s and 1990s the decline resumed. Nowadays, economic history as such as has all but disappeared in (almost) all PhD programs in economics. In contrast, the recent wave of Historical Economics is spearheaded by economists who deal with economic history issues, but as we said, are not necessarily interested in historical knowledge.

Cioni et al. (2021) provide quantitative evidence with regards to this narrative. They trace the success of the Cliometric revolution and of the new wave of Historical economics by looking at the publication record in top field journals, measuring the status of economic history as the share of all articles in the major economics journals. In a companion paper (Cioni et al., 2019) these authors document the large differences between top economics and top field journals in terms of issues and patterns as well as of citation numbers. Above all, they show that there is limited overlapping between the new wave of Historical Economics and the more traditional (post-Cliometric) economic history, and not only in the research questions. Even if all Historical Economists share the same methodological approach, few of them publish in both top field and general interest economics journals.[6]

The chapter by Nathan Nunn (Nunn, 2021) foresees the innovation of Historical Economics as pushing for a novel interpretation of historical phenomena. He argues that history should be interpreted along with a theory of biological and cultural evolution. This theory is well-developed in terms of formal models and Nunn (2021) argues that it provides for sharp implications in terms of our understanding of human capital, innovation, gender roles, the consequences of warfare, the effects of market competition, and more. Most generally, the theory of biological and cultural evolution has great explanatory power with respect to the historical persistence of several socio-economic phenomena and hence it may be useful to address at its core the fundamental question of economic development, why is sustained economic growth often so elusive.

2.2 Part 2: Sources, methods, and models

The development and discovery of new data sources are a fundamental component of the contributions of Historical Economics. In recent years, scholars have collected and estimated a large number of new economic series, with a major effort to make them internationally comparable and easily available. On-line data-bases provide data on trade by country at constant and current prices since 1800 (Federico and Tena-Junguito, 2019) and on bilateral trade at current prices since the 1830s (Dedinger and Girard, 2017) Following the seminal work by Robert Allen (Allen, 2001) and (Allen, 2019), real wages are now routinely expressed in welfare ratios a simple and intuitive measure which can be compared across time and countries. Arguably, the most relevant contribution is the so called Maddison project, which continues the pioneering work by Angus Maddison (Bolt and Van Zanden, 2014; Fouquet and Broadberry, 2015; Broadberry, 2021) He started to collect series of national income since the 1980s (Maddison, 1991) and later converted them in 1990-PPP dollars (Maddison et al., 1995). Economic historians have since substantially increased the number of countries and have extended the series back in time to the Middle Ages. The work is going on, and new or revised series are added as soon as they available. In recent times Historical economists have widened the range of available data, as shown in the chapter by Giuliano and Matranga (2021). First, they show how modern technology has charged new versions of traditional sources, such as censuses and maps. Censuses have always been

---

[6] These differences will play a central role in our critical analysis of Historical Economics as a discipline, in Section 3, where we will explicitly make a distinction between "economic historians" and "economists" tout court.

used as sources of aggregate data but the use of records was limited by their sheer size.[7] The great increase in computing power has all but abolished this constraint, allowing researchers to link records from multiple U.S. censuses and trace the life pattern of individuals; see Abramitzky et al. (2019b,a). Similarly, geo-referencing has transformed maps from a visual static help into a source of information and variables for regression analysis. But Giuliano and Matranga (2021) show also the potential of 'new' qualitatively different sources, to address new research questions. Scientific research, for instance, offers a lot of new information on climate via tree rings and glaciers (Guiot et al., 2010) and on economic activity via lead deposits in glaciers (McConnell et al., 2018, 2019), even if publication in science journals might reduce their impact on the scholarly debate.

Matranga and Pascali (2021) provide a review of the data and the empirical methodologies developed to study the persistent effects of the very distant past on e.g., present-day living conditions and economic prosperity. Much of recent research in Historical Economics argues that these effects manifest themselves in local institutions and cultural traits which go back millennia. The scarcity of written records, as we move back in time, has pushed Historical Economists to study archaeological and paleoanthropological data. In this respect, Matranga and Pascali (2021) show e.g., how archeological data have been successfully used to shed light on Neolithic revolution, the origins of state, and long-distance trade.[8]

For a number of reasons, the geographic coverage of archeological research is patchy: there are very many sites in Europe and the Mediterranean, some in Asia, but few in the America and very few in Sub-Saharian Africa. Furthermore, even when available, the archeological sources cannot document a wide range of activities, institutions, and beliefs. Thus, scholars have widely resorted to ethnographic data, as Lowes (2021) shows and discusses in her chapter. The most notably source is Murdock's Ethnographic Atlas (Murdock (1967)), which collects information about primitive, historical, and contemporary societies, mostly from Africa and Northern America. More recently, Lowes (2021) reports, several economists working in Historical Economics have resorted to collect their own ethnographic data, following the practice and methods of anthropologists in the field; see e.g., De la Sierra et al. (2014), Lowes et al. (2017), and Lowes and Montero (2020).

Besides new sources, Historical Economics has brought new statistical and econometric methods to historical analysis, borrowing them from the causal inference literature in e.g., labor and development economics; see Angrist and Pischke (2008, 2014) and Cunningham (2021) for book treatments of this literature. The identification of causal relationships across history is central to Historical Economics, especially in the case of Persistence studies. The empirical focus of these studies centers, in the jargon of the causal inference literature, on the effects of a treatment variable taken-up in the historical past but whose effects persist in the present; e.g., high-quality norms or institutions. An exogenous historical factor may be available that directly affects the treatment variable and can be exploited as an instrument to identify causal effects. From the point of view of formal statistical and econometric theory and practice, these exogenous historical factors can be studied with the use distinct methodologies; notably, *Regression discontinuity* design, *Instrumental Variable* analysis, and *Natural Historical Experiments*.

---

[7] The pioneering Gallman-Parker sample, for instance, was widely used in the early work on slavery but referred to only 405 cotton-producing counties from the 1860 U.S. Census.

[8] Archeological sources are also widely used in the current revival of Roman economic history, after having long been crippled by the disappearance of archives during barbaric invasions (Erdkamp, 2016).

The chapter by Valencia Caicedo (2021) surveys the research in Historical Economics employing either a Regression discontinuity design or Instrumental Variables, distinguishing between the seminal articles published from 2001 to 2011 and those belonging to second wave of studies, from 2012 to today (2020), which have introduced various refinements of these causal identification strategies. The studies surveyed in this chapter are quite impressive in terms of their breadth, studying the effects of several historical phenomena like the development of independent city-states in Italy from the 12th century, the historical variation in land tenure patterns in colonial India, the redrawing of African national boundaries, the operation of the "Mita" forced labor system in colonial Peru and Bolivia, the invention and spread of the printing press, the role of media in support of democratic institutions, the bombing and counterinsurgency operations in Vietnam, the introduction of the steamship during the first wave of trade globalization.

Cantoni and Yuchtman (2021) survey instead the literature on Natural Historical Experiments.[9] Consistently with the reading of Historical Economics we have given in this Introduction, they provide a useful taxonomy distinguishing experiments *i) to understand history* - a traditional staple of economic historians, revised with the tools of modern econometrics; and experiments *ii) to understand economics* - where history supplies observations to test some economic theory to understand contemporary outcomes - i.e., Persistence Studies focusing on the effects of specific events in the past rather than on general economic characteristics.[10] The breadth of the analyses and results surveyed in this chapter is also impressive: from the effects of historical phenomena like the Neolithic Revolution, the Columbian Exchange, the Marshall Plan, colonialism, and slavery; to tests of the efficacy of infant industry protection, the existence of urban agglomeration effects, the incorporation of news in asset prices.

The chapters by Voth (2021) and Bisin and Moro (2021) take up the methodological challenge of extending the statistical and econometrics methods of causal inference to Historical Economics, and to Persistence Studies in particular. Voth (2021) makes two major points. The first is that persistence studies differ according to the similarity between the (current) outcomes and the (past) treatment. The causal inference is strong when the two measure the same feature ("apples and apples"), such as anti-semitism, which inspired Middle Ages pogroms in Germany and 20th century Holocaust. However, many studies ("apples and oranges"), relate different (past) treatments and (current) outcomes and thus their statistical results are more convincing if supported by modeling ("apples and oranges with theory"). Then Voth (2021) addresses the forceful critique of Persistence Studies recently put forth by Morgan Kelly (Kelly, 2019), arguing that it overstates the concerns about spatial correlation. Voth (2021) shows that most of the papers which Kelly (2019) quotes do control for spatial correlation by adding fixed geographical effects in at least one specification, without causing the results to become insignificant.

---

[9] See Diamond et al. (2010) for an interesting divulgative account of this method, containing various interesting examples. More generally, one can think of the current interest Natural Historical Experiments as an evolution of comparative history, whereby the exogeneity of the experiment is more formally addressed. An interesting example in this respect is the article by O'Rourke on the "Grain Invasion" of the European economy of the 1880s O'Rourke (1997). A sharp drop in transport costs caused the supply prices of American wheat all over Europe to collapse but European countries reacted differently. Some kept import free while others imposed heavy duties. O'Rourke estimates the impact of protection with a structural CGE model by comparing potential (under free trade) and actual (with protection) changes in functional distribution of income.

[10] See also Cantoni and Yuchtman (2020) for a complementary survey of this literature.

Bisin and Moro (2021) look at different methodological aspects of Persistence Studies. More specifically, they analyze the implications of allowing for heterogeneous treatment effects in Persistence Studies. More specifically, when treatment effects are heterogeneous, the research design identifies a Local Average Treatment Effect (LATE), rather than the Average (subject-level) Treatment Effect (ATE); see Angrist and Imbens (1995). Explicit models of the causal relationships to be studied in the context of the specific empirical analysis, help to clarify the interpretation of the identified causal effects and to put forward relevant new sets of questions, which can be addressed empirically, possibly with new data. In this respect Bisin and Moro (2021) propose minimal abstract models that help interpret results and guide the development of empirical strategies to uncover the mechanisms generating the effects, bridging causal inference studies and structural estimation methods in economics; along the lines, notably, of Heckman and Urzua (2010).

It would be easy to conclude from our discussion up to this point that structural estimation methods are still not as extensively used in Historical Economics as they are e.g., in several sub-fields of economics, from industrial organization (Reiss and Wolak, 2007) and labor economics (Keane, 2010); to political economy (Merlo, 2005). But the realm of applications of structural methods in Historical Economics is quite vast in the context of traditional dynamic macroeconomic questions. Early pathbreaking attempts, such as the books by Jeffrey Williamson on American economic growth and inequality in Britain (Williamson et al., 1974; Williamson, 1985) might have had relatively little following, methodologically. In more recent times, however, Historical economists have used structural estimation and calibration methods, exploiting interesting historical datasets. These works shed new light on important historical episodes by using diagnostic methods that help identify potential classes of models for evaluating important historical events and by quantifying the impact of different shocks on macroeconomic activity during historical periods. The chapter by Hansen et al. (2021) surveys these methods, with two important historical episodes as examples of their applicability: the Industrial Revolution and the U.S. economy from 1889-1929, forty crucial years which featured World War I, two major financial panics, the diffusion of electricity and the internal combustion engine and the 'Roaring Twenties", which immediately preceded the Great Depression.

The survey by Monnet and Velde (2021) on the applications of Historical Economics to the study of money, banking, and financial intermediation, points to the prevalence of structural models also in this sub-field structural models are prevalent. They construct a straw man of Historical Economics as dominated by causal inference, lacking structural methods, and argue that this is not - and should not be - the case in their field. The study of the effects of monetary policy, in particular, is mostly about identifying the data generating process over time, that is, typically a stochastic dynamic general equilibrium model, rather than identifying marginal effects of specific events.[11] Monnet and Velde (2021) notably highlights the evolution of the literature, especially on financial development and financial crises. Recent works display trend towards understanding the diversity of development models and financial systems and the microeconomic sources of aggregate fluctuations. Structural models appear particularly central in their review of the literature on the roots of high inflation in the 1970s.

Finally, the explanatory power of structural models is very promising in the study of the role of institutions on economic prosperity. As we already noticed, institutions have been at the core of Historical Economics; and much empirical work has been indeed devoted to the study of their effect on economic

---

[11] They grant Friedman and Schwartz (1963) with the early formulation of their methodological take on monetary history.

growth and prosperity, starting from the seminal papers by Acemoglu et al. (2001), Acemoglu et al. (2002). While this empirical work does not yet exploit structural models, a large theoretical literature has developed to address several fundamental questions which arise naturally in the empirical study of institutions in Historical Economics. Several chapters in this Handbook are devoted to surveying this theoretical literature.

Acemoglu et al. (2021) illustrate the issues involved in understanding institutional persistence and change by means of a simple conceptual game-theoretic framework which encompasses much of the authors' and others' theoretical work on the subject. This conceptual framework illustrates the strategic stability of institutions by identifying the forces behind "institutional stasis" and the potential drivers of institutional change. Importantly, the theoretical analysis exemplified in this chapter provides an important justification for much of the empirical work on the Historical Economics of institutions by providing the rationale for why current institutions are shaped by past institutional choices, thus exhibiting "path-dependent change" whereby initial conditions determine both the subsequent trajectories of institutions and how they respond to shocks.

In the class of "top-down" models studied by Acemoglu et al. (2021) institutional change is deliberately implemented by political elites either acting as a centralized authority or interacting with other competing political groups. In contrast Bowles et al. (2021) survey the "bottom-up" models, where changes in cultures and/or conventions are the result of the unintended and uncoordinated actions of a large numbers of actors with sparse information. This type of institutional change is akin to the transition from one equilibrium to another in an evolutionary equilibrium selection process. The dynamics in this class of models is illustrated by Bowles et al. (2021) with applications to a series of historic cases, including the emergence of private property and of the national bureaucratic state and the demise of serfdom. Most notably, they explore a key issue in world history, the Neolithic revolution – i.e., the transition from foraging to agriculture. This epoch-making change could be easily explained if agriculture were more productive and population was growing, as in the 'standard model' (Weisdorf, 2005; Brooke, 2014), or if climate change made it more productive (Dow et al., 2009; Matranga, 2017). Bowles et al. (2021) aim to explain the stability of foraging societies and, above all, transition if agriculture were not more productive than foraging. They argue that, under some well defined conditions, societies shifted to agriculture because it offered better defined property rights and thus reduced internal conflicts.

Levine and Modica (2021) also study models of institutional dynamics or, more generally, of social organizations. They however concentrate their analysis on the long run changes brought about by one specific, but historically very important, mechanism: external competition and conflict. Indeed, historically, institutional success has occurred in the aftermath of invasion, warfare, and other form of conflict. The chapter by Levine and Modica (2021) then provides an analysis of models of conflict driven evolutionary theory, centered on their dynamic and stochastic properties, used to motivate the analysis of a broad range of historical phenomena. Evolutionary models are useful to select which of many feasible institutions and arrangements are persistent and hence observed in the long-run. They show, for instance that the simplest configuration resulting from conflict is a hegemony of the winner, with a single society ruling over an isolated geographical area. This is because of a form of complementarity of success in conflict: conquering a city or a province strengthens the winner and weakens the loser. They then argue that i) hegemonies have in fact been more common and persistent in the last two millennia than one would expect; ii) where and when they have not been prevalent (e.g., in Europe and India), outsider societies have played a decisive role. Furthermore, the models studied by Levine and Modica (2021) have explanatory power to distinguish conditions under which, in the absence of hegemony, competing societies are extractive or rather inclusive.

While several earlier empirical studies in Historical Economics appeared to run races between the explanatory power of institutions and culture (as well as history, geography, and other factors) for economic growth and prosperity, it is now more common to stress the importance of the interaction between institutions and culture to this effect. Both Persson and Tabellini (2021) and Bisin and Verdier (2021) take this view in their chapters. They define culture as individual values and preferences and model its dynamics in a society as the outcome of evolutionary selection mechanism, along the lines of the models of the models surveyed by Bowles et al. (2021). Both chapters also consider institutional change as the result of the interactions between elites and other political groups, along the lines of the models surveyed instead by Acemoglu et al. (2021). Persson and Tabellini (2021) construct their survey gradually building layers of complex interactions on one specific simple model of political agency. It highlights the joint effects of culture and institutions on policy outcomes by studying the mechanisms politicians adopt to extract rents from the political process at the voters expense. More specifically, in this context, institutions are represented by formalized rules of the socio-economic interaction between political groups, such as the rules for political and judicial procedures.

Bisin and Verdier (2021) take instead a more abstract approach to the study of the interaction of culture and institutions, showing how the combination of models of institutional dynamics with models of cultural dynamics can generally be projected into a useful representation of these interactions, as a system of differential/difference equations represented by a phase diagram. They focus on some general properties of these systems which matter for the comparative dynamics of culture and institutions and for the response of the system to exogenous shocks, e.g., natural historical experiments. Indeed, Bisin and Verdier (2021) show how these general properties depend in a fundamental way on whether culture and institutions are complementary or substitutes in the dynamical system. The chapter also illustrates these methods and concepts by means of a simple analytical example from Bisin and Verdier (2017), studied and solved in some detail. It singles out conditions under which the cultural and institutional dynamics, between groups with different propensities to act violently in a conflictual society, favor or hinder the development of a legal system for the protection of property rights.

2.3 Part 3: Topics

There are dozens of interesting and exciting topics in Historical Economics worthy of a survey in the Handbook. In an attempt to avoid expanding the size of the Handbook well above the reasonable, we have selected just a few which we deem representative of the different strains of the field and of their distinctive methods. Furthermore, we have selected topics which have not been recently surveyed in other published material - to which we explicitly refer here instead[12]: Meissner (2014) on globalization and growth, Deng (2014) on China, Johnson and Koyama (2017) on state capacity, Abramitzky and Boustan (2017) on immigration in United States, and Crafts and Woltjer (2020) on productivity growth.

The chapter on development of markets (Federico, 2021) bridges two literatures: the well-established one on trade and trade policies and the fast growing one on market integration. So far

---

[12] The massive Handbook of Cliometrics (Haupert and Diebolt (2019)) surveys almost all major subjects in economic history (and also some minor ones), but it pays comparatively little attention to Persistence Studies and to non economic issues in the Historical Economics literature.

they have remained separate and indeed they are the subject of two separate chapters in the Handbook of Cliometrics (Lampe and Sharp, 2015; Federico, 2019). In the chapter for this Handbook, Federico (2021) argues that these two literatures deal with the same process with different measures, depending on available sources, respectively quantities, or prices. He also argues that these literatures share strengths and weaknesses. For instance, we know a lot about trends (for trade, only since about 1800) and we have identified the causes of important changes in the process of development of markets, e.g., technological progress in transportation and political decisions about trade, but we have made few inroads about the effects of these changes. Conventional wisdom argues that development of markets and specialization have been a major source of (Smithian) growth but scholars are still struggling to find a way to measure their dynamic benefits.

After many decades of neglect by economic historians, Africa has become a hot issue in Historical Economics. Several Persistence Studies deal with the long term effects of historical events such as the slave trade (Nunn and Wantchekon (2011)) and the diffusion of missions (Nunn (2014)). Other study the effects of culture and institutions on socio-economic development, e.g., in the Kuba Kingdom (Lowes et al. (2017)). The survey by Michalopoulos and Papaioannou (2020) and the chapter by Fourie et al. (2019) in the Handbook of Cliometics, deal extensively with this literature. The chapter by Frankema (2021) brings a different perspective. He questions the African exceptionalism which ultimately motivates much of Persistence Studies. The recent economic history literature has shown that Sub-Saharan Africa was not uniformly poor and stagnant and has stressed the agency role of local population as opposed to the Eurocentric view of earlier works.

Becker et al. (2021) show how much Judaism, Christianity, and Islam have shaped the economic and social life of Europe and the Middle East. The study of the socio-economic effects of religion is a booming field in Historical Economics, with a strong empirical turn, but the literature is "eclectic" and "fractionalized" (Becker et al. (2021)). Becker et al. (2021) in their survey stress the multiple interactions between religion and politics at the roots of differences in economic performance among religions and consequently among regions. The list of potential channels of transmission in this respect is quite varied: prosperity of Jews, Jewish persecutions, Protestant-Catholic differences, Muslim-Christian differences, human capital development, cultural attitudes, doctrinal differences, legal development, and financial development. In this respect, various recent contributions in Historical Economics pertain to the study of the causes of the "Long Divergence" between Middle Eastern and Western European economies from about the year 1000CE. In this respect, e.g., Kuran (2012) stresses the inability of the Muslim world to create or adopt those fundamental commercial and financial institutions which were responsible for significant socio-economic growth in the West, such as banking, the corporation (and corporate law), and institutions supporting impersonal exchange; Rubin (2017) centers on the use of Islamic religion by Middle Eastern rulers to consolidate their power stifling innovation (most notably the printing press) and economic growth.[13]

Last but not least, the chapter by Malis et al. (2021) is an example of the interdisciplinary bent of much of recent Historical Economics. As the authors note, interventions have been studied in "comparative politics, international relations, development economics, and political economy" - but historical economics offers something additional. They focus on a clear research question (was foreign intervention a failure) and conclude that, although failures were very frequent, they were not the

---

[13] See also, Blaydes and Chaney (2013) and Bisin et al. (2019, 2020).

pre-determined outcome of interventions. The more pessimistic conventional wisdom depends to some extent on methodological flaws of some quantitative studies.

A series of other chapters we have selected to be added to this part of the Handbook offer topical reinterpretations of key topics in Historical Economics.

The research agenda of outlined in Ashraf et al. (2021) is a novel (some would say provocative) and controversial version of Persistence Studies. They argue that economic performance has been ultimately determined, in substantial part, by genetic heritage. They substantiate this claim by studying two historical drivers of genetic evolution. First of all, they show that migration of early humans out of Africa determined the amount of genetic diversity of different ethnic groups and hence of the different regions these ethnicities established themselves in. They then identify a causal relationship between genetic diversity and economic performance in the present. They argue that an intermediate level of diversity maximizes the chances of economic growth: too much diversity reduced trust, too little impacts negatively on the potential for innovation. The second driver of evolution studied by Ashraf et al. (2021) is the Neolithic revolution. After the birth of agriculture, natural selection favored individuals with pro-growth genetic characteristics who were more likely to survive and have many offsprings. They argue that this selection mechanism has favored various traits - e.g., a predisposition towards child quality, time preference, loss aversion, and entrepreneurial spirit, which in turn contributed to differential paths of technological progress, human-capital formation, and economic development across societies.

The chapter by Gregory Clark (2021) is also an analysis of pro-growth behavior in societal development. Even though Clark refrains from a strictly genetic interpretation of behavior, a key component of his interpretation of the escape from Malthusian structures of pre-industrial society stands on the effects of differential fertility (Clark, 2007). The focus of his chapter Clark (2021) is on social mobility and, in this respect, the higher fertility of the rich has contrasting effects: it is good for the economy at large, because it increases the proportion of pro-growth individuals in the population; but it is not necessarily good for the offspring of the rich, as it made difficult for all of them to keep the high status of their forebears - i.e., it caused downward social mobility for the former elites. To better understand this process Clark (2021) measures social mobility with the diffusion of rare (elite) surnames. He finds that this diffusion has been much slower than commonly assumed and has not accelerated after the Industrial revolution (Clark, 2014). But, as shown in this chapter, the process did work in the very long run: 'surnames of Norman origin, for example, had high status in England still in 1200-1400, but now are just slightly above average social status'.

The Industrial Revolution constitutes the second major watershed in world history, after the Neolithic revolution, and hence it represents one of the most intensely studied and interesting topics in economic history; see Crafts (2021) for a recent survey. The Handbook offers three different views of its origins.

Broadberry (2021), building on his earlier estimate of English GDP in the very long term Broadberry et al. (2015), highlights two peculiarities of England. It did not experience, unlike the rest of Europe (except Holland), a fall in GDP per capita when population recovered from the Black Death and the onset of the Industrial Revolution in the late 18th century was preceded by at least a century of slow growth in GDP per capita and of structural change, with a massive shift of occupation towards manufacturing and services: industrialization before the industrial revolution. Mokyr (2021) looks for the intellectual roots of the revolution in the early diffusion of the scientific method in Europe, which resulted in the subjection of all conventional wisdom to empirical testing. He argues that this intellectual approach was not just the prerogative of a small number of scientists, but it extended to practical inventors ("tweakers"). These latter were able to implement their ideas thanks to a large number of skilled artisans, trained in a quite efficient apprenticeship system.

The Industrial Revolution (1770-1867) is the key watershed of the narrative in Allen (2021), relating changes in technology, wages, and the functional income distribution in the very long run. Allen (2021) argues that the high pre-industrial wages (relative to the cost of coal) stimulated labor-saving and energy-intensive technological change, which increased profits while wages stagnated. Then the tide turned, and for about a century capital-intensive technological progress in manufacturing raised wages for all workers. In the latest half a century, the rise of low-productivity low-wage services shifted again the distribution against workers, with exception at the very top of skill distribution. We have selected the three final research chapters to highlight the wide range of issues and methodologies of research in Historical Economics.

Hall and Sargent (2021) explore the sources of government financing for eight American wars and two insurrections, between 1812 and 1975, by the decomposing the changes in debt/GDP ratio between tax, debt (i.e., future taxation), and money creation (i.e., ultimately a reduction in the ex-post real returns to debt). They look at the data very closely through the eyes of two classic formal models of optimal government financing of (more or less permanent) surges of government expenditures. The two models (Barro, 1979; Lucas and Stokey, 1983) differ in terms of the set of financing instruments the government is assumed to have access to and have different implications regarding the composition of tax collection, adjustment of ex-post returns to government creditors and quantities of government debt, which are optimal after a fiscal shock: Barro (1979) requires an increase in both tax and debt (in fractions which depend on how permanent is the fiscal shock) but constant ex-post real returns; while in Lucas and Stokey (1983) all the adjustment operates through ex-post returns to government creditors. By and large, the U.S. adopted an optimal tax smoothing policy (increase debt during wars and pay it later with taxation) and without affecting the returns to bondholders, in line with Barro (1979). But the U.S. has also seen negative wartime bond returns followed by positive postwar returns in the War of 1812, the Civil War, World War I, and the Korean War as prescribed by Lucas and Stokey (1983). In conclusion Hall and Sargent (2021) give us a positive view of the explanatory power of even stylized formal economic models as narratives for how "policy makers over two centuries confront [...] their predicaments by combining their recollections of histories with their theories, [... how they...] struggle over and over again with the same economic and political forces."

The chapter by Stasavage (2021) on the origins of state is a typical example of the empirical turn in Historical Economics. The origin of the state is one of the oldest topics in history, but historians have not gone much beyond narratives with some plausible generalizations, such as states developed where agricultural surplus was greater. Stasavage (2021) instead contrasts a well-defined hypothesis of the origin of the state, the prevalence of storable cereals as main food staple which gives rise to the fundamental economic potential to support the economy of the state (Mayshar et al., 2019), with the invention, adoption, and diffusion of writing, as a technology central to governance ability.[14] He finds that both hypotheses have explanatory power as factors for the origin of state, increasing roughly by the same amount (10-15%) the likelihood of having a state. The main conclusion is that economic potential and governance ability have been complementary factors in the formation and development of states, from the earliest to modern nation-states.

---

[14] Writing is believed to have originated independently in Ancient Sumeria, among the Olmecs in Mesoamerica, and in China under the Shang dynasty.

Last but not least Greenwood et al. (2021) is a great example of the power of formal economic models in tracing the dynamics of the effects of technological changes on various socio-economic aspects of human life. The ramifications of the effects of large technological shocks are generally far from confined to strict realm of economics.[15] These complicated chains of effects call for "quantitative-theoretical history," that is, the use of structural models allowing for an analysis of both the qualitative and the quantitative effects of technological shocks.[16] The chapter by Greenwood et al. (2021) illustrates this line of research exploring specifically the effects of the transformation in contraceptive technologies and their take up from 1900 to 2000. This transformation has led to a sexual revolution, which witnessed a rise in premarital sex and out-of-wedlock births, and a decline in marriage. These demographic phenomena in turn have had important effects on many aspects of social and economic interactions, e.g., in labor markets. The calibrated model fits well various empirical moments, including e.g., the decline of proportion of married people, the increase in out-of-wedlock births, and the rise in the share of sexually active single females.

3 The challenges of Historical Economics

In the previous discussion we aimed to show how methodologically rigorous and innovative the field of Historical Economics is and how interesting and promising its results are. However there are sizeable differences in topics and attitude to research between "economic historians" in the Cliometric tradition and the new wave of "historical economists" (or "economists" tout court) engaging in economic history (especially in Persistence Studies). In this section we better delineate these differences so that we can suggest strategies to merge them.

Economic historians tend to be inward looking: even when they take up important questions and issues, they tend to deal with them as part of the ongoing discourse within the discipline which seldom resonates outside it. A good example is the debate on Allen's view of England as a 'high wage economy', which is the cornersone of his interpretation of the causes of the industrial revolution Allen (2021). The hypothesis has triggered a lively debate among economic historians about the level of wages (Humphries, 2013; Allen, 2015), which has attracted very little interests among economists, in spite of its implications for a major issue in economic history. Economists on the other hand tend to favor big questions with clear present-day relevance. Some of their work spans literally thousands of years (Ashraf and Galor, 2013) and puts forward broad generalizations. As a consequence, they expose themselves to the criticisms to neglect the historical context while designing natural experiments (Dippel and Leonard, forthcoming) and to "compress history" (Austin, 2008), viewing it as just a repository of events and/or as a source of instruments.

---

[15] The Second Industrial Revolution (which brought electricity, the petrochemical industry, and the internal combustion engine) at the beginning of the twentieth century, for instance, arguably encouraged the rise of cities and suburbs and allowed women to enter the labor force, providing a catalyst for women's rights. A similar narrative applies regarding the advent of the Information age; see Greenwood (1997).

[16] Greenwood et al. (2021) refer to an extensive literature in "quantitative-theoretical history;" it suffices to cite Greenwood et al. (2005) on secular decline in fertility; Hansen and Prescott (2002) on the transition from the pre-industrial to the industrial era, from land-intensive to capital-intensive production technologies; Kopecky and Suen (2010) on the impact of the automobile on suburbanization between 1910 and 1970; and the literature surveyed by Hansen et al. (2021) in this Handbook.

The sociology of history and economics as academic disciplines has amplified this cleavage between economic historians and historical economists, giving rise to what we have interpreted as attempts at the methodological *acquisition* of one discipline by the other. This cleavage played out most evidently in defining the study of institutions (Acemoglu et al., 2005b; Ogilvie and Carus, 2014). Institutions have been a main concern of economic historians since its beginning in the 19th century, with two widely different approaches. Some scholars described, with as many details as possible given the sources, the rules, and the evolution of specific institutions, guilds, merchant companies etc. Others, more often than not inspired by Marxism, put forward broad generalizations about economics and politics. The early Cliometricians disliked both approaches, respectively as antiquarian and not scientific, and retreated towards strictly economic issues. Douglass North, himself a prominent member of the Cliometrician group, brought institutions back to the limelight, with two books (North and Thomas, 1973; North, 1981). His call for action was only slowly heeded by economic historians. They were reluctant to use quantitative methods for the study of institutions, arguably because they felt it very difficult to translate broad generalizations (e.g., extractive/inclusive, particularized/generalized institutions) and models of institutional change in terms of source-compatible research questions. Indeed, many original documents on institutions have been lost and anyway written sources are unlikely to shed light on key features (tacit knowledge, network effects, cultural influences etc.). Economic historians thus preferred a softer rhetoric, based on general statements supported by selected examples. If pressed to generalize, they painted broad historical canvases. Economists, on the contrary, often deemed the price in terms of historical accuracy worth paying if the evidence is consistent with theoretical generalizations. A good example is the analysis of origin of the economic decline of the Venetian Republic (the Serenissima), which Acemoglu and Robinson (2012) see in its turn into a oligarchic institutional system from the Serrata del Gran Consiglio (1297). While consistent with theory of the role of the extractive/inclusive institutions dichotomy to explain economic growth Acemoglu et al. (2001, 2005b), this narrative is in contrast with the evidence that the institutions of the Serenissima lead its transition from a commercial to an industrial power in the Seventeen century (Rapp, 1976).[17] Another significant example of the difference is the debate on guilds, a quintessential economic institution of pre-industrial European cities. Guilds were formal associations of merchants or craftsmen which enjoyed monopoly of a specific activity (wholesale trade or production of goods and services for consumers). Conventional wisdom since the Enlightenment and Adam Smith was that their monopoly was economically harmful. Avner Greif (Greif, 1989, 1993) disagreed and argued that merchant guilds performed some useful tasks and buttressed this claim with the analysis of business practices of the (Jewish) Maghribi traders in medieval Cairo and Genoese merchants. He argues that the Maghribi traders were a closely-knit group who enforced contracts via reputational effects, contrasting them with Genoese traders, who settled business controversies in courts. Ogilvie contested Greif's general views on merchant guilds in a book (Ogilvie, 2011) and his reconstruction of the business practices of the Maghribi traders in an article (Edwards and Ogilvie, 2012); Greif refuted the criticism and presents additional pieces of evidence supporting his analysis (Greif, 2012). Ogilvie and Greif use the same set of business letters, but

---

[17] The origin of the decline of Venice can then be identified with the plague of 1630, which hit Northern Italy with special strength (Alfani, 2013; Alfani and Murphy, 2017). Another competing narrative has the discovery of the Americas as a fundamental cause of the decline of the economic power of Venice (Borlandi, 1964; Braudel, 1972; O'Rourke and Williamson, 2009).

Greif looks at the general pattern in the documents, guided by his theoretical structure, while Edwards and Ogilvie focus on the details of interpretation of some of them.

Without taking a stand, we would like to highlight how this debate points to a silver lining in the cleavage between different approaches we have identified. Indeed there are a promising signs of methodological convergence - a path to a fruitful methodological *merger* of disciplines. For instance, while in her earlier book Ogilvie relies, in the traditional approach to institutions taken by economic historians, on generalizations supported by anecdotal evidence, in her more recent book on artisanal corporations (Ogilvie, 2019), she has made an admirably massive effort to collect qualitative and quantitative information on the rules and activities of these institutions, a total of over 17,000 pieces. She is thus able to construct systematic tables of statistics, which may fall short of the requirements for econometrics analysis but are much more convincing for an economist than a single example.[18] More generally, beyond this instance, the economists' demand for quantification of institutions (and not only of institutions) is pushing economic historians out of their comfort zone, with very promising results. For instance, they have succeeded to measure the influence of Parliaments in Medieval and early modern Europe. They were assemblies of representatives of the elites, which had some power to authorize the ruler(s) to impose new taxes, and thus could act as a constraint to the executive.[19] Van Zanden et al. (2012) measure the Parliaments' power with the number of years of their meeting per century and find a positive relation with economic growth, as measured by city growth. Their proxy shows that power of parliaments grew all over Europe until the 16th century, while afterwards it continued to rise in North-Western Europe and declined sharply elsewhere (the French Etats Generaux were not convened from 1688 to 1789). Henriques et al. (2019) use a more precise measure of parliamentary activity, as well as information on fiscal conditions of the state, to compare England with Spain and Portugal. They find, in contrast with Acemoglu et al. (2005a), that English institutions were not better than Spanish and Portuguese ones until the late 17th century. The case of the Polish parliament (Seijm) shows that too much constraint to the executive may be counterproductive as well (Malinowski, 2019): since 1652, each member had a veto power and this progressively paralyzed the legislative activity of the parliament. The uncertainty in property rights reduced the integration of domestic market, with negative consequences for the economy. The Polish-Lithuanian commonwealth became politically and militarily weaker and weaker in the 17th and 18th centuries and was ultimately carved between Russian, Prussian, and Habsburg empires.

Economists, on their part, have been very creative and innovative in the use of interesting variables as instruments (formally and metaforically) for their analysis of the effects institutional change. In this respect, the real game changer has been the publication of Acemoglu et al. (2001) who came from different traditions. They were not surely the first to argue that colonial institutions had an important effect on economic growth, especially in Africa, nor they buttressed this claim with any structural modeling. The real novelty was the use of econometrics to test their claim - and especially of an Instrumental Variable approach to tackle the issue of endogeneity. The Instrumental Variable they used is 'settlers' mortality,' a measure of the pattern of settlement of Western colonists which determined

---

[18] Nonetheless, this does open issue of representativeness: Paris had 100 guilds in 1261-71 and 133 in 1766; if all information referred to Paris guilds only, which is clearly not the case, it would amount to one piece every four years.

[19] Notably, North and Weingast (1989) argued that the conditions imposed by the English Commons to the new king William III in 1688 marked a watershed in protection of property rights and the credibility of state commitments and that this institutional change fostered the development of financial system and of the military power of the kingdom.

the quality of colonial institutions. In their interpretation, higher settlers' mortality encodes for low-quality (extractive) institutions. This combination of wide ranging plausible hypothesis and empirical testing with panel regression has become the standard in the recent work by historical economists on institutional change, with the introduction of an innovative and interesting series of instruments, including: genetic diversity for social conflict and trust in Ashraf and Galor (2013), pogroms for anti-semitism in Voigtländer and Voth (2012), plow-suitability of the terrain for gender roles in Alesina et al. (2013), and the list could continue a long way. Not all the instruments and data used by economists would pass a stringent test for historical accuracy, but this work should constitute at least valuable food for thought for more traditional economic historians (Dippel and Leonard, forthcoming).

The issue of quantity and quality of data emerges from this sketch as the key challenge for historical economists. Without data, you cannot address a lot of highly significant questions for the interpretation of the past and of its effect on the present and thus all historical economists agree that some compromise about their quality is necessary. However, economic historians tend to be more knowledgeable about the limitation of specific data. The most egregious example is the Atlas of World Population History (Jones, 1978), which is still widely and often a-critically used in Historical economics. It reports crude estimates, with almost no support reference, at long term intervals. By the time of publication it was a bold venture: we still have very limited and crude data on population before the 19th century for advanced countries and before the second half of the 20th for most of the others. However, at least for some countries, we have more fine-grained and reliable data. For instance, Broadberry et al. (2015) estimate a yearly series of the British population from 1270 onwards, based on twelve benchmark estimates between 1250 and 1522 and on the monumental work by Wrigley et al. (1981) from 1541.

Economic historians would call for some caution in using two other standard sources, the Ethnographic Atlas (Murdock, 1967) and the data-base for Global Agro-economic zones, built by FAO and IIASA (Fischer et al., 2012). As said, the data from Ethnographic Atlas have been essential for many recent works on Africa. Lowes (2021) reports the positive and reassuring results of some attempts to validate its information (most notably on the mapping of ethnic groups) with independent sources. However, this work leaves out other reasons for caution, most notably the lack of knowledge about who was collecting the information (Western travelers vs. professional anthropologists), for which purposes (scholarly endeavors versus tax collection) and how common were substantial forms of misunderstanding or outright misleading on the part of surveyed populations. Just to take an extreme example, would a village head disclose to a British colonial administrator their slave holding, knowing that slavery was strongly disapproved or even forbidden? The GAEZ maps the suitability of world soils to different crops at very high geographical detail and thus is widely used as totally exogenous instrument in historical analysis (Alesina et al., 2013; Galor and Özak, 2014; Nunn and Qian, 2014). It is a really impressive work. It relies on data on temperature, amount of water, quality of soil, slopes, and so on to estimate the suitability under five systems of water provision, rain-fed, rain-fed with conservation and three different irrigation systems. The low-input is meant to refer to traditional technology, without fertilizers or machinery and thus it is used in Historical Economics. As Giuliano and Matranga (2021) correctly point out, the present-day low input technology may not be representative of past one: the historical varieties of seeds could be less (more) suitable to a given environment. One might add that millennia of cultivation and specific investments might have altered some features of the soil and the present-day climate might not be representative of the past one. During the Younger Dryas (about 12900 to 11700 before present), climate was decidedly cooler than nowadays (Bowles and Choi, 2019) and thus GAEZ is bound to overstate the suitability of land during the Neolithic transition.

The issue of reliability of data extends to proxies, which are widely used in all Historical Economics literature. In his chapter Federico (2021) discusses at length the potential bias from using distance as proxy for transport costs and the ratio of custom revenues to imports as proxy for protection in gravity model of trade. The former assumes constant transport cost, while the latter tends to understate protection. Taken jointly, they give relatively more weight to technology than to policy decisions in determining barriers to trade. Another example is the use of urbanization rates as proxy for GDP in pre-industrial societies, as popularized by Acemoglu et al. (2005a). The relation was indeed positive until 1910, but it seems rather unstable in its strength between the Sixteen and the Nineteen centuries (Jedwab and Vollrath, 2015).[20]

In general, assessing the reliability of any specific set of data and keeping abreast of the fast progress in historical research is difficult. In a seminal and unfortunately overlooked paper, Feinstein and Thomas (2002) argued that producers of historical series should attach to their figures an explicit assessment of margin of errors. Following this advice, Federico and Tena-Junguito (2019) estimate the overall margin of error of their series of world trade as sum of the (independent) variance of individual country-series. Also, Broadberry (2021) gives some examples for estimates of GDP per capita from the Maddison project, with margin of errors ranging from the almost negligible (Netherlands 1650-1750) to the humongous (Japan 750-1150). In our opinion any systematic effort along these lines, requiring the joint work of economic historians and historical economists, would be extremely valuable for the discipline.

4 Conclusions

Historical Economics is a very promising and important field. As all interdisciplinary endeavors, it differs from its parent-fields. It differs from economic history for the breadth of research questions, which include political and social issues, and above all for its statistical methods, which rely heavily on causal inference and at times on structural modeling. Historical Economics differs also from economics in that the availability of data is a serious constraint. Economists have showed remarkable ingenuity in overcoming the constraint, but they could be more aware of the fundamental trade-off: dealing with 'large' issues with weak (to say the least) data vs limiting oneself to 'small' issues with accurate and reliable data.

The obvious winning strategy is a *merger* of disciplines, putting together economists, political scientists, and economic historians (as well as, in specific instances, anthropologists, sociologists, evolutionary biologists). Good Historical Economics needs a combination of the knowledge of sources and detailed historical events and phenomena, the capability of distilling complex historical processes into a model to put forward alternative testable hypotheses, the statistical/econometric skills for identification, causal inference, structural estimation, and testing, the detailed knowledge of specific political and socio-economic institutions, an understanding of the role of cultural traits, e.g., ethnic/religious, and of their evolution.

---

[20] The relationship has become negative after World War Two, with cities growing relatively more in poorer countries, but this has no relevance for the use of the proxy, for pre-industrial times.

This book is a step in this direction, and this Introduction written jointly by an economist and an historian, discussing the pitfalls of their own disciplines, should serve as a suggestion that the *merger* can be done, leaving aside *acquisition* attempts.

References

Abramitzky, R., Boustan, L., 2017. Immigration in American economic history. Journal of Economic Literature 55 (4), 1311–1345.

Abramitzky, R., Boustan, L.P., Eriksson, K., Feigenbaum, J.J., Pérez, S., 2019a. Automated linking of historical data. National Bureau of Economic Research.

Abramitzky, R., Boustan, L.P., Jácome, E., Pérez, S., 2019b. Intergenerational Mobility of Immigrants in the US over Two Centuries. Technical report. National Bureau of Economic Research.

Acemoglu, D., 2012. Introduction to economic growth. Journal of Economic Theory 147 (2), 545–550.

Acemoglu, D., De Feo, G., De Luca, G.D., 2020. Weak states: causes and consequences of the Sicilian Mafia. The Review of Economic Studies 87 (2), 537–581.

Acemoglu, D., Egorov, G., Sonin, K., 2021. Institutional change and institutional persistence. In: Bisin, A., Federico, G. (Eds.), The Handbook of Historical Economics. Elsevier. Chapter 13 (in this book).

Acemoglu, D., Johnson, S., Robinson, J.A., 2001. The colonial origins of comparative development: an empirical investigation. The American Economic Review 91 (5), 1369–1401.

Acemoglu, D., Johnson, S., Robinson, J.A., 2002. Reversal of fortune: geography and institutions in the making of the modern world income distribution. The Quarterly Journal of Economics 117 (4), 1231–1294.

Acemoglu, D., Johnson, S., Robinson, J., 2005a. The rise of Europe: Atlantic trade, institutional change, and economic growth. The American Economic Review 95 (3), 546–579.

Acemoglu, D., Johnson, S., Robinson, J.A., 2005b. Institutions as a fundamental cause of long-run growth. In: Handbook of Economic Growth, vol. 1, pp. 385–472.

Acemoglu, D., Robinson, J.A., 2012. Why Nations Fail: The Origins of Power, Prosperity, and Poverty. Currency.

Adena, M., Enikolopov, R., Petrova, M., Santarosa, V., Zhuravskaya, E., 2015. Radio and the rise of the Nazis in prewar Germany. The Quarterly Journal of Economics 130 (4), 1885–1939.

Alesina, A., Giuliano, P., Nunn, N., 2013. On the origins of gender roles: women and the plough. The Quarterly Journal of Economics 128 (2), 469–530.

Alfani, G., 2013. Plague in seventeenth-century Europe and the decline of Italy: an epidemiological hypothesis. European Review of Economic History 17 (4), 408–430.

Alfani, G., Murphy, T.E., 2017. Plague and lethal epidemics in the pre-industrial world. The Journal of Economic History 77 (1), 314–343.

Allen, R.C., 2001. The great divergence in European wages and prices from the Middle Ages to the First World War. Explorations in Economic History 38 (4), 411–447.

Allen, R.C., 2015. The high wage economy and the industrial revolution: a restatement. The Economic History Review 68 (1), 1–22.

Allen, R.C., 2019. Poverty and the labor market: today and yesterday. Annual Review of Economics 12.

Allen, R.C., 2021. The interplay among wages, technology, and globalization: the labor market and inequality, 1620-2020. In: Bisin, A., Federico, G. (Eds.), The Handbook of Historical Economics. Elsevier. Chapter 26 (in this book).

Angrist, J.D., Imbens, G.W., 1995. Identification and estimation of local average treatment effects. Technical report. National Bureau of Economic Research.

Angrist, J.D., Pischke, J.-S., 2008. Mostly Harmless Econometrics: An Empiricist's Companion. Princeton University Press.

Angrist, J.D., Pischke, J.-S., 2014. Mastering 'metrics: The Path from Cause to Effect. Princeton University Press.

Ashraf, Q., Galor, O., 2013. The 'Out of Africa' hypothesis, human genetic diversity, and comparative economic development. The American Economic Review 103 (1), 1–46.

Ashraf, Q.H., Galor, O., Kemp, M., 2021. The ancient origins of the wealth of nations. In: Bisin, A., Federico, G. (Eds.), The Handbook of Historical Economics. Elsevier. Chapter 22 (in this book).

Austin, G., 2008. The 'reversal of fortune' thesis and the compression of history: perspectives from African and comparative economic history. Journal of International Development: The Journal of the Development Studies Association 20 (8), 996–1027.

Barro, R.J., 1979. On the determination of the public debt. Journal of Political Economy 87 (5, Part 1), 940–971.

Barro, R.J., Sala-i Martin, X., et al., 1995. Economic Growth.

Bechtel, M.M., Hangartner, D., Schmid, L., 2016. Does compulsory voting increase support for leftist policy? American Journal of Political Science 60 (3), 752–767.

Becker, S.O., Rubin, J., Woessmann, L., 2021. Religion in economic history: a survey. In: Bisin, A., Federico, G. (Eds.), The Handbook of Historical Economics. Elsevier. Chapter 20 (in this book).

Becker, S.O., Woessmann, L., 2009. Was Weber wrong? A human capital theory of Protestant economic history. The Quarterly Journal of Economics 124 (2), 531–596.

Bisin, A., Moro, A., 2021. LATE for history. In: Bisin, A., Federico, G. (Eds.), The Handbook of Historical Economics. Elsevier. Chapter 10 (in this book).

Bisin, A., Rubin, J., Seror, A., Verdier, T., 2020. Culture, Institutions and the Long Divergence. New York University. Mimeo.

Bisin, A., Seror, A., Verdier, T., 2019. Religious legitimacy and the joint evolution of culture and institutions. In: Advances in the Economics of Religion. Springer, pp. 321–332.

Bisin, A., Verdier, T., 2017. On the joint evolution of culture and institutions. Working Paper 23375. National Bureau of Economic Research.

Bisin, A., Verdier, T., 2021. Phase diagrams in historical economics: culture and institutions. In: Bisin, A., Federico, G. (Eds.), The Handbook of Historical Economics. Elsevier. Chapter 17 (in this book).

Blaydes, L., Chaney, E., 2013. The feudal revolution and Europe's rise: political divergence of the Christian West and the Muslim world before 1500 CE. American Political Science Review 107 (1), 16–34.

Bolt, J., Van Zanden, J.L., 2014. The Maddison Project: collaborative research on historical national accounts. The Economic History Review 67 (3), 627–651.

Borlandi, F., 1964. L'età delle scoperte e la rivoluzione economica nel secolo XVI. Nuove questioni di Storia moderna.

Bowles, S., Choi, J.-K., Hwang, S.-H., Nadu, S., 2021. How institutions and cultures change: an evolutionary perspective. In: Bisin, A., Federico, G. (Eds.), The Handbook of Historical Economics. Elsevier. Chapter 14 (in this book).

Bowles, S., Choi, J.-K., 2019. The Neolithic agricultural revolution and the origins of private property. Journal of Political Economy 127 (5), 2186–2228.

Braudel, F., 1972. La Méditerranée et le Monde Méditerranéen à l'Epoque de Philippe II (1949) (The Mediterranean and the Mediterranean World in the Age of Philip II). Harper, New York.

Broadberry, S., 2021. The Industrial Revolution and the Great Divergence: recent findings from historical national accounting. In: Bisin, A., Federico, G. (Eds.), The Handbook of Historical Economics. Elsevier. Chapter 24 (in this book).

Broadberry, S., Campbell, B.M.S., Klein, A., Overton, M., Van Leeuwen, B., 2015. British Economic Growth, 1270–1870. Cambridge University Press.

Brooke, J.L., 2014. Climate Change and the Course of Global History: A Rough Journey. Cambridge University Press.

Cantoni, D., Yuchtman, N., 2020. Historical Contingencies, Econometric Problems: The Analysis of Natural Experiments in Economic History. Working paper. National Bureau of Economic Research.

Cantoni, D., Yuchtman, N., 2021. Historical natural experiments: bridging economics and economic history. In: Bisin, A., Federico, G. (Eds.), The Handbook of Historical Economics. Elsevier. Chapter 8 (in this book).

Cioni, M., Federico, G., Vasta, M., 2021. The two revolutions in economic history. In: Bisin, A., Federico, G. (Eds.), The Handbook of Historical Economics. Elsevier. Chapter 2 (in this book).

Cioni, M., Federico, G., Vasta, M., 2019. Three Different Tribes: How the Relationship between Economics and Economic History Has Evolved in the 21st Century.

Clark, G., 2007. The long march of history: farm wages, population, and economic growth, England 1209–1869. The Economic History Review 60 (1), 97–135.

Clark, G., 2014. The Industrial Revolution. In: Handbook of Economic Growth, vol. 2. Elsevier, pp. 217–262.

Clark, G., 2021. Social mobility in historical economics. In: Bisin, A., Federico, G. (Eds.), The Handbook of Historical Economics. Elsevier. Chapter 23 (in this book).

Conrad, A.H., Meyer, J.R., 1958. The economics of slavery in the ante bellum South. Journal of Political Economy 66 (2), 95–130.

Crafts, N., 2021. Understanding productivity growth in the industrial revolution. The Economic History Review.

Crafts, N., Woltjer, P., 2020. Growth accounting in economic history: findings, lessons and new directions. Journal of Economic Surveys.

Cunningham, S., 2021. Causal Inference: The Mixtape. Yale University Press.

Dedinger, B., Girard, P., 2017. Exploring trade globalization in the long run: the RICardo project. Historical Methods: A Journal of Quantitative and Interdisciplinary History 50 (1), 30–48.

Dell, M., 2010. The persistent effects of Peru's mining mita. Econometrica 78 (6), 1863–1903.

Dell, M., Querubin, P., 2018. Nation building through foreign intervention: evidence from discontinuities in military strategies. The Quarterly Journal of Economics 133 (2), 701–764.

Deng, K., 2014. A survey of recent research in Chinese economic history. Journal of Economic Surveys 28 (4), 600–616.

Diamond, J., Robinson, J.A., et al., 2010. Natural Experiments of History. Harvard University Press.

Dippel, C., Leonard, B., forthcoming. Not-so-natural experiments in history. Journal of Historical Political Economy.

Dow, G.K., Reed, C.G., Olewiler, N., 2009. Climate reversals and the transition to agriculture. Journal of Economic Growth 14 (1), 27–53.

Edwards, J., Ogilvie, S., 2012. Contract enforcement, institutions, and social capital: the Maghribi traders reappraised. The Economic History Review 65 (2), 421–444.

Erdkamp, P., 2016. Economic growth in the Roman Mediterranean world: an early good-bye to Malthus? Explorations in Economic History 60, 1–20.

Federico, G., 2019. Market integration. In: Diebolt, C., Haupert, M. (Eds.), Handbook of Cliometrics. Springer, Berlin-Heidelberg.

Federico, G., 2021. The economic history of commodity market development. In: Bisin, A., Federico, G. (Eds.), The Handbook of Historical Economics. Elsevier. Chapter 18 (in this book).

Federico, G., Tena-Junguito, A., 2019. World trade, 1800-1938: a new synthesis. Revista de Historia Económica-Journal of Iberian and Latin American Economic History 37 (1), 9–41.

Feinstein, C.H., Thomas, M., 2002. A plea for errors. Historical Methods: A Journal of Quantitative and Interdisciplinary History 35 (4), 155–165.

Fischer, G., Nachtergaele, F.O., Prieler, S., Teixeira, E., Tóth, G., Van Velthuizen, H., Verelst, L., Wiberg, D., 2012. Global Agro-Ecological Zones (GAEZ v3. 0)-Model Documentation.

Fogel, R.W., 1964. Railroads and American Economic Growth. Johns Hopkins Press, Baltimore.

Fogel, R.W., Engerman, S.L., 1974. Time on the Cross: The Economics of American Negro Slavery, vol. 1. WW Norton & Company.

Fouquet, R., Broadberry, S., 2015. Seven centuries of European economic growth and decline. The Journal of Economic Perspectives 29 (4), 227–244.

Fourie, J., Obikili, N., et al., 2019. Decolonizing with data: the cliometric turn in African economic history. In: Handbook of Cliometrics, pp. 1–25.

Frankema, E., 2021. Why Africa is not *that* poor. In: Bisin, A., Federico, G. (Eds.), The Handbook of Historical Economics. Elsevier. Chapter 19 (in this book).

Friedman, M., Schwartz, A.J., 1963. A Monetary History of the US 1867-1960. Princeton University Press.

Galor, O., Özak, Ö., 2014. DP10122 The Agricultural Origins of Time Preference.

Giuliano, P., Matranga, A., 2021. Historical data: where to find them, how to use them. In: Bisin, A., Federico, G. (Eds.), The Handbook of Historical Economics. Elsevier. Chapter 4 (in this book).

Greenwood, J., 1997. The Third Industrial Revolution: Technology, Productivity, and Income Inequality. No. 435. American Enterprise Institute.

Greenwood, J., Guner, N., Kopecky, K., 2021. The wife's protector: a quantitative theory linking contraceptive technology with the decline in marriage. In: Bisin, A., Federico, G. (Eds.), The Handbook of Historical Economics. Elsevier. Chapter 29 (in this book).

Greenwood, J., Seshadri, A., Vandenbroucke, G., 2005. The baby boom and baby bust. The American Economic Review 95 (1), 183–207.

Greif, A., 1989. Reputation and coalitions in medieval trade: evidence on the Maghribi traders. The Journal of Economic History 49 (4), 857–882.

Greif, A., 1993. Contract enforceability and economic institutions in early trade: the Maghribi traders' coalition. The American Economic Review, 525–548.

Greif, A., 2012. The Maghribi traders: a reappraisal? The Economic History Review 65 (2), 445–469.

Guiot, J., Corona, C., et al., 2010. Growing season temperatures in Europe and climate forcings over the past 1400 years. PLoS ONE 5 (4), e9972.

Hall, G., Sargent, T., 2021. Debt and taxes in eight U.S. wars and two insurrections. In: Bisin, A., Federico, G. (Eds.), The Handbook of Historical Economics. Elsevier. Chapter 27 (in this book).

Hansen, G.D., Prescott, E.C., 2002. Malthus to Solow. The American Economic Review 92 (4), 1205–1217.

Hansen, G., Ohanian, L., Ozturk, F., 2021. Dynamic general equilibrium modeling of long and short-run historical events. In: Bisin, A., Federico, G. (Eds.), The Handbook of Historical Economics. Elsevier. Chapter 11 (in this book).

Haupert, M.J., Diebolt, C., 2019. Handbook of Cliometrics. Springer.

Heckman, J.J., Urzua, S., 2010. Comparing IV with structural models: what simple IV can and cannot identify. Journal of Econometrics 156 (1), 27–37.

Henriques, A., Pedro, N., Palma, G., 2019. Comparative European Institutions and the Little Divergence, 1385-1800.

Humphries, J., 2013. The lure of aggregates and the pitfalls of the patriarchal perspective: a critique of the high wage economy interpretation of the British industrial revolution. The Economic History Review 66 (3), 693–714.

Jedwab, R., Vollrath, D., 2015. Urbanization without growth in historical perspective. Explorations in Economic History 58, 1–21.

Johnson, N.D., Koyama, M., 2017. States and economic growth: capacity and constraints. Explorations in Economic History 64, 1–20.

Jones, C.M., 1978. Richard. Atlas of World Population History.

Juhász, R., 2018. Temporary protection and technology adoption: evidence from the Napoleonic blockade. The American Economic Review 108 (11), 3339–3376.

Keane, M.P., 2010. Structural vs. atheoretic approaches to econometrics. Journal of Econometrics 156 (1), 3–20.

Kelly, M., 2019. The standard errors of persistence. Working Paper DP13783, CEPR.

Kopecky, K.A., Suen, R.M.H., 2010. A quantitative analysis of suburbanization and the diffusion of the automobile. International Economic Review 51 (4), 1003–1037.

Kuran, T., 2012. The Long Divergence: How Islamic Law Held Back the Middle East. Princeton University Press.

La Porta, R., Lopez-de Silanes, F., Shleifer, A., Vishny, R.W., 1998. Law and finance. Journal of Political Economy 106 (6), 1113–1155.

Lampe, M., Sharp, P., 2015. Cliometric approaches to international trade. In: Handbook of Cliometrics, pp. 295–330.

Levine, D., Modica, S., 2021. State power and conflict driven evolution. In: Bisin, A., Federico, G. (Eds.), The Handbook of Historical Economics. Elsevier. Chapter 15 (in this book).

Li, X., Bleakley, C.J., Bober, W., 2012. Enhanced beacon-enabled mode for improved IEEE 802.15. 4 low data rate performance. Wireless Networks 18 (1), 59–74.

Lowes, S., 2021. Ethnographic and field data in historical economics. In: Bisin, A., Federico, G. (Eds.), The Handbook of Historical Economics. Elsevier. Chapter 6 (in this book).

Lowes, S., Montero, E., 2020. Concessions, violence, and indirect rule: evidence from the Congo free state. Technical report. National Bureau of Economic Research.

Lowes, S., Nunn, N., Robinson, J.A., Weigel, J.L., 2017. The evolution of culture and institutions: evidence from the Kuba Kingdom. Econometrica 85 (4), 1065–1091.

Lucas, R.E. Jr, Stokey, N.L., 1983. Optimal fiscal and monetary policy in an economy without capital. Journal of Monetary Economics 12 (1), 55–93.

Maddison, A., et al., 1995. Monitoring the World Economy, 1820-1992.

Maddison, A., 1991. Dynamic Forces in Capitalist Development: A Long-Run Comparative View. Oxford University Press, USA.

Malinowski, M., 2019. Economic consequences of state failure—legal capacity, regulatory activity, and market integration in Poland, 1505–1772. The Journal of Economic History 79 (3), 862–896.

Manioudis, M., Milonakis, D., 2020. Smith's Wealth of Nations and the economic past: setting the scene for economic history? The European Journal of the History of Economic Thought, 1–22.

Margo, R., 2021. The economic history of economic history: the evolution of a field in economics. In: Bisin, A., Federico, G. (Eds.), The Handbook of Historical Economics. Elsevier. Chapter 1 (in this book).

Malis, M., Querubin, P., Satyanath, S., 2021. Persistent failure? International interventions since World War II. In: Bisin, A., Federico, G. (Eds.), The Handbook of Historical Economics. Elsevier. Chapter 21 (in this book).

Matranga, A., 2017. The Ant and the Grasshopper: Seasonality and the Invention of Agriculture. https://mpra.ub. uni-muenchen.de/76626/1/MPRA_paper_76626.pdf.

Matranga, A., Pascali, L., 2021. The use of archaeological data in economics. In: Bisin, A., Federico, G. (Eds.), The Handbook of Historical Economics. Elsevier. Chapter 5 (in this book).

Mayshar, J., Moav, O., Neeman, Z., Pascali, L., 2019. The Origin of the State: Land Productivity or Appropriability? Technical report, mimeo. Hebrew University of Jerusalem, University of Warwick, Tel-Aviv . . . .

McConnell, J.R., Chellman, N.J., Wilson, A.I., Stohl, A., Arienzo, M.M., Eckhardt, S., Fritzsche, D., Kipfstuhl, S., Opel, T., Place, P.F., et al., 2019. Pervasive Arctic lead pollution suggests substantial growth in medieval silver production modulated by plague, climate, and conflict. Proceedings of the National Academy of Sciences 116 (30), 14910–14915.

McConnell, J.R., Wilson, A.I., Stohl, A., Arienzo, M.M., Chellman, N.J., Eckhardt, S., Thompson, E.M., Pollard, A.M., Steffensen, J.P., 2018. Lead pollution recorded in Greenland ice indicates European emissions tracked plagues, wars, and imperial expansion during antiquity. Proceedings of the National Academy of Sciences 115 (22), 5726–5731.

Meissner, C.M., 2014. Growth from globalization? A view from the very long run. In: Handbook of Economic Growth, vol. 2. Elsevier, pp. 1033–1069.

Merlo, A., 2005. Whither political economy? Theories, facts and issues.

Michalopoulos, S., Papaioannou, E., 2017. The Long Economic and Political Shadow of History Volume I. A Global View. Centre for Economic Policy Research.

Michalopoulos, S., Papaioannou, E., 2020. Historical legacies and African development. Journal of Economic Literature 58 (1), 53–128.

Mokyr, J., 2021. Attitudes, aptitudes, and the roots of the great enrichment. In: Bisin, A., Federico, G. (Eds.), The Handbook of Historical Economics. Elsevier. Chapter 25 (in this book).

Monnet, E., Velde, F.R., 2021. Money, banking, and old-school historical economics. In: Bisin, A., Federico, G. (Eds.), The Handbook of Historical Economics. Elsevier. Chapter 12 (in this book).

Murdock, G.P., 1967. Ethnographic atlas.

North, D.C., 1981. Structure and Change in Economic History. Norton.

North, D.C., Thomas, R.P., 1973. The Rise of the Western World: A New Economic History. Cambridge University Press.

North, D.C., Weingast, B.R., 1989. Constitutions and commitment: the evolution of institutions governing public choice in seventeenth-century England. The Journal of Economic History 49 (4), 803–832.

Nunn, N., 2014. Historical development. In: Handbook of Economic Growth, vol. 2. Elsevier, pp. 347–402.

Nunn, N., 2020. The historical roots of economic development. Science 367 (6485).

Nunn, N., 2021. History as evolution. In: Bisin, A., Federico, G. (Eds.), The Handbook of Historical Economics. Elsevier. Chapter 3 (in this book).

Nunn, N., Qian, N., 2014. US food aid and civil conflict. The American Economic Review 104 (6), 1630–1666.

Nunn, N., Wantchekon, L., 2011. The slave trade and the origins of mistrust in Africa. The American Economic Review 101 (7), 3221–3252.

Ogilvie, S., 2011. Institutions and European Trade: Merchant Guilds, 1000–1800. Cambridge University Press.

Ogilvie, S., 2019. The European Guilds: An Economic Analysis. Princeton University Press.

Ogilvie, S., Carus, A.W., 2014. Institutions and economic growth in historical perspective. In: Handbook of Economic Growth, vol. 2. Elsevier, pp. 403–513.

O'Rourke, K.H., 1997. The European grain invasion, 1870-1913. The Journal of Economic History, 775–801.

O'Rourke, K.H., Williamson, J.G., 2009. Did Vasco da Gama matter for European markets?. The Economic History Review 62 (3), 655–684.

Persson, T., Tabellini, G., 2021. Culture, institutions, and policy. In: Bisin, A., Federico, G. (Eds.), The Handbook of Historical Economics. Elsevier. Chapter 16 (in this book).

Rapp, R.T., 1976. Industry and Economic Decline in Seventeenth-Century Venice. Cambridge, Mass.

Reiss, P.C., Wolak, F.A., 2007. Structural econometric modeling: rationales and examples from industrial organization. In: Handbook of Econometrics, vol. 6, pp. 4277–4415.

Rubin, J., 2017. Rulers, Religion, and Riches: Why the West Got Rich and the Middle East Did Not. Cambridge University Press.

Satyanath, S., Voigtländer, N., Voth, H.-J., 2017. Bowling for fascism: social capital and the rise of the Nazi Party. Journal of Political Economy 125 (2), 478–526.

De la Sierra, R.S., et al., 2014. On the Origin of States: Stationary Bandits and Taxation in Eastern Congo. University of Chicago, Chicago.

Squicciarini, M.P., Voigtländer, N., 2015. Human capital and industrialization: evidence from the age of enlightenment. The Quarterly Journal of Economics 130 (4), 1825–1883.

Stasavage, D., 2021. Biogeography, writing, and the origins of the state. In: Bisin, A., Federico, G. (Eds.), The Handbook of Historical Economics. Elsevier. Chapter 28 (in this book).

Townsend, R.M., 1993. The Medieval Village Economy: A Study of the Pareto Mapping in General Equilibrium Models. Princeton University Press, Princeton, NJ.

Valencia Caicedo, F., 2021. Historical Econometrics: Instrumental Variables and Regression Discontinuity Designs. In: Bisin, A., Federico, G. (Eds.), The Handbook of Historical Economics. Elsevier. Chapter 7 (in this book).

Van Zanden, J.L., Buringh, E., Bosker, M., 2012. The rise and decline of European parliaments, 1188–1789. The Economic History Review 65 (3), 835–861.

Voigtländer, N., Voth, H.-J., 2012. Persecution perpetuated: the medieval origins of anti-semitic violence in Nazi Germany. The Quarterly Journal of Economics 127 (3), 1339–1392. https://doi.org/10.1093/qje/qjs019.

Voigtländer, N., Voth, H.-J., 2014. Highway to Hitler. National Bureau of Economic Research.

Voth, J., 2021. Persistence – myth and mystery. In: Bisin, A., Federico, G. (Eds.), The Handbook of Historical Economics. Elsevier. Chapter 9 (in this book).

Weisdorf, J.L., 2005. From foraging to farming: explaining the Neolithic Revolution. Journal of Economic Surveys 19 (4), 561–586.

Williamson, J.G., et al., 1974. Late Nineteenth-Century American Development: A General Equilibrium History. CUP Archive.

Williamson, J.G., 1985. Did British Capitalism Breed Inequality? Allen and Unwin.

Wrigley, E.A., Schofield, R.S., 1981. The Population of England 1541–1871–A Reconstruction. Arnold, London.

Alberto Bisin[a,b,d] **and Giovanni Federico**[c,d]
[a]New York University, New York, NY, United States
[b]NBER, Cambridge, MA, United States
[c]NYUAD, Abu Dhabi, United Arab Emirates
[d]CEPR, London, United Kingdom

What is historical economics

The economic history of economic history: the evolution of a field in economics

Robert A. Margo[a]

Boston University, Boston, MA, United States

1.1 Introduction

Academic disciplines divide up into sub-disciplines or fields, and economics is no exception. Most fields in economics are self-contained – for example, public economics or macroeconomics. Economic history is different, however, in that it belongs to two broader academic disciplines, economics and history. This chapter reflects on the evolution of economic history as a field in economics, drawing on my previous and ongoing work (Margo, 2011, 2018a, 2018b). To be clear upfront, the analysis, particularly of recent trends, applies mainly to economic history as it is practiced in economics departments in the United States; the changes described in the chapter are considerably less dramatic elsewhere in the world (Cioni et al., 2020, 2021). However, the market for economics scholarship (and scholars) is now global, and there are good reasons to believe that the style and content of economics scholarship has and will continue to converge across countries.

In the early twentieth century, when economics was still a very young discipline, professional activity in economic history was very similar in departments of history or economics. Back then, it was one of the most popular fields in economics, accounting for the large share of economics PhDs prior to World War One. Over time, economics turned more mathematical and quantitative. Other fields grew disproportionately and economic history's share of economics PhD's declined. The trend of greater use of mathematics and statistics accelerated after World War Two, at a time when the economics profession was expanding in size.

Economic historians were swept up in these trends, and "cliometrics" was born after World War Two. There is an urban legend that cliometrics diffused quickly and resolutely in economic history – it was Revolution, not Evolution. The urban legend, however, is just that – a legend. Compared with the analogous "human capital" revolution in labor economics, the cliometrics revolution was more protracted (Margo, 2018a; Cioni et al., 2020, 2021).

The comparative slowness of the cliometrics revolution reflected the influence of two schools of thought about how so-called "new" economic historians should conduct their business within eco-

---

[a] Robert A. Margo is Professor of Economics at Boston University, Boston MA, and a Research Associate in the Development of the American Economy Program at the National Bureau of Economic Research. He is the author, co-author, or co-editor of 6 books, and over 150 articles, book chapters, and book reviews.

The Handbook of Historical Economics. https://doi.org/10.1016/B978-0-12-815874-6.00009-5

nomics. One school argued that traditional economic history was insufficiently scientific and needed the mathematical and statistical tools of post-war economics to make it more rigorous. Here, the idea was not so much to create new questions for inquiry but, instead, to reinterpret conventional wisdom in light of new data and new methods; classic examples are Fogel and Engerman (1971) and Davis et al. (1972). Economics proper found this compelling for a time because the broader discipline was in ascendance and openly imperialistic in its goals to be the "queen" of the social sciences. However, to win over more traditional economic historians, cliometricians had to be respectful of scholarly norms in the history profession. It is convenient to associate these this first school of thought with one of the two economic historians who later received the Nobel Prize in Economics, Robert Fogel, although the vast majority of early cliometricians agreed with this line of reasoning.

The second school of thought was quite different. It viewed economic history as a bulwark against narrow theorizing in economics about the underlying sources of long run growth and development. Growth theory came to the fore in the 1950s, as did development economics. Both turned to economic history for stylized facts and useful metaphors (for example, Rostow's (1960) "stages of growth"). Anathema to the second school was that the most popular growth model, namely Solow (1956), abstracted from institutions and institutional change. Growth would occur in the steady state if the rate of technical change was sufficiently positive, but technical change would not occur unless institutions were present in a society that encouraged and enabled it to take place. The role of the economic historian was to remind mainstream economics of its shortcomings, drawing on the historical record for telling examples. The second school I associate with Douglass North – although, again, there were many others who made similar arguments (and still do).

Cliometrics in its two flavors attracted new entrants to the field. Initially, this entry stabilized the long-term decline in the economic history share of economics PhDs. By the mid-1990s, there were many articles by economic historians (and even some economists) celebrating cliometrics, along with the intellectual validation of two Nobel Prizes. However, a more careful look reveals a field largely in isolation from the broader world of economics that no longer viewed cliometrics as novel. Even earlier, academic history had lost interest in cliometrics along with "quantitative" history more generally.

From the perspective of the survival of economic history as a field within economics this situation was not tenable in the medium run, let alone the long run. However, the seeds for another reinvention were in place that ultimately led to the present status, in which economic history as it is practiced in the United States is largely indistinguishable from other empirical fields within economics – a feature that I have called elsewhere the "integration" of economic history into economics (Margo, 2018a). The central feature of this integration is that scholarly identities are more fluid than in previous (scholarly) generations. Leading scholars who self-identify as economic historians – for example, by listing economic history as a field on their CV, or membership in the Economic History Association –publish in field journals other than those specializing in economic history and, increasingly, in mainstream, general-interest journals.

The other side of the coin is that scholars who self-identify as labor economists or macroeconomists or development economists work on topics in which historical evidence or argument is integral or, less often, on recognized issues in the literature of economic history. Among many examples, the most prominent involve research inspired, directly or indirectly, by the various papers by Daron Acemoglu and co-authors (for example. Acemoglu et al., 2001) that investigate how transient events or factors in the distant past could still shape economic outcomes in the present. This entire body of scholarship has little in common with traditional economic history or cliometrics. Aside from its substantive contribution, it is crucial in providing a (very) high profile example of the value of historical evidence in economics scholarship and, as such, has made mainstream economists accepting of the analysis of historical evidence as a routine part of the economic toolkit.

The main challenge posed by the integration of economic history into economics is the long-run viability of economic history as a separate field in economics. This may seem like an odd observation, if use of historical evidence in economics is becoming more popular. However, this new popularity does not appear to be generating an increase in the demand for specialists in the field *per se*. As foreseen a quarter century ago by Romer (1994), recent trends could put an "end" to economic history in the sense that individuals no longer specialize in the field, but instead specialize in the use of historical evidence in other fields of economics. That is, there are (or will be) labor economists whose general area of expertise might be wage inequality and whose knowledge extends to the long-run history of inequality, as opposed to just recent trends. At its extreme, this would mean no more generalists in economic history within economics, but rather only specialists in the economic history of relevant topics within fields. Sunk costs being what they are, something is lost if there are no longer generalist economic historians, because the whole is greater than the sum of the parts. For example, if there were no more generalists, it seems highly unlikely there would be generalist courses in economic history taught in economics departments, either at the undergraduate or graduate level. In turn, this may reduce the likelihood that economists will engage with scholars in other fields involved in research in economic history, to the detriment of all concerned.

1.2 Economics and economic history in the United States before World War Two

My narrative begins in the late nineteenth century, when economics had just been born as an academic discipline in the United States. Founded in the late 1880s, the American Economic Association (AEA) was slow at first to develop into a viable professional organization (see Margo, 2011). At the turn of the century, the AEA provided a variety of services to its members, but it was not until 1911 that the American Economic Review (AER) would appear as the organization's flagship journal. By the time the AER launched its first issue, the Quarterly Journal of Economics (QJE) had already been publishing for a quarter century, and the Journal of Political Economy (JPE) for just under two decades.

Like that of economics, the economic history of economic history in the United States begins in the late nineteenth century (Mejia, 2015; Lamoreaux, 2016). At the time, economic history was a popular field within both economics and history, more or the less the same in content and method in both disciplines. Although always in the minority, articles in economic history appeared regularly in the AER, QJE, JPE, and the American Historical Review (AHR), and there is little, if anything to distinguish between them from a disciplinary point of view. Max Ferrand's "The Taxation of Tea, 1767-1773" which was published in the AHR in the January 1898 issue, could have appeared in the JPE of the 1890s just as Ella Caroline Lapham's "The Industrial Status of Women in Elizabethan England," which the JPE published in 1901, would have been right at home in the AHR of the early 1900s.

By today's standards economic history attracted a remarkably high share of PhDs in economics in the early twentieth century. In 1904 the AEA began collecting and publishing information on PhDs awarded in economics. This information included the name of the student, title of the dissertation, institution, and most important, a classification by subject matter. A convenient summary analysis of these early reports is Froman (1930), who produced several useful tables showing the distribution of economics PhDs over time by school and subject matter.

Froman's Table VI (1930, p. 241) covers 3,117 economics PhDs granted from 1904 to 1928. From the institutional perspective, production was extraordinarily unequal; just three schools (Chicago, Columbia, and Wisconsin) awarded half of the PhDs.[1] The rate of PhD production was steadily increasing over time; 1,471 PhD's were awarded from 1924 to 1928, compared with just 199 PhDs from 1904 to 1908.

Overall, economic history was the most popular subject for a dissertation in economics, accounting for 12.5 percent of all economics theses over the period (1904-28) studied by Froman. This popularity, however, was declining over time – the history share declined from 18.6 percent in 1904-08 to 9.5 percent in 1924-28. The decline occurred discretely, dropping in the early 1910s and then in the late 1920s. The falling off in popularity was relative because, while the absolute number of economic history PhDs increased, this did not keep pace with the rapid growth of economics PhDs overall.

The topics of economics dissertations do not emerge in a vacuum but rather from the coursework that students undertake along the way. To the best of my knowledge, historians of economic thought have not traced the aggregate evolution of coursework at the doctoral level – in the present case, courses in economic history. However, for one important department – the University of Chicago – Mitch (2007, 2011, 2014) has produced a time line. Here I discuss Mitch's chronology before World War Two.

Founded in 1892, the Chicago economics department immediately offered graduate instruction in economic history – narrow courses on the tariff and financial history of the United States, as well as general courses in "Economic and Social History" and "Industrial and Economic History". Chicago was far from atypical – of the 23 US institutions that offered graduate instruction in economics in the late 1890s, 15 regularly programmed courses in economic or financial history (Collier, 2015).

There were no specific course requirements in economic history at Chicago for the degree nor, for that matter, an explicit requirement to exhibit mastery of the field in some other manner (for example, an exam). This changed in 1920, when the Chicago department declared that its PhD students were supposed to have a basic knowledge of the economic history of England and the United States. By 1925, specific courses could satisfy this knowledge requirement. By the early 1940s, PhD requirements at Chicago were refined further. Graduate students had to show competence in ten specific areas, two of which were American and European economic history.

As Chicago and (presumably) other departments were strengthening their graduate requirements, economic history continued to slide in popularity relative to other fields in attracting PhD students. The AEA's methods of collecting and classifying dissertations changed over time and it is difficult to construct a consistent time series. Nevertheless, it is clear that the decrease extended into the 1930s. Point estimates that I have made for the second half of the 1930s from the AEA's reports of dissertations granted in economics suggest that around 6 percent of dissertations were on topics in economic history, which is below the level for the late 1920s (Froman, 1930, Table VI). Continued secular erosion before the war in economic history's relative share is not surprising. The bright lights of economics

---

[1] Harvard was fourth but one must keep in mind that this does not include Radcliffe, which was a separate degree-granting institution at the time. If Radcliffe's PhD production is added to Harvard, the total share is 10.3 percent, approximately the same as the Wisconsin's.

– Friedman, Samuelson, among others – were embracing new methods or else confronting the pressing policy issues of the Depression and impending conflict in Europe, rather than studying economic history.

1.3 **The cliometrics revolution**

World War Two transformed the economics profession in the United States. Economists were deeply involved in wartime planning and their role in government expanded after the war with the passage of the Full Employment Act of 1946. Veterans took advantage of the GI Bill, and large numbers enrolled in college economics courses. The prewar trend in greater use of mathematics and statistics continued unabated, indeed, accelerated after 1945. Academic economists allocated more time to producing research, and submissions to the AER and other general interest journals increased sharply in the late 1950s and early 1960s (Margo, 2011).

The early postwar years were a defining moment for economic history. As discussed earlier, the field had been losing "market share" among economics PhDs before the war but there were hopeful signs on the horizon. The field had its own flagship outlet in the United States, the Journal of Economic History (JEH). Established in 1941, the JEH was a joint venture of the AEA and the Organization of American Historians, acknowledging the "interdisciplinary" character of the field. Regular issues of the JEH appeared three times a year, with a fourth devoted to the "The Tasks of Economic History" consisting of papers given at the annual convention of the Economic History Association (EHA), along with discussant comments. A typical regular issue had three main articles; a similar number of shorter notes, comments, or review articles; and book reviews – roughly 100 pages in length, including front and back matter.

Another hopeful sign was the emergence of a specific intellectual demand from economics for historical evidence on development and growth. This demand had three sources.

The first was the National Bureau of Economic Research. Established in 1920, the Bureau immersed itself in the development of national income accounting, including the extension of national accounts back in historical time for the United States. This research was under the direction of Simon Kuznets. In the very first issue of the JEH, Kuznets (1941) published an important article arguing for closer collaboration between economic historians and "statistical economists" (Kuznets' phrase), in order to achieve what he called "the final goal of economic study". Kuznets trained many PhD students – most famously, Robert Fogel, but also Richard Easterlin and Robert Gallman, who, like Fogel, front and center of the cliometrics revolution and who were to become towering figures in economic history as their respective careers unfolded. Easterlin's early work provided estimates of regional national income in the United States for various census years beginning in 1840. Gallman's dissertation and early papers provided detailed figures on aggregate output and its components and the capital stock, also beginning in 1840 (Gallman and Rhode, 2019). Later researchers (see, for example, Atack and Margo, 2019) would revise these early estimates but, to this day, they remain part of the data infrastructure used daily by American economic historians.

The second source was the Cold War, which created a pressing need in the West to provide policy advice to developing nations lest they fall into the Soviet orbit. Here, as noted earlier, the classic example is Rostow (1960). Today, Robert Fogel's dissertation-*cum*-monograph (Fogel, 1964), is remembered mainly for his estimate of the social savings of the railroad but his Chapter 4 and related

Chapter 5 offered deep and compelling critiques of Rostow's "take-off" hypothesis. In doing so, Fogel demonstrated the value of cliometrics in validating – or, in this case, not – the use of historical evidence in economic argument in contemporary development economics.

The third source was growth theory. This originated before the war but received an enormous intellectual boost with the publication of Solow's (1956, 1957) fundamental papers. The assumptions of Solow's model as well as the application to growth accounting opened up major topics of research in economic history that, to this day, attract scholarly attention.

Another hopeful sign was that, despite the long run downward trend in the field's share of new economics PhDs, a numerically significant share of graduate students took courses in economic history ca. 1950 and a solid majority of graduate faculty felt that knowledge of economic history should be a required part of graduate training. We know this from an important, if neglected study of graduate education in economics, which I refer to as the Bowen (1953) study.

The impetus for the Bowen study was a prior report on undergraduate education in economics, commissioned by the AEA in the late 1940s. Impressed by the undergraduate study as it was nearing completion, the AEA's Executive Committee decided that a second study focusing on graduate education would also be valuable. An ad-hoc committee of four individuals, one of whom was Milton Friedman, was appointed to study the feasibly of a report on graduate education. The ad-hoc group was in favor, so the next step was for the Executive Committee to seek funding, which they did successfully from the Rockefeller Foundation.

The principal investigator of the AEA study was Howard R. Bowen. Born in 1908, Bowen received his BA and MA degrees from Washington State University and his PhD in economics from Iowa in 1935, followed by post-doctoral work at Cambridge and LSE. He began his career teaching at the University of Iowa but quickly moved into government service and the private sector. After World War Two, he became dean of the College of Commerce at the University of Illinois, but was forced to resign in a dispute over his efforts to reform the business curriculum to include discussion of "social responsibility". Bowen was a faculty member at Williams College when the AEA hired him to conduct the study. He later moved back to Iowa where he served as president of Grinnell College and the University of Iowa. During his academic career Bowen published 14 books, 12 on the economics of higher education, on which he was a leading authority. He spent the 1951-52 academic year working on the AEA study.

Bowen used three principal sources in researching and writing his report. The first was the extant literature on graduate education, almost all of which was general rather than specific to economics and not much at that. The second, and the heart of the study, was a series of twelve questionnaires on a variety of issues sent to deans, department chairs, faculty members, and former and current graduate students. Bowen reported the statistical results from the questionnaires in simple one-way tables throughout the book. Lastly, Bowen conducted personal interviews.

The fundamental goal of Bowen's study was to make recommendations about whether PhD instruction in economics should include a "core" – that is, required courses in the first and second year – and if so, what those courses should be. Indeed, one of Bowen's questionnaires asked faculty what they thought on this very point – 72 percent were in favor of a core and another 9 percent were willing to consider one (depending on the details). Of those in favor of a core, there was near universal agreement – 98 percent – that there should be courses in microeconomic theory. Beyond micro-theory, however, there was less consensus but a solid majority – 55 percent – felt that economic history should be part of the core, slightly higher than the fraction that favored econometrics (53 percent).

How did faculty attitudes correspond with practice at the time? Bowen's (1953, p. 105) Table 25 gives the proportion of programs requiring, for example, courses in economic theory as well as the proportion in which students "usually" electing said courses if not required. A little more than two-thirds (65 percent) of programs had required courses in economic theory, but even if these were not required, the courses were routinely offered and almost always taken by students, for a total proportion of 95 percent. At 49 percent, almost half of the programs had a course requirement in history of thought; of the 51 percent that did not have a requirement, students usually took such courses in slightly more than half (53) of the programs for a combined total of 76 percent. Thus, around the middle of the twentieth century, Bowen's survey results suggest that PhD students in economics had universal exposure to doctoral level microeconomic theory and a large majority received instruction in the history of thought.

On the remaining elements of Bowen's prospective core, there was more variation. A little more than a fifth (22 percent) of programs had a course requirement in statistics. Among the 78 percent that did not, students rarely took it up on their own (7 percent of the time). Regarding economic history, 14 percent of programs had a history requirement but of the 86 percent that did not, students routinely took economic history in 22 percent of programs. The combined proportion is 33 percent – among PhD students in economics in the US in the early 1950s, one-third took some graduate instruction in economic history. As I discuss later, this is approximately twice as high as my best guess of the proportion today.

The circumstances just described set the stage for the cliometrics revolution. Cliometrics is an invented word combining "Clio" (for the Greek goddess of history) with "metrics," meaning measurement. Conventional wisdom dates the revolution from professional meetings held in the late 1950s and various manifestos published at the time. The movement picked up steam in the 1960s and, allegedly, generated a full-blown takeover by the early 1970s, leading to a marked, immediate change in intellectual orientation within economic history towards economics, including regular and widespread use of formal models, econometrics, and hypothesis testing.

As with all conventional wisdom, there is some truth but the revolutionary aspect is overblown. Margo (2018a) conducted a text analysis of articles in five economics journals from the early 1950s through 2009. Two of these are economic history journals, the JEH and Explorations in Economic History (EEH), two are labor economics, Industrial and Labor Relations Review (ILRR) and the Journal of Human Resources (JHR); and one is a "top-five", the AER. The JEH and ILRR were already in existence at the end of World War Two; EEH and JHR came into existence in the 1960s. My text analysis looks for instances of econometric language (e.g. "regression") in empirical articles (defined as articles in which one or more tables appear). The comparison of economic history and labor economics is relevant because both were effectively non-quantitative in the early 1950s. Economic history had its cliometric revolution and labor economics, its "human capital" revolution. Which came quicker?

The AER was already routinely publishing articles with econometrics in the 1950s but there was essentially no econometrics in either the JEH or the ILRR during the decade. Then, in the 1960s, the content of ILRR begins to change and it rapidly converges on the AER in terms of usage of econometrics. The JHR, which began publishing during the second half of the 1960s, embraced modern empirical methods almost immediately. By intellectual standards, the human capital revolution in labor economics happened overnight.

By contrast, economic history was much slower to adopt modern econometric techniques. Change came faster in EEH but even so, it was not until the 1980s that the journal caught up with labor economics or the economics profession more broadly (for a similar conclusion, see also Cioni et al., 2020, 2021). The extent of econometrics in the JEH was always below EEH and the pace of change slower, although consistent with a weak revolutionary metaphor, the trend was definitely upward.

A deep dive into the JEH articles published in the 1960s that used any econometrics confirms the tepid pace of change evident in the formal text analysis. By "deep dive" I read every relevant article closely – quite a bit less work than it might be imagined, as, there were only 16 of them, or roughly 5 percent of the articles, notes, comments, and so on published in the JEH in the decade. It is not simply that there are few articles. Rather, the use of econometrics is defensive, as if authors feel they have to apologize to some portion of their audience. Results are discussed briefly and often only in footnotes.

The relatively slow pace of adoption of econometrics suggests that, while cliometrics might have been a revolutionary in a certain sense, its goals were not entirely consonant with the analogous revolution in labor economics. Margo (2018a) confirms this through an analysis of the publication histories of successive PhD cohorts of prominent economic historians. A remarkable feature of those who received their degrees in the late 1960s and early 1970s is that many did little or no publishing whatsoever outside of economic history journals in the first decade of their professional careers; included in this statement are such prominent economic historians as Claudia Goldin and Joel Mokyr. This is not the case with similarly prominent labor economists, who not only published in, say, the JHR or ILRR, but routinely published in top mainstream journals like the AER, QJE, or JPE.

What accounts for the different publication strategies? In Margo (2018a) I argue that one should view intellectual academic revolutions through the lens of an "overlapping generations" model of academic labor markets. New entrants to a field, even those who arrive at a time of intellectual formant, are evaluated for tenure and promotion by an older generation of scholars. New methods and new questions may diffuse fairly quickly or may not, depending on the equilibrium of the model.

The model suggests that there are good reasons to expect the cliometrics revolution to be slow. Although the initial demand for a "new" economic history may have originated in economics, the revolution quickly morphed into providing general "reinterpretation" of past work in the field informed by economic methods. In part, this reflected a reaction to the prevailing content of graduate courses in economic history in the early 1950s, as documented in the AEA report. Although a majority of graduate faculty felt that instruction in economic history was necessary, students were less favorable, complaining that the courses emphasized dates and places – a common criticism of history courses at the time – and made insufficient use of economic reasoning. Indeed, when the first generation of cliometricians took a careful look at the economic history literature they realized there were intellectual holes, often profound, wherever they looked. The pickings were ripe, not slim.

At the same time, however, the early cliometricians were not in a position to obliterate the traditional opposition, even if that had been their public goal (Diebolt and Haupert, 2018). Pointedly, it was not – rather, the idea was to supplement the traditional tools of the economic historian with the tools of economics. This required much more than lip service to professional norms. Early cliometricians were expected to learn foreign languages if they studied a non-English speaking country, read professional history journals, write books in addition to journal articles. Most important, they were to wear their economics lightly when engaging with professional historians –hence, the character and tone of the "econometrics" articles in the JEH in the 1960s.

Although the attempt to make traditional economic history more like economics is understandable in context, with the benefit of hindsight it is far from obvious that it deserved to go on for as long as it did. Ultimately, the majority of economists did not care very much if cliometricians were successful in proselytizing among traditional economic historians. Adherence to scholarly norms in history, such as writing monographs to gain tenure, ultimately had little or no import in economics. For a while, historians played along with "quantification" but began to lose interest, especially after the divisive controversies over economics scholarship on slavery (Fogel and Engerman, 1974) but also because, by the 1980s, articles and books written by economic historians in economics departments were too technical for the average historian.

The impulse in early cliometrics to make traditional economic history more scientific is usually associated with Robert Fogel although, as pointed out earlier, it was routinely accepted by other cliometricians. However, there was another school of thought that was also present. This school of thought saw economic history as a way to discipline economists in theorizing about development and growth.

The notion that economic history places significant limitations on economic modeling about growth and development is often associated with the other Nobelist, Douglass North, but it has a long intellectual tradition in the field. North was a card-carrying cliometrician in the early years of the revolution but by the late 1960s and 1970s his views had changed, evolving towards the work on institutions and institutional change for which he is remembered today. North certainly believed that economics had powerful tools, but he also believed that the prevailing models omitted first order causal factors, largely because economic theory lacked the tools to describe these adequately. He was also frequently critical of his fellow economic historians for playing too nice with the rest of economics. For a long time North was a voice crying in the wilderness. Some of this reflects that fact that disciplinary criticism is rarely successful in real time. But a deeper reason is that North was not able to come up with technical or econometric tools on his own that would have persuaded the rest of economics. Of course, economics did eventually buy into the idea that institutions "matter" and North's contributions were celebrated in his Nobel. But the requisite tools to truly further the research agenda did not come from North, his students, or elsewhere in economic history but rather from outside the field. These tools were dynamic games and the development and application of causal identification strategies from econometrics.

The two schools of thought carved out an intellectual pace in which economic historians with PhDs in economics could function professionally – teach, do research, publish, and gain tenure. All fields have such spaces but economic history was different. The publication records of successive cohorts of economics PhDs in their first ten years of professional life reveal these differences. Economic historians with economics PhDs who began in the 1970s were far more likely to write books, articles in economic history or interdisciplinary history journals than articles in economics journals. 1980s and 1990s PhD cohorts began to move towards economics but the changes were relatively modest (Margo, 2018a).

By the early to mid-1990s cliometrics was at a crossroads. On the one hand, cliometricians believed their revolution to be successful, especially after the awarding of the Nobel Prizes to Fogel and North. Cliometrics can also claim credit for stabilizing the long-run decline in share of economic history PhDs in economics, albeit at a very low level; according to estimates I have made from dissertations reported to the AEA, the economic history share of new PhDs in economics fluctuated between 1 and 2 percent from the mid-1960s to mid-1990s, On the other hand, and ominously, the field functioned largely in isolation from the rest of Economics. In one of his most remarkable articles, George Stigler (1995, published posthumously with Stephen J. Stigler and Claire Friedland as co-authors) measured the extent to which different sub-fields in economics cited each other. In contrast to other fields, economic history was essentially an island. It "imported" results from other fields to some extent – that is, cited articles in economics outside of economic history – but rarely "exported" its findings – economic history articles were cited rarely outside the field.

However, with the arrival of the post-2000 PhD cohorts arrive on the scene, there was the stirring of a revival. Evidence is found in a strong divergence in publication patterns (Margo, 2018a). Post-2000 cohorts are much less likely to publish books, and more likely to publish articles in economics journals outside of economic history and in top-five mainstream economics journals.

Why does the structural break happen? One straightforward explanation is cohort succession. By the early 2000s the earliest cliometricians were already leaving the research scene through life-cycle declines in productivity, retirement, and death. Even earlier, there were second or third generation PhDs who began to engage directly with other fields in economics. One of the most successful is Claudia Goldin, whose earliest work was totally within cliometrics but whose second book (Goldin, 1990) resonated strongly with a broader audience in labor economics. Additional examples include Barry Eichengreen, Christina Romer, Alan Taylor, among many others.

While I believe this "role model" story to be important, it is not the full story. Intellectual developments outside of economic history have dramatically raised the profile and acceptance of use of historical evidence in economic analysis.

There are three principal developments. The first and arguably most important is research on the (very) long roots of contemporary differences in per capita income around the world. The idea is that, in the distance past, events led to differences in institutions with very different growth potentials that, because of sunk costs, persisted for a very long time or even to the present. As mentioned earlier, this type of argument is quite alien from the point of view of traditional economic history or cliometrics but fits naturally into economics, creating a clear reason for studying the economic past for those not predisposed to do so (Cioni et al., 2021). The well-known and astonishingly well-cited papers by Daron Acemoglu and his various coauthors (e.g. Acemoglu et al., 2001) essentially jump-started this area of research some two decades ago, quickly went into orbit and continues to attract new researchers to this day.

The second and third are related to advances in modeling in growth theory and macroeconomics. Growth theory was re-invigorated by endogenous growth models that quite naturally invoke certain kinds of historical evidence (see Galor and Weil, 2000). Macroeconomists realized that dynamic general equilibrium models were a powerful tool for exploring long run changes in aggregate economic outcomes, such as the shift of labor out of agriculture, long run changes in fertility, and changes in labor force participation. By itself, the use of general equilibrium models in economic history was not new. But the dynamic models were far more sophisticated and, perhaps most importantly, internally consistent and, therefore, more persuasive as theoretical constructs, even as debates arose over particular applications.

What is perhaps equally critical is that the various economists leading the charge had little or no interest in persuading card-carrying economic historians by publishing their research in economic history journals. Rather, they sought to persuade economists by targeting and succeeding in publishing in top-five journals. In turn, this opened up space for historical argument in field journals outside of economic history (for example, in development or macroeconomics). The post-2000 cohort of PhDs in economic history were paying attention because they too began to craft articles intended for publication in top-five and non-economic history field journals – collectively, a much larger audience than just economic history (Margo, 2018a).

In thinking about these changes it is essential to keep in mind that it is not simply a matter of who does economic history and where economic history is published. The motivation of research in the field has also fundamentally changed. Certainly it is still possible to write a paper that is "traditional" cliometrics, on a topic that would not have seemed unusual in the 1970s or 1980s (see, for example, Atack and Margo, 2019). However, to a significant extent, papers being written today in economic history routinely follow the logic of modern empirical economics especially the emphasis on identification of causal parameters. This is true whether or not the paper is written originally for an economic history journal, or finds its way to an economic history journal after being submitted to a mainstream journal or a field journal outside of economic history.

1.4 **Not your father's economic history**

Economic history appears to be enjoying a professional rebirth. Compared with just a few decades ago scholarly identity in the field falls on a continuum. Well known economic historians are visible in other sub-fields of economics and there are many economists who, from time to time, pursue historical evidence or historical topics. Young scholars can work on research projects in economic history and be confident that their work will get a hearing. Overall, these are welcome changes. At the end of the day, there are only two types of empirical evidence in economics – experimental or observational. All observational data in economics sit in an historical context. A central feature of economic method is, when necessary, to abstract from historical context, often to argue in favor or against a particular theoretical model of behavior. The special gift of economic history to economics is the constant reminder that historical context is always present, either in the background or front and center. Broader recognition of the fundamental role of historical evidence and argument in economics can only improve and enrich the discipline overall.

At the same time, there are costs as well as benefits to the recent changes in the field. All fields in economics have specialized knowledge and, within fields, some economists are more specialized than others. For economic history, the issue is whether the specialized knowledge can be reproduced within other sub-fields or whether there is some benefit to keeping it "in-house". There are two reasons why this issue is important. First, within economics, the number of new PhDs specializing in economic history in the United States is, once again, dwindling sharply. The AEA's records indicate that, between 2006 and 2015, the economic history share of new PhDs in economics in the United States averaged around 0.8 percent per year. In absolute terms, the number is tiny. For example, in the year 2015, 1,080 PhDs in economics were awarded in the United States. The AEA classified just 7 of these into economic history. Sustaining a field with just 7 new entrants per year seems impossible.

How did this happen, one might wonder, if economic history is increasing in popularity? The answer is that individuals who do historical work increasingly identify with the *topical* subfield, rather than economic history *per se*. A young scholar who writes articles on topics in historical labor economics, in other words, calls herself, first and foremost, a labor economist rather than an economic historian. This possibility was foreseen by Romer (1994) – instead of economic historians for whom the Great Depression was a topic to be mastered along with others in American economic history, there are macroeconomists who write articles on the economics of the 1930s, along with other topics in the field.

The second reason is related to the first. As I documented earlier in this paper, approximately a third of PhD students in economics took classes in economic history in the early 1950s. In Margo (2018b; see also Jaremski, 2020) I make an estimate of this number for today's graduate students. In the United States currently there are approximately 120 active PhD programs in economics. Just 12 of these have an economic history requirement (loosely defined) as part of the core and perhaps another 8 or so offer PhD courses in the field but do not have a formal requirement (my own department, Boston University, is an example). As a consequence, students in perhaps only one sixth (17 percent) of today PhD programs are at risk of *ever* taking a PhD course in economic history in their home department. Earlier in the paper I estimated that ca. 1950 one-third of economics PhD students took a graduate course in economic history as part of their training. Today's fraction, therefore, is half that at the mid-twentieth century. Taking a PhD-level course is neither necessary nor sufficient to ultimately doing professional level research in any field of economics but it would difficult to argue that, on average, the treatment effect of such a course is anything but positive.

As a thought experiment, imagine a counterfactual discipline in which economics is still divided into fields but economic history is not one of them. Instead, within other fields, there are economists who specialize in historical topics – public finance economists whose role is to study the economic history of taxation, macroeconomists who study the economic history of business cycles, and so on. In this counterfactual, there is a tradeoff between general and specific. On the assumption that, on average, specialization is a good thing, we might learn more about relatively few, but important (to economics) topics in economic history, as opposed to a little about a lot. It is not obvious which is "better", but if we lose the economics take on the generalist perspective in economic history there are implications for scholarship, not necessary positive.

One implication is ceding the "big picture" to history or other fields (e.g. political science). The early cliometricians, by and large, saw themselves as generalists who maintained at least some links to professional history. This is far less true today, and will only become less true in the future if present trends continue. A labor economist who is deeply knowledgeable about the economic history of, say, immigration but little else in the economic past is not really a full-fledged economic historian.

Professional history lost interest in cliometrics many years ago and shows few signs of interest in the new strands of historical scholarship emerging in economics. However, it does not follow that historians have lost interest in economic history *per se*. Those historians who were displaced by cliometrics and who have little interest or incentive to follow developments in economics have long since migrated to greener pastures, such as the Business History Conference. However, the failure to follow economic history research in economics can negatively affect the quality of scholarship in history.

An important current example is the so-called "History of Capitalism". Historians of capitalism are interested in many of the same topics that economic historians are interested in, but largely eschew or dismiss relevant research in cliometrics or economic more generally. Cliometricans who have looked carefully at articles and books by historians of capitalism find numerous and egregious errors (Olmstead and Rhode, 2018; Hilt, 2017). As a result, one could be dismissive of the entire enterprise but I believe this to be an overreaction. Fortunately, while the disciplinary gaps are yawning, s there have been recent attempts on both sides to bridge them and engage in productive dialog.

The upshot, and my closing observation, is very simple. No one owns the past. The present state of economic history research is a consequence of long run trends that, in my opinion, are not going to change course. I wish that historians had more incentives to do good economics but I also wish that economists who venture into economic history had strong incentives to do good history. In the final analysis, the best and most durable economic history combines the best of both worlds (Collins, 2018).

Acknowledgments

I am grateful to Jeremy Atack, Martha Bailey, Alberto Bisin, William Collins, Giovanni Federico, Matthew Jaremski, David Mitch, and participants at the 2019 ASSA meetings in Atlanta for helpful comments.

References

Acemoglu, D., Johnson, S., Robinson, J., 2001. The colonial origins of comparative economic development. The American Economic Review 91 (5), 1369–1401.

Atack, J., Margo, R.A., 2019. Gallman revisited: blacksmithing and American manufacturing, 1850–1870. Cliometrica 13 (1), 1–23.

Bowen, H.R., 1953. Graduate education in economics. The American Economic Review 43 (4), ii–243.

Cioni, M., Federico, G., Vasta, M., 2020. The long term evolution of economic history: evidence from the five top field journals. Cliometrica 14 (1), 1–39.

Cioni, M., Federico, G., Vasta, M., 2021. The two revolutions in economic history. In: Bisin, A., Federico, G. (Eds.), The Handbook of Historical Economics. Elsevier. Chapter 2 (in this book).

Collier, I., 2015. Graduate economics courses: 23 universities, 1898-99, economics in the rear-view mirror: archival artifacts from the history of economics. http://www.irwincollier.com/graduate-economics-courses-23-us-universitites-1898-99/. (Accessed 23 July 2020).

Collins, W.J., 2018. Publishing economic history. In: Colvin, C., Blum, M. (Eds.), An Economist's Guide to Economic History. Palgrave MacMillan, Switzerland, pp. 347–353.

Davis, L.E., Easterlin, R.A., Parker, W.N., Brady, D.S., Fishlow, A., Gallman, R.E., et al., 1972. American Economic Growth: An Economist's History of the United States. Harper and Lee, New York.

Diebolt, C., Haupert, M., 2018. We are all Ninjas: How Economic History has Infiltrated Economics. Association Française de Cliométrie Working Paper No. 4.

Fogel, R.W., 1964. Railroads and American Economic Growth: Essays in Econometric History. Johns Hopkins Press, Baltimore.

Fogel, R.W., Engerman, S. (Eds.), 1971. The Reinterpretation of American Economic History. Harper and Row, New York.

Fogel, R.W., Engerman, S., 1974. Time on the Cross: The Economics of American Negro Slavery. Little, Brown, New York.

Froman, L.A., 1930. Graduate students in economics, 1904 to 1928. The American Economic Review 20 (2), 235–247.

Gallman, R.E., Rhode, P.W., 2019. Capital in the Nineteenth Century. University of Chicago Press, Chicago.

Galor, O., Weil, D., 2000. Population, growth, and technology: from Malthusian stagnation to the demographic transition and beyond. The American Economic Review 90 (4), 806–828.

Goldin, C., 1990. Understanding the Gender Gap: An Economic History of American Women. Oxford University Press, New York.

Hilt, E., 2017. Economic history, historical analysis, and the new 'History of capitalism'. The Journal of Economic History 77 (2), 511–536.

Jaremski, M., 2020. Today's economic history and tomorrow's scholars. Cliometrica 14 (1), 169–180.

Kuznets, S., 1941. Statistics and economic history. The Journal of Economic History 1 (1), 26–41.

Lamoreaux, N.R., 2016. Beyond the old and new: economic history in the United States. In: Boldizzoni, F., Hudson, P. (Eds.), Routledge Handbook of Global Economic History. Routledge, New York, pp. 35–54.

Margo, R.A., 2011. The economic history of the "American economic review": a century's explosion of economics research. The American Economic Review 101 (1), 9–35.

Margo, R.A., 2018a. The integration of economic history into economics. Cliometrica 12 (3), 377–406.

Margo, R.A., 2018b. The Economic History Requirement: Past, Present, Future. Department of Economics, Boston University. Unpublished manuscript.

Mejia, J., 2015. The evolution of economic history since 1950: from cliometrics to cliodynamics. Tiempo y economia 2 (2), 79–103.

Mitch, D., 2007. A Student Eye View: Requirements and Dissertation Work in Economic History at Chicago. Department of Economics, University of Maryland-Baltimore County. Unpublished manuscript.

Mitch, D., 2011. Economic history in departments of economics: the case of the University of Chicago, 1892 to the present. Social Science History 35 (2), 237–271.

Mitch, D., 2014. Chicago and economic history. In: Emmet, R.B. (Ed.), The Elgar Companion to the Chicago School of Economics. Edward Elgar, Northampton MA, pp. 114–127.

Olmstead, A., Rhode, P.W., 2018. Cotton, slavery, and the new history of capitalism. Explorations in Economic History 67 (1), 1–17.

Romer, C., 1994. The end of economic history. The Journal of Economic Education 25 (1), 49–66.

Rostow, W.W., 1960. The Stages of Economic Growth: A Non-Communist Manifesto. Cambridge University Press, Cambridge UK.

Solow, R., 1956. A contribution to the theory of economic growth. The Quarterly Journal of Economics 70 (1), 65–94.

Solow, R., 1957. Technical change and the aggregate production function. Review of Economics and Statistics 39 (3), 312–320.

Stigler, G., Stigler, S.M., Friedland, C., 1995. The journals of economics. Journal of Political Economy 103 (2), 331–359.

The two revolutions in economic history

2

Martina Cioni[a]**, Giovanni Federico**[b,c]**, and Michelangelo Vasta**[a,c]

[a]*Department of Economics and Statistics, University of Siena, Siena, Italy*
[b]*Division of Social Sciences, NYUAD, Abu Dhabi, United Arab Emirates*
[c]*CEPR, London, United Kingdom*

2.1 Introduction

Historical economics was born in the 1960s, but economic history has a long tradition. The first chair of Economic history at the University of Harvard was established in 1892 and the first field journal, the *Vierteljahrschrift für Sozial und Wirtschaftsgeschichte*, was published in German since 1903. The two professional associations, the English Economic History Society and the American Economic History Association were established respectively in 1926 and 1940, and they started to publish their journals, the *Economic History Review* and the *Journal of Economic History*, the following year. Economic history articles had been published in economics and history journals even before. The second issue of the *Quarterly Journal of Economics* included a history of land sales in the United States from 1785 onwards (Hart, 1887) and the third issue of the *Journal of Political Economy* a historical sketch of shipping in Scandinavia (Kiaer, 1893). The *American Economic Review* started its publications only in 1911, but the presidential address for 1912 dealt with the 'Economic utilization of history' (Farnam, 1912) – i.e. with history as source of quasi natural experiments (he quotes Erode's slaughtering of boys born in Bethlehem as an example).

In its first seventy years economic history was largely a historical discipline with little or no use of formal economic reasoning. Its nature started to change in 1958, with the publication in the *Journal of Political Economy* of an article by two Harvard economists on the efficiency of slavery (Conrad and Meyer, 1958). This event triggered the so called Cliometric Revolution and the marked the birth of Historical economics. Scholars such as the Nobel laureate Fogel harnessed economic theory and econometrics to address traditional issues in economic history, such as the contribution of railways to American economic growth (Fogel, 1962). Now, arguably, a Second Revolution is on-going. Unlike the Cliometric revolution, it features a change in the research questions, beyond the traditional boundaries of economic history, in two different (but partly overlapping) directions. First, scholars have started to look for the historical origins of current outcomes, hence persistence studies (henceforth PS). The idea of path dependency had first been put forward in a famous paper by David (1985) on the QWERTY keyboard, but arguably the Second Revolution was started by the publication of the seminal paper by Acemoglu et al. (2001) on the effect of colonial institutions on levels of development in 1995. Second, economists have extended to historical issues their interest in 'non-economic outcomes studies' (henceforth NEOS), which dates back at least to the seminal work by Becker (1957, 1978, 1981) on

The Handbook of Historical Economics. https://doi.org/10.1016/B978-0-12-815874-6.00008-3

17

the economics of discrimination and human behavior. This two pronged movement has attracted much attention from economists, also because the research questions of the Second Revolution fit well into recent trends in economics. Nowadays, economists are much more interested in empirical work, as opposed to pure theory, and in issues, such as growth and inequality, which lend themselves to historical perspective (Hamermesh, 2013; Cioni et al., 2020a). Moreover, PS tally well with the economists' instrumental view of history, as outlined by Abramitzky (2015: 1242): 'The typical modern economist does not share the view that history is interesting for its own sake [as economic historians]. Most economists care about the past only to the extent it sheds light on the present'. Actually, as argued more than one century ago by the Italian philosopher Benedetto Croce (1915), history is always useful to understand the present, but for most 'traditional' economic history literature the connection is loose and anyway left to the reader. In contrast, the persistence studies aim at establishing a direct and measurable connection between the past and the present (Voth, 2021). In the words of one the pioneers of this approach: 'The most enlightening papers are able to trace the full impact of a historical event through time, while examining specific channels and mechanisms' (Nunn, 2014: 347). Likewise, the diffusion of NEOS in economic history can be seen as a modern version of the 'imperialism' of economics on issues which often are related to the current political agenda (Angrist et al., 2020). The novelty here is the massive resort to econometric testing rather than to modelling as in the Becker tradition.

This chapter compares, as far as we know for the first time, these two revolutions. The literature on the Cliometric Revolution is extensive (e.g. Andreano, 1970; Fogel and Elton, 1983; Drukker, 2006; Lyons et al., 2007 and, for recent updated surveys, Haupert, 2019 and Margo, 2021). The literature on the Second Revolution is smaller, as one would expect for a more recent intellectual movement, but growing fast (Nunn, 2009, 2020; Spolaore and Wacziarg, 2013; Ashraf and Galor, 2018; Michalopoulos and Papaioannou, 2020; Voth, 2021). Yet, we feel that this chapter fills a major gap. First, as far as we know, the surveys focus on persistence studies, neglecting the NEOS. Second, and more importantly, the existing works on the two revolutions deal mostly with their methodological innovation and with only selected empirical results. In contrast, this chapter focuses on measurable characteristics, such as the share of 'revolutionary' articles on total, the affiliations of authors and the number of citations as a proxy for their scientific impact. We feel that the comparison with the successful first Cliometric Revolution can highlight some key features of the Second Revolution and its prospects.

Our quantitative analysis relies on two databases. The first one, which we have collected for our paper on the development of economic history as profession (Cioni et al., 2020b), includes all articles published in the top five economic history journals, the *Economic History Review* (EHR), the *Journal of Economic History* (JEH), *Explorations in Economic History* (EEH), the *European Review of Economic History* (EREH), and *Cliometrica* (CLIO). The second database, which we use in this chapter and in a companion paper (Cioni et al., 2020a), includes all articles on economic history issues published from 2001 to 2019 in thirteen economics journals: the top five, three other major generalist journals, two 'history-friendly' journals and three top field ones. The top five are of course the *American Economic Review* (AER), *Econometrica* (ECMA), the *Journal of Political Economy* (JPE), the *Quarterly Journal of Economics* (QJE), and the *Review of Economic Studies* (RESTUD). The second group, selected according to three rigid criteria,[1] includes other three generalist journals – the *Economic Journal* (*E J*),

---

[1] These criteria deal with the 'generalist nature' of the journal, the beginning of publication before 2001 and the high position in a set of ten recent rankings of economics journals, based on Bornmann et al. (2018). For a precise description of these criteria, see Cioni et al. (2020a, particularly Table A1, in the Appendix).

the *Journal of Economic Literature* (*JEL*), and the *Review of Economics and Statistics* (*RESTAT*). We have selected as 'history friendly' the two journals which were at the top of the rankings for economics journals in terms of number of citations made and received by economic history journals in 2017, according to the *Journal Citation Reports* (*JCR*) after *AER, JEL, QJE* and *JPE*: the *Journal of Development Economics* (*JDE*), the *Journal of Economic Growth* (*JEG*). Last but not least, we have included the three highest ranked field journals in the classification by (Kalaitzidakis et al., 2011, Table 1): the *Journal of Economic Theory* (*JET*), the *Journal of Monetary Economics* (*JME*), the *Journal of Public Economics* (*JPUB*).[2] We realize that, although extensive, our database cannot capture the whole development of the two revolutions. Our sample of journals is unavoidably limited. It does not include specialized and country/area economic history journals, which could have been useful to trace the success of the Cliometric Revolution outside Anglo-Saxon countries, nor other major economics journals which has published relevant work, such as the article by Guiso et al. (2016) on the long term effect of Medieval self-government on civic capital in Italy and by Grosjean (2014) on the transmission of the culture of violence among generations in the south of the United States. Furthermore, we do not include books or book chapters. Nowadays, they are generally used to illustrate wide research projects (Williamson, 2011) or to present general interpretations (Rosenthal and Wong, 2011), while they present first-hand research only in few cases, such as the chapter by Nunn (2015) on the persistent effects of exposition to missions on educational attainments in Africa. In contrast, books were very important during the Cliometric Revolution: both Fogel and North published their Nobel-winning work in books (Fogel, 1964, 1989; North, 1981, 1990).

In the next Section, we measure the world-wide diffusion of the Cliometric Revolution, and in Section 2.3, we outline very briefly the evolution of economic history in the two decades between the two revolutions. In the two following sections, we deal with the Second Revolution, tracing its evolution (Section 2.4), outlining its distinctive features with a simple taxonomy of articles and measuring their success in terms of citations (Section 2.5). Section 2.6 concludes with some musings about the future of the discipline.

2.2 The Cliometric Revolution

There is no need to delve in much detail about the origins and diffusion of the Cliometric Revolution. It suffices to recall that the key methodological innovation relative to the prevailing historical approach (rebranded 'traditional' by cliometricians in their aggressive campaigning) was the use of economic theory and statistical testing. Thus, in this Section, we trace its diffusion by measure separately the use of 'theory' and quantitative tools. We try to capture the use of theory by looking, with the advanced search tool of *Google Scholar*, for ten typical economic words (counterfactual, opportunity cost, demand elasticity, supply elasticity, consumer surplus, market equilibrium, equilibrium price, social savings, utility function, and total factor productivity) and we single our articles using three categories of quantitative tools (tables, figures - historical graphs, representations of market equilibria and so on - and econometric tests – regressions). We consider all the 3,552 articles published in the *EHR*,

---

[2] We have compiled this database by selecting articles by looking at their abstracts and/or content. See for details Cioni et al. (2020a).

JEH, and *EEH*, from their establishment to 2000.[3] We plot the results in Fig. 2.1, adding a vertical line in 1958, to mark the beginning of the Cliometric Revolution.

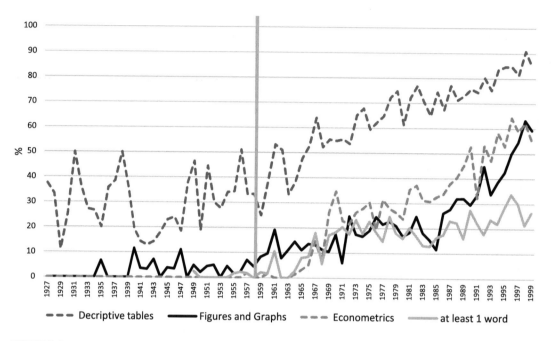

FIGURE 2.1

The use of 'theory' and quantitative tools in the three top economic history journals, *EHR, JEH*, and *EEH* (1927-2000). *Source*: Our own elaborations.

As expected, before the 1960s almost no articles in economic history journals used econometrics and very few contained 'Cliometric' words. Yet, quantitative economic history did exist. Admittedly, the share of articles with figures was low, but in all likelihood this reflected the high costs of reproduction rather than a hostility to visual presentations per se. In contrast, about one third of articles tabulated data, and the share was more than double in the British *EHR* (40.7%) than in the American *JEH* (19.6%). According to the influential opinion of Charles Feinstein "I've always thought that the Americans needed the Cliometric Revolution because their work had lacked quantitative analysis entirely; whereas in Britain, we'd had a very long tradition of it. This was not Cliometric in the shiny sense that it developed in America, with neoclassical economics and econometrics at its core, but it was deeply quantitative in terms of measuring what happened and making the numbers the basis for any analysis" (Thomas, 2007: 293).

---

[3] We have chosen 2000 as end date to avoid overlapping with our conventional dating of the Second Revolution. The database for this Section includes the *EHR* and *JEH* since the start of their publication, respectively in 1927 and 1941 and the *EEH* since the re-start of publication in 1969.

The onset of the Revolution seems to have boosted only the share of articles with tables. The shares of articles with figures and with econometrics changed very little in the late 1960s and rose decidedly only since the 1980s, possibly because of editorial constraints to publishing figures and to access to computing. There was no such constraint in the use of theory words and yet the share of articles with at least one 'Clio' word rose very slowly and remained fairly low to the end of the period, in spite of the abundant anecdotal evidence on the success of the Revolution. This gap might reflect the shortcomings of the word-based approach and/or a too conservative choice of words.[4] Indeed, our selection excludes seminal 'Cliometric' articles by Abramovitz (1986) on the determinants of convergence in productivity, and by Feinstein (1998) on standard of living and real wages in Britain. The share would have been much higher if we had included words such as 'productivity' or 'price', which however were widely used also by non-Cliometric authors.

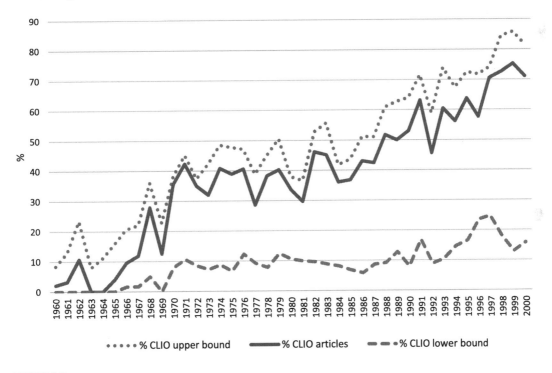

FIGURE 2.2

The diffusion of the Cliometric Revolution in the three top economic history journals, *EHR, JEH*, and *EEH* (1960-2000). *Source*: Our own elaborations.

In our baseline estimate (Fig. 2.2) we define as 'Cliometric' any article featuring either a 'theory' word or some econometric testing. The share of such articles did increase sharply in the late 1960s,

---

[4] The most common 'Clio' word was 'opportunity cost' – quoted a total of 215 times, followed by 'counterfactual' (205), 'total factor productivity' (154), 'demand elasticity', and 'supply elasticity' (respectively, 64 and 61 times), 'utility function' (60), 'market equilibrium' (40), 'social saving' (26), 'equilibrium price' (25), and 'consumer surplus' (24).

but then it hovered around two fifths until the mid-1980s (Fig. 2.2). At the turn of the 20th century, there were still a third of 'non-Cliometric' articles, at least in our definition, in the top three economic history journals. Fig. 2.2 plots also two alternative estimates as robustness check.

The upper bound adds articles with a figure and clearly does not make much difference. The lower bound refers to 'pure Cliometric' articles, featuring both a 'theory' word and some econometrics. They still accounted for less than a fifth of total articles even in the 1990s. This is clearly implausible and strongly suggests that the lower bound is too restrictive. Anyway, the key message from Fig. 2.2 seems to be that the Cliometric Revolution developed more slowly than one would expect from the ex-post accounts. The share of 'Cliometric' articles increased quite fast in the second half of the 1960s to about two fifths, but then it remained broadly stable for fifteen to twenty years.

One might explain the slow world-wide progress of the revolution with the stubborn resistance of non-American economic historians to the invasion of 'barbarians' (McCloskey, 1976), but, as Figs. 2.3 and 2.4 show, this is not entirely the case.

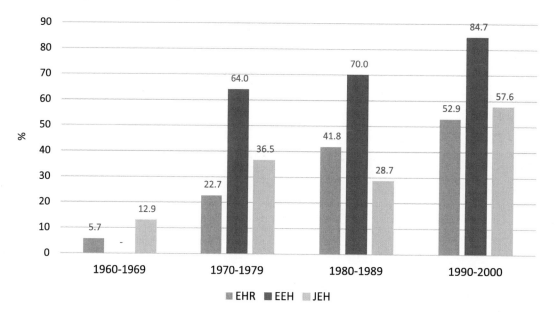

FIGURE 2.3

The share of Cliometric articles by journal (1960-2000). *Source*: Our own elaborations.

The proportion of 'Clio' articles (Fig. 2.3) was as expected by far the highest in *EEH*, which had been transformed in 1969 in an explicitly Cliometric journal.[5] Actually, the substantial share of non Cliometric articles in *EEH* further confirms that our definition is conservative. The share of 'Clio'

---

[5] The journal had been established in 1949 as *Explorations in Entrepreneurial History*, with Hugh G.J. Aitken as editor. It ceased in 1958 and restarted in 1963 with second series edited by Ralph L. Andreano. In 1969, the journal was renamed as *Explorations in Economic History*. Thus, we include it only since 1969, when it took the current denomination (personal communication by Ralph L. Andreano, March 2019).

articles in the 1960s and 1970s in the *JEH* remained low and indeed there is ample evidence of strong clashes within the Economic History Association and the editorial board on the publication strategy of the journal (Diebolt and Haupert, 2018). Less than a fifth of articles in *JEH* used econometrics or had a 'theory' word. As expected, these shares were even lower for *EHR* (respectively 10% and 6%), although over a half of articles had tables, consistently with Feinstein's remark about the use of data by British authors. The gap between *JEH* and *EHR* reversed in the 1980s and disappeared in the 1990s.

The slow diffusion of the Revolution emerges also by looking at the share of 'Cliometric' articles by country/area of affiliation of (fractionalized) authors (Fig. 2.4).[6]

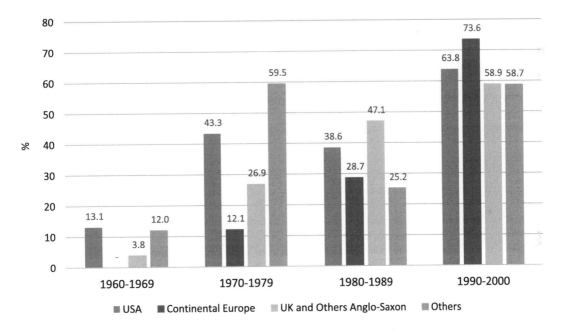

FIGURE 2.4

The share of Cliometric articles by country of affiliation (1960-2000). *Source*: Our own elaborations.

As expected, most of the early 'Cliometric' articles were published by American authors (77% in the 1960s, 71% in the 1970s) but even in the United States they did not account for the majority of contributions until the 1990s. The diffusion of 'Cliometric' articles in Great Britain and other Anglo-Saxon countries (including Canada) was very limited in the 1960s but their share rose substantially in the 1970s and the gap with the United States disappeared in the 1980s. There is no evidence of a flow of British Cliometricians seeking outlets in American journals for their work: the share of British

---

[6] Each author (and thus her institution and, ultimately, her country) is assigned the inverse of the number of authors of the article (0.5 if there are two authors, 0.33 if there are three and so on). We collect the affiliation as stated in the article at the time of publication and we use 'American' (or 'British') to refer to the institution and not to the nationality of the author.

authors in the two American journals (*EEH* and *JEH*) fluctuated around 5% in until the 1980s and reached a tenth of the total in the 1990s. Until 1990, very few authors from Continental Europe and from the rest of the world published any type of article, Cliometric or traditional, in American and British journals and thus the higher share of 'Cliometric' articles is hardly representative. The 1990s witnessed a sudden flourishing of the community of Cliometric economic historians in Continental Europe, who wrote about 8% of the 608 articles published in the three journals. Indeed, the growing supply of Cliometric articles in Continental Europe was a key factor in the establishment of two new journals, the *EREH* (since 1997) and the aptly named Cliometrica (*CLIO*) since 2007 (Cioni et al., 2020b).

Even if our conservative measure may not capture all true 'Cliometric' articles, one might conclude that by the turn of the 20th century, the Cliometric Revolution had won, at least in the most advanced countries. The approach was dominant in economics departments in the USA and, with some exception, in the United Kingdom and other Anglo-Saxon countries and had made huge inroads in (Western) Continental Europe.

2.3 Intermezzo: economic history at the turn of the 20th century

The optimistic conclusion of the previous section must be qualified. The situation differed in the rest of the world. Authors of articles in the top international field journals were, and still are, a minority of economic historians.[7] The qualitative account by Boldizzoni and Hudson (2016) reminds that a sizeable number of non-Cliometric economic historians are still active in many countries. Furthermore, there was a large number of business historians in all countries, with their own journals. Furthermore, in the cradle of the Revolution, historians and economists were losing interest for economic history in spite of optimism by Sutch (1991). The so-called cultural turn in history destroyed any common ground with economic history, while the economists' interests moved away from long-term growth and other history-related issues towards micro-founded research with strong policy implication (Heckman, 1997). This trend had been detected as early as in the mid-1970s by McCloskey (1976) and continued, in spite of the valiant attempts of some prominent economists, including two Nobel prize winners, Arrow and Solow, to convince fellow economists of the relevance of economic history (Parker, 1986).

In Fig. 2.5, we proxy the impact of economic history on economics with the share of articles on historical issues in the three oldest of the top five journals, the *AER*, the *JPE*, and the *QJE* since 1925, with data from McCloskey (1976), Abramitzky (2015), and our own.

The comparison between shares in 1925-1944 and 1945-1974 shows clearly the loss in status of economic history, likely as a result of the mathematization of economics (Debreu, 1991). The long-run averages may hide any short term rise in the early stages of the Cliometric Revolution, but it is striking how low the share was already in the second half of the 1970s. It did rise in the late 1990s and early 2000s and this increase has been interpreted as a renewed integration of economic history into economics (Abramitzky, 2015; Margo, 2018). In our companion paper (Cioni et al., 2020a), we

---

[7] Baten and Muschallik (2012) estimate that in 2010 there were up 10,700 economic historians active in the world in 2010 and less than one quarter of them have published an article in the top five economic history journals (Cioni et al., 2020b).

argue that this claim is excessive. There we use a reduced version of our database, which includes only the top five and three other major generalist economics journals (using the other journals for the robustness checks only) for the period 2001-2018. We base this statement on four sets of results.

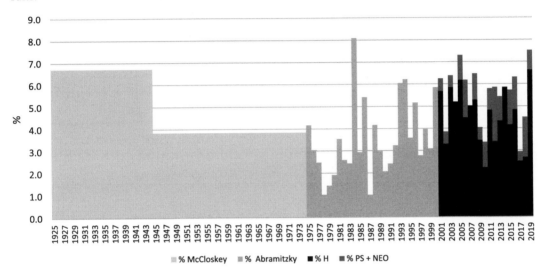

FIGURE 2.5

Share of economic history articles in the three top economics journals (*AER, JPE, QJE*), 1925-2019. *Source*: 1925-1974: McCloskey (1976), 1975-2000: economic history articles (Abramitzky, 2015) and total articles (Card and DellaVigna, 2013, Appendix); 2001-2019: our own data.

i) the share of economic history articles in the top ten economics journals has remained pretty stable around 4% over the whole period 2001-2018, without any clear upward trend. The share of economic history articles is substantially higher and growing in time only in the two 'history-friendly' journals (*JDE, JEG*). They have published a total of 101 articles in economic history, accounting for 5.8% of the total in the whole period, but for 0.8% in 2001-2004 and for 12% in 2015-2018. However, they have been selected exactly for this reason: it would be easy to find equally prestigious journals with hardly any article in economic history;

ii) there are statistically significant differences in topics, periods, methods, and geographical area between economic history articles in top field and in economics journals.[8] Articles in economics journals deal more frequently with institutions with than any other topic, focus more on recent past (and on the very long run), are technically more sophisticated and deal more with any area except the United Kingdom, which is the subject of many papers in the *EHR*;

iii) there is very little overlapping between authors of articles in economic history journals and in economics journals. Out of the 2,040 authors included in the database, 1,529 have published only

---

[8] These results are obtained by running a set of multinomial logistic regressions with the number of articles for each different category as dependent variable.

in economic history journals, 372 only in economics journals and a mere 139 (6.8% of the total) in both economic history and economics journals. Furthermore, the distribution of authors by country of affiliation is heavily skewed towards the United States in economics journals and much more balanced in economic history journals. American affiliations account for two thirds of authors in economics journals and for a third in field journals, as many as British and Continental European universities;

iv) last but not least, publishing in economics journals yielded more citations than in economic history journals, about 4.6 citations per year.[9] However, the gap was really huge only with the top five (5.8 more citations per year) and relatively small with the three other generalist economics journals (3.2). Remarkably, these latter got less citations than the best articles, here defined as the top decile of the distribution, in economic history journals.

2.4 The Second Revolution: a general view

Overall, our two databases include a total of 2,888 articles on economic history issues, published from 2001 to 2019 in the top five economic history journals (2,286) and in the thirteen economic journals selected (602) – in the top five economics journals (220), in the other three major generalist economics journals (186), in the two 'history friendly' journals (118), and in the three top field ones (78). In this Section, we focus on PS and on NEOS, labelling all others as 'traditional' economic history articles. We have classified as PS any article that relates a present outcome to some specific event which had happened at least one century earlier. We have classified as NEOS any article which deals with a non-economic outcome, including domestic political events (elections, state-building and so on), international political events (wars, etc.), religion, and some types of personal behavior, such as divorce. These are arguably quite conservative definitions, both in the length of the period between the event and its outcome and in our definition of 'non-economic' event. This latter excludes, as economic outcomes, education, human capital, urbanization, migration, mortality, and also trust/social capital. A fortiori, we do not include the very many articles which explain economic outcomes with political or social causes. In both cases, a less conservative definition (e.g. a lower span of time between the event and the outcome for the PS or the inclusion of education among the non-economic outcomes) would have boosted the impact of the Second Revolution.

In Fig. 2.5, we distinguish the PS and NEOS from 'traditional' economic history articles published by plotting them in red (dark gray in print version). The figure makes it quite clear that the Second Revolution is a recent phenomenon and that the publication of a growing number of PS and NEOS has prevented the share of economic history articles to slide down again. Table 2.1 extends the comparison to all eighteen journals.[10]

The Table highlights two stylized facts. First, the Second Revolution has made very little inroads in economic history journals. No PS have been published until 2019, and the share of NEOS is almost

---

[9] This figure is obtained from a regression with number of citations per year explained by dummies for groups of journals (reference group: economic history journals), controlling for topic, period, year of publication, length, number of authors, gender, affiliation and so on.

[10] The sum of columns PS and NEOS exceeds the total because ten articles, such as Bertocchi and Dimico (2019) on the determinants of female in HIV infection in Africa, look for roots of a non-economic outcome in the distant past and thus belong to both categories.

Table 2.1 The total number of PS and NEOS (2001-2019).

	PS	%	NEOS	%	Total	%
Economics	45	9.6	53	11.3	92	19.7
Economics (history-friendly journals)	21	15.7	10	7.5	27	20.1
Economic history	–	–	33	1.4	33	1.4
Total	66	2.3	96	3.3	152	5.3

Source: Our own elaborations.

negligible both on the aggregate of all five journals and also on each of them, the highest share being 2% for *EEH* (a total of eleven articles). These low figures are hardly surprising, given the strong incentives for economists to publish in economics journals and possibly some perplexity among editors of economic history journals about unconventional topics. Second, the overall number of PS and NEOS is small and indeed they account for less than 1% of all articles published in the thirteen journals. However, their combined share on economic history articles only is not so tiny, and, above all, it is unevenly distributed between journals, as Table 2.2 shows. Six journals (*AER, QJE, RESTAT, EJ, JDE,* and *JEG*) account for more than 80% of the PS and NEOS, and also separately for the two categories. The share of the Second Revolution articles in these journals is correspondingly higher, up to almost a third for the *JEG*.[11]

Table 2.2 Number and share PS and NEOS, by journal (2001-2019).

Journal	PS	NEOS	PS+NEOS[*]	% on PS+NEOS	% on economic history articles
AER	9	7	16	13.4	15.5
ECMA	4	5	9	7.6	75.0
JPE	–	2	2	1.7	5.9
QJE	9	9	17	14.3	26.6
RESTUD	1	1	2	1.7	28.6
E J	11	16	23	19.3	25.3
JET	–	–	–	–	–
JME	1	–	1	0.8	2.1
JPUB	–	5	5	4.2	17.9
RESTAT	10	8	17	14.3	21.5
JDE	9	7	13	10.9	17.1
JEG	11	3	13	10.9	31.0
JEL	1	–	1	0.8	6.3
Total	66	63	119	100	19.8

[*] *The total is not equal to the sum of the PS and NEOS because 10 articles belong to both categories.*
Source: Our own elaborations.

---

[11] The very high share of PS and NEOS in *ECMA* is due to the very limited number of economic history articles.

Fig. 2.6 adds a time dimension to the data of Table 2.1. The shares of PS and NEOS in economics journals fluctuated widely in the short term, as a consequence of their small number, but their trend is unmistakeably upward, from 6.2% in the first five years to 21% in 2010-14 and to 33% in 2015-19. Over half both of the PS (37 out of 66) and the NEOS (37 out of 63) have been published in the last five years. By definition, this rise has widened the gap between the journals more open to the Second Revolution and the rest.

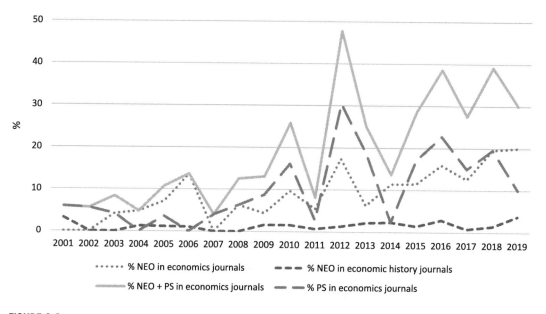

FIGURE 2.6

Share of PS and NEOS on economic history articles, by group of journal (2001-2019). *Source*: Our own elaborations.

The 602 economic history articles published in the thirteen economics journals from 2001 to 2019 have been written by a total of 843 authors: who were they?

First, as Fig. 2.7 shows, they were predominantly affiliated to American universities: these latter accounted for the majority of (fractionalized) contribution both for 'traditional' economic history articles and for PS and NEOS in all the thirteen economics journals and for three quarters of contributions in the top five (76% for 'traditional' economic history, 78.2% for PS and NEOS combined). This contrasts with the current almost perfectly balanced distribution among the three main areas in economic history journals, as a result of the evolution outlined in Section 2.3. Note that Americans prevailed, though less clearly, also among the authors of NEOS on economic history journals. The Second Revolution, as the Cliometric one, is an American movement but its success in getting articles published in prestigious economics journals does not depend much on their typology. Authors from American universities are comparatively more successful than British and other Europeans in publishing economic history articles in top economics journals, whatever the nature of the article.

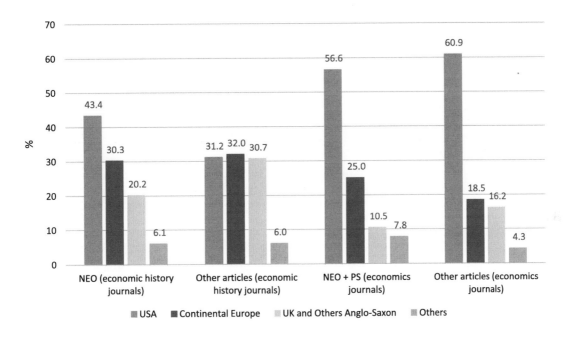

FIGURE 2.7

Affiliation's area by contributions (2001-2019). *Source*: Our own elaborations.

Second, divisions between specialized 'tribes' (Cioni et al., 2020b) run deep also among economists, as shown in Fig. 2.8.[12]

Over nine tenths of authors in economics journals (779 out of 843) have published only one category of article. Most of the remaining 64 have authored a PS or a NEOS and a 'traditional' economic history article, while the overlap between PS and NEOS is minimal (8 authors). This suggests a specialization along research questions and methods rather than on history per se. This is quite clear for authors of PS – they are mostly economists who deal with other issues and publish in economics journals.

The case is somewhat more nuanced for authors of NEOS, as shown by their overall publication pattern. From one hand, publishing NEOS in economics journals was clearly not their main focus. Almost all of them (96) have authored only one NEOS, 15 two and only one (Voth) three. Almost all authors of NEOS are economists, few of them economic historians, while only four out of 112 authors are clearly political scientists. A substantial number of authors of NEOS (41) have zero articles in journals of political science and related fields. They were scholars who studied non-economic outcomes in history as part of their own research agenda in economics, which may of course include non-economic

---

[12] Consistently with our overall view about the separation of 'tribes' (Cioni et al., 2020b), Fig. 2.8 omits authors of NEOS in economic history journals.

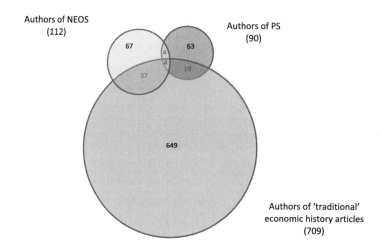

FIGURE 2.8

Authors publishing in economics journals (2001-2019). *Source*: Our own elaborations.

outcomes in the present. However, eleven of them have also published their research in one of the top economic history journals. In contrast, about half of authors (53) of NEOS seems to have a composite research agenda. Indeed, they publish in journals of political science or related fields (e.g. law and economics and public choice). Almost a quarter of them (12) have also published in at least one of the top three generalist science journals (Nature, Science, and Proceedings of National Academy of Science), and twelve of them have also published in the top economic history journals. Finally, other 14 authors, although have not published in political science and related fields, show a composite publication record since they have published in social science journals, medicine journals, and/or in the top three generalist science journals.

Last but not least, the Second Revolution, as almost all new intellectual movements, started in a specific location. The early cliometricians were affiliated to universities all over the United States, but since 1960 they gathered in an annual conference in Purdue University. The birthplace of PS was Massachusetts Institute of Technology (MIT), or Boston at large. The first four PS over time in our database were published by MIT authors (Acemoglu et al., 2001, 2002; Acemoglu et al., 2003; Banerjee and Iyer, 2005), the fifth by two Harvard University graduates (Gennaioli and Rainer, 2007) and the sixth by Nunn (2008). Boston still wields a huge influence in PS. Harvard and MIT account for a sixth of all (fractionalized) PS in the database, for more than one third in the top five, and have at least one author in almost two thirds of PS (vs. 40% for NEOS and 'traditional' economic history articles). However, the Revolution has spread well beyond the banks of the river Charles. The ten top world universities, as ranked by Quacquarelli and Symonds (www.qs.com) in 2019, for economics account for 30.7% of (fractionalized) PS, double of the share for the NEOS (17.4%).[13] Actually, the number

---

[13] The share of top universities were decidedly lower for 'traditional' economic history articles, both if published in economics journals (19.4%) and in economic history ones (13.4%) The top universities are: Harvard University, Massachusetts Institute of

of total contributions is so small that having one or two prominent scholars in the field is sufficient to rank in the list of the top ten universities for PS. Indeed, this includes only four universities (Harvard, MIT, University of Oxford, and London School of Economics and Political Science) ranked in the top ten by Quacquarelli and Symonds and we find also other two European universities such as University of Gothenburg and Universitat Pompeu Fabra, and one South American, the Pontificia Universidad Catolica de Chile. From this point of view, the NEOS are slightly different: Harvard remains by far the most prolific producer of contributions (7.4% of the total), but all the other nine top universities account jointly for 10.1% and only one of them, University of California Berkeley (UCB), appears in the list in the tenth position. However, also in this case the top ten list is geographically diversified, featuring two European universities (Stockholm University and University of Munich) and one Asian, the Hong Kong University of Science and Technology (see Table A.1 in the Appendix for the complete list for all three categories of articles).

These results are not really earth-shattering – it is well known that many authors of articles on the most important journals hail from top research universities. The question is whether the share of latter for PS or NEOS differs from the percentage for economics at large. For this comparison, we rely on the data by Heckman and Moktan (2020: tab. 8) which refers to the (non-fractionalized) share of authors from slightly different list of top twelve universities in 2001-2016.[14] With these criteria, authors from top universities account for 31% of PS (vs. 30.7% with our criteria) and for 28.6% of NEOS (vs. 17.4% with our criteria): both percentages are decidedly lower than the figure for all articles published in the top five (48.2%). This is a consequence of the unbalanced geographical distribution of authors of PS and NEOS. By definition, authors from all top universities in Heckman and Moktan (2020) list have published widely in top five journals, but no affiliate of some of them, such as Columbia University, Northwestern University, or UCL have so far published a PS or a NEOS.

Summing up, the Second Revolution is a prevalently an American movement, which is developing in few top universities and has got a firm foothold in prestigious economics journals but it is still comparatively small. Jointly, NEOS and PS still account for a minority of economic history articles even in economics journals, and so far have made almost no inroad in economic history ones. Thus, it can be regarded as somewhat less successful than the Cliometric Revolution in a comparable stage of its development. One might argue that comparison is to some extent unfair. First, the competition for publication in economics journals is very tough and the early cliometricians seem to have not been very successful in top economics journals either (see Fig. 2.3). Furthermore, our work does not cover the most recent publications in journals (in 2020 and early view) as well as the vast body of on-going research, so far available only in working papers and early drafts. Of course, it is impossible to predict how many of these works will be published in one of the thirteen journals we cover.

Technology (MIT), Stanford University, University of California Berkeley (UCB), University of Chicago, the London School of Economics and Political Science (LSE), Princeton University, Yale University, University of Oxford, and University of Cambridge.

[14] The twelve universities in Heckman and Moktan paper (2020) are: Chicago University, Columbia University, Harvard University, MIT, New York University, Northwestern University, Princeton University, Stanford University, University of California Berkeley (UCB), University of Pennsylvania, Yale University, and University College London.

2.5 The Second Revolution: beyond the traditional boundaries of economic history

The discussion so far has considered jointly PS and NEOS in opposition to 'traditional' economic history, but they are really two different categories of articles by different authors. The limited number of articles makes an econometric analysis impossible, thus we will highlight the distinctive features of the two approaches with a simple taxonomy, focusing on the main outcome (i.e. the dependent variable of the main regression of the article), time period, and geographical area.

In a nutshell, our classification shows that the typical NEOS deals with 'domestic politics' issues in 'modern' period in 'OECD countries' (Table 2.3).

Table 2.3 The NEOS and their citation success (2001-2019).

	Number of articles	Average Citations per year	Median Citations per year
Main outcome			
Personal behavior	26	2.5	1.5
Domestic politics	50	4.0	2.2
International politics	20	2.8	1.4
Time period			
Early modern and medieval	15	2.5	2.2
Modern	68	3.2	1.1
Long run	13	5.0	5.1
Geographical area			
Africa	6	2.7	2.4
America	1	1.6	1.6
Asia	6	5.1	4.7
OECD countries	66	3.4	1.2
World	17	3.1	1.8
Total	*96*	*3.4*	*1.8*

Source: Our own elaborations.

About half (26) of the articles on domestic politics deal with 20th century issues and three quarters (40) on OECD countries. Unsurprisingly, given the affiliation of authors, a particular attention is paid to the United States which account for one fourth (23) of all articles. Quite a few articles deal with persecutions and authoritarian regimes (10), with a fascination for the rise to power of Nazi party in Germany, with articles on the role of social capital (Satyanath et al., 2017), of the radio (Adena et al., 2015), and of the economic policies of the last governments of the Weimar republic (Stögbauer and Komlos, 2004). Outside the core issue of 'domestic politics' articles, there are quite a few articles on religion (see, Becker et al., 2021), dealing with issues such as the characteristics of State religion (Barro and McCleary, 2005) or with the role of the Protestant Reformation on secularization (Cantoni et al., 2018). The works labelled as 'international politics' focus mainly on conflicts. Harrison and Wolf (2012) deal with factors determining the frequency of wars in general, while others deal with more specific issues, such as the effects of fluctuations in rainfall on nomadic incursions in the Heavenly empire (Bai and Kung, 2011) or of different American bombing strategies on Vietnam insurgency (Dell and Querubin, 2018). The category 'personal behavior' is a very mixed bunch, with topics such as the behavior of soldiers during the American civil war (Costa and Khan, 2003), the effects of unilateral divorce laws on the divorce rates (Wolfers, 2006), and the origins of culture of violence against women in Spain (Tur-Prats, 2019).

Table 2.3 shows also that NEOS have not been particularly successful in terms of citations, without much difference among issues.[15] Each of them got on average about twice the citations of articles in economic history journals (mean 1.4 and median 1.0), but half those of 'traditional' economic history articles in economics journal (mean 6.2 and median 3.2). These figures are negatively affected by the poor performance of the 33 NEOS in economic history journals, which received on average only 1.0 citations. The most successful of them, the article by Engermann and Sokoloff (2005) on the evolution of suffrage in the New world, has received 7.6 citations per year (118 altogether) and the second most cited only 2.8 citations per year. For a comparison, the two most successful NEOS in economics journals, Wolfers on divorce (2006) and Becker et al. (2016) on trust and corruption on Habsburg Empire, received respectively 19.7 and 18.2 citations per year. Omitting them from the computation increase somewhat the performance of NEOS, but the 63 articles published in the economics journals have still been cited less (average 4.6 citations per year, median 3.2) than 'traditional' economic history articles. In other words, the NEOS approach seems to be still a niche one, which struggles to attract attention outside economics, particularly within the community of political scientists.

In contrast with the NEOS, the PS have been extremely successful in term of citations (Table 2.4). The figures are biased upwards by the outstanding success of the articles by Acemoglu Johnson and Robinson, the already quoted seminal paper on the colonial roots of underdevelopment (2001) and the other on reversals of fortunes (2002), which have received respectively 205.8 and 84.7 citations per year. Without them, the average and median number of citations reduces to 10.9 and 5.2, still well above the figures for 'traditional' economic history articles, let alone the NEOS. The top NEOS has been cited less than thirteen PS, including the famous articles on the effect of slave trade on trust and growth (Nunn, 2008; Nunn and Wantchekon, 2011), and on origins of gender roles in agriculture (Alesina et al., 2013).

The paper by Acemoglu et al. (2001) is not only the most highly cited in the whole database: it has had and still has a strong influence on the entire research agenda of persistence studies. They set out to explain the level of development in 1995, and GDP or its proxies, such as urbanization rate or earth lightning, as the outcome in about a half of the PS. Most articles on other outcomes, such as 'well-being' and 'institutions', focus on some limited geographical areas and this might explain their relatively low impact. For instance, Akçomak et al. (2016) deal with the beneficial effects of the Brethren of the Common Life (a late 14th century religious sect), on literacy, book production, and city growth in the Netherlands in the following century. Again following Acemoglu et al. (2001, 2002), most PS deal with former colonial areas: Africa alone is the subject of more articles than all OECD countries, and jointly with Asia and Latin America, accounts for two thirds of area-specific articles. The strong interest in colonization and in Africa explains the high number of entries in the 'modern' category, but several PS in the 'early modern and medieval' one refer to long run effects of colonial institutions and policies. Dell (2010) argues that the mita, a type of forced labor for silver mines in Peru,

---

[15] In the model from Cioni et al. (2020a), after controlling for type of journal, the dummy for PS, and the interaction term with top five are both positive but not significant. Re-running with a dummy for NEOS yields a striking result: a NEOS is likely to get 1.3 citations per year less than other articles.

Table 2.4 The PS and their citation success (2001-2019).

	Number of articles	Average Citations per year	Median Citations per year
Main outcome			
GDP level or growth	21	27.6	7.8
Proxies of GDP (Urbanization, pop. density, etc.)	10	10.4	5.2
Institutions	7	6.2	5.1
Well-being (health, education)	16	5.0	3.1
Other	12	14.8	7.0
Time event			
Early modern and medieval	25	10.2	5.3
Modern	25	22.2	6.4
Long run	16	11.0	4.7
Type event			
Pre-colonial institutions	12	14.3	6.5
Colonialism (colonial institutions and policies)	20	28.3	8.7
Religious institutions	11	4.4	3.1
Permanent characteristics	14	11.8	5.0
Other	9	3.9	2.3
Geographical area			
Africa	15	13.6	8.6
Asia	5	8.5	5.6
America	8	15.4	2.9
OECD countries	14	5.4	3.0
World	24	22.6	6.2
Total	66	*14.9*	5.5

Source: Our own elaborations.

established in 1573, still affects welfare of the Peruvian communities, but her results are controversial (Arroyo Abad and Maurer, 2019). Quite a few 'early modern and medieval' articles deal with the slave trade (officially abolished in 1807) or with pre-colonial states or institutions, such as the Kuba Kingdom of the central Africa (Lowes et al., 2017). In contrast, only six PS deal with the long-term effect of events in OECD countries and all of them with on religion. Andersen et al. (2017) trace the origins of Protestant values (hard work, thrift and so on) to the predication of the Circestians in early Medieval Europe and Voigtländer and Voth (2012) look for medieval origins of anti-semitic violence in Nazi Germany. The category 'long run' is reserved to articles on effects of 'events' very far in time - such as the migration of early humans or the Neolithic revolution, respectively on genetic diversity and ethnofractionalization (Ashraf and Galor, 2013; Ahlerup and Olsson, 2012) and on the adoption of collectivist values (Olsson and Paik, 2016). Last but not least, the legacy of Acemoglu, Johnson and Robinson lives also in the type of event. One third of articles deals with colonial institutions and policies, and another one third with issues, such as the effects of missions ('religious institutions') and slave trade ('pre-colonial institutions'), which are naturally related to the colonial past. The 'permanent characteristics' include pre-historical events, such as the already quoted migrations out of Africa, and environmental features such as the suitability of land to different crops (Alesina et al., 2013) or the susceptibility to weather shocks, which according to Ashraf and Michalopoulos (2015) determined the Neolithic transition from hunting gathering to agriculture. Actually, hardly any PS article deals with a specific historical 'event' in the narrow meaning of the word.

2.6 Conclusions

This chapter has highlighted a deep difference between the two revolutions. The Cliometric Revolution was initiated by young economic historians who aimed at transforming the field, arguing that their combination of formal theory and econometrics would yield better results than the traditional historical methods of the previous generation. Indeed, they were successful and achieved intellectual dominance of economic history, at least in the Anglo-Saxon countries and, some years later, in Western Europe too. In contrast, the Second Revolution has been started by economists and does not entail any methodological innovation. The typical PS or NEOS tend to use more extensively advanced econometrics techniques, within the constraints of the available data, but the real novelty is in the research questions they address. The NEOS extend their gaze well beyond the traditional boundaries of economic history, while for PS history is a canvas which authors paint with images of their interest.

The Second Revolution has not escaped criticism, even if there is nothing comparable to the Methodenstreit which engulfed the Cliometric one. Predictably, the discussion has focused on the PS, as the NEOS, as an extension to history of a consolidated approach within economics, do not imply any major intellectual breakthrough. Some critics have focused on specific technical issues, such as data handling by Acemoglu and his co-authors (Albouy, 2012; Acemoglu et al., 2012; Kopsidis and Bromley, 2016), the omission of control for spatial autocorrelation in many well-known PS studies (Kelly, 2019) and the possibility that historical instruments weight too much a subset of observations (Bisin and Moro, 2021). However, there are two more general methodological points. First, Austin (2008) has questioned the very idea of a measurable connection between events in the past and present day-outcomes. In his view, neglecting the effects of other historical development in the meanwhile imply a 'compression of history', and thus ultimately produces spurious correlation. Voth (2021) introduces an insightful distinction among PS which speaks to this criticism. Some of them 'regress outcomes (today) on historical variables that are quite different from the past', while in other the outcome and the past variables are 'identical or very close' (e.g. cultural beliefs). Of course, the former category ('apples and oranges') is much more open to the risk of spurious correlation than the latter ('apples on apples'), unless the hypothesized causal relation is based on some independent theoretical framework ('apples and oranges with theory').

It is too early to predict whether the Second Revolution will succeed as the Cliometric one and how this will shape the future of economic history. There might be a new synthesis, with scholars integrating a wider range of research questions, 'traditional', PS, and NEOS, with (in all likelihood) new and more sophisticated econometric techniques, using whenever possible big data. Or perhaps the field will splinter, with persistence economists invoking more and more events to explain a limited set of relevant outcomes (or a large set of much less relevant ones) in economics departments, economists interested in political science issues (or in NEOS in general) in political science departments, and economic historians publishing 'traditional' papers in field journals trying to convince the economists that economic history research questions are still worth of attention.

2.7 **Appendix**

Table A.1 Top 10 institutional affiliations by number of contributions by category of articles.

#	H		PS		NEOS	
	Institutions	*%*	*Institutions*	*%*	*Institutions*	*%*
1	Harvard University	4.5	Harvard University	9.4	Harvard University	7.4
2	University of Chicago	3.1	Massachusetts Institute of Technology	8.0	University of Pennsylvania	5.1
3	University of California Los Angeles	2.7	Brown University	7.2	Hong Kong University of Science and Technology	3.4
4	University of California Berkeley	2.3	University of California Merced	3.3	George Mason University	3.1
5	London School of Economics and Political Science	2.1	University of Oxford	3.3	University of Pittsburgh	2.8
6	University of Michigan Ann Arbor	2.1	Pontificia Universidad Catolica de Chile	3.3	University of Munich	2.7
7	Stanford University	2.1	London School of Economics and Political Science	3.0	Stockholm University	2.6
8	Columbia University	1.9	University of Gothenburg	3.0	Bar-Ilan University	2.6
9	New York University	1.9	Universitat Pompeu Fabra University of Michigan Ann Arbor Southern Methodist University	2.5	University of California Los Angeles	2.3
10	Massachusetts Institute of Technology	1.7			University of California Berkeley	2.3

Acknowledgments

We are grateful to Mattia Bertazzini, Samuel Bowles, Gabriele Cappelli, Robert Margo, and Tiziano Razzolini for helpful comments and suggestions. A special thanks is due to Ran Abramitzky and Stefano DellaVigna for sharing their data with us. We also thank Sara Pecchioli for her excellent research assistance. This paper has benefited from the comments of all participants at the Riccardo Faini CEIS seminars held in Rome (Tor Vergata, 2019), at the Galatina Summer Meeting (Galatina, 2019), at the European Historical Economics Society Conference (Paris, 2019), and at the 2019 Handbook of Historical Economics Conference (New York, 2019). The usual disclaimer applies.

References

Abramitzky, R., 2015. Economics and the modern economic historian. The Journal of Economic History 75 (4), 1240–1250.

Abramovitz, M., 1986. Catching up, forging ahead, and falling behind. The Journal of Economic History 46 (2), 385–406.

Acemoglu, D., Johnson, S., Robinson, J.A., 2001. The colonial origins of comparative development: an empirical investigation. The American Economic Review 91 (5), 1369–1401.

Acemoglu, D., Johnson, S., Robinson, J.A., 2002. Reversal of fortune: geography and institutions in the making of the modern world income distribution. The Quarterly Journal of Economics 117 (4), 1231–1294.

Acemoglu, D., Johnson, S., Robinson, J.A., 2012. The colonial origins of comparative development: an empirical investigation: reply. The American Economic Review 102 (6), 3077–3110.

Acemoglu, D., Johnson, S., Robinson, J.A., Thaicharoen, Y., 2003. Institutional causes, macroeconomic symptoms: volatility, crises and growth. Journal of Monetary Economics 50 (1), 49–123.

Adena, M., Enikolopov, R., Petrova, M., Santarosa, V., Zhuravskaya, E., 2015. Radio and the rise of the Nazis in prewar Germany. The Quarterly Journal of Economics 130 (4), 1885–1939.

Ahlerup, P., Olsson, O., 2012. The roots of ethnic diversity. Journal of Economic Growth 17 (2), 71–102.

Akçomak, İ.S., Webbink, D., ter Weel, B., 2016. Why did the Netherlands develop so early? The legacy of the brethren of the common life. The Economic Journal 126 (593), 821–860.

Albouy, D.Y., 2012. The colonial origins of comparative development: an empirical investigation: comment. The American Economic Review 102 (6), 3059–3076.

Alesina, A., Giuliano, P., Nunn, N., 2013. On the origins of gender roles: women and the plough. The Quarterly Journal of Economics 128 (2), 469–530.

Andersen, T.B., Bentzen, J., Dalgaard, C.J., Sharp, P., 2017. Pre-reformation roots of the protestant ethic. The Economic Journal 127 (604), 1756–1793.

Andreano, R., 1970. The New Economic History: Recent Papers on Methodology. John Wiley and Sons, Oxford.

Angrist, J., Azoulay, P., Ellison, G., Hill, R., Feng Lu, S., 2020. Inside job or deep impact? Extramural citations and the influence of economic scholarship. Journal of Economic Literature 58 (1), 3–52.

Arroyo Abad, L., Maurer, N., 2019. The long shadow of history? The impact of colonial labor institutions on economic development in Peru. SSRN: https://ssrn.com/abstract=3559510.

Ashraf, Q.H., Galor, O., 2013. The 'Out of Africa' hypothesis, human genetic diversity, and comparative economic development. The American Economic Review 103 (1), 1–46.

Ashraf, Q.H., Galor, O., 2018. The macrogenoeconomics of comparative development. Journal of Economic Literature 56 (3), 1119–1155.

Ashraf, Q.H., Michalopoulos, S., 2015. Climatic fluctuations and the diffusion of agriculture. Review of Economics and Statistics 97 (3), 589–609.

Austin, G., 2008. Resources, techniques, and strategies south of the Sahara: revising the factor endowments perspective on African economic development, 1500-2000. Economic History Review 61 (3), 587–624.

Bai, Y., Kung, J., 2011. Climate shocks and sino-Nomadic conflict. Review of Economics and Statistics 93 (3), 970–981.

Banerjee, A., Iyer, L., 2005. History, institutions and economic performance: the legacy of colonial land tenure system in India. The American Economic Review 95 (4), 1190–1213.

Barro, R.J., McCleary, R.M., 2005. Which countries have state religions? The Quarterly Journal of Economics 120 (4), 1331–1370.

Baten, J., Muschallik, J., 2012. The global status of economic history. Economic History of Developing Regions 27 (1), 93–113.

Becker, G.S., 1957. The Economics of Discrimination Chicago. University of Chicago Press, Chicago.

Becker, G.S., 1978. The Economic Approach to Human Behavior. University of Chicago Press, Chicago.

Becker, G.S., 1981. Treatise on the Family. Harvard University Press, Cambridge.

Becker, S.O., Boeckh, K., Hainz, C., Woessmann, L., 2016. The empire is dead, long live the empire! Long-run persistence of trust and corruption in the bureaucracy. The Economic Journal 126 (590), 40–74.

Becker, S.O., Rubin, J., Woessmann, L., 2021. Religion in economic history: a survey. In: Bisin, A., Federico, G. (Eds.), The Handbook of Historical Economics. Elsevier. Chapter 20 (in this book).

Bertocchi, G., Dimico, A., 2019. The long-term determinants of female HIV infection in Africa: the slave trade, polygyny, and sexual behavior. Journal of Development Economics 140, 90–105.

Bisin, A., Moro, A., 2021. LATE for history. In: Bisin, A., Federico, G. (Eds.), The Handbook of Historical Economics. Elsevier. Chapter 10 (in this book).

Boldizzoni, F., Hudson, P. (Eds.), 2016. Routledge Handbook of Global Economic History. Routledge, London.

Bornmann, L., Butz, A., Wohlrabe, K., 2018. What are the top five journals in economics? A new meta-ranking. Applied Economics 50 (6), 659–675.

Cantoni, D., Dittmar, J., Yuchtman, N., 2018. Religious competition and reallocation: the political economy of secularization in the protestant reformation. The Quarterly Journal of Economics 133 (4), 2037–2096.

Card, D.E., DellaVigna, S., 2013. Nine facts about top journals in economics. Journal of Economic Literature 51 (1), 144–161.

Cioni, M., Federico, G., Vasta, M., 2020a. Three tribes: the uneasy relations between economics and economic history. Department of Economics and Statistics Working Paper, University of Siena, n. 842.

Cioni, M., Federico, G., Vasta, M., 2020b. The long-term evolution of economic history: evidence from the top five journals (1927-2017). Cliometrica 14 (1), 1–39.

Conrad, A.H., Meyer, J.R., 1958. The economics of slavery in the Ante Bellum South. Journal of Political Economy 66 (2), 95–130.

Costa, D.L., Khan, M.E., 2003. Cowards and heroes: group loyalty in the American Civil War. The Quarterly Journal of Economics 118 (2), 519–548.

Croce, B., 1915. Teoria e storia della storiografia. Laterza, Bari.

David, P.A., 1985. Clio and the economics of QWERTY. The American Economic Review 75 (2), 332–337.

Debreu, G., 1991. The mathematization of economic theory. The American Economic Review 81 (1), 1–7.

Dell, M., 2010. The persistent effects of Peru's mining mita. Econometrica 78 (6), 1863–1903.

Dell, M., Querubin, P., 2018. Nation building through foreign intervention: evidence from discontinuities in military strategies. The Quarterly Journal of Economics 133 (2), 701–764.

Diebolt, C., Haupert, M., 2018. We are ninjas: how economic history has infiltrated economics. Association Française de Cliométrie (AFC) Working Papers No. 4.

Drukker, J.W., 2006. The Revolution That Bit Its Own Tail. Aksant, Amsterdam.

Engermann, S.L., Sokoloff, K.L., 2005. The evolution of suffrage institutions in the New World. The Journal of Economic History 65 (4), 891–921.

Farnam, H., 1912. The economic utilization of history: annual address of the president. The American Economic Review 2 (1), 5–18. Supplement, Papers and Proceedings of the Twenty-fourth Annual Meeting of the American Economic Association.

Feinstein, C.H., 1998. Pessimism perpetuated: real wages and the standard of living in Britain during and after the industrial revolution. The Journal of Economic History 58 (3), 625–658.

Fogel, R.W., 1962. A quantitative approach to the study of railroads in American economic growth: a report of some preliminary findings. The Journal of Economic History 22 (2), 163–197.

Fogel, R.W., 1964. Railroads and American Economic Growth: Essays in Econometric History. Johns Hopkins Press, Baltimore.

Fogel, R.W., 1989. Without Consent or Contract. The Rise and Fall of American Slavery. W.W. Norton and Company, New York.

Fogel, R.W., Elton, G.R., 1983. Which Road to the Past? Two Views of Scientific and Traditional History. Yale University Press, New Haven.

Gennaioli, N., Rainer, I., 2007. The modern impact of precolonial centralization in Africa. Journal of Economic Growth 12 (3), 185–234.

Grosjean, P., 2014. A history of violence: the culture of honor and homicide in the US South. Journal of the European Economic Association 12 (5), 1285–1316.

Guiso, L., Sapienza, P., Zingales, L., 2016. Long term persistence. Journal of the European Economic Association 14 (5), 1401–1436.

Hamermesh, D.S., 2013. Six decades of top economics publishing: who and how? Journal of Economic Literature 51 (1), 162–172.

Harrison, M., Wolf, N., 2012. The frequency of wars. Economic History Review 65 (3), 1055–1076.

Hart, A.B., 1887. The disposition of our public lands. The Quarterly Journal of Economics 1 (2), 169–183.

Haupert, M., 2019. History of cliometrics. In: Diebolt, C., Haupert, M. (Eds.), Handbook of Cliometrics, 2nd edition. Springer, Berlin-Heidelberg.

Heckman, J.J., 1997. The value of quantitative evidence on the effect of the past on the present. The American Economic Review 87 (2), 404–408.

Heckman, J.J., Moktan, S., 2020. Publishing and promotion in economics: the tyranny of the top five. Journal of Economic Literature 58 (2), 419–470.

Kalaitzidakis, P., Mamuneas, T.P., Stengos, T., 2011. An updated ranking of academic journals in economics. Canadian Journal of Economics 44 (4), 1525–1538.

Kelly, M., 2019. The standard errors of persistence. CEPR Discussion Paper DP13783.

Kiaer, A.N., 1893. Historical sketch of the development of Scandinavian shipping. Journal of Political Economy 1 (3), 329–364.

Kopsidis, M., Bromley, D., 2016. The French revolution and German industrialization: dubious models and doubtful causality. Journal of Institutional Economics 12 (1), 161–190.

Lowes, S., Nunn, N., Robinson, J.A., Weigel, J., 2017. The evolution of culture and institutions: evidence from the Kuba Kingdom. Econometrica 85 (4), 1065–1091.

Lyons, J.S., Cain, L.P., Williamson, S.H. (Eds.), 2007. Reflections on the Cliometrics Revolution. Conversations with Economic Historians. Routledge, London and New York.

Margo, R., 2018. The integration of economic history into economics. Cliometrica 12 (3), 377–406.

Margo, R., 2021. The economic history of economic history: the evolution of a field in economics. In: Bisin, A., Federico, G. (Eds.), The Handbook of Historical Economics. Elsevier. Chapter 1 (in this book).

McCloskey, D., 1976. Does the past have useful economics? Journal of Economic Literature 14 (2), 434–461.

Michalopoulos, S., Papaioannou, E., 2020. Historical legacy and African development. Journal of Economic Literature 58 (1), 53–128.

North, D.C., 1981. Structure and Change in Economic History. W.W. Norton and Company, New York.

North, D.C., 1990. Institutions, Institutional Change, and Economic Performance. Cambridge University Press, New York.

Nunn, N., 2008. The long term effects of Africa's slave trade. The Quarterly Journal of Economics 123 (1), 139–176.

Nunn, N., 2009. The importance of history for economic development. Annual Reviews of Economics 1, 65–92.

Nunn, N., 2014. Historical development. In: Aghion, P., Durlauf, S. (Eds.), Handbook of Economic Growth, vol. 2. North Holland, Amsterdam, pp. 347–402.

Nunn, N., 2015. Gender and missionary influence in colonial Africa. In: Akyeampong, E., Bates, R., Nunn, N., Robinson, J. (Eds.), Africa's Development in Historical Perspective. Cambridge University Press, Cambridge, pp. 489–512.

Nunn, N., 2020. The historical roots of economic development. Science 367 (6485), eaaz9986. https://doi.org/10.1126/science.aaz9986.

Nunn, N., Wantchekon, L., 2011. The slave trade and the origins of mistrust in Africa. The American Economic Review 101 (7), 3221–3252.

Olsson, O., Paik, C., 2016. Long-run cultural divergence: evidence from the neolithic revolution. Journal of Development Economics 122, 197–213.

Rosenthal, J.L., Wong, R.B., 2011. Before and Beyond Divergence. Harvard University Press, London and Cambridge (Mass.).

Parker, W.N. (Ed.), 1986. Economic History and the Modern Economist. Basil Blackwell, Oxford.

Satyanath, S., Voigtländer, N., Voth, H.J., 2017. Bowling for fascism: social capital and the rise of the Nazi Party. Journal of Political Economy 125 (2), 478–526.

Spolaore, E., Wacziarg, R., 2013. How deep are the roots of economic development? Journal of Economic Literature 51 (2), 325–369.

Stögbauer, C., Komlos, J., 2004. Averting the Nazi seizure of power: a counterfactual thought experiment. European Review of Economic History 8 (2), 173–199.

Sutch, R., 1991. All things reconsidered: the life-cycle perspective and the third task of economic history. The Journal of Economic History 51 (2), 271–288.

Thomas, M., 2007. Charles, H. Feinstein, interviewed by Mark Thomas. In: Lyons, J.S., Cain, L.P., Williamson, S.H. (Eds.), Reflections on the Cliometrics Revolution. Conversations with Economic Historians. Routledge, London and New York, pp. 286–300.

Tur-Prats, A., 2019. Family types and intimate partner violence: a historical perspective. Review of Economics and Statistics 101 (5), 878–891.

Voigtländer, N., Voth, H.J., 2012. Persecution perpetuated: the medieval origins of anti-semitic violence in Nazi Germany. The Quarterly Journal of Economics 127 (3), 1339–1392.

Voth, H.J., 2021. Persistence – myth and mystery. In: Bisin, A., Federico, G. (Eds.), The Handbook of Historical Economics. Elsevier. Chapter 9 (in this book).

Williamson, J.G., 2011. Trade and Poverty. When the Third World Fell Behind. MIT Press, Cambridge (Mass).

Wolfers, J., 2006. Did unilateral divorce laws raise divorce rates? A reconciliation and new results. The American Economic Review 96 (5), 1802–1820.

History as evolution[☆]

3

Nathan Nunn[a,b]
aHarvard University, Cambridge, MA, United States
bCanadian Institute for Advanced Research (CIFAR), Toronto, ON, Canada

3.1 Introduction

To many economic historians, the benefit of an evolutionary perspective for studying economic history or long-term economic growth may seem limited. Evolution is typically viewed as only being relevant in well-defined subfields within economics that study the importance of genetics for economic outcomes.[1] In this chapter, I will argue that an evolutionary perspective can provide useful insights that are widely relevant for the study of economic history and long-run economic growth.[2] My goal is to bridge the divide between research done within the field of economic history and that done within the evolutionary social sciences – i.e., evolutionary biology, evolutionary psychology, and particularly evolutionary anthropology.

The aspect of evolutionary research that is the most relevant for economic history is the study of cultural evolution. This line of inquiry is motivated by a desire to better understand human psychology, human societies, human behavior, and their evolution over time. The first contributions were theoretical, consisting of studies that adapted and extended models from evolutionary biology and applied them to cultural evolution (e.g., Cavalli-Sforza and Feldman, 1981; Boyd and Richerson, 1985).[3]

I begin the chapter by first providing a conceptual and theoretical overview of culture and its evolution. An important part of this is to describe the theory and evidence behind the benefits of culture. This, in turn, explains why culture is ubiquitous and why it is such a central part of human decision making. The first benefit is that by relying on traditions that are passed down over generations, culture allows individuals to make decisions efficiently in complex environments where figuring out the

---

[☆] I am particularly grateful to Joseph Henrich for numerous insightful discussions. I also thank Ran Abramitzky, Alberto Bisin, Robert Boyd, Ben Enke, Michele Gelfand, Nicholas Khaw, Michael Muthukrishna, James Robinson, and Felipe Valencia Caicedo for helpful comments and/or discussions. I also thank Vafa Behnam, Aditi Chitkara, Rumi Khan, and Laura Kincaide for excellent RA work.

[1] Examples of this line of research include geneoeconomics (Benjamin et al., 2012), macro-level analyses of the effects of genetic distance and genetic diversity (Spolaore and Wacziarg, 2009; Ashraf and Galor, 2013), micro-level studies on the importance of genetics relative to the environment for economic outcomes (Sacerdote, 2007; Cesarini et al., 2008, 2009), or empirical and theoretical research that takes a Darwinian perspective to understand economic growth (Galor and Moav, 2002; Clark, 2007).

[2] I make no claims to being the first person to make this point. For previous discussions along these lines, see for example Mokyr (1991) and Mokyr (1998). I view this chapter as adding to this line of thinking, with particular emphasis on advances made in the evolutionary literature in the past two decades.

[3] For an overview and introduction into the field of cultural evolution, see Chudek et al. (2015). For a description of the history of the field, see Mesoudi (2016).

optimal action with certainty is costly or even impossible. As long as a society's environment is fairly stable over time, then reliance on evolved cultural traditions is an effective strategy. The second benefit of cultural evolution arises from the fact that it is cumulative. Culture allows societies to build an evolved body of knowledge that is greater than any single individual could learn within their lifetime or fit within their mind. By taking as given the cultural wisdom of previous generations, societies do not need to 'reinvent the wheel' and instead can focus their efforts on adding to and improving upon the existing body of culturally-accumulated knowledge of the society.

After describing the conceptual foundations of cultural evolution and its benefits, I then turn to a series of examples aimed at showing how an evolutionary perspective of human behavior can provide insight into the study of economics in general and economic history in particular. I do this in three ways. The first is to show that the differences between evolutionary thinking and traditional economic thinking are often much smaller than one might think. There are many cases where the same logic, the same evidence, and similar narratives are developed, but using different terminology, empirical methods, and data. I hope to make these commonalities more apparent.

The second is to highlight cases where insights from the evolutionary literature can be used by economic historians to gain a better understanding of certain historical processes. Using a few cases that have become apparent to me over the years, I discuss how evolutionary insights, such as environmental mismatch, the collective brain, cumulative improvements, kludges, group-level selection, sexual dimorphism, and reproduction strategies provide a deeper understanding of a diverse set of aspects of human history, including human capital, innovation, warfare, state formation, cooperation, social structure, gender roles, kinship, social structure, path dependence, and comparative economic development. To me, these are the most obvious examples of the insights that emerge from an evolutionary perspective. However, my sense is also that they are just the tip of the iceberg.

The third is to highlight cases in which historical research within economics has contributed to the cultural evolution literature. As I will discuss, a sizeable and quickly growing area of research within economics, that takes a historical (and often cultural) perspective, has been successful at contributing, both theoretically and empirically, to evolutionary fields outside of economics.

I now turn to the first step in this process, which is to describe the mechanisms that form the foundation of the benefits of culture.

3.2 **The benefits of cultural evolution**

The standard definition of 'culture' from evolutionary anthropology defines culture as the knowledge, technology, values, beliefs, and norms that can be transmitted across generations and between individuals (e.g., Boyd and Richerson, 1985). There are numerous examples of cultural traits that vary by context: religious/supernatural beliefs, views about morality, norms about giving and cooperation, gender norms, food preferences, taboos, and traditions and skills regarding farming, house-building, hunting, etc.

An important question is the extent to which cultural values affect our behavior. Within economics, this is not something that we take for granted. When one views human behavior from the traditional economic perspective of 'rationality', a series of questions arise. Why does culture exist? Why would someone be influenced by what they are told by their teachers, their parents, friends, church leaders, celebrities, etc.? Why wouldn't individuals just figure out what is best by using some form of rational calculus? For example, if cheating, stealing, or lying yields a higher payoff, then why would someone be influenced by the fact that religious leaders, parents, teachers, or friends might tell them that this behavior is wrong and should be avoided? These are important questions. To understand the logic behind culture and why it affects our behavior, I now turn to a theoretical literature where culture is not taken as given, but its influence is derived endogenously. An important contribution of this class of models is that they show how and why culture is beneficial and, therefore, why it emerges and guides our behavior.

3.2.1 Cultural evolution saves on information costs

To understand the primary benefits of culture, one must first recognize an important fact: As human beings, we have cognitive limits. Acquiring and processing information is not free; it has an opportunity cost. In the face of these limits, we have developed culture and cultural learning, and with them cultural values and beliefs. These serve as tools that are "fast and frugal" and allow us to make decisions more efficiently than if we were an economist's traditional version of 'rational' (e.g., Gigerenzer and Goldstein, 1996; Todd and Gigerenzer Peter, 1999).

3.2.1.1 Theory

The formal theory behind culture and its evolution has been thoroughly developed in the cultural evolution literature and began with seminal models by Boyd and Richerson (1985) and Rogers (1988) among others.[4] The authors model situations where an action must be made in a setting without perfect (costless) certainty. The payoff of each action depends on the environment, which is variable. Individuals can either collect information and figure out the optimal action on their own or they can rely on the traditions that have evolved up until the previous generation. They do this by copying the action of a person from the previous generation. In other words, their behavior is determined by cultural values that are learned from the prior generation.

The models show that, under fairly general conditions, we should observe the presence of culture i.e., decision-making based on socially-transmitted cultural values. There are two primary benefits that culture provides over rationality. First, culture-based decision-making provides a quick and easy way to make decisions. To the extent that rational decision-making (narrowly defined) requires costs due to information acquisition or cognitive processing, then acting on one's transmitted cultural traditions and values saves on these costs. The second benefit is that relying on culture allows for cumulative learning. By following the culture of the previous generations, individuals do not have to reinvent the wheel and re-learn everything that has already been figured out during the history of the society in question. For example, if the society has already learned how to effectively hunt, which plants are not poisonous, and what rituals and beliefs help the society to exist in harmony, then taking these as given and trying to improve upon them may be a better strategy than having individuals try to figure these things out again.

I now present a simple model that focuses on the first of the two benefits and shows how culture can emerge in equilibrium. Following this, I discuss the second benefit of culture, the fact that it is cumulative, in Section 3.2.2.

---

[4] For a related paper within economics, see Bisin and Verdier (2001a). The models are very similar, except that what we think of as a reliance on culture/tradition in the description below they interpret (and model) as imperfect empathy on the part of the parents.

The model is taken from Giuliano and Nunn (2021) and reproduces the basic logic of Rogers (1988), which is one of the first and simplest models of this aspect of cultural evolution. The players of the game consist of a continuum of members of a society. Each period, a new generation is born and the previous generation dies. When a player is born, they make a once-and-for-all choice of two possible actions, which we denote a and b. Which of the two actions yields a higher payoff depends on the state of the world (i.e., the environment), which can be either A or B. If the state is A, then action a yields the payoff $\beta > 0$ and action b yields a payoff of $-\beta$. If the state is B, then action a yields a payoff of $-\beta$ and action b yields the payoff $\beta > 0$. Thus, in each state, one of the two actions is better than the other.

In each period, with probability $\Delta \in [0, 1]$, there is a shock that results in a new draw of the state of the environment. It is equally likely that the draw results in the new environment being in state A or state B. The state of the world is unknown to the players. However, as I explain below, it is possible to engage in learning (at a cost) to determine the state of the world.

There are two potential types of players. Each uses a different method to choose their action. The first type, "Traditionalists (T)," value tradition and place strong importance on the actions of the previous generation. They choose their action by following the action of a randomly chosen person from the previous generation. Thus, the model allows for both vertical and oblique transmission.[5] The second type, "Non-Traditionalists (NT)," do not value tradition and ignore the actions of the previous generation. They obtain the optimal action with certainty for the current period, but there is a cost of learning, $\kappa \in (0, \beta)$. Thus, although the cost is positive, it is assumed to be fairly modest. Let x denote the proportion of the population that is a traditionalist.

I now turn to the payoffs of both types of players, starting with the non-traditionalists. In each generation, they incur the cost κ to learn the optimal action. This action is chosen and they obtain β. Therefore, the payoff to a non-traditionalist is given by:

$$\Pi^{NT} = \beta - \kappa.$$

To calculate the expected payoff of a traditionalist, consider the following sequence of possibilities, each of which results in a traditionalist choosing the right action for her environment, thus, receiving β. First, a traditionalist copies a non-traditionalist from the previous generation; and the environment did not experience a shock between the last and current generation. Since the non-traditionalist from the previous generation chose the action that was optimal in her environment and since a shock did not occur, then this action will also be optimal in the current environment and the traditionalist receives β. This scenario occurs with probability $(1 - x)(1 - \Delta)$. Second, a traditionalist copies a traditionalist from the previous generation, who had copied a non-traditionalist from the previous generation. No shocks occurred during this time. The traditionalist receives β and this occurs with probability $x(1 - x)(1 - \Delta)^2$. Third, a traditionalist copies a traditionalist, who copied a traditionalist, who copied a non-traditionalist. No shocks occurred during this time. This occurs with probability $x^2(1 - x)(1 - \Delta)^3$.

One can continue this sequence of possibilities infinitely. The sum of the probabilities is given by $\sum_{t=1}^{\infty} x^{t-1}(1 - x)(1 - \Delta)^t$. With probability equal to one minus this sum, a traditionalist does not necessarily obtain the correct action. In these cases, there has been at least one shock to the environment

---

[5] Vertical transmission is transmission from parents to children. Oblique transmission is all other forms of transmission of those from an older generation to the younger generation.

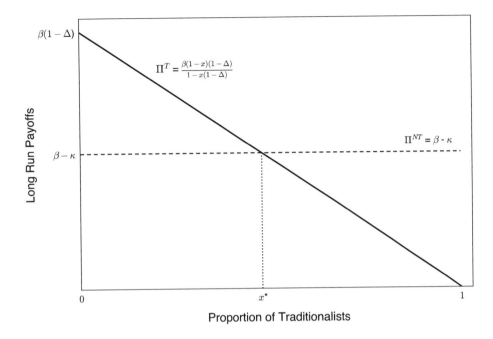

FIGURE 3.1

The equilibrium proportion of traditionalists (T) and non-traditionalists (NT).

since the most recent non-traditionalist was copied. Because the consequence of a shock is an equal probability of being in either state, a traditionalist still has a 50% chance of receiving β, a 50% chance of receiving $-\beta$, and her expected payoff is 0. Putting this together, and using the formula for an infinite geometric sequence gives:

$$\Pi^T = \frac{\beta(1-x)(1-\Delta)}{1-x(1-\Delta)}.$$

The payoffs to traditionalists and non-traditionalists as a function of the proportion of traditionalists in the society, x, are shown in Fig. 3.1. The expected payoff of a traditionalist, Π^T, is decreasing in x. Intuitively, as the fraction of traditionalists increases, it is less likely that a traditionalist will copy a non-traditionalist who is more likely to have chosen the correct action. At the extreme, where everyone in the population is a traditionalist ($x = 1$), each traditionalist copies another traditionalist and the expected payoff is 0.

At the other extreme, where everyone is a non-traditionalist ($x = 0$), a (mutant) traditionalist will copy the correct action from someone in the previous generation and as long as there was not a shock to the environment between the two generations, she will obtain the right action. Thus, with probability $1 - \Delta$, a traditionalist's payoff is β. If, on the other hand, the environment did change, which occurs with probability Δ, then there is an equal probability that the environment is in either state and the expected payoff is 0. Therefore, the expected payoff to a traditionalist when $x = 0$ is $\beta(1 - \Delta)$.

In an equilibrium with both types present, the expected payoffs to both types must be equal. In an equilibrium with only one type, its average payoff must be no less than that of the other type. Thus, the equilibrium proportion of traditionalists x^* is given by:

$$x^* = \begin{cases} \frac{\kappa - \Delta\beta}{\kappa(1-\Delta)} & \text{if} \quad \Delta \in [0, \frac{\kappa}{\beta}] \\ 0 & \text{if} \quad \Delta \in [\frac{\kappa}{\beta}, 1] \end{cases} \tag{3.1}$$

From Fig. 3.1, it is clear that under fairly general conditions ($\kappa > \Delta\beta$), traditionalists are present in society. Their emergence is due to the benefit of cultural transmission, which provides a fairly accurate way of making decisions at a low cost.

It is straightforward to show that the equilibrium is stable under the standard assumption that the relative payoffs of types affect their fitness and/or survival. Formally, this can be modeled using the standard replicator dynamic (e.g., Gintis, 1997). In the polymorphic equilibrium, where both types are present, a small perturbation of $x > x^*$ causes the payoff of traditionalists to be lower than that of non-traditionalists and x will decrease until x^* is reached. If $x < x^*$, the payoff of traditionalists is higher than that of non-traditionalists, and x will increase until x^* is reached. In the monomorphic equilibrium with $x^* = 0$, a perturbation of $x > x^*$ causes the payoff of traditionalists to be lower than that of non-traditionalists and x will decrease until there is convergence to x^*.

3.2.1.2 Evidence

In the model, the presence of culture in equilibrium is due to the benefit of cultural transmission, which provides a fairly accurate way of making decisions at a low cost. Anthropologists have documented numerous real-world examples of functional cultural traits being followed despite the population not knowing their benefits.[6] One of the best-known examples is the alkali processing of maize, which is the traditional method of preparing maize in many parts of Latin America. During the process, dried maize is boiled in a mixture of water and limestone or ash, before being mashed into a dough called 'masa'. Although it was unknown at the time, putting limestone, or ash in the water before boiling prevents pellagra, a disease resulting from niacin deficiency, which is common in diets that consist primarily of maize. The alkaline solution that is created when limestone or ash is added increases the body's absorption of niacin (Katz et al., 1974).

Another example of the benefits of culture and tradition is documented in Billing and Sherman (1998). The authors examine data for 43 spices from 4,578 meat-based recipes in 93 cookbooks from 36 countries. They document several empirical regularities that are consistent with the use of spices as antimicrobials even though this benefit was unknown. They show that spices that are more commonly used are the ones that are more antimicrobial. Societies in hotter climates tend to use more antimicrobial spices. Spices are used in ways, and in combinations, that appear to maximize their antimicrobial properties. For example, onions are not effective unless they are cooked and cilantro is not effective if it is cooked. In most recipes, onions are cooked and cilantro is not. Another example is chili powder (e.g., red pepper, onion, garlic, cumin, etc.), which contains a combination of spices that generates complementarities and maximizes their effectiveness.

Another well-known example of a tradition with unknown benefits is from the Naskapi, an indigenous First Nations society who traditionally lived on land that today is in Quebec, Newfoundland and

---

[6] For an excellent overview and many examples, see chapter 7 of Henrich (2016).

Labrador (Speck, 1935). The primary form of subsistence of the Naskapi was caribou hunting. Deciding where to hunt was an important decision. The hunters would like to hunt in the locations where the caribou are. By contrast, the caribou would like to avoid the locations where the hunters are. Effectively, this is a two-dimension version of the game "matching pennies."[7] We know that in such a game, the only Nash equilibrium is a mixed strategy equilibrium where one randomly chooses each direction with equal probability. The difficulty is that human beings are notoriously bad at randomizing and instead would tend to follow certain patterns, which could be detected by the Caribou. The Naskapi developed a ritual that they undertook prior to hunting expeditions. They would put the shoulder blade of a caribou in the fire. It would then burn and crack and the patterns of these told the hunters where they should hunt. Although this was unknown, the ritual was effective because it provided a method to randomly select the location of the next hunting expedition.

The basic logic described above has been tested and confirmed in numerous studies. One clear prediction of the model above, which is common to most models in the literature, is that we should observe a stronger reliance on culture and tradition when the environment is more stable. This is because evolved traditions are more likely to still be useful in the current environment. Within the evolutionary literature, this prediction has been tested using experimental tools (Galef and Whiskin, 2004; McElreath et al., 2005; Toelch et al., 2009).

Most recently, the prediction that tradition and cultural persistence should be weaker in more unstable environments was tested by Giuliano and Nunn (2021). The study uses paleoclimatic data, combined with information on the historical locations of ethnic groups, to construct estimates of the variability of the ancestral environment across generations for ethnic groups and countries. They find that ancestral climatic stability is associated with greater self-reported importance placed on tradition, and more persistence in cultural traits over time, including among the descendants of immigrants to the United States and the Indigenous populations of the United States and Canada.

3.2.2 Cultural evolution is cumulative

3.2.2.1 Theory

An important characteristic of the model discussed above, which has long been recognized in the literature, is that, in the end, the existence of culture and tradition does not make the society better off. In the long-run, regardless of the extent to which culture is present, the society-wide payoff is $\beta - \kappa$. This is contrary to the conventional wisdom that humans are more successful than other animals because we have culture, which leads to greater group-level success (Henrich, 2016). Subsequent theoretical work has shown that this characteristic of Rogers' model is not due to its simplicity. Instead, it is general and found in a large class of models where the only benefit of culture is to save on individual-level information acquisition (Boyd and Richerson, 1995, 2005).

This has led to an emphasis on 'cumulative cultural evolution' as a key benefit of culture. It is related to the benefit of information acquisition, highlighted in the model above but conceptually distinct. To put it simply (and to use multiple clichés), an important benefit of culture is that it means that we do not have to 'reinvent the wheel' and that we can 'stand on the shoulders of giants.' We can take as given

---

[7] Matching pennies is a two-player zero-sum game in which each player chooses either heads or tails. One player obtains a higher payoff when the players' choices are the same. The other player obtains higher payoffs if the players' choices are different.

the knowledge or traditions of the previous generation, without necessarily understanding them fully, and build on them, continuing the process of incremental cultural innovation.

To see the logic of this, consider the following variant of the model above, which is detailed in Boyd and Richerson (1985, 1995). The setup is the same except there is a continuum of states. As before, in each period, there is a probability that the environment switches to a new state. There is also a continuum of behaviors, with one behavior yielding the highest payoff for each possible state. In addition, the payoff of a behavior in a particular state is decreasing in the distance from the state's optimal behavior. We will see examples below, but concretely one can think of the behavior as being the technology used to build tools or houses, or strategies used to forage for food or hunt for game. The further one deviates from the optimal strategy or technology, the lower is one's expected payoff.

Unlike the model above, it is now assumed that all individuals can modify their behavior by learning. Individuals start with an initial guess and then through costly trial and error modify their behavior. Following the same logic as above, there are two types: traditionalists and non-traditionalists. Traditionalists adopt the behavior of a randomly chosen individual from the previous generation and use this as the starting point from which they experiment. By contrast, non-traditionalists ignore the behavior from the previous generation and use a fixed behavior as their starting point and they always acquire the optimal behavior given the current state. Relative to non-traditionalists, traditionalists invest much less in changing their behavior and thus they improve upon their initial behavior much less than a non-traditionalist.

The logic of the equilibrium of this model is similar to the prior model. As long as the environment doesn't change too frequently, traditionalists will slowly converge to the optimal behavior over time. The movement is not as rapid as for non-traditionalists, who accomplish this in one generation, but learning costs are reduced. In this model, each new generation of non-traditionalists 'reinvents the wheel' and obtains the optimal action. By contrast, traditionalists build on the knowledge accumulated by the previous generation. Their behavior does not track the environment as optimally as non-traditionalists, but they save on information acquisition costs. In this model, the average payoff in society is increasing in the share of traditionalists in the population. Thus, the model is consistent with cultural evolution increasing the effective knowledge and wellbeing of the society.

The benefits of cumulative cultural evolution become even more clear when one recognizes that the world is much more complicated than the stylized models that we use in economics. We typically model settings where the number of determinants is modest, payoff functions are smooth and continuous, and therefore, equilibria are typically unique and nicely behaved.[8] However, reality is much more complicated. There are often many equilibria. Our wellbeing is affected by a very large number of determinants, including our own actions, the actions of others, and exogenous shocks. In addition, there are complicated interactions between each of these factors. Unlike our simplified models that feature smooth and well-behaved payoff functions that generate an optimal action that is easily calculated, in reality, payoff functions are not smooth and are highly irregular. (We will see examples of this below.) In such a setting, calculating the optimal action is literally impossible. Cumulative cultural evolution reduces these much larger optimization problems into smaller, more manageable chunks, where cumulative learning can take place. This allows each generation to 'tinker' and develop small

---

[8] If our models do have multiple equilibria, then we usually simplify the setting by using a selection criterion such as choosing the Pareto superior equilibrium.

piecemeal improvements to the current values, beliefs, or technologies (i.e., culture) of a society. These simpler chunks feature simpler problems and smoother surfaces. As Boyd et al. (2013, p. 136) put it:

> *In a small neighborhood in design space, the performance surface is approximately flat, so that even if small changes are made at random, half of them will increase the payoff (unless the design is already at the optimum). Large changes will improve things only if they are in the small cone that includes the distant optimum. Thus, we expect it to be much harder to design a useful bow from scratch than to tinker with the dimensions of a reasonably good bow.*

Thus, an important characteristic of culture is that it makes optimization problems that cannot be solved by any single individual solvable by society as a whole when the problem is tackled in an incremental manner over many generations.

3.2.2.2 Evidence

In many ways, the best evidence of the importance of cumulative cultural evolution is the technological sophistication developed by humans compared to other animals including non-human primates. As early as 10,000 years ago, humans moved into and were able to subsist in diverse, and often remote, parts of the earth. Living in these environments necessitated the development of new technologies. "Spears, atlatls, and later bow and arrow are used to acquire game; flaked stone tools are necessary to process kills and to shape wood, bone, and process hides; clothing and shelter are crucial for thermoregulation; fire making paraphernalia is necessary for cooking, heat, and light. Slings, baskets, and pottery facilitate transport and storage; boats expand foragers; ranges to include lakes and oceans; fishhooks and cordage make coastal habitats rich sources of protein." (Boyd et al., 2013, p. 142).

Another important source of evidence for the value of cumulative cultural evolution is from numerous natural experiments where explorers (usually European) arrived in a new location with more advanced technology but no cumulative knowledge of the local environment. These "lost explorer experiments" have a remarkably similar storyline (Boyd et al., 2013; Henrich, 2016). European explorers arrive at a new location inhabited by smaller-scale societies. These are societies that the explorers perceived as being less sophisticated with technology that was much less advanced. The expedition experiences unexpected circumstances which require the explorers to remain in the new lands longer than their provisions allow for, which forces them to live off the land as the indigenous population does. Despite having more scientific knowledge and more resources, including manufactured survival equipment, the explorers never fair well and often die. Without the benefits of cumulative cultural evolution, they are not able to survive let alone thrive in the new setting.

One of the more notable examples among these natural experiments is the Franklin Expedition of 1846 in which the explorers starved to death on King William Island, where indigenous Inuit had lived successfully for over 700 years (Boyd et al., 2013). Two particularly telling examples are the 1860 Burke and Wills expedition in Australia and the Narvaez expedition in what today is Florida. They show that an exception to the standard story appears to only occur when the lost European explorers engage in cumulative cultural evolution, learning the culture of local populations. In the case of the Burke and Wills expedition, at one point the explorers were saved by indigenous hunter-gatherers, who showed them how to make bread from a seed called 'nardoo,' which could be pounded, made into flour, and baked as bread. However, the explorers didn't follow the indigenous cultural practices of preparing the nardoo precisely. They did not leach the flour with water extensively, they did not expose the flour to ash during heating, and they did not eat the nardoo from mussel shells. It turns out that each of these was an important detoxification practice that combats the high levels of thiaminase in nardoo. In the end, despite the presence of abundant food around them, Burke and Wills both died. There was one additional person, named King, on the expedition who survived long enough to be saved. How did he do it? By living among the local population. In other words, by completely relying on their cumulative cultural knowledge (Henrich, 2016, pp. 27–30). In the Narvaez expedition, of the 300 original conquistadors that were part of the expedition, four individuals were able to survive, but again, this was only because they lived among the local indigenous population (Henrich, 2016, pp. 30–31).

Another source of evidence for the benefits of cumulative cultural evolution is from experiments intended to test for the benefits of this mechanism. Muthukrishna et al. (2014) designed an experiment where participants are asked to undertake a difficult task that they have no prior experience with. The experiment was designed to mimic the process of cumulative cultural evolution and to vary its presence. All versions of the experiment had 10 generations and information sharing across generations. The experiment was incentivized so that participants' payoffs were increasing in their performance and in the performance of subsequent generations. In one treatment, which was intended to model greater access to cumulative cultural evolution, participants in generations 2 to 10 had access to guidance from all five participants of the previous generation. In the other, which was intended to model less cumulative cultural evolution, the participants only had access to information from one of the five participants of the previous generation.

There were two versions of the experiment, each with a different task. In one, participants had to create an image using software on a computer. The information that was transmitted between generations was the created image and two pages of written notes/tips from one or five participants (depending on treatment) from the previous generation. In the other, participants had to tie a system of knots using rock-climbing equipment. In this experiment, participants had access to an instructional video created by one or five participants from the previous generation.

The authors find strong evidence that performance on the tasks was better in the versions of the experiment that allowed for greater cumulative cultural evolution. These participants had more information when starting and therefore didn't need to 'reinvent the wheel.' In this setting, learning from an accumulated body of knowledge helped them avoid common pitfalls and to gain important insights more easily than if they were learning on their own.

As I will discuss below, a number of findings within the economics literature regarding puzzling aspects of technology and innovation provide evidence in support of models of cumulative cultural evolution. Or put differently, models of cumulative cultural evolution provide a useful framework that can help economists make sense of the process of innovation. I return to this in Section 3.3.2.

3.3 Insights from a recognition of history as evolution

I now turn to a discussion of how an evolutionary framework provides a range of insights relevant for economics. At this point, a few caveats are in order. Although I have organized these insights into subsections, the ideas do not necessarily flow from one subsection to the next. These should be thought of as disparate insights that have come to me from reading the cultural evolution and economic history literature in tandem. In addition, in no way do I think that the insights and connections described below are complete or even representative. My sense is that they are still just the tip of the iceberg in terms of fruitful ideas and research that will emerge from a more evolutionary perspective within economics.

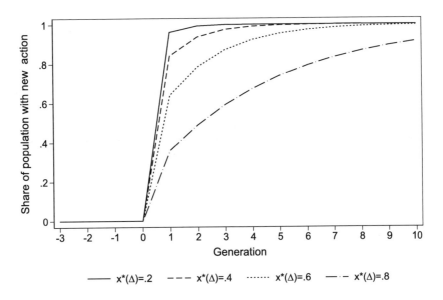

FIGURE 3.2

The adoption of a new (optimal) action following a shock depends on the proportion traditionalists in the society x^*.

3.3.1 Environmental mismatch

An important consequence of cultural evolution is that it can result in environmental mismatch. To see this, we return to the model of Rogers (1988). In the model, the benefit of culture is that it saves on information acquisition costs. However, the cost is that when the environment changes, traditionalists (i.e. those who rely on culture for decision making) do not choose actions that respond as quickly to the environment as non-traditionalists do. To see this, consider Fig. 3.2, which shows how the actions chosen in society respond to a change in the state of the world that occurs between periods 0 and 1. Different paths are reported, each for a society with a different equilibrium proportion of traditionalists (which is due to differences in the underlying Δ). As shown, societies with fewer traditionalists (low x^*) respond more quickly and more fully to a change in the environment.

In the model, many individuals continue to choose the old action after the state changes. This is an example of environmental mismatch. These individuals are choosing an action that is optimal for a past environment but not for the current environment. When actions are chosen based on culture, episodes of mismatch can occur.

The most well-known examples of mismatch are actually from evolutionary biology. One is sea turtles. The mothers leave the ocean, come to shore, and bury their eggs on sandy beaches. Once the sea turtles hatch, they need to make their way back to the ocean. They have evolved a method that allows them to do this simply. After they are born, at night, they head directly towards any bright light. In their natural environment, the only bright light is the reflection of the moon off of the water. By moving in the direction of the moon's reflection, sea turtles are able to navigate towards the water (Ehrenfeld and Carr, 1967). This evolved mechanism worked extremely well until the environment changed. In the modern world, where cities and freeways with bright lights are often located next to

FIGURE 3.3

An example of environmental mismatch: The dodo bird (*raphus cucullatus*). Sketch by Roelandt Savery, 1626. *Source*: Figure 10 of Hume (2006).

beaches, this biological heuristic works less well. Instead of heading towards the ocean, baby turtles move towards city lights which are in the opposite direction of the ocean (Salmon et al., 1995). This is an example of mismatch. A trait that worked well in the environment in which it evolved works poorly in the current environment.

Another commonly cited example is the dodo bird (*raphus cucullatus*), which is a bird that lived on the Island of Mauritius. A sketch of the bird from 1626 is shown in Fig. 3.3. Because of a scarcity of berries and other food during certain times of the year, dodo birds developed accumulations of fat on their bodies. They lost the ability to fly but developed a keen sense of smell that allowed them to track down the limited amounts of berries that existed during seasonal scarcity. Because there were no predators on the islands, they didn't develop special strategies to hide or protect their eggs. In all, they were well-adapted to their environment (Claessens et al., 2015; Gold et al., 2016). However, after human contact, predators like pigs, rats, and dogs were brought to the islands. The unprotected eggs and the flightless birds did not fare well and the species soon became extinct.

The notion of mismatch provides a framework that provides a deeper understanding of recent empirical findings from the historical economics literature. For example, the finding that Africa's slave trades reduced contemporary levels of trust from Nunn and Wantchekon (2011), combined with the evidence that increased trust is associated with higher incomes at both the country- and individual-level (Algan and Cahuc, 2010; Butler et al., 2016), suggests that the current levels of trust within Africa may be suboptimal. They may have been well-suited to the 400-year period of intensive slave raiding that the continent experienced, but they are likely lower than optimal in the current environment.

One of the nicest historical examples of mismatch is from Avner Greif's (1989, 1993, 1994) studies of the Maghribi and Genoese merchants of the Medieval Mediterranean. One group, the Maghribi traders, were Jewish traders who had migrated from Baghdad to Tunis and had adopted the values of Muslim society. They began trading in the early 11th Century. According to Greif, their merchant-agent relationships relied on information sharing. If an agent cheated a merchant, then no other merchants would hire the agent. This created a form of collective punishment, which required information sharing and the formation of dense information networks. The other group of traders in the region at the time were traders from Genoa, who did not engage in the same form of collective punishment of cheating agents. Instead, they were highly individualistic and did not engage in information sharing. The wage that had to be paid to keep an agent from cheating was lower in the collectivist regime of the Maghribi than under the individualistic regime of the Genoese.[9]

From the early 11th to 12th Centuries, trade between Spain and Constantinople expanded significantly. In response, the Genoese expanded by creating new merchant-agent relationships with non-Genoese. A consequence of this is that formal organizations and legal practices developed to facilitate these forms of cross-group exchange. The institutions that emerged were helpful for longer-term economic development (Greif, 1994). By contrast, the Maghribi, because of the equilibrium they were in, could only expand by creating new merchant-agent relationships within their own group. Thus, more formal institutional structures did not develop and commerce continued to rely on informal enforcement mechanisms such as social norms of group punishment.

Another example of mismatch is highlighted by the recent study by Alesina et al. (2013a), which measures perceptions of intergenerational mobility in Sweden, Italy, France, the U.K., and the United States. The authors find that the sample from the United States has, by far, the most optimistic perceptions of the amount of economic mobility in their country. This is particularly striking since the United States has the lowest mobility of the countries studied. In addition, for the other countries, the measures of perceived mobility and actual mobility are pretty similar. For the United States, perceived mobility is far from actual mobility. Thus, the United States appears to be a clear outlier in terms of its perceptions about mobility.

While this has yet to be studied thoroughly, the origins of this misperception are most likely due to the fact that in the 19th Century, the United States was a settler economy with very high levels of mobility, and much higher than other comparable countries, like Great Britain, at the time (Long and Ferrie, 2013). It was likely this environment that generated some of the values and beliefs that are particularly American, such as a belief in the American Dream (anyone can make it if they work hard enough), a desire to have limited government, and a limited set of policies that economically support the population and/or redistribute income, such as universal health care or high-quality public schooling. While other factors are clearly important, such as the history of race relations, a key determinant of these beliefs is likely the high mobility experienced in the U.S. historically. While these beliefs may

---

[9] In addition, the Maghribi system also featured other benefits. Merchants could use each other as agents. If a merchant-agent was dishonest, then other merchants could punish the merchant-agent by not punishing agents who had cheated that merchant. This additional threat meant that the efficient wage need to pay a merchant-agent to keep them from cheating was even lower (Greif, 1994).

have been accurate and well-suited for the historical setting, it is less clear that they are well-suited to the current environment.

Viewing the world through the lens of mismatch also generates insights that are important for policy. One example of this is the recent paper by Heller et al. (2017), which examines the effectiveness of a series of interventions from 2009 to 2015 aimed at improving the outcomes of disadvantaged youth from Chicago. One was a one-year program called 'Becoming a Man' (BAM), which was developed by the Chicago nonprofit Youth Guidance. The other was a version of the same program that was stretched out over two years. The programs comprised 2,740 and 2,064 randomly-chosen youth, respectively. Both versions of the program had significant effects. They reduced total arrests by 28–35%, arrests for violent crime by 45–50%, and arrests for other crimes by 37–43%. The authors also found persistent effects on schooling outcomes: graduation rates increased by 6–9 percentage points. The third program had many of the same elements of BAM but was implemented among high-risk juvenile arrestees by the Cook County, Illinois Juvenile Treatment Detention Center. This program was also very successful, reducing readmission rates to the detention center by 21%.

The authors also study potential mechanisms that could explain the results. They find that the evidence points to one aspect of the interventions being particularly important. To understand the mechanism, we must first recognize that much of our behavior is driven by automatic impulses – what Daniel Kahneman (2011) calls 'system 1'. (For cultural economists and those studying cultural evolution, system 1 is closely associated with transmitted cultural values and beliefs.) This is also true for the youth in the programs, who are from distressed neighborhoods where being aggressive and fighting is often necessary to save one's reputation. However, these automatic responses, although generally adaptive to the youth's environment, may not be the best response in many situations, like in school. The programs helped students develop the mental tools necessary to switch from an automatic reaction based on system 1 responses to one that is more thoughtful, takes into account the specifics of the situation, and relies on system 2 thinking, which is more slow and deliberative. According to the authors, a key consequence of the experiments is that they teach "a greater sense of occasion" (Heller et al., 2017, p. 6).

This example illustrates that one solution to cultural mismatch is to attempt to reduce the reliance of decision-making on the cultural trait. In this case, there was a reduction in the reliance on system 1 and an increase in the use of system 2. The study also provides an excellent example of how knowing the cultural and psychological roots of behavior can help design policy that can effectively improve the actions and outcomes of those involved.

Another example of mismatch and its implications for policy is explored in the recent study by Bursztyn et al. (2020). The authors study Saudi Arabia, a setting that is much less supportive of female employment outside of the home than the rest of the world. The authors study a sample of 500 college-educated, married men, aged 18–35, from the city of Riyadh. Participants were divided into groups of 30 individuals from the same neighborhood. They were then asked whether or not they agree that "women should be allowed to work outside the home," as well as their guess about the number of members of their group who hold this view. The authors found that individuals systematically underestimated the support for women working outside the home. This mismatch between beliefs of the norms held by others and actual norms in the population can be understood as a form of mismatch. Within

Saudi Arabia, in recent decades beliefs about women's work have been changing.[10] Thus, beliefs about norms, which evolved in a previous environment, are not accurate in the current setting.

The authors then test whether the perceived and actual norms of others can be more closely aligned by providing participants with information about the survey-based self-reported beliefs of others within their group. For a randomly-selected half of the sample, this was done. They find that the information provision increased the likelihood that participants signed their wives up for a job-matching service, and that their wives had applied for a job or had interviewed for a job 3–5 months after the experiment. Not surprisingly, the effects are greater for those who had larger initial misperceptions. Thus, the study documents the presence of mismatch and shows how information provision can reduce its severity.

3.3.1.1 Endogenous mismatch

Recent research on the origins of the Industrial Revolution can be viewed through the lens of mismatch where the change in the environment is endogenous to the strength of tradition in society. To see this, we again return to the model from Rogers (1988). In the model, the stability of the environment Δ was exogenously given. However, in reality, there are many examples of the external environment – such as economic conditions, politics, technology, etc. – being determined by human actions. Further, the rate of technological innovation, economic growth, and political change, itself, can be endogenous to the tradition in society.

Joel Mokyr (2018), in his book *Culture of Growth*, argues that a crucial determinant of the 18th Century Industrial Revolution in Western Europe was the novel belief that it was acceptable for younger generations to question the wisdom of the previous generations. This change in thinking resulted in a cultural belief that it is possible and desirable to understand how the natural world works. This, in turn, resulted in innovation and knowledge creation, which created the productivity gains of the Industrial Revolution. Mokyr (2018) argues that the presence of this new cultural trait – a weakening of the importance placed on traditional ways of thinking – was present in Western Europe but not China, which explains why, despite similar levels of economic development, the Industrial Revolution did not occur in China. He argues that "the heavy hand of the respect for the 'ancients' was felt through much of Chinese history" (p. 298). According to his argument, a weakening of tradition, and the resulting cultural change, are key determinants of the Industrial Revolution and the World's current economic prosperity.

Within this model, this means that in addition to instability Δ affecting tradition x^*, tradition x^* can also affect instability Δ. We can extend the Rogers model to incorporate this mechanism by assuming that the rate of change Δ is decreasing in the proportion of traditionalists in the economy x: $\Delta(x)$ and $\Delta'(x) < 0$.

We can also add technological progress to the model by altering the payoffs such that the payoff to a matching state and action is $\pi + \beta$ (rather than β) and to a mismatching state and action is $\pi - \beta$ (rather than $-\beta$), where π can be thought of as the level of technology in the society. Following the logic of Mokyr (2018), assume that increases in π occur as a by-product of the information acquisition of non-traditionalists. Therefore, the growth of π is a decreasing function of the proportion of traditionalists in the economy: $\frac{\dot{\pi}}{\pi}(x)$ and $\frac{\dot{\pi}}{\pi}'(x) < 0$. Further, assume that instability is driven solely by technological

---

[10] For example, according to the Global Gender Gap Index, the 'economic participation and opportunity' score for Saudi Arabia increased from 0.24 in 2006 to 0.38 in 2020. In addition, if one looks at the data for Saudi Arabia from the Arab Barometer, one finds strong evidence that individuals born in more recent years have views that are more supportive of women's employment.

innovation and, therefore, instability is increasing in the rate of technological change: $\Delta\left(\frac{\dot{\pi}}{\pi}(x)\right)$ and $\Delta'\left(\frac{\dot{\pi}}{\pi}(x)\right) > 0$. From this it follows that instability Δ is a decreasing function of the prevalence of tradition x in society: $\Delta(x)$ and $\Delta'(x) < 0$.

This setting gives rise to multiple stable equilibria. To see this, first consider an equilibrium where the proportion of traditionalists is high. As a consequence, there is little technological change and the environment is stable. Because of the stability of the environment, the relative benefit of tradition is high, which sustains the high proportion of traditionalists. Thus, such an equilibrium is stable. Second, consider an equilibrium where the proportion of traditionalists is low (even zero). In such an equilibrium, there is a lot of trial-and-error learning, which generates rapid technological change and a highly unstable environment. This in turn results in a relatively low benefit of tradition, which sustains the low proportion of traditionalists. Thus, such an equilibrium is also stable.

To see this more formally, recall the payoffs of the two types:

$$\Pi^T = \pi + \frac{\beta(1-x)(1-\Delta)}{1 - x(1-\Delta)}$$

$$\Pi^{NT} = \pi + \beta - \kappa.$$

Assume that the probability that there is no shock in a generation, $1 - \Delta$, is given by the following function: $1 - \Delta(x) = x^\theta$ for $\theta \in [0, 1]$. With this, the expected payoff of a traditionalist then becomes:

$$\Pi^T = \pi + \frac{\beta(1-x)x^\theta}{1 - x^{\theta+1}}.$$

The payoffs of the two types are shown in Fig. 3.4 for the case where $\theta = 1/2$.[11] The payoffs to non-traditionalists remain unchanged since they do not depend on Δ. The payoffs to traditionalists are now increasing in the proportion of traditionalists x. This is because the higher the proportion of traditionalists in the economy, the less innovation, the more stable the environment, and the greater the benefits of tradition. From the figure it is also clear that the level of technology, π, does not affect the equilibrium. This is because π affects the payoffs of both types symmetrically and additively.

The figure also shows that, with endogenous Δ, there can be multiple equilibria. In one equilibrium, $x^* = 1$. Since the proportion of traditionalists is high, economic growth is low, and the environment is stable. This can be thought of as a traditional low-growth equilibrium. In the other equilibrium, $x^* = 0$, since the proportion of traditionalists is low, there is rapid economic growth, and the environment is more dynamic. In the figure, x^B denotes the boundary of the basins of attraction of the two equilibria. Any initial population distribution of traditionalists greater than x^B eventually converges to the $x^* = 1$ equilibrium. Initial population distributions less than x^B converge to the $x^* = 0$ equilibrium.

A necessary condition for multiple equilibria to arise is that the cost of information acquisition, κ, must be sufficiently high; namely, $\kappa > \frac{\beta\theta}{1+\theta}$. If this is not satisfied, then the equilibrium with $x^* = 0$ is unique. Intuitively, if acquiring information is sufficiently easy, then traditionalists are not present in equilibrium.

---

[11] The payoffs shown are for the scenario where information acquisition costs are sufficiently high; namely, $\kappa > \beta/3$ (or $\kappa > \beta\theta/(1+\theta)$ in the more general case). This condition is discussed further below.

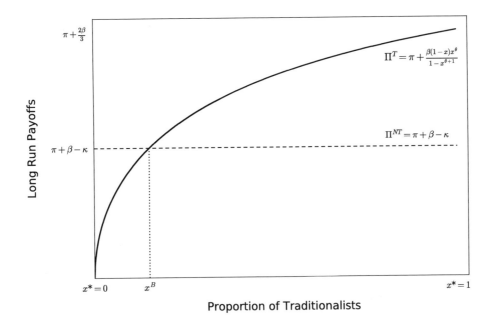

FIGURE 3.4

The equilibrium proportion of traditionalists (T) and non-traditionalists (NT), assuming the instability of the environment is endogenous to learning by NT (and $\theta = 1/2$).

Mokyr's description of the industrial revolution is one where society transitioned out of the $x^* = 1$ equilibrium, which featured no (or little) information acquisition and strong importance placed on following the beliefs and actions of previous generations. Because of the strong reliance on tradition, the external environment was stable, which meant that reliance on tradition was efficient.

In this setting, a society transitioning from the former to the latter equilibrium requires a reduction in the number of traditionalists below x^B. Once this occurs, economic growth increases and the environment becomes less stable, which further reduces the benefits to tradition.

3.3.2 Education and cultural evolution

I now turn to a discussion of how cultural evolution provides a deeper and more realistic understanding of education, human capital, and innovation. To see this, I return to the definition of culture. Within the cultural evolution literature, the standard definition is something like: "[culture is] the transmission from one generation to the next, via teaching and imitation, of knowledge, values, and other factors that influence behavior. Cultural transmission may have a variety of structures... For example, parents may enculturate their offspring or peers may enculturate each other." (Boyd and Richerson, 1985, p. 2). This definition is very similar to the standard definition that has emerged in the field of historical development and cultural economics. For example, Guiso et al. (2006) define culture as "customary beliefs and values that ethnic, religious, and social groups transmit fairly unchanged from generation to generation." (p. 23).

At first glance, the two definitions of culture appear essentially identical, which is not surprising since the cultural economics literature builds upon the cultural evolution literature. Both definitions describe the transmission of values and beliefs from one generation to the next.[12] A small but important difference is that "knowledge" and its transmission is mentioned in the definition of Boyd and Richerson (1985) but not Guiso et al. (2006). This is actually an important difference in how culture is defined in the two fields. Within economics, the accumulation and transmission of knowledge within or across generations is not culture. That is human capital. When I first came across the definition from evolutionary anthropology, my immediate reaction was likely the same as your reaction now. Knowledge and technology are conceptually very different from culture. They are examples of human capital and not of culture. But, I have come to realize that, in general, the difference is not clear and making a conceptual distinction between the two is often problematic and not particularly helpful.

Take the example of how to create arrows that are used for hunting. Henrich (2016) describes this process for the indigenous hunter-gatherers of Tierra del Fuego. This production process is relatively simple, requiring only fourteen steps and six material inputs. Henrich (2016, p. 107) describes some of the steps and I quote him directly:

- *The process begins by selecting the wood for the shaft, which preferably comes from chaura, a bushy, evergreen shrub. Though strong and light, this wood is a nonintuitive choice since the gnarled branches require extensive straightening. (Why not start with straighter branches?)*
- *The wood is heated, straightened with the craftsman's teeth, and eventually finished with a scraper. Then, using a preheated and grooved stone, the craftsman presses the shaft into the grooves and rubs it back and forth, pressing it down with a piece of fox skin. The fox skin becomes impregnated with the dust, which prepares it for the polishing stage. (Does it have to be fox skin?)*
- *Bits of pitch, gathered from the beach, are chewed and mixed with ash. (What if you don't include ash?)*
- *The mixture is then applied to both ends of a heated shaft, which must then be coated with white clay. (What about red clay? Do you have to heat it?) This prepares the ends for the fletching and arrowhead.*
- *Two feathers are used for the fletching, preferably from the left wing of the bird, and vice versa for the lefties. (Does this really matter?)*
- *The feathers are lashed to the shaft with sinews from the back of the guanaco, after they are smoothed and thinned with water and saliva. (Why not sinews from the fox that I had to kill for the aforementioned skin?)*

Learning how to successfully create arrowheads requires years of apprenticing. The knowledge, much of which is tacit, is taught over an extended period of time and much of it is codified in terms of tradition. The underlying mechanics and reasons that a certain feather is used or a certain type of wood is used are not understood. Instead, the learning is of culture and traditions. In this case, culture is synonymous with knowledge and human capital.

There are numerous examples where the accumulation of human capital is really cultural transmission – i.e., information and knowledge that is transferred through cultural learning. Such examples are

---

[12] It is true that the definition of Guiso et al. (2006) does not mention transmission between those of the same generation (horizontal transmission). However, it is clear that the cultural economics literature does not exclude this form of transmission.

also present within the economics literature, although this is often referred to as 'tacit knowledge' acquisition rather than cultural transmission. One example is the famous case of Desh Garments, where as part of a 1980 joint venture agreement between South Korea's Daewoo and Bangladesh's Desh garments, 130 workers from Desh garments were brought to a Daewoo garment plant located in Busan, South Korea (Easterly, 2001). This episode of cultural transmission had a dramatic effect on garment production in Bangladesh. Annual production increased from 43,000 shirts in 1980 to 2.3 million in 1987. Of the 130 Desh workers who had traveled to South Korea, 115 of them left Desh garments to start their own garment companies at some point in the 1980s.

Another example, but in a more controlled setting is from an experiment that intentionally varied the amount of cultural transmission to textile firms in India (Bloom et al., 2013, 2020). The authors study 17 firms that comprise 28 medium-sized (100-1,000 employees) family-owned textile plants, located in Maharashtra, India. Fourteen of the 28 plants received five months of extensive management consulting, which was valued at $250,000. The consulting was intended to improve management and operations within the plants. They found that in the months following the study, the treatment resulted in fewer defects, inventory savings, and higher total factor productivity. Nine years after treatment, they found that although about half of the previously adopted management improvements had been abandoned, the treated plants still were much more productive than the non-treatment plants. In addition, they found additional forms of cultural transmission. The practices had fully spread to non-treatment plants (even those not involved in the experiment at all) that belonged to the same company (i.e., firm) as a treatment plant. Thus, cultural knowledge was transmitted fully within the company.

A theoretical model of such processes of cultural transmission was developed by Henrich (2004b). To anthropologists, the model is one of cultural transmission. To economists, it is one of human capital accumulation. In the model, in each period there is a role model. Depending on the setting, this person could be a master craftsman, the village sage, or even a professor of economics. There are N pupils who learn from the role model, who is the most prolific and highly skilled individual of their generation. After learning from this teacher, the cultural knowledge / human capital of the pupils is determined from a draw from a distribution. The person with the highest draw then becomes the next role model who conveys their knowledge to the next generation.

Let z_i denote the level of cultural knowledge and human capital of individual i. The role model's z is denoted z_{max} and is shown by the vertical line in Fig. 3.5. Also shown is the probability distribution of draws of z. In the original model, it is assumed that the distribution is Gumbel (α, β), but subsequent studies find that the predictions hold for a large class of distributions (Vaesen, 2012).[13] Because the role model is the individual with the highest skill in the previous generation, as shown in Fig. 3.5, each student's z_i tends to be lower than that of the role model.

Because the frontier of knowledge of the next generation, measured by the z_{max}, is governed by the maximum draw of z in that generation, a larger population (and therefore more draws), will result in a higher level of skill for the role model. For the Gumbel distribution, the level of skill of the role model is given by

$$z_{max} = \alpha + \beta(\gamma + \ln N),$$

---

[13] Also see Kobayashi and Aoki (2012) for various extensions of the model, including allowing for the more-realistic assumption that role models are chosen from an individual's network of acquaintances.

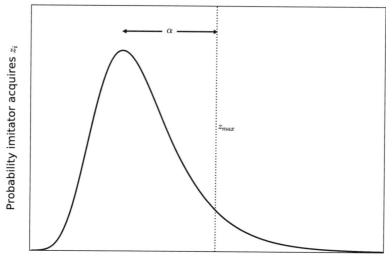

FIGURE 3.5

Illustration of the model of cumulative culture / human capital developed by Henrich (2004b).

where γ is the Euler-Mascheroni constant, which is approximately 0.5772. In addition, the growth in the average level of human capital in the economy is given by

$$\Delta \bar{z} = -\alpha + \beta(\gamma + \ln N).$$

In other words, for sustained knowledge growth (or cumulative cultural evolution), the population has to be sufficiently large. In addition, if the population is below a threshold size, then it can experience technological regress. Henrich (2004b) uses these predictions to explain the technological regress observed in Tasmania after it was separated from Australia due to the rising sea levels during the Holocene glacial retreat.

The important point here is that a model of cultural evolution is isomorphic to a model of human capital accumulation. In this sense, given that human capital has been at the core of our discipline for centuries, it turns out that we have been believers in culture all along.

3.3.2.1 Innovation and the collective brain

To drive home the similarity of cultural transmission and knowledge accumulation, both empirically and theoretically, I will compare two ways of thinking about knowledge. One will be familiar to the reader and is at the center of endogenous growth theory. The other, which will be less familiar, is from evolutionary anthropology and emphasizes the fact that knowledge creation occurs through a process of cumulative cultural evolution and cultural transmission.

As a conceptual framework to aid in the discussion, consider the following setting. Society has a population of size L. Assume that the fraction γ of the population L is exposed to a role model and thus has the opportunity to innovate. For those with this opportunity, innovation occurs with probability μ.

The extent to which an innovation diffuses into the aggregate economy (e.g., through social learning or cultural transmission), which raises knowledge growth $\dot{A}/A$, is increasing in the connectivity and cohesiveness of the population θ. Thus, knowledge growth is given by:

$$\frac{\dot{A}}{A} = \gamma \mu \theta L. \tag{3.2}$$

This is a highly-simplified version of an endogenous growth model with scale effects (meaning that the rate of innovation is increasing in the population size). However, it can also be interpreted as a representation of the notion of the 'collective brain' from evolutionary anthropology (Muthukrishna and Henrich, 2016). (I return to a detailed discussion of this concept below.)

Research within the field of economics has tended to focus on two terms in Eq. (3.2). The first is population size, L. The (initially surprising) prediction that the rate of technological change should be increasing in the size of the population, L, was famously tested and confirmed by Kremer (1993).[14] The second area of focus has been on the level of human capital (e.g., health or education) which is an important determinant of μ (Mankiw et al., 1992).

While research within cultural evolution has recognized the importance of scale effects (e.g., Derex et al., 2013), it has also emphasized the importance of parameters associated with cultural transmission of ideas; namely the amount of connectivity and social learning within a population: γ and θ. The parameter γ captures aspects of a society that influence the extent to which all individuals are able to participate in the innovative process. Inclusivity can be along the lines of gender, socioeconomic status, race, ethnicity, place of birth, etc. The parameter θ can be thought of as capturing how cohesive or connected a population is, which facilitates the diffusion of existing knowledge and the creation of new innovations. Within the literature, this is viewed as the first-order determinant of a society's success. As Joseph Henrich (2004b, p. 214) puts it: "If you want to have cool technology, it's better to be social than smart." The focus on these determinants of aggregate knowledge, which are inherently social, has been developed within a conceptual framework called the 'collective brain' (Muthukrishna and Henrich, 2016). Within this framework, the key to knowledge creation is cumulative cultural evolution and social learning. This is what effectively allows humans to have access to a larger repertoire of knowledge and technology that could ever fit into any one individual's brain. This larger network of knowledge is our 'collective brain'.

This perspective provides insight into findings from recent research within economics that seeks to understand the determinants of innovation within the United States. Bell et al. (2019) use data from 1.2 million inventors linked to tax records to document the determinants of innovation within the United States, paying particular attention to factors related to the childhood environment. They document significant variation across the United States, with the U.S. South having particularly low levels of innovation. While a modest portion of this is explained by educational attainment, they find other factors to be even more important, including race, gender, and parental income. Interestingly, these effects are most pronounced for the most highly educated children, suggesting that education may be a necessary but not sufficient condition for innovation. There appears to be a missing ingredient that is

---

[14] Interestingly, this prediction was also confirmed by anthropologists who found a strong positive relationship between population size and the number and complexity of pre-industrial marine tools across Polynesian islands (Kine and Boyd, 2010).

needed beyond education and one that is correlated with observables like race, income, or residential location.

The study then attempts to better understand this missing ingredient. Although they do not use this terminology, the patterns they find are exactly those that are predicted by models of the 'collective brain' that feature cumulative cultural evolution. They find that the children of inventors are more likely to be inventors themselves. This itself is not particularly surprising, but they also find that the innovation of the children tends to occur within the same fine-grained technology class as their father. The most likely explanation for this is role-model effects and the transfer of cultural knowledge from fathers to sons. The evidence is not consistent with this being the intergenerational transmission of more general human capital or knowledge which is more relevant for certain technology classes. Child innovation plummets drastically within technology classes that are only one or two classes away from those of the parents' innovations, which is consistent with specific knowledge being transmitted from parents to children.

These findings may be surprising when one is working within the traditional view of innovation in economics, where an innovator is tinkering in their garage and comes up with a new invention. However, the collective-brain framework has cumulative culture and social learning at its core. Because innovation is social and cumulative, it will not occur unless an individual is exposed to ideas, beliefs, values, and mental models taught by another individual. Since vertical transmission of culture from parents to children is the core mode of cultural transmission, it is not surprising that a child's ability to innovate depends on the cultural knowledge of their parents. As Muthukrishna and Henrich (2016, p. 4) put it: "The most basic structure of the collective brain is the family. Young cultural learners first gain access to their parents, and possibly a range of alloparents (aunts, grandfathers, etc.)."

Bell et al. (2019) also test for the importance of another form of cultural transmission – oblique transmission – although the authors do not use this terminology and instead refer to this as transmission from "parents' coworkers to children." They calculate the patent rate among workers in the father's (NAICS 6-digit) industry of employment. They find that the rate of innovation in their father's industry of employment is strongly predictive of child innovation as an adult. In addition, they also find that, here too, the child's innovation tends to occur within the same technology class as the innovation of the parents' coworkers.

Although the paper does not have a theoretical framework, the authors' conceptualization of the mechanisms at play is described as follows: "the data point to mechanisms such as transmission of specific human capital, access to networks that help children pursue a certain subfield, acquisition of information about certain careers, or role model effects." (Bell et al., 2019, pp. 688–689). In other words, the authors are describing a model of the collective brain, where knowledge and innovation occur through cumulative cultural evolution and social learning.

Complementary evidence for the importance of social learning for innovation can be found in a recent study by Andrews (2019) that looks at the effects of U.S. prohibition against alcohol in the early 20th Century. Recognizing the importance of bars, taverns, and saloons for building network connections that facilitated knowledge flow, he estimates the effects that prohibition, which legally penalized these establishments, had on inventive activity as measured by patenting rates. He finds that after the imposition of state-level prohibition, previously wet counties had 8–18% fewer patents per year relative to consistently dry counties. Thus, removing these locations of connectivity had sizeable detrimental effects on innovative activity.

The logic of cultural evolution, and its connection with technology, innovation, and productivity, helps us to understand the long-term permanent effects of historical events that (temporarily) reduced a population's inclusiveness. An example is slavery within the United States, where a large proportion of the population was restricted from basic rights and freedoms. Even following the abolition of slavery, intimidation, violence, fear, and discriminatory policies were used to further exclude Americans of African descent. The relationship between slavery and long-term underdevelopment has been well-documented (e.g., Mitchener and McLean, 2003; Nunn, 2008). More specific to the mechanisms of cultural evolution and innovation, Cook (2014) studies the effects of race riots and lynching on the patent rates of African Americans. According to her estimates, these acts of violence reduced African American patenting by 15% annually between 1882 and 1940. This is a sizeable effect and its persistence is a likely determinant for the racial differences in innovation documented by Bell et al. (2019). According to the logic of the 'collective brain', when a group is excluded or discouraged from participating in cumulative knowledge creation, this decreases innovation not only in the current period but also in all future periods.

A potentially important factor affecting a society's level of connection and cohesion – θ in Eq. (3.2) – is generalized trust. There is a strong positive relationship between generalized trust and per capita income. This is found whether one looks across countries, U.S. states, or European regions, and has shown to be causal (Algan and Cahuc, 2010, 2013). We also know that part of the effect of trust on income is due to the effect of trust on innovation and knowledge creation. Micro-level evidence for this is found in a recent study by Nguyen (2018) that studies the CEOs of 3,598 public firms in the United States. She collects information on the ancestry of the CEO and of all inventors within the firm and finds that across firms, innovation is more rapid and of higher quality if the CEO is from a place with higher levels of trust in general and with higher levels of trust in the ancestral origins of the inventors in the firm.

The economic benefits of trust raise the question of why all countries do not have higher levels of trust than they do. One explanation for this is that historical events can have persistent adverse effects on trust (Nunn and Wantchekon, 2011; Alsan and Wanamaker, 2018; Lowes and Montero, 2017). Alternatively, societies may be stuck in 'distrust traps,' where economic activity is low because trust is low which maintains low levels of trust (Guiso et al., 2008).

A third explanation for this is more subtle and stems from the fact that the positive relationship between trust and income is only found at the society level – e.g., regions or countries. When one looks at the individual level, the relationship is actually not positive and monotonic but hump-shaped (Butler et al., 2016). That is, too high a level of trust is associated with less, and not more, income. Thus, while high levels of trust are associated with better outcomes at the society level, this is not necessarily the case at the individual level. This suggests that trust, like other prosocial cultural traits, is subject to a trade-off between what is optimal for the individual and what is optimal for society.

Another example of the connection between models of the collective brain and research in economic history can be found in studies of international contact and migration, which can be thought of as ways to increase the size, diversity, and connectivity of the collective brain. Consistent with theory, immigration has been shown empirically to be associated with higher incomes, more innovation, and stronger international business connections, in the short-, medium-, and long-runs (Burchardi et al., 2019; Sequeira et al., 2020). The effects that connectivity can have on economic activity were recently studied by Campante and Yanagizawa-Drott (2018), who document a strong effect of the presence of direct flights between cities on foreign ownership links between these locations.

3.3.3 How and why history matters

As we have noted, an important aspect of cultural evolution is that it is cumulative. As with biological evolution, the benefit of any possible mutation (and what the optimal next improvement is) depends on the current state of the organism and the environment. In addition, progress must be made in a series of incremental steps (one is not able to jump to a completely different configuration), and each incremental step has to be one that improves the well-being (i.e., fitness) of the organism.

To convey the basic logic of this, Richard Dawkins (1996) in his well-known book *Climbing Mount Improbable* uses the analogy of climbing hills and mountains. One's location on a slope is the product of a set of cumulative and incremental steps. An additional requirement in an evolutionary setting is that one is only able to move uphill. Since elevation represents the payoff or fitness of an organism, the next step is only taken (i.e., the change made) if it results in an improvement and moves you uphill. Thus, one is not able to move downhill.

An example of this process is shown in Fig. 3.6, which provides a visual metaphor of the evolution of the eye drawn by neurobiologist Michael F. Land (Dawkins, 1996, p. 195). The figure shows a series of peaks, which represent groupings of the types of eyes that have developed in various parts of the animal kingdom. It is estimated that eyes have independently evolved between forty and sixty times (Dawkins, 1996, p. 139). The figure shows numerous peaks, the heights of which provide some sense of how well-functioning the eyes are. The lower peaks represent the presence of photocells that detect light by capturing photons with a pigment and translating them into nerve impulses. The highest ranges are the most complex eyes found in the animal kingdom that provide fine-grained and precise sight.

Two types of peaks are shown: those on the left that represent compound eyes and those on the right representing camera-type eyes. Camera eyes are the eyes that evolved among many mammals including humans. They comprise light-sensitive photocells forming a cup, a pinhole, and a lens (or a curved mirror, denoted by lower peaks). Another completely different type of eye is the compound eye, which is common among insects, crustaceans, and some worms. The main difference here is in how photocells are organized to receive photons. With camera eyes, photo cells are organized as if on the inside of a cup backed by an opaque screen so that they look inwards to each other. By contrast, with compound eyes, the photocells are placed on the outside of the cup, causing them to look outwards in different directions.

In Fig. 3.6, the peaks represent different equilibrium outcomes or effective steady states. It is only at these peaks that there are no additional steps to be taken. No additional movement can put one further up a slope. The compound eye peaks are drawn to be lower than the camera eyes. This is because compound eyes are not able to see in as much detail as camera eyes unless they are extremely large. For example, for humans to see as well with a compound eye as with our camera eye, the compound eye would have to be 24 meters in diameter (Dawkins, 1996, p. 181).

Now imagine that one is at one of the compound-eye peaks in Fig. 3.6. Can one move to one of the even higher peaks within the camera-type eye mountain range? The answer is no. This would require one to move downhill which is not allowed with evolution. Effectively, there is a valley between the two peaks that cannot be crossed.

To see why the 'no-downhill' rule has bite, let's consider a concrete example. One characteristic of camera eyes is that the image that is formed is upside down. With compound eyes, the image is right-side up. Thus, if an organism that had compound eyes evolved to have camera eyes, its image-processing nervous apparatus would no longer match its eyes and it would be worse off. Such an innovation would not survive. The only way that a switch could be made is if an animal completely

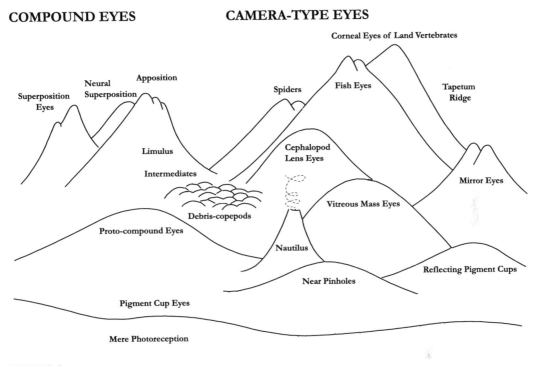

COMPOUND EYES   CAMERA-TYPE EYES

FIGURE 3.6

Illustration of a mountain landscape dictating the evolution of the eye as described by Dawkins (1996).

lost its image processing nervous apparatus so that with a switch from compound to camera eyes the organism is no worse off.

The analogy of climbing mountains is overly simplistic since it has reduced evolution to three dimensions. In reality, fitness and payoffs depend on many factors, resulting in a setting with very high dimensionality. However, the analogy still provides important insights into path dependence and why sometimes it is very difficult to undo the consequences of previous paths.

I now turn from biological evolution to historical or cultural evolution. As I will show, the same logic applies. Consider an example drawn from a stylized model by Nunn (2007). The model features two cultural types, those who produce and those who engage in predation, stealing from those who produce. Each type has a bundle of cultural traits, including accumulated experience, that supports the activity. The model assumes that each period a thief can steal from at most one producer and producers can only be robbed once. There is perfect information and no search costs. If a producer is robbed, the thief steals a fraction q of the producer's output, which is given by A. We let x denote the fraction of the population with a culture of theft.

The payoffs to the two cultural traits are shown in Fig. 3.7a for different values of x. Despite the extreme simplicity of the setting, the model yields multiple equilibria, which are denoted in Fig. 3.7a by x_0^*, x_B^* and x_1^*. When $x = 0$, the payoff to the cultural trait of hard work is greater than to the trait of theft and this is an equilibrium, x_0^*. Here, the only cultural trait that exists is one of hard work. There

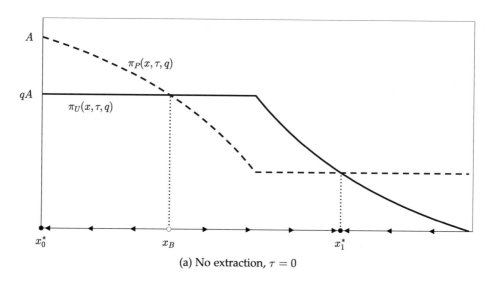

(a) No extraction, $\tau = 0$

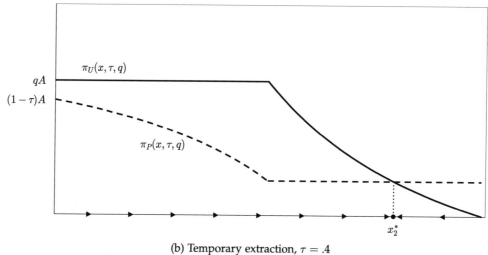

(b) Temporary extraction, $\tau = .4$

FIGURE 3.7

Temporary historical events and permanent effects.

are also two additional equilibria, where both cultural traits exist, and the payoffs to the two traits are equal, x_B^* and x_1^*.

Now consider the fact that cultural evolution is cumulative and that only innovations that improve one's payoff are adopted. That is, you can only 'walk uphill'. Such a restriction can be micro-founded by assuming that in each period each individual, with some probability α, has an experience that potentially changes their cultural values.[15] As part of this experience, the individual learns the cultural value and payoff of another randomly chosen individual and compares it to their own. If the other person has a different cultural value and a higher payoff is observed, the individual adopts that value with a probability that is equal to γ times the difference between the payoffs. As shown by Gintis (1997), given these assumptions one finds that cultural traits grow over time if and only if their average payoffs are higher than the average payoff in the whole population. That is, cultural traits that tend to do better than average grow and those that tend to do worse shrink. Within the model of Nunn (2007), the cultural evolution is given by:

$$\frac{\dot{x}}{x} = \alpha \gamma \left\{ \Pi^R(x) - \overline{\Pi}(x) \right\}, \tag{3.3}$$

where $\overline{\Pi}(x)$ is the average payoff for the whole population, i.e., $x \Pi^R(x) + (1-x) \Pi^E(x)$.

Given this dynamic, which formalizes the notion that cultural evolution is incremental and cumulative, a number of insights emerge. The first is that one of the three Nash equilibria above is unstable. This is the equilibrium marked x^B. It is straightforward to verify that a slight change in x either above or below x^B will generate movements in x away from this equilibrium. Thus, x^B is not a peak, but actually a valley that divides two peaks.

The second insight the model offers is a deeper understanding of why it is so hard for a society stuck in a socially-suboptimal equilibrium to switch to another more socially-beneficial equilibrium. Consider a society, in equilibrium x_1^*. This could describe the low-income situation in many developing countries. Here, average payoffs are comparatively low. Everyone is optimizing. In other words, those at this peak cannot climb any higher. Just as developing countries can see the wealth of rich countries, those at this peak see another higher peak far off in the distance. However, they are not able to get there. Doing so would require individuals to move downhill, adopting behaviors that make them worse off. In this case, this is switching from rent-seeking to production. In popular media, and even journal articles, one regularly observes writers asking the question "why do poor countries stay poor?" Without an evolutionary perspective, particularly one rooted in cultural evolution, this question may appear as a puzzle. However, with this perspective, the reason for this is clear and the question itself seems kind of odd.

Another insight that emerges involves the importance of history. What determines which equilibrium of the two a society is located in? The answer in this setting is history. This is due to the cumulative and incremental nature of evolution. To see this, consider two examples. The first is one where there is stability such that no parameters change over the history of the society. In such a setting, the long-run equilibrium is determined by the value of x during the very first time period, x_0. This uniquely determines the equilibrium in the long-run. If $x_0 < x_B$, then in the long-run the equilibrium is the socially optimal equilibrium where $x = x_0^*$. If $x_0 > x_B$, then the long-run equilibrium is the socially suboptimal one where $x = x_1^*$. Thus, history, meaning the historical conditions of a society, can matter for long-term outcomes. Within an evolutionary framework, this fact is obvious. Rather than asking 'why history matters?', we should ask 'why wouldn't history matter?'.

---

[15] This assumption is consistent with the existing evidence that events within a person's lifetime, whether it is attending celebrations, watching certain television programs, or shocks to the macro environment, can affect a person subsequent cultural values and beliefs (e.g., Madestam and Yanagizawa-Drott, 2011; La Ferrara et al., 2012; Giuliano and Spilimbergo, 2014; Cornelson, 2018; Bursztyn et al., 2020).

Next, consider a scenario where the parameters of the model change. Fig. 3.7b shows the effects of a temporary historical event that reduces the payoffs of those who engage in production relative to those who steal. As shown, the payoffs are tilted so much that the x_0^* equilibrium disappears leaving a unique equilibrium, denoted x_2^* where a high proportion of the population has a culture of theft. For a society initially in the x_0^* equilibrium, over time, in accordance with cultural evolution governed by Eq. (3.3), those with a culture of work slowly adopt a culture of theft. This occurs as the society converges to the x_2^* equilibrium. In other words, the change in the environment caused one of the two peaks to disappear leaving a path upwards to a single peak that is relatively low.

Even if the episode is short-lived and the society has not fully converged to the new equilibrium, as long as the culture of theft has become sufficiently prevalent by the end of the episode, i.e., $x > x^B$, then the temporary event will have permanently moved the society from the equilibrium where everyone has a culture of work, x_0^*, to one where most of the population has a culture of theft, x_1^*. Returning again to the analogy, if the trek upwards towards the low peak has progressed sufficiently, even after the high peak returns, it is impossible to get to it. This is because it would require first going downhill to then climb back up. All that can be done is to continue upwards to the smaller peak.

This example illustrates another way in which historical events can matter, even if the event is only temporary. Nunn (2007) argues that such a sequence of events potentially explains the long-term effects that colonialism and the slave trade appear to have had on many African societies.

3.3.3.1 Kludges

In the example above, when one is to the right of x_B movement towards the lower-peaked equilibrium x_1^* as individuals switch from production to theft is making those who switch better off. They are optimizing. However, each subsequent step in this direction is making things worse as one moves further away from the higher peak. The further one moves up the path towards the low peak, the harder it is to get back to the high peak (even if one were allowed to move downhill).

Such situations have been termed 'kludges.' A commonly cited example of a kludge is the bony flatfish (e.g., Dawkins, 1986, 1996). The ancestors of the flatfish used to swim vertically in the ocean. At some point in their evolutionary history, the fish began living on the ocean floor, lying on one side, leaving one eye looking directly at the sand. Over time and through evolutionary processes, the eye migrated to the top of the head so that the two eyes were on one side of the fish and looking up (Friedman, 2008). An example of the modern flatfish is shown in Fig. 3.8, which is the first drawing in Norman's (1934) collection of flatfish sketches. This incremental innovation solved an inefficiency given the situation at the time but resulted in a design that was suboptimal overall. If one were to completely redesign the bony flatfish, one would have the fish lie on its stomach so that neither eye would be in the ground and symmetry could be maintained. The more the flatfish evolved to its current form, the further away from this ideal it became.

Although the insight this provides for the social sciences is still under-explored, there are a few studies within economics that attempt to make progress in this direction. One is a theoretical analysis by Ely (2011), who provides a formal framework to understand kludges, which he defines as "an improvement upon a highly complex system that solves an inefficiency but in a piecemeal fashion and without addressing the deep-rooted underlying problem ... the kludge itself – because it makes sense only in the presence of the disease it is there to treat – intensifies the internal inefficiency, necessitating either further kludges in the future or else eventually a complete revolution." (p. 211)

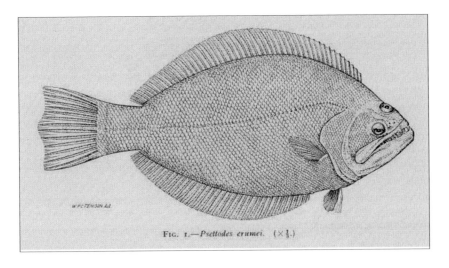

FIG. 1.—*Psettodes erumei.* (×⅓.)

FIGURE 3.8

An example of a kludge: the bony flatfish. *Source*: Figure 1 of Norman (1934).

A subsequent paper takes a more applied approach and uses the notion of kludges to better understand the evolution of laws or policies (Kawai et al., 2018). The paper models the emergence of kludges in policy in a world with two political parties. In this setting, when a new political party comes into power, they can add or remove previous rules in an incremental manner. An interesting aspect of the model is that rules can be deleted. That is, it is possible to move 'downhill'. However, the model shows how despite this ability, the political parties choose not to move 'downhill' removing old rules, but instead only choose to add new rules. This occurs because as policies become more complex – i.e., with a longer path of rules being added on – the rules become entangled in one another. And so removing an unfavorable rule involves also removing favorable rules if they are entangled. Thus, when policy complexity is high, there is entanglement and a bias towards adding rather than deleting rules, generating further additions and complexity.

The model shows that even in settings that are different from that of biological evolution where one can undo innovations, in equilibrium, the environment mirrors biological evolution and kludges emerge. Interestingly, the theory shows that policy is more likely to exhibit kludges if political power is balanced, electoral terms are short, and legislative frictions are high, which are all characteristics of the U.S. political system. The model also predicts that with a kludged public policy, the policy outcomes are moderate, which is also consistent with the reality of the United States.

There are many examples of cultural evolution that can be described as kludges. Consider the issue of paternity certainty. While men can create multiple children during a short period of time, women have biological limits on how quickly they can have children. Thus, the main concern for women is to ensure that the father of her children invests in them sufficiently. That is, she does not want him to employ a strategy where he is choosing quantity over quality. The concern of a potential father is that he may invest heavily in a child thinking that it is his but it may not be. For biological reasons, while a woman is certain that a child is her offspring, there is much less certainty for men. If there is sufficient paternity uncertainty, then he will be less likely to invest in his mate's child.

This is a fundamental issue related to reproductive success that is driven by the nature of reproduction and the biological differences between men and women. The existing evidence indicates that societies came up with different innovations to improve upon this. Much like Dawkins' (1996) analogy of reaching peaks by climbing uphill one step at a time, different societies climbed different hills; customs and traditions evolved that served to improve upon this issue.

Among certain groups, matrilineal kinship developed. Here kinship is traced through the women. Men belong to the lineage of their sisters and mother and children belong to the lineage of their mother. This means that a father does not belong to the same lineage as his children. The children belong to their mother's lineage and their father belongs to his mother and sister's lineage. Because of this, the father is not the most important male adult in a child's life and he is not the one providing primary financial support. The people who fill this role are the mother's brothers (i.e., the child's maternal uncles). The logic behind this is that with paternity uncertainty, there is no guarantee that the father is genetically related to a child. However, it is certain that the mother's brother is related to the child. The child came from their mother and so is related to her. The mother and her brother came from the same mother and so they are related. Thus, the child must be related to their uncle. By contrast, there is no guarantee that the child is related to their father.

Thus, one innovation in the face of paternity uncertainty is matrilineal kinship, where family/clan membership is traced through women. The results of such an innovation are far reaching and can be difficult to undo. In this case, it is natural that family members live in close proximity to one another, and, thus, there is matrilocality, where the nuclear family lives near the woman's family.

An alternative incrementally-designed set of innovations that has emerged is as follows. Rather than having matrilineal kinship, a society has patrilineal kinship. Lineage is traced through the father's line. At the time of marriage, the wife leaves her lineage and joins her husband's lineage. Due to the tendency of lineages to live within close proximity, patrilocality develops where families live close to the husband's parents.

This then presents another problem. If daughters leave their parent's lineage and move away from them when they are married, what incentive is there for the parents to invest resources in raising someone who they will never see again and no longer be part of their family after marriage? The incremental innovation that emerged to overcome this issue is bridewealth, where a sizeable transfer of resources is made from the husband's family to the wife's family at marriage. This is given as a gift of appreciation and incentivizes the parents' investment in their daughter even knowing that she will not be a member of the family in the future. The practice of bridewealth is common in patrilineal societies but not in matrilineal societies.

The two evolved solutions to the problem of paternity uncertainty and paternal investment in children are very different and take societies along different paths with a different set of incremental improvements. There is evidence that one path may be better than the other. Lowes (2018) finds that within matrilineal households, due to the greater empowerment of women, children are healthier and more educated. Thus, it is plausible that this evolutionary path is better for fitness. However, once society has progressed down the patrilineal path, jumping to the matrilineal equilibrium is no easy task. This would involve undoing existing customs, leading to a lower payoff to then be able to travel along the matrilineal path. One would need to undo bridewealth, patrilocality, and fundamentally alter society's perception of kinship.

This is potentially an example of a kludge. As the cultural innovations accumulate, the society is locked in more and more deeply into a suboptimal equilibrium. The case for a kludge among patrilineal societies is particularly strong for those who have developed additional cultural innovations that are harmful to women but are meant to resolve the issue of paternity uncertainty. As has been documented, in societies that practice nomadic pastoralism, where men are often absent for long periods of time, the problem of paternity uncertainty is particularly acute. In these societies, it appears as if additional innovations are required. It is not possible to move 'downhill' and then back 'uphill' to the higher matrilineal 'peak'. Instead one must continue upward on the existing path.

As documented in Becker (2019), female genital cutting and infibulation developed as customs that helped husbands ensure greater paternity certainty. With these extreme forms of female circumcision, sex becomes painful, reducing the temptation to have sexual relations outside of the marriage, even when the husband is away for extended periods of time. In other parts of the world, other customs emerged that also served the purpose of controlling women's autonomy and sexuality, such as the veil or burqa, restrictions on women's mobility, and limits on the decisions that women could make.

3.3.4 Group-level selection

Our discussion up to this point has implicitly assumed that the success of a cultural trait depends on the wellbeing of the individuals with the trait. However, historically a big part of cultural evolution occurs through the rise and fall of societies. In other words, the fate of individuals and their success is as much tied to the success of their community as to their own relative success within the community. Thus, what may also be important for the adoption of cultural traits is how they affect the society as a whole. This is called group-level selection and is often used as one explanation for why prosocial cultural traits (ones that are costly for the individual but beneficial for the group), like altruism or proclivity to cooperate, can emerge (Henrich, 2004a; Richerson et al., 2016).

This insight has the potential to improve our understanding of the historical process, particularly at the society level. To see this, recall the famous quote from Charles Tilly (1990) that "war made the state, and the state made war" (p. 42). While generally not viewed in this light, Tilly's famous argument that war lies at the heart of the economic rise of Europe is actually an argument about group-level selection. Those groups, namely states, with characteristics that were beneficial were able to outcompete other states with less beneficial characteristics. He writes that "states having access to a combination of large rural populations, capitalists, and relatively commercialized economies won out...their form of state became the predominant one in Europe. Eventually European states converged on that form: the nation states." (p. 15).

While recent studies have examined the effects of warfare within the European context on taxation, urbanization, and state formation (e.g., Gennaioli and Voth, 2015; Dincecco and Onorato, 2017), group-level selection has yet to be examined, even though the famous Tilly effect can be interpreted through this lens.[16] With the formation of groups, such as villages, kingdoms, empires, or nation-states, the wellbeing of the citizens of each entity are intricately connected. If a kingdom is conquered, everyone in the kingdom is conquered. Thus, warfare and interstate conflict are a form of group-level competition.

---

[16] The most extensive research undertaken along these lines is from the evolutionary biologist Peter Turchin, who applies insights from evolutionary biology to understand the course of human history, including warfare and the rise and fall of empires. For a sampling of this ambitious research agenda, see Turchin (2003, 2006, 2016) and Turchin et al. (2013).

This is important because this, in turn, leads to group-level selection.[17] When an individual's survival is, to a large extent, determined by the success of the group rather than their own success, then cultural traits that are not individually optimal but are socially beneficial can arise. An example of such a trait is altruism. Giving to others when they are in need reduces one's material wellbeing. However, if everyone in society does this, then the society will be better off. Of course, just because traits are socially beneficial does not mean they will arise in equilibrium. This depends on the trade-offs between group-level benefits and individual-level costs. The stronger group-level selection is, the more likely it is that the former prevails over the latter (Henrich, 2004a).

The prediction that arises from the framework of group-level selection is that, all else equal, conflict should be associated with more prosocial traits (i.e., traits that are individually costly but socially beneficial). Several recent studies have stumbled across the finding that conflict appears to be associated with higher levels of prosociality and greater social cohesion. This was confirmed in a recent meta-analysis Bauer et al. (2016). The finding is counter-intuitive if one expects that conflict would cause the breakdown of social capital. However, viewed through the lens of intergroup competition, these relationships make perfect sense. Evolutionary theory predicts an association between conflict and prosocial behavior if conflict activates prosocial psychology which is particularly beneficial in that setting due to group-level selection forces.

Another explanation for the relationship comes from very recent research in social psychology that emphasizes the effect that 'threat' has on the extent to which norms are adhered to (i.e., on the 'tightness' of norms). According to Gelfand (2018), external threat increases the importance of norm following and therefore tightness increases. If conflict is a form of threat and society's baseline norms are ones of cooperation and prosociality towards in-group members, then past experience with conflict will lead to greater prosociality. Consistent with this interpretation, subsequent research by Henrich et al. (2019) shows that past experience with conflict is associated with greater religiosity, which can be interpreted as a tightening of traditional norms. The study uses a survey of 1,709 individuals from three post-conflict societies: Uganda, Sierra Leone and Tajikistan. They find that conflict exposure is associated with an increased likelihood of identifying as Christian or Muslim and with more frequent participation in religious gatherings and rituals.

A case study illustrating the logic of group-level competition is provided by Nunn and Sanchez de la Sierra (2017). The authors describe recent events in a village in the Eastern Democratic Republic of the Congo. The village had a history of being regularly pillaged by a Hutu militia group called the FDLR. The raiding and pillaging had occurred multiple times per year for well over a decade. This was until 2012 when an elderly man in the village, through a dream, learned how to bulletproof the people of the village by having them undertake a specific ritual. Beliefs in bulletproofing are common in the region and are connected to traditional religious beliefs. As is common, this form of bulletproofing came with conditions that had to be followed for the protection to work. Thus, if someone who had been known to have been bulletproofed died, then it must be the case that they did not follow the necessary conditions. Due to the bulletproofing, the villagers, particularly the young men, were able to fight back when they were attacked. Over the course of multiple years, the FDLR eventually gave up

---

[17] To be precise, there are two conditions that are needed for warfare to cause cultural group selection. The first is that variation in cultural traits between groups causes success in warfare. The second is that success in warfare affects the spread of the cultural traits (Richerson et al., 2016).

trying to attack the village and concentrated their efforts elsewhere. For the first time in over a decade, the village had been liberated.

In their analysis, Nunn and Sanchez de la Sierra (2017) try to understand these events. They interpret the production function of producing the village's freedom as one with team production, meaning there are strong complementarities to effort. As is well known, the equilibrium level of effort is lower than is socially optimal in such settings. Beliefs in bulletproofing serve to reduce the perceived cost of effort and to raise the equilibrium level of effort so that it is closer to the socially-optimal level. Thus, these beliefs, even if false, are beneficial for society. However, this benefit does not guarantee the existence of such beliefs. As discussed above, socially-beneficial traits that are individually suboptimal only arise with strong group-level selection. The authors argue that the Eastern DRC, which has experienced decades of sustained conflict, is a setting where group-level selection is expected to be strong. Thus, in their setting, conflict generated group-level competition, which resulted in bulletproofing beliefs, which although individually suboptimal are socially beneficial. This interpretation is consistent with the fact that beliefs about bulletproofing appear to be common in many conflict-ridden areas, not only in the contemporary period but also historically (Kamarck, 2009, ch. 4; Sinclair-Thomas and Challis, 2017).

The best evidence for whether historical warfare would have been significant enough to generate group-level selection is from a recent study by Samuel Bowles (2009). In it, he takes a historical perspective and asks whether the group-level selective pressures due to intergroup conflict during Late Pleistocene and early Holocene could have been strong enough to affect the evolution of prosocial cultural traits. The study combines models of group-level selection, archaeological data from the period, and ethnographic data from contemporary hunter-gatherers. It finds that the levels of mortality associated with intergroup warfare would have been sizeable enough to have a large effect on prosocial traits, promoting behaviors that while individually costly would have been beneficial for the group overall.

While the examples discussed to this point have focused on warfare as the source of group-level competition, the exact same logic applies to competition that occurs through market forces. While this form of competition might not be particularly important for studying cultural evolution over the course of human history, it is highly relevant for the field of economics where markets are central. One of the few pieces of research along these lines is the recent study by Francois et al. (2018), which examines selection arising from firm competition. They begin by first showing a relationship between the competitiveness of an industry and the level of trust of individuals who work in that industry. Their analysis looks at the United States and Germany and estimates the relationship in the cross-section and also over time for workers who switch industries.

In this setting, firms are the group and firm competition is the form of group-level competition. Given this, group-level selection is expected to facilitate the emergence of group-level beneficial traits, like generalized trust. Firms with trusting employees perform better and are more likely to survive. This is true despite evidence that suggests that if trust is too high it can lower individual income (Butler et al., 2016). In other words, even though high trust is socially beneficial, it is not necessarily individually optimal.

The authors confirm these findings and their interpretation by undertaking an event study that exploits the increase in competition that arose from a series of bank deregulations that occurred across U.S. states in the 1980s. Lastly, the authors are able to replicate the effects of group-level selection on generalized trust using a behavioral experiment involving 220 French participants. Participants were placed in groups of 20 and played a series of one-shot anonymous public goods games with other participants from their group. In one treatment arm, payoffs were determined by the relative performance of a participant's group compared to other groups. In the other treatment arm, payoffs were determined in the standard manner, by the earnings of the participant him/herself. They find that the group-level selection treatment resulted in higher contributions and importantly in higher levels of self-reported trust at the end of the experiment.

The study is important because it provides valuable evidence that market competition can result in group-level selection. This provides a new perspective from which one can think about market competition and its effects.

3.3.5 Biology, sex, and gender

There are well-known biological differences between men and women. One difference is that the two sexes have very different roles in reproduction. The role of men is to fertilize an egg, while that of women is to carry the egg as it develops, give birth, and (typically) breastfeed the newborn for the first years of life. As a consequence, women can have only one offspring (ignoring the case of twins) per 1–2 year period. By contrast, men can have a much larger number of offspring during this same time. However, due to the nature of sex and childbirth, men have much less certainty that a child that is born is related to them biologically. By contrast, women have near-perfect certainty that a child is her offspring.

It has been argued that the different biological constraints faced by men and women result in different optimal mating strategies (e.g., Trivers, 1972; Buss and Scmitt, 1993; Buss, 1994). As we will see, these strategies have implications for gender relations and social structure more generally. For women, the concern is that men will choose a quantity-over-quality mating strategy and not invest sufficient resources into the child. For men, the concern is that the child is not actually theirs and they are allocating resources to another person's child.

These concerns have important social consequences. As mentioned, Becker (2019) studies how the fundamental issue of paternity uncertainty differs depending on ecological conditions. Her study shows that societies that engage in pastoralism tend to exhibit greater control over women's sexuality by men. This can take the form of norms about female autonomy and practices such as infibulation and veiling. This is because, in a pastoral society, grazing requires men to be absent from the community as their herds move to new pastures. These prolonged periods of absence raised concerns of infidelity, which resulted in the evolution of restrictions on female sexuality.

Another evolved response to the issue of paternal uncertainty has been matrilineal kinship. Rather than the father being the primary supporter of a child, it is the mother's brother (i.e., the maternal uncle). With matrilineal kinship, lineage is traced through women. Men belong to the lineage of their sisters and mothers, and children belong to the lineage of their mother. Thus, a father does not belong to the same lineage as his children. The children belong to their mother's lineage and the father belongs to his mother and sister's lineage. As a consequence, the father is not the most important male adult in his children's lives and, often, he is not the one who provides primary financial support. Instead, this is the mother's brothers (i.e., the children's maternal uncles). As explained above, the logic behind this is that while there is no guarantee that the father is genetically related to the children, it is certain that the mother's brother is related to the children. Thus, the fundamental problem of how to incentivize the father to invest in his children if perceived paternal uncertainty is high is solved by having developed norms and customs where maternal uncles are the ones who invest in children.

As we have discussed, matrilineal kinship and control over women's sexuality are two different evolutionary paths that serve to address the same fundamental biologically-based problem. A testable prediction of this evolutionary perspective is that since the two sets of customs are solutions to the same problem, they are substitutes and the presence of one should be negatively associated with the presence of the other. If one looks at ethnographic data, one finds that matrilineal kinship is associated with weaker control of women's sexuality. Although data are limited, there is some information on these cultural traits in the *Ethnographic Atlas*. Within the database, there are 244 patrilineal and 59 matrilineal ethnic groups for which data are available on societal norms about the premarital sexual behavior of girls, which we take to be an indicator of sexual norms more generally. For matrilineal groups with data, only 6.7% (4 of 59) have norms that prohibit any sex before marriage. Among patrilineal groups with data, the same statistic is 34% (82 of 244). By contrast, among matrilineal groups with data, 54% (32 of 59) have norms that fully permit premarital sex, while among patrilineal groups with data, this figure is only 33% (80 of 244).[18]

Another biological difference between men and women lies in their body size and strength, which is an example of a more general phenomenon referred to as sexual dimorphism. Relative to women, men tend to be taller, larger in stature, and have greater upper body strength (Gustafsson and Lindenfors, 2004). These differences have also been fairly stable (i.e., a 15% difference in body mass) for *Homo sapiens* since at least the Pleistocene (Ruff, 2002). Recent research within economics has studied the consequence of sexual dimorphism for modern gender norms and how it is mediated by historical technologies that made the physical differences more or less important. Alesina et al. (2013b) provide evidence that the greater physical size and strength of males was an important determinant of a gender-based division of labor historically, but primarily in agricultural societies that had adopted intensive plow agriculture. With this form of agriculture, significant upper body strength was needed to control or pull the plow. As a consequence, in these societies, there was a gendered division of labor where men worked outside the home in agriculture and women tended to work within the home. As shown by Alesina et al. (2013b), this division generated norms about the appropriate role of women in society, which persist in the modern era and affect female employment outside the home today. The form of traditional agriculture has even been found to affect preferences for sons over daughters, which results in male-biased sex-ratios (Alesina et al., 2018).

3.4 Contributions of economics to cultural evolution

The study of cultural evolution is a recent area of research, with the bulk of findings emerging in the last few decades. The field began with a small number of scholars who adapted models from evolutionary biology to cultural evolution (e.g., Cavalli-Sforza and Feldman, 1981; Boyd and Richerson, 1985). An important contribution of economics has been to use these theoretical foundations to build more elaborate models that remain tractable and provide insight into a range of economic issues, including preference heterogeneity and segregation (Bisin and Verdier, 2000, 2001b), entrepreneurship (Doepke and Zilibotti, 2014), occupational choice (Doepke and Zilibotti, 2008), female labor force

---

[18] Also consistent with this is the finding from Lowes (2018) that matrilineal kinship is associated with greater female empowerment.

participation (Fernandez, 2013), parenting strategies (Bisin and Verdier, 2001a; Doepke and Zilibotti, 2017), or domestic institutions (Tabellini, 2008; Bisin and Verdier, 2017). A related area of research that has developed within economics is theoretical work that exploits the dynamics of natural selection to understand various aspects of economic growth over the very long-run (e.g., Galor and Moav, 2002; Galor and Michalopoulos, 2012; Galor and Ozak, 2016; Galor and Savitskiy, 2018).

One way to think about the difference between theoretical studies of culture within evolutionary anthropology and economics is that the prior has tended to focus on studying the emergence of culture and its transmission between individuals. Thus, culture and its evolution is the outcome of interest in the models. By contrast, within economics, culture and its transmission are taken as given and the analysis follows based on this.[19] Thus, the theoretical work within evolutionary anthropology provides the micro-foundations for the assumptions used in a wide range of models within cultural economics.

While the origins of the study of cultural evolution were primarily theoretical, the field has subsequently become increasingly quantitative (Mesoudi, 2016). It is this line of analysis to which economic historians and growth economists have made the greatest contributions. A large body of evidence documents how the historical environment or historical shocks – what other disciplines would call ecological factors – affects the long-term evolution of cultural traits.[20] For the interested reader, an overview of this body of evidence is provided in Table 3.1. The table reports the citation, the cultural trait that is being explained, the determinant of interest, the unit of observation, the sample, and the primary statistical methods used. Although the list is far from exhaustive, it still shows that economists have made important contributions to a deeper understanding of the historical and ecological factors that have shaped the evolution of cultural traits.

Recently, there has been a push for multidisciplinary research that takes a historical/evolutionary perspective and involves both economists and evolutionary anthropologists. An example is a recent collaboration between anthropologist Joseph Henrich and three economists (Schulz et al., 2019). Together, the authors study the historical origins of Western European psychology. They document how the policies of the medieval Roman Catholic Church, such as the prohibition on cousin marriage, weakened extended kinship ties and led to a more individualistic social structure and psychology. To do this, the authors use data from a range of disciplines, including historical data on the duration of exposure to the medieval Western church, ethnographic data on the traditional prevalence of kinship practices like cousin marriage and polygamy, and contemporary survey and experimental data that measure a range of cultural and psychological traits.

Another way that economics has contributed to the study of cultural evolution is by evidence for the effects that shorter-term factors can have on cultural traits. This literature is summarized in Table 3.2. It has the same structure as Table 3.1 except that it summarizes studies that estimate the more-immediate effects of the factors of interest; namely, effects that are felt within a person's lifetime rather than multiple generations into the future.

An additional contribution that economics has made is to estimate the effects that cultural traits have on economic outcomes. Research has shown that culture affects a host of outcomes, including trade, foreign direct investment, political turnover, conflict, innovation, savings, investment, and economic growth. An overview of the key studies from this body of research is provided in Table 3.3.[21]

---

[19] An exception is Bisin and Verdier (2001a).

[20] See Nunn (forthcoming) for a summary of this literature.

[21] For a review of the early literature documenting the economic consequences of culture see Guiso et al. (2006).

Table 3.1 Summary of the literature on the long-term determinants of cultural traits.

Study	Trait being explained	Determinant being tested	Unit of observation	Scope of sample	Statistical strategy
Alesina and Fuchs-Schundeln (2007)	Preferences for government redistribution	Communism	Individuals	East & West Germany	Natural experiment, OLS
Alesina et al. (2013b)	Gender roles & gender attitudes	Plough agriculture	Individuals, ethnicities, countries	Global	OLS, IV
Alesina et al. (2018)	Male-female sex ratio if children	Plough agriculture	Countries	Global	OLS, IV
Alsan and Wanamaker (2018)	Trust of medical system	Tuskegee experiment	Individuals	United States	DD
Andersen et al. (2016)	Work ethic	Catholic Order of Cistercians	Counties	England	OLS
Ang and Fredriksson (2017)	Individualism	Labor intensive agriculture	Countries, ethnicities	Global	OLS
Ang and Fredriksson (2017)	Strength of family ties	Wheat agriculture	Individuals, districts, countries	United States and Global	OLS, IV
Baranov et al. (2018)	Attitudes about gay marriage	19th Century sex ratios	Individuals, counties	Australia	OLS, DD, IV
Bazzi et al. (2018)	Individualism/collectivism	Frontier experience	Counties	United States	OLS, IV
Becker (2019)	Female genital cutting	Pastoralism	Individuals, ethnic groups	Africa, Global	RD
Becker et al. (2016)	Trust of state bureaucracy	Habsburg empire	Individuals	Eastern Europe	OLS
BenYishay et al. (2017)	Matrilineal inheritance	Presence of coral reefs	Islands and ethnic groups	Global	Natural experiment, OLS
Blouin (2018)	Interpersonal trust	Colonial production quotas	Counties	Rwanda	OLS, DD
Brodeur and Haddad (2018)	Attitudes towards homosexuality	19th Century gold rush	Individuals	United States	IV, RD, DD
Campa and Serafinelli (2019)	Attitudes towards gender equality	Communism	Women, cohorts	Germany, Central & E. Europe	Natural experiment, IV
Campante and Yanagizawa-Drott (2016)	Authoritative parenting style	Father's war experience	Individuals	United States	OLS
Cervellati et al. (2019)	Ethnic affiliation, endogamy	Prevalence of malaria	Individual, ethnic groups	Africa	Natural experiment
Chaudhary et al. (2018)	Cooperation (contribution to a public good)	Colonial rule (direct vs. indirect)	Individuals, villages	Rajasthan, India	DD, IV
Cornelson (2018)	African American educational attainment	Role models from Cosby Show	Cities & birth cohorts	United States	OLS
Couttenier et al. (2017)	Homicides	Timing of mineral discoveries	Counties	United States	RD
Dell et al. (2018)	Cooperation	Dai Viet Kingdom	Villages, individuals	Vietnam	RD
Dell and Querubin (2018)	Attitudes towards the U.S.	Military bombing	Villages, Individuals	Vietnam	OLS, IV
Enke (2019)	Universal/limited morality	Strength of kinship ties	Individuals, ethnic groups, countries	Global	OLS, IV
Fenske (2014)	Polygyny	Historical mission stations and education	Individuals	Africa	OLS, IV
Fernandez et al. (2004)	Gender attitudes	Female wartime employment during WWII	Married women	United States	OLS, DD
Fouka and Schlapfer (2020)	Work ethic	Marginal returns to labor of crop mix	Individuals, districts, countries	Europe	OLS
Galor and Ozak (2016)	Patience	Agricultural suitability of traditional crops	Individuals, countries	Global	OLS, DD
Galor and Savitskiy (2018)	Loss aversion	Climatic volatility	Individuals, ethnic groups, countries	Global	OLS
Gershman (2019)	Supernatural beliefs	Trans-Atlantic slave trade	Individuals, ethnic groups, regions	Africa & Latin America	OLS, IV
Giuliano and Nunn (2013)	Support for democracy	Traditional village leadership	Individuals, countries	Global	OLS

continued on next page

Table 3.1 (*continued*)

Study	Trait being explained	Determinant being tested	Unit of observation	Scope of sample	Statistical strategy
Giuliano and Nunn (2021)	Importance of tradition	Similarity of environment across generations	Individuals, ethnic groups, countries	Global	Natural experiment, OLS
Grosjean (2014)	A culture of honor	Scotch-Irish Immigration	Counties	United States	OLS
Grosjean and Khattar (2018)	Attitudes about gender equality	18th Century male-biased sex ratios	Counties	Australia	IV
Guiso et al. (2016)	Self-efficacy, civic mindedness	Medieval independent city states	Individuals, villages	Italy	IV, DD, OLS
Heldring (2021)	Obedience to state	State formation	Individuals	Rwanda	Natural experiment
Karaja and Rubin (2017)	Interpersonal trust	Habsburg vs. Ottoman/Russian state	Individuals, villages	Region of Romania	Natural experiment
Lowes et al. (2017)	Rule following	State formation	Individuals	Province in the Dem. Rep. Congo	Natural experiment
Lowes and Montero (2017)	Trust in Western medicine	Colonial medical Campaigns	Individuals, districts	French Colonial Africa	IV, OLS
Lowes and Montero (2019)	Social cohesion	Forced rubber collection	Individuals, villages	Democratic Republic of the Congo	RD, OLS
Michalopoulos (2012)	Ethnic affiliation	Variation in agricultural suitability	Grid cells	Global	OLS
Michalopoulos et al. (2018)	Adherence to Islam	Trade routes, land suitability	Countries, ethnic groups	Global	OLS
Moscona et al. (2017)	Ingroup and outgroup trust	Traditional segmentary lineage organization	Individuals, ethnic groups	Africa	OLS
Nunn (2010)	Belief in Christianity	Colonial mission stations	Individuals, ethnic groups, villages	Africa	OLS
Nunn and Wantchekon (2011)	Trust	Slave trades	Individuals	Sub-Saharan Africa	IV
Okoye (2017)	Trust	18th Century Christian missions	Individuals, ethnic groups	Nigeria	OLS
Olken (2009)	Social cohesion	Introduction of tv & radio	Villages, individuals	Indonesia	OLS
Ramos-Toro (2019)	Prosociality, in-group bias, trust in medicine	Ancestors being kept in a leper colony	Individuals	Colombia	OLS
Rubin (2014)	Religious beliefs (Protestantism)	Early access to printing press	Cities	Europe	OLS
Rustagi (2019)	Conditional cooperation	Medieval democracy	Individuals, municipalities	Switzerland	OLS, IV
Schulz (2017), Schulz et al. (2019)	Kinship ties	Catholic Church's medieval policies	Cities, regions, countries	Europe and Global	DD, OLS
Teso (2019)	Gender roles	Slave trades	Individuals, ethnic groups	Sub-Saharan Africa	OLS, IV
Tur-Prats and Valencia Caicedo (2020)	Interpersonal trust	Spanish Civil War	Individuals	Spain	OLS, RD, IV
Xue (2018)	Gender roles	Cotton weaving	Counties	China	IV

Notes: The statistical strategies list in the last column of the table include: natural experiments, instrumental variables (IV), regression discontinuity (RD), difference-in-difference estimates (DD), or randomized control trials (RCT). Natural experiments are cases where the determinant of interest occurs in locations or to individuals in an idiosyncratic manner that is close to randomly assigned. Instrumental variables are employed when one can find a variable (i.e., instrument) that is correlated with the determinant of interest and only affects the outcome of interest through the determinant. In such cases, the instrument can be used to obtain a consistent causal estimate of the effect of the determinant on the outcome. Regression discontinuity can be employed when the treatment of interest has strict idiosyncratically determined borders delineating the treated group from untreated group. In such cases, differences in the outcome of interest can be compared at the boundary and this provides an unbiased causal estimate of the treatment of interest. Difference-in-difference estimates exploit variation in a treatment over time and estimate effects by looking at how the outcome changes for the treatment group relative to the control group after, relative to before, the treatment occurs. Another strategy is for the researcher to manipulate the implementation of a treatment of interest so that the implementation is done randomly (RCT). This allows the researcher to obtain causal estimates by comparing the randomly chosen treatment group to the randomly chosen control group. Lastly, OLS refers to ordinary least squares, which indicate that the study relies on evidence from conditional correlations.

Table 3.2 Overview of the economics literature on the shorter-term determinants of cultural traits.

Study	Trait being explained	Determinant tested	Unit of observation	Scope of sample	Statistical strategy
Alesina and Fuchs-Schundeln (2007)	Changing preferences for government redistribution	Unification of Germany	Individuals	East & West Germany	Natural experiment, OLS
Bau (2019)	Differential child preference	Government pension	Individuals	Indonesia & Ghana	DD
Bauer et al. (2014)	Prosociality & in-group bias	Civil conflict	Individuals	Rep. of Georgia & Sierra Leone	OLS
Beaman et al. (2009)	Attitudes about women and politics	Reservation of position for women	Individuals	India	Natural experiment
Bentzen (2019)	Religiosity	Earthquakes	Individuals	Global	Natural experiment, DD
Bergh and Ohrvall (2018)	Trust	Movement to new country	Individuals	Swedish Expatriates	Natural experiment, OLS
Booth et al. (2019)	Competitiveness	Growing up under communism	Women	Beijing & Taipei	Natural experiment, DD
Bursztyn et al. (2020)	Attitudes about gender equality	Information provision	Men	Saudi Arabia	RCT
Campante and Yanagizawa-Drott (2015)	Religiosity & subjective well-being	Ramadan fasting	Individuals	Global	Natural experiment, DD
Cassar et al. (2013)	Trust	Civil conflict	Individuals	Tajikistan	OLS
Cassar et al. (2017)	Risk aversion, prosociality & patience	Tsunami	Individuals	Rural Thailand	Natural experiment, OLS
Cantoni et al. (2017)	Political beliefs & attitudes	School curricula	Students	China	DD
Clingingsmith et al. (2009)	Attitudes about gender equality	Hajj pilgrimage	Individuals	Global (all visa applicants)	Natural experiment
Della Vigna and Kaplan (2007)	Political preferences (voting)	Access to Fox News	Towns	United States	Natural experiment, DD
Depetris-Chauvin et al. (2020)	National identity vs. coethnic identity	National soccer team victories	Individuals	Africa	Natural experiment, RD
Fernandez et al. (2019)	Openness to homosexuality	AIDS epidemic	Individuals	United States	OLS, DD
Fouka (2020)	Cultural assimilation	Language restrictions	Individuals	German immigrants in the U.S.	Natural experiment, DD
Francois et al. (2010)	Trust	Firm competition	Workers, industries	United States	OLS
Francois et al. (2018)	Trust	Banking deregulation, firm competition	Workers, industries	United States, Germany	OLS, DD
Giuliano and Spilimbergo (2014)	Luck vs. effort, preferences for redistribution	Childhood recession	Individuals	United States & 37 Countries	DD
Henrich et al. (2019)	Religiosity	War	Individuals	Uganda, Sierra Leone, Tajikistan	OLS
Jakiela and Ozier (2019)	Exposure to election violence	Risk aversion	Individuals	Kenya	Natural experiment, DD, IV
Jensen and Oster (2009)	Gender norms, female empowerment	Cable & satellite television	Villages	India	DD
Kosse et al. (2019)	Altruism, trust, & other-regarding behavior	Mentor program	Children	Germany	RCT
La Ferrara et al. (2012)	Norms about fertility	Television soap operas	Women	Brazil	Natural experiment, DD
Madestam and Yanagizawa-Drott (2011)	Political preferences	Fourth of July festivities	Individuals	United States	Natural experiment, DD
Madestam et al. (2013)	Political preferences	Tea Party protests	Counties	United States	Natural experiment, DD
Mitrunen (2019)	Assimilation & patriotism	Compulsory patriotic acts in schools	Children	United States	Natural experiment, OLS
Qian (2008)	Gender bias (sex imbalance)	Female income	Individuals	China	DD
Rao (2019)	Altruism toward outgroup	School integration polities	Children	Private schools in Delhi, India	Natural experiment, DD
Riley (2017)	Educational success	Watching inspirational movie	Secondary school students	Schools in Uganda	RCT

Notes: The statistical strategies list in the last column of the table include: natural experiments, instrumental variables (IV), regression discontinuity (RD), difference-in-difference estimates (DD), or randomized control trials (RCT). Natural experiments are cases where the determinant of interest occurs in locations or to individuals in an idiosyncratic manner that is dose to randomly assigned. Instrumental variables are employed when one can find a variable (i.e., instrument) that is correlated with the determinant and only affects the outcome of interest through die determinant In such cases, the instrument can be used to obtain a consistent causal estimate of the effect of die determinant on the outcome. Regression discontinuity can be employed when the treatment of interest has strict idiosyncratically determined borders delineating the treated group from untreated group. In such cases, differences in the outcome of interest can be compared at the boundary and this provides an unbiased causal estimate of the treatment of interest Difference-in-difference estimates exploit variation in a treatment over time and estimate effects by looking at how the outcome changes for the treatment group relative to the control group after, relative to before, the treatment occurs. Another strategy is for the researcher to manipulate the implementation of a treatment of interest so that the implementation is done randomly (RCT). This allows the researcher to obtain causal estimates by comparing the randomly chosen treatment group to the randomly chosen control group. Lastly, OLS refers to ordinary least squares, which indicate that the study relies on evidence from conditional correlations.

Table 3.3 Overview of the economics literature on the consequences of differences in cultural traits.

Study	Outcome being affected	Trait being examined	Unit of observation	Scope of sample	Statistical strategy
Aghion et al. (2010)	Government regulation	Distrust	Individuals, countries	Global	OLS
Algan and Cahuc (2010)	Economic growth	Generalized trust	Individuals, countries	Global	Natural experiment, IV
Ashraf et al. (2020)	Education	Bride price	Individuals, ethnic groups	Indonesia & Zambia	OLS, DD
Atkin (2016)	Malnutrition	Food preferences	Households	India	Natural experiment, OLS
Becker and Woessmann (2008)	Female education, gender gap	Religious beliefs (Protestantism)	Counties	Prussia	OLS, IV
Becker and Woessmann (2009)	Education & economic growth	Religious beliefs (Protestantism)	Counties	Prussia	OLS, IV
Butler et al. (2016)	Income	Generalized trust	Individuals	Global	OLS
Campante and Chor (2017)	Industrial specialization of production	Workplace obedience	Countries & industries	Global	OLS, DD
Campante and Yanagizawa-Drott (2015)	Happiness, economic output	Religiosity due to fasting	Individuals, countries	Islamic countries	Natural experiment
Corno et al. (2019)	Early marriage and fertility differences due to drought	Bride price or dowry	Women	Sub-Saharan Africa & India	OLS
Dohmen et al. (2018)	Capital accumulation & economic growth	Patience	Countries	Global	OLS
Enke (2020)	Voting in U.S. Presidential elections	Universal vs. group-based morality	Counties	United States	OLS
Enke (2019)	Economic growth	Kinship tightness, universal morality	Ethnic groups, countries	Global	OLS
Enke et al. (2019)	Political preferences	Universal vs. group-based morality	Individuals, countries	United States & Europe	OLS
Figlio et al. (2019)	Educational performance	Long-term orientation	Immigrant students in U.S.	Global	OLS
Gorodnichenko and Roland (2011, 2017)	Economic growth	Individualism vs. collectivism	Countries	Global	OLS, IV
Gorodnichenko and Roland (2015)	Autocratic vs. democratic national government	Individualism vs. collectivism	Countries	Global	OLS, IV
Gorodnichenko et al. (2018)	Foreign outsourcing vs. foreign direct investment	Cultural difference between countries	Country pairs	Global	OLS, DD
Guiso et al. (2009)	Bilateral trade & foreign direct investment	Trust between countries	Countries	European countries	OLS
Jayachandran and Pande (2017)	Childhood stunting	Son preference	Children	India & Africa	OLS
Lowes (2018)	Household cooperation, female, and child wellbeing	Matrilineal kinship	Individuals, ethnic groups	Dem. Republic of the Congo	OLS, RD
Moscona et al. (2019)	Conflict	Segmentary lineage systems	Ethnic groups, grid cells	Africa	OLS, RD
Nguyen (2018)	Innovation	Interpersonal trust	CEOs, workers, companies	United States	OLS
Nunn et al. (2019)	Political turnover	Generalized trust	Countries, U.S. counties	Global & United States	DD

Notes: The statistical strategies list in the last column of the table include: natural experiments, instrumental variables (IV), regression discontinuity (RD), difference-in-difference estimates (DD), or randomized control trials (RCT). Natural experiments are cases where the determinant of interest occurs in locations or to individuals in an idiosyncratic manner that is close to randomly assigned. Instrumental variables are employed when one can find a variable (i.e., instrument) that is correlated with the determinant and only affects the outcome through the determinant In such cases, the instrument can be used to obtain a consistent causal estimate of the effect of the determinant on the outcome. Regression discontinuity can be employed when the treatment of interest has strict idiosyncratically determined borders delineating the treated group from untreated group. In such cases, differences in the outcome of interest can be compared at the boundary and this provides an unbiased causal estimate of the treatment of interest Difference-in-difference estimates exploit variation in a treatment over time and estimate effects by looking at how the outcome changes for the treatment group relative to the control group after, relative to before, die treatment occurs. Another strategy Is for the researcher to manipulate the Implementation of a treatment of Interest so that the implementation Is done randomly (RCT). This allows the researcher to obtain causal estimates by comparing the randomly chosen treatment group to the randomly chosen control group. Lastly, OLS refers to ordinary least squares, which indicate that the study relies on evidence from conditional correlations.

A particularly noteworthy aspect of the body of economic research summarized in Tables 3.1–3.3 is that the scope of societies studied is relatively broad. This can be seen with a quick glance at the 'Scope of sample' column in the three tables. There are many studies of non-Western societies. This is important since it is now well-recognized that the cultural traits of Western European societies – what Henrich et al. (2010b) famously term 'WEIRD' societies – are not the modal or even median traits of the World. Instead, they appear to be highly exceptional (Henrich et al., 2010b; Henrich, 2020; Muthukrishna et al., 2020). Many disciplines that seek to better understand human culture and human behavior, most notably psychology, have a very strong tendency to focus almost exclusively on Western societies (Henrich et al., 2010a). In addition, because they are not particularly interested in cross-cultural variation, they then do not ask the question of where this variation is from, which would then cause them to look at history for answers. Thus, there is also a tendency for analysis to be ahistorical (Muthukrishna and Slingerland, 2020). While behavioral economics often shares the same 'WEIRD' bias, research within cultural economics generally considers a broad cross-section of societies and takes a historical perspective. The reason for this approach is likely due to the origins of the field, which lie in economic history, economic development, and economic growth, each of which has traditionally been historical and/or global in their focus. In the future, I expect research in this area to continue to become increasingly interdisciplinary, particularly as fields like psychology begin to look beyond WEIRD societies and then seek to understand the historical origins of cross-societal differences on culture and psychology.

An important contribution that I can envision economists – particularly economic historians and political economists – making to evolutionary research is a greater emphasis on power and coercion and an explicit inclusion of states and state actors into theory and empirics. In standard evolutionary models, the evolution of particular cultural traits depends on their relative success. However, in reality, the success of different groups also depends on the institutions and power structures within societies. While there are existing evolutionary studies that incorporate power, coercion, and institutions (e.g., Vehrencamp, 1983), there is scope for a greater and more explicit focus on these aspects of human society within evolutionary frameworks. While there has already been important progress using an evolutionary perspective to think about states and institutions (e.g., Bowles and Gintis, 1998b,a; Gintis, 2000; Platteau, 2000; Aoki, 2001; Bowles and Gintis, 2002; Bowles, 2004; Tabellini, 2008; Bisin and Verdier, 2017; Besley and Persson, 2019), there is much more that remains to be done.

A recent example of research along these lines is the theoretical study by Tabellini (2008) which models the interplay of culture and institutions. In the model, a cooperative cultural trait evolves through vertical transmission. He then introduces institutions, which are 'rules of the game' that affect the payoffs to the different cultural types in the model. The institutions are determined by majority voting. A potential equilibrium in the model is one where there are a large number of non-cooperative types. They vote for institutions that do not punish those who do not cooperate, which in turn increases the payoffs to non-cooperators. In another equilibrium, the number of cooperators is high, and they are able to implement institutions that punish deviations from cooperation, which reduce the payoff to non-cooperators and increase the payoffs to cooperators, thus sustaining this equilibrium. The model, therefore, shows how culture, which is endogenous to the institutional structure, underpins the type of institutions that emerge.

While I expect research on the interplay between culture and institutions to develop further – see Bisin and Verdier (2017) for a more recent example – I also expect the empirical research on these questions to progress. There are a few examples of recent papers that have sought to understand the effect of states and institutions on the evolution of cultural traits, but much more remains to be understood. For example, the effect of state presence appears to be different in the limited number of settings that have been studied and we really don't have a clear sense of why yet (e.g., Becker et al., 2016; Lowes et al., 2017; Dell et al., 2018; Heldring, 2021).

3.5 Conclusions

In this chapter, I provided an overview of the insights that emerge when history is viewed through an evolutionary lens. The first part of the chapter discussed the theory and empirical evidence for the benefits of cultural evolution. The primary advantage of culture is that it allows one to conserve on information acquisition costs and to tap into the accumulated body of knowledge that has evolved during previous generations. Thus, culture allows the collective knowledge of society to be much greater than the information that any one person could learn in their lifetime. The theoretical models and empirical evidence that I reviewed show that societies can be made better off when decision-making occurs through cultural processes.

I then turned to a discussion of how an evolutionary perspective provides insights into a range of phenomena that are important within economics. I discussed insights into human capital and innovation that can be gained by thinking of these as cumulative cultural processes. I explained how thinking about the nature of cultural evolution helps us better understand historical persistence, path dependence, and the determinants of successful societies. I described a series of evolutionary insights that can be used to provide a deeper understanding of human history. I showed how concepts such as environmental mismatch, the collective brain, cumulative improvements, kludges, group-level selection, sexual dimorphism, and reproduction strategies provide insights into key aspects of economic history, including human capital, innovation, warfare, state formation, cooperation, social structure, gender roles, kinship, social structure, path dependence, and comparative economic development.

I ended the chapter by describing the recent wave of research within economic history and growth economics that studies, both theoretically and empirically, cultural evolution and its importance for social and economic outcomes. I discussed the way this research has contributed to the field of cultural evolution and how I expect this to continue in the future.

References

Aghion, P., Algan, Y., Cahuc, P., Shleifer, A., 2010. Regulation and distrust. The Quarterly Journal of Economics 125 (3), 1015–1049.

Alesina, A., Fuchs-Schundeln, N., 2007. Good-bye Lenin (or not?): the effect of communism on people's preferences. The American Economic Review 94 (4), 1507–1528.

Alesina, A., Teso, E., Stantcheva, S., 2013a. Mobility and preferences for redistribution. The American Economic Review 108 (2), 521–554.

Alesina, A., Giuliano, P., Nunn, N., 2013b. On the origins of gender roles: women and the plough. The Quarterly Journal of Economics 128 (2), 469–530.

Alesina, A., Giuliano, P., Nunn, N., 2018. Traditional agricultural practices and the sex ratio today. PLoS ONE 13 (1), e0190510.

Algan, Y., Cahuc, P., 2010. Inherited trust and growth. The American Economic Review 100 (5), 2060–2092.

Algan, Y., Cahuc, P., 2013. Trust and growth. Annual Review of Economics 5, 521–549.

Alsan, M., Wanamaker, M., 2018. Tuskegee and the health of black men. The Quarterly Journal of Economics 133 (1), 407–455.

Andersen, T.B., Bentzen, J., Dalgaard, C.-J., Sharp, P., 2016. Pre-reformation roots of the protestant ethic. The Economic Journal 127 (604), 1756–1793.

Andrews, M., 2019. Bar Talk: Informal Social Interactions, Alcohol Prohibition, and Invention. Working paper.

Ang, J.B., Fredriksson, P.G., 2017. Wheat agriculture and family ties. European Economic Review 100, 236–256.

Aoki, M., 2001. Towards a Comparative Institutional Analysis. MIT Press, Cambridge.

Ashraf, N., Bau, N., Nunn, N., Voena, A., 2020. Bride price and female education. Journal of Political Economy 128 (2), 591–641.

Ashraf, Q., Galor, O., 2013. The "Out of Africa" hypothesis, human genetic diversity, and comparative economic development. The American Economic Review 103 (1), 1–46.

Atkin, D., 2016. The caloric costs of culture: evidence from Indian migrants. The American Economic Review 106 (4), 1144–1181.

Baranov, V., De Haas, R., Grosjean, P., 2018. Men. Roots and Consequences of Masculinity Norms. Working paper. University of Melbourne.

Bau, N., 2019. Can Policy Change Culture? Government Pension Plans and Traditional Kinship Practices. Working paper. University of California, Los Angeles.

Bauer, M., Cassar, A., Chytilova, J., Henrich, J., 2014. War's enduring effects on the development of egalitarian motivations and in-group biases. Psychological Science 25 (1), 47–57.

Bauer, M., Blattman, C., Chytilova, J., Henrich, J., Miguel, E., Mitts, T., 2016. Can war foster cooperation? The Journal of Economic Perspectives 30 (3), 249–274.

Bazzi, S., Fiszbein, M., Gebresilasse, M., 2018. Frontier Culture: The Roots and Persistence of "Rugged Individualism" in the United States. Working paper. Boston University.

Beaman, L., Chattopadhyay, R., Duflo, E., Pande, R., Topalova, P., 2009. Powerful women: does exposure reduce bias? The Quarterly Journal of Economics 124 (4), 1497–1540.

Becker, A., 2019. On the Economic Origins of Restrictions on Women's Sexuality. Working Paper. Harvard University.

Becker, S.O., Woessmann, L., 2008. Luther and the girls: religious denomination and the female education gap in nineteenth-century Prussia. Scandinavian Journal of Economics 110 (4), 777–805.

Becker, S.O., Woessmann, L., 2009. Was Weber wrong? A human capital theory of protestant economic history. The Quarterly Journal of Economics 124 (2), 531–596.

Becker, S.O., Boeckh, K., Hainz, C., Woessmann, L., 2016. The empire is dead, long live the empire! Long-run persistence of trust and corruption in the bureaucracy. The Economic Journal 126 (590), 40–74.

Bell, A., Chetty, R., Jaravel, X., Petkova, N., Van Reenen, J., 2019. Who becomes an inventor in America? The importance of exposure to innovation. The Quarterly Journal of Economics 134 (2), 647–713.

Benjamin, D.J., Cesarini, D., Chabris, C.F., Glaeser, E.L., Laibson, D.I., Guonason, V., Harris, T.B., Launer, L.J., Purcell, S., Vernon Smith, A., Johannesson, M., Magnusson, P.K.E., Beauchamp, J.P., Christakis, N.A., Atwood, C.S., Hebert, B., Freese, J., Hauser, R.M., Hauser, T.S., Grankvista, A., Hultman, C.M., Lichtenstein, P., 2012. The promises and pitfalls of genoeconomics. Annual Review of Economics 4, 627–662.

Bentzen, J.S., 2019. Acts of God? Religiosity and natural disasters across subnational world districts. The Economic Journal 129 (622), 2295–2321.

BenYishay, A., Grosjean, P., Vecci, J., 2017. The fish is the friend of matriliny: reef density and matrilineal inheritance. Journal of Development Economics 127, 234–249.

Bergh, A., Ohrvall, R., 2018. A sticky trait: social trust among Swedish expatriates in countries with varying institutional quality. Journal of Comparative Economics 46 (4), 1146–1157.

Besley, T., Persson, T., 2019. Democratic values and institutions. American Economic Review – Insights 1 (1), 59–76.

Billing, J., Sherman, P.W., 1998. Antimicrobial functions of spices: why some like it hot. The Quarterly Review of Biology 73 (1), 3–49.

Bisin, A., Verdier, T., 2000. Beyond the melting pot: cultural transmission, marriage and the evolution of ethnic and religious traits. The Quarterly Journal of Economics 115, 955–988.

Bisin, A., Verdier, T., 2001a. Agents with imperfect empathy may survive natural selection. Economics Letters 71, 277–285.

Bisin, A., Verdier, T., 2001b. The economics of cultural transmission and the dynamics of preferences. Journal of Economic Theory 97, 298–319.

Bisin, A., Verdier, T., 2017. On the Joint Evolution of Culture and Institutions. NBER Working Paper 23375.

Bloom, N., Mahajan, A., McKenzie, D., Roberts, J., 2020. Do management interventions last? Evidence from India. American Economic Journal: Applied Economics 12 (2), 198–219.

Bloom, N., Eifert, B., Mahajan, A., McKenzie, D., Roberts, J., 2013. Does management matter? Evidence from India. The Quarterly Journal of Economics 128 (1), 1–51.

Blouin, A., 2018. Culture and Contracts: The Historical Legacy of Forced Labour. Working Paper. University of Toronto.

Booth, A., Fan, E., Meng, X., Zhang, D., 2019. Gender differences in willingness to compete: the role of culture and institutions. The Economic Journal 129 (618), 734–764.

Bowles, S., 2004. Microeconomics: Behavior, Institutions, and Evolution. Princeton University Press, Princeton.

Bowles, S., 2009. Did warfare among ancestral hunter-gatherers affect the evolution of human social behaviors? Science 324, 1293–1298.

Bowles, S., Gintis, H., 1998a. How communities govern: the structural basis of prosocial norms. In: Ben-Ner, A., Putterman, L. (Eds.), Economics, Values, and Organization. Cambridge University Press, Cambridge, pp. 206–230.

Bowles, S., Gintis, H., 1998b. The moral economy of communities: structured populations and the evolution of pro-social norms. Evolution and Human Behavior 19, 3–25.

Bowles, S., Gintis, H., 2002. Social capital and community governance. The Economic Journal 112, F419–F436.

Boyd, R., Richerson, P.J., 1985. Culture and the Evolutionary Process. University of Chicago Press, London.

Boyd, R., Richerson, P.J., 1995. Why does culture increase human adaptability? Ethology and Sociobiology 16, 125–143.

Boyd, R., Richerson, P.J., 2005. The Origin and Evolution of Cultures. Oxford University Press, London.

Boyd, R., Richerson, P.J., Henrich, J., 2013. The cultural evolution of technology: facts and theories. In: Richerson, P.J., Christiansen, M. (Eds.), Cultural Evolution: Society, Technology, Language, and Religion, Strungmann Forum Reports. MIT Press, Cambridge, MA, pp. 119–142.

Brodeur, A., Haddad, J., 2018. Institutions, Attitudes and LGBT: Evidence from the Gold Rush. University of Ottawa. Mimeo.

Burchardi, K.B., Chaney, T., Hassan, T.A., 2019. Migrants, ancestors, and investments. The Review of Economic Studies 86 (4), 1448–1486.

Bursztyn, L., Gonzalez, A., Yanagizawa-Drott, D., 2020. Misperceived social norms: female labor force participation in Saudi Arabia. The American Economic Review 110 (10), 2997–3029.

Buss, D., 1994. The Evolution of Desire: Strategies of Human Mating. Basic Books, New York.

Buss, D.M., Scmitt, D.P., 1993. Sexual strategies theory: an evolutionary perspective on human mating. Psychological Review 100, 204–232.

Butler, J.V., Giuliano, P., Guiso, L., 2016. The right amount of trust. Journal of the European Economic Association 14 (5), 1155–1180.

Campa, P., Serafinelli, M., 2019. Politico-economic regimes and attitudes: female workers under state-socialism. Review of Economics and Statistics 101 (2), 233–248.

Campante, F., Yanagizawa-Drott, D., 2015. Does religion affect economic growth and happiness? Evidence from Ramadan. The Quarterly Journal of Economics 130 (2), 615–658.

Campante, F., Yanagizawa-Drott, D., 2016. The Intergenerational Transmission of War. Working paper. Harvard Kennedy School.

Campante, F., Yanagizawa-Drott, D., 2018. Long-range growth: economic development in the global network of air links. The Quarterly Journal of Economics 133 (3), 1395–1458.

Campante, F., Chor, D., 2017. "Just Do Your Job": Obedience, Routine Tasks, and the Pattern of Specialization. Working paper. Harvard Kennedy School.

Cantoni, D., Chen, Y., Yang, D.Y., Yuchtman, N., Zhang, Y.J., 2017. Curriculum and ideology. Journal of Political Economy 125 (2), 338–392.

Cassar, A., Healy, A., von Kessler, C., 2017. Trust, risk, and time preferences after a natural disaster: experimental evidence from Thailand. World Development 94, 90–105.

Cassar, A., Grosjean, P., Whitt, S., 2013. Legacies of violence: trust and market development. Journal of Economic Growth 18, 285–318.

Cavalli-Sforza, L.L., Feldman, M.W., 1981. Cultural Transmission and Evolution: A Quantitative Approach. Princeton University Press, Princeton.

Cervellati, M., Chiovelli, G., Esposito, E., 2019. Bite and Divide: Malaria and Ethnolinguistic Diversity. Working paper. University of Bologna.

Cesarini, D., Dawes, C.T., Fowler, J.H., Johannesson, M., Lichtenstein, P., Wallace, B., 2008. Heritability of cooperative behavior in the trust game. Proceedings of the National Academy of Sciences 105 (10), 3721–3726.

Cesarini, D., Dawes, C.T., Fowler, J.H., Johannesson, M., Lichtenstein, P., Wallace, B., 2009. Genetic variation in preferences for giving and risk taking. The Quarterly Journal of Economics 124 (2), 809–842.

Chaudhary, L., Iyer, S., Rubin, J., Shrivastava, A., 2018. Culture and Colonial Legacy: Evidence from Public Goods Games. Working paper. Naval Postgraduate School.

Chudek, M., Muthukrishna, M., Henrich, J., 2015. Cultural evolution. In: Buss, D.M. (Ed.), Handbook of Evolutionary Psychology, 2nd edition. Wiley, New York.

Claessens, L.P.A.M., Meijer, H.J.M., Hume, J.P., 2015. The morphology of the Thirioux dodos. Journal of Vertebrate Paleontology 35, 29–187.

Clark, G., 2007. A Farewell to Alms: A Brief Economic History of the World. Princeton University Press, Princeton.

Clingingsmith, D., Khwaja, A.I., Kremer, M., 2009. Estimating the impact of the Hajj: religion and tolerance in Islam's global gathering. The Quarterly Journal of Economics 124 (3), 1133–1170.

Cook, L., 2014. Violence and economic growth: evidence from African American patents, 1870–1940. Journal of Economic Growth 19 (2), 221–257.

Cornelson, K., 2018. Media Role Models and Black Educational Attainment: Evidence from the Cosby Show. Working paper. University of Notre Dame.

Corno, L., Hildebrandt, N., Voena, A., 2019. Age of marriage, weather shocks, and the direction of marriage payments. Econometrica 88 (3), 879–915.

Couttenier, M., Grosjean, P., Sangnier, M., 2017. The wild West is wild: the homicide resource curse. Journal of the European Economic Association 15 (3), 558–585.

Dawkins, R., 1986. The Blind Watchmaker: Why the Evidence of Evolution Reveals a Universe Without Design. W.W. Norton, New York.

Dawkins, R., 1996. Climbing Mount Improbable. W.W. Norton, New York.

Dell, M., Querubin, P., 2018. The historical state, local collective action, and economic development in Vietnam. The Quarterly Journal of Economics 133 (2), 701–764.

Dell, M., Lane, N., Querubin, P., 2018. The historical state, local collective action, and economic development in Vietnam. Econometrica 86 (6), 2083–2121.

Della Vigna, S., Kaplan, E., 2007. The Fox News effect: media bias and voting. The Quarterly Journal of Economics 122, 1187–1234.

Depetris-Chauvin, E., Durante, R., Campante, F.R., 2020. Building nations through shared experiences: evidence from African football. The American Economic Review 110 (5), 1572–1602.

Derex, M., Beugin, M.-P., Godelle, B., Raymond, M., 2013. Experimental evidence for the influence of group size on cultural complexity. Nature 503, 389–391.

Dincecco, M., Onorato, M.G., 2017. From Warfare to Wealth. Cambridge University Press, Cambridge.

Doepke, M., Zilibotti, F., 2008. Occupational choice and the spirit of capitalism. The Quarterly Journal of Economics 123 (2), 747–793.

Doepke, M., Zilibotti, F., 2014. Culture, entrepreneurship, and growth. In: Aghion, P., Durlauf, S. (Eds.), Handbook of Economic Growth. Elsevier, New York, pp. 1–48.

Doepke, M., Zilibotti, F., 2017. Parenting with style: altruism and paternalism in intergenerational preference transmission. Econometrica 67 (5), 1331–1337.

Dohmen, T., Falk, A., Huffman, D., Sunde, U., 2018. Patience and Comparative Development. Working paper. University of Bonn.

Easterly, W., 2001. The Elusive Quest for Growth: Economists? Adventures and Misadventures in the Tropics. MIT Press, Cambridge, MA.

Ehrenfeld, D.W., Carr, A., 1967. The role of vision in the sea-finding orientation of the green turtle (Chelonia myadas). Animal Behavior 15 (1), 25–26.

Ely, J.C., 2011. Kludged. American Economic Journal: Microeconomics 3, 210–231.

Enke, B., 2019. Kinship, cooperation, and the evolution of moral systems. The Quarterly Journal of Economics 134 (2), 953–1019.

Enke, B., 2020. Moral values and voting. Journal of Political Economy 128 (10), 3679–3729.

Enke, B., Rodriguez-Padilla, R., Zimmerman, F., 2019. Moral Universalism and the Structure of Ideology. Working paper. Harvard University.

Fenske, J., 2014. African polygamy: past and present. Journal of Development Economics 117, 58–73.

Fernandez, R., 2013. Cultural change as learning: the evolution of female labor force participation over a century. The American Economic Review 103 (1), 472–500.

Fernandez, R., Fogli, A., Olivetti, C., 2004. Mothers and sons: preference formation and female labor force dynamics. The Quarterly Journal of Economics 119, 1249–1299.

Fernandez, R., Parsa, S., Viarengo, M., 2019. Coming Out in America: AIDS, Politics, and Cultural Change. Working paper. New York University.

Figlio, D., Giuliano, P., Ozek, U., Sapienza, P., 2019. Long-term orientation and educational performance. American Economic Journal: Economic Policy 11 (4), 272–309.

Fouka, V., 2020. Backlash: the unintended effects of language prohibition in U.S. schools after World War I. The Review of Economic Studies 87 (1), 204–239.

Fouka, V., Schlapfer, A., 2020. Agricultural returns to labor and the origins of work ethics. The Economic Journal 130 (628), 1081–1113.

Francois, P., Fujiwara, T., van Ypersele, T., 2010. Competition Builds Trust. Working paper. University of British Columbia.

Francois, P., Fujiwara, T., van Ypersele, T., 2018. The origins of human prosociality: cultural group selection in the workplace and the laboratory. Science Advances 4 (9), eaat2201.

Friedman, M., 2008. The evolutionary origin of flatfish asymmetry. Nature 454, 209–212.

Galef, B.G., Whiskin, E.E., 2004. Effects of environmental stability and demonstrator age on social learning of food preferences by young Norway rats. Animal Behavior 68 (4), 897–902.

Galor, O., Moav, O., 2002. Natural selection and the origin of economic growth. The Quarterly Journal of Economics 117 (4), 1133–1191.

Galor, O., Michalopoulos, S., 2012. Evolution and the growth process: natural selection of entrepreneurial traits. Journal of Economic Theory 147 (2), 759–780.

Galor, O., Ozak, O., 2016. The agricultural origins of time preference. The American Economic Review 106 (10), 3064–3103.

Galor, O., Savitskiy, V., 2018. Climatic Roots of Loss Aversion. Working paper. Brown University.

Gelfand, M., 2018. Rule Makers, Rule Breakers. Simon & Schuster Inc., New York.

Gennaioli, N., Voth, H.J., 2015. State capacity and military conflict. The Review of Economic Studies 82, 1409–1448.

Gershman, B., 2019. Witchcraft Beliefs as a Cultural Legacy of the Atlantic Slave Trade: Evidence from Two Continents. Working paper. American University.

Gigerenzer, G., Goldstein, D.G., 1996. Reasoning the fast and frugal way: models of bounded rationality. Psychological Review 103 (4), 650–669.

Gintis, H., 1997. A Markov model of production, trade, and money: theory and artificial life simulation. Computational and Mathematical Organization Theory 3, 19–41.

Gintis, H., 2000. Game Theory Evolving. Princeton University Press, New Jersey.

Giuliano, P., Nunn, N., 2013. The transmission of democracy: from the village to the nation state. The American Economic Review: Papers and Proceedings 103 (3), 86–92.

Giuliano, P., Nunn, N., 2021. Understanding cultural persistence and change. The Review of Economic Studies. https://doi.org/10.1093/restud/rdaa074.

Giuliano, P., Spilimbergo, A., 2014. Growing up in a recession. The Review of Economic Studies 81 (3), 787–817.

Gold, M.E.L., Bourdon, E., Norell, M.A., 2016. The first endocast of the extinct dodo (Raphus cucullatus) and an anatomical comparison amongst close relatives (Aves, Columbiformes). Zoological Journal of the Linnean Society 177, 950–963.

Gorodnichenko, Y., Roland, G., 2011. Individualism, innovation, and long-run growth. Proceedings of the National Academy of Sciences 108 (4), 21316–21319.

Gorodnichenko, Y., Roland, G., 2015. Culture, Institutions, and Democratization. Working paper. University of California Berkeley.

Gorodnichenko, Y., Roland, G., 2017. Culture, institutions, and the wealth of nations. Review of Economics and Statistics 99 (3), 402–416.

Gorodnichenko, Y., Kukharskyy, B., Roland, G., 2018. Cultural Distance, Firm Boundaries, and Global Sourcing. Working paper. University of California Berkeley.

Greif, A., 1989. Reputation and coalitions in medieval trade: evidence on the Maghribi traders. The Journal of Economic History 49, 857–882.

Greif, A., 1993. Contract enforceability and economic institutions in early trade: the Maghribi traders' coalition. The American Economic Review 83 (3), 525–548.

Greif, A., 1994. Cultural beliefs and the organization of society: a historical and theoretical reflection on collectivist and individualist societies. Journal of Political Economy 102 (5), 912–950.

Grosjean, P., 2014. A history of violence: the culture of honor as a determinant of homicide in the U.S. South. Journal of the European Economic Association 12 (5), 1285–1316.

Grosjean, P., Khattar, R., 2018. It's raining men! Hallelujah? The long-run consequences of male-biased sex ratios. The Review of Economic Studies 86 (2), 723–754.

Guiso, L., Sapienza, P., Zingales, L., 2006. Does culture affect economic outcomes? The Journal of Economic Perspectives 20 (2), 23–48.

Guiso, L., Sapienza, P., Zingales, L., 2008. Social capital as good culture. Journal of the European Economic Association 6 (2–3), 295–320.

Guiso, L., Sapienza, P., Zingales, L., 2009. Cultural biases in economic exchange. The Quarterly Journal of Economics 124 (3), 1095–1131.

Guiso, L., Sapienza, P., Zingales, L., 2016. Long-term persistence. Journal of the European Economic Association 14 (6), 1401–1436.

Gustafsson, A., Lindenfors, P., 2004. Human size evolution: no evolutionary allometric relationship between male and female stature. Journal of Human Evolution 47 (4), 253–266.

Heldring, L., 2021. The origins of violence in Rwanda. The Review of Economic Studies. https://doi.org/10.1093/restud/rdaa028.

Heller, S.B., Shah, A.K., Guryan, J., Ludwig, J., Mullainathan, S., Pollack, H.A., 2017. Thinking, fast and slow? Some field experiments to reduce crime and dropout in Chicago. The Quarterly Journal of Economics 132 (1), 1–54.

Henrich, J., 2004a. Cultural group selection, coevolutionary processes and large-scale cooperation. Journal of Economic Behavior & Organization 53 (1), 3–35.

Henrich, J., 2004b. Demography and cultural evolution: how adaptive cultural processes can produce maladaptive losses – the Tasmanian case. American Antiquity 69 (2), 197–214.

Henrich, J., 2016. The Secret of Our Success. Princeton University Press, Princeton.

Henrich, J., 2020. The Weirdest People in the World: How Westerners Became Psychologically Peculiar and Particularly Prosperous. McMillan, New York.

Henrich, J., Bauer, M., Cassar, A., Chytilova, J., Purzycki, B.G., 2019. War increases religiosity. Nature Human Behavior 3, 129–135.

Henrich, J., Heine, S.J., Norenzayan, A., 2010a. Most people are not WEIRD. Nature 466 (29).

Henrich, J., Heine, S.J., Norenzayan, A., 2010b. The weirdest people in the world. Behavioral and Brain Sciences 33 (2/3), 1–75.

Hume, J.P., 2006. The history of the dodo Raphus cucullatus and the penguin of Mauritius. Historical Biology 18 (2), 69–93.

Jakiela, P., Ozier, O., 2019. The impact of violence on individual risk preferences: evidence from a natural experiment. Review of Economics and Statistics 101 (3), 547–559.

Jayachandran, S., Pande, R., 2017. Why are Indian children so short? The role of birth order and son preference. The American Economic Review 107 (9), 2600–2629.

Jensen, R., Oster, E., 2009. The power of TV: cable television and women's status in India. The Quarterly Journal of Economics 124 (3), 1057–1094.

Kahneman, D., 2011. Thinking, Fast and Slow. Macmillan, London.

Kamarck, A.M., 2009. Culture Under Cross-Examination: International Justice and the Special Court for Sierra Leone. Cambridge University Press, New York.

Karaja, E., Rubin, J., 2017. The Cultural Transmission of Trust Norms: Evidence from a Lab in the Field on a Natural Experiment. Working paper. Chapman University.

Katz, S.H., Hediger, M.L., Valleroy, L.A., 1974. Traditional maize processing techniques in the New World. Science 184 (4138), 765–773.

Kawai, K., Lang, R., Li, H., 2018. Political kludges. American Economic Journal: Microeconomics 10 (4), 131–158.

Kine, M.A., Boyd, R., 2010. Population size predicts technological complexity in Oceania. Proceedings of the Royal Society B.

Kobayashi, Y., Aoki, K., 2012. Innovativeness, population size, and cumulative cultural evolution. Theoretical Population Biology 82, 38–47.

Kosse, F., Deckers, T., Schildberg-Horisch, H., Falk, A., 2019. The formation of prosociality: causal evidence on the role of the social environment. Journal of Political Economy 128 (2), 434–467.

Kremer, M., 1993. Population growth and technological change: one million B.C. to 1990. The Quarterly Journal of Economics 108 (3), 681–716.

La Ferrara, E., Chong, A., Duryea, S., 2012. Soap operas and fertility: evidence from Brazil. American Economic Journal: Applied Economics 4 (4), 1–31.

Long, J., Ferrie, J., 2013. Occupational mobility in Great Britain and the United States since 1850. The American Economic Review 103 (4), 1109–1137.

Lowes, S., 2018. Matrilineal Kinship and Spousal Cooperation: Evidence from the Matrilineal Belt. Working paper. Stanford University.

Lowes, S., Montero, E., 2017. Mistrust in Medicine: The Legacy of Colonial Medicine Campaigns in Central Africa. Working paper. Bocconi University.

Lowes, S., Montero, E., 2019. Concessions, Violence and Indirect Rule: Evidence from the Congo Free State. Working paper. Stanford University.

Lowes, S., Nunn, N., Robinson, J.A., Weigel, J., 2017. The evolution of culture and institutions: evidence from the Kuba Kingdom. Econometrica 85 (4), 1065–1091.

Madestam, A., Yanagizawa-Drott, D., 2011. Shaping the Nation: The Effect of the Fourth of July on Political Preferences and Behavior in the United States. Working paper. Harvard University.

Madestam, A., Shoag, D., Veuger, S., Yanagizawa-Drott, D., 2013. Do political protests matter? Evidence from the Tea Party movement. The Quarterly Journal of Economics 128 (4), 1633–1685.

Mankiw, N.G., Romer, D., Weil, D.N., 1992. A contribution to the empirics of economic growth. The Quarterly Journal of Economics 107, 407–437.

McElreath, R., Lubell, M., Richerson, P.J., Waring, T.M., Baum, W., Edstein, E., Efferson, C., Paciotti, B., 2005. Applying evolutionary models to the laboratory study of social learning. Evolution and Human Behavior 26, 483–508.

Mesoudi, A., 2016. Cultural evolution: a review of theory, findings and controversies. Evolutionary Biology 43, 481–497.

Michalopoulos, S., 2012. The origins of ethnolinguistic diversity. The American Economic Review 102 (4), 1508–1539.

Michalopoulos, S., Naghavi, A., Prarolo, G., 2018. Trade and geography in the spread of Islam. The Economic Journal 128 (616), 3210–3241.

Mitchener, K.J., McLean, I.W., 2003. The productivity of U.S. states since 1880. Journal of Economic Growth 8, 73–114.

Mitrunen, M., 2019. Can you Make an American? Compulsory Patriotism and Assimilation of Immigrants. Working paper. University of Chicago.

Mokyr, J., 1991. Evolutionary biology, technological change, and economic history. Bulletin of Economic Research 43 (2), 127–149.

Mokyr, J., 1998. Science, Technology, and Knowledge. Working paper. Northwestern University.

Mokyr, J., 2018. A Culture of Growth: The Origins of the Modern Economy. Princeton University Press, Princeton.

Moscona, J., Nunn, N., Robinson, J.A., 2017. Keeping it in the family: lineage organization and the scope of trust in Sub-Saharan Africa. The American Economic Review: Papers and Proceedings 107 (5), 565–571.

Moscona, J., Nunn, N., Robinson, J.A., 2019. Segmentary lineage organization and conflict in sub-Saharan Africa. Econometrica 88 (5), 1999–2036.

Muthukrishna, M., Bell, A.V., Henrich, J., Curtin, C.M., Gedranovich, A., McInerney, J., Thue, B., 2020. Beyond western, educated, industrial, rich, and democratic (WEIRD) psychology: measuring and mapping scales of cultural and psychological distance. Psychological Science 31 (6), 678–701.

Muthukrishna, M., Henrich, J., 2016. Innovation and the collective brain. Philosophical Transactions B 371, 20150192.

Muthukrishna, M., Slingerland, E., 2020. Psychology as a historical science. Annual Review of Psychology 72, 717–749.

Muthukrishna, M., Shulman, B.W., Vasilescu, V., Henrich, J., 2014. Sociality influences cultural complexity. Proceedings of the Royal Society B 281, 20132511.

Nguyen, K.-T., 2018. Trust and Innovation within the Firm: Evidence from Matched CEO-Firm Data. Working paper. London School of Economics.

Norman, J.R., 1934. A Systematic Monograph of the Flatfishes (Heterosomata). Vol. 1. Psettotidae, Bothidae, Pleuronectidae. The Trustees of the British Museum, London.

Nunn, N., 2007. Historical legacies: a model linking Africa's past to its current underdevelopment. Journal of Development Economics 83 (1), 157–175.

Nunn, N., 2008. Slavery, inequality, and economic development in the Americas: an examination of the Engerman-Sokoloff hypothesis. In: Helpman, E. (Ed.), Institutions and Economic Performance. Harvard University Press, Cambridge, MA, pp. 148–180.

Nunn, N., 2010. Religious conversion in colonial Africa. The American Economic Review: Papers and Proceedings 100 (2), 147–152.

Nunn, N., forthcoming. On the causes and consequences of cross-cultural differences: an economic perspective, volume 8. In: Gelfand, M.J., Chiu, C.-Y., Hong, Y.-Y. (Eds.), Advances in Culture and Psychology. Oxford University Press, Oxford.

Nunn, N., Wantchekon, L., 2011. The slave trade and the origins of mistrust in Africa. The American Economic Review 101 (7), 3221–3252.

Nunn, N., Sanchez de la Sierra, R., 2017. Why being wrong can be right: magical warfare technologies and the persistence of false beliefs. The American Economic Review: Papers and Proceedings 107 (5), 582–587.

Nunn, N., Qian, N., Wen, J., 2019. Distrust and Political Turnover. Working paper. Harvard University.

Okoye, D., 2017. Things Fall Apart? Missions, Institutions, and Interpersonal Trust? Working paper. Dalhousie University.

Olken, B., 2009. Do television and radio destroy social capital? American Economic Journal: Applied Economics 1 (4), 1–33.

Platteau, J.-P., 2000. Microeconomics: Behavior, Institutions, and Evolution. Harwood Academic Publishers, Singapore.

Qian, N., 2008. Missing women and the price of tea in China: the effects of sex-specific income on sex imbalance. The Quarterly Journal of Economics 123 (3), 1251–1285.

Ramos-Toro, D., 2019. Social Exclusion and Social Preferences: Evidence from Colombia's Leper Colony. Working paper. Brown University.

Rao, G., 2019. Familiarity does not breed contempt: diversity, discrimination, and generosity in Delhi schools. The American Economic Review 109 (3), 774–809.

Richerson, P., Baldini, R., Bell, A.V., Demps, K., Frost, K., Hillis, V., Mathew, S., Newton, E.K., Naar, N., Newson, L., Ross, C., Smaldino, P.E., Waring, T.M., Zefferman, M., 2016. Cultural group selection plays and essential role in explaining human cooperation: a sketch of the evidence. Behavioral and Brain Sciences 39, e30.

Riley, E., 2017. Increasing Students' Aspirations: The Impact of Queen of Katwe on Students' Educational Attainment. CSAE Working Paper WPS/207-13.

Rogers, A.R., 1988. Does biology constrain culture? American Anthropologist 90 (4), 819–831.

Rubin, J., 2014. Printing and protestants: an empirical test of the role of printing in the reformation. Review of Economics and Statistics 96 (2), 270–286.

Ruff, C., 2002. Variation in human body size and shape. Annual Review of Anthropology 31, 211–232.

Rustagi, D., 2019. Historical Self-Governance and Norms of Cooperation. Working paper. Brown University.

Sacerdote, B., 2007. How large are the effects from changes in family environment? A study of Korean American adoptees. The Quarterly Journal of Economics 122 (1), 119–157.

Salmon, M., Tolbert, M.G., Painter, D.P., Goff, M., Reiners, R., 1995. Behavior of loggerhead sea turtles on an urban beach. II. Hatchling orientation. Journal of Herpetology 29 (4), 568–576.

Schulz, J., 2017. The Churches' Bans on Consanguineous Marriages, Kin Networks and Democracy. Working paper. Yale University.

Schulz, J., Bahrami-Rad, D., Beauchamp, J., Henrich, J., 2019. The church, intensive kinship, and global psychological variation. Science 366 (6466), eaau5141.

Sequeira, S., Nunn, N., Qian, N., 2020. Immigrants and the making of America. The Review of Economic Studies 87 (1), 382–419.

Sinclair-Thomas, B., Challis, S., 2017. The 'bullets to water' belief complex: a Pan-Southern African cognate epistemology for protective medicines and the control of projectiles. Journal of Conflict Archaeology 12 (3), 192–208.

Speck, F.G., 1935. Naskapi: The Savage Hunters of the Labrador Peninsula. University of Oklahoma Press, Norman.

Spolaore, E., Wacziarg, R., 2009. The diffusion of development. The Quarterly Journal of Economics 124 (2), 469–529.

Tabellini, G., 2008. The scope of cooperation: values and incentives. The Quarterly Journal of Economics 123 (3), 905–950.

Teso, E., 2019. The long-term effects of demographic shocks on the evolution of gender roles: evidence from the trans-Atlantic slave trade. Journal of the European Economic Association 17 (2), 497–534.

Tilly, C., 1990. Coercion, Capital and European States, A.D. 990–1990. Blackwell Publishers, Cambridge.

Todd, P.M., Gigerenzer, G., The ABC Research Group, 1999. Simple Heuristics That Make Us Smart. Oxford University Press, Oxford.

Toelch, U., van Delft, M.J., Bruce, M.J., Donders, R., Meeus, M.T.H., Reader, S.M., 2009. Decreased environmental variability induces a bias for social information use in humans. Evolution and Human Behavior 30 (1), 32–40.

Trivers, R.L., 1972. Parental investment and sexual selection. In: Campbell, B. (Ed.), Sexual Selection and Descent of Man, 1871–1971. Aldine, Chicago, pp. 136–179.

Tur-Prats, A., Valencia Caicedo, F., 2020. The Long Shadow of the Spanish Civil War. Working paper. University of British Columbia.

Turchin, P., 2003. Historical Dynamics: Why States Rise and Fall. Princeton University Press, Princeton.

Turchin, P., 2006. War and Peace and War: The Life Cycles of Imperial Nations. Pi Press, New York.

Turchin, P., 2016. How 10,000 Years of War Made Humans the Greatest Cooperators on Earth. Beresta Books, Chaplin, Connecticut.

Turchin, P., Currie, T.E., Turner, E.A.L., Gavrilets, S., 2013. War, space, and the evolution of Old World complex societies. Proceedings of the National Academy of Sciences 110, 16384–16389.

Vaesen, K., 2012. Cumulative cultural evolution and demography. PLoS ONE 7 (7), e40989.

Vehrencamp, S.L., 1983. A model for the evolution of despotic versus egalitarian societies. Animal Behavior 31, 667–682.

Xue, M.M., 2018. High-Value Work and the Rise of Women: The Cotton Revolution and Gender Equality in China. Working paper. Northwestern University.

Sources and methods

Historical data: where to find them, how to use them[☆]

Paola Giuliano[a,b,c,d] **and Andrea Matranga**[e]

[a]*UCLA, Los Angeles, CA, United States*
[b]*NBER, Cambridge, MA, United States*
[c]*CEPR, London, United Kingdom*
[d]*IZA, Bonn, Germany*
[e]*Chapman University, Orange, CA, United States*

4.1 Introduction

The use of historical data has become a standard tool in economics. The use of these data poses several challenges. Historical data are collected by different people, at different times, using different units of analysis. Especially when looking at long periods of time, not only the quality can vary but also the geographical unit needs to be adjusted, for example because borders across geographical units are not constant. The composition of populations can also change due to migration, natural disasters, and many other forces.

This chapter describes the main data sources that have been profitably used in economics research, and their most prominent applications. We broadly classify them in geographical data, ethnographic data, and Censuses. We also describe other commonly used historical data. For each group, we outline the issues they raise and also point out which methodological advances allow economists to overcome or minimize these problems.

The chapter starts with the description of geographical data. Exploiting the geographical element of the data to match different variables over time, is the most common task economic historians have to perform before even starting to analyze their data. We start by describing how original sources should be evaluated: before going through the time and effort of digitizing a map, for example it is important to do a preliminary step and considers capabilities and motives of the individual or entity who compiled the map. We proceed by showing how to use a geographical information systems software (GIS) to convert historical maps in modern format and how to analyze and integrate the data obtained using spatial locations. After digitizing different maps, one of the difficulties is that both the number and the geographical boundaries can change over time. Take the case of the United States: there were only 250 counties in 1790, whereas the number in 2000 is well above 3000. The chapter describes in details different potential ways of linking counties across the different census years. We finally describe other

---

☆ We thank seminar participants at the Handbook of Historical Economics Conference at New York University. All remaining errors are ours.

geographical data commonly used in economics, which, unlike old maps that need to be digitized, are already available and ready to use, simply outlining potential issues in using them.

The chapter proceeds by describing the use of ethnographic data. A prolific strand of the economic literature has documented a strong persistence of economic outcomes over time, including economic growth, political development and a variety of cultural traits (Putternam and Weil, 2010; Spolaore and Wacziarg, 2013; Michalopoulos and Papaioannou, 2013; Alesina et al., 2013; Voigtländer and Voth, 2012). The most comprehensive information about societal characteristics going back to pre-industrial times is the *Ethnographic Atlas*, assembled by Murdock (1967a), containing information on political, economic, and cultural traits of societies. Economists vastly used this dataset to document persistence in political, economic, or cultural outcomes (Gennaioli and Rainer, 2007; Michalopoulos and Papaioannou, 2013; Giuliano and Nunn, 2013; Alesina et al., 2013; Becker, 2019 to quote just few studies). The challenge faced by researchers when using this important source is how to connect historical characteristics of pre-industrial societies to current outcomes: the further back into the past one goes, the more the population composition of a given place tends to diverge from people who currently live there, because ethnicities moved over time or even disappeared. For example, the ethnicities reported in the *Ethnographic Atlas* for the case of the United States were Native-American populations, mostly involved in hunting, fishing, and horticultural communities and organized in small, pre-state political units. By contract, if one looks at the actual composition of the population in the United States today, a large fraction comes from ethnicities that lived in settled agricultural societies organized in large states. The chapter describes different ways used in literature to link the past to the present, using historical geographical locations (Alsan, 2015; Mayshar et al., 2015), current distribution of languages or ethnicities across the world (Alesina et al., 2013; Giuliano and Nunn, 2018), a migration matrix (Putternam and Weil, 2010) or individual data at the ethnicity level (Alesina et al., 2013; Becker, 2019).

Recent advances in economic history came from the use of historical complete census data (mostly for the United States), whose biggest advantage has been to link individuals' names over time, therefore allowing researchers to provide new and more precise answers to topics such as social mobility (Abramitzky et al., 2014). Contrary to modern administrative data, which contains social security numbers, historical censuses can only be linked using name, presenting a huge challenge especially for individuals with common names. The chapters present the different methods used to match individuals over time (and their limitations): from direct match (Ferrie, 1996 and Abramitzky et al., 2012, 2014, 2019a) to a more sophisticated machine-learning (Feigenbaum, 2016) or fully automated probabilistic algorithm (Abramitzky et al., 2019b, 2020).

The paper is organized as follows: Section 4.2 describes the use of geographical data. Section 4.3 is dedicated to ethnographic data. Sections 4.4 and 4.5 describe Census data and other historical data, whereas Section 4.6 concludes.

4.2 Geographical data

Researchers using historical datasets often need to exploit the geographical element of their data to match the different variables to each other. Economic historians are much more likely to use data that were collected by different people at different times, using different units of analysis. For example, an economic historian who wants to study the effect of wars on contemporary outcomes might be using the amount of wars engaged in by German principalities in the 15th century, but might need to cross-reference them with the population levels of German provinces a few centuries later, which have completely different borders. The only way to do so is exploiting the geographic overlap in the two sets of jurisdictions.

The common way of dealing with geographical data is a geographic information system (GIS) which allows to analyze and integrate different types of data, using spatial locations. Any GIS data one can find will be of one of two kinds, shapefiles, and rasters. Most kinds of data can be represented in either format, and it is possible to convert between the two, but different types of data and collection processes generally call for one or the other.

i. *Shapefiles* are vector formats, that give precise coordinates for specific points, which might represent distinct features such as villages or wells, or be strung together in lines or polygons to describe borders, roads, canals, etc. For example if we were interested in using the border between Colorado and Wyoming (a straight line along the 41st parallel North) for an RDD along the lines of Card and Krueger (1994), we could summarize it in the following very short shapefile giving only the two endpoints $(41, -109.5; 41, -102.05)$. Even relatively complicated borders (or other linear features) can be summarized by files that are quite small. Shapefiles can be similarly used to describe point features, such as villages, wells, or homicides.

ii. The second way of representing geographical data is through *rasters*. Rasters are image files that have been georeferenced, i.e. have been tagged with information on the geographic location of the corners of the image, and the precise way the flat image should be stretched to conform to the curved surface of the earth. For the case of the border between Wyoming and Colorado, one would have to create a raster covering the entire states of Wyoming and Colorado with cells small enough to record the data with the precision required. The difficulty with creating a border using a raster file is the creation of a large number of records coded as "Not a Border" for all the points in the interior of the two states, which could easily result in a file be several gigabytes in size.

Generally different types of data are better suited for storage using one of the two methods. Data originally created as a rectangular grid of points, for example scanned maps, aerial photographs, or satellite imagery and its many derived products (e.g. cloud cover, rainfall, landcover) are normally saved as raster files, whereas data indicating just specific locations, such as borders, wells, or villages, are more conducive to the use of shapefiles. All GIS packages provide many tools for converting data from raster to shapefile and vice versa.

Below we provide a concrete example on how to convert historical data using the GIS tools. Often economic historians need to work with scanned maps, whose quality can vary. Suppose that the researcher needs to convert a paper map of medieval borders in Europe, which might show each country with a different color. Once scanned each country will in fact be composed of pixels that slightly differ in shade, because of imperfections in the paper and printing technique, as well as random fluctuations in the acquisition process.

Esri ArcGIS provides the "Classify" tool that allows researchers to collapse all these similar colors to a raster of unique values, which can then be used as is, or converted to polygons. Generally, such a dataset will still need to be cleaned to remove objects within each country that are of a different color, such as rivers, cities, and printed text.[1]

---

[1] This process can often be partially automated by running the "Zonal Statistics" tool with the Median option, and a radius larger than the thickness of the largest feature that should be ignored. For example if the problem is a network of rivers that are

4.2.1 Assessing the suitability of geographic data

Before going through the time and effort of digitizing a paper map, it is necessary to do a preliminary step and consider the capabilities and motives of the individual or entity who compiled the map. To warrant use, the map should have been compiled by people that had the technical and resource capability to collect the data, and the incentives to do so accurately (unless of course reporting biases are themselves being studied!).

How was the map created?

It is often useful to have at least a rough understanding of how the map was compiled. For example, if a 19th cartographer was asked to produce a map of UK counties by population density, the best procedure will involve two steps. In the first step one could use the map to simply trace out the borders of the British counties. In the second step, the researcher could use data from the UK census to convert the population densities into shades, and color in the counties appropriately. Since this tracing process inevitably introduces errors, digitizing this map directly would import those errors into the dataset. It would therefore be better to instead digitize the county borders from a large scale map directly into a shapefile, and then assign to each county the correct values from the population density map.

Other issues can arise when maps are compiled by cartographers based on accounts from explorers. The report might have said simply that after crossing to the left bank of River X, she encountered population Y. In absence of further details, the cartographer might have generalized this observation by assigning the entire left bank of the river to population Y, which may or may not have been true. If the area under study is an entire continent, it is perhaps acceptable to use a map with such generalizations, since over a large sample size many sources of error will even out. But if we are interested in estimating the long run persistence of the effect of the institutions of the single population Y, such a map could not be reasonably be taken at face value. Tracking down the exact history of how a map was made could be too laborious (particularly if it is not the variable of interest, but one of dozens of controls), but a diligent researcher will seek contact with experts on the history of population Y, that could point out what controversies might exist over the precise borders of their territory.

How to deal with interpolated data

Another common issue in digitizing a map is the use of interpolated data, especially common when one has to deal with weather data. Suppose one is interested in converting point data for rainfall to a raster file. The first step before using such a point dataset, would be to go to the original point dataset and interpolate the data yourself with a known method rather than using the historical interpolation. If the variable in question can be expected to change very discontinuously, it might be advisable to eliminate observations that are too far away from an actual sampling point. For example, if a researcher was using data from pollution that was interpolated based on data from a collection of measurement stations, it would be wise to check whether (as it is likely) these stations are more commonly placed in populated centers, which are likely to also be major sources of pollution. If that is the case, the researcher would be wise to eliminate interpolated observations that were more than a fixed distance from each actual measurement.

As a best practice to make the assessment of the original quality of the data transparent, one could add some explanation on the quality of the original data. For example "The map was compiled by the

---

5 pixels wide, a radius of 10 pixels will usually work well. These routines are sufficiently powerful to generally pick out roads, forests, or other similar uniformly colored features from satellite imagery.

Engineer Corps of India to facilitate movement of troops, based on an extensive survey conducted over the course of 10 years. Since they had the technical capability, and the incentives to record the land accurately, we can assume that the location of the villages was accurately recorded".

4.2.2 Projections, inaccurate or sketched maps, distance measures

Map projections describe mathematically how an Earth's curved surface is conceptually flattened for representation in maps or their digital equivalent. To be an ideal representation of geographic reality, a map would have to be conformal, equal area, and equidistant. *Conformal* means that the map is not stretched locally. *Equal area* implies that areas on the map are proportional to areas on the planet. And *equidistant* means that distances are preserved, though unfortunately this is possible only between two points.

Unfortunately, while projections can have any of these properties, no projection can have all of them at the same time. So economic historians have to pick the best compromise depending on the area depicted by the map, and its intended use. For example, if we are interested in using a shapefile of country borders and a raster of total annual rainfall to calculate average rainfall within different countries, it's important to ensure that the calculation is performed using an *equal area* projection. This will ensure that each pixel in the precipitation raster represents the same geographic extent, and will avoid certain areas of each country being incorrectly weighted more.

Universal Transverse Mercator projection (UTM)

For areas up to a few hundred kilometers in extent, the easiest solution is to use the appropriate Universal Transverse Mercator (UTM) projection. The UTM projection is a family of projections each covering a slice of the Earth that is 6 degrees wide in longitude. The area within each slice can be treated as essentially flat, and coordinates are given in meters East or North of an arbitrary point. Specifically the size of the slices was chosen so that any errors in distance would be at most 0.1% which is essentially negligible for most economic history projects.

Below we describe a workflow to digitize historical maps.

Approaches to digitization

Let's assume a researcher is interested in creating a shapefile with the borders of the Holy Roman Empire in 1786, and the territories of imperial cities, based on the following map, which uses an unknown projection (Fig. 4.1).

One would first load some already georeferenced data for the same area, to which points from the scanned map can then be matched. For example in this case our base-map consisted of data on country borders (and coastlines) and major rivers. We first need to click on a point to geo-reference on the scanned map, and then on the corresponding spot on our base-map. Two is the minimum number of point pairs, but this will only be precise if one knew or correctly guessed the projection. More points help average out some inaccuracies and will allow for progressively more flexible transformations such as polynomials up to order three.

In our example, given the European setting and the fact that the meridians converge towards North, we first guessed that the map had been projected using some sort of conic projection.[2] We then matched

---

[2] In this case we chose the Europe Albers Equal Area Conic as the base projection. This projection is a conic, equal area map projection that uses two standard parallels. With this projection, although scale and shape are not preserved, the distortion

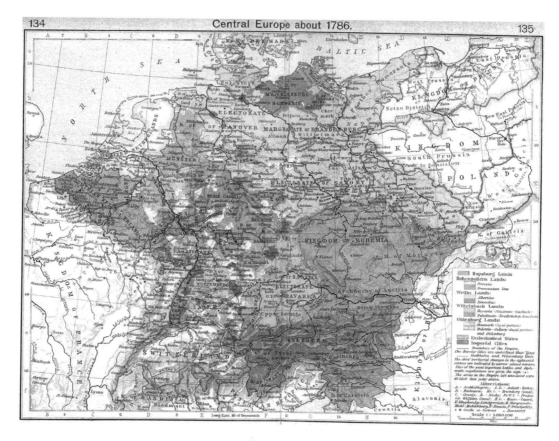

FIGURE 4.1

The Holy Roman Empire in 1786.

the locations of a number of prominent points on each map. Note that in this case, since a graticule was available in the scanned map (Fig. 4.2), it would have been more accurate to match the intersections of the latitude and longitude lines, but since these are not always available we wanted to show how points could be selected. Instead in this case the two graticules can be compared to show the inaccuracies introduced by this process (most prominent in the North Sea).

Using more points is generally better for older, hand traced maps, since they average out the inevitable inaccuracies. After selecting each point, one should check if the general fit of the two maps improves, and remove the point if it does not (this usually means the compiler of the map made a tracing error). If older maps that appear to be locally distorted are used, it is better to use the *spline*

---

between the two chosen parallels is minimal. If an incorrect projection had been chosen, the geo-referencing would still have worked, but it would have been necessary to specify more points, and use a third order polynomial or spline stretching to ensure a good fit.

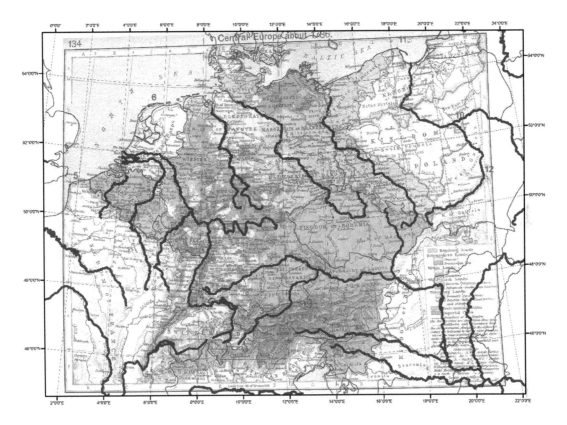

FIGURE 4.2

The Holy Roman Empire in 1786, georeferenced using coastlines and rivers.

function. This forces each pair of points to fit exactly, and then stretches the parts in between to make them fit. One should continue by adding points until all visible features match. Again, if adding a particular point makes the fit visibly worse, that point should be deleted, and other reference points used. This can happen if for example the cartographer was inaccurate in placing a particular village which is being used as a reference point.

Once the researcher is satisfied with the fit between the map being georeferenced and the reference map, they can either create polygons to represent the features manually, or use the "Classify" tools described above to partially automate the process. To do so, the researcher will have to select some areas of the map that are of the colors that she wants to extract. The algorithm will then select all pixels that have colors similar to those chosen. This will generally create rasters that have holes in them due to the presence of text, which is not the same color as the area of interest. These holes can be filled using for example the *Zonal Statistics* tool with the *Median option*, and a radius large enough to span the holes to be filled (Fig. 4.3).

The following map shows the end result. The black and white line delineates the areas owned by the Hapsburg Monarchy, plus the territories of the Imperial Cities (Fig. 4.4).

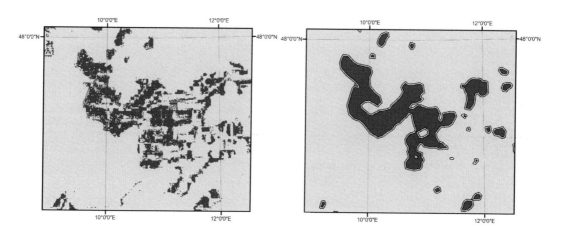

FIGURE 4.3

Classification tool results and after Median smoothing.

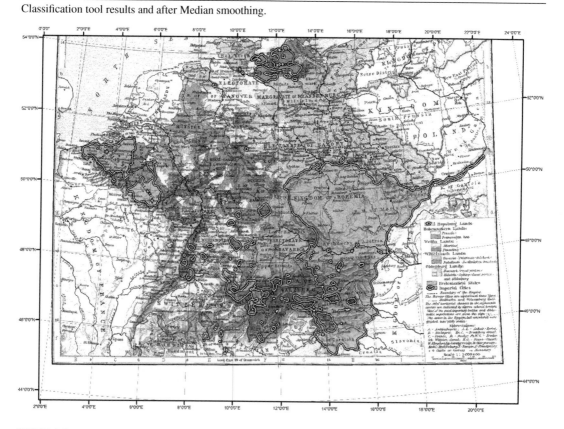

FIGURE 4.4

The automatically generated borders of the Hapsburg Lands and Imperial Cities.

4.2.3 Reconciling changing unit boundaries

After digitizing different maps, one of the difficulties of using historical data at the geographical level is that both the number and the geographic boundaries can change over time. For the case of the United States, one of the most systematically studied countries, the number and location of the counties changed frequently and significantly since 1790. The difficulty is creating a consistent panel of spatial units, which are consistent over time. The most used source for historical geographical data of the United States is the National Historical Geographic Information System (NHGIS). This website is rich in terms of information, but provides data with geographical identifiers at the time of data collection. The number of counties changed a lot over time. For example, there were only 250 counties in 1790, and the number is higher than 3000 in 2000.

There are different ways of linking counties across all the different census years. Horan and Hargis (1995) published a County Longitudinal template in order to allow for an inter-temporal comparison of fixed county groups between 1840 and 1990. At the time of publication, ARCGIS was not much used. What the authors did was to aggregate counties, as defined by their boundaries in 1990, into larger units on the basis of earlier historical county boundary configurations. These clusters are larger the further one goes back in time.

The most commonly used approach is the one followed by Eckert et al. (2018). They provide a crosswalk from historical county boundaries in every decade from 1790-2000 to the 1900 county borders. Eckert et al. (2018) used ArcGIS to provide a crosswalk that disaggregate historical counties into 1990 county boundaries based on their land area. They overlaid historical county shape files with the 1990 county shape files and then calculate the share of land of each historical county that forms part of a given recent county. Using such land partitions as weights, researchers can directly aggregate historical information to spatial units as defined by the recent boundaries. The advantage compared to Horan and Hargis (1995) is that the number of counties stay constant over time.

A different approach has been followed by Hornbeck (2010) who started with historical U.S. county boundary files (Carville et al., 1999) and intersected county borders in later decades with historical county borders. When later counties fall within more than one 1870 county, data for each piece are calculated by multiplying the later county data by the share of its area in the 1870 county. For these later periods, each 1870 county is then assigned the sum of all pieces falling within its area.

4.2.4 Detailed data presentation: a practical guide using GIS

Maps serve many uses in papers.

Presenting summary statistics as maps

One frequent use of maps is to locate the area of interest, particularly when discussing areas that the reader cannot be expected to be immediately familiar with. This is perhaps more frequent in presentations than in papers, since the audience can't easily check reference material in a seminar room.

Generally speaking, most economics papers that include historical content could benefit from the inclusion of one summary map. This can help the reader locate the area of the study in the world, familiarize himself with any location names that are important in the story and see visually the relevant sources of geographical variation. If the dataset contains less than a few hundred observations, it is usually feasible to show all the observations at this stage.

If understanding the story requires displaying multiple types of geographic data, it is generally possible to consolidate into a smaller number of combined maps. For example instead of showing side by side maps of waterways, it might be better to combine them into a single map showing both types of data in different colors.

Where the map is only used to show the geography of the area in question, such as a handful of cities with some associated borders, backgrounds like Gray Earth (pictured in Fig. 4.5)[3] can be more informative than showing just the coastlines and land borders. The map is ideal for many uses because it exaggerates elevation in flatter areas. This allows e.g. the Himalayas and the much less prominent Appalachians to be visible on the same map.

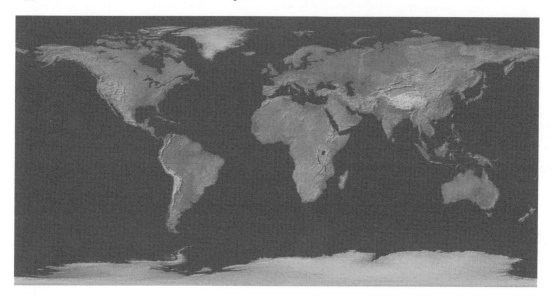

FIGURE 4.5

The map of Gray Earth.

Showing all of the observations in a dataset as a map is also useful in that it can preempt readers' doubts as to the representativeness of the sample.

Showing causal effects using maps and integrating maps and scatterplots

Communicating causal relationships through maps is often difficult. This is particularly true in situations where both the independent and dependent variables are most easily represented by a raster, since both can't be simultaneously visible. For example if we wanted to show with a map the relationship between rainfall and population density, the simplest approach would be to show the two maps side by side (Fig. 4.6). This works reasonably well, since the relationship is generally strong (e.g. in the US the area west of Texas is very dry and very unpopulated until you reach the Pacific Coast).

However if we did the exercise for only e.g. the San Francisco Bay Area, the relationship might no longer be as obvious, since for example mountain areas will have more rainfall, but less population. As

---

[3] The Gray Earth background, including versions with rivers and sea floor relief, is available from https://www.naturalearthdata.com/downloads/10m-raster-data/10m-gray-earth/.

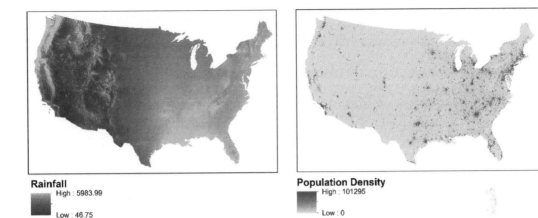

Rainfall
High : 5983.99

Low : 46.75

Population Density
High : 101295

Low : 0

FIGURE 4.6

Comparison of rainfall and population map.

a side-by-side comparison might now be difficult to read, in this case it might be better to transform the rainfall raster into a simple binary raster showing if rainfall is above or below a specific threshold. This could then be overlaid over the vegetation map, to show more clearly how the preponderance populated areas are in the locations with lower precipitations, i.e. population density is lower in the mountains (Fig. 4.7).

Mapping as a research tool

So far we have assumed that the paper has already been written, and the researcher is simply deciding how to best present her results to the profession. However, making maps can also be a powerful tool at every step of the research process.

For example, while conducting their literature review, researchers can make simple maps, e.g. they can drop pins on every important city mentioned in the text, draw lines along the trade routes mentioned, and start finding and adding potentially important variables to the map. Besides improving their understanding of the historical events being studied, this can help them recognize patterns that might be significant for their research, and will eventually make it easier to transition to the hypothesis testing phase of the project.

Once the results are ready, these same place-markers can be used as needed for any of the maps necessary for the working paper.

4.2.5 Other geographical data

In this subsection we describe geographical data commonly used in economic research. Unlike old maps that need to be digitized, most of these data are already available and ready to use. We therefore just outline potential issues in using them.

4.2.5.1 *FAO GAEZ*

The FAO's Global Agro-Ecological Zones dataset (GAEZ) (Fischer et al., 2002) was created to document the extent to which agriculture is possible, and performed all over the world. It provides freely

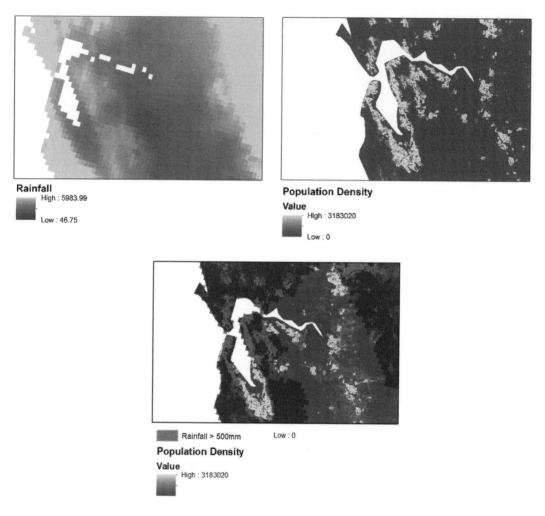

FIGURE 4.7

Comparison of rainfall and population density for the San Francisco Bay Area.

accessible data in five main areas: land and water resources, agro-climatic resources, suitability and potential yield for 280 crops under a variety of farming technologies, actual production data for the main crops, and information on the gap in yield and production.

As an illustration for the use of these data we can describe the application to the introduction of the potato in Europe (Nunn and Qian, 2011). The idea being that while actual modern production or productivity of potatoes is endogenous to current economic conditions, the soil and climate suitability of different European regions to a crop which had never been cultivated in the Old World before is plausibly exogenous. Similarly, Alesina et al. (2013) used the relative suitability for either plough positive or plough negative crops to instrument for the relative productivity of women's labor. As the

FAO GAEZ data covers an enormous variety of crops and cultivation techniques, a wide range of hypothesis can be tested, such as the importance of irrigation in developing state capacity (Bentzen et al., 2017), the role of subsistence versus cash crops (Nunn and Qian, 2011), the implications of improved agricultural technology for structural transformation (Bustos et al., 2016), and agriculture vs pastoralism (Voigtländer and Voth, 2013a).

The model documentation is well written and worth reading, particularly if the GAEZ data is central to the research project. For example, soil suitability for various crops is recorded for low, intermediate, and high input levels. These levels correspond to using traditional methods and seeds, improved methods and seeds, or fully mechanized agriculture.[4]

So if we use the increase in production going from low to high input levels, we will be largely exploiting variation in the ratio of nutrient retention to nutrient availability. If any of these geological factors are connected with our variable of interest in another way, for example greater risk of landslides, higher slope, or mineral deposits, the analysis will naturally be invalid.

The dataset also includes an enormous array of gridded geographic data, such as weather, geology, and soil cover. Furthermore these data have already been harmonized across countries, and derived consistently. They are therefore a natural first place to look for such data when needed. These can be used for data analysis directly, or as derived measures tailored to specific empirical purposes.

One important aspect to consider is that the FAO calculated the crop potentials for the purpose of determining how the world could be fed today, under a variety of scenarios. This means that care must be exercised when using the data in a historical context, as today's crops and techniques are of course very different from those of the past.

The usual workaround is to use the suitability using "low input levels", i.e. only hand power and unimproved variety. While this assumption is often perfectly reasonable, it might become invalid if this modern data is used to proxy for conditions many centuries or even millennia into the past.

Over these extended timeframes, we can expect a certain degree of coevolution between the crops and their farmers, as more efficient cultivation techniques are developed, and the plants themselves adapt to their new conditions through both artificial and natural selection.

For example, imagine we are interested in measuring the effect of the introduction of coffee to a hypothetical Pacific archipelago in the 18th century on present day urbanization. We might be tempted to use the FAO GAEZ productivity level with low inputs as a proxy for the exogenous suitability for coffee before its introduction. Let us imagine that we find that in fact high suitability for coffee production is a significant predictor of urbanization, which we attribute to agglomeration economies and persistence of urban settlements.

However, there is a potential confounding factor. The FAO is calculating present day productivity. Even the traditional cultivars available today are very different from those that would initially have been brought over on the ship. For example, it could be that the coffee available at the time grew best at higher altitudes, but that due to transportation issues the plantations were initially created close to

---

[4] The documentation tells how these values were calculated: nutrient availability is of utmost importance for low level input farming; nutrient retention capacity is most important for high level inputs; nutrient availability and nutrient retention capacity are considered of equal importance for intermediate level inputs farming; nutrient availability and nutrient retention capacity are strongly related to rooting depth and soil volume available, and oxygen available to roots, excess salts, toxicity, and workability are regarded as equally important soil qualities, and the combination of these four soil qualities is best achieved by multiplication of the most limiting rating with the average of the ratings of the remaining three soil qualities.

the harbor used for export. Over time, the local cultivars would have adapted to their new conditions, and farmers would have learned how to coax the most output in the soil and weather they were familiar with. By the time that transportation to the highlands became feasible, coffee cultivation may in fact have become more productive in the lowlands, which is what we measure now.

Therefore, if we had the true soil suitability for coffee in 1700, we would have found the opposite effect — that greater suitability led to less urbanization. The reason for finding a positive effect was that the presence of a harbor drove both the location of cities, and of the first plantations. In turn, the decision to plant those first coffee trees in a particular location ensured that the local cultivars adapted to those conditions in the long run.

Whether this scenario applies to particular historical instances is something that must be determined by researchers on a case by case basis. What must be avoided are cases in which (a) enough time has elapsed since crop introduction to expect significant learning by doing and (b) there is a potential factor that could have both influenced the initial decision to plant a particular crop and independently had an effect on the variable of interest.

4.2.5.2 Rivers

Data on rivers is frequently included in economic history regressions, either as a variable of interest, or as a control. Depending on the historical context, rivers have had remarkably varied impacts on human societies. They are used as sources of irrigation and drinking water, transportation (Bleakley and Lin, 2012), fish, mechanical energy (Caprettini and Voth, 2020), and obstacles to be crossed by both traders and armies (Matranga and Nathkov, 2019).

Depending on the specific factor being analyzed, different types of data on rivers are most appropriate. If the water source aspect is the primary interest, it is obviously necessary to know how much water is actually in the river. For many regions, the annual water flow of rivers can be obtained only at its mouth, and perhaps at a few of the important forks. If finer grained data is necessary, ground elevation and precipitation data can be combined to calculate the Flow Accumulation, which is the amount of water that should theoretically flow through each pixel of the map given its slope and precipitation totals: While this methodology excludes the role of evaporation and ground water transport, it should in most cases produce results that are at least ordinally consistent, particularly in smaller areas (e.g. the Po's plain in Italy).

From a transportation standpoint, besides the actual river network, the extent of each river's watershed can also be used. Since river transport of bulk goods was generally much cheaper than overland transport by pack or draft animal, the patchwork of watersheds will often be a reasonable description of the areas that can form integrated markets for the major staple crops, or other bulky trade items such as lumber. Historically important examples of such areas are the Po' Valley, the Rhineland, the Yangtze and Yellow River basins, the Mississippi Valley, and the Indus and Ganges Valley.

While the tracks of rivers are generally fairly stable on human timescales, the lower portions of many rivers (such as the Mississippi and the Yellow River) have experienced multiple changes in their tracks during historical times, sometimes swinging by hundreds of miles. It is important therefore to not accept data on river location blindly, but to instead check whether the data reflects the actual location of the rivers at the time of the study.

Data on modern rivers is available from Hydrosheds (Lehner et al., 2008). More detailed data can generally be acquired by the various national geological offices.

4.2.5.3 Elevation

Elevation is another frequently used variable in economic analysis. Higher elevations areas are generally colder, wetter, and harder to travel in. This has major impacts on the organization of production of the human societies which inhabit it. High altitude areas are also much harder for armies to conduct offensive operations in, giving an advantage to the defenders. In particular, since Nunn and Puga (2012), the de facto standard for measuring the impenetrability of an area is the Terrain Ruggedness Index (TRI) of Riley et al. (1999). The TRI is simply the power mean of the differences in altitude between each cell and the neighboring eight cells. Note that in general, ruggedness calculations will give different results depending on the resolution of the raster being used, therefore consistency is key to obtaining a valid dataset.

4.2.5.4 Climate data

Many economic history papers have used climate data, as either variable of interest or control (see Dell et al., 2014 for a review). The two most frequently used variables are temperature and rainfall. These variables have been used as instruments for warfare or agricultural productivity (Miguel et al., 2004; Dell et al., 2012; Burke and Leigh, 2010). These two measures are also part of the de facto standard set of controls for regressions in economic history, where available.

If only cross sectional variation is required, it is sometimes appropriate to use modern climatic averages as proxies for past average climatic conditions. This is easier to justify if the units of observation are widely scattered in various climate zones and if the period of interest is not too remote, or part of a known climatic anomaly. For example modern temperature averages could plausibly proxy for past temperature in world national capitals in 1750. They would, however, likely not be a good proxy for the temperatures of different cities on the shore of Lake of Geneva during a specific year of the Little Ice Age.

4.3 Ethnographic data

A prolific strand of the economics literature has documented a strong persistence of economic outcomes over time, including economic growth, political development and a variety of cultural traits (Putternam and Weil, 2010; Spolaore and Wacziarg, 2013; Michalopoulos and Papaioannou, 2013; Alesina et al., 2013; Giuliano and Nunn, forthcoming; Voigtländer and Voth, 2012).

The historical dataset containing the most comprehensive information about societal characteristics going back to pre-industrial times is the *Ethnographic Atlas*, assembled by Murdock (1967a). The original dataset is collected at the ethnicity level and contains information on 1265 ethnic groups, all observed prior to industrialization or European contact. The earliest observation dates are for groups in the Old World where early written evidence is available. For the parts of the world without a written history, the information is from the earliest observers of these cultures. Overall, 23 ethnicities are observed during the seventeenth century or earlier, 16 during the eighteenth century, 310 during the nineteenth century, 876 between 1900 and 1950, and 31 after 1950. For nine ethnicities an exact year is not provided. The dataset contains information on political, economic and cultural traits of societies, and it has been used in various papers to analyze the long-term effects of historical characteristics.[5] The variable in the original database are names *v1*, *v2*, etc. There are 115 variables in the dataset. The type of variables present in the dataset is provided in Table 4.1.

Table 4.1 Ethnographic Atlas, variables.

Variables	Societal characteristics
	Economic characteristics
v1-v5	Main form of economic subsistence (agriculture, husbandry, fishing, hunting, and gathering)
v39-v42	Animals and plough cultivation, type of animal husbandry
v44-v65	Sex and age occupational specialization
v79-v88	Type of dwelling
	Political and societal characteristics
v32-v35, v72, v94	Political organization and religion (jurisdictional hierarchy of local community and beyond the local community, the presence of high gods and which types of games the society was practicing), succession to the office of local headman
v66-v69	Class stratification
v70-v71	Type of slavery
v73-v77	Inheritance rules
v90	Political integration
	Cultural characteristics
v6-v27, v43	Various forms of societal organization, mostly related to marriage practices, and type of descent
v36-v38, v78	Societal behavior of boys and girls such as male genital mutilation, post-partum sex taboos, pre-marital sexual behavior
v97-v99	Linguistic Affiliation (by language continent, language phylum, subfamilies)
	Geographical characteristics
v91-v92	Region (Africa, Mediterranean, East Eurasia, Insular Pacific, North and South America) and area within region
v95-v96	Climate
v103-v106	Latitude, longitude
	Miscellaneous
v89, v93	Inclusion in summary atlas volume, ethnographic atlas number
v100-v102	Date (millennium, century, year with century)
v107-v111	Society name (first, second…nine letters)

---

[5] One issue with the original *Ethnographic Atlas* is that European groups are under-represented, the information about these groups was available but anthropologists were interested in studying ethnicities that could actually be observed. Giuliano and Nunn (2018) created an extended version of the *Ethnographic Atlas*, adding several additional ethnicities. Specifically, they use three sources. Two sources are data collections, one containing 17 ethnic groups from Eastern Europe (Bondarenko et al., 2005) and the other containing information from Siberia (Korotayev et al., 2004). The third source, the World Ethnographic Sample, was also assembled by Murdock (1967b), and it contains additional 17 European ethnicities not included in the original *Ethnographic Atlas*. The complete sample contains information on 565 ethnic groups. Giuliano and Nunn (2018) construct three versions to link the past to the present. One using only information contained in the *Ethnographic Atlas*, one adding the Eastern European and Siberian identities, and the third one including the 17 additional ethnicities contained in the World Ethnographic Sample.

4.3.1 Political characteristics

The *Ethnographic Atlas* contains several measures of political and institutional characteristics. One of the most widely used variable is the level of jurisdictional hierarchy beyond the local community. The variable, which is generally interpreted as a measure of political centralization or political sophistication, measures the level of political authority when one moves beyond the local authority. It attributes the value of 0 to groups lacking any form of centralized political organization, 1 to petty chiefdoms, 2 to large paramount chiefdoms/small states and 3 or 4 to large states. For example, if the local village chief is the highest level of authority, and he or she does not answer to anyone above them, then the variable would take on a value of zero. If above the chief there was a district leader, and above this the paramount chief, then this variable would take on the value of four. Gennaioli and Rainer (2007) documents a strong correlation between the provision of public goods (education, health, and infrastructure) in Africa and the centralization of their ethnic groups' precolonial institution.

Michalopoulos and Papaioannou (2013) also use the degree of centralization and study whether it matters for contemporary economic performance, as proxied by satellite images of light density at night. They find a strong correlation, which also holds within pairs of adjacent ethnic homelands, with different legacies of pre-colonial institutions.

Mayshar et al. (2015) argue that hierarchies and states were related to differences in the appropriability of agricultural surplus, rather than to differences in land productivity. They provide empirical evidence supporting the theory that the presence of cereals (a type of crop much easier to appropriate than other crops) is strongly related to political hierarchy, calculated using data from the *Ethnographic Atlas*.

Another measure present in the *Ethnographic Atlas* is the extent of village democracy during the pre-industrial period. This variable reports the traditional form of succession of the local headman (or close equivalent such as clan chief). More specifically, the categories recorded in the data are: patrilineal heir, matrilineal heir; appointment by a higher authority; seniority or age; influence, wealth, or social status; formal consensus (including elections); and informal consensus. A given society has a tradition of democracy if the appointment of the local headman was through either formal consensus or informal consensus. Giuliano and Nunn (2013) show that having experienced local democracy in the past makes it more likely to develop democratic institutions today. The evidence provided by the authors suggests that the persistence comes from the development of more supportive beliefs of national democracy today.

4.3.2 Economic characteristics

Alesina et al. (2013) test the hypothesis that traditional agricultural practices influenced the historical division of labor and the evolution of gender norms. They find that societies that traditionally practiced plough agriculture in the past, today have less equal gender norms, measured using reported gender-role attitudes and female participation in the workplace, politics, and entrepreneurial activities. They use a measure from the *Ethnographic Atlas* to calculate the historical reliance on plough agriculture, and proxy plough agriculture using the agroclimatic suitability for crops that benefit from the plough. The data is provided by the FAO GAEZ project (see Section 4.2.5.1).

Becker (2019) studies how reliance on pastoralism has been relevant in determining restrictions on women's sexuality, such as female genital cutting, restrictions on women's freedom of mobility, and norms about their sexual behavior. For pastoralists it was hard to check paternity due to extended periods of male absence from the settlement. Using within-country variation across 500,000 women, Becker (2019) shows that women coming from pastoral societies are more likely to have undergone infibulation, adhere to more restrictive norms about women's promiscuity, are more restricted in their freedom of mobility.

She constructs a measure on historical dependence on pastoralism, by combining two variables from the *Ethnographic Atlas:* the degree to which a society depended on animal husbandry (from 0 to 100%) combined with the predominant type of animal in that specific society. For the predominant animals she defines a dummy if the societies have a herding animal (sheep, cattle, horses, reindeer, alpacas, or camels) and 0 otherwise (pigs, dogs or poultry or not animals at all).

Another commonly used variable is the measure of complexity of settlements. Ethnic groups are classified as belonging to categories going from nomadic to having complex settlements.[6] This variable has been used by a number of scholars as a measure of traditional economic development by assigning each non-missing category an integer value from 1 to 8 (Alesina et al., 2013; Giuliano and Nunn, forthcoming, and Michalopoulos and Papaioannou, 2013).

4.3.3 Cultural characteristics

Enke (2019) studies the long-term effect of different societal organization, based on how tight the kinship structure was. He finds that societies with a historically tight kinship structure regulate behavior through communal moral values, revenge taking, emotions of external shame, and notions of purity and disgust. In loose kinship societies, cooperation is enforced through universal moral values, internalized guilt, altruistic punishment, and the appearance of moralizing religions.

He constructs an index measuring the extent to which people in preindustrial societies were embedded in large, interconnected extended family networks. He follows Henrich (2020) and relies on information on local family structures and descent systems. More specifically he identifies two societal characteristics in the *Ethnographic Atlas* that reflect strong extended family networks: the presence of extended family systems and post-marital residence with parents (family structure) and the presence of lineages and localized clans (descent systems).

For family structure, he creates a variable that equals 1 if the domestic organization is around independent nuclear families and 0 otherwise. The idea is that living in extended family systems is an indication of the presence of large interconnected family networks. He also creates a variable equal to 1 if the wife is expected to move in with the husband's group or vice versa, and 0 otherwise. Strong kinships are indicated by norms that prescribe residence with the husband or wife group.

On the descent systems, the distinction is between unilineal or bilateral descent, and between segmented communities and localized clans. Unilineal descent systems track descent primarily through one line (maternal or paternal) as opposed to through both lines, and induce strong and cohesive in-groups. For segmented communities and localized clans, he defines a variable equal to 1 if people are part of localized clans that live as segmented communities and 0 otherwise. Clans are important to build very large extended family networks because they allow very distantly related people to feel connected.

---

[6] Categories in between are: Semi-nomadic, semi-sedentary, compact but not permanent settlements, neighborhoods of dispersed family homesteads, separate hamlets forming a single community, compact and relatively permanent settlements.

Another cultural practice that has received considerable attention in recent research is the practice of bride price, which is a transfer of money and/or other valuable assets that is made at marriage from the groom and/or his parents to the bride's parents. The importance of this tradition for female educational investments has recently been studied by Ashraf et al. (2020), Corno and Voena (2016), and Corno et al. (2017).

The *Ethnographic Atlas* categorizes the marriage customs of pre-industrial societies into the following groups: Bride price, which is also known as bride wealth and is a transfer of a substantial consideration in the form of goods, livestock, or money from the groom or his relative to the kinsmen of the bride; token bride price is a small or symbolic payment only; bride service, which is a substantive material consideration in which the principal element consists of labor or other services rendered by the groom to the bride's kinsmen; gift exchange, which is a reciprocal exchange of gifts of substantial value between the relatives of the bride and groom, or a continuing exchange of good and services in approximately equal amounts between the groom or his kinsmen and the bride's relatives; female relative exchange, which is a transfer of a sister or other female relative of the groom in exchange for the bride; dowry, which is a transfer of a substantial amount of property from the bride's relative to the bride, the groom, or the kinsmen of the latter; and no significant consideration, which is an absence of any significant consideration, or giving of bridal gifts only.

4.3.4 Connecting the past to the present

There are various ways in which researchers could link the historical characteristics of pre-industrial societies to current outcomes. We review the main ones used in literature.

Linking historical characteristics using the historical geographical location

The *Ethnographic Atlas* records the centroid of each society (longitude and latitude in degree). The question is how to associate the historical characteristics to current territory. One possibility is to use a circular "buffer zone" of various distances around the centroid. For example, Mayshar et al. (2015) use a circle of 20 mile radius around the centroid. This approach is shown in Fig. 4.8A.

There are several potential problems with this approach. If the buffer zones are chosen too large, they overlap, making it difficult to allocate territory to mutually exclusive ethnic groups. If the buffer zones are too small, they will be a poor approximation of the actual boundaries. An alternative approach (Alsan, 2015) is to construct Thiessen polygons, which more nearly approximate boundaries. The starting point to construct the Thiessen polygons is the centroids of the ethnic groups as reported in the *Ethnographic Atlas*. For a set of points S in Euclidean space, a Thiessen polygon (also known as a Voronoi diagram) is one such that every point in the constructed polygon is closer to one such point p than to any other point in S. Within Africa, Thiessen polygons have a higher correlation with the boundaries of ethnicities (that for this continent was provided by Murdock) than the buffer zone technique.

Linking historical characteristics using the current distribution of languages or ethnicities across the world

Both the buffer zone and the Thiessen polygons techniques are valid if the current location of the historical society is very similar to the current location of the society today. The further back into the past one goes, the more the economic history of a given place tends to diverge from the economic history of the people who currently live there. For example, the ethnicities reported in the *Ethnographic*

Panel A. Map   Panel B. Thiessen polygons   Panel C. Buffer zones

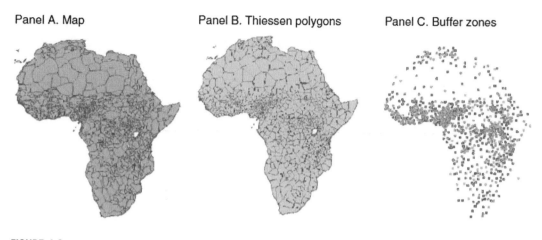

FIGURE 4.8

Thiessen polygons and buffer zones (from Alsan, 2015).

Atlas for the case of the United States were Native-American populations, mostly involved in hunting, fishing, and horticultural communities and organized into small, pre-state political units. By contrast, if one looks at the actual composition of the population in the United States a large fraction comes from ethnicities that lived in settled agricultural societies organized in large states. For the case of the United States, therefore, if one would link current outcomes using the geographical method this would lead to a misleading representation as the current distribution of population is very different than the one represented in the *Ethnographic Atlas*.

A better approach has been to link the historical information of the *Ethnographic Atlas* to the current population distribution. We describe in detail the approach followed by Giuliano and Nunn (2018).

To link the historical ethnicities with the current distribution of ethnicities, Giuliano and Nunn (2018) use the sixteenth edition of the *Ethnologue: Languages of the World* (Gordon, 2009) a data source that maps the current geographic distribution of over 7000 different languages and dialects, which were manually matched to one of the ethnic groups from the ethnographic data sources.

The *Ethnologue* provides a shape file that divides the world's land into polygons, with each polygon indicating the location of a specific language/dialect as of the data of publication. The *Ethnologue* shapefile is combined with data on the global distribution of the world's population taken from the Landscan 2007 database. The source reports estimates of the world's population in 2007 for 30 arc-second by 30 arc-second (roughly 1 km by 1 km) grid-cells globally. Combining these two sources of data provides an estimate of the distribution of populations' mother-tongue and, hence, the ancestral characteristics of populations across the globe today at a 1-km resolution. By combining these data sources, the authors construct country-level estimates of the average ancestral characteristics of populations for each modern country. The procedure can also be used to construct average ancestral characteristics at the subnational level.

We use the example of the authors to illustrate their procedure. In Alesina et al. (2013) the authors' research question was to look at the historical persistence of plough agriculture on current female labor force participation.

The first step is to look at the distribution of languages in a given country. Fig. 4.9A shows a map of Ethiopia with the land inhabited by different ethnic groups, i.e. groups speaking different languages. Each polygon represents the approximate borders of a group as found in the *Ethnologue*. The map also shows the *Landscan* estimate of the population of each cell within the country. A darker share indicates greater population.

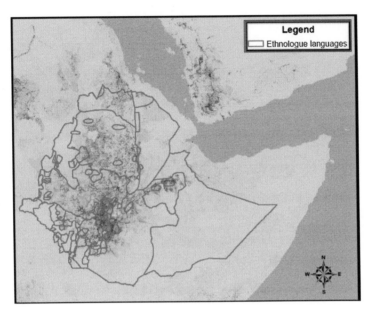

FIGURE 4.9A

Map of Ethiopia from Alesina et al. (2013), Ethnologue.

The second step in their procedure is to manually match each of the 7612 *Ethnologue* language groups to one of the 1265 *Ethnographic Atlas* Ethnic groups. From the *Ethnographic Atlas*, they then know whether a given ethnic group used the plough historically. Fig. 4.9B shows whether the ancestors of a given language group engaged in plough agriculture or not.

The third step consists in overlaying political districts and construct, using the *Landscan* population data (Fig. 4.9C), and finally estimate for each district (or country) the fraction of the population living that descends from ancestors that traditionally engaged in plough agriculture (Fig. 4.9D).

While the use of the *Ethnologue* constitutes an improvement compared to the matching using a geographical radius, it has its own drawbacks. The first one is that the information is missing for some part of the world. This is due to uncertainty or a lack of information about the boundaries of some language groups, a problem particularly pronounced for Latin America.

For those countries or districts in which the information is missing, a potential strategy is to construct alternative measures, by making different assumptions regarding the missing language data. The first is to assume that the inhabitants of unclassified territories all speak the official national language of the country. The second strategy is to impute the missing data using information on the spatial distribution of the ethnic groups taken from the *Geo-Referencing of Ethnic Group* (*GREG*) database

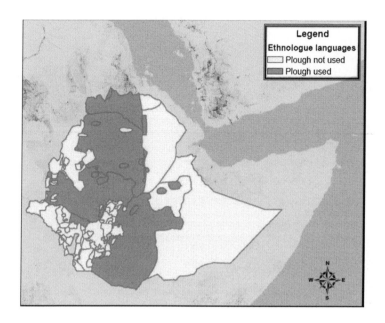

FIGURE 4.9B

Map of Ethiopia with plough/no plough.

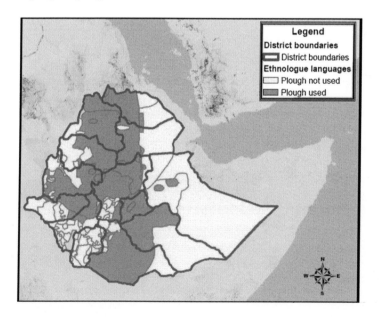

FIGURE 4.9C

Map of Ethiopia with political districts.

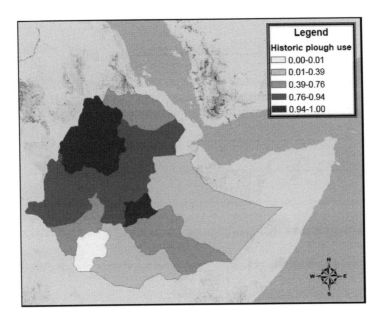

FIGURE 4.9D

Map of Ethiopia, plough use at the district level.

(Weidmann et al., 2010). Like the *Ethnologue*, the *GREG* database provides a shape file that divides the world's land into polygons, with each polygon indicating the location of a specific ethnicity. The shortcoming of the GREG database is that ethnic groups are much less finely identified relative to the *Ethnologue* database.[7] The big advantage if this dataset is that provides a better distribution of ethnicities for Latin America, where the *Ethnologue* provide only the official language.

Linking historical characteristic using a migration matrix

An alternative approach to account for migration is to follow Putternam and Weil (2010). The authors use this measure to re-examine the hypothesis that early development of agrarian societies (and states, their socio-political correlate) conferred development advantages that remain relevant today. The authors formally address the issue of migration by constructing a matrix detailing the year-1500 origins of the current population of almost every country in the world. Before them, Acemoglu et al. (2001, 2002) calculated the share of the population that is of European descent for 1900 and 1975. Putternam and Weil (2010) was an improvement because they broke down ancestor populations much more finely than Europeans and non-Europeans.

Putternam and Weil (2010) use 1500 as a rough starting point for the era of European coloniza-tion of other continents. To estimate the proportion of the ancestors of today's inhabitants they use a wide range of secondary sources. A crucial challenge in their methodology is the attribution of mixed populations (for instance mestizos) to their original source countries. The authors, whenever possible,

---

[7] The GREG database identifies 1364 ethnic groups, while the *Ethnologue* identifies 7612 language groups.

use genetic evidence as the basis for dividing the ancestry of modern mixed groups that account for large fractions of their country's population. In cases where genetic evidence on the ancestry of mixed groups was not available, the authors rely on textual accounts and generalizations from countries with similar histories for which genetic data were available.

The authors construct a matrix of migration since 1500. The matrix has 165 rows, each for a present-day country, and 172 columns (the same 165 countries plus seven other source countries with current populations of less than one half million). Using the authors' example: Malaysia has five entries, corresponding to the five source countries for the current Malaysian population: Malaysia (0.6), China (0.27), India (0.075), Indonesia (0.04), and the Philippines (0.025).

Linking historical characteristics using individual level data at the ethnicity level

The final way of linking current outcomes to ancestral characteristics is to use individual level information on the ethnicity or language spoken by the person. Each current ethnicity/language can be manually matched to the historical ethnicity name. This procedure has the advantage that one can control for county and also finer geographical fixed effects. The direct link has been used in different papers, including Alesina et al. (2013) and Becker (2019).

4.4 Censuses

4.4.1 The use of complete count population censuses

Research in economic history has advanced very recently with the use of historical complete count population censuses, mostly for the United States. Besides the enormous sample size, an important advantage of these datasets is that they provide individuals' names, allowing researchers to link information across time, creating large panel datasets, which can then be used to answer questions on intergenerational mobility or immigrant assimilations, often with illuminating results. For example, cross-sectional work had concluded that immigrants to the United States started from lower-paid positions than U.S. born workers but converged over time. Abramitzky et al. (2014) instead used individual-linked, and find that even recent immigrants to the U.S. earned just as much as the native born, and further that their wages then grew at similar rates.

Linking historical data across censuses present various challenges. For modern data, administrative datasets contain social security numbers (SSN), allowing researchers to link individuals using SSN, names, and place of birth. Social security numbers are however not present in historical records. Without SSN linking individuals with census frequency is extremely challenging especially for individuals with common names. Various methods have been developed to improve the matching. Abramitzky et al. (2019b) provide a detailed overview. Here we briefly describe each them, together with their advantages and disadvantages.

One approach is to try to match individuals by using their name and last name directly, as initially done by Ferrie (1996), and later improved by Abramitzky et al. (2012, 2014, 2019a). The second is a machine-learning approached developed by Feigenbaum (2016). The third one is a fully automated probabilistic algorithm (Abramitzky et al., 2020).

4.4.2 Linking historical information using names

This method has been followed by Ferrie (1996) and more recently by Abramitzky et al. (2012, 2014, 2019a). The algorithm consists in uniquely identifying a name in a given Census Year. In their case the name is identified using first and last name, place, and date of birth. The information is further restricted to individuals who are unique. They then search for these unique individuals in the following Census-year. If there is unique match, this is considered a match. If there are multiple matches, this information is discarded. If there are no matches, the algorithm searches for matches within two years of reported birth (one year before or one year after) first, and if this is unsuccessful within 4 years (two years before and two years after). Only unique matches are accepted. If there are no unique matches the observation is discarded. The procedure is then repeated for each record in the second database. Finally the intersection of the two matched samples is taken.[8]

Abramitzky et al. (2020) developed a probabilistic approach. For each observation in a given dataset, they identify a set of potential matches in the second dataset. The potential matches are identified by looking for individuals with the same place of birth, the same estimated year of birth (plus/minus five years), and the same first letter in their first and last names. For each pair of potential matches, they compute a measure of similarity in the reported year of birth and name, where they use the Jaro-Winkler score for the first and last names. Similarity in age is calculated using the absolute value of the difference in reported years of birth. They then look at the combination of distances in reported names and ages, which is a good approximation of the probability that both records belong to the same individual.

4.4.3 Machine learning algorithm

Feigenbaum (2016) uses a machine learning algorithm which train the algorithm using hand linked data. The procedure has the following steps. First, for each observation in dataset A, he identifies a set of potential matches in dataset B (see Feigenbaum for the specific rule followed). Second, a human researcher helps with the construction of a training dataset on a small share of the possible links. This training dataset is used for the matching algorithm, by using a probit model, taking the value of 1 if the human researcher matched these records and 0 if not. The fitted model is then applied to the full data and generates a predicted probability of being a match for each pair of records in A and B (see Feigenbaum, 2016, for details).

Abramitzky et al. (2020) describe in details the accuracy of the different methods and the trade-off that they have between type I and type II errors, where the trade-off is between low discrepancy rates (their false positive) at the cost of having a relatively low true match rate. The other option is to have higher true match rates but also higher discrepancy rates. Finally, the authors also discuss how different automated linking methods can affect inferences.

---

[8] The authors also propose additional strategies to improve the match. For example, to limit the possibility of misspelling, they use the New York State Identification and Intelligence System (NYSIIS) standardized names, rather than actual names (this system standardizes names based on their pronunciation). Another possibility is to use the Jaro-Winkler string distance adjustment which gives a measure of the similarity of two strings, placing more weight on characters at the beginning of the strings.

4.5 Other historical data

In this section we describe some other historical data commonly used by economic historians.

4.5.1 Military history

Understanding the causes and consequences of wars, and their outcomes, has been one of the perennial objective of historiography since its very inception. A number of economic historians have contributed to this area, some focusing on the causes (Gennaioli and Voth, 2015), and others on the effects (Voigtländer and Voth, 2013b).

If the number of conflicts is needed, one approach is to digitize the battles cataloged in reference material, such as Chandler (1987) or Jaques (2006). In more localized settings, specialized sources should be sought where possible. For example, in their paper on the long run effects of Sherman's March to The Sea in the US Civil War, Feigenbaum et al. (2019) digitized maps of the US Army's routes of advance prepared by the US Department of War. Indeed the US government edited an entire War of the Rebellion Atlas, comprising over 1000 such maps, detailing the war at both the strategic and tactical scale.

In reading contemporaneous accounts of specific campaigns, or the memoirs of their combatants, researchers should always maintain some level of skepticism. The participants of every conflict are keen to embellish their successes and hide or dismiss their defeats. Before using such data, researchers should ask themselves whether the source would have had an interest to misreport in ways that could be significant to the analysis, and whether it would have been likely to be caught if they had tried to do so.

4.5.2 Transportation networks

The economic history of transportation was of course one of the first fields to receive modern cliometric techniques (Fogel, 1964). For more recent times, data is often already available digitized, or at least contemporaneous maps are available to be scanned and geocoded. For example, the US Military has mapped enormous areas of the world at a high level of detail, and many of the maps from the WWII era are freely available online from the Perry Castadena Library Map Collection at the University of Texas, Austin. All these maps include many features of potential economic interest, such as roads (often separated by surface type, canals, railways, ports, and airfields). For many important European and North American areas, maps of similar quality were being made already in the 19th century, but for earlier periods researchers will typically have to rely on maps that were prepared well after the fact, usually by historians or archaeologists basing themselves on the lay of the land, archaeological remains, narrative knowledge of which cities were connected, and other contextual factors.

Often the researcher has to guess about the historical nature of roads. For example, if the compiler knew that cities A and B were connected by a road, but did not know its exact lay, she might guess that it probably followed more or less the track of the modern road. This guess would be fairly accurate only when the location of transportation routes is extremely persistent, for example, the Roman road network is known with very high precision for the vast majority of its extent.

4.6 Conclusions

The use of historical data has become a standard tool in economics. This chapter describes the main sources of data used by economic historians, specifically looking at geographical data, ethnographic data, and censuses. For each group, we describe where to obtain these data, how to use or manipulate them and the main methodologically advances which allow economists to overcome or minimize the problems in using them. We finally discuss a variety of issues that they raise, such as the constant change in national and administrative borders; the reshuffling of ethnic groups due to migration, colonialism, natural disasters, and many other forces.

References

Abramitzky, R., Boustan, L., Eriksson, K., 2012. Europe's tired, poor, huddled masses: self-selection and economic outcomes in the age of mass migration. The American Economic Review 102 (5), 1832–1856.

Abramitzky, R., Boustan, L., Eriksson, K., 2014. A nation of immigrants: assimilation and economic outcomes in the age of mass migration. Journal of Political Economy 112 (3), 467–717.

Abramitzky, R., Boustan, L., Eriksson, K., 2019a. To the new world and back again: return migrants in the age of mass migration. Industrial & Labor Relations Review 72 (20), 300–322.

Abramitzky, R., Boustan, L., Erikson, K., Feigenbaum, J., Perez, S., 2019b. Automated Linking of Historical Data. Stanford University. Mimeo.

Abramitzky, R., Mill, R., Perez, S., 2020. Linking individuals across historical sources: a fully automated approach. Historical Methods 53 (2), 94–111.

Acemoglu, D., Johnson, S., Robinson, J., 2001. The colonial origins of comparative development: an empirical investigation. The American Economic Review 91 (5), 1369–1401.

Acemoglu, D., Johnson, S., Robinson, J., 2002. Reversal of fortunes: geography and institutions in the making of the modern world income distribution. The Quarterly Journal of Economics 117 (4), 1231–1294.

Alesina, A., Giuliano, P., Nunn, N., 2013. On the origins of gender roles: women and the plough. The Quarterly Journal of Economics 128 (2), 469–530.

Alsan, M., 2015. The effect of the TseTse fly on African development. The American Economic Review 105 (1), 382–410.

Ashraf, N., Bau, N., Nunn, N., Voena, A., 2020. Bride price and female education. Journal of Political Economy 128 (2), 591–641.

Becker, A., 2019. On the Economic Origins of Restrictions on Women's Sexuality. Harvard Mimeo.

Bentzen, J.S., Kaarsen, N., Wingender, A.M., 2017. Irrigation and autocracy. Journal of the European Economic Association 15 (1), 1–53.

Bleakley, H., Lin, J., 2012. Portage and path dependence. The Quarterly Journal of Economics 127 (2), 587–644.

Bondarenko, D., Kazankov, A., Khaltourina, D., Korotayev, A., 2005. Ethnographic Atlas XXI: people of eastermost Europe. Ethnology 44, 261–289.

Burke, P.J., Leigh, A., 2010. Do output contractions trigger democratic change? American Economic Journal: Macroeconomics 2 (4), 124–157.

Bustos, P., Caprettini, B., Ponticelli, J., 2016. Agricultural productivity and structural transformation: evidence from Brazil. The American Economic Review 106 (6), 1320–1365.

Caprettini, B., Voth, H.-J., 2020. Rage against the machines: labor-saving technology and unrest in England, 1830-32. American Economic Review: Insights 2 (3), 305–320.

Card, D., Krueger, A., 1994. Minimum wages and employment: a case study of the fast-food industry in New Jersey and Pennsylvania. The American Economic Review 84 (4), 772–793.

Carville, E., Heppen, J., Otterstrom, S., 1999. HUSCO 1790-1999: Historical United States County Boundary Files. Louisiana State University, Baton Rouge.

Chandler, D.G., 1987. Dictionary of Battles: The World's Key Battles from 405 BC to Today. Ebury Press.

Corno, L., Voena, A., 2016. Selling daughters: age of marriage, income shocks, and the bride price tradition. IFS W16/08. Institute for Fiscal Studies.

Corno, L., Hildebrandt, N., Voena, A., 2017. Age of Marriage, Weather Shocks, and the Direction of Marriage Payments. NBER WP 23604.

Dell, M., Jones, B.F., Olken, B.A., 2012. Temperature shocks and economic growth: evidence from the last half century. American Economic Journal: Macroeconomics 4 (3), 66–95.

Dell, M., Jones, B.F., Olken, B.A., 2014. What do we learn from the weather? The new climate-economy literature. Journal of Economic Literature 52 (3), 740–798.

Eckert, F., Gvirtz, A., Peters, M., 2018. A Consistent County-Level Crosswalk for US Spatial Data Since 1790. Yale University. Mimeo.

Enke, B., 2019. Kinship, cooperation, and the evolution of moral systems. The Quarterly Journal of Economics 134 (2), 953–1019.

Feigenbaum, J.J., 2016. Automated census record linking: a machine learning approach. WP. https://open.bu.edu/handle/2144/27526.

Feigenbaum, J.J., Lee, J., Mezzanotti, F., 2019. Capital Destruction and Economic Growth: the Effects of Sherman's March, 1850-1920. NBER WP 25392.

Ferrie, J.P., 1996. A new sample of males linked from the public use microdata sample of the 1850 US federal census of population to the 1860 US federal census manuscript schedules. Historical Methods 29 (4), 141–156.

Fischer, G., van Nelthuizen, H., Shah, M., Nachtergaele, F., 2002. Global Agro-Ecological Assessment for Agriculture in the 21st Century: Methodology and Results. Food and Agriculture Organization of the United Nations, Rome.

Fogel, R.W., 1964. Railroads and American Economic Growth. Johns Hopkins Press, Baltimore.

Gennaioli, N., Rainer, I., 2007. The modern impact of precolonial centralization in Africa. Journal of Economic Growth 12 (3), 185–234.

Gennaioli, N., Voth, H.J., 2015. State capacity and military conflict. The Review of Economic Studies 82 (4), 1409–1448.

Giuliano, P., Nunn, N., 2013. The transmission of democracy: from the village to the nation-state. The American Economic Review: Papers and Proceedings 103 (3), 86–92.

Giuliano, P., Nunn, N., forthcoming. Understanding cultural persistence and change. The Review of Economic Studies. https://doi.org/10.1093/restud/rdaa074.

Giuliano, P., Nunn, N., 2018. Ancestral characteristics of modern populations. Economic History of Developing Regions 33 (1), 1–17.

Gordon, R.G., 2009. Ethnologue: Languages of the World, 16th ed. SIL International, Dallas.

Henrich, J., 2020. The WEIRDest People in the World: How the West Became Psychologically Peculiar and Particularly Prosperous. Princeton University Press, Princeton, NJ.

Horan, P.M., Hargis, P.G., 1995. County Longitudinal Template, 1840-1990. Inter-University Consortium for Political and Social Research, Ann Arbor, MI.

Hornbeck, R., 2010. Barbed wire: property rights and agricultural development. The Quarterly Journal of Economics 125 (2), 767–810.

Jaques, T., 2006. Dictionary of Battles and Sieges: Vol. 3. P-Z. Greenwood Publishing Group.

Korotayev, D., Kazankov, A., Borinskaya, S., Khaltourina, D., Bondarenko, D., 2004. Ethnographic Atlas XXX: people of Siberia. Ethnology 43, 83–92.

Lehner, B., Verdin, K., Jarvis, A., 2008. New global hydrography derived from spaceborne elevation data. Transactions - American Geophysical Union 89 (10), 93–94.

Matranga, A., Nathkov, T., 2019. All Along the Watchtower: Linear Defenses and the Introduction of Serfdom in Russia. Chapman University Mimeo.

Mayshar, J., Moav, O., Neeman, Z., Pascali, L., 2015. Cereals, Appropriability and Hierarchy. CEPR WP 10742.

Michalopoulos, S., Papaioannou, E., 2013. Pre-colonial ethnic institutions and contemporary African development. Econometrica 81, 113–152.

Miguel, E., Satyanath, S., Sergenti, E., 2004. Economic shocks and civil conflict: an instrumental variables approach. Journal of Political Economy 112 (4), 725–753.

Murdock, G.P., 1967a. Ethnographic Atlas. University of Pittsburgh Press.

Murdock, G.P., 1967b. World ethnographic sample. American Anthropologist 59, 664–687.

Nunn, N., Puga, D., 2012. Ruggedness: the blessing of bad geography in Africa. Review of Economics and Statistics 94 (1), 20–36.

Nunn, N., Qian, N., 2011. The potato's contribution to population and urbanization: evidence from a historical experiment. The Quarterly Journal of Economics 126 (2), 593–660.

Putternam, L., Weil, D., 2010. Post-1500 population flows and the long-run determinants of economic growth and inequality. The Quarterly Journal of Economics 125, 1627–1682.

Riley, S.J., De Gloria, S.D., Elliot, R., 1999. A terrain ruggedness index that quantifies topographic heterogeneity. Intermountain Journal of Science 5 (1–4), 23–27.

Spolaore, E., Wacziarg, R., 2013. How deep are the roots of economic development? Journal of Economic Literature 51, 325–369.

Voigtländer, N., Voth, J., 2012. Persecution perpetuated: the medieval origins of anti-semitic violence in Nazi-Germany. The Quarterly Journal of Economics 127, 1339–1392.

Voigtländer, N., Voth, H.-J., 2013a. How the West "invented" fertility restriction. The American Economic Review 103 (6), 2227–2264.

Voigtländer, N., Voth, H.-J., 2013b. The three horsemen of riches: plague, war, and urbanization in early modern Europe. The Review of Economic Studies 80 (2), 774–811.

Weidmann, N.B., Rod, J.K., Cederman, L.-E., 2010. Representing ethnic groups in space: a new dataset. Journal of Peace Research 47 (4), 491–499.

The use of archaeological data in economics

5

Andrea Matranga[a] **and Luigi Pascali**[b]

[a]*Chapman University, Orange, CA, United States*
[b]*Pompeu Fabra University, Barcelona, Spain*

5.1 Introduction

Why are some countries or regions characterized by better living conditions than others? The usual answer in economics relates differences in economic prosperity to variation in local institutions and culture (e.g. property rights protection, civil vs common law, trust, individualism etc.). A body of research has now established that many of these differences are explained by historical factors that go back millennia. The scarcity of written records for this earlier period has motivated economists to look at datasets developed in archaeology and paleoanthropology. The purpose of this study is to provide a review of both the data and the empirical methodologies developed in economics to study this distant past and relate it to contemporary economic outcomes. As an illustration of the importance of archaeology to understand persistent differences in economic prosperity, we will consider five fundamental topics. Section 5.2 examines the empirical economic work on the very earliest periods of our species existence, the Paleolithic and Neolithic. Section 5.3 discusses a series of papers documenting the exceptional persistence of economic disparities across regions and countries. Section 5.4 examines the origin and the role of the first states in explaining the emergence and the persistence of these disparities. Section 5.5 focuses on the role of ancient trade. Section 5.6 provides a primer to other databases of archaeological interests, including skeletal remains, paleoclimate, structures, and inscriptions. Finally, Section 5.7 concludes.

5.2 The stone age
5.2.1 The Paleolithic

The earliest human behavior to be studied by economists is the dispersal of *H. Sapiens* from Africa into the other continents, which started around 100,000 years ago and was substantially complete by 10,000 years ago. Ashraf and Galor (2013), argued that as humans radiated from Africa, the serial founder effect resulted in declining amounts of genetic diversity, as each area was populated by descendants of a smaller and smaller subset of the populations that migrated out of Africa. They find that long run economic development was faster in areas that had an intermediate level of genetic diversity, and they argue that this is because both very low and very high levels of diversity reduce growth.

Another paper investigating the long run impact of deep prehistory is Ashraf et al. (2010), which documents how areas that were more isolated in the Paleolithic, when our ancestors could only travel over land, are actually more developed today. They argue that being comparatively more isolated contributed to a society that was more conducive to innovation, because it was both less able to freeride on inventions made elsewhere, and less likely to be invaded and dispossessed of the fruits of its labor. To confirm that this finding is indeed driven by the very distant past, rather than by trade during more recent times, the authors show that the effect of walking-only distance persists even after controlling for isolation using straight line distance. This is informative since in later periods the availability of sea travel made straight line distances much more indicative of transportation costs.

5.2.2 The Neolithic

Agriculture was independently invented at least seven times, starting with the Levant, around 12,000 years ago. During the so-called Neolithic Revolution, our ancestors abandoned nomadic hunting and gathering and became settled farmers. This new lifestyle spread rapidly, averaging about a kilometer per year from the Middle East into Europe (Pinhasi et al., 2005), and eventually became by far the dominant lifestyle of humans on all continents, wherever there was enough rainfall and sunshine to support a crop.

The most important change was of course agriculture itself. As long as our ancestors had remained hunter gatherers, their food supply had been ultimately limited by the amount available naturally. They could become more efficient in collecting it, or learn to consume new sources, but decreasing returns to extra effort set in rather early. With farming, humans had a way of transforming labor into food, most obviously by planting some of the previous year's crops in suitable conditions, but also by removing competing inedible weeds, or diverting small streams to irrigate dry land. This meant that food production could expand almost linearly with population size, at least as long as there was new land to put into cultivation.

Once land in a particular location became scarce, part of the population could take some of those seeds and set up a new farming village in a new location. If the chosen destination was inhabited, farmers could use their greater numbers to push aside the previous occupants. In some cases, perhaps the expansion could occur through intermarriage, with the offspring of farmers bringing the seeds and farming techniques, and the current inhabitants providing the land. These twin processes led to the rapid expansion of agriculture into virtually all lands that could support it. As this was going on, rapid coevolution of farmers and their crops meant that the cultivated species soon became domesticated, meaning that their genetics changed to make them easier to cultivate and harvest (Harlan, 1998).

The Neolithic Revolution is of interest to economists for a number of reasons. First of all, unlike most inventions of comparable importance, agriculture was invented multiple times (Purugganan and Fuller, 2009), which means that it is possible to gain some idea of what characteristics made this crucial discovery more likely. Second, the arrival of agriculture made densely populated civilizations, with highly hierarchical institutions possible. The period is therefore a logical starting point for studies of the long run persistence of institutions and culture. Third, in most cases, the first farmers were noticeably shorter than the last hunter-gatherers, and also showed a decrease in general health (Cohen and Armelagos, 1984), a finding that has prompted a number of explanations.

The earliest modern theory for the Neolithic (based on actual archaeological excavations rather than theoretical speculation) was arguably presented by Vere Gordon Childe (1936). He posited that due to a drier climate at the end of the last glacial period, humans, plants, and animals had to necessarily live in much closer proximity, and that this cohabitation made agriculture possible, and ultimately inevitable.

After WWII, work by Braidwood showed that the desiccation event, which Childe had found limited evidence for, had not in fact occurred in the areas with the earliest evidence for agriculture. Boserup (1965) theorized that as population densities increased, humans had to adapt by finding new sources of food, and some of these efforts resulted in agriculture. Note that in this formulation, population growth is essentially constant.

In contrast, later work by Binford (1968) and Flannery (1973) assumed that a population of hunter-gatherers would over time reach an equilibrium with its environment, leveling off at a fixed sustainable population size. Under these conditions, there was no pressure to develop agriculture. This pressure came instead in the wake of climate change, which forced the local populations to move into more marginal zones. These areas were locally overpopulated and had the right incentives for developing farming.

Diamond's Guns, Germs, and Steel (1997) proposed a different climate change story, ascribing the birth of agriculture to the abundance of plants that could be domesticated easily, which became more abundant at the end of the last Ice Age. As described in Section 5.4 below, he then extended this reasoning into a theory for the different development paths undertaken by civilizations on different continents.

A parallel research program has investigated the wellbeing of our ancestors as agriculture was invented and adopted. Until the mid 1960s, researchers thought hunting and gathering was a universally precarious subsistence strategy, and agriculture therefore a clear improvement. In 1966, Marshall Sahlins introduced his Original Affluent Society hypothesis, which noted that most hunter gatherers that had survived to be studied by anthropologists appeared anything but precarious in their day to day life. Indeed, they appeared to be able to satisfy their primary needs with a three-day workweek, which left them time to socialize and play. Further, he argued that this was also likely to be true for primitive hunter gatherers. While he conceded that some hunters in marginal locations were indeed at times at risk of starvation, humanity is still all too acquainted with starvation, so that hunger can hardly be said to be a trait distinctive of hunter gatherers.

The comparatively leisurely conditions were largely confirmed by Cohen and Armelagos (1984), which collected and analyzed skeletal evidence from a number of distinct excavation campaigns in both the New and Old World covering the transition from hunting and gathering to agriculture in each location. The nearly unanimous finding was that as agriculture was adopted, our ancestors became shorter and in worse general health, suggesting that they ate less, worked more, and were more exposed to infectious diseases. Diamond (1997) argued that the initial increase in food availability was more than matched by runaway population growth, which resulted in worse health conditions.

Economists have tested these theories for the reduction in average standard of living and proposed their own. Since this chapter focuses on archaeological data, we are going to focus mainly on the contributions with an explicitly empirical component (this however covers the vast majority of the economic literature of the Neolithic of the last two decades).[1]

The literature on the Neolithic transition can be divided into two parts: the first one focuses on the factors that made the invention and the adoption of agriculture more likely and is discussed below

---

[1] A discussion of some earlier theoretical contributions can be found in Weisdorf (2005).

while the second part investigates the long-term impact of agriculture on human political and economic disparities and will be discussed in the next section.

The Diamond (1997) hypothesis, as stated in the book, relied on a fairly general overview of the data on domesticable species by comparing Eurasia with Africa, the Americas, and Australasia. Olsson and Hibbs (2005) sought to systematically test this hypothesis at the country level, using a sample of 112 countries. The data on plant domestication (the same used by Diamond) comes from Blumler (1992). It should be noted that this data is specified for only nine macro regions worldwide and is therefore only appropriate for very large-scale analysis such as this one.

Ashraf and Michalopoulos (2015) were able to use much finer grained data to test their novel theory for the Neolithic Revolution, which built on features of the Broad-Spectrum Revolution and climate change hypotheses. As in the theories of Binford and Flannery discussed above, they argue that where there was too little climate variability at the scale of decades or centuries, human populations would have little incentive to innovate. But as in e.g. Richerson et al. (2001), too much climate variability made it too risky to farm, since harvests of individual species would have been too variable. They therefore reason that farming was more likely to be invented in areas that were experiencing intermediate climatic volatility, and they test this hypothesis at the global scale using gridded climate data for the period 1901-2000 CE, as provided by Mitchell et al. (2004),[2] and using the country data on Neolithic adoption from Putterman and Trainor (2006). They find that, as predicted, areas with intermediate levels of volatility were the first to adopt agriculture. The analysis is then repeated, with similar results, for the 765 archaeological sites in Western Eurasia with C14 dates reported in the Pinhasi et al. (2005) dataset. Their datasets are available online from the journal website and are a logical entry point for researchers interested in probing the causes for the differential timing of the Neolithic.

Matranga (2020) also argues that climate volatility was the driving factor for the invention and spread of agriculture, but focuses on predictable seasonal changes *within* a year, rather than random differences *across* years. The difference is important because seasonal changes can be rather easily smoothed by storing food, as long as a suitable storage technology is present. The author shows that well understood cyclical changes in the parameters of Earth's orbit caused a marked increase in climate seasonality around the time when humans first became sedentary, and then started to farm. He argues that this was caused by climate seasonality making it essential to store wild foods for winter, even before agriculture was developed. Since food stores are too heavy to carry on nomadic migrations, this meant they had to become sedentary, which in turn facilitated the development of agriculture. The empirical part uses the same outcome data as Ashraf and Michalopoulos (2015),[3] but uses reconstructed panel climate data for the last 22,000 years from He (2011) for the explanatory variables, instead of cross-sectional climate data from the present. The author shows that agriculture first appeared at times and in places where climate was very seasonal, and that more seasonality also favored the spread of farming techniques. Further, he shows that areas that had a lot of different microclimates in a very short radius (accessible by a sedentary population) started farming earlier.

---

[2] This data is cross-checked against historical data of the past 500 years from Luterbacher et al. (2004), to show that climatic volatility is persistent at the timescales for which we have data.

[3] I.e. the Putterman and Trainor (2006) country dataset at the global scale, and the archaeological site data from Pinhasi et al. (2005) for Western Eurasia.

5.3 **Persistent economic disparities**

There are two striking facts when looking at the spatial concentration of economic activities during the last millennia. First, research has highlighted an exceptional persistence in the levels of economic, technological, and political development around the world until 1500 AD. Second, although the European colonization created a "reversal of fortunes" among European colonies, once accounting for migration between countries, ancient economic disparities are still explaining a large portion of current economic disparities.

Comin et al. (2010) show that worldwide technological differences are surprisingly persistent over long periods of time. The basis of this empirical work is a new country-level dataset on the history of technology over 2500 years of history prior to the era of European colonization. Specifically, data on technology for 1000 BC and 0 AD are derived from Peregrine's (2003) Atlas of Cultural Evolution,[4] while data for 1500 AD are coded from the Encyclopedia of Prehistory (Peregrine and Ember, 2001a,b),[5] one of the most comprehensive overviews of human history from two million years ago to the historic period. Using this novel dataset, Comin et al. (2010) document a significant technological persistence from 1000 BC to 0 AD and from 0 AD to 1500 AD. Ashraf and Galor (2011) take a step forward and provide evidence of persistence of technological disparities since at least the invention of agriculture, 11,000 years ago. This work uses a country-level dataset on the year of transition to agriculture developed by Putterman and Trainor (2006)[6] and documents that countries that experienced an earlier Neolithic transition were still characterized by more sophisticated technologies and higher levels of population density and urbanization up to 1500 AD.

When looking at the last 5 centuries, the evidence on the persistence of regional disparities becomes blurrier. For instance, when looking at ex-European colonies, Acemoglu et al. (2002) show that those that were relatively rich in 1500 AD are now relatively poor. Among these societies, the European intervention appears to have created an institutional reversal with the European elite promoting institutions of property rights protection in regions that were relatively less densely populated and less urbanized to incentivize European immigration and investments. However, once accounting for migration between countries, there is ample evidence that the persistence of regional disparities from the Neolithic transition has survived until today. Putterman and Weil (2010) and Chanda et al. (2014) use data on

---

[4] The Atlas of Cultural Evolution provides basic data on the evolution of cultural complexity using "archaeological traditions" as the units of analysis. These units are defined as a "group of populations sharing similar subsistence practices, technology, and forms of socio-political organization, which are spatially contiguous over a relatively large area and which endure temporally for a relatively long period". Comin et al. (2010) re-organized "archaeological traditions" into countries by assigning to each country the most advanced tradition within his current border in a certain period. For example, technologies used by the Aztecs during colonial times are coded as the ones used by Mexico in 1500 AD.

[5] The Encyclopedia of Prehistory is organized regionally with entries on each major archaeological tradition, written by noted experts in the field. The volumes follow a standard format and employ comparable units of description and analysis, making them easy to use and compare different historical periods and populations.

[6] Putterman and Trainor (2006) determine the date of transition using the first attested date within the country's border as stated by various specialized archaeological sources. This cross-country dataset has been widely used in the comparative development literature and is available for free download: https://www.brown.edu/Departments/Economics/Faculty/Louis_Putterman/agricultural%20data%20page.htm. An alternative data source that has been used by the literature (e.g. Ashraf and Michalopoulos (2015) and Olsson and Paik (2020)) to determine the timing of Neolithic transition is the list of 750 early Neolithic settlements in Europe and the Middle East from Pinhasi et al. (2005). These sites are carbon dated allowing to construct a more granular measure of the diffusion of agriculture.

large-scale migration since 1500 AD, constructed using a mix of modern census data and genetic data, to translate modern-day countries into their ancestral populations.[7] They then show that five different proxies of the levels of economic development of ancestral populations in 1500 AD are strongly positively correlated with modern development. Other contributions have documented the persistence of regional disparities until nowadays both when excluding countries interested by massive migration movements and when looking at within-country variation. After excluding neo-Europes from the sample, Hibbs and Olsson (2004); Olsson and Hibbs (2005) find that geographic factors that predict the timing of the Neolithic Revolution in a region also predict current per-capita income. Maloney and Valencia Caicedo (2015) establishes within-country persistence of economic activity in the New World over the last millennium: within American countries, pre-colonial population density is strongly and robustly correlated with population density today (and, to lesser extent, to current per-capita income). Subnational data on the density of indigenous people before colonization are drawn from a long tradition of academic research, with the most comprehensive source being Denevan's (1992) *"The Native Population in the Americas in 1492"*. Davis and Weinstein (2002) examine the distribution of regional economic activity in Japan from the Stone Age to the modern era. They use two proxies for economic activity in the past: archaeological site density and population density. Data on the number of archaeological sites come from Koyama (1978) and cover the modern Japanese prefectures in the Jomon period (6000 BC to 300 BC) and the Yayoi period (300 BC to 300 AD). Population data comes from Kito (1996) and are based on censuses beginning in 725 AD. This work provides evidence of an exceptional persistence in Japanese population concentration over the last eight thousand years, and despite recent massive wartime devastation.

An exception to this persistence literature showing overwhelming positive serial correlation in economic variables comes from Olsson and Paik (2020), who use the Pinhasi et al. (2005) dataset to document a reversal of fortunes within Western Eurasia. They show that while *across* macro regions, areas that adopted early are on average more densely populated and wealthy today (as documented by Ashraf and Galor, 2011), *within* Western Eurasia, the early adopters are instead on average poorer than those that delayed. This finding is robust to the use of either output or population density, as well as to the inclusion of a variety of controls variables. The authors further show that the effect is likely to work at least partially through a delayed adoption of democracy in areas with a long history of agriculture. In this section, we highlighted the most recent works that have documented an exceptional persistence of regional disparities back from the Neolithic Revolution. In the following sections, we will look at the ways in which economists have discussed the emergence of these disparities. We will consider, in particular, two events that shaped the organization of human societies, the emergence of the first states and the rise of long-distance trade.

5.4 The rise of the state

Approximately 3000 BCE, the first two states emerge in Egypt and Mesopotamia. In the following millennia pristine states arose in the Indus Valley, the Yellow River, Mesoamerica, and the Andes. This

---

[7] A revised version of the dataset on large scale population movements for migration is available for free download: https://www.brown.edu/Departments/Economics/Faculty/Louis_Putterman/world%20migration%20matrix.htm.

was a turning point in human history. In all areas where the state emerged, population increased and so did land productivity. The first cities appeared, together with a more complex division of labor, and with a hierarchical administrative structure composed of religious and military leaders and parts of the population specialized in the production of manufacturers. A new class of rulers took power, organized around aristocratic lineages, while centrally codified laws took the place of consensual normative regulations of small local communities (Chase-Dunn and Lerro, 2014).

What caused the transition of these societies from simple tribes to complex states? The usual answer relates the first large states to the Neolithic transition.[8] But how did farming trigger this change? Why is it that, once farming arrived, some regions developed complex hierarchies while some others did not? This is a fundamental question in comparative development as state history has been shown to explain an important variation of current differences in economic development (Ang (2013); Bockstette et al. (2002); Michalopoulos and Papaioannou (2013, 2014); Borcan et al. (2018a); Putterman and Weil (2010)).

We can divide the theories that aim at answering these questions into four groups.

The first set of theories, which goes back to Adam Smith and Gordon Childe, relates the emergence of the state to an increased productivity of labor that came with agriculture. The Neolithic transition increased the calories that could be extracted by one worker from the same acre of land: the resulting food surplus made it possible to have an elite that did not need to produce for his own subsistence. These theories naturally predict that regions blessed by a more productive agriculture will experience an earlier onset of the state. For instance, Diamond (1997) famously argued that the early state development of Eurasia lies in a series of environmental advantages, which resulted in a larger variety of domesticated crops and animals, and ultimately in both an earlier transition to farming and a more productive agriculture. These advantages include the larger size of Eurasia, its initial biological endowments (the availability of domesticable crops and animals), and its East-West orientation (which made it easier the spread of domesticates). The Diamond hypothesis has been tested in different contexts using a mix of data on biogeography and archaeological evidence. Ashraf and Galor (2011), a work that we already discussed in the previous section, show that those countries characterized by a larger number of native domesticable species of wild plants and animals experienced earlier the Neolithic transition and were still characterized by a more sophisticated technology up to at least 1500 CE. The data on domesticable species of wild plants come from Blumler (1992), briefly discussed in Section 5.2 above. Data on domesticable animals comes from Nowak's (1991) *Walker's Mammals of the World*, an encyclopedia which provides the native distribution of domesticable mammals. Using the same data on the biogeographical environment, a growing empirical literature has shown that a richer prehistoric availability of domesticates is an important predictor of an early presence of a macro-level polity (Borcan et al. (2018b); Petersen and Skaaning (2010)), independence from colonial powers post 1500 CE (Ertan et al. (2016)) and higher per-capita GDP today (Bleaney and Dimico (2011), Hibbs and Olsson (2004); Olsson and Hibbs (2005)). Within this context, the most widely used dataset on state

---

[8] The idea that the Neolithic Revolution paved the way to civilization has been criticized by Testart et al. (1982), who argued that the adoption of storing technologies provided the basis for the emergence of social classes and exploitation of food producers well before the Neolithic Revolution. By looking at 40 hunter-gatherer societies, Testart et al. show that storing societies present three characteristics, sedentarism, high population density, and large socioeconomic inequalities that have been considered typical of agricultural societies. Kuijt (2008) argued that food storage served as an economic and nutritional foundation for a period of rapid population growth in Southern Levantine, several thousand years before domestication.

antiquity comes from Bockstette et al. (2002) and has been recently updated by Borcan et al. (2018a). This dataset provides an index of state presence, scale, and home-based character to 160 present-day countries for every half-century since 3500 CE.[9]

The second set of theories relates the origin of the state to the conflicts generated by population growth and the resulting population pressure (e.g. Johnson and Earle, 2000; North et al., 2009; Dow and Reed, 2013). Within these theories, a famous contribution goes back to Carneiro circumscription theory. The theory is based on 3 assumptions: (1) population growth naturally leads to warfare, (2) warfare usually disperses people, (3) in areas with high agricultural productivity surrounded by less productive areas, like mountains, desert, or sea (circumscribed areas) the losers in warfare cannot migrate. When population is growing in a circumscribed area, the frequency and intensity of warfare increases as villages are competing for scarcer and scarcer land. The ultimate effect of this warfare is to change the political structure of the enclosed population: the political autonomy of tribes and small villages breaks down, while supra-village polities emerge.[10] In a recent working paper, Schonholzer (2020) provides systematic evidence in support for the circumscription theory of state formation using a mix of geographical and archaeological data. Schonholzer created a global proxy for the circumscription of 1/4 degree land cells (28 km at the equator) by comparing the land suitability of the cell to those of its neighbors within various radii. Data on the potential production capacity of each cell come from the FAO's Global Agricultural Zones (GAEZ) database (Fischer et al., 2008).[11] Archaeological data documenting the rise of civilizations across different regions of the world comes from *The Atlas of World Archaeology*, edited by Paul Bahn (2000). This is a large collection of archaeological sites spanning Paleolithic sites, Neolithic sites, sites indicative of an initial state formation process, and finally sites indicative of a process of state consolidation. The estimates show that circumscription is strongly correlated with the location of the first states. Interestingly the intensity of circumscription is also correlated with the timing of the formation of the state even within the Pristine states. Finally, when looking at modern country boundaries, Schonholzer shows that the average level of circumscription is positively correlated with the length of time an independent state existed. Mayoral and Olsson (2019) provide a test for the circumscription theory in the context of ancient Egypt. They show that political stability increased in the times of high circumscription, that is in periods in which agricultural productivity was relatively high around the Nile banks and relatively low in the hinterland regions. To this purpose they exploit the fact that the annual land productivity in these two areas depends on two independent weather systems. The agricultural productivity along the Nile depends on the Nile floods, which are in turn regulated by the African summer monsoons, while the productivity in the hinterland is regulated by the Mediterranean winter rainfalls. To capture rainfall variability in the distant past, the authors use two paleoclimate archives: Ethiopian monsoon precipitations and the Mediterranean winter precipitations are calculated by measuring the oxygen isotope content from stalagmites in the

---

[9] The dataset is available for free download: https://sites.google.com/site/econolaols/extended-state-history-index.

[10] Allen (1997) developed a variant of the circumscription theory to explain the rise of the state in Egypt. While agreeing that the desert bordering the Nile limited the chances of escaping taxation by leaving the river, he noted that state formation happened in a moment in which population density was low and farmers could avoid taxation by moving South along the river. Eventually, Upper Egypt solved the labor mobility problem by conquering Lower Egypt. Only then, the Egyptian state was able to tie peasants to the land and implement a uniform system of agricultural taxation.

[11] This database provides potential yields in terms of t/ha of the major crops under different types of agriculture (subsistence vs modern and rain-fed vs irrigated). It is available for download at: http://www.fao.org/nr/gaez/programa/es/.

Qunf cave (Southern Oman) and in the Soreq cave (Israel).[12] Political stability and state capacity in ancient Egypt are measured by the frequency of rule changes, the construction of pyramids and the geographical extent of the Egyptian state.[13,14]

The third set of theories suggests that state formation is linked to expropriation by emerging elites. Mancur Olson (1993, 2000) famously argued that the rise of early hierarchies is related to roving bandits turning stationary and permanently monopolizing expropriation in a given location. To maximize the revenues from expropriation, these bandits have incentives to encourage some degree of economic success in the local population and, accordingly, provide a series of basic public goods, like protection and order. These theories generally imply that states are more likely to emerge in regions in which the output of workers can be easily taxed or stolen.[15] Mayshar et al. (2019) suggest a test for this "appropriability" theory by exploiting the fact that some agricultural crops are easier to tax and expropriate than others. Specifically, cereal grains are storable and easy to transport, making it relatively easy for an elite to confiscate them from farmers and transport them to distant centers of power. On the other hand, roots and tubers are perishable and their high-water content hampers the efficient transportation of their nutritional content. Using a mix of biogeographical and archaeological evidence, the authors argue that states developed first in regions in which agriculture was limited to cereal crops, either because they were substantially more productive than roots and tubers, or because they were the only crop available. The evolution of hierarchy on a global scale is captured by data either on the location and demographic evolution of ancient cities (Reba et al., 2016),[16] or on archaeological evidence of complex civilizations (Whitehouse and Whitehouse, 1975).[17] The productivity advantage of cereals is captured by the GAEZ FAO's dataset on potential yields of different crops under rain-fed subsistence agriculture, while the availability of crops is proxied either by the local availability of wild relatives of domesticated cereals, roots, and tubers or by the distance from the areas of independent domestication of these crops.[18]

The final set of theories relate the origin of the state with a series of functions that the state provides. Prominent "functionalist" theories focus on the demand for construction and maintenance of hydraulic

---

[12] Data on the Qunf cave comes from Fleitmann et al. (2003), while data from the Soreq cave comes from Bar-Matthews et al. (2003); Bar-Matthews and Ayalot (2011).

[13] Data on the ruler tenure list in ancient Egypt come from Shaw (2000), data on the timing and volume of pyramid construction come from Lehner (1997). Data on the geographical extent of the Egyptian state comes from the Geacron World History data and are available for download at: http://geacron.com/home-en/.

[14] The approach of Mayoral and Olsson (2019) shares important similarities with Chaney (2013) and Manning et al. (2017). Chaney (2013) focuses on Egypt in the years AD 1169-1425 and documents that during periods in which Nile flood levels were deviating substantially from the annual average, religiosity and social unrest increased. This result is confirmed by Manning et al. (2017), which illustrates that the suppression of Nile floods related to volcanic activity in Ptolemaic Egypt (1305-30 BC) led to more frequent revolts against the elite.

[15] See Sanchez de la Sierra (2020) and Arjona et al. (2015) for a test of these theories applied on modern state formation.

[16] Reba et al. (2016) provide data on the location of urban settlements from 3700 BC. The dataset is based on historical, archaeological, and census-based urban population data previously published in separate contributions by Chandler and Modelski.

[17] David and Ruth Whitehouse's *Archaeological Atlas of the World* is a database of the most relevant radiocarbon dated global prehistoric and proto-historic archaeological sites. Mayshar et al. (2019) complemented this (admittedly dated) dataset with the archaeological collections provided by the portals http://ancientlocations.net and https://www.megalithic.co.uk.

[18] Larson et al. (2014) provide data on the 20 centers in which domestication of at least one plant or animal most likely took place and the list of domesticated in each of these areas.

infrastructure or storage facilities, on the demand for law and order to facilitate trade, and on the demand for protection from roving bandits.

The most prominent functionalist theory relates the formation of the state to the need to construct and manage large-scale irrigation systems. In his book *Oriental Despotism*, Karl August Wittfogel (1957) argued that absolutist states arose in Mesopotamia, Egypt, Rome, China, India, and Peru because despotic governments were necessary for irrigation and flood control. Managing the water for agriculture required coordination and specialized bureaucracies, which ended up dominating the economy and the religious life and monopolizing the political power.[19] Bentzen et al. (2017) provide a test for this theory using Murdock's (1967) *Ethnographic Atlas*, a database that contains information on several cultural, institutional, and economic features for 1200+ pre-modern societies from around the world. For each of these societies, the authors construct a measure for the productivity advantage from irrigation in agriculture using the FAO data on crop productivities discussed above. The cross-sectional regressions show that societies for which irrigated agriculture was substantially more productive than rain-fed agriculture had a higher probability of presenting "an elite class that derives its superior status from, and perpetuates it through, control over scarce resources, particularly land". Interestingly, it turns out that a higher potential for irrigation is also correlated with more modern autocratic states, suggesting a long-term persistence mechanism that goes from ancient hydraulic empires to higher historical inequality to a barrier to the diffusion of democracy today.

A second functionalist theory relates the state to the need to protect trade. On the basis of evidence from Africa, Bates (1983) argues that ecologically diverse environments increase the returns from trade. He concludes that "the origins of the state, then, lie in the welfare gains that can be reaped through the promotion of markets".[20] Bates supports this view by showing that, on a set of 34 agrarian societies, the proportion of societies with central monarchs was higher around ecological boundaries. Fenske (2014) provides further supportive evidence for this theory. He measures the gains from trade in a region calculating different indexes of its ecological diversity. Using data from the *Ethnographic Atlas* on the hierarchical complexity of societies, he then shows that African societies in ecologically diverse environments were characterized by relatively more complex hierarchical structures.

The third functionalist theory relates the emergence states to the need for security, peace, and stability as means to increase the productivity of workers.[21] In a recent work Dal Bó et al. (2019) argue that pristine civilizations emerged in areas in which conditions were favorable for food production and the state could protect the food surplus. Their theory predicts that the areas of the world that are going to develop long-lasting civilizations are those where returns to productive investments are high enough to allow for growth, and security is guaranteed by either high natural defense or an initial productivity sufficient to fund artificial defense. The theory is validated by an empirical exercise in which returns to investments are measured using the productivity advantage from irrigation as in Bentzen et al. (2017),

---

[19] Also Steward (1949) related the rise of the first states to the need to manage irrigation and other communal projects.

[20] Algaze (2008) proposes an analogous theory to explain the emergence of ancient Sumer.

[21] In the *Leviathan*, Thomas Hobbes postulates that the natural state of humankind in the absence of the state would be a "war of all against all". "In such condition, there is no place for industry; because the fruit thereof is uncertain: and consequently no culture of the earth; no navigation, nor use of the commodities that may be imported by sea; no commodious building; no instruments of moving, and removing, such things as require much force; no knowledge of the face of the earth; no account of time; no arts; no letters; no society; and which is worst of all, continual fear, and danger of violent death; and the life of man, solitary, poor, nasty, brutish, and short". Hobbes set out his doctrine of the foundation of states, in which all individuals cede some rights to a sovereign authority for the sake of protection.

the productivity of the land is measured with the FAO GAEZ data, and the rise of civilization is measured using data on ancient cities from Reba et al. (2016).

5.5 The emergence of long-distance trade

The flourishing of city states and empires alike, as well as advances in navigation, caused a rapid intensification of trade, which was widespread within western Eurasia by the late Bronze Age. Reconstructing the extent and shape of this first trade network has been proven particularly difficult as systematic archaeological evidence on trade relationships is limited. Most research in economic history infers trade intensity in a certain location using geographical characteristics or pollen data, while actual trade data are rarely available. One of the fundamental research questions within this context is whether early trade opportunities can explain the distribution of historical population and current patterns of economic development.

Bakker et al. (2018) analyze the coastline of the Mediterranean and the Black Sea and find that better connected locations are associated with a larger number of archaeological sites dating to the Iron Age. Connectedness is interpreted as a measure of market access and is measured as the number of other coastal locations that can be reached within a fixed maritime travel distance of each site, while archaeological data comes from the Pleiades dataset.[22] Dalgaard et al. (2018) focus on the area under the dominion of the Roman Empire at its zenith and show that the location of Roman roads predicts not only the number of Roman settlements in 500 CE but also greater economic activity in 2010.[23] Data on Roman roads come from the Digital Atlas of Roman and Medieval Civilization (DARMC) project,[24] while data on Roman settlements comes from the Digital Atlas of the Roman Empire (DARE).[25] The long-term impact of the Roman road network is confirmed by Wahl (2017). Wahl concentrates on Germany and, using a regression discontinuity design, shows that areas dominated by the Romans are still more developed (as measured by night luminosity) today than those that did not enter the Roman empire. This relationship is at least partially explained by the road network developed by the Romans: in fact, the differences between the two parts of the long-gone Roman Empire border are only noticeable for areas along ancient Roman roads.

The majority of studies seem to point towards a positive impact of geographic proximity and trade on the development of early settlements and on a long-term positive impact on economic development. There is a notable exception: the study of Ashraf et al. (2010) discussed in Section 5.2.

Until now, we reviewed a series of works that use geographic proximity as proxies for trade opportunities or trade intensity. A different, but still indirect, measure of trade is analyzed by Izdebski et al.

---

[22] The Pleiades dataset has extensive coverage of the Greek and Roman world and is currently being extended back into the ancient Near East, and forwards as far as the Early Medieval period. Outside of Western Eurasia, data is also available for specific areas, but we are unaware of a comparable database covering entire continents systematically.

[23] The identifying assumption here is that Roman roads were built mainly for military reasons, and therefore connected the military colonies the Romans built to occupy a newly conquered area, rather than the existing population centers. Interestingly, the positive impact of Roman roads was concentrated in the Western part of the Empire, where carts remained the dominant form of land transport until the industrial revolution. In the parts of the Roman empire where trade switched to camels (the Middle East and North Africa), the roads became unimportant, and the track of the Roman roads no longer predicts development.

[24] http://darmc.harvard.edu.

[25] https://dh.gu.se/dare/.

(2020), who use ancient pollen data for cereals, olive trees, and vines, from six different sites in Greece to document a trend towards greater geographic specialization (oil in the South, cereals in the North) from 1000 BCE to 480 BCE. The study of pollen in lake and peat sediments, known as palynology, is a reliable way to study landscape changes in the past. In this case data come from the European Pollen Database,[26] the most comprehensive dataset on paleoecological records for Eurasia.

A limitation of the pollen data is that they do not measure trade directly: trade is inferred instead from the changes in the regional agricultural specialization. The quantitative evidence on the movements of goods coming from archaeological sites is generally limited. There are two notable exceptions, however.

The first exception is the work of Barjamovic et al. (2019), which studies the role of trade in the history of Assyria. In this case, the empirical analysis is based on a large dataset of commercial records produced by Assyrian merchants in the 19th century BCE: a collection of 12,000+ tablets that were excavated at the archaeological site of Kultepe, in Turkey, and then deciphered and translated. Using this source, a measure of bilateral commercial interactions is computed based on the number of mentions of cargo shipments traveling between two cities. The empirical result points toward large cities emerging at the intersection of natural transport routes as indicated by topography. Additionally, the authors attempt to locate lost ancient cities by estimating a gravity model on these bilateral trade data (and interestingly, in many cases the location predicted by the gravity model is in line with the conjectures of historians following very different methodologies).

Finally, in a recent working paper, Flueckiger et al. (2019) constructed a dataset on bilateral trade in the Roman Empire using the Samian Research Database.[27] This source provides information for approximately 250,000 excavated potsherds of Roman fine tableware. A unique characteristic of these ceramics is that the production sites are clearly identifiable: once the production sites are paired with the location of archaeological excavation sites, the dataset is able to capture the volume of interregional trade volumes within Western Europe during the Roman era. Using these novel data in a gravity regression, the authors document that trade patterns were strongly influenced by the connectivity within the multi-modal Roman transport network. Moreover, the trade Roman trade network can explain the spatial pattern of firm ownership today. In the words of the authors this "continuity is largely explained by selective infrastructure routing and cultural integration due to bilateral convergence in preferences and values. Both plausibly arise from network-induced history of repeated socio-economic interaction."

5.6 Other available databases

In this section we will discuss in greater detail some of the datasets most commonly used in economic history. In turn, we will discuss skeletal data, paleoclimatic data, structures, and inscriptions.

---

[26] http://www.europeanpollendatabase.net/index.php.

[27] The database collects information on the terra sigillata, produced and distributed through the provinces of the North Western Roman Empire and the adjacent Barbaricum. The database can be consulted at: http://www.rgzm.de/samian.

5.6.1 Skeletal data

While soft tissues are easily lost, and only very sporadically available, bones are much more commonly preserved, and allow a range of insight into the lives of our ancestors. Unless otherwise noted, we will rely on the information from *The Cambridge Encyclopedia of Human Paleopathology* (Aufderheide et al., 1998).

The most commonly available measure taken from skeletons is height, which is convenient because it can be calculated based on even an incomplete skeleton. Unlike most other skeletal data source, it also has the added advantage of being directly comparable to readily available height data from modern times e.g. military records. Height is generally used as a nonspecific marker for average health status, since a wide variety of stresses such as hunger, pathogens, or emotional trauma can slow down growth in the child and result in a shorter adult. Given the importance of genes in determining height, researchers should be wary of directly comparing the height of individuals from different cultural contexts.

Some datasets include the estimated age at death of the individual skeletons. This measurement is conceptually trickier, and its accuracy will depend on how complete the skeleton is. If the skull is preserved, the pattern of dentition will generally allow anthropologists to age a child to within a year, until at least the age of 16. After that, a number of different markers such as toot wear will give some indication of age, but it will be increasingly difficult to separate actual age from various biological stresses, such as having to eat gritty foods.

If the skull is not present, age can be estimated thanks to bone length, and some more subtle indicators such as hip enlargement in females reaching puberty, or the sealing of the epiphyseal plate (which signals the end of long bone growth). However, in these cases it will often be impossible to estimate age and height for age independently.

Once an individual is past the age of about 20, their body stops changing in a predictable fashion, and wear and tear take over. Unless the age is recorded on cultural artifacts associated with the grave (e.g. headstones), the age of fully developed adults will have to be inferred by such markers as bone remodeling, tooth wear, joint diseases, and evidence of thoroughly healed fractures or wounds. While this data can still be used to some extent to construct age curves for different populations, they are by construction correlated with the health conditions they are based on. Such data is also unreliable when trying to compare very different populations, where the speed at which these processes accumulate in the body may vary.

Researchers are often interested in knowing the sex of individuals, either because it is one of the main variables of interest, or because they need it as a control variable or to stratify the sample. There are no generally adopted, widely applicable ways of sexing humans before puberty, and the best results are achieved with complete skeletons of individuals over 20 years old. Some datasets might record presumptive sex for adolescentes based on height for age, but of course such an approach would completely invalidate any research design on sexual dimorphism. In short any sex determination in a dataset must be traced back to the methodology employed, in order to ensure it is well matched to the needs of the chosen empirical strategy.

The presence and nature of diseases is another economically relevant data source. For example, Porotic Hyperostosis are spongy sections found in bones that should be smooth and are caused by excess growth in bone marrow in response to a sudden demand for blood cells. Archaeologists have traditionally attributed these lesions to an iron deficiency, either due to malnourishment or parasite load. However newer research (Walker et al., 2009) has suggested megaloblastic anemia as a more likely environmental cause of Porotic Hyperostosis. This is caused by a lack of either Vitamin B12 (animal products) or Folate (vegetables, legumes), and would imply that the lesions could be a marker for having a narrow diet, instead of a scarce one.

Data on the quantity and character of trauma evident in the skeletons can also be used. Often only the affected bone is mentioned, or even just the total number of fractures. Occasionally the examining anthropologists have also noted the likely cause of the injury, whether accidental or violent. Such data can be particularly interesting for studying changing patterns of violence in prehistoric societies.

Another potentially important markers are the Harris Lines, or Growth Arrest Lines. These forms in the long bones of children if they are subjected to starvation or disease, followed by a rapid return to normal conditions. Under these conditions, body growth will first stop to conserve energy, but assuming the diet then improves rapidly, there will be a period of catchup growth, which will leave a layer of denser tissue in the long bones. These layers are visible as lines in the X-Rays of the long bones and can be used as a marker of volatility in consumption over a time frame of weeks or months. This is useful since the other measures are generally a marker for average conditions, while reflecting relatively little information on the variability of conditions.

A convenient data source for North America is The Western Hemisphere Project[28] describes more than 12,000 individual observations with data such as age, sex, height, ancestry, society, dental health, and the presence of a variety of diseases such as anemia, joint damage, and trauma. Note that since not all skeletons are complete or equally preserved, some variables are missing in many observations.

The data comes from 65 sites, though very bad coverage of most of South America, and overrepresentation of North America.

Chronologically the data covers the past 8000 years, though only seven sites are 3000 years or older. It can be used to test a variety of hypotheses across space and time. The best way of appreciating the potential of this dataset is the edited volume that accompanied the release of the dataset (Steckel and Rose, 2002). It contains both an overview of the science behind the calculation of the variables available, a thorough discussion of the main stylized facts apparent from the data, and how they relate to what was already known about the population history of the Americas.

Cohen and Armelagos (1984) document health just before and after the adoption of agriculture. The underlying data is not available, and each chapter author contributed data from their own excavations. Some variables are universally reported (e.g. height), and there are chapters summarizing the data across sites. However, some variable and cross tabulations are reported only by a subset of studies.

5.6.2 Paleoclimatic data

Data on past climates comes from a variety of sources and methodologies. Ice cores, pollen records, and tree rings, are some of the more common sources of information on past climates.

Ice cores are informative because ice contains tiny air bubbles, from which scientists can determine the chemistry of Earth's atmosphere at the time that it formed. In particular the Vostok Ice Core (Petit et al., 2001) from Antarctica has yielded data on temperature and CO_2 concentration going back 400k years, at variable intervals of around 2k years. However, these values reflect average conditions all around the world, and are therefore not particularly useful for understanding the geographical distribution of conditions.

---

[28] The project webpage is https://economics.osu.edu/western-hemisphere-project.

If cross sectional or panel data is instead required, paleopalynology (the study of ancient pollen) can be of service. Most conifers and about 12% of flowering plants are wind pollinated, releasing massive amounts of pollen each year, some of which ends up preserved, often by sinking to the bottom of lakes. Archaeologists have been able to collect these stratified samples, determine the age of each layer through ^{14}C, and measure the frequency of pollen grains from different kinds of plants. This allows archaeologists to reconstruct which plants were present at various points in the past, and to therefore reconstruct the sort of climates that were present.

A particular sample might show that over time, grasses become relatively more abundant compared to trees. Depending on whether data for precise species is available, and on the general archaeological context, this might either be due to a decrease in rainfall, or the arrival of farming, or even other causes. It is therefore essential that before using this data, a thorough review of the relevant archaeological literature is performed, to determine what is the consensus interpretation for specific patterns in pollen concentration. However, once a particular interpretation is established as credible, pollen stratigraphy from multiple sites within a region can be compared over time to reconstruct panel data for the variables of interest.

Tree rings are another important source of panel climate data. The width of each ring is an indication of the growth conditions in the year it was formed, so that depending on the species and location, the series of widths can be used as a proxy for either temperature or rainfall. The International Tree Ring Data Bank[29] has data on raw ring width, wood density, and isotope measurements, plus site growth index chronologies, from over 4000 sites on six continents.

For example, Landon-Lane et al. (2009) use data from tree rings to extend weather data for the Great Plains state into the mid 19th century, allowing them to measure the effect of weather shocks on financial variables before rainfall data for the region became reliable. Besides indicating weather conditions, timbers taken from historical buildings can also be used to date them to within a few years. This allowed Ljungqvist et al. (2018) to collect a dataset of 50,000 dated tree fellings from between 1250 to 1699. They use this proxy for construction activity to document that construction activity decreased in response to plague outbreaks, high grain prices, the Thirty Years' War, and economic crisis already starting half a century *before* the Black Death.

5.6.3 Structures

Given that buildings are generally preserved much better than their contents, data on construction activities is generally one of the most universally available indicators of human activity. In particular the character and location of public works can tell us a lot about the societies that built them. For example, analysis of the road network layout can help us rank urban centers by centrality or understand the character of trade. The distribution of fortifications can tell us about the alliances, long-standing feuds, and contested regions. And the mere location of the settlements can inform our understanding of how production was organized.

Settlement data for the Paleolithic period tends to be more dispersed than the equivalent data for the Neolithic and later periods. One very useful reference for Western Eurasia is Tallavaara et al. (2015), which collect radiocarbon dates for the archaeological sites within the region between 30,000 and

---

[29] https://www.ncdc.noaa.gov/data-access/paleoclimatology-data/datasets/tree-ring.

13,000 years ago, and make clever use of period climate data, population density estimates, and site distribution to reconstruct human population dynamics around the end of the Ice Age. The dataset used in the study is available online and is an excellent resource for researchers interested in the period. The climate variables available are potential evotranspiration (a proxy for the potential for plant growth that combines temperature and precipitation), mean temperature of the coldest month, and water balance (that is precipitation minus evotranspiration). The paper also provides references to the source datasets, and the method used to construct the data.

The Canadian Archaeological Radiocarbon Database (CARD, Gajewski et al., 2011) provides C-14 dates for more than 25,000 sites, with excellent coverage of North America, and Europe (including reasonable coverage of the asian portion of Russia), and Australia, and a few sites around the African Great Lakes. Unfortunately, Central and South America, Africa, and Asia have only smattering of sites. Each site can have more than one sample, so for many sites a minimum duration of occupation can be inferred.

As an example of the potential of this dataset, Broughton and Weitzel (2018) leverage the data of CARD to show that different regions of North America have different timing of megafauna extinction relative to human arrival and population growth. Besides being interesting in its own right, the paper has full R code and data available on the Nature website and is therefore also useful as a way to learn how this data source can be used.

The Pleiades dataset[30] has extensive coverage of the Greek and Roman world and is currently being extended back into the ancient Near East, and forwards as far as the Early Medieval period. This data was used by the Bakker et al. (2018) paper discussed in the section on trade. Outside of Western Eurasia, data is also available for specific areas, but we are unaware of a comparable database covering entire continents systematically. One useful resource for locating potentially interesting local or regional datasets is *the Digital Archaeological Record* (tDAR, www.tdar.org), which provides a search engine for locating documents, pictures, sensor data, and a variety of datasets for sites all over the world (though these are all independent datasets prepared by different archaeologists for various research projects, rather than an integrated and harmonized dataset).

The transportation network connecting urban centers is itself of great interest to economic historians. The most well documented road network of the ancient world is of course that of the Romans, which relied on their mastery of the Mediterranean to quickly move people or supplies from one end of the Empire to the other, and to a network of well-maintained roads to provide reach into the interior. The canonical source for Roman transportation infrastructure data is the Barrington atlas of the Greek and Roman world (Talbert and Bagnall, 2000). The road data component of the atlas has been digitized and is available online.[31]

If the research project requires not just the location of roads, but actual travel time, then the ORBIS project gives users an interface to calculate travel times and costs between any two cities in the Roman Empire, under a variety of assumptions, such as season of the year, transshipment cost, and type of locomotion. Unfortunately, the underlying codebase and data cannot be exported, but the documentation is extremely clear and can be used to recreate the parts of the transportation model that are of interest for any particular project. In particular there is excellent sourcing for reasonable costs and speeds of various types of transportation, under a variety of conditions.

---

[30] https://pleiades.stoa.org/home.
[31] https://darmc.harvard.edu/data-availability.

5.6.4 Inscriptions

Archaeological excavations from the Bronze Age onwards inevitably generate a multitude of written texts, ranging all the way from inscriptions on coins, to entire volumes. Temin (2002) used a unique data series from Babylonian clay tablets showing various astronomical observations, and what were suspected to be the prices for six commodities, from 464 to 78 BCE. He was able to confirm that these were indeed market prices, as they had the same statistical properties as modern prices, specifically they were random walks, and they spiked when social order broke down. He inferred from this that the Babylonian economy was highly dependent on political conditions.

Kaiser's (2007) paper on the Athenian Trierarchy used inscriptions on wealthy Athenian families to test a model describing the system of public good provisions used in classical times.

Finally, as discussed above, the Barjamovic et al. (2019) paper used the frequency of city name pairs in Assyrian commercial letters to reconstruct the trade network at the time and estimates a gravity trade model to confirm or disprove various theories for the names of lost cities.

5.7 **Conclusion**

In this chapter, we have reviewed a recent literature in economics that has found evidence of persistence in economic activity over thousands or even tens of thousands of years. This literature highlights the importance of distant history to answer one of the most relevant questions in development economics: why is it that some regions are characterized by better living conditions than others? Economists are now realizing that understanding the current world is impossible without understanding this distant past. The scarcity of written records as we move back in time has pushed the profession to look for datasets developed in the field of archaeology and paleoanthropology. We illustrated the main datasets and empirical methodologies used to document this persistence of fates, explain the rise of the state and the emergence of long-distance trade. We think that this guide will serve to economists as a base to start scraping the gigantic set of data produced by archaeologists over these last decades.

References

Acemoglu, D., Johnson, S., Robinson, J.A., 2002. Reversal of fortune: geography and institutions in the making of the modern world income distribution. The Quarterly Journal of Economics 107 (4), 1231–1294.

Algaze, G., 2008. Ancient Mesopotamia at the Dawn of Civilization: The Evolution of an Urban Landscape. University of Chicago Press.

Allen, R.C., 1997. Agriculture and the origins of the state in ancient Egypt. Explorations in Economic History 34, 135–154.

Ang, J., 2013. Institutions and the long-run impact of early development. Journal of Development Economics 104, 1–18.

Arjona, A., Kasfir, N., Mampilly, Z., 2015. Rebel Governance in Civil War. Cambridge University Press.

Ashraf, Q., Galor, O., 2011. Dynamics and stagnation in the Malthusian epoch. The American Economic Review 101 (5), 2003–2041.

Ashraf, Q., Galor, O., 2013. The 'out of Africa' hypothesis, human genetic diversity, and comparative economic development. The American Economic Review 103 (1), 1–46.

Ashraf, Q.H., Galor, O., Özak, O., 2010. Isolation and development. Journal of the European Economic Association 8 (2), 401–412.

Ashraf, Q.H., Michalopoulos, S., 2015. Climatic fluctuations and the diffusion of agriculture. Review of Economics and Statistics 97, 589–609.

Aufderheide, A.C., Rodríguez-Martín, C., Langsjoen, O., 1998. The Cambridge Encyclopedia of Human Paleopathology, Vol. 478. Cambridge University Press, Cambridge.

Bahn, P.G., 2000. The Atlas of World Archaeology. Checkmark Books.

Bakker, J.D., et al., 2018. Of mice and merchants: Trade and growth in the Iron Age. No. w24825. National Bureau of Economic Research.

Bar-Matthews, M., et al., 2003. Sea-land isotopic relationships from planktonic foraminifera and speleothems in the Eastern Mediterranean region and their implications for paleorainfall during interglacial intervals. Geochimica Et Cosmochimica Acta 67 (17), 3181–3199.

Bar-Matthews, M., Ayalot, A., 2011. Mid Holocene climate variations revealed by high-resolution speleothem records from Soreq Cave, Israel, and their correlation with cultural changes. Holocene 21 (1), 163–171.

Barjamovic, G., Chaney, T., Coşar, K., Hortaçsu, A., 2019. Trade, merchants, and the lost cities of the bronze age. The Quarterly Journal of Economics 134 (3), 1455–1503.

Bates, R.H., 1983. Essays on the Political Economy of Rural Africa. University of California Press.

Bentzen, J.S., Kaarsen, N., Wingender, A.M., 2017. Irrigation and autocracy. Journal of the European Economic Association 15 (1), 1–53.

Binford, L.R., 1968. Post-Pleistocene adaptation. In: Binford, S.R., Binford, L.R. (Eds.), New Perspectives in Archaeology. Aldine, Chicago, pp. 313–341.

Bleaney, M., Dimico, A., 2011. Biogeographical conditions, the transition to agriculture and long-run growth. European Economic Review 55, 943–954.

Blumler, M., 1992. Seed Weight and Environment in Mediterranean-Type Grasslands in California and Israel. Unpublished Dissertation.

Bockstette, V., Chanda, A., Putterman, L., 2002. The advantage of an early start. Journal of Economic Growth 7, 347–369.

Borcan, O., Olsson, O., Putterman, L., 2018a. State history and economic development: evidence from six millennia. Journal of Economic Growth 23, 1–40.

Borcan, O., Olsson, O., Putterman, L., 2018b. Transition to Agriculture and First State Presence: a Global Analysis. Mimeo.

Boserup, E., 1965. The Conditions of Agricultural Growth: The Economics of Agrarian Change Under Population Pressure. G. Allen and Unwin, London; Aldine, Chicago, 1965. 124 pp.

Broughton, J.M., Weitzel, E.M., 2018. Population reconstructions for humans and megafauna suggest mixed causes for North American Pleistocene extinctions. Nature Communications 9, 5441.

Chanda, A., Cook, C.J., Putterman, L., 2014. Persistence of fortune: accounting for population movements, there was no post-Columbian reversal. American Economic Journal: Macroeconomics 6 (3), 1–28.

Chaney, E., 2013. Revolt on the Nile: economic shocks, religion, and political power. Econometrica 81 (5), 2033–2053.

Chase-Dunn, C., Lerro, B., 2014. Social Change. Routledge.

Childe, V.G., 1936. Man Makes Himself. Watts & Co.

Cohen, M.N., Armelagos, G.J. (Eds.), 1984. Paleopathology at the Origins of Agriculture. Academic Press, Orlando, FL. 615 pp.

Comin, D., William, E., Gong, E., 2010. Was the wealth of nations determined in 1000 BC? American Economic Journal: Macroeconomics 2, 65–97.

Dal Bó, E., Hernández, P., Mazzuca, S., 2019. The Paradox of Civilization: Pre-Institutional Sources of Security and Prosperity.

Dalgaard, C.-J., Kaarsen, N., Olsson, O., Selaya, P., 2018. Roman roads to prosperity: persistence and non-persistence in public good provision. CEPR Discussion Paper 12745. Mimeo.

Davis, D.R., Weinstein, D., 2002. Bones, bombs, and break points: the geography of economic activity. The American Economic Review 92 (5), 1269–1289.

Denevan, W., 1992. The Native Population of the Americas in 1492. University of Wisconsin Press, Madison, WI.

Diamond, J., 1997. Guns, Germs and Steel: The Fates of Human Societies. Norton, New York.

Dow, G.K., Reed, C.G., 2013. The origins of inequality: insiders, outsiders, elites, and commoners. Journal of Political Economy 121, 609–641.

Ertan, A., Martin, F., Putterman, L., 2016. Who was colonized and when? A cross-country analysis of determinants. European Economic Review 83, 165–184.

Fenske, J., 2014. Ecology, trade, and states in pre-colonial Africa. Journal of the European Economic Association 12 (3), 612–640.

Fischer, G., Nachtergaele, F., Prieler, S., Van Velthuizen, H.T., Verelst, L., Wiberg, D., 2008. Global Agro-Ecological Zones Assessment for Agriculture (GAEZ2008). Technical report. IIASA/FAO, Laxenburg, Austria/Rome, Italy.

Flannery, K.V., 1973. The origins of agriculture. Annual Review of Anthropology 2, 271–310.

Fleitmann, D., et al., 2003. Holocene forcing of the Indian Monsoon recorded in a stalagmite from Southern Oman. Science 300, 1737–1739.

Flueckiger, M., Hornung, E., Larch, M., Ludwig, M., Mees, A., 2019. Roman Transport Network Connectivity and Economic Integration. CEPR Discussion Paper 13838.

Gajewski, K., Munoz, S., Peros, M., Viau, A., Morlan, R., Betts, M., 2011. The Canadian archaeological radiocarbon database (Card): archaeological 14C dates in North America and their paleoenvironmental context. Radiocarbon 53 (2), 371–394. https://doi.org/10.1017/S0033822200056630.

Harlan, J.R., 1998. The Living Fields: Our Agricultural Heritage. Cambridge University Press, United Kingdom.

He, F., 2011. Simulating Transient Climate Evolution of the Last Deglaciation with CCSM3. Ph.D. thesis. University of Wisconsin - Madison.

Hibbs, D.A., Olsson, O., 2004. Geography, biogeography and why some countries are rich and others are poor. Proceedings of the National Academy of Sciences 101 (10), 3715–3720.

Izdebski, A., Słoczyński, T., Bonnier, A., Koloch, G., Kouli, K., 2020. Landscape change and trade in ancient Greece: evidence from pollen data. The Economic Journal 130 (632), 2596–2618.

Johnson, A.W., Earle, T., 2000. The Evolution of Human Societies: From Foraging Group to Agrarian State, second edition. Stanford University Press.

Kaiser, B., 2007. The Athenian trierarchy: mechanism design for the private provision of public goods. The Journal of Economic History 67 (2), 445–480. Available at SSRN: https://ssrn.com/abstract=2559630.

Kito, H., 1996. [Chosa] Meiji Izen Nihon no Chiiki Jinko (The Regional Population of Japan before the Meiji Period). Jochi Keizai Ronsyu 41 (1–2), 65–79.

Koyama, S., 1978. Jomon Subsistence and Population. Senri Ethnological Studies, vol. 2.

Kuijt, I., 2008. Demography and storage systems during the Southern Levantine neolithic demographic transition. In: Bocquet-Appel, J.-P., Bar-Yosef, O. (Eds.), The Neolithic Demographic Transition and Its Consequences. Springer, pp. 287–313.

Landon-Lane, J., Rockoff, H., Steckel, R., 2009. Droughts, Floods, and Financial Distress in the United States. NBER Working Paper No. 15596: 6.

Larson, G., et al., 2014. Current perspectives and the future of domestication studies. Proceedings of the National Academy of Sciences 111 (17), 6139–6146.

Lehner, M., 1997. The Complete Pyramids. Thames & Hudson, London.

Ljungqvist, F.C., Tegel, W., Krusic, P.J., Seim, A., Gschwind, F.M., Haneca, K., et al., 2018. Linking European building activity with plague history. Journal of Archaeological Science 98, 81–92. https://doi.org/10.1016/j.jas.2018.08.006.

Luterbacher, J., Dietrich, D., Xoplaki, E., Grosjean, M., Wanner, H., 2004. European seasonal and annual temperature variability, trends, and extremes since 1500. Science 303 (5663), 1499–1503.

Maloney, W.F., Valencia Caicedo, F., 2015. The persistence of (subnational) fortune. The Economic Journal 126, 2362–2401.

Manning, J., et al., 2017. Volcanic suppression of Nile summer flooding triggers revolt and constraints interstate conflict in ancient Egypt. Nature Communications 8-9.

Matranga, A., 2020. The Ant and the Grasshopper: Seasonality and the Invention of Agriculture. Working Paper.

Mayoral, L., Olsson, O., 2019. Pharaoh's Cage: Environmental Circumscription and Appropriability in Early State Development. Mimeo.

Mayshar, J., Moav, O., Pascali, L., 2019. The Origin of the State: Land Productivity or Appropriability? Mimeo.

Michalopoulos, S., Papaioannou, E., 2013. Pre-colonial ethnic institutions and contemporary African development. Econometrica 81, 113–152.

Michalopoulos, S., Papaioannou, E., 2014. National institutions and subnational development in Africa. The Quarterly Journal of Economics 129, 151–213.

Mitchell, T.D., et al., 2004. A comprehensive set of high-resolution grids of monthly climate for Europe and the globe: the observed record (1901–2000) and 16 scenarios (2001–2100). Tyndall centre for climate change research working paper 55.0, 25.

Murdock, G.P., 1967. Ethnographic Atlas. University of Pittsburgh Press, Pittsburgh.

North, D.C., Wallis, J.J., Weingast, B.R., 2009. Violence and Social Orders: A Conceptual Framework for Interpreting Recorded Human History. Cambridge University Press.

Nowak, R., 1991. Walker's Mammals of the World. Johns Hopkins University Press, Baltimore.

Olson, M., 1993. Dictatorship, democracy, and development. American Political Science Review 87, 567–576.

Olson, M., 2000. Power and Prosperity. Outgrowing Communist and Capitalist Dictatorships. Basic Books, New York.

Olsson, O., Hibbs Jr., D.A., 2005. Biogeography and long-run economic development. European Economic Review 49, 909–938.

Olsson, O., Paik, C., 2020. A western reversal since the neolithic? The long-run impact of early agriculture. The Journal of Economic History 80 (1), 100–135.

Peregrine, P.N., 2003. Atlas of cultural evolution. World Cultures 14 (1), 1–75.

Peregrine, P.N., Ember, M. (Eds.), 2001a. Encyclopedia of Prehistory, Volumes 1–8. Kluwer Academic/Plenum Publishers, New York.

Peregrine, P.N., Ember, M. (Eds.), 2001b. Encyclopedia of Prehistory, Volume 9. Kluwer Academic/Plenum Publishers, New York.

Petersen, M.B., Skaaning, S.-E., 2010. Ultimate causes of state formation: the significance of biogeography, diffusion, and neolithic revolutions. Historical Social Research 35 (3), 200–226.

Petit, J.R., et al., 2001. Vostok Ice Core Data for 420,000 Years. IGBP PAGES/World Data Center for Paleoclimatology Data Contribution Series #2001-076. NOAA/NGDC Paleoclimatology Program, Boulder, CO, USA.

Pinhasi, R., Fort, J., Ammerman, A.J., 2005. Tracing the origin and spread of agriculture in Europe. PLoS Biology 3, E410.

Purugganan, M., Fuller, D., 2009. The nature of selection during plant domestication. Nature 457, 843–848.

Putterman, L., Trainor, C.A., 2006. Agricultural transition year country. Data set. Available at http://www.econ.brown.edu/fac/Louis_Putterman.

Putterman, L., Weil, D.N., 2010. Post-1500 population flows and the long run determinants of economic growth and inequality. The Quarterly Journal of Economics 125 (4), 1627–1682.

Reba, M., Reitsma, F., Seto, K.C., 2016. Spatializing 6,000 years of global urbanization from 3700 BC to AD 2000. Scientific Data 3, 160034.

Richerson, P.J., Boyd, R., Bettinger, R.L., 2001. Was agriculture impossible during the Pleistocene but mandatory during the Holocene? A climate change hypothesis. American Antiquity 66 (3), 387–411.

Sanchez de la Sierra, R., 2020. On the origin of states: stationary bandits and taxationin Eastern Congo. Journal of Political Economy 128 (1), 32–74.

Schonholzer, D., 2020. The origin of incentive compatible state: environmental circumscription. Mimeo.

Shaw, I., 2000. The Oxford History of Ancient Egypt. Oxford University Press.

Steckel, R.H., Rose, J.C. (Eds.), 2002. The Backbone of History: Health and Nutrition in the Western Hemisphere. Cambridge University Press, New York. ISBN 0-521-80167-2. xx + 633 pp. $75 (cloth).

Steward, J.H., 1949. Cultural causality and law: a trial formulation of the development of early civilizations. American Anthropologist 51, 1–27.

Talbert, R.J.A., Bagnall, R.S., 2000. Barrington Atlas of the Greek and Roman World. Princeton University Press, Princeton, NJ.

Tallavaara, M., Luoto, M., Korhonen, N., Järvinen, H., Seppä, H., 2015. Human population dynamics in Europe over the Last Glacial Maximum. Proceedings of the National Academy of Sciences of the United States of America 112 (27), 8232–8237.

Temin, P., 2002. Price behavior in ancient Babylon. Explorations in Economic History 39, 46–60.

Testart, A., et al., 1982. The significance of food storage among hunter-gatherers: residence patterns, population densities and social inequalities. Current Anthropology 23, 523–537.

Wahl, F., 2017. Does European development have Roman roots? Evidence from the German limes. Journal of Economic Growth 22 (3), 313–349.

Walker, P.L., Bathurst, R.R., Richman, R., Gjerdrum, T., Andrushko, V.A., 2009. The causes of porotic hyperostosis and cribra orbitalia: a reappraisal of the iron-deficiency-anemia hypothesis. American Journal of Physical Anthropology 139 (2), 109–125.

Weisdorf, J.L., 2005. From foraging to farming: explaining the Neolithic Revolution. Journal of Economic Surveys 19, 561–586. https://doi.org/10.1111/j.0950-0804.2005.00259.x.

Whitehouse, D., Whitehouse, R., 1975. Archaeological Atlas of the World. Thames and Hudson.

Wittfogel, K.A., 1957. Oriental Despotism: A Comparative Study of Total Power. Yale University Press.

Ethnographic and field data in historical economics[☆]

Sara Lowes[a,b,c]
[a]*UC San Diego, La Jolla, CA, United States*
[b]*NBER, Cambridge, MA, United States*
[c]*Canadian Institute for Advanced Research (CIFAR), Toronto, ON, Canada*

6.1 Introduction

Research in historical economics naturally often relies on access to historical data. However, this has tended to limit the extent to which regions without much historical data can be studied. The result is that economic research focuses on areas for which there are good archival records, neglecting those areas for which there are limited data.

However, there has been a growing interest in alternative approaches to studying historical economics. These approaches include incorporating datasets compiled outside of economics and the collection of novel survey and experimental data. These approaches offer an opportunity to both increase the geographic coverage of research as well as the types of questions that can be answered. Often, these data sources and strategies focus on measuring various aspects of culture and preferences.

This article will first introduce various ethnographic data sources that can be used to study cultural traits. These datasets, generally compiled by anthropologists and historians, provide new potential sources of cultural and historical data for economic historians. They cover a diverse set of topics, from cultural practices, historic state formation, and religious beliefs. The relevance of these datasets for economists highlights the growing inter-disciplinary nature of research in historical economics and the links between economics and history, sociology, psychology, and evolutionary anthropology.

I will then review recent research using alternative data sources and strategies – such as original survey data collection within and across countries and lab-in-the-field experiments – to explore questions in historical economics. I describe existing cross-cultural data sets and how they have been used.

I will argue that lab-in-the-field experiments expand the types of questions that can be answered within economics. I describe how they are being used in a growing literature combining economic history with lab-in-the-field experiments. These papers build off of a deep lab experimental literature, and apply these methods and measurement strategies to new contexts and research questions. I distinguish between papers in which the experimental results are the key outcomes and those where the experimental results are used to understand persistence mechanisms. Finally, I will describe some of the practical challenges of administering lab-in-the-field experiments, particularly for work in historical economics.

[☆] I thank Nathan Nunn for helpful feedback. I thank Vafa Behnam for excellent research assistance.

6.2 Ethnographic data sources
6.2.1 Ethnographic Atlas, Standard Cross Cultural Survey, and Murdock map

There are several ethnographic data sources – data on the customs and cultures of particular groups – that economists frequently use. The most commonly used data sets are the Ethnographic Atlas (Murdock, 1957, 1967) and the related Standard Cross Cultural Survey (Murdock and White, 1969).

The Ethnographic Atlas (EA) is an ethnicity level database with pre-industrial characteristics on 1265 ethnic groups from around the world. The EA was compiled by Murdock (1967), based on his own reading and coding of available ethnographies. The EA bibliographies contain the information for the underlying ethnographies, as well as suggestions on which authors were deemed to be the authority on the particular subject.

The information in the database is meant to represent the earliest date for which there is reliable information; this means that the earliest observations are from the Old World. For places without many written records, the data in the EA are intended to reflect a society's characteristics prior to European contact; however, the observations were generally recorded by Europeans upon contact. The EA contains a rich variety of data on economic activities, political and social organization, and cultural practices. Examples of the variables present in the EA are: location (latitude and longitude); major subsistence activities (gathering, hunting, fishing, animal husbandry, agriculture); cultural practices (marriage payments, family organization, practice of polygyny); and political organization (jurisdictional levels, succession rules for local leaders, class structure). See Fig. 6.1 for the geographic distribution of societies included in the EA.

The Standard Cross Cultural Survey (SCCS) is a sample of 186 ethnic groups, chosen from cultural groupings in the EA (Murdock and White, 1969). Ethnic groups in the EA were classified into "independent" cultural clusters, and approximately one ethnic group per cluster was chosen to be included in the SCCS. Criteria for inclusion in the sample were either that the ethnic group had good ethnographic coverage or that it was particularly distinctive in some respect (Murdock and White, 2006). The goal was to both represent cultural variation but to also eliminate cases where similarities across groups were due to cultural diffusion or common origin (referred to as "Galton's problem").[1] While fewer groups are represented in the SCCS, there are over 2000 variables in the data set. The groups in red x's (gray in print version) in Fig. 6.1 are the subset of ethnic groups that are both in the EA and the SCCS.

For work on Africa, the EA is often paired with the Murdock ethnic group boundary map (Murdock, 1959), in which Murdock outlines the historical boundaries of ethnic groups as of the nineteenth century. There are 835 ethnic group boundaries in the Murdock map. In the EA, there are data on approximately 527 ethnic groups in Africa. However, there is not a perfect 1:1 matching between the EA and the Murdock map boundaries. First, not all ethnic groups represented on the Murdock map are present in the EA. Second, some groups present in the EA are not identified on the map. Third, ethnic group names can be spelled differently across the data sets. Finally, the geographic coordinates provided in the EA at times do not align with the boundaries of the ethnic group in the map. Because of these concordance difficulties, there are multiple strategies for matching across the EA and the Murdock map. Additionally, there are multiple approaches to interpolating the data for ethnic groups

---

[1] Some anthropologists have objected to the attempt at identifying "independent" cultural groups. See Mace and Pagel (1994), who advocate for the construction of phylogenies to map patterns of cultural descent.

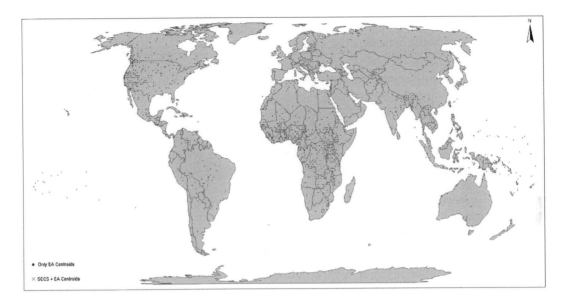

FIGURE 6.1

Societies in the Ethnographic Atlas and SCCS.

without an exact match (e.g. through cultural proximity, language groups, or geographic proximity). Fenske (2013) provides detailed information on matches between the EA and map for cases where there is not an exact name match. AfricaMap (2020) also provide a shapefile with a concordance between the Murdock map and data from the Ethnographic Atlas.

The EA has been used in many papers in economics. Perhaps one of the earliest uses is from Gennaioli and Rainer (2007), who examine the relationship between jurisdictional hierarchy – defined as the number of jurisdictional levels above the village level – and economic performance. The authors find a strong positive association between an ethnic group's precolonial centralization and education, health, and infrastructure today. Nunn (2008) and Nunn and Wantchekon (2011) also make use of the EA and Murdock boundaries. Nunn (2008) estimates the number of slaves exported during the slave trades by country. He finds that exposure to the slave trades is negatively associated with economic development. He then examines the effects of exposure to the slave trade on state development, finding a negative correlation between the slave trade and centralization. Subsequently, Nunn and Wantchekon (2011) use ethnicity level estimates of slave trade intensity to examine the effects of the slave trade on trust levels; they find that greater exposure to the slave trade leads to lower levels of trust in others.

Many subsequent papers use the EA data, SCCS data, or Murdock map boundary data, including: Alesina et al. (2013); Michalopoulos and Papaioannou (2013, 2014); Fenske (2014); Alsan (2015); Fenske (2015); Michalopoulos and Papaioannou (2016); Enke (2019). These papers explore a wide variety of questions on the long run development of Africa. See Table 6.1 for examples of papers in economics that use the EA, SCCS, Murdock boundaries, or Ancestral Characteristics data. See Bahrami-Rad et al. (2018) for published papers in anthropology that also use the EA.

Table 6.1 Examples of economics papers that use the EA, SCCS, Murdock map, Ethnologue or Ancestral Characteristics data.

Authors	Journal	Dataset	Explanatory variable	Outcome variable
Ahmed and Stasavage (2020)	American Political Science Review	SCCS	Agricultural Suitability	Council Governance
Akbari et al. (2019)	J. of Econ. Behavior & Organization	E, EA	In-Marriage vs Out-Marriage	Corruption
Alesina et al. (2011)	American Economic Review: P&P	E, EA, SCCS	Plough Agriculture	Fertility
Alesina et al. (2013)	Quarterly Journal of Economics	E, EA, SCCS	Plough Agriculture	Gender Roles
Alesina et al. (2018)	PLoS ONE	E, EA	Plough Agriculture	Male-Female Sex Ratio
Alsan (2015)	American Economic Review	E, EA, M	TseTse Fly	Political Centralization, Population
Anderson (2007)	Journal of Economic Perspectives	EA	Class Stratification	Incidence of Dowries
Anderson (2018)	American Economic Review	M	Legal Origins	Female HIV Rates
Ashraf et al. (2020)	Journal of Political Economy	E, EA	Existence of Bride Price Practices	Female Education
Baker (2008)	Journal of Economic Growth	SCCS	Population, Technological Diffusion	Incidence of Agriculture
Baker and Miceli (2005)	J. of Econ. Behavior & Organization	SCCS	Population, Social Stratification	Inheritance
Becker (2019)	Mimeo	AC, E, EA	Pastoralism	Female Mobility, Infibulation
Becker et al. (2020)	American Economic Association P & P	E	Ancestral Migration Patterns	Economic Preferences
BenYishay et al. (2017)	Journal of Economic Dev.	E, EA, SCCS	Reef Density	Incidence of Matriliny
Botticini and Siow (2003)	American Economic Review	EA	Post-Marital Residence	Incidence of Dowries
Buggle (2020)	Journal of Economic Growth	AC, E, EA, M	Irrigation Agriculture	Collectivist Norms
Desmet et al. (2020)	Journal of Development Economics	AC, E, EA	Ethnolinguistic Diversity	Public Goods
Dippel (2014)	Econometrica	EA	Shared Governance	Income
Enke (2019)	Quarterly Journal of Economics	AC, E, EA	Kinship Tightness	In-group Loyalty, Norm Adherence
Fenske (2013)	The Economic Journal	EA, M	Suitability for Agriculture	Land Rights, Slavery, Polygyny
Fenske (2014)	J. of European Econ. Association	EA, M	Ecological Diversity	Pre-colonial Centralization
Fenske (2015)	Journal of Development Economics	EA, M	Gender Roles, Class Stratification	Polygamy
Gennaioli and Rainer (2007)	Journal of Economic Growth	EA, SCCS	Precolonial Centralization	Public Goods Provision
Giuliano and Nunn (2013)	American Economic Review P&P	EA	Historical Democratic Institutions	Modern Democratic Institutions
Giuliano and Nunn (forthcoming)	Review of Economic Studies	AC, E, EA	Intergenerational Enviro. Similarity	Cultural Persistence
Gomes (2020)	Journal of Economic Growth	E	Cultural Distance	Health
Lowes (2018a)	Mimeo	EA, M,	Lineage and Inheritance by Gender	Competition
Lowes (2018b)	Mimeo	EA, M	Lineage and Inheritance by Gender	Spousal Cooperation
Michalopoulos (2012)	American Economic Review	E	Geographic Land Endowments	Ethnolinguistic Diversity
Michalopoulos and Papaioannou (2013)	Econometrica	EA, M	Precolonial Centralization	Local Light Density
Michalopoulos and Papaioannou (2014)	Quarterly Journal of Economics	EA, M	Colonial Border Design	Night Lights
Michalopoulos and Papaioannou (2016)	American Economic Review	EA, M	Colonial Border Design	Political Violence, Income
Michalopoulos et al. (2019)	J. of European Econ. Association	EA, M	Historical Dependence on Agriculture	Income, Education
Mayshar et al. (2020)	Mimeo	EA, SCCS	Cereal Appropriability	Hierarchy
Moscona et al. (2020)	Econometrica	M	Segmentary Lineage	Conflict
Moscona et al. (2017)	American Economic Review P & P	M	Segmentary Lineage	Trust in Relatives vs. Non-Relatives
Nunn (2008)	Quarterly Journal of Economics	EA, M	Trans-Atlantic Slave Trade	Precolonial Centralization
Nunn and Wantchekon (2011)	American Economic Review	EA, M	Trans-Atlantic Slave Trade	Trust
Obikili (2016)	Economic History Review	EA, M	Trans-Atlantic Slave Trade	Number of Decision Making Entities
Schulz (2017)	Mimeo	AC, E, EA	Kinship Organization	Political Participation
Teso (2019)	J. of European Econ. Association	EA, M	Trans-Atlantic Slave Trade	Gender Norms
Corno et al. (2020)	Econometrica	EA	Bride Price vs Dowry	Early Marriage

AC is the Ancestral Characteristics database (Giuliano and Nunn, 2018). E is the Ethnologue (Gordon, 2009). EA is the Ethnographic Atlas (Murdock, 1957, 1967). M is the Murdock map (Murdock, 1959). SCCS is the Standard Cross Cultural Survey (Murdock and White, 1969).

6.2.2 Validation and extension of the Ethnographic Atlas

Despite the heavy reliance on the EA, there are several potential shortcomings of the data. First, ethnic groups are sampled at different time periods. The dates for which the data are recorded span a millennium. However, the majority of observations are from the 19th and 20th centuries. It is also difficult to ascertain the historical depth of the observed characteristics – for example, the EA does not speak to whether an ethnic group has always practiced matrilineal kinship or if it is a recent practice. Second, coverage in the EA is almost certainly non-random, perhaps due to availability of information, accessibility, and group prominence. This issue is perhaps more clear with the SCCS, in which the selected sub-sample of groups was chosen based on data availability. Third, the underlying data for the EA come from ethnographies; it can be challenging to codify this richer set of data systematically, and subtle distinctions across places can be lost. Finally, European groups are under-represented in the EA sample. Relatedly, the Murdock map boundaries, which are often taken as a given in many of the analyses presented above, are almost certainly noisy and over-simplified representations of reality. In practice, ethnic group boundaries overlap and shift over time.

6.2.2.1 Validation of the Ethnographic Atlas

There have been several recent efforts to validate the data in the Ethnographic Atlas and build upon the data available in the EA. Bahrami-Rad et al. (2018) seek to validate the EA data against nationally representative contemporary data from the Demographic and Health Surveys (DHS) (ICF, 2020). The DHS data include individual level data for more than 790,000 individuals from 300 ethnic groups in 43 countries. The authors identify variables that can be matched across the EA (or SCCS) and the DHS – such as patrilocality, polygyny, reliance on animal husbandry, and breastfeeding duration. Reassuringly, across many dimensions, the authors find a positive and significant correlation between the historical characteristics and the present day data. Rijpma and Carmichael (2016) compare data in the EA on family structure with country level data from Todd (1985), who classifies practices related to endogamy, co-residence, and inheritance, and in general, they find concordance. However, the Todd data are much less granular since they are at the country level.

Other validation efforts seek to examine the extent to which an individual's self-reported ethnicity coincides with the ethnic group homeland they are located in on the Murdock map. For example, Moscona et al. (2020) show that the share of individuals whose self-reported ethnicity in the Afrobarometer corresponds with the Murdock ethnic group homeland is substantially higher within the ethnic group homeland relative to an adjacent ethnic group homeland at the boundary border. This analysis is done on a sample of 80 ethnic groups for which a segmentary lineage society is adjacent to a non-segmentary lineage group.

However, there appears to be substantial heterogeneity in the extent to which there is concordance between an individual's self-reported ethnic group and the ethnic group homeland they are located in. Fig. 6.2 presents data from Afrobarometer rounds 3 to 6. Ethnic group names were matched between the Murdock map and the Afrobarometer using the following steps. First, names were matched exactly between the two data sets. This resulted in a match rate of 42 percent. To increase the match rate, I digitized the index of the Murdock (1959), in which all the ethnic groups covered in the book are assigned cultural codes. Murdock assigns culturally proximate groups the same cultural code and also provides alternative names for the same group. The digitized index is then used to increase Afrobarometer and Murdock matches, as groups sharing the same code are then matched using the name that is on the Murdock map. This results in a match rate of 54 percent.

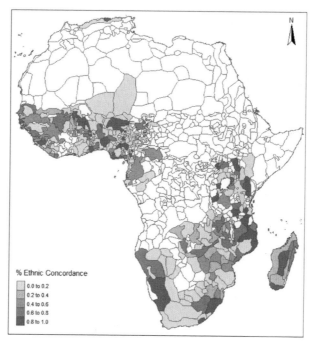

(a) Share of respondents with same ethnicity as Murdock homeland.

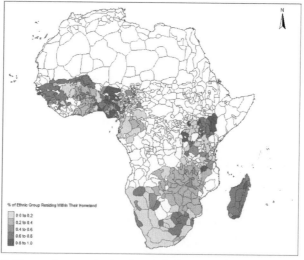

(b) Share of respondents of an ethnic group that are in their Murdock homeland.

FIGURE 6.2

Afrobarometer respondents and Murdock homeland. The figure uses data from Afrobarometer Rounds 3-6 (Afrobarometer Data, 2020) and the Murdock Index (Murdock, 1959). The ethnic group boundaries are the Murdock Map boundaries digitized from Murdock (1959).

For those ethnic groups for which it was possible to construct a match, Fig. 6.2a presents the share of respondents with a self-reported ethnicity that corresponds with the ethnic homeland where they are located. It is clear that there is substantial heterogeneity in the extent to which individuals randomly sampled for the Afrobarometer have an ethnicity that corresponds with the Murdock boundary where they are located. For example, in Southern Africa, only a small share of those sampled have a self-reported ethnicity that concords with the Murdock ethnic group boundary.

Fig. 6.2b undertakes a slightly different exercise. It presents the share of individuals with a self-reported ethnicity that are actually located in that ethnicity's homeland boundary. Again, there is quite a lot of variation in the mobility of groups. While some ethnic groups seem to be quite mobile, such that only a small percentage of individuals with that self-reported ethnicity live within their ethnic homeland, individuals from other groups are almost entirely located within their ethnic homeland boundaries. Thus, while the Murdock map boundaries do appear to be meaningful, there is also substantial variation in the diversity of some areas and the mobility of various groups.

6.2.2.2 Extensions of the Ethnographic Atlas

Giuliano and Nunn (2018) augment the data in the Ethnographic Atlas with several additional data sources. First, they use data from Korotayev et al. (2004), which has information on groups in Siberia and Bondarenko et al. (2005), which has data on groups in Eastern Europe. They also include data on European groups from Murdock (1957). Additionally, data from the Ethnologue: Languages of the World (Gordon, 2009) provide information on the current geographic distribution of over 7000 languages and dialects. Finally, Giuliano and Nunn include various geographic variables, such as climate, ruggedness, and distance to the coast. The ethnographic data are matched to the present day data on the distribution of language groups at the grid-cell level – effectively assuming that the transmission of ancestral traits is correlated with language. This comprehensive data set is described in detail in Giuliano and Nunn (2018). See Fig. 6.3 for the distribution of the cultural group boundaries in the Giuliano and Nunn (2018) data.

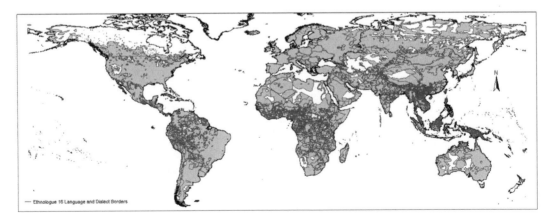

FIGURE 6.3

Ancestral characteristics of modern populations. This map is constructed using the shapefile provided by Giuliano and Nunn (2018).

There are other efforts to improve the quality, coverage, and historical depth of the data in the Ethnographic Atlas. This can be done by supplementing from other ethnographic data sources. One potentially rich data source for Africa is the Ethnographic Survey of Africa, a series of books edited by Daryll Forde and published by the International Africa Institute between 1950 and 1977 (and recently re-issued by Routledge). The series includes 50 books with detailed ethnographies on many groups (Forde, 2017). Often, this includes data outside of what is reported in the EA. For example, Moscona et al. (2020) use the books to code whether 145 ethnic groups have the practice of segmentary lineages, a form of kinship structure characterized by unilineal descent, a shared ancestor, and sub-units within the broader lineage. They use this newly coded data to test whether segmentary lineage systems increase conflict.

Lowes (2018b) uses detailed ethnographic data on the Democratic Republic of Congo from Vansina (1966). This allows her to digitize a more granular ethnic group boundary map for the DRC that may more accurately reflect ethnic group boundaries – as it allows for multiple groups to be present in one area and represents more granular cultural groups. She then assigns each group to matrilineal or patrilineal kinship status. Her resulting data has information on over 380 groups for DRC. She finds that matrilineal kinship structure undermines spousal cooperation but has benefits for investment in children and the well-being of women.

An alternative strategy for addressing the lack of historical depth for some of these traits is to construct measures that take into account changes over time. For example, Depetris-Chauvin (2016) examines how long-run exposure to statehood at a sub-national level affects conflict. To do this, he compiles a list of historical states, their boundaries, and their chronologies. This allows him to construct the fraction of years that a territory was exposed to a state-like institution between 1000 and 1850 CE. He finds that exposure to historical state-hood reduces conflict.

6.3 Additional data sources
6.3.1 Alternative culture and ethnographic data sets

There are many other cultural and ethnographic data sets that have yet to be widely used within economics. I briefly describe these various data sets, many of which are currently used in anthropology. Table 6.2 provides a summary of these data sources and the links to access them. Slingerland et al. (2020) describe the challenges associated with constructing and maintaining these types of cross-cultural databases. Some of the key challenges include how to choose a unit of analysis, appropriately coding data, managing uncertainty, and the sustainability of the databases.

6.3.1.1 Human relations area files

Human Relations Area Files (HRAF) are a collection of ethnographies that have been subject coded. While the original collection is in paper and microfiche, HRAF maintains two online databases: eHRAF World Cultures and eHRAF Archaeology. The eHRAF databases are online collections of ethnographic and archaeological texts that have been subject-indexed at the paragraph level. The indexing relies on the "Outline of Cultural Materials" – a classification system of social and cultural life developed by Murdock. The subject classification system has a hierarchical structure so that searches can be broadened or refined within a subject. The second index is the "Outline of World Cultures," also created by Murdock, which indexes cultures by region and country. It covers over 2500 cultures. All cultures

Table 6.2 Additional sources of cultural data.

Panel A: Culture databases

Name	URL	Subject	Overview
Database of Places, language, culture and environment (D-Place) (Kirby et al., 2016)	d-place.org	Culture, environment, language	Cultural, environment, linguistic, geographic for over 1400 societies.
Database of Religious History (DRH) (Slingerland and Sullivan, 2017)	religiondatabase.org	Religion	Approx. 400 entries for religious groups.
eHRAF World Cultures (eHRAF) (Ember, 2012)	ehrafworldcultures.yale.edu	Culture	Approx. 320 cultures; searchable subject indexed database.
eHRAF Archaeology (eHRAF) (Ember, 2012)	ehrafarchaeology.yale.edu	Culture	Approx. 100 archaeological traditions; searchable subject indexed database.
Ethnographic Survey of Africa (ESA) (Forde, 2017)	NA	Culture (Africa)	A series of 50 books on African ethnic groups and culture.
Pulotu: Database of Pacific Religious Beliefs and Practices (Pulotu) (Watts et al., 2015)	pulotu.shh.mpg.de	Religion (Austronesia)	Over 100 Austronesian cultures; 62 variables on religion, history, society, and the natural environment.
Seshat: Global History Databank (Seshat) (Turchin et al., forthcoming)	seshatdatabank.info	Culture	Historical political, economic and religious variables for 30 "natural geographic areas" around the world.

Panel B: Cross-national data

Name	URL	Subject	Overview
Cohn et al. (2019)	dataverse.harvard.edu/dataverse/honesty/	Honesty	Cross national experiment with wallets.
Global Preferences Survey (Falk et al., 2018)	briq-institute.org/global-preferences	Preferences	Cross national data set of 80,000 people from 76 countries with time and risk preferences, altruism, positive reciprocity, negative reciprocity, and trust.
Gachter and Schulz (2016)	https://datadryad.org/stash/dataset/ https://doi.org/10.5061/dryad.9k358	Honesty	Die rolling experiment across 23 countries.
Values Survey Module (Hofstede, 1980)	geerthofstede.com	Cultural Values	Survey instrument for cross cultural value measurement. Country level values dataset.
Folklore (Michalopoulos and Xue, 2019) (Berezkin, 2015)	NA	Folklore motifs	Motifs from folklore for 1000 societies. Linked to EA.
newspapers.com (2020)	newspapers.com	Digitized newspapers	18,000 + newspapers from 1700s to 2000s.
Xu et al. (2020)	projectimplict.com	IATs	Materials for and data from IATs.

that are covered in the SCCS are also included in the eHRAF World Cultures database. Approximately 300 cultures are in the eHRAF World Cultures database (with new cultures added each year), covering nearly 600,000 pages of ethnographies. Topics covered include information on the economy, history, family and kinship, sociopolitical organization and religion. The eHRAF Archaeology data indexes archaeological traditions for over 100 societies. Data include culture name, region and sub region, subsistence type, and beginning and end dates.

Recent work using the eHRAF World Cultures database is Jackson et al. (2020) who examine the relationship between ecological threats and cultural tightness. The hypothesis is that ecological threats increase the need for coordination and cooperation. Societies that face these types of challenges will respond by creating "tighter" norms that more harshly punish deviant behavior. Using the eHRAF data, the authors find evidence that cultural tightness is associated with ecological threat.

6.3.1.2 Seshat: global history databank

Seshat is a database of human polities over time. It was established in 2011 and was compiled by scholars in the social sciences and humanities. The goal of the database is to systematically collect data on the social and political organization of societies and to document how they have changed over time. In particular, the database is intended to facilitate understanding the evolution of societies and the processes that generate cultural change. The Seshat data covers the time period between the Neolithic and Industrial Revolutions (approximately 4000 BCE to 1900 CE). The unit of analysis is a polity, which is defined as an independent political unit and can vary in scale from a village to a complex state. To construct a sample, the researchers divided the world into 10 regions. They define three "natural geographic areas" (NGA) within each region by identifying a polity that emerged early, a polity that emerged in an intermediate time period, and a polity that emerged relatively late. The resulting 30 NGAs serve as the initial sample, from which polities are tracked over time. The resulting database has over 1500 variables for 400 polities. The dataset includes variables on social complexity, warfare, religion, institutions, technology, and public goods provision. For more information on the dataset's construction, see Turchin et al. (forthcoming).

A recent paper that uses the Seshat data set is Whitehouse et al. (2019), who examine whether moralizing gods precede or follow the creation of complex societies. They argue that moralizing gods follow the creation of complex societies. This is in contrast to other theories that suggest moralizing gods help facilitate large scale cooperation and thus may promote complex societies (Norenzayan et al., 2016). However, Beheim et al. (2019) argue that data quality issues are driving these results. Missing data are treated as known absence of moralizing gods, representing 61 percent of the data in the analysis. The results reverse when this is recoded. Beheim et al. (2019) also suggest that the coding of Seshat data has some systematic inaccuracies and inadequate data quality management, highlighting the challenges of creating and maintaining these types of databases.

6.3.1.3 Database of religious history

The Database of Religious History (DRH) is a database that is intended to bring together the best scholarly opinions on historical religious traditions (Slingerland and Sullivan, 2017). The database includes qualitative and quantitative historical data that are contributed by field experts and are peer-reviewed. Unlike the SCCS or eHRAF, the unit of analysis is not a cultural group but a "religious group". The focus is on religious groups from the pre-modern period; the data are for groups up to 1700 CE, prior to Western colonialism. Religious scholars submit information on the attributes of these various religious groups – such as beliefs and practices. The database relies on experts to synthesize their knowledge on a particular religious group and construct binary standardized data. Entries on religious groups are often accompanied with photos, manuscripts, and links to primary and secondary data sources. As of 2017, the DRH had 230 priority variables and 220 non-priority variables. There are approximately 400 entries. The selection of priority variables is driven by the observation that religions are associated with certain beliefs and practices and may extend pro-social behavior. Examples of variables include: presence of supernatural beings, size and structure of the religious group, scripture, presence of moral norms, and level of social complexity.

6.3.1.4 Others

I briefly describe several other cultural and ethnographic databases.

Pulotu: Database of Pacific Religions is a database of Austronesian supernatural beliefs and practices for 116 cultures. The data set includes 62 variables related to religion, history, society, and the natural environment. The data can be matched with Austronesian language phylogenies (Watts et al., 2015).

D-PLACE: Database of Places, Language, Culture and Environment (D-PLACE) is a database with information on geography, language, culture and environment for over 1400 human societies (Kirby et al., 2016). The data for D-PLACE combines data from the Ethnographic Atlas, the Binford Hunter-Gatherer dataset (Binford, 2001; Binford and Johnson, 2006), the Standard Cross Cultural Sample, and the Western North American Indians dataset (Jorgensen, 1980, 1999b,a). The Binford Hunter-Gather set describes cultural practices for 338 hunter-gather groups, a third of which are not included in the EA. The Western North American Indian dataset codifies cultural practices for 172 societies in Western North America, approximately 20 of which are not in the previous data sets.

The data are at the cultural group level at a given location and time. For each data point, D-PLACE includes reference to the original primary sources and comments regarding coding choices. D-PLACE links to eHRAF. D-PLACE also includes information on language affiliation, following the classifications of Glottolog (Hammarström et al., 2020). The data include a wide variety of environmental data: e.g. ecoregion, biome, elevation, slope, precipitation, and temperature.

6.3.2 Cross-national data

There has been increasing interest and ability to create cross-national data sets that measure cultural variation. Many of these efforts involve survey and experimental measures across cultures.

6.3.2.1 Hofstede's values survey module

The Values Survey Module (VSM) is a way to measure values across societies. The instrument was introduced in Hofstede (1980), where he proposes several key dimensions on which cultures vary: power distance, uncertainty avoidance, individualism versus collectivism, and masculinity versus femininity. Power distance is the extent to which less powerful individuals are willing to accept unequal power distributions. Uncertainty avoidance captures a willingness to tolerate uncertainty and ambiguity. Individualism versus collectivism is the extent to which individuals feel independent rather than being part of a collective whole. Masculinity is the extent to which emotional gender roles are distinct – in which men are supposed to be assertive and tough (Hofstede, 2013). Subsequent versions of the VSM measure additional attributes: long term orientation, the extent to which a culture is future oriented, and indulgence, in which freedom rather than duty is valued. The survey instruments are publicly available and have been translated into many languages.

6.3.2.2 Global preferences survey

Falk et al. (2018) explore cultural variation by collecting survey data from 80,000 people across 76 countries. These countries represent approximately 90 percent of the world's population. The samples within each country are representative. The sample includes 15 countries in the Americas, 25 in Europe, 22 in Asia and the Pacific, and 15 in Africa. The median sample size per country was 1000 respondents. The survey includes questions to measure: time and risk preferences, altruism, positive reciprocity, negative reciprocity, and trust. While the survey questions are not incentivized, the survey modules were experimentally validated prior to the survey's administration. This minimizes the cost associated with collecting the data, as implementing experiments is expensive. The process of validation and the exact survey questions are described in detail in Falk et al. (2018). The authors then map the distribution of global preferences, how preferences vary by gender, age, and cognitive ability, examine geographic correlates, and show that the survey measures are correlated with relevant outcomes, such as savings.

6.3.2.3 Honesty

Gachter and Schulz (2016) explore the relationship between intrinsic honesty and a society level measure of "prevalence of rule violations" (PRV) based on 2003 country-level data on corruption, tax evasion, and fraudulent politics. Across 23 countries, they conduct a die rolling experiment with 2568 students as a measure of intrinsic honesty. In the die rolling experiment, individuals are asked to roll a six-sided die and to report the number they observe. Their payment is tied to the outcome of the die roll: if they roll a one they receive one money unit, a two they receive two money units etc. However, if they roll a six they receive nothing. In a fully honest society, the average money claimed would be 2.5; in a fully dishonest society it would be 5. They find that intrinsic honesty as measured in the die rolling task is higher in societies that have a lower PRV.

Cohn et al. (2019) conduct an experiment to measure honesty in 355 cities across 40 countries. The authors "turned in" over 17,000 wallets to one of five types of societal institutions: banks, cultural establishments, post offices, hotels, or public offices. The authors experimentally varied whether the wallet contained money (approximately US $13.45). The key outcome was whether the recipient of the wallet contacted the owner, whose fictitious contact information was on a business card in the wallet. The first key outcome is that wallets are much more likely to be reported when they had money in them. Second, there is substantial variation across countries in the rates at which wallets are reported. In some countries more than 70 percent are reported (e.g. Denmark, Sweden) while in others less than 20 percent are reported (e.g. Kenya and Mexico). For a sub-sample of countries, the authors increase the amount of money in the wallet to $94.15. They find even higher rates of wallet reporting when there is more money in the wallet.

6.3.2.4 Folklore

Michalopoulos and Xue (2019) compile a folklore database based off of the life work of anthropologist Yuri Berezkin (Berezkin, 2015, 2016). The authors define folklore as "the collection of traditional beliefs, customs, myths, legends, and stories of a community". The database codes the spatial distribution of thousands of motifs – the unit of analysis in a tale or myth – across 1000 societies. The authors link the Berezkin database to the EA. They show that motifs are associated with the natural environment and institutional setting. For example, groups with more earthquake related motifs live closer to earthquake areas. They also show that motifs are predictive of historical norms and how they are correlated with present day attitudes.

6.3.2.5 Names

Knudsen (2019) examines the relationship between emigration and individualism. Using emigration data from Scandinavia between 1850 and 1920, she first documents that those who are more individualistic are more likely to migrate. To overcome the challenge of measuring individualism, she constructs a measure based on the commonness of first names; those who chose more unique first names are considered more individualist. She validates this measure of individualism and collectivism against historical and present day data. She finds that as a result of this type of selective migration sending areas from Scandinavia are more collectivist. A similar strategy is employed in Bazzi et al. (2020), who examine the relationship between frontier culture and individualism in the US.

6.3.2.6 Implicit association tests

Implicit Association Tests (IATs) are intended to measure a subject's implicit attitude toward a subject, particularly those that a subject may be unable or unwilling to report. The idea is to measure the strength of an individual's association between various concepts (e.g. black people or women) and evaluations or stereotypes (e.g. good and bad). Individuals are shown words or stimuli related to the concept of interest and must sort those with the evaluation. The intuition is that if a subject has a stronger association between an object and an evaluation, then the subject will be able to more quickly sort the object and the evaluation together. For example, if an individual has a strong association between "women" and "the humanities", it will be easier to sort words related to women with words related to "the humanities" than with words related to "science".

Project Implicit is a non-profit organization that allows individuals to take IATs, administer their own IATs, and use the data from the IATs that have been administered on the website. Examples of the IATs available include: age IAT, Gender-Science IAT, Race IAT, Weapons IAT (Greenwald et al., n.d.; Nosek et al., 2007; Xu et al., 2020).

6.3.2.7 Newspapers

A potentially rich source of information on culture is newspapers.com, a digital archive of historical and present day newspapers (newspapers.com, 2020). It is one of the largest online newspaper archives, with more than 18,400 newspapers from the 1700s to the 2000s. It has digitized over 600 million pages of newspapers, for which it is possible to do keyword searches.

One example of how this data can be used comes from Ottinger and Winkler (2020), who examine the relationship between political threat and the use of anti-Black propaganda in the U.S. South following the 1892 presidential elections. To measure anti-Black propaganda, the authors develop an automated script that accesses the database and records keyword frequencies. Specifically, they proxy for anti-Black propaganda by searching for the presence of the words "rape" and "negro". The keyword frequencies can then be linked to data on the newspaper's location and the date of publication. They find that where Democrats faced more of a threat from the Populist Party there is an increase in anti-Black propaganda.

6.3.2.8 Public attitude surveys

Finally, there are several publicly available public attitude surveys that measure various cultural traits. These are periodic surveys conducted across many countries. Some of the key surveys are: the World Values Survey (WVS), Afrobarometer, AmericasBarometer, Arab Barometer, Eurobarometer, Latinobarometer, and Asian Barometer (World Values Survey Data, 2020; Afrobarometer Data, 2020; AmericasBarometer Data, 2020; Asian Barometer Data, 2020; Arab Barometer Data, 2020; Eurobarometer Data, 2020; Latinobarometer Data, 2020). The Pew Research Center also conducts surveys, particularly related to civic culture and religious beliefs (Pew Research Center, 2020). The associated websites for these organizations have detailed information on sampling, survey instruments, and available data.

6.4 Lab-in-the-field experiments

A complementary strategy to the use of pre-existing ethnographic and cultural data is the collection of new survey and experimental data. While this is still relatively infrequent – given the high costs of data collection – it is an important tool for examining mechanisms and outcomes in places with limited historical data.

6.4.1 What are lab-in-the-field experiments?

Lab-in-the-field experiments are lab experiments that are conducted in a "naturalistic" setting (Gneezy and Imas, 2017). Lab-in-the-field experiments may help address some of the key concerns with lab experiments. First, lab experiments are often conducted with populations of convenience, such as students. These populations may not be broadly representative, particularly given that most of these experiments are conducted with so-called "WEIRD" (Western, Educated, Industrialized, Rich and Democratic) populations.

Second, while lab experiments are often conducive to precise measurement because they are conducted in a highly controlled environment, the setting may be too abstract. Lab-in-the-field experiments may help address these issues by using validated lab experiments with relevant populations in a more naturalistic environment. Gneezy and Imas (2017) suggest that lab-in-the-field experiments be used as part of a randomized controlled trial (RCT) at baseline to test whether treatment depends on measured behavior or as an outcome of a RCT. See Gneezy and Imas (2017) for a detailed overview of the benefits of lab-in-the-field experiments, their relationship to RCTs, and a discussion of recent lab-in-the-field papers.

Common lab experiments are the dictator game, ultimatum game, public goods game (or voluntary contribution mechanism), measures to elicit time and risk preferences, random allocation game, cheating game, and joy of destruction game. Other measures include IATs, which measure an individual's implicit view towards a target object or person.

There is a growing interest in the use of lab experiments to complement work in historical economics. This is particularly appealing in settings with limited historical data. As of yet, there are few papers that combine lab-in-the-field work with historical economics. In historical economics, lab-in-the-field experiments are either used as outcomes or as a way of understanding mechanisms. In contrast,

Gneezy and Imas focus on lab-in-the-field experiments as a way of measuring social preferences or helping to design and target policies.

I will review the work in historical economics that makes use of lab-in-the-field experiments (see Table 6.3). The first set of papers are those that use the lab-in-the-field measures as the primary outcomes of interest, asking how a historical event or treatment shapes the experimental outcome. The second set of papers use the experimental measures as a way of understanding cultural or institutional mechanisms.

6.4.2 Lab-in-the-field experiments as outcomes

6.4.2.1 States, institutions, and colonialism

Lowes et al. (2017) examine the effects of the historical Kuba state on present day norms of rule following. The Kuba Kingdom was a historical Kingdom in Central Africa, what is today the Democratic Republic of Congo. The Kuba Kingdom had well developed state institutions, including an unwritten constitution, a capital city, separation of powers, a judiciary, a police force, and the provision of public goods. The Kingdom was created by an innovative outsider, who united multiple groups, including the Kuba, on one side of a river, but left other culturally similar groups, primarily the Lele, outside of the Kingdom on the other side of the river. This provides a natural experiment in which groups that had a similar history and culture were differentially exposed to the state.

The authors were interested in understanding how exposure to the state affects norms of rule following. However, there was no pre-existing data would have allowed them to answer this question. Therefore, the authors went to Kananga, the major city closest to the Kuba Kingdom's capital, Mushenge. In Kananga, they sampled individuals from the Kuba and Lele ethnic groups, as well as other culturally proximate groups in the region.

Respondents participated in a series of lab experiments intended to measure an individual's propensity to follow rules. The primary experiment was the Resource Allocation Game (RAG). In this task, individuals are given thirty 100 CF bills to allocate between themselves and another player. They are told that in order to allocate the bills, they must roll a die that has three white sides and three black sides. Before each roll, they decide in their heads which color to associate with themselves and which color to associate with the other player. They then roll the die, and make the allocation of the 100 CF bill based on the outcome of the die roll. However, given that the association made by the individual is not observable to the researcher, the respondent can choose to deviate from the rules and allocate to themselves if they wish. While this is not verifiable at the individual level, it is possible to assess whether on average groups deviate from the fifty-fifty split that should result from members of a group following the rules. Participants made allocation decisions with real money in the privacy of a tent. Instructions were administered in the local languages. See Fig. 6.4 for a depiction of the "mobile lab" set up and of enumerator training.

By comparing individuals from just inside the Kuba Kingdom to those just outside the Kuba Kingdom, the paper finds that Kuba individuals are less likely to follow the rules in the RAG, which is interpreted as less strong norms of rule following among the Kuba. This result is consistent with models in which strong states crowd out parental investment in the norm of rule following. They find that Kuba parents are also more likely to report that it is less important to teach values related to rule following to children.

Table 6.3 Historical economics and lab-in-the-field.

Authors	Journal	Location	Treatment	Experiments	Outcome variable
Bergeron (2020)	Mimeo	DRC	Missionaries	Referral Task	Kinship ties, universal morality
Blouin (2019)	Mimeo	Rwanda, Burundi	Forced Labor	TG	Trust, Contracts
Chaudhary et al. (2020)	J. of Econ. Behavior & Organization	India	British/Princely State	PG	Cooperation
De Juan and Koos (2019)	World Development	DRC	Bushi Kingdom	DG	Cooperation
Gangadharan et al. (2018)	Mimeo	Cambodia	Genocide	JOD, DG, honesty, TG, Risk	Pro-social
Gneezy et al. (2009)	Econometrica	India & Tanzania	Matrilineal Kinship	Competition Task	competitiveness
Heldring (forthcoming)	Review of Economic Studies	Rwanda	Nyiginya kingdom	RAG	Violence, Obedience
Hruschka et al. (2014)	Human Nature	Various	Pathogen Stress Material Security	RAG	Favoring In-group
Karaja and Rubin (2017)	Mimeo	Romania	Habsburg/Ottoman institutions	TG	Trust
Lowes (2018b)	Mimeo	DRC	Matrilineal kinship	DG, UG, PG, IAT Risk, Time, Stress	Cooperation, Health, Education
Lowes and Montero (2020)	Mimeo	DRC	Rubber Concessions	DG, RDG	Development, Pro-social
Lowes et al. (2017)	Econometrica	DRC	Kuba Kingdom	RAG, UG, IAT	Rule Following
Ramos-Toro (2019)	Mimeo	Colombia	Leper colony	DG	Pro-social, Trust
Rustagi (2020)	Mimeo	Switzerland	Institutions	PG	Cooperation
Schulz et al. (2019)	Science	Global	Medieval Church	PG	Individualism, Conformity, Impartial Pro-sociality
Valencia Caicedo and Voth (2018)	Mimeo	Paraguay	Missionaries	LOC, Cheating game, DG, TG, Risk	Non-cognitive Skills
Walker (2020)	J. Comparative Economics	Romania	Habsburg/Ottoman institutions	Risk, Time	Pro-social, Trust

DG is the dictator game. IAT is the implicit association test. JOD is the joy of destruction game. LOC is locus of control. PG is the public goods game. RAG is the resource allocation game. TG is the trust game.

(a) Enumerator Training

(b) Experimental Setup

FIGURE 6.4

Lab-in-field training and enumeration. These images depict an example of enumerator training and the experimental set up for administering lab-in-the-field in DRC.

In addition to experimental data, the authors collected other complementary data. For example, the respondents completed IATs to measure their implicit association towards Joseph Mobutu Sese-Seko, the president of DRC from 1965 to 1997. The concern was that perhaps the effect observed in the lab experiment was driven by differential treatment of the Kuba during Mobutu's rule. However, it is difficult to measure exposure to Mobutu's policies. The IAT thus served as proxy for the experience under Mobutu. See Fig. 6.5 for an example of an IAT screenshot.

FIGURE 6.5

Screenshot of Mobutu IAT. This is a screenshot of the Mobutu IAT in which images related to Mobutu would be sorted to the left side of the screen along with "happy" images.

A related paper, De Juan and Koos (2019), explores how the pre-colonial Bushi state in Eastern Congo shapes cooperation. The Bushi Kingdom emphasized social integration and the creation of broad horizontal networks. The authors collect survey and experimental data from 1000 participants across 100 villages near the historical Bushi Kingdom border. Their primary outcome is participation in community works programs as reported by respondents. They find that individuals from villages from inside the Bushi Kingdom report participating more in these community work programs. As a behavioral measure, the authors give the respondents the opportunity to donate part of the compensation they receive for participating in the survey to an education program. They find that individuals from inside the former kingdom are more likely donate, which they interpret as evidence of more pro-social behavior.

Rustagi (2020) also examines the role of institutions for cooperation. He focuses on Switzerland, where during the middle ages some Swiss municipalities acquired self-governance while others remained under feudalism for an additional 600 years. He combines survey and experimental data to examine how historical self-governance affects cooperation. He conducts an online one-shot anonymous public goods game with 262 individuals from 174 municipalities. The experimental results suggest greater experience with self-governance increases conditional cooperation – e.g. willingness to increase public goods contributions as the other player increases their contribution. He finds a similar increase in cooperative attitudes in World Values Survey data and data from the Swiss Household Panel.

Blouin (2019) explores how historical forced labor shapes ethnic relations in Rwanda and Burundi. During the colonial era, Belgian authorities implemented a coffee production quota. Additionally, the Belgians encouraged Tutsi chiefs to coerce Hutu farmers to produce coffee to meet the quota. Given that there was variation in coffee suitability but the quota was uniform there is variation in the extent to which meeting the quota would benefit from forced labor.

To examine the legacy of forced labor for inter-ethnic relations, he collects lab-in-the-field data with Hutu and Tutsi farmers in Rwanda and Burundi. Given that Rwanda prohibits explicit mention of ethnic affiliation, ethnic identity is inferred through eligibility for the genocide survivor fund (which is understood to mean Tutsi). He conducts in-person trust games with 869 farmers from 143 different villages. In the trust game, a player 1 is given an endowment. They can send part of that endowment to a player 2; any amount sent to the player 2 is doubled. Player 2 can then choose to return some of that increased amount to the player 1. Generally, the amount sent by player 1 to player 2 is interpreted as a measure of trusting behavior and the share returned by player 2 to player 1 as a measure of trustworthiness. Additionally, he conducts a "partner selection task", in which individuals can choose other participants in the session as their partner. The outcome of interest is the share of those chosen that are from the other ethnic group. Finally, he collects data on real world agricultural insurance contracts – as a measure of real world cooperation. Hutu from areas that experienced forced labor send less in the trust game when paired with a Tutsi, are less likely to choose a Tutsi partner, and make fewer agricultural agreements. The results suggest that the Belgian policy of manipulating social identity has had long run effects on inter-ethnic relations.

Chaudhary et al. (2020) examine how exposure to British colonialism relative to Princely States in India affects present day norms of cooperation. The hypothesis is that the institutions of British India may have affected cooperative norms because these individuals were exposed to taxation and had a longer history of living with outsiders relative to individuals in Princely States. The authors conduct public goods games with 554 individuals from three towns, one of which was formerly part of British India. They also vary the identity of the other members of the group in the public goods game; in some cases groups are mixed and include individuals from another town, in other cases other players are from the same town. They find that relative to a neighboring town in a Princely State, individuals from the town that was part of British India cooperate more with others, regardless of the other players' identities. The results are driven by individuals whose parents are from the town.

In a related paper, Karaja and Rubin (2017) compare towns that are along the former Habsburg/Austrian and Ottoman/Russian border in Romania. The Habsburg administration was relatively less corrupt and more efficient than the Ottoman administration. The authors hypothesize that the more rapacious Ottoman institutions may have undermined trust, particularly in outsiders. They take advantage of a natural experiment because the border between the Ottomans and Habsburgs was somewhat arbitrary. They conduct trust games with individuals in three towns along this historical border. They find that individuals from the former Habsburg side whose grandparents are from the town are more trusting of outsiders – i.e. they send more in the first stage of the trust game.

6.4.2.2 Environment

Hruschka et al. (2014) examine how pathogen stress affects willingness to favor an in-group member. The hypothesis is that greater pathogen stress leads individuals to be more likely to favor in-group members. To test this, they administer lab-in-the-field experiments across eight different societies with 223 individuals. The experiment is the Resource Allocation Game (RAG), described above. In one version the allocations are made between an in-group and out-group member; in a second version the individual allocated between themselves and an anonymous out-group member. They find no evidence for the pathogen stress hypothesis. Rather, individuals are more likely to follow the impartial allocation rule when there is better institutional quality and material security.

6.4.2.3 The Church and missionaries

Schulz et al. (2019) explore how the Western Church (which became the Roman Catholic Church) shaped European kinship structures. The authors hypothesize that by undermining kin-based institutions (e.g. by banning cousin marriage), the Western Church encouraged the development of independent nuclear (or stem) families. This in turn led to social norms less dominated by in-group loyalty and conformism and to greater individualism and impersonal cooperation. To test this hypothesis, the authors compile a wide variety of surveys and lab experiments to measure their outcomes of interest: individualism, conformity, and impersonal pro-sociality. Some of the key lab experimental measures are a public goods games and a die rolling task, for which payments are linked to the reported outcome of the die roll as a measure of honesty. They find that greater exposure to the Western Church is associated with less intensive kinship, greater individualism, less conformity, and more fairness towards strangers.

Building on work that finds that the Guarani Jesuit missionaries have had a long-run impact on education and income in Argentina, Brazil, and Paraguay (Valencia Caicedo, 2019), Valencia Caicedo and Voth (2018) use a series of lab-in-the-field experiments and surveys to measure the effects of the Jesuit missionaries on non-cognitive skills. They collect data from approximately 500 individuals in Paraguay from areas with low and high presence of missionaries to examine the effect of missionary presence. They implement the Rotter Locus of Control Scale, which is a series of questions intended to measure the extent to which individuals feel that they have agency in their lives. They also conducted the dictator game, trust game, a cheating game (as in Hanna and Wang (2017); Lowes et al. (2017)) and implemented questions measuring time and risk preferences. They find that areas with greater exposure to the missionaries report having more of an internal locus of control, allocate more to the other player in a dictator game, return more money in the trust game to the other player, cheat less in the rule following game, and are more risk averse.

Related work explores how exposure to missionaries in the Democratic Republic of Congo is associated with the scope of cooperation (Bergeron, 2020). The paper examines the extent to which exposure to missionaries increases cooperation beyond kin (i.e. family members or co-ethnics) and whether individuals have more universal moral systems. To examine this question, he digitizes historical maps of missionary presence in the DRC and collects survey and lab-in-the-field data with 1000 individuals presently residing in the city of Kananga. He measures exposure to missionaries based on the distance of an individual's village of origin to the nearest mission station. He measures kin preference with a series of survey questions and with a lab experiment. The survey questions elicit attitudes toward various other groups including nuclear family members, extended family, coethnics, non-coethnics, foreigners etc. As part of the survey, participants are asked to refer social network members for paid and unpaid activities. This allows him to examine whether respondents are more likely to recommend kin relative to non-kin for the paid tasks. He finds that exposure to missionaries is associated with weaker kin ties and individuals are less likely to refer kin in the lab experiment. The survey responses are consistent with missionary exposure encouraging more universal moral values.

6.4.2.4 Social exclusion and violence

Ramos-Toro (2019) examines how social exclusion impacts social preferences. The setting is a former leper colony in Colombia. Historically, individuals with leprosy were forcibly isolated at specific locations, as the disease was mistakenly believed to be highly contagious. Treatment in the leper colony was characterized by isolation from family and friends and loss of citizenship. These policies were enforced by the colony physicians. By the 20th century, approximately 8000 lepers were living in the Agua de Dios colony. The author collects data from individuals living in and around Agua de Dios. Individuals participated in two dictator games, one in which the other player is from the same municipality (i.e. an in-group member) and one in which the other player is from a different municipality (an out-group member). He finds that individuals living in the former leper colony are more generous in the dictator game. However, they also demonstrate a larger in-group preference, suggesting greater identity awareness. He also collects data on how social exclusion affects views towards modern medicine. He finds that individuals from Agua de Dios are less likely trust physicians and less likely to believe the HPV vaccine is safe. This translates into lower infant vaccination rates.

To examine the transmission of these social preferences, he collects data to measure how aware individuals are of the history of exclusion. Additionally, he experimentally manipulates knowledge of the non-medical history of exclusion or the history of the role of medicine and physicians. The history of exclusion information increases in-group preferences and the medical history information decreases trust in modern medicine. A placebo treatment with information on trees has no significant effect. The results suggest long lasting effects of social exclusion on preferences, that this experience shapes views of the group that is associated with implementing the exclusion, and that knowledge of this history is an important transmission mechanism.

A large literature documents the effects of exposure to violence on pro-social preferences, suggesting that exposure to violence may actually increase pro-social preferences (see Bauer et al. (2016) for a review of this literature). However, few papers examine the long-run impact of exposure to violence. Gangadharan et al. (2018) examine the effect of exposure to the Cambodian genocide on anti-social behavior. During the Cambodian genocide an estimated 1.7 million Cambodians were killed by the Khmer Rouge. Most individuals that survived the Khmer Rouge rule were either directly affected by this violence or witnessed violence. The authors use variation in intensity of estimated deaths to measure exposure to violence. They collect data from 492 individuals across districts with estimated differential exposure to Khmer Rouge violence. They find that those directly exposed to Khmer Rouge violence in areas with a greater Khmer Rouge mortality rate are less altruistic, are more likely to destroy another player's endowment, and are more dishonest than those from areas with less exposure.

6.4.2.5 Kinship structure

In matrilineal societies, lineage is traced through female members rather than male members. This may have implications for a wide variety of social preferences. Gneezy et al. (2009) explore the effects of matrilineal relative to patrilineal kinship structure on preference for competition. Using a task where individuals can choose whether to compete or be paid in a piece-rate scheme, they find that there is a gap between men and women's preference for competition among a patrilineal group in Tanzania, where men compete more. However, among a matrilineal group in India, there is no longer a gap in preference for competition. Subsequent papers have built on this work, but test this hypothesis with more groups (Anderson et al., 2013; Flory et al., 2017). Other work examines how various other preferences vary between matrilineal and patrilineal groups, including altruism and risk preferences (Gong and Yang, 2012; Gong et al., 2015; Lowes, 2018a). See Lowes (2020) for a review of this literature.

6.4.3 Lab-in-the-field experiments as mechanisms

Lowes and Montero (2020) examine how private concessions granted during the colonial era affect present day development in the DRC. The Congo Free State, which was the personal colony of King Leopold II of Belgium between 1892 and 1908, was divided into concessions where private companies were given monopoly rights over resource extraction. The most infamous of these concessions, Abir and Anversoise, focused on the extraction of rubber (see Fig. 6.6 for a map of concession granted in the CFS). The concession companies used extreme violence to force villages to meet rubber quotas and indirect rule – coopting local leaders – to enforce the rubber quotas. They examine the effects of exposure to these concessions using the arbitrarily defined borders of the two northern most concessions and a geographic regression discontinuity design. Using data from the Demographic and Health Surveys for DRC, they find that exposure to these concessions is associated with worse development outcomes: lower levels of education, health, and wealth.

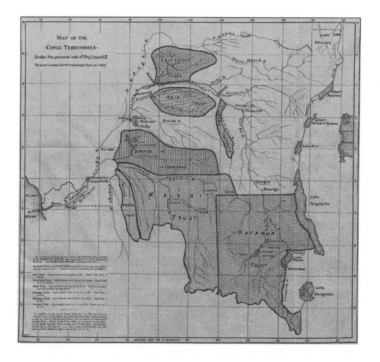

FIGURE 6.6

Congo free state concessions. This is a map of the concessions granted in the CFS as of 1904. Abir and Anversoise are the two Northern concessions.

To understand mechanisms, they collected survey and experimental data from Gemena, a town along the boundary of one of the former concessions. They collect data on the role of culture and institutions for shaping present day development outcomes. They sample over 500 individuals from Gemena, whose ancestors come from in and outside the former concession boundary. They collect survey data on local institutional quality, how chiefs are chosen, public goods provision, and trust and closeness in a wide variety of others. They also conduct two lab-in-the-field experiments including a dictator game and a reverse dictator game. In the reverse dictator game individuals decide how much of another individual's earned endowment to allocate to themselves. They also complete the earnings task, once they have already made the allocation decision. This is meant to capture the extent an individual is willing to redistribute for themselves and tax another's earned income.

They find two key sets of results. First, individuals with ancestors from inside the former concessions come from villages with less accountable leaders. These leaders are less likely to be elected and more likely to be hereditary. They also provide fewer public goods. This suggests that local institutions inside the former concessions are of lower quality. Second, they find evidence of more pro-social norms and more acceptance of sharing and redistribution. Individuals from the former concessions report feeling more trusting of and close to others. They self-report believing sharing and redistribution are important, and also reallocate more of another's earned endowment to themselves. They find no significant differences in allocations in the dictator game, which is a measure of altruism. They interpret these results as consistent with the concession system undermining local institutions and with social norms responding to the weakened institutions.

Heldring (forthcoming) examines how exposure to the precolonial state affects violence and norms of rule following in Rwanda. The hypothesis is that states inculcate norms of rule following and that greater exposure to the state will lead to more obedience to state policy. To test this hypothesis, he leverages the slow expansion of the precolonial Rwandan state – the Nyiginya kingdom – which expanded over several centuries. He combines data on length of exposure to the precolonial state with data on violence perpetrated during the genocide and with lab-in-the-field data. He finds that greater exposure to the Nyiginya kingdom is associated with more violence during the genocide. To provide evidence on mechanisms, he conducts a lab-in-the-field experiment with individuals from areas with differential exposure to the historical state. He implements the RAG (as in Lowes et al. (2017)). He finds that those individuals from areas with longer exposure to the pre-colonial state are more likely to follow the rules – i.e. to not cheat for material gain – than those with less exposure. He interprets this as evidence that the historical state inculcates norms of obedience, which also led to greater violence during the genocide as individuals followed orders to participate in the killings.

Lowes (2018b) examines how kinship structure affects outcomes for women and children and spousal cooperation. The DRC is intersected by the so-called matrilineal belt, which describes the distribution of matrilineal ethnic groups across the center of Africa. See Fig. 6.7 for a map of matrilineal groups in Africa. In matrilineal systems lineage and inheritance are traced through female group members rather than through male group members. This means that children are part of their mother's kin group and that women in matrilineal systems generally have greater support from their kin. Anthropologists had hypothesized that matrilineal systems may improve outcomes for women, but that women's empowerment may also lead to decreased spousal cooperation. Using data from the DHS and a geographic regression discontinuity design along the matrilineal belt border, she finds that women from matrilineal areas are less likely to support domestic violence and less likely to experience domestic violence. Children of matrilineal women also fare better; they are more educated and healthier, with many of these benefits accruing to girl children.

FIGURE 6.7

Matrilineal belt in Africa.

To examine mechanisms she collected survey and experimental data from 320 couples in the city of Kananga. About 40 percent of the sample are from ethnic groups that practice matrilineal kinship. While the individuals have villages of origin along the matrilineal belt, they are all presently located in the same institutional environment. The individuals in the sample complete a dictator game, an ultimatum game, and a modified public goods game with their spouse and with a stranger of the opposite sex. In the public goods game, individuals roll a die with three white sides and three black sides. If they see a black side, they get an additional 500 CF to their public goods game endowment of 1000 CF. They are then asked to allocate their endowment across an envelope for themselves and a "shared" envelope. Any contributions to the shared envelope are increased by 1.5 or by 2. For a household to maximize earnings in the experiment, each individual should contribute all of their endowment to the shared envelope. In practice, couples rarely allocate more than half of their endowment to the shared envelope. Matrilineal individuals allocate even less than patrilineal individuals to the shared envelope. This is particularly the case when they win the unobserved bonus and it becomes relatively easier to be less cooperative with the spouse. This differential behavior of matrilineal individuals is specific to being paired with a spouse; matrilineal individuals no longer differentially contribute less when they win the bonus and are paired with a stranger of the opposite sex. The results are robust to controlling for altruism, as measured in the dictator game. The results are consistent with matrilineal kinship undermining spousal cooperation. However, by being less cooperative, women may retain more control over their earnings in the experiment.

Walker (2020) exploits the former Habsburg-Ottoman boundary discontinuity to explore how these imperial legacies shape savings behavior. The Habsburg Monarchy was more financially developed and more decentralized relative to the Ottomans. The Habsburg legal institutions were also known to be relatively less corrupt. She collects experimental and survey data with 331 semi-subsistence farmers along the former border. She measures risk preferences with choices between lotteries and time preferences by asking individuals to choose between smaller amounts in a near period and larger amounts in a later period. All of these experiments were incentivized. Using survey data, she finds that individuals from the former Habsburg side save more. However, she finds no evidence that this is driven by time or risk preferences. Instead, financial access seems to drive the results, with individuals on the former Habsburg side have greater access to financial institutions.

6.4.4 Practical issues

Implementing lab-in-the-field experiments presents a wide variety of practical challenges. While not all of these challenges are specific to lab-in-the-field experiments in historical economics, some of these challenges become particularly important when dealing with historical treatments. I highlight a few of these challenges and potential solutions.

There are several potential challenges with sample selection. Sample selection will likely take place in two parts. First, it will be important to choose a location or locations from which to collect data. Second, individuals must be recruited to participate in the study.

Choosing a location from which to collect data will likely be driven by the historical episode of interest and the identification strategy. For example, in Lowes et al. (2017), where they are interested in how the Kuba state affects norms of rule following, they focus on individuals living in a major city near the Kuba Kingdom. They sample individuals within the city of Kananga, some of whose ancestors come from the Kuba Kingdom and others whose ancestors come from outside the Kingdom. There are several benefits to this strategy. It is analogous to the epidemiological approach in which individuals from different cultural (or historical) backgrounds share a common institutional environment (Fernández, 2011). This helps separate institutions from internalized cultural norms. In the context of data collection and developing countries, it is also a very practical approach in that it decreases implementation costs and eases data collection demands. The historical treatment variable is then linked to where an individual is from, rather than to their current location (for other examples see e.g. Lowes (2018b); Lowes and Montero (2020); Bergeron (2020) where respondents' village of origin are mapped to the historical treatment variable).

A potential challenge, however, is addressing selection into migration based on the historical treatment of interest. The concern is that the historical variable itself may affect migration choices, making the sample of individuals in that location a selected sample and potentially not representative of the group of interest. Note, this issue applies to many lab experiments where convenience samples are used.

There are several strategies to deal with this. In Lowes et al. (2017) they collect detailed migration information, including reasons for migration and timing of migration. This allows them to show that the Kuba do not report different reasons for migration – for example, they are not more likely to have migrated because they were asked to leave their village of origin. An additional strategy is to use other data to show how the sample selected in the location of choice differs from a potential broader and more representative sample for whom you may have only limited demographic data rather than detailed survey and experimental data.

The second strategy for choosing locations to sample would be to randomly select villages that meet a particular inclusion criteria. For example, Heldring (forthcoming) collects data in villages along a border that designated a longer period of time under the pre-colonial state. This strategy helps diminish the issue of selection into migration. However, it can be costly and logistically challenging, particularly in places with limited infrastructure. It also makes it more difficult to disentangle cultural and institutional variables.

The second part of sample selection is to recruit individuals to participate in the lab experiment. There may not be a pre-existing sampling frame from which to select individuals. This is often the case in developing countries where there may be limited administrative or public survey data available. One method of addressing this issue is to set up a sampling frame, perhaps by using satellite data, and a method of randomly choosing geographic units, and then randomly sampling individuals within these units. It may be important to record refusal data to be able to show individuals are not differentially refusing to participate based on the treatment of interest. Again, whether individuals are statistically representative of the group of interest is a challenge for lab experiments more broadly, but becomes more salient with lab-in-the-field experiments, as one of the benefits of lab-in-the-field experiments is working with the group of interest.

Finally, another practical consideration is writing and submitting a pre-analysis plan for the project prior to field work. Initially, primarily randomized controlled trials were expected to have pre-analysis plans. However, it is now common place for researchers to submit pre-analysis plans for lab experiments as well. A common repository for these pre-analysis plans is the AEA randomized controlled trial registry.[2]

6.5 Conclusion

Work in historical economics has relied on existing historical data. However, ethnographic data sets, lab-in-the-field experiments, and survey methods increase the scope of the research questions that can be empirically explored in historical economics. These approaches are particularly helpful in cases where there is limited written historical records and increase the representation of non-"WEIRD" societies in economics research.

This article first reviewed some of the most commonly used ethnographic data sources, including the Ethnographic Atlas and the Standard Cross Cultural Survey. I discuss how these data were constructed, potential limitations of the data, and efforts to validate and improve upon these data sets. Additionally, I provide examples of how these datasets have been used in economics research. I then describe alternative ethnographic data sources that have been compiled by anthropologists and historians, but have yet to be widely used in economics. I also discuss other survey and experimental resources that can be used to measure cultural traits across cultures.

---

[2] The web address for the AEA RCT registry is https://www.socialscienceregistry.org/.

Finally, I discuss the use of lab-in-the-field experiments in historical economics. There are still few papers that combine historical economics and experimental methods. Lab-in-the-field experiments have been used both as outcomes and as a way of understanding persistence. I highlight some of the benefits of these methods, potential problems, and practical implementation issues. These data sets and methods offer an opportunity for future research in the realm of historical economics and to increase the connections between work in historical economics and other disciplines.

References

AfricaMap, 2020. https://worldmap.harvard.edu/africamap/.

Afrobarometer Data, 2020. afrobarometer.org.

Ahmed, A.T., Stasavage, D., 2020. Origins of early democracy. American Political Science Review 114 (2), 502–518.

Akbari, M., Bahrami-Rad, D., Kimbrough, E.O., 2019. Kinship, fractionalization and corruption. Journal of Economic Behavior & Organization 166, 493–528.

Alesina, A., Giuliano, P., Nunn, N., 2011. Fertility and the plough. The American Economic Review: Papers and Proceedings 101 (3), 499–503.

Alesina, A., Giuliano, P., Nunn, N., 2013. On the origins of gender roles: women and the plough. The Quarterly Journal of Economics 128 (2), 469–530.

Alesina, A., Giuliano, P., Nunn, N., 2018. Traditional agricultural practices and the sex ratio today. PLoS ONE 13 (1).

Alsan, M., 2015. The effect of the TseTse fly on African development. The American Economic Review 105 (1), 382–410.

AmericasBarometer Data, 2020. vanderbilt.edu/lapop.

Anderson, S., 2007. The economics of dowry and brideprice. The Journal of Economic Perspectives 21 (4), 151–174.

Anderson, S., 2018. Legal origins and female HIV. The American Economic Review 108 (6), 1407–1439.

Anderson, S., Ertac, S., Sneezy, U., List, J.A., Maximiano, S., 2013. Gender, competitiveness, and socialization at a young age: evidence from a matrilineal and a patriarchal society. Review of Economics and Statistics 95 (4), 1438–1443.

Arab Barometer Data, 2020. www.arabbarometer.org.

Ashraf, N., Bau, N., Nunn, N., Voena, A., 2020. Bride price and female education. Journal of Political Economy 128 (2), 591–641.

Asian Barometer Data, 2020. asianbarometer.org.

Bahrami-Rad, D., Becker, A., Henrich, J., 2018. Tabulated Nonsense? Testing the Validity of the Ethnographic Atlas and the Persistence of Culture. Working Paper. Harvard University.

Baker, M.J., 2008. A structural model of the transition to agriculture. Journal of Economic Growth 13.

Baker, M.J., Miceli, T.J., 2005. Land inheritance rules: theory and cross-cultural analysis. Journal of Economic Behavior & Organization 56 (1), 77–102.

Bauer, M., Blattman, C., Chytilová, J., Henrich, J., Miguel, E., Mitts, T., 2016. Can war foster cooperation? The Journal of Economic Perspectives 30 (3), 249–274.

Bazzi, S., Fiszbein, M., Gebresilasse, M., 2020. Frontier culture: the roots and persistence of "rugged individualism" in the United States. Econometrica 88 (6), 2329–2368.

Becker, A., 2019. On the Economic Origins of Restrictions on Women's Sexuality. Mimeo.

Becker, A., Enke, B., Falk, A., 2020. Ancient origins of the global variation in economic preferences. AEA Papers and Proceedings 110, 319–323.

Beheim, B., Atkinson, Q., Bulbulia, J., Gervais, W., Gray, R.D., Henrich, J., Lang, M., Monroe, M.W., Muthukrishna, M., Norenzayan, A., Purzycki, B.G., Shariff, A., Slingerland, E., Spicer, R., Willard, A.K., 2019. Corrected analyses show that moralizing gods precede complex societies but serious data concerns remain.

BenYishay, A., Grosjean, P., Vecci, J., 2017. The fish is the friend of matriliny: reef density and matrilineal inheritance. Journal of Development Economics 127, 234–249.

Berezkin, Y.E., 2015. Folklore and mythology catalogue: its layout and potential for research. In: Lukin, F., Lukin, K. (Eds.), Between Text and Practice: Mythology, Religion, and Research, Vol. 10 The Retrospective Methods Network Newsletter Folklore Studies/Department of Philosophy, History, Culture and Art Studies. University of Helsinki, Helsinki.

Berezkin, Y.E., 2016. Peopling of the New World in light of the data on distribution of folklore motifs. In: Kenna, R., Carron, M.M., Carron, P.M. (Eds.), Maths Meets Myths: Quantitative Approaches to Ancient Narratives, Vol. 10. Springer-Verlag, pp. 71–89.

Bergeron, A., 2020. Religion and the Scope of Morality: Evidence from Exposure to Missions in the D.R. Congo.

Binford, L.R., 2001. Constructing Frames of Reference: An Analytical Method for Archaeological Theory Building Using Ethnographic and Environmental Data Sets. University of California Press.

Binford, L.R., Johnson, A., 2006. Documentation for Program for Calculating Environmental and Hunter-Gatherer Frames of Reference (ENVCALC2).

Blouin, A., 2019. Culture and Contracts: the Historical Legacy of Forced Labor.

Bondarenko, D., Kazankov, A., Khaltourina, D., Korotayev, A., 2005. Ethnographic Atlas XXXI: peoples of easternmost Europe. Ethnology 44 (3), 261–289.

Botticini, M., Siow, A., 2003. Why dowries? The American Economic Review 93, 1385–1398.

Buggle, J., 2020. Growing collectivism: irrigation, group conformity and technological divergence. Journal of Economic Growth 25 (2), 147–193.

Chaudhary, L., Rubin, J., Iyer, S., Shrivastava, A., 2020. Culture and colonial legacy: evidence from public goods games. Journal of Economic Behavior & Organization 173, 107–129.

Cohn, A., Marechal, M.A., Tannenbaum, D., Zund, C.L., 2019. Civic honesty around the globe. Science 365, 70–73.

Corno, L., Hildebrandt, N., Voena, A., 2020. Age of marriage, weather shocks and the direction of marriage payments. Econometrica 88 (3), 879–915.

De Juan, A., Koos, C., 2019. The historical roots of cooperative behavior: evidence from eastern Congo. World Development 116, 100–112.

Depetris-Chauvin, E., 2016. State History and Contemporary Conflict: Evidence from Sub-Saharan Africa.

Desmet, K., Gomes, J.F., Ortuño Ortín, I., 2020. The geography of linguistic diversity and the provision of public goods. Journal of Development Economics 143.

Dippel, C., 2014. Forced coexistence and economic development: evidence from native American reservations. Econometrica 82 (6), 2131–2165.

Ember, C.R., 2012. Leadership in Science and Technology: A Reference Handbook, Vol. 2. Sage, Los Angeles.

Enke, B., 2019. Kinship, cooperation, and the evolution of moral systems. The Quarterly Journal of Economics 134 (2), 953–1019.

Eurobarometer Data, 2020. gesis.org/en/eurobarometer-data-service/home.

Falk, A., Becker, A., Dohmen, T., Enke, B., Huffman, D., Sunde, U., 2018. Global evidence on economic preferences. The Quarterly Journal of Economics 133 (4), 1645–1692.

Fenske, J., 2013. Does land abundance explain African institutions? The Economic Journal 123 (573), 1363–1390.

Fenske, J., 2014. Ecology, trade and states in pre-colonial Africa. Journal of the European Economic Association 12 (3), 612–640.

Fenske, J., 2015. African polygamy: past and present. Journal of Development Economics 117, 58–73. Mimeo. Oxford University.

Fernández, R., 2011. Does culture matter? In: Jackson, M.O., Benhabib, J., Bisin, A. (Eds.), Handbook of Social Economics, Vol. 1A. Elsevier, pp. 481–510. Chapter 11.

Flory, J., Leonard, K.L., Tsaneva, M., Vasilaky, K., 2017. Changes in Competitiveness with Motherhood Stages and Culture: Evidence from Patrilocal and Matrilocal Society.

Forde, D., 2017. Ethnographic Survey of Africa. Routledge.

Gachter, S., Schulz, J.F., 2016. Intrinsic honesty and the prevalence of rule violations across societies. Nature 531.

Gangadharan, L., Islam, A., Ouch, C., Wang, L.C., 2018. The Long-term effects of genocide on antisocial preferences.

Gennaioli, N., Rainer, I., 2007. The modern impact of precolonial centralization in Africa. Journal of Economic Growth 12 (3), 185–234.

Giuliano, P., Nunn, N., 2013. The transmission of democracy: from the village to the nation state. The American Economic Review: Papers and Proceedings 103 (3), 86–92.

Giuliano, P., Nunn, N., 2018. Ancestral characteristics of modern populations. Economic History of Developing Regions 33 (1), 1–17.

Giuliano, P., Nunn, N., forthcoming. Understanding cultural persistence and change. The Review of Economic Studies.

Gneezy, U., Imas, A., 2017. Lab in the field: measuring preferences in the wild. In: Banerjee, A., Duflo, E. (Eds.), Handbook of Field Experiments, Vol. 1. Elsevier, North Holland.

Gneezy, U., Leonard, K.L., List, J.A., 2009. Gender differences in competition: evidence from a matrilineal and a patriarchal society. Econometrica 77 (5), 1637–1664.

Gomes, J.F., 2020. The health costs of ethnic distance: evidence from Sub-Saharan Africa. Journal of Economic Growth 25, 95–226.

Gong, B., Yang, C.-L., 2012. Gender differences in risk attitudes: field experiments on the matrilineal Mosuo and the patriarchal Yi. Journal of Economic Behavior & Organization 83 (1), 59–65.

Gong, B., Yan, H., Yang, C.-L., 2015. Gender differences in the dictator experiment: evidence from the matrilineal Mosuo and the patriarchal Yi. Experimental Economics 18, 302–313.

Gordon, R.G., 2009. Ethnologue: Languages of the World, 16th edition. SIL International.

Greenwald, T., Banaji, M., Nozek, B., n.d. https://www.projectimplicit.net.

Hammarström, H., Forkel, R., Haspelmath, M., Bank, S., 2020. Glottolog 4.2.1. Max Planck Institute for the Science of Human History, Jena.

Hanna, R., Wang, S.-Y., 2017. Dishonesty and selection into public service: evidence from India. American Economic Journal: Economic Policy 9 (3), 262–290.

Heldring, L., forthcoming. The origins of violence in Rwanda. The Review of Economic Studies.

Hofstede, G., 1980. Culture's Consequences: International Differences in Work-Related Values. Sage, Beverly Hills, CA.

Hofstede, G., 2013. Replicating and extending cross-national value studies: rewards and pitfalls - an example from middle East studies. Academy of International Business Insights 13 (2), 5–7.

Hruschka, D., Efferson, C., Jiang, T., Falleta-Cowden, A., Sigurdsson, S., McNamara, R., Sands, M., Munira, S., Slingerland, E., Henrich, J., 2014. Impartial institutions, pathogen stress, and the expanding social network. Human Nature 25, 567–579.

ICF, 2020. Demographic and Health Surveys.

Jackson, J.C., Gelfand, M., Ember, C.R., 2020. A global analysis of cultural tightness in non-industrial societies. Proceedings of the Royal Society of London. Series B, Biological Sciences 287, 20201036.

Jorgensen, J.G., 1980. Western Indians: Comparative Environments, Languages, and Cultures of 172 Western American Indian Tribes. WH Freema, San Francisco.

Jorgensen, J.G., 1999a. Codebook for western Indians data. World Cultures 19 (2), 144–293.

Jorgensen, J.G., 1999b. An empirical procedure for defining and sampling culture bearing units in continuous geographic areas. World Cultures 10 (2), 139–143.

Karaja, E., Rubin, J., 2017. The Cultural Transmission of Trust: Evidence from a Lab in the Field on a Natural Experiment.

Kirby, K.R., Gray, R.D., Greenhill, S.J., Jordan, F.M., Gomes-Ng, S., Bibiko, H.-J., Blasi, D.E., Botero, C.A., Bowern, C., Ember, C.R., Leehr, D., Low, B.S., McCarter, J., Divale, W., Gavin, M.C., 2016. D-PLACE: a global database of cultural, linguistic and environmental diversity. PLoS ONE 11 (7), e0158391.

Knudsen, A.S.B., 2019. Those Who Stayed: Selection and cultural change during the Age of Mass Migration.

Korotayev, A., Kazankov, A., Borinskaya, S., Khaltourina, D., Bondarenko, D., 2004. Ethnographic Atlas XXX: peoples of Siberia. Ethnology 43, 83–92.

Latinobarometer Data, 2020. latinobarometro.org.

Lowes, S., 2018a. Kinship Structure, Stress, and the Gender Gap in Competition.

Lowes, S., 2018b. Matrilineal Kinship and Spousal Cooperation: Evidence from the Matrilineal Belt. Mimeo.

Lowes, S., 2020. Kinship structure and women: evidence from economics. Daedalus.

Lowes, S., Montero, E., 2020. Concessions, Violence, and Indirect Rule: Evidence from the Congo Free State.

Lowes, S., Nunn, N., Robinson, J.A., Weigel, J.L., 2017. The evolution of culture and institutions: evidence from the Kuba Kingdom. Econometrica 85 (4), 1065–1091.

Mace, R., Pagel, M., 1994. The comparative method in anthropology. Current Anthropology 35 (549–557).

Mayshar, J., Moav, O., Pascali, L., 2020. The Origin of the State: Land Productivity or Appropriability? Mimeo.

Michalopoulos, S., 2012. The origins of ethnolinguistic diversity. The American Economic Review 102 (4), 1508–1539.

Michalopoulos, S., Papaioannou, E., 2013. Precolonial ethnic institutions and contemporary African development. Econometrica 81 (1), 113–152.

Michalopoulos, S., Papaioannou, E., 2014. National institutions and subnational development in Africa. The Quarterly Journal of Economics 129 (1), 151–213.

Michalopoulos, S., Papaioannou, E., 2016. The long-run effects of the scramble in Africa. The American Economic Review 106 (7), 1802–1848.

Michalopoulos, S., Xue, M., 2019. Folklore.

Michalopoulos, S., Putterman, L., Weil, D., 2019. The influence of ancestral lifeways on individual economic outcomes in Sub-Saharan Africa. Journal of the European Economic Association 17 (4), 1186–1231.

Moscona, J., Nunn, N., Robinson, J.A., 2017. Keeping it in the family: lineage organization and the scope of trust in Sub-Saharan Africa. The American Economic Review: Papers and Proceedings 107 (5), 565–571.

Moscona, J., Nunn, N., Robinson, J.A., 2020. Social structure and conflict: evidence from Sub-Saharan Africa. Econometrica 88 (5).

Murdock, G.P., White, D.R., 2006. Standard Cross-Cultural Sample: online edition. UC Irvine Working Paper.

Murdock, G.P., 1957. World ethnographic sample. Ethnology 59 (4), 664–687.

Murdock, G.P., 1959. Africa: Its Peoples and Their Cultural History. McGraw-Hill Book Company, New York.

Murdock, G.P., 1967. Ethnographic Atlas. University of Pittsburgh Press, Pittsburgh.

Murdock, G.P., White, D.R., 1969. Standard cross-cultural sample. Ethnology 8 (4), 329–369.

newspapers.com, 2020. newspapers.com.

Norenzayan, A., Shariff, A.F., Gervais, W.M., Willard, A.K., McNamara, R.A., Slingerland, E., Henrich, J., 2016. The cultural evolution of prosocial religions. Behavioral and Brain Sciences 39, 1–65.

Nosek, B.A., Smyth, F.L., Hansen, J.J., Devos, T., Linder, N.M., Ratliff (Ranganath), K.A., Smith, C.T., Olson, K.R., Chugh, D., Greenwald, A.G., Banaji, M.R., 2007. Pervasiveness and correlates of implicit attitudes and stereotypes. European Review of Social Psychology 18, 36–88.

Nunn, N., 2008. The long-term effects of Africa's slave trades. The Quarterly Journal of Economics 123 (1), 139–176.

Nunn, N., Wantchekon, L., 2011. The slave trade and the origins of mistrust in Africa. The American Economic Review 101 (7), 3221–3252.

Obikili, N., 2016. The trans-Atlantic slave trade and local political fragmentation in Africa. The Economic History Review 69 (4), 1157–1177.

Ottinger, S., Winkler, M., 2020. Political Threat and Propaganda: Evidence from the U.S. South.

Pew Research Center, 2020. pewresearch.org.

Ramos-Toro, D., 2019. Social Exclusion and Social Preferences: Evidence from Colombia's Leper Colony.

Rijpma, A., Carmichael, S.G., 2016. Testing Todd and matching Murdock: global data on historical family characteristics. Economic History of Developing Regions 31 (1), 10–46.

Rustagi, D., 2020. Historical Self-Governance and Norms of Cooperation.

Schulz, J., 2017. The Churches' Bans on Consanguineous Marriages, Kin Networks and Democracy. Mimeo. Yale University.

Schulz, J.F., Bahrami-Rad, D., Beauchamp, J.P., Henrich, J., 2019. The Church, intensive kinship, and global psychological variation. Science 707.

Slingerland, E., Sullivan, B., 2017. Durkheim with data: the database of religious history. Journal of the American Academy of Religion 85 (2), 312–347.

Slingerland, E., Atkinson, Q.D., Ember, C.R., Sheehan, O., Muthukrishna, M., Bulbulia, J., Gray, R.D., 2020. Coding culture: challenges and recommendations for comparative cultural databases. Evolutionary Human Sciences 2 (29).

Teso, E., 2019. The long-term effect of demographic shocks on the evolution of gender roles: evidence from the transatlantic slave trade. Journal of the European Economic Association 17 (2), 497–534.

Todd, E., 1985. The Explanation of Ideology: Family Structures and Social Systems. Blackwell Publishers, Oxford.

Turchin, P., Whitehouse, H., Francois, P., Hoyer, D., Alves, A., Baines, J., Baker, D., Bartkowiak, M., Bates, J., Bennett, J., Bidmead, J., Bol, P., Ceccarelli, A., Christakis, K., Christian, D., Covey, A., De Angelis, F., Earle, T.K., Edwards, N.R., Feinman, G., Grohmann, S., Holden, P.B., Juliusson, A., Korotayev, A., Kradin, N., Kristinsson, A., Larson, J., Litwin, O., Mair, V., Manning, J.G., Manning, P., Marciniak, A., McMahon, G., Miksic, J., Garcia, J.C.M., Morris, I., Mostern, R., Mullins, D., Oyebamiji, O., Peregrine, P., Petrie, C., Preiser-Kapeller, J., Rudiak-Gould, P., Sabloff, P., Savage, P., Spencer, C., Stark, M., ter Haar, B., Thurner, S., Wallace, V., Witoszek, N., Xie, L., forthcoming. An introduction to seshat: global history databank. Journal of Cognitive Historiography.

Valencia Caicedo, F., 2019. The mission: human capital transmission, economic persistence, and culture in South America. The Quarterly Journal of Economics 134 (1), 507–556.

Valencia Caicedo, F., Voth, H.-J., 2018. Christ's Shadow: Non-Cognitive Skills and Prosocial Behavior Amongst the Guarani.

Vansina, J., 1966. Introduction a l'Ethnographie du Congo, Centre de Recherche et d'Information Socio-Politiques.

Walker, S., 2020. Historical legacies in savings: evidence from Romania. Journal of Comparative Economics 48 (1), 76–99.

Watts, J., Sheehan, O., Greenhil, S.J., Gomes-Ng, S., Atkinson, Q.D., Bulbulia, J., Gray, R.D., 2015. Pulotu: database of Austronesian supernatural beliefs and practices. PLoS ONE 10 (9), e0136783.

Whitehouse, H., Francois, P., Savage, P.E., Currie, T.E., Feeney, K.C., Cioni, E., Purcell, R., Ross, R.M., Larson, J., Baines, J., ter Haar, B., Covey, A., Turchin, P., 2019. Complex societies precede moralizing gods throughout world history. Nature 568 (7751), 226–229.

World Values Survey Data, 2020. worldvaluessurvey.org.

Xu, K., Nosek, B.A., Greenwald, A.G., Ratliff, K.A., Bar-Anan, Y., Umansky, E., Banaji, M.R., 2020. Project implicit demo website datasets. https://osf.io/y9hiq/.

Historical Econometrics: Instrumental Variables and Regression Discontinuity Designs[☆]

Felipe Valencia Caicedo[a,b,c]

[a]*Vancouver School of Economics, University of British Columbia, Vancouver, BC, Canada*
[b]*CEPR, London, United Kingdom*
[c]*IZA, Bonn, Germany*

7.1 Introduction

This chapter surveys two econometric tools—Instrumental Variables (IVs) and Regression Discontinuity Designs (RDDs)—in economic history, in what I term Historical Econometrics. For the actual history of IVs, see Stock and Trebbi (2003) and for the historical application of RDDs in psychology, statistics, and economics, see Cook (2008). Along with natural experiments (surveyed in this book by Cantoni and Yuchtman, 2021), these econometric techniques have played an important role in the modern development of economic history. In fact, I argue here that such methods have been instrumental in what Margo (2018) has called the "integration of economic history into economics."

The usage of modern econometric techniques in economic history, did not occur in a vacuum and parallels the broader developments in economics. One essential origin can be traced back to the so-called Identification or Credibility Revolution, emanating from Labor Economics and Applied Microeconomics. Seminal papers from the IV camp of this movement include Angrist (1990), Imbens and Angrist (1994), Angrist and Imbens (1995), Angrist et al. (1996), Angrist and Krueger (2001), Acemoglu and Angrist (2000), and Card (2001). Notably, some of these papers exploited sources of historical variation, coming from compulsory schooling laws and the Vietnam War lottery, though by no means were they seen as purely economic history contributions. In turn, RDDs in economics were developed, and popularized, in articles such as Angrist and Krueger (1991), Angrist and Lavy (1999), Imbens and Lemieux (2008), and Lee and Lemieux (2010). These modern econometric methods were later incorporated into the standard economics toolkit, of any Economics PhD program, with books such as Angrist and Pischke (2008).

Economic history had also lived a revolution of its own, before the arrival of IVs and RDDs, through the advent of Cliometrics. Though a proper survey of this phenomenon is beyond the scope of this chapter (see Margo, 2021, in this book), the usage of historical data and quantitative methods for decades,

[☆] I thank the editors, Alberto Bisin and Giovanni Federico for their comments and encouragement, Giovanni Federico for kindly sharing his data, participants at the 2019 book conference at NYU, Ellora Derenoncourt, Juliana Jaramillo, and Nathan Nunn for comments, and Fernando Secco for impeccable research assistance. The usual disclaimer applies.

paved the field for the usage of ever more sophisticated econometric techniques. The data requirements for properly computing regression discontinuities non-parametrically, for instance, remains large. Already by 2010, Diamond and Robinson argued for the usage of "Natural Experiments" from history for causal identification. Perhaps a final push in economic history came from what was termed "Historical Development" by Nunn (2014). In a pair of surveys, Nunn (2009, 2014) stressed the importance of history for the better understanding of economic development. Nunn not only captured the state of the art in this literature, but coalesced the existing articles into a new sub-discipline. In his surveys, Nunn emphasizes the particular role of causal identification in the recent wave of economic history papers. This approach provides an important counterpoint to the Randomized Control Trial (RCT) revolution that reshaped economic development, and was recognized with the 2019 Nobel Prize in Economics. The quest for the "deep roots" of comparative economic development were later summarized by Spolaore and Wacziarg (2013), Michalopoulos and Papaioannou (2017), and Nunn (2020). This book offers a new synthesis of knowledge, of a rapidly evolving field.

As opposed to the comprehensive articles just mentioned, the chapter at hand is meant to be more illustrative in terms of econometric methodologies—focusing on IV and RDD methods. To this end the rest of the article is organized as follows. In the next section, I discuss the problem of econometric identification, as it relates to economic history. Next, I review some of the main trends in the economic history literature in terms of econometric methods. I then describe individual papers, and how they tackled key identification challenges, dividing them between the pioneering studies and a more recent "second wave" of papers. More technical sections discuss recent refinements in the IV and RDD camps, with the idea of providing some potentially useful tools and practical guide for researchers in the field. I offer some concluding thoughts along with potential avenues for future research.

7.2 Identification in economic history

Identification plays a special role in modern economic history. Many studies, especially those related to historical persistence (surveyed by Voth, 2021, in this book), are aided by the arrow of time. It is essentially impossible to have reverse causality, from an event occurring in the future to an event that happened in the past. This is not to say, that there could still be *other* econometric threats to identification, such as measurement error and omitted variable bias. The first could be especially relevant for historical studies, where data can be spotty, inaccurate, and in many cases, simply missing. Omitted variables, in turn, might be correlated with a given historical determinant, that can still drive modern outcomes today. These can include geographic and weather characteristics, as well as other historical episodes, including events that occurred in the periods between the main historical event of interest and the current time. This "compression of history" is perhaps the main criticism of persistence papers, coming from the economic history field (Austin, 2008). To be fair, economists and economic historians are well aware of many of these issues and are now rather trying to better understand when persistence occurs, and why (see, for instance, Giuliano and Nunn, 2020).

Identification issues have been tackled in various ways in the recent literature. Historical variation can be simply taken as given, as the persistence of a given trait is established. Notably, this has been shown for cultural traits such as trust (described later) and antisemitism in Germany, from medieval to Nazi times (Voigtländer and Voth, 2012); but also in documenting the persistence of human populations from ancient to modern times (Davis and Weinstein, 2002; Chanda et al., 2014; Maloney and Valencia

Caicedo, 2016). In other cases, researchers have studied "Natural Experiments" from history for identification. Diamond and Robinson (2010) provide a pioneering summary of this approach, and Cantoni and Yuchtman (2021) survey the more recent contributions to this agenda in this book. Though the specific policies and events are diverse, the European colonization of vast swaths of land, often provides a plethora of natural experiments in terms of legal and political regimes, labor arrangements, religious, military, and medical campaigns (see Nunn, 2020).

Lastly, economic historians have recurred to standard econometric tools, such as Instrumental Variables and Regression Discontinuity Designs for identification—which is the focus of this chapter. I make here the distinction between IVs and RDDs for organization purposes, as econometrically fuzzy RD is equivalent to IV estimation. For IVs the main identification assumptions are relevance (strong first stage), excludability (the effect is working through the regressor of interest only), and monotonicity (compliers move in the "right" direction). Though the first one is relatively easy to test, the other two are less so, with some technical exceptions (Huber and Mellace, 2015; Kitagawa, 2015). For RDDs, the precise assumptions differ between fuzzy and sharp designs, but essentially the discontinuity in the running variable should be accompanied by smooth covariates (not "jumping" at the given threshold). There should not be any bunching at the threshold either, which I discuss further later. Under these assumptions, these methods allow for the recovery of a Local Average Treatment Effect (LATE). So even under this ideal scenario, IVs and RDDs do *not* recover an Average Treatment Effect (ATE). This is an important limitation, not only in terms of inference, but also interpretation (see, for instance the critiques by Heckman, 1999 and Deaton, 2010). IVs and RDDs are by no means the only available econometric techniques available to researchers in the field, which also include differences-in-differences, placebos, randomized controlled experiments, and propensity score matching. Still, as this chapter shows, the progress made with IVs and RDs has been substantial, leading to important insights, and holds promise for the other methods as well.

7.3 General trends: 2000-2020

In order to see the evolution of IV and RD papers in economic history, I use three different empirical vantage points. The first is a dataset containing all the articles in this discipline in top 20 general economic journals, none of which include economic history journals. The second one looks at articles in the top five economic history journals, employing "advanced econometric methods", as compiled by Cioni et al. (2020). The third one looks at articles published in economic history, using IV and RDDs, in the top five economics general interest journals. All of these datasets take into account approximately the last 20 years of research production, starting in 2000.

A first way to see the evolution of Instrumental Variables and Regression Discontinuity papers in economic history is presented in Fig. 7.1. The figure plots the number of papers in this field in top twenty general interest journals (according to Ideas) employing these techniques from 2000 to 2018.[1]

---

[1] These are, ranked, the *Quarterly Journal of Economics, Journal of Political Economy, American Economic Review, Econometrica, Journal of Economic Literature, Journal of Financial Economics, Review of Economic Studies, Journal of Finance, Journal of Monetary Economics, Journal of Economic Growth, Journal of Economic Perspectives, Review of Financial Studies, Journal of Econometrics, Review of Economic and Statistics, Journal of Labor Economics, AEJ: Macroeconomics, Journal*

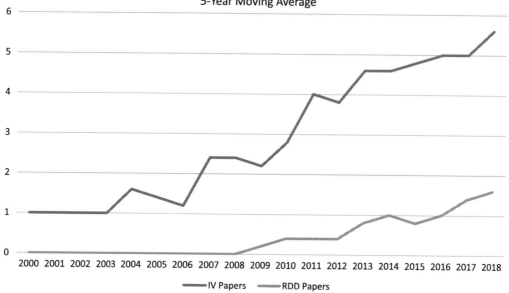

FIGURE 7.1

The figure depicts the evolution of the number of IV (blue [dark gray in print version]) and RD (orange [gray in print version]) papers in top 20 economic journals, according to Ideas from 2000 to 2018. The trends are smoothed using five year moving averages. Own calculations.

A five-year moving average is used to smooth the data.[2] We can see some of the first papers in the discipline employing Instrumental Variables appearing at the beginning of year 2000 and how this number increases to more than five papers a year in 2018 (blue [dark gray in print version] line). The evolution of Regression Discontinuity papers (orange [gray in print version] line) in economic history starts almost a decade later, around 2008. It reaches two papers per year at the end of the sample period. By 2018, there are on average ten IV and RD economic history papers (the actual number is 11) published in the discipline's top twenty most prestigious journals. In total, there are almost a hundred such economic history papers published in these top outlets during the last two decades. The positive trend mimics that documented by Abramitzky (2015), of economic history papers increasingly addressing causal questions.

Fig. 7.2A provides another way to see a similar pattern to the one just shown. Now the figure plots the number of papers in the top five field journals in economic history employing "advanced econo-

---

of International Economics, Economic Journal, Journal of Public Economics, Brookings Papers on Economic Activity. Own calculations.

[2] Technically, the sample starts earlier, to be able to calculate the moving average. But given the practical absence of articles before the 2000s, the results remain virtually unchanged. Using a three-year moving average instead, leaves the results almost unchanged, not shown.

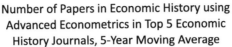

Number of Papers in Economic History using
Advanced Econometrics in Top 5 Economic
History Journals, 5-Year Moving Average

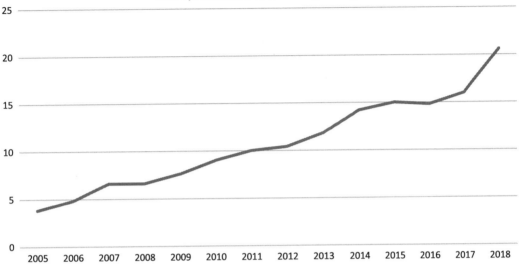

FIGURE 7.2A

The figure depicts the evolution of the number of papers using advanced econometrics in top five economic history journals from 2000 to 2018. The trends are smoothed using five year moving averages. Own calculations, based on see Cioni et al. (2020), see their article for details.

metrics". The top five journals are the *Economic History Review*, the *Journal of Economic History*, *Explorations in Economic History*, the *European Review of Economic History*, and *Cliometrica*. This allows us to see the evolution of econometric techniques from within the field, covering the period from 2001-2018. In this case the definition of "advanced econometrics" is more ample and now also includes differences in differences, panel regression, propensity score matching, vector auto regression, and vector error correction models.[3] As before, we use a five-year moving average to smooth the data (a three-year moving average leaves the results unchanged). Despite the broader definition, the pattern remains clear, the number of papers in economic history using more sophisticated econometric techniques goes from almost zero (literally zero in 2002) at the beginning of the 2000s to more than twenty papers a year, almost twenty years later. Cioni et al. (2020) note that the first paper with Instrumental Variables in their data was Newell (1973). The higher number of papers, might be due to the fact that now other techniques are included, as well as the potentially larger number of papers published in these field specific journals.[4] To correct for this possibility, Fig. 7.2B plots the percentage of papers

---

[3] I thank Giovanni Federico from making available this data. The definition was not disaggregated further in this case. Please see Cioni et al. (2020) for more details on this data.

[4] For comparison, about 100 articles are published per year in these five journals, whereas, the average number of articles in economic history in the top five general interest journal described next was slightly below twenty.

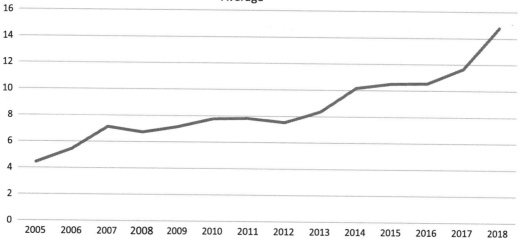

FIGURE 7.2B

The figure depicts the evolution of the percentage of papers using advanced econometrics in top five economic history journals, over the total number of papers in these journals. The trends are smoothed using five year moving averages. Own calculations, based on see Cioni et al. (2020), see their article for details.

in economic history using advanced econometrics over the total number of papers in economic history journals. This rate goes from 0% at the beginning of the 2000s to almost a sixth by 2018. The number is much higher, reaching 40%, when looking at the sub-set of papers using Econometrics (Appendix Fig. A.1). Altogether, the recent upward trajectory of articles employing advanced econometrics is also clear from using this alternative dataset.

One last way of seeing the evolution of IV and RDD papers in economic history is by looking at publications in the "top five" economic journals in Economics. These are the *Quarterly Journal of Economics*, the *Journal of Political Economy*, the *American Economic Review*, *Econometrica*, and the *Review of Economic Studies*. Abramitzky (2015) already documented a positive trend of economic history publications in these journals. Articles are selected here if they report using one of the *Journal of Economic Literature* codes for economic history (category N). The sample is further restricted to papers that include the words or expressions "instrumental variables", "instrument" or "2SLS" for this econometric technique. For regression discontinuity, this same word is used, along with "discontinuity", "discontinuities", or "RDD" at least once. Finally, we manually checked the context in which the words were used, differentiating between a mention in passing of such words, for instance referring to another article, or the actual usage of these estimation methods for identification.[5] Only the latter

---

[5] I gratefully acknowledge the work of Fernando Secco in constructing this dataset. Papers are technically until 2019, as 2020 and forthcoming papers are not yet included in EconLit.

were kept in the final dataset and are presented in Tables 7.1 and 7.2. Papers that used IVs mainly for robustness are presented in the Appendix (Table A.1). This might be an indication that the endogeneity problem was not that severe in those cases. Interestingly, there are no papers that employ RDDs only for robustness. Overall, there are almost fifty papers employing Instrumental Variables for identification in Table 7.1 and around one fifth of that number using Regression Discontinuity. Only very few papers employ both techniques. Though these tables serve as primary reference to IV/RDD studies in economic history, I describe specific studies in more detail next.

7.4 **First generation studies: 2001-2011**

Some of the first articles to use Instrumental Variables from history in economics were the seminal institutional pieces of Acemoglu et al. (2001, 2002).[6] To better understand the importance of these articles and how they coalesced existing knowledge in various fields of economics, see Cantoni and Yuchtman (2021, in this book). The main identification concern in this set up is that institutions could be endogenous to income, as famously argued by Lipset (1959). To get around this challenge, the authors instrument institutions using a measure of settler mortality in former colonies. The idea is that European colonizers established different institutions depending on their likelihood of survival in various places. Colonies with worse disease endowments led to the establishment of more extractive institutions, while those with better endowments led to settler colonies with more favorable regimes, as argued by Engerman and Sokoloff (1997). Acemoglu, Johnson, and Robinson document a robust negative first stage in the relationship between the logarithm of settler mortality and average expropriation risk from 1985 to 1995. In the second stage, they find a large (causal) impact of this institutional measure on GDP per capita in 1995. These influential set of articles helped put institutions at the center stage of economics, and also gave a boost to the economic history field.

As is often the case with major intellectual contributions, Acemoglu et al. (2001, 2002) have also received scholarly attention scrutinizing some of their findings. I discuss here some of the main criticisms and threats to identification, as they related to identification in an IV context. An obvious confounder is the direct impact of geography through the disease environment on income (see Gallup and Sachs, 2001; Sachs and Malaney, 2002). Aware of this potential issue, Acemoglu et al. (2001) show that their estimates are robust to controlling for malaria prevalence and various indicators of health. In a comment, Albouy (2012) questions the validity of the settler mortality data, raising issues of interpolation and, potentially, selection. Acemoglu et al. (2012) provide their own response to these criticisms and restate the robustness of their results. Glaeser et al. (2004) employ the same settler mortality instrument for their preferred measure of human capital (years of schooling). Beyond econometrics, their point is that it is hard to disentangle whether the effect of colonizers is working through institutions or education: what they brought with themselves. Easterly and Levine (2016) look instead at the direct impact of European settlement on development, expanding on the settler mortality variable. They find a finding a positive relationship between early European settlements and subsequent growth. It is fair to conclude that settler mortality is by now one of the most famous—and hotly contested instruments—employed in economic history.

---

[6] For an earlier example of instrumental variables not coming from history, to study global differences in productivity, see Hall and Jones (1997).

Table 7.1 Papers in top five economics journals in economic history, using Instrumental Variables as the main identification method from 2000 to 2020.

	Title	Author	Journal	Year	Explanation
1	The Colonial Origins of Comparative Development: An Empirical Investigation	Acemoglu, Daron; Johnson, Simon; Robinson, James A.	AER	2001	Modern institutions instrumented with colonial settler mortality
2	Endogenous Matching and the Empirical Determinants of Contract Form	Ackerberg, Daniel A.; Botticini, Maristella	JPE	2002	Crop choice instrumented by tenant's wealth and town dummies
3	How Do Sex Ratios Affect Marriage and Labor Markets? Evidence from America's Second Generation	Angrist, Josh	QJE	2002	Sex ratio in labor market instrumented by number of immigrants
4	Reversal of Fortune: Geography and Institutions in the Making of the Modern World Income Distribution	Acemoglu, Daron; Johnson, Simon; Robinson, James A.	QJE	2002	Population in 1500 instrumented by the population in 1000 and modern institutions instrumented with colonial settler mortality
5	Bones, Bombs, and Break Points: The Geography of Economic Activity	Davis, Donald R.; Weinstein, David E.	AER	2002	Population growth rate from 1940-47 instrumented by number of deaths and number of buildings destroyed per capita
6	Consequences of Bank Distress during the Great Depression	Calomiris, Charles W.; Mason, Joseph R.	AER	2003	Loan supply instrumented by bank size, real estate owned relative to loans and bank net worth relative to total assets
7	Radio's Impact on Public Spending	Stromberg, David	QJE	2004	Access to radio instrumented by geological features that affect the quality of radio reception
8	Women, War, and Wages: The Effect of Female Labor Supply on the Wage Structure at Midcentury	Acemoglu, Daron; Autor, David H.; Lyle, David	JPE	2004	Female labor supply instrumented by military mobilization rates in WWII
9	Does Local Financial Development Matter?	Guiso, Luigi; Sapienza, Paola; Zingales, Luigi	QJE	2004	Financial development instrumented by local banking structure in 1936
10[a]	The Relationship between Education and Adult Mortality in the United States	Lleras-Muney, Adriana	RESTUD	2005	Years of education instrumented by compulsory education laws
11	The Great Leap Forward: Anatomy of a Central Planning Disaster	Li, Wei; Yang, Dennis Tao	JPE	2005	Retained grain per capita instrumented by weather characteristics
12	History, Institutions, and Economic Performance: The Legacy of Colonial Land Tenure Systems in India	Banerjee, Abhijit; Iyer, Lakshmi	AER	2005	Proportion of non-landlord districts instrumented by British conquest between 1820-56

continued on next page

Table 7.1 (*continued*)

	Title	Author	Journal	Year	Explanation
13	Child Labor and the Labor Supply of Other Household Members: Evidence from 1920 America	Manacorda, Marco	AER	2006	Child labor instrumented by child labor laws
14	Did Highways Cause Suburbanization?	Baum-Snow, Nathaniel	QJE	2007	Number of roads built instrumented by number of roads planned in the 1947 national interstate highway
15	The Long-Term Effects of Africa's Slave Trades	Nunn, Nathan	QJE	2008	Number of slaves instrumented by the distance between the country of origin and their destination port
16	Inequality in Landownership, the Emergence of Human-Capital Promoting Institutions, and the Great Divergence	Galor, Oded; Moav, Omer; Vollrath, Dietrich	RESTUD	2009	Land share of large land owners instrumented by state-specific climatic conditions interacted with changes in the price of cotton relative to the price of corn
17	Branch Banking as a Device for Discipline: Competition and Bank Survivorship during the Great Depression	Carlson, Mark; Mitchener, Kris James	JPE	2009	Introduction of a bank branch in a city instrumented by its population in 1922, dummy indicating if the city is in the North and population in the county in 1910
18	Was Weber Wrong? A Human Capital Theory of Protestant Economic History	Becker, Sascha O.; Woessmann, Ludger	QJE	2009	County's share of Protestants instrumented by distance to Wittenberg
19	Asymmetric Information and Adverse Selection in Mauritian Slave Auctions	Dionne, Georges; St-Amour, Pascal; Vencatachellum, Desire	RESTUD	2009	Seller and buyer dummy instrumented by number of Heirs
20	Harvests and Business Cycles in Nineteenth-Century America	Davis, Joseph H.; Hanes, Christopher; Rhode, Paul W.	QJE	2009	Cotton, wheat and corn harvest instrumented by precipitation and temperature
21	Quality Matters: The Expulsion of Professors and the Consequences for PhD Student Outcomes in Nazi Germany	Waldinger, Fabian	JPE	2010	Average faculty quality and student faculty ratio instrumented by the dismissal of faculty
22	Dynamics and Stagnation in the Malthusian Epoch	Ashraf, Quamrul; Galor, Oded	AER	2011	Number of years since the Neolithic Revolution instrumented by number of prehistoric domesticable species of plants and animals
23	Information Technology and Economic Change: The Impact of the Printing Press	Dittmar, Jeremiah E.	QJE	2011	Adoption of the printing press instrumented by distance to Mainz

continued on next page

Table 7.1 (*continued*)

	Title	Author	Journal	Year	Explanation
24	The Slave Trade and the Origins of Mistrust in Africa	Nunn, Nathan; Wantchekon, Leonard	AER	2011	Number of slaves instrumented by the distance between the country of origin and their destination port
25	The Consequences of Radical Reform: The French Revolution	Acemoglu, Daron; Cantoni, Davide; Johnson, Simon; Robinson, James A.	AER	2011	Institutions instrumented by number of years of French presence
26	Compulsory Licensing: Evidence from the Trading with the Enemy Act	Moser, Petra; Voena, Alessandra	AER	2012	Number of licensed patents in the US instrumented by number of patents from the enemies in WWI
27	Forced Coexistence and Economic Development: Evidence from Native American Reservations	Dippel, Christian	ECON	2014	More centralized reservations instrumented by historical mining rushes
28	Peer Effects in Science: Evidence from the Dismissal of Scientists in Nazi Germany	Waldinger, Fabian	RESTUD	2012	Average peer quality and number of peers instrumented by the dismissal of scientists
29	Urban Growth and Transportation	Duranton, Gilles; Turner, Matthew A.	RESTUD	2012	Number of highways in 1983 instrumented by number of 1947 planned interstate highway kilometers, 1898 kilometers of railroads and an index of 1528-1850 exploration routes
30	The 'Out of Africa' Hypothesis, Human Genetic Diversity, and Comparative Economic Development	Ashraf, Quamrul; Galor, Oded	AER	2013	Genetic diversity instrumented by migratory distance from East Africa
31	On the Origins of Gender Roles: Women and the Plough	Alesina, Alberto; Giuliano, Paola; Nunn, Nathan	QJE	2013	Historical plough use instrumented by geoclimatic conditions
32	How the West 'Invented' Fertility Restriction	Voigtlander, Nico; Voth, Hans-Joachim	AER	2013	Percentage of land use for pastore in 1290 instrumented by number of days during which grass can grow
33	Immigration and the Diffusion of Technology: The Huguenot Diaspora in Prussia	Hornung, Erik	AER	2014	Share of Huguenots in a city instrumented by population loss in the Thirty year war
34	Local Economic Development, Agglomeration Economies, and the Big Push: 100 Years of Evidence from the Tennessee Valley Authority	Kline, Patrick; Moretti, Enrico	QJE	2014	Manufacturing wages instrumented by Changes in the spline components of manufacturing density lagged by two decades

continued on next page

Table 7.1 (*continued*)

	Title	Author	Journal	Year	Explanation
35	Valuing the Vote: The Redistribution of Voting Rights and State Funds following the Voting Rights Act of 1965	Cascio, Elizabeth U.; Washington, Ebonya	QJE	2014	Presidential turnout growth instrumented by interaction between having a literacy test and percent of black people in the population
36	German Jewish Emigres and US Invention	Moser, Petra; Voena, Alessandra; Waldinger, Fabian	AER	2014	Number of emigree patents between 1920-1970 instrumented by pre-1933 patents of dismissed scientists
37	The Impact of the Great Migration on Mortality of African Americans: Evidence from the Deep South	Black, Dan A.; Sanders, Seth G.; Taylor, Evan J.; Taylor, Lowell J.	AER	2015	Migration to urban areas instrumented by distance from the birthplace to railroad lines
38	Democratization under the Threat of Revolution: Evidence from the Great Reform Act of 1832	Aidt, Toke S.; Franck, Raphael	ECON	2015	Number of riots in a constituency instrumented by travel time distance to Sevenoaks (initial place of riots)
39	Financial Asset Holdings and Political Attitudes: Evidence from Revolutionary England	Jha, Saumitra	QJE	2015	Overseas joint investor instrumented by having 21 years in an IPO year
40	Radio and the Rise of the Nazis in Prewar Germany	Adena, Maja; Enikolopov, Ruben; Petrova, Maria; Santarosa, Veronica; Zhuravskaya, Ekaterina	QJE	2015	Change in radio subscription instrumented by change in the signal strength
41	Elite Recruitment and Political Stability: The Impact of the Abolition of China's Civil Service Exam	Bai, Ying; Jia, Ruixue	ECMTA	2016	Quota for public service instrumented by number of rivers in the region and the change in the exam before the quotas being installed
42	Railroads and American Economic Growth: A 'Market Access' Approach	Donaldson, Dave; Hornbeck, Richard	QJE	2016	Changes in the market access instrumented by water market access
43	Investment Banks as Corporate Monitors in the Early Twentieth Century United States	Frydman, Carola; Hilt, Eric	AER	2017	Intensity of bank firm relationship in 1920 instrumented by intensity of bank firm relationship in 1913
44	The Wind of Change: Maritime Technology, Trade, and Economic Development	Pascali, Luigi	AER	2017	Exports instrumented by geographic isolation of a country, calculating using shipping distances and wind patterns
45	The Economic Effects of the Abolition of Serfdom: Evidence from the Russian Empire	Markevich, Andrei; Zhuravskaya, Ekaterina	AER	2018	Share of serfs instrumented by share of monasterial serfs and land reform implementation instrumented by gentry's level of debt

continued on next page

Table 7.1 (*continued*)

	Title	Author	Journal	Year	Explanation
46	Temporary Protection and Technology Adoption: Evidence from the Napoleonic Blockade	Juhasz, Reka	AER	2018	Location of cotton industry Napoleonic blockade trade cost shock
47	Migrants, Ancestors, and Foreign Investments	Burchardi, Konrad B., Chaney, Thomas; Hassan, Tarek A.	RESTUD	2019	Present day ancestry composition instrumented by historical migratory waves
48	Religion, Division of Labor, and Conflict: Anti-semitism in Germany over 600 Years	Becker, Sascha O.; Pascali, Luigi	AER	2019	Jewish lending activity instrumented by city's specialization in trade industries and share of Protestants instrumented by distance to Wittenberg
49	Exit, Voice, and Political Change: Evidence from Swedish Mass Migration to the United States	Karadja, Mounir; Prawitz, Erik	JPE	2019	Immigration from Sweden to the US instrumented by interaction term between frost shocks and distance to emigration ports

[a] *Paper 10 is an IV/RD paper.*

Table 7.2 Papers in top five economics journals in economic history, using Regression Discontinuity Designs as the main identification method from 2000 to 2019.

	Title	Author	Journal	Year	Explanation
1	The Persistent Effects of Peru's Mining Mita	Dell, Melissa	ECMTA	2010	Spatial discontinuity comparing places with and without mita
2	Pre-colonial Ethnic Institutions and Contemporary African Development	Michalopoulos, Stelios; Papaioannou, Elias	ECMTA	2013	Spatial discontinuity comparing places inside and outside ethnic boundaries
3	National Institutions and Subnational Development in Africa	Michalopoulos, Stelios; Papaioannou, Elias	QJE	2014	Spatial discontinuities from national borders of African countries
4	Democracy, Redistribution, and Political Participation: Evidence from Sweden 1919-1938	Hinnerich, Bjorn Tyrefors; Pettersson-Lidbom, Per	ECMTA	2014	Population threshold for political representation
5	The Long-Run Effects of the Scramble for Africa	Michalopoulos, Stelios; Papaioannou, Elias	AER	2016	Spatial discontinuities from national borders of African countries
6	The Evolution of Culture and Institutions: Evidence from the Kuba Kingdom	Lowes, Sara; Nunn, Nathan; Robinson, James A.; Weigel, Jonathan L.	ECMTA	2017	Spatial discontinuity comparing places inside and outside Kuba Kingdom
7[a]	Nation Building through Foreign Intervention: Evidence from Discontinuities in Military Strategies	Dell, Melissa; Querubin, Pablo	QJE	2018	Uses discontinuities in military strategies
8	The Historical State, Local Collective Action, and Economic Development in Vietnam	Dell, Melissa; Lane, Nathan; Querubin, Pablo	ECMTA	2018	Spatial discontinuity comparing places inside and outside Dai Viet areas

[a] *Paper 7 is an RD/IV paper.*

Guiso et al. (2016) constitutes a seminal piece in the cultural economics literature.[7] In it the authors take Robert Putnam seriously and investigate whether social capital can be a driver of economic performance. The key idea is that self-governing cities, mostly in the North of Italy, perform better institutionally and economically because of their underlying social fabric. To instrumentalize this notion, the authors collect data on non-profit organizations, organ donations and cheating in math exams. They find that areas within Italy that have been independent for longer have higher social capital and are more financially developed (see also, Guiso et al., 2004). Because the first variable might be endogenous, the authors instrument it with Bishoprics and the presence of Etruscan settlements. The findings for Italy have been extended for regions in Europe (Tabellini, 2010) and across the globe. For instance, Algan and Cahuc (2010), use the inherited trust of migrants to the US to conclude that trust *causes* growth. Guiso et al. (2016) not only vigorously advocated for the importance of culture for economic performance, but also helped initiate the long-term persistence literature.

In another important institutional paper, Banerjee and Iyer (2005) exploit historical variation from colonial India. In their analysis they look at the legacy of historical land tenure patterns, differentiating between landlords and cultivators. In particular, they compare areas, within the country, where the British took over tax collection from 1820 to 1856. These areas resulted in higher prevalence of non-landlord systems. They find that such systems led to higher agricultural investment and productivity. They also find that landlord areas have lower health and education levels today. In a similar vein, Iyer (2010) looks at the long-term impact of direct versus indirect colonial rule in India. She finds that territories that experienced direct rule during colonial times have lower access to schools, health facilities and public roads in modern times.[8] These papers provide concrete within country evidence about the role of European colonialism in Asia, complementing previous cross-country studies.

Focusing on Latin America, in a landmark study, Dell (2010) looked at the long-term impact of the *mita* colonial labor system in Peru and Bolivia. This mining tribute system, existed in the Andean region from 1573 to 1812. The author exploits econometrically the specific boundaries of the *mita* catchment area. To this end, Dell employs a geographic Regression Discontinuity Design, the first of its kind in economics. Hence this paper was an important contribution not only in economic history and the institutional economics literature, but also methodologically. Employing this new econometric technique, on household surveys, Dell finds that the *mita* significantly reduced consumption and increased stunting in modern times. In terms of mechanisms, she looks at land tenure (*haciendas*), public good provision and sectoral composition. It is surprising that the effects persisted, even though the *mita* as an institution has been long abolished. As will be discussed later, this initial geographic RDD has been refined econometrically in different ways.

In turn, Nunn (2008) and Nunn and Wantchekon (2011) empirically test whether Africa's regional development patterns could be partly explained by transatlantic slavery. The authors use shipping records and match them to the original ethnicities of slaves, using Murdock's 1959 map.[9] As instruments for shipments, they use distance to the coast and sailing distances to the nearest slave ports. Nunn (2008) finds that indeed, countries where more slaves were taken from are significantly poorer

---

[7] I include this article in the first wave, since even though it was published in 2016, the widely circulated and cited working paper version is from 2008. Guiso et al. (2008).

[8] In another famous piece, Jha (2013) looks at how trade and institutions related to ethnic tolerance in India.

[9] Digitizing this map was an important contribution in it of itself, which has led to many articles in economics, some of them summarized later in this chapter.

today. In terms of mechanisms, Nunn and Wantchekon (2011) find that this is mainly due to decreased trust. For this they use geo-located individual level data from the Afrobarometer. In terms of transmission channels, they stress cultural norms, beliefs and values. These influential papers helped cement the importance of economic history for explaining current (under) development, as well as the usage of standard econometric techniques in the economic history field.

In the culture and religion realms, Becker and Woessmann's (2009) testing of Max Weber's hypothesis represented a watershed in the usage of instrumental variables in economic history. A key question in this paper is whether Protestant areas do better economically than Catholic ones. To answer it, the authors focus on Prussia and use data from the 1871 census. The key problem here is that religion could be endogenously chosen, so regressing Protestantism directly on income could lead to biased estimates. To solve this problem, they use the concentric spread of Protestantism, emanating out of Wittenberg, where Martin Luther posted his famous 95 theses in 1517. Using this instrument, the authors find a causal, positive impact of Protestantism on proxies for income in 1871. Furthermore, in a 3SLS framework the authors find that literacy is the main channel of transmission of the religion to income effect.[10] Meaning that Protestant areas are indeed richer, but that this is due to the fact that they invested heavily in education, in accordance to the new religious doctrines. In the paper, the authors explore the exogeneity of the instrument and provide some bounds for their baseline estimates. Econometrically, Becker and Woessmann (2009) helped propel the usage of distance-based instruments in economic history.[11]

In a similar econometric vein, Dittmar (2011) quantified the economic impact of the printing press, one of the most important technological innovations in history. As before, the main challenge in terms of identification is that the adoption of new media could be endogenous to economic growth, responding to demand and not just supply considerations. To get around this issue, the author exploits the fast spread of the printing technology, originating from Johannes Gutemberg's workshop in Mainz, in 1440. Using distance to Mainz, as an instrument for the adoption of printing, Dittmar finds a positive and sizable effect on subsequent population growth of European cities. Importantly, this effect is not present from 1450 to 1500, but kicks off after this later year. Relating his findings to Becker and Woessmann's (2009) piece, Dittmar (2011) finds no effect of distance to Wittenberg on the adoption of the printing press. Following this line of argument in the opposite direction—and using distance to Mainz as an instrument—Rubin (2014) finds a positive impact of the printing press on the spread of Protestantism.

Lastly, Ashraf and Galor (2013) advance and empirically test the hypothesis that genetic diversity is a pillar of comparative economic development. The problem with this genetic measure is that it could be endogenous to income, due, for instance, to historical waves of migration. To get around this problem, they look at the first wave of migration in human history, that of Homo sapiens out of Africa. Due to a serial founder effect, the farther away a human population is from Addis Ababa, Ethiopia (the cradle of humankind) the lower its genetic diversity. Using this first stage, the authors are able to predict levels of genetic diversity for countries where ancestral population genetic data is not available. Employing this instrument they find a hump-shaped relationship with income, reflecting how low levels of genetic diversity are bad for innovation, while high levels can foster conflict (Arbatlı et al., 2020 expand on this second dimension). The optimal level of diversity, according to the authors,

---

[10] To the best of my knowledge, this is one of the only papers to employ 3SLS in the economic history literature. For an alternative view of the Weberian effect see Cantoni (2015) and for the cultural channel, Spenkuch (2017).

[11] For a more recent application, see Becker and Pascali (2019).

corresponds to that of Japan in 1500 AD and the United States in 2000, adjusting for later waves of migration (following Putterman and Weil, 2010 and Ashraf et al., 2021, this book). This important—and provocative—article put genetics in the center stage of the debate on the "deep rooted" causes of growth. As other articles covered in this section, it was a seminal piece in the genetics and economics field, just as other contributions covered in this section helped to jumpstart the economic literatures on institutions, culture, religion, human capital, and technology.

7.5 A second wave: 2012-2020

A "second wave" of papers in economic history appeared during the second decade of the twenty first century, employing ever more sophisticated econometric techniques. I showcase here some emblematic examples, which are meant to be more illustrative in capturing the zeitgeist. Though still employing Instrumental Variables and Regression Discontinuity Designs, the papers covered next enhanced these methods, alleviating concerns of excludability and identification more generally. Recall that it is precisely during this time period that we saw an acceleration in the publication of economic history papers in some of the top economics journals (a trend echoed in Margo, 2018 and Abramitzky, 2015).

A good illustration of the second generation papers is the series of articles by Michalopoulos and Papaioannou (2013, 2014, 2016). Though they look at different outcomes separately, the key identification strategy holds across the three studies. Historically, they exploit the haphazard redrawing of African national boundaries, resulting from the scramble for Africa. When European representatives met during the 1884-1885 Berlin conference, they established new borders for Africa that obeyed more their own colonial interests that the traditional pre-colonial ethnic boundaries, which had been developed for centuries. Econometrically, this leads to a two-way partition of space: one coming from the ethnic homelands mapped by Murdock and another from the newly drawn national boundaries for Africa. The authors argue that this second partition is "exogenous" and could have had long-term consequences. Using a Regression Discontinuity Design, they find three important results. First, *precolonial* ethnic homelands are important predictors of contemporary economic development, as proxied by nightlights (Michalopoulos and Papaioannou, 2013). Second, *national* borders or institutions are less important predictors of economic prosperity in the African continent (Michalopoulos and Papaioannou, 2014). And, third, partitioned ethnicities resulted in higher levels of conflict later on (Michalopoulos and Papaioannou, 2016). These three papers all employ an RDD to establish causality. To the best of my knowledge, no other paper has yet exploited such a two way partition of space in economic history.

On the IV front, Alsan (2015) studies the impact of the TseTse fly on African development. It has long been hypothesized that this disease could be another cause for African underdevelopment, but no one had empirically tested this claim. Again, the problem is that the TseTse fly could be endogenous to other correlates of income, such as weather characteristics. To instrument for the presence of this insect, Alsan develops her own suitability index, using models from entomology. This novel approach follows a well-established literature of using other types of suitabilities as instruments, reviewed in the next subsection.[12] She finds that the fly, which affects animals more than people, results in lower usage of animal husbandry. Moreover, this led to less precolonial political centralization, an important institutional variable, following the studies reviewed above.

In the political economy arena, Adena et al. (2015) look at the role of the media in supporting democratic institutions. The authors focus on Weimar Germany during the 1920s and 1930s. They use the radio, which was a key mass media technology at the time. Because access to this technology is potentially endogenous, they use as instrument radio signal strength (following Strömberg, 2004). With this instrument, they find that the effect is positive during the democratic period, but that when the Nazis came to power, the same communication technology was used as propaganda. A similar identification strategy has been used by Gagliarducci et al. (2020) during WWII in Italy with BBC radio. This identification strategy, using radio signals, has also been used in other contexts—in political economy and the economics of mass media.

In the conflict space, Dell and Querubin (2018) examine the impact of bombing and counterinsurgency operations in Vietnam. Since bombing is a strategic (and costly) choice, they use two different identification strategies to estimate its causal effect. In particular, they use rounding thresholds in the algorithm used to target air strikes. This is almost an ideal instrument in terms of exogeneity and excludability. Moreover, they exploit a spatial discontinuity design on the types of American counterinsurgency operations: predominantly firepower versus "hearts and minds". Armed with these tools, they find that bombing increased anti-American sentiment, both politically and militarily. This paper is also novel econometrically, as it employs two different types of identification strategies (IV and geographic RDD) to empirically test their claim.

The historical international trade literature has also experienced a revival in terms of modern econometric techniques. A good example of this is Pascali's (2017) work on the introduction of the steamship during the first wave of trade globalization (1870-1913). What is key in this paper, in terms of identification, is that the new technology reduced transportation costs differentially across the globe. Pascali builds an instrument based on wind patterns to calculate optimal routes.[13] The author finds that the expansion of trade led to *negative* economic outcomes for most countries. Only a few countries with good institutions were able to profit from the trade boom, exacerbating global economic divergence.

Also in the trade field, Juhász (2018) exploits a natural experiment to empirically test the validity of the infant industry argument—whereby governments provide temporary protection to crucial industries. Namely, she analyzes the Napoleonic blockade of 1803-1815. The confrontation with the United Kingdom generated a trade shock to France, effectively providing protection to incipient spinning industries. The author uses this shock as an instrument for the post-blockade location of the cotton industries. She finds that the temporary shock changed the structure of textile production in the long run, providing a tangible case where (unintended) infant industry protection coming from conflict was largely effective.

In a follow up paper, Juhász and Steinwender (2019) focus instead on communication technology and fragmented production chains. The idea is that some products are more easily "codifiable" than others (yarn vs. printed clothes), and hence would benefit differentially from new communication

---

[12] Technically, she reports a reduced form approach, given the lack of historical data on TseTse presence, so we exclude the paper from Table 7.1 and present it in Table A.1 only.

[13] This paper can be seen as a more modern version of Feyrer and Sacerdote (2009), who first employed wind as an instrument for colonization, covered later.

techniques such as the introduction of the telegraph.[14] Since the adoption of this technology is itself endogenous, the authors use submarine ruggedness as an instrument, which is both relevant and presumably excludable. They estimate a Poisson IV model and find that communication improvements enhanced upstream production (of yarn) and increased fragmentation. These last three papers have in common that they combine key historical variation to study important trade questions, aided with modern econometric techniques. Arguably the construction of the different instruments makes these contributions stand out from previous work, to reach at causal evidence on long-standing debates in the literature.

Lastly, in a recent contribution, Becker et al. (2020) examine the link between forced migration and human capital (for a summary of this topic see Becker and Ferrara, 2019). They focus on former Polish territories after World War II, when Poles and Germans were forced to migrate, with the redrawing of national boundaries. In particular, they exploit the borders of the Kresy territories, where Poles were forced to move out due to the Soviet occupation. Migrants resettled in the newly acquired Western Territories, where Germans had been previously expelled. Zooming on the border, and using a spatial RDD, they find that forced migration resulted in one extra year of schooling. These results speak to the portability of human capital investments, and preference towards them, which they test using a household survey. Again, what stands out in this recent paper is not a new method (RDD) as such, but a clean employment of this technique to answer a meaningful economic question, in a historical context.

7.5.1 Classes of instruments

Having covered numerous papers, it might be helpful now to categorize now certain classes of instruments in other notable studies. As in some of the articles previously mentioned, later contributions have used *geographic* instruments such as distance (Naidu and Yuchtman, 2013), proximity to rivers (Bai and Jia, 2016), and the slope of the terrain (Ashraf et al., 2018). Other researchers have focused on *weather* characteristics such as wind (Feyrer and Sacerdote, 2009), rainfall (Dell, 2012), or temperature shocks (Franck and Michalopoulos, 2017). Others have used different types of *suitability*, be it agricultural (Nunn and Qian, 2011; Alesina et al., 2013), or marine (Dalgaard et al., 2015). Some papers have further decomposed these agricultural measures, looking at the interaction with heavy soils (Caprettini and Voth, 2018) or the relative values for different crops (Lowes and Montero, 2018). Chen et al. (2019) use a fully *interactive* instrument, looking at the combination of different forests (bamboo and pines). Following the migration literature, some papers have used Bartik type instruments in historical contexts (most notably, Karadja and Prawitz, 2019; Burchardi et al., 2019; Nunn et al., 2020, and Tabellini, 2020).[15] Others have exploited econometrically variation coming from expulsions and ethnic minorities, as in the case of Waldinger (2010, 2012), Moser et al. (2014), Hornung (2014), and Pascali (2016). Many of these papers are referenced in Table 7.1, along with a short description of the instrument used.

---

[14] Though not exactly an IV or RD paper, this joint contribution follows the earlier article by Steinwender (2018) documenting the drop of the price dispersion between the UK and the US after the advent of the telegraph.

[15] In such studies, measures for larger units (such as state) or historical aggregates are used to predict those for smaller ones (such as counties) or modern times (see Goldsmith-Pinkham et al., 2018 for a survey).

7.5.2 Other regression discontinuity designs

On the regression discontinuity front, scholars have used variation coming from imperial boundaries, battlefronts, pre-colonial boundaries, colonial partitions, and assignment thresholds. Though not exactly an RDD, Becker et al. (2016) exploited imperial boundaries to show that corruption is lower today in areas that were historically controlled by the Habsburgs. More recently, Dell et al. (2018) use divisions between the Dai Viet and the Cambodian Empire within Vietnam, to show the long-term impact of state centralization. In the conflict arena, Fontana et al. (2017) use the Gothic line to look at political extremism in Italy and Tur-Prats and Valencia Caicedo (2019) exploit the Aragon Front to look at voting behavior in Spain. In terms of pre-colonial boundaries, Lowes et al. (2017), study political centralization in the Kuba Kingdom, Lowes (2018) analyzes spousal cooperation in the matrilineal belt, and Moscona et al. (2020) show the roles of clans in conflict. Studying colonial times, Dell and Olken (2020) use a spatial discontinuity design to measure the impact of the Dutch cultivation system in Java, and Lowes and Montero (2018) the negative long-term effect of rubber concessions in the Belgian Congo. More recently, Montero (2018) exploits an acreage threshold in the 1970s Salvadorian land reform to study the impact of cooperative property rights. Several of these papers are still working papers, recent job market papers or forthcoming in general interest journals. Though hard to predict—based on the existing trend—the eventual publication of these pieces would increase the number of RDD papers in economic history in top economics journals, perhaps even relative to IV articles.

7.6 Technical refinements and regression diagnostics
7.6.1 Instrumental variables

Since the time of writing of some of the papers described so far, there have been some technical refinements in the econometrics literature, which provide potentially useful tools for economic history. One example of that is the work on Plausibly Exogenous instruments by Conley et al. (2012). In this paper, the authors depict a tradeoff for instruments between relevance and exogeneity. Given this fact, they then present some bounding corrections for second stage estimates.[16] Since in many cases instruments from history might not be entirely excludable, this could be a useful tool for such studies, though it applies more broadly to other set-ups.

Focusing on functional form, Dieterle and Snell (2016) examine non-linear misspecification in two stage models. They suggest using non-linear first stages, employing emblematic examples from the economic history literature, such as Acemoglu et al. (2001) and Becker and Woessmann (2009), described here. One paper employing this newly suggested method is Riaño and Valencia Caicedo (2020) to instrument for the strategic bombing of Laos. Antoine and Lavergne (2019) suggest using instead a more generalized "Integrated Conditional Moment" for non-linear instruments. Casey and Klemp (2020) propose an econometric IV model, which is precisely geared towards estimating causal effects in the long run—when the outcome of interest is available at different points in time. Using a canonical example from the institutional literature, this correction leads to smaller, but more reliable estimates.

---

[16] Dippel et al. (2017) propose a mediation tool for instrumental variables.

Perhaps one of the most promising, and increasingly popular, method is the usage of LASSO for control variables and instrument selection (Belloni et al., 2014). A recent application of this method is Derenoncourt (2019).[17] In her job market paper, the author analyzes the Great Migration from the US South to Northern American cities during the 1940s. Derenoncourt uses a Bartik-type instrument, as is standard in the migration literature, but crucially improves the prediction of the second stage, using LASSO to select the relevant variables. With this correction, she finds that this massive internal migration wave led to *less* upward mobility in destination counties, especially for black men, potentially via racial segregation and urban decline. This paper is a good example of the forefront of the economic history literature. See also Bisin and Moro (2021, in this book) for a more in-depth discussion of these issues.

7.6.2 Regression discontinuity designs

In the RDD camp a series of technical refinements have also followed the publication of the seminal papers in the literature, see Melly and Lalive (2020) for a recent review. Perhaps the most important advances have been a set of papers on non-parametric RDDs, local randomization and optimal bandwidth selection by Calonico et al. (2014), Cattaneo et al. (2016), and Calonico et al. (2020), respectively. Such non-parametric estimation methods have been used widely in the economics literature and are making inroads into economic history, even in the geographic discontinuity designs, enhancing the original method introduced by Dell (2010). There has also been a discussion about the usage, or not, of polynomials in the parametric framework. Gelman and Imbens (2019), argue that higher-order polynomials should *not* be used in RDDs, contradicting previous practice. Card et al. (2018) further explore the problem of local polynomial order in RDDs.

Barreca et al. (2011), in turn, employ a Donut RDD to address the problem of sorting on thresholds in the context of low birthweight. They then propose a way to go around one of the most common pitfalls in RDDs. In Fujiwara et al. (2020) we use this method to look at the impact of the Tordesillas Treaty between Spain and Portugal, on the prevalence of slavery and modern-day income inequality in Brazil. Our usage of this method arises from the uncertainty arising from the implementation of this landmark treaty on the Portuguese and Spanish colonies in the Americas.

Card et al. (2015) propose a Regression Kink (RK) Design identifying off changes in slopes, even if the running variable has no discontinuities.[18] Though this is by now a fairly standard method in labor economics and public finance, to the best of my knowledge, the only paper in economic history employing this method so far is Milner (2019). In his job market paper, on the 1870 Education Act, Milner employs an RK Design at the 1/6 children population threshold that was used to assign school boards. He finds a significantly positive and statistically significant effect of 13.5% of new schools on high-skilled occupations. This econometric refinement holds promise for economic history, in cases where discontinuities might be less apparent.

---

[17] Maloney and Valencia Caicedo (2017) use instead LASSO for the selection of controls, refining the Land Grant Colleges education instrument for the technical training of engineers.

[18] This framework can also be implemented non-parametrically, with the rdrobust command in Stata. The command also allows for the option of using the alternative "IK" bandwidth selector of Imbens and Kalyanaraman (2012).

7.6.3 Regression diagnostics: a guide to practice

I provide in this section some regression diagnostics, as a practical guide for identification in economic history. This is by no means an authoritative set of instructions, but exemplifies some common identification problems and provides some (potentially) useful solutions. Perhaps the most basic form of identification, comes from controlling for observables. Though usually not the ultimate econometric specification, a basic correlation between the variable of interest with controls, goes a long way in at least knowing where some of the potential biases might emerge from, and provides a good baseline comparison for better identified estimates. In some cases, OLS and IV estimates even change sign! To test more formally whether coefficients are stable when controls are added, one can further use Altonji/Oster ratios (Altonji et al., 2005; Oster, 2019). This is a good way also for testing for the potential role of unobservables in biasing the results. For some notable applications, see Bellows and Miguel (2009) and in economic history, Nunn and Wantchekon (2011). In many cases, fixed effects can soak variation coming from national factors or state level policies (see Maloney and Valencia Caicedo, 2016, 2017). Short of identification, using this estimation method could at least narrow the potential set of confounders by investigating within country or state variation.

If the IV route is taken, one would want to test the validity of the instrument, where the usual rule of thumb is an F-statistic of more than 10 (Stock and Yogo, 2005), though this is now actively debated in the literature. For the actual estimation, 2SLS is often implemented, though LIML could offer some advantages (for jackknife IV estimation, see Angrist et al., 1999). In practice, in many cases the IV estimates end up being larger than OLS estimates. This could happen for many reasons, such as the fact that only LATEs and not ATEs are recovered (Imbens and Angrist, 1994). In other cases, instruments might be weak, which is an active area of study in econometrics (surveyed recently by Andrews et al., 2019). One might also want to look at the "reduced form" effect—directly regressing the instrument on the outcome of interest—as is often done in labor and education economics. If more than one instrument is available, it is helpful to use over identification tests, such as Sargan. Still, IVs are no panacea, as there might be a violation of the exclusion restriction. Becker (2016) provides a good econometric guide to practice for IVs to establish causality.

In the RDD front, perhaps the best guides to practice are provided by Imbens and Lemieux (2008) and Angrist and Pischke (2008). They cover topics such as sharp versus fuzzy designs, bandwidth selection and estimation. One might want to conduct a McCrary test to see if there is sorting on the threshold (for actual bunching estimation, exploiting this feature of the data, see Kleven, 2016). It is also standard and advisable to test whether other covariates are smooth or also jumping at the threshold. Aside from some of the technical refinements already covered (non-parametric estimation, optimal bandwidth, and local randomization) other tools such as line segment fixed effects and simulations have been employed. Yet another econometrics literature has focused on standard errors, for the state of the art, see Colella et al. (2019). Overall, IVs and RDs are a constantly evolving field in econometrics, often bringing useful tools for researchers in economic history and other fields.

7.6.4 Other sources of identification

Before concluding, it is important to note that even though this chapter focused on IVs and RDDs, these are clearly not the only tools available for identification in economic history (and economics as a whole). I only provide some illustrative examples here. In a classic study, Ciccone and Hall (1996) looked at the role of economic density for productivity. To instrument for the first, they used population density in the 1850s. Given the later persistence literature, simply taking a lagged variable as instrument now presents challenges in terms of potential threats to the exclusion restriction. The instrument could still be valid, but working through ways other than the intended channel of interest. In many cases, researchers have found placebos and natural experiments from history, which often provide quasi experimental variation to test economic theories. For instance, history often provides some placebos or at least relevant control groups (Belloc et al., 2016; Valencia Caicedo, 2019; Angelucci et al., 2020). As mentioned before, other papers have used standard econometric techniques such as differences-in-differences, neighborhood fixed effects, matching and synthetic controls (see, for instance, Voigtländer and Voth, 2012; Dell and Olken, 2020). Though it is often hard or plainly impossible to use Randomized Control Trials (RCTs) in history, some economic history papers have complemented their findings using lab-in-the-filed experiments (surveyed by Lowes, 2021, in this book). With the advent of census linking and the wider availability of data sources, many papers have opted to describe some broad and important patterns in the data. Notably, this can be seen in the study of inequality and historical finance (Piketty, 2014; Schularick and Taylor, 2012). These papers take Shiller's (2017) narrative economics approach seriously. One such case in economic history is Michalopoulos and Xue (2019). It is not only the case that other econometric approaches are valid, but that sometimes the endogeneity problems are not as severe to merit an identification strategy altogether.

7.7 Concluding remarks

This chapter surveys the usage of Instrumental Variables and Regression Discontinuity Designs in economic history, in what I term "Historical Econometrics", paralleling the title of this handbook. I argue that it is in part due to the appropriate usage of these methods that some economic history papers were successful in terms of publication venues and became influential in the broader economics literature. I document the positive trends of economic history articles employing these methods using three different samples: top 20 journals in economics, top 5 journals in economic history, and top five general interest journals in economics. I detail two broad phases: (1) pioneering articles appearing from 2001 to 2011, which became seminal contributions in their respective literatures and (2) a second wave of studies refining these techniques appearing from around 2012 to today (2020). I also discuss some methodological refinements that have appeared more recently in the econometrics field in the IV and RDD camps. I then present a guide to practice with respect to regression diagnostics, acknowledging that there are other useful sources of identification such as differences-in-differences, placebos, randomized controlled experiments and propensity score matching.

Having concluded this summary, it seems that the time was ripe for writing such a survey piece. This is due to the large number of papers and the interesting recent trends. Though it is hard to speculate, the number of RD studies in economic history will possibly grow in the future, perhaps competing with the corpus of IV papers. There are also some studies now combining different identification strategies, a trend that could become more common in the future. There seems to be too a broader shift in the literature from cross country to within county studies, in part searching for better identification. There also appears to be more emphasis on mechanisms of transmission (following Dell, 2010; Nunn and Wantchekon, 2011). These include new (often non-instrumented) variables, or meaningful sample splits. Some of these trends echo the criticism voiced by Deaton (2010) on the validity of instruments and randomization.

Generally speaking, economic history has profited from recent advances and refinements coming from the econometrics realm, which could possibly spur new research. Still, the economic history discipline has not moved yet to a more model based or structural approach, as is increasingly seen in other areas such as international trade, urban, health, and education economics, and is also discussed throughout this book (see Donaldson and Hornbeck, 2016; Donaldson, 2018; Hornbeck and Rotemberg, 2019; Allen and Donaldson, 2018 for important exceptions). Yet it appears that the advent of Historical Econometrics, just as Cliometrics before, is here to stay. Though this was a methodological chapter aimed to capture the spirit of the times, by no means does it advocate for a particular identification strategy. Ultimately, the right tool depends on the question being asked and the nature—if any—of the endogeneity problem at hand.

7.8 **Appendix**

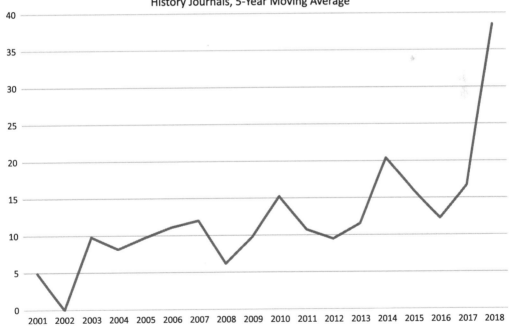

Percentage of Papers in Economic History using
Advanced Econometrics in Top 5 Economic
History Journals, 5-Year Moving Average

FIGURE A.1

The figure depicts the evolution of the percentage of papers using advanced econometrics in top five economic history journals, over the total number of papers in these journals using econometrics. The trends are smoothed using five year moving averages. Own calculations, based on see Cioni et al. (2020), see their article for details.

Table A.1 Economic history papers where the IVs are in the robustness section from 2000 to 2020.

	Title	Author	Journal	Year	Explanation
1	Charity and the Bequest Motive: Evidence from Seventeenth-Century Wills	McGranahan, Leslie Moscow	JPE	2000	Number of family members instrumented by number of members in the testator's parish of residence
2	Race, Roosevelt, and Wartime Production: Fair Employment in World War II Labor Markets	Collins, William J.	AER	2001	Number of cases docketed in each city instrumented by presence of FEPC office, number of ES-270 filled and war-type industry earnings
3	Exchange-Rate Regimes and International Trade: Evidence from the Classical Gold Standard Era	Lopez-Cordova, J. Ernesto; Meissner, Christopher M.	AER	2003	Gold standard dummy instrumented by the product of each country's ratio of gold reserves to bank notes in circulation and Monetary union instrumented by common language
4	The Rise and Fall of World Trade, 1870-1939	Estevadeordal, Antoni; Frantz, Brian; Taylor, Alan M.	QJE	2003	Gold standard dummy instrumented by product of the logarithm of each partner country's average distance from all countries on gold standard
5	Desegregation and Black Dropout Rates	Guryan, Jonathan	AER	2004	Decade of desegregation in high schools instrumented by decade where the district received filed the first legal opinion on that matter and the decade of the first integration plan
6	Surviving Andersonville: The Benefits of Social Networks in POW Camps	Costa, Dora L.; Kahn, Matthew E.	AER	2007	Number of friends (members of the same company) instrumented by if a prisoner was transferred and number of net transfers into a camp
7	Betting on Hitler—The Value of Political Connections in Nazi Germany	Ferguson, Thomas; Voth, Hans-Joachim	QJE	2008	Firm's affiliation with the Nazi Party instrumented by percentage of votes for the Communist party in the firm's region
8	Luther and Suleyman	Iyigun, Murat	QJE	2008	Number of conflicts between Ottoman empire and European powers instrumented by sultan's characteristics
9	Portage and Path Dependence	Bleakley, Hoyt; Lin, Jeffrey	QJE	2012	Log population density instrumented by portrage variables (proximity to a river dummy and interaction of portage site with the log of land area in the watershed upstream of the fall line)
10	Coercive Contract Enforcement: Law and the Labor Market in Nineteenth Century Industrial Britain	Naidu, Suresh; Yuchtman, Noam	AER	2013	Employment share in textiles instrumented by distance to Lancashire and pig iron production instrumented by Iron ore production

continued on next page

Table A.1 (*continued*)

	Title	Author	Journal	Year	Explanation
11	Revolt on the Nile: Economic Shocks, Religion, and Political Power	Chaney, Eric	ECON	2013	Judge changes instrumented by Nile river shocks
12	The Enduring Impact of the American Dust Bowl: Short- and Long-Run Adjustments to Environmental Catastrophe	Hornbeck, Richard	AER	2012	Erosion in counties instrumented by droughts
13	The Anatomy of a Credit Crisis: The Boom and Bust in Farm Land Prices in the United States in the 1920s	Rajan, Raghuram; Ramcharan, Rodney	AER	2015	Number of banks in 1920 instrumented by number of banks in 1910
14	In the Name of the Son (and the Daughter): Intergenerational Mobility in the United States, 1850-1940	Olivetti, Claudia; Paserman, M. Daniele	AER	2015	Father's earnings instrumented by first name of sons dummies
15	The Effect of the TseTse Fly on African Development	Alsan, Marcela	AER	2015	Uses the TSI (TseTse suitability index) as an instrument, reduced form
16	State Capacity and Military Conflict	Gennaioli, Nicola; Voth, Hans-Joachim	RES	2015	Fiscal revenue of a country instrumented by their war frequency and war frequency instrumented by war frequency in neighboring states
17	The Institutional Causes of China's Great Famine, 1959-1961	Meng, Xin; Qian, Nancy; Yared, Pierre	RES	2015	Retained grain per capita instrumented by production gap
18	Adapting to Climate Change: The Remarkable Decline in the US Temperature-Mortality Relationship over the Twentieth Century	Barreca, Alan; Clay, Karen; Deschenes, Olivier; Greenstone, Michael; Shapiro, Joseph S.	JPE	2016	Electricity prices instrumented by US census division indicator
19	Bowling for Fascism: Social Capital and the Rise of the Nazi Party	Satyanath, Shanker; Voigtlander, Nico; Voth, Hans-Joachim	JPE	2017	Number of associations in 1920 instrumented by number of associations in 1860
20	Real Effects of Information Frictions: When the States and the Kingdom Became United	Steinwender, Claudia	AER	2018	Difference between export and changes in stock prices instrumented by exports

References

Abramitzky, R., 2015. Economics and the modern economic historian. The Journal of Economic History 75 (4), 1240–1251.

Acemoglu, D., Angrist, J., 2000. How large are human-capital externalities? Evidence from compulsory schooling laws. NBER Macroeconomics Annual 15, 9–59.

Acemoglu, D., Autor, D.H., Lyle, D., 2004. Women, war, and wages: the effect of female labor supply on the wage structure at midcentury. Journal of Political Economy 112 (3), 497–551.

Acemoglu, D., Cantoni, D., Johnson, S., Robinson, J.A., 2011. The consequences of radical reform: the French revolution. The American Economic Review 101 (7), 3286–3307.

Acemoglu, D., Johnson, S., Robinson, J.A., 2001. The colonial origins of comparative development: an empirical investigation. The American Economic Review 91 (5), 1369–1401.

Acemoglu, D., Johnson, S., Robinson, J.A., 2002. Reversal of fortune: geography and institutions in the making of the modern world income distribution. The Quarterly Journal of Economics 117 (4), 1231–1294.

Acemoglu, D., Johnson, S., Robinson, J.A., 2012. The colonial origins of comparative development: an empirical investigation: reply. The American Economic Review 102 (6), 3077–3110.

Ackerberg, D.A., Botticini, M., 2002. Endogenous matching and the empirical determinants of contract form. Journal of Political Economy 110 (3), 564–591.

Adena, M., Enikolopov, R., Petrova, M., Santarosa, V., Zhuravskaya, E., 2015. Radio and the rise of the Nazis in prewar Germany. The Quarterly Journal of Economics 130 (4), 1885–1939.

Aidt, T.S., Franck, R., 2015. Democratization under the threat of revolution: evidence from the great reform act of 1832. Econometrica 83 (2), 505–547.

Albouy, D.Y., 2012. The colonial origins of comparative development: an empirical investigation: comment. The American Economic Review 102 (6), 3059–3076.

Alesina, A., Giuliano, P., Nunn, N., 2013. On the origins of gender roles: women and the plough. The Quarterly Journal of Economics 128 (2), 469–530.

Algan, Y., Cahuc, P., 2010. Inherited trust and growth. The American Economic Review 100 (5), 2060–2092.

Allen, T., Donaldson, D., 2018. The Geography of Path Dependence. Working Paper.

Alsan, M., 2015. The effect of the Tsetse fly on African development. The American Economic Review 105 (1), 382–410.

Altonji, J., Elder, T., Taber, C., 2005. Selection on observed and unobserved variables: assessing the effectiveness of Catholic schools. Journal of Political Economy 113 (1), 151–184.

Andrews, I., Stock, J.H., Sun, L., 2019. Weak instruments in instrumental variables regression: theory and practice. Annual Review of Economics 11, 727–753.

Angelucci, C., Meraglia, S., Voigtländer, N., 2020. How Merchant Towns Shaped Parliaments: from the Norman Conquest of England to the Great Reform Act. Working Paper.

Angrist, J.D., 1990. Lifetime earnings and the Vietnam era draft lottery: evidence from social security administrative records. The American Economic Review 80 (3), 313–336.

Angrist, J.D., 2002. How do sex ratios affect marriage and labor markets? Evidence from America's second generation. The Quarterly Journal of Economics 117 (3), 997–1038.

Angrist, J.D., Imbens, G.W., 1995. Two-stage least squares estimation of average causal effects in models with variable treatment intensity. Journal of the American Statistical Association 90 (430), 431–442.

Angrist, J.D., Imbens, G.W., Rubin, D.B., 1996. Identification of causal effects using instrumental variables. Journal of the American Statistical Association 91 (434), 444–455.

Angrist, J.D., Krueger, A.B., 1991. Does compulsory school attendance affect schooling and earnings? The Quarterly Journal of Economics 106 (4), 979–1014.

Angrist, J.D., Krueger, A.B., 2001. Instrumental variables and the search for identification: from supply and demand to natural experiments. The Journal of Economic Perspectives 15 (4), 69–85.

Angrist, J.D., Lavy, V., 1999. Using Maimonides' rule to estimate the effect of class size on scholastic achievement. The Quarterly Journal of Economics 114 (2), 533–575.

Angrist, J.D., Pischke, J.-S., 2008. Mostly Harmless Econometrics: An Empiricist's Companion. Princeton University Press.

Angrist, J.D., Imbens, G.W., Krueger, A.B., 1999. Jackknife instrumental variables estimation. Journal of Applied Econometrics 14 (1), 57–67.

Antoine, B., Lavergne, P., 2019. Identification-Robust Nonparametric Inference in a Linear IV Model. TSE Working Paper, N. 19-1004.

Arbatlı, C.E., Ashraf, Q., Galor, O., Klemp, M., 2020. Diversity and conflict. Econometrica 88 (2), 727–797.

Ashraf, Q., Galor, O., 2011. Dynamics and stagnation in the Malthusian Epoch. The American Economic Review 101 (5), 2003–2041.

Ashraf, Q., Galor, O., 2013. The 'out of Africa' hypothesis, human genetic diversity, and comparative economic development. The American Economic Review 103 (1), 1–46.

Ashraf, Q.H., Cinnirella, F., Galor, O., Gershman, B., Hornung, E., 2018. Capital-skill complementarity and the emergence of labor emancipation.

Ashraf, Q.H., Galor, O., Kemp, M., 2021. The ancient origins of the wealth of nations. In: Bisin, A., Federico, G. (Eds.), The Handbook of Historical Economics. Elsevier. Chapter 22 (in this book).

Austin, G., 2008. The 'reversal of fortune' thesis and the compression of history: perspectives from African and comparative economic history. Journal of International Development 20 (8), 996–1027.

Bai, Y., Jia, R., 2016. Elite recruitment and political stability: the impact of the abolition of China's civil service exam. Econometrica 84 (2), 677–733.

Banerjee, A., Iyer, L., 2005. History, institutions, and economic performance: the legacy of colonial land tenure systems in India. The American Economic Review 95 (4), 1190–1213.

Barreca, A.I., Guldi, M., Lindo, J.M., Waddell, G.R., 2011. Saving babies? Revisiting the effect of very low birth weight classification. The Quarterly Journal of Economics 126 (4), 2117–2123.

Baum-Snow, N., 2007. Did highways cause suburbanization? The Quarterly Journal of Economics 122 (2), 775–805.

Becker, S.O., 2016. Using instrumental variables to establish causality. IZA World of Labor 250.

Becker, S.O., Boeckh, K., Hainz, C., Woessmann, L., 2016. The Empire is dead, long live the Empire! Long-run persistence of trust and corruption in the bureaucracy. The Economic Journal 126 (590), 40–74.

Becker, S.O., Ferrara, A., 2019. Consequences of forced migration: a survey of recent findings. Labour Economics 59, 1–16.

Becker, S.O., Grosfeld, I., Grosjean, P., Voigtlaender, N., Zhuravskaya, E., 2020. Forced migration and human capital: evidence from post-WWII population transfers. The American Economic Review 110 (5), 1430–1463.

Becker, S.O., Pascali, L., 2019. Religion, division of labor, and conflict: anti-Semitism in Germany over 600 years. The American Economic Review 109 (5), 1764–1804.

Becker, S.O., Woessmann, L., 2009. Was Weber wrong? A human capital theory of protestant economic history. The Quarterly Journal of Economics 124 (2), 531–596.

Belloc, M., Drago, F., Galbiati, R., 2016. Earthquakes, religion, and transition to self-government in Italian cities. The Quarterly Journal of Economics 131 (4), 1875–1926.

Belloni, A., Chernozhukov, V., Hansen, C., 2014. High-dimensional methods and inference on structural and treatment effects. The Journal of Economic Perspectives 28 (2), 29–50.

Bellows, J., Miguel, E., 2009. War and local collective action in Sierra Leone. Journal of Public Economics 93 (11–12), 1144–1157.

Bisin, A., Moro, A., 2021. LATE for history. In: Bisin, A., Federico, G. (Eds.), The Handbook of Historical Economics. Elsevier. Chapter 10 (in this book).

Black, D.A., Sanders, S.G., Taylor, E.J., Taylor, L.J., 2015. The impact of the great migration on mortality of African Americans: evidence from the deep South. The American Economic Review 105 (2), 477–503.

Burchardi, K.B., Chaney, T., Hassan, T.A., 2019. Migrants, ancestors, and foreign investments. The Review of Economic Studies 86 (4), 1448–1486.

Calomiris, C.W., Mason, J.R., 2003. Consequences of bank distress during the great depression. The American Economic Review 93 (3), 937–947.

Calonico, S., Cattaneo, M.D., Farrell, M.H., 2020. Coverage Error Optimal Confidence Intervals for Local Polynomial Regression. Working Paper.

Calonico, S., Cattaneo, M.D., Titiunik, R., 2014. Robust nonparametric confidence intervals for regression-discontinuity designs. Econometrica 82 (6), 2295–2326.

Cantoni, D., 2015. The economic effects of the protestant reformation: testing the Weber hypothesis in the German lands. Journal of the European Economic Association 13 (4), 561–598.

Cantoni, D., Yuchtman, N., 2021. Historical natural experiments: bridging economics and economic history. In: Bisin, A., Federico, G. (Eds.), The Handbook of Historical Economics. Elsevier. Chapter 8 (in this book).

Caprettini, B., Voth, H.-J., 2018. Rage against the machines: labor-saving technology and unrest in England, 1830-32. CEPR Discussion Papers 11800.

Card, D., 2001. Estimating the return to schooling: progress on some persistent econometric problems. Econometrica 69 (5), 1127–1160.

Card, D., Lee, D.S., Pei, Z., Weber, A., 2015. Inference on causal effects in a generalized regression kink design. Econometrica 83 (6), 2453–2483.

Card, D.E., Lee, D.S., Pei, Z., Weber, A.M., 2018. Local Polynomial Order in Regression Discontinuity Designs. Princeton University.

Carlson, M., Mitchener, K.J., 2009. Branch banking as a device for discipline: competition and bank survivorship during the great depression. Journal of Political Economy 117 (2), 165–210.

Cascio, E.U., Washington, E., 2014. Valuing the vote: the redistribution of voting rights and state funds following the voting rights act of 1965. The Quarterly Journal of Economics 129 (1), 379–433.

Casey, G., Klemp, M., 2020. Instrumental Variables in the Long Run. Working Paper.

Cattaneo, M.D., Titiunik, R., Vazquez-Bare, G., 2016. Inference in regression discontinuity designs under local randomization. Stata Journal 16 (2), 331–367.

Chanda, A., Cook, C.J., Putterman, L., 2014. Persistence of fortune: accounting for population movements, there was no post-Columbian reversal. American Economic Journal: Macroeconomics 6 (3), 1–28.

Chen, T., Kung, J.K.-s., Ma, C., 2019. Long Live Keju! The Persistent Effects of China's Imperial Examination System. Working Paper.

Ciccone, A., Hall, R.E., 1996. Productivity and the density of economic activity. The American Economic Review 86, 54–70.

Cioni, M., Federico, G., Vasta, M., 2020. The long-term evolution of economic history: evidence from the top five field journals (1927–2017). Cliometrica 14 (1), 1–39.

Colella, F., Lalive, R., Sakalli, S.O., Thoenig, M., 2019. Inference with arbitrary clustering.

Conley, T.G., Hansen, C.B., Rossi, P.E., 2012. Plausibly exogenous. Review of Economics and Statistics 94 (1), 260–272.

Cook, T.D., 2008. "Waiting for life to arrive": a history of the regression-discontinuity design in psychology, statistics and economics. Journal of Econometrics 142 (2), 636–654.

Dalgaard, C.-J., Knudsen, A.S.B., Selaya, P., 2015. The Bounty of the Sea and Long-run Development. Working Paper.

Davis, D.R., Weinstein, D.E., 2002. Bones, bombs, and break points: the geography of economic activity. The American Economic Review 92 (5), 1269–1289.

Davis, J.H., Hanes, C., Rhode, P.W., 2009. Harvests and business cycles in nineteenth-century America. The Quarterly Journal of Economics 124 (4), 1675–1727.

Deaton, A., 2010. Understanding the mechanisms of economic development. The Journal of Economic Perspectives 24 (3), 3–16.

Dell, M., 2010. The persistent effects of Peru's mining mita. Econometrica 78 (6), 1863–1903.

Dell, M., 2012. Path Dependence in Development: Evidence from the Mexican Revolution. Working Paper. Harvard University.

Dell, M., Lane, N., Querubin, P., 2018. The historical state, local collective action, and economic development in Vietnam. Econometrica 86 (6), 2083–2121.

Dell, M., Olken, B.A., 2020. The development effects of the extractive colonial economy: the Dutch cultivation system in Java. The Review of Economic Studies 87 (1), 164–203.

Dell, M., Querubin, P., 2018. Nation building through foreign intervention: evidence from discontinuities in military strategies. The Quarterly Journal of Economics 133 (2), 701–764.

Derenoncourt, E., 2019. Can you move to opportunity? Evidence from the Great Migration. Working Paper.

Diamond, J., Robinson, J.A. (Eds.), 2010. Natural Experiments of History. Harvard University Press.

Dieterle, S.G., Snell, A., 2016. A simple diagnostic to investigate instrument validity and heterogeneous effects when using a single instrument. Labour Economics 42, 76–86.

Dionne, G., St-Amour, P., Vencatachellum, D., 2009. Asymmetric information and adverse selection in Mauritian slave auctions. The Review of Economic Studies 76 (4), 1269–1295.

Dippel, C., 2014. Forced coexistence and economic development: evidence from native American reservations. Econometrica 82 (6), 2131–2165.

Dippel, C., Gold, R., Heblich, S., Pinto, R., 2017. Instrumental variables and causal mechanisms: Unpacking the effect of trade on workers and voters. No. w23209. National Bureau of Economic Research.

Dittmar, J.E., 2011. Information technology and economic change: the impact of the printing press. The Quarterly Journal of Economics 126 (3), 1133–1172.

Donaldson, D., 2018. Railroads of the Raj: estimating the impact of transportation infrastructure. The American Economic Review 108 (4–5), 899–934.

Donaldson, D., Hornbeck, R., 2016. Railroads and American economic growth: a "market access" approach. The Quarterly Journal of Economics 131 (2), 799–858.

Duranton, G., Turner, M.A., 2012. Urban growth and transportation. The Review of Economic Studies 79 (4), 1407–1440.

Easterly, W., Levine, R., 2016. The European origins of economic development. Journal of Economic Growth 21 (3), 225–257.

Engerman, S., Sokoloff, K., 1997. Factor endowments, institutions and differential paths of growth among the New World economies. In: Haber, S. (Ed.), How Latin America Fell Behind. Stanford University Press, Stanford.

Feyrer, J., Sacerdote, B., 2009. Colonialism and modern income: islands as natural experiments. Review of Economics and Statistics 91 (2), 245–262.

Fontana, N., Nannicini, T., Tabellini, G., 2017. Historical Roots of Political Extremism: the Effects of Nazi Occupation of Italy. Working Paper.

Franck, R., Michalopoulos, S., 2017. Emigration During the French Revolution: Consequences in the Short and Longue Durée. No. w23936. National Bureau of Economic Research.

Frydman, C., Hilt, E., 2017. Investment banks as corporate monitors in the early twentieth century United States. The American Economic Review 107 (7), 1938–1970.

Fujiwara, T., Laudares, H., Valencia Caicedo, F., 2020. Tordesillas, Slavery and the Origins of Brazilian Inequality. Working Paper.

Gagliarducci, S., Onorato, M.G., Sobbrio, F., Tabellini, G., 2020. War of the waves: radio and resistance during World War II. American Economic Journal: Applied Economics 12 (4), 1–38.

Gallup, J.L., Sachs, J.D., 2001. The economic burden of malaria. The American Journal of Tropical Medicine and Hygiene 64 (1_suppl), 85–96.

Galor, O., Moav, O., Vollrath, D., 2009. Inequality in landownership, the emergence of human-capital promoting institutions, and the great divergence. The Review of Economic Studies 76 (1), 143–179.

Gelman, A., Imbens, G., 2019. Why high-order polynomials should not be used in regression discontinuity designs. Journal of Business & Economic Statistics 37 (3), 447–456.

Giuliano, P., Nunn, N., 2020. Understanding cultural persistence and change. The Review of Economic Studies, rdaa074. https://doi.org/10.1093/restud/rdaa074.

Glaeser, E.L., La Porta, R., Lopez-de-Silanes, F., Shleifer, A., 2004. Do institutions cause growth? Journal of Economic Growth 9 (3), 271–303.

Goldsmith-Pinkham, P., Sorkin, I., Swift, H., 2018. Bartik instruments: What, when, why, and how. No. w24408. National Bureau of Economic Research.

Guiso, L., Sapienza, P., Zingales, L., 2004. Does local financial development matter? The Quarterly Journal of Economics 119 (3), 929–969.

Guiso, L., Sapienza, P., Zingales, L., 2008. Long Term Persistence. No. w14278. National Bureau of Economic Research.

Guiso, L., Sapienza, P., Zingales, L., 2016. Long-term persistence. Journal of the European Economic Association 14 (6), 1401–1436.

Hall, R.E., Jones, C.I., 1997. Levels of economic activity across countries. The American Economic Review 87 (2), 173–177.

Heckman, J.J., 1999. Instrumental variables: response to Angrist and Imbens. The Journal of Human Resources 34 (4), 828–837.

Hinnerich, B.T., Pettersson-Lidbom, P., 2014. Democracy, redistribution, and political participation: evidence from Sweden 1919–1938. Econometrica 82 (3), 961–993.

Hornbeck, R., Rotemberg, M., 2019. Railroads, Reallocation, and the Rise of American Manufacturing. No. w26594. National Bureau of Economic Research.

Hornung, E., 2014. Immigration and the diffusion of technology: the Huguenot diaspora in Prussia. The American Economic Review 104 (1), 84–122.

Huber, M., Mellace, G., 2015. Testing instrument validity for LATE identification based on inequality moment constraints. Review of Economics and Statistics 97 (2), 398–411.

Imbens, G.W., Angrist, J.D., 1994. Identification and estimation of local average treatment effects. Econometrica 62 (2), 467–475.

Imbens, G., Kalyanaraman, K., 2012. Optimal bandwidth choice for the regression discontinuity estimator. The Review of Economic Studies 79 (3), 933–959.

Imbens, G.W., Lemieux, T., 2008. Regression discontinuity designs: a guide to practice. Journal of Econometrics 142 (2), 615–635.

Iyer, L., 2010. Direct versus indirect colonial rule in India: long-term consequences. Review of Economics and Statistics 92 (4), 693–713.

Iyigun, M., 2008. Luther and Suleyman. The Quarterly Journal of Economics 123 (4), 1465–1494.

Jha, S., 2013. Trade, institutions, and ethnic tolerance: evidence from South Asia. American Political Science Review 107 (4), 806–832.

Jha, S., 2015. Financial asset holdings and political attitudes: evidence from revolutionary England. The Quarterly Journal of Economics 130 (3), 1485–1545.

Juhász, R., 2018. Temporary protection and technology adoption: evidence from the Napoleonic blockade. The American Economic Review 108 (11), 3339–3376.

Juhász, R., Steinwender, C., 2019. Spinning the Web: the Impact of ICT on Trade in Intermediates and Technology Diffusion. Working Paper.

Karadja, M., Prawitz, E., 2019. Exit, voice, and political change: evidence from Swedish mass migration to the United States. Journal of Political Economy 127 (4), 1864–1925.

Kitagawa, T., 2015. A test for instrument validity. Econometrica 83 (5), 2043–2063.

Kleven, H.J., 2016. Bunching. Annual Review of Economics 8, 435–464.

Kline, P., Moretti, E., 2014. Local economic development, agglomeration economies, and the big push: 100 years of evidence from the Tennessee Valley authority. The Quarterly Journal of Economics 129 (1), 275–331.

Lee, D.S., Lemieux, T., 2010. Regression discontinuity designs in economics. Journal of Economic Literature 48 (2), 281–355.

Li, W., Yang, D.T., 2005. The great leap forward: anatomy of a central planning disaster. Journal of Political Economy 113 (4), 840–877.

Lipset, S.M., 1959. Political man: the Social Bases of Politics.

Lleras-Muney, A., 2005. The relationship between education and adult mortality in the United States. The Review of Economic Studies 72 (1), 189–221.

Lowes, S., 2018. Matrilineal kinship and gender differences in competition. Working Paper. Harvard University.

Lowes, S., 2021. Ethnographic and field data in historical economics. In: Bisin, A., Federico, G. (Eds.), The Handbook of Historical Economics. Elsevier. Chapter 6 (in this book).

Lowes, S., Nunn, N., Robinson, J.A., Weigel, J.L., 2017. The evolution of culture and institutions: evidence from the Kuba Kingdom. Econometrica 85 (4), 1065–1091.

Lowes, S.R., Montero, E., 2018. The legacy of colonial medicine in Central Africa.

Maloney, W.F., Valencia Caicedo, F., 2016. The persistence of (subnational) fortune. The Economic Journal 126 (598), 2363–2401.

Maloney, W.F., Valencia Caicedo, F., 2017. Engineering growth: innovative capacity and development in the Americas.

Manacorda, M., 2006. Child labor and the labor supply of other household members: evidence from 1920 America. The American Economic Review 96 (5), 1788–1801.

Margo, R.A., 2018. The integration of economic history into economics. Cliometrica 12 (3), 377–406.

Margo, R.A., 2021. The economic history of economic history: the evolution of a field in economics. In: Bisin, A., Federico, G. (Eds.), The Handbook of Historical Economics. Elsevier. Chapter 1 (in this book).

Markevich, A., Zhuravskaya, E., 2018. The economic effects of the abolition of serfdom: evidence from the Russian Empire. The American Economic Review 108 (4–5), 1074–1117.

Melly, B., Lalive, R., 2020. Estimation, Inference, and Interpretation in the Regression Discontinuity Design. No. dp2016. Universitaet Bern, Departement Volkswirtschaft.

Michalopoulos, S., Papaioannou, E., 2013. Pre-colonial ethnic institutions and contemporary African development. Econometrica 81 (1), 113–152.

Michalopoulos, S., Papaioannou, E., 2014. National institutions and subnational development in Africa. The Quarterly Journal of Economics 129 (1), 151–213.

Michalopoulos, S., Papaioannou, E., 2016. The long-run effects of the scramble for Africa. The American Economic Review 106 (7), 1802–1848.

Michalopoulos, S., Papaioannou, E., 2017. Series introduction: historical legacies and contemporary development. In: The Long Economic and Political Shadow of History.

Michalopoulos, S., Xue, M.M., 2019. Folklore. No. w25430. National Bureau of Economic Research.

Milner, B., 2019. The Impact of State-Provided Education: Evidence from the 1870 Education Act. Mimeograph. University of British Columbia.

Montero, E., 2018. Cooperative Property Rights and Development: Evidence from Land Reform in El Salvador. Working Paper. Harvard.

Moscona, J., Nunn, N., Robinson, J.A., 2020. Segmentary lineage organization and conflict in sub-Saharan Africa. Econometrica 88 (5), 1999–2036.

Moser, P., Voena, A., 2012. Compulsory licensing: evidence from the trading with the enemy act. The American Economic Review 102 (1), 396–427.

Moser, P., Voena, A., Waldinger, F., 2014. German Jewish Émigrés and US invention. The American Economic Review 104 (10), 3222–3255.

Newell, W.H., 1973. The agricultural revolution in nineteenth-century France. The Journal of Economic History 33 (4), 697–731.

Nunn, N., 2008. The long-term effects of Africa's slave trades. The Quarterly Journal of Economics 123 (1), 139–176.

Nunn, N., 2009. The importance of history for economic development. Annual Review of Economics 1 (1), 65–92.

Nunn, N., 2014. Historical development. In: Handbook of Economic Growth, Vol. 2. Elsevier, pp. 347–402.

Nunn, N., 2020. The historical roots of economic development. Science 367 (6485), eaaz9986.

Nunn, N., Qian, N., 2011. The potato's contribution to population and urbanization: evidence from a historical experiment. The Quarterly Journal of Economics 126 (2), 593–650.

Nunn, N., Qian, N., Sequeira, S., 2020. Immigrants and the making of America. The Review of Economic Studies 87 (1), 382–419.

Nunn, N., Wantchekon, L., 2011. The slave trade and the origins of mistrust in Africa. The American Economic Review 101 (7), 3221–3252.

Oster, E., 2019. Unobservable selection and coefficient stability: theory and evidence. Journal of Business & Economic Statistics 37 (2), 187–204.

Pascali, L., 2016. Banks and development: Jewish communities in the Italian renaissance and current economic performance. Review of Economics and Statistics 98 (1), 140–158.

Pascali, L., 2017. The wind of change: maritime technology, trade, and economic development. The American Economic Review 107 (9), 2821–2854.

Piketty, T., 2014. Capital in the 21st Century. The Belknap Press of Harvard University Press, Cambridge Massachusetts.

Putterman, L., Weil, D.N., 2010. Post-1500 population flows and the long-run determinants of economic growth and inequality. The Quarterly Journal of Economics 125 (4), 1627–1682.

Riaño, J.F., Valencia Caicedo, F., 2020. Collateral Damage: the Legacy of the Secret War in Laos. Working Paper.

Rubin, J., 2014. Printing and protestants: an empirical test of the role of printing in the reformation. Review of Economics and Statistics 96 (2), 270–286.

Sachs, J., Malaney, P., 2002. The economic and social burden of malaria. Nature 415 (6872), 680–685.

Schularick, M., Taylor, A.M., 2012. Credit booms gone bust: monetary policy, leverage cycles, and financial crises, 1870-2008. The American Economic Review 102 (2), 1029–1061.

Shiller, R.J., 2017. Narrative economics. The American Economic Review 107 (4), 967–1004.

Spenkuch, J.L., 2017. Religion and work: micro evidence from contemporary Germany. Journal of Economic Behavior & Organization 135, 193–214.

Spolaore, E., Wacziarg, R., 2013. How deep are the roots of economic development? Journal of Economic Literature 51 (2), 325–369.

Steinwender, C., 2018. Real effects of information frictions: when the states and the kingdom became united. The American Economic Review 108 (3), 657–696.

Stock, J., Yogo, M., 2005. Asymptotic distributions of instrumental variables statistics with many instruments. In: Identification and Inference for Econometric Models: Essays in Honor of Thomas Rothenberg, pp. 109–120.

Stock, J.H., Trebbi, F., 2003. Retrospectives: who invented instrumental variable regression? The Journal of Economic Perspectives 17 (3), 177–194.

Strömberg, D., 2004. Radio's impact on public spending. The Quarterly Journal of Economics 119 (1), 189–221.

Tabellini, G., 2010. Culture and institutions: economic development in the regions of Europe. Journal of the European Economic Association 8 (4), 677–716.

Tabellini, M., 2020. Gifts of the immigrants, woes of the natives: lessons from the age of mass migration. The Review of Economic Studies 87 (1), 454–486.

Tur-Prats, A., Valencia Caicedo, F., 2019. Trust Unraveled: the Long Shadow of the Spanish Civil War. Working Paper.

Valencia Caicedo, F., 2019. The mission: human capital transmission, economic persistence, and culture in South America. The Quarterly Journal of Economics 134 (1), 507–556.

Voigtländer, N., Voth, H.-J., 2012. Persecution perpetuated: the medieval origins of anti-semitic violence in Nazi Germany. The Quarterly Journal of Economics 127 (3), 1339–1392.

Voigtländer, N., Voth, H.-J., 2013. How the West "invented" fertility restriction. The American Economic Review 103 (6), 2227–2264.

Voth, H.-J., 2021. Persistence – myth and mystery. In: Bisin, A., Federico, G. (Eds.), The Handbook of Historical Economics. Elsevier. Chapter 9 (in this book).

Waldinger, F., 2010. Quality matters: the expulsion of professors and the consequences for PhD student outcomes in Nazi Germany. Journal of Political Economy 118 (4), 787–831.

Waldinger, F., 2012. Peer effects in science: evidence from the dismissal of scientists in Nazi Germany. The Review of Economic Studies 79 (2), 838–861.

Appendix References

Barreca, A.I., Clay, K., Deschenes, O., Greenstone, M., Shapiro, J.S., 2016. Adapting to climate change: the remarkable decline in the US temperature-mortality relationship over the twentieth century. Journal of Political Economy 124 (1), 105–159.

Bleakley, H., Lin, J., 2012. Portage and path dependence. The Quarterly Journal of Economics 127 (2), 587–644.

Chaney, E., 2013. Revolt on the Nile: economic shocks, religion, and political power. Econometrica 81 (5), 2033–2053.

Collins, W.J., 2001. Race, Roosevelt, and wartime production: fair employment in World War II labor markets. The American Economic Review 91 (1), 272–286.

Costa, D.L., Kahn, M.E., 2007. Surviving Andersonville: the benefits of social networks in POW camps. The American Economic Review 97 (4), 1467–1487.

Estevadeordal, A., Frantz, B., Taylor, A.M., 2003. The rise and fall of world trade, 1870–1939. The Quarterly Journal of Economics 118 (2), 359–407.

Ferguson, T., Voth, H.-J., 2008. Betting on Hitler: the value of political connections in Nazi Germany. The Quarterly Journal of Economics 123 (1), 101–137.

Gennaioli, N., Voth, H.-J., 2015. State capacity and military conflict. The Review of Economic Studies 82 (4), 1409–1448.

Guryan, J., 2004. Desegregation and black dropout rates. The American Economic Review 94 (4), 919–943.

Hornbeck, R., 2012. The enduring impact of the American dust bowl: short- and long-run adjustments to environmental catastrophe. The American Economic Review 102 (4), 1477–1507.

Lopez-Cordova, J.E., Meissner, C.M., 2003. Exchange-rate regimes and international trade: evidence from the classical gold standard era. The American Economic Review 93 (1), 344–353.

McGranahan, L.M., 2000. Charity and the bequest motive: evidence from seventeenth-century wills. Journal of Political Economy 108 (6), 1270–1291.

Meng, X., Qian, N., Yared, P., 2015. The institutional causes of China's great famine, 1959–1961. The Review of Economic Studies 82 (4), 1568–1611.

Naidu, S., Yuchtman, N., 2013. Coercive contract enforcement: law and the labor market in nineteenth century industrial Britain. The American Economic Review 103 (1), 107–144.

Olivetti, C., Paserman, M.D., 2015. In the name of the son (and the daughter): intergenerational mobility in the United States, 1850-1940. The American Economic Review 105 (8), 2695–2724.

Rajan, R., Ramcharan, R., 2015. The anatomy of a credit crisis: the boom and bust in farm land prices in the United States in the 1920s. The American Economic Review 105 (4), 1439–1477.

Satyanath, S., Voigtländer, N., Voth, H.-J., 2017. Bowling for fascism: social capital and the rise of the Nazi Party. Journal of Political Economy 125 (2), 478–526.

Historical natural experiments: bridging economics and economic history[☆]

Davide Cantoni[a,b,c] **and Noam Yuchtman**[d,b,c]

[a] *Ludwig-Maximilians-Universität Munich, Munich, Germany*
[b] *CEPR, London, United Kingdom*
[c] *CESifo, Munich, Germany*
[d] *LSE, London, United Kingdom*

8.1 Introduction

The last 20 years have seen an extraordinary rise in the prominence of historical analysis in the broader economics profession (Abramitzky, 2015; Margo, 2018). It is easy to pick out historical work among the highest-impact research across fields in recent years, and much of this work relies on historical natural experiments: from economic growth and development (e.g., Acemoglu et al., 2001; Banerjee and Iyer, 2005; Nunn, 2008b; Dell, 2010), to health (Bleakley, 2007; Alsan, 2015), environmental economics (Hornbeck, 2012), economic geography (Davis and Weinstein, 2002; Bleakley and Lin, 2012), to macroeconomics (Imbens et al., 2001; Fuchs-Schündeln and Schündeln, 2005), and beyond.[1]

From the perspective of economic historians, the examination of historical natural experiments allows one to make causal arguments about historical processes using the language and empirical methods of applied economists more generally. From the perspective of economists across applied fields, historical variation provides a laboratory in which there exist unique opportunities to test hypotheses that cannot be tested using naturally-occurring contemporary variation or experimental methods. The study of specifically *historical* natural experiments also allows sufficient time to pass to observe general equilibrium effects. Natural experiments in history are a methodological "bridge" between economic history and other fields: historians' empirical methods have converged toward those in other applied microeconomic fields; scholars in other fields have developed the archival research skills of the economic historian.

We believe this bridge between fields has been extraordinarily valuable: historical natural experiments have allowed economic historians, development economists, and economists more generally to

---

[☆] We thank the editors, Alberto Bisin and Giovanni Federico, for their advice and encouragement. Helpful and much appreciated suggestions and critiques were provided by Sascha Becker, Mathias Bühler, James Fenske, Joel Mokyr, Torsten Persson, and many seminar and conference participants.

[1] Of course, economic history continues to be influential beyond the application of historical natural experiments. Recent, important descriptive historical work exists e.g. in finance (Frydman and Saks, 2010), labor (Abramitzky et al., 2012), and public economics (Piketty and Saez, 2003; Piketty et al., 2006), among others.

The Handbook of Historical Economics. https://doi.org/10.1016/B978-0-12-815874-6.00016-2

pose big questions while still attaining the identification of causal effects that is emphasized in modern empirical microeconomics (Angrist and Krueger, 1999; Angrist and Pischke, 2010). Perhaps in no field has the examination of historical quasi-experimental variation been more influential than in economic growth and development: historical natural experiments have allowed scholars to identify plausibly fundamental factors — for example, political institutions and culture — using the causal, experimental language central to empirical work in (micro)economic development (as pioneered by Duflo, 2001; Miguel and Kremer, 2004, and Gertler, 2004, among others). The combination of big questions and careful causal identification explains this approach's impact across fields.

In this chapter we begin by tracing the development and increasing application of the natural historical experiment methodology, both from the perspective of economic historians and from the perspective of economists in other subdisciplines. Interestingly, the rise of the historical natural experiment reflects changes in fields as diverse as labor economics, economic history, and economic development.

Building on this intellectual history of the methodology, we propose a taxonomy of three primary motives for examining historical natural experiments. The taxonomy divides the literature into categories that reflect different priorities and objectives in different fields. The different objectives are reflected in the breadth and depth of the historical analysis, as well as in the empirical challenges facing different analyses.

(1) Experiments to understand history. A first set of research, typically conducted by economic historians, is primarily motivated to understand a *specific* historical episode or process. Scholars producing this sort of research will naturally seek historical experiments *within* their pre-specified setting. Rather than aiming at testing a general economic hypothesis, they aim to make more compelling causal arguments about the setting or process of interest (perhaps with more general implications). Examples of this sort of work are the research by Heldring et al. (2017), who study R.E. Tawney's famous hypothesis about the "Rise of the Gentry" and its relationship to industrialization, or our own work on medieval universities (Cantoni and Yuchtman, 2014), aiming to understand the causal effect of universities and legal institutions on the Commercial Revolution. A study of the historical context helps identifying plausibly exogenous variation — variation in the presence of dissolved monasteries in England, or variation in university establishment in 14th century Germany resulting from the Papal Schism.

(2) Experiments to understand economics. A second set of research, produced by economists across fields, aims primarily to answer a theoretical or empirical question in an economics subdiscipline, then identifies a historical source of variation that can test theory or provide a clean estimate of an empirical parameter. The specific historical setting is not of interest *per se*, but one must carefully apply historical methods to identify and collect data and — most importantly — to argue for the exogeneity of the historical treatment. Examples of this work include Bernhofen and Brown (2004, 2005), who test the theory of comparative advantage examining the forced opening of the Japanese economy in the late 1850s. Their work is not written as an economic history of the Japanese economy, but as a remarkably clean test of trade theory.

(3) Experiments to understand contemporary outcomes. Finally, a third set of research, produced mainly by growth and development economists, aims to understand contemporary economic development outcomes by looking at the past.[2] Identifying the causal role of past events — whether directly, or through an intermediating variable — requires identifying historical quasi-experimental variation. While scholars typically have a specific set of historical factors they wish to understand, their interest is primarily in linking variation in the past to outcomes in the present. Specific sources of historical variation are selected both for their possible long-term impact and for the plausibility of the assumptions needed to identify causal effects. An example of this is the work of Dell (2010), which identifies the persistent effect of a coercive labor institution (colonial Peru's mining *mita*) on contemporary economic development outcomes. Dell's work includes an extremely rich historical analysis of its setting; yet it is the sharp geographical variation in institutions which makes the context of the *mita* particularly suitable for this study, compared to other — possibly equally important, but less sharply bounded — instances of extractive colonial institutions in the Americas.

It is important to highlight two characteristics of our taxonomy: first, it is not exclusive, as there are no bright lines dividing work into the three categories we describe. We apply the taxonomy in the belief that most research more naturally fits into a single category, rather than the others, but many papers will have elements of multiple categories. For example, work in category (1) is characterized by a primary motivation to understand a specific historical process. But, work in this category may well speak to some general economic questions, which are the primary driver of work in category (2). Work in categories (2) and (3), including Dell's (2010) work, makes significant contributions to our understanding of a specific historical process even if the research may not have initially been motivated by the desire to understand the specific historical setting on which the author focuses.

A second important note about our taxonomy is that the existence of *different* motives for undertaking the study of historical natural experiments does not imply in any way the existence of better or worse motives. All of the work we highlight here makes deep, important social science contributions by combining careful applied econometric analysis of natural experiments with careful historical research. The emphasis on understanding historical episodes themselves versus general phenomena, versus contemporary outcomes varies, but we learn a great deal from all three categories of work (including about *history*).

Research in each category has made important contributions, which will be reviewed below. Economic history research in category (1) has produced important steps forward in our analysis of historical experiences, from the Neolithic Revolution (Matranga, 2017), to the Columbian Exchange (Nunn and Qian, 2011), to the Marshall Plan (Giorcelli, 2019). Research in category (2) has provided some of the cleanest tests of economic theory: from evidence of the efficacy of infant industry protection (Juhász, 2018), to the existence of urban agglomeration effects (Bleakley and Lin, 2012), to the incorporation of news in asset prices (Koudijs, 2016). Finally, research in category (3) has significantly broadened economic development research beyond the (valuable) work conducted implementing randomized controlled trials (RCT's) and has also impacted development policy. Not only do scholars and

---

[2] Scholarship identifying deep historical roots of contemporary development shares its methods with work documenting the persistence of historical cultural traits. Among other important findings are: persistence of anti-Semitism (Voigtländer and Voth, 2012); persistence of gender norms (Alesina et al., 2013); and, persistence of fundamental economic preferences (Galor and Özak, 2016). Research in this field is focused on linking spatial (or cross-group) patterns of cultural traits and historical features across time, and relies less on historical natural experiments changing cultural traits (though exceptions exist, e.g. the work by Nunn and Wantchekon, 2011 on the effect of the slave trade on trust in Africa).

practitioners now have a better appreciation for the historical legacy of colonialism and slavery (see, e.g., Acemoglu et al., 2001, 2002; Nunn, 2008b; Feyrer and Sacerdote, 2009; Iyer, 2010; Lowes and Montero, 2018); but they also are more focused on the importance of historically-rooted culture and political institutions, and their expression in contemporary state governance.[3]

In what follows, we first offer a brief intellectual history of the rise to prominence of the historical natural experiment. Next, we provide a review of the research contributions made in each category of our taxonomy. We then provide a brief discussion of empirical challenges facing each category of work (which we develop further in Cantoni and Yuchtman, 2020), then offer some concluding thoughts.

8.2 How did we get here?

We see the increased analysis of historical natural experiments as the outcome of changes across multiple fields in economics. We first discuss these changes in the fields of labor economics, economic history, and growth and development economics, and we argue that they can be mapped to the three types of papers based on historical natural experiments delineated in the taxonomy above. We then describe a particularly influential strand of research — on the causal effect of political institutions on economic development — which brought these three developments together.

Labor economics and the credibility revolution

The "credibility revolution" (Angrist and Pischke, 2010) across applied microeconomics has pushed economists across fields to find credible sources of (experimental or quasi-experimental) variation to answer their research questions. Some of the earliest "quasi-experimental" work in labor economics had the flavor of studying historical natural experiments. Angrist (1990) identified the causal effect of military service on earnings by exploiting the Vietnam-era draft of US men, which implemented a lottery across men's birth dates. Angrist and Krueger (1991) study the effects of compulsory schooling laws — in conjunction with quasi-random variation in individuals' birth dates — to estimate the causal effect of schooling on earnings.

Both of these papers are the outcomes of searching the past and present for variation that can identify the causal effects of interest. Quite simply, historical variation in public policies, historical human-made events, and historical natural processes all provide sources of variation that may provide cleaner tests of theory or better opportunities to estimate an important empirical causal parameter than any contemporary variation allows for. This was recognized early on by labor economists, then increasingly appreciated across applied microeconomic fields. The labor economics-led credibility revolution was thus a driving force of the analysis of historical natural experiments across the discipline. Research in our taxonomic category (2) very naturally arises from the credibility revolution across the discipline: economists are increasingly looking across space *and* time to identify the ideal source of variation to test a hypothesis or estimate a causal parameter.

---

[3] In planning its post-2015 development agenda, the United Nations writes that its framework "must be based on an understanding of the importance of, and a commitment to further promote, resilient, legitimate, and inclusive national and local institutions, as well as inclusive participation in public processes. It must address institutional and governance bottlenecks to ensure transformative and sustainable development." This echoes the arguments of Acemoglu and Robinson (2012). Development research on governance more generally is summarized in Finan et al. (2017). The UN report can be found at https://www.un.org/millenniumgoals/pdf/Think%20Pieces/7_governance.pdf, last accessed October 10, 2019.

Economic history beyond the cliometric revolution

The decades leading up to the increased application of historical natural experiments saw the convergence of empirical work in economic history toward the practices of applied microeconomics more generally. This convergence dates back to the cliometric revolution of the 1960s, which brought quantitative analysis and regressions into economic history research (see perhaps its best-known example, Fogel and Engerman's, 1974, *Time on the Cross*). The convergence has continued with the increasing availability of data due to digitization; this set the stage for the adoption of the credibility revolution within economic history itself.[4] Research in our taxonomic category (1) thus arises from the incorporation of the credibility revolution into quantitative economic history: economic historians trained in economics will naturally try to make causal arguments about the past using the quasi-experimental methods taught in all major graduate programs, and applied in other fields.

Economic development and the randomization revolution

The early 2000's saw the rise of randomized controlled trials (RCTs) and impact evaluation as the "gold standard" in empirical economic development research (Gertler, 2004; Miguel and Kremer, 2004; Banerjee and Duflo, 2009). While RCTs were undoubtedly a huge step forward in the analysis of economic development, there was a tendency for something of a "streetlight effect" (Deaton, 2010): a focus on the types of questions that could be answered by conducting an RCT. This can lead to the neglect of explanatory variables of interest that *cannot* be randomized because of ethical constraints; funding constraints; or logistical constraints. In such a setting, identifying the causal effects of some of these difficult to randomize variables of interest by examining *natural* experiments provided by history held the promise of answering big questions with credible identification. There was thus a gap in the development and growth literature that the analysis of historical natural experiments could fill. Research in our taxonomic category (3) is closely linked to this desire to identify the ultimate drives of economic growth, while adhering as closely as possible to the causal identification standards expected by development economists, whose benchmark was the RCT.

The confluence of these currents

The application of the historical natural experimental methodology in the subfield of economic growth and development reflects all three of the trends above, and has produced one of the most influential economics articles of recent decades: Acemoglu, Johnson, and Robinson's (2001), "The Colonial Origins of Comparative Development" (over 13,000 Google Scholar citations as of January 2020).

A crucial precursor to economists' use of the historical natural experiment to understand the causes of economic development was Jared Diamond's (1997) *Guns, Germs, and Steel*. This work asked deep questions about fundamental drivers of economic success across societies, pointing to ancient historical roots of contemporary riches and poverty. The work also took something of an "experimentalist" approach to understanding historical development: Eurasia differed from the Americas and Africa in having an orientation on the x-axis; Eurasia also happened to have more species of domesticable plants and animals in its natural resource endowment than other continents. This "historical natural exper-

---

[4] See Abramitzky (2015), Margo (2018), and Jaremski (2020), for a discussion of recent changes in the position of economic history within the economics discipline; see also Mitchener (2015), Abramitzky et al. (2019), and Zhang et al. (2019) on the promise of digitized historical data for economic history. A prior, optimistic assessment of the integration of economic history into the economics profession is contained in Romer (1994), contrasting the older, more pessimistic view of McCloskey (1976).

iment" — the quasi-random assignment of species across space; of geographic connections across space — arguably shaped paths of human development for thousands of years.[5]

From the perspective of economics and economic history, taking a similar approach, Engerman and Sokoloff (1997), too, argue that contemporary development outcomes were fundamentally shaped by geography and historical experience. Working within the cliometric tradition, they provide a richer social science structure for linking geography to development, highlighting the path from geographical endowments (e.g., suitability for plantation agriculture in the Americas) to political and economic institutions (e.g., slavery) to contemporary poverty. They, too, apply an experimental lens to the analysis of history and development, viewing the Americas' colonization as an experiment in which agricultural suitability varies, allowing for the identification of causal forces.

Drawing from these early analyses of historical natural experiments, Acemoglu et al. (2001) examine the impact of (arguably exogenous) historical settler mortality across space on contemporary development, working through the historical and contemporary political institutions developed in different colonies.[6] Acemoglu et al. (2001) build on Engerman and Sokoloff's work by: *(i)* examining a global sample of countries; *(ii)* applying a canonical, large-*n*, quantitative analysis (i.e., the cross-country growth regression pioneered by Barro, 1991, and Mankiw et al., 1992); and, *(iii)* explicitly formulating a quasi-experimental (instrumental variables) identification strategy for studying the causal effect of contemporary political institutions (resulting from historical variation in settler mortality and thus colonial settlement strategies and historical political institutions) on development.

This work powerfully unites the three currents described above. First, the developments of quantitative economic history: its reference to the cliometric literature of Engerman and Sokoloff (1997) and its archival research on settler mortality. Second, the implementation of credible, quasi-experimental research design emphasized in modern applied microeconomics. Third, a compelling fusion between the big picture, cross-country macroeconomic analysis of growth (e.g., Barro, 1991), and the experimental emphasis in recent microeconomic work on economic development (summarized in, e.g., Banerjee and Duflo, 2009).

8.3 What have we learned?

As described in the introduction above, we propose a taxonomy of papers relying on historical natural experiments, based on their major focus and their epistemological objective: *(1)* papers that seek to understand a specific historical episode or process; *(2)* papers that aim to answer a (theoretically-founded) question in economics through a historical episode; *(3)* papers that aim to understand contemporary development by examining historical factors. Each category of work in our taxonomy has yielded a range of powerful insights: teaching us about history, about economic processes, and about the sources of income variation across countries. Importantly, boundaries between these categories are fluid, and many

---

[5] Kremer (1993) similarly exploits natural quasi-experimental variation across human societies in where they settle to study the causal effect of population size on technological progress. The concept of historical natural experiments, and in particular the use of humankind's expansion across the world as a major experiment, is further explored in Diamond and Robinson (2010) from the perspectives of various social science disciplines.

[6] This work is then developed in Acemoglu et al. (2002) and generalized in Acemoglu and Robinson (2012).

of the papers in this literature will provide different layers of insights, and not fall unambiguously into exactly one of the categories.

In the following, we sketch out some of the most impactful work in each of areas. The work we cite implements a variety of empirical strategies: from differences in differences, to instrumental variables, to regression discontinuity. Our definition of what constitutes a "(historical) natural experiment" is thus not limited to a narrow set of econometric methods, but rather encompasses any historical imposition of a "treatment", evaluated relative to some counterfactual or control group.[7] The sources of quasi-experimental variation also vary: from literal lotteries to historical policies, to natural events, to spatial variation, sometimes smooth and sometimes sharp.

8.3.1 Experiments to understand history

We present work falling into this category chronologically, in historical order, illustrating the remarkable scope of this body of work.

The Neolithic Revolution

Matranga (2017) studies the effects of seasonality on the development of settled agricultural societies, exploiting natural variation in seasonality across space — which sharply increased as a result of exogenous oscillations in Earth's axis around 12,000 years ago. He finds that greater seasonality is, indeed, associated with the development of settled agricultural societies. He argues that this is due to the need to store food when climate is highly seasonal: a given crop will grow in a location in a particular season, but during other seasons, stored food may be needed. Providing corroborating evidence for a mechanism emphasizing the need to store food in highly seasonal environments, Matranga exploits the fact that local crop diversity (and thus year-round food availability) is greater when there is more local variation in elevation. Consistent with his theory, seasonal areas with more variation in elevation are not as likely as other seasonal areas to develop settled agricultural societies. Matranga's work provides a compelling causal argument for one of human society's most important developments.

The Commercial Revolution

In our work on medieval universities (Cantoni and Yuchtman, 2014) we aimed to understand the causal effect of universities and legal institutions on the European Commercial Revolution. Exploiting the exogenous establishment of the first universities in Germany — a result of the Papal Schism — we show that greater access to a university increased human capital accumulation, particularly legal human capital, and also increased the rate of market establishment. The rise of an urban, commercial European economy, we argue, was causally shaped by Europe's universities, and the legal training they provided. Legal training reduced the costs of trade and contract enforcement in an environment that was highly politically fragmented.

---

[7] Sometimes the "treatment" consists of the abolition of a pre-existing form of variation: e.g., the eradication of hookworm (Bleakley, 2007). In this case, variation in the intensity of the treatment comes not from the application of the treatment itself, but from the pre-existing distribution of the condition. The treatment can thus be interpreted as a historically-contingent effect of a pre-existing feature. We discuss the econometric challenges of this, and related, empirical research designs in Cantoni and Yuchtman (2020).

The invention of the printing press

The invention of the printing press by Gutenberg was arguably among the most important single innovations in world history. But identifying its causal effects proved difficult for economic historians. Dittmar (2011) provides credible evidence that the printing press caused European cities to grow. He exploits the quasi-random diffusion of the press from its initial location, in Mainz. Building on this work, Dittmar and Seabold (2018) aim to study the impact of the quantity of printing on both economic and cultural change in early modern Europe. They discovered that printers' deaths *increased* printed output due to the unraveling of collusion among printers. Exploiting the quasi-random increase in printing following printers' deaths, they show that increased printed output increased economic activity (likely working through the spread of business knowledge) and induced social change (the adoption of the Reformation). In addition to Dittmar's work (and exploiting similar variation), Rubin (2014) presents evidence that the printing press supported the rapid spread of the Protestant Reformation across Europe.

The Protestant Reformation

As one of the turning points of Western European history, the Protestant Reformation naturally lends itself to be examined as a historical natural experiment. Cantoni et al. (2018) present evidence that the Reformation led to the reallocation of economic resources from religious uses (e.g., the construction of churches and monasteries) to secular uses (e.g., the construction of administrative buildings). Hornung (2014) shows that the Protestant Huguenots expelled from France produced a more productive industrial sector in Prussia in the 18th century.[8]

Other work has tackled one of the best-known theories in social science, the Weber Hypothesis, postulating that Protestant regions were richer than Catholic ones due to a specific work ethic. Exploiting the quasi-random diffusion of Protestantism from Luther's home of Wittenberg, Becker and Woessmann (2009) find that Protestantism was associated with economic development in late 19th century Prussia, but contrary to Weber's argument, this was likely not due to cultural differences. Differences in economic development are instead accounted for by the greater human capital in Protestant regions.[9] Cantoni (2015) finds no difference in economic development between Catholic and Protestant cities across the entire period from 1500–1900.

The Columbian Exchange

One of the most important transfers of people, plants, animals, and microorganisms in human history was the "Columbian Exchange" between the Old World and the New World following Europeans' conquest of the Americas. Nunn and Qian (2011) argue that among the most profound consequences of this exchange was the adoption of the potato in Old World agriculture. The potato is an extremely inexpensive source of nutrition, where it can be grown. Exploiting quasi-random geographic variation in potato crop suitability, Nunn and Qian (2011) show that potato-suitable regions differentially grew compared to other regions, specifically after potato adoption occurred — the potato can account for one-quarter of the growth in Old World population between 1700 and 1900. Jia (2014b) presents evidence that the adoption of the sweet potato in China (another crop introduced from the new world)

---

[8] In related work, Iyigun (2008) finds that religious conflict with the Islamic World reduced conflict between Protestants and Catholics in Europe.

[9] In other work on the economic consequences of religion, Botticini and Eckstein (2007) examine the historical roots of the Jewish people's economic specialization and emphasis on human capital accumulation.

mitigated the effects of adverse agricultural productivity shocks and thus reduced the frequency of civil conflict.

The French Revolution

The French Revolution and subsequent Napoleonic Wars have long been viewed by historians as among the most consequential historical episodes in European history. Acemoglu et al. (2011a) identify the causal effect of Napoleon's conquest of much of Europe by examining quasi-random, within-Germany variation in the extent of French occupation. They find that the reforms introduced by Napoleonic conquest causally shaped economic development trajectories. Specifically, radical institutional reform established conditions that led to more rapid growth following the onset of the Industrial Revolution.

The Industrial Revolution

The Industrial Revolution is one of the most studied episodes in the field of economic history, but its unique status in history — arising only once — has made it challenging to study as a "large-n" historical natural experiment. Recent work exploiting historical natural experiments has provided some insight into the Industrial Revolution's rise and spread, as well as how the Industrial Revolution economy functioned.

Fernihough and O'Rourke (2014), with an empirical approach explicitly modeled on the work of Nunn and Qian (2011), find a significant causal effect of coal availability on city growth during the time of the Industrial Revolution, suggesting an important geographic component to the distribution of industrial development. Heldring et al. (2017) find that the presence of "gentry" elites, rather than the traditional aristocracy, was associated with more industrial employment and mills during the Industrial Revolution in England and Wales. Squicciarini and Voigtländer (2015), collecting data on the regional distribution of subscribers to Diderot's *Encyclopédie*, identify the role of upper tail human capital in driving France's industrialization. Naidu and Yuchtman (2013) study the functioning of labor markets in Industrial Revolution Britain, regulated by Master and Servant law, which limited labor mobility. They find that exogenous labor demand shocks strongly increased prosecutions, but did not produce monotonic effects on wages: prosecutions under Master and Servant law reduced mobility and thus limited the variation in wages.[10]

The Progressive Era's investments in public health

The late nineteenth and early twentieth century US saw many "Progressive Era" public health initiatives, and scholars have exploited quasi-experimental variation arising from these to shed light on their consequences. Examining variation across the US South in exposure to hookworm infection, Bleakley (2007) finds that eradication of the hookworm disease in the early twentieth century significantly increased educational investments. Alsan and Goldin (2019) study the consequences of sewerage and clean water infrastructure for mortality. They exploit variation across Boston-area municipalities in their timing of joining the (Boston) Metropolitan Sewerage District, and find that the combination of

---

[10] An often-cited precondition for the British Industrial Revolution was the ability of merchants to protect their property rights from the monarch (Acemoglu et al., 2005). Jha (2015) studies the process through which property rights protection was achieved, presenting evidence that individuals with a (quasi-randomly assigned) stake in overseas trading companies differentially opposed the extractive Charles I during the English Civil War.

sewerage and clean water was a major factor in reducing child mortality in turn of the 20th century Massachusetts.[11]

The Great Migration

Hornbeck and Naidu (2014) identify the causal effect of one of the great demographic shifts in American history: the Great Migration of Black Americans northward from the US South. To identify the causal effect, they exploit quasi-random variation in the intensity of the Great Mississippi flood of 1927. More intensely flooded areas saw significantly more Black outmigration. Whites attempted to restrict Black outmigration, but in the long run adjusted by adopting new agricultural technologies. Interestingly, technology adoption made more affected regions more productive than less flooded regions in the long run. Boustan (2010) studies the impact of the Great Migration on the residential segregation of American cities. Implementing a shift-share approach that relies on pre-existing black populations in Northern cities and variation in economic conditions across the US South, she estimates large effects of black migration on "white flight" from the inner cities.[12]

The Great Depression

Work on the Great Depression was among the first to explicitly exploit natural experiments to understand important historical episodes. Most famously, Friedman and Schwartz (1963) examined policy experiments that varied the money supply and used them to argue for a "monetarist" interpretation of the Depression's severity. Richardson and Troost (2009) exploit the division of the state of Mississippi between two Federal Reserve banks — which differed in their monetary policy in response to a 1930 bank crisis — to identify the importance of regional Federal Reserve policies to the Depression. Hausman et al. (2019) exploit variation across space in agricultural production to identify the effect of dollar devaluation on crop prices, incomes, and consumption. They find that the "farm channel" played an important role in the 1933 recovery from the Depression. Finally, Kline and Moretti (2014) study the effects of the Tennessee Valley Authority (TVA), a major public works program enacted in response to the Depression. Comparing TVA counties to counties in *proposed, but not enacted* regional authorities, they find a significant, persistent effect of this major economic stimulus program on manufacturing.

The Holocaust

The Holocaust was one of the worst atrocities of the 20th century. Acemoglu et al. (2011b) show that the effect of murdering Jews was not only a humanitarian catastrophe, but also had persistent economic costs. The wiping out of the disproportionately "middle class" Jewish population distorted Russia's social structure and economy, and made Russian regions persistently poorer decades later.

The Marshall Plan

The economic recovery of Europe following World War II (WWII) was one of the first-order facts of the postwar era. Giorcelli (2019) identifies the causal effect of one program through which the United States helped stimulate the European economy: management and technology transfers to Italian firms.

---

[11] Unintended consequences arising from public health programs include exposing individuals to lead (studied by Clay et al., 2014) and allowing studies such as the infamous "Tuskegee Study of Untreated Syphilis in the Negro Male," which (in addition to its horrific direct consequences from leaving Syphilis untreated) generated persistent adverse health consequences for Black men (Alsan and Wanamaker, 2018).

[12] In related work, Fouka et al. (2019) find that the Great Migration fostered the integration of previously-marginalized recent immigrants from Southern and Eastern Europe.

Exploiting the quasi-random restriction of the program (resulting from an unexpected budget cut), she finds that firms exposed to the management and technology transfer had higher performance than comparison firms for more than a decade.[13]

Social movements in the post-WWII US

The post-WWII US saw the rise of the Black Civil Rights movement, which culminated in the Civil Rights Act of 1964 and the Voting Rights Act of 1965. Cascio and Washington (2014) show that the enfranchisement of Black Americans under the 1965 Voting Rights Act produced a shift in public expenditure towards counties with more Black citizens. Aneja and Avenancio-Leon (2019) show that the Voting Rights Act led to greater hiring of Blacks into public offices, which contributed to Black-White wage convergence.[14]

The post-War era also saw great strides toward socioeconomic equality for US women. Goldin and Katz (2002), Bailey (2006), and Bailey (2010) document that a key cause of greater socioeconomic equality was access to contraception technology, specifically "the Pill." Exploiting cross-cohort, cross-region variation in access to contraception, they find that it reduced and deferred women's fertility; increased educational attainment; and led to greater selection of women into the highly-skilled professions.

8.3.2 Experiments to understand economics

Work in this category primarily aims at the empirical verification of a fundamental economic theory or concept (often in the form of an "existence" proof), or estimating a specific causal parameter (either of theoretical interest or policy relevance). To illustrate the breadth of the contributions made in this category of work, we will organize this section by economics subfield.

General economic theory

Fundamental economic theories have been tested by scholars exploiting historical natural experiments. The importance of secure property rights — whether enforced privately or by the state — for incentivizing investment has been examined by various scholars. Hornbeck (2010) exploits quasi-experimental variation in the adoption of barbed wire to enforce property rights across space; Bühler (2019) shows that regulating access rights to grazing districts increases productivity relative to open-access rangeland, using a discontinuity generated by the 1934 Taylor Grazing Act. The work by Libecap and Lueck (2011) and by Bleakley and Ferrie (2014) reveals the importance of initial allocations of property rights, and their effects on land values.

How does the arrival of new, private information get incorporated into prices? Koudijs (2016) exploits variation in the arrival of information to the 18th century Amsterdam stock market, arising from variation in wind that delayed the arrival of information-bearing boats from England. Koudijs finds that

---

[13] Another notable post-WWII program was the US GI Bill, which paid for higher education for returning American soldiers. Stanley (2003) presents evidence that exposure to the GI Bill had economically significant effects on postsecondary schooling.

[14] Aaronson and Mazumder (2011) study an earlier episode of Black-White socioeconomic convergence, the effects of the Rosenwald School initiative, which constructed 5000 schools for Black children in the US South. Exploiting quasi-random variation in exposure to the schools across cohorts and counties, they find that the Rosenwald program produced meaningful socioeconomic impacts for affected Black students: school attendance, literacy, years of schooling, cognitive test scores, and northern migration all increased.

share prices significantly react to information arrival, consistent with financial economic theory. Dube et al. (2011) also find that new information sharply moves stock prices, exploiting a different source of information: leaks of classified information about American covert operations — planned coups — that had the potential to produce high returns to companies in the targeted countries.[15]

Another area of research considering basic questions in economic theory regards preference formation. An active area of research examines historical natural experiments to study whether individual experience shapes preferences. Exploiting the division of Germany between East and West, Alesina and Fuchs-Schündeln (2007) show that the experience of Communism persistently shaped preferences for redistribution and state intervention in the economy. Malmendier and Nagel (2011) show that the experiences of high stock returns (to which individuals are exposed quasi-randomly depending on their cohort) affect one's willingness to take financial risks. Koudijs and Voth (2016) show that (quasi-random) personal exposure to risk of significant losses affected 18th century Dutch investors' willingness to take subsequent financial risks. Giuliano and Spilimbergo (2014) show that experiencing a recession in one's formative years affects one's beliefs about the world and preferences for redistribution.

Labor economics

In one of the earliest papers exploiting a credibly causal research design based on a historical natural experiment, Angrist (1990) studies the causal effect of military service on earnings. To overcome the endogeneity of military service, he exploits the Vietnam War draft lottery that randomly increased the probability that men with certain birthdates would serve. Angrist finds that military service is causally associated with a significant earnings penalty for white men. To study the effects of low-skilled immigration on local wages, Card (1990) exploits the arrival of over one hundred thousand Cuban migrants' arrival in Miami as part of the Mariel Boatlift in 1980. He compares Miami's labor market outcomes following this "natural experiment" to those in other cities and finds very small effects. Angrist and Krueger (1991) study the effects of compulsory schooling laws — in conjunction with quasi-random variation in individuals' birth dates — to estimate the causal effect of schooling on earnings (see also Stephens and Yang, 2014).

Determinants of human capital investments have also been studied by exploiting historical natural experiments. Santavirta (2012) studies the role of families in shaping human capital outcomes by exploiting quasi-random variation in children's adopted families in World War II era Scandinavia. Exploiting variation across US states in the legal minimum working age, Manacorda (2006) studies the effects of local labor market opportunities for children on their siblings, finding that working children improve their siblings' educational outcomes. Using an almost archetypal natural experiment — Georgia's Cherokee Land Lottery of 1832 — Bleakley and Ferrie (2016) show that substantial wealth transfers do *not* lead the children of lottery winners to obtain better outcomes in terms of wealth, income, or literacy.

A large literature studies the determinants of health and the consequences of variation in health — an important dimension of human capital — and historical natural experiments have proved to be

---

[15] The value of private information has also been studied in the context of research on auctions incorporating historical natural experiments (Hendricks and Porter, 1988 and Hendricks et al., 2003). Craft (1998) and Feigenbaum and Rotemberg (2014) identify the value of greater access to information in the context of the creation of the US Weather Bureau and Postal Service, respectively.

particularly useful to study the "Fetal Origins" hypothesis. Almond (2006) finds that fetal exposure to the 1918 flu epidemic worsened a range of human capital and economic outcomes. Examining individuals who experienced the eradication of malaria in India during their early childhood, Cutler et al. (2010) find small, positive effects on income in adulthood, but only mixed results on educational attainment. Banerjee et al. (2010) identify the effect of a temporally and spatially varying agricultural productivity shock (phylloxera, which destroyed vineyards in nineteenth century France and reduced farmers' incomes) on height outcomes, finding large effects. Baten et al. (2014) study the impact of high food prices in early 19th-century Britain, caused by bad harvests and the interruption of grain imports from France during the Continental Blockade, on cognitive outcomes in adulthood. They find that individuals born in years with high food prices had lower levels of numeracy and worked in occupations with lower earnings. Exploiting Sweden's rich administrative data, Almond et al. (2009) find that fetal exposure to fallout from the Chernobyl disaster affected academic performance; Grönqvist et al. (2020) find significant effects of fetal exposure to lead; and, Nilsson (2017) finds significant effects of fetal exposure to alcohol. Exploiting changes in air pollution driven by the 1970 Clean Air Act, Isen et al. (2017) find that labor market outcomes are affected by exposure to air pollution in the first year of life.

Marriage markets have also been studied by exploiting historical natural experiments. Scarcity of men induced by military casualties has been studied by Abramitzky et al. (2011) and Brainerd (2017), among others. In different contexts, theoretical predictions about male scarcity are confirmed: men achieve better matches; women's marriage rates fall; and, out of wedlock births rise. Goñi (2018) considers the "London Season", in which aristocratic bachelors were introduced to "eligible" debutantes. The exogenous interruption of this matching technology (e.g., due to the death of Prince Consort Albert) reduced the extent of sorting in the marriage market.

Finally, personnel economics questions have been answered using historical natural experiments. Xu (2018) exploits variation at the top of the British Colonial Office to study the effects of patronage on bureaucrat performance. He finds that a patron leading the Colonial Office produces more desirable placements, and worse performance. In a different historical context, the British Royal Navy, Voth and Xu (2020) find that patronage produces promotion, but in this case *better* selection and better performance.

Public finance

The causal effects of the introduction of major social welfare programs have been evaluated exploiting historical natural experiments. Aizer et al. (2016) consider the effects of the Mothers' Pension program — one of the first government-sponsored welfare programs in US history. Using individual-level administrative records of applicants to the program they show that children of the beneficiaries have improved health and higher income in the long run. Gelber et al. (2016) study the effects of additional Social Security income on earnings, exploiting a sharp change in benefits depending on birth year. Goodman-Bacon (2018) studies the effects of Medicaid's introduction, exploiting variation across states in the *ex ante* eligible population, and finding that it significantly reduced child mortality. Fetter and Lockwood (2018) exploit variation in Old Age Assistance Programs across US states and find that these programs significantly reduced older men's labor force participation rates. Combining the study of the "Fetal Origins" hypothesis with the evaluation of a major welfare program, Almond et al. (2011) find that the rollout of the Food Stamp Program improved birth outcomes, especially among the African American population. Studying Bismarck's health insurance — the oldest compulsory health insurance program — Bauernschuster et al. (2020) find that its introduction reduced mortality rates from infectious diseases.

In addition to studying government expenditure programs, several studies have examined major historical tax reforms to estimate the impact of tax rates on labor supply (e.g., Feldstein, 1995 and Bianchi et al., 2001).

Trade economics

The theory of comparative advantage is central to trade theory, yet it is difficult to test. Bernhofen and Brown (2004) and Bernhofen and Brown (2005) identify a setting of exogenous trade opening: the forced opening of the Japanese economy in the late 1850s. They provide the cleanest empirical evidence available on the causal effect of openness on trade volume (exports and imports), prices, and welfare. They also confirm the predictions of one of the most important theories in economics.

The relationship between distance and trade volume is at the heart of empirical trade research. Feyrer (2009) exploits the closure of the Suez Canal between 1967 and 1975 — and the resulting sharp change in shipping distances between trading partners — to identify the causal effect of distance on trade and incomes. He finds that greater distance reduces trade, and thus income. Pascali (2017) exploits the invention of the steamship and consequent variation in the reduction of trade costs to show that in the first era of globalization, trade promoted economic development in locations with more inclusive political institutions.

Whether temporary trade protections can support industrial development is an important question for both trade economists and policymakers. Providing an "existence result" — protection can promote industrial development — Juhász (2018) exploits the Napoleonic blockade, which protected textile producers in northern France from English competition. She finds that the temporary protection provided by the blockade led to mechanization and production in the textile sector. In related work, exploiting historical variation in South Korea and Finland, respectively, Lane (2019) and Mitrunen (2019) present evidence of successful industrial policy.

The impact of access to markets on prices, output, trade volumes, and welfare is among the core empirical questions in trade, and has been studied exploiting quasi-random historical variation in the diffusion of transportation networks. Fogel (1962) and Fogel (1964) famously studied the impact of the railroad (relative to a *counterfactual*) on the historical development of the US. Building on this work, and incorporating modern trade theory, Donaldson (2018) structurally estimates the impact of market access exploiting variation in the construction of railroads in British Colonial India. Donaldson and Hornbeck (2016) estimate large effects of railroad-provided market access on US land values in the late nineteenth century. Redding and Sturm (2008) find large effects of lost market access in the context of the division of Germany into East and West.[16]

Urban economics

What determines the spatial pattern of urban development? Davis and Weinstein (2002) find evidence consistent with locational fundamentals being very important, finding significant persistence in Japanese city sizes, even in the face of massive shocks. To identify a causal effect of a short-term locational advantage, Bleakley and Lin (2012) exploit the existence of specific portage sites on US rivers. These sites were crucial points for *historical* trade as goods moving on water needed to be transported on land at precisely these sites (e.g., at rapids or water falls). Bleakley and Lin (2012) find that these

---

[16] In related work, Burchardi and Hassan (2013) identify the value of *social* linkages for economic activity by exploiting quasi-random variation across West German cities in linkages to the East, then observing differential growth following Germany's reunification.

sites were *persistently* more densely populated up through the year 2000. This represents compelling evidence of path-dependence in urban development. Redding et al. (2011) provide evidence that spatial equilibria can be shifted, exploiting variation in airport traffic in Germany following reunification. Constraints to urban growth arising from existing construction are studied by Hornbeck and Keniston (2017). They interpret the rapid reconstruction after the Great Boston Fire of 1872 as a sign that prior, outdated buildings imposed negative spillovers and dampened growth.

How transportation networks affect the spatial distribution of economic activities is another empirical question that has been answered using historical natural experiments. Baum-Snow (2007) studies residential sorting between central cities and suburbs, finding that highway construction in the US played a significant role in the declining population in US central cities. Ahlfeldt et al. (2015) use the separation of Berlin by the Wall (1961–1989) to estimate parameters that govern agglomeration and dispersion forces in a model of urban production and commuting. Heblich et al. (2018) find that the construction of the London Underground was a crucial contributor to the spatial distribution of housing, employment, and the overall growth of Greater London.

Political economy

Core political economy questions have been answered using historical natural experiments. The role of the media in influencing public opinion, as well as turnout and voting, is a central area of research in this broad field. Several recent papers examine the impact of quasi-random changes in access to information on political outcomes. Strömberg (2004) exploits variation in access to radio to show that better-informed citizens receive more favorable policies. Gentzkow et al. (2011) find that local newspaper entry increased voter turnout, while Gentzkow (2006) finds that the introduction of television reduced voter turnout in the US (due to the crowding out of local news). Adena et al. (2015) study the impact of radio in Weimar and Nazi Germany, finding that exposure to pro-government radio increased support of the democratic regime in the Weimar era, but increased support for the Nazis as well as anti-Semitic acts once the Nazis took power.

Several papers exploit historical natural experiments to study the consequences of political institutions on economic outcomes. Hinnerich and Pettersson-Lidbom (2014) exploit a sharp population threshold determining whether Swedish local governments function as direct or representative democracies. They find that direct democracies spend less on public welfare than representative democracies, perhaps due to elite capture. Miller (2008) considers the importance of who has the right to vote. Exploiting sharp variation in timing of state-level women's suffrage laws, he shows that granting women the right to vote significantly increased public health spending and improved children's health outcomes. Dal Bó and Rossi (2011) examine the impact of legislators' term lengths on their performance in office, exploiting two natural experiments that randomly assigned term lengths in the Argentine Congress. They find that longer term lengths increase legislators' effort, because effort takes time to yield payoffs: a longer time horizon in office means a higher likelihood of reaping returns on effort.

Dippel (2014) examines the consequences of the composition of the state — whether a state is made of a homogeneous ethnic group or consists of several different groups. The latter sort of state was often the consequence of colonial policies that forced coexistence upon distinct ethnicities. Exploiting variation in the composition of US Native American reservations, Dippel finds that forced coexistence is associated with significantly worse economic outcomes. Finally, Chaney (2013) considers the importance of the threat of revolt on the allocation of resources and the balance of power, an important parameter in formal political economy models of institutional change. Specifically, he studies religious and military authorities in Egypt in the centuries following the establishment of the Ayyubid dynasty in

1169. In this context, Chaney finds that major floods of the Nile were associated with more transfers to the religious authority and a lower likelihood of replacement. This is consistent with a model in which floods increased the power of religious authorities due to their ability to coordinate a revolt against the military authority.

The economics of science and innovation

In a series of papers examining the consequences for German science of the expulsion of Jewish scientists under the Nazi regime, Fabian Waldinger is able to shed light on the importance for scientific production of faculty quality (Waldinger, 2010) and peer effects (Waldinger, 2012). The outbreak of WWII provides Waldinger and co-authors with a source of variation allowing them to identify the importance of physical capital (Waldinger, 2016) as well as access to frontier knowledge (Iaria et al., 2018) in scientific production. The arrival of German scientists in the US is also a useful source of variation to study the impact of frontier scientists on innovation (Moser et al., 2014).

The importance of intellectual property rights for scientific output — and creative output more generally — has been examined in a series of papers by Petra Moser. She and he co-authors find that stringent protection of intellectual property rights involves a clear trade off. On the one hand, intellectual property rights can encourage creative activity (Giorcelli and Moser, 2019); on the other hand, intellectual property rights can limit follow-on innovation (Moser and Voena, 2012), as well as scientific output (Moser and Biasi, forthcoming). Watzinger et al. (2020) show that in 1956, when the antitrust authorities forced Bell to license all its existing patents royalty-free, this had a positive effect on innovation, but only in sectors where Bell did not maintain a monopolistic position.

Hanlon (2015) provides an empirical test of one of the most influential theories of technical change: technology should be developed *endogenously* to complement abundant inputs (as argued in the work of Hicks, 1932, and Habbakuk, 1962, and more recently by Acemoglu, 2002). In his work, Hanlon (2015) identifies a causal effect of input relative abundance on complementary directed technical change by exploiting the sharp decline in (Southern) American cotton imports to Britain during the US Civil War. Hanlon finds that the sharp, unanticipated change in relative Indian cotton abundance indeed induced the development of complementary technology — perhaps the clearest example of directed technical change that economists have identified.

Macroeconomics

Fundamental questions in macroeconomics have been answered by exploiting historical natural experiments (see also Fuchs-Schündeln and Hassan, 2016 for a review of this literature). The impact of monetary policy on real economic outcomes has been identified from sharp historical variation in the money supply, argued by the researchers to have been exogenous (see Friedman, 2005 and Velde, 2009). Romer and Romer (2004) identify plausibly exogenous changes in monetary policy by closely examining narrative records from Federal Open Market Committee meetings. All of this work finds large effects of monetary policy on real economic outcomes.

The impact of fiscal policy on output has been studied by Barro and Redlick (2011) and Ramey (2011), who exploit variation in government spending arising from (arguably exogenous) war needs. They find significant crowding out of private economic activity by government spending. Relying on a close reading of the narrative record (presidential speeches and Congressional reports), Romer and Romer (2010) find large contractionary effects of plausibly exogenous tax increases.

Preferences driving savings and consumption decisions have been estimated from historical quasi-experimental variation as well. Hausman (2016) exploits quasi-random variation in eligibility for US military veterans' payments to identify the marginal propensity to consume during the Great Depression. Imbens et al. (2001) study the impact of windfall earnings on consumption and savings by examining the behavior of lottery winners. Fuchs-Schündeln and Schündeln (2005) exploit exogenous variation in income risk produced by the reunification of Germany to estimate precautionary savings accounting for self-selection into riskier occupations.

8.3.3 Experiments to understand contemporary outcomes

Work in this category of papers aims to identify historical determinants of contemporary outcomes, often contemporary economic development. We organize this section by the historical causal driver, thus illustrating the broad range of factors studied using historical natural experiments (a large part of this literature is also reviewed by Nunn, 2009).

Colonial experience

A range of work establishes causal effects of the colonial experience on contemporary development outcomes. As discussed above, Acemoglu et al. (2001) and Acemoglu et al. (2002) provide evidence that settler mortality shaped subsequent political institutions, and thus economic growth. Feyrer and Sacerdote (2009) exploit quasi-random variation in wind direction and wind speed — which affected *when* an island would be colonized, and thus *who* was likely to colonize it — to provide evidence that the identity of the colonist matters for subsequent development. Iyer (2010), Bruhn and Gallego (2012), and Banerjee and Iyer (2005) argue that specific policy choices of colonists affected long run development. This work is closely related to the research of La Porta et al. (1998) and La Porta et al. (2008), who argue that a country's legal tradition — common law or civil — is significantly shaped by the colonial experience, and has important consequences for economic outcomes.

Dell (2010) and Lowes and Montero (2018) examine sharp geographic discontinuities in exposure to specific colonial extractive institutions (the Potosí mining *mita* and the Congo's extractive rubber concessions, respectively). Regression discontinuity evidence suggests that colonial practices persistently, negatively affected development outcomes in these settings. Not all colonial action was harmful to economic activity in the long-run. In a within-country analysis, Dell and Olken (2020) find that greater extraction by the Dutch on Java is associated with greater economic development today; Jia (2014a) finds that the colonial treaty ports in China (forcibly extracted by Western Powers from the Chinese) exhibit greater economic development today than very similar locations that were not established as treaty ports.

The slave trade

The slave trade was unquestionably devastating for peoples and societies in Africa and in the New World. One naturally wonders: did this immense economic extraction persistently affect economic outcomes in Africa today? One can imagine different relationships between slavery and development: on the one hand, slaving may have destroyed local institutions (formal and informal) and disincentivized long-term investments (in physical or human capital), reducing wealth, with persistent negative consequences. On the other hand, if slaving was associated with local investments in political, economic, and commercial infrastructure, locations with intense slaving might have performed better than areas in the neighboring hinterlands (though, to be clear, perhaps worse than in a counterfactual scenario with no slaving at all).

Nunn (2008b) identifies a significant, negative causal effect of the intensity of the slave trade on contemporary economic development in Africa. To measure the intensity of the slave trade at the country level, he first collects historical data on the ethnicities of slaves shipped and traded. He then links these data to ethnic homelands, and ethnic homelands to contemporary country boundaries. He finds that countries from which more slaves were extracted (relative to land area) remained significantly poorer in the year 2000 (Nunn and Wantchekon, 2011 present evidence that contemporary levels of trust in Africa have also been affected by the slave trade). To more credibly identify a causal relationship, Nunn exploits variation in distance to the major slave-receiving ports: some locations in Africa were intensely traded not because of their own innate characteristics, but because they happened to be closer to the slave-receiving ports. Using distance to slave-receiving ports as an instrument for the intensity of the slave trade, Nunn continues to find a negative effect of the slave trade on economic development. Related work by Nunn studies the impact of slave holding in the US on long-run economic outcomes (Nunn, 2008a).

Disease environment

The impact of geography and the associated disease environment on development has been argued perhaps most famously by Jeffrey Sachs (see, for example, Bloom and Sachs, 1998). Acemoglu and Johnson (2007) show that the worldwide improvement of life expectancy starting in the 1940s, due to more effective public health measures and pharmaceuticals, has produced population growth but *not* improvements in income per capita. Recent work by Marcella Alsan (2015) has provided some of the clearest causal evidence of Africa's specific disease environment affecting economic development. Alsan exploits geographic variation in the suitability of the environment for the Tze Tze fly, which carries a parasite that sickens humans and kills livestock. She finds that disease environment shaped technological progress and political organization in Sub-Saharan Africa, with persistent consequences for economic development.

Leadership

The role of individual leaders in shaping economic outcomes, and shaping the course of history more generally, is an important question across the social sciences. While it is easy to find anecdotal evidence linking individual political leaders to important policy choices and economic development outcomes (e.g., Deng Xiaoping's decision to open the Chinese economy), it is difficult to identify a credible causal link from individuals to economic outcomes (perhaps Deng Xiaoping's choice was endogenous with respect to the economic opportunities facing the Chinese economy). To identify a causal effect of leaders, Jones and Olken (2005) exploit the quasi-random deaths of leaders. They find that when a leader happens to die, growth trajectories significantly change — this is particularly true, as one would expect, for autocrats, who did not face tight formal political constraints. Besley et al. (2011) exploit similar variation to show that leaders' education matters for economic growth as well.

Genetic diversity

Ashraf and Galor (2013) advance the hypothesis that economic development outcomes reflect deeply rooted genetic differences across societies. They argue that a moderate level of genetic diversity should promote economic development: on the one hand, more diversity makes it more likely that the right traits are available to develop or adopt a particular technology. On the other hand, too much diversity can generate distrust and conflict among differing people. To test their hypothesis, the authors exploit the natural (quasi-experimental) variation in genetic diversity across societies arising from humans' spread around the world "Out of Africa". As founders left the original human groups to establish new groups, these groups would be ever less diverse. Thus, the homeland of humans (Africa) is extremely diverse — too diverse according to the authors, and thus relatively poor. Eurasia is moderately diverse — and relatively rich. And, the Americas (i.e., native American societies) are very genetically homogeneous — too homogeneous according to the authors, and again, relatively poor.

Historical political experience of one's ancestors

Several recent papers exploit historical natural experiments to identify the persistent effects of ancestors' historical political experiences on contemporary culture and economic development outcomes. Guiso et al. (2016) identify a historical source of variation in local culture ("civic capital"): the experience of self-governance in the city-states of medieval Italy. They exploit a source of quasi-random historical variation in self-governance: the presence of a bishop in the year 1000, which made self-governance more likely in northern Italian towns. Lowes et al. (2017) show that historical experience of a centralized state (the Kuba Kingdom) persistently affected the social norms of the descendants of its inhabitants. Heldring (forthcoming) finds that villages that had a longer experience of a historical centralized state in Rwanda exhibit more adherence to state policy. This produced differentially more violence when the Rwandan government mobilized citizens for mass killing and less violence when the government pursued peace.

Putterman and Weil (2010) show that countries with longer histories of developed states are richer today and that individuals descended from regions with a longer experience of organized states are higher in their current home countries' income distributions. Michalopoulos and Papaioannou (2013) find that pre-colonial political centralization of local ethnic groups is positively associated with regional development in Africa.

8.4 Challenges to the analysis of historical natural experiments

Each category of work in our taxonomy is subject to particular, historically relevant empirical critiques.

8.4.1 Experiments to understand history

Research in our category (1) aims to exploit quasi-experimental variation to make more credible causal statements about historical processes. This sort of work, we believe, is particularly susceptible to the critique of "looking under the lamppost": the economic historian may miss important aspects of the historical process of interest due to the study a component of it that exhibits useful identifying variation. Our work (Cantoni and Yuchtman, 2014) is one target of such critique: while we aim to study the Commercial Revolution — a process beginning in Northern Italy in the Middle Ages — we study market establishment in the Holy Roman Empire several centuries after the Commercial Revolution began. We argue for the applicability of our findings to the broader process of the Commercial Revolution, but the critique is well-taken.

Another concern specific to this category of work is that establishing the exogeneity of a quasi-experimental treatment can amount to arguing for the *inexplicability* of the precise historical variable of interest. The work of Squicciarini and Voigtländer (2015) is exposed to this critique: the authors link upper-tail human capital — which is measured using the proxy variable of subscriptions to Diderot's *Encyclopedie* — to industrialization and growth in France. Yet, the precise explanatory variable of interest varies in a manner that is unexplained. The authors show that the distribution of subscribers is "balanced" on many dimensions suggesting that they can identify a causal effect — much to the experiment's benefit, but not to the benefit of the historian wishing to understand the distribution of human capital across France.

8.4.2 Experiments to understand economics

Research in category (2) is subject to the sorts of concerns raised by Heckman (2005) and Deaton (2010) about quasi-experimental work more generally. One can identify a causal effect from a clean experiment, but to understand socioeconomic processes, one typically needs to go beyond estimating a single causal effect to understand how that effect relates to economic theory. Work in category (2) thus often offers very nice "existence" results, without necessarily providing insight into the mechanisms producing a particular empirical finding. For example, the work of Juhász (2018) provides an extremely important finding, indicating the potential for temporary trade protection to promote industrial development. However, it does not tell us why protection worked in this case, while it appears to fail in other cases (only a short discussion is provided in the paper).

Whether causal parameter estimates from a particular historical natural experiment are useful or interesting to an economist interested in contemporary policy questions is also likely to vary significantly across settings and applications. For example, labor supply elasticities estimated from a "clean" historical experiment (e.g., the introduction of a new tax) may not be relevant for contemporary policy recommendations, in very different institutional and cultural settings. While clean parameter estimates and existence results such as those in Bernhofen and Brown (2004) or by Davis and Weinstein (2002) can inform broad classes of models, economic theory and an understanding of institutional details are needed to draw general conclusions from specific historical settings.

8.4.3 Experiments to understand contemporary outcomes

Research in category (3), *causally* linking past variation to contemporary outcomes (either directly or through single endogenous regressors in an instrumental variables model), is subject to a range of threats from *historical contingency*. As we discuss in more detail in Cantoni and Yuchtman (2020), the arrival of time-varying shocks makes it very difficult to trace out simple causal effects from even the cleanest natural experiment. Estimated treatment effects are typically historically-contingent, or in some cases, mix up time-contingent effects of instrument, regressor of interest, and perhaps intermediate outcomes. While there is much to like, and learn from, work linking past variation to the present, it requires extremely careful historical work all along the causal chain, not merely understanding the moment of randomization itself.

All of these critiques are best resolved by applying economic theory and deep historical understanding to one's quasi-experimental research. This helps one generalize a local average treatment effect; it helps one understand how historical mechanisms act over time.

8.5 Concluding thoughts

In this piece we have traced out the development of a methodology, the historical natural experiment, that has stimulated work in the field of economic history and also provided a tool that is applied across fields in economics. It has produced some of the most influential recent empirical work not only in economic history but also in subfields from economic development, to trade, to urban economics, labor economics, macroeconomics, and beyond.

We have described the accomplishments of this large body of research, and briefly raised concerns with the application of the methodology. Both strengths and weaknesses, we believe, have their roots in the intellectual history of the rise of the historical natural experiment as an empirical tool. The strengths lie in the linking of extraordinary ambition in asking fundamental research questions with sharp research design that allows for more credible causal statements. The weaknesses lie in the temptation to conduct very reduced form empirical analysis, and thus very narrow historical analysis, once a (seemingly) clean source of historical variation is identified. The weaknesses, we note, are ironically reinforced by the incorporation of economic history papers into an ever-wider range of economics field course syllabi — while concomitantly stand-alone economic history courses (once required in PhD programs around the world) disappear. We emphasize that the analysis of historical natural experiments is a *bridge*: historians must learn to do good applied econometrics, *and* non-historians must cross over and develop tools of historical analysis.

References

Aaronson, D., Mazumder, B., 2011. The impact of Rosenwald schools on black achievement. Journal of Political Economy 119 (5), 821–888.

Abramitzky, R., 2015. Economics and the modern economic historian. The Journal of Economic History 75 (4), 1240–1251.

Abramitzky, R., Boustan, L.P., Eriksson, K., 2012. Europe's tired, poor, huddled masses: self-selection and economic outcomes in the age of mass migration. The American Economic Review 102 (5), 1832–1856.

Abramitzky, R., Boustan, L.P., Eriksson, K., Feigenbaum, J.J., Pérez, S., 2019. Automated linking of historical data. NBER Working Paper Series, 25825.

Abramitzky, R., Delavande, A., Vasconcelos, L., 2011. Marrying up: the role of sex ratio in assortative matching. American Economic Journal: Applied Economics 3 (3), 124–157.

Acemoglu, D., 2002. Directed technical change. The Review of Economic Studies 69 (4), 781–809.

Acemoglu, D., Cantoni, D., Johnson, S., Robinson, J.A., 2011a. The consequences of radical reform: the French Revolution. The American Economic Review 101 (7), 3286–3307.

Acemoglu, D., Hassan, T.A., Robinson, J.A., 2011b. Social structure and development: a legacy of the Holocaust in Russia. The Quarterly Journal of Economics 126 (2), 895–946.

Acemoglu, D., Johnson, S., 2007. Disease and development: the effect of life expectancy on economic growth. Journal of Political Economy 115 (6), 925–985.

Acemoglu, D., Johnson, S., Robinson, J.A., 2001. The colonial origins of comparative development: an empirical investigation. The American Economic Review 91 (5), 1369–1401.

Acemoglu, D., Johnson, S., Robinson, J.A., 2002. Reversal of fortune: geography and institutions in the making of the modern world income distribution. The Quarterly Journal of Economics 117 (4), 1231–1294.

Acemoglu, D., Johnson, S., Robinson, J.A., 2005. The rise of Europe: Atlantic trade, institutional change, and economic growth. The American Economic Review 95 (3), 547–579.

Acemoglu, D., Robinson, J.A., 2012. Why Nations Fail: The Origins of Power, Prosperity, and Poverty. Crown, New York.

Adena, M., Enikolopov, R., Petrova, M., Santarosa, V., Zhuravskaya, E., 2015. Radio and the rise of the Nazis in prewar Germany. The Quarterly Journal of Economics 130 (4), 1885–1939.

Ahlfeldt, G.M., Redding, S.J., Sturm, D.M., Wolf, N., 2015. The economics of density: evidence from the Berlin wall. Econometrica 83 (6), 2127–2189.

Aizer, A., Eli, S., Ferrie, J., Lleras-Muney, A., 2016. The long-run impact of cash transfers to poor families. The American Economic Review 106 (4), 935–971.

Alesina, A., Fuchs-Schündeln, N., 2007. Good bye Lenin (or not?): the effect of communism on people's preferences. The American Economic Review 97 (4), 1507–1528.

Alesina, A., Giuliano, P., Nunn, N., 2013. On the origins of gender roles: women and the plough. The Quarterly Journal of Economics 128 (2), 469–530.

Almond, D., 2006. Is the 1918 influenza pandemic over? Long-term effects of in utero influenza exposure in the post-1940 U.S. population. Journal of Political Economy 114 (4), 672–712.

Almond, D., Edlund, L., Palme, M., 2009. Chernobyl's subclinical legacy: prenatal exposure to radioactive fallout and school outcomes in Sweden. The Quarterly Journal of Economics 124 (4), 1729–1772.

Almond, D., Hoynes, H.W., Schanzenbach, D.W., 2011. Inside the war on poverty: the impact of food stamps on birth outcomes. Review of Economics and Statistics 93 (2), 387–403.

Alsan, M., 2015. The effect of the Tsetse fly on African development. The American Economic Review 105 (1), 382–410.

Alsan, M., Goldin, C., 2019. Watersheds in child mortality: the role of effective water and sewerage infrastructure, 1880–1920. Journal of Political Economy 127 (2), 586–638.

Alsan, M., Wanamaker, M., 2018. Tuskegee and the health of black men. The Quarterly Journal of Economics 133 (1), 407–455.

Aneja, A.P., Avenancio-Leon, C.F., 2019. The effect of political power on labor market inequality: evidence from the 1965 Voting Rights Act. Unpublished. UC Berkeley.

Angrist, J.D., 1990. Lifetime earnings and the Vietnam era draft lottery: evidence from Social Security administrative records. The American Economic Review 80 (3), 313–336.

Angrist, J.D., Krueger, A.B., 1991. Does compulsory school attendance affect schooling and earnings? The Quarterly Journal of Economics 106 (4), 979–1014.

Angrist, J.D., Krueger, A.B., 1999. Empirical strategies in labor economics. In: Orley, A., Card, D. (Eds.), Handbook of Labor Economics, Vol. 3A. Elsevier. Chapter 23.

Angrist, J.D., Pischke, J.-S., 2010. The credibility revolution in empirical economics: how better research design is taking the con out of econometrics. The Journal of Economic Perspectives 24 (2), 3–30.

Ashraf, Q., Galor, O., 2013. The 'Out of Africa' hypothesis, human genetic diversity, and comparative economic development. The American Economic Review 103 (1), 1–46.

Bailey, M.J., 2006. More power to the pill: the impact of contraceptive freedom on women's life cycle labor supply. The Quarterly Journal of Economics 121 (1), 289–320.

Bailey, M.J., 2010. 'Momma's got the pill': how Anthony Comstock and Griswold V. Connecticut shaped US childbearing. The American Economic Review 100 (1), 98–129.

Banerjee, A.V., Duflo, E., 2009. The experimental approach to development economics. Annual Review of Economics 1 (1), 151–178.

Banerjee, A.V., Duflo, E., Postel-Vinay, G., Watts, T., 2010. Long-run health impacts of income shocks: wine and phylloxera in nineteenth-century France. Review of Economics and Statistics 92 (4), 714–728.

Banerjee, A.V., Iyer, L., 2005. History, institutions, and economic performance: the legacy of colonial land tenure systems in India. The American Economic Review 95 (4), 1190–1213.

Barro, R.J., 1991. Economic growth in a cross section of countries. The Quarterly Journal of Economics 106 (2), 407–443.

Barro, R.J., Redlick, C.J., 2011. Macroeconomic effects from government purchases and taxes. The Quarterly Journal of Economics 126 (1), 51–102.

Baten, J., Crayen, D., Voth, H.-J., 2014. Numeracy and the impact of high food prices in industrializing Britain, 1780–1850. Review of Economics and Statistics 96 (3), 418–430.

Bauernschuster, S., Driva, A., Hornung, E., 2020. Bismarck's health insurance and the mortality decline. Journal of the European Economic Association 18 (5), 2561–2607.

Baum-Snow, N., 2007. Did highways cause suburbanization? The Quarterly Journal of Economics 122 (2), 775–805.

Becker, S.O., Woessmann, L., 2009. Was Weber wrong? A human capital theory of protestant economic history. The Quarterly Journal of Economics 124 (2), 531–596.

Bernhofen, D.M., Brown, J.C., 2004. A direct test of the theory of comparative advantage: the case of Japan. Journal of Political Economy 112 (1), 48–67.

Bernhofen, D.M., Brown, J.C., 2005. An empirical assessment of the comparative advantage gains from trade: evidence from Japan. The American Economic Review 95 (1), 208–225.

Besley, T., Montalvo, J.G., Reynal-Querol, M., 2011. Do educated leaders matter? The Economic Journal 121 (554), F205–F227.

Bianchi, M., Gudmundsson, B.R., Zoega, G., 2001. Iceland's natural experiment in supply-side economics. The American Economic Review 91 (5), 1564–1579.

Bleakley, H., 2007. Disease and development: evidence from hookworm eradication in the American South. The Quarterly Journal of Economics 122 (1), 73–117.

Bleakley, H., Ferrie, J., 2014. Land openings on the Georgia frontier and the Coase Theorem in the short- and long-run. Unpublished. Northwestern University.

Bleakley, H., Ferrie, J., 2016. Shocking behavior: random wealth in Antebellum Georgia and human capital across generations. The Quarterly Journal of Economics 131 (3), 1455–1495.

Bleakley, H., Lin, J., 2012. Portage and path dependence. The Quarterly Journal of Economics 127 (2), 587–644.

Bloom, D.E., Sachs, J.D., 1998. Geography, demography, and economic growth in Africa. Brookings Papers on Economic Activity 1998 (2), 207–295.

Botticini, M., Eckstein, Z., 2007. From farmers to merchants, conversions and diaspora: human capital and Jewish history. Journal of the European Economic Association 5 (5), 885–926.

Boustan, L.P., 2010. Was postwar suburbanization "White Flight"? Evidence from the Black migration. The Quarterly Journal of Economics 125 (1), 417–443.

Brainerd, E., 2017. The lasting effect of sex ratio imbalance on marriage and family: evidence from World War II in Russia. Review of Economics and Statistics 99 (2), 229–242.

Bruhn, M., Gallego, F., 2012. Good, bad and ugly colonial activities: do they matter for economic development? Review of Economics and Statistics 94 (2), 433–461.

Bühler, M., 2019. Property rights, resources, and wealth: the public grazing solution in the United States. Unpublished. University of Munich.

Burchardi, K.B., Hassan, T.A., 2013. The economic impact of social ties: evidence from German reunification. The Quarterly Journal of Economics 128 (3), 1219–1271.

Cantoni, D., 2015. The economic effects of the Protestant Reformation: testing the Weber hypothesis in the German lands. Journal of the European Economic Association 13 (4), 561–598.

Cantoni, D., Dittmar, J., Yuchtman, N., 2018. Religious competition and reallocation: the political economy of secularization in the Protestant Reformation. The Quarterly Journal of Economics 133 (4), 2037–2096.

Cantoni, D., Yuchtman, N., 2014. Medieval universities, legal institutions, and the commercial revolution. The Quarterly Journal of Economics 129 (2), 823–887.

Cantoni, D., Yuchtman, N., 2020. Historical contingencies, econometric problems: the analysis of natural experiments in economic history. Unpublished Working Paper. University of Munich.

Card, D., 1990. The impact of the Mariel boatlift on the Miami labor market. Industrial & Labor Relations Review 43 (2), 245–257.

Cascio, E.U., Washington, E., 2014. Valuing the vote: the redistribution of voting rights and state funds following the Voting Rights Act of 1965. The Quarterly Journal of Economics 129 (1), 379–433.

Chaney, E., 2013. Revolt on the Nile: economic shocks, religion, and political power. Econometrica 81 (5), 2033–2053.

Clay, K., Troesken, W., Haines, M., 2014. Lead and mortality. Review of Economics and Statistics 96 (3), 458–470.

Craft, E.D., 1998. The value of weather information services for nineteenth-century Great Lakes shipping. The American Economic Review 88 (5), 1059–1076.

Cutler, D., Fung, W., Kremer, M., Singhal, M., Vogl, T., 2010. Early-life malaria exposure and adult outcomes: evidence from malaria eradication in India. American Economic Journal: Applied Economics 2 (2), 72–94.

Dal Bó, E., Rossi, M.A., 2011. Term length and the effort of politicians. The Review of Economic Studies 78 (4), 1237–1263.

Davis, D.R., Weinstein, D.E., 2002. Bones, bombs, and break points: the geography of economic activity. The American Economic Review 92 (5), 1269–1289.

Deaton, A., 2010. Instruments, randomization, and learning about development. Journal of Economic Literature 48 (2), 424–455.

Dell, M., 2010. The persistent effects of Peru's mining mita. Econometrica 78 (6), 1863–1903.

Dell, M., Olken, B.A., 2020. The development effects of the extractive colonial economy: the Dutch cultivation system in Java. The Review of Economic Studies 87 (1), 164–203.

Diamond, J., 1997. Guns, Germs, and Steel: The Fates of Human Societies. W.W. Norton, New York.

Diamond, J., Robinson, J.A. (Eds.), 2010. Natural Experiments of History. Harvard University Press, Cambridge, Mass.

Dippel, C., 2014. Forced coexistence and economic development: evidence from Native American reservations. Econometrica 82 (6), 2131–2165.

Dittmar, J., 2011. Ideas, technology, and economic change: the impact of the printing press. The Quarterly Journal of Economics 126 (3), 1133–1172.

Dittmar, J., Seabold, S., 2018. New media and competition: printing and Europe's transformation after Gutenberg. Unpublished. London School of Economics.

Donaldson, D., 2018. Railroads of the Raj: estimating the impact of transportation infrastructure. The American Economic Review 108 (4–5), 899–934.

Donaldson, D., Hornbeck, R., 2016. Railroads and American economic growth: a "market access" approach. The Quarterly Journal of Economics 131 (2), 799–858.

Dube, A., Kaplan, E., Naidu, S., 2011. Coups, corporations, and classified information. The Quarterly Journal of Economics 126 (3), 1375–1409.

Duflo, E., 2001. Schooling and labor market consequences of school construction in Indonesia: evidence from an unusual policy experiment. The American Economic Review 91 (4), 795–813.

Engerman, S.L., Sokoloff, K.L., 1997. Factor endowments, institutions, and differential paths of growth among New World economies: a view from economic historians of the United States. In: Haber, S. (Ed.), How Latin America Fell Behind. Stanford University Press, Palo Alto, Calif.

Feigenbaum, J.J., Rotemberg, M., 2014. Information and investment: impacts of the introduction of rural free delivery. Boston University Working Paper.

Feldstein, M., 1995. The effect of marginal tax rates on taxable income: a panel study of the 1986 tax reform act. Journal of Political Economy 103 (3), 551–572.

Fernihough, A., O'Rourke, K.H., 2014. Coal and the European Industrial Revolution. NBER Working Paper Series, 19802.

Fetter, D.K., Lockwood, L.M., 2018. Government old-age support and labor supply: evidence from the old age assistance program. The American Economic Review 108 (8), 2174–2211.

Feyrer, J., 2009. Distance, trade, and income – the 1967 to 1975 closing of the Suez Canal as a natural experiment. NBER Working Paper Series, 15557.

Feyrer, J., Sacerdote, B., 2009. Colonialism and modern income: islands as natural experiments. Review of Economics and Statistics 91 (2), 245–262.

Finan, F., Olken, B.A., Pande, R., 2017. The personnel economics of the developing state. In: Abhijit, B., Esther, D. (Eds.), Handbook of Field Experiments, Vol. 2. North Holland.

Fogel, R.W., 1962. A quantitative approach to the study of railroads in American economic growth: a report of some preliminary findings. The Journal of Economic History 22 (2), 163–197.

Fogel, R.W., 1964. Railroads and American Economic Growth: Essays in Econometric History. Johns Hopkins Press, Baltimore.

Fogel, R.W., Engerman, S.L., 1974. Time on the Cross: The Economics of American Negro Slavery. W.W. Norton, New York.

Fouka, V., Mazumder, S., Tabellini, M., 2019. From immigrants to Americans: race and assimilation during the Great Migration. Unpublished. Stanford University.

Friedman, M., 2005. A natural experiment in monetary policy covering three episodes of growth and decline in the economy and the stock market. The Journal of Economic Perspectives 19 (4), 145–150.

Friedman, M., Schwartz, A.J., 1963. A Monetary History of the United States, 1867–1906. Princeton University Press, Princeton, NJ.

Frydman, C., Saks, R.E., 2010. Executive compensation: a new view from a long-term perspective, 1936–2005. The Review of Financial Studies 23 (5), 2099–2138.

Fuchs-Schündeln, N., Hassan, T.A., 2016. Natural experiments in macroeconomics. In: Taylor, J.B., Uhlig, H. (Eds.), Handbook of Macroeconomics, Vol. 2a. Elsevier, pp. 923–1012.

Fuchs-Schündeln, N., Schündeln, M., 2005. Precautionary savings and self-selection: evidence from the German reunification "experiment". The Quarterly Journal of Economics 120, 1085–1120.

Galor, O., Özak, Ö., 2016. The agricultural origins of time preference. The American Economic Review 106 (10), 3064–3103.

Gelber, A.M., Isen, A., Song, J., 2016. The effect of pension income on elderly earnings: evidence from Social Security and full population data. UC San Diego Working Paper.

Gentzkow, M., 2006. Television and voter turnout. The Quarterly Journal of Economics 121 (3), 931–972.

Gentzkow, M., Shapiro, J.M., Sinkinson, M., 2011. The effect of newspaper entry and exit on electoral politics. The American Economic Review 101 (7), 2980–3018.

Gertler, P., 2004. Do conditional cash transfers improve child health? Evidence from PROGRESA's control randomized experiment. The American Economic Review 94 (2), 336–341.

Giorcelli, M., 2019. The long-term effects of management and technology transfers. The American Economic Review 109 (1), 1–33.

Giorcelli, M., Moser, P., 2019. Copyright and creativity: evidence from Italian operas. NYU Working Paper.

Giuliano, P., Spilimbergo, A., 2014. Growing up in a recession. The Review of Economic Studies 81 (2), 787–817.

Goldin, C., Katz, L.F., 2002. The power of the pill: oral contraceptives and women's career and marriage decisions. Journal of Political Economy 110 (4), 730–770.

Goñi, M., 2018. Assortative matching at the top of the distribution: evidence from the world's most exclusive marriage market. Unpublished.

Goodman-Bacon, A., 2018. Public insurance and mortality: evidence from medicaid implementation. Journal of Political Economy 126 (1), 216–262.

Grönqvist, H., Nilsson, J.P., Robling, P.-O., 2020. Understanding how early lead exposure affect children's life-trajectories. Journal of Political Economy 128 (9), 3376–3433.

Guiso, L., Sapienza, P., Zingales, L., 2016. Long-term persistence. Journal of the European Economic Association 14 (6), 1401–1436.

Habbakuk, H.J., 1962. American and British Technology in the Nineteenth Century: Search for Labor Saving Inventions. Cambridge University Press, Cambridge.

Hanlon, W.W., 2015. Necessity is the mother of invention: input supplies and directed technical change. Econometrica 83 (1), 67–100.

Hausman, J.K., 2016. Fiscal policy and economic recovery: the case of the 1936 veterans' bonus. The American Economic Review 106 (4), 1100–1143.

Hausman, J.K., Rhode, P.W., Wieland, J.F., 2019. Recovery from the great depression: the farm channel in spring 1933. The American Economic Review 109 (2), 427–472.

Heblich, S., Redding, S.J., Sturm, D.M., 2018. The making of the modern metropolis: evidence from London. LSE Working Paper.

Heckman, J.J., 2005. The scientific model of causality. Sociological Methodology 35 (1), 1–97.

Heldring, L., forthcoming. The origins of violence in Rwanda. The Review of Economic Studies.

Heldring, L., Robinson, J.A., Vollmer, S., 2017. The long-run impact of the Dissolution of the English monasteries. Unpublished.

Hendricks, K., Pinkse, J., Porter, R.H., 2003. Empirical implications of equilibrium bidding in first-price, symmetric, common value auctions. The Review of Economic Studies 70 (1), 115–145.

Hendricks, K., Porter, R.H., 1988. An empirical study of an auction with asymmetric information. The American Economic Review 78 (5), 865–883.

Hicks, J.R., 1932. The Theory of Wages. Macmillan, New York.

Hinnerich, B.T., Pettersson-Lidbom, P., 2014. Democracy, redistribution, and political participation: evidence from Sweden 1919-1938. Econometrica 82 (3), 961–993.

Hornbeck, R., 2010. Barbed wire: property rights and agricultural development. The Quarterly Journal of Economics 125 (2), 767–810.

Hornbeck, R., 2012. The enduring impact of the American Dust Bowl: short- and long-run adjustments to environmental catastrophe. The American Economic Review 102 (4), 1477–1507.

Hornbeck, R., Keniston, D., 2017. Creative destruction: barriers to urban growth and the Great Boston Fire of 1872. The American Economic Review 107 (6), 1365–1398.

Hornbeck, R., Naidu, S., 2014. When the levee breaks: black migration and economic development in the American South. The American Economic Review 104 (3), 963–990.

Hornung, E., 2014. Immigration and the diffusion of technology: the Huguenot diaspora in Prussia. The American Economic Review 104 (1), 84–122.

Iaria, A., Schwarz, C., Waldinger, F., 2018. Frontier knowledge and scientific production: evidence from the collapse of international science. The Quarterly Journal of Economics 133 (2), 927–991.

Imbens, G.W., Rubin, D.B., Sacerdote, B.I., 2001. Estimating the effect of unearned income on labor earnings, savings, and consumption: evidence from a survey of lottery players. The American Economic Review 91 (4), 778–794.

Isen, A., Rossin-Slater, M., Walker, W.R., 2017. Every breath you take — every dollar you'll make: the long-term consequences of the clean air act of 1970. Journal of Political Economy 125 (3), 848–902.

Iyer, L., 2010. Direct versus indirect colonial rule in India: long-term consequences. Review of Economics and Statistics 92 (4), 693–713.

Iyigun, M., 2008. Luther and Suleyman. The Quarterly Journal of Economics 123 (4), 1465–1494.

Jaremski, M., 2020. Today's economic history and tomorrow's scholars. Cliometrica 14 (1), 169–180.

Jha, S., 2015. Financial asset holdings and political attitudes: evidence from revolutionary England. The Quarterly Journal of Economics 103 (3), 1485–1545.

Jia, R., 2014b. Weather shocks, sweet potatoes and peasant revolts in historical China. The Economic Journal 124 (575), 92–118.

Jia, R., 2014a. The legacies of forced freedom: China's treaty ports. Review of Economics and Statistics 96 (4), 596–608.

Jones, B.F., Olken, B.A., 2005. Do leaders matter? National leadership and growth since World War II. The Quarterly Journal of Economics 120 (3), 835–864.

Juhász, R., 2018. Temporary protection and technology adoption: evidence from the Napoleonic blockade. The American Economic Review 108 (11), 3339–3376.

Kline, P., Moretti, E., 2014. Local economic development, agglomeration economies, and the big push: 100 years of evidence from the Tennessee Valley authority. The Quarterly Journal of Economics 129 (1), 275–331.

Koudijs, P., 2016. The boats that did not sail: asset price volatility in a natural experiment. The Journal of Finance 71 (3), 1185–1226.

Koudijs, P., Voth, H.-J., 2016. Leverage and beliefs: personal experience and risk-taking in margin lending. The American Economic Review 106 (11), 3367–3400.

Kremer, M., 1993. Population growth and technological change: one million B.C. to 1990. The Quarterly Journal of Economics 108 (3), 681–716.

La Porta, R., Lopez-de-Silanes, F., Shleifer, A., 2008. The economic consequences of legal origins. Journal of Economic Literature 46 (2), 285–332.

La Porta, R., Lopez-de-Silanes, F., Shleifer, A., Vishny, R.W., 1998. Law and finance. Journal of Political Economy 106 (6), 1113–1155.

Lane, N., 2019. Manufacturing revolutions – industrial policy and industrialization in South Korea. Unpublished. Monash University.

Libecap, G.D., Lueck, D., 2011. The demarcation of land and the role of coordinating property institutions. Journal of Political Economy 119 (3), 426–467.

Lowes, S., Montero, E., 2018. Concessions, violence, and indirect rule: evidence from the Congo Free State. Unpublished. Bocconi University.

Lowes, S., Nunn, N., Robinson, J.A., Weigel, J.L., 2017. The evolution of culture and institutions: evidence from the Kuba Kingdom. Econometrica 85 (4), 1065–1091.

Malmendier, U., Nagel, S., 2011. Depression babies: do macroeconomic experiences affect risk taking? The Quarterly Journal of Economics 126 (1), 373–416.

Manacorda, M., 2006. Child labor and the labor supply of other household members: evidence from 1920 America. The American Economic Review 96 (5), 1788–1801.

Mankiw, N.G., Romer, D., Weil, D.N., 1992. A contribution to the empirics of economic growth. The Quarterly Journal of Economics 107 (2), 407–437.

Margo, R.A., 2018. The integration of economic history into economics. Cliometrica 12 (3), 377–406.

Matranga, A., 2017. The ant and the grasshopper: seasonality and the invention of agriculture. Unpublished. New Economic School.

McCloskey, D.N., 1976. Does the past have useful economics? Journal of Economic Literature 14 (2), 434–461.

Michalopoulos, S., Papaioannou, E., 2013. Pre-colonial ethnic institutions and contemporary African development. Econometrica 81 (1), 113–152.

Miguel, E., Kremer, M., 2004. Worms: identifying impacts on education and health in the presence of treatment externalities. Econometrica 72 (1), 159–217.

Miller, G., 2008. Women's suffrage, political responsiveness, and child survival in American history. The Quarterly Journal of Economics 123 (3), 1287–1327.

Mitchener, K.J., 2015. The 4D future of economic history: digitally-driven data design. The Journal of Economic History 75 (4), 1234–1239.

Mitrunen, M., 2019. Structural change and intergenerational mobility: evidence from the Finnish war reparations. Unpublished. IIES Stockholm.

Moser, P., Biasi, B., forthcoming. Effects of copyright on science: evidence from the WWII Book Republication Program. American Economic Journal: Microeconomics.

Moser, P., Voena, A., 2012. Compulsory licensing: evidence from the Trading with the Enemy Act. The American Economic Review 102 (1), 396–427.

Moser, P., Voena, A., Waldinger, F., 2014. German Jewish emigres and US invention. The American Economic Review 104 (10), 3222–3255.

Naidu, S., Yuchtman, N., 2013. Coercive contract enforcement: law and the labor market in nineteenth century industrial Britain. The American Economic Review 103 (1), 107–144.

Nilsson, J.P., 2017. Alcohol availability, prenatal conditions, and long-term economic outcomes. Journal of Political Economy 125 (4), 1149–1207.

Nunn, N., 2008a. Slavery, inequality, and economic development in the Americas: an examination of the Engerman-Sokoloff hypothesis. In: Helpman, E. (Ed.), Institutions and Economic Performance. Harvard University Press, Cambridge, Mass, pp. 148–180.

Nunn, N., 2008b. The long term effects of Africa's slave trades. The Quarterly Journal of Economics 123 (1), 139–176.

Nunn, N., 2009. The importance of history for economic development. Annual Review of Economics 1 (1), 65–92.

Nunn, N., Qian, N., 2011. The potato's contribution to population and urbanization: evidence from a natural experiment. The Quarterly Journal of Economics 126 (2), 593–650.

Nunn, N., Wantchekon, L., 2011. The slave trade and the origins of mistrust in Africa. The American Economic Review 101 (7), 3221–3252.

Pascali, L., 2017. The wind of change: maritime technology, trade, and economic development. The American Economic Review 107 (9), 2821–2854.

Piketty, T., Postel-Vinay, G., Rosenthal, J.-L., 2006. Wealth concentration in a developing economy: Paris and France, 1807–1994. The American Economic Review 96 (1), 236–256.

Piketty, T., Saez, E., 2003. Income inequality in the United States, 1913-1998. The Quarterly Journal of Economics 118 (1), 1–41.

Putterman, L., Weil, D.N., 2010. Post-1500 population flows and the long-run determinants of economic growth and inequality. The Quarterly Journal of Economics 125 (4), 1627–1682.

Ramey, V.A., 2011. Identifying government spending shocks: it's all in the timing. The Quarterly Journal of Economics 126 (1), 1–50.

Redding, S.J., Sturm, D.M., 2008. The costs of remoteness: evidence from German division and reunification. The American Economic Review 98 (5), 1766–1797.

Redding, S.J., Sturm, D.M., Wolf, N., 2011. History and industry location: evidence from German airports. Review of Economics and Statistics 93 (3), 814–831.

Richardson, G., Troost, W., 2009. Monetary intervention mitigated banking panics during the great depression: quasi-experimental evidence from a federal reserve district border, 1929–1933. Journal of Political Economy 117 (6), 1031–1073.

Romer, C.D., 1994. The end of economic history? The Journal of Economic Education 25 (1), 49–66.

Romer, C.D., Romer, D.H., 2004. A new measure of monetary shocks: derivation and implications. The American Economic Review 94 (4), 1055–1084.

Romer, C.D., Romer, D.H., 2010. The macroeconomic effects of tax changes: estimates based on a new measure of fiscal shocks. The American Economic Review 100 (3), 763–801.

Rubin, J., 2014. Printing and protestants: an empirical test of the role of printing in the Reformation. Review of Economics and Statistics 96 (2), 270–286.

Santavirta, T., 2012. How large are the effects from temporary changes in family environment: evidence from a child-evacuation program during World War II. American Economic Journal: Applied Economics 4 (3), 28–42.

Squicciarini, M.P., Voigtländer, N., 2015. Human capital and industrialization: evidence from the age of enlightenment. The Quarterly Journal of Economics 130 (4), 1825–1883.

Stanley, M., 2003. College education and the midcentury GI Bills. The Quarterly Journal of Economics 118 (2), 671–708.

Stephens, M., Yang, D.-Y., 2014. Compulsory education and the benefits of schooling. The American Economic Review 104 (6), 1777–1792.

Strömberg, D., 2004. Radio's impact on public spending. The Quarterly Journal of Economics 119 (1), 189–221.

Velde, F.R., 2009. Chronicle of a deflation unforetold. Journal of Political Economy 117 (4), 591–634.

Voigtländer, N., Voth, H.-J., 2012. Persecution perpetuated: the medieval origins of anti-semitic violence in Nazi Germany. The Quarterly Journal of Economics 127 (3), 1339–1392.

Voth, H.-J., Xu, G., 2020. Patronage for productivity: selection and performance in the Age of Sail. Unpublished. UC Berkeley.

Waldinger, F., 2010. Quality matters: the expulsion of professors and the consequences for PhD student outcomes in Nazi Germany. Journal of Political Economy 118 (4), 787–831.

Waldinger, F., 2012. Peer effects in science: evidence from the dismissal of scientists in Nazi Germany. The Review of Economic Studies 79 (2), 838–861.

Waldinger, F., 2016. Bombs, brains, and science: the role of human and physical capital for the production of scientific knowledge. Review of Economics and Statistics 98 (5), 811–831.

Watzinger, M., Fackler, T.A., Nagler, M., Schnitzer, M., 2020. How antitrust enforcement can spur innovation: Bell Labs and the 1956 Consent Decree. American Economic Journal: Economic Policy 12 (4), 328–359.

Xu, G., 2018. The costs of patronage: evidence from the British Empire. The American Economic Review 108 (11), 3170–3198.

Zhang, K., Shen, Z., Zhou, J., Dell, M., 2019. Information extraction from text regions with complex tabular structure. In: Conference Proceedings, NeurIPS Document Intelligence Workshop.

Persistence – myth and mystery[☆]

Hans-Joachim Voth[a,b]

[a]*University of Zurich, UBS International Center of Economics in Society, Zurich, Switzerland*
[b]*CEPR, London, United Kingdom*

How deep are the historical roots of the present? All around us, the world we live in echoes with the footsteps of the past – from the houses we inhabit to the structure of the cities in which we dwell, the languages we speak and the religions many of us practice. Overwhelmingly, the cultural universe and the built environment we inhabit were created before our time. The novelist William Faulkner famously observed: "The past is never dead. It's not even past." The notion that history can evolve in a particular direction, and not merely repeat itself, is relatively recent (Koselleck, 2003). While cultural anthropologists and sociologists have long emphasized the sluggishness with which many important aspects of our lives change from generation to generation, economics has only recently become interested in the general stickiness of life – *homo oeconomicus*, as he emerges from most textbooks, has no past.

Once economists began to look, a growing number of rigorous studies uncovered a startlingly wide range of phenomena with deep roots. From gender attitudes, trust, investments in human capital, and within-country variation in riches to racial prejudice, the shadows of the past seem to loom large in every corner of intellectual inquiry pursued by economists (Dell, 2010; Alesina et al., 2010; Nunn and Wantchekon, 2011; Guiso et al., 2016; Valencia Caicedo, 2019). At the same time, many historians (and economic historians) see persistence studies as "ahistorical". Persistence studies now form a distinct group of scholarly papers (Cioni et al., 2020). Like many labels that gain wider currency for a research program, it refers to a range of different approaches and research ideas.

The *Oxford English Dictionary* defines persistence as the "continued or prolonged existence of something." Persistence papers typically measure some variable in the past and then relate it to a later-day outcome, often in the present or recent past. The articles with the longest 'range' argue for historical dependence over millennia. Such long-term persistence seems surprising not least because of our everyday experience of massive and often rapid changes – both in economic outcomes and cultural traits. Countries like South Korea or Italy were poor two generations ago, but rank amongst the richest today. Attitudes towards homosexuality, corporal punishment, smoking, women's work, and pre-marital sex have changed beyond all recognition in the last 40 years or so, a mere blink of an eye in the history of mankind.

How can we understand the juxtaposition of rapid change and remarkable persistence over the long run? If persistence is indeed a fact, and common across a wide range of outcomes, the implications for economic policy – and even for philosophical questions such as the concept of free will – can be

---

[☆] For detailed comments, I thank Sascha Becker, Joel Mokyr, and Felipe Valencia Caicedo. Excellent research assistance by Marcel Caesmann is gratefully acknowledged.

profoundly disturbing. If, for example, a country's riches today were determined by its use of technology 1000 BC, its chances for development may be limited – at least as long as time travel remains a technological challenge.

This essay's purpose is to first clarify the meaning of persistence before providing an overview of what insights the buoyant literature has produced in the last decade. I will then discuss critically the empirical and conceptual challenges, and propose methods and standards for assessing the plausibility of persistence studies.

The range of historical variables used in persistence studies is wide – from the self-governance of Italian city-states to plough usage, medieval pogroms, and the adoption of Protestantism to gold discoveries, large numbers of different explanatory variables have been examined in persistence papers. The types of dependent variables used are also large, ranging from GDP per capita, city growth, human capital investment, and institutional quality to anti-Semitic violence, trust, and gender attitudes. Since this chapter cannot survey every combination of variables that has been tried in the domain of persistence studies, it will aim to illustrate key themes and challenges.

9.1 Conceptual challenges

Persistence studies arguably come in at least two and a half different "flavors". Since the mechanisms underlying them are distinct, it would be misguided to conflate them by using the same rubric. The first "flavor" takes modern-day output or a related variable, and regresses it on a historical variable. Conceptual problems arise where the origin of the historical treatment is unclear – many shocks and outcomes in the past can create self-perpetuating equilibria. Numerous papers in this category can be classified as 'apples-and-oranges' papers – meaning that they regress outcomes (today) on historical variables that are quite different in nature. Many papers of this kind have economic outcomes on the left-hand side, and some non-economic variable on the right – not only arguing, in effect, that the past influences the economic presence, but that non-economic variables are key drivers. While some of hypothesized linkages can seem ad-hoc, the more promising papers in this literature use theoretical frameworks from pre-existing studies to discipline the empirical analysis ('apples-and-oranges-with-theory'). This can help to alleviate concerns over extensive specification searches, with large numbers of combinations of variables being tried out until a significant result emerges.

A second flavor of persistence study focuses on cultural characteristics such as attitudes and beliefs, using non-economic factors as explanatory and dependent variable. I will refer to these as 'apples-on-apples' papers, using left-and-right-hand side variables that are conceptually close. This can seem more compelling. This second category of papers, while arguably easier to conceptualize, may suffer from possible confounders "along the way": many of the driving variables have direct economic effects; by influencing economic conditions in the past, their link with outcomes today may be intermediated by other, unrelated variables, creating a spaghetti-tangle of causal relationships.

9.1.1 The "history curse" – an illustration

The bible, in the book of Matthew (13:12), already had a view on the importance of persistence: "For whosoever hath, to him shall be given, and he shall have more abundance; but whosoever hath not, from him shall be taken away even that he hath." The biblical idea applies to individuals. It implies not just an enormous predictive power of starting positions, but even increasing polarization over time.

A first glance at long-run patterns in output per capita suggests that the Matthew principle broadly holds in the cross-section of countries. Fig. 9.1 shows a scatterplot of per capita incomes in 1500, 1700, 1820, and 1998. While the correlation is not perfect, correlation coefficients are high. Past riches explain up to 64% of modern-day riches. While the effect of the past fades, it does so surprisingly slowly – per capita income in 1500 still explains 20% of the variation in incomes in 1998.

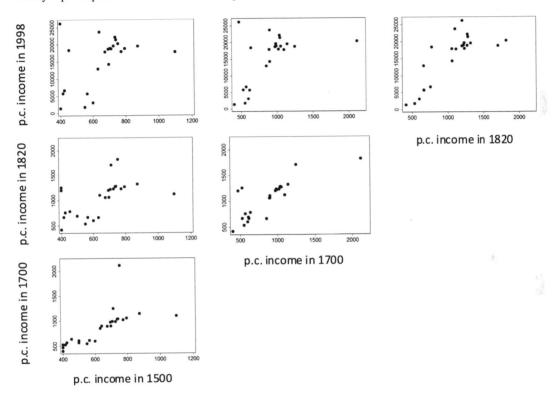

FIGURE 9.1

Scatterplot of per capita incomes in 1500, 1700, 1820, and 1998. *Source*: Voigtländer, N., Voth, H.-J., 2013. Gifts of Mars: warfare and Europe's early rise to riches. The Journal of Economic Perspectives 27 (4), 165–186. Copyright American Economic Association; reproduced with permission of the Journal of Economic Perspectives (Voigtländer and Voth, 2013a).

The strong grip of the past is startling because it is hard to rationalize in workhorse models of economic growth. In the Solow-Swan model, for example, convergence between rich and poor countries should be relatively rapid. With low capital, the return to savings should be high. Consequently, in poor countries, high savings will drive a massive expansion of the capital stock, which in turn should create catch-up vis-a-vis leading countries in short order. Most of the convergence should occur within a few decades at most (Pritchett, 1997).

First, the Matthew effect needs to be put into perspective – dramatic reversal can and have occurred over the course of history. China used to dominate most of the world in terms of the sophistication of its technology, the quality of its bureaucracy, and the effectiveness of its highly centralized state. Why it nonetheless failed to develop economically is at the heart of the so-called "Needham Puzzle", which is the subject of substantial recent research interest (De la Croix et al., 2018; Voigtländer and Voth, 2013b; Landes, 2006; Lin, 1995). Similarly, Islamic countries used to lead in terms of technology and science relative to European ones for centuries (Mokyr, 1990), before falling behind. Engerman and Sokoloff (1997) showed how in the Americas, formerly rich areas like the sugar islands of the Caribbean saw sharp declines in their relative economic standing (Sokoloff and Engerman, 2000). Acemoglu et al. (2002) argue that among the areas colonized by Europeans, those that were richest in 1500 are now particularly poor as the colonizers set up institutions designed to exploit natural resources.[1] Finally, a considerable number of once-poor East Asian countries have successfully escaped the "history curse" (Young, 1995; Kim and Lau, 1994; Hsieh, 2002).

Despite these important exceptions, the Matthew effect holds on average, as Fig. 9.1 shows. Generically, there can only be two broad classes of explanation for it – high incomes in the past may themselves facilitate growth, or the same factors that helped countries grow rich in the past are still important determinants of per capita income today.

Persistence studies overwhelmingly argue for the latter channel, but not all long-range results are equally plausible. In a widely-cited paper, Comin et al. (2010) ask "Was the wealth of nations determined 1000 BC?". The authors create indicators of technological development for different regions of the world, for 1000 BC, the year 0, and 1500, based on a detailed encyclopedia of archaeology (for pre-historical times). These they use to explain income levels today. The authors find a high degree of predictability – technologically advanced countries in 1000 BC, 0, or 1500 are all richer today. The finding is puzzling at several levels. First, because the predictive power of technology in 1000 BC for income and technology in 0 or 1500 is limited – why would technology before the age of Homer predict incomes today if it is a poor predictor of incomes at the time of Christ or Luther? Second, it is challenging to think through underlying mechanisms because the authors use geographical units, not populations, as units of observation. Since not many descendants of the people living in Germany at the time of Tacitus are still living there today, it is difficult to see how technology adoption by the ancient tribe called the Cimbri could influence technology use in modern-day Denmark, where they originated. The same is true of large parts of Greece, France, Eastern Europe, to name but a few areas.

Some of the coding that drives results can be questioned. The authors, for example, award a point to countries building ships that cross the Atlantic, another point for crossing the Indian Ocean, another for the Pacific. This is, of course, not "technology" in the strict sense of the word – building large, ocean-going ships is a technological feat. To cross various oceans with them is an outcome driven by a combination of political, economic, and cultural factors. Relatedly, the 1500 coding awards a large number of points for firearms (small, large, mounted on large ships, etc.). These choices stack the odds in favor of finding technological advantages for European powers. The main puzzle pointed out by historians of technology over the last millennium is arguably not why China was consistently behind Europe in technology – but how it came to fall behind, having been ahead for so long (Needham, 1976).

One of the earliest, path-breaking studies of history's long reach illustrates how challenging it is to untangle cause and effect. In their paper "Long-term persistence", Guiso et al. (2016) examine income differences across municipalities in modern-day Italy. They argue that the medieval experience

---

[1] Relatedly, Maloney and Valencia Caicedo (2016) show that at the sub-national level across Latin America, the persistence of fortunes is the rule – but that extractive institutions (and in particular, slavery) reduce local persistence.

of self-governance ("communes") is an important determinant of productivity today – cities that became independent created a culture of civic responsibility and self-reliance, which pays dividends to the present day. They document a persistent influence of commune status on an impressive range of outcomes – from reduced cheating on national math exams to better financial intermediation, medieval self-governance is closely associated with desirable outcomes today.

There are indeed strong reasons to assume that self-governance would have affected efficiency and output in medieval times already – as the literature on the importance of institutions would predict (Fig. 9.2). Correlated outcomes creating a new, self-reinforcing equilibrium, however, will often create a good deal of stability in state variables over time.

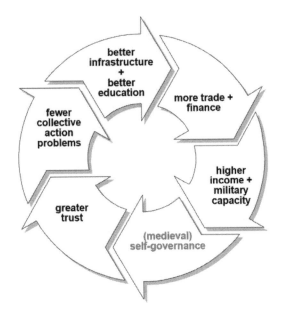

FIGURE 9.2

A medieval wheel of fortune – self-governance and economic success.

Several studies argue in favor of seemingly deep roots of comparative development but base their analysis on theoretical predictions from an earlier literature. One important example is Putterman and Weil (2008). The authors begin with the well-known connection between income per capita on the one hand, and state antiquity time as well as time since the agricultural revolution on the other – where state-like structures have existed for centuries or millennia, incomes are higher. The same is true for the length of time since the invention of sedentary agriculture in a particular country. Putterman and Weil make the important point that state antiquity in a location is not necessarily relevant – on the territory of the modern-day United States and Canada, there were no state-like structures until quite recently. However, the people living in the US today mostly come from countries where the state is quite old. Some 97 percent of the population of the New World is descended from people whose ancestors lived elsewhere. In other places, almost no adjustment is necessary – the vast majority (97.5%) of Europeans are descendants of people who already lived in Europe in 1500.

What happens if we adjust state antiquity and time since the start of agriculture by the effects of migration? Remarkably, their predictive power increases by leaps and bounds – not state antiquity in a location matters, but the exposure to the existence of a state, transmitted from generation to generation. This points the finger at a plausible mechanism – the internalization of norms that comes from abundant state power, leading to the growing "domestication" of humans along the lines of Pinker (2012) and Elias (1994).[2] Once "rendering unto Caesar" has become an ingrained habit, and the state can enforce the monopoly of violence, it is easier for growth to occur and riches to last. In this way, the results by Putterman and Weil do not only add credibility to an earlier persistence result but provide additional insight into factors driving "stickiness".[3]

This finding is in line with within-country evidence by Dell et al. (2018). They show that in areas of Vietnam that were – for plausibly exogenous reasons – not brought under the control of the centralized Northern Dai Viet state, both civic society and local governance are better at creating public goods and redistribution. Just as in Africa (Gennaioli and Rainer, 2007), pre-colonial centralization of state authority is systematically associated with better development outcomes, arguably because better governance crowds in pro-social attitudes and behaviors. The idea of "internalizing" good social norms as a result of prolonged exposure to state power is examined more closely in a recent paper by Lowes et al. (2017). However, they find that among descendants of people who lived under the Kuba kingdom in the Central African Republic, honesty was no greater than amongst study participants from other areas. Whether this reflects the specificities of state-building under the Kuba kings or the idiosyncrasies of the setting (examining migrants to Kananga instead of locals under Kuba and alternative rule) is an open question.

A similarly spectacular illustration of long-term persistence is Ashraf and Galor's (2013) argument that genetic diversity – largely determined at the time of mankind's migration out of Africa – is a prime determinant of riches today. The authors first show that migration distances from Addis Abeba are a good predictor of genetic diversity today. Since there is ample archaeological evidence to suggest that humans first appeared in Africa and then spread in small groups to the rest of the world, this is a plausible argument – reinforced by the fact distance to other locations has no predictive power. Genetic variation today is greatest in Africa, and it is lowest amongst native tribes of the Amazon.

Ashraf and Galor don't only show that genetic variation – and the part of the variation driven by the "out of Africa" component – predict income. They demonstrate that the relationship is non-linear, with intermediate levels of genetic diversity being best for GDP p.c. in 2000. Both too much and too little diversity can be bad for productivity. The argument is that 'excessive' ethnic diversity is bad because it undermines social cohesion and makes it more difficult for a capable state to emerge. Low levels of genetic diversity, on the other hand, are a barrier to creativity and technological progress. The ideal level of diversity follows a goldilocks logic – not too much and not too little.[4]

Two features distinguish the Ashraf and Galor study in methodological terms. First, they show that their mechanism is already at work in 1500. Using population density as a measure of production in the Malthusian epoch, they find the same effects of diversity and diversity squared. The fact that the same

---

[2] The separate effect for agriculture is a little harder to explain. However, since the size of states historically increased rapidly once sedentary agriculture was invented, it may be hard to tell these two factors apart.

[3] An even broader interpretation of Western European divergence and technological creativity argues that unusually high incomes led to greater individualism, pro-social attitudes, and higher rates of innovation (Baumard, 2019).

[4] The paper has been criticized by anthropologists, who contest the validity of the underlying data and assumptions about human behavior (d'Alpoim Guedes et al., 2013), and declare themselves troubled by the potential social and political effects.

pattern is visible for incomes in 1500 and 2000 increases the likelihood that Ashraf and Galor have identified a deep parameter of the development process. Second, they show evidence consistent with these mechanisms: the number of scientific articles is higher in places with greater genetic diversity, but the level of interpersonal trust is lower. The value of the Ashraf and Galor study is in showing how one 'deep' parameter – genetic diversity – can lead to similar relative outcomes over the very long run, and in documenting plausible mechanisms. In other words, Ashraf and Galor's implied explanation of the Matthew paradox is that the key driving variable for incomes has remained the same since *Homo sapiens* left Africa some 150,000 years ago.

In contrast to papers that present long-run persistence in economic outcomes as a black box, the Putterman-Weil and Ashraf-Galor papers have the benefit of documenting a detailed causal chain. Its plausibility derives from a well-documented literature demonstrating the importance of state capacity for economic development (Besley and Persson, 2010, 2009; Diamond, 1997; Spolaore and Wacziarg, 2009) and the deleterious effects of ethnic heterogeneity on the size and strength of states (Alesina et al., 2001).

9.1.2 Like father, like son

A second category of persistence studies is arguably more humble in ambition. Papers with this flavor ('apples-on-apples') employ variables on the left- and right-hand side that measure the same (or very similar) traits. There is little doubt that persistence in the strict sense of the word exists – with the same attitude or belief passed down the generations. When the variables in question are cultural features, such as attitudes and beliefs, the idea of persistence rests on relatively strong micro-foundations. This is what could be called "pure cultural persistence", especially in cases where there are no intervening or re-enforcing economic factors.

Important work by Dohmen et al. (2012) demonstrates that fundamental psychological characteristics show high correlations between parents and children. They use data from the German socio-economic panel (SOEP), and examine risk taking and trust of children as a function of parental responses. The authors find a highly significant relationship – even in narrowly defined domains, such as risk taking when driving, as opposed to risk taking in financial matters. The average child in Dohmen et al.'s study is 25 years old, meaning that results are not driven by highly impressionable young children (who may change their views in later life). Both mothers' and fathers' attitudes matter for trust, while others are primarily transmitted only via one of the parents. Overall explanatory power is not particularly high, ranging from 7 to 11% of overall variation – but parents' attitudes on average matter a great deal. Both cultural and genetic factors could be driving such dependence. In either case, long-term transmission may be higher than implied by simple correlations across two generations – for example, if latent genetic factors are activated by circumstances, or if cultural beliefs become relevant in particular contexts. A similar pattern is visible in intergenerational mobility of income and socio-economic status, where grandparents/grandchildren are more alike than is implied by parent-child transmission.

Similarly, Fernandez and Fogli (2009) pioneered the use of data on immigrants' behavior, showing striking correlations of migrants' fertility outcomes with fertility levels in the country of parental origin. Because the offspring of immigrants grew up in a very different environment than their parents, it is much more likely that we observe true cultural transmission and not a feedback effect from the environment to attitudes ("epidemiological approach"). How long attitudes can persist through vertical transmission is, however, not clear. Fuchs-Schundeln and Alesina (2007) in "Good-bye Lenin or Not?"

argue that Germans who grew up under the Communist regime are much more likely to favor redistribution and social support (and to downplay individual responsibility) than their countrymen who grew up in the West. The more time Germans spent under Communist influence, the more pro-government people became. Because the environment changed radically after 1989, with the fall of the wall, the attitudes of young people growing up in the eastern part of Germany today are converging towards the West German norm – but such convergence is relatively slow, and will take one to two generations to be complete.

The assumption that assignment to treatment in the past is often as "good as random" is unfortunately often wrong. Implicitly, the Alesina and Fuchs-Schündeln paper assumes that pre-1945, East and West Germany were largely identical in attitudes – and hence, any differences that appear today must be the result of the Communist "treatment". This assumption is prima facie sensible, in the absence of evidence to the contrary – after all, they had formed part of the same country since 1871. However, there is strong evidence that the area of Germany that became the GDR was already strongly different in a number of important dimensions prior to 1945 – church attendance was already lower, female labor force participation was higher, and electoral support for the Communists was higher in the East in the interwar period (Becker et al., 2020). In other words, the 'treatment' of Communist rule and Soviet occupation may only have preserved or amplified pre-existing differences. This does not imply that there was no persistence – it implies that it was so strong in this particular case that even the cultural and social effects of a brutal, long-lasting dictatorship did little more than to leave intact differences that existed long ago.

Both the Dohmen et al. and the Fernandez and Fogli studies provide conceptual microfoundations for *cultural* persistence – with attitudes and beliefs staying the same. Along the same lines, the *amplification* of existing prejudice through synergy with policy can strengthen beliefs and biases, as Voigtländer and Voth (2015) show in the case of exposure to Nazi schooling and anti-Semitism. Historical studies that have studied such persistence over the long run have often focused on human capital. Here, however, the possible 'contamination' with economic feedback effects is not trivial.

In one recent study, Chen et al. (2020) examine the long-run effects of keju, China's imperial exam system. They show that in areas of China where more citizens passed the highest exams (jinshi), educational attainment today is markedly higher. The imperial exam system itself first appeared in the Han Dynasty (206BC-220AD). Its core elements lasted for more than two millennia. The authors argue that social capital, educational infrastructure, and interactions with political elites led to continued investments in one trait – the value given to education. The fact that local continuity is visible in China despite the massive institutional, cultural, and economic discontinuity of the Chinese civil war and the Communist takeover after 1948 is remarkable. A similar result emerges from recent work on earnings differences between descendants of elite and non-elite families, based on social stratification prior to the Communist take-over. Despite the best efforts of the Chinese Communist party to eliminate intergenerational transmission of status and wealth, descendants of China's pre-revolutionary elite have higher education and higher earnings than the average Chinese (Alesina et al., 2020).[5]

Valencia Caicedo (2019) examines educational outcomes in modern-day Paraguay, Brazil, and Argentina. In areas inhabited by Guaraní tribesmen, he finds that areas where the Jesuits proselytized, levels of education (and income) are markedly higher today. The Jesuits were more keenly interested in educating converts than other Catholic orders, building massive schools in the middle of the

---

[5] This finding echoes results by Clark on the long-term transmission of status in English society (Clark, 2014).

South-American rainforest. Similar effects do not exist for, say, areas of Guaraní settlement where the Franciscans, another order, built missions. Persistence of educational outcomes over 250 years is remarkable, not least because the Jesuits were expelled from South America, following an agreement between the Spanish and Portuguese crowns in 1759. In other words, just as in the Chinese case studied by Kung et al., Valencia finds that educational persistence is high over the very long run – despite the fact that in his case, the intervention leading to high investments in the past was itself relatively short-lived, compared with the prolonged Chinese exposure to a high-education environment in the past.

Both the Valencia and the Kung et al. studies have the advantage of studying the same variable's long-term evolution. At the same time, factors such as intellectual aptitude and the importance of education are typically passed down from parent to child within families, having both a genetic and cultural component – making for a plausible transmission mechanism. Along the same lines, Voigtländer and Voth (2012) analyze anti-Semitic attitudes and acts in Germany, comparing outcomes in the 1920s and 1930s with the geography of medieval pogroms. In these three cases, the variable on the left-hand side of the regression is essentially the same as the one that is on the right-hand side, or the implicit model of causation is relatively straightforward. Sometimes, the concept itself is not straightforward to measure ("anti-Semitism"; "education"), requiring the use of multiple outcome indicators to confirm the similarity of basic patterns across time. Persistence papers in this vein are unlikely to suffer from the problem of multiple hypothesis testing and the attendant inflation of test statistics. They also – implicitly or explicitly – are based on a clear, micro-evidence based model of causation.

A second category of papers examining the roots of attitudes and beliefs relies on well-specified theoretical connections between historical and modern-day outcomes to guide and inspire statistical analysis. Here, the link is often indirect, but made plausible by a pre-existing narrative or guiding theory. One example of this is Alesina et al. (2010). They argue that plough adoption, with its need for greater upper-body strength, increased men's bargaining power within the household. This led to greater inequality between the sexes, with men being favored in terms of social status, access to food and education, and legal standing. The hypothesis goes back to Esther Boserup, whose book *Women's Role in Economic Development* (Boserup, 2007) spelled out the idea that ancient agricultural practices influence gender roles today.

Alesina et al. then go on to show that plough usage in pre-modern agriculture correlates with lower labor force participation of women today – long after the role of agriculture as a source of employment has declined to low levels. To avoid issues of omitted variable bias, the authors use data on soil suitability for different crop types to show that the variation in plough usage driven by exogenous factors predicts gender roles today. Where productive agriculture required men to work long and hard in the fields, it is still the case that women mostly stay at home today. Attitudes in the past were probably changed by a new tool – the plough – and then perpetuated themselves over time. Additional evidence that gender roles already were unequal in the past would have strengthened results still further. If, say, in 1900 countries with heavy plough usage did not show much evidence of traditional gender roles, and the correlation only emerged in the period after 1950, the plausibility of persistence as a vital driver of the gender division of labor today could be called into question.

Similarly, Nunn and Wantchekon (2011) argue that slave catching in Africa from the 17th to the 19th century is a cause of lower trust today. Slave catching was pre-dominantly an activity that pitted Africans against Africans – few Europeans survived African disease environments before the 19th century. Groups that suffered from greater enslavement may have evolved traditions of distrusting outsiders, fellow tribesmen, and family, in order to avoid capture. Where slave catching was intense and long lasting, this should have created a strong incentive for parents to pass on distrustful attitudes to children. The idea is not novel, but part of a long tradition of historical writings on slavery and its effects on African countries.

The Nunn and Wantchekon study has the advantage of a setting where the causal connection is highly plausible, coming from a rich historical literature. At the same time, because of the well-known feed-back effect between income and trust may affect each other, it is harder to think of slavery's effect on trust as persistence in its simplest form. If slave catching lowered trust historically, and thereby also incomes in the past, thinking about causal effects becomes more challenging. Since low income environments typically breed distrust (arguably because people do not have the resources to invest in the social connections maintain exchange among equals), the continued co-existence of low incomes and low trust in areas with massive slave hauls in the past is harder to interpret. Instead of showing pure cultural persistence (perhaps as a result of parent to child or horizontal transmission), it could be part of an equilibrium outcome, with two variables reinforcing each other. Here, Nunn's and Wantchekon's use of the epidemiological approach is crucial. By showing that Africans who migrated to other areas still show lower trust today if they came from areas historically affected by slave catching, they can rule out much of the effect of contemporaneous poverty on trust. What remains is the transmission of the effects of both poverty and trust "back home" on an individual's attitudes.[6]

The most questionable category of persistence papers regresses a modern-day outcome on some variable from past, and then argues that a significant coefficient is a sign of persistence. This is all the more problematic if the explanatory variable is multi-faceted, touching on many beliefs and attitudes, like Protestantism. Since culture travels in packages – as a set of interrelated characteristics – the actual insight gained by such regressions is limited. For example, a recent paper (Kenyon and Fatti, 2020) asked "Thank Martin Luther that ciprofloxacin could cure your gonorrhoea?" The paper examines the consumption of antimicrobial medicine in 30 European countries and shows a strong 'effect' of Protestantism – which is then rationalized by uncertainty avoidance and a preference for cooperation over performance in Catholic countries are to blame (Kenyon and Fatti, 2020). Apart from the doubts one might reasonably have about a cross-country study with 30 observations, it is clear that the association with (historical) Protestantism does not create particular insight into the origins of resistant "super-bugs".

9.1.3 Mistakes and mechanisms

For a whole class of persistence papers, there is a readily available alternative interpretation – economic geography. This is because cross-sectional differences are the main source of variation exploited in persistence studies. As long as data cannot be supplemented by information on movers, as in the epidemiological approach, telling cultural persistence apart from stable patterns due economic geography is fundamentally hard. For example, if geography spelled riches for some Italian cities, but not others in the Middle Ages, then similar factors may still be at work today. While the exact set of geographical characteristics that lead to high incomes may have shifted over the centuries, basic features like coastal

---

[6] Note that the solution is necessarily imperfect – because we know that people's attitudes are more malleable at a young age. If, say, the transmission from income was strong and took place entirely before age 10, looking at movers only would not attenuate the reflection problem.

access, centrality in a network of cities, and a terrain suitable for housing an expanding population could all influence economic performance at the same moment in time. Given that both economic geography and cultural traits are often highly persistent, good practice arguably requires a concerted effort to rule out one in favor of the other. Allen and Donaldson (2020) build a model of spatial externalities showing under what conditions history matters for the distribution of economic activity. Calibrating parameters to US data from 1800 to the present, they show that even small differences in the past can have repercussions for the location and efficiency.

Few papers explicitly try to explain (let alone model) the geographical distribution of their deep-rooted explanatory variable. In economic geography, the location of economic activity can be explained by two alternative approaches – either by increasing returns interacting with random shocks, as in the work by Krugman (1991) and Fujita et al. (1999), or by locational fundamentals. Davis and Weinstein's (2002) study of Japanese population and production after 1945 shows that even a shock as large as the atomic bombing of Hiroshima and Nagasaki did not shift the distribution of economic activity significantly. This suggests that locational fundamentals are first-order. At the same time, numerous studies have found that temporary shocks can cause long-term shifts in economic activity. Bleakley and Lin's (2012) study of portage sites in the US, Redding et al.'s (2011) work on the location of airports in Germany – fundamentally transformed by the country's partition – and Kline and Moretti's (2014) analysis of the Tennessee Valley Authority (TVA) all document that geographically well-defined, local shocks can severely affect economic activity over the long term.

Where such well-defined shocks are not a source for identification, the claim that 'persistence' (of cultural traits) is to blame can be hard to substantiate. For example, Fritsch et al. (2019) analyze patterns of self-employment in Kaliningrad – the formerly German city of Königsberg, today an exclave of the Russian Federation. Comparing data from 1925 and 2010, they find that patterns of self-employment within each industry have remained broadly similar. This is striking because the area around Königsberg suffered heavily during the final phase of World War II. A high proportion of the housing stock, and of industrial installations, was completely destroyed. What remained of the original German population either fled the Soviets or was quickly expelled after 1945. The paper then argues that in areas where small German firms adopted advanced technology (in the form of electric motors), the historical success of small firms was self-perpetuating. As the authors put it:

"The most likely explanation for this persistence is the historical experience with entrepreneurship in a certain industry. In the case of the Kaliningrad area, this experience led to an awareness of the region-specific scope and viability of entrepreneurship among the new population. If this awareness was passed on across generations, then it is likely to lead to a re-emergence of entrepreneurship after the dissolution of the Soviet Union, which implies high shares of small firms and self-employment rates."

The authors apparently rationalize the continued importance of self-employment as a form of updating in the minds of the new residents – the Soviet citizens looking around the ruins of Königsberg in 1945 decided, in some places more than in others, that in this environment, self-employment is promising. This insight then lays dormant for half a century, before becoming relevant and useful once the Soviet Union fell. The authors conclude that cultural transmission from Germans to Soviets is an unlikely explanatory factor, as new Russian residents hardly overlapped with previous German inhabitants; but that the awareness of entrepreneurial activity was passed down the generations.

The effects of economic geography are a more likely interpretation. The authors argue that controlling for economic geography (which they proxy by coastal access) does not alter their results. A richer set of controls would likely capture more of the relevant variation. What is being produced where is often driven by regional specialization plus the stickiness of past infrastructure. While population changed entirely, existing factories and infrastructure did not. The Soviets repaired destroyed structures and production equipment on a considerable scale. The fact that industrial structures in 2010 are similar to those in 1925 is therefore not surprising – not even the atomic blasts of Hiroshima and Nagasaki had major long-term effects on the distribution of economic activity across space in Japan (Davis and Weinstein, 2002).[7] As Fritsch et al.'s regressions show, adding a measure of industrial structure in 1925 already renders historical shares of self-employment insignificant predictors of self-employment in 2010.

Some useful insight into the role of economic geography comes from an innovative paper by Michaels and Rauch (2018). They examine changes in the urban structure of Britain and France after the end of the Roman Empire. While Britain saw a wholesale decline of her cities after the Roman legions withdrew, French cities never disappeared. The "reset" of the British urban system allowed for the creation of new centers in favorable locations during the Middle Ages. In contrast, French cities were "locked in"; the one-off cost of moving to more favorable locations was never paid. This was costly in the long run. As urban centers re-emerged in medieval Europe, British cities were much more likely to be in places that facilitated rapid growth, with good coastal or river access.

Michaels and Rauch's paper suggests that the shadows of history can be long indeed, and cause major inefficiency. However, if a major shock provides an opportunity for a "reset", locational fundamentals can reassert themselves, becoming key explanatory variables for the location of economic activity in space. The exact circumstances under which persistence is either strong, or fades away, have yet to be established.

9.1.4 Change and re-emergence

Persistence – defined as the continued or prolonged existence of something – also sits uncomfortably with the seeming re-emergence of historical traits and features. Individual human memory is not fundamentally different from that of other primates; but collective memory is a cultural construct: By definition, it is not based on the sensory experience of individuals, but an act of cultural production (Nora, 1989). Many Israeli conscripts used to take their induction oath at Masada, where Sicarii rebels defied the Romans towards the end of the First Jewish-Roman war. Modern-day recruits could never have met anyone whose living memory included the siege, which concluded in 74 AD – but it nonetheless defined their country's identity and outlook during the decades after 1948. Reinterpreting situations later in life through the lens of transmitted cultural focal points such as this one, there is 'persistence' – but in the form of a latent trait or concept that can be activated when current circumstances are reminiscent of a situation in the past (imagined, collectively recalled, or personally experienced). In other words, Masada acquired relevance for Jews living in Palestine once more when faced with the overwhelmingly hostile environment of the Middle East after the Jewish state's founding.

One good example of the more complex interaction of political choices and a remembered past is Ochsner and Roesel's (2017) paper on the Turkish sieges of Vienna. Turkish advances into central Europe in the 16th and 17th centuries were defining moments, not just for the affected areas, but for Europe as a whole. As was the case with all early modern armies, the Ottoman Empire's invasion of

---

[7] In related research, Grosfeld and Zhuravskaya (2015) demonstrate that the quality of historical infrastructure in Poland in the 19th century still has predictive power for modern infrastructure and economic prosperity.

the Austrian lands was accompanied by arson and plunder, rape and pillage. Many cities and towns commemorate the hardships of Turkish occupation to the present day. Heraldic crests recall how cities were burned down; in other locations, street names remind citizens of the horrors of the Turkish invasion.

Interestingly, towns and cities affected by the Turkish advance on Vienna were not more right-leaning than others during the 20th century. This changed radically once the far-right freedom party of Austria began to campaign against a potential Turkish membership of the EU in 2005. While a remote political prospect, the perceived threat of such a move solidified support for the FPÖ – and all the more so in locations that had suffered at the hands of the Turks. Hence, what appears like a clear case of persistence is actually the result of complex interactions. Instead of suffering at the hands of one group, which then leads to enmity, a long-forgotten incident is revived in public consciousness only if and when doing so is propitious for one political player – in this case "hate entrepreneurs" along the lines of Glaeser's (2005) classic paper. The standard persistence analysis, a simple regression of FPÖ voting on Turkish occupation in 1529 and 1683, would show a high correlation – but there is no direct continuity. Instead, as the authors carefully document, it was collective recall, carefully engineered by far-right politicians in the FPÖ, that is created an effect as a result of being part of an "imagined community", in the words of Benedikt Anderson (2006).

Some insightful studies look at change and persistence jointly. Bazzi et al. (2020), for example, test the "Turner hypothesis" about the American frontier experience. Turner and Bogue (1893) had famously argued that living in the newly-settled areas of the American West was instrumental in creating a culture of rugged self-dependence, and that greater scepticism about the role of the government compared to other countries was a direct consequence of the frontier. Bazzi et al. now examine one indicator of individualism – naming patterns. They show that in counties on the frontier, defined as those with population density below a low threshold of six people per square mile, rare first names back then and today are much more common. In other words, naming patterns reflected a willingness to stand out rather than blend in. Areas that experienced the frontier for a long time believe that the government should not redistribute income, prefer public spending cuts for the poor and welfare, oppose a ban on assault rifles and raising the minimum wage, and prefer to reduce public debt. Bazzi et al. then go on to show that in these places, there is more support for the Republican party, and greater distrust of government intervention, than in parts of the US without the frontier experience.

The frontier could have attracted people who were already more individualistic; and these could then have stayed, with their descendants still believing in the same values. This would be a case of direct cultural persistence. While transmission over a century alone would be interesting, it would not greatly shift priors relative to other papers. Importantly, Bazzi et al. also show that the frontier experience itself made people more individualistic – families that moved to the frontier increasingly gave highly unusual names to their children, and stopped using the names of fathers and mothers to name their children. Children whose parents moved to the frontier when they were young were much more likely to be highly individualistic in naming their children, too. Interestingly, they also find that individualists (based on their measure) did better economically in 19th century America – on the frontier. The combination of documenting cultural change, selection, and persistence makes the Bazzi et al. paper a particularly compelling contribution, offering insights into mechanisms, economic feedback effects, and long-term cultural transmission.

9.2 **Econometric challenges**

Recently, both the size and significance of statistical persistence results have come to be questioned. I first discuss general challenges before turning to recent work on persistence and spatial autocorrelation, and the effect of long-term dependence on parameter estimates.

Potential econometric problems in persistence studies abound. Publication bias compounds some of them. Few papers estimate precisely estimated zero effects – in contexts where persistence might have been plausible – or show that some seemingly immutable characteristics disappear. There are many historical events and features that could be investigated, and their effect on modern-day outcomes examined. Take, for example, the role of women in society today, and the geography of witch-hunting. Every argument made for why anti-Semitism might persist over long time periods could apply here; areas with more witch persecution will have had more negative views of women, on average, but will also have induced women to be less assertive, less insistent on equal rights, and less inclined to question traditional gender roles. Some of these mechanisms may have perpetuated themselves even without actual witch persecutions (the last of which still occurred in the 19th century). At the level of entire countries, the argument may have some empirical support – the country with the most intense persecution of witches, Germany, has remarkably low rates of labor force participation, for example. In other words, there are strong reasons to argue that gender attitudes today should reflect witch-hunting – but there are no papers making this point. Given the importance of the topic, this may well indicate that the link cannot be proven – and yet, in surveys of persistence, non-results hardly play any role.

The very range of different variables and analytical categories employed creates the potential for false positives. If there are N different historical variables whose impact might be explored, and M modern-day outcomes that can be analyzed, researchers could theoretically run N∗M regressions. At standard levels of statistical significance, 0.1∗(N∗M) or 0.05∗(N∗M) regressions will find an effect that is different from zero. Of course, there are standard ways to adjust for multiple hypothesis testing, such as Bonferroni corrections. One problem is that for any one paper, it is hard to assess what the set of plausible variables is. Researchers will typically iterate over different variables, looking for significant patterns. Once a pattern emerges, it becomes easier to think of a set of explanations why historical variable x is related to modern-day outcome y.

One simple way to address the multiple hypothesis testing problem would be to pre-register empirical analyses, as is common in development economics. Researchers would have to state ex ante which patterns in the data they expect, and why. They could even register the range of additional variables they expect to try, should the main hypothesized relationship not materialize. Researchers might start with the hypothesis that gold discoveries in an area lead to higher discount rates today, because gold mining rewards immediate effort and attracts the impatient. If this regression turned out to be insignificant, but the researchers had moved on to demonstrate that there were larger gay communities in areas of great mineral wealth of any kind (rationalized by the after-effects of a sizeable gender imbalance), it would become immediately apparent that authors were fishing for significance.[8] Because the number of possible explanatory/dependent variables is specified ex ante, the appropriate adjustment could be applied, raising the bar for statistical significance.

---

[8] After this section was written, I was made aware of a recent paper by Brodeur and Haddad (2018). In no way do I wish to imply that the authors followed this path of discovery – this is an illustrative example only.

The vast majority of persistence papers use geographical variation of a variable at some point in the distant past to explain a later – often modern-day – outcome. In a paper that has attracted substantial attention, Kelly (2019) argues that these papers severely understate the size of standard errors because of spatial correlation – adjacent observations are not truly independent from each other, but display a great deal of dependence. Kelly examines the extent of spatial correlation analyzing the residuals of the key regressions in 23 papers, using Moran's I. He finds a significant degree of spatial dependence, which he takes to imply that significance levels have been severely overstated. To assess the extent of the problem, Kelly then uses spatial noise as both dependent and independent variable. Regressions using both produce levels of significance that in many cases exceed those for the main regression in the papers in question. While a few papers still show significance at standard levels, the vast majority do not.

None of Kelly's analysis is specific to persistence studies as such – any paper using spatial variation will potentially suffer from the same problem.[9] The potential problem of spatial correlation is also widely known, and subject of a large literature in econometrics that has developed a standard set of tools to deal with it. There appear to be no compelling reasons to cast aside the standard econometricians' toolbox for dealing with spatial error correlations. Equally importantly, there are strong reasons to reject the conclusions drawn by Kelly (2019). Several aspects of his implementation bias results in favor of finding overstated significance levels. First, where authors used a range of variables to capture outcomes, he invariably picks the one that makes results look more fragile. One example is the paper by Voigtländer and Voth (2012) about the link between medieval pogroms and anti-Jewish persecution in Germany. Kelly picks only one of the five different dependent variables used by the authors – a regression with the percentage of Nazi votes in 1928 on the left-hand side. The paper uses another four additional outcomes that also measure interwar anti-Semitism – anti-Jewish pogroms before 1933, the share of Jews deported, letters to the anti-Semitic newspaper *Der Stürmer*, and attacks during the Night of Broken Glass in 1938. For each of these, results even in the baseline specification are markedly stronger when using the Kelly method. As Fig. 9.5 shows, for the example of synagogue attacks, using the Kelly method of simulated spatial noise yields only a 2% probability of noise outperforming.

Equally problematic is the fact that Kelly only picks the first specification presented in each paper. While this allows a certain degree of standardization, it creates a false impression of fragility – the first regression in empirical papers typically shows only a simple bivariate relationship, demonstrating the strength of basic patterns. Papers that do not show such a basic relationship, but instead rely on saturated specifications to find significant coefficients, are often on shaky empirical grounds – but according to Kelly's analysis, they will appear superior. All papers on Kelly's list as a matter of course conduct more sophisticated analysis using more extensive specifications. This matters because, if other explanatory variables capture a significant share of the spatial correlation, the error term itself may be largely free of spatially correlated noise.

Almost all of the papers in question also consider the possibility of spatially correlated variables directly.[10] Standard remedies like regional fixed effects and clustered standard errors are common in many research papers on persistence. I will next illustrate the strength of the bias introduced by Kelly's focus on the first specification in each paper. Becker and Woessmann (2009) argue that early adoption of Lutheranism led to higher levels in education in 19th century Prussia. In other words, while

---

[9] Note that Kelly implicitly acknowledges as much, applying a related approach to non-historical papers (Kelly, 2020a).

[10] For example, Nunn and Wantchekon (2011) report three different types of standard errors including Conley standard errors. Other papers (Michalopoulos and Papaioannou, 2013, 2016) use the multi-way clustering approach by Cameron et al. (2011).

Max Weber's famous hypothesis about the economic benefits of Protestantism looks right in the cross-section, the reasons for it may well be different – since Protestants put particular emphasis on reading the bible, human capital was simply higher. In Kelly's exercise, spatial noise (used as an explanatory variable) outperforms the basic regression by Becker and Woessmann 56 percent of the time. This, taken at face value, would suggest that there is no explanatory power at all in their explanatory variable – the share of Protestants in a Prussian county. Of course, Becker and Woessmann estimate full specifications including latitude and longitude, an interaction of latitude and longitude to control for non-linearities, plus distance to Berlin (Table 2, col 3), to which they add 35 district dummies (col 4). In the saturated specification, their coefficient on percentage Protestant improves from 0.08 to 0.11, and the t-statistic from 5.15 to 10. Whatever overall similarity there may be in each district in terms of the share of Protestants is absorbed by the fixed effect. Put another way, when the authors effectively compare two counties in the same district with different shares of Protestants, holding constant latitude, longitude, latitude x longitude, and distance to Berlin, they find even larger effects. At the same time as their coefficient strengthens, the R2 increases from 0.057 to 0.81, moving from the basic OLS to the saturated specification. In the spirit of Altonji et al./Oster, this implies that unobservables are unlikely to account for the main finding (Oster, 2019; Altonji et al., 2005).

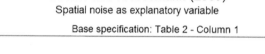

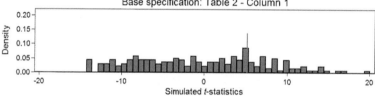

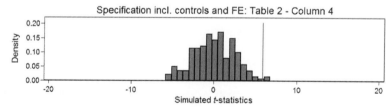

Notes: Vertical red line indicates t-statistic of observed explanatory variable.
Correlation range = 4

FIGURE 9.3

Simulated regression coefficients, education regressed on Protestantism, baseline regression and saturated specification, Kelly (2019) method.

Once we re-estimate the Kelly approach with the full specification, including Becker and Woessmann's controls and fixed effects, noise only outperforms in one percent of simulations. The seeming problem of spatial correlation is well-addressed by what the authors of the original paper already did. Fig. 9.3 gives an overview of the significance of the share of simulations outperforming the paper's estimated coefficient. The distribution of simulated coefficients shrinks as controls and fixed effects are added. Since the coefficient estimated by Becker and Woessmann barely changes, its significance relative to the distribution of simulated coefficients increases sharply. This means that the overall conclusion in Becker and Woessmann is robust even when using Kelly's method to assess significance.

Fig. 9.4 illustrates why including geographical fixed effects is a very effective tool to control for spatial correlation. It uses variation in Nazi voting in interwar Germany in 1928, and tries to explain it by the density of clubs and associations (Satyanath et al., 2017). The upper panel plots the residuals in the naive regression, simply using a bivariate regression. There is a good deal of spatial dependence. Most of the Ruhr area shows positive deviations, meaning that there was more voting for the NSDAP than expected; the opposite is true in the Eastern part of Germany. The lower panel shows the effect of including province fixed effects. Now, both in the Ruhr and in Saxony positive and negative deviations at the local level sit side-by-side. As is readily apparent from eyeballing the residuals, spatial autocorrelation is well-controlled, with red (light gray in print version) and blue (dark gray in print version) dots (indicating above and below average levels of Nazi support) alternating in close geographical proximity.

Fig. 9.5 shows that most papers included in Kelly (2019) register a marked improvement once we use the more sensible, "full" specifications included in the original papers. In other words, the majority of researchers working on persistence were perfectly aware of the potential problems arising from spatial correlation, and already took effective steps to sidestep its impact. In doing so, they overcame most of the upward bias in significance; almost no paper suffers from results that become insignificant in the key specification, once spatial dependence is properly controlled for. What remains are minor disagreements about the exact magnitude of statistical significance.[11]

There are also major doubts about the conceptual usefulness of Kelly's approach – the percentage of cases where noise outperforms the OLS estimation in Fig. 9.5 is not an accurate guide to the validity of the estimation technique. Monte Carlo simulations by Colella et al. (2019) demonstrate that his horserace of spatial noise regressed on spatial noise is too restrictive, leading to a substantial exaggeration of any existing bias. The standard Conley correction of standard errors for spatial correlation is sufficient to assess the significance of findings. If randomization inference is to be used, it should only be used with spatial noise as the exogenous variable – a test which most persistence papers pass with flying colors. In other words, most of the problem identified by Kelly (2019) is a myth. His paper overestimates the scale of the problem, creates an artificially high bar for overcoming it; it is also not compelling in its insistence that persistence papers are particularly prone to suffer from spatial dependence to the point of insignificance.[12]

---

[11] The code and data for regressions and simulations in this essay are freely available at http://www.jvoth.com/data/replication/handbook and at the ICSPR data repository.

[12] A recent extension adds claims that many regression results in the persistence papers are fragile, and become insignificant once estimation methods are changed and outliers stopped (Kelly, 2020b). Again, most papers already study exactly these alleged sources of 'fragility', and demonstrate that there is no serious fragility. For example, Acemoglu et al. (2002), criticized by Kelly (2019) for using continent fixed effects, actually already reported specifications with them. Most of the fragility critique appears to be a case of 'reverse p-hacking', where out of the N specifications in a paper, a single one is singled out and subjected to every possible permutation, until a coefficient drops below standard significance levels. A fair-minded approach would instead consider the overall pattern of coefficient size and significance, including all that papers have already done to address issues of robustness and sensitivity to outliers.

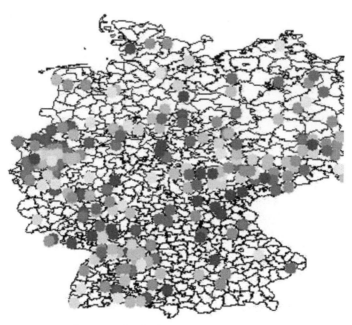

Panel a: Residuals, baseline OLS regression

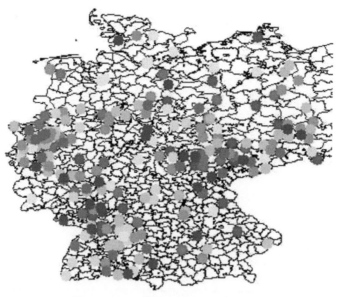

Panel b: Residuals after using geographical fixed effects and controls

FIGURE 9.4

Spatial correlation in Nazi voting, residuals after baseline OLS specification (panel a), or with fixed effects (panel b). Data from Satyanath et al. (2017).

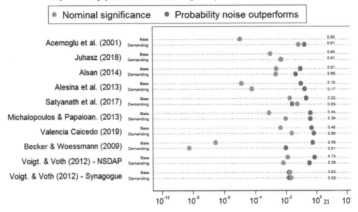

FIGURE 9.5

Significance of main parameter estimates, baseline vs full specification, OLS vs Kelly (2019) method. *Note:* The graph shows the statistical significance of the main variable of interest, for two estimation methods and two specifications (4 outcomes per paper) – simple OLS and the Kelly random noise method, using the baseline specification in the paper and the most demanding specification used. *Example:* In the Becker & Woessmann paper, using the baseline specification, spatial noise outperforms the estimated coefficient 56% of the time. In the most demanding specification, this is only the case 1% of the time.

A different potential objection concerns the size of parameter estimates. Casey and Klemp (2020) argue that the coefficients in persistence regressions suffer from systematic upward bias – and the more so, the longer the period over a which a trait's persistence is being examined. Their argument is simple. If we are interested in the effect of A on B. A is changing as time goes by. If A is potentially endogenous, we need an instrument to estimate the causal effect of A on B. Now, A is often not observed in the past: instead, we measure A', contemporaneous values of the variable. Crucially, historical values of A can influence modern-day values of A'. Casey and Klemp now argue that the OLS coefficient will over-estimate the effect of modern-day A if historical values of A' are not very similar to modern-day ones, i.e. if persistence is low. The intuition for this result is that the OLS coefficient indicates the long-run effect of an increase in historical A that leads to a unit rise in modern-day A. If persistence of A is low, then estimating with IV will systematically overestimate the size of effects.

Casey and Klemp make a conceptually valid point. At the same time, the corrections necessary appear relatively small. They apply their approach to deriving correct estimates to the Becker and Woessmann study, for example, and find a coefficient that is only 9% smaller than the one estimated by conventional IV. For the case of Acemoglu et al.'s (2001) famous study of settler mortality, institutions and income, the correction is somewhat larger – reducing the main coefficient by 45%. However, conceptual challenges appear a potentially greater issue (Albouy, 2012).

9.2.1 Summary

Econometric challenges in persistence studies undoubtedly have to be taken seriously. In 'apples-and-oranges' studies, there is a real risk of p-hacking because of the wide range of variables that can appear on the left-hand side of an econometric equation. This is especially true when modern-day surveys are used to generate dependent variables, since they typically contain dozens of questions. The potential effect of spatial correlation, on the other hand, has been exaggerated. The problem of autocorrelated spatial residuals biasing standard errors downwards is not specific to persistence studies, and is well-known. Recent work examining various persistence papers with this problem in mind (Kelly, 2019) appears to overstate its severity by several orders of magnitude, and offers no diagnostics that are conceptually or empirically superior to well-established routines (Colella et al., 2019).

9.3 Conclusion: vanishing for understanding

'My future will not copy fair my past'
- Elizabeth Barret-Browning

To escape one's origins, to leave behind the binding ties of family, place, class and gender, is a dream as old as mankind – as the quote by Barret-Browning implies. The rapidly growing literature showing a surprising predictive power of the past touched a nerve within economics and beyond, because it seems to question this dream. Nothing can today be done to change a country's technology, or its government institutions, in 1000 BC; nor can African nations exposed to the slave-trade shed their past. One view is that, the tighter the handcuffs of the past shackle the present, the more fatalistic – and less hopeful – economics as a science will have to be. An alternative interpretation is that a deeper understanding of the determinants of riches and poverty can guide policy interventions towards more realistic 'levers of riches' (Mokyr, 1990).[13]

A significant share of papers claiming to find evidence of persistence regress some historical variable on a modern-day outcome. Many are almost entirely "black box", and do not go beyond finding a significant coefficient, or invoking vertical transmission from parent to child as a likely interpretation. This may make sense when the same trait, preference or attitude is measured historically and in modern times – but this is arguably the case in only a minority of papers. As the conceptual distance between the historical and the modern-day measure increases, the passing on of culture from parent to child becomes less and less likely, and alternative mechanisms become more probable – such as new equilibria driven by an interaction of economic outcomes with historical characteristics, or the simple stickiness of economic geography and man-made infrastructure. Many persistence studies invoke culture as an arguably plausible mechanism, but it is rare that its role is demonstrated in a rigorous fashion. Where complex interactions between historical variables combined to create differences in initial outcomes, the further scientific value-added of "reduced form" estimates, derived from regressing modern-day outcomes on past indicators, is going to be limited.

As in other areas of empirical work in economics, more work on mechanisms will be helpful. To understand persistence of this (more narrow) kind, we arguably need to look at what it takes to make it

---

[13] A similar point is made by Nunn (2020).

go away. This will allow a better understanding of the mechanisms driving it in the first place. An ambitious paper that attempts to accomplish this is Giuliano and Nunn (2017). They argue that the stability of a group's environment encourages a high degree of vertical transmission. In particular, they examine whether areas that experienced considerable shifts in climatic conditions are more conservative in their attitudes, giving greater weight to the opinions of elders and the like. In each generation, people have a choice of either copying from previous generations, or of experimenting with new technologies, agricultural practices, or forms of interaction. The more stable the environment, the greater the similarity of conditions today relative to those of the previous generation. The extent of variability then affects the degree of stability of preferences and practices. To measure stability of the environment, Giuliano and Nunn (2017) look at climatic change over the period 500-1900. Across a range of empirical settings, they find support for their basic prediction: In the World Value Survey, people from countries with greater climatic variation in the past show less regard for tradition. When looking at immigrants to the US, there is also less outgroup marriage for those who come from countries where climate stayed large the same over the last 1500 years. Similarly, immigrants from countries with stable climates were also less likely to speak English at home after migrating to the US. They then go on to examine stability of the same traits over time, and the extent to which this is attenuated by climatic variability. For three variables – cousin marriage, polygamy, and female labor force participation – they find a high degree of persistence, as well as an attenuating effect of climatic instability. Giuliano and Nunn conclude that persistence is an outcome, which can be rationalized based on the costs and benefits associated with it.

Along similar lines, Voigtländer and Voth (2012) document that the predictive power of medieval anti-Semitism in Germany in general was high for persecution in the interwar period. However, persistence is lower in towns and cities with more immigration during the 19th century. In other words, where modern-day inhabitants were largely unrelated to the people living in a location centuries ago, persistence – narrowly defined – vanishes. The same is true in old trading cities, where there was a particularly strong trade-off between prejudices on the one hand, and economic success on the other. Differential migration and its effect on the composition in general is arguably underappreciated as a driver of cultural change: Ichino and Maggi (2000) demonstrate that in Italy, the more reliable employees gravitated towards the North, where they would find co-workers with similar characteristics. Similarly, East Germany's continued underperformance after reunification may echo the size of the brain drain prior to 1961 (Becker et al., 2020).[14] Such findings reconnect with some of the theoretical work on the trade-offs involved in cultural transmission – in this case, the canonical Bisin-Verdier model of parental investment in children's attitudes (Bisin and Verdier, 2000, 2001).[15]

The second meaning of "persistence" highlighted by the *Oxford English Dictionary* is the "fact of continuing in an opinion or course of action in spite of difficulty or opposition." To make progress, persistence studies will have to grapple not just with scepticism by professional historians, but to find ways of dealing effectively with the challenges highlighted in this essay. In 'apple-on-apple' analyses, where the *same* or near-identical variables are on the right- and left-hand side, and where attitudes, beliefs, cultural preferences or social arrangements are often the focus, we can speak of persistence in its basic form. Going forward, a greater focus on persistence in this stricter sense, and on mechanisms creating it, may be helpful.

---

[14] At the same time, if migration is slow enough, even substantial turnover may go hand-in-hand with stable cultural preferences, if horizontal transmission is sufficiently powerful (Becker et al., 2016).

[15] For a related approach exploring interactions with economic incentives, cf. Doepke and Zilibotti (2008).

References

Acemoglu, D., Johnson, S., Robinson, J.A., 2001. The colonial origins of comparative development: an empirical investigation. The American Economic Review 91 (5), 1369–1401.

Acemoglu, D., Johnson, S., Robinson, J.A., 2002. Reversal of fortune: geography and institutions in the making of the modern world income distribution. The Quarterly Journal of Economics 117 (4), 1231–1294.

Albouy, D.Y., 2012. The colonial origins of comparative development: an empirical investigation: comment. The American Economic Review 102 (6), 3059–3076.

Alesina, A., Giuliano, P., Nunn, N., 2010. On the Origins of Gender Roles: Women and the Plough. Mimeo.

Alesina, A., Glaeser, E., Sacerdote, B., 2001. Why doesn't the United States have a European-style welfare state? In: Brookings Papers on Economic Activity, pp. 187–278.

Alesina, A.F., Seror, M., Yang, D.Y., You, Y., Zeng, W., 2020. Persistence through Revolutions. NBER Working Paper Series, No. 27053. National Bureau of Economic Research, Cambridge, Mass.

Allen, T., Donaldson, D., 2020. Persistence and Path Dependence in the Spatial Economy. NBER Working Paper Series, No. 28059. National Bureau of Economic Research, Cambridge, Mass.

Altonji, J.G., Elder, T.E., Taber, C.R., 2005. Selection on observed and unobserved variables. Journal of Political Economy 113 (1), 151–184.

Anderson, B., 2006. Imagined Communities: Reflections on the Origin and Spread of Nationalism. Verso Books.

Ashraf, Q., Galor, O., 2013. The "out of Africa" hypothesis, human genetic diversity, and comparative economic development. The American Economic Review 103 (1), 1–46.

Baumard, N., 2019. Psychological origins of the industrial revolution. Behavioral and Brain Sciences 42.

Bazzi, S., Fiszbein, M., Gebresilasse, M., 2020. Frontier culture: the roots and persistence of "rugged individualism" in the United States. Econometrica 88 (6), 2329–2368.

Becker, S.O., Boeckh, K., Hainz, C., Woessmann, L., 2016. The Empire is dead, long live the Empire! Long-run persistence of trust and corruption in the bureaucracy. The Economic Journal 126 (590), 40–74.

Becker, S.O., Mergele, L., Woessmann, L., 2020. The separation and reunification of Germany: rethinking a natural experiment interpretation of the enduring effects of communism. The Journal of Economic Perspectives 34 (2), 143–171.

Becker, S.O., Woessmann, L., 2009. Was Weber wrong? A human capital theory of protestant economic history. The Quarterly Journal of Economics 124 (2), 531–596.

Besley, T., Persson, T., 2009. The origins of state capacity: property rights, taxation, and politics. The American Economic Review 99 (4), 1218–1244.

Besley, T., Persson, T., 2010. State capacity, conflict, and development. Econometrica 78 (1), 1–34.

Bisin, A., Verdier, T., 2000. "Beyond the melting pot": cultural transmission, marriage, and the evolution of ethnic and religious traits. The Quarterly Journal of Economics 115 (3), 955–988.

Bisin, A., Verdier, T., 2001. The economics of cultural transmission and the dynamics of preferences. Journal of Economic Theory 97 (2), 298–319.

Bleakley, H., Lin, J., 2012. Portage and path dependence. The Quarterly Journal of Economics 127 (2), 587–644.

Boserup, E., 2007. Woman's Role in Economic Development. Earthscan.

Brodeur, A., Haddad, J., 2018. Institutions, Attitudes and LGBT: Evidence from the Gold Rush.

Cameron, A.C., Gelbach, J.B., Miller, D.L., 2011. Robust inference with multiway clustering. Journal of Business & Economic Statistics 29 (2), 238–249.

Casey, G., Klemp, M., 2020. Historical instruments and contemporary endogenous regressors. Journal of Development Economics. Forthcoming.

Chen, T., Kung, J.K.-s., Ma, C., 2020. Long live keju! The persistent effects of China's imperial examination system. The Economic Journal 130 (631), 2030–2064.

Cioni, M., Federico, G., Vasta, M., 2020. The long-term evolution of economic history: evidence from the top five field journals (1927–2017). Cliometrica 14 (1), 1–39.

Clark, G., 2014. The Son also Rises: Surnames and the History of Social Mobility. Princeton University Press.

Colella, F., Lalive, R., Sakalli, S.O., Thoenig, M., 2019. Inference with Arbitrary Clustering. IZA Discussion Paper.

Comin, D., Easterly, W., Gong, E., 2010. Was the wealth of nations determined in 1000 BC? American Economic Journal: Macroeconomics 2 (3), 65–97.

d'Alpoim Guedes, J., Bestor, T.C., Carrasco, D., Flad, R., Fosse, E., Herzfeld, M., Lamberg-Karlovsky, C.C., Lewis, C.M., Liebmann, M., Meadow, R., 2013. Is poverty in our genes? A critique of Ashraf and Galor, "The 'out of Africa' hypothesis, human genetic diversity, and comparative economic development," American Economic Review. Current Anthropology 54 (1), 71–79.

Davis, D.R., Weinstein, D.E., 2002. Bones, bombs, and break points: the geography of economic activity. The American Economic Review 92 (5), 1269–1289.

De la Croix, D., Doepke, M., Mokyr, J., 2018. Clans, guilds, and markets: apprenticeship institutions and growth in the preindustrial economy. The Quarterly Journal of Economics 133 (1), 1–70.

Dell, M., 2010. The persistent effects of Peru's mining mita. Econometrica 78 (6), 1863–1903.

Dell, M., Lane, N., Querubin, P., 2018. The historical state, local collective action, and economic development in Vietnam. Econometrica 86 (6), 2083–2121.

Diamond, J.M., 1997. Guns, Germs, and Steel: The Fates of Human Societies. Norton.

Doepke, M., Zilibotti, F., 2008. Occupational choice and the spirit of capitalism. The Quarterly Journal of Economics 123 (2), 747–793.

Dohmen, T., Falk, A., Huffman, D., Sunde, U., 2012. The intergenerational transmission of risk and trust attitudes. The Review of Economic Studies 79 (2), 645–677.

Elias, N., 1994. The Civilizing Process, Vol. 2. Blackwell, Oxford.

Engerman, S., Sokoloff, K., 1997. Factor endowments, institutions, and differential growth paths among New World economies. In: How Latin America Fell Behind: Essays on the Economic Histories of Brazil and Mexico by Haber S., Vol. 89. Stanford University Press.

Fernandez, R., Fogli, A., 2009. Culture: an empirical investigation of beliefs, work, and fertility. American Economic Journal: Macroeconomics 1 (1), 146–177.

Fritsch, M., Sorgner, A., Wyrwich, M., Zazdravnykh, E., 2019. Historical shocks and persistence of economic activity: evidence on self-employment from a unique natural experiment. Regional Studies 53 (6), 790–802.

Fuchs-Schundeln, N., Alesina, A., 2007. Good-bye Lenin (or not?): the effect of communism on people's preferences. The American Economic Review 97 (4), 1507–1528.

Fujita, M., Krugman, P.R., Venables, A., 1999. The Spatial Economy: Cities, Regions, and International Trade. MIT Press.

Gennaioli, N., Rainer, I., 2007. The modern impact of precolonial centralization in Africa. Journal of Economic Growth 12 (3), 185–234.

Giuliano, P., Nunn, N., 2017. Understanding Cultural Persistence and Change. 0898–2937. National Bureau of Economic Research.

Glaeser, E.L., 2005. The political economy of hatred. The Quarterly Journal of Economics 120 (1), 45–86.

Grosfeld, I., Zhuravskaya, E., 2015. Cultural vs. economic legacies of Empires: evidence from the partition of Poland. Journal of Comparative Economics 43 (1), 55–75.

Guiso, L., Sapienza, P., Zingales, L., 2016. Long term persistence. Journal of the European Economic Association 14 (6), 1401–1436.

Hsieh, C.T., 2002. What explains the industrial revolution in East Asia? Evidence from the factor markets. The American Economic Review 92 (3), 502–526.

Ichino, A., Maggi, G., 2000. Work environment and individual background: explaining regional shirking differentials in a large Italian firm. The Quarterly Journal of Economics 115 (3), 1057–1090.

Kelly, M., 2019. The Standard Error of Persistence. UCD Working Paper.

Kelly, M., 2020a. Direct Standard Errors for Regressions with Spatially Autocorrelated Residuals. UCD Working Paper.

Kelly, M., 2020b. Understanding Persistence. UCD Working Paper.

Kenyon, C., Fatti, G., 2020. Thank Martin Luther That Ciprofloxacin Could Cure Your Gonorrhoea? Ecological Association between Protestantism and Antimicrobial Consumption in 30 European Countries. Mimeo.

Kim, J.-I., Lau, L.J., 1994. The sources of economic growth of the East Asian newly industrialized countries. Journal of the Japanese and International Economies 8 (3), 235–271.

Kline, P., Moretti, E., 2014. Local economic development, agglomeration economies, and the big push: 100 years of evidence from the Tennessee Valley Authority. The Quarterly Journal of Economics 129 (1), 275–331.

Koselleck, R., 2003. Wiederholungsstrukturen in der Geschichte. Divinatio 17, 17–32.

Krugman, P., 1991. Increasing returns and economic geography. Journal of Political Economy 99 (3), 483–499.

Landes, D.S., 2006. Why Europe and the West? Why not China? The Journal of Economic Perspectives 20 (2), 3–22.

Lin, J.Y., 1995. The Needham puzzle: why the industrial revolution did not originate in China. Economic Development and Cultural Change 43 (2), 269–292.

Lowes, S., Nunn, N., Robinson, J.A., Weigel, J.L., 2017. The evolution of culture and institutions: evidence from the Kuba Kingdom. Econometrica 85 (4), 1065–1091.

Maloney, W.F., Valencia Caicedo, F., 2016. The persistence of (subnational) fortune: geography, agglomeration, and institutions in the New World. The Economic Journal 126 (198), 2363–2401.

Michaels, G., Rauch, F., 2018. Resetting the urban network: 117–2012. The Economic Journal 128 (608), 378–412.

Michalopoulos, S., Papaioannou, E., 2013. Pre-colonial ethnic institutions and contemporary African development. Econometrica 81 (1), 113–152.

Michalopoulos, S., Papaioannou, E., 2016. The long-run effects of the scramble for Africa. The American Economic Review 106 (7), 1802–1848.

Mokyr, J., 1990. The Lever of Riches: Technological Creativity and Economic Progress. Oxford University Press, New York.

Needham, J., 1976. Science and Civilisation in China, Vol. 5. Cambridge University Press.

Nora, P., 1989. Between memory and history: les lieux de mémoire. Representations, 7–24.

Nunn, N., 2020. The historical roots of economic development. Science 367 (6485).

Nunn, N., Wantchekon, L., 2011. The slave trade and the origins of mistrust in Africa. The American Economic Review 101, 3221–3252.

Ochsner, C., Roesel, F., 2017. Activated History-the Case of the Turkish Sieges of Vienna.

Oster, E., 2019. Unobservable selection and coefficient stability: theory and evidence. Journal of Business & Economic Statistics 37 (2), 187–204.

Pinker, S., 2012. The Better Angels of Our Nature: Why Violence Has Declined. Penguin Group, USA.

Pritchett, L., 1997. Divergence, big time. The Journal of Economic Perspectives 11 (3), 3–17.

Putterman, L., Weil, D.N., 2008. Post-1500 population flows and the long run determinants of economic growth and inequality. The Quarterly Journal of Economics 125 (4), 1627–1682.

Redding, S.J., Sturm, D.M., Wolf, N., 2011. History and industry location: evidence from German airports. Review of Economics and Statistics 93 (3), 814–831.

Satyanath, S., Voigtländer, N., Voth, H.-J., 2017. Bowling for fascism: social capital and the rise of the Nazi party. Journal of Political Economy 125 (2), 478–526.

Sokoloff, K.L., Engerman, S.L., 2000. History lessons: institutions, factors endowments, and paths of development in the New World. The Journal of Economic Perspectives 14 (3), 217–232.

Spolaore, E., Wacziarg, R., 2009. The diffusion of development. The Quarterly Journal of Economics 124 (2), 469–529.

Turner, F.J., Bogue, A.G., 1893. The Frontier in American History. Courier Corporation.

Valencia Caicedo, F., 2019. The mission: human capital transmission, economic persistence, and culture in South America. The Quarterly Journal of Economics 134 (1), 507–556.

Voigtländer, N., Voth, H.-J., 2012. Persecution perpetuated: the medieval origins of anti-semitic violence in Nazi Germany. The Quarterly Journal of Economics 127 (3), 1339–1392.

Voigtländer, N., Voth, H.-J., 2013a. Gifts of Mars: warfare and Europe's early rise to riches. The Journal of Economic Perspectives 27 (4), 165–186.

Voigtländer, N., Voth, H.-J., 2013b. The three horsemen of riches: plague, war, and urbanization in early modern Europe. The Review of Economic Studies 80 (2), 774–811.

Voigtländer, N., Voth, H.-J., 2015. Nazi indoctrination and anti-semitic beliefs in German. Proceedings of the National Academy of Sciences of the United States of America 112 (26), 7931–7936.

Young, A., 1995. The tyranny of numbers: confronting the statistical realities of the East Asian growth experience. The Quarterly Journal of Economics 110 (3), 641–680.

LATE for history[☆]

Alberto Bisin[a,b,c] **and Andrea Moro**[d]

[a]*Department of Economics, New York University, New York, NY, United States*
[b]*NBER, Cambridge, MA, United States*
[c]*CEPR, London, United Kingdom*
[d]*Department of Economics, Vanderbilt University, Nashville, TN, United States*

10.1 Introduction

Many studies in Historical Economics document the persistence of some historical phenomenon, while others leverage this persistence to identify causal relationships of interest in the present. These are generally referred to as *Persistence studies* (Voth, 2021, in this book). In this chapter, we analyze the implications of allowing for *heterogeneous treatment effects* in these studies, we delineate their common empirical structure, argue that heterogeneous treatment effects are likely in their context, and propose simple abstract models that help interpret results and guide the development of empirical strategies to uncover the mechanisms generating the effects.

Persistence studies focus empirically on the effects of a treatment variable in the present, assuming its persistence from the historical past. Consider as an illustration the effects of cultural norms or institutions, e.g., on economic development. The adoption of cultural norms or the process of institutional change can be viewed, using the language of the causal inference literature, as taking-up treatment in the past. High-quality norms or institutions may then persist over time and thereby realize their effects on economic development in the present. An exogenous historical factor may be available that directly affects the treatment variable and can be exploited as an instrumental variable to identify a causal effect of norms or institutions on development.

The adoption of norms or institutions may be correlated with the returns in terms of economic development. If these returns are heterogeneous across countries - that is, if treatment effects are heterogeneous - countries with higher returns may be more likely to have adopted higher quality institutions or norms.[1] Heterogeneous treatments may then change the interpretation of the identified relationship between norms or institutions and economic development. For example, if higher values of the instrument induce countries with relatively higher returns to adopt higher quality norms or institutions, then the instrumental variable procedure identifies the effects produced only in high-return countries, possibly overstating the average returns of all countries. Similarly, the instrument could activate institutional and cultural changes over time, interacting with successive independent historical phenomena, inducing a special selection of heterogeneous treatment effects. Finally, even if the impact of institutions

---

[☆] We thank Thierry Verdier for countless exchanges on these topics over the years. We also thank Jess Benhabib, Giovanni Federico, Atsushi Inoue, Franco Peracchi and Pedro Sant'Anna for their helpful comments.

[1] This is often labeled a "selection on returns" or "selection on gains," see Heckman et al. (2010).

The Handbook of Historical Economics. https://doi.org/10.1016/B978-0-12-815874-6.00018-6

and norms in the present is homogeneous, the persistence of institutional and cultural changes in the historical past activated by treatment can be heterogeneous, affecting the interpretation of the nature of persistence.

When treatment effects are heterogeneous, therefore, the causal arguments remain generally unaffected; but the interpretation of estimated coefficients may pose new empirical questions to analyze further the mechanisms underlying the identified causal relationships. More specifically, when treatment effects are heterogeneous, the research design identifies a *Local Average Treatment Effect* (LATE), rather than the Average (subject-level) Treatment Effect (ATE); see Imbens and Angrist (1994). In the investigation of the effects of cultural norms or institutions, for example, the *local* effect identified by the instrumental variable procedure is the effect in countries that take-up treatment (higher quality institutions or norms) only when instrumented.[2]

Heterogeneous effects are bound to be important in Persistence studies. In fact, the persistent variable in Persistence studies is typically a cultural (or genetic) trait or an institutional feature or norm.[3] Because these variables are often defined by such sweeping concepts such as institution quality, cultural, or civic norms, they are likely affected by several underlying heterogeneous mechanisms. Furthermore, because treatment is generally taken-up in the historical past, various complex and heterogeneous dynamical processes may affect it, intervening in the determination of the objective of the analysis in the present.

Since heterogeneous treatment effects do not generally affect the causal identification argument, in this chapter we shy away from discussing the validity of the data and econometric procedures adopted in these studies.[4] We focus instead on the interpretation of the estimated coefficients under heterogeneous treatment effects. While the identification of causal effects in Persistence studies has produced significant first-order results, it has also highlighted how little we know about the mechanisms driving these effects. The paucity of data in historical contexts makes mechanisms hard to identify both with a quasi-experimental design and with a structural econometrics approach. For the same reason, it is hard to identify the distribution of treatment heterogeneity.

To guide our understanding about what moments of this treatment parameters distribution the estimates identify, it is therefore important to study the relationship between the instrument and treatment

---

[2] In environments where this *essential heterogeneity* is present Heckman and Vytlacil (2005) show that the IV procedure identifies a weighted average of the returns and characterize the weights in terms of the relationship between the IV and the returns. In the Appendix we introduce a simple, informal primer on the distinction between LATE and ATE in the context of labor economics, to level the field between historians, economists, and other social scientists who might not be uniformly attuned to these concepts.

[3] Recent examples have exploited variation in a wide range of historical variables: from colonial settlers' mortality to the self-governance of Italian cities, the adoption of the plow in agriculture, medieval pogroms, the size of the slave trade from Africa. Some of these studies have identified causal relationships between phenomena of interest in the present, for example, the effect of institutional quality or civic capital on economic performance. Others have documented the persistence of various dimensions of institutional and cultural characteristics, including trust, gender attitudes, and anti-semitism. Persistence studies are a sizeable component of Historical Economics, about 10%, according to Cioni et al. (2021, in this book)'s classification; see their Table 2 and 4.

[4] Persistence studies have been the subject of great scrutiny. The credibility of the causal parameter estimates stands on the reliability of historical data, assumptions about the econometric model's error structures, and, in most cases, on the adoption of a valid instrumental variable (Casey and Klemp, 2021). Because most of these studies exploit variation across geographic dimensions, spatial correlations of residuals can be a severe econometric issue; see Kelly (2019) and Voth (2021, in this book).

and how the mechanism responsible for the persistence of treatment over time correlates with the values of treatment effects. Explicit models of these relationships and mechanisms, in the context of the specific empirical analysis, help to clarify the interpretation of the identified causal effects and help the formulation of interesting new sets of questions, which can be addressed empirically, possibly with new data. To this end, we develop simple abstract models linking treatment take-up and treatment's persistence over history with treatment effects. These models delineate the underlying causal relationships and the role of the research design in the identification problem. Explicit models of these relationships and mechanisms represent the outcome of political equilibrium processes or the aggregation of individuals' relevant behavioral choices. This is typically the case, in particular, when treatment involves institutional change or change in cultural attitudes and traits as just described. To illustrate the role of these models in the abstract, without imposing a fully developed structure (which would be necessarily context dependent), we will construct minimal reduced-form models of treatment take-upwithout being explicit about their behavioral and equilibrium micro-foundations. These models provide us with interpretations of the estimated parameters, opening new empirical questions, possibly with new data.

We proceed, in the next section, by formalizing Persistence studies' common structure. In Section 10.3 we apply this framework to persistence studies whose main goal is to identify the causal relationship between variables in the present. These studies exploit the persistence of a variable in the historical past to provide an instrument. In Section 10.4, we focus instead on a set of persistence studies that are directly interested in investigating the persistence of historical variables.

10.2 Persistence studies

In this section, we introduce the issue of identification of causal relationships in Persistence studies. We delineate their common empirical structure by constructing a simple formal framework that encompasses most papers in the literature.[5]

10.2.1 Empirical model

Let any variables measured in present time be indexed by t and any historical variables by $t - h$, where h is the historical lag considered. Let $i = 1, 2, \ldots, N$ index the cross-section in the data, typically defined along political or geographic dimensions: countries, cities, ethnic groups, etc... Consider the following cross-sectional relationship between variables at present time t:

$$y_t = \alpha + \beta x_t + u_t, \tag{10.1}$$

where y_t, x_t, u_t are $N-$dimensional vectors indexed by location $i = 1, 2, \ldots, N$; the parameter β is also an $N-$dimensional vector: distinct β_i, across locations $i = 1, 2, \ldots, N$, represent the heterogeneous effects which are the focus of our analysis.[6] The explanatory variable x_t is generally endogenous, e.g., because of a common factor affecting both x_t and y_t or because of two-way causation between y_t and x_t.

---

[5] For a book-length treatment of causal analysis in econometrics, see Angrist and Pischke (2008, 2014). For a more abstract approach to causality, see Pearl (2009); Pearl et al. (2016).

[6] We abuse notation by not distinguishing the random variables in the population from their sample realizations. Also, in our notation, products between vectors are to be intended as Hadamard products; so that, in Eq. (10.1), $\beta x_t = \left[\beta_i x_{i,t} \right]_{i=1}^{N}$.

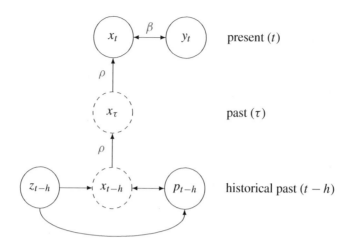

FIGURE 10.1

Persistence studies: general case. *Note*: Circles indicate variables observed by the investigator. Dashed circles indicate unobserved variables. Solid arrows indicate directions of causality. Double arrows indicate endogeneity or any other factor preventing the identification of a causal effect (omitted variables, selection bias, etc...).

History enters the empirical model through the underlying (unobservable) historical dynamics of the explanatory variable x_t, governed by a stochastic process, $\{x_\tau\}_{\tau \in T}$, where T denotes the historical sequence of time until the present $\{t - h, \ldots, \tau, \ldots t\}$. We model the persistence of the process $\{x_\tau\}$ assuming

$$cov(x_{t-h}, x_t) = \rho; \tag{10.2}$$

where ρ is also an $N-$dimensional vector, allowing for heterogeneity of persistence across locations $i = 1, 2, \ldots, N$ (for simplicity we assume that ρ does not depend on h or t).

The econometrician observes an instrument for x_t that we will assume to be valid throughout the chapter, in the sense defined below (Assumption 10.1). The characterizing feature of Persistence studies is that the instrument, an $N-$dimensional vector z_{t-h}, is realized in the historical past, at $t - h$. The empirical structure underlying the IV strategy depends crucially on the historical persistence of the instrumented variable, x_t. The instrument z_{t-h} is assumed to affect causally and directly x_{t-h} and hence indirectly x_t through the persistence of the process $\{x_\tau\}_{\tau \in T}$ in history. This structure does not require the econometrician to observe the realizations of the stochastic process at any time other than t; in particular, x_{t-h} is generally not observable to the econometrician. However, if a proxy p_{t-h} for x_{t-h} is observable, z_{t-h} can be an instrument for p_{t-h}, even though p_{t-h} might be endogenous with respect to x_{t-h}. Fig. 10.1 illustrates the relationship between variables in this empirical model.[7]

---

[7] It is difficult to represent models with endogenous, equilibrium relationships, or to represent the distinction between LATE and ATE, using Directed Acyclic Graphs (see Imbens (2019)). This chart and the next ones are meant to illustrate the relationships

The examples from the literature that we study in the rest of the paper focus on two separate objectives of the empirical analysis. One is to estimate some moment of the cross-section of treatment effects, β_i, or another relevant feature of their distribution. When data on a proxy p_{t-h} for x_{t-h} are available, another objective of the analysis is to estimate some relevant feature of the distribution of the cross-section of persistence effects, ρ_i.

10.2.2 Heterogeneity and LATE effects

Allowing for heterogeneous treatment effects might have important implications with respect to how these effects, as they are identified in Persistence studies, are interpreted. Consider the empirical model delineated in Section 10.2.1 and represented in Fig. 10.1. Assume that either the relationship between x_t and y_t and/or the persistence effects from x_{t-h} to x_t are heterogeneous; that is, β, ρ are heterogeneous across locations $i = 1, 2, \ldots, N$. As long as z_{t-h} is a valid instrument for x_t or for p_{t-h}, the IV procedure identifies a causal effect; that is, the causal arguments which are the objective of Persistence studies remain unaffected. But consider the case in which the mechanism inducing location i to take-up treatment after being instrumented, or to maintain the treatment over time, depends on the values of β and ρ assumed by that location. In this case, heterogeneity matters for the interpretation of the identified causal effect. For instance, if locations taking-up treatment have on average high β, e.g., because a high β lowers the cost of treatment, then the IV procedure will tend to identify a high β; that is, the *local* effect of treatment for those locations in fact induced by the instrument to adopting treatment (the *complier* locations in the jargon of LATE studies; see later).

To push the empirical analysis of Persistence studies forward it is therefore important to study the relationship between the instrument z_{t-h} and treatment x_t and how this relationship can be filtered through the values of β and/or ρ. Similarly, it is important to study how the mechanism responsible for the persistence of treatment over time, from x_{t-h} to x_t, correlates with the values of β and/or ρ. Explicit models of these relationships and mechanisms, in the context of the specific empirical analysis, help clarifying the interpretation of the identified causal effects and help the formulation of interesting new sets of questions, which can be addressed empirically, possibly with new data. To this end, we develop below minimal abstract models linking treatment take-up in a location, and the treatment's persistence over history with the location's value of β and/or ρ.

Importantly, the mechanisms leading to treatment take-up and its persistence over history cannot generally be represented by behavioral choice problems because the units of observation in most of these studies are countries, cities, ethnic groups. Consequently, whether treatment is adopted or not, and whether it persists over history, rests on the outcome of political equilibrium processes or on the aggregation of the relevants behavioral choices of individuals. This is typically the case when treatment involves institutional change or change in characteristic cultural attitudes and traits. For the sake of simplicity and abstraction, our analysis will be limited to reduced-form models of treatment take-up, without being explicit about their equilibrium micro-foundations. Furthermore, since the context determines the appropriate modeling assumptions, we will illustrate our approach in the context of several classic Persistence studies.

---

between variables in the various empirical models, not as a tool to discuss the causal identification designs, which we study analytically in the text.

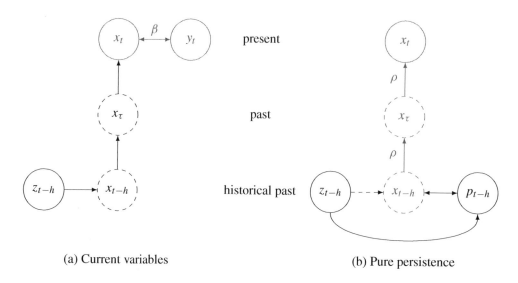

| | (a) Current variables | | (b) Pure persistence |

FIGURE 10.2

Persistence studies: empirical models. *Note*: Circles indicate variables observed by the investigator. Dashed circles indicate unobserved variables. Solid arrows indicate directions of causality. Double arrows indicate endogeneity or any other factor preventing the identification of a causal effect (omitted variables, selection bias, etc...). Dashed arrows indicate potential causal links. Highlighted in red (gray in print version) are the relationships of interest.

In the next two sections, we introduce two empirical models, special cases of the model introduced above, to highlight different strands of the literature.[8] In Section 10.3 we consider first the special case of the empirical model in Section 10.2.1 in which the econometrician aims at uncovering a causal relationship between current variables. The instrument in the historical past and the persistence of the independent variable are, in a sense, means to this end. The relationships between variables in this class of models are represented in Fig. 10.2(a). As an illustration of this empirical model it will be useful to consider two classic papers among the most-well known in the field: Acemoglu et al. (2001) on the colonial origins of economic development, and Ashraf and Galor (2013) on the effect of human genetic diversity on development. These papers provide distinct causal explanations of comparative economic development (affected by different dependent variables). Acemoglu et al. (2001) focus on the effect of the quality of institutions; specifically, the level of protection of property rights. Ashraf and Galor (2013) study how human genetic diversity affects economic development through the contrasting effect of social conflict and innovation or creativity.

Next, in Section 10.4 we consider the special case of the empirical model in Section 10.2.1 in which the econometrician aims at uncovering the relationship between the same variable at two distant times in history. The instrument in the historical past identifies the persistence of a relevant variable, which is, in a sense, the objective of the analysis; see Fig. 10.2(b). As an illustration of this type of models we

---

[8] This categorization is related to the distinction between *apples-on-apples* and *apples-on-oranges* models by Voth (2021, in this book).

will consider four other classic well-known papers providing evidence for the persistence of some form of either institutions or cultural traits over the long-run historical past: Voigtländer and Voth (2012), Nunn and Wantchekon (2011), Guiso et al. (2016), and Alesina et al. (2013), studying, respectively, the persistence of anti-semitism, social trust, civic capital, and gender attitudes.

10.3 Persistence studies that analyze relationships between current variables

Consider the special case of the empirical model of Section 10.2.1 in which the econometrician does not observe any proxy p_{t-h} for x_{t-h} and z_{t-h} is an instrument for x_t, through the persistence of the process $\{x_\tau\}_{\tau \in T}$. We assume that z_{t-h} is a valid instrument to concentrate our analysis on the interpretation of the estimates of β or ρ when they are allowed to be heterogeneous across locations $i = 1, 2, \ldots, N$. Besides requiring that z_{t-h} be correlated with x_t, validity also requires z_{t-h} to be as good as randomly assigned and to satisfy the exclusion restriction, that is, z_{t-h} affects y_t only through x_t.[9]

Assumption 10.1. *z_{t-h} is a valid instrument for x_t; in particular,*

$$cov\,(z_{t-h}, x_t) \neq 0$$
$$cov\,(z_{t-h}, y_t \mid x_t) = 0.$$

In Acemoglu et al. (2001), for instance, the process $\{x_\tau\}_{\tau \in T}$ represents the quality of institutions, from colonial times $t - h$ to the present t. The instrument z_{t-h} is settler's mortality: the authors argue that low settlers' mortality facilitated the set-up of inclusive institutions by colonial powers, whereas high settlers' mortality caused extractive institutions. The parameter β represents the returns to institutional quality in terms of economic development, measured by current per capita GDP. In Ashraf and Galor (2013) the process $\{x_\tau\}_{\tau \in T}$ is human genetic diversity, from the first migration of *Homo sapiens* "Out of Africa" until the present. The instrument is distance of the current geographical location from East Africa, which is causal to human genetic diversity as a consequence of the *serial-founder effect*, whereby genetic diversity is reduced at any successive migration event. The parameter β represents the returns to human genetic diversity in terms of economic development, measured by population density in 1500. The underlying hypothesis, confirmed by their empirical analysis, is that diversity has a hump-shaped effect on development, because it has both beneficial and detrimental effects by increasing social conflict, but fostering innovation or creativity. Table 10.1 presents concisely the variables adopted in the main specifications of these studies.[10]

---

[9] See Angrist and Pischke (2008), ch. 4.4.1 for formal assumptions.

[10] These examples illustrate well how heterogeneous treatment effects may play a role in the analysis. Acemoglu et al. (2001), e.g., interpret their measure of institutional quality a "cluster of institutions, including constraints on government expropriation, independent judiciary, property rights enforcement, and institutions providing equal access to education and ensuring civil liberties, that are important to encourage investment and growth. Expropriation risk is related to all these institutional features." This interpretation allows for different mechanisms connecting expropriation risk to economic performance, leading naturally to the possibility of heterogeneous effects, which depend on which mechanism is activated. This is the case in Ashraf and Galor (2013) as well, where genetic diversity, or lack thereof, affects development by a combination of creativity, increased cooperation, trust, socioeconomic order, adaptability, specialization, and so on.

Table 10.1 Variables in selected current relationship studies.

Article	y_t	x_{t-h}	z_{t-h}
AJR (2001)	GDP per capita, $t = 1995$	Property rights	Settlers' mortality
AG (2013)	Population density, $t = 1500$	Genetic diversity	Distance from Africa

Note: See Fig. 10.2(a) for relationships between variables. Abbreviations: AJR: Acemoglu et al. (2001), AG: Ashraf and Galor (2013).

To simplify the intuition and to present results with minimal algebra (the argument generalizes without these assumptions), consider an environment where both the instrument z_{t-h}, and the treatment x_τ, for any $\tau \in T$, are binary. Under these assumptions, the instrumental variable estimator coincides with the Wald estimator, whose population analog is:

$$\frac{E(y_t|z_{t-h}=1) - E(y_t|z_{t-h}=0)}{E(x_t|z_{t-h}=1) - E(x_t|z_{t-h}=0)} = \beta \tag{10.3}$$

This representation of the IV estimator has an intuitive interpretation: assuming the instrument is random with respect to the treatment, the effect of the instrument on the dependent variable (the *Reduced form*) divided by the effect of the instrument on the treatment (the *First stage*) uncovers the causal effect of a unit change of the independent variable on the treatment.

Allowing for β to be heterogeneous across locations $i = 1, 2, \ldots, N$ opens the door for the possibility that the relationship between the instrument z_{t-h} and the independent variable, the treatment x_t, is filtered through the effect of β. Instrumented locations, with $z_{i,t-h} = 1$, might take treatment or not, $x_{i,t} = 1$ or $= 0$, depending on β_i. This is the fundamental factor inducing relevant LATE effects that are different from ATE effects. Importantly, note that this does not affect the validity of the instrument.[11] To formalize the result we want to focus on, assume β_i affects differently the relationship between $z_{i,t-h}$ and the treatment $x_{i,t}$ across locations $i = 1, 2 \ldots, N$. Then we can categorize four conceptually different types of locations, which we label, following the causal identification literature, *Always takers, Never takers, Compliers, and Defiers*:

Always takers: all i such that $x_{i,t} = 1$ for all values of $z_{i,t-h}$;
Never takers: all i such that $x_{i,t} = 0$ for all values of $z_{i,t-h}$;
Compliers: all i such that $x_{i,t} = 1$ when $z_{i,t-h} = 1$ and $x_{i,t} = 0$ when $z_{i,t-h} = 0$;
Defiers: all i such that $x_{i,t} = 1$ when $z_{i,t-h} = 0$ and $x_{i,t} = 0$ when $z_{i,t-h} = 1$.

The instrumental variables estimator in Eq. (10.3) identifies the LATE effects of the instrument, that is, the effect of the instrument for the Compliers:

---

[11] Validity is guaranteed if $x_t|_{z_{t-h}=1} \neq x_t|_{z_{t-h}=0}$ and $y_t|_{x_t,z_{t-h}=0} = y_t|_{x_t,z_{t-h}=1}$, where $x_t|_{z_{t-h}}$ and $y_t|_{x_t,z_{t-h}}$ indicate, respectively, the random variable x_t conditional to the realization of z_{t-h} and y_t conditional to the realization of x_t, z_{t-h}. Weaker conditions in terms of conditional means are sufficient.

Theorem 10.1. *(Imbens and Angrist, 1994) Suppose Assumption 10.1 holds and that the treatment induces no Defiers, then*

$$\frac{E(y_t|z_{t-h}=1) - E(y_t|z_{t-h}=0)}{E(x_t|z_{t-h}=1) - E(x_t|z_{t-h}=0)}$$
$$= E\left(y_{i,t}\,|_{x_{i,t}=1} - y_{i,t}\,|_{x_{i,t}=0}|\ i \in\ compliers\right)$$
$$= E(\beta_i\ |\ i \in\ compliers)$$

This theorem helps qualifying the interpretation of the estimate of β in the empirical implementation of Persistence studies when reasonable structures can be hypothesized which separate Compliers as a subset of all the locations and on whether in these structures Compliers can be characterized by a distinct distribution of β with respect to the other types.

10.3.1 Abstract models of treatment take-up and persistence

To identify Complier locations and their characteristics it is generally useful to model how the mechanisms which induces treatment take-up and persistence, so that $x_t = 1$, can be filtered through β. We illustrate this generally, by developing four minimal abstract models linking z_{t-h} to x_t via β. These models represent reduced-form behavioral-equilibrium relationships, as we already noticed, without explicit micro-foundations. It is our aim to show how this analysis is especially relevant in an historical context and how it may guide the development of empirical strategies to uncover the mechanisms underlying the identified causal effect. We associate these models narratively to the papers we have selected as an example in this section.

10.3.1.1 Treatment take-up at t − h

Let b_i denote the benefits of treatment for location i in historical times, $t - h$; that is, the benefits of $x_{i,t-h} = 1$ relative to $x_{i,t-h} = 0$. Assume b_i represents a relevant parameter which characterizes location i, but is not observable to the econometrician. Let $c(z_{t-h})$ denote the cost of treatment at $t - h$; and let the effect of the instrument be a reduction in the cost of treatment,

$$c(z_{i,t-h} = 1) < c(z_{i,t-h} = 0).$$

In Acemoglu et al. (2001) lower settler mortality, which we denote with $z_{t-h} = 1$, is assumed to lower the cost of creating and maintaining inclusive institutions that protect property rights in the colony. In Ashraf and Galor (2013) the distance from East Africa affects treatment because a shorter distance facilitates higher genetic diversity being associated with fewer migration events after the original one "Out of Africa."

Consider a behavioral-equilibrium relationship postulating treatment at $t - h$ to be determined by a simple cutoff condition: each location $i = 1, 2, \ldots, N$ takes-up treatment if its benefit is greater than the cost:

$$x_{i,t-h} = \begin{cases} 1 & \text{if } b_i \geq c(z_{i,t-h}) \\ 0 & \text{otherwise} \end{cases}.$$

To focus on the relationship between z_{t-h} and x_t, assume that the persistence of the explanatory variable is homogeneous (and perfect); that is, $\rho_i = 1$, for all $i = 1, 2 \ldots, N$, and

$$x_{i,\tau} = x_{i,\tau-1}, \quad t - h \leq \tau \leq t.$$

Treatment can only occur at $t - h$ and is never undermined in the course of history. Consequently, locations can be categorized depending on their characteristic b_i. *Always takers* are all those locations i such that $b_i \geq c(z_{i,t-h} = 0) > c(z_{i,t-h} = 1)$; and *Never takers* are all i such that $c(z_{i,t-h} = 0) > c(z_{i,t-h} = 1) > b_i$. Most importantly, the *Compliers* whose effect is identified by the IV are those locations whose benefits of treatment b_i are higher than the cut-off when treated by the instrument, but lower when not-treated:

$$c(z_{i,t-h} = 1) \leq b_i < c(z_{i,t-h} = 0).$$

Finally, there are no *defiers* (as required by Theorem 10.1).

According to this abstract behavioral-equilibrium model of treatment, for LATE effects to be distinct from ATE it is sufficient to hypothesize that β_i and b_i are correlated, i.e. that the benefits of treatment b_i are at least in part obtained through the effects of treatment on the relevant dependent variable $y_{i,t}$, β_i. In the context of the effects of institutional quality on economic development in Acemoglu et al. (2001), it seems natural to think of the returns of institutional quality in terms of economic development for a country i, β_i, as a measure of the benefits of treatment b_i for this country. In this context, this simple behavioral-equilibrium model of institutional formation can be used to explicit conditions, that may in principle be validated empirically, and refine the interpretation of the IV estimate of the returns of institutional quality by identifying the mechanisms leading different locations to take up treatment or not.

Consider the following somewhat extreme case as further illustration.[12] Assume for simplicity that there are two types of countries, l, h with $\beta_h > \beta_l$, and that their proportions are π_h, $\pi_l = 1 - \pi_h$ respectively. Further, assume that $c(z_{i,t-h})$ satisfies $c(z_{i,t-h} = 1) < \beta_l < c(z_{i,t-h} = 0) < \beta_h$. High settlers' mortality, $z_{t-h} = 0$, increases the cost for the colonial power to implement the inclusive institutions that reduce future expropriation risk. Under this assumption, this cost is generally lower than the benefit, with the exception of l countries when settlers' mortality is high, which represent then the *compliers*.[13] In this example, therefore, the Wald estimator identifies

$$\frac{E(y_t|z_{t-h} = 1) - E(y_t|z_{t-h} = 0)}{E(x_t|z_{t-h} = 1) - E(x_t|z_{t-h} = 0)} =$$
$$\frac{\beta_h \pi_h + \beta_l \pi_l - \beta_h \pi_h}{1 - \pi_h} = \beta_l \qquad (10.4)$$

i.e., the gains for countries with low values of β, the average value of β among the *compliers*:

$$E\left(\beta_i \mid i : c(z_{i,t-h} = 0) > b_i \geq c(z_{i,t-h} = 1)\right) = \beta_l.$$

---

[12] We follow Rosenzweig and Wolpin (2000) who use a similar approach to interpret IV estimates in several labor economics studies; see the Appendix for an illustrative example.

[13] All that is needed in general is for settlers' mortality to affect disproportionately one group of countries. Note that settlers' mortality only affects economic performance by changing institutional quality directly and therefore is by assumption a valid instrument.

Note however that, with a different cost structure, for example in the opposite extreme case where high-quality institutions are adopted only by h countries and only when their settlers' mortality is low, the instrumental variable analysis would on the contrary identify β_h. We conclude that this analysis of a simple behavioral-equilibrium model of treatment take-up, while extremely stylized, suggests the importance of evaluating various specific dimensions institutional change. It suggests notably the importance of proposing an empirical strategy that tries to test empirically the underlying assumptions regarding the benefits from institutional change to better understand what effects are identified. It also provides some nuance about the interpretations of the contemporaneous effects of institutional quality, because different "instruments" favoring improvements in institutional quality may operate on a different set of compliers.

Related arguments can be used to illustrate the possible role of heterogeneous treatment effect in the context of Ashraf and Galor (2013). The interesting difference, in this case, consists in the fact that the treatment (genetic diversity) is not directly the result of a political economy equilibrium choice, but is rather the (perhaps unintended) consequence of the migration process via the *serial founder effect*. This mechanism cannot be directly conceived as the outcome of an equilibrium model. On the other hand, genetic diversity can also be thought of as the consequence of evolutionary processes, for example driven by mating patterns in society. Assortative mating along any phenotypical trait, notably e.g., along ethnic dimensions, may reduce genetic diversity by producing ethnic cleavages which might turn into distinct homogeneous populations.

Consider then a behavioral-equilibrium model of mating patterns along migration events after the original one "Out of Africa" as an illustration. Let instrumented locations i, such that $z_{i,t-h} = 1$, be those which are at the economic development-maximizing level distance from East Africa.[14] These locations, by construction, are treated by the *serial founder effect*: their genetic diversity is $x_{i,t} = 1$; that is, genetic diversity is such that the combination of innovation and creativity, on the one side, and conflict and trust, on the other, induces the highest economic development. Suppose there are two types of populations defined by their ethnicities, culture, etc... Type h has a hump-shaped benefit from diversity, type l also has hump-shaped benefits, but with smaller effects. Let the benefits at the peak be denoted b_h and b_l, respectively. Suppose that mating strategies conducive to genetic diversity $x_t = 1$ are costly - say they have a cost c - and assume that $b_l < c < b_h$. Therefore,

$$x_{i,t-h} = \begin{cases} 1 & \text{if } z_{i,t-h} = 1; \text{ or if } z_{i,t-h} = 0 \text{ and } b_i \geq c \\ 0 & \text{otherwise} \end{cases}.$$

Consequently, the locations with benefits b_h are *Always takers*: they achieve "optimal diversity" regardless of location. Locations with returns b_l are instead *Compliers*; that is, they obtain the optimal diversity $x_{i,t} = 1$ only if moving "Out of Africa." As in Acemoglu et al. (2001), it seems natural to hypothesize that β_i and b_i are correlated, that the benefits of treatment b_i are at least in part obtained through the effects of treatment on the relevant dependent variable $y_{i,t}$, β_i. In this case, the IV strategy identifies the LATE effect, that is, the average β_i of the locations that have a different adoption rule

---

[14] This is just an innocuous change-of-variable re-normalization of the IV procedure.

when z_{t-h} changes value[15]:

$$E\left(\beta_i \mid i : b_i = b_l\right) = \beta_l.$$

Indeed, in the context Ashraf and Galor (2013), as in Acemoglu et al. (2001), conditions can be assumed (in this case on the costs and benefits of evolutionary selection through mating patterns) which give rise to distinct implications with respect to LATE effects. If for instance evolutionary selection towards the optimal diversity does not operate unless migration occurs, and if even with migration it occurs only when there are high incentives to do so, then it is the combined effect of migration and high incentives that generates development. In this case, the IV would identify β_h, even if diversity may have low or zero effects on development for some populations. We conclude that this simple behavioral-equilibrium model in the context of Ashraf and Galor (2013) suggests the importance of empirically evaluating different mating patterns, and how the structure of benefits (e.g., from isolating ethnically) depends on migration, to shed light on the mechanisms linking genetic diversity to economic development. While the stylized model we used for illustration abstracts from fertility, fertility patters would also relate to marriage and migration patters in fundamental ways affecting the interpretation of the identified causal effects of genetic diversity.

10.3.1.2 Treatment take-up at τ

In this section we leverage even more than in the previous one the particular role of history in the understanding of LATE effects. Consider the abstract behavioral-equilibrium models delineated in the previous section but assume now that locations can enter treatment at any time τ, with $t - h \leq \tau \leq t$, that is, after the realization of the instrument. One way to introduce the role of history in the determination of treatment take-up is to let the cost of treatment depend on the instrument z_{t-h} as well as on the

---

[15] The Wald arithmetic is identical to (10.4). In fact, the running hypothesis in Ashraf and Galor (2013), documented in the data, is more nuanced. Genetic diversity has a hump-shaped effect on economic development, reflecting a combination of beneficial and detrimental factors: diversity is associated with a higher likelihood of innovation and creativity, but also increases conflict and decreases trust. The simple model we have delineated can be extended to an environment in which the instrument and the treatment take three values for x_{t-h} and z_{t-h}, say $0, 1, 2$, representing respectively ordered distances from East Africa and measures of genetic diversity. Under the assumptions that locations with benefits b_h have the evolutionary incentive to converge to the genetic diversity which induces the highest economic development, independently of their distance from East Africa, and that b_i and β_i are correlated, the IV strategy identifies β_l. In this case, the benefits are identified by calculating the Wald estimator, comparing pairwise locations. First consider locations i with $z_{i,t-h} = 0, 1$:

$$\frac{E(y_t|z_{t-h} = 1) - E(y_t|z_{t-h} = 0)}{E(x_t|z_{t-h} = 1) - E(x_t|z_{t-h} = 0)}$$
$$= \frac{(\pi_l \beta_l + \pi_h \beta_h) - (\pi_l 0 + \pi_h \beta_h)}{1 - \pi_h} = \beta_l$$

Similarly, calculate the benefit comparing locations i with $z_{i,t-h} = 1, 2$:

$$\frac{E(y_t|z_{t-h} = 2) - E(y_t|z_{t-h} = 1)}{E(x_t|z_{t-h} = 2) - E(x_t|z_{t-h} = 1)}$$
$$= \frac{(\pi_h \beta_h + \pi_l 0) - (\pi_l \beta_l + \pi_h \beta_h)}{\pi_h + 2\pi_l - 1} = -\beta_l$$

Suggesting that under the assumptions made on the cost structure, the strategy identifies the least pronounced hump-shaped relationship between diversity and development.

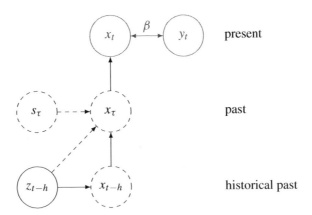

FIGURE 10.3

Current variables empirical model: interacting historical process. *Note*: Circles indicate variables observed by the investigator. Dashed circles indicate unobserved variables. Solid arrows indicate directions of causality. Double arrows indicate endogeneity or any other factor preventing the identification of a causal effect (omitted variables, selection bias, etc...). Dashed arrows indicate potential causal links. Highlighted in red (gray in print version) is the relationships of interest.

realization of a stochastic process $\{s_\tau\}_{\tau \in T}$: $c_\tau = c(z_{t-h}, s_\tau)$. The empirical model, with the addition of the effects of the stochastic process $\{s_\tau\}_{\tau \in T}$ is represented in Fig. 10.3.

In the context of the effects of institutional quality on economic development, for instance, it is natural to assume the process $\{s_\tau\}_{\tau \in T}$ capturing the dynamics of relevant cultural variables interacting with the dynamics of institutions.[16] Importantly, the validity of the instrument z_{t-h}, via the exclusion restrictions, is not hindered by the correlation of z_{t-h} with the cultural process $\{s_\tau\}_{t-h \leq \tau \leq t}$, as long as culture does not have a direct effect on economic development, that is, as long as s_τ affects y_t only through $\{x_\tau\}_{t-h \leq \tau \leq t}$. Let again the effect of the instrument be a reduction in the cost of treatment,

$$c(z_{i,t-h} = 1, s_{i,\tau}) < c(z_{i,t-h} = 0, s_{i,\tau}).$$

Maintain the assumption that the benefits of treatment across locations i, b_i, are correlated with β_i; i.e., that the returns of institutional quality in terms of economic development are a measure of the benefits of treatment. Suppose for simplicity a form of perfect persistence, where treatment is never reversed in the course of history,

$$x_{i,\tau} = 1, \ \tau \in T, \ \text{implies } x_{i,\tau'} = 1, \ \tau < \tau' \leq t.$$

Treatment is then still determined by a simple cutoff condition, for each location $i = 1, 2, \ldots, N$:

$$x_{i,\tau} = \begin{cases} 1 & b_i \geq c(z_{i,t-h}, s_{i,\tau}) \text{ or if } x_{i,\tau-1} = 1 \\ 0 & \text{otherwise} \end{cases}.$$

---

[16] Bisin and Verdier (2017) model these interactions in related contexts.

Treatment could occur at any $t - h < \tau \leq t$. The Compliers whose effect is identified by the IV are those locations whose benefits of treatment b_i are higher than the cut-off when treated by the instrument, but lower when not-treated; but whether this is the case might depend in general on the dynamics of s_τ. As in the previous case, since β_i and b_i are correlated, the IV strategy identifies the LATE effect, that is, the average β_i of the compliers. In this case, however, the instrument z_{t-h} interacts with the process $\{s_\tau\}_{\tau \in T}$. In general, b_i and the process $\{s_{i,\tau}\}_{\tau \in T}$ will be correlated. Interpreting β as a measure of the returns of institutional quality effectively disregards the effect of the dynamics of s_τ, which could represent, as we have already noted, cultural traits or social capital in the historical process of institutional change.[17] The IV strategy identifies in this case the returns to the institutional quality of the compliers that are activated by the historical processes. Different, counterfactual histories may have activated processes with different returns.

To illustrate the role of the interaction between different processes in the course of history, consider the analysis of the economic development of the sample of countries colonized by European powers after 1500 in Acemoglu et al. (2002). This paper documents how i) colonial powers developed high-quality institutions disproportionally in initially poorer countries, (a "Reversal of Fortune"); ii) the inclusive institutions developed by colonial powers manifested their effects on economic development only after the Industrial Revolution in 1800-1900, and not before.

Consider the two following possible interpretations of these results.[18] One, assuming wealth in 1500 as exogenous with respect to economic development, is that historical poverty causes growth. Another interpretation, considering poverty in 1500 as an instrument for beneficial institutional change, is that inclusive institutions established by colonies cause economic growth. Both interpretations are valid in principle as long as they are qualified in terms of their effect being *local*. Poverty in 1500 acted *locally*, through institutional change in colonial times. But institutional change in colonial time acted *locally* on economic development through the Industrial Revolution.[19] Both of these *local* effects in principle have selected a subset of Compliers whose effect the empirical analysis identifies and which depend on both institutional quality and the Industrial Revolution. More specifically, the heterogeneity of the effects could be intrinsic to the quality of institutions as we argued in Section 10.3.1.1. But could also be due to the different nature of industrialization in time or place.[20] Even if the mechanism generating development from good institutions had homogeneous effect, heterogeneity could arise from different returns to industrialization.[21]

---

[17] In fact, s_τ could also be thought of as a contributing causal factor, e.g., if a different realization of $s_{i,\tau}$ would have induced an instrumented location i not to set-up high quality institutions $x_{i,\tau} = 1$. In this case we could say that x_τ, s_τ are jointly causal to y_t.

[18] See Cantoni and Yuchtman (2021, in this book) for a related argument.

[19] Following the logic exposed in Footnote 17, we could reasonably consider institutional quality and the Industrial Revolution as jointly causal.

[20] In fact, in Acemoglu et al. (2002), the identifying variation in the regression between post-industrialization production per capita and the interaction of institutions quality and opportunities to industrialize is the variation of U.K. industrial output over time, between 1750 and 1980.

[21] A similar discussion could pertain, for instance, to the negative relationship between past slave exports and economic performance within Africa, uncovered by Nunn (2008), if this effect appears when the dependent variable, economic performance, is measured in 1980, but not when measured in 1960, as suggested by Bottero and Wallace (2013). This would indicate the interaction of the effects of slave trade with a more recent phenomenon, like e.g., de-colonization.

We conclude that this analysis suggests that the interpretation of the causal effects in Persistence studies depends in a fundamental manner not only from the historical process of the treatment variable but also from any other intervening historical process correlated with treatment. While generally difficult, this calls for the importance of historical narratives to identify possibly important intervening processes. This is exactly what Acemoglu et al. (2002) do in their study of the effects of colonization, isolating the Industrial Revolution as the main intervening factor in the process of development. The introduction of possible heterogeneous treatment effects adds a layer of complexity and interest, suggesting the importance to better identify the relationship between the returns to institutional change and industrialization and their interaction in the development process.

10.3.1.3 *Treatment take-up and reversals*

In this section we suggest the existence of circumstances in Persistence studies when one of the assumptions of Theorem 10.1 may not hold, namely the absence of Defiers, and study how this changes the interpretation of the estimates. In the previous sections we have developed minimal abstract behavioral-equilibrium models of Treatment take-up that consist of simple cutoff conditions: each location $i = 1, 2, \ldots, N$ is treated if the benefits b_i are greater than the cost of adoption, which is reduced by the treatment and possibly an interacting process, as in the previous section. In these examples, as we observed, there are no Defiers: a Defier-location i would have to be characterized by benefits b_i such that $c(z_{i,t-h} = 0) \leq b_i < c(z_{i,t-h} = 1)$, which contradicts $c(z_{i,t-h} = 1) < c(z_{i,t-h} = 0)$.[22]

Consider as in the previous subsection the case where treatment can be adopted at $t - h \leq \tau < t$ and the cutoff cost are also affected by an interacting process $\{s_\tau\}_{\tau \in T}$. Suppose the instrument z_{t-h} - and possibly the treatment x_{t-h} - affect $\{s_{i,\tau}\}_{\tau \in T}$. In this case, interestingly, non-monotonic effects of z_{t-h} are possible, without impinging on the validity of z_{t-h} as an instrument for x_t. These relationships in the empirical model are represented in Fig. 10.4.

For instance, it is possible for the process $\{s_{i,\tau}\}_{\tau \in T}$ to act selectively on locations with $z_{i,t-h} = 0$, fostering high-quality institutions in a subset of these, against historical odds. E.g., in the context of Acemoglu et al. (2001), extractive institutions at $t - h$ could foster, by a mechanism of substitutability between culture and institutions, the development of cultural traits which over time lead to a reduction of the cost of high-quality institutions and hence to treatment even location with relatively low benefits b_i.[23] In this case, $b_i < c(z_{i,\tau} = 1, s_{i,\tau})$ for any $\tau \in T$ but $b_i > c(z_{i,\tau} = 0, s_{i,\tau})$ for some $\tau \in T$. Keeping our assumption of correlation between β_i and b_i would induce the estimate $\hat{\beta}$ to weigh both Compliers and Defiers (but not Always-takers and Never-takers). Let π_c and π_d denote the proportion of Compliers and Defiers in the population. Then, the estimator identifies:

$$\frac{E(y_t|z_{t-h} = 1) - E(y_t|z_{t-h} = 0)}{E(x_t|z_{t-h} = 1) - E(x_t|z_{t-h} = 0)}$$

$$= E(\beta_i \mid i \in \text{Compliers}) \frac{\pi_c}{\pi_c - \pi_d} + E(\beta_i \mid i \in \text{Defiers}) \frac{-\pi_d}{\pi_c - \pi_d}. \tag{10.5}$$

---

[22] The existence of *Defiers* is ruled out by assumption in Theorem 10.1, a special case of the *Monotonicity* assumption in Imbens and Angrist (1994). To be precise, what is required is that Defiers be simultaneously present with Compliers: Defiers would be Compliers after reversing the definition of treatment.

[23] See Bisin and Verdier (2017) for a formal discussion of substitutability between culture and institutions.

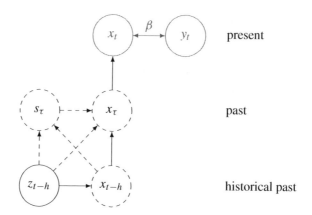

FIGURE 10.4

Current variables empirical model: non-linear interacting historical process. Note: Circles indicate variables observed by the investigator. Dashed circles indicate unobserved variables. Solid arrows indicate directions of causality. Double arrows indicate endogeneity or any other factor preventing the identification of a causal effect (omitted variables, selection bias, etc...). Dashed arrows indicate potential causal links. Highlighted in red (gray in print version) are the relationships of interest.

Expression (10.5) is a weighted average of the treatment effects, but note that one of the two weights must be negative, therefore the procedure estimates not a return, but a net effect which is difficult to interpret.[24]

Examples of the possible role of Defiers in historical contexts typically include cases of historical reversals in development. Consider Acemoglu et al. (2002) once again, for instance. Relative wealth in 1500 might have fostered future growth, in and of itself, but relative poverty as well, through institutional change in colonial times and the Industrial revolution. In this interpretation, countries which have maintained growth from 1500 would be Compliers, while the protagonists of the *reversal of fortunes* would be Defiers. Another interesting case of reversal is documented in Ashraf et al. (2010), when it is shown that more isolated locations in the Paleolithic are more developed today. It is argued that isolation was more conducive to innovation, through a mechanism combining less free-riding on inventions elsewhere and lower predisposition to being invaded. More generally, we conclude that the interpretation of causal effects in Persistence studies requires a careful analysis of the distribution of treatment take-up over historical time, once again suggesting an important role for historical narratives to guide the formal econometric IV strategy.

10.3.1.4 Persistence of treatment

In this subsection we entertain the analysis of the role of heterogeneous treatment effects operating through the persistence mechanisms itself rather than directly through treatment take-up as in the

---

[24] See Heckman et al. (2006) for a discussion of the implications of violations to the monotonicity assumption. Heckman and Vytlacil (2005) show in a general framework that the IV identifies a weighted average of the treatment effects. In the absence of Monotonicity the weights may be negative. Eq. (10.5) characterizes this average in the context of our simple model.

previous sections. Consider a behavioral-equilibrium model in which treatment at $t - h$ is perfectly determined by the instrument, $x_{t-h} = z_{t-h}$, but persistence is heterogeneous and depends on the value of x_τ: for instance treatment is more persistent than lack of treatment. Continuing our parallel with colonial origins in Acemoglu et al. (2001), this could occur for example because inclusive institutions, for example, are less costly to maintain once established.[25] In the context of (our interpretation of) Ashraf and Galor (2013), where the persistence of human genetic diversity is the result of the composition of mating patterns and the serial founder effect, heterogeneity of persistence could be the consequence of mating patterns depending on the number of migration events, e.g., because of the resulting distribution of phenotypical diversity, e.g., ethnic fractionalization.

A simple formalization of heterogeneous treatment effects operating through the persistence mechanisms is obtained if the transition matrix $\Pr(x_\tau \mid x_{\tau-1})$ depends on β. This could induce different compliance across values of β_i. To illustrate, assume β_i only takes two values, $\beta_1 < \beta_2$, respectively in fractions $\pi_1, \pi_2 = 1 - \pi_1$ of locations, and the correlation between x_t, x_{t-h} with $\Pr(x_t \mid x_{t-h})$ is as in Table 10.2.

Table 10.2 Heterogeneous persistence with binary x: $\Pr(x_t \mid x_{t-h})$.

		β_1		β_2	
	x_t	0	1	0	1
x_{t-h}	0	p_1	$1 - p_1$	p_2	$1 - p_2$
	1	$1 - q_1$	q_1	$1 - q_2$	q_2

The population analog of the Wald estimator is:

$$\frac{E(y_t \mid x_{t-h} = 1) - E(y_t \mid x_{t-h} = 0)}{E(x_t \mid x_{t-h} = 1) - E(x_t \mid x_{t-h} = 0)} =$$

$$\frac{(\beta_1 \pi_1 q_1 + \beta_2 \pi_2 q_2) - (\beta_1 \pi_1 (1 - p_1) + \beta_2 \pi_2 (1 - p_2))}{\pi_1 q_1 + \pi_2 q_2 - (\pi_1 (1 - p_1) + \pi_2 (1 - p_2))} =$$

$$\frac{\sum_{i=1,2} \pi_i \beta_i (p_i + q_i - 1)}{\sum_{i=1,2} \pi_i (p_i + q_i - 1)}.$$

It follows that, as long as $p_1 + p_2 \neq q_1 + q_2$, the LATE effect is different from the ATE. In particular, consider the (natural) case in which if the persistence of the treatment is correlated with the returns of the treatment β, that is, $\Pr(x_\tau = 1 \mid x_{\tau-1} = 1)$ increases with β. In the example of the table this would be the case if, e.g., $q_2 > q_1$ and $p_2 = p_1$. In this case, the Wald estimator would identify a LATE effect β greater than the ATE effect, $\sum_{i=1,2} \pi_i \beta_i$.[26] We conclude that a formal behavioral-equilibrium model of persistence suggests dimensions and directions of inquiry useful to better qualify the mechanisms driving the causal relationships identified in Persistence studies that rely on the persistence of the treatment effect in history.

---

[25] See Przeworski (2004) for evidence regarding the heterogeneity of institutional persistence over historical times.

[26] If $p_1 = p_2 = 1/2$ the LATE effect would be β_2.

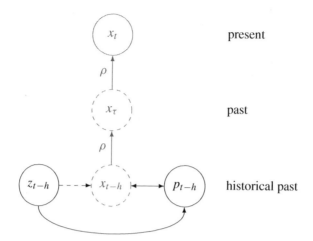

FIGURE 10.5

Pure persistence empirical model. *Note*: Circles indicate variables observed by the investigator. Dashed circles indicate unobserved variables. Solid arrows indicate directions of causality. Double arrows indicate endogeneity or any other factor preventing the identification of a causal effect (omitted variables, selection bias, etc...). Dashed arrows indicate potential causal links. Highlighted in red (gray in print version) is the relationships of interest.

10.4 Pure persistence studies

In this section we consider the special case of the empirical model in Section 10.2.1 in which the objective of the analysis is to prove the persistence over time of a variable x_τ. In these studies, the econometrician observes a proxy p_{t-h} for x_{t-h}, and, possibly, z_{t-h}, an instrument for p_{t-h}. This empirical model is illustrated in Fig. 10.2(b) which is reproduced here for convenience, as Fig. 10.5. We assume that z_{t-h} is a valid instrument for p_{t-h} to concentrate our analysis on the interpretation of the estimates of ρ when they are allowed to be heterogeneous across locations $i = 1, 2, \ldots, N$. Besides requiring that z_{t-h} be correlated with p_{t-h}, validity also requires z_{t-h} to be as good as randomly assigned and to satisfy the exclusion restriction, that is, z_{t-h} affects x_t only through p_{t-h}.

Assumption 10.2. z_{t-h} *is a valid instrument for* p_{t-h}*; in particular,*

$$cov\,(z_{t-h}, p_{t-h}) \neq 0$$
$$cov\,(z_{t-h}, x_t \mid p_{t-h}) = 0.$$

The examples of empirical studies that represent this model and we use as an illustration are listed in Table 10.3. All of these papers are interested in demonstrating the persistence in history of important factors related to current socio-economic performance: anti-semitism (Voigtländer and Voth (2012)), the role of women in society Alesina et al. (2013), civic trust (Nunn and Wantchekon (2011)), and social capital Guiso et al. (2016).

While it is possible to find or collect detailed measures of these variables in current times, the values of these variables in the past can only be measured with proxies. In addition, in some cases,

Table 10.3 Variables in selected Pure persistence studies.

Article	x_t	p_{t-h}	z_{t-h}
VV (2012)	Anti-semitism	Pogroms in 1349	-
AGN (2013)	Gender attitudes	Plow use	Plow suitability
NW (2011)	Trust	Slave trade	Distance from sea
GSZ (2016)	Civic capital	City-state	Bishop city

Note: See Fig. 10.2(b) for relationships between variables. Abbreviations: VV: Voigtländer and Voth (2012), AGN: Alesina et al. (2013), NW: Nunn and Wantchekon (2011), GSZ: Guiso et al. (2016).

the proxies are endogenous to the process and an historical instrument is introduced to disentangle the causal effect.

Consider for simplicity (but the arguments extend) an environment where both z_{t-h}, and p_{t-h}, are binary and assume that z_{t-h} is a valid instrument for p_{t-h}.[27] The Instrumental Variable estimator coincides with a Wald estimator:

$$\frac{E(x_t|z_{t-h}=1) - E(x_t|z_{t-h}=0)}{E(p_{t-h}|z_{t-h}=1) - E(p_{t-h}|z_{t-h}=0)} = \rho. \tag{10.6}$$

Analogously to the cases in Section 10.3, we distinguish:

Always takers: All i such that $p_{i,t-h} = 1$ for all values of $z_{i,t-h}$;
Never takers: All i such that $p_{i,t-h} = 0$ for all values of $z_{i,t-h}$;
Compliers: All i such that $p_{i,t-h} = 1$ when $z_{i,t-h} = 1$ and $p_{i,t-h} = 0$ when $z_{i,t-h} = 0$;
Defiers: All i such that $p_{i,t-h} = 1$ when $z_{i,t-h} = 0$ and $p_{i,t-h} = 0$ when $z_{i,t-h} = 1$.

A version of Theorem 10.1 can be stated in this case.

Theorem 10.2. *(Imbens and Angrist, 1994) Suppose that Assumption 10.2 holds and that the treatment induces no Defiers, then*

$$\frac{E(x_t|z_{t-h}=1) - E(x_t|z_{t-h}=0)}{E(p_{t-h}|z_{t-h}=1) - E(p_{t-h}|z_{t-h}=0)}$$
$$= E\left(x_{i,t}\,|_{p_{i,t-h}=1} - x_{i,t}\,|_{p_{i,t-h}=0}|\, i \in compliers\right)$$
$$= E(\rho_i\,|\, i \in compliers)$$

The estimated parameter is generally different from $E(\rho_i)$ when persistence ρ_i is heterogeneous across locations. We analyze two special cases.

---

[27] The validity of the instrument assumption is formally guaranteed by the following assumption:

$$E\left(p_{t-h}\,|\, z_{t-h}=1\right) \neq E\left(p_{t-h}\,|\, z_{t-h}=0\right) \qquad \text{First stage}$$
$$x_t\,|_{p_t,z_{t-h}=0} = x_t\,|_{p_t,z_{t-h}=1} \qquad \text{Exclusion restrictions.}$$

10.4.1 Abstract models of persistence of treatment

In this section we follow the analysis of Section 10.3.1.4, studying in some detail the role of heterogeneous treatment effects operating through persistence mechanism. We develop behavioral-equilibrium models in which the persistence of the treatment at $t - h$ is heterogeneous. We distinguish environments with and without a valid observed instrument z_{t-h}.

10.4.1.1 No instrument

Consider first the simplest case in which the econometrician does not observe any instrument in historical time z_{t-h}. Being interested in documenting persistence ρ in the process $\{x_\tau\}_{\tau \in T}$, the econometrician only observes x_t and a proxy p_{t-h} for x_{t-h}. Suppose for simplicity the underlying process for x_t takes the form

$$x_t = \rho x_{t-h} + \epsilon,$$

where ϵ is a random shock.[28] Voigtländer and Voth (2012)'s investigation of the historical persistence of anti-semitism in German cities serves well as an illustration of this type of Persistence studies. Lacking detailed evidence of anti-semitism in history, this article uses pogroms in 1348-50CE in a cross-section of cities as an imperfect proxy for it. The presumption is that the Black Death of 1348-50CE lowered the threshold for violence which resulted in Jews being blamed and in some cases being mass-executed in pogroms as a result. The study finds that pogroms in 1348-50CE are indeed positively correlated with various detailed measures of anti-semitism in the 20th century in the cross-section of cities (vote shares for the Nazi Party, number of deportees from each city, anti-semitic letters to newspapers, etc...). In this context, the shock ϵ captures all determinants of anti-semitism not operating through its cultural persistence.

Consider a behavioral-equilibrium cut-off model of the relationship between proxy p_{t-h} and treatment x_{t-h}:

$$p_{t-h} = \begin{cases} 1 & \text{if } x_{t-h} > \widetilde{x} \\ 0 & \text{if } x_{t-h} \leq \widetilde{x} \end{cases}; \tag{10.7}$$

that is, activation of the proxy is associated to treatment being sufficiently high, even though the relationship is not necessarily causal. In the context of Voigtländer and Voth (2012), indeed following their logic, pogroms $p_{t-h} = 1$ occur in cities with high anti-semitism x_{t-h}. But it is not excluded that pogroms might have induced a reinforcement of anti-semitic attitudes. Lacking data on x_{t-h} it is only possible to estimate

$$x_t = \alpha^R + \rho^R p_{t-h}, \tag{10.8}$$

which identifies

$$\begin{aligned} \rho^R &= E(x_t|p_{t-h} = 1) - E(x_t|p_{t-h} = 0) \\ &= \rho \cdot (E(x_{t-h}|x_{t-h} > \widetilde{x}) - E(x_{t-h}|x_{t-h} \leq \widetilde{x})); \end{aligned} \tag{10.9}$$

---

[28] Recall that $\rho x_{t-h} = [\rho_i x_{i,t-h}]_{i=1}^N$.

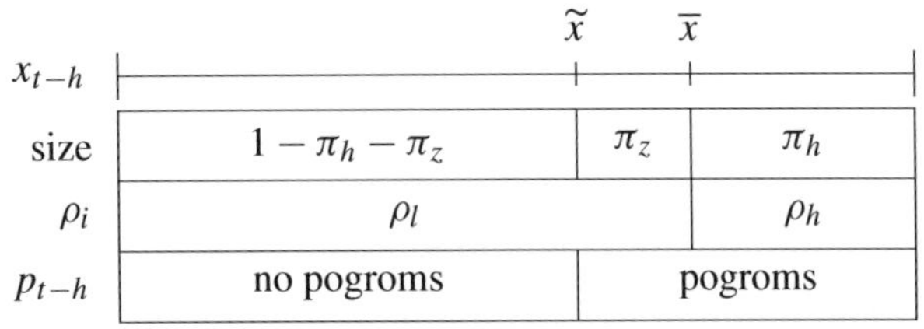

FIGURE 10.6

A model of Voigtländer and Voth (2012) with heterogeneous persistence.

that is, the true persistence parameter ρ times the difference in treatment between locations with $p_{t-h} = 1$ and $p_{t-h} = 0$. This kind of empirical analysis therefore reaches its objective of identifying the presence of long-run persistence: a positive estimate of ρ^R is obtained only if $\rho > 0$. As long as pogroms are positively correlated with anti-semitism x_{t-h}, using the pogroms variable produces an estimate of ρ^R that converges, in limit probability, to a positive number. The estimated ρ^R can be interpreted as the difference between treated and non-treated locations on the average level of x_t which is due to the persistence effect of x_{t-h}.

This interpretation of the estimate of ρ^R can be refined if we allow persistence to be heterogeneous; that is, if we allow ρ_i to differ across locations $i = 1, 2, \ldots, N$. As in the examples from the previous section, heterogeneity may occur because persistence is somehow correlated with the occurrence of pogroms, or because some other variable s_τ affects persistence itself over time. Allowing for heterogeneity in ρ_i across locations, estimating (10.8) identifies

$$\rho^R = E(\rho_i x_{t-h} | x_{t-h} > \widetilde{x}) - E(\rho_i x_{t-h} | x_{t-h} \leq \widetilde{x}). \tag{10.10}$$

An abstract behavioral-equilibrium model of the inter-generational transmission of cultural traits is helpful in interpreting (10.10) to illustrate the implications of heterogeneous persistence. Suppose cultural traits survive when they are sufficiently strongly held in the population; more specifically, e.g., a fraction of locations i, π_h with $x_{t-h} > \overline{x}$ have a high $\rho_i = \rho_h$ so that the trait persists more easily over time than in the remaining $(1 - \pi_h)$ cities, with persistence $\rho_l < \rho_h$ (see Fig. 10.6).[29] In this case (10.10) reduces to

$$\rho^R = \rho_l E(\widetilde{x} < x_{t-h} \leq \overline{x}) + \rho_h E(x_{t-h} > \overline{x}) - \rho_l E(x_{t-h} < \widetilde{x}) \tag{10.11}$$

It follows then that the identified effect of persistence ρ^R can still be interpreted as a difference between treated and non-treated cities of the average level of x_t due to the persistence of x_{t-h}. On the other hand, the size of the effect depends on the distribution of x_{t-h} and on the relationship between x_{t-h} and persistence ρ across locations. For instance, assuming instead $\widetilde{x} > \overline{x}$, we obtain

$$\rho^R = \rho_h E(x_{t-h} > \widetilde{x}) - (\rho_l E(x_{t-h} < \overline{x}) + \rho_h E(\overline{x} < x_{t-h} \leq \widetilde{x}))$$

---

[29] See Bisin and Verdier (2001, 2011) for models of inter-generational cultural transmission with implications along these lines.

Under different hypotheses, which, e.g., in Voigtländer and Voth (2012)'s context can ultimately be reduced to how high anti-semitism in the XIVth century needed to be to trigger a pogrom, the size of the identified effect changes. Pogroms identify the persistence of anti-semitism in cities where they took place, not the persistence in cities where they did not occur, because they did not occur in a random sample of cities.[30] We conclude that while it might be difficult to distinguish a priori between the different process we have hypothesized drive persistence of anti-semitism in relations to pogroms, it would be interesting in principle and with additional historical evidence we may be able to support one case over the other to improve our understanding of the nature of persistence. More generally, the simple behavioral-equilibrium model indicates novel and interesting empirical directions to pursue the analysis of the persistence of cultural traits and values.

10.4.1.2 Instrumenting for persistence

Consider now the case in which the econometrician does observe an instrument in historical time z_{t-h} for p_{t-h}. That is, consider the case where z_{t-h} affects causally x_{t-h} and p_{t-h}, while x_{t-h} and p_{t-h} are in principle linked by two-way causation, as in the empirical model in Fig. 10.2(b). The econometrician, interested in measuring the process' persistence ρ, observes x_t and a proxy p_{t-h} for x_{t-h} (but not x_{t-h} directly).

Three examples from the literature clarify this empirical model. Nunn and Wantchekon (2011) study the persistence of social trust, an important determinant of current development, using data from African regions. Modern surveys, such as the Afrobarometer, provide measures of trust in the present. The historical proxy is the size of slave trade, which varies by location and ethnicity, and may have affected local trust in the past by generating "an environment of ubiquitous insecurity caused individuals to turn on others". Reverse causality may also hold, however, because communities with lower trust may experience a lower cost to "kidnap, trick or sell each other to slave"). To address this endogeneity the geographical distance from the coast is used as an instrument for the size of trade. Distance from the coast correlates with the size of slave trade and, arguably, does not affect directly current levels of trust. The study finds that the level of social trust can be traced back to the slave trade.

In Guiso et al. (2016) the process $\{x_\tau\}_{\tau \in T}$ represents civic capital in Italian cities, measured, in modern times, with indicators such as the proportion of student cheating in mathematics tests, the prevalence of non-profit associations, or measures of blood donations. The proxy for this variable in the past is whether the city experienced self-government in the middle ages, which arguably generated a culture of cooperation and trust that persists until current times. Indeed, the evidence shows that cities that experienced self-government have better measures of current social capital. Because this correlation may be due to omitted endogenous factors, the paper supports these results by showing that the correlation remains when instrumenting self-government with the presence of a bishop seat in the city before 1400 CE. The instrument's validity is motivated by the argument (advanced by several historians) that bishops facilitated the adoption of self-government by morally sanctioning the citizens'

---

[30] This model's assumptions can be mapped into the assumptions we used to build the model in Subsection 10.3.1.4. In that model, the persistent variable is binary, but the correlation between variables over time is more general than the correlations that are possible imposing the structure of Fig. 10.6. For example, in the model in this subsection, assume there is an underlying continuous latent variable χ_{t-h} that determines both p_{t-h} and $x_{t-h} \in \{0, 1\}$ according to different thresholds. Then, knowing the distribution of χ_{t-h} one can derive the conditional probabilities that are analog to $\{p_i, q_i\}$, $i = 1, 2$ in Table 10.2 and compute what magnitudes the Wald estimator identifies.

agreement. The presence of bishops lowers the coordination cost required to achieve independence without affecting modern social capital directly. The study finds that indeed, self-government in the late middle ages determines higher civic capital today.

In our last example of papers that conform to this framework, Alesina et al. (2013), trace the origin of current cross-cultural differences regarding the role of women in society (measured by labor-force participation, political representation, and women entrepreneurship, x_t) to agricultural practices in pre-industrial periods, proxied by plow cultivation (p_{t-h}). The process $\{x_\tau\}_{\tau \in T}$ represents gender attitudes and the proxy p_{t-h} is the adoption of plow cultivation in pre-industrial times. The argument is that practices requiring more physical strength encouraged specialization of production by gender, affecting the perception of gender roles, which persisted in current times even if modern market production does not require a physical strength advantage. The adoption of plow agriculture is therefore a proxy for the perception of gender roles, but could be affected by it, because societies that believe women should be confined to home production are more prone to adopt agricultural practices that comparatively advantage men. The study addresses this endogeneity using the suitability of locations for plow cultivation as an instrument. Plow suitability disproportionally induces the adoption of the plow, arguably without affecting the perception of gender roles.

In all these examples, because a valid instrument is observed for the adopted proxy, the empirical model leads to the identification of

$$\frac{E(x_t|z_{t-h}=1) - E(x_t|z_{t-h}=0)}{E(p_{t-h}|z_{t-h}=1) - E(p_{t-h}|z_{t-h}=0)} = \rho. \tag{10.12}$$

Following the logic of our discussion of Voigtländer and Voth (2012), an instrument is not necessary to identify a positive ρ. As long as $p_{i,t-h} = 1$ and $x_{i,t-h}$ are correlated, the estimate ρ will have the correct sign. The endogeneity of the adoption of the plow in Alesina et al. (2013), for instance, does not invalidate the fact that locations which adopted the plow in $t - h$ are characterized by more conservative gender attitudes at t: locations i with $p_{i,t-h} = 1$ have higher $x_{i,t}$. These attitudes in the present are the consequence of the persistence of cultural traits and attitudes. The same is true for the identification of the persistence of trust in Nunn and Wantchekon (2011) and of civic capital in Guiso et al. (2016), that we argued have the same structural relationship between variables.

However, the IV estimate of ρ can be interpreted as a LATE estimate of the persistence of the process $\{x_\tau\}_{\tau \in T}$; that is, a *local* effect through the specific instrument adopted. For instance, the IV in Nunn and Wantchekon (2011), identifies the persistence of community trust. Assume the benefits of trust b_i are heterogeneous across ethnic groups, for simplicity assume two levels $b_h > b_l$. Trust is then the consequence of a behavioral-equilibrium outcome: adopted when its benefits are greater than the benefits from slave trade. Let the benefit of slave trade be denoted by $d(z_{t-h})$ and denote with $z_{t-h} = 1$ high distance from the coast, with $d(1) < d(0)$. Assume $b_l < d(1) < b_h < d(0)$ so that the ethnic groups with low value of trust $b_i = b_l$ always experience slave trade, whereas groups with $b_i = b_h$ experience trade only if they are close to the coast. In this case distance from coast induces a change in treatment only for ethnic groups with the highest returns to trust, those where, presumably, incentives for trust to persist are higher.[31] This would imply that the IV parameter identifies the per-

---

[31] For example assume that the cost of acquiring trust is random, but on average higher than the average cost of maintaining it once acquired. Then ethnic groups with higher benefits will display higher persistence of trust.

sistence of trust in locations where trust is more beneficial and consequently where its persistence is higher.

Similarly, consider Guiso et al. (2016), and assume cities have different returns to civic capital, and persistence is higher when returns are higher. Further, assume that cities with high returns adopt self-government in the middle ages regardless of the triggering effect of a coordinating factor (the presence of a bishop, z_{t-h}), whereas cities with $b_i = b_l$ adopt self-government only through the coordination from a bishop (if $z_t = 1$). In this case Compliers are cities with a low return, which arguably are less likely to experience persistence otherwise. In this case, the instrument identifies persistence in cities with relatively low returns and consequently low persistence.

Finally, in Alesina et al. (2013) the instrument identifies the persistence of gender attitudes as affected by the exogenous adoption of the plow. It is conceivable that some locations are Always Takers, that they have adopted the plow motivated by their previous gender attitudes - independently of whether their land were suitable for plow agriculture. If these locations are characterized by stronger persistence of these attitudes, the instrument identifies persistence in location with relatively lower persistence.

10.5 Conclusions

In this chapter, we have argued that it is often natural for heterogeneous effects to occur in the context of Persistence studies: if different mechanisms affect the variable of interest with different intensity over locations over time, then different combinations of mechanisms that aggregate into the same value of the treatment variable generate heterogeneous effects.

Behavioral-equilibrium models can help the interpretation of the causal effects uncovered in Persistence studies when treatment effects are heterogeneous and the LATE parameter identified in quasi-experimental designs differs from the Average Treatment Effect. In this context, we have shown, even minimal models of treatment take-up may shed some light on what information the estimated effects provide, at least conditionally on assumptions that sometimes can be empirically tested. Adding structure, as recent and current research on the dynamics of institution and culture is doing, can only be of help; see Acemoglu et al. (2021, in this book); Bisin and Verdier (2021, in this book); Persson and Tabellini (2021, in this book). Importantly, these arguments are independent of the soundness of econometric techniques and of data reliability.

The interpretation of the estimated parameters is important when Persistence studies have policy implications. If multiple slow-moving mechanisms (with heterogeneous effects) underlie long-run correlations, then policies motivated by the estimated parameters, which are not necessarily the average treatment effect, may produce unexpected outcomes if they do not operate through the channels that are *locally* identified by the research design.

The correct interpretation of the estimated parameters is important not only for policy implications, but also when the researcher is interested in counterfactual historical analysis. When treatment effects are heterogeneous, the instrument operates by identifying a specific historical path whose effects may be different from those that may have been generated in a counterfactual.

Pushing the arguments of this chapter forward, this line of analysis sheds doubts on the notion of *origin*, often used in these studies. A causal relationship realized in history at time τ with effects at time t does not preclude another historical causal relationship realized prior to τ.[32] In many cases the relevant question is not what was the origin of a phenomenon, but what are the counterfactual *quantitative* effect that results from changing variables in the historical past on variables in the present. Each variable at different points in the past may affect the present differently. This paper highlights how the empirical implications of Persistence studies may be interpreted using simple models that inform how these mechanisms affect the variable of interest suggesting directions for future research.

10.6 Appendix LATE for school

The clearest applications of the distinction between LATE and ATE are in labor/education economics. In this Appendix we exploit Rosenzweig and Wolpin (2000)'s comment on Angrist and Krueger (1991)'s instrumental variable approach to estimating returns to schooling.[33]

Consider the relationship between schooling attainment and earnings. A simple regression fails to identify the causal effect of schooling because an omitted variable bias: for example, children of higher ability may earn higher wages for given schooling and also choose a higher schooling attainment. A valid instrument for schooling may be adopted to identify the causal effect. Angrist and Krueger (1991) propose to use Quarter of birth. The birth date cutoffs for school-entry age combined with minimum compulsory schooling ages induce some children born during the last months of the year to complete more years of schooling relative to children born at the beginning of the year, because they are induced to start schooling at an earlier age (this is true for example if they intend to leave school at the mandatory minimum age). The arguably random variation in date of birth provides a "natural" instrument for estimating the return to schooling.[34]

Consider the case in which the treatment effect is heterogeneous, that is, returns to schooling vary in the cross-section of students; for instance, they increase with the underlying unobservable ability. To illustrate the difference between LATE and ATE, limit the students' choice to one extra year of schooling after mandatory schooling age, and assume that high ability students attain an extra year of education regardless of their Quarter of birth, but low-ability students always intend to drop out of school at mandatory age, and can only be "forced" to undertake an extra year of education if, by being born late in the year, they start attending school one year younger.

The instrumental variable technique "works" by randomly inducing a subset of students, low-ability students, to undertake an extra year of education. The extra earnings gained by students not born in the first quarter, relative to the earnings of those born during the rest of the year, are generated only by

---

[32] For instance, the origin of the Mafia in Sicily has been reduced with good arguments to the rise of socialist Peasant Fasci organizations at the end of the 19th century (Acemoglu et al., 2020); to a price shock on sulphur and lemon in the 1850's (Buonanno et al., 2015; Dimico et al., 2017); to the lack of city states in the XIV'th century - in turn a consequence of Norman domination (Guiso et al., 2016); to the Paleolithic split into nomadic pastoralism in 7th millenium B.C. (Alinei, 2007).

[33] Underlying this analysis is the debate in econometrics regarding identification power in reduced-form causal inference design: see Angrist and Krueger (1991); Imbens and Angrist (1994); Angrist and Imbens (1999); Deaton (2010, 2020); Heckman (1997, 1999); Heckman and Urzua (2010); Imbens (2010).

[34] In fact, the validity of quarter of birth as an instrument has been questioned, see Buckles and Hungerman (2013), but for the purposes of this introduction, we assume the instrument to be valid from an econometric standpoint.

low-ability students that attend an extra year of education. All other students have the same schooling attainment regardless of the date of birth, therefore the instrumental variable estimate only identifies the returns for low-ability students (a LATE effect), not the return of high-ability students, nor the average return of all students (the ATE).

While the estimated parameter remains of great interest, this interpretation is consequential in that it suggests that the specific IV procedure adopted, while valid, under-estimates the returns to schooling. Furthermore, it suggests caution when considering the policy implications of the estimates, because a different policy with the goal of inducing higher schooling attainment may not induce the same subset of students to comply.

This stylized model highlights how the Quarter of birth instrument is likely to identify the returns of the low-ability students, because arguably these students are the most likely to leave schooling at the minimum compulsory age. It is both a logically reasonable assumption, and an empirically testable implication that could provide additional evidence about the interpretation of the estimated returns. It is in this spirit that we proceed, in this paper, to formalize stylized models of persistence studies.

References

Acemoglu, D., De Feo, G., De Luca, G.D., 2020. Weak states: causes and consequences of the Sicilian mafia. The Review of Economic Studies 87 (2), 537–581.

Acemoglu, D., Egorov, G., Sonin, K., 2021. Institutional change and institutional persistence. In: Bisin, A., Federico, G. (Eds.), The Handbook of Historical Economics. Elsevier. Chapter 13 (in this book).

Acemoglu, D., Johnson, S., Robinson, J.A., 2001. The colonial origins of comparative development: an empirical investigation. The American Economic Review 91 (5), 1369–1401.

Acemoglu, D., Johnson, S., Robinson, J.A., 2002. Reversal of fortune: geography and institutions in the making of the modern world income distribution. The Quarterly Journal of Economics 117 (4), 1231–1294.

Alesina, A., Giuliano, P., Nunn, N., 2013. On the origins of gender roles: women and the plough. The Quarterly Journal of Economics 128 (2), 469–530.

Alinei, M., 2007. Origini pastorali e italiche della camorra, della mafia e della'ndrangheta: un esperimento di Archeologia Etimologica. In: Origini pastorali e italiche della camorra, della mafia e della'ndrangheta, pp. 1000–1039.

Angrist, J.D., Imbens, G.W., 1999. Comment on James J. Heckman, "Instrumental variables: a study of implicit behavioral assumptions used in making program evaluations". The Journal of Human Resources, 823–827.

Angrist, J.D., Krueger, A.B., 1991. Does compulsory school attendance affect schooling and earnings? The Quarterly Journal of Economics 106 (4), 979–1014.

Angrist, J.D., Pischke, J.-S., 2008. Mostly Harmless Econometrics: An Empiricist's Companion. Princeton University Press.

Angrist, J.D., Pischke, J.-S., 2014. Mastering 'Metrics: The Path from Cause to Effect. Princeton University Press.

Ashraf, Q., Galor, O., 2013. The 'Out of Africa' hypothesis, human genetic diversity, and comparative economic development. The American Economic Review 103 (1), 1–46.

Ashraf, Q., Özak, Ö., Galor, O., 2010. Isolation and development. Journal of the European Economic Association 8 (2–3), 401–412.

Bisin, A., Verdier, T., 2001. The economics of cultural transmission and the dynamics of preferences. Journal of Economic Theory 97 (2), 298–319.

Bisin, A., Verdier, T., 2011. The economics of cultural transmission and socialization. In: Benhabib, J., Bisin, A., Jackson, M.O. (Eds.), Handbook of Social Economics, vol. 1. Elsevier, pp. 339–416.

Bisin, A., Verdier, T., 2017. On the joint evolution of culture and institutions. Working Paper 23375. National Bureau of Economic Research.

Bisin, A., Verdier, T., 2021. Phase diagrams in historical economics: culture and institutions. In: Bisin, A., Federico, G. (Eds.), The Handbook of Historical Economics. Elsevier. Chapter 17 (in this book).

Bottero, M., Wallace, B., 2013. Is There a Long-Term Effect of Africa's Slave Trades? Economic History Working Paper 30. Bank of Italy.

Buckles, K.S., Hungerman, D.M., 2013. Season of birth and later outcomes: old questions, new answers. Review of Economics and Statistics 95 (3), 711–724. https://ideas.repec.org/a/tpr/restat/v95y2013i3p711-724.html.

Buonanno, P., Durante, R., Prarolo, G., Vanin, P., 2015. Poor institutions, rich mines: resource curse in the origins of the Sicilian mafia. The Economic Journal 125 (586), F175–F202.

Cantoni, D., Yuchtman, N., 2021. Historical natural experiments: bridging economics and economic history. In: Bisin, A., Federico, G. (Eds.), The Handbook of Historical Economics. Elsevier. Chapter 8 (in this book).

Casey, G., Klemp, M., 2021. Historical instruments and contemporary endogenous regressors. Journal of Development Economics 149, 102586. https://doi.org/10.1016/j.jdeveco.2020.102586.

Cioni, M., Federico, G., Vasta, M., 2021. The two revolutions in economic history. In: Bisin, A., Federico, G. (Eds.), The Handbook of Historical Economics. Elsevier. Chapter 2 (in this book).

Deaton, A., 2010. Instruments, randomization, and learning about development. Journal of Economic Literature 48 (2), 424–455.

Deaton, A., 2020. Randomization in the Tropics Revisited: A Theme and Eleven Variations. Working Paper 27600. National Bureau of Economic Research.

Dimico, A., Isopi, A., Olsson, O., 2017. Origins of the Sicilian mafia: the market for lemons. The Journal of Economic History 77 (4), 1083–1115.

Guiso, L., Sapienza, P., Zingales, L., 2016. Long-term persistence. Journal of the European Economic Association 14 (6), 1401–1436. https://doi.org/10.1111/jeea.12177.

Heckman, J., 1997. Instrumental variables: a study of implicit behavioral assumptions used in making program evaluations. The Journal of Human Resources, 441–462.

Heckman, J.J., 1999. Instrumental variables: response to Angrist and Imbens. The Journal of Human Resources 34 (4), 828–837.

Heckman, J.J., Lochner, L.J., Todd, P.E., 2006. Earnings functions, rates of return and treatment effects: the Mincer equation and beyond. In: Handbook of the Economics of Education, vol. 1, pp. 307–458.

Heckman, J.J., Schmierer, D., Urzua, S., 2010. Testing the correlated random coefficient model. Journal of Econometrics 158 (2), 177–203.

Heckman, J.J., Urzua, S., 2010. Comparing IV with structural models: what simple IV can and cannot identify. Journal of Econometrics 156 (1), 27–37.

Heckman, J.J., Vytlacil, E., 2005. Structural equations, treatment effects, and econometric policy evaluation 1. Econometrica 73 (3), 669–738.

Imbens, G.W., 2010. Better LATE than nothing: some comments on Deaton (2009) and Heckman and Urzua (2009). Journal of Economic Literature 48 (2), 399–423.

Imbens, G., 2019. Potential Outcome and Directed Acyclic Graph Approaches to Causality: Relevance for Empirical Practice in Economics. Working Paper 26104. National Bureau of Economic Research.

Imbens, G.W., Angrist, J.D., 1994. Identification and estimation of local average treatment effects. Econometrica 62 (2), 467–475. http://www.jstor.org/stable/2951620.

Kelly, M., 2019. The standard errors of persistence. Working Paper DP13783, CEPR.

Nunn, N., 2008. The long-term effects of Africa's slave trades. The Quarterly Journal of Economics 123 (1), 139–176.

Nunn, N., Wantchekon, L., 2011. The slave trade and the origins of mistrust in Africa. The American Economic Review 101 (7), 3221–3252.

Pearl, J., 2009. Causality. Cambridge University Press.

Pearl, J., Glymour, M., Jewell, N.P., 2016. Causal Inference in Statistics: A Primer. John Wiley & Sons.

Persson, T., Tabellini, G., 2021. Culture, institutions, and policy. In: Bisin, A., Federico, G. (Eds.), The Handbook of Historical Economics. Elsevier. Chapter 16 (in this book).

Przeworski, A., 2004. The last instance: are institutions the primary cause of economic development? Archives Européennes de Sociologie/European Journal of Sociology/Europäisches Archiv für Soziologie, 165–188.

Rosenzweig, M.R., Wolpin, K.I., 2000. Natural "natural experiments" in economics. Journal of Economic Literature 38 (4), 827–874.

Voigtländer, N., Voth, H.-J., 2012. Persecution perpetuated: the medieval origins of anti-semitic violence in Nazi Germany*. The Quarterly Journal of Economics 127 (3), 1339–1392. https://doi.org/10.1093/qje/qjs019.

Voth, H.-J., 2021. Persistence – myth and mystery. In: Bisin, A., Federico, G. (Eds.), The Handbook of Historical Economics. Elsevier. Chapter 9 (in this book).

Dynamic general equilibrium modeling of long and short-run historical events

11

Gary D. Hansen[a,b]**, Lee E. Ohanian**[a,b]**, and Fatih Ozturk**[a]

aUCLA, Los Angeles, CA, United States
bNBER, Cambridge, MA, United States

11.1 Introduction

Macroeconomists have increasingly been studying historical events using quantitative general equilibrium tools, with a focus on important historical episodes that previously had been studied using traditional historical methods (see for example Ohanian (1997), Cole and Ohanian (1999, 2004), Kehoe and Prescott (2007), McGrattan (2012)). The application of general equilibrium analysis is shedding new light on important historical episodes by using diagnostic methods that help identify potential classes of models for evaluating these events, and by quantifying the impact of different shocks on macroeconomic activity during historical periods within fully articulated general equilibrium models.

The recent integration of macroeconomics with economic history involves the practice of combining general equilibrium analytical methods and historical narratives with existing and recently constructed historical datasets. This is creating new insights about long-run growth and cyclical fluctuations.

This chapter advances the use of quantitative general equilibrium tools within the field of historical economics to study two important and very different historical episodes that have received little attention using general equilibrium macroeconomic growth models. The first is the Industrial Revolution, which captures the transition of Western economies from the Malthusian era, in which there was little, if any growth in per-capita income, to that of the era of Modern Economic Growth, which has featured persistent, long-run per capita growth and rising living standards, all of which took place around the middle of the 18th century. This analysis uses Hansen and Prescott (2002) model of the Industrial Revolution to analyze newly constructed data from Britain that dates back to 1245 (Clark (2010)).

Clark's data include total factor productivity (TFP), real output, population, factor prices, and capital stocks, among other variables, which allow us to provide the first quantitative-theoretic analysis of the transition from the Malthusian era to the modern growth era. Our main finding advances our quantitative understanding of the timing of the transition to modern economic growth that occurred in the 1700s.

We find that this transition realistically could never have occurred much before that time, as the productivity of the Malthusian sector peaked around 15th century, virtually guaranteeing that the nascent capital-intensive technologies of that time would not be close to being competitive. Instead, a 300 year stagnation of the Malthusian sector implicitly allowed the newer capital-intensive production methods to catch up, become viable alternatives to the Malthusian technology, and ultimately dominate the labor and land-intensive Malthusian technologies. Moreover, we find that the timing of this catchup is robust to plausible amounts of historical TFP mismeasurement.

The second episode studied is the U.S. economy from 1889-1929. This is a particularly striking period in the history of the U.S., involving World War I, two major financial panics, the diffusion of several important new technologies, including electricity and the internal combustion engine, and the "Roaring Twenties", one of the most rapid growth decades in U.S. history, and the period which immediately preceded the Great Depression. This section uses variants of Business Cycle Accounting (Cole and Ohanian (2002), Chari et al. (2007), and Brinca et al. (2016)), a general equilibrium diagnostic tool, to study this period in its entirety, and well as analyze individual events, including World War I and the Panics of 1893 and 1907, and the "Roaring Twenties".

One main finding is that technology shocks are remarkably important drivers of economic activity between 1889 and 1916, including the Panics of 1893 and 1907. This finding stands in sharp contrast to the perception that technology shocks today are quantitatively unimportant. Our second main finding is that labor is substantially depressed during World War I, and this labor depression continues through the 1920s, one of the highest growth decades in U.S. history. We find that a large labor wedge is the key factor depressing growth during the 1920s, and that output per capita should have been about 15 percent higher by 1929 in the absence of the increased labor wedge. We find that standard factors, such as tax rates, do not account for the post-1916 labor wedge, and that future research should study this decade to gain a better understanding of the specific factors that created this wedge.

The chapter is organized as follows. Section 11.2 presents the analysis of the Industrial Revolution. Section 11.3 presents the analysis of the U.S. economy between 1889-1929. Section 11.4 concludes.

11.2 Growth in the very long run

In this section, we use the model studied in Hansen and Prescott (2002) to interpret data from Clark (2010). In particular, this model features an endogenous transition from Malthusian stagnation to sustained growth. Malthusian stagnation is the result of firms choosing to use a production process where land's share of income is positive, and hence there are decreasing returns to capital and labor. Another important feature required for Malthusian stagnation is that the population growth rate is an increasing function of living standards. Sustained growth begins when a production process is employed that exhibits constant returns to capital and labor.

Perhaps the most important feature of this model is that both production processes are available throughout history and the choice to employ one or both processes is made by firms in response to the total factor productivity associated with each of these processes. In the early stages of development, when TFP for the second production process is low, only the land intensive technology is used. Eventually, if TFP associated with the second production process grows over time, that process will inevitably begin to be employed. At this point an "industrial revolution" occurs and the economy converges to a standard Solow type balanced growth path.

The approach followed by Hansen and Prescott (2002) differs from other contributions to the literature using dynamic general equilibrium models to understand the industrial revolution in two respects. First, Hansen and Prescott (2002) study the consequences of technological progress while papers such as Galor and Weil (2000) or Lucas (2018) aim to explain technological progress itself. Second, the transition to sustained growth happens in the Malthus to Solow model when a production process with a lower land share becomes profitable and is adopted. In the other two papers, sustained growth results from an increase in the rate of return to human capital that leads to a demographic transition resulting from endogenous fertility decisions of the sort modeled in Becker and Barro (1988). Doepke (2004) develops a model that aims to unify these two approaches.

11.2.1 The "Malthus to Solow" model

The model of Hansen and Prescott (2002) is a version of the Diamond (1965) overlapping generations growth model. Households live for two periods. They earn labor income when young which is used to finance consumption, investment in physical capital and land. In the second period of life, households are the owners of capital and land and finance consumption from renting these assets to firms, who use them along with labor as inputs in production. At the end of the period, old households sell their land to the young, which also helps finance their consumption. An additional important feature of the model is that population growth is a function of living standards as is generally assumed in a Malthusian growth model.

11.2.1.1 Technology

This is a one-good economy in which the single consumption good can be produced from two available production processes that are assumed to be accessible throughout time. The first is called the Malthus process and requires capital, labor, and land (K_M, N_M, and L) to produce output according to the following Cobb-Douglas technology:

$$Y_{Mt} = A_{Mt} K_{Mt}^{\phi} N_{Mt}^{\mu} L_M^{1-\phi-\mu} \tag{11.1}$$

The second production process uses only capital and labor (K_S and N_S):

$$Y_{St} = A_{St} K_{St}^{\theta} N_{St}^{1-\theta} \tag{11.2}$$

Given that these two processes are always available and that Y_M and Y_S are the same good, the aggregate production function can be described as follows:

$$Y = F(K, N, L) = \max_{K_M, K_S, N_M, N_S} \left\{ A_M K_M^{\phi} N_M^{\mu} L^{1-\phi-\mu} + A_S K_S^{\theta} N_S^{1-\theta} \right\} \tag{11.3}$$

$$\text{subject to } K_M + K_S \leq K$$
$$N_M + N_S \leq N$$

Here, A_M is total factor productivity specific to the Malthus production process and A_S is total factor productivity specific to the Solow process.

Land is in fixed supply, it can't be produced and does not depreciate. Its only use is for production employing the Malthus process. Hence we normalize this to be one ($L_M = L = 1$).

Total output, $Y_t = Y_{Mt} + Y_{St}$, can be consumed or invested to produce capital productive the following period. Capital depreciates fully in the period it is used in production. Hence, the resource constraint is

$$C_t + K_{t+1} = Y_{Mt} + Y_{St} \tag{11.4}$$

One way of decentralizing this economy is to assume that one firm, called the Malthus firm, operates the Malthus production process (11.1) and another operates the Solow process (11.2).[1] Let w be the wage rate, r_K be the capital rental rate and r_L be the rental rate for land. Given these factor rental prices and values for A_M and A_S, each firm maximizes profit,

$$\max_{N_j, K_j, L_J} \left\{ Y_j - wN_j - r_K K_j - r_L L_j \right\}, \ j = M, S \tag{11.5}$$

11.2.1.2 Households

We assume that N_t households are born in period t live for two periods. A household born in period t consumes c_{1t} units of consumption in the first period of his life and $c_{2,t+1}$ units in the second. His utility is given by

$$U(c_{1t}, c_{2,t+1}) = \log c_{1t} + \beta \log c_{2,t+1} \tag{11.6}$$

The number of new households born in a given period is assumed to grow at rate that is a function of living standards. Living standards at date t are assumed to be given by c_{1t} and N_t evolves as follows:

$$N_{t+1} = g(c_{1t})N_t \tag{11.7}$$

The initial old at date t_0 are assumed to be endowed equally with land ($\frac{1}{N_{t_0-1}}$ units) and capital ($\frac{K_{t_0}}{N_{t_0-1}}$ units). In addition, each young household is endowed with one unit of labor that is supplied inelastically. Old households are assumed to rent land and capital to firms and then sell their land to the young at the end of the period. This finances consumption in the second period of life, c_2. The young supply labor and earn labor income which is used to finance c_1, investment (k_{t+1}), and the purchase of land from the old. The price of land is denoted by q. Hence, a household born in period t will choose consumption, investment, and land purchase to maximize (11.6) subject to the following budget constraints:

$$c_{1t} + k_{t+1} + q_t l_{t+1} = w_t \tag{11.8}$$

$$c_{2,t+1} = r_{K,t+1} k_{t+1} + (r_{L,t+1} + q_{t+1}) l_{t+1} \tag{11.9}$$

11.2.1.3 Competitive equilibrium

Given N_{t_0}, N_{t_0-1}, and K_{t_0}, as well as a sequence of sector specific total factor productivities $\{A_{Mt}, A_{St}\}_{t=t_0}^{\infty}$, a competitive equilibrium consists of sequences of prices $\{q_t, w_t, r_{Kt}, r_{Lt}\}_{t=t_0}^{\infty}$, firm allocations $\{K_{Mt}, K_{St}, N_{Mt}, N_{St}, Y_{Mt}, Y_{St}\}_{t=t_0}^{\infty}$, and household allocations $\{c_{1t}, c_{2t}, k_{t+1}, l_{t+1}\}_{t=t_0}^{\infty}$ such that

- Given the sequence of prices, the firm allocations solve the problems specified in Eq. (11.5).
- Given the sequence of prices, the household allocation maximizes (11.6) subject to (11.8) and (11.9). Recall that the old in period t_0 are endowed with $\frac{1}{N_{t_0-1}}$ units of land and $\frac{K_{t_0}}{N_{t_0-1}}$ units of capital.

---

[1] Given constant returns to scale, the number of firms does not matter.

- Markets clear:
  - $K_{Mt} + K_{St} = N_{t-1}k_t$
  - $N_{Mt} + N_{St} = N_t$
  - $N_{t-1}l_t = 1$
  - $Y_{Mt} + Y_{St} = N_t c_{1t} + N_{t-1}c_{2t} + N_t k_{t+1}$
- $N_{t+1} = g(c_{1t})N_t$

11.2.1.4 Characterizing the equilibrium

Here we briefly summarize how we solve for an equilibrium sequence of prices and quantities. More details are provided in Hansen and Prescott (2002) and Greenwood (2020). The key results show that the Malthus sector will always operate, but the Solow sector will only operate if A_S is sufficiently large. In particular, the papers cited establish the following results:

1. For any w_t and r_{Kt}, the Malthus sector will operate. That is, $Y_{Mt} > 0$ for all t.
2. Given values for w_t and r_{Kt}, maximized profit per unit of output in the Solow sector is positive if and only if

$$A_{St} > \left(\frac{r_{Kt}}{\theta}\right)^{\theta} \left(\frac{w_t}{1-\theta}\right)^{1-\theta} \tag{11.10}$$

Profits are zero if Eq. (11.10) holds with equality. Hence, the Solow firm will only produce output ($Y_{St} > 0$) if A_{St} is greater than or equal to the right hand side of (11.10).

Given values for A_{Mt}, A_{St}, K_t, and N_t for some t, define w_t^M and r_{Kt}^M as follows:

$$w_t^M \equiv \mu A_{Mt} K_t^{\phi} N_t^{\mu-1} \tag{11.11}$$

$$r_{Kt}^M \equiv \phi A_{Mt} K_t^{\phi-1} N_t^{\mu} \tag{11.12}$$

Our solution procedure involves first evaluating the right hand side of Eq. (11.10) at w_t^M and r_{Kt}^M each period. If A_{St} is less than or equal to this value, only the Malthus sector will operate. In this case, in equilibrium $w_t = w_t^M$, $r_{Kt} = r_{Kt}^M$, and $r_{Lt} = (1 - \phi - \mu)A_{Mt} K_t^{\phi} N_t^{\mu}$. If A_{St} is greater than this value, both sectors will operate and the marginal product of labor and capital will be equated across sectors (see problem (11.3)). Hence, the equilibrium rental rates are as follows:

$$w_t = \begin{cases} w_t^M & \text{if } A_{St} \leq \left(\frac{r_{Kt}^M}{\theta}\right)^{\theta} \left(\frac{w_t^M}{1-\theta}\right)^{1-\theta} \\ \mu A_{Mt} K_{Mt}^{\theta} N_{Mt}^{\mu-1} = (1-\theta)A_{St} K_{St}^{\theta} N_{St}^{-\theta} & \text{if } A_{St} > \left(\frac{r_{Kt}^M}{\theta}\right)^{\theta} \left(\frac{w_t^M}{1-\theta}\right)^{1-\theta} \end{cases} \tag{11.13}$$

$$r_{Kt} = \begin{cases} r_{Kt}^M & \text{if } A_{St} \leq \left(\frac{r_{Kt}^M}{\theta}\right)^{\theta} \left(\frac{w_t^M}{1-\theta}\right)^{1-\theta} \\ \phi A_{Mt} K_{Mt}^{\phi-1} N_{Mt}^{\mu} = \theta A_{St} K_{St}^{\theta-1} N_{St}^{1-\theta} & \text{if } A_{St} > \left(\frac{r_{Kt}^M}{\theta}\right)^{\theta} \left(\frac{w_t^M}{1-\theta}\right)^{1-\theta} \end{cases} \tag{11.14}$$

$$r_{Lt} = (1 - \phi - \mu)A_{Mt} K_{Mt}^{\phi} N_{Mt}^{\mu} \tag{11.15}$$

The first order conditions for choosing k_{t+1} and l_{t+1} in the household's problem can be written

$$c_{1t} = \frac{w_t}{1+\beta} \tag{11.16}$$

$$q_{t+1} = q_t r_{K,t+1} - r_{L,t+1} \tag{11.17}$$

Finally, the budget constraints and market clearing conditions imply that

$$K_{t+1} = N_t(w_t - c_{1t}) - q_t \tag{11.18}$$

Given a value for q_{t_0}, $\{A_{Mt}, A_{St}\}_{t=t_0}^{\infty}$, K_{t_0}, and N_{t_0}, Eqs. (11.3), (11.7) and (11.13) - (11.18) determine the equilibrium sequence of prices and quantities,

$$\{Y_t, w_t, r_{Kt}, r_{Lt}, c_{1t}, q_{t+1}, K_{t+1}, N_{t+1}\}_{t=t_0}^{\infty} .$$

The initial price of land, q_{t_0}, is not given but is also determined by the equilibrium conditions of the model. In particular, q_{t_0} turns out be uniquely determined by the requirement that iterations on Eq. (11.17) do not cause q_t to eventually become negative or K_{t+1} (determined by Eq. (11.18)) to become negative. We use a numerical shooting algorithm to find this value of q_{t_0}.

11.2.1.5 Calibration of population growth function

In the application carried out here, we interpret one model time period to be 25 years. We use the same population growth function, $g(c_{1t})$, as in Hansen and Prescott (2002). This function, which was based on data from Lucas (1988) on population growth rates and per capita income, has the following properties: (1) the population growth rate increases linearly in living standards until population doubles every 35 years or 1.64 periods; (2) at the point where population doubles every 35 years, living standards are twice the Malthusian level; (3) the population growth rate decreases linearly from this point until living standards are 18 times the Malthusian level at which point the growth rate of population is zero; and (4) population is constant as living standards continue to rise. Here, c_{1M} is the Malthusian steady state level of c_{1t} and γ_M is the growth factor of A_{Mt} in a Malthusian steady state. This will be characterized fully in the next subsection.

$$g(c_{1t}) = \begin{cases} \gamma_M^{1/(1-\mu-\phi)}\left(2 - \frac{c_{1t}}{c_{1M}}\right) + 1.64\left(\frac{c_{1t}}{c_{1M}} - 1\right) & \text{for } c_{1t} < 2c_{1M} \\ 1.64 - 0.64\frac{c_{1t}-2c_{1M}}{16c_{1M}} & \text{for } 2c_{1M} \leq c_{1t} \leq 18c_{1M} \\ 1 & \text{for } c_{1t} > 18c_{1M} \end{cases} \tag{11.19}$$

11.2.1.6 The Malthusian steady state

As in Hansen and Prescott (2002), we will assume that this economy begins in a Malthusian steady state, which is the asymptotic growth path for a version of the model with only the Malthus production process available or where A_S is sufficiently low for all t that Eq. (11.10) is never satisfied. Also, prior to period t_0, A_M is assumed to grow at a constant rate equal to $\gamma_M - 1$, $c_{1t} < 2c_{1M}$, and the population growth rate is determined according to the first segment of the function g in Eq. (11.19). In this case, the Malthusian steady state growth rate of population will be $g_N = \gamma_M^{1/(1-\mu-\phi)}$. Both the price of land and the stock of capital will also grow at this same rate on this steady state growth path.

It will be useful for our empirical exercise if we choose a value for steady state income per capita, call it y_M, and compute the rest of the steady state to be consistent with that value. From steady state versions of Eqs. (11.11) and (11.16), we can compute c_{1M} as

$$c_{1M} = \frac{w_M}{1+\beta} = \frac{\mu}{1+\beta} y_M \,. \tag{11.20}$$

Next, the following three equations, which are steady state versions of Eqs. (11.14), (11.17), and (11.18), can be solved to obtain the rental rate of capital, $r_{K,M}$, the steady state capital to labor ratio, $\hat{k}_M$, and the steady state land price to labor ratio, $\hat{q}_M$:

$$r_{K,M} = \phi \frac{\hat{y}}{\hat{k}} \tag{11.21}$$

$$\left(\frac{r_{K,M}}{g_N} - 1 \right) \hat{q} = (1 - \mu - \phi) \hat{y} \tag{11.22}$$

$$g_N \hat{k} = \left(\mu - \frac{\mu}{1+\beta} \right) \hat{y} - \hat{q} \tag{11.23}$$

11.2.2 Quantitative exercise: England from 1245 to 1845

The model presented in the last subsection is now used to interpret time series taken from Clark (2010).[2] Clark uses a variety of sources to construct data that can be used in a quantitative general equilibrium model, including TFP, national income, the capital stock, and payments to capital and labor. This allows us to study the Industrial Revolution in much more quantitative detail than previously possible.

Given that one model time period is interpreted to be 25 years, we use 25 year averages of annual data on total factor productivity, output per capita, and population constructed by Clark using the methodology described in Clark (2010). In particular, data for a given year, say 1845, is actually an average constructed from annual data from 1845 to 1870.[3]

Fig. 11.1 shows Clark's total factor productivity series from 1245 to 1845. The series is extended to 2020 by allowing it to grow from 1845 according to the value we assign to the parameter γ_M. Twenty five year averages of Clark's estimate of England's population from 1245 to 1845 are shown in Fig. 11.2 and his estimate for real per capita income is in Fig. 11.3.

11.2.2.1 Model calibration

The model parameter values we used were $\mu = 0.65$ and $\phi = 0.1$ for the Malthus production process and $\theta = .35$ for the Solow process. These values imply that labor's share of income is the same (0.65)

---

[2] Clark (2010) provides data at ten year intervals on a variety of macroeconomic aggregates. The data we actually use was received from the author and includes annual data that enabled us to compute 25 year averages.

[3] Specifically, total factor productivity is from the third column of Table 33 in Clark (2010), which was constructed using a price index of domestic expenditures. An alternative measure is provided using the price of net domestic output. Similarly, we chose to measure per capita output using real national income that was also constructed using domestic expenditure prices. This series is contained in Table 28 of Clark (2010). The population series we use is from Table 7 of that paper.

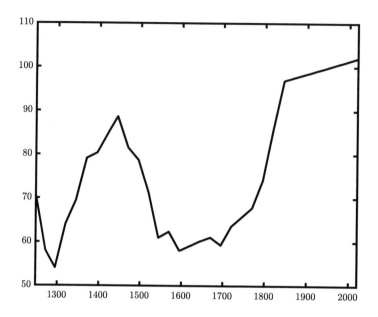

FIGURE 11.1

Malthusian TFP (A_M).

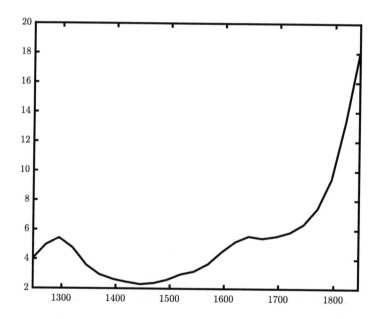

FIGURE 11.2

Population of England, 1245-1845 (millions of people).

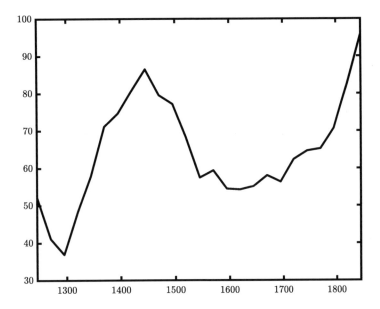

FIGURE 11.3

Real national income per capita of England, 1245-1845 (average from 1860-69 = 100).

for both production processes, following Hansen and Prescott (2002). Land's share in the Malthus process is 0.25. The growth factor for Malthus total factor productivity prior to 1245 and after 1845, when our measured data series ends, is given by $\gamma_M = 1.0074$. This was set to match the average population growth rate from 1245 to 1745 and characterizes our Malthusian steady state. Similarly, the growth factor for Solow total factor productivity beginning in 1895 is $\gamma_S = 1.27$. This implies an asymptotic growth rate of real output per capita equal to 1.5 percent per year. The value of the discount factor, β, was set equal to one following Hansen and Prescott.

The value of y_M used is equal to 55. The movements in per capita income exhibited by our model economy are both the direct result of TFP movements and the Malthusian dynamics associated with the economy converging back to steady state following a given change in TFP. We chose y_M by simply trying different values above and below the mean of per capita income from 1245 to 1745 and taking the one that allowed our model to best fit the time series on per capita income during that period.

The final calibration issue to be resolved, other than initial conditions K_{t_0} and N_{t_0}, is a time series for A_S prior to 1895. Recall that the Solow production process will be employed only when A_S satisfies Eq. (11.10). We construct our A_S time series so that this happens for the first time in the year 1745. Prior to that, the value of A_S is perhaps growing at a slow rate, but is irrelevant to the computation of an equilibrium. We set $A_{S,1745}$ equal to 25, which is the smallest integer value that satisfies Eq. (11.10). Following that, A_S grows 10 percent each period until 1870. This value was chosen so that a demographic transition would not occur until at least this date given that the rate of population in our data sample continues to raise with living standards. That is, we chose this value so that the population growth rate would continue to be determined by the first branch of Eq. (11.19).

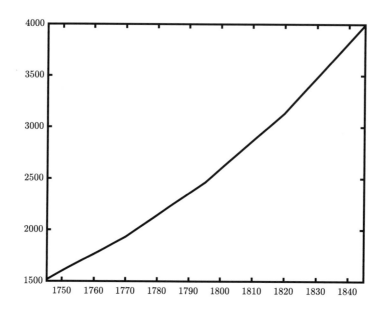

FIGURE 11.4

Solow TFP (A_S).

Fig. 11.4 is a plot of our assumed A_S series from 1745 to 1845.

11.2.2.2 Benchmark simulation

We assume that the economy was in a Malthusian steady state at date $t_0 - 1 = 1220$. Given $y_M = 55$ and $N_{t_0-1} = 5$, we obtain $K_{t_0-1} = \hat{k} N_{t_0-1}$. Also, so that $y_{1220} = y_M$, we set $A_{M,1220} = A_{M,1245}$ and normalize the A_M sequence so that $y_{t_0-1} = Y_M = A_{M,t_0-1} K_{t_0-1}^{\phi} N_{t_0-1}^{\mu-1}$. In this case, our initial conditions for 1245 are $N_{t_0} = g_N N_{t_0-1}$ and $K_{t_0} = \hat{k} N_{t_0}$.

We also add an additional element in our benchmark simulation that is not part of the model described so far. In particular, England suffered from a series of plagues that decimated its population for three centuries from 1345 (the Black Death) to 1645 (the Great Plague of London). In particular, there is a downward sloping portion in Fig. 11.2 that shows that population was declining from 1320 to 1470.[4] We capture this by replacing Eq. (11.7) with

$$N_{t+1} = P_t g(c_{1t}) N_t , \tag{11.24}$$

where P_t, which we interpret as a "plague shock", is equal to one for all t except for $t = 1295 - 1445$. For these dates, we set $P_t = 0.8$.

Fig. 11.5 shows that our benchmark simulation successfully captures the decline in population from 1295 to 1445. After that, England's actual population increased more rapidly than in the model

---

[4] We will discuss how the model would respond to the plagues beyond 1470 in subsequent experiment.

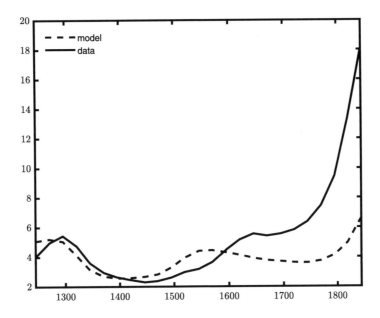

FIGURE 11.5

Population from Benchmark experiment.

economy. This is particularly true after 1750. Fig. 11.6 shows that the model economy captures the fluctuations in per capita income quite well.

The transition from employing all inputs in the Malthus production process to having almost all of the capital and labor assigned to the Solow process is shown in Fig. 11.7. In particular, in the first period of the industrial revolution, 1745, 31 percent of capital and 12 percent of labor is employed in the Solow process. The fraction of inputs employed in Solow production increases over time and exceeds 95 percent in 1895 for labor and in 1870 for capital. At this point, the economy has come close to converging to a standard neoclassical steady state growth path where real output per capita is growing by 1.5 percent per year.

11.2.2.3 No plagues

As a counterfactual experiment, we recompute the benchmark under the assumption that $P_t = 1$ for all t. In this case, as shown in Fig. 11.8, model population is as much as three times larger than in the actual data during the period of plagues from 1345 to 1645. Similarly, Fig. 11.9 shows that per capita income in our model is significantly lower than in the actual data during this period due to population in the model economy being so high.

11.2.2.4 More plagues

As mentioned previously, England suffered plagues pretty continuously from 1245 to 1645. In this experiment, we set $P_t = 0.8$ for $t = 1295 - 1620$. As shown in Fig. 11.10, this leads to model population being as much as a third of what is observed in the actual data from 1550 to 1750. This result is simply

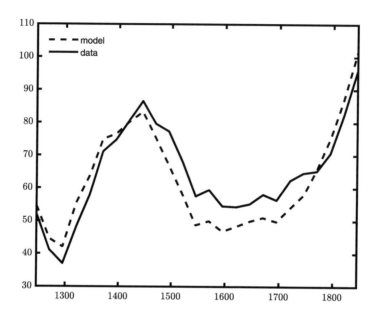

FIGURE 11.6

Output per capita from Benchmark experiment.

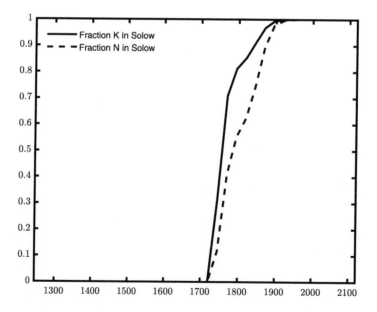

FIGURE 11.7

Fraction of inputs employed in Solow.

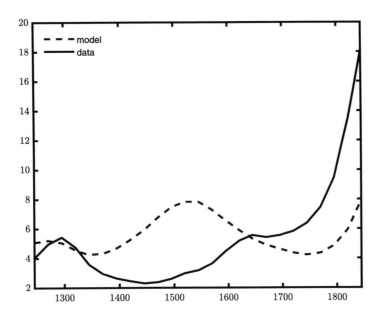

FIGURE 11.8

Population from "No Plagues" experiment.

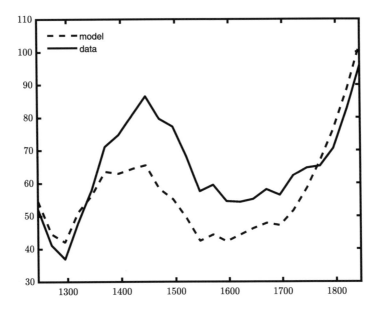

FIGURE 11.9

Output per capita from "No Plagues" experiment.

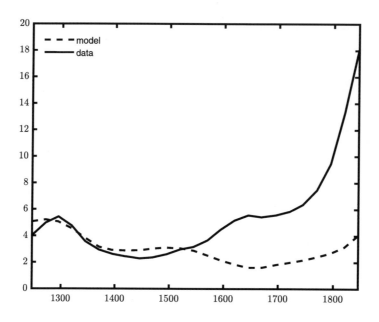

FIGURE 11.10

Population from "More Plagues" experiment.

a more extreme version of what is observed with population in the benchmark simulation. Model and data series for per capita income look fairly similar in this experiment as shown in Fig. 11.11. Clearly there is something happening with population during the period 1550-1750 that is not captured solely by plagues and Malthusian dynamics.

11.2.2.5 Timing of the industrial revolution

In the experiments done so far, we constructed the A_S sequence so that the Solow production process is initially adopted in 1745. Note that in Fig. 11.12, A_M (the solid line) reaches a peak in 1445 and then drops significantly. In this counterfactual experiment, we assume this drop never occurred and that A_M simply grew at rate $\gamma_M - 1$ after 1445 (see dotted line in Fig. 11.12). Will this relative success of the Malthusian production process, given the same sequence for A_S as in the benchmark, cause the Industrial Revolution to happen at a later date? Turns out that the adoption of the Solow process begins at exactly the same date as in the benchmark (1745). Fig. 11.13 shows the right hand side of Eq. (11.10) for both the benchmark and this counterfactual case from 1245 to 1745. We see that while this threshold is very high when A_M reached its peak in 1450 in both cases, the threshold falls very quickly in the benchmark due to declines in A_M. In the counterfactual, however, Malthusian dynamics dominate. As A_M continues to grow, population also grows (see Fig. 11.14). This causes income per capita to decline as it converges to the Malthusian steady state of $y_M = 55$ (see Fig. 11.15). These same dynamics cause the Solow threshold to decline and, as it turns out, it is still profitable to adopt the Solow process in 1745 when A_S is equal to 25.

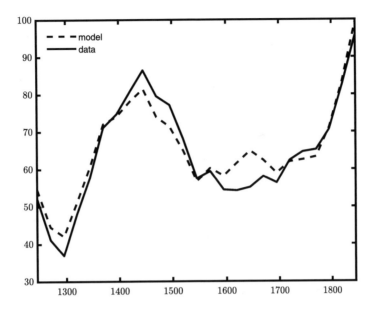

FIGURE 11.11

Output per capita from "More Plagues" experiment.

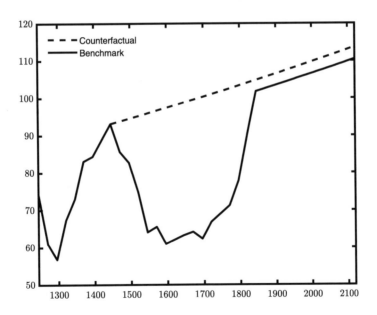

FIGURE 11.12

A_M for "Timing of Industrial Revolution" and Benchmark experiments.

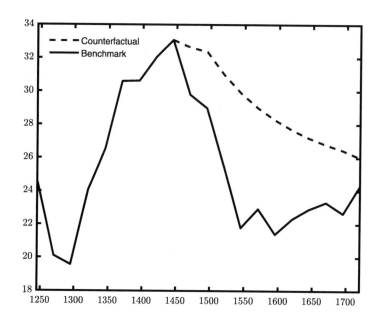

FIGURE 11.13

Solow threshold from "Timing of Industrial Revolution" and Benchmark experiments.

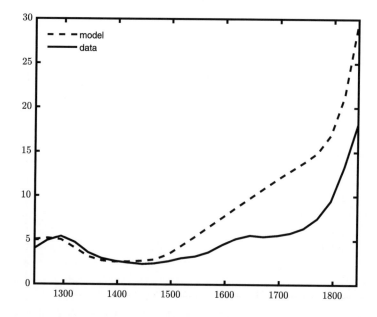

FIGURE 11.14

Population from "Timing of Industrial Revolution" experiment.

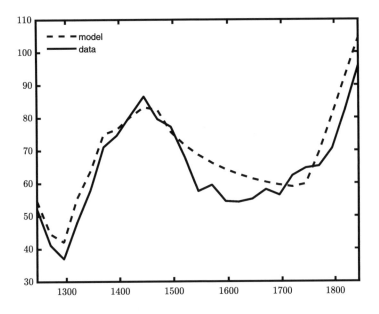

FIGURE 11.15

Output per capita from "Timing of Industrial Revolution" experiment.

The key here is that in the Malthusian steady state, the right hand side of Eq. (11.10) is a constant. This threshold might deviate from this steady state due to short run fluctuations in A_M, but over time will converge back to this constant. Hence, while we chose the A_S sequence in the benchmark so that the Solow production process would be adopted in 1745, this result turns out to be robust in the absence of significant upward movements in the A_M process in the period near 1745.

11.3 Business cycle accounting of the 1889-1929 U.S. economy

To apply Business Cycle Accounting (BCA) for this period, we use data constructed by John Kendrick (1961). Kendrick constructed data from 1869-1957 for the U.S. economy using NIPA principles. These data include real measures of consumption, private and government fixed investment, inventories, government consumption, and exports and imports. The data also have consistent measures of labor and capital input that are aggregated from sectoral measures of these variables. These data are considered to be high quality and the best available for this time period. The data are decennial from 1869-1889, and are annual from 1889 onwards, which leads us to begin in 1889.

The period from 1889-1929 is striking from a macroeconomic perspective because of a number of short-run events and also because of it its importance in the long-run evolution of the American economy. This period includes the "Roaring Twenties", well-known for its high economic growth rate and as the runup to the Great Depression. It also includes World War I, in which government consumption rose enormously, taking away resources from the private sector. There were also two very famous financial panics, the Panic of 1893 and the Panic of 1907.

More broadly, 1889-1929 is a period of enormous technological change, including the diffusion of electrification and the expansion of the internal combustion engine, which transformed production methods (electrification) and transportation (internal combustion engine). 1889-1929 also includes the heyday of American monopolies, including the famous Standard Oil trust and John D. Rockefeller, and Andrew Carnegie's U.S. Steel trust, both of which motivated the passage of the country's major antitrust acts, the Sherman Act in 1890 and the Clayton Act in 1914.

To our knowledge, neither this period in its totality, nor any of the individuals events within the period, have been analyzed using quantitative general equilibrium tools. This chapter thus provides the first such evaluation of this remarkable period. BCA, first used in Cole and Ohanian (2002), and Chari et al. (2002), and then developed further in Chari et al. (2007), and Brinca et al. (2016), henceforth BCKM, is ideally suited for investigating this period, because it is the leading diagnostic general equilibrium framework for identifying a set of possible factors affecting macroeconomic performance and for measuring the quantitative importance of these factors for output, consumption, investment, and hours worked. Moreover, we show that BCA is not only useful for analyzing fluctuations at the business cycle frequency (e.g. four years), but also is useful for studying lower frequency phenomena that evolve over a decade or more.

1889-1929 represents a period of unique long-run economic evolutions that are overlayered with several large short-run fluctuations that are of interest in their own right. As we show below, BCA highlights a number of key factors that are striking and surprising relative to the literature, and surprising relative to findings from postwar business cycles and the Great Recession. They also will suggest specific theoretical classes of models for understanding this important episode.

We summarize BCA and its application protocol here, and refer the reader to BCKM for details. BCA begins with a standard optimal growth model. Each period t, a random event s_t is realized. Let $s^t = (s_0, \ldots, s_t)$ denote the history of events up through and including period t and $\pi_t(s^t)$ be the probability of history s^t being realized at period t. Preferences are defined over expected sequences of consumption and leisure. There is a standard Cobb-Douglas constant returns to scale production function with labor-augmenting technological change. Output is divided between consumption, investment, and government consumption. There is a standard law of motion for capital, and the household time endowment is normalized to unity:

$$\max E_0 \sum_{t=0}^{\infty} \sum_{s^t} \beta^t \pi_t(s^t) U(C_t(s^t)/N_t, 1 - l_t(s^t))$$

subject to:

$$F(K_t(s^{t-1}), (1+\gamma)^t N_t l_t(s^t)) \geq C_t(s^t) + X_t(s^t) + G_t(s^t)$$

and the capital accumulation law:

$$K_{t+1}(s^t) = X_t(s^t) + (1-\delta)K_t(s^{t-1})$$

All variables except for time allocated to market production are then divided by technological progress $(1+\gamma)^t$ and population $N_t = (1+\gamma_n)^t$ to induce stationarity, and the transformed variables are denoted by lower case letters. The optimality conditions for this problem (assuming that transversality is satisfied) are given by[5]:

$$U_{lt}(s^t) = U_{ct}(s^t) f_{lt}$$

$$U_{ct}(s^t)(1+\gamma) = \beta^* \sum_{s^{t+1}} \pi_t(s^{t+1}|s^t) U_{ct+1}(s^{t+1})\{f_{kt+1} + 1 - \delta\}$$

$$f(k_t(s^{t-1}), l_t(s^t)) \geq c_t(s^t) + k_{t+1}(s^t)(1+\gamma)(1+\gamma_n)$$
$$- (1-\delta)k_t(s^{t-1}) + g_t(s^t)$$

To use this model for diagnostic purposes, we first augment these optimality conditions with multiplicative terms known as "wedges", that are functions of state s^t. The wedges will allow this model to completely account for the data. As you will see below, several of the wedges appear to be tax rates, though we do not give the wedges structural interpretations at this stage of analysis. The augmented first order conditions are below:

$$U_{lt}(s^t) = U_{ct}(s^t)[1 - \tau_{lt}(s^t)]A_t(s^t) f_{lt}$$

$$A_t(s^t) f(k_t(s^{t-1}), l_t(s^t)) \geq c_t(s^t) + k_{t+1}(s^t)(1+\gamma)(1+\gamma_n) - (1-\delta)k_t(s^{t-1}) + g_t(s^t)$$

$$U_{ct}(s^t)(1+\gamma)[1 + \tau_{xt}(s^t)]$$
$$= \beta^* \sum_{s^{t+1}} \pi_t(s^{t+1}|s^t) U_{ct+1}(s^{t+1})\{A_{t+1}(s^{t+1}) f_{kt+1} + (1-\delta)[1 + \tau_{xt+1}(s^{t+1})]\}$$

We begin with the wedge $A_t(s^t)$, which multiplies the production function. This wedge is observationally equivalent to the Solow Residual, and thus accounts for movements in output not due to movements in capital and labor. This is called an *efficiency wedge*. Next, consider the first order condition for allocating time between market work and leisure. The wedge here is denoted as $1 - \tau_{lt}(s^t)$, and is written in this way because it is observationally equivalent to a tax on labor income. This is called the *labor wedge*, and as noted above, is not given a structural interpretation at this stage. The economy's intertemporal condition is augmented with a wedge denoted as $1/[1 + \tau_{xt}(s^t)]$, and is written in this way because it is similar to a tax on investment. It is called the *investment wedge*. The last wedge is called the *government consumption wedge*, which accounts for the sum of government consumption and net exports. With a Markovian implementation there is one to one and onto mapping from the event s_t to the wedges $(A_t, \tau_{lt}, \tau_{xt}, g_t)$.

The stochastic process for the event $s_t = (A_t(s^t), \tau_{lt}(s^t), \tau_{xt}(s^t), g_t(s^t))$ is governed by a first-order VAR:

$$s_{t+1} = P_0 + P s_t + \varepsilon_{t+1}, \quad E(\varepsilon\varepsilon') = V$$

in which P_0 and P are matrices of autoregressive coefficients to be estimated, ε is a vector of innovations, and V is the variance-covariance matrix of the innovations. As BCKM show, it is straightforward to estimate the coefficients and the elements of the variance-covariance matrix using maximum likelihood after log-linearizing the model, setting it up in state space form, and using the Kalman Filter.

---

[5] We will be using log utility, therefore β^* denotes $\beta(1+\gamma_n)$.

With these wedges, which equal the number of endogenous variables, the augmented model fits the data perfectly, and therefore the model is used as an *accounting device*. To do this, we first measure the wedges as realizations from their stochastic process, and we then use the wedges within the linearized model to conduct various experiments, including quantifying the contribution of one or more wedges in accounting for the endogenous variables. We then use the results from these experiments to evaluate different classes of structural models. Below, we report some very surprising findings from this analysis in comparison from findings from postwar analyses, and from the perspective of narrative historical studies about this period.

11.3.1 Business cycle accounting findings

Real GNP and its components, and labor input, measured as hours worked, are from Kendrick (1961). Following standard practice, all variables are first divided by the population, 16 years old and over.[6] As is standard practice, we divide all growing variables by a common trend, in which we use 1.6 percent annually. We divide government spending into government consumption and government investment, in which the latter is put in the investment category, and following BCKM and Hansen and Ohanian (2016), we add net exports to government consumption.

Fig. 11.16 shows these data. There are several noteworthy features. One is the very large increase in government consumption during World War I, which suggests potentially large effects of the war on the economy. Ohanian (1997) and McGrattan and Ohanian (2010) quantitatively analyze how well a neoclassical model can account for the World War II economy, and how much government fiscal policy affected output, labor input, investment and consumption. Applying BCA to this period will provide an assessment of the neoclassical model for the World War I economy which will be a natural complement to the existing World War II studies.

Another notable feature is the behavior of the economy around the two major financial panics, the Panic of 1893 and the Panic of 1907. Both episodes feature above-normal economic growth for some years prior to the panic, followed by a drop in real GDP and hours worked, then followed by a rapid rebound in economic activity.

But perhaps the most striking feature of these data is the pattern of hours worked. These average around 1/3 of the households time endowment from the mid-1890s up to the mid-teens, but then hours drop around the end of World War I and remain at that low level through the booming 1920s. This raises an important question: Why do hours worked remain so low during an economic boom with sharply rising investment and productivity? Standard theory indicates that hours should be higher than average during the 1920s, not lower than average.

To quantitatively evaluate these three issues, we log-linearize the model, set it up in state space form, and estimate the parameters of the wedge stochastic process using maximum likelihood via the Kalman Filter. To model the stochastic process for the wedges, we use a VAR. We use one lag for the VAR because the data are annual.

Fig. 11.17 reports the four wedges between 1889-1929. Panel A shows the efficiency wedge over time. This shows large and stationary movements until World War I, then it rises substantially through the 1920s, likely reflecting the rapid diffusion of electricity and the internal combustion engine. Given

---

[6] The data are available from 1900 to 1929. Linear interpolation is used to construct the data from 1889 to 1899 using the data on the population 15 years old and over. Details are available upon request.

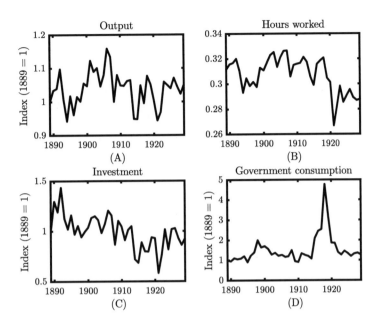

FIGURE 11.16

Detrended macro aggregates.

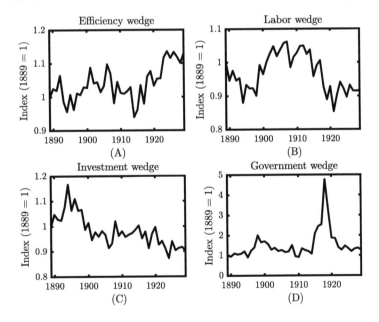

FIGURE 11.17

Estimated wedges.

the large literature on 1920s productivity growth and innovation diffusions, we refer to the efficiency wedge during this period as productivity growth.

The investment wedge shows a large trend decline, which is observationally equivalent to a continuously declining tax on investment goods. It also features temporary increases around the times of the Panics of 1893 and 1907. The World War I spending increases dwarfs all other movements in the government wedge, as government spending rises by about a factor of four during the war. The labor wedge declines in the early teens, which is equivalent to a higher labor income tax. This higher labor wedge continues through World War I and the 1920s.

11.3.1.1 Contribution of the wedges

Fig. 11.18 shows the contribution of the efficiency wedge to output, hours worked, and investment. This is the model prediction for these variables over time with only the efficiency wedge included, and the other wedges set to their steady state values. We have split the graph between the period 1889-1916 and 1917-1929. We do this because the findings are so remarkably different between these two periods, and these large differences are economically very interesting.

Note that between 1889 and 1916, the efficiency wedge accounts very closely for output fluctuations which is just before the U.S. entered World War I in 1917. The figure shows this very close relationship between data and the model, in which the detrended model economy is driven just by stationary productivity shocks. Table 11.1 provides complementary information on goodness of fit by presenting what is analogous to an R^2 statistic for this procedure. Known as the "ϕ-statistic" within the literature, this R^2-type measure is given by:

$$\phi_i^Y = \frac{1/\sum_t (y_t - y_{it})^2}{\sum_j (1/\sum_t (y_t - y_{jt})^2)},$$

where ϕ_i^Y is the percentage of variable y accounted for by wedge $i = (A, \tau_l, \tau_x, g)$. In the numerator, y is the individual variable, i is the wedge individually driving the system, and y_{it} is the model prediction of variable y at date t using wedge i. In the denominator, the summation over j indicates that all wedges are included, which delivers a perfect fit of the model net of approximation error. The statistic lies between 0 and 1, in which a perfect fit is 1.

The efficiency wedge accounts for 83 percent of the squared model deviations from trend (see Table 11.1). This is high when compared to similar calculations made for different episodes and across countries. BCKM calculate this statistic for the Great Recession across 25 countries, including the U.S., and find an average of 64 percent. For the U.S, it was just 16 percent during the Great Recession.

After that, however, there is a significant disconnect between efficiency variations and output variations, as the efficiency wedge accounts for much less of output. Throughout the 1920s, the efficiency wedge is rising (see Fig. 11.18), and by 1929, these large increases in the efficiency wedge alone drive output about 19 percent above its trend growth path within the model. This stands in sharp contrast to actual output, which is about 4 percent above its trend growth path in 1929.

These findings are striking when viewed within the context of the literature on twentieth century economic growth and the context of BCA. There is a broad consensus that the 1920s was one of the most striking decades of U.S. economic growth in its history, and that this growth was fostered by an unusual wave of technological advances, including the diffusion of electrification, which transformed production methods, and the internal combustion engine, which revolutionized transportation.

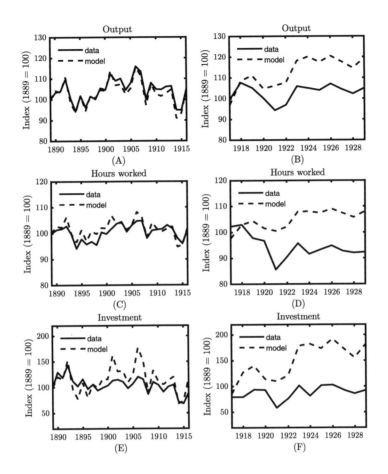

FIGURE 11.18

Efficiency wedge only economy.

The BCA efficiency wedge only economy result presented here indicates that the famous 1920s economic boom is much weaker than it should have been relative to the technological improvements that took place.

As a related point, we are unaware of any other period, in the U.S. or in other countries, in which the efficiency wedge accounts for so much of output (83 percent), and is then followed by an immediate and large change in this accuracy, in which the efficiency wedge accounts for so little of output. Note that the efficiency wedge accounts for only about 10 percent of output following 1916.

The post-1916 figure and the associated ϕ-statistic indicate that some other factor changed substantially around this time, and it persistently depressed the economy relative to what it could have achieved with the measured, positive efficiency wedge realizations. The figure also shows the accounting of labor and investment using just the efficiency wedge, and these patterns reveal more about the pre and post-1916 economy.

Table 11.1 ϕ-statistics for output, labor, and investment.

Samples	Output				Labor				Investment			
	ϕ_A^Y	$\phi_{\tau_l}^Y$	$\phi_{\tau_x}^Y$	$\phi_{\tau_g}^Y$	ϕ_A^L	$\phi_{\tau_l}^L$	$\phi_{\tau_x}^L$	$\phi_{\tau_g}^L$	ϕ_A^X	$\phi_{\tau_l}^X$	$\phi_{\tau_x}^X$	$\phi_{\tau_g}^X$
1889-1916	0.83	0.07	0.04	0.06	0.46	0.22	0.05	0.27	0.26	0.27	0.10	0.37
1917-1929	0.09	0.19	0.18	0.54	0.02	0.75	0.16	0.07	0.02	0.29	0.13	0.56
1889-1929	0.29	0.25	0.16	0.30	0.09	0.56	0.12	0.23	0.07	0.32	0.12	0.49

Note that the efficiency wedge's accuracy in accounting for hours is also very different between these two sub-periods. Table 11.1 shows that the efficiency wedge accounts for about 46 percent of hours worked between 1889 and 1916, which is very high relative to similar calculations in the real business cycle literature. In particular, much of the criticism of real business cycle models is that productivity shocks account for very little of hours worked in post-1983 data (Kehoe et al. (2018)).

The fraction of hours worked that the model accounts for declines from 46 percent to about two percent, in which the large positive efficiency wedge changes of the 1920s generate much higher labor than what actually occurs. This predicted large rise in labor reflects increases in both labor demand and in labor supply, both of which are driven by higher efficiency which raises worker productivity.

The pattern for investment (bottom Fig. 11.18 panels) is qualitatively similar to that of hours, in that the model with just the efficiency wedge generates much higher investment than observed. Quantitatively, the deviation between model and data is much larger. By 1929, the model driven just by the efficiency wedge predicts investment that is about 70 percent above trend, compared to the actual value which is modestly above trend.

Fig. 11.19 provides complementary information about the impact of the efficiency wedge by plotting the model predictions including all wedges *except* the efficiency wedge. Note that the prediction of the model with all other wedges is far from the data for output, and surprisingly, also for labor through the 1916 period. This latter finding is particularly noteworthy given that the labor wedge is included in making this prediction.

The post-1916 deviations present a consistent pathology about the 1920s. Rapidly growing efficiency should have led to higher labor input, which in turn should have led to much higher investment, given the complementarity between capital and labor in production. The fact that the post-1916 prediction errors are so large and of a consistent pattern suggests that a quantitatively important factor emerged around this time to simultaneously depress labor, investment, and output, and that was sufficiently large to negatively offset much of the expansionary effect of higher efficiency.

Simulating the model in response to just the labor wedge provides important information about this factor. Fig. 11.20 shows that the labor wedge captures nearly all of the movement in labor after 1916. Recall that Fig. 11.17 Panel B showed that the labor wedge, which is observationally equivalent to a labor income tax, becomes larger (more negative) around the time of World War I through the 1920s. Driven by just the labor wedge alone, the model predicts that the 1920s would have been one of the *worst* growth decades for the U.S. economy, with output remaining about six percent below trend through the decade, and with labor averaging about seven percent below trend through the decade.

This indicates the key reason why output was low was because labor was low, and while the labor wedge alone doesn't account for the fluctuations in investment, it does accurately predict that investment was depressed below its normal level during the 1920s. Since the labor wedge creates a wedge between the marginal rate of substitution between consumption and leisure, and high productivity, this

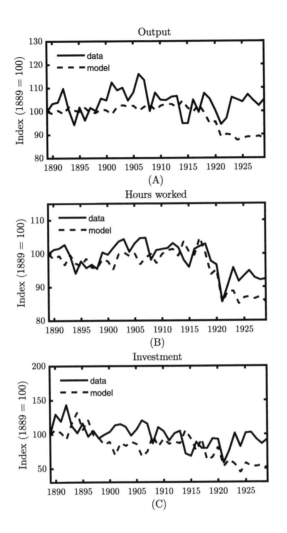

FIGURE 11.19

All wedges except efficiency wedge economy.

suggests that the economic factor(s) behind the rising importance of the labor wedge during this period depressed either the incentives and/or the opportunities for individuals and firms to trade labor services.

Figs. 11.21–11.22 show the model's ability to account for output, labor, and investment from the investment wedge individually, and the government wedge individually. The figures suggest that neither of these wedges are broadly important for understanding output, labor, or investment over the full period. The ϕ-statistics indicate that government accounts for more than 50 percent of output and investment after 1916, but that largely reflects the very large increase in government spending in 1917-19. Ohanian (1997) and McGrattan and Ohanian (2010) show that neoclassical models driven by large

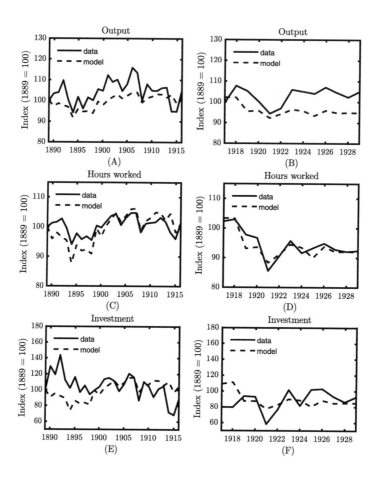

FIGURE 11.20

Labor wedge only economy.

fiscal shocks closely account for the World War II economy. The World War I fiscal shock generates higher hours worked, higher output, and lower investment, all of which are qualitatively similar to the actual World War I economy. The model is not as quantitatively accurate for World War I as World War II, which likely reflects the fact that the World War I shock is not nearly as large as the World War II shock.

11.3.2 Business cycle accounting and the Panics of 1893 and 1907

The years 1889-1912 occurred under the National Banking Era, a monetary and financial system created by the National Banking Act of 1863. As a precursor to the Federal Reserve system, the National Banking Era featured nationally chartered banks that were under the oversight of the Comptroller of

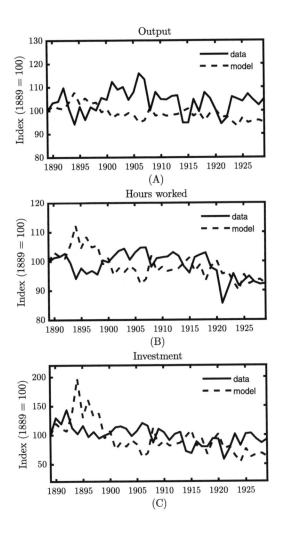

FIGURE 11.21

Investment wedge only economy.

the currency. The goal was to create a de facto national currency in which national chartered banks would accept each other's currency. The system had flaws, however, and panics occurred frequently.

The Panics of 1893 and 1907 were two of the most severe panics in the history of the U.S. Previous research by Jalil (2015) as well as earlier studies of these panics, dates them consistently, with the Panic of 1893 occurring around the middle of the year, and the Panic of 1907 beginning around October of 1907. This section uses BCA to study these episodes and compares them to the most recent findings within the historical literature. BCA findings show that these two episodes differ regarding the

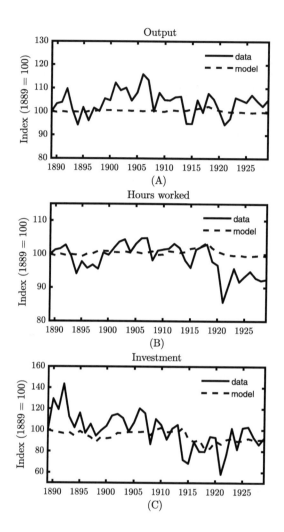

FIGURE 11.22

Government wedge only economy.

importance of wedges, particularly regarding the labor market, and we find very different contributions of the panics on economic activity relative to the literature.

11.3.2.1 The Panic of 1893

The Panic of 1893 features large declines in output, hours worked, and investment, which began declining before the panic. Other authors have noted in higher frequency data that the economic decline began before the run on banks, and this makes it in principle difficult to evaluate how much of the panic

Table 11.2 ϕ-statistics for the Panic of 1893.

Samples	Output			Labor			Investment		
	ϕ_A^Y	$\phi_{\tau_l}^Y$	$\phi_{\tau_x}^Y$	ϕ_A^L	$\phi_{\tau_l}^L$	$\phi_{\tau_x}^L$	ϕ_A^X	$\phi_{\tau_l}^X$	$\phi_{\tau_x}^X$
1889-1890	0.65	0.01	0.30	0.42	0.03	0.25	0.47	0.03	0.46
1889-1891	0.86	0.01	0.09	0.47	0.03	0.31	0.57	0.03	0.36
1889-1892	0.95	0.01	0.02	0.22	0.04	0.52	0.83	0.03	0.10
1889-1893	0.88	0.02	0.05	0.41	0.06	0.14	0.72	0.05	0.14
1889-1894	0.92	0.02	0.02	0.61	0.10	0.03	0.65	0.11	0.06
1889-1895	0.92	0.02	0.02	0.51	0.11	0.04	0.66	0.10	0.06

was a symptom of economic weakness compared to its potential depressing effect on the economy by disrupting the financial system.

A recent assessment of the National Banking era panics by Jalil finds very large and persistent effects. He fits a VAR to Davis's (2004) constructed industrial production series, along with indicator variables that are based on how the financial press of that time viewed the panic. By reading the financial newspapers at that time, he grades a panic on a 1-3 scale as to the extent that the panic was an independent event, or whether it was more a symptom of the downturn. He constructs another indicator variable regarding the state of the economy at the time of the panic, also on a 1-3 scale, depending on its underlying strength. He finds that a panic has very large and persistent effects on industrial production during this period, with a one-unit change in the financial indicator variable leading to a 10 percent change in industrial production, and that the impact of the shock persists roughly unchanged for at least 3 years.

BCA provides a different, and complementary analysis to Jalil's VAR study. We find the efficiency wedge plays a very important role in the 1893 panic. The left panel of Fig. 11.23 shows the predicted movements from the efficiency wedge alone from 1889 to 1905. The figure shows a close correspondence between predicted and actual changes, particularly for output, which fits nearly perfectly.

The efficiency wedge also captures the qualitative features of labor and investment movements. For labor, it predicts a somewhat smaller increase before the panic, but predicts an overall decline in labor over the downturn in percentage terms that is very close to the actual decline. Table 11.2 shows the ϕ-statistics for the efficiency wedge, which accounts for 92%, 51%, and 66% of the movements, respectively. This episode looks like it was generated largely by a classic real business cycle model, as the efficiency wedge substantially accounts for changes in output, labor, and investment.

This real business cycle interpretation of the Panic of 1893 is consistent with some earlier research. Sprague (1910) presents evidence of declining economic activity prior to the panic, including slowing investment in railroad expansion and building construction, and in silver production (see Fig. 11.24). Davis (2004) shows that a broader-based index of industrial production declined in 1893 (see Fig. 11.25). Moreover, the real investment to output ratio did not drop in 1893, which stands in contrast to what should have occurred if an impaired financial system was substantially impacting the economy. These data support the view that the Panic of 1893 was more of a symptom of the downturn, rather than a primary contributing factor, and that the downturn partially reflects a natural slowing of business following a boom.

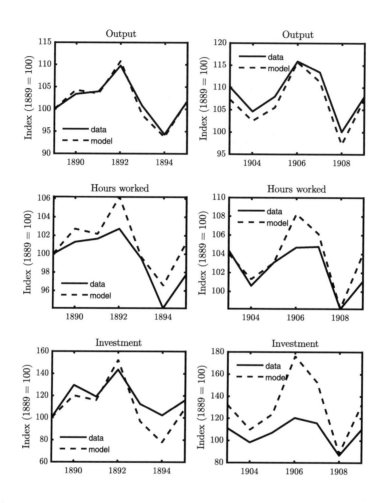

FIGURE 11.23

Efficiency wedge only economy in the Panics of 1893 and 1907.

11.3.2.2 The Panic of 1907

The Panic of 1907 is similar in that the efficiency wedge accounts largely for output, but differs in that it doesn't account as closely for labor or investment. The right panel of Fig. 11.23 shows the predicted movements from the efficiency wedge alone from 1903 to 1909. Table 11.3 shows the ϕ-statistics for the Panic of 1907. It shows that the labor wedge plays a central role in the Panic of 1907 (see also Fig. 11.26). The labor wedge accounts for 73% and 82% of the movements in labor and investment, respectively, while the efficiency wedge accounts for 73% of the movements in output.

A hint about the factors that generated the rising labor wedge during the Panic of 1907 may lie in the labor market and a failure for wages to adjust to slowing economic conditions at this time. Fig. 11.27 shows an index of composite wages from 1889 to 1909. The figure shows that wages decline considerably around the 1893 downturn, but decline much less around the time of the 1907 downturn.

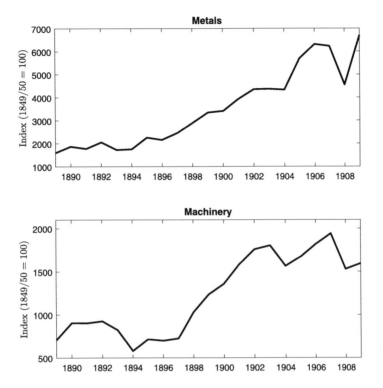

FIGURE 11.24

Industrial production of metals and machinery for United States, 1889-1909.

Table 11.3 ϕ-statistics for the Panic of 1907.

	Output			Labor			Investment		
Samples	ϕ_A^Y	$\phi_{\tau_l}^Y$	$\phi_{\tau_x}^Y$	ϕ_A^L	$\phi_{\tau_l}^L$	$\phi_{\tau_x}^L$	ϕ_A^X	$\phi_{\tau_l}^X$	$\phi_{\tau_x}^X$
1903-1904	0.73	0.14	0.05	0.65	0.31	0.01	0.05	0.78	0.03
1903-1905	0.73	0.14	0.05	0.71	0.27	0.01	0.04	0.83	0.02
1903-1906	0.87	0.06	0.02	0.18	0.75	0.01	0.02	0.90	0.01
1903-1907	0.88	0.06	0.02	0.24	0.69	0.01	0.01	0.92	0.01
1903-1908	0.85	0.08	0.02	0.25	0.69	0.01	0.03	0.83	0.02
1903-1909	0.86	0.07	0.02	0.18	0.73	0.01	0.03	0.82	0.02

This suggests that labor market imperfections around that time that slowed nominal wage adjustment may have significantly depressed employment during 1907.

The fact that we find a significant labor wedge in the Panic of 1907 is intriguing because this makes it similar to the Great Recession, in which a large labor wedge is also quantitatively important (see Ohanian (2010) and Brinca et al. (2016)). This comparison also emerges among economic historians comparing the two periods, including Bernanke (2013) and Tallman (2013). They argue that the Panic

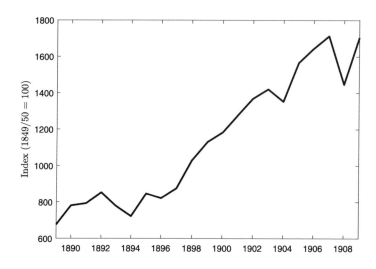

FIGURE 11.25

Index of industrial production for United States, 1889-1909.

of 1907 is similar to the Great Recession from the perspective of lightly regulated financial intermediaries. For example, one can think of trust companies in 1907, which were relatively less regulated, and not part of the New York Clearinghouse, like shadow banks during the Great Recession, which were also less regulated and did not have immediate access to the Federal Reserve System.

11.3.3 Potential interpretations of the 1920s BCA findings

The BCA results after 1916 indicate very large changes in either the shocks hitting the economy relative to the pre-1916 period, and/or how these shocks affected the economy. The findings stand in sharp contrast to the literature, which focuses on relatively rapid 1920s economic growth that was driven by the increased diffusion of new technologies, specifically electricity and the internal combustion engine. The BCA findings show that technology did rise rapidly during this period, but that its large and positive contribution was substantially attenuated by some factor(s) creating a labor wedge that is observationally equivalent to a rising labor income tax distortion. This section considers some possibilities that may have created the large increase in the labor wedge.

The post-1916 findings regarding rapidly rising productivity in conjunction with a sizable labor market imperfection are similar to findings from studies that have analyzed why the recovery from the Great Depression was not stronger. Cole and Ohanian (1999) showed that the efficiency wedge rose rapidly after 1933, which should have promoted strong growth and returned hours worked back to normal after a few years. However, similar to 1917-1929, hours worked remained depressed as productivity increased. Cole and Ohanian analyzed a number of possible factors that could have depressed hours worked, including labor and capital income taxes, and financial market stability and monetary policy. They concluded that neither monetary policy, which eliminated deflation, nor financial markets,

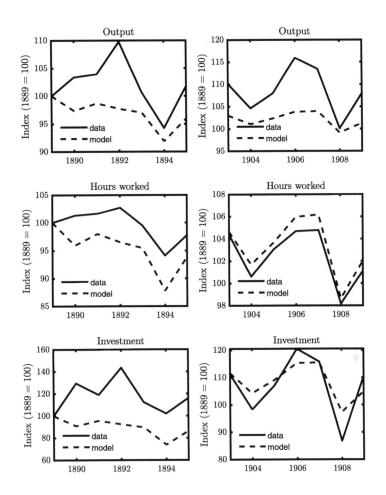

FIGURE 11.26

Labor wedge only economy in the Panics of 1893 and 1907.

which were stabilized by new legislation, were at fault. They found that modestly higher labor and capital income taxes were minor factors. This led them (Cole and Ohanian (2004)) in subsequent research to study how much industry-labor cartel policies depressed hours worked, and found that it accounted for most of continuation of low hours worked. Chari et al. (2007) found that a very large labor wedge was responsible for the continuation of depressed hours, and also cited industry-labor cartels.

We now apply a similar approach as used in Cole and Ohanian (1999) to evaluate potential factors that could have kept labor depressed after 1917. Regarding tax rates, statutory tax rates declined substantially after World War I, which would motivate higher hours worked, ceteris paribus. Average tax rates were low, and did not change much over the period. Barro and Sahasakul (1983) construct average tax rates and find an average tax rate of about 0.5 percent in 1916, which rises to about two percent

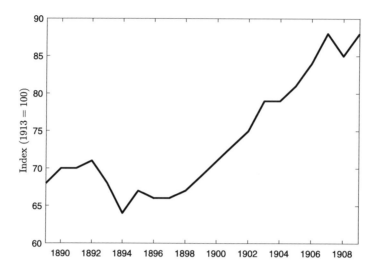

FIGURE 11.27

Index of composite wages for United States, 1889-1909.

during the war, and then declines to about one to 1.5 percent during the 1920s. These data indicate that changes in taxes were quantitatively unimportant in accounting for the 1920s labor wedge.

Immigration slowed in the 1920s, as the population rose about 15 percent in the decade compared to about 21 percent in the two decades before that. This is frequently discussed in the literature on the 1920s as an important factor (Smiley (1994)). However, a relative decline in the labor force should motivate *higher* hours per worker, because hours per worker are a substitute for workers. A relative decline in labor should also lead to higher wages, ceteris paribus. Smiley notes that manufacturing wages for men rose 5.3 percent for semi-skilled males to 8.7 percent for unskilled males, but manufacturing output per hour worked rose 29 percent this same period. These data indicate that reduced immigration is not a promising candidate in accounting for the labor wedge.

The data on real manufacturing wages, and real manufacturing output per hour, suggest another issue within the labor market, and one that may be related to the 1920s labor wedge. The standard model of labor supply and demand predicts that the real wage will move closely with worker productivity. This is not the case in the 1920s, with manufacturing output per hour rising 29 percent, but real wages rising only between 5.3 and 8.7 percent. Why didn't competitive pressure increase wages? Why didn't comparatively low wages stimulate more hiring?

These observations about the 1920s labor market reveal dysfunction that is more difficult to identify than that of the Great Depression. During the 1930s, wages were far above trend, while labor was far below trend. This naturally suggested excess supply, in which labor market policies prevented the wage from falling and clearing the labor market. In this case, both the relative price of labor and the quantity of labor hired are below trend, despite the fact that productivity was high. Given these findings, future research should consider addressing these important questions about the 1920s.

11.4 Conclusion

This chapter provides quantitative general equilibrium analyses of the Industrial Revolution and the period of 1889-1929 in the United States. These episodes were selected because of their importance and interest, the lack of existing quantitative general equilibrium studies of these episodes, and the simplicity of applying quantitative general equilibrium models and methods.

Previous discussions about the Industrial Revolution have focused on inventions such as the steam engine and the Spinning Jenny. But this analysis shows that these developments are only half of the story. These new, capital intensive technologies were substitutes for the older, less capital-intensive technologies. The new technologies, which improved over time, would only be implemented if they were competitive with the alternatives. Given TFP data from that time, there was no chance that the Industrial Revolution could have taken place in the 1500s, or before, as the productivity of the Malthusian technologies were temporarily high around that time. After that, the Malthusian productivity stagnated, which meant that it was only a matter of time before the Solow technologies ultimately caught up and became profitable to adopt over the alternative, land-intensive Malthusian technologies.

In addition, our analysis of the period from 1245 to 1845 reveals some puzzling issues concerning population movements during this period that deserve additional study.

Moving from the very long-run to a shorter horizon, we studied the remarkable 1889-1929 period in the U.S., one of the most important episodes in American economic history. In particular, the decade of the 1920s is known as perhaps the greatest peacetime growth decade. The research presented here shows that growth could easily have been much higher, given the remarkable productivity growth of the decade.

Instead, puzzlingly low labor input depressed the economy by a cumulative 15 percent relative to predicted model output driven by just productivity shocks. The decade reveals a large labor wedge, and we find that the labor wedge does not have an obvious interpretation. The coincidence of a large labor wedge, low labor input, and low wages suggest a labor market puzzle more challenging to identify that the labor market dysfunction that occurred just a decade later. What factor depressed employment in such a booming economy? Why didn't wages grow at nearly the same rate as productivity? Why didn't firms hire more labor, given its low relative price? These are open and important questions for future research.

Acknowledgments

We thank Jaeyoung Jang and Greg Clark for very helpful discussions, Greg Clark for providing historical data, Xiaoxia Ye for computational help, and Pedro Brinca and Francesca Loria for advice and for providing us with their Business Cycle Accounting programs. Abhi Vemulapati provided outstanding research assistance.

References

Barro, R.J., Sahasakul, C., 1983. Measuring the average marginal tax rate from the individual income tax. The Journal of Business 56 (4), 419–452.

Becker, G.S., Barro, R.J., 1988. A reformulation of the economic theory of fertility. The Quarterly Journal of Economics 103 (1), 1–25.

Bernanke, B.S., 2013. The crisis as a classic financial panic, 11 2013. Remarks by Ben S. Bernanke Chairman Board of Governors of the Federal Reserve System at Fourteenth Jacques Polak Annual Research Conference Sponsored by the International Monetary Fund, Washington, D.C. (Accessed 15 October 2020).

Brinca, P., Chari, V.V., Kehoe, P.J., McGrattan, E., 2016. Accounting for Business Cycles. Handbook of Macroeconomics, vol. 2. Elsevier, pp. 1013–1063.

Chari, V.V., Kehoe, P.J., McGrattan, E.R., 2002. Accounting for the great depression. The American Economic Review 92 (2), 22–27.

Chari, V.V., Kehoe, P.J., McGrattan, E.R., 2007. Business cycle accounting. Econometrica 75 (3), 781–836.

Clark, G., 2010. The macroeconomic aggregates for England, 1209–2008. In: Research in Economic History, vol. 27. Emerald Group Publishing Limited, pp. 51–140.

Cole, H.L., Ohanian, L.E., 1999. The great depression in the United States from a neoclassical perspective. Quarterly Review 23, 2–24.

Cole, H.L., Ohanian, L.E., 2002. The U.S. and U.K. great depressions through the lens of neoclassical growth theory. The American Economic Review 92 (2), 28–32.

Cole, H.L., Ohanian, L.E., 2004. New deal policies and the persistence of the great depression: a general equilibrium analysis. Journal of Political Economy 112 (4), 779–816.

Davis, J.H., 2004. An annual index of U. S. industrial production, 1790–1915. The Quarterly Journal of Economics 119 (4), 1177–1215.

Diamond, P.A., 1965. National debt in a neoclassical growth model. The American Economic Review 55 (5), 1126–1150.

Doepke, M., 2004. Accounting for fertility decline during the transition to growth. Journal of Economic Growth 9 (3), 347–383.

Galor, O., Weil, D.N., 2000. Population, technology, and growth: from Malthusian stagnation to the demographic transition and beyond. The American Economic Review 90 (4), 806–828.

Greenwood, J., 2020. Numerical methods for macroeconomists. Department of Economics, University of Pennsylvania. Manuscript.

Hansen, G., Ohanian, L., 2016. Neoclassical models in macroeconomics. In: Taylor, J.B., Uhlig, H. (Eds.), Handbook of Macroeconomics, vol. 2. Elsevier, pp. 2043–2130.

Hansen, G.D., Prescott, E.C., 2002. Malthus to Solow. The American Economic Review 92 (4), 1205–1217.

Jalil, A.J., 2015. A new history of banking panics in the United States, 1825-1929: construction and implications. American Economic Journal: Macroeconomics 7 (3), 295–330.

Kehoe, P.J., Midrigan, V., Pastorino, E., 2018. Evolution of modern business cycle models: accounting for the great recession. The Journal of Economic Perspectives 32 (3), 141–166.

Kehoe, T., Prescott, E., 2007. Great Depressions of the Twentieth Century. Research Department, Federal Reserve Bank of Minneapolis.

Kendrick, J.W., 1961. Productivity Trends in the United States. National Bureau of Economic Research, Inc.

Lucas, R.E., 1988. On the mechanics of economic development. Journal of Monetary Economics 22 (1), 3–42.

Lucas, R.E., 2018. What was the industrial revolution? Journal of Human Capital 12 (2), 182–203.

McGrattan, E.R., 2012. Capital taxation during the U.S. great depression. The Quarterly Journal of Economics 127 (3), 1515–1550.

McGrattan, E.R., Ohanian, L.E., 2010. Does neoclassical theory account for the effects of big fiscal shocks? Evidence from World War II. International Economic Review 51 (2), 509–532.

Ohanian, L.E., 1997. The macroeconomic effects of war finance in the United States: World War II and the Korean War. The American Economic Review 87 (1), 23–40.

Ohanian, L.E., 2010. The economic crisis from a neoclassical perspective. The Journal of Economic Perspectives 24 (4), 45–66.

Smiley, G., 1994. The American Economy in the Twentieth Century. College Division, South-Western Publishing Company.

Sprague, O., 1910. History of Crises Under the National Banking System. U.S. Government Printing Office.

Tallman, E., 2013. The panic of 1907. In: Randall, E.P., Whaples, R. (Eds.), Routledge Handbook of Major Events in Economic History. Routledge.

Money, banking, and old-school historical economics[☆]

Eric Monnet[a] and François R. Velde[b]
[a]Paris School of Economics, Paris, France
[b]Federal Reserve Bank of Chicago, Chicago, IL, United States

A great merit of the examination of a wide range of qualitative evidence, so essential in a monetary history, is that it provides a basis for discriminating between these possible explanations of the observed statistical covariation. We can go beyond the numbers alone and, at least on some occasions, discern the antecedent circumstances whence arose the particular movements that become so anonymous when we feed the statistics into the computer.

Friedman and Schwartz (1963, 686)

12.1 Introduction

How has the quantitative research in monetary and financial history over the last twenty years changed our understanding of historical and economic processes? What methods have been used to achieve new results?

Our conclusions differ from the premises of the editors of this Handbook. First, monetary and financial historians continue to study financial development and investigate the past for the sake of historical knowledge rather than "looking at the effect of past events on the current situation." Second, they continue to use models, "structural economic reasoning" and narrative methods to address key issues in the field. Although monetary and financial history has also been revolutionized by access to new microeconomic data, it makes limited use of statistical inference methods associated with recent development in applied microeconometrics. Difference in differences, quasi-natural experiments or discontinuity regressions are sometimes used successfully, but they have not become the gold standard.

There are good reasons for this. The description of sequences of events and general equilibrium perspectives remain key methods, rather than the identification of marginal effects, for studying the course of history (development and crises), building narratives and examining how the present has been shaped by history. Recent work also shows that important political and economic conclusions can be drawn from historical studies, without necessarily studying the direct effect of past events on current outcomes.

[☆] The views presented here do not necessarily reflect those of the Federal Reserve of Chicago or the Federal Reserve System. We thank Gadi Barlevy, Michael Bordo, Benjamin Chabot, Marc Flandreau, Eric Hilt, Gary Richardson, Tom Sargent; errors and omissions remain our own.

The Handbook of Historical Economics. https://doi.org/10.1016/B978-0-12-815874-6.00020-4

335

The history of financial development and financial crises remains the cornerstone of this field. Although these are old research topics, the recent work reviewed in sections 2 and 3 has gone considerably beyond traditional perspectives.[1] The basic chronology and typology of financial development has been questioned, leading to an approach that gives much more weight to the diversity of development models, financial systems, or central bank frameworks. The literature now focuses more on documenting and explaining this variety, recognizing that previous studies obsessed with the question of efficiency were often subject to a strong survival bias and centered on US and UK perspectives. The history of financial crises has benefited above all from a renewal of approaches that view the financial system as a network, making extensive use of the mass digitization of information on financial intermediaries. Rather than simply comparing aggregates, monetary history now focuses on the microeconomic sources of aggregate fluctuations.

In reviewing this literature, we identify three different types of causal statements used by economic historians. Section 12.4 compares them: (i) *process tracing* (causality is identified by the description of the chain of events), (ii) the *"experimentalist" view of causality*—familiar to applied microeconomists and revolving around the ideal of a random experiment—and (iii) *structural or model-based causality*, which has a long tradition in macroeconomics and relies on historically informed theoretical relationships to construct counterfactuals.

Section 12.5 expands on this structural approach, explaining why it is essential for historical macroeconomics and how models are used in this case. Models are used for their narratives, whether to inform current debates or to better understand the past. From this perspective, a key question is whether the model used by the researcher is—and should be—consistent with the model that agents had in mind when making decisions. We illustrate this point with a review of the literature on the roots of high inflation in the 1970s.

In the course of our investigation, we realize that most of the discussion of the research topics and methods examined here can be traced back to Friedman and Schwartz (1963). They studied most of the topics and formulated most of the hypotheses currently common in the literature. They alternately used the three different definitions of causality that we still observe. Whether one disagrees with their conclusions or not, they still shape the how and why of our writings today.

12.2 Financial development

Historians of finance and money have devoted much energy over the last twenty years to debunking myths about the causes and typology of financial development. If we must name a common characteristic of these different studies, it has been to highlight the diversity of modes of financial development and not to consider that what has survived today is a good starting point for investigating the past.

12.2.1 The impact of legal regimes

Institutions matter for economic and financial development, but it is challenging to identify which ones really made the difference. The danger of a-historical methods is to look for institutions that were

---

[1] We have focused on money and financial intermediation while setting aside related but vast areas such as public finance, sovereign debt, and exchange rates.

essential to the economy in the past through the lens of contemporary views about what is or is not important. As recently restated by Lamoreaux (2015), this creates a major survival bias, also named retrospective illusion, where much of the course of history is attributed to institutions that have survived or whose effects are likely to still matter.[2]

Legal regimes change only slowly, which makes them a plausible candidate to explain cross-country variations in financial systems. The "law and finance" theory of La Porta et al. (1998) argued that legal systems that protect investors will foster financial development, and found that common law countries have the strongest investor protections while Civil law countries have the weakest. The ensuing debate had a great influence on the development of financial history over the last twenty years, although the initial argument has ended up being almost universally rejected (see the survey by Musacchio and Turner 2013). Detailed studies of the way legal systems framed business and financial practices have shown that the development of financial institutions did not conform to the predictions of the theory on law and finance. Sgard (2006); Coyle et al. (2019); Acheson et al. (2019) show that the English financial market took off and achieved a high level of development in the 18th and 19th centuries without formal shareholder protection, against the argument that common law was better suited for creditors' right and spurred financial development. Lamoreaux and Rosenthal (2005); Sgard (2006); Musacchio and Turner (2013); Coyle et al. (2019); Acheson et al. (2019) demonstrate that countries with civil law could in fact had greater flexibility in business laws and forms of corporations than countries with common law. Focusing on bond markets and creditor protections, Musacchio (2008) showed large variations over time in bond market size, creditor protections, and court enforcement of bond contracts, within the *same* legal system; too large to support a direct causal link between a legal system and future financial development. Social and economic factors that shaped financial systems historically may have disappeared, such that their effect might be captured today by legal regimes in econometric estimations, although there was no actual direct relationship between the legal regime and financial development. Consider, for example, that colonialism played a key role in the development of the London financial market in the 19th century, in a context of weak protection of property rights (despite the common law). While economists seeking to prove historical causal effects tend to focus on sample size and exogeneity, economic historians point out that exogeneity is not sufficient to prove causality if there is no evidence of the transmission of the effect over time.

12.2.2 The many paths of financial development

Another instance of survival bias was the implicit belief that extinct forms of financial intermediation must have been inherently inefficient. The work carried out over the last two decades to reassess the traditional distinction between bank-based and market-based financial systems (Gershenkron, 1963; Goldsmith, 1969; Kindleberger, 1984) has highlighted the importance of certain forms of financial intermediation that had disappeared or been neglected by previous studies. The view that emerges emphasizes the variety of financial development paths without reducing it to a simple dichotomy between two opposing models. The literature not only documents the role of intermediaries that were

---

[2] She writes (in a paragraph about the research that focuses on the long-term economic effects of institutions): "The literature ignores cultural practices and institutions that do not have lasting effects, even though they may have been important shapers of economic behavior for long periods of time. At the same time, the literature simply assumes that practices and institutions that have significant associations with outcomes in the present were always important." (Lamoreaux, 2015, 1255).

neither banks nor financial markets. It also shows that systems that were thought to be bank-based relied heavily on markets (as in Germany), whereas the role of markets in market-based systems must be reconsidered (as in the US).

In this area, the work of Guinnane (2001) on German credit cooperatives and of Hoffman et al. (2000, 2019) on French notaries have provided seminal references for further studies (see Cull et al. 2006 for a mid-term review). Drawing on different perspectives and studying different periods and countries, these studies show that, in many cases, long-term loans to households and businesses were granted or negotiated by institutions that were neither commercial (or universal) banks nor stock markets. Numerous studies have followed: Wandschneider (2015) on Prussian mortgage cooperatives, Gelderblom et al. (2016) on direct finance and notaries in the Netherlands, Colvin and McLaughlin (2014) on credit cooperatives in the Netherlands and Ireland, Monnet (2018) on public credit institutions in France, etc. As Cull et al. (2006); Monnet (2018); Hoffman et al. (2019) and others point out, lending institutions different from banks and stock markets are still very important today in emerging markets (where peer lending and government credit still account for a large share of total lending, especially long-term lending), although their role has diminished in Western economies. It is also striking that this type of institution has been extremely different from country to country. Summarizing historical research on financial systems, Fohlin (2012) thus concludes that new studies written since the early 2000s (in contrast to previous literature on financial systems) have undoubtedly shown that there is no "one size fits all" solution for the design of financial systems. Various forms of institutions have developed in response to local needs and in a way that is strongly influenced by specific economic and political contexts. Financial institutions that have succeeded in one context would not have succeeded in another. German cooperative banking, for example, prospered in the Netherlands because they could operate in niche markets without long-established incumbents, whereas they failed in Ireland where other institutions already performed similar functions in rural areas Colvin and McLaughlin (2014).

A large part of this new literature developed to modify the standard narrative of financial development that was based primarily on the expansion of financial markets in England and the United States. For this reason, researchers have devoted much effort to searching elsewhere, that is, outside the US and British cases and outside stock markets. But recent research on stock markets and on the US has also emphasized institutional diversity and the limitations of the standard narrative on financial developments.

Thus Hautcoeur and Riva (2012) points out that a highly regulated monopolistic stock market (the official Paris stock exchange in the 19th century) provided security and transparency in spot transactions while a free, innovative secondary market focused on forward liquidity, and that the two markets provided complementarity for investors. In examining the development of the Amsterdam Stock Exchange in the 18th century, Gelderblom and Jonker (2004, 2011) challenges the widely held view—based on the English example—that a liquid market for public debt was necessary for the development of financial markets. Lehmann-Hasemeyer and Streb (2016) shows the importance of the Berlin Stock Exchange in financing innovative technologies in a country previously characterized as bank-based. In the 19th century, large banks and the development of the stock exchange were not contradictory. The German case—among others—also shows the role of banks in the development of stock and bond markets through underwriting of securities (Lehmann, 2014). In the international private and public debt markets, underwriters were also key players—although, in contrast to the German example, they were mainly investment banks (prominently Rothschild) rather than commercial or universal banks (Flandreau and Flores, 2009). As for the US stock exchange, O'Sullivan (2016) has contested its role in the direct financing of US industrial development before the First World War, showing that it was in fact limited to the financing of the railways. This contrasted sharply with the London Stock Exchange, where industrial securities were widely traded.

12.2.3 The role of regulation

Calomiris and Haber (2015) remind us how banking systems have been shaped by politics. Financial systems differ in part because they are subject to different regulations. In turn, regulation and state intervention have shaped financial weaknesses or strengths, as well as responses to crises.

Bordo et al. (2015) investigate why the US suffered from more banking crises than Canada in the 1930s. They demonstrate that most of the differences between the Canadian and US banking systems during the Great Depression were explained by the structure of the banking system and its supervisory policy (large oligopolistic banks in Canada versus unitary branches in the US). Likewise, within the US, the differences in bank suspensions in the 1930s were also partly explained by the differences in bank supervision (Mitchener, 2005). These differences in US banking supervision can themselves be attributed to the legacy of 19th century policies and crises (Mitchener and Jaremski, 2015). On the contrary, outside North America, bank regulation and supervision rarely existed before the Great Depression. This can be explained by the politics of the banking system and especially by the fact that politics created central banks on the one hand—providing liquidity during crises (Grossman, 2010; Toniolo and White, 2015)—and savings institutions on the other—protecting long-term savings (Degorce and Monnet, 2020). Until the Great Depression, this was considered sufficient to protect savings and ensure banking stability.

The absence of banking regulation is not only studied as an historical phenomenon to be explained. Braggion et al. (2017) study the almost unregulated English banking system in the 19th century in order to test predictions of economic theory on the impact of bank competition on bank lending. They compare bank lending in areas with high and low bank concentration. A theory of lending with asymmetric information led them to examine loan quality, in order to establish whether the observed lower level of bank lending in highly concentrated countries is the result of higher credit rationing or lower demand. They assess loan quality by reading the bank's comments on each loan, which are kept in archival records. The finding that loan quality increases as loan volume decreases leads them to conclude that the correlation between higher bank concentration and lower lending volumes is the result of higher credit rationing.

The history of banking regulation continues to be a very active area of research. Numerous recent articles aim at estimating the effect these regulation on economic outcomes. Carlson et al. (2018) exploit a discontinuity in bank capital requirements during the 19th century National Banking era in the United States to investigate how banking competition affects credit provision and growth. Anderson et al. (2019) use original data on bank balance sheets and a network model to show that the introduction of the reserve requirements by the National Banking Acts of 1863 and 1864 in the US changed the nature of the financial links between banks. Calomiris and Jaremski (2019) also use a discontinuity in regulation (i.e. difference in regulation between similar groups of banks) to study the impact of deposit insurance prior to the creation of the FDIC, and Park and Van Horn (2015) to study the effect of reserve requirements in the 1930s. The discontinuity approach is particularly well suited to the history of the US banking system because banking regulation in the US is much older than anywhere else and notoriously multilayered, with different supervisors and rules applied to different institutions and locations (Toniolo and White, 2015).

Although the case of pre-World War II United States has received much more attention than other countries in this literature, there is also a growing body of work on the post-war period and heavy banking regulation in countries where banks were nationalized and credit was mainly state-directed (Calomiris and Haber, 2015; Monnet, 2018; Musacchio and Lazzarini, 2014). This kind of work also comes back to general questions about the relationship between financial development, regulation and policy, which are usually left aside in the US literature that focuses on the marginal effect of specific regulations. Calomiris and Haber (2015) build an analytical framework to explain how differences in financial development and financial fragility correspond to different political regimes and relationships between these regimes and the domestic banking sector. They apply their framework to the history of banking systems in the US, UK, Canada, Brazil and Mexico since the 19th century. The nature of the government-banker partnership varies among different types of political systems defined by the authors as "weakly centralized" or "centralized" autocracies, "populist" or "liberal" democracies. Since "banks need states" and "states need banks", there is a conflict of interest inherent in government-banker partnerships that makes the banking systems of most countries "fragile by design". But the sources of fragility depend on the type of relationship between the government and the banks. From this point of view, regulating or bailing out banks can reduce risk in the short term, but increase overall financial fragility by changing the relationship between the government and the banks and creating, for example, moral hazard or vested interests.

12.2.4 Central banking

The literature on central banking has changed considerably in the last two decades. Hitherto it was largely conducted through the lens of modern, interest rate-setting central banks. To the extent that the past central banks were investigated, the focus had been mostly on the Bank of England as a prototype, and the late 19th-century gold standard as a regime in which the banks' role was to set interest rates. By contrast, much effort has been devoted in recent years to documenting and understanding the different models and operational frameworks of past central banks, and how they eventually influenced the fate of financial development.

As central banks entered a world of quantitative easing and credit policies after 2008, economic historians turned to the archives to show that central banking was not fully captured by interest rate management. Rather, quantitative tools and collateral policies were an integral part of central bank history (Cerretano, 2009; Monnet, 2014, 2018; Jaremski and Mathy, 2018). This opened the door to examining the variety of practices and how monetary authorities adapted their balance sheet policies to the needs of banks with which they had relationships. A more functional view of central banking has also led to study institutions that might not be central banks in the modern sense, but exercised the functions that are now in central banks' remit. Likewise central banks have in the past played roles that differ from theirs today. For example, in many countries central banks drove financial development by setting up nationwide branches and fostering local credit markets (Bazot, 2014; Klovland and Øksendal, 2017).

The mid-2010s brought a wave of bicentennial celebrations of central banks founded after the Congress of Vienna in 1815 that renewed interest in case studies outside the UK and the US (Bordo et al., 2016; Edvinsson et al., 2018; Jobst and Kernbauer, 2016). Several comprehensive surveys (Roberds and Velde, 2016a,b,c; Ugolini, 2017; Bindseil, 2020) have adopted a broad view of central banks and their predecessors the public banks of Europe, as institutions fulfilling a bundle of economic functions: not just setting monetary policy, but also the provision of liquidity services and reliable means of payment to the private sector, and of financing to the public sector. Another important lesson of this long-term history is that this last function made relations with governments perilous; survival often required these institutions to maintain a "gentlemanly distance" with their sponsors (see Karaman et al. 2020 for similar considerations in the case of monetary debasements). But to appreciate the inventiveness of these proto-central banks requires in-depth archival research, guided by a sharp understanding of the bundle of functions. Thus Quinn and Roberds (2007, 2014, 2019) have shown how the Bank of Amsterdam, the most advanced of its time, provided an irredeemable central bank money in the late 17th century and managed its value through open-market operations and the issue of repos. Quinn and Roberds (2015) found that it provided liquidity and prevented bankruptcies of major actors during the European crisis of 1763 described by Schnabel and Shin (2004).

Our understanding of the variety of lender of last resort policies has also tremendously progressed in the last decade. Economic historians have especially highlighted the various institutional arrangements of these policies: collateral requirements (Bignon et al., 2011), lifeboat operations vs. liquidity provision (Hautcoeur et al., 2014), secrecy on the identity of rescued banks (Gorton and Tallman, 2018), etc. Investigations into the political economy of these policies are still in their infancy, however, and deserve to be deepened, especially on how private interests and social networks may have dictated the choice of collateral and the identity of the rescued institutions.

The history of central banking does not only involve central banks. Costabile and Neal (2018) show how early modern Naples had a small and stable group of banks owned by charitable institutions providing the payments services that public banks had been created elsewhere in Europe to provide. The banks weathered successfully two hundred years of vicissitudes and were later merged to become the central bank of the Two Sicilies. The function of lender of last resort was not restricted to central banks, although only the latter exercised it on a large scale. Moen and Tallman (2000); Gorton and Tallman (2018) highlight the quasi-central bank function of clearing houses in the US before the creation of the Federal Reserve. They limited counterparty risk and provided liquidity during crises. Bernstein et al. (2019) examine the effect of a clearing house on the stock market by looking at the creation of a clearing house on the New York Stock Exchange (NYSE) in 1892. At that time, the NYSE's largest shares were also listed on the Consolidated Stock Exchange (CSE), which already had a clearing house. Using identical securities on the CSE as a control, they find that the introduction of clearing reduced the annualized volatility of NYSE returns and increased asset values. Jaremski (2018) presents a more mixed picture of the clearing houses, showing that their introduction in the US states created negative externalities for banks that were not members of the clearing houses.

12.3 Banking and financial crises

In recent years, the literature on the sources and consequences of financial crises has undergone four important developments that are partly interrelated. First, financial networks have been the focus of interest in order to identify how crises become systemic. Second, new digital technologies have revolutionized access to historical financial data (Mitchener, 2015), allowing a more global view of financial systems and their interconnections. Third, investigations of the cost of crises—and of central bank policies mitigating or aggravating them—have relied more extensively on econometric identification and large microeconomic datasets. Fourth, in contrast with the monetarist approach of Friedman and Schwartz (1963), recent studies examine both the assets and liabilities of the balance sheets of financial intermediaries. Broad lending conditions and interbank markets are investigated together. Studies on the microeconomic sources and transmission of financial and banking crises are therefore consistent with the "credit view" highlighted in long-term perspective by Schularick and Taylor (2012).[3]

For economic historians, financial crises are a familiar phenomenon. Even before the 2008 global financial crash, few historians could have been tempted by the illusion that "this time is different". On the contrary, an abundant literature flourished in the 1990s, drawing parallels between the crises of the first era of globalization (at the end of the 19th century) and those of the new era of financial internationalization that followed the collapse of the communist world in the 1990s (Bordo et al., 2001; Bordo and Flandreau, 2003; Obstfeld and Taylor, 2005; Meissner et al., 2006; Esteves and Khoudour-Castéras, 2009) The upheavals of the 1990s, from the Latin American debt crisis to the dot-com bubble, confirmed that the world had returned to a world of frequent financial crises, even though—looking back to the early 2000s—none of them had yet become fully global and as severe as the Great Depression of the 1930s. Credit booms and busts, asset price bubbles, sovereign debt crises and international contagion were the subject of landmark studies in international economic history in the years leading up to the 2008 crisis (Bordo and Meissner, 2006; Schnabel, 2004; Schnabel and Shin, 2004; Neal and Weidenmier, 2003; Eichengreen and Mitchener, 2004). The banking and stock market crises of the Great Depression of the 1930s, particularly those in the United States, continued to be the subject of lively research (Rappoport and White, 1994; Klug et al., 2005; Calomiris and Mason, 2003; Mitchener, 2005; Richardson, 2007a,b). Yet, the 2008 financial crash has considerably renewed the approach of financial and monetary historians and broadened the scope of their investigations.

12.3.1 Network and contagion

As in many fields, the past is read through the lens of the present. The global financial crash of 2008, as well as the European sovereign debt problems of 2010-2012, prompted researchers to shed new light on past crises (by focusing on mechanisms or institutions that had been neglected before), often with the intention of fueling current debates. Important works on the causes and transmission of crises mainly use financial documents to reconstruct the links in the chain that led from a spark in the financial system to a systemic crisis. Thus, the new literature on financial crises after 2008 devotes much attention to the importance of financial networks and contagion. This approach is mainly based on very detailed archival research on the financial exposures of major banks (Richardson and Van Horn, 2009; Accominotti, 2012; Postel-Vinay, 2016; Straumann et al., 2017; Richardson and Van Horn, 2018), or on microeconomic data allowing to reconstruct the links between networks and financial flows (Richardson, 2007b; Carlson and Wheelock, 2018; Mitchener and Richardson, 2019; Anderson et al., 2019; Baubeau et al., 2020).

The focus on international contagion has renewed the study of the 1931 crisis, which was the main driving force behind the Great Depression. By examining the balance sheets of English merchant banks

---

[3] Although the historical macroeconomic literature has highlighted the strong link between financial crises and public debt crises, we keep the history of public debt out of the scope of this paper. A survey of the international historical macro literature on financial and fiscal crises is already written by Bordo and Meissner (2016).

and the archives of the Bank of England, Accominotti (2012) shows that the devaluation of the pound sterling in September 1931 followed an exchange rate crisis whose roots were the financial exposure of London merchant banks to German merchants. The banking and economic crisis in Germany thus caused the pound sterling crisis, which in turn was a huge shock to the world economy. In the same vein, Straumann et al. (2017) note that the banking crisis in Sweden was also triggered by Germany's insolvency because Swedish banks had accumulated short-term foreign assets. By contrast, detailed archival research led Richardson and Van Horn (2009, 2018) to find that New York banks were not affected by the Eastern European banking crises in the same year. This body of research is both instructive on the mechanics of a crisis in general and valuable in understanding one of the most dramatic economic crises in history.

The study of the links in a crisis chain through a detailed examination of the financial network is not limited to international contagion. Mitchener and Richardson (2019) examine the key role of the interbank network in transmitting deposit withdrawals through the US banking system and amplifying the contraction of lending during the Great Depression. The peculiar structure of the US banking system prompted hinterland banks to deposit certain reserves in large correspondent banks in financial centers. When hinterland banks began to experience withdrawals from depositors, they also withdrew their funds from correspondent banks. Although banks in the major financial centers did not face a run of depositors, they did face withdrawals from other banks, forcing them to reduce their lending. The authors show that the reduction in lending was in fact from two distinct sources. First, there was a general reduction in the assets of correspondent banks from which hinterland banks withdrew funds. Second, in response to liquidity risk, correspondent banks changed the composition of their assets and reduced the share of loans relative to the share of safe assets (government securities, cash and central bank reserves). Because of this change in behavior and asset composition, the volume of loans did not resume after the panic, when funds were returned to the correspondent banks. The essence of their argument is based on a detailed examination of the financial mechanics and interconnectedness. It is complemented by econometric analysis showing that indeed, interbank deposits and loans reacted after a bank panic.

12.3.2 Mass digitization

Easier access to historical records and, more importantly, the lower cost of digitization and data management have significantly changed the way economic historians can assess the macroeconomic effects of financial crisis. An unprecedented collection of microeconomic data on financial institutions or individuals enables researchers to adopt a holistic view of the financial system.[4] The article by Mitchener and Richardson (2019) cited above is only one study among many showing how more data can help tracking the chain of events. It is only a first step because this article did not make a full use of the geographic information contained in the data (Mitchener, 2015). The data revolution was not a necessary condition for the increasing attention being paid to the financial network, but it is changing the game. Rather than simply comparing aggregates, monetary history now focuses on the microeconomic sources of aggregate fluctuations.

---

[4] In an area different from that of financial crises, Flandreau and Jobst (2005) had preliminary used a network approach—also relying on a vast amount of data—to graph the connections between financial centers within the international monetary system. They present data on each currency quoted in each stock market around the world in the 19th century.

Compared to previous studies of financial crises, wider access to data allows researchers to see the financial system as a network. It has at least two important implications for a renewed historiography. First, as Mitchener and Richardson (2019) clearly show, it is a means of decomposing the transmission channels, which makes it possible to understand why macroeconomic variables evolve together. In this case, the authors renew the literature on the Great Depression because data on interbank linkages lead them to reinterpret the causal link between money (deposits), credit and real activity that was at the heart of landmark studies such as those of Friedman and Schwartz (1963) and Bernanke (1983). Second, the wealth of data gives researchers a comprehensive view of the financial system while previous studies were often limited to one specific segment of the financial system.

The study of French banking crises during the Great Depression illustrates how this new holistic approach of the financial system can renew the historiography. Baubeau et al. (2020) start from a fundamental—but rarely addressed—question for the history of banking crises: where do deposits go when depositors in a bank run withdraw them? For this country, the use of statistics of bank balance sheets was all the more limited because there was no banking regulation. Absent a banking supervisor, the article relies on private sources to collect the balance sheets of all major French commercial banks. Without comprehensive statistics, previous studies usually adopted a biased perspective focusing on the few large banks that did not fail. The availability of new data overturns previous knowledge: while the country's four largest banks were not affected (in fact, like the major banks in New York during the US crisis), the rest of the banking system experienced severe waves of withdrawals and a sharp drop in activity.

The authors then track the fate of deposits that were withdrawn from banks by panicked depositors. The approach is similar to the reconstruction of a flow of funds accounts. A necessary first step is to estimate whether cash hoarding was the main counterpart of withdrawals from bank deposits. Using a wealth of data from court records on bank liquidation and bankruptcies, the article then finds that the vast majority of depositors managed to withdraw their deposits before the bank closed, so that "frozen deposits" (i.e., losses to depositors) were small. Only one type of financial institution saw a significant increase in the flow of deposits during the crisis: government-guaranteed savings institutions (*Caisses d'épargne*). Overall, the nominal increase in *Caisses d'épargne* deposits was greater than the nominal decrease in bank deposits, but the two phenomena may have been unrelated and had independent causes. A mixture of estimates based on balance of payments statistics and qualitative records on the identity of depositors finally led the authors to conclude that during the two years of banking panic (1930-1931), the decrease in bank deposits was almost entirely due to withdrawals and transfers to the accounts of the *Caisses d'épargne*.

It is hard to imagine how this type of study could have been achieved without the recent significant reduction in the cost of digitizing archival data. In many ways, this is the continuation of the work undertaken by Friedman and Schwartz (1963) on the monetary history of the US, although their data were still limited and especially missed microeconomic information that helps to understand why macroeconomic aggregates move. The monetary histories of many other countries that followed the seminal publication of Friedman and Schwartz usually relied on even more limited data and focused on estimating money aggregates. By contrast, the new generation of studies that use digitized microeconomic data on banks and financial institutions has the means to go back to the questions initially raised by Friedman and Schwartz on the causes of large movements in monetary and financial aggregates. This is done primarily through reconstructing the linkages between the different parts of the financial and monetary network.

12.3.3 The cost of crises

While the studies mentioned above construct a narrative of the crisis by dissecting the sources and transmission of financial risk, another line of research aims to assess the economic impact of banking or financial difficulties. Rather than working at a general equilibrium level, this often means focusing on a narrower window to estimate this impact by identifying differences between a group affected by the crisis and a group not affected. These identification methods, also popular in empirical finance (Rajan and Zingales, 1998; Khwaja and Mian, 2008), have mainly used the fact that some firms or households were exposed differently to the financial turmoil than others. The source of the financial turmoil is not seen as exogenous to the overall economy, but the reason why some borrowers are affected differently from others by the crisis is deemed to be unrelated to the characteristics of the borrowers. It remains difficult for this literature, however, to link estimates of well-identified marginal effects to broad narratives of the crisis that take a holistic view of the financial system.

Recent papers study the effect of the US banking crises during the Great Depression using the identification method of Rajan and Zingales (Benmelech et al., 2019; Gorton et al., 2019. 1930): firms that relied more on external financing were more affected by banking crises than others. The challenge of this empirical method is to control for all the characteristics of firms that can be jointly associated with the choice of the composition of liabilities and the performance of firms. Xu (2018) applies the same type of identification procedure to measure the consequences of the English banking crisis of 1866 on international trade: all other things being equal, countries exposed to banks with headquarters in London that failed in 1866 exported less in the following decades.

Frydman et al. (2015) go further by using information on financial networks as a source of identification. They study the consequences of a run on trust companies in New York during the 1907 panic. Their identification is based on the fact that the withdrawals were caused by the identity of the trust company but were not related to the financial health of the companies financed by the trust. Based on qualitative and quantitative archival information, they establish that much of the variation in deposit losses among the New York financial trusts was due to their associations with individuals involved in speculation in the shares of a mining company (United Copper Company). When stock prices of this company fell, households feared that their deposits were threatened and ran on trusts whose directors had been involved in the speculation. The cause of these withdrawals was therefore not related to the financial health of the trust companies' corporate clients. The companies that borrowed from the trusts that suffered from the rush are akin to a treated group, whose main access to long-term credit was suddenly cut off. The authors find that companies affiliated with the most affected trusts made fewer capital investments in the years following the panic.

12.3.4 Central banks to the rescue

As the history of the 1930s reminds us, crises are all the more costly without emergency liquidity provision by a central bank. Richardson and Troost (2009) used a quasi-natural experiment to support this interpretation. The experiment is based on Mississippi (United States) being divided into two Federal Reserve districts, which followed different policies of lender of last resort during the banking panic of 1930. In the district of Atlanta, the central bank provided liquidity to banks in trouble, whereas the central bank in the district of St Louis did not. The two parts of Mississippi were similar and the distinct policies of Atlanta and St Louis were not motivated by different characteristics of these two parts. The authors find that the failing rate of banks was lower and commercial activity remained higher in the part of Mississippi that was in the district of Atlanta. This is a rare example of an historical policy that is akin to a controlled experiment with one group that receives a treatment while the other do not. In this case, econometrics evidence provides important robustness checks but the effect was immediately observable by comparing the means of the two groups.

In another article about the lender of last resort role of the Federal Reserve, Carlson et al. (2011) study how the Federal Reserve Bank of Atlanta halted the spread of a banking panic in 1929 by rushing currency to member banks. The panic was caused by an exogenous event (a fruit fly infestation that created bank runs in citrus growing regions) so that the intervention of the central bank is viewed as independent from pre-crisis characteristics. The authors use simple models to predict the failure rate of banks during the panic. Building on these counterfactuals, they conclude that bank failure rates would have been twice as high in Florida without the Atlanta Fed's decision to provide funds to the key correspondents in Tampa that were facing runs. Contrary to Richardson and Troost (2009), this paper does not rely on a comparison between two groups but on a counterfactual, using a simple estimated model to simulate what would have happened without central bank intervention. This counterfactual has important policy implications because it implies that if the Federal Reserve System had reacted in 1930 and 1931 as the Atlanta Fed did in 1929, it could have mitigated the consequences of banking panics during the Great Depression.

12.4 Different types of causal identification

How do financial and monetary historians deal with causality? Most of the literature reviewed in the previous sections makes little use of the methods associated with the "credibility revolution" in applied microeconomics (Angrist and Pischke (2010)). This is sometimes the case when studying the effect of banking regulation or banking crises. In these cases, economic historians have successfully relied on instrumental variables, discontinuity regressions, quasi-natural experiments, or difference in differences to identify exogenous variations and estimate the marginal effect of a crisis or policy intervention on one specific group, relative to another. Yet this is not a dominant trend of research. Economic historians also use other methods to study the effect of policy interventions and crises, such as narratives or model-based counterfactuals. More importantly, when it comes to key topics such as the sources and characteristics of financial development and financial crises, the literature relies on other methods and definitions of causality than those used in applied microeconomics.

Below we distinguish three main types of causality used in the literature in financial and monetary history (and more generally in economic history). We begin by "process tracing", which is a common method for introducing causal reasoning into narrative analysis. Then we compare this method to the "experimentalist" or "interventionist" definition of causality that is currently familiar to microeconomists. Third, we present the structural approach that is mainly defended in macroeconomics and that is still widely used by historians of money and finance. The following sections of this chapter will explore in more detail how this structural, or model-based, approach to causality is used in history and how it is combined with narratives.

12.4.1 Process tracing

The above-mentioned studies on financial development and financial contagion use causal statements when reconstructing the chain of events. Detailed qualitative and quantitative information on the timing and volume of financial flows as well as financial exposure, for example, allow researchers to assert that one event or set of events was instrumental in triggering other events. Other assumptions or confounding factors are considered, but are eventually rejected by information on how the process actually unfolded. This definition of causality is common in history and the social sciences and corresponds to what Salmon (1998) calls a theory of process causality, or what has recently been reframed as "process tracing" by political scientists (Collier, 2011; Bennett and Checkel, 2015). As explained by Salmon (1998), the identification of such causality does not imply a counterfactual. It relies on the description of the chain of transmission.

In the studies by Richardson and Van Horn (2009); Accominotti (2012); Straumann et al. (2017); Richardson and Van Horn (2018), the authors are thus able to determine whether a crisis in one country triggered a crisis in another country by examining financial linkages. In a very different context, Bordo et al. (2019) examine the dual crisis of the pound sterling and the US dollar in 1967, by exploiting both series of foreign exchange interventions and archival information on buyers of gold at the US 'gold window' to demonstrate that sterling crisis triggered the dollar crisis. By contrast, standard studies on financial contagion that merely examine the correlation between asset prices are not able to distinguish between correlation and causality. Only a precise description of the sequence of financial and political events can assess the direction of causation in this case. Similarly, by reconstructing financial flows and establishing a detailed chronology of bank panics, Mitchener and Richardson (2019) show that bank panics in the US hinterland were one of the causes of bank distress in large cities (through the interbank system).

The most popular definition of causality in microeconomics is based on the identification of an exogenous shock and the maintenance of constant characteristics between groups (see below), without necessarily observing the sequence from shock to outcome. In contrast, process tracing is a descriptive inference where a precise characterization of the sequence is the key to asserting causality. The scientific criteria used to evaluate sequence description depend on the type of material available to researchers. In political science and international relations, for example, qualitative information on the decision-making process of policy makers is essential for adequate description and identification (Collier, 2011; Bennett and Checkel, 2015). In financial and monetary history, as the examples above show, evidence of financial linkages between institutions is central to identification. By examining these linkages, researchers are able to assess causality (i.e. the chain of events) rather than simply observing the correlation between macroeconomic aggregates. It can also be supplemented with information on policy decisions where relevant.

In their comparative study of politics and financial development in history, Calomiris and Haber (2015, 451) justify their approach to causality in the following way in order to distinguish it from the standard identification restrictions that guide causal inference in microeconomics:

> *At the same time, we believe that the country histories in this book illustrate the usefulness of an alternative, complementary approach, based on the study of the sequence of events in particular countries over long periods of time. Such narratives can be uniquely useful for identifying causal patterns, so long as they are more than a string of facts. [...] Our approach, therefore, is to develop "structural narratives," which combine the logic of economics and political bargaining with a careful examination of the specific historical events in individual countries.*

An interesting avenue for further research, raised by Calomiris and Haber (2015) among others, is to evaluate the use of economic theory in characterizing the chain of events. In other words, how much does process tracing need theory to order the facts? When examining a sequence of financial flows, economic historians often start from theoretical considerations. For example, both Mitchener and Richardson (2019) and Baubeau et al. (2020) have used standard monetarist theory as a starting point to guide their empirical research and test alternative hypotheses, even if they end up showing their limitations. In a paper that exploits individual data on the exposure of lenders to a syndicate that went bankrupt in Amsterdam in 1772, Koudijs and Voth (2016) used a model to interpret the change in investor behavior, namely the impact of risk on haircuts and interest rates. They show that only those who were at risk of losing money changed their behavior significantly (they lent at much higher haircuts). Although the links of the chain and individual financial exposure are adequately described, the authors need the predictions of financial theory to infer the consequences of individual behavior from the data.

12.4.2 Credibility revolution and interventionist causality

When possible, detailed historical research on financial linkages also follows the definition and identification of causality put forward in the applied microeconomics literature (recently labeled "credibility revolution" by Angrist and Pischke (2010)), and known in the epistemology literature as "interventionist", "manipulationist" or "experimentalist" causality (Reiss, 2005; Heckman and Pinto, 2014; Bourgeois-Gironde and Monnet, 2017). The use of these terms is nevertheless sometimes confusing because other authors use the term "interventionist" to denote definitions of causality that are model-based (see below). Contrary to structural models, the "interventionist" or "manipulationist" definition of causality associated with applied microeconomics and natural experiments relies on the agency of the researcher rather than on model-based relationships. The randomized experiment ideal is the guiding principle of this definition of causality. In this perspective, causation can be identified because the researcher is able to design an experiment, give a treatment and observe its effects. In the absence of controlled or natural experiments similar to the one used in Richardson and Troost (2009), economic historians study the differences (all else being equal) between the institutions that were most likely to suffer from a crisis, for example. The main disadvantage of this approach is that if it is not complemented by a detailed account of the crisis, or supported by a structural model, there is no understanding of the mechanics of the crisis and thus no possibility of making it interesting for historians of a given period, nor any means of generalizing the conclusions.

This type of causal identification can nevertheless be combined with a detailed narrative of the sequence of events and, in this case, be illuminating for historians. The study of Frydman et al. (2015) mentioned above is a good example of microeconomic identification based first on a detailed analysis of the sequence of a financial crisis and the links between financial institutions and firms. It combines a causal analysis based on process tracing to highlight the cause of the crisis, and then uses an interventionist definition of causality to examine how the crisis had different effects on different groups.

12.4.3 Structural causality

Another definition of causality that is widely used in macroeconomics and economic history is structural or model-based causality. It will be discussed further in the next section. This type of causality relies on a model of structural equations that specifies the relationship between variables (for an introduction to the large literature on structural causality in philosophy of sciences, see Heckman and Pinto 2014; Hitchcock 2020). Although a variable is usually endogenous in the model, the researcher can simulate an exogenous shock to one of these variables. This is where the causal process originates. The model, through the structural equations, predicts the impact of this shock on other variables. Several events in history can be interpreted as "shocks" if it can be proven that they are not mere consequences of the changes in other variables of the model. The researcher can either use the model to assess the historical consequences of this shock, or, alternatively, compare the historical outcomes (if directly observable) to the ones predicted by the model. Counterfactual reasoning is essential to this definition of causality.

Contrary to "process tracing", the causality is assessed through theoretical relationships rather by a full description of the sequence. When the researcher does not have access to sufficient empirical material to document the sequence of events, it is by relying on a model and theoretical assumptions that she can fill in the gaps between unrelated a priori facts. Contrary to difference-in-difference or natural experiments, there is no control group: the counterfactual is specified by the model rather than by the existence of two groups (treated vs. untreated).

Anderson et al. (2019) provide a recent landmark investigation of the link between banking regulation and financial stability using a structural network model on the US banking system in the 19th century. Thanks to unique data on bank balance sheets, they reconstruct linkages between banks, before and after the passage of the National Banking Acts (NBAs) of 1863 and 1864. The NBAs established legal reserve requirements that allowed banks to maintain a large portion of interbank deposits in designated cities, thereby creating a reserve pyramid. In a second step, they build a structural network model of the system that they calibrate using historical data. Then, they simulate financial shocks in the model and assess how the transmission of liquidity shocks differs before and after the NBAs. Contrary to Mitchener and Richardson (2019), the authors do not reconstruct the precise sequence of events during a crisis. They do not in fact study actual crises. Instead, they use a calibrated model to simulate crises in order to study how banking regulation changed liquidity transmission. It provides important conclusions on both the process of US financial development and current issues for banking regulators: concentration of interbank deposits facilitated diversification but contagion was thus more likely when financial center banks faced large shocks.

As it will become clear in the next section, the application of structural models to history requires the use of a lot of qualitative information to justify the hypotheses and main structural relationships on which a model relies. For this reason, major works in monetary and financial history have combined the use of theory and of narratives based on archival evidence to make sense of a particular historical period of event.

12.5 **Historical macroeconomics and the science of story-telling**

Our survey shows that the "modern methods" have found limited use in monetary, banking, and financial history. Broadly speaking, researchers in this subfield of historical economics have used the methods to shed strong but narrow light on a particular piece of a broader mechanism. There is very little emphasis on natural experiments and differences-in-differences estimation, as well as a general absence of long-run regressions stretching over centuries.

Why? Setting aside the hypothesis that those researchers respond less to obvious incentives, the rest of this chapter speculates on the reasons. Macroeconomics in general has embraced these methods to a lesser degree, and used them differently when it has, than the rest of economics. We think the reasons apply as well, if not more, to historical macroeconomics where models have structured narratives for a long time and continue to do so.

12.5.1 The macroeconomic tradition

Modern macroeconomics is built on tradition. The econometric theory of Haavelmo (1944), Marschak (1953), and the Cowles Commission in the 1940s and 1950s gave the first scientific foundation for the analysis of economic data. The ultimate goal of the program, which began during the Great Depression, was to provide sound policy advice, that is, credible counterfactuals.

The first step is to separate the *explananda*, the endogenous variables we are in the business of explaining, from the *explanantia*, the exogenous variables we do not try to explain and take from engineers, psychologists, lawyers, historians.

> *For the economy as a whole, endogenous variables can be roughly identified with what are often called "economic variables." These are usually the quantities (stocks or flows) and prices of goods and services, or their aggregates and averages, such as national income, total investment, price level, wage level, and so on. The exogenous variables and the structural parameters are, roughly, "noneconomic variables" (also called "data" in the economic literature) and may include the weather and technological, psychological, and sociological conditions as well as legal rules and political decisions. But the boundary is movable. Should political science ever succeed in explaining political situations (and hence legislation itself) by economic causes, institutional variables like tax rates would have to be counted as endogenous Marschak (1953, 10).*

Macroeconomics differs from the rest of economics in its concern for economy-wide aggregates and its natural framework is the general equilibrium theory of Arrow and Debreu (1954), Debreu (1959), and McKenzie (1954)—indeed, it may be the last field of economics where general equilibrium theory is still cherished. In that framework Marschak's "non-economic variables" are specified as preferences of agents defined over a space of goods, their endowments of goods, and the available means to turn goods into more or other goods (technology). His "legal rules and political decisions" can be described in the constraints on agents' choices and transactions (taxes) or in the resource constraints (government spending, money creation, etc). The model is solved by a set of endogenous variables that satisfies the conditions expressing the purposeful behavior of agents and the coherence of their actions. These conditions involve the structural parameters θ that characterize the exogenous objects of the model, and the endogenous variables p to be predicted. The equilibrium conditions $F(p, \theta) = 0$ implicitly define the vector p as a function of the vector θ.

What is causality in this framework? As Heckman (2000, 46) puts it:

> *Just as the ancient Hebrews were "the people of the book," economists are "the people of the model." Formal economic models are logically consistent systems within which hypothetical "thought experiments" can be conducted to examine the effects of changes in parameters and constraints on outcomes. Within a model, the effects on outcomes of variation in constraints facing agents in a market setting are well defined. Comparative statics exercises formalize Marshall's notion of a ceteris paribus change which is what economists mean by a causal effect.*

Thus, while $F(p, \theta)$ only defines a mapping from the complete vector θ to the complete vector p, one can conceivably vary only one element of θ to trace its effect on one or more elements of p. Causality is postulated by the equations of the model, and causal effects are the outcomes of thought experiments. But the general equilibrium framework, and its implication that all elements of p are simultaneously determined, places the problem of simultaneous equations (Haavelmo, 1943) at the heart of econometric work.

Time and uncertainty do not change the notion of causality although they complicate the interpretation of observed outcomes (Lucas and Sargent, 1981). Exogenous variables must now be specified as stochastic processes whose whole future paths enter into agents' calculations, and the model needs to take a stand on agents' information sets and beliefs.

Macroeconomics, whether in the DSGE tradition, or in the multivariate time series models restricted by economic reasoning (Sims, 2010), has remained much more structural in nature than other areas of economics (see the survey in Nakamura and Steinsson 2018). To the extent that quasi-experiments are useful, it is to illuminate one particular "block" or portion of a model, or to derive estimates of a parameter that can be then used in a fully structural model. The tradition of using historical narrative to identify exogenous shocks, in the spirit of Friedman and Schwartz (1963), and use them to evaluate competing models, continues (Romer and Romer, 2004). But "natural" experiments have their "natural" limits outside of models (Fuchs-Schündeln and Hassan, 2016).

12.5.2 History and macroeconomics

When history and economics meet, particular challenges arise.

There are two broad, not mutually exclusive modes of interaction between history and economics. The first is to think of the historical record as a large warehouse of data on which we can draw to test our theories, more or less formally. This can be useful for macroeconomics, since observations about aggregate economies are necessarily fewer than for particular microeconomic questions, and particularly useful for infrequent phenomena such as large-scale financial crises. The confrontation with past experiences can also expand our thinking by presenting us with events, arrangements, or outcomes that we might not have thought of in the first place (Abramitzky, 2015).

The two disciplines can interact in a second way. If historians want to be more than annalists, instill some order into apparent chaos, and shape a jumble of disconnected facts with a narrative then a causal process can serve as an organizing device for the flow of history.[5] When the events are economic in nature, economic theory provides the logical structure of that process.

Historical analysis, however, creates particular challenges for the framework used by macroeconomics, and details that were set aside become prominent.

First, history unfolds in the flow of time, and in that flow agents look forward. Their expectations or beliefs become salient. Second, that flow must always be interrupted (the narrative has a starting point) but in truth there is no pure $t = 0$, endowments and beliefs are products of $t < 0$. In a simple Markovian world, we know all we need to know at $t = 0$ to understand the future. But chains of causation can run through these products. The counterfactual that necessarily follows from quasi-experiments must be

---

[5] "On fait la science avec des faits comme une maison avec des pierres; mais une accumulation de faits n'est pas plus une science qu'un tas de pierres n'est une maison" [Science is built up with facts, as a house is with stones; But an accumulation of facts is no more a science than a heap of stones is a house] Poincaré (1902), cited by Calomiris and Haber (2015, 451).

compatible with the chain of events for $t < 0$: e.g., what would Germany have been if history had been such that the French Revolution did not happen? This is particularly true when the quasi-experiment is in fact run by a purposeful agent such as the government, which often looms large in macroeconomic models (see also Chemla and Hennessy, 2020).

Second, while the partition between endogenous and exogenous is fairly straightforward for the first elements in Marschak's list (preferences, endowments, technology, delivered by psychologists and engineers), matters become more complicated when we come to the offerings of the lawyers and historians. We have to specify details about information (who knows what and when), timing (who moves first), market structure (who trades with whom, outside of complete markets), which promises can be made and will be enforced. In the case of monetary, banking, and financial history this is simply because in a complete markets model there is neither need nor room for money, banks, or finance (except the anonymous trading of perfectly safe Arrow securities).

Much of this has been labeled "institutions," even outside of money, banking, and finance, for a natural heuristic reason. The concept of causality relies on generalization: as Hume famously said, "the same cause produces the same effects," but with historical macroeconomics we do not have myriads of instances where the "same" cause is readily identified. For the inductive method to work, a collection of events $\{x_i\}$ must become a class X. The challenge is to do so while remaining sensitive to the specificity of each history–generalize just enough to function in the "middle terrain" between economics and history identified by Lamoreaux (2015). "Institutions" serve that heuristic purpose of generalization, without necessarily having recourse to a model.

But what are institutions? The simplest model is a set of constraints on agent behavior, or an exogenous collection of payoffs: this can be an explicit penal code or norms of behavior, that is, exogenously restricted sets of expectations about other agents' actions. A more subtle interpretation would make the constraints endogenous, i.e., spell out the game in which agents find it in their interest to abide what seem to be constraints when only equilibrium paths are observed (e.g., Chari and Kehoe, 1990).

Remarkably, while many of the long-run effects studies in historical economics rely crucially on institutions and have appealed to the so-called "New Institutional Economics" (NEI) to play up their importance, the concept plays an ambiguous role. NEI often burrows (perhaps too) deeply into the logic of institutions: why do they exist, what purpose do they serve, why do they change. For the purposes of quasi-experiments their role is exogenous: an institution is randomly changed, and the consequences are observed. Yet the motivation is typically interventionist in nature: policy-oriented conclusions are drawn on the merits of the institutions, implicitly at least to argue that some institutions are preferable to others. But if institutions can change as a result of the researcher's policy advice because some are better than others, could they not have changed in the course of history, for the same reason? As Marschak noted in the quotation above, institutions are near the shifting boundary between exogenous and endogenous. The boundary can shift (permanently) because of scientific progress, but it will also shift depending on the topic and its time-frame.

Institutions are, by nature, stable: we wouldn't call them by that name if they weren't. Yet vary across space and change over time, slowly or abruptly: that's why they are used as vectors of causation. Setting institutions as exogenous and taking small, partial variations as quasi-random may well be adequate for very short horizons. But the appropriate time frame for historical macroeconomics in money, banking, and finance is awkward: too short to ignore them altogether as background noise, too long to see them as fixed. In this time scale, institutions can both matter and change at the same time. If they change durably, the first suspicion must be that they change for some solid reason. Even when the change is prompted by an event that might look random if one doesn't look too closely (say, being invaded by French armies), the next suspicion must be that the change stuck for some reason. It is not enough to drop a legal code onto a defeated nation to create a natural experiment. Nor can changes be always summarized by a crisp list of enacting dates, as if institutions were a panel of toggles and switches.

12.5.3 Models to structure a narrative: some examples

The nature and tradition of macroeconomics, as well as the added challenges of historical macroeconomics, help understand which tools have been used or not. Historical macroeconomics has its own tradition as well.

Friedman and Schwartz (1963) remains one of the most important texts for modern macroeconomists. They used high-powered money and two ratios (the deposit-to-reserve ratio, and the deposit-to-currency ratio, broadly capturing the behavior of the banking system and the public respectively) as "proximate determinants" of the stock of money. The core theoretical principle that makes it possible to construct a ninety-year history of the US macroeconomy on this basis, is the non-neutrality of money in the short run, and its neutrality on the long run. Variations in the money stock are used to account for departures from a trend impervious to those variations, in other words business cycles, and the proximate determinants are used to trace these variations either to monetary authorities or to shocks in the private sector (such as banking panics). But the book is not just a collection of tables and graphs: a detailed history is woven onto that frame, using as threads the documented motives and actions of the players. The normative implication is strong: whatever the source of monetary contraction (endogenous or exogenous), it would have been preferable for monetary authorities to counteract it. While the theoretical apparatus was incomplete, as Tobin (1965) pointed out, its impact was long-lasting because "it served the purpose that any narrative history must serve: it told a coherent story, and told it well" (Lucas, 1994).

The study of hyperinflations by Sargent (1983) came at a time when the rational expectations hypothesis was increasingly used to account for agents' expectations. In models with time and uncertainty, agents' perceptions about future events could not be ignored, and assuming rational expectations was a way to specify them in a coherent way: agents know the model no less than the modeler. The implications for current debates about the costs of bringing inflation under control were crisply summarized by Paul Samuelson: the proponents of the rational expectations hypothesis "are optimistic that inflation can be wiped out with little pain if only the government makes credible its determination to do so. But neither history nor reason tempt one to bet their way" (cited by Sargent 1983). Sargent took up the challenge: what did history have to say? Cagan (1956) and Sargent (1977) had studied the four post-World War I hyperinflations of Austria, Hungary, Poland, and Germany: Sargent (1983) studied their ends, and also considered the absence of hyperinflation in Czechoslovakia. He showed that the hyperinflations stopped abruptly once fiscal regimes had been changed and central banks prevented from financing deficits. Money stocks continued to grow but exchange rates and price levels stabilized nearly overnight.

In another broad narrative in monetary history, stretching over centuries, Sargent and Velde (2002) use a model to understand why the dysfunctions of commodity money systems in medieval and early modern Europe. Money consisted of gold and silver coins of various sizes. The coins were supplied by mints operating under specific rules: coins were provided on demand in exchange for metal at a stated price, providing an upper bound on their value. The ability to melt coins in excess of the transaction needs provided a lower bound. The system did not seem to supply coins of various denominations in adequate quantities, as recurrent shortages of small change indicated. Yet the solution, making all coins but the largest into tokens and pegging their value, was not widely known and adopted by the end of the 19th century. The model has the fewest elements necessary: it relies on two cash-in-advance constraints to generate distinct demands for small and large coins for the purchase of small and large goods. A shortage of small change is modeled as a binding "penny-in-advance" constraint. The model generates surprising results: when a shortage occurs, the large coin appreciates: the capital gain on the large coin compensates for its reduced usefulness in transactions, relative to the small coin. The prediction accounts for a secular trend of large coin appreciation relative to the small coin that is borne out in the data. The model can also account for instances when the solution was partially implemented: small coins made into tokens but without pegging their value, with resulting inflation. The simplicity of the solution contrasts with the time it took to implement it, and directs attention to the possible impediments: the concept of token coinage (or fiat money) and the technology to make counterfeit-proof tokens both had to be invented.

Velde and Weber (2000) study the existence and desirability of bimetallism as a monetary system, questions raised by Friedman (1990). Their model shows that bimetallism was not a knife-edge system oscillating between gold and silver, but allowed the two metals to circulate as money at an indeterminate (within bounds) parity. Their calibration suggests that bimetallism was not doomed to disappear when it did in 1873, in spite of the recent gold discoveries. The model they construct, in the tradition of Walras (1889) and Fisher (1911), also allows them to compute welfare, and they find that the steady state welfare cost of bimetallism (the value of metal in monetary form) is higher than that of monometallism.

12.5.4 Experiments?

The language of experiments permeates the tradition of historical macroeconomics. Friedman (1953, 11) (cited by Bordo and Rockoff 2013) uses it explicitly:

> *Occasionally, experience casts up evidence that is about as direct, dramatic, and convincing as any that could be provided by controlled experiments. Perhaps the most obviously important example is the evidence from inflations on the hypothesis that a substantial increase in the quantity of money within a relatively short period is accompanied by a substantial increase in prices. Here the evidence is dramatic, and the chain of reasoning required to interpret it is relatively short.*

Likewise, in their conclusion (Friedman and Schwartz, 1963, 696) write:

> *The varied character of U.S. monetary history renders this century of experience particularly valuable to the student of economic change. He cannot control the experiment, but he can observe monetary experience under sufficiently disparate conditions to sort out what is common from what is adventitious and to acquire considerable confidence that what is common can be counted on to hold.*

And Sargent (1983) also concludes: "The four incidents we have studied are akin to laboratory experiments in which the elemental forces that cause and can be used to stop inflation are easiest to spot."

The metaphor can be misleading: the process remains one of abstraction, in order to generate visible patterns. Sometimes the historical circumstances sharpen the focus and simplify the pattern, making abstraction easier. This is not, however, fundamentally different from the tradition of business cycle analysis from Burns and Mitchell (1946) through Prescott (1986) and Galí (2008), which abstracts from specific time paths to discern patterns: but the quest for patterns remains guided by a model.

Velde (2009), perhaps misleadingly, also uses the language of experiment in describing particular monetary policy actions taken in 1724 France.[6] Specifically, the actions formed a sequence of three overnight, unannounced reductions of the money supply in exact proportion to agents' money balances. The response of prices and output, and the reactions of contemporaries, are documented from archival sources. Although the word "experiment" is used repeatedly, there is no claim whatsoever that the 1724 episode is "natural", let alone plausibly exogenous or quasi-random: the policy was clearly not exogenous (it was a response to elevated prices) and it was unannounced but not necessarily unanticipated—indeed, expectations play a prominent role in contemporary explanations of price movements, and in the government's own rationale for the last of the three reductions. There is no control group and no cross-sectional variation to exploit: the whole country was subjected at once to the same policy, and the government took care that the policies be announced at exactly the same time everywhere.

The government's experiment was carefully designed, but not to simulate a pharmaceutical study. If it serves us, researchers, as an experiment, it does so in the sense of a thought experiment, such as those that Hume used to elucidate his reasoning about monetary non-neutralities (citing the same 1724 episode). What makes the story interesting is that the response of prices was not the one predicted by the government of the time, nor is it the one that follows from many standard models. Additionally, the circumstances do not satisfy assumptions (such as menu costs or rational inattention) commonly used to generate monetary non-neutralities. In short, the contribution, if any, is not to establish causation: it exists only within the context of models.

12.5.5 Off-the-rack or bespoke models

The examples of the previous section have in common that they use models of their time for their narratives, whether to shed light on current debates or to better understand the past. There are recent examples in this vein. Chen and Ward (2019) use a fairly standard macroeconomic approach to understand why economies under the gold standard (i.e., fixed exchange rates) responded to external shocks with little output loss. They include several possible channels (flexible prices, labor mobility, monetary policy) in an otherwise standard model, calibrate some parameters, estimate the others, and simulate the estimated model economy while counterfactually shutting down some channels to assess their relative importance. Price flexibility turns out to be the most important channel, and the primary sector, with the most flexible prices, dominated exports. Palma and Silva (2016) calibrate a general equilibrium model of the world economy to understand trade and metal flows between Asia and the rest of the world in the early modern period, and find that the metal discoveries in the New World vastly outweigh the lower trading costs to explain the increased trade.

This strategy is not always available. A strong theme of our survey is the diversity of arrangements, institutions, policies, and outcomes; unsurprising given that money, banking, and financial intermediation all presume some market incompleteness. Lucas (2013, 272) famously paraphrased Tolstoy's

---

[6] Angrist and Pischke (2010, 19) say it is as close to their sort of quasi-experimental work and one of the "rays of sunlight" poking through the "grey clouds" of DSGE. The author might be allowed to plead that it is, in fact, a counter-example.

observation about happy families to say that "complete market economies are all alike, but each incomplete market economy is incomplete in its own individual way." By "in its own way" Tolstoy, if not Lucas, meant that each has a different history.[7] There are examples of scholars using bespoke models in macroeconomic and financial history: Anderson et al. (2019) on bank networks in late 19th century US, Börner and Hatfield (2017) on medieval fairs, Koudijs (2015) on insiders in 18th century financial markets. The common approach is to tailor carefully a model built on standard theory in order to understand a set of events or a particular institution. The placement of such papers should be an encouraging sign for those not quite committed to the methods of quasi-experiments and long-run regressions. But more off-the-shelf, well-worn models of banks, markets, and financial systems will help.

12.5.6 Models arguing: the Great Inflation debate

In the 1990s and early 2000s there was an active debate about the so-called "Great Inflation" in the US, namely the rise and fall of inflation from the 1960s to the 1980s. While this might not qualify as quite historical (since macro-history seems to start with quarterly NIPA accounts in 1946), it involved some of the most prominent macroeconomists, yet its focus was a single sequence of events and its goal is to understand the process driving them.

Based on a broad narrative (mixing analyses of speeches, writings of policymakers and economists), De Long (1996) argued that the Great Inflation was due to the very high weight assigned to unemployment by monetary policy ("The memory left by the Depression predisposed the left and center to think that any unemployment was too much"). The measures to fight inflation starting 1979 are thus interpreted as a shift in beliefs.

Sargent (1999) took up De Long's idea, deepened the narrative and built a model to account for the change in policymakers beliefs and their impact on economic outcomes. Orphanides (2002) brought "archival material" into play to argue that policy actions can be explained by misinterpretations of the current data. Romer and Romer (2002) used extensively the archives of the Fed to provide evidence of the change in policymakers' beliefs over time. Based on records of the discussions at the Fed, they emphasized that it was not so much a too high weight on unemployment that led the Fed to run inflationary policies in the 1970s (because they adopted early the natural rate of unemployment theory) but an underestimation of the natural rate of unemployment.

In his discussion of Romer and Romer (2002), Sargent (2002) acknowledged the usefulness of their work but criticized the main conclusion based on the narrative approach because it lacked the kind of quantitative analysis that could take into account other parameters, especially the variety of shocks hitting the economy. That being said, Sargent included himself in the "Berkeley" view, together with the Romers and De Long, for emphasizing the importance of the changes in beliefs as an explanation of the Great Inflation. Cogley and Sargent (2005) responded to Romer and Romer (2002) by incorporating model uncertainty. They built a model where the central bank chooses (with uncertainty) at each period between several models of the world/Phillips curve and NAIRU.

Primiceri (2006) modeled and estimated directly the changes in beliefs of policymakers about the NAIRU over time. Sims and Zha (2006) criticized the literature by showing that, when accounting for

---

[7] Tolstoy was inspired by the French proverb that happy people have no history, which in turn seems to derive from the dictum of D'Alembert (1779, vii): "happy [fortunate] are the people with a boring history!" Over time the implication was reversed; then Tolstoy, as a novelist, redirected the statement from aggregates to households and from history to stories.

a wide range of shocks, they did not estimate drastic regime shift in the coefficients of the monetary policy rule over time. In turn, this literature continued to influence economic historians working with a qualitative or narrative approach. For example, Meltzer (2010) in his history of the Fed, Bordo and Eichengreen (2013), Weise (2012) emphasized that, besides internal beliefs and NAIRU estimates of the Fed, the pressures from the Treasury to keep interest rates low were of key importance.

The debate died out with the Great Recession and was left somewhat unresolved. Three views remained: a story based on luck (Sims and Zha, 2006); exogenous changes in policy that moved from a region of indeterminacy to determinacy (Lubik and Schorfheide, 2004); and the learning story (also Orphanides and Williams 2013), either about parameters of a model as in Primiceri (2006) or between different models as in Cogley and Sargent (2005).

The question throughout this literature is a simple, historical one: "Why did X happen?" At first sight this history for history's sake, arguing over a single data point without any attempt at establishing a causal relationship. But the debate was fruitful because models (more or less fleshed out, more or less confronted with observations) were arguing with each other and fighting to claim the data point. Whether or not a winner came out is of little importance: our knowledge and understanding of the (recent) past is deeper, our theoretical insights are sharper. Everyone gained.

12.6 Summary and conclusion

Money and banking is an important subfield of historical economics: it represents twelve out of sixty-five chapters in the recent *Handbook of Cliometrics* (Diebolt and Haupert, 2019) and was an important part of the earlier cliometrics revolution. Its own "bible" (Friedman and Schwartz, 1963) already contained the language of causality and "controlled experiments," long before the so-called credibility revolution (Angrist and Pischke, 2010). But this subfield has little embraced the two trends identified by the editors of the present volume, namely the search for long-run effects in persistence studies and the reduced-form empirics targeted at causality through quasi-random experiments. The latter method has been used in some papers to study local effects, but the subfield still relies on traditional approaches: long narratives, large data collection to document long-term trends, and the construction of arguments and narratives through monographs and not just sharply focused articles. It is also a subfield with, in our experience, meaningful interactions between historians and economists, which may not be typical of historical economics in general (Lamoreaux, 2015).

We speculated on the reasons for this difference. The new methods are ill-suited to answer the traditional questions of money and banking history: Why markets and financial institutions developed as they did? Why do monetary and financial institutions differ so much across time and space? Is capital efficiently allocated? Wherefore financial crises? There are no natural experiments to answer these questions. Other large questions, such as the impact of monetary shocks, have been addressed with different methods (Sims, 2010).

The interesting studies that use methods of empirical microeconomics rely on group comparisons rather than genuine natural experiment, and examine local and short-term effects. They are context-specific and difficult to generalize. This is consistent with the ongoing tradition of macroeconomics (Leamer, 2010; Sims, 2010) that highlights the difficulties left aside in the new "historical economics" literature but cannot be evaded in a general equilibrium setting.

It does not mean that causation is ignored, but it is understood differently: causality identified with a chain of events or relations, hence particular attention to the provision of plausible transmission mechanisms. Better yet, it is understood within a structural model, where causality has been explicitly asserted by the modeler, and where counterfactuals, the ultimate meaning of causality, are truly meaningful.

In the end, says Leamer (2010, 44), "we seek patterns and tell stories." He spoke as a macroeconomist, but those of the historical persuasion tend to agree (Antipa and Bignon, 2018). Are we, then, any better than epic poets? Not a bad thing to be, in our opinion. We have our prosody too: writing models and testing against data is our rhyme and meter. And if indeed we are just telling stories, we shouldn't fool ourselves that we aren't, yet we should fool ourselves, constantly, to tell better ones.

References

Abramitzky, R., 2015. Economics and the modern economic historian. The Journal of Economic History 75 (4), 1240–1251.

Accominotti, O., 2012. London Merchant Banks, the Central European Panic, and the Sterling Crisis of 1931. The Journal of Economic History 72 (1), 1–43.

Acheson, G.G., Campbell, G., Turner, J.D., 2019. Private contracting, law and finance. The Review of Financial Studies 32 (11), 4156–4195.

Anderson, H., Paddrik, M., Wang, J.J., 2019. Bank networks and systemic risk: evidence from the national banking acts. The American Economic Review 109 (9), 3125–3161.

Angrist, J.D., Pischke, J.-S., 2010. The credibility revolution in empirical economics: how better research design is taking the con out of econometrics. The Journal of Economic Perspectives 24 (2), 3–30.

Antipa, P., Bignon, V., 2018. Whither economic history? Between narratives and quantification. Revue de l'OFCE 157 (3), 17–36.

Arrow, K.J., Debreu, G., 1954. Existence of an equilibrium for a competitive economy. Econometrica 22 (3), 265.

Baubeau, P., Monnet, E., Riva, A., Ungaro, S., 2020. Flight-to-safety and the credit crunch: a new history of the banking crises in France during the Great Depression. Economic History Review.

Bazot, G., 2014. Local liquidity constraints: what place for central bank regional policy? The French experience during the belle epoque (1880–1913). Explorations in Economic History 52, 44–62.

Benmelech, E., Frydman, C., Papanikolaou, D., 2019. Financial frictions and employment during the Great Depression. JFE Special Issue on Labor and Finance. Journal of Financial Economics 133 (3), 541–563.

Bennett, A., Checkel, J.T. (Eds.), 2015. Process Tracing: From Metaphor to Analytic Tool. Cambridge University Press, Cambridge, New York.

Bernanke, B.S., 1983. Nonmonetary effects of the financial crisis in the propagation of the Great Depression. The American Economic Review 73 (3), 257–276.

Bernstein, A., Hughson, E., Weidenmier, M., 2019. Counterparty risk and the establishment of the New York stock exchange clearinghouse. Journal of Political Economy 127 (2), 689–729.

Bignon, V., Flandreau, M., Ugolini, S., 2011. Bagehot for beginners: the making of lender-of-last-resort operations in the mid-nineteenth century. The Economic History Review 65 (2), 580–608.

Bindseil, U., 2020. Central Banking Before 1800: A Rehabilitation. Oxford University Press, Oxford.

Bordo, M.D., Eichengreen, B., 2013. Bretton Woods and the Great Inflation. In: Bordo, M.D., Orphanides, A. (Eds.), The Great Inflation: The Rebirth of Modern Central Banking. University of Chicago Press, pp. 449–489.

Bordo, M.D., Eichengreen, B., Klingebiel, D., Martinez-Peria, M.S., 2001. Is the crisis problem growing more severe? Economic Policy 16 (32), 52–82.

Bordo, M.D., Eitrheim, Ø., Flandreau, M., Qvigstad, J.F., 2016. Central Banks at a Crossroads: What Can We Learn from History? Cambridge University Press, Cambridge and New York.

Bordo, M.D., Flandreau, M., 2003. Core, periphery, exchange rate regimes, and globalization. In: Globalization in Historical Perspective. University of Chicago Press, pp. 417–472.

Bordo, M.D., Meissner, C.M., 2006. The role of foreign currency debt in financial crises: 1880–1913 versus 1972–1997. Journal of Banking & Finance 30 (12), 3299–3329.

Bordo, M.D., Meissner, C.M., 2016. Fiscal and financial crises. In: Handbook of Macroeconomics, vol. 2. Elsevier, pp. 355–412.

Bordo, M.D., Monnet, E., Naef, A., 2019. The Gold Pool (1961–1968) and the fall of the Bretton Woods system: lessons for central bank cooperation. The Journal of Economic History 79 (4), 1027–1059.

Bordo, M.D., Redish, A., Rockoff, H., 2015. Why didn't Canada have a banking crisis in 2008 (or in 1930, or 1907, or...)? The Economic History Review 68 (1), 218–243.

Bordo, M.D., Rockoff, H., 2013. Not just the great contraction: Friedman and Schwartz's a monetary history of the United States 1867 to 1960. The American Economic Review 103 (3), 61–65.

Börner, L., Hatfield, J.W., 2017. The design of debt-clearing markets: clearinghouse mechanisms in preindustrial Europe. Journal of Political Economy 125 (6), 1991–2037.

Bourgeois-Gironde, S., Monnet, É., 2017. Expériences naturelles et causalité en histoire économique: Quels rapports à la théorie et à la temporalité? Annales. Histoire, Sciences Sociales 72 (4), 1087–1116.

Braggion, F., Dwarkasing, N., Moore, L., 2017. Nothing special about banks: competition and bank lending in Britain, 1885–1925. The Review of Financial Studies 30 (10), 3502–3537.

Burns, A.F., Mitchell, W.C., 1946. Measuring Business Cycles. NBER, New York.

Cagan, P., 1956. The monetary dynamics of hyperinflation. In: Friedman, M. (Ed.), Studies in the Quantity Theory of Money. Chicago University Press, Chicago, pp. 25–117.

Calomiris, C.W., Haber, S.H., 2015. Fragile by Design: The Political Origins of Banking Crises and Scarce Credit. Princeton University Press, Princeton, NJ.

Calomiris, C.W., Jaremski, M., 2019. Stealing deposits: deposit insurance, risk-taking, and the removal of market discipline in early 20th-century banks. The Journal of Finance 74 (2), 711–754.

Calomiris, C.W., Mason, J.R., 2003. Fundamentals, panics, and bank distress during the depression. The American Economic Review 93 (5), 1615–1647.

Carlson, M.A., Correia, S., Luck, S., 2018. The effects of banking competition on growth and financial stability: evidence from the national banking era. SSRN Electronic Journal.

Carlson, M., Mitchener, K.J., Richardson, G., 2011. Arresting banking panics: Federal Reserve liquidity provision and the forgotten panic of 1929. Journal of Political Economy 119 (5), 889–924.

Carlson, M., Wheelock, D.C., 2018. Did the founding of the Federal Reserve affect the vulnerability of the interbank system to contagion risk? Journal of Money, Credit, and Banking 50 (8), 1711–1750.

Cerretano, V., 2009. The treasury, Britain's postwar reconstruction, and the industrial intervention of the bank of England, 1921–91. The Economic History Review 62, 80–100.

Chari, V.V., Kehoe, P.J., 1990. Sustainable plans. Journal of Political Economy 98 (4), 783–802.

Chemla, G., Hennessy, C.A., 2020. Rational expectations and the paradox of policy-relevant natural experiments. Journal of Monetary Economics 114, 368–381.

Chen, Y., Ward, F., 2019. When do fixed exchange rates work? Evidence from the Gold Standard. Journal of International Economics 116, 158–172.

Cogley, T., Sargent, T.J., 2005. The conquest of US inflation: learning and robustness to model uncertainty. Review of Economic Dynamics 8 (2), 528–563.

Collier, D., 2011. Understanding process tracing. PS: Political Science and Politics 44 (4), 823–830.

Colvin, C.L., McLaughlin, E., 2014. Raiffeisenism abroad: why did German cooperative banking fail in Ireland but prosper in the Netherlands? The Economic History Review 67 (2), 492–516.

Costabile, L., Neal, L. (Eds.), 2018. Financial Innovation and Resilience: A Comparative Perspective on the Public Banks of Naples (1462-1808). Palgrave Macmillan, London.

Coyle, C., Musacchio, A., Turner, J.D., 2019. Law and finance in Britain c.1900. SSRN Electronic Journal.

Cull, R., Davis, L.E., Lamoreaux, N.R., Rosenthal, J.-L., 2006. Historical financing of small- and medium-size enterprises. Journal of Banking & Finance 30 (11), 3017–3042.

D'Alembert, 1779. Éloges lus dans les séances publiques de l'Académie française. Pancoucke, Moutard, Paris.

De Long, J.B., 1996. America's Only Peacetime Inflation: The 1970s. Technical report.

Debreu, G., 1959. Theory of Value: An Axiomatic Analysis of Economic Equilibrium. Yale University Press, New Haven, CT and London.

Degorce, V., Monnet, E., 2020. The Great Depression as a Saving Glut. Discussion paper 15287. CEPR.

Diebolt, C., Haupert, M. (Eds.), 2019. Handbook of Cliometrics. Springer, Berlin, Heidelberg.

Edvinsson, R., Jacobson, T., Waldenström, D., 2018. Sveriges Riksbank and the History of Central Banking. Cambridge University Press.

Eichengreen, B., Mitchener, K.J., 2004. The Great Depression as a credit boom gone wrong. Research in Economic History 22, 183–238.

Esteves, R., Khoudour-Castéras, D., 2009. A fantastic rain of gold: European migrants' remittances and balance of payments adjustment during the Gold Standard period. The Journal of Economic History 69 (4), 951–985.

Fisher, I., 1911. The Purchasing Power of Money; Its Determination and Relation to Credit, Interest and Crises. The Macmillan Company, New York.

Flandreau, M., Flores, J.H., 2009. Bonds and brands: foundations of sovereign debt markets, 1820–1830. The Journal of Economic History 69 (3), 646–684.

Flandreau, M., Jobst, C., 2005. The ties that divide: a network analysis of the international monetary system, 1890-1910. The Journal of Economic History 65 (4), 977–1007.

Fohlin, C., 2012. Mobilizing Money: How the World's Richest Nations Financed Industrial Growth. Cambridge University Press, Cambridge, New York.

Friedman, M., 1953. The methodology of positive economics. In: Essays in Positive Economics. University of Chicago Press, Chicago and London, pp. 3–42.

Friedman, M., 1990. Bimetallism revisited. The Journal of Economic Perspectives 4 (4), 85–104.

Friedman, M., Schwartz, A.J., 1963. A Monetary History of the United States, 1867–1960. Princeton University Press, Princeton, NJ.

Frydman, C., Hilt, E., Zhou, L.Y., 2015. Economic effects of runs on early "Shadow Banks": trust companies and the impact of the panic of 1907. Journal of Political Economy 123 (4), 902–940.

Fuchs-Schündeln, N., Hassan, T.A., 2016. Natural experiments in macroeconomics. In: Handbook of Macroeconomics. Elsevier, pp. 923–1012.

Galí, J., 2008. Monetary Policy, Inflation, and the Business Cycle: An Introduction to the New Keynesian Framework. Princeton University Press, Princeton, NJ.

Gelderblom, O., Jonker, J., 2004. Completing a financial revolution: the finance of the Dutch East India trade and the rise of the Amsterdam capital market, 1595–1612. The Journal of Economic History 64 (3), 641–672.

Gelderblom, O., Jonker, J., 2011. Public finance and economic growth: the case of Holland in the seventeenth century. The Journal of Economic History, 1–39.

Gelderblom, O., Jonker, J., Kool, C., 2016. Direct finance in the Dutch Golden Age. The Economic History Review 69 (4), 1178–1198.

Gershenkron, A., 1963. Economic Backwardness in Historical Perspective: A Book of Essays. Bellknap Press of Harvard University Press, Cambridge, MA.

Goldsmith, R., 1969. Financial Structure and Development. Yale University Press, New Haven, CT.

Gorton, G.B., Tallman, E.W., 2018. Fighting Financial Crises: Learning from the Past. University of Chicago Press, Chicago.

Gorton, G., Laarits, T., Muir, T., 2019. 1930. First Modern Crisis. Working paper 25452. National Bureau of Economic Research.

Grossman, R.S., 2010. Unsettled Account: The Evolution of Banking in the Industrialized World Since 1800. Princeton University Press, Princeton, NJ.

Guinnane, T.W., 2001. Cooperatives as information machines: German rural credit cooperatives, 1883-1914. The Journal of Economic History 61 (2), 366–389.

Haavelmo, T., 1943. The statistical implications of a system of simultaneous equations. Econometrica 11 (1), 1–12.

Haavelmo, T., 1944. The probability approach in econometrics. Econometrica 12, iii–vi, 1–115.

Hautcoeur, P.-C., Riva, A., 2012. The Paris financial market in the nineteenth century: complementarities and competition in microstructures. The Economic History Review 65 (4), 1326–1353.

Hautcoeur, P.-C., Riva, A., White, E.N., 2014. Floating a "lifeboat": the Banque de France and the crisis of 1889. Journal of Monetary Economics 65, 104–119.

Heckman, J.J., 2000. Causal parameters and policy analysis in economics: a twentieth century retrospective. The Quarterly Journal of Economics 115 (1), 45–97.

Heckman, J., Pinto, R., 2014. Causal analysis after Haavelmo. Econometric Theory 31 (1), 115–151.

Hitchcock, C., 2020. Causal models. In: Zalta, E.N. (Ed.), The Stanford Encyclopedia of Philosophy, Summer 2020. Metaphysics Research Lab, Stanford University.

Hoffman, P.T., Postel-Vinay, G., Rosenthal, J.-L., 2000. Priceless Markets: The Political Economy of Credit in Paris, 1660-1870. University of Chicago Press.

Hoffman, P.T., Postel-Vinay, G., Rosenthal, J.-L., 2019. Dark Matter Credit: The Development of Peer-to-Peer Lending and Banking in France. Princeton University Press, Princeton, NJ.

Jaremski, M., 2018. The (dis)advantages of clearinghouses before the Fed. Journal of Financial Economics 127 (3), 435–458.

Jaremski, M., Mathy, G., 2018. How was the quantitative easing program of the 1930s unwound? Explorations in Economic History 69, 27–49.

Jobst, C., Kernbauer, H., 2016. The Quest for Stable Money: Central Banking in Austria, 1816-2016. Campus Verlag.

Karaman, K.K., Pamuk, Ş., Yıldırım-Karaman, S., 2020. Money and monetary stability in Europe, 1300–1914. Journal of Monetary Economics 115, 279–300.

Khwaja, A.I., Mian, A., 2008. Tracing the impact of bank liquidity shocks: evidence from an emerging market. The American Economic Review 98 (4), 1413–1442.

Kindleberger, C.P., 1984. A Financial History of Western Europe. Allen & Unwin, London and Boston.

Klovland, J.T., Øksendal, L.F., 2017. The decentralized central bank: bank rate autonomy and capital market integration in Norway, 1850–1892. European Review of Economic History 21 (3), 259–279.

Klug, A., Landon-Lane, J.S., White, E.N., 2005. How could everyone have been so wrong? Forecasting the great depression with the railroads. Explorations in Economic History 42 (1), 27–55.

Koudijs, P., 2015. Those who know most: insider trading in eighteenth-century Amsterdam. Journal of Political Economy 123 (6), 1356–1409.

Koudijs, P., Voth, H.-J., 2016. Leverage and beliefs: personal experience and risk-taking in margin lending. The American Economic Review 106 (11), 3367–3400.

La Porta, R., Lopez-de-Silanes, F., Shleifer, A., Vishny, R.W., 1998. Law and finance. Journal of Political Economy 106 (6), 1113–1155.

Lamoreaux, N., 2015. The future of economic history must be interdisciplinary. The Journal of Economic History 75 (4), 1251–1257.

Lamoreaux, N.R., Rosenthal, J.-L., 2005. Legal regime and contractual flexibility: a comparison of business's organizational choices in France and the United States during the era of industrialization. American Law and Economics Review 7 (1), 28–61.

Leamer, E.E., 2010. Tantalus on the road to asymptopia. Journal of Economic Perspectives 24 (2), 31–46.

Lehmann, S.H., 2014. Taking firms to the stock market: IPOs and the importance of large banks in Imperial Germany, 1896–1913. The Economic History Review 67 (1), 92–122.

Lehmann-Hasemeyer, S., Streb, J., 2016. The Berlin stock exchange in Imperial Germany: a market for new technology? The American Economic Review 106 (11), 3558–3576.

Lubik, T.A., Schorfheide, F., 2004. Testing for indeterminacy: an application to U.S. monetary policy. The American Economic Review 94 (1), 190–217.

Lucas Jr, R.E., 1994. Review of Milton Friedman and Anna J. Schwartz's 'a monetary history of the United States, 1867–1960'. Journal of Monetary Economics 34 (1), 5–16.

Lucas Jr, R.E., 2013. Collected Papers on Monetary Theory. Harvard University Press.

Lucas Jr, R.E., Sargent, T.J., 1981. Introduction. In: Rational Expectations and Econometric Practice: Volume 1, NED - new edition. University of Minnesota Press, pp. xi–xl.

Marschak, J., 1953. Economic measurements for policy and prediction. In: Hood, W.C., Koopmans, T.C. (Eds.), Studies in Econometric Method. John Wiley & Sons, Inc., London, pp. 1–27.

McKenzie, L., 1954. On equilibrium in Graham's model of world trade and other competitive systems. Econometrica 22 (2), 147.

Meissner, C.M., Taylor, A.M., et al., 2006. Losing our Marbles in the New Century? The Great Rebalancing in Historical Perspective. Technical report. National Bureau of Economic Research, Inc.

Meltzer, A.H., 2010. A History of the Federal Reserve. University of Chicago Press, Chicago.

Mitchener, K.J., 2005. Bank supervision, regulation, and instability during the Great Depression. The Journal of Economic History 65 (1), 152–185.

Mitchener, K.J., 2015. The 4D future of economic history: digitally-driven data design. The Journal of Economic History 75 (4), 1234–1239.

Mitchener, K.J., Jaremski, M., 2015. The evolution of bank supervisory institutions: evidence from American States. The Journal of Economic History 75 (3), 819–859.

Mitchener, K.J., Richardson, G., 2019. Network contagion and interbank amplification during the Great Depression. Journal of Political Economy 127 (2), 465–507.

Moen, J.R., Tallman, E.W., 2000. Clearinghouse membership and deposit contraction during the panic of 1907. The Journal of Economic History 60 (1), 145–163.

Monnet, E., 2014. Monetary policy without interest rates: evidence from France's Golden Age (1948 to 1973) using a narrative approach. American Economic Journal: Macroeconomics 6 (4), 137–169.

Monnet, E., 2018. Controlling Credit: Central Banking and the Planned Economy in Postwar France, 1948–1973. Cambridge University Press.

Musacchio, A., 2008. Can civil law countries get good institutions? Lessons from the history of creditor rights and bond markets in Brazil. The Journal of Economic History 68 (1), 80–108.

Musacchio, A., Lazzarini, S.G., 2014. Reinventing State Capitalism: Leviathan in Business, Brazil and Beyond. Harvard University Press, Cambridge, MA.

Musacchio, A., Turner, J.D., 2013. Does the law and finance hypothesis pass the test of history? Business History 55 (4), 524–542.

Nakamura, E., Steinsson, J., 2018. Identification in macroeconomics. The Journal of Economic Perspectives 32 (3), 59–86.

Neal, L.D., Weidenmier, M.D., 2003. Crises in the global economy from tulips to today. In: Globalization in Historical Perspective. University of Chicago Press, pp. 473–514.

Obstfeld, M., Taylor, A.M., 2005. Global Capital Markets: Integration, Crisis, and Growth. Cambridge University Press.

Orphanides, A., 2002. Monetary-policy rules and the Great Inflation. The American Economic Review 92 (2), 115–120.

Orphanides, A., Williams, J.C., 2013. Monetary policy mistakes and the evolution of inflation expectations. In: Bordo, M.D., Orphanides, A. (Eds.), The Great Inflation: The Rebirth of Modern Central Banking. University of Chicago Press, pp. 449–489.

O'Sullivan, M.A., 2016. Dividends of Development: Securities Markets in the History of US Capitalism, 1866–1922. Oxford University Press.

Palma, N., Silva, A.C., 2016. Spending a Windfall: American Precious Metals and Euro-Asian Trade 1531-1810. GGDC Research Memorandum, vol. 165. University of Groningen, Groningen.

Park, H., Van Horn, P., 2015. Did the reserve requirement increases of 1936-37 reduce bank lending? Evidence from a quasi-experiment. Journal of Money, Credit, and Banking 47 (5), 791–818.

Poincaré, H., 1902. La Science et l'Hypothèse. Ernest Flammarion, Paris.

Postel-Vinay, N., 2016. Debt dilution in 1920s America: lighting the fuse of a mortgage crisis. The Economic History Review 70 (2), 559–585.

Prescott, E.C., 1986. Theory ahead of business-cycle measurement. Carnegie-Rochester Conference Series on Public Policy 25, 11–44.

Primiceri, G.E., 2006. Why inflation rose and fell: policy-makers' beliefs and U. S. postwar stabilization policy. The Quarterly Journal of Economics 121 (3), 867–901.

Quinn, S., Roberds, W., 2007. The Bank of Amsterdam and the leap to Central Bank money. The American Economic Review 97 (2), 262–265.

Quinn, S., Roberds, W., 2014. The Bank of Amsterdam through the lens of monetary competition. In: Financial and Monetary Policy Studies. Springer International Publishing, pp. 283–300.

Quinn, S., Roberds, W., 2015. Responding to a shadow banking crisis: the lessons of 1763. Journal of Money, Credit, and Banking 47 (6), 1149–1176.

Quinn, S., Roberds, W., 2019. A policy framework for the Bank of Amsterdam, 1736–1791. The Journal of Economic History 79 (3), 736–772.

Rajan, R.G., Zingales, L., 1998. Financial dependence and growth. The American Economic Review 88 (3), 559–586.

Rappoport, P., White, E.N., 1994. Was the crash of 1929 expected? The American Economic Review 84 (1), 271–281.

Reiss, J., 2005. Causal instrumental variables and interventions. Philosophy of Science 72 (5), 964–976.

Richardson, G., 2007a. Categories and causes of bank distress during the great depression, 1929–1933: the illiquidity versus insolvency debate revisited. Explorations in Economic History 44 (4), 588–607.

Richardson, G., 2007b. The check is in the mail: correspondent clearing and the collapse of the banking system, 1930 to 1933. The Journal of Economic History, 643–671.

Richardson, G., Troost, W., 2009. Monetary intervention mitigated banking panics during the great depression: quasi-experimental evidence from a Federal Reserve district border, 1929–1933. Journal of Political Economy 117 (6), 1031–1073.

Richardson, G., Van Horn, P., 2009. Intensified regulatory scrutiny and bank distress in New York city during the Great Depression. The Journal of Economic History 69 (2), 446–465.

Richardson, G., Van Horn, P., 2018. In the eye of a storm: Manhattan's Money Center Banks during the international financial crisis of 1931. Explorations in Economic History 68, 71–94.

Roberds, W., Velde, F.R., 2016a. Early public banks I: ledger-money banks. In: Fox, D., Ernst, W. (Eds.), Money in the LEgal Western Tradition: Middle Ages to Bretton Woods. Oxford University Press, Oxford, pp. 321–355.

Roberds, W., Velde, F.R., 2016b. Early public banks II: banks of issue. In: Fox, D., Ernst, W. (Eds.), Money in the LEgal Western Tradition: Middle Ages to Bretton Woods. Oxford University Press, Oxford, pp. 465–488.

Roberds, W., Velde, F.R., 2016c. The descent of central banks. In: Bordo, M.D., Eitrheim, Ø., Flandreau, M., Qvigstad, J.F. (Eds.), Central Banks at a Crossroads: What Can We Learn from History? Cambridge University Press, New York, pp. 18–61.

Romer, C.D., Romer, D.H., 2002. The evolution of economic understanding and postwar stabilization policy. In: Rethinking Stabilization Policy. Federal Reserve Bank of Kansas City, Kansas City, MO, pp. 11–78.

Romer, C.D., Romer, D.H., 2004. A new measure of monetary shocks: derivation and implications. The American Economic Review 94 (4), 1055–1084.

Salmon, W.C., 1998. Causality and Explanation. Oxford University Press, New York.

Sargent, T.J., 1977. The demand for money during hyperinflations under rational expectations: I. International Economic Review 18 (1), 59–82.

Sargent, T.J., 1983. The ends of four big inflations. In: Hall, R.E. (Ed.), Inflation. University of Chicago Press, Chicago.

Sargent, T.J., 1999. The Conquest of American Inflation. Princeton University Press, Princeton, NJ.

Sargent, T.J., 2002. Commentary: the evolution of economic understanding and postwar stabilization policy. In: Rethinking Stabilization Policy. Federal Reserve Bank of Kansas City, Kansas City, MO.

Sargent, T.J., Velde, F.R., 2002. The Big Problem of Small Change. Princeton University Press, Princeton, NJ.

Schnabel, I., 2004. The German twin crisis of 1931. The Journal of Economic History, 822–871.

Schnabel, I., Shin, H.S., 2004. Liquidity and contagion: the crisis of 1763. Journal of the European Economic Association 2 (6), 929–968.

Schularick, M., Taylor, A.M., 2012. Credit booms gone bust: monetary policy, leverage cycles, and financial crises, 1870–2008. The American Economic Review 102 (2), 1029–1061.

Sgard, J., 2006. Do legal origins matter? The case of bankruptcy laws in Europe 1808–1914. European Review of Economic History 10 (3), 389–419.

Sims, C.A., 2010. But economics is not an experimental science. The Journal of Economic Perspectives 24 (2), 59–68.

Sims, C.A., Zha, T., 2006. Were there regime switches in U.S. monetary policy? The American Economic Review 96 (1), 54–81.

Straumann, T., Kugler, P., Weber, F., 2017. How the German crisis of 1931 swept across Europe: a comparative view from Stockholm. The Economic History Review 70 (1), 224–247.

Tobin, J., 1965. The monetary interpretation of history. The American Economic Review 55 (3), 464–485.

Toniolo, G., White, E.N., 2015. The Evolution of the Financial Stability Mandate: from its Origins to the Present Day. Working paper 20844. National Bureau of Economic Research.

Ugolini, S., 2017. The Evolution of Central Banking: Theory and History. Palgrave Macmillan, UK.

Velde, F.R., 2009. Chronicle of a deflation unforetold. Journal of Political Economy 117 (4), 591–634.

Velde, F.R., Weber, W.E., 2000. A model of bimetallism. Journal of Political Economy 108 (6), 1210–1234.

Walras, L., 1889. Éléments D'Économie Politique Pure ou Théorie de la Richesse Sociale, 2nd ed. F. Rouge, Guillaumin & Cie, Duncker & Humblot, Lausanne, Paris, Leipzig.

Wandschneider, K., 2015. Landschaften as credit purveyors—the example of East Prussia. The Journal of Economic History 75 (3), 791–818.

Weise, C.L., 2012. Political pressures on monetary policy during the US Great Inflation. American Economic Journal: Macroeconomics 4 (2), 33–64.

Xu, C., 2018. Reshaping Global Trade: The Immediate and Long-Run Effects of Bank Failures. Technical report. Working paper.

Institutional change and institutional persistence

Daron Acemoglu[a], Georgy Egorov[b,c], and Konstantin Sonin[d]
[a]*Massachusetts Institute of Technology, Cambridge, MA, United States*
[b]*Northwestern University–Kellogg School of Management, Evanston, IL, United States*
[c]*NBER, Cambridge, MA, United States*
[d]*University of Chicago, Chicago, IL, United States*

13.1 Introduction

A central question of social science is the way in which history influences current outcomes. This is doubly true for institutional investigations, since institutions, as constraints on human behavior and a framework for coordinating expectations, are only meaningful if they are at least to some degree durable.[1] Few commentators or social scientists doubt that the U.S. Constitution, ratified on June 21, 1788, and its first 10 amendments, the Bill of Rights, adopted on December 15, 1791, have shaped U.S. institutions and society ever since (Holton, 2008). But why and how have they had this lasting effect? They could have been completely cast aside or ignored. Indeed, every newly independent South American country also adopted a constitution, in many cases a few decades after and often modeled on the American one (Billias, 2009). But all of them have been superseded by new constitutions, in most cases very different in intent or form than the original one.

Indeed, change is as much a part of our experience as is persistence. Though the U.S. is an exemplar of institutional persistence, there is little similarity between how politics worked in the United States at the end of the 18th century and how it is organized today, and even the laws look very different. So how and why have U.S. institutions persisted? More importantly, what determines when institutions persist and when they change?

This is partly an empirical question. The persistence of the U.S. Constitution has many peculiarities. It originally specified, among other things, that slavery was legal, and slaves could be owned and had no rights, certainly no voting rights. And yet they would count as 3/5th of a free person when it came to apportioning voting power and resources across the 13 original colonies. Fortunately, these provisions have since been thrown out, even if we all think that the Constitution has had a durable impact on our politics. The Constitution has persisted partly because of the Union's victory in the Civil War in 1865, which did fundamentally change some of its provisions (but at the same time also reaffirmed the unity of the country against the secessionist South). The broad consensus on the persistence of the U.S. Constitution notwithstanding, these provisions have since been thrown out. So even in this canonical example of institutional durability, persistence, and change have been interwoven.

---

[1] See below for the most common definitions of "institutions" in the literature.

The Handbook of Historical Economics. https://doi.org/10.1016/B978-0-12-815874-6.00021-6

In fact, the story of American institutional persistence is even more complex than that. The Civil War was fought largely on the question of slavery, and even before the Confederate armies were defeated, on September 22, 1862, President Abraham Lincoln issued the Emancipation Proclamation, declaring that slavery would end. Following victory, the Thirteenth, Fourteenth, and Fifteenth amendments freed the slaves, granted citizenship and equal protection to all freedmen, and made the denial of the vote on the basis of "race, color, or previous condition of servitude" illegal — as radical a change in institutions as one can imagine. Though these amendments and the stationing of Northern troops in the South ushered in the period of Reconstruction, during which Blacks made important economic, social, and political progress, this was short-lived. Reconstruction was replaced by Redemption, in which the reactionary forces set about to "redeem" the South. This meant the reimposition of many of the slavery-era economic practices, forcing Blacks into low-wage, low-skill, and coercive labor relations on large plantations (Wiener, 1978). Redemption turned into Jim Crow, in which an extreme form of social and economic discrimination was coupled with systematic economic subjugation and complete political disenfranchisement of Blacks, the Fifteenth amendment notwithstanding (Woodward, 1955; Wright, 2013).

The peculiarities of American persistence and change are the subject matter of a voluminous history literature, as are many other questions of institutional persistence. Nevertheless, a conceptual framework is useful for orienting ourselves. Though no other historical episode has the same exact features as the circuitous history of slavery in the U.S. South, we can understand the economic and political reasons for why certain groups wanted to reimpose coercive labor relations on Southern Blacks and why and how they succeeded (and why and how, ultimately, their project failed with the sweeping changes of the Civil Rights era).

The aim of this essay is to provide conceptual tools for clarifying some of the factors underpinning institutional persistence and institutional change. Our purpose is to present a simple framework that can help elucidate the channels of persistence and change in institutions across a range of historical episodes. For this reason, we eschew mathematical formalism and refer the reader to Acemoglu et al. (2015, 2018) for more formal treatments (as well as to Roberts (2015), Lagunoff (2001), Battaglini and Coate (2007), Acemoglu et al. (2008), and Acemoglu and Robinson (2008) for related and complementary frameworks) as background to the more informal discussion here.

Our framework is a simple dynamic game-theoretic model, with society consisting of a number of groups of individuals who have preferences over policy and over institutional arrangements (which determine what types of economic relations are possible, for example). Individuals are potentially forward-looking and may care not just about current outcomes but also the future. Institutions (most closely corresponding to political institutions, though they may have social elements as well) determine the distribution of political power in society. This generates another indirect preference over institutions — individuals would be better off with institutional arrangements that empower their group in both policy choices and decisions over future institutional decisions. This desire to influence future institutions is of course related to the reason why Southern elites in the mid-19th century were willing to secede from the rest of the U.S. and when that was not possible, fight a major war, in order to have a say on future institutions (Potter, 1976; Weingast, 1998).

Using this framework, we first highlight the simplest type of institutional persistence, which we call "institutional stasis". This is an unchanging institutional equilibrium: the same institutional arrangement we start with repeats itself over and over again. There are several reasons for institutional stasis, but the most important one is that power begets power. That is, groups that are empowered by current institutions benefit from these institutions and thus use their power in order to maintain them, in the process reproducing their own power over the future institutions. In the case of the U.S. South, these dynamics were certainly important. Large plantation owners were the group that held the greatest power in the antebellum period, and this group was both fairly cohesive and convinced that the political and economic institutions undergirding slavery were in their best interest. Their grip on power and cohesiveness were sufficiently powerful that even after Reconstruction, they were able to maintain much of their political power (Wiener, 1978).

Nevertheless, as our discussion so far has already indicated, when people informally talk of the U.S. Constitution having had a durable effect, this type of stasis is not necessarily what they have in mind — the U.S. society has been anything but unchanging, and the institutional changes in Latin America or the Caribbean have been even more sweeping. Yet, many social scientists' views of institutional persistence are shaped by this type of institutional stasis and the power-begets-power dynamics. For example, Engerman and Sokoloff's famous thesis on the institutional problems of Latin America emphasizes how colonial practices created economic inequality, and this economic inequality empowered the rich segments of society, leading to institutional persistence (Engerman and Sokoloff, 1997). There are certainly examples of this type of institutional stasis, including some in Latin America (see below our discussion of Guatemala), in the U.S. South itself before the Civil War, and in North Korea today. However, as we discuss below, most institutional persistence in Latin America did not take this form, and even when inequality was persistent and had institutional roots, this was neither because the same elites kept power nor because the economic system perpetually remained the same. In practice, persistence often takes a much richer and varied form than institutional stasis.

To understand these richer institutional dynamics, we begin with an evaluation of the forces that lead to change in the first place. We emphasize two interlinked factors and how our framework sheds light on their functioning. First, there may be an incongruence between political and economic arrangements. Stasis does not follow simply from the fact that power begets power; it also requires that those who are so empowered want to maintain the current institutional arrangements. But imagine that groups that are empowered under current institutions prefer a different set of institutional arrangements. This could be, for example, because of economic reasons: repressive institutions may create major economic costs, which even the group controlling political power may want to avoid. An example of this phenomenon from recent history is the (political) elite-driven reform movement in the Soviet Union that gathered steam in the 1980s. There was no necessity that the Soviet Union would start unwinding and ultimately collapse in three short years between 1989 and 1991. The Communist Party certainly had sufficient political control and coercive power to keep things as they were, and there were many who wanted to do so. But sufficiently powerful constituencies became convinced that the economic costs of this strategy would be prohibitive and decided to engineer a reform process instead. Their plan was to undertake limited reform, modernizing the economy but maintaining the communist regime more or less intact (Roland, 1991). But the reality of institutional change was more complicated, as we discuss below.

A classic historical example of this type of institutional reform is North and Weingast's theory of the Glorious Revolution as an institutional commitment to repaying government debt, which then unleashed a process of deeper political change (North and Weingast, 1989). Many Marxist theories of the transition from feudalism to capitalism also fall within this broad category, emphasizing the internal contradictions of the feudal system, especially once towns and proto-industries started flourishing.[2] Yet another example of this logic is the theory of democracy in Lizzeri and Persico (2004), where the elites may decide to broaden the franchise because within-elite competition in a regime with a narrow franchise becomes increasingly costly to themselves.

Second, even if the politically powerful have no direct economic benefits from initiating institutional change, the threat of political reactions from non-elites can induce them to do so. Economic and political conditions in almost every society are in constant flux. This is particularly true in nondemocratic political systems, where the control of elites over the political system depends on the inability of the disempowered majority to organize and solve their collective action problem. Changes in the *de facto* power of non-elites occur occasionally, however, and both such changes themselves and their anticipation can become powerful drivers of institutional change. For instance, following episodic periods of unrest or revolutionary fervor, major institutional changes may be imposed upon the elites (as the imperial aristocracy of Russia experienced in the midst of the Russo-Japanese war in 1904-05 and even more starkly, after the Bolshevik revolution in 1917, see Service, 2005). Alternatively, the elites may realize that they need to initiate reform themselves in order to prevent even worse outcomes. Acemoglu and Robinson (2000, 2006b) argue that the emergence of democracy in many countries in Europe and some in Latin America during the 19th and early 20th centuries illustrates this logic. In their theory, when citizens solve their collective action problem during temporary windows of opportunity, they acquire *de facto* power to challenge the prevailing system. Elites may then wish to make a commitment to a political system that will be more responsive to their demands as a way of placating these actions. Democratization is an effective commitment device of this sort, because it distributes political power more equally in society (Acemoglu and Robinson, 2006b).

These sources of incongruence between economic and political considerations do not always lead to institutional change, however. This is because of the possibility of what we call "strategic stability": politically powerful groups may refrain from institutional change because they are concerned about subsequent institutional dynamics. This idea has emerged in the literature in a number of distinct forms. Fernandez and Rodrik (1991) pointed out that inability to ensure *ex post* redistribution of gains may induce risk-averse agents to block reforms that have uncertain returns, thus ensuring institutional stability. Acemoglu and Robinson (2006a) argued that what they call the "political loser effect" (the fear of losing political power) can often be a paralyzing force against institutional reform, even when such reform can bring economic benefits and even military improvements. Acemoglu et al. (2012) provide a general theory of "slippery slopes" that formalizes this type of strategic stability. Our framework provides a simple way of thinking about strategic stability and its implications. Several historical examples, as we discuss in greater detail below, feature this type of strategic considerations in the institutional calculus of powerful groups. An obvious case is the process of reform in the Soviet Union, which we mentioned above. The reformers' plan was to limit political change, while modernizing the economy and improving the allocation of resources within the communist system. But once the process of reform was underway, it went much further and faster than the communist reformers wished or could have foreseen (Fischer, 1994; Treisman, 2011). Thus, if preserving the Soviet Union and its

---

[2] In the Introduction to *A Contribution to the Critique of Political Economy,* Marx formulated the theory of revolutions as follows (Marx, 1911): "At a certain stage of development, the material productive forces of society come into conflict with [...] the property relations within the framework of which they have operated hitherto." See also Aston and Philpin (1987).

political system was an important priority for the reformers, they might have had reason to strategically block the early reforms, even if these were beneficial, because they would have been a first step towards a slippery slope. Indeed, many of the autocratic leaders of the former Soviet republics, such as Azerbaijan, Belarus, Turkmenistan or Uzbekistan, have been reluctant to embrace deep economic reforms, perhaps learning from Russia's experience.

Acemoglu and Robinson (2006a) also emphasized that the unwillingness of many elites in absolutist Russia and Hapsburg Empires in the early 19th century to embrace industrialization and railroads was related to their concerns about losing political power once the process of industrialization was underway. Similarly, as argued by Acemoglu et al. (2010a), many African leaders may have refrained from building strong armies, despite their need for military power against uprisings and internal enemies, because they viewed this as a first step towards a slippery slope in which the military would become more powerful or even capable of engineering a coup against them.

One other interesting set of circumstances that can lead to institutional persistence is miscoordination. Even though institutional change that may be beneficial to many citizens and organized groups may be possible, it often requires some trust and coordination between groups, especially trust that nobody will try to hijack the process. This dynamic leads to multiple equilibria: when trust is missing, the process of institutional change may never get off the ground, creating a form of institutional stasis. If the different groups trusted each other, a better institutional arrangement, with power sharing between groups, would be an equilibrium as well.

Our discussion so far has followed much of the economics and political science literatures, focusing on institutional stasis (extreme institutional persistence) as the (typical) conceptual model for thinking about the durability of institutions. Reality is much more complex, however. Institutions are subject to continuous change as very few societies experience immutable conditions for even short periods of time. Thinking of institutional persistence as stasis is thus unsatisfactory at best and potentially misleading at worst.

What might institutional persistence mean then? A more general notion of persistence is proposed in works on path dependence (Pierson, 2000; Mahoney, 2000; Thelen, 1999). We follow these studies, and especially Acemoglu and Robinson (2012), by using their notion of "path-dependent change" as another, often more relevant, notion of persistence in institutions. By path dependence we mean that the process of institutional change is shaped by historical conditions and initial institutional choices. Two societies that start with somewhat different institutions (potentially similar, but still with small differences) may end up with very different trajectories. This may entail distinct institutional dynamics and possibly divergent economic outcomes.

We distinguish two types of path-dependent change: intrinsic and extrinsic. Intrinsic path-dependent change results from internal dynamics. Small differences can put a society in the basin of attraction of very different institutional equilibria. Yet even more interesting may be extrinsic path-dependent change, whereby small differences are amplified by shocks. We discuss several examples of path-dependent change, emphasizing how they provide a more nuanced and useful notion of persistence than the more dominant institutional stasis view in the economics literature. In particular, we illustrate extrinsic path-dependent change with brief discussions of: Brenner (1976)'s thesis about why the Black Death and the subsequent population collapse had very different effects on institutions in different parts of Europe (Aston and Philpin, 1987); Acemoglu et al. (2002)'s discussion of industrialization opportunities leading to a huge divergence across former European colonies with different institutional structures in the 19th century; Acemoglu and Robinson (2019)'s discussion of the divergent trajectories of Guatemala and Costa Rica following improvements in shipping technology that enabled a coffee boom in both economies; and Putnam (1993)'s arguments about divergence between the north and the south of Italy.

We end the paper with a brief discussion of three related major topics, which we cannot do justice to in this essay, but can briefly touch up on. These are:

(1) Designing persistence in institutions: Since institutions can be both persistent and on their way to change, powerful coalitions may wish to introduce additional institutional safeguards to slow down or prevent change. We discuss both theoretical ideas and some applications in this context.

(2) Social mobility and institutional dynamics: Another force that can either destabilize institutions or contribute to their stability is the interplay between social mobility and institutional preferences. When those who do not have political power in an institutional arrangement expect to be upwardly mobile and benefit from the same institutional structure that is now keeping them down, they may be less willing to take action against it. This would be an example of anticipated social mobility further stabilizing existing institutions. Building on Acemoglu et al. (2018), we show, however, that anticipated social mobility may also destabilize certain regimes, in particular democracy. This would happen, for example, when the current median voter expects to be in a different social position in the future and may then want to initiate a process for shifting political power towards their future position.

(3) Culture and institutions: There has been a resurgence in research on the role of cultural factors in economic and institutional development in recent decades (see Roland, 2004, Alesina and Giuliano, 2015, and Tabellini, 2010, for overviews). The interplay between culture and institutions is another potent force that can generate both institutional change and persistence. On the one hand, when cultural change naturally occurs under the auspices of a given institution, it may be a force towards undermining the same institutions. On the other hand, culture may adapt to an institutional environment, further cementing its hold in society. We explain how these ideas can be embedded into our simple framework.

While this essay is not a survey, it is still useful to mention some of the approaches to institutions we build upon.[3] Our work, as well as much of the literature in this area, builds on Douglass North's seminal work on institutions. North (1990) defined institutions as "the rules of the game in a society, or more formally, are the humanly devised constraints that shape human interaction", which is the perspective we adopt in this essay.[4] Also relevant to our focus here is Ostrom (2005)'s distinction between "operational rules", which correspond to policy choice in our model, "collective choice rules", which govern the change of operational rules, and "constitutional rules", which govern the change of collective choice rules.[5]

In adopting a dynamic game-theoretic approach, we do not mean to deny the importance of other factors, including evolutionary forces and bounded rationality considerations, in shaping institutions. The evolutionary perspective dates back to Veblen (1899), who argued that "the evolution of social

---

[3] See, for example, Acemoglu et al. (2005), Persson and Tabellini (2000), Kingston and Caballero (2009), Besley and Ghatak (2010), and Brousseau et al. (2011) for overviews of recent work in this area.

[4] A more encompassing definition of institutions is provided in Aoki (2001), who defined them as systems of beliefs over possible actions of others; effectively, an institution is a focal point in a coordination game. This perspective is also adopted in Greif (2006). Such definitions are less well adapted to formal game-theoretic analyses and do not make it easy to distinguish the role of institutions as setting rules from the equilibrium play.

[5] Other game-theoretic analyses that build on a similar distinction include Acemoglu and Robinson (2001, 2008), Barbera and Jackson (2004), Lizzeri and Persico (2004), and Acemoglu et al. (2012), all of which model collective choices on both policies and future institutions.

structure has been a process of natural selection of institutions", and is today more often associated with Hayek (1973), who argued that institutions (rules of conduct) "have evolved because the groups who practiced them were more successful and displaced others". Williamson (2000)'s seminal work emphasizes the role of bounded rationality and the use of simple rules to help in this context. Hodgson (2004) combines bounded rationality and evolutionary considerations. Though these approaches constitute important directions for the literature, they significantly multiply the set of institutions that can be stable, and as such do not provide as natural a starting point for our analysis as fully game-theoretic models, where individuals and groups can secure institutional change if they can build a sufficiently powerful coalition to support it.

The rest of the paper is organized as follows. In Section 13.2, we introduce our general framework. In Section 13.3 we discuss institutional stasis through the lenses of our model. Section 13.4 turns to various factors that push towards institutional change and illustrates these with a variety of historical examples. Section 13.5 introduces our notion of strategic stability and explains how such considerations can stem institutional change. Section 13.6 turns to the issue of path-dependent change, explaining both how institutional stasis is often an imperfect model of how institutions persist and how and why path-dependent change takes place in practice. Sections 13.7, 13.8, and 13.9 discuss designing persistence, social mobility, and culture and institutions, while Section 13.10 concludes.

13.2 General framework

In this section, we present a(n informal) framework that will help us exposit the main ideas of this essay. The framework draws on our previous work, in particular, Acemoglu et al. (2015), but here we suppress all but the most essential technical aspects to simplify the exposition.

Consider a society consisting of n groups of individuals such that group i has share α_i. We represent economic preferences with a policy space, and preferences of all individuals within a group are the same and do not change over time, and we assume that they have bliss point b_i and utility function from policy p given by:

$$u_i(p) = -(p - b_i)^2 + a_i, \tag{13.1}$$

where a_i is a term that depends on the institutional arrangement currently prevailing that may impact individual payoffs (see below). Later, we will allow these preferences to change over time, either because the economic structure changes (e.g., what a landowner may think about industrialization may change over time with developments in agricultural markets and relative prices) or because of social mobility. We also allow for political shocks that shift power from one group to another. We do not introduce expectations and stochastic events explicitly to simplify the notation.

Total individual payoffs are given by a discounted sum of (13.1), with discount factor $\beta \in [0, 1)$.

Suppose that $\{b_i\}$ is increasing in i, which implies that groups are ordered, for example from left to right or on some other ideological or economic dimension. Our focus is on institutions that determine decision-making rules and constraints. We denote these institutions by s^j, and model them in the simplest possible way, by assuming that under each institution, different groups receive a certain "weight" in collective decision-making. Namely, under institution s^j, group i has weight w_i^j; we might think of an institution where all weights are equal as democracy, whereas an institution where only one group, say group i, has positive weight as the dictatorship of group i. It is often sufficient to look at the case where these weights are indicators 0 or 1, i.e., some groups are enfranchised and some are not.

As explained in Acemoglu et al. (2015), one could look for the Markov Perfect Equilibria of this game, or more simply (and essentially equivalently), focus on Markov Voting Equilibria (MVE), which are, loosely speaking, given by effective median voters' choices over institutions anticipating the decisions of future effective median voters. In that paper, we showed that such MVE exist and are well-behaved under relatively weak assumptions, and here we do not get into these technical details.

Suppose that we start with institution s^j in the beginning of period t and that both policy decisions and institutional choices (for example, whether there will be an institutional reform) will be determined with the power distribution implied by the institution. We simplify the discussion here by assuming that both decisions are taken by the "effective median voter", i.e., by an individual from group $k = k(s^j)$ such that neither the groups to the left of k nor the groups to its right constitute a weighted majority (with weights given by the current institution s^j). Observe that because policy is not a state variable, policy choices will always be dictated by the preferences of the effective median voter. In other words, given the effective median voter group k, we will have policy given by this group's bliss point, $p = b_k$. Institutional choice is generally more complicated.

Institutions matter for individual payoffs through two channels. First, institutions determine the distribution of political power and thus who will set policy today and in the future. Second, they may also matter directly for payoffs, for example because they set the rules of economic interactions or enable different types of innovations or investments. This can be captured in our framework by making the term a_i above a function of the current institution, i.e., $a_i(s^j)$.

13.3 Institutional stasis: power begets power

The simplest form of institutional persistence, and the one that most discussions of persistence gravitate around, is one in which once an institution gets put in place (either by design or randomly), it self-replicates — creating a type of stasis, lack of any meaningful change. The most obvious reason why this would happen in the model is because of a close congruence between political power and economic interests (combined with a lack of shocks that disrupts this congruence). The next result informally summarizes this possibility:

Result 13.1 (Institutional stasis). Suppose that under institution s^* the effective median voter is in group i^*,[6] with bliss point b_{i^*} and $a_{i^*}(s^*) \geq a_{i^*}(s)$ for all other s, then we will have institutional stasis — group i^* will always choose to remain with institutions s^* and thus continue to be the effective median voter.

In other words, the group that is in power is happy with the current institutions and thus uses its power to maintain these institutions. There are certainly examples of such institutional stasis in history (and these examples and this type of reasoning often shape the way that many economists think about persistence). For example, the U.S. South before the Civil War had an institutional structure that both

---

[6] More explicitly, s^* empowers a set of groups $I = \{i_1, \ldots, i_n\}$, and the (weighted) median voter within this set of politically active groups is in group i^*.

economically and politically empowered the planter elite, who owned the largest plantations and the greatest number of slaves (Potter, 1976). Until the Civil War (and to some degree thereafter), this elite was able to maintain the same institutional structure, thus retaining its power (Acemoglu and Robinson, 2008; Wiener, 1978). As mentioned in the Introduction, this was because the planter elite was cohesive and well organized, had its political power reinforced by the slavery system, and had a clear interest in perpetuating that system (Genovese, 1976; Fogel, 1994). The case of institutional persistence in Guatemala is even more extreme, with the descendents of the original conquistadors of the area retaining political power and maintaining a similarly coercion-based economy well into the 20th century (Acemoglu and Robinson, 2012, Chapter 11). Feudal institutions, which lasted well into the 19th century in some parts of Europe, are another example of an arrangement empowering a narrow elite, which then worked hard to maintain this system from which it benefited economically and politically (Bloch, 1964).

Result 13.1 gives the simplest form of stasis — from the fact that power begets power. Another reason for this type of institutional persistence would be multiplicity of equilibria (and miscoordination), which we discuss later.

Though institutional stasis is simple to understand and may be what many think of when they start imagining institutional persistence, it is not the most common or most interesting form of persistence. This is for the obvious reason that institutions, like much else, never remain completely stationary. This motivates the rest of our inquiry in this essay, attempting to understand how institutional change and in what ways initial institutional choices shape later outcomes.

Before we delve deeper into different types of institutional persistence, we also make an important observation:

Observation. Meaningful institutional persistence necessitates multiple steady-state institutions.

This observation is very intuitive.[7] If there was a unique steady-state institution, meaning that ultimately all institutional equilibria converge to some unique s_∞, then we would not have any notion of institutional persistence, because all institutions would converge to s_∞. This is not a statement about multiple equilibria — whereby, starting from a given state, multiple equilibrium paths are possible. There might be multiple steady states, but the equilibrium path starting from any institution may be unique (Matsuyama, 1991; Krugman, 1991). For example, starting with highly autocratic government forms, there may be a unique equilibrium in which society converges to an oligarchic institution, while starting with more participatory institutions, the unique equilibrium may involve convergence to democracy (Acemoglu et al., 2015). Or there may be multiple equilibria as we will see below. We will return to the importance of multiple steady states below, but it already highlights an important issue: it is not possible to talk of institutional persistence in models that do not admit multiple steady states.

In the next section, we start with a number of departures from the institutional stasis outcome outlined in Result 13.1. We then introduce a more subtle form of institutional persistence, based on strategic considerations. We subsequently explore various mechanisms for institutional change, and then return to "path-dependent" institutional change.

---

[7] Some care is necessary here. There may also be institutional persistence if the limit of equilibrium sequence of institutions is a non-steady-state arrangement, such as a limit cycle, fluctuating between different types of institutions. To keep technicalities to a minimum, in this observation we focus on "multiple steady states".

13.4 Institutional change

Why would the institutional stasis outcome and Result 13.1 not apply? We outline two possible reasons for this in the next two results.

Result 13.2 (Incongruence between political and economic power). Suppose that under institution s^* the effective median voter is in group i^*, with bliss point b_{i*}, but there exists s' such that $a_{i*}(s')$ is sufficiently larger than $a_{i*}(s^*)$. Suppose in addition that β is small, so individuals are sufficiently myopic. Then starting from institution i^*, we will transition to another institution.

The reason for institutional change in this case is that the group in power under current institutions, group i^*, prefers an alternative institutional arrangement. This could be, for example, because aristocrats who hold political power in a monarchic regime may realize that their economic interests will be better served by bringing new groups into political power. The most famous example of this type of institutional change is discussed in North and Weingast (1989), who argued that the emergence of parliamentary institutions in England were in part a commitment to financial markets that government debt would be repaid. A related example is proposed in Acemoglu and Wolitzky (2020) as an explanation for the emergence of rule of law. In this account, current elites use the rule of law (in particular, relinquishing their own above-the-law status) as a commitment that they will themselves not exploit non-elites and thus encourage greater effort from them. Acemoglu and Wolitzky (2020) give the example of the Meiji Restoration in Japan to illustrate this possibility (see also Ravina, 2020). Threatened by foreign forces, especially the American fleet led by Commodore Perry, Japanese elites decided to defensively modernize their economy. This was deemed impossible as long as the very unequal treatment of elites and non-elites in Japan remained, so important steps towards equality before the law were introduced as part of this modernization drive.

Yet another set of historical examples illustrating Result 13.2 would be the instances in which economic change inexorably (albeit sometimes slowly) shifts political power, thus generating such an incongruence. The early Marxist theories of the collapse of feudalism, and thus rise of early capitalism, fall within this category. Following some of Marx's comments (Marx, 2019), these theories argued that the development of towns and craft industries slowly shifted political power away from the feudal hierarchy (see below on this).

From a theoretical point of view, the two conditions in this result are important. First, we need the alternative institution to be sufficiently better than the current one in order to make sure that the potential loss of political power, and together with it the deviation of current policy from group i^*'s bliss point, is compensated for. Otherwise, this group may prefer to stay in the current institutional environment in order to enjoy policy privileges, even if there are better institutional arrangements for them. Second, the condition that β is small is important as well. Without this condition group i^* may worry about subsequent institutional changes, and this fear may in turn lead to what we are going to call "strategic stability". The requirement that β is small ensures that future, potentially adverse consequences from current change are not going to be the dominant factor influencing decisions, and thus the group that is currently politically powerful will resolve the incongruence between their current economic and future political interests in favor of their economic interests.

Lizzeri and Persico (2004)'s theory of democratization provides another illustration of Result 13.2. In their theory, with limited suffrage, taxes are low, but intra-elite conflict leads to wasteful patronage. Franchise extension increases taxes but also leads to the redirection of spending towards public goods,

Example 13.1. Suppose there are three groups and that group 1 is the initial elite (monarchy or an oligarchy). We start in an initial institution s^1, in which this group is the dictator and maintains political power by repression. Because of this repression, the payoffs of all groups are lowered under institution s^1. An alternative institutional arrangement is s^2, where political power is shared between this initial elite and industrial interests. In this institutional arrangement, repression is reduced, and payoffs for all groups are higher than under s^1. But political power may now shift to industrial interests. Suppose, for example, that at each date, with probability $q > 0$, industrial interests will make the political decisions. What they want for their economic interests is to undertake rapid industrialization, by building factories and railways. This however further empowers the third group, the workers, who make up the majority. Once they are sufficiently powerful, then they are able to force a transition to democracy, denoted by s^3. Suppose that democracy empowers workers, who make up the majority of the population and are thus the effective median voter. Suppose also that democracy gives the workers the highest feasible payoff, which makes democracy a steady-state (stable) institutional arrangement. However, the traditional elite has lower payoff in democracy than under s^1. This then implies that when the discount factor β is sufficiently large, the initial elite would not like to undertake institutional change starting from s^1. This implies that there is another steady-state institutional arrangement: s^1. Intuitively, even though a move from s^1 to s^2 improves the initial elite's payoffs in the short run, the power sharing with industrial interests will ultimately pave the way to rapid industrialization and thus to the emergence of democracy. Because democracy itself is a steady-state institutional arrangement, the initial elite recognizes that democracy arrives, it will last forever. When they pay sufficient attention to future payoffs (β sufficiently large), this makes the initial move unattractive. Notice that it is the combination of strategic reasoning and high discount factor that makes s^1 a steady-state institutional arrangement here. In addition, we can also observe that even though both institutional arrangements s^1 and s^3 are steady states, the equilibrium path is always unique. When we start in one of these institutions, we stay there (and hence there is institutional stasis).

Example 13.1 thus illustrates how strategic stability, or slippery slope concerns, may generate a very strong form of some optimality — Pareto inefficiency. Even institutions that provide higher utility to all groups may not be attractive enough because of (expected) subsequent changes. Another simple historical illustration of these ideas is the role of the army in many less developed economies. Despite multiple internal and external security challenges, many nations, especially those in Africa, have armies that are weak, underprovisioned, and disarrayed. Acemoglu et al. (2010a) suggest that this is because civilian leaders, who are themselves weak, are afraid that strengthening the military further would undercut their own power or even leave them exposed to coups. The logic is again one of strategic stability: the current elite sacrifices the benefits that they can reap from a stronger army because they do not want to risk the institutional trajectory that would leave them with lower power or deposed.

Example 13.1 is one with multiple steady-state institutions, but a unique equilibrium path — meaning that starting from any initial institution, there is a unique equilibrium sequence of institutions and policies. Strategic stability is not confined to such situations. It can also arise when there are multiple equilibrium paths supporting multiple limiting equilibria. The next example illustrates this possibility:

Example 13.2. Suppose there are n groups, and there are $n + 1$ institutional arrangements. One of those corresponds to democracy, which gives the highest utility to all groups. The other n institutions correspond to the dictatorship of one of the groups. The dictatorship of group i gives a somewhat lower utility to this group but a very low utility to all other groups. On the other hand, if society is democratic, then at each date there is a random variable determining which one of the n groups can undertake a coup and set up its own dictatorship. It can be verified that there are multiple equilibria in this case. In one equilibrium, the group that is first picked sets up its dictatorship and maintains it forever, because it is afraid that, if it chooses to transition to democracy, other groups will undertake a coup, setting up their own dictatorship. Another equilibrium is one in which all groups trust each other and nobody attempts a coup, even when they have the chance.

This example thus provides another form of strategic stability of institutions, but differently from the previous example, miscoordination and trust-related issues matter greatly because there is a multiplicity of equilibria. Consequently, institutions that persist in the absence of between-group trust may make way to better institutional arrangements if there is coordination or trust. This example also further qualifies the meaning of institutional stasis: though we may stay in the dictatorship of one of the groups, say group 1, in an equilibrium in which no group trusts others, it is possible for beliefs to change (for example, because of an unanticipated exogenous shocks to beliefs or a new vision or rhetoric) and a very different type of equilibrium behavior to be realized thereafter.

We end this section with another result, which further clarifies the nature of strategic stability and will then be useful in our discussion of designing constitutional provisions in order to increase the stability of institutions.

Result 13.5 (More stable institutions). Institutional arrangements that preclude small changes tend to be more durable.[9]

The intuition for this result is an illustration of the general principle highlighted in Acemoglu et al. (2012): institutions are made stable by the absence of alternative stable institutions that receive sufficient support from powerful constituencies. Hence, stability is made more likely when forming such a coalition supporting alternative institutions becomes more difficult. When small institutional reforms are feasible, they are likely to be less threatening to powerful constituencies, and coalitions in favor of such reforms are more likely to form. But this in turn makes existing institutions less stable. The alternative is an institutional framework that can only be changed in more radical directions. In that case, except under exceptional circumstances, there will be powerful groups trying to block the change, rendering existing institutions more stable.

One illustration of these ideas is from the U.S. Constitution, which has changed little since the Civil War (there have been only a handful of amendments, mostly minor except those leading to the direct election of Senators and the federal income tax). Mittal and Weingast (2013) interpret the post-1877 U.S. Constitution as "self-enforcing". In fact, the general interpretation among constitutional scholars and politicians has been that the overarching framework imposed by the Constitution is not up for discussion, thus helping with the notion that any meaningful change in the Constitution will be a relatively major one. As a result, Elkins et al. (2009) state: "The United States presents a constitution with formal inflexibility but much informal flexibility", and conjecture that "... a moderate level of flexibility seems to be a necessary condition for enduring constitutions."

---

[9] Formally, we can express this result as follows: Suppose that institution s^* has the effective median voter in group i^*. Suppose, furthermore, that there are institutions s^*_{-1} and s^*_{+1} where the effective median voter is in the neighboring groups $i^* - 1$ and $i^* + 1$, respectively. Then s^* is more likely to be stable when it is not possible to transition to these neighboring institutions, s^*_{-1} and s^*_{+1}.

13.6 Path-dependent change

In contrast to institutional stasis, most institutional persistence does not involve lack of change, but the possibility that initial institutions shape how that change takes place. This is what Acemoglu and Robinson (2012) refer to as "path-dependent change". There are two aspects to this definition. The first is a form of path dependence, meaning that initial conditions matter (Pierson, 2000; Mahoney, 2000; Thelen, 1999).[10] The second is that there is actual institutional change. In particular, institutional stasis, though it involves dependence on initial conditions, is not path-dependent change.

To explain these ideas more systematically, let us introduce some notation. Suppose that starting from some institution s, the equilibrium path of institutions can be represented by the stochastic sequence $\{s_1 = s, s_2, \ldots\}$. In contrast, suppose that starting from a different institution $s' \neq s$, it is $\{s_1' = s', s_2', \ldots\}$. If $\lim_{t \to \infty}(s_t - s_t') = 0$ with probability one, then we say that there is no path dependence. On the other hand, if this is not the case, then there is path dependence.

Clearly, institutional stasis is an example of path dependence. For instance, if $s_t = s$ and $s_t' = s'$ for all t, we have a simple example of institutional stasis, and by our definition this is path dependent. But it is not path-dependent *change*, since there is no change. Hence, we say that there is path-dependent change so long as $s_t \neq s_{t-1}$ and $s_t' \neq s_{t-1}'$ with positive probability for all $t \leq T$ for some large T. This does not rule out the possibility that as $t \to \infty$, there may be convergence to a limiting institutional equilibrium, but it requires that, with positive probability, institutions change at least along the transition path.

Why would there be path-dependent change? There are two distinct but related reasons for this. The first is because of internal dynamics, which create change that intricately depends on initial conditions. We refer to this as "intrinsic path-dependent change". The second is because of the arrival of shocks, so we refer to it as "extrinsic path-dependent change". In this case, it is the differential response of institutions to a common shock depending on where they currently are that undergirds path-dependence.

The next result explains one set of conditions under which extrinsic path-dependent change arises.

Result 13.6 (Path-dependent change). Suppose that starting from institution s, the equilibrium path of institutions is given by the deterministic sequence $\{s_1 = s, s_2, \ldots\}$ and starting from $s' \neq s$, it is given by deterministic sequence $\{s_1' = s', s_2', \ldots\}$. There is intrinsic path-dependent change if $s_t' \neq s_t$ for all t and $\lim_{t \to \infty}(s_t - s_t') \neq 0$. On the other hand, there will be extrinsic path-dependent change, under the following circumstances: suppose that $s_t' \neq s_t$ for all t and $\lim_{t \to \infty}(s_t - s_t') \neq 0$, but at each date t, with probability $q_t > 0$ the environment changes, and following this environment change at time T, the resulting sequence of institutional equilibria takes the form $\{\tilde{s}_T = s_T, \tilde{s}_{T+1}, \ldots\}$ or $\{\tilde{s}_T' = s_T', \tilde{s}_{T+1}', \ldots\}$. Then there will be extrinsic path-dependent change if $\lim_{t \to \infty}(\tilde{s}_{T+t} - \tilde{s}_{T+t}') \neq 0$.

In other words, intrinsic path-dependent change leads to a different evolution of institutions starting from different initial conditions. In fact, this is true even though there are no shocks and thus we are looking at a deterministic sequence of institutional equilibria. Extrinsic path-dependent change is defined for the case where there is no intrinsic-path dependent change and thus without shocks, equilibrium paths starting from different initial conditions will converge towards the same steady states.

---

[10] We refer to this as a simple form of path dependence, because it is distinct from some of the more intricate possibilities, for example what Page et al. (2006) refers to as "phat dependence", obtained from path dependence by changing the order of letters to emphasize that the exact sequence of realizations of random variables matters for long-run outcomes.

Yet, the arrival of some shocks on the way to institutional convergence may disrupt the convergence and usher in divergence instead, because the institutional differences at the time the shock hits will fundamentally shape the response to it.

One historical illustration of path-dependent change comes from Acemoglu and Robinson (2019). Despite the many similarities between Costa Rica and Guatemala in the 19th century (which used to be part of the same Kingdom of Guatemala), faced with new maritime trade opportunities, especially for coffee, created by advances in shipping technology, the two countries sharply diverged. When this "shock" took place, there were some small but relevant differences. Guatemala had a more monolithic elite that was able to dominate the economy and politics of the country. They were then able to monopolize most of the coffee-suitable land and set up coercive coffee plantations. In contrast, the somewhat different political equilibrium in Costa Rica, where the landed elite was a little weaker and different urban centers competed against each other, did not enable this type of elite monopolization. Rather than large-scale plantations, in Costa Rica smallholder coffee production took off (Paige, 1998). These economic institutions in turn generated very different political institutional paths, with Guatemala becoming more and more repressive and authoritarian, while Costa Rica developed more participatory institutions, and eventually reached a consolidated democracy. The contrast of Guatemala and Costa Rica therefore provides an example of extrinsic path-dependent change under the presumption that without this major shock, Costa Rica and Guatemala would have remained similar and perhaps at some point achieved institutional convergence, but this potential convergence was disrupted, paving the way to institutional divergence. Acemoglu and Robinson (2012) also interpret the divergent paths of North and South America following the collapse of colonial empires as another example of path-dependent change. After independence, in most of Latin America the old colonial elites and their allies weakened and disappeared (Guatemala and El Salvador are exceptions in this). But their place was not filled by more participatory institutions and more inclusive economic arrangements, but by new elites who took power and set up a different, yet similarly extractive economics system (Coatsworth, 2008).

Some of the theories of transition away from feudalism in Europe also fall within this category. The so-called neo-Malthusian historians (e.g., Postan, 1973; North and Thomas, 1973) emphasized the role of the population declines brought about by the black death and its aftermath in Europe as a major force destabilizing the feudal regime. These theories were criticized by Brenner (1976), who pointed out that similar demographic changes led to different outcomes throughout Europe (Aston and Philpin, 1987). Brenner's thesis can be interpreted as an example of path-dependence change. Brenner argued that a key variable was the balance of power between lords and peasants, and the shock created by demographic change played out very differently depending on this balance of power. In terms of our framework, this amounts to relatively small differences in the institutional structure (in particular in terms of the ability of lords to dominate peasants) leading to divergent institutional trajectories after a major shock, such as the one generated by the black death episode (see Acemoglu and Wolitzky, 2011 for a formalization of these ideas in the context of an equilibrium model of labor coercion). Finally, another example is provided by Putnam (1993)'s account for the further divergence of the south and the north of Italy from the 1970s onwards, based on differences in culture, social capital and institutions in these two parts of the country reacting differently to the greater autonomy and resources given to local governments.

We conclude this section with a brief mention of a complementary result from Acemoglu et al. (2010b), who study the flexibility advantage of more democratic governance structures. In particular, in this paper we show that increasing the ability of political insiders to block change does not necessarily lead to worse static outcomes, but reduces the flexibility of institutions to adapt to change. As a result of this lack of flexibility, in the presence of sufficiently frequent shocks, political systems that empower insiders more will significantly underperform, thus illustrating another facet of path-dependent change — differences in initial power distribution can lead to a divergence because it determines whether or not adaptation to this change is possible. A historical example with this flavor is given by Runciman (2017), who suggests that the more democratic British government was able to adapt to the changing conditions of World War I better than the more autocratic German government and military, which found it difficult to switch away from their early strategies that later proved inadequate.

13.7 **Designing persistence**

Institutional change is often costly for current political incumbents. This raises the possibility that they may try to design new institutional provisions (or attempt "institutional innovations") in order to create stability, in the process solidifying their privileged position. History is full of examples of such efforts, though not all of them have succeeded.

One canonical approach to this problem is Barbera and Jackson (2004), who introduce (in a two-period setting) the choice of the constitution which determines future voting rules. They observe that simple and desirable decision-making procedures such as a majority rule may result in good policy outcomes, but they may be unstable in that a majority may vote to get rid of a majority rule. On the other hand — and this is the key idea — the rules that determine policy and the rules that determine institutional change may be distinct, and if the constitutional rules the support of a supermajority for institutional change, they may help make an institution stable. Indeed, a typical constitution requires a much higher burden on amendments and constitutional changes than on deciding ordinary policies. Barbera and Jackson (2004) show that majority rule can be made stable if it is coupled with a constitutional unanimity requirements to change it, because there will never be unanimous agreement to change majority rule as there are always some groups that expect to benefit from this decision-making procedure.

This idea can be generalized and applied in our dynamic setting. In the extreme, when there are no constraints on designing constitutional requirements, current incumbents can always design a constitution that replicates their most preferred outcomes by requiring that a change of institutions requires unanimity, thereby granting themselves veto power on institutional change. The next result summarizes one way of formalizing these ideas:

Result 13.7 (Constitutions). Suppose that group i^* is the effective median voter under institution s^* and prefers some other institution s' to s^* (because $a_{i*}(s')$ is much greater than $a_{i*}(s^*)$). Suppose also that s^* is the most preferred institution for some other group i'. Then a constitution consisting of institution s^* as the decision-making rule, coupled with a unanimity requirement to change the constitution, is always stable.

The problem of design of constitutions becomes more realistic and interesting when there are constraints on what types of super majority or unanimity requirements can be imposed for constitutional change or when there are changes in the environment for which we cannot write complete contracts (Aghion and Bolton, 2003). For example, there may be significant uncertainty about the conditions that will arise in the future. In such situations, full unanimity may be prohibitively costly (precluding very beneficial changes necessary to adapt to new environments), but some amount of institutional stability can be achieved by introducing constitutional requirements that necessitate the formation of relatively large coalitions to implement change. One example is provided by the famous Missouri compromise (Weingast, 1997). This compromise tried to create a balance between free and slave states in the U.S. Senate and a critical component of this balance was that in the future free and slave states would be admitted in pairs, so that power would not shift in favor of one of the two constituencies. The breakdown of this compromise, with the admission of Kansas as a free state into the Union in January 1861, paved the way to the Civil War.

Similarly, the National Pact of 1943 in Lebanon stipulated that the most important political positions in the country be held by individuals with certain religious affiliation: the president would have to be a Maronite Catholic, the prime minister a Sunni Muslim, and the speaker of the parliament a Shia Muslim. On top of that, 55% of seats in the parliament would be occupied by Christians and the rest by Muslims. This agreement, even if highly distortionary for selecting good governments, economic policy-making and public good provision, was maintained until demographic changes substantially increased the share of Muslim population. It took a civil war for the factions to renegotiate the pact. The Taif agreement that ended the civil war in 1989 gave equal representation to Christians and Muslims in the parliament and curtailed the power of the Maronite president, but did not dismantle the segmented system that apportions political power across sectarian groups in Lebanon (Bogaards, 2019).

These examples highlight the two major problems with designing stable institutions by increasing the hurdle for changes. The first is that it may make common sense changes more difficult. These changes may reflect omissions or oversights in the original design of an institution. For example, prior to the Twelfth Amendment the U.S. Constitution all but guaranteed that the president and the vice president would represent opposing factions, making effective governance and federal policy much more difficult. Another fallout from creating hurdles for change is the subsequent difficulties that society will face when confronted with a changing environment. In addition to the Lebanese case, the structure of the Sejm (parliament) of the Polish-Lithuanian Commonwealth, which required unanimity for making decisions, illustrates this problem. This unanimity rule made the oligarchic regime of Poland-Lithuania highly stable, but also generated a severe political gridlock (Roháč, 2008). Even in less extreme circumstances, the trade-off between flexibility and stability could be a complex one.

Finally, we can apply some of the lessons highlighted by Result 13.5 above. This result emphasized that institutional arrangements that make small changes infeasible may be more stable. This suggests that, under certain circumstances, ruling out small changes and only allowing radical ones could be one way of increasing the stability of institutions. One way of achieving this may be to create an immutable constitution, so that any significant reforms in laws will necessitate a new constitutional arrangement, which could then lead to sweeping changes. Though not as extreme, the U.S. Constitution, which occupies an almost sacred position in American life and politics, can be considered as an illustration of this principle.

13.8 Social mobility and institutional change

An interesting set of economic and political forces are rooted in social mobility. In terms of our framework, social mobility can be thought of as a pattern of individuals changing their preferences, because their economic station in life is changing. Upward social mobility of some is typically associated with downward social mobility of others, so forward-looking players should also anticipate changes in their own preferences and the preferences of others. These issues are studied in Acemoglu et al. (2018). Here we provide one result on how anticipation of social mobility alters the nature of political equilibria and can be a force towards either institutional change or institutional inertia.

Suppose, in particular, that individual bliss points, the b_i's, change over time. This could take the form of each of those following a Markov chain. If the cross-section of preferences starts in the stationary distribution of this Markov chain, then this process of social mobility would be stationary — meaning that the stationary distribution would replicate itself, so for every agent moving up from the bottom to the top, there will be another one that moves down from the top to the bottom. Alternatively, we could start from an arbitrary initial condition, so that the entire distribution of economic (and thus political) preferences would evolve, generating predictable aggregate changes (we may still eventually converge to a stationary distribution, at least in the absence of other shocks).

The analysis of political dynamics in the presence of social mobility considerations is somewhat more intricate, but some of the main ideas can be conveyed with the following result:

Result 13.8 (Social mobility). Suppose that group i^* is the effective median voter under institution s^* and their most preferred institutional arrangement is s^*. Consider social mobility that will change the economic position of individuals in this society. If social mobility is such that members of other groups expect to have preferences close to b_{i^*} in the future, then it makes institution s^* more likely to persist (relative to the case of no social mobility). If, on the other hand, social mobility is such that members of group i^* expect their preferences to shift close to the bliss point $b_{i'}$ of some other group i' (and the discount factor β is not too large), then social mobility makes institution s^* less stable.

The idea that social mobility can help ensure institutional (democratic) stability goes back to the classic work of de Tocqueville (2000) on U.S. democracy. De Tocqueville argued that America had greater social mobility than Europe and people expected their children or grandchildren to be part of the middle class, and singled this out as an important reason why democracy worked better in America than in his home country, France, where the democratic governments that emerged after the 1789 revolution was short-lived. In terms of our Result 13.8, De Tocqueville's theory makes sense when the rich and the poor find it likely that their children will be part of a large middle class that will benefit from and will have political voice in democracy. This idea is also closely related to the role that the perception of upward social mobility can play in shoring up support for pro-rich or pro-middle-class policies among the poor (Benabou and Ok, 2001). However, Result 13.8 also shows that social mobility can destabilize prevailing institutions. In the context of democracy, for example, this may happen because the middle class expects to be poorer in the future, making it less willing to support democracy. One application of the ideas in Acemoglu et al. (2018) is the disenfranchisement of Blacks after Reconstruction in the U.S. postbellum South, which was aided by the belief among the poor Whites that they were themselves upwardly mobile and would benefit from separating their political fortunes from those of Blacks (and would also benefit from the discrimination against Blacks).

Of course, institutions also affect social mobility. This two-way interaction between institutions and social mobility raises many other interesting possibilities. For example, politically powerful groups may actively try to reduce social mobility not just for economic reasons (to maintain their economic a privileged position) but also for political reasons (e.g., if they expect social mobility to destabilize the current institutional arrangement). Conversely, (capitalist or rich) elites may have an interest in either increasing social mobility or creating the impression of greater social mobility in order to build support for policies that favor capital or reduce the taxation of high incomes.

13.9 Culture and institutions

There has recently been a resurgence in research on the role of cultural factors in economic and political development (Roland, 2020, Alesina and Giuliano, 2015, and Tabellini, 2010, and see Acemoglu and Robinson, 2020 for a critique). Our purpose here is not to review this literature, but to highlight another set of factors that can contribute to institutional persistence or institutional change.

The conceptual framework we have is related to Bisin and Verdier (2017), as well as Tabellini (2008), who provide models in which both institutions and culture (interpreted as values children inherit from parents and society) are endogenous and respond to each other.

For simplicity, let us again focus on the a terms in the payoff functions in (13.1) (as before, one could also endogenize the b terms). Suppose that these can change slowly in response to the political, social, and economic incentives generated by institutions.[11] Since our purpose here is to communicate the basic ideas (rather than build a micro-founded framework), we summarize these responses by the mappings $\phi_i(a_i(\cdot), s)$ for each $i = 1, \ldots, n$.[12] Namely, these mappings specify how the current preferences of members of group i, given by $a_i(\cdot)$, change as a function of the prevailing institutions, s. We will say that the collection of mappings $\{\phi_i(\cdot, \cdot)\}$ is "concordant", if the $a_i(\cdot)$'s change such that each group's utility from the current state, $a_i(s)$, increases relative to payoffs from other institutions. This collection is "discordant", if on the other hand the direction of cultural change is such that the $a_i(s)$'s decline relative to payoffs from other institutions.

The next result summarizes how cultural change can be a force towards stabilizing a given set of institutions or one that sows the seeds of further institutional evolution.

Result 13.9 (Change and persistence from culture). If cultural change is concordant, then existing unstable institutions can be transformed into steady-state institutions. If, on the other hand, cultural change is discordant, potentially stable institutional arrangements can be made unstable and initiate a process of institutional change.

The intuition for this result is simple but important. Let us start with an institutional arrangement, which as in our Results 13.2 or 13.3 above, is unstable and is expected to make way to different institutions. If this process is slow and culture adapts in the process, it may stabilize these otherwise unstable institutional arrangements. Consider a very hierarchical society, such as the one based on the caste system in India (Ghurye, 1969). When lower castes, which make up the majority of the population, would like to overthrow the rule of the higher caste groups, long-run stability may be impossible to achieve. But this process could be very slow, for example, because lower castes are disorganized or are subject to repression. Nevertheless, without any other adaptations, their political power will grow at some point and the current institutional arrangements will start unwinding. Now imagine that these lower cast members can be convinced that such change is not in their interest, for example, because the hierarchy is divinely ordained or higher castes are better able to rule and will look after their interests. If they are swayed by these ideas, this would be an example of concordant cultural

---

[11] In the economics literature, most recent research builds on the mechanism proposed in Bisin and Verdier (2001), which endogenizes culture during the formative years of children, due to parental or societal influences. Both this mechanism or others that endogenize post-childhood values and norms could be important in the context of our discussion here.

[12] A major simplification here is to make cultural change a function of current institutions, rather than the future path of institutions. We adopt this simplification to facilitate our current discussion.

change: their preferences may endogenously evolve to be satisfied with the current configuration, even though they are economically exploited and politically voiceless under these institutions.

This example highlights how culture can be a stabilizing force for prevailing institutions. But this not the only possibility: discordant cultural change could alter values and attitudes away from those that support existing institutions. An example of this would be women's liberation movement (Wollstonecraft, 1891; Pankhurst, 2019). Women were in a subservient economic and political position in almost all of the Western world throughout the Middle Ages and early modern period. The prevailing cultural values of the time also convinced many women that this was a tolerable situation (even if many suffered and were unhappy with material or nonmaterial aspects of their lives). Nevertheless, in the course of the 19th century, many women (and some men) started to recognize the injustice of these arrangements and began a campaign of social and political organization for women. This can be interpreted as an example of discordant cultural change, as people started to view the subjugation of women as less and less acceptable, triggering a process of major institutional transformation.

Another interesting example comes from Iraq after the collapse of Saddam Hussein's regime, which had started as a secular dictatorship but had then heavily exploited religious themes in order to gain additional legitimacy (see Bacevich, 2016, and the discussion in Acemoglu and Robinson, 2019). The power vacuum left after Saddam's fall created room for different types of cultural changes. The early sectarian conflicts under the American-imposed quasi-democratic system may have strengthened religious commitments, making the same institutions and cross-community cooperation much harder to maintain. These factors became more extreme after the rise of the Islamic State, which imposed harsher religious controls in parts of the country it controlled (and reactions to the presence of American soldiers may have contributed as well). This example also illustrates an aspect we have not incorporated into our model: beyond current institutions, the expectations of how future institutions will evolve may also impact cultural choices. Hence, choices of religious observance and education may have been influenced by expectations concerning how durable the rule of the Islamic State and other religious groups would be.

13.10 **Conclusion**

Much of social science and historical analysis of social, economic, and political arrangements builds on the idea that institutions persist. But we are far away from a comprehensive framework that elucidates the rich mechanisms for persistence and change in institutions. In this essay, we provided a simple conceptual framework for clarifying why and how institutions persist and change. The reasons and pathways via which institutions become durable are varied and depend on the historical circumstances facing the country or region in question. Our essay is motivated by the belief that, this richness in detail notwithstanding, there are certain major commonalities that can be useful to highlight.

We developed a dynamic game-theoretic model to organize these ideas. Different groups care both about current policies and institutions and future policies, which are themselves determined by current institutional choices. The discount rate of different groups is a measure of how forward-looking they are and how much they care about the future. Equilibria in this game take the form of (stochastic or deterministic) paths of institutions. Institutional change can happen because of internal dynamics or because of shocks to the economic environment or political power of different groups.

We used this framework first to clarify the simplest form of institutional persistence, which we called "institutional stasis", whereby a given set of institutions persist over time. One of the most natural reasons for this is that "power begets power", meaning that existing institutions reproduce the dominance of currently powerful groups, which could then choose to keep these institutions in place.

We emphasized that, though there are examples of this type of stasis and the thinking of many economists and political scientists is shaped by such dynamics, institutional stasis is rare; rather, most institutions are in a constant state of flux. A better approach is provided by the notion of "path-dependent change", whereby current institutions determine the future trajectory of institutional change, both because of internal dynamics and because even small differences can cause big divergences in the response to shocks. We provided several historical examples illustrating the workings of path-dependent change as well.

We also explored how our framework sheds light on different mechanisms for institutional change, once again illustrating several possibilities through historical examples. But incumbent political groups are not powerless against such change. One aspect of their ability to withstand such change comes from our notion of "strategic stability": anticipating the subsequent institutional changes, which may go in directions that are detrimental to their interests, can motivate the formation of coalitions opposed to change — because they are concerned about the "slippery slope" that this will create. This type of strategic reasoning, clarified by our game-theoretic setup, has also many examples in history.

Another strategy incumbents can use is to design new institutions in order to bolster existing arrangements, which we also studied using our framework.

Our framework provides new perspectives on the rich interactions between social mobility and institutions as well. The extent of social mobility is determined by prevailing institutions, but influences the evolution of these institutions, too. For example, expectations of upward social mobility may motivate disadvantaged groups to put up with current institutions in the hope that they will be their beneficiaries in the near future. On the other hand, social mobility can also destabilize current institutions, because people expect to have very different preferences in the future and thus may not protect current institutions or they may even actively work to undermine them.

Finally, we used our framework to discuss the interplay between culture and institutions. Among the multitudes of such interactions, we focused on one aspect of this relationship and discussed how different types of cultural change can stabilize or destabilize existing institutional arrangements.

We view our essay as a contribution to the growing and flourishing field of institutional economics. We hope that the general framework we have outlined can be useful to historical and empirical investigations in specific contexts. Such investigations will undoubtedly reveal new forces and may highlight the limits of some of the mechanisms we have summarized here.

References

Acemoglu, D., Wolitzky, A., 2011. The economics of labor coercion. Econometrica 79 (2), 555–600.

Acemoglu, D., Wolitzky, A., 2020. A Theory of Equality Before the Law. Working paper.

Acemoglu, D., Egorov, G., Sonin, K., 2008. Coalition formation in non-democracies. The Review of Economic Studies 75 (4), 987–1009.

Acemoglu, D., Ticchi, D., Vindigni, A., 2010a. A theory of military dictatorships. American Economic Journal: Macroeconomics 2 (1), 1–42.

Acemoglu, D., Egorov, G., Sonin, K., 2010b. Political selection and persistence of bad governments. The Quarterly Journal of Economics 125 (4), 1511–1575.

Acemoglu, D., Egorov, G., Sonin, K., 2012. Dynamics and stability of constitutions, coalitions, and clubs. The American Economic Review 102 (4), 1446–1476.

Acemoglu, D., Egorov, G., Sonin, K., 2015. Political economy in a changing world. Journal of Political Economy 123 (5), 1038–1086.

Acemoglu, D., Egorov, G., Sonin, K., 2018. Social mobility and stability of democracy: reevaluating de Tocqueville. The Quarterly Journal of Economics 133 (2), 1041–1105.

Acemoglu, D., Robinson, J.A., 2000. Why did the West extend the franchise? Democracy, inequality, and growth in historical perspective. The Quarterly Journal of Economics 115 (4), 1167–1199.

Acemoglu, D., Robinson, J.A., 2001. A theory of political transitions. The American Economic Review 91 (4), 938–963.

Acemoglu, D., Robinson, J.A., 2006a. Economic backwardness in political perspective. American Political Science Review 100 (1), 115.

Acemoglu, D., Robinson, J.A., 2006b. Economic Origins of Dictatorship and Democracy. Cambridge University Press.

Acemoglu, D., Robinson, J.A., 2008. Persistence of power, elites, and institutions. The American Economic Review 98 (1), 267–293.

Acemoglu, D., Robinson, J.A., 2012. Why Nations Fail: The Origins of Power, Prosperity, and Poverty. Crown Publishers, New York.

Acemoglu, D., Robinson, J.A., 2019. The Narrow Corridor: States, Societies, and the Fate of Liberty. Penguin.

Acemoglu, D., Robinson, J., 2020. Culture, Institutions and Social Equilibria: A Framework. Working paper.

Acemoglu, D., Johnson, S., Robinson, J.A., 2002. Reversal of fortune: geography and institutions in the making of the modern world income distribution. The Quarterly Journal of Economics 117 (4), 1231–1294.

Acemoglu, D., Johnson, S., Robinson, J.A., 2005. Institutions as a fundamental cause of long-run growth. In: Handbook of Economic Growth. Elsevier, pp. 385–472.

Aghion, P., Bolton, P., 2003. Incomplete social contracts. Journal of the European Economic Association 1 (1), 38–67.

Aidt, T.S., Franck, R., 2015. Democratization under the threat of revolution: evidence from the Great Reform Act of 1832. Econometrica 83 (2), 505–547.

Aidt, T.S., Jensen, P.S., 2014. Workers of the world, unite! Franchise extensions and the threat of revolution in Europe, 1820–1938. European Economic Review 72, 52–75.

Alesina, A., Giuliano, P., 2015. Culture and institutions. Journal of Economic Literature 53 (4), 898–944.

Aoki, M., 2001. Toward a Comparative Institutional Analysis. MIT Press Books, vol. 1. The MIT Press.

Åslund, A., 2019. Russia's Crony Capitalism: The Path from Market Economy to Kleptocracy. Yale University Press.

Aston, T.H., Philpin, C.H.E., 1987. The Brenner Debate: Agrarian Class Structure and Economic Development in Pre-Industrial Europe. Cambridge University Press.

Bacevich, A.J., 2016. America's War for the Greater Middle East: A Military History. Random House.

Barbera, S., Jackson, M.O., 2004. Choosing how to choose: self-stable majority rules and constitutions. The Quarterly Journal of Economics 119 (3), 1011–1048.

Battaglini, M., Coate, S., 2007. Inefficiency in legislative policymaking: a dynamic analysis. The American Economic Review 97 (1), 118–149.

Benabou, R., Ok, E.A., 2001. Social mobility and the demand for redistribution: the POUM hypothesis. The Quarterly Journal of Economics 116 (2), 447–487.

Besley, T., Ghatak, M., 2010. Property rights and economic development. In: Handbook of Development Economics, vol. 5. Elsevier, pp. 4525–4595.

Billias, G.A., 2009. American Constitutionalism Heard Round the World, 1776-1989: A Global Perspective. NYU Press.

Bisin, A., Verdier, T., 2001. The economics of cultural transmission and the dynamics of preferences. Journal of Economic Theory 97 (2), 298–319.

Bisin, A., Verdier, T., 2017. On the joint evolution of culture and institutions. Technical report. National Bureau of Economic Research.

Black, J.L., 2014. The Russian Presidency of Dmitry Medvedev, 2008-2012: The Next Step Forward or Merely a Time Out? Taylor & Francis.

Bloch, M., 1964. Feudal Society.

Bogaards, M., 2019. Formal and informal consociational institutions: a comparison of the national pact and the Taif agreement in Lebanon. Nationalism and Ethnic Politics 25 (1), 27–42.

Brenner, R., 1976. Agrarian class structure and economic development in pre-industrial Europe. Past & Present 70 (1), 30–75.

Brousseau, E., Garrouste, P., Raynaud, E., 2011. Institutional changes: alternative theories and consequences for institutional design. Journal of Economic Behavior & Organization 79 (1–2), 3–19.

Coatsworth, J.H., 2008. Inequality, institutions and economic growth in Latin America. Journal of Latin American Studies 40 (3), 545–569.

de Tocqueville, A., 2000. Democracy in America (H.C. Mansfield & D. Winthrop, Trans.). University of Chicago Press, Chicago (Original work published 1835).

Elkins, Z., Ginsburg, T., Melton, J., 2009. The Endurance of National Constitutions. Cambridge University Press.

Engerman, S., Sokoloff, K., 1997. Factor Endowments, Institutions, and Differential Paths of Growth Among New World Economics. Stanford University Press, Stanford, CA, pp. 260–304.

Fernandez, R., Rodrik, D., 1991. Resistance to reform: status quo bias in the presence of individual-specific uncertainty. The American Economic Review, 1146–1155.

Fischer, S., 1994. Russia and the Soviet Union Then and Now. University of Chicago Press, pp. 221–258.

Fogel, R.W., 1994. Without Consent or Contract: The Rise and Fall of American Slavery. American Studies Collection Norton.

Genovese, E.D., 1976. Roll, Jordan, Roll: The World the Slaves Made, vol. 652. Vintage.

Gershenkron, A., 1962. Economic Backwardness in Historical Perspective. Belknap, Cambridge, MA.

Ghurye, G.S., 1969. Caste and Race in India. Popular Prakashan.

Greif, A., 2006. Institutions and the Path to the Modern Economy: Lessons from Medieval Trade. Cambridge University Press, Cambridge.

Hayek, F., 1973. Economic Freedom and Representative Government. Wincott Foundation, London.

Hodgson, G.M., 2004. The Evolution of Institutional Economics. Routledge.

Holton, W., 2008. Unruly Americans and the Origins of the Constitution. Hill and Wang.

Kingston, C., Caballero, G., 2009. Comparing theories of institutional change. Journal of Institutional Economics 5 (2), 151–180.

Krugman, P., 1991. History versus expectations. The Quarterly Journal of Economics 106 (2), 651–667.

Lagunoff, R., 2001. A theory of constitutional standards and civil liberty. The Review of Economic Studies 68 (1), 109–132.

Lizzeri, A., Persico, N., 2004. Why did the elites extend the suffrage? Democracy and the scope of government, with an application to Britain's "Age of Reform". The Quarterly Journal of Economics 119 (2), 707–765.

Mahoney, J., 2000. Path dependence in historical sociology. Theory and Society 29 (4), 507–548.

Marx, K., 1911. A Contribution to the Critique of Political Economy. CH Kerr.

Marx, K., 2019. Capital: Volume One. Dover Publications.

Matsuyama, K., 1991. Increasing returns, industrialization, and indeterminacy of equilibrium. The Quarterly Journal of Economics 106 (2), 617–650.

Mittal, S., Weingast, B.R., 2013. Self-enforcing constitutions: with an application to democratic stability in America's first century. Journal of Law, Economics, & Organization 29 (2), 278–302.

North, D., 1990. Institutions, Institutional Change and Economic Performance Cambridge University Press. Cambridge University Press.

North, D.C., Thomas, R.P., 1973. The Rise of the Western World: A New Economic History. Cambridge University Press, Cambridge.

North, D.C., Weingast, B., 1989. Constitutions and commitment: the evolution of institutions governing public choice in seventeenth-century England. The Journal of Economic History 49 (4), 803–832.

Ostrom, E., 2005. Doing institutional analysis digging deeper than markets and hierarchies. In: Handbook of New Institutional Economics. Springer, pp. 819–848.

Page, S.E., et al., 2006. Path dependence. Quarterly Journal of Political Science 1 (1), 87–115.

Paige, J.M., 1998. Coffee and Power: Revolution and the Rise of Democracy in Central America. Harvard University Press.

Pankhurst, E.S., 2019. The Suffragette: The History of the Women's Militant Suffrage Movement, 1905-1910. Good Press.

Persson, T., Tabellini, G., 2000. Political Economics: Explaining Economic Policy. MIT Press, Cambridge, MA.

Pierson, P., 2000. Increasing returns, path dependence, and the study of politics. American Political Science Review, 251–267.

Postan, M.M., 1973. The Medieval Economy and Society: An Economic History of Britain, 1100-1500, vol. 1. Univ. of California Press.

Potter, D., 1976. The Impending Crisis, 1848-1861. Harper & Row.

Putnam, R.D., 1993. Making Democracy Work: Civic Traditions in Modern Italy. Princeton University Press.

Roberts, K., 2015. Dynamic voting in clubs. Research in Economics 69 (3), 320–335.

Roháč, D., 2008. The unanimity rule and religious fractionalisation in the Polish-Lithuanian Republic. Constitutional Political Economy 19 (2), 111–128.

Roland, G., 1991. The political economy of transition in the Soviet Union. European Economy 49, 197–216.

Roland, G., 2004. Understanding institutional change: fast-moving and slow-moving institutions. Studies in Comparative International Development (SCID) 38, 109–131.

Roland, G., 2020. Culture, Institutions, and Development. Princeton University Press.

Runciman, D., 2017. The Confidence Trap: A History of Democracy in Crisis from World War I to the Present-Revised Edition. Princeton University Press.

Service, R., 2005. A History of Modern Russia from Nicholas II to Vladimir Putin. Harvard University Press.

Tabellini, G., 2008. Institutions and culture. Journal of the European Economic Association 6 (2–3), 255–294.

Tabellini, G., 2010. Culture and institutions: economic developpent in the regions of Europe. Journal of the European Economic Association 8 (4), 677–716.

Thelen, K., 1999. Historical institutionalism in comparative politics. Annual Review of Political Science 2 (1), 369–404.

Treisman, D., 2011. The Return: Russia's Journey from Gorbachev to Medvedev. Free Press.

Veblen, T., 1899. The Theory of the Leisure Class: An Economic Study of Institutions.

Weingast, B.R., 1997. The political foundations of democracy and the rule of law. American Political Science Review 91 (2), 245–263.

Weingast, B., 1998. Political Stability and Civil War: Institutions, Commitment, and American Democracy. Princeton University Press, pp. 148–193.

Wiener, J.M., 1978. Social Origins of the New South: Alabama, 1860-1885. Louisiana State University Press.

Williamson, O.E., 2000. The new institutional economics: taking stock, looking ahead. Journal of Economic Literature 38 (3), 595–613.

Wollstonecraft, M., 1891. A Vindication of the Rights of Woman: With Strictures on Political and Moral Subjects. Fisher Unwin.

Woodward, C.V., 1955. The Strange Career of Jim Crow. Oxford University Press.

Wright, G., 2013. Sharing the Prize. Harvard University Press.

How institutions and cultures change: an evolutionary perspective

Samuel Bowles[a], **Jung-Kyoo Choi**[b], **Sung-Ha Hwang**[c], **and Suresh Naidu**[d,e]

[a]*Sante Fe Institute, Santa Fe, NM, United States*
[b]*Kyungpook National University, Daegu, Republic of Korea*
[c]*Korean Advanced Institute of Science and Technology (KAIST), Seoul, Republic of Korea*
[d]*Columbia University, New York, NY, United States*
[e]*NBER, Cambridge, MA, United States*

14.1 Introduction

Changes in institutions and cultures are often attributed to decisions of governments or other authoritative bodies: the end of slavery in the U.S. South by the Emancipation Proclamation in 1863, the prohibition of polygyny by the Catholic Church at the mid 16th century Council of Trent, or Benito Mussolini's 1939 requirement that the more informal "voi" replace "Lei" in official spoken language and in schools. But the relationship between these three edicts and changes in the de facto structure of social interactions differs dramatically. The Emancipation Proclamation fundamentally altered the institutional structure of the southern economy and society; but the Council of Trent's prohibition confirmed a process that had effectively eliminated polygyny from Europe at least a half a millennium earlier, and the limited effect of Mussolini's language policy was erased upon his death.

To understand the processes by which social structures change, economists have adopted what we call the political economy approach, treating "institutions as collective choices that are the outcome of a political process" and cultural and institutional change as the outcome of bargaining between farsighted representatives of a small number of groups—a political elite and the citizenry, for example, as in Acemoglu and Robinson (2008) or Acemoglu et al. (2020) in this book. An important contribution of this approach is its focus on societal level conflict between classes and between political elites and commoners. Institutions considered in this literature are most often state-enforced "rules of the game" as exemplified by U.S. slavery and its eventual prohibition in 1863. But the early demise of European polygyny and the failure of the Partito Nazionale Fascista to foster less hierarchical forms of address suggest that other dynamic processes are also at work.

Here we make the case that these are best studied by combining the focus on group conflict of the political economy approach with evolutionary game theory, which has been used extensively for modeling and selecting among equilibria that emerge from decentralized interactions in a large population of boundedly rational individuals. Models of cultural evolution in this literature draw on analogies from population genetics, exemplified by Cavalli-Sforza and Feldman (1981) and Boyd and Richerson (1988).

The Handbook of Historical Economics. https://doi.org/10.1016/B978-0-12-815874-6.00022-8

Nunn (2020) in this book updates the Boyd and Richerson approach to cultural change as an evolutionary process. The literatures inspired by these works have focused for the most part on cross-group variation in cultural traits, like "trust", rather than on the evolution of rules of the game governing conflictual relationships between classes or other groups.[1] Exceptions among studies applied to empirical questions include the study of crop sharing conventions (Young and Burke, 2001) and linguistic markers of superior and subordinate status (Clyne et al., 2009) as well as studies of between-population conflicts that could support the genetic evolution of altruism by group selection (Bowles, 2006).

Evolutionary game theory is particularly well suited to model the evolution of institutions and cultures where these are not maintained by the state or negotiated among a few collective actors, but instead emerge at the population level from a decentralized process. An illustration is the dramatic effect on relations between men and women that was set in motion by the adoption of animal traction and the plough (Boserup, 1970), an entirely uncoordinated process that apparently transformed the gender division of labor, inducing gender inequalities that persist even today, for example, in lower female labor force participation and more unequal gender norms (Alesina et al., 2013).

Other examples of these substantially decentralized processes involving conflicts of interest among groups include community standards for female labor force participation and customs governing inheritance (Goody et al., 1976), conventions of wage-setting (Bewley, 1999; Dube et al., 2018), informal economic norms of property (Silbey, 2010), legal contracting (Gulati and Scott, 2012), and the evolution of linguistic conventions concerning, what are termed "pronouns of power and solidarity" (illustrated by the asymmetrical use of "vous" and "tu" (Naidu et al., 2017)), building on classic work in the socio-linguistics of inequality (Brown and Gilman, 1960).

Before proceeding, let us clarify our use of terms. Both institutions and cultures are attributes not of individuals but of groups of people. *Institutions* are the durable rules of the game governing social interactions in a population. Conformity to these rules may be secured by centralized enforcement ("laws"), by social sanctioning of deviations ("social norms"), or by common expectations, where conformity is a best response conditional on most others conforming ("beliefs").[2] A *culture* is constituted by learned (not genetically transmitted) behaviors and is described by the distribution of the preferences motivating these behaviors in a population.

Here we illustrate the evolutionary approach to understanding how cultures and institutions change. Although we retain the political economy focus on conflict, cultures and institutions in our model are not directly chosen by forward-looking actors, but rather emerge as the largely unintended consequence of individual actions of large numbers of myopic people using local information, none of whom is powerful enough to make choices over society-wide outcomes (David, 1985; Greif, 1994; Sugden, 1989; Young, 1998b; Hayek, 1960).

Four empirically motivated building blocks are the foundation of our model. First, both the information available to actors and their cognitive capacities and predispositions are limited; people take actions in light of what they may reasonably be expected to have learned from their own and others' recent past experiences. Second, for both accidental and intentional reasons, people sometimes do not

---

[1] Nunn interprets a number of empirical "persistence" results, where differences between cultures persist long after the source of differentiation has disappeared, in light of an evolutionary model. He notes that the evolutionary literature rarely addresses power, coercion, and inequality.

[2] A social norm – against eating pork or selling your vote, for example – can constitute part of the rules of the game if it becomes what Amartya Sen calls a "commitment", effectively truncating the action set of the members of a population.

act in ways that maximize their expected payoffs. Third, we represent cultural-institutional configurations as conventions, that is, mutual best responses. These multiple stable equilibria arise because of the positive feedbacks arising from the strategic complementarities associated with conforming to a set of institutions or a societal culture. Fourth, changes in cultures and institutions occur as a result of both transitions among conventions within populations and competition between populations, modeled jointly as a single dynamical system.

Our strategy is to discipline our modeling by confronting a series of historical cases. In the next section, we illustrate this unified dual evolutionary selection mechanism with an agent-based model of one of the most fundamental cultural-institutional shifts experienced by humanity, the Neolithic revolution. Sections 14.3–14.6 provide a unified model of both between-population competition and within-population cultural-institutional transitions. Then we illustrate the approach by an analysis of the demise of serfdom and the emergence of the national state in Europe. Further historical illustrations (in Section 14.7) come from the inverted-U-shaped trajectory of union density among private sector workers in the 20th-century United States.

14.2 Evolutionary selection: the origin of private property

For most of the epoch in which anatomically modern humans have lived—the 150,000 or so years before the end of the last ice age—our ancestors interacted without the aid of any institutions even remotely resembling contemporary states or private property. The mobile foraging bands then making up the common form of human social organization apparently did not, however, suffer the chaos of the Hobbesian state of nature. Rather, in a manner similar to contemporary mobile hunter-gatherers, there is good reason to believe that their lives were regulated by social norms (often including resource-sharing) enforced by collective peer punishment.

Beginning around eleven thousand years ago at perhaps a dozen independent sites around the world, our hunter–gatherer ancestors radically altered both the technologies by which they secured their livelihood and the rules of the game governing its production and distribution. Food was now produced rather than foraged, and individual or family possession-based private property rights replaced a system of widespread sharing of food and other resources.[3]

The magnitude of these changes and their occurrence long before there were state structures or other forms of elite power that could have implemented them by some kind of "top-down" process make the Neolithic revolution an apt illustration of the joint decentralized dynamics of within- and between-population institutional selection. Any convincing model of this process must be consistent with the extraordinary persistence of the hunter–gather conventions prior to 11,000 years ago. Here we show how the dual evolutionary selection process mentioned above can help explain both the persistence of the collectivist and egalitarian hunter–gatherer cultural-institutional convention and its eventual replacement by a more unequal private-property-based convention.

---

[3] This section draws on the models, evidence, and simulations reported by Bowles and Choi (2013, 2019).

Table 14.1 The row player's expected payoff in the Bourgeois–Sharer–Civic game in a foraging economy.
Foragers acquire V_h and then play the game to distribute the product. Because possession of a foraged product is difficult to establish, Bourgeois always claim the product regardless of possession and play exactly like Hawk in the Hawk–Dove game. Sharers are identical to Dove. The winning probability of Civic player, $f((1 - \alpha - \beta)N))$, is larger the greater is the number of the Civics in the group $((1 - \alpha - \beta)N)$, where N is the total population size. For example, we could assume that $f = \frac{1}{2} + \frac{1}{2}(1 - \alpha - \beta)$. C is the cost that the loser of the contest bears.

	Bourgeois	Sharer	Civic
Bourgeois	$\frac{1}{2}(V_h - C)$	V_h	$-fC + (1 - f)V_h$
Sharer	0	$\frac{1}{2}V_h$	$\frac{1}{2}V_h$
Civic	$\frac{fV_h - (1-f)C}{(1-\alpha-\beta)N}$	$\frac{1}{2}V_h$	$\frac{1}{2}V_h$

14.2.1 The long-term persistence of the hunter–gatherer convention

To explain the persistence of this convention and also its eventual demise in a common model, we study the distribution of behaviors among individual members of distinct populations that occasionally engage with other populations in some kind of conflict or contest for resources. We begin with interactions within a particular population.

After acquiring foraged resources, each individual is randomly paired with another member of their group for an interaction in which they distribute the consumption of their products, which we model as a modified version of Maynard Smith's Bourgeois–Hawk–Dove game (Maynard Smith, 1974).

The strategies that an individual may adopt reflect patterns of sharing, aggrandizement, and collective discipline found in ethnographic studies of hunter–gatherers and horticulturalists (Kaplan and Hill, 1985; Kaplan et al., 2005; Gintis et al., 2005; Boehm, 2009; Wiessner, 2005). Similar to the Dove in the Hawk–Dove game, the first behavioral type, the Sharer, concedes half of the product to the other, or the whole product if the other claims it. Bourgeois individuals claim the entire product if it is in their possession or where possession is ambiguous. Let α and β be the fraction of Sharers and Bourgeois, respectively, in the population.

The third behavioral type, the Civics, act exactly like Sharers when they meet a fellow Civic or a Sharer (i.e., they share), but when paired with an individual who refuses to share (a Bourgeois), they join with any other Civics in the population to contest the claims of the Bourgeois, succeeding with a probability $f((1 - \alpha - \beta)N)$ that is increasing with their numbers $(1 - \alpha - \beta)N$, where $1 - \alpha - \beta$ is the fraction of the Civics and N is the total population size. If they succeed, then they distribute the Bourgeois' product among all the Civics, whereas the losing Bourgeois bears a cost. If, instead, the Civics fail, then they equally bear the losers' cost.[4] Two Bourgeois may engage in contests with each other with negative expected payoffs if possession of the product is ambiguous and contestable (as we assume it to be in a foraging economy).

Individuals are occasionally paired with a cultural model (e.g., an elder) and have the opportunity to update their strategy. If the two are the same type, then no updating occurs. However, if they differ,

---

[4] The civic strategy is based on ethnographic studies of the maintenance social order in stateless societies (Wiessner, 2005; Boehm, 2009) so as to allow a more realistic coordinated rather than individual punishment process (Boyd et al., 2010).

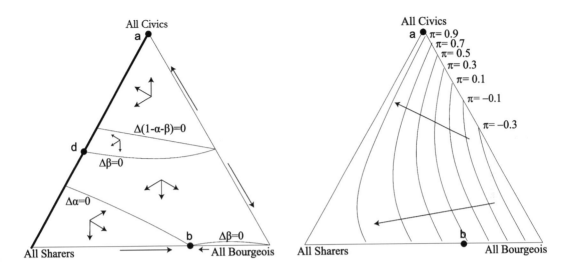

FIGURE 14.1 Within-population and between-population dynamics in the foraging economy.

In both panels the coordinates of a point in the simplex sum to one, giving the distribution of strategies. Point **d** in the left panel, for example, is a state with half of the populations being Civics and half Sharers, with no Bourgeois. Point **a** is a state with only Civics. The vectors (arrows) in the left panel show the change in the fraction playing each strategy that is implied by the payoff monotonic updating process applied to the distribution of strategies given by the root of the arrow. An arrow pointing toward a vertex means that the strategy labeled at the vertex is increasing its population share; an arrow pointing away from a vertex means the opposite. In the right panel the contours show states with equal population average payoffs. For the parameters used ($V_h = 2, C = 3$), any state like point **d** in the left panel along the left edge of the simplex in which the Bourgeois strategy has not been adopted by anyone will have an average payoff of 1, whereas a state like point **b** in the right-hand panel – the Bourgeois–Sharer equilibrium – has an average payoff of one-third. The arrows in the right panel indicate the direction of increasing average payoffs.

and if the model's payoff in the previous period was higher than that of the updating individual, then he or she switches to the type of the model. Thus strategies with higher than average playoffs tend to increase in frequency within the population. The payoff matrix of this game appears in Table 14.1.

In addition to within-group individual interactions and updating, populations interact in contests. These could be outright violent conflicts (the case we model here); but a contest could also be with nature for the survival of the group facing a climate shock, in which the surviving group occupies and populates the site of the failed group. The payoffs of members of the losing group are reduced for one period following the contest.

In groups that have not lost a contest with another group, the cultural model is selected from the group's own population as above. But in groups that have lost a contest in the previous period, updating individuals are paired with models drawn from the winning group, thereby tending to spread those behavior types that are common in the winning group. The key is that the group with the higher total payoff becomes a cultural model for the less successful group.

Using the model, we ask how the forager-cum-resource sharing convention might have endured over long periods. For every population state in the simplex in the left-hand panel of Fig. 14.1, we determine the changes of the population share of each of the behavioral types from period to period. We can do this because the current fraction of each behavior type uniquely determines the expected payoffs of each type and, hence, given the updating process just described, the expected change in population frequencies of the types in the next period. Thus the replicator equations describing this dynamic give the expected movement of each frequency of three strategies (i.e., behavioral types) on the simplex (the arrows in the left panel in Fig. 14.1).

In the figure we identify two equilibria. One is located on the bottom edge of the simplex, where Civics are entirely absent, and Sharers' and Bourgeois' population shares are $1 - V_h/C$ and V_h/C, respectively (point **b**). This equilibrium is analogous to the equilibrium of the standard Hawk–Dove game, and it is evolutionarily stable. Both strategies are represented because in the absence of Civics, neither Bourgeois nor Sharer is an evolutionary stable strategy: given the ambiguity of possession in a foraging economy, Bourgeois will invade an all Sharer population (claiming the goods of the Sharers), and Sharers will invade an all Bourgeois population in which the expected payoff to Bourgeois is negative (because their interactions are entirely with other Bourgeois). We call this the Hobbesian equilibrium as it is characterized by frequent fighting over the product and Bourgeois seizures of the products of Sharers.

The other equilibrium is the set of population states located on the left edge of the simplex, where no Bourgeois exist in the population. This equilibrium combines unconditional sharing (by Sharers) and collective upholding of social norms (by Civics). We call this decentralized and egalitarian convention the Rousseauian equilibrium. It is neutrally stable and subject to drift along the edge of the simplex because Sharers and Civics are behaviorally identical in the absence of Bourgeois.

Because of drift, the Rousseauian equilibrium is prone to unraveling and in the absence of between group competition will not persist over long periods. To see this, suppose that initially only Civics are present ($\alpha = \beta = 0$), then an invading bourgeois will with virtual certainty lose contests with the Civics ($f = \frac{1}{2} + \frac{1}{2}(1 - \alpha - \beta) \approx 1$), receiving zero payoffs. Due to migration across groups or nonbest-response play, both Bourgeois and Sharers will be introduced into the population. Initially, Bourgeois players will still not be able to successfully invade the population because they will be outnumbered by Civics in the group and hence will lose interactions with Civics. But as there will be no selective pressures operating against the Sharers, the number of Civics will occasionally decline below point **d**. When the Civics become too few to punish Bourgeois when they claim the Civic's product, the Bourgeois types will successfully invade the population and, as the vectors in Fig. 14.1 show, propel the population to the Hobbesian equilibrium.

By contrast, the Hobbesian equilibrium is asymptotically stable and thus will not be subject to the chance-induced drift that eventually unravels the Rousseauian equilibrium. Invasion by a lone Civic will be repelled because it would frequently engage in one-on-one attempts to punish the many Bourgeois, and costs of occasional losses in these contests would deter others from copying the Civic strategy in the updating process. Of course, this Hobbesian equilibrium may itself be displaced: sooner or later a bunching of chance events may displace the population into the basin of attraction of the Rousseauian equilibrium. But the fact that the Hobbesian equilibrium is not subject to drift means that its displacement will be unlikely in any given period and hence will be infrequent.

If the Rousseauian equilibrium is more vulnerable to chance events than the Hobbesian equilibrium as our model shows, why and how did most of human prehistory witness a social order more akin to the Rousseauian equilibrium? To explain its evolutionary success, refer to the right panel in Fig. 14.1 giving iso-average-payoff loci showing the population states with equal average payoffs. Higher payoff all-Civic populations or mixed Civic Sharer populations will win between-population contests, and this will periodically create populations with substantial Civic populations in place of defeated populations that were at the Hobbesian equilibrium.

If the between-population competition—occasionally converting Bourgeois–Sharer populations to largely Civic—is sufficiently frequent and contest outcomes are strongly dependent on average payoffs, then this could account for the long-term persistence of the hunter–gatherer convention. We will explore this possibility and the demise of the Rousseauian equilibrium using a simulation of the model just described based on empirically plausible parameters.[5]

14.2.2 The Neolithic revolution: a puzzle

Douglass North and Paul Thomas explained what they called "the first economic revolution" by some combination of "a decline in the productivity of labour in hunting, a rise in the productivity of labour in agriculture, or [an] ... expansion of the size of the labour-force" (North and Thomas, 1977, 232). The puzzle arises because recent evidence (Bowles, 2011) suggests that it is very unlikely that farming was more productive than foraging at the time, and the first domestications occurred following periods of population decline (Bowles and Choi, 2019).

Recall that the Bourgeois–Sharer convention is characterized by frequent within group conflicts between Bourgeois players and hence low average payoffs compared to the Civic convention. These conflicts arise because the sources of the forager livelihood—dispersed and wild resources—make it difficult to establish the unambiguous possession that would eliminate conflicts between Bourgeois types. Farming reduced this problem because it raised the average product of land, so that a relatively small, easily demarcated and defended plot or set of domesticated animals could be the basis of a family's livelihood.[6]

The payoffs to the three behavioral types conditional on the product being farmed rather than foraged are given in Table 14.2.

In the Bourgeois–Sharer–Civic game in farming economy, there are two equilibria. As in the forager economy, one is the Rousseauian equilibrium, where only two behavioral types, Sharer and Civic, coexist. The second equilibrium is an all-Bourgeois equilibrium, where Bourgeois respect the other's possession and avoid any conflicts because there is no ambiguity of possession. The change in technology—to food production—makes Bourgeois an evolutionary stable strategy.

The key result of the advent of farming is that between-population conflicts no longer strongly favor the Rousseauian equilibrium: the difference in two conventions' average payoffs is now limited to the somewhat inferior productivity of the farming economy rather than including also the frequency of costly within-group conflicts, which occurred when possession was ambiguous. Given the difference

---

[5] If contest success is based on some concave function of the payoffs of the members of the group, then the Rousseauian equilibrium will be additionally favored because payoffs in the all Civic state are equal, whereas in the Bourgeois equilibrium, payoffs to both Sharers and Bourgeois are highly unequal as they depend critically on whether they are matched with a Bourgeois or a Sharer. For example, if contest success resources of an individual are a concave function such as $\ln(1+$ the individual's payoffs) and the probability that the Civic population wins a contest is its share of total contest resources of the two contestants, then with $V_h = 2$ and $C = 3$, the Civic population's win probability goes from 75 percent in the linear case to virtually certainty (98 percent) in the concave case. We return to the possibility that contest success is concave in members' payoffs in Section 14.5.

[6] Amy Bogaard has estimated that under the wheat-farming methods used during the early Neolithic in Europe, a single hectare of land could provide more than two-thirds of the calories required annually for a family of five (Bogaard, 2004, Table 2.2).

Table 14.2 The row player's expected payoff in the Bourgeois–Sharer–Civic game in a farming economy.

Farmers obtain V from the production stage. Because the possession of farmed products is readily determined and defended, a Bourgeois respects ownership of the product by other Bourgeois. As before, $f((1 - \alpha - \beta)N)$ is the winning probability of a Civic player engaged in a contest with a Bourgeois, which is increasing with the number of the Civics in the group. Note that farming requires a prior investment z, so that a farmer bears a cost of $-z$ irrespective of the pairing. When a Bourgeois meets either a Sharer or a Civic, she will be a possessor half the time.

	Bourgeois	Sharer	Civic
Bourgeois	$\frac{1}{2}V - z$	$\frac{3}{4}V - z$	$\frac{1}{2}(-fC + (1-f)V) + \frac{1}{4}V - z$
Sharer	$\frac{1}{4}V - z$	$\frac{1}{2}V - z$	$\frac{1}{2}V - z$
Civic	$\frac{fV-(1-f)C}{(1-\alpha-\beta)N} + \frac{1}{4}V - z$	$\frac{1}{2}V - z$	$\frac{1}{2}V - z$

in the stability properties of the two equilibria – asymptotically stable for the new Bourgeois convention (we no longer call it Hobbesian because within-group conflict is absent) and only neutrally stable for the Rousseauian convention – that was therefore subject to unraveling by drift, as we saw above.

This opened a possible pathway for the emergence of the farming-cum-private property convention, even if on a calories-per-hour basis food production initially fell short of foraging. But a would-be farmer would have had little incentive to engage in the required investments in clearing, cultivation, animal tending, and storage if a harvested crop or slaughtered domesticated animal would be distributed under the forager system of sharing.

The resulting chicken-and-egg puzzle might be resolved if farming had been much more productive than foraging, but initially it very likely was not. The highly volatile climate conditions of the Late Pleistocene (that is prior to about 11,500 years ago; see Fig. 14.2) made the choice of farming particularly unlikely, even were most members of some group to adopt the Bourgeois strategy. It also dictated highly mobile foraging strategies, also militating against the build up of a domain of privately owned things of value, such as homes, which could later be a property-rights template that could be extended to farming. The warming and moderation of climate variations at the end of the Pleistocene allowed a more sedentary living and reduced but did not eliminate the productivity disadvantage of farming.

How, then, did this new technology and novel system of property rights emerge and proliferate? We propose that the new property rights and the new way of making a living coevolved, neither being viable alone, but each providing the conditions permitting the advance of the other. This coevolution hypothesis is based on two empirically motivated premises: that farming required a novel system of property rights and that (in the absence of exceptional circumstances) this system of farming-friendly possession based property rights was not viable in an economy based on dispersed and irregularly occurring wild plant and animal species. This is why coevolution was possible and independent evolution unlikely.

Because the complexity of our unified between and within population updating dynamics do not allow informative analytical solutions, we use an agent-based simulation to examine how the transition might have occurred (Bowles and Choi, 2013). Our results summarized in Fig. 14.2 show both the long persistence of resource-sharing norm enforced by collective punishments in foraging economy and the eventual coevolution of farming and private property-rights system. Despite being an unlikely

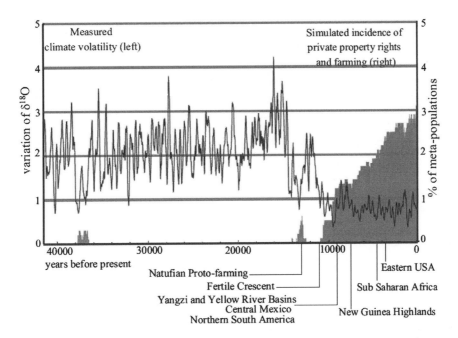

FIGURE 14.2 Transition to possession-based farming economy.

Based on simulations by Bowles and Choi (2013), the grey vertical bars indicate for the year given the number of simulated populations (of the 1,000 simulated) in which more than half of the entire population have adopted the Bourgeois behavioral strategy and the farming technology. The solid line indicates year-to-year variability in surface temperatures measured by levels of $\delta^{18}O$ from Greenland ice cores. The labels below the horizontal axis give the dates of some well documented transitions to farming. Parameter values: group size per generation=20; migration rate=0.2; nonbest-response play=0.25; group interaction=once every generation.

event, farming and a new system of farming-friendly property rights nonetheless jointly emerged in the simulations.

Though the only time series data used in the simulation is the measure of climate volatility, the simulations replicate the archaeological record, indicated below the horizontal axis by the dates at which the best studied transitions from foraging to farming took place. Recall also that the independent occurrence of the Neolithic revolution is an extraordinarily rare event, and our simulations replicate this too: fewer than 3% of our simulations result in a transition from the foraging-Civic equilibrium to the farming-cum-private property. Note that the brief climate amelioration around 37,000–35,000 and 15,000–13,000 years ago are associated in the simulations with short-lived experiments with farming, the latter coinciding exactly with the well-documented Natufian proto-farming episode in the Levant.[7]

---

[7] There is no archaeological evidence that humans experimented with farming or private property in the earlier climate ameliorating period, but there are cases of false starts other than the Natufian in the later period.

If our interpretation is correct, then, the Neolithic revolution was not induced by a superior technology. It occurred because possession of the products of farmers could be unambiguously demarcated and defended. This created a new asymptotically stable private property equilibrium to which the forager-Civic populations would switch frequently enough (due to drift) to more than offset the modest disadvantages (due to lower productivity) of the farming groups in between-group competition.

14.3 Wars and revolutions: a unified model of equilibrium selection

Our interpretation of the Neolithic revolution addressed a specific question about an actually occurring historical event, and we borrowed from the ethnographic and archaeological evidence to develop a model of sufficient complexity to capture what may have been the critical dynamics. But partly as result, our analytical results thus far have been confined to identifying stable equilibria in the space of choices of behavioral strategies and technologies. The analytically intractable dynamics of the dual process of equilibrium selection, operating both within- and between-populations, has been explored using a simulation.

Agent-based simulations are important tools for modeling complex systems. The natural formal analogue of an agent-based model is stochastic evolutionary game theory, where agents play strategies with some "noise" enabling transitions across equilibria. We now propose to explicitly model the dynamical process resulting from within- and between-population institutional and cultural transitions illustrated by the Neolithic revolution.

We will also modernize the setting somewhat by introducing classes, that is, sets of people occupying differing positions defined by the rules of the game governing the economy. We also modify the stochastic element in the choice of strategies by requiring agents to only play "intentionally" when they are engaging in nonbest-response play.

14.3.1 A dual process equilibrium selection mechanism

In our model, two classes of actors (rich and poor) make up distinct populations (e.g., nations or firms) that jointly constitute a metapopulation. The model has two basic ingredients. The first is a simultaneous move game ("stage game") played between the members of two classes in a large population to select one of two alternative contracts to govern their interaction. As in our model of the Neolithic revolution, the population fractions of a strategy will increase if the payoffs to that strategy are higher than the population mean. A stable equilibrium of this process is a Nash equilibrium of the game.

An attractive feature of evolutionary game theory is that it provides an explicit mechanism by which an equilibrium is obtained (without empirically dubious assumptions on rationality and common knowledge) based on the explicit modeling of out-of-equilibrium dynamics. This feature is essential to the second ingredient, equilibrium selection. Because institutions are modeled as conventions, the stage games typically have multiple equilibria. Rather than seeing this as an unattractive "bug" of the model, we see them as real features of the data we seek to explain. Transitions between otherwise long-enduring social arrangements that occur rapidly (on historical or archaeological timescales) are real phenomena to be explained. A model of transitions between equilibria capture these dynamics naturally without the ad hoc introduction of exogenous aggregate shocks.

Two processes make up the equilibrium selection mechanism in our model. Within a population, a transition from one stable equilibrium to another may occur as the result of the rare bunching of nonbest-response (idiosyncratic) play. Here we extend models due to Young (1993, 1998b) by introducing (as in Bowles (2004) and Naidu et al. (2010)) both intentional deviations from the status quo convention (rather than mutation-like random errors in the conventional set up) and by allowing for subpopulations—our classes—to differ in size.[8] The second equilibrium selection process is between-population competition, in which populations at equilibria supporting higher payoffs prevail over other populations, imposing their cultural-institutional convention on the losers.

Both of these selection processes—idiosyncratic play and between population selection—have natural analogues in biology. Group selection is a force that can account for the emergence of individually costly behaviors (e.g., altruistic cooperation) that raise the fitness of other members of a population group. Institutional change by idiosyncratic play is analogous to the emergence of new species or novel characteristics due to mutation in population genetics (Wright, 1935; Bowles et al., 2003; Pagano, 2001).

14.3.2 The stakes of the game are the rules of the game

We consider a large population consisting of two classes whose members play the asymmetric contract game shown in Table 14.3 with two pure-strategy Nash equilibria. These are the cultural-institutional conventions of interest. A convention is a state in which virtually all members of both classes play the same strategy because it is a best response given the strategies they believe that others will adopt.[9]

The strategy sets for players of both classes are committing to one of two contracts, E in which the payoffs of the two classes (sub-populations) are equal and U in which the members of one class receive more than half of the total payoffs. Both conventions are Pareto-efficient. But they differ in the distribution of the payoffs that they implement: the rich (Rs) do better in the unequal contract and the poor (Ps) do better in the equal contract.

To illustrate the kinds of contracts among which decentralized selection may take place, suppose the Rs (column players in our game matrix) are landowners, men, whites, or employers, whereas Ps (row players) are tenants, women, African-Americans, or workers. Contract E is an equal sharecropping or profit-sharing contract, yielding payoff 1 to both poor and rich agents, whereas Contract U is an unequal fixed rental or wage contract, yielding payoffs $\sigma\rho$ and $(1-\sigma)\rho$ to the poor and rich agents, respectively, with $\sigma < \frac{1}{2}$ and $\sigma\rho < 1 < (1-\sigma)\rho$, so that Rs prefer the unequal contract U, whereas Ps prefer the equal contract E.

We refer to the class receiving the less-than-one-half share in the unequal contract as "poor" even though their share is one-half in the equal contract. This is a convenience motivated by that fact that for the class structures we illustrate here, there are more poor than rich. For example, the crop share may be

---

[8] We contrast our model of within-population convention transitions with the more standard evolutionary game theory model in Section 14.4.4.

[9] We provide formal results in our associated papers (Bowles and Choi, 2013, 2019; Bowles et al., 2003; Naidu et al., 2010; Hwang et al., 2018); here we describe the foundational intuitions about the stochastic stability of cultural-institutional conventions and transitions among them (Belloc and Bowles, 2013, 2017; Bowles and Choi, 2013, 2019; Naidu et al., 2010; Hwang et al., 2018; Naidu et al., 2017).

Table 14.3 Payoffs in the Contract Game.
Note that because $\sigma\rho < 1 < (1-\sigma)\rho$, Rs strictly prefer the unequal contract (U, U), whereas Ps strictly prefer the equal contract (E, E). The off-diagonal terms are zero because while we represent payoffs as shares of total output, the players are bargaining over the rules of the game governing their interaction rather simply over distributional shares. Agreement on the rules of the game is a necessary condition for positive payoffs.

	U	E
U	$\sigma\rho, (1-\sigma)\rho$	$0, 0$
E	$0, 0$	$1, 1$

one half, but under this "equal" contract, the landlord with ten sharecroppers will be correspondingly richer than each of his tenants.

We term the Nash equilibria of this game conventions because they are mutual best responses: if almost all of one class are playing U, then the best response for members of the other is to play U as well, stabilizing the unequal convention.

In this model, cultural-institutional change is represented by a population shifting from one of the Nash equilibria to another, which takes place by means of two selection processes working simultaneously. The first, internal, process occurs if the members of one class deviate from the strategy defining the status quo convention in sufficient numbers to make it a best response for the members of the other class to switch strategies.

The second selection process is external. Each population is occasionally paired with another population in some kind of competition in which the group's total payoffs and their distribution compared to that of the other group will determine the outcome of the competition. Analogously to the model of the Neolithic revolution, if the conventions of the two population differ, then the losing population switches to the convention in the winning population.

The most obvious form of competition is war—as in the example of the emergence of the European national state that we model in Section 14.7—and this is the metaphor we will use in modeling the process. Other well-documented empirical cases of cultural and institutional change, as a result of between-population contests and assimilation, are the conquest of the Dinka by the Nuer in the upper Nile basin (Kelly, 1985) and the process of cultural evolution in New Guinea (Soltis et al., 1995). Another example is the meteoric spread of Islam in the century following Mohammed's death encompassing a broad swath from beyond the Indus River in the east to the Douro River in Spain in the West. This was possible because (according to Levy (1957, p. 3)) the faith in Allah provided "a bond far stronger though more subtle than that of kinship" and facilitated more inclusive systems of taxation and military recruitment and alliance. Thus the process of group conflict followed by cultural assimilation or physical extinction appears to be quite general.

The between-population selection process can be based on any form of competition including demographic and emulation (e.g., religious or linguistic conversions) that is sufficiently decisive to result in a convention switch. The same model can be applied to economic competition among alternative forms of business organization (e.g., firms, unionized firms, and cooperatives).

We first consider the internal convention-switching process.

14.4 **Within-population transitions**

14.4.1 **Best response and intentional deviations from the status quo**

Within each population, in every period, rich and poor members are randomly paired to play the game shown in Table 14.3. The updating process is not forward looking but instead responds to recent play of members of the other class. With probability $1 - \epsilon$, members select a strategy that is a best response to the distribution of the other class's strategies played in the previous period. With some small probability ϵ, the rate of nonbest-response (that is, idiosyncratic) play, they choose the strategy that would give them a higher payoff if sufficiently many other members of their class were to do the same. Our updating rule is termed myopic best response with intentional idiosyncratic play. The relative size of the poor class is η, so if N^R is the size of the rich class, then $N^P = \eta \times N^R$ is the size of the poor class.

A state is given by a number for each class (p, q), where p is the fraction of poor that adopted strategy E in the previous period, and q is the fraction of the rich that played U. Members of each class are randomly matched to play the game, so that everyone in each class has an equal probability of interacting with every member in the other class each round. Thus given the distribution of play by the other class in the previous period, p and q, the payoffs expected from a single interaction for a rich person (π_R) and a poor person (π_P) were they to play U and E respectively, are

$$\pi_R(U, p) = (1 - p)(1 - \sigma)\rho \quad \text{and} \quad \pi_R(E, p) = p$$

and

$$\pi_P(U, q) = q\sigma\rho \quad \text{and} \quad \pi_P(E, q) = 1 - q.$$

The best responses are denoted as $B_P(q)$ and $B_R(p)$ and given by

$$B_P(q) := \arg\max_{i \in \{U,E\}} \pi_P(i, q) \quad \text{and} \quad B_R(p) := \arg\max_{j \in \{U,E\}} \pi_R(j, p).$$

In the absence of idiosyncratic play (i.e., for $\epsilon = 0$), the evolutionary dynamics within the population is governed by a set of monotonic best-response replicator equations with two recurrent (stable) states, (U, U) and (E, E).

$$P \text{ agent chooses} \begin{cases} B_P(q) & \text{with probability } 1 - \epsilon, \\ E & \text{with probability } \epsilon; \end{cases}$$
$$R \text{ agent chooses} \begin{cases} B_R(p) & \text{with probability } 1 - \epsilon, \\ U & \text{with probability } \epsilon. \end{cases} \tag{14.1}$$

This means that when the population is at or near the (E, E) equilibrium so that playing E is a best response for poor members, they always play E, whether best responding or not; similarly, near the (U, U) equilibrium, all rich players play U, whether best responding or playing idiosyncratically.

The kinds of intentional deviance that we are consider here include Rosa Parks' refusal to bow to racial segregation and give up her seat at the front of the bus, the Soweto school children who boycotted classes in protest of apartheid, and the 14th-century British villeins who simply refused to perform the labor duties owed to their lord. These actions are idiosyncratic not because they are literally random, but because they occur for reasons outside the model. We are not attempting to model the complex process of collective action in social movements; instead, we examine what conventions are stochastically stable when the process generating transitions between conventions resemble social movements.

As a result, we do not explore these reasons—intentional idiosyncratic play is a primitive of our modeling strategy—but they include outrage, a quest for personal dignity through opposition to injustice and other motives not necessarily tied to the objective of inducing a transition (Wood, 2003). The intentionality we introduce is simply directional: the 14th-century farmers did not deviate by insisting on providing more than the conventional labor services to the lord.

14.4.2 Decentralized transitions and stochastically stable states

The cultural-institutional conventions in our model are stochastically stable states, meaning that the population spends virtually the whole of some long period in that state as the rate of idiosyncratic play goes to zero. Here we also introduce the concept of isostochastic stability (from Bowles (2004)) by exploring the conditions under which transitions from the U to the E convention are equally as likely as transitions in the opposite direction, so that over a suitably long period of time the population will spend half the time in each. Isostochastic stability is a device for exploring how the degree of inequality, the level of overall productivity, the rate of idiosyncratic play, and the relative size of the two classes will alter the equilibrium selection process.

To find the stochastically stable convention, we need to determine the so-called resistances to a transition: R^{UE}, the minimum number of the poor adopting the E contract sufficient to induce a transition from the status quo unequal to the equal convention, and R^{EU}, the resistance to a transition in the opposite direction, defined analogously. These are just the critical *fraction* of the poor and of the rich sufficient to induce a transition to the convention they prefer, p^{UE} and q^{EU}, respectively, multiplied by the respective *class sizes*, namely N^P and N^R.

The critical fractions in Fig. 14.3 are given by the intersection of the two expected profit lines in each figure. Suppose in panel a of the figure that the status quo convention is U, the unequal convention that favors the rich. From Eq. (14.1) you can see that if sufficiently many idiosyncratically playing poor were to demand contract E rather than the status quo contract U, then best responding rich players would concede, switching to offering contract E in the subsequent period. We can see that the R class members will play E as their best responses if $p > p^{UE}$ or

$$p > \frac{(1 - \sigma)\rho}{1 + (1 - \sigma)\rho} = p^{UE}. \tag{14.2}$$

This will propel a transition from the unequal to the equal convention.

In the right panel of Fig. 14.3, we show the analogous case, with the equal contract the status quo. We see that if the fraction of Rs deviating from the convention and playing U exceeds q^{EU}, then the best responding poor members will switch to playing U, propelling a transition to the unequal contract preferred by the rich. The critical value q^{EU} is the boundary between the two basins of attraction, defined for transitions from E to U induced by the idiosyncratic play of the rich class with

$$q > \frac{1}{1 + \sigma\rho} = q^{EU}. \tag{14.3}$$

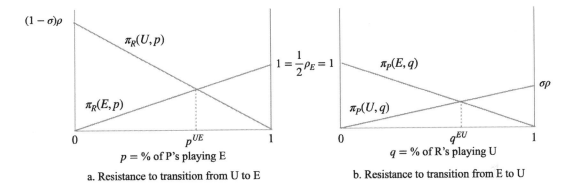

FIGURE 14.3 Critical population fractions of idiosyncratic play for transitions among conventions.

In the left panel we show p^{UE}, the minimum fraction of poor people idiosyncratically demanding the equal contract that is sufficient to induce the best responding rich in the next period to concede to interacting under the equal contract. The right panel shows q^{EU}, the analogous minimum fraction of idiosyncratically playing rich sufficient to induce the best responding poor to concede to interacting under the unequal contract. Note that both critical fractions are greater than one-half; this is because those playing idiosyncratically are seeking to induce the other class to abandon the contract they prefer.

Taking account of the size of the two classes, using Eqs. (14.2) and (14.3), the critical numbers of deviants to induce a convention switch are[10]:

Resistance for a transition from U to E: $R^{UE} = \eta N^R p^{UE} = \underbrace{\eta N^R \dfrac{(1-\sigma)\rho}{(1-\sigma)\rho + 1}}_{\text{Minimum number of deviant poor}}$,   (14.4)

Resistance for a transition from E to U: $R^{EU} = N^R q^{EU} = \underbrace{N^R \dfrac{1}{1+\sigma\rho}}_{\text{Minimum number of deviant rich}}$.   (14.5)

Which of the two states will be stochastic stable depends intuitively on the expected waiting time for a transition to that convention. The one with the shorter waiting time will be the stochastic stable state. The expected waiting times (also termed first passage time) depend in turn on the probability that in a given period a switch will occur. This requires us to establish the probabilities that the number of people in the class that would benefit from a transition who deviate is sufficient to induce the best responding members of the other class to switch strategies. For sufficiently small ϵ, these probabilities

---

[10] Throughout we assume that N^R and N^P are sufficiently large so that we can ignore the fact that R^{UE} and R^{EU} will not generally be integers.

are approximated by[11]:

$$\text{Pr}(U \text{ to } E \text{ transition}): \quad \lambda_{UE}^I(\sigma, \rho, \eta N^R) \approx \epsilon^{R^{UE}}, \tag{14.6}$$

$$\text{Pr}(E \text{ to } U \text{ transition}): \quad \lambda_{EU}^I(\sigma, \rho, N^R) \approx \epsilon^{R^{EU}}, \tag{14.7}$$

where the superscripts I denote internally induced transitions (in the next section, we introduce switches induced externally, that is, by group competition, with superscripts X).[12]

14.4.3 Equilibrium selection by productivity, inequality, and class size

Intuitively, the stochastically stable state is the convention in which those who prefer the other convention face more resistance in inducing a transition. Thus the stochastically stable state is the convention i for which $R^{ij} > R^{ji}$, that is, the convention that requires more nonbest-response play to displace (see Young (1998a)). We say that conventions i and j are isostochastically stable if $R^{ij} = R^{ji}$.

The device of isostochastic stability allows us to characterize the nature of cultural-institutional conventions and associated class structures that are favored by the within-population evolutionary dynamics that we have modeled. We will see that evolution selects conventions that are more productive (larger ρ) and preferred by the least numerous class. We also show that if class sizes are equal, then evolutionary selection favors the more equal convention unless the unequal convention has a sufficiently great productivity advantage; but the more equal convention need not be evolutionarily advantaged if the poorer class is sufficiently numerous.

To understand these results, recall that our equal contract is characterized by $(\rho_E = 2, \sigma_E = \frac{1}{2})$. For a given level ϵ of idiosyncratic play among members of the two classes, we now ask what is the set of other conventions that is isostochastically stable with the equal contract? (As in Table 14.3, we use ρ and σ without subscripts to refer to the unequal contract.)

The isostochastically stable set of contracts, relative to the equal contract, is the set of contracts for which the probabilities of transitions from U to E and from E to U are equal, that is,

$$\text{Pr}(U \text{ to } E \text{ transition}) = \lambda_{UE}^I(\sigma, \rho, \eta N^R) = \lambda_{EU}^I(\sigma, \rho, N^R) = \text{Pr}(E \text{ to } U \text{ transition}). \tag{14.8}$$

This is equivalent to the equality of two resistances to transition, that is,

$$R^{UE} = \underbrace{\eta N^R \frac{(1-\sigma)\rho}{(1-\sigma)\rho + 1}}_{\text{Minimum number of deviant poor}} = \underbrace{N^R \frac{1}{1 + \sigma\rho}}_{\text{Minimum number of deviant rich}} = R^{EU}. \tag{14.9}$$

For given values of the class sizes, Eq. (14.9) is our iso-SSS locus in (ρ, σ) space, shown in Fig. 14.4. We begin by considering the case of equal class sizes, shown by the upper curve. Unequal contracts

---

[11] Here we follow the set-up in Belloc and Bowles (2017, 2013) in which convention switches are the result of "one-step transitions," as in Kandori et al. (1993, p. 52), where "an equilibrium is upset by large jumps (from the equilibrium to the basin of attraction of the other equilibrium)" or as in Binmore et al. (2003, 309), where "single burst of mutations" are considered.

[12] These probabilities will vary inversely with the rates of idiosyncratic play in the two classes. While there is no reason to expect them to be the same (and we have elsewhere ((Bowles, 2004; Naidu et al., 2017)) incorporated class differences in this regard), we here assume identical rates.

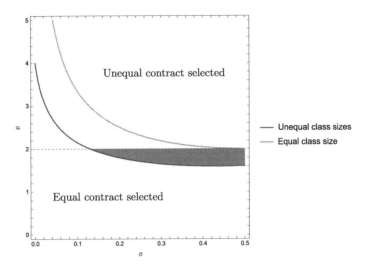

FIGURE 14.4 Isostochastic stability for different shares received by the poor in the unequal contact, for equal and unequal class sizes.

The two loci show the set of contracts characterized by pairs (σ, ρ) such that the unequal contract is isostochastically stable with the equal contract. Contracts represented by the pairs (ρ, σ) above and the right of the loci will be selected over the equal contract $(\rho_E = 2, \sigma_E = \frac{1}{2})$. The equation for the upper locus, based on equal class size, is $\rho^2\sigma(1 - \sigma) = 1$, so contracts below or to the left of it are risk dominated by the equal contract. For the lower locus, $N^R = 8$, and $N^P = 10$. The shaded area represents unequal contracts that, when the poor are more numerous than the rich, will be evolutionarily selected over the equal contract despite being less efficient $(\rho < 2.0)$.

above the locus are sufficiently productive to be selected over the equal contract, whereas the reverse is the case for contracts below the locus.

The fact that evolution selects more productive contracts (ceteris paribus) is hardly surprising. The more notable feature of this iso-SSS locus for the equal class size case is that for an unequal contract to be selected over the equal contract by this evolutionary process, it must be more productive (higher ρ), and more unequal conventions require a greater productivity advantage.

This can be seen, first, by the fact that the locus is uniformly above $\rho = 2$ (the productivity of the equal contract) and, second, by comparing contracts horizontally rather than vertically. This shows that contracts to the left of the locus are sufficiently unequal so that, notwithstanding their productivity advantage over the equal contract, they will be out-competed in the long run by the more equal contract.

To understand this penalty imposed on unequal conventions in the evolutionary equilibrium selection process, remember that the degree of inequality at the unequal convention affects the critical population fractions (p^{UE} and q^{EU}) required to induce a convention switch, and these along with the size of the two classes determine the minimum number of deviants from the status quo convention.

Evolution favors greater equality in the equal class size case because, while greater inequality increases the critical population fraction required for a transition in either direction, it increases q^{EU} more than p^{UE}. Because we consider the case in which class sizes are identical, this means that relatively fewer of the poor must deviate to induce a transition away from the unequal convention to the convention they prefer.

This is clear from Eq. (14.9), from which we see that

$$\sigma \to 0 \quad \Rightarrow \quad R^{EU} = N^R q^{EU} \to N^R, \tag{14.10}$$

which means that as the share received by the poor in the unequal contract goes to zero, to induce a transition away from the equal convention, all of the rich must deviate from the convention. But the same equation shows that

$$\sigma \to 0 \quad \Rightarrow \quad R^{UE} = \eta N^R p^{UE} \to \eta N^R \frac{\rho}{\rho + 1}, \tag{14.11}$$

meaning that if $\eta = 1$ (equal class sizes), then the minimum number of the poor deviating from the unequal convention sufficient to destabilize it is fewer than N^R, the minimum number of deviating rich sufficient to destabilize the equal convention. The result is that as the share received by the poor in the unequal contract falls, the equal contract becomes increasingly "unravel-proof" compared to the unequal contract.

This egalitarian aspect of evolutionary selection is strengthened if the poor class is less numerous than the rich. But if instead $\eta > 1$, evolution need not be propoor, particularly if the poor greatly outnumber the rich and the level of inequality in the unequal contract is limited. In Fig. 14.4, we also show the effects of unequal class sizes: The lower iso-SSS locus is for an economy in which $N^R = 8$ and $N^P = 10$, so $\eta = 1.25$.

As a result, if the "unequal" contract were barely distinguishable from the equal contract, then almost twenty five percent more poor would have to deviate from the unequal convention to displace it, than would be required for the rich to displace the equal convention. This is why as $\sigma \to \frac{1}{2}$, the value of the productivity of the unequal contract that would make it isostochastically stable with the equal contract falls from $\rho = 2$ (the value for the equal class sizes case) to $\frac{2}{\eta} = 1.6$.

The evolutionary disadvantage of being in a more numerous class arises for the following reason. Because we have assumed that the rate of idiosyncratic play is less than the critical fraction required to induce a transition in either direction (which, recall is always greater than one-half), the expected number of deviations is less than the critical value. So transitions occur only as the result of extreme realizations of the stochastic process governing deviations. Due to a phenomenon similar to sampling error, these extreme transition-inducing realizations of deviating are more likely in a smaller group.[13]

The (negative of the) slope of the iso-SSS locus can be interpreted as the evolutionary cost of inequality: it is the increase in the productivity of the unequal contract that is required to offset a small decrease in the share going to the poor, so that the modified unequal contract remains isostochastically stable with the equal contract. Differentiating Eq. (14.9) totally with respect to ρ and σ and setting the result equal to zero, we find this quantity:

$$\text{Evolutionary cost of inequality} \quad \equiv -\frac{d\rho}{d\sigma} = \frac{\rho(\eta - 1) + \eta \rho^2 (2\sigma - 1)}{(1 - \sigma)(1 - \eta - 2\eta\rho\sigma)}. \tag{14.12}$$

---

[13] If the critical fraction of deviants required to induce a transition were less than the rate of idiosyncratic play, then larger numbers would be an advantage. We do not consider this case because if idiosyncratic play is intentional, then the critical fractions are never lass than one-half.

If the classes are equal in size ($\eta = 1$), then Eq. (14.12) tells us (given that the denominator is negative) that unequal contracts are penalized by evolutionary selection. But the same equation shows that if the poor outnumber the rich — more sharecroppers than landlords, for example, arguably the more relevant case — for limited levels of inequality (σ close to one-half), more unequal contracts are favored. This means that an unequal contract that is also less efficient (lower ρ) may out-compete the equal contract.

This occurs for the following reason. Recall that increased inequality (a lower value of σ) raises the critical fraction of idiosyncratic players required to induce a convention switch in either direction. But given that there are more poor than rich ($\eta > 1$), for not very unequal contracts, this increases the critical *number* of deviant players among the poor required to induce a switch from U to E more than it increases the numbers of deviant rich players required for them to destabilize the equal contract. The iso-SSS locus for unequal class sizes in Fig. 14.4 shows that for very unequal contracts, the differential effect of inequality on the critical populations shares – raising q^{EU} more than p^{UE} – becomes dominant and in the unequal class size case, this outweighs the differential numbers effect — $\eta > 1$ – so that the cost of inequality (the negative of the slope of the iso-SSS locus) is positive: unequal contracts are selected even with efficiency levels inferior to the equal contract.

Superior numbers are thus an evolutionary disadvantage. Moreover, it is evident from Eq. (14.12) that a decline in the size of the poorer class (η) steepens the iso-SSS locus, increasing the evolutionary cost of inequality, a result to which we will return. This can be seen in Fig. 14.4 from the fact that the upper iso-SSS locus (equal population size) is steeper for all values of σ than the iso-SSS locus for $\eta > 1$.[14]

14.4.4 Contrast with the undirected model of transitions within populations

The inspiration for the analysis of within-group transitions outlined above is the model already cited due to Young, which we have adapted and extended. The primary difference is that in his model, deviance from the best response is analogous to mutation in a population genetics model, that is, an undirected chance event. For many, perhaps most, applications to historical transitions, we find this formulation unsatisfactory for two reasons. First, as we will see further, the implied process of change—which actors' deviant actions induce a transition—is empirically implausible. Second, historical transitions between conventions have been driven not so much by mistakes but instead by what we have termed intentional idiosyncratic play, namely, actions that are not a best response to the status quo as modeled, but that would benefit the actor if sufficiently many members of his class were to do the same.

In the standard case, transitions from unequal to equal conventions are always driven by the nonbest-response play of the better-off group, that is, those who, as a group, would lose from the transition, not by the deviance from the unequal norm by the poor, who would benefit (Bowles, 2004). Whereas one can imagine a transition resulting, for example, from landlords idiosyncratically asking

---

[14] We have

$$-\frac{d^2\rho}{d\eta d\sigma} = -\frac{\sigma^2}{(1-\sigma)(1-\eta-2\eta\rho\sigma)^2}.$$

So, if the slope of iso-SSS is negative, then a decrease in η will steepen it, whereas if the slope is positive, then a decrease in η will flatten it. Effectively, a reduction in the size of the poor group raises and rotates clockwise the iso-SSS locus.

their tenants to pay less than the conventional crop share, we think that the empirically more relevant case would be where the tenants deviate from the convention and insist on paying less than the norm. In our model, transitions from more to less unequal conventions arise from deviations of the disadvantaged group, more in line with historical experience.

The evolutionary disadvantage of the unequal contract was first demonstrated in Young's contract theorem (Young, 1998b). This is a consequence, as he put it, of the fact that highly unequal conventions are easily unraveled: "[I]t does not take many stochastic shocks to create an environment in which members of the dissatisfied group prefer to try something different." (Young, 1998b, p. 137). This mechanism in the standard model (which reminds us of Marx's claim that the working class has "nothing to lose but your chains") is not the basis of the evolutionary disadvantage of a highly unequal contract in our model. In Young's illustration, as in the discussion above, it is the idiosyncratic play of the privileged group that unravels the unequal convention, that is, the convention from which they benefit disproportionately.

Introducing intentional idiosyncratic play alters the equilibrium selection processes in the standard bargaining games as well. In an asymmetric coordination game between members of different groups bargaining over conventional contracts (e.g., segregation norms or crop shares), Young (1998b) shows that evolution favors conventions that are risk dominant. We can recover this result from our Eq. (14.9) by making the class sizes equal (setting $\eta = 1$) to show that in this case the unequal contract will be evolutionarily selected if $\rho^2 \sigma (1 - \sigma) > 1$, that is, if the unequal contract risk dominates the equal contract.

In contrast, we have demonstrated (Naidu et al., 2010; Hwang et al., 2018) the stochastic stability of risk-dominated conventions, which can be both unequal and inefficient (in the sense of a lower value of ρ) relative to the alternate convention. When idiosyncratic play is intentional and the relative size of the less well-off group is sufficiently great, a risk-dominated convention can be stochastically stable. In Fig. 14.4 the set of such inefficient and unequal contacts that would be selected over the equal and more efficient contract are those above the lower iso-SSS locus with values of $\rho < 2$.

14.5 Evolutionary selection within and between populations

To represent the between-population dynamics illustrated by our analysis of the Neolithic revolution, we now introduce pairwise contests between populations. The effect of between-population competition on the evolutionary selection of alternative cultural-institutional conventions depends on both the frequency and decisiveness of contests and also on the manner in which the values of ρ and σ characterizing a population's convention affect the level of contest success resources of the population. The importance of large conscripted armies for between-nation contest success in the 19th and 20th centuries, for example, elevated the importance of the well-being of the poor for contest success. This would favor nations that managed to implement a modicum of equality, e.g. the French Republic, and, later, the Prussian Empire.

By contrast, some forms of inter-group competition may impose little penalty on highly unequal populations, a case illustrated by the "Great Stirrup Controversy" concerning the role of the cavalry in the rise of European feudalism. White (1962) advanced the view that the stirrup made the contribution of mounted cavalry (knights) to military success paramount. Beginning with Charles Martel in the 8th-century Francia, this provided military advantages to political entities that implemented feudal property rights ensuring that knights had the resources (including serf labor) required to field armored mounted cavalry.

14.5.1 Equilibrium selection by between-population competition

In any period, we let α be the probability that a given population will be paired for a contest with a population governed by a different convention. Since ϵ is small, we can assume that almost all populations will be very near to the U or E convention. This allows us to treat each of the populations making up the metapopulation as if it were an individual, characterized by one or the other convention (U or E), which may be switched as the result of a contest because when two groups with different conventions compete, the winner replaces the strategy mix in the one that loses.[15]

The outcome of the contest depends on what we term the total contest resources available to the populations at the unequal and equal conventions Π_U and Π_E, respectively, where these are determined by the total payoffs and their distributions of the two groups. Thus the probability that the population governed by convention U will switch conventions as a result of the contest is

$$\text{Probability that group with } U \text{ convention adopts } E, \text{ given conflict } = \beta(\frac{\Pi_E}{\Pi_U}), \qquad (14.13)$$

where β is a contest success function (e.g., logistic), increasing in its argument, such that if the populations' contest resources are equal so that $\Pi_U = \Pi_E$, then the probability of a switch is $\frac{1}{2}$.

It remains to define the relation between the payoffs of the classes and the contest resources available to the group. We illustrate the model with two cases. The first defines contest resources simply as total payoffs irrespective of which class receives them. This, noting that the rich may engage in more interactions than the poor because $\eta \geq 1$, is

$$\Pi^l(\sigma, \rho) = N^P \times \sigma\rho + N^R \times (\frac{N^P}{N^R}(1-\sigma)\rho) \qquad (14.14)$$

$$= \rho N^P. \qquad (14.15)$$

The superscript l refers to the linear aggregation in this definition of contest resources.

A possibly more empirically grounded alternative would recognize that insufficient nutrition and other resources among the poor can significantly reduce population's contest success capabilities. For this case (already raised in our discussion of the Neolithic revolution), contest resources can be represented as a concave function of the payoffs of the poor and the rich. We illustrate this concave aggregation function using a logarithmic function (the superscript c is for concave):

$$\Pi^c(\sigma, \rho) = N^P \times \ln(\sigma\rho) + N^R \times \ln(\frac{N^P}{N^R}(1-\sigma)\rho). \qquad (14.16)$$

With the two conventions defined as before in Table 14.3, we can now define the probabilities that in any period a group governed by the unequal convention will switch to the equal convention and the

---

[15] This dynamic can be formalized by a standard replicator equation in a cultural evolution model, treating entire populations as individuals adopting or abandoning some behavioral trait, which in this case are conventions.

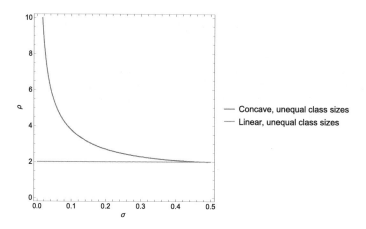

FIGURE 14.5 The effect of group competition.

The two loci show sets of unequal contracts (characterized by their σ and ρ) that are isostochastically stable with the equal contract (with $\rho_E = 2, \sigma_E = \frac{1}{2}$) such that $\lambda_{UE}^X = \lambda_{EU}^X$, where these transition probabilities are given by Eqs. (14.18) and (14.17), that is, in the absence of internal transitions. The upper locus is the case in which contest resources are concave in payoffs, so that unequal contracts bear a penalty. The horizontal locus is the case in which the outcome of the conflict depends on the (linear) sum of payoffs (and hence on ρ alone, independently of σ).

reverse, as a result of interpopulation competition (signaled by the X superscript), or, respectively,

$$\lambda_{EU}^X(\sigma, \rho, N^R, N^P) = \alpha\beta(\frac{\Pi_U}{\Pi_E}), \tag{14.17}$$

$$\lambda_{UE}^X(\sigma, \rho, N^R, N^P) = \alpha(1 - \beta(\frac{\Pi_U}{\Pi_E})). \tag{14.18}$$

Fig. 14.5 shows the set of isostochastically stable contracts when between-population competition is the only selection mechanism. As expected, if contests tend to be won by groups with higher total payoffs (illustrated by the horizontal line), then any contract with $\rho > 2$ will be selected over the equal contract (for which $\rho_E = 2$). But where the marginal contest-success benefit of contest resources is decreasing, as in the concave (logarithmic) function above, highly unequal groups will tend to lose contests unless their contract has substantially greater total productivity (as is shown by the upper locus).

14.5.2 A unified model of cultural-institutional change

To unify the within- and between-population dynamics, we assume that the discrete time periods we use are sufficiently limited so that we can ignore the small probability that a transition by both internal and external dynamics would coincide. Then we have two probabilities, namely, a population at an unequal convention switching to the equal convention, and the reverse transition:

Probability $U \rightarrow E$: $\lambda^{UE} = \lambda_{UE}^I(\sigma, \rho, N^P) + \lambda_{UE}^X(\sigma, \rho, N^R, N^P), \tag{14.19}$

Probability $E \to U$: $\lambda^{EU} = \lambda^I_{EU}(\sigma, \rho, N^R) + \lambda^X_{EU}(\sigma, \rho, N^R, N^P)$.   (14.20)

The I superscripted probabilities give the within-group transition probabilities from U to E or E to U, which depend on the resistances R^{UE} and R^{EU}. The X superscripted probabilities give the transition probabilities from one convention to another as functions of the group payoffs, which in turn depend on the efficiency of the unequal contract ρ and (for the case where contest resources are concave in payoffs) on the relative equality of the unequal contract σ.

To find the set of unequal contracts that are isostochastically stable with the equal contract ($\rho_E = 2, \sigma_E = \frac{1}{2}$), we equate the above two transition probabilities giving us the equation for the isostochastic stability locus:

Isostochastic stability of U and $E \Rightarrow \lambda_{UE} = \lambda^I_{UE} + \lambda^X_{UE} = \lambda^I_{EU} + \lambda^X_{EU} = \lambda_{EU}$.   (14.21)

We have depicted the internal and between-population process separately in Figs. 14.4 and 14.5. When integrated into a unified dynamic, as in Eqs. (14.19), (14.20), and (14.21), the relative influence of the internal and external processes on the evolutionary selection mechanism vary with the parameters of the unified model. Increasing the rate of idiosyncratic play and decreasing population size (of both classes) raise the probability of within-population transitions in both directions and so increase the weight of the internal process. Increasing the frequency of between-population contests or elevating the effect of differences in contest resources on contest success probabilities increase the importance of the between-population process.

But the strength of the two processes will vary endogenously as well. We know that decreasing σ increases the resistance to a switch in both directions, reducing the contribution of the internal process to the overall selection dynamics. If the share received by the poor in the unequal contract is close to zero, then, as a result, the predominant selection mechanism will be between rather than within populations. However, if the level of disparity in the unequal contract is modest, then the internal selection process will be relatively more important.[16]

In Fig. 14.6, for ease of comparison, we show the iso-SSS locus for the within-population dynamics (with unequal class sizes) along with the iso-SSS locus for the internal and between-population dynamics combined as above for both concave and linear contest resource functions (also with unequal class sizes). The effect of adding between-population competition to the within-population dynamics favors the equal convention when effective contest resources are concave in the payoffs of the rich and the poor (the upper curve), and also increases the evolutionary cost of inequality, the steepness of the iso-SSS locus, as can be seen from the figure.

If the unequal contract awards a very small share to the poor, then the equality-favoring effect is particularly strong, a consequence of the fact that in this case within-population transitions both

---

[16] The absolute strength of the between population selection process is also endogenous. This is because the likelihood that the randomly selected groups paired for contest are at different conventions (α in Eqs. (14.17) and (14.18)) varies with the distribution of conventions in the metapopulation, though here we do not model that. Recall that when populations are paired for a contest, switches will not occur if the two populations are at the same convention. If g is the fraction of populations at or near the equal contract, then this will occur with probability $2g(1 - g)$, which will approach zero as g goes to either zero or 1 and will reach its maximum when $g = \frac{1}{2}$. As a result, the evolutionary force of between-population competition as a selection mechanism is self-limiting because the frequency of convention switches due to contests goes to zero as the metapopulation becomes homogeneous, composed entirely of populations governed by either the equal or the unequal convention.

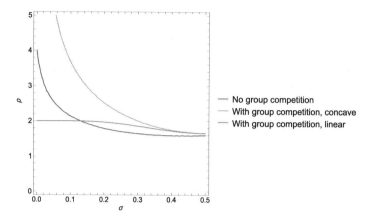

FIGURE 14.6 Evolutionary selection of institutions: Within- and between-population dynamics combined.

The three loci show the sets of unequal contracts (characterized by their σ and ρ) that are isostochastically stable with the equal contract. Class sizes are $N^R = 8$ and $N^P = 10$. We set $\epsilon = 0.1$ and α at 10^{-5}.

into and out of highly unequal conventions are rare, effectively placing more weight on the between-population selection process.

The iso-SSS locus of the combined selection process for the case in which contest resources are simply payoffs (so there is no penalty for unequal shares) is also equality-favoring (by comparison to the within-population dynamics taken alone) except for highly unequal contracts. This is shown by the flatter iso-SSS locus labeled 'With group competition, linear' being above the iso-SSS locus labeled 'No group competition' for most of the range of unequal contracts except for the most unequal.

The reason that even total payoff-based contest success favors the equal contract is that where disparities are modest in the unequal contract and the poor are more numerous than the rich, as we have seen, the internal process if operating singly favors inequality. So, comparatively inefficient contracts ($\rho < 2$) can out-compete the equal convention in the absence of between-population competition.

As a result, even in the case where the between-population dynamics is selecting entirely for efficiency, adding it to the within-population dynamics is equality-favoring, as it selects against these inefficient and unequal contracts, increasing the space of unequal contracts that will be out-competed by the equal contract (i.e., the lens between two iso-SSS loci labeled 'With group competition, linear' and 'No group competition' in the figure).

However, if the poor receive virtually nothing in the unequal contract, as we have already seen, then the within-population dynamics is dominated by between-population competition. And if contest resources are simply payoffs (the linear case), then all that matters is efficiency. The result is that highly unequal contracts with ρ barely exceeding 2 are now selected over the equal contract.

14.6 Darwin, Marx, and the evolutionary selection of institutions

Our model also allows us to pose some enduring questions about institutional evolution in a new way.

14.6.1 "Efficient design" in biology and history

A celebrated result in biology, Fisher's fundamental theorem, is commonly interpreted to show that under appropriate conditions, natural selection generates increasing average fitness levels (Fisher, 1930; Price, 1972). Analogous reasoning is common in the social sciences. Douglass North (1981) summarized this view as follows: "Competition in the face of ubiquitous scarcity dictates that the more efficient institution ... will survive and the inefficient ones perish. (p. 7)" Just as fitness maximization suggests certain features of species design in distinct ecologies, the axiomatic status of efficient outcomes in some economic models supports strong propositions about the types of institutions one would expect to find in particular economic environments (Williamson, 1985; Ouchi, 1980).

Similarly, a core idea in Marx's historical materialism is that the advance of knowledge and its embodiment in new technology may make status quo institutions anachronistic. When this happens, they are eventually overthrown by social revolution, introducing institutions better able to coordinate economic activity, given what he called the new "forces of production." (Marx, 1904; Cohen, 1978). A similar technology-led view is common in the property rights school in institutional economics, expressed by Harold Demsetz: "the emergence of new ... property rights will be in response to changes in technology" (Demsetz, 1974, 350). The difference between the historical materialist and property rights theory version is that the process of change is abrupt—resulting in a "punctuated equilibrium dynamic"—in the former and gradual in the latter (Eldridge and Gould, 1972). The similarity of the two views and why it makes sense to consider them jointly is because, as Pagano (2001) has pointed out, the creation of novel institutions is akin to the emergence of new species; it requires the confluence of a large number of improbable variations in the status quo.

But analytical models based on the idea that this unlikely process of innovation in either biological or social variants would result in "efficient design" are rarely offered and difficult to develop. Ever since Darwin grappled with the problem in *On The Origin of Species*, the production of novel designs through random variation has remained a puzzle. We know from both biology and economics that optimization at the level of the individual or gene does not in general support equilibria that are efficient unless epistatic gene interactions and (the equivalent in economics) uncompensated external effects are ruled out.

Notwithstanding these analytical challenges, our model does provide a mechanism by which the efficient design idea could be applied to cultural-institutional conventions. Suppose, given the technologies, preferences, and other relevant data in some historical period, there is a set of feasible contracts defined in (σ, ρ) space. The contract set is constituted by the contracts (i.e., ρ, σ pairs) that could possibly be implemented at some place and time, independently of any considerations of the process by which this implementation might take place. In our analysis of the early Neolithic property rights revolution, for example, hunting and gathering, would be represented by a point in the set with limited inequality and substantial productivity, whereas early farming would appear as a point in the interior of the set with somewhat less productivity and greater inequality. This poses the puzzle of the Neolithic revolution in a framework taking account of both within- and between-population evolutionary selection.

The left panel of Fig. 14.7 illustrates a contract set and an isostochastic stability map. Think of the set of iso-SSS loci as evolutionary selection's indifference map. Contracts with the (σ, ρ) pairs on the iso-SSS loci higher and to the right will be selected over contracts on lower or to the left iso-SSS loci. Evolutionary selection is "indifferent" between any two points on a given iso-SSS locus: a population

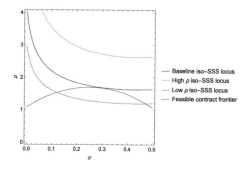
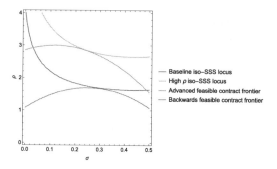

FIGURE 14.7

The loci that are concave to the origin show sets of unequal contracts (characterized by their σ and ρ) that are isostochastically stable. Group sizes are $N^R = 8$ and $N^P = 10$. The feasible contract frontier is the boundary of the set of contracts that are technically feasible.

will spend an equal amount of a very long run at each. In the left panel the convention indicated by the tangency of an iso-SSS locus and the feasible contract frontier, is selected.[17]

Is there a process by which the most efficient contract in the contract set would be selected? We have already seen that it could be if the between-population selection process were sufficiently dominant over the within-population dynamics and if contest success resources were linearly related to individual payoffs, rather than concavely. In this case, the isostochastic stability loci would be approximately horizontal over the entire range of σ, effectively selecting the contract with the greatest ρ.

14.6.2 A new contract set

The advance of technology can shift the feasible contract set. Sticking with the Neolithic narrative for an illustration, later in the Neolithic and in the Bronze Age in Western Eurasia, a dramatic transformation of farming technology occurred: the introduction of ox teams drawing ploughs, a highly productive and labor saving innovation. The adoption of the new technology was associated with a substantial increase in wealth inequality between households (Bogaard et al., 2019). Two pieces of evidence point to associated changes in relationships among men and women as well. Ancient DNA evidence suggests a dramatic increase in inequality among men (but not women) in the number of children surviving to reproductive age consistent with increased polygynous mating among a small class of wealthy males (Karmin et al., 2015; Lippold et al., 2014). Recent ethnographic evidence finds a robust association between the use of plough agriculture in the past and women's contemporary lower levels of labor force participation and leadership in politics (Alesina et al., 2013).

A set of new feasible contracts similar to the ox team/plough innovation are shown in the right panel of the figure. Our model leads us think it likely that a new contract would eventually emerge, one

---

[17] The slope of the feasible contract frontier can be understood as the marginal rate of transformation of more equal shares into a level of efficiency. The (negative of the) slope of an iso-SSS locus is the evolutionary marginal rate of substitution, that is, the opportunity cost of greater inequality: the increase in ρ required to offset a decrease in σ, the share received by the poor.

that would outcompete the less unequal but also less productive early Neolithic labor intensive farming methods.

14.6.3 Collective action and the evolution of institutions

Finally, we can use the same apparatus to study how collective action affects the process of evolutionary selection. To do this, we refine our model by defining the effective size of a class as the number of decision making units.[18] If all members of a nuclear family necessarily play the same strategy, then the effective size is the number of families. Similarly, if all employees of a firm belong to a trade union that makes a single offer or demand to the employer, then the effective size of the working class is the number of firms, not the number of workers. For concreteness, we illustrate our model for the case $\eta > 1$, that is, there are more sharecroppers than landlords, more employers than employees, and so on.

In Fig. 14.4, for example, the lower iso-SSS locus represents the equilibrium selection process for classes of 8 employers and 10 workers in the absence of trade unions with seven employers hiring a worker each and the eighth employer hiring the remaining three workers. The upper iso-SSS (for the case $N^R = 8$, $N^P = 8$) would then reflect the change in the evolutionary equilibrium selection, that would result if the three workers employed by the same employer formed a labor union and bargained collectively with the employer, always choosing the same strategy. The effect would be to cause many previously selected unequal contracts to be no longer evolutionary competitive with the equal contract.

Fig. 14.8 shows a detail from the previous figures, with two iso-SSS loci. The less steep one is a member of a family of such "evolutionary indifference curves" summarizing the selection process for a population in which there are 10 poor and 6 rich. The steeper locus is part of the iso-SSS map of a population with 10 poor and 8 rich.

From Eq. (14.12) we know that the evolutionary cost of inequality (the negative of the slope of the iso-SSS locus) is greater the smaller is the size of the poor class. From Fig. 14.8 we see that given the contract set shown, the evolutionarily selected contract with the larger class of the poor would give them 18% of the total payoffs; reducing the size of the poorer class would raise this to 23%. We return to the case of collective action, illustrated by trade unions, in Section 14.8.

14.7 The demise of serfdom and the rise of the national state

To illustrate our equilibrium selection model, we consider two examples, one concerning a decentralized transition within a population and the other a change arising from between group competition.

14.7.1 The demise of serfdom

The distinction between the political economy and evolutionary approaches is evident in two very different empirical cases of the demise of European feudalism. Consistent with the centralized top-

---

[18] The term is due to biologists Ronald Fisher and Sewall Wright as the number of individuals (different from a census count) such that the model under consideration would capture the evolutionary dynamics of the population under study. For example, in a highly polygynous population with substantial fraction of nonreproductive males, the effective male population size may be substantially less than the census size.

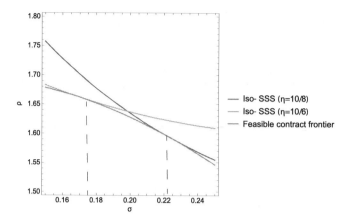

FIGURE 14.8 Lesser effective class size favors the selection of more equal contracts from a given contract set.

The feasible contract frontier is the boundary of the set of contracts that are technically feasible.

down approach, the emancipation of Russia's serfs by Tsar Alexander II in 1863 was a deliberate choice to implement a new set of institutions resulting from bargaining within Russia's elite (Blum, 1971).

In contrast, English serfdom was never formally repealed by law in England, and indeed all legal labor restrictions were arguably not abolished until the 1875 repeal of Master and Servant criminal fines (Naidu and Yuchtman, 2013). But, in practice, agricultural serfdom had disappeared centuries earlier. As the historian E.B. Fryde (1996, p. 6) writes:

> throughout the 1380s and long beyond them ... the servile villeins refused with ever increasing persistence to accept the implications of serfdom, ... In this atmosphere of frequent local disorder and of continuous tension between lords and tenants, the direct exploitation of domanial estates would largely disappear from England in the fifty years after the [1381] Great Revolt.

The practice of serfdom in England had been centered on customary villeinage, whereby serfs (villeins) were tied to lords on inherited customary contracts and had labor obligations (e.g., tallage, the land tax) as well as tax obligations like merchet (dues for marriage of a daughter), heriot (death taxes), childwite (fine for illegitimate pregnancy), and chevage (head taxes paid to the lord).

Beyond these economic claims, serfdom came with a distinct inequality in status, with the chevage being "psychologically burdensome, signifying, ... the yoke of servitude." (Bailey, 2014, p. 46). The inferior status of the villeins was sustained by "a bewildering variety of practices ... a mosaic of variable bargains even within the same locality or upon the same seigniorial estate." (Bailey, 2014, p. 23). Between 1350 and 1450, this entire system disappeared after centuries of persistence, replaced by shorter leases (either copyhold or leasehold), where rents were fixed in cash, status was no longer inherited, and no feudal dues were collected.

The most immediate candidate explanation for the substantial institutional and cultural changes during this period is the mid 14th century Black Death, which lowered population by 30% across Europe and substantially more in some areas. North and Thomas (1971) provided an economic interpretation of the change. Essentially, the fall in the labor-land ratio increased the value of labor, and competition among manors for scarce villeins induced a change in customs. North and Thomas do not describe the role of idiosyncratic deviations by peasants as mediating the effect of labor scarcity on changes away from feudal relationships. Indeed, the timing of the decline of serfdom occurs a full generation after the Black Death, largely during a period of falling real wages, and with considerable local variation, North and Thomas point out that were changes simply the result of increased labor scarcity alone, it would be difficult to account for the simultaneous change of so many customs together, rather than a simple change in the terms of various obligations.

The transition required a change in tenant–landlord cultural-institutional conventions, rather than simply a renegotiation of the terms of a contract.[19] In addition, the mechanism is not simply manorial competition for labor: there was a wave of peasant unrest in the decades after the Black Death, culminating in the Great Peasant Revolt of 1381, ranging from conspiracies to not pay merchet to physical attacks on lords and the destruction of land records.

Though highly localized, bargaining was more collective than individual, as whole groups of villeins simultaneously demanded better terms: In Holywell-cum-Needingworth, there were large strikes in 1353 and 1386, along with 191 cases of individual refusal to perform labor services between 1353 and 1403 (compared to 21 such instances between 1288 and 1339) (Bailey, 2014). In 1379 Essex county, "the tenants [collectively] offered their lord 40 (shillings) to set fixed monetary sums for rents and services." (Poos, 1991, pp. 247). There is also evidence of a "seigniorial reaction", where lords attempted to squeeze more servile dues out of their tenants, as well as using powers granted to them by the 1351 Statute of Labourers.

Nonetheless, by the mid-15th century, the panoply of feudal norms was extinct, with little change in formal law. Beyond the changes in economic conventions, the cultural norms regulating the interactions between peasants and lords also changed. For example, Bailey (2014) notes that the language used in manor records to describe relationships with peasants was upgraded from "bondage" and "villeinage" to more dignified modes of address.

Similarly, in France, a protracted agrarian conflict culminated in the 1789 peasant rebellions, forcing local lords to abandon many of their feudal privileges well before any legislation was passed (Markoff, 1996, p. 509). The abolition of seigniorial dues by the Estates General in 1789 confirmed the new order, it did not introduce it. Instead, a series of actions by dispersed peasants, each taking the grievances of the entire group as their own and coordinated at most at the local not the global level, had induced the aristocratic class to change conventions governing agricultural labor and rural life.

14.7.2 The emergence of the national state

Our second example illustrates the process by which a novel institutional form, the national state, and an associated civic culture was the emergent property of a half-millennium long process of competition among distinct modes of rule among a large number of now-defunct sovereign entities rather than the result of constitutional design by a centralized authority.

The growth in state capacity that was part of the rise of powerful governments in Europe is illuminated by our model. Consider a large population of nobles, functionaries, or tax-farmers ("state

---

[19] North and Thomas (p. 799) write that "When a change of parameters offers potential gains from establishing new secondary institutional arrangements, these may not be directly realizable simply because they run counter to the basic rules of society." Although North and Thomas stress common law changes, recent research shows that the changes in customs predated the legal changes by at least a century (Hatcher and Bailey, 2001).

agents") who are matched randomly each period with citizens. Following Acemoglu (2005) and Besley and Persson (2009), we suppose that citizens can either produce taxable or nontaxable (more precisely, difficult to tax) output and that government officials can either allocate tax revenue to provide public goods that are strongly complementary with tradable goods (e.g., contract enforcement or transportation infrastructure) or keep it for themselves.

We describe the emergence of the national state as a transition from a state with a tax farming elite providing no public goods along with unproductive and tax evading commoners to a state with the bureaucratic elite devoting tax revenues to the provision of public goods supporting a highly productive economy of tax compliant commoners.

The citizens' strategies are a) T, to produce tradable goods worth y that have no value unless public goods are provided and that are readily taxed at a fixed tax rate $\tau = \frac{1}{2}$ or b) U, to produce ϕy units of a subsistence good where $\phi < 2/3$ that does not depend on the provision of public goods. Tax obligations are difficult to enforce on producers of the U good, yielding an effective rate $\tau = \frac{1}{4}$.

The state agents' strategies include a) P (for public goods), to collect taxes at a rate τ and turn them over entirely to the public good provisioning, receiving a fixed wage of w. This can be thought of as respecting the rule of law and behaving as a rule-following salaried bureaucrat. The other strategy is b) K (for "keep") where the bureaucrat spends none on the public good, receives no fixed wage, and instead pockets the tax revenue as income.

The resulting payoffs are in the game matrix in Table 14.4. Citizens get $\frac{y}{2}$ if they produce taxable output and the government provides public goods, whereas the tax collector gets wage w. If the citizens produce taxable output and the tax collector supplies no public good, then payoffs are 0. If the citizens produce difficult-to-tax output, then they produce ϕy units of output, of which the tax-collector gets one quarter. If the tax collector gives that quarter to the public good, then they get wage w, whereas the citizen gets $\frac{3\phi y}{4}$. We assume the bureaucrat's wage is sufficiently low, $w < \frac{\phi y}{4}$, so that even when the citizen produces a difficult-to-tax good, the tax farmers prefer to consume the tax for themselves rather than contribute to the public good and receive their wage.

Table 14.4 Payoffs in the State-Capacity Game.

Note that we fix $\phi < \frac{2}{3}$ and $\frac{\phi y}{4} < \frac{y}{6}$, which ensures that citizens strictly prefer the high-productivity equilibrium with public goods and taxable output. Since $w < \frac{\phi y}{4}$, the tax collectors strictly prefer the weak state, where little tax is collected, and no public goods are provided. The top off-diagonal term captures the fact that with no public good (e.g., no transportation infrastructure or no contract enforcement), the taxable output cannot be traded, and hence 0 output is produced. The bottom off-diagonal captures the fact that the public good does not complement the nontaxable good and the tax-collector receives only the wage, w.

		Tax-collector	
		public good (P)	keep (K)
Citizen's	taxable (T)	$\frac{y}{2}, w$	0,0
Output	untaxable (U)	$\frac{3\phi y}{4}, w$	$\frac{3\phi y}{4}, \frac{\phi y}{4}$

This game has two conventions. One is that citizen engage in high-productivity readily taxed production, are taxed by honest officials who contribute the proceeds to the central government, and are paid a wage, securing public goods that are valuable for production. The other convention is that citizens engage in low-productivity hard-to-tax activities that do not benefit at all from public goods, and tax-officials keep what little they collect.

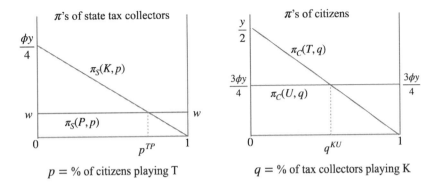

FIGURE 14.9 Critical population fractions of idiosyncratic play for transitions to and from the national state convention.

In the left panel, we show p^{TP}, the minimum fraction of citizens idiosyncratically producing the taxable good (T) that is sufficient to induce the best responding tax collectors (state officials, S) in the next period to concede to give up tax farming and devote tax revenues to the provision of public goods (P). The right panel shows q^{KU}, the analogous minimum fraction of idiosyncratically playing tax collectors (keeping the tax revenues for themselves and providing no public goods) to induce the best responding citizens to shift to producing the U good (which does not require a complementary public good).

Under the parameter restrictions described above, transitions out of the "weak state" equilibrium occur as citizens innovate with new forms of taxable production despite the absence of public goods from the state. Craftsmen produce tradable goods in the absence of a port, and insurers sell contracts despite the absence of a court. These attempts will fail until enough of them occur to induce the agents of the state to best-respond by complying with their duties toward the state (which will be facilitated, i.e., the resistance will be lower, by the state paying a high wage w).

The critical fractions of the two classes, tax collectors and citizens, deviating from the status quo convention that are sufficient to induce the best responding members of the other class to best respond by switching strategies are shown in Fig. 14.9.

This decentralized model of state capacity is similar to the framework in Acemoglu and Robinson (2020). The K, U equilibrium is the "paper leviathan", where a weak state predates on its citizens, who respond by sticking with low-productivity activities, whereas the T, P equilibrium is the "shackled leviathan", where the state takes more in taxes but also provides public goods and has a competent and rule-following bureaucracy. But our model gives more scope for the decentralized behavior of state agents and citizens, and how a convention of bureaucratic compliance could emerge due to the accumulation of novel forms of production that require public goods. As woolens, and later, textile mills increase in productivity, the pressure on the British state to provide ports and merchant marine could have increased, motivating tax officials to pocket less of their collections and become more obedient employees of the Crown.

We also have in mind the large literature on the importance of bureaucratic norms and "cultures of corruption" (see Finan et al. (2017) for a survey of the microeconomic evidence on the management of bureaucrats). In the historical accounts of the rise of state capacity, an important role is given to the emergence of rule-following bureaucrats (what Weber termed "bureaucracy as a vocation") in increasing the size and efficacy of government organizations.

This model of the conflict between the "state" and "society" does not require any representative agents and generates transitions from "weak-state/low-output" equilibria to "strong-state/high-output" equilibria based on the idiosyncratic play of citizens who stand to benefit. When enough citizens insist on producing tradeable goods, government officials switch from unhelpful bribe-taking to public good provision and wage-taking.

But intrastate bargaining between political agents and citizens is not the only or even primary force in the rise of European state capacity. Between-group competition, in this case, military and geopolitical competition, played an important role in winnowing the set of institutional configurations. Brewer (1990) is the classic account of how military pressures generated fiscal capacity in England. Societies where elites could not engineer a transition to the taxable income equilibrium would be readily conquered and assimilated by those that could.

Eight centuries ago in what is now Italy, there were two to three hundred distinct city-states and other sovereign political entities.[20] In South Germany, a half-millennium ago, there were sixty-nine free cities in addition to numerous bishoprics, principalities, duchies, and other state-like entities (Brady, 1985). The whole of Europe at that time was governed by about five hundred sovereign bodies.

But by the First World War, fewer than thirty states remained. This culling of states not only thinned the number of sovereign bodies, but it radically reduced the heterogeneity of forms of governance. A single political form, the national state, emerged, where once had ruled, according to Charles Tilly (1990, 5), "[e]mpires, city states, federations of cities, networks of landlords, religious orders, leagues of pirates, warrior bands, and many other forms of governance." Unlike the competing forms it eclipsed, the national state exhibited a centralized bureaucratic structure maintaining order over a defined territory, with the capacity to raise substantial amounts revenue in the form of taxation and to deploy permanent armed forces.

What explains the competitive success of this novel form of rule? The simple answer is that when national states warred with other forms of governance, they tended to win. But, Tilly writes, "No monarch could make war without securing the acquiescence of nearly all of his subject population, and the active cooperation of at least a crucial few" (Tilly, 1990, p. 75). A system of taxation paid in money, coupled with the capacity to borrow large sums, allowed rulers of national states to make war without resort to more unpopular measures such as the direct seizure of food, weapons, and animals.

The establishment of well-defined private property rights and markets facilitated this taxation- and debt-based approach to mobilizing the coercive resources needed to win wars. Market environments favored state formation in a less obvious way, too, by inducing tax compliance. Tilly further comments: "Participants in markets already do a significant share of the requisite surveillance thorough the recording of prices and transfers. Properly socialized citizens, furthermore, come to attach moral value to the payment of taxes; they monitor themselves and each other, blaming tax evaders as free riders." (p. 89)

---

[20] In addition to Tilly (1990), here we draw here on Gellner (1983); Bright and Harding (1984); Tilly (1975); Smith (1959); Wallerstein (1974); Anderson (1974, 2013); Gintis and Bowles (1984).

Successful national states assimilated the populations they absorbed, and, over the period, they promoted and eventually required a common pattern of childhood socialization through schooling.[21]

In part as a result of its success in Europe, replicas of the European national state were exported (often at gun point) and flourished throughout the world, extinguishing competing forms of organization. Under the auspices of the national state and the emerging capitalist economy, European populations grew rapidly, multiplying 15-fold in Britain in the four centuries after 1500 after having grown hardly at all over the previous four centuries, and eclipsing population growth elsewhere in the world (except, perhaps, for eighteenth-century China).

As a result, the global diffusion of the national state was promoted not only by competitive pressures on the states of the European periphery and beyond, but also by the substantial emigration of bearers of the European cultural traits and military capacities that had favored state-building in Europe. In sum, the national state evolved because it won wars with competing organizations, and the ability to win wars depended on its peculiar ability to raise taxes and mobilize soldiers. This ability depended on the extent of commerce, administrative capacity, the availability of credit, tax compliance, and the willingness to serve rulers in war.

These, in turn, were fostered by the diffusion of norms guiding individual behaviors that, although not (at least initially) individually advantageous, contributed to group success in war on the above reasoning. Among these are bureaucratic professionalism, voluntary tax compliance, willingness to risk danger in war for a ruler or nation, and respect for property rights.

Of course, national states eventually created legal and cultural environments in which those adhering to the norms that enhanced state war-making capacities suffered little or no material loss by comparison to those rejecting these norms. But the emergence and early diffusion of the national state may have relied critically on group-advantageous but individually costly norms.

14.8 The 20th-century evolution of collective bargaining in the U.S.

A more recent application of our decentralized approach lies in the evolution of collective bargaining practices in the United States. It is well known that union density and inequality are inversely correlated at the aggregate time-series level. Farber et al. (2020) provide a wide variety of evidence that unions reduce inequality and argue that the U-shape in inequality that is mirrored by the inverse U-shape in union density is not simply a correlation, but also reflects a causal relationship.

As with the case of the demise of serfdom and the rise of the national state in Europe, most empirical work has focused on the role of changes in the formal legal structure, such as the Wagner Act and the Taft–Hartley Act as well as right-to-work laws. But historical accounts of both the sharp 20th century increase in private-sector unionization and the subsequent slow decline in union density also document decentralized transitions driven by small numbers of union activists during the up-swing and by an accumulation of antiunion practices by employers together with fierce competition facing unionized firms during the decline.

---

[21] Weber (1976) describes the assimilation of distinct populations by the French national state. Gellner (1983) develops the connection between the rise of commerce, the national state, and the rise of what he terms "exo-education," that is, childhood socialization by specialists who are not members of one's family or group of close associates.

14.8.1 Collective bargaining and equilibrium selection

In the language of our model the firm corresponds to our "population", and the two "classes" are workers and managers/employers in a given workplace. Workers can ask for a "strong union contract", which limits management authority, holds employers liable for violations of contracts, and secures higher wages and benefits, all of which result in an more equal division of rents within the firm corresponding to our E, E contract. The unequal convention can be thought of as either a nonunion or weak union workplace, with employers having the freedom to introduce new technologies and organization, pay lower wages, and unconstrained by scheduling or seniority restrictions in a union contract.

The basis for identifying a strong union contract with our equal convention is the abundant evidence, which shows that unions transfer income from employers and managers to workers (Abowd, 1989; Abowd and Lemieux, 1993; DiNardo et al., 1997; Frydman and Saks, 2010). So the share of total output σ received by workers will be larger in the strong union workplace. There is also some evidence that unions reduce output or efficiency (Hirsch, 2008), so we can impose that overall productivity ρ is higher in the nonunion firm.[22] The off-diagonal zeros of our model's payoff matrix correspond to absenteeism/strikes and lockouts/terminations: when workers refuse to work except under a strong union contract, both sides get 0, and the same happens when managers refuse to employ unionized workers i.e. a lockout.

In our model, within-firm transitions are driven by the idiosyncratic play of either workers or managers. Idiosyncratic play inducing a transition between nonunion and union conventions could include workers simply not showing up to work. Individual absenteeism deprives both workers and employers of their shares of output, but collective absenteeism, a strike, can induce management to change from a nonunion contract to a unionized one. Similarly, managers in unionized firms can either terminate an individual worker or (at least, during bargaining) lockout a whole group of workers. This is costly to the firm but could induce workers to concede to a nonunion (or weak union) convention.

We represent the strong union and weak (or no) union states as conventions because unionization is more akin to bargaining over the "rules of the game" than bargaining over the wage, as a unionized workplace comes along with a large set of de facto and de jure workplace governance practices. While a great deal of what unions do is encoded in legally binding collective bargaining agreements that cover the entire workplace, even with these formal contracts, enforcement of these contracts takes place on a case-by-case basis. Further, when workers and management disagree about the conditions of workplace governance, no production can occur, motivating (as a simplification) the 0 off-diagonal payoffs.

To summarize, a within-firm transition in our model would occur when workers at a single nonunion plant went on strike, refusing to work until they were granted a collective bargaining agreement and a recognized union. The managers and owners dealing with these workers would not respond until a sufficient number of workers went on strike, but then once they transitioned to the new norm, the firm would treat all its workers under the new norm.

The presence of many firms, some union and some not, in the metapopulation also creates opportunities for convention switching if firms' market share or probability of failure differs across union and nonunion states. The role of market competition in shrinking or eliminating unionized firms has been widely discussed (Hirsch, 2008). The union state may also be favored by between-firm migration. Workers committed to the prounion norm would also work for nonunion employers eventually,

---

[22] The regression discontinuity-based evidence is also mixed: little impact on wages, some impact on firm closure, but significant and large impacts on workers benefits. See Frandsen (2020) and Knepper (2020).

possibly increasing the ranks of those willing to play idiosyncratically to induce a switch to a union workplace.

14.8.2 The rise and demise of private sector trade unions in the U.S.

We can use our model to interpret the 20th-century pattern of unionization in the U.S. Numerous scholars (see Farber et al. (2020) for a recent survey) have documented low union density until the 1935 Wagner Act and its being upheld in 1937 by the United States Supreme Court. Density increased sharply by around 5–10 percentage points before World War II, and importantly, included the largest firms in the U.S. economy (e.g., General Motors and US Steel). Density then increased again quite rapidly during World War II, where unions were protected by the National War Labor Broad. But after the rapid growth through the 1935–1950 period, private sector unionization began a slow but steady decline, which accelerated in the late 1970s and early 1980s, falling from a high of around 30% of the nonagricultural workforce to around 6% in 2019.

The importance of small numbers of activists during the 1930s increase in union density is apparent from historical accounts. Lynd and Lynd (2014) present numerous biographical stories of workers who tried (and often failed and were fired) to organize unions in their shops. These workers held out for the E strategy in our model, who would usually get the 0 payoff, but would occasionally succeed. Friedlander (1975) documents in an oral history the decentralized process that led to the emergence of a United Auto Workers local at the "Detroit Parts Company" between 1936 and 1938. He shows that the presence of a prounion floor inspector who managed to avoid getting fired was instrumental in the percolation of union sentiment across the different parts of the plant.

Indicative of the highly localized process of change, Friedlander also shows how different parts of the plant informally secured collective representation at different times, well before the formal establishment of the union. Other historical accounts of the emergence of unions in the 1930s are consistent with this story.[23]

The Wagner Act appears to have raised the rate at which nonunion firms became unionized, both by protecting recognition strikes (so that the off diagonal payoffs were no longer zero) and by allowing representation elections by which workers could win union recognition. The recognition election formalized process by which in our model best responding employers would switch strategies, causing firms to tip at an increasing rate from nonunion to union.

The rapid increase in union density at firms created by the Wagner Act was then consolidated by the National War Labor Board, which altered between-firm competition so that the union convention was favored in competition for war production. Then for a brief window, increase of idiosyncratic play by workers within firms together with a favorable between-firm selection environment generated almost all sustained increases in private-sector union density in the 20th-century United States.

Note that the "labor peace" norm persisted for almost 30 years despite the considerable antiunion legal devices at the disposal of employers. Supreme Court decisions along with the Taft–Hartley Act altered the legal architecture put in place by the Wagner Act and the National Labor Relations Board eliminating many prounion provisions. Further, the Supreme Court had weakened the National Labor Relations Act protections of strikers almost immediately after the passage of the Wagner Act, allowing

---

[23] In a review of an account of autoworker organizing by Kruchko (1972), David Montgomery (1973) writes "the union was forged by a network of local activists, spreading strikes like those of 1935 and 1937 by raising demands over local grievances."

employers to fire workers permanently during strikes in the *NLRB vs Mackay* case, thereby reinstating the zero offdiagonal payoffs for workers deviating from the nonunion convention.

Our model also illustrates the forces driving the decline of unions. Taft–Hartley and anticommunist purges lowered the idiosyncratic play of workers, and the ending of war conditions removed the prounion aspects of between-firm competition. Then the decline of unions also occurs on the same two dimensions: within-firm transitions from unionized conventions to nonunion (or greatly weakened union) conventions, with between-firm competition, also reducing the ability of unionized firms to avoid bankruptcy or acquisition. Globalization and deregulation, by further intensifying between-firm competition, further narrowed the space for high σ and low ρ union contracts to persist in cases where the union contract reduced overall productivity.

Within-firm transitions out of the union convention are driven by idiosyncratic play of managers and owners. Despite the legality of many antiunion practices following 1947, they were not widely used throughout the 1947–1975 period. But employers were deliberately experimenting with these devices, often failing to overcome resistance of union members. The increase in antiunion practices still remained sporadic until after the 1970s economic crisis (in particular the 1970s oil shocks and subsequent inflation).

An example of the new environment from the 1980s on was the fate of prounion convention concerning the firing of strikers. Until the mid-1970s, strikes at many unionized firms were routine affairs, where workers could expect their jobs back after a strike. Although employers occasionally experimented with replacing striking workers permanently, they did not succeed in establishing it as a new convention, generally because unions successfully demanded rehiring of such workers as conditions of a new contract.

Wachter and Carter (1989) write that "Until the late 1970s or 1980s, firms rarely made use of their rights under Mackay Radio to hire permanent replacements." In the terms of our model, both workers and managers adhered to the "no-permanent-replacement" convention prior to the mid-1970s. A 1980s management handbook (cited in Canzoneri (1993)) wrote "Prior to the 1980s management usually chose not to operate during a strike..... Plant operation [during a strike] is a departure from the norm in union-management relations ... it represents a clear escalation of conflict ... in its relationship to a union." Gramm (1991) in a small survey of the mid-1980s strikes found that while 16% (24% in New York) of employers used permanent replacement workers during the strike, 100% said that this was the first time they had used them, leading Gramm to conclude that "employer willingness to hire permanent replacements has increased during the 1980s."

The convention then tipped toward one where firing of striking workers became acceptable (no doubt facilitated by Ronald Reagan's very public termination of the air traffic controllers). Alongside this change in strike costs, unions reacted to the increased willingness to lockout and permanently replaced strikers by surrendering many privileges once ensconced in collective bargaining agreements. Explicitly named as "concession bargaining", unions agreed to conditions like no-strike pledges, exemptions of select groups of new workers, and mandatory arbitration. Over the 1980s, the unionized part of manufacturing, especially, not only shrank in terms of absolute size and density, but also a newly unequal set of shopfloor conventions and contract terms prevailed.

Although the idiosyncratic play of managers driving unionized workplaces into less equal contracts is important, another potentially even more important force operating is market competition between union and nonunion firms, the analog of between-population competition in our model. Since between-firm competition favors efficiency, inefficient unionized firms can be eliminated even in the absence of management-driven transitions from union to nonunion. That is, the between-group selection can favor nonunion firms even if within-firm transitions of unionized to nonunion are few.

Fierce market competition could favor unequal firm governance structures that were too costly in terms of output. Efficient nonunion firms would out compete union firms on the market. If on the other hand, they were insulated from that competition (as they had been during World War II), then a highly unequal within-firm distribution of output could make the nonunion firm vulnerable to being tipped into a unionized convention by the collective action of workers.

To recap, a summary of the 20th-century trajectory of union density in the vocabulary of our model would be that a spurt of collective action at large firms in the 1930s generated transitions to unionized firms, and union-biased firm selection in the 1940s wartime economy enabled these union firms to dominate their markets. The National War Labor Board concluded procurement contracts that were conditional on union recognition amidst quite tight and competitive labor markets. But then, with the end of WW2, both antiunion activity of managers (which did not pay off at first) and a between-firm selection dynamics that favored firm efficiency over within-firm equality together deunionized already union firms and shrank the market shares of those unionized firms that remained.

A limitation of this account is that it leaves no role for laws and formal institutions, even though historical narratives of the rise and decline of unions emphasize the role of laws such as the Wagner Act and the Taft–Hartley Act. We next address this omission in our formal model above.

14.8.3 Formal vs informal institutions

None of our historical or theoretical analysis implies that the formal laws were unimportant or merely window dressing on the changing conventions. Indeed, a richer model would consider the joint evolution of the formal and informal institutions (Bisin and Verdier, 2017; Belloc and Bowles, 2013, 2017).

We can think of the formal institutions as affecting the payoffs from different strategies, which alters the size of the basin of attraction of the two conventions. Antiunion laws could make idiosyncratic play by workers costly (the off-diagonal $E - U$ payoffs to workers negative), for example, allowing workers to be fired for union activity or criminally punishing striking workers. Antiunion laws could also lower the payoffs to having a union contract, for example, by restricting what employers have a "duty to bargain" over. Further antiunion laws could increase the payoffs to employers from lockouts and other antiunion activity (making the off-diagonal $U - E$ payoffs to employers positive).

It is important what these antiunion laws alter the resistances to transitions by raising R^{UE} and lowering R^{EU}. The actual transition to this equilibrium will depend on the timing of the idiosyncratic play, relative population size, and, more generally, the network of interaction. Thus we would not expect immediate effects of laws that affect the out-of-equilibrium payoffs in the contexts where idiosyncratic play is low or where the network structure leads to slow percolation of changes in the population.[24]

An empirical example of this kind of policy effect can be seen in the effect of the National Labor Relations Act (NLRA or Wagner Act) on union density. As Freeman (1998) points out, the NLRA

---

[24] For example, right-to-work laws have a difficult-to-detect effect on union density in difference-in-difference specifications (Farber et al., 2020; Fortin et al., 2020). But if our model is correct, then it would take some time for a new equilibrium to emerge, as unionization is dispersed across many industries and many establishments. The dynamics of idiosyncratic play and best-responses would only play out over some time before manifesting in new equilibria, and as such would not show up in short-run variation.

resulted in a big increase in union density, *not* only via the newly formed recognition process, but instead via recognition strikes. Farber et al. (2020, pp. 143) in Figure G.6 show that recognition strikes were generally at a constant level throughout the 1930s, but with the Wagner Act, the fraction of the successful strikes changed. In the lens of our model, this is akin to the basin of attraction of the "union" equilibrium getting larger, so that a given strike is more likely to induce a set of employers or managers to concede recognition.

14.9 Conclusion

Our model, while retaining the focus on class and other forms of group conflict of the political economy approach, is based on three departures. First, we have integrated within- and between-population conflicts and institutional transitions into a common model. Second, our explicit dynamical system allows us to study (albeit in a rudimentary manner) the out-of-equilibrium movements of a system, that is, the process of institutional change itself. Third, our actors are not fictive representatives of unitary groups, but instead individuals whose substantially uncoordinated actions are based (realistically) on sparse information, limited cognitive capacities, and (for the most part) local rather than global objectives.

Our variant of the stochastic evolutionary game theory approach allows predictions of the cultural-institutional conventions governing a population in the very long run and provides a rather strong characterization of the nature of these stochastically stable states. The approach thus provides one account of how the institutions termed "evolutionary universals" by Talcott Parsons might come to be recurrent historically and ubiquitous at any given point in time. These conventions having the status of stochastically stable states would have been, as Parsons (1964, 340) put it, "likely to be 'hit upon' by various systems operating under different conditions" and to persist over long periods.

We were able to show, for example, that when class sizes are not very unequal, the within-population equilibrium selection mechanism we have modeled favors more egalitarian conventions (even if they are less productive) and especially if the alternative to an egalitarian convention is a highly unequal one. Our between-population mechanism may also favor egalitarian conventions (as long as they are not too unproductive) and will more likely do so if the resources that determine success in between-population contests are subject to diminishing returns in the payoffs to individual group members.

We have used this model to illuminate historical phenomena such as the demise of serfdom and the rise of the national state in Europe, the emergence of private property during the Neolithic, and the evolution of 20th-century U.S. union density. These transitions have been relatively rapid and were driven at least partly by decentralized accumulation of novel practices, often long prior to formal institutional recognition. Thus our model provides a prediction about the dynamic of change: Although cultural-institutional endure for long periods, they also can change quite suddenly for entirely endogenous reasons.

There are a number of directions for future work, both conceptual and empirical. Our model of intentional but myopic idiosyncratic play avoids the extremes of the mutation-like noise in standard evolutionary models and prescient forward-looking decision-making in the classical game theory models. But we have not found a similar half-way house between our entirely decentralized dynamic and the more standard top-down approach. We would like to be able to take account of the fact that switches in best response are often highly coordinated often by law, for example, by requiring that employers bargain collectively with workers a majority of whom have voted pro-union in a recognition election. A balance of integrating actions taken by group members as the outcome of collective decisions would be vital to a complete model, as we have sketched in Section 14.8.3.

We have made the level and direction of idiosyncratic play endogenous (actors do not play idiosyncratically when at their favored convention) but in a very rudimentary way. Progress along these lines could be made following Van Damme and Weibull (2002) and by modeling a collective decision to play idiosyncratically by some members of a class (as in Bowles (2004)). A better empirical understanding of the Rosa Parks', the Soweto schoolchildren, the Gdansk shipyard workers, and others who sought to upset a status quo convention could suggest new approaches.

Finally, our evolutionary model provides explicit out-of-equilibrium dynamics that might be tested and calibrated with time-series data. Although this is rarely done in historical economics, we can imagine that high-frequency data could be used to distinguish theories of institutional persistence and change.

References

Abowd, J.M., 1989. The effect of wage bargains on the stock market value of the firm. The American Economic Review, 774–800.

Abowd, J.A., Lemieux, T., 1993. The effects of product market competition on collective bargaining agreements: the case of foreign competition in Canada. The Quarterly Journal of Economics 108 (4), 983–1014.

Acemoglu, D., 2005. Politics and economics in weak and strong states. Journal of Monetary Economics 52 (7), 1199–1226.

Acemoglu, D., Egorov, G., Sonin, K., 2020. Institutional change and institutional persistence. In: Bisin, A., Federico, G. (Eds.), The Handbook of Historical Economics. Elsevier. Chapter 13 (in this book).

Acemoglu, D., Robinson, J., 2008. Persistence of power, elites and institutions. The American Economic Review 98 (1), 267–293.

Acemoglu, D., Robinson, J., 2020. The Narrow Corridor: States, Societies, and the Fate of Liberty. Penguin Books.

Alesina, A., Giuliano, P., Nunn, N., 2013. On the origins of gender roles: women and the plough. The Quarterly Journal of Economics 128 (2), 469–530.

Anderson, P., 1974. Lineages of the Absolutist State. New Left Books.

Anderson, P., 2013. Passages from Antiquity to Feudalism. Verso Books.

Bailey, M., 2014. The Decline of Serfdom in Late Medieval England: From Bondage to Freedom. Boydell & Brewer Ltd.

Belloc, M., Bowles, S., 2013. The persistence of inferior cultural-institutional conventions. American Economic Association, Papers and Proceedings, 93–98.

Belloc, M., Bowles, S., 2017. Persistence and change in culture and institutions under autarchy, trade, and factor mobility. American Economic Journal: Microeconomics 9 (4), 245–276.

Besley, T., Persson, T., 2009. The origins of state capacity: property rights, taxation, and policy. American Economic Review 99 (4), 1218–1244.

Bewley, T.F., 1999. Why Wages Don't Fall During a Recession. Harvard University Press.

Binmore, K., Samuelson, L., Young, P., 2003. Equilibrium selection in bargaining models. Games and Economic Behavior 45 (2), 296–328.

Bisin, A., Verdier, T., 2017. On the joint evolution of culture and institutions. Technical report. National Bureau of Economic Research.

Blum, J., 1971. Lord and Peasant in Russia. Princeton University Press.

Boehm, C., 2009. Hierarchy in the Forest: The Evolution of Egalitarian Behavior. Harvard University Press.

Bogaard, A., 2004. Neolithic Farming in Central Europe: An Archaeobotanical Study of Crop Husbandry Practices. Routledge.

Bogaard, A., Fochesato, M., Bowles, S., 2019. The farming-inequality nexus: new insights from ancient Western Eurasia. Antiquity 93 (371), 1129–1143.

Boserup, E., 1970. Woman's Role in Economic Development. George Allen & Unwin.

Bowles, S., 2004. Microeconomics: Behavior, Institutions, and Evolution. Princeton University Press.

Bowles, S., 2006. Group competition, reproductive leveling, and the evolution of human altruism. Science 314, 1569–1572.

Bowles, S., 2011. Cultivation of cereals by the first farmers was not more productive than foraging. Proceedings of the National Academy of Sciences 108 (12), 4760–4765.

Bowles, S., Choi, J.-K., 2013. Coevolution of farming and private property during the early Holocene. Proceedings of the National Academy of Sciences 110 (22), 8830–8835.

Bowles, S., Choi, J.-K., 2019. The neolithic agricultural revolution and the origins of private property. Journal of Political Economy 127 (5), 2186–2228.

Bowles, S., Choi, J.-K., Hopfensitz, A., 2003. The coevolution of individual behaviors and group level institutions. Journal of Theoretical Biology 223 (2), 135–147.

Boyd, R., Gintis, H., Bowles, S., 2010. Coordinated punishment of defectors sustains cooperation and can proliferate when rare. Science 328, 617–620.

Boyd, R., Richerson, P.J., 1988. Culture and the Evolutionary Process. University of Chicago Press.

Brady, T.A., 1985. Turning Swiss: Cities and Empire, 1450–1550. Cambridge Univ. Press.

Brewer, J., 1990. The Sinews of Power: War, Money, and the English State, 1688-1783. Harvard University Press.

Bright, C., Harding, S.F., 1984. Statemaking and Social Movements: Essays in History and Theory. University of Michigan Press.

Brown, R., Gilman, A., 1960. The pronouns of power and solidarity. In: Sebeok, T.A. (Ed.), Style in Language. MIT Press, pp. 253–276.

Canzoneri, J.J., 1993. Management's attitudes and the need for the workplace fairness act. Buffalo Law Review 41, 205–243.

Cavalli-Sforza, L.L., Feldman, M.W., 1981. Cultural Transmission and Evolution: A Quantitative Approach. Princeton University Press.

Clyne, M., Norrby, C., Warren, J., 2009. Language and Human Relations: Styles of Address in Contemporary Language. Cambridge University Press.

Cohen, G., 1978. Karl Marx's Theory of History: A Defence. Princeton University Press.

David, P., 1985. Clio and the economics of QWERTY. The American Economic Review 75 (2), 332–337.

Demsetz, H., 1974. Toward a Theory of Property Rights. Springer.

DiNardo, J., Hallock, K., Pischke, J.-S., 1997. Unions and managerial pay. Technical report. National Bureau of Economic Research.

Dube, A., Manning, A., Naidu, S., 2018. Monopsony and employer mis-optimization explain why wages bunch at round numbers. Technical report. National Bureau of Economic Research.

Eldridge, N., Gould, S.J., 1972. Punctuated equilibria: an alternative to phyletic gradualism. In: Schopf, T.J.M. (Ed.), Models in Paleobiology, pp. 82–115.

Farber, H.S., Herbst, D., Kuziemko, I., Naidu, S., 2020. Unions and inequality over the twentieth century: new evidence from survey data. Technical report. National Bureau of Economic Research.

Finan, F., Olken, B.A., Pande, R., 2017. The personnel economics of the developing state. In: Banerjee, A., Duflo, E. (Eds.), Handbook of Economic Field Experiments, pp. 467–514.

Fisher, R., 1930. The Genetical Theory of Natural Selection. Clarendon Press.

Fortin, N., Lemieux, T., Lloyd, N., 2020. Labor market institutions and the distribution of wages: the role of spillover effects. Technical report. National Bureau of Economic Research.

Frandsen, B.R., 2020. The surprising impacts of unionization: evidence from matched employer-employee data. Economics Department, Brigham Young University. Mimeo.

Freeman, R.B., 1998. Spurts in union growth: defining moments and social processes. In: Bordo, M., Goldin, C., White, E. (Eds.), The Defining Moment: The Great Depression and the American Economy in the Twentieth Century, pp. 265–296.

Friedlander, P., 1975. The Emergence of a UAW Local, 1936–1939: A Study in Class and Culture. University of Pittsburgh Press.

Fryde, E., 1996. Peasants and Landlords in Later Medieval England, C. 1380-C.1525. Alan Sutton Publishing.

Frydman, C., Saks, R.E., 2010. Executive compensation: a new view from a long-term perspective, 1936–2005. The Review of Financial Studies 23 (5), 2099–2138.

Gellner, E., 1983. Nations and Nationalism. Cornell University Press.

Gintis, H., Bowles, S., 1984. State and class in European feudalism. In: Bright, C., Harding, S. (Eds.), Statemaking and Social Movements: Essays in History and Theory, pp. 19–51.

Gintis, H., Bowles, S., Boyd, R.T., Fehr, E., et al., 2005. Moral Sentiments and Material Interests: The Foundations of Cooperation in Economic Life. MIT Press.

Goody, J.R., Thirsk, J., Thompson, E.P. (Eds.), 1976. Family and Inheritance: Rural Society in Western Europe, 1200-1800. Cambridge University Press.

Gramm, C.L., 1991. Empirical evidence on political arguments relating to replacement worker legislation. Labor Law Journal 42 (8), 491–496.

Greif, A., 1994. Cultural beliefs and the organization of society: a historical and theoretical reflection on collectivist and individualist societies. Journal of Political Economy, 912–950.

Gulati, M., Scott, R.E., 2012. The Three and a Half Minute Transaction: Boilerplate and the Limits of Contract Design. University of Chicago Press.

Hatcher, J., Bailey, M., 2001. Modelling the Middle Ages: The History and Theory of England's Economic Development. Oxford University Press.

Hayek, F.V., 1960. The Constitution of Liberty. University of Chicago.

Hirsch, B.T., 2008. Sluggish institutions in a dynamic world: can unions and industrial competition coexist? The Journal of Economic Perspectives 22 (1), 153–176.

Hwang, S.-H., Naidu, S., Bowles, S., 2018. Social conflict and the evolution of unequal conventions. Available at http://tuvalu.santafe.edu/~snaidu/papers/class_dyn_forcirculation.pdf.

Kandori, M.G., Mailath, G., Rob, R., 1993. Learning, mutation, and long run equilibria in games. Econometrica 61, 29–56.

Kaplan, H., Gurven, M., Hill, K., Hurtado, A.M., 2005. The natural history of human food sharing and cooperation: a review and a new multi-individual approach to the negotiation of norms. In: Gintis, H., Bowles, S., Boyd, R., Fehr, E. (Eds.), Moral Sentiments and Material Interests: The Foundations of Cooperation in Economic Life, pp. 75–113.

Kaplan, H., Hill, K., 1985. Hunting ability and reproductive success among male ache foragers: preliminary results. Current Anthropology 26 (1), 131–133.

Karmin, M., Saag, L., et al., 2015. A recent bottleneck of Y chromosome diversity coincides with a global change in culture. Genome Research 25, 459–466.

Kelly, R.C., 1985. The Nuer Conquest: The Structure and Development of an Expansionist System. University of Michigan Press.

Knepper, M., 2020. From the fringe to the fore: labor unions and employee compensation. Review of Economics and Statistics 102 (1), 98–112.

Kruchko, J.G., 1972. The Birth of a Union Local: The History of UAW Local 674, Norwood, Ohio, 1933 to 1940. ILR Press.

Levy, R., 1957. The Social Structure of Islam. Taylor & Francis.

Lippold, S., Xu, H., et al., 2014. Human paternal and maternal demographic histories: insights from high-resolution Y chromosome and mtDNA sequences. Investigative Genetics 5 (13).

Lynd, A., Lynd, R.S., 2014. Rank and File: Personal Histories by Working-Class Organizers. Princeton University Press.

Markoff, J., 1996. The Abolition of Feudalism: Peasants, Lords, and Legislators in the French Revolution. Pennsylvania State Univ. Pr.

Marx, K., 1904. A Contribution to the Critique of Political Economy. C. H. Kerr.

Maynard Smith, J., 1974. The theory of games and the evolution of animal conflicts. Journal of Theoretical Biology 47, 209–221.

Montgomery, D., 1973. Review of "The Birth of a Union Local: The History of UAW Local 674, Norwood, Ohio, 1933 to 1940 by John G. Kruchko". Journal of American History 60 (2), 498.

Naidu, S., Hwang, S.-H., Bowles, S., 2010. Evolutionary bargaining with intentional idiosyncratic play. Economics Letters 109 (1), 31–33.

Naidu, S., Hwang, S.-H., Bowles, S., 2017. The evolution of egalitarian sociolinguistic conventions. The American Economic Review: Papers and Proceedings 107 (5), 572–577.

Naidu, S., Yuchtman, N., 2013. Coercive contract enforcement: law and the labor market in nineteenth century industrial Britain. The American Economic Review 103 (1), 107–144.

North, D.C., 1981. Structure and Change in Economic History. W. W. Norton and Co.

North, D.C., Thomas, R.P., 1971. The rise and fall of the manorial system: a theoretical model. The Journal of Economic History 31 (04), 777–803.

North, D.C., Thomas, R.P., 1977. The first economic revolution. The Economic History Review 30 (2), 229–241.

Nunn, N., 2020. History as evolution. In: Bisin, A., Federico, G. (Eds.), The Handbook of Historical Economics. Elsevier. Chapter 3 (in this book).

Ouchi, W., 1980. Markets bureaucracies and clans. Administrative Science Quarterly 25, 129–141.

Pagano, U., 2001. The Origin of Organizational Species. In: Nicita, A., Pagano, U. (Eds.), The Evolution of Economic Diversity. Routledge, pp. 21–43.

Parsons, T., 1964. Evolutionary universals in society. American Sociological Review 3 (29), 339–357.

Poos, L.R., 1991. A Rural Society After the Black Death: Essex 1350–1525. Cambridge University Press.

Price, G., 1972. Fisher's 'fundamental theorem' made clear. Annals of Human Genetics 36, 129–140.

Silbey, S.S., 2010. J. Locke, op. cit.: invocations of law on snowy streets. Journal of Comparative Law 5, 66.

Smith, D.M., 1959. Italy: A Modern History. University of Michigan Press.

Soltis, J., Boyd, R., Richerson, P.J., 1995. Can group-functional behaviors evolve by cultural group selection?: an empirical test. Current Anthropology 36 (3), 473–494.

Sugden, R., 1989. Spontaneous order. The Journal of Economic Perspectives 3 (4), 85–97.

Tilly, C., 1975. Western state-making and theories of political transformation. In: Tilly, C. (Ed.), The Formation of National States in Western Europe. Princeton University Press, pp. 601–686.

Tilly, C., 1990. Coercion, Capital, and European States, A.D. 990–1990. Blackwell.

Van Damme, E., Weibull, J.W., 2002. Evolution in games with endogenous mistake probabilities. Journal of Economic Theory 106 (2), 296–315.

Wachter, M.L., Carter, W.H., 1989. Norm shifts in union wages: will 1989 be a replay of 1969? Brookings Papers on Economic Activity 1989 (2), 233–264.

Wallerstein, I., 1974. The Modern World-System I: Capitalist Agriculture and the Origins of the European World-Economy in the Sixteenth Century. University of California Press.

Weber, E., 1976. Peasants into Frenchmen: The Modernization of Rural France, 1870-1914. Stanford University Press.

White, L., 1962. The act of invention: causes, contexts, continuities and consequences. Technology and Culture 3 (4), 486–500.

Wiessner, P., 2005. Norm enforcement among the Ju/'hoansi Bushmen. Human Nature 16 (2), 115–145.

Williamson, O., 1985. The Economic Institutions of Capitalism. Free Press.

Wood, E., 2003. Insurgent Collective Action and Civil War in El Salvador. Cambridge University Press.

Wright, S., 1935. Evolution in populations in approximate equilibrium. Journal of Genetics 30 (2), 257.

Young, H.P., 1993. An evolutionary model of bargaining. Journal of Economic Theory 59 (1), 145–168.

Young, H.P., 1998a. Conventional contracts. The Review of Economic Studies 65 (4), 773–792.

Young, H.P., 1998b. Individual Strategy and Social Structure: An Evolutionary Theory of Institutions. Princeton University Press.

Young, H.P., Burke, M., 2001. Competition and custom in economic contracts: a case study of Illinois agriculture. The American Economic Review 91 (3), 559–573.

State power and conflict driven evolution[☆]

David K. Levine[a,b] and Salvatore Modica[c]

aDepartment of Economics, RSCAS European University, San Domenico di Fiesole, Italy
bDepartment of Economics, WUSTL, St. Louis, MO, United States
cDepartment of Economics, Business and Statistics (SEAS), Università di Palermo, Palermo, Italy

15.1 Introduction and historical contest

The goal of this chapter is to examine the implications of the evolution of social organizations due to external competition. There are a variety of models of external competition. Models such as Ely (2002) examine voluntary migration - these models tend to efficient outcomes as people are drawn to locations with high per capita income. Historically, however, institutional success has not been through voluntary immigration into the arms of welcoming richer neighbors. Rather people and institutions have generally spread through invasion and conflict: the Carthaginians did not emigrate to Rome. Large institutional change has often occurred in the aftermath of the disruption caused by warfare and other conflicts. Hence it seems worthwhile studying external competition through conflict, which is the focus of this chapter.

It is common to develop fact driven theories: a historical fact or laboratory anomaly is observed and a theory is introduced to explain that fact. Here we focus on using theory to analyze facts and particularly facts it was not designed to explain. The theory as indicated is external competition through conflict. The theory itself tells us what facts and data to look for.

In a dynamic setting of a game or mechanism in which punishments and rewards are possible most social arrangements arise as equilibrium - this finds sharp definition in the folk theorem of repeated games (see Fudenberg and Maskin (1986)) but is a much broader observation. The goal of evolutionary game theory is to ask which of these many feasible institutions and arrangements are persistent, which are durable, which will we see in the long-run. Here we preview our results.

15.1.1 Geography

The starting point of any evolutionary theory of conflict must be to specify the geographical area over which conflict takes place. There is no point in arguing about why historically India did not conquer China or vice versa - even a brief glance at the map show the Himalayan mountains in between, and a closer look shows as well the dense jungles of Southeast Asia separating the two. Hence a theory of conflict must focus on a region in which societies are able to fight. Over the sweep of recorded history

---

☆ We gratefully acknowledge support from the EUI Research Council and MIUR (PRIN 2017H5KPLL).

The Handbook of Historical Economics. https://doi.org/10.1016/B978-0-12-815874-6.00025-3

the bulk of human population has lived in the Eurasian continent (including North Africa). There are three distinct geographical subregions which undoubtedly had trading relations but were not in conflict: China, India, and Europe (including North Africa). For geographical as well as cultural reasons, in each of them history shows different societies competing on a more or less level playing field, and most of our historical data is from these three regions treated separately.

None of these areas, however, is completely isolated, and in addition to the contestants there have always been annoying "outsiders:" Mongols, Afghans, Vikings, English and so forth. Each of these groups has in common that while they can and do play a military role in the region of conflict they themselves are largely immune from the consequences. Hence Mongols in their deserts, Afghans in their mountain strongholds, and Vikings and English protected by their seas are all able to raid and fight and even conquer in China, India, and (continental) Europe, but are themselves largely immune to invasion. As the strength of these outsiders does not depend on events in the central area of conflict we model them as exogenous; and as their strength waxes and wanes - due to, for example, to climate change and migration - we examine what impact this has on the evolution of societies in the main areas of conflict.

15.1.2 Hegemony

In conflict luck matters, but success begets success. Conquering a city or a province strengthens the winner and weakens the loser. Hence as war and invasion unfold we expect that eventually one side gets lucky enough, strong enough, and faces opponents weak enough, that it wins outright. In this sense the conquest and destruction of Carthage by Rome (or vice versa) was inevitable. This argues that the natural state of mankind is hegemony, with a single society ruling over an isolated geographical area: that is China, India, and (continental) Europe should naturally and commonly be found under the rule of one strong central state.

To a surprising extent this is true. The fact is that hegemonies have been much more frequent and long lasting than one may think: over roughly two millennia prior to the industrial revolution, in India, China, and Europe (comprising 85% of world population during the period) about 37% of the time hegemonies prevailed.[1] On the other hand while hegemonies were common in China, they were infrequent in Europe and non-existent in India.[2] We find the answer in the role of outsiders - and ultimately with the fully developed theory - we can explain well not only when we see a hegemony and when not, but also why in the absence of hegemony we sometimes see competing societies that are extractive and sometimes competing societies that are inclusive.

On the grounds it is better to walk before running, we begin by explaining the simple theory: here weak outsiders lead to hegemony, but there is little to say about the structure of non-hegemonic regions when outsiders are strong. With the simple theory evolution not surprisingly selects societies with high state power - the ability to prevail in conflict over rivals. Never-the-less this simple theory has significant implications which we outline next.

---

[1] See Levine and Modica (2013) for data and sources. Here we take the population weights of India and China as 1 and Europe as 1/2.

[2] For unclear reasons in all the theorizing about China versus Europe few have thought to ask how their theory fares in the third (and second largest) center of world population, India. We do.

15.1.3 Malthus

One of the most fundamental economic aspects of a society is its population and prosperity. Here Malthus casts a long shadow. It is an amazing triumph of theory over fact that such a thoroughly discredited theory still maintains its grip on the imagination of the economics profession. Malthusian theory asserts that in the long-run population will adjust so that society should be at a subsistence level of prosperity. In our reading of economic history we have been unable to identify any study of any society in any place or at any time for which this is the case. Modern anthropological research argues that ancient hunter-gatherer societies were more prosperous than subsequent agricultural societies - so presumably above subsistence.[3] Ancient agricultural societies may have largely consisted of peasants at subsistence level - but also had elites well above subsistence so on average they must have been above subsistence. The entire history of the industrial revolution - the well known fact of the demographic transition - all starkly contradict Malthusian theory.[4] Yet despite the fact that every observed society is above subsistence some economic historians continue to assume that any society for which data is lacking are at subsistence.[5] Historically, the subsistence level meant "the physical requirements to survive and reproduce." To deal with the obvious contradictions in the data modern economic historians such as Clark (2007) have introduced the slippery idea that "subsistence" means "some socially determined level of per capita income above which population decreases and below which it increases."[6] This is somewhat awkward as the cross-sectional evidence is clear that rich countries reproduce at much lower rates than poor ones.

Rather than tweaking an obviously wrong theory we instead ask what happens when social evolution is driven by conflict. As Malthus himself recognized that there can be incentive compatible social arrangements that stabilize the population at a low level, he still thought that in some long-run evolutionary sense these low-population equilibria were unstable. Evolution through conflict argues the opposite - that societies at subsistence level are unstable. Specifically, our intuition can be captured by the following conceptual experiment. Imagine a "Malthusian" society with farmers living at the edge of subsistence. Next door live their less numerous but richer neighbors who control their population. What happens when the few but rich neighbors invade the nearly starving farmers? For the farmers to spend time fighting is to take time from farming - that is, to starve. The outcome of this conflict is easy to see. In place of the discredited Malthusian theory arguing that every technological improvement should be met with population increase driving income back to subsistence, we develop a theory of when and how per capita income increases and decreases with technological change.

---

[3] See, for example, Bowles et al. (2021).

[4] See for example Hansen and Prescott (2002).

[5] See for example Maddison (2007).

[6] A close reading of the literature reveals serious problems in the way data is collected to support these theories. The most central problem is that at best what is computed is median per capita income - that is, the typical income of a poor person. Of course, as we noted, the upper classes consume considerably more than subsistence so the mean must also be above subsistence. A typical example of this problem is in the classical and much cited Ladurie (1974) study of Languedoc peasants in France. Ignored in this study are the facts that the nobles live above subsistence; that the entire area made substantial payments to the King - and indeed the ability of France to conduct continual wars throughout this period indicates that substantial resources above subsistence were available. More serious students of historical per capita GDP such as Maddison (2007) point out the Malthusian bias implicit in conclusions of this type.

15.1.4 Theory motivated analysis of facts

As indicated our goal is to use theory to motivate the analysis of facts. Hence we ask: given the theory what should be true? For example: Why should Spain now more than 300 years after ceding it to the British still wish to regain Gibraltar? Why would the UK be concerned to retain the Falkland Islands and Scotland? Why should Spain care about Catalan succession? Nobody thinks to answer these questions because their theories do not suggest these facts are relevant. Our theory prompts looking at these facts and suggests that the answer to these question lies in the nature of societies selected by evolutionary pressure. In particular, we show that those societies that simply seek to defend their territory are doomed to domination by those who aggressively seek expansion. Hence successful societies such as Spain and England have survived and thrived precisely because they are aggressive.

15.1.5 Gradual versus stochastic evolution

The economics profession is often accused by ignoramuses in the popular press of "physics envy." In this imaginary world of economic theory we supposedly think of economies as following predictable trajectories like planetary orbits. Nowhere is the contrast with such supposed theories greater than in modern evolutionary game theory. In conflict driven evolutionary theory the economy does not gradually converge to a long-run state - the economy is dynamic and stochastic. Random events play a central role, and eventually bad luck leads to too many things going wrong at once.

As a case in point: hegemonies are persistent, but they also rise and fall. The dynamics of the fall is interesting. Our model predicts that a hegemony does not gradually deteriorate as imagined by historians such as Gibbon (1776). It is rather under constant attack: there are rebellions, invasions - many of them. Most fail, a few succeed for a long period of time and then also fail. And eventually when the fall comes it is abrupt. This happens when the hegemony is at low ebb - in a recession or depression or suffering some other sort of temporary setback from which it has recovered many times. Success driven by luck enables rebels or invaders to overthrow the existing hegemony before it has time to regroup and assert its strength. The picture is of many failed attempts, most short, a few long, followed by a sudden and rapid success.

This theoretical description then directs us to the data. Is it true? What is the nature of the fall of hegemony? To answer this we look for a well documented case study and find it in the story of the fall of the Qing dynasty in China. Indeed, as we show, the history of that fall has precisely the characteristics predicted by the theory.

15.1.6 Balance of power

After taking the first steps with a simple model we next analyze more carefully the role of strong outsiders. Here a non-hegemonic state of affairs - a balance of power - can persist for a long period. The point is a simple one: while there is a natural tendency for one side to win a conflict, this tendency is offset by outsiders whose interests may conflict with the existence of a hegemon and may therefore intervene on the weaker side, or who may simply take advantage of foreign commitments to stab the hegemon in the back. We examine this theory in two stages.

We first present the basic result which establishes that outside intervention prolongs conflicts. We examine a large dataset on interventions and modern conflict and show that indeed, when there is no outside intervention (think of the US Civil War, or the two World Wars) conflict ends relatively quickly

- in four or five years - with one side winning. By contrast when there is outside intervention conflicts drag on for decades or even centuries, and often there is no clear victor.

Next we develop a careful model of the role of social institutions in creating and resolving conflict, examining the motivations of elites and masses and their ability to influence policy under more or less inclusive institutions. On the basis of economic incentives we develop a theory that takes into account the strength of outsiders but also the advancement of military technology to understand when we are likely to see hegemony, when we are likely to see a balance of power and in case there is a balance of power whether the competing societies are likely to be inclusive or exclusive. We then apply this to two millennia of historical data from the three great regions of China, India, and Europe. The theory provides a clear and compelling accounting for the facts. If we accept as economic historians say that it was the development of competing inclusive institutions in Europe in the late Medieval period that was responsible for the subsequent industrial revolution, our theory provides a clear answer to the question: why Europe and not China or India?[7] The answer we offer is Ghengis Khan, the cannon, and the English. Ghengis Khan accomplished two things: he brought cannons to Europe and he depopulated Mongolia. In China the removal of the outside threat of the Mongols led - as the theory asserts - to an extractive hegemony. In Europe the advent of the cannon together with the preying of the English on the French and the Spanish resulted - as the theory asserts - in an inclusive balance of power. Here as is often asserted the English played a key role in the industrial revolution - albeit a rather different one than is commonly assumed.

15.2 A model

We start by presenting a formal model which yields predictions about institutional change brought about by conflict driven evolution. We call our competing social organizations *societies,* of which there are a finite number $j \in J$. Time is discrete, $t = 1, 2, \ldots$. A society can be *inactive,* representing a template for a possible form of social organization, or it can be *active,* controlling resources. We assume that there are a positive integral number of resources L representing land, capital, people and so forth. For simplicity we simply refer to this as land. An active society j controls a positive amount of land $L_{jt} > 0$ while an inactive society controls no land $L_{jt} = 0$. Evolution will take place as land changes hands due to conflict. Total resources are fixed: $\sum_j L_{jt} = L$ at all t.

In the simplest version of the theory each society has a fixed structure. It does not evolve internally and institutions do not change, but evolution takes place as societies gain and lose land through conflict and perhaps are driven into extinction. In this scheme evolution follows a Markov process. A state $z_t \in Z$ is a list of land holding, $z_t = (L_{1t}, L_{2t}, \ldots, L_{Jt})$. External evolution is modeled as changes of ownership over land due to conflict. We assume that at most one unit of land changes hands each period - this can be taken to mean that time periods are "short enough."

We initially use a mechanical model of conflict. We assume that there is a simple scalar index of the potential ability of a social organization to resist and influence other societies. This depends on institutional characteristics of the society, including stability of the government and the ability to collect taxes and conscript soldiers, which depend in turn on the law-abidingness of citizens, the efficiency of

---

[7] Not that anyone besides us tries to account for India.

the courts, and the overall economic strength of the society. We refer to this as "state power" and denote it by γ_j. The overall ability to prevail in conflict will depend upon state power, but also upon resources L_{jt}.

We recognize as well that institutions and behavior must be learned. At any moment of time there is no reason to assume that a society is internally in equilibrium. There are models of varying complexity of how this may work (see Levine and Modica (2013)) but here we take a very simple approach. We assume that there are two types of societies indexed by a stability index $b_j \in \{0, 1\}$ with 1 indicating stability. Stable societies are those with robust incentive compatible institutions and behavior. By contrast unstable societies represent short-term behavior that may not be sustainable but tend nonetheless to generate short-term power. To wit, a strong leader may inspire fanatical soldiers, but as they age fanatical soldiers tend to become less interested in fighting in sketchy environments and more interested in wine and song - and surely that is true of their descendants. Our formal assumption is that the strongest unstable society is stronger than the strongest stable society: specifically we assume that $\max_{j|b_j=0} \gamma_j > \max_{j|b_j=1} \gamma_j$.

As indicated our model of evolution is a Markov model - indexed, however, by a parameter ϵ which in this context should be thought of as "the importance of luck in warfare." Specifically there are transition probabilities $P_\epsilon(z_{t+1}|z_t)$. We are going to be interested in the case where ϵ is small, which will have the interpretation that a very weak society will have little chance of prevailing over a strong one. This enables us to make use of the mathematical concept of resistance. Specifically we make three basic assumptions about P_ϵ:

1. P_ϵ is ergodic
2. There exists $\lim_{\epsilon \to 0} P_\epsilon = P_0$
3. For all $z_{t+1}, z_t \in Z$ there is a resistance function $0 \le r(z_t, z_{t+1}) \le \infty$ and constants $0 < C < 1 < D < \infty$ such that $C\epsilon^{r(z_t,z_{t+1})} \le P_\epsilon(z_{t+1}|z_t) \le D\epsilon^{r(z_t,z_{t+1})}$.

Here $r(z_t, z_{t+1})$ is the *resistance* of the transitions from z_t to z_{t+1}; observe that zero resistance means strictly positive probability for all ϵ hence positive probability with respect to P_0; on the other hand infinite resistance is zero probability in all P_ϵ's. Resistance measures speed of convergence of $P_\epsilon(z_{t+1}|z_t)$ to zero; roughly speaking higher resistance means lower probability. In the final section we will see how such a resistance function can emerge from a model in which conflict is endogenous.

Our assumptions about conflict are stated in terms of resistances. The probability that society j loses a unit of land is given by a conflict resolution function with resistance $r_j(z) < \infty$ to j losing one unit of land - this is the resistance of a transition from z to a state where j has one less unit of land. If j looses land the probability the land goes to society k has *land gain resistance* $\lambda_{jk}(z)$ where $\lambda_{jj} = \infty$ but if $k \ne j$ then $\lambda_{jk} < \infty$. Note that when an active society loses a unit of land new institutions may be introduced in that land - that is to say, an inactive society may gain the land.

We make several specific assumptions about the conflict resolution and land gain resistance.

1. r and λ depend only on the land holdings, state power and stability of the different societies; since they are just templates for societies, we assume that the state power of inactive societies does not matter.

2. resistance to losing land r is monotone in the sense that the resistance of j losing land is increasing in its own state power and land, and decreasing in that of other societies.

3. for stable societies resistance to losing land r is strictly increasing in state power and land when non-zero.

4. the weakest stable society with positive land holding has zero resistance to losing a unit of land.

5. unstable societies have zero resistance to losing a unit of land.

6. for given land holding, resistance to losing land is greater when facing more than one opponent with positive land holding than when all enemy land is in the hands of the strongest land holding opponent - also this is strict if resistance is positive.

7. for land gain resistance active societies all have zero resistance to gaining land, that is if $k \neq j$ and $L_k > 0$ then $\lambda_{jk}(z) = 0$.

Our last assumption involves *outsiders* - forces which are not societies in J but which may still influence the evolution of the z_t process. Outsiders are assumed to be protected by geography, climate, or sheer strength from action by the region in question. One example is Great Britain with respect to continental Europe from roughly the 14th to 20th centuries. Currently the U.S. and Russia are outside forces with respect to the Middle East, being protected by distance, the ocean (in the case of the U.S.) and by military strength from Middle Eastern societies. The strength of the outsiders is modeled simply as a real number $0 \leq y \leq 1$. The idea is that outsiders are antithetical to concentration of power in J. To state this formally, for any stable society j let z_j be the *hegemonic* state in which $L_j = L$ and define the *hegemonic resistance* as $h(\gamma_j, y) = r_j(z_j)$. Under our assumptions $h(\gamma_j, y)$ is strictly increasing in γ_j when positive. We postulate that h depends on y as follows:

8. $h(\gamma_j, y)$ is continuous and strictly decreasing in y when positive. There is a $\overline{y}$ sufficiently large that $h(\gamma_j, \overline{y}) = 0$ for all γ_j.

A stochastically stable state z is defined to be absorbing for $\epsilon = 0$ and such that the resistance of the unique limiting ergodic probability as $\epsilon \to 0$ is positive.[8]

15.2.1 A theory of hegemony

The next results, proven in Levine and Modica (2016), characterize the stochastically stable sets of the system.

Theorem 15.1. *If $y < \overline{y}$ then the stochastically stable states consist of hegemonies of stable societies with maximal state power. If $y > \overline{y}$ all states are positive recurrent for $\epsilon = 0$.*

This theory says we should often see hegemony. The idea of history being dominated by hegemonic states may seem a strange one, but the fact is that hegemonies have been much more frequent and long lasting than one may think: over roughly two millennia prior to the industrial revolution, in India, China, and Europe (comprising 85% of world population during the period) about 37% of the time hegemonies prevailed.[9]

Next, letting μ^ϵ denote the ergodic probability of P^ϵ (as in footnote 8), the next result says that hegemonies with higher state power (and hence higher hegemonic resistance) are more likely (hence more persistent).

---

[8] It is proven in Young (1993) that the ergodic probability μ^ϵ (such that $\mu^\epsilon P^\epsilon = \mu^\epsilon$) has a unique limit μ^0 as $\epsilon \to 0$; formally, a state z is stochastically stable if $\mu^0(z) > 0$.

[9] See Levine and Modica (2013) for data and sources. Here we take the population weights of India and China as 1 and Europe as 1/2.

Theorem 15.2 (Hegemonies with more state power are more persistent). *Let z_j and z_k be hegemonic states of j and k respectively. Then $\mu^\epsilon(z_j)/\mu^\epsilon(z_k) = 1/\epsilon^{h_j - h_k}$.*

15.3 The fall of Malthus[10]

The theory so far is one of evolution that favors higher state power. Our first goal is to examine what this implies about the organization of society. In general in order to disrupt neighbors or defend against disruption it is important to have resources that are not being used for other purposes: we refer to these as *free resources*. We first explore this idea in a setting with endogenous population and show how this leads to a theory of endogenous population size. In this discussion we focus on a single society hence we drop the j subscript.

In the *Malthusian Game* there are N families $i = 1, \ldots, N$ and each family chooses family size $M^i \in \{1, 2, \ldots, M\}$. Families utility comes from their children: utility is taken equal to family size. However, the society may act collectively to choose a social norm $v \in \{1, 2, \ldots, M\}$ for the maximum size of families and impose a penalty P on any family that fails to adhere to the social norm. If $v \geq M - P$ the society is incentive compatible and family size will be v; otherwise family size will be M. Define $\pi = Nv$ if $v \geq M - P$ and $\pi = MN$ otherwise. We take π as the immutable characteristic defining the society. Our goal is to relate state power γ to π.

Here there are many incentive compatible social norms: some with large populations and some with small. In real societies, long before the advent of birth control, population was controlled - largely, of course, by abstinence from intercourse. One possible implementation of this is: women are limited to a certain number of children, and anyone who attempts to violate the norm is put to death along with her children. As extreme as it may appear, in practice societies often used methods not so different than this. Marriage was limited and delayed through requirements of substantial accumulation of capital or side-payments as a prerequisite to get married, and unwed mothers were severely punished, in many cases through capital punishment. This seems to be understood by demographic historians such as Bacci (2006). We will show that evolution through conflict favors neither the poorest nor the richest societies, but those which generate in aggregate the greatest level of income above subsistence.

Our first economic assumption is that population produces output according to a production function $\alpha Y(\pi)$ where α is a scalar technology parameter. We assume that $Y(\pi)$ is smooth that $Y(0) = 0$ and $Y'(0) > 0$. We assume decreasing returns in the sense that when $Y'(\pi) \neq 0$ that $Y''(\pi) < 0$. As it seems compelling that only so many people can fit on a particular plot of land before production becomes impossible due to overcrowding we assume that output is bounded above and denote by $\overline{Y}$ the least such upper bound. We allow but do not require that for large enough π output may actually be decreasing due to congestion.

Our second economic assumption is that output is needed to sustain the population so we assume that there is a subsistence level which we normalize to 1. That is, to sustain a population of π requires at least that amount of output. Here we eschew the modern slippery concepts of subsistence as used, for example, by Clark (2007) in favor of the traditional notion of subsistence as requirements for survival and reproduction.

---

[10] Based on Levine and Modica (2013).

Note that since population is at least $\pi \geq M$ for sufficiently small α it will be impossible to meet the subsistence requirement. In particular if $\alpha \overline{Y} < M$ subsistence is impossible. Hence we define $\underline{\alpha} > 0$ to be the smallest value of α such that $\max_\pi \alpha Y(\pi) - \pi \geq 0$. We assume hereafter that $\alpha \geq \underline{\alpha}$.

Free resources are resources in excess of subsistence, that is $\alpha Y(\pi) - \pi$. As these can be used for warfare, assume that they give state power γ directly: $\gamma = \alpha Y(\pi) - \pi$. Then (unless outsiders are very strong) the long-run stochastically stable outcome will maximize free resources. By contrast recall the usual Malthusian case where population is so large that income per capita is at subsistence level, that is the value of π for which output per capita settles at subsistence level for each α: $\alpha Y(\pi)/\pi = 1$.

We can now highlight how different is evolution through conflict from Malthusian evolution. In Malthusian theory technological change is always squandered as population grows pushing per capita output back to subsistence. Hence improved technology in the long-run leaves per capita income unchanged and only leads to an increase in population. In our theory we have

Proposition 15.1. *The population size $\hat{\pi}$ that maximizes free resources is non-decreasing in α. As $\alpha \to \infty$, however, per capita output $Y(\hat{\pi})/\hat{\pi}$ grows without bound.*

The first result is a Malthusian one: improved technology does increase population. The second result is anti-Malthusian - population does not grow so much as to keep the population poor: sufficiently great technological improvement will increase per capita output. In the special case in which there is a satiation level for output, that is $Y(\overline{\pi}) = \overline{Y}$ the latter result is easy to establish: once the upper bound on population is reached there is no point in adding more people regardless of the state of technology. The only way to take advantage of improved technology to get more free resources is through increased per capita output.[11]

Proof. For the first result the value $\hat{\pi}$ is defined implicitly by the equation $\alpha Y'(\hat{\pi}) - 1 = 0$, so $d\hat{\pi}/d\alpha = -Y'(\hat{\pi})/\alpha Y''(\hat{\pi})$. This is positive for $Y''(\hat{\pi}) < 0$.

For the second result, we have already dealt with the case where $\hat{\pi}$ is bounded above by $\overline{\pi}$. Suppose instead that $\hat{\pi} \to \infty$. If this is to be possible it must be that $Y(\pi) < \overline{Y}$ for all π so $\overline{Y} - Y(\pi) \to 0$ as $\pi \to \infty$ (by definition of $\overline{Y}$).

Observe that $\alpha Y(\hat{\pi}) - \hat{\pi} \geq \alpha Y(\hat{\pi}/2) - \hat{\pi}/2$ so that $\hat{\pi} \leq 2\alpha \left(Y(\hat{\pi}) - Y(\hat{\pi}/2) \right) \leq 2\alpha \left(\overline{Y} - Y(\hat{\pi}/2) \right)$. Hence

$$\alpha Y(\hat{\pi})/\hat{\pi} \geq \frac{Y(\hat{\pi})}{2\left(\overline{Y} - Y(\hat{\pi}/2)\right)}.$$

Since $\hat{\pi}$ is non-decreasing so is $Y(\hat{\pi})$. As $\hat{\pi} \to \infty$ so $\hat{\pi}/2 \to \infty$, so $\overline{Y} - Y(\hat{\pi}/2) \to 0$ so it must be that $\alpha Y(\hat{\pi})/\hat{\pi} \to \infty$.   □

Although high levels of technology will result in increased per capita income, it is by no means the case that the relation needs to be monotone. A simple example makes the point. Suppose that near $\pi = M$ we have $Y(\pi) = A + (\pi/K) - (\pi/K)^2/2$ where $A > 0$ and $K > M$.[12] Then we may easily

---

[11] The mechanism here is not dissimilar to that discussed in Hansen and Prescott (2002), where the exhaustion of land forces a change to a capital based technology that increases per capita income.

[12] Note that this cannot hold globally.

solve for $\hat{\pi} = K(1 - \alpha^{-1})$. Then in this region output per capita is

$$\frac{Y(\hat{\pi})}{\hat{\pi}} = \frac{\alpha A}{K(1 - \alpha^{-1})} + (\alpha/2 + 1/2).$$

Differentiating with respect to α we get

$$\frac{d(Y(\hat{\pi})/\hat{\pi})}{d\alpha} = \frac{A\alpha}{K(\alpha - 1)^2}(\alpha - 2) + 1/2,$$

which is negative for α near 1, that is for small α. This is consistent with the often made claim that farming societies were worse off than hunter gatherers, while of course for large α the theory predicts the certainly true fact that industrial societies are much better off.

15.3.1 Jewelry versus swords

Free resources, that is output above subsistence, can be used to improve utility and also to improve the chances of success in conflict. There can be complementarity between those goals - for example a good court system can both improve commerce and improve chances of success in conflict. There can also be substitutability between them. As an example, consider families who must choose whether to take their share of surplus output as either jewelry or as swords - the former representing things that raise individual utility, the latter things that improve the chances of success in conflict. Left to themselves individuals will clearly choose jewelry, however as is the case with family size societies can enforce social norms which require the acquisition of swords rather than jewelry.

The basic point is a simple one: greater state power requires free resources be spent on swords, and so evolution pushes in this direction. We shall see later that the time span over which societies fall is long - on the order of hundreds of years - so swords have little value even as a public good, the chances of losing a conflict being very low. This observation reflects a basic bias in conflict driven evolution. It is not benevolent. It favors systems that are better able to defend themselves regardless of the impact on individual utility. Consider for a moment defense expenditures in the USA versus what would actually be needed to defend the country from realistic threats. Given the geographical isolation from strong rivals the answer is surely very little. Yet evolutionary pressure is towards societies such as the USA that grossly overspend on the military.

Free resource maximization is a lot like profit maximization and indeed our formal models has a strong similarity with models of profit maximization. Moreover, from an empirical standpoint, this connection may explain the historical importance of monarchies that can only be described as profit maximizing. But as the jewelry and swords example makes clear, this connection is not perfect: the residual - profits if you will - may be turned to many uses and only some of these uses - swords not jewelry - enhance state power. Hence a profit maximizing monarchy that through social norms is bound to use its profit for fighting and conflict is the type we expect to survive: a profit maximizing monarchy that spends its profits on large and beautiful palaces has less of a future.

15.3.2 Wolves versus sheep

Societies vary by their inclination to export their ideas and social norms. The model we have presented is one of expansionary societies - always ready to grab some land from their neighbors. Expansion may have many forms and motivations: two examples are conquest through warfare or religious conversion, but others are the desire to explore new territory, contact other societies and mix with them, propose values and possibly learn from outside communities. The Roman empire is a strong example of the first type of expansion; more modern expansions have often involved religious conversion - for example, the sending of religious missionaries, although this has often occurred in the context of warfare, for example the conversion of the South and Central American Indian populations to Christianity through a combination of conquest and missionary activity. Equally relevant is influence through exchange of goods spurred by explorations (think of Marco Polo), or the more modern culture spreading through the sale of goods ranging from Coca-Cola to television sets. Or going to the other extreme, we may think of the "curiosity", that is the expansionism, of the primitive hunters-gatherers.

Regardless of the form of expansion, expansionary institutions are not universal.[13] Religions such as Christianity and Islam have historically been expansionary trying actively to convert nonbelievers. By contrast since the diaspora Judaism has been relatively insular in this respect, and the same has been true of other groups such as the Old Believers in Czarist Russia. To our model we may add an additional type of society, non-expansionary ones which have resistance to losing land, but also very high resistance to gaining land.

Without going through the details, societies that are non-expansionary are never stochastically stable. Although they may be part of an absorbing state for $\epsilon = 0$ they face the problem that they can be whittled away: a unit of land is lost and the new situation is also an absorbing state. Ellison (2000) shows that absorbing states like these are not stochastically stable.

This observation helps us understand a puzzle. Why should Spain now more than 300 years after ceding it to the British still wish to regain Gibraltar. Why would the UK be concerned to retain the Falkland Islands and Scotland? Why should Spain care about Catalan succession? The answer to all these questions is: this is the nature of societies selected by evolutionary pressure. By contrast to the successfully independent UK and Spain the area currently comprising Czechia and Slovakia historically has not been independent - for centuries being part of the Habspurg Empire. Hence we should be less surprised at the division of Czechoslovakia into Czechia and Slovakia.

15.3.3 The weakest link

We have made assumptions that a society can only be in one state. In fact societies wax and wane, sometimes being strong and other times weak. We can add to the model internal states $\xi_{jt} \in \Xi$ for each society. As long as these evolve according to a fixed Markov process with transition probability $\Pi_j(\xi_{jt}|\xi_{j,t-1}) > 0$ independent of land holdings we can easily do the evolutionary analysis. State power will now depend upon internal state $\gamma_j(\xi_{jt})$. The overall state will now be $z_t = (L_{1t}, \xi_{1t}, L_{2t}, \xi_{2t}, \ldots, L_{Jt}, \xi_{Jt})$. Instead of stochastically stable states in Z we will now have stochastically stable sets corresponding to the different points in Ξ. Theorem 15.1 remains intact except that instead of maximizing state power it is the weakest internal state that matters, that is, it is the hegemony of the largest value of $\underline{\gamma}_j = \min_\xi \gamma_j(\xi)$ that is stochastically stable.

Two examples illustrate what this is about. One case could be the model in Acemoglu and Robinson (2000) where the voting franchise is extended or contracted. As the system oscillates back and forth

---

[13] Our notion of expansionism is connected to the theory of the transmission of innovations in Aoki et al. (2011).

between civilian and military rule what counts is state power in the weaker of those two internal states. In that model oscillations are driven by recessions - and recessions themselves have implications, state power presumably being greater in a boom than a recession. Hence from an evolutionary point of view what matters is that the worst possible recession be relatively mild. Even if from the point of view of welfare it might not be worth engaging in stabilization policy that lowers the variance of recessions because the reduction in mean consumption is too great, it could never-the-less be a strategy favored by evolution if the stabilization policy moderates the worse possible recession. Here perhaps lies an explanation for why government institutions are obsessed with recession and often seem to carry out stabilization policy to an excessive degree. Although it might be wrong from a welfare point of view, it may also be the strategy favored by evolutionary forces.

15.4 The fall of the Qing dynasty[14]

So far we have dealt with stochastically stable states or sets - behavior in the very long-run. As $\epsilon > 0$ the Markov process has rich dynamics and the theory provides a great deal of information about fluctuations near stochastically stable states and transitions between stochastically stable states. Suppose that $\hat{z}$ is absorbing in the limit dynamic where $\epsilon = 0$. The main result proven in Levine and Modica (2016) is that the system will typically moving repeatedly out of $\hat{z}$ and back, and finally exiting to reach the absorbing state $\tilde{z}$ which is achievable with the least resistance.[15] The likelihood of transition paths is greater the less their resistance. This implies that monotone paths in which a society repeatedly gains land without losing it are far more likely than one where it suffers temporary setbacks.

For our model the least resistance of leaving a hegemony is to have it attacked by a most powerful society which repeatedly gains land until it becomes hegemonic. We have already said the most powerful society is unstable, and we call it a society of *zealots*. Their hegemony has zero resistance to losing land, so the next least resistance phase is invasion of the zealots by a stable society which in turn conquers all land period after period.

With respect to fluctuations near a stochastically stable state $\hat{z}$ Levine and Modica (2016) prove that the largest fraction of time will be spent at the stochastically stable state but there will be a large number of periods during which the system will move to nearby states that are not absorbing and falls back again. The relative likelihood of these states is given by the resistance of getting there. For example the hegemony may use a unit of land then get it back again; this happens many times, and many times more often than the number of times it loses two units of land before falling back. Eventually the system will breach what is called the inner basin - it will be sufficiently far from $\hat{z}$ that there is no longer probability 1 of returning when $\epsilon = 0$. These states are the set of warring states. During this period there will be many societies which may rise and fall, and swap land back and forth - it is a chaotic and turbulent phase. Eventually a new hegemony will rise. The rise of the new hegemony is in some respects opposite of the fall. Once a stable society has enough land that it has positive resistance to land least resistance implies it can only gain land and not lose it.

---

[14] Based on Levine and Modica (2016).

[15] The resistance of a path is just sum of the resistances of its transitions.

Levine and Modica (2016) show that the entire period of transition is short relative to the length of the hegemony, and of course that must be true individually for each of the three phases. Under some additional assumptions Levine and Modica (2016) also show that the warring states phase where land trades chaotically back and forth is long relative to the initial invasion by zealots and the subsequent rise of a new hegemony.

Finally, Levine and Modica (2016) show that the longest departures from an absorbing $\hat{z}$ that result in a return are typically much longer than the final transition to a new absorbing state.

As the model has many implications for the details of the dynamics it seems useful to examine a case study to see if these details are reflected in reality. The fall of the final Qing dynasty in China (early 20th century) is a good case study because we have good data about those details.

15.4.1 China

We compare the theoretical predictions of the model with the fall of the final Qing dynasty in China and the subsequent rise of the communist hegemony - a case study for which there is quite a bit of historical information.[16] The basic fact, as we shall see, is that Chinese institutions that lasted from roughly the introduction of the Imperial Examination System in 605 CE until 1911 CE were swept away in less than a year. At the beginning of the nineteenth century, before the First Opium War, the Qing dynasty held a hegemony over China proper.[17]

Several independent sources of instability concurred to the fall of the hegemony. In the early 1800s China fell into a severe economic depression from which it did not recover prior to the fall of the hegemony. Outsiders, most notably the English, French, and Japanese actively intervened in China, sometimes fighting for and other times against the Qing, but in any case certainly piling on pressure. Opium consumption, induced by the English to correct trade imbalances, increased as well.

From 1839 to 1910 there were a series of unsuccessful attempts to overthrow the Qing dynasty including local rebellions and acts of defiance by committed revolutionaries. During this time the outlying territories were lost: Korea became independent, Indochina was lost to the French, and Taiwan to the Japanese further weakening the hegemon. Roughly speaking the state ξ_j became increasingly worse. However, each internal rebellion was successfully repressed, each war brought to an end, and in each case the Qing hegemony over China proper - tax collecting authority, control of institutions local and global - remained intact. Although it is hard to measure the relative frequency of failed rebellions before and after the economic weakness of the 19th Century, in the earlier periods there seem not to have been such dramatic episodes as the Boxer rebellion and the less known Duggan revolt (which lasted for fifteen years). As our discussion of the weakest link suggests, before the actual fall the state ξ_j is very bad, and there are many and probably increasing failed attempts at rebellion.

The actual fall of the Qing occurred in 1911 and it was very quick - as predicted the least-resistance results we mentioned above. There were again a series of revolts - now however they succeeded. Also as the theory suggests the length of the successful revolt - less than a year - is considerably shorter than the longest failed rebellions - the Boxer and Duggan rebellion lasting many years. The final successful revolt is coordinated by Sun Yat Sen. The groups carrying out the various revolts can reasonably be

---

[16] There are of course many accounts of this period, and while they sometimes disagree on exactly who did what to whom when, all agree on the basic facts we describe below. One readable account by a journalist is that of Fenby (2008).

[17] That is excluding the Korean Peninsula, Indochina, and Taiwan.

described as zealots: they share in common a dedication to overthrowing the Qing, they are willing to suffer severe risk and live under unpleasant circumstances in order to achieve that goal. Such behavior is power maximizing, but is not stable in the sense that no society has ever lasted very long based on the fanatical devotion of its members - nor was it the case in China. Hence the theoretical description of the fall of the hegemony is relatively accurate: zealots quickly capture the land, and do so without a serious setback. In some cases land is seized by other groups, but they quickly join Sun Yat Sen as the theory suggests. By the end of 1911 the Qing Emperor abdicated and Sun Yat Sen became the provisional President of China, which however no longer was hegemonic in any reasonable sense of the word.

Next is the period of warring states, both in theory and in fact. The theory says that there can be many competing societies, land may be lost and gained, zealots may or may not play a role. Again, this is an accurate description of the situation in China between 1911 and 1946. Sun Yat Sen was quickly deposed by a less fanatical and more materialistic warlord Yuan Shikai, but until about 1927, and even after, there are many warlords in various parts of China who rise and fall, many revolutions, some successful and other unsuccessful. Basically the theory predicts chaos (in a non-technical sense) and that is what we see. Beginning in about 1927 things settle down slightly with two relatively more powerful groups, the Nationalists and the Communists, fighting a civil war - but there remain many warlords who continue to rise and fall, at times forming alliances or professing allegiance to the two more significant groups. The two major groups, unlike the earlier revolutionaries, appear to have coherent and potentially stable institutions. Then in 1936 the Japanese seize control of most of the country, an occupation that lasts until 1945. Notice that as the theory suggests the length of this warring states period - 35 years - is much longer than either the fall (less than a year) and the rise (about three years).

The final stage of a least resistance transition is the rise of the new hegemon. Now we are in the basin of the new hegemony so the least resistance path consists of the hegemony gaining territory - without losing any - until hegemony is again established. Notice that since in this model once the basin is left there are zero resistance transitions to any particular hegemony breaching the threshold, the model makes no prediction about which hegemony eventually emerges - in particular there is a non-negligible probability that even a very weak hegemony emerges. In China, the threshold appears to be reached about 1946 when the Communists controlled about a quarter of the country and about a third of the population. They quickly overran the remaining areas held by the Nationalists, who retreated to Taiwan in 1949.

15.5 Peace[18]

While hegemonies are common in history, there are two glaring exceptions, namely India and continental Europe. Indeed the situation, especially in Europe, can better be described as a balance of power between competing societies. Clearly the theory presented so far is deficient: it says that as one side gains an advantage it becomes more likely to gain additional advantage. To see what might happen the example of the Korean war is useful. In September 1950 North Korea was on the verge of dominating the South. On the 15th of September the United Nations led by the United States launched an am-

---

[18] Based on Levine and Modica (2018).

phibious invasion reversing the situation. But rather than gaining resources and weakening the North Koreans the result of this success was the entry of China into the war on the side of North Korea - resulting in the United Nations forces being pushed back and ultimately in a stalemate. The key point is: gaining land leads to greater weakness of the opponent only if it does not draw outside intervention.

The intervention of outsiders - protected typically by their own strong geographic barriers so not at risk in the conflict - is common in history. In Europe following the fall of Rome and up to around 1066 we have the continued interference of northerners - the Vikings and later Swedes were especially well protected by their own geography. Following 1066 we have the constant interference of England - also safe behind a water barrier: during this period we observe that England constantly intervened in continental conflicts but always to support the weaker side, and eventually this policy of balance of power became explicit.[19] India also was subject to repeated invasion from central Asia - protected not by water but by difficult desert and mountain terrain.[20]

To further advance the theory and understand the role of outside intervention in the balance of power we need to model outside intervention more closely.

15.5.1 Two competing societies

With this aim we now focus on a conflict between two societies so that $j \in 1, 2$. Here we have $y_j = \varphi(\gamma_j, L_j)$. We write resistance of j losing a unit of land as $r(y_j, y_{-j})$ omitting the land argument; monotonicity in land is always assumed.

The purpose of the section is to examine how intervening outsiders change the course of the conflict, depending on the strength of their involvement. The starting point is of course to look at the no-intervention benchmark, so we shall start with that and introduce outsiders later. In that case, since victory in battle weakens the opposition making further victories easier, typically one side achieves enough success that it is ultimately able to win the war in a relatively short period of time. This leads to the peace of the strong ruling the weak. The problem with outside intervention is that supporting the weak may result in much longer and bloody conflicts (think of the Vietnam war or the more recent Syrian hell). The results we are going to present in this section provide some suggestions as to "how to intervene if you must," *given* outsiders' goals. The qualification is important since we do not intend to address the issue of the relative desirability of short term peace versus long-term conflict, but instead try to develop a useful model of the length and nature of conflict and how it depends upon outside intervention. If protecting the weak from the strong is a priority, we will see that the level of intervention is a relevant determinant of the nature and length of the conflict, with stronger intervention being generally preferable towards the goal of minimizing casualties.

---

[19] It is not completely correct to view England and Scandinavia as "outsiders" as at various time they had continental interests and conversely, but the key point is that they had a core area relatively safe from invasion. In a different direction Hoffman (2013) argues a role also for the Western Catholic church which in Europe acted as a balancing force much akin to the outsiders of our model.

[20] The exact nature of the asymmetry in the physical geographical barrier is uncertain, but it is a fact that India has been invaded numerous times successfully from Central Asia, but there have been no successful conquests of Central Asia from India. Phil Hoffman in a private communication suggests that part of the answer may lie in the fact that the area of Central Asia is well suited for raising horses and India is not, and that horses play a central military role in conflict between Central Asia and India.

15.5.2 Outside intervention and the balance of power

Outside forces can reinforce society j and we focus on the case in which only one party to the conflict is the beneficiary of outside intervention at any moment of time. If society j is reinforced its *combined power* is $\phi_j = y_j + y$, otherwise it is $\phi_j = y_j$. Hence resistance is given by $r(\phi_j, \phi_{-j})$.

The behavior of outside forces is determined by an intervention policy which we initially take to be exogenous. We study a simple but important intervention: intervention on behalf of the weak. Specifically we assume the there exist thresholds $\overline{L}_j, \overline{L}_k$ with $\overline{L}_j + \overline{L}_k < L$ and such that if $L_{jt} \leq \overline{L}_j$ then outsiders reinforce society j. The inequality $\overline{L}_j + \overline{L}_k < L$ means that $\overline{L}_j$ appears on the left of $\overline{L}_k$ in the land line (measuring j's land from left to right). The assumption that the size of intervention y is the same on both sides is a simplification enabling us to focus on $\overline{L}_j$ as a measure of the strength of intervention.

It is useful at this point to denote combined power of j as $\phi_j(L_{jt})$ since state power y_j is determined by j while intervention is determined by L_{jt} (because $L_{kt} = L - L_{jt}$).

With outside intervention in addition to hegemonic states that are stochastically stable there may also be stable *balance of power segments* consisting of a contiguous collection of states not including hegemonies.[21] To analyze segments we extend the idea of an absorbing state to that of an *absorbing set* - meaning that as $\epsilon \to 0$ the probability of escaping from the set goes to zero, but the probability of moving about within the set remains positive. Hence segments are absorbing if at the left end society j has positive resistance; at the right end society k has positive resistance; and in the interior, if nonempty, both have zero resistance to losing land.[22] From the general results of Young (1993) discussed above only absorbing segments can be stochastically stable.

There may be no absorbing segments at all, a situation we refer to as *hegemony*. In addition two (and only two) types of absorbing segments are possible that we refer to as *hot peace* and *prolonged war*. To motivate these terms we make two claims.

First, either the left endpoint of the segment is the intervention threshold for j or the right endpoint of the segment is the intervention threshold for k. To see this suppose the left endpoint is not an intervention threshold. Society j cannot have zero resistance otherwise we move left without resistance and we are not really at the left endpoint of an absorbing segment. Therefore society k must have zero resistance; then as it loses land it continues to have zero resistance at least until the intervention threshold is reached. If at the intervention threshold the outsiders are strong enough to protect society k then this terminates the absorbing segment - we cannot escape to the right. If the outsiders are not strong enough then resistance is zero until hegemony is reached so there is no balance of power segment at all.

Our second claim is that the segment must either run the entire length between the intervention thresholds or it must have length one. To see this, suppose that the segment starts at the left intervention threshold. If moving a second step to the right has resistance then the segment has length one. If it does not have resistance then moving further to the right continues to have no resistance at least until we encounter the right intervention threshold and the outsiders come in to prop up society k.

This gives rise then to the above classification of absorbing segments:

---

[21] This is proved in Levine and Modica (2018).

[22] We always measure the land of j from the left and the land of k from the right.

Hot peace is a segment of length one at one of the intervention thresholds - that is either $L_j = \overline{L}_j, \overline{L}_j + 1$ or $L_k = \overline{L}_k, \overline{L}_k + 1$ (inclusive). Here a single unit of land changes hands back and forth. As well as a single hot peace segment there can be a pair of hot peace segments, one at each intervention threshold.

Prolonged war is a segment running from one intervention threshold to the other, that is from $L_j = \overline{L}_j$ to $L_j = L - \overline{L}_k$ inclusive. We also require that the intervention thresholds not be adjacent, $\overline{L}_j + \overline{L}_k < L - 1$, so that the segment is longer than one and is not a hot peace.

The two types give rise to considerably different scenarios. Indeed, if we were to subdivide the units of land the length of hot peace segments would shrink while the length of prolonged war segments would not. Hot peace can be thought of concretely as a relatively low key and "peaceful" conflict, with border skirmishes going on without land actually being gained or lost - for example, the recent conflict between Israel and Lebanon which occasionally flares into the firing of rockets over the border or a small border incursion. The point is that while a hot peace is not peace the level of conflict and casualties are low as the fighting is extremely limited. The case of prolonged war is on the contrary a real, bloody war where the two sides fight back and forth losing and gaining substantial amounts of land and not merely skirmishing at the border. The civil war in Syria in the last years is a case in point.

Whether we see hot peace, prolonged war or hegemony depends on the strength of intervention. We distinguish four levels of intervention *on behalf of j*:

Definition 15.1 (Intervention strength). 1. *Strong.* Intervention takes place when resistance is positive in the absence of intervention: $r(y_j(\overline{L}_j), y_k(L - \overline{L}_j)) > 0$

2. *Ineffective.* Intervention is insufficient to give positive resistance: $r(y_j(\overline{L}_j) + y, y_k(L - \overline{L}_j)) = 0$; this includes the case where there is no intervention.

For the remaining cases we assume that #1 and #2 do not hold, that is $r(y_j(\overline{L}_j), y_k(L - \overline{L}_k)) = 0$ and $r(\phi_j(\overline{L}_j), \phi_k(L - \overline{L}_j)) > 0$:

3. *Medium.* When j gains a unit of land above the threshold (thus losing support) the opponent has zero resistance to losing land: $r(\phi_k(L - \overline{L}_j - 1), \phi_j(\overline{L}_j + 1)) = 0$ and $\overline{L}_j + \overline{L}_k < L - 1$.

4. *Weak.* When j gains a unit of land above the threshold the opponent has positive resistance to losing land: $r(\phi_k(L - \overline{L}_j - 1), y_j(\overline{L}_j + 1)) > 0$

Depending on the level of intervention some segments are absorbing and others are not. In Levine and Modica (2018) we characterize the relationship between intervention and the existence of absorbing segments of different types. The results are reported in the following

Theorem 15.3. *Existence, if any, of absorbing segments depending on the type of intervention on behalf of societies j and k can be summarized in Table 15.1 (where land is expressed in units of L_j).*

Stochastic stability of these segments depends on the strength of the outside forces. The formal result, see Levine and Modica (2018), is the following:

Theorem 15.4. *There exist $\infty \geq \overline{y} \geq \underline{y} > 0$ such that if $y > \overline{y}$ and if intervention thresholds are positive on both sides there are stochastically stable balance of power segments but not stochastically stable hegemonies, while if $y < \underline{y}$ there are stochastically stable hegemonies but not stochastically stable - or even absorbing - balance of power segments.*

Table 15.1 Intervention and Peace.

	Strong k	Medium k	Weak k	Ineffective k
strong j	hegemony	hegemony	hot peace at $L - \overline{L}_k$	hegemony of j
medium j	hegemony	prolonged war or hot peace at $\underline{\overline{L}}_j = L - \overline{L}_k - 1$	hot peace at $L - \overline{L}_k$	hegemony of j
weak j	hot peace at $\overline{L}_j$	hot peace at $\overline{L}_j$	hot peace at both $\overline{L}_j$ and $L - \overline{L}_k$	hot peace at $\overline{L}_j$
ineffective j	hegemony of k	hegemony of k	hot peace at $L - \overline{L}_k$	hegemony

15.5.3 Peace and war

Theorem 15.3 shows that there is a non-monotonicity in the consequences of intervention - roughly, one can see this by scanning the above table going up left. To understand this non-monotonicity it is useful to consider a simple case. Suppose that j and k are equally strong so that $\gamma_j = \gamma_k = \gamma$, and that the intervention policy is symmetric so that $\overline{L}_j = \overline{L}_k$. Hence intervention policy is indexed by a single scalar, the land threshold for intervention on behalf of both contenders. We assume for the present discussion that the number of units of land L is odd.[23] Finally we assume that the strength of the intervenor(s) φ_0 is high enough that strong intervention is possible, but that it is ineffective for $\overline{L}_j$ sufficiently small.

Now increase the intervention threshold for both sides at the same time. Start with $\overline{L}_j$ small. In this case as we have noted intervention is ineffective - there is no point in intervening when j has become so weak that they have lost even with outside help. In this case there is no balance of power segment, but rather a hegemony of one society: we refer to this as the *peace of the strong over the weak*. As $\overline{L}_j$ increases, eventually the point is reached where intervention is weak. As we indicated we now have a hot peace in which the weaker side survives by virtue of outside support and the stronger side by virtue of their strength.

The key transition to understand is that from weak to medium intervention, since it is medium intervention that leads to a prolonged war. Why is this? As the intervention threshold increases the side receiving support is propped up when it is relatively strong: eventually strong enough that the opposition no longer has resistance to losing land. At this point intervention becomes medium and when launched from behind the shield of foreign protection success is now possible and may sometimes range until intervention occurs on the side of the opponent. As an example of this we might consider the second Vietnam war until the withdrawal of the United States in 1973: here we have the United States intervening to prevent the fall of South Vietnam and the Soviet Union intervening to prevent the fall of North Vietnam. The war ranged for nearly twenty years with substantial battle deaths and loss and gain of territory on both sides and no doubt would have gone longer had the United States not withdrawn its intervention.

As the strength of intervention $\overline{L}_j$ increases further the length of the prolonged war segment shrinks reducing the scale of the conflict until eventually $\overline{L}_j$ reaches the center and we are again at a hot peace. As an example of this we might consider the intervention of the United States on both sides of the Israel/Egypt conflict at the Camp David accords in 1978: in effect the United States provides arms

---

[23] So it is feasible for the two thresholds $\overline{L}_j, \overline{L}_k$ to be adjacent; this would be ruled out by symmetry if L is even.

and support to both armies to stare at each other across a border that will bring quick intervention in response to a violation.

We want to emphasize the non-monotonicity of the consequences of intervention in its strength: a weak or strong intervention leads to hot peace, but a medium intervention leads to prolonged war and it is the costliest in terms of lives and distress to the peoples and economies involved. No intervention brings about peace relatively quickly but with the strong dominating the weak. What the model suggests is that if the goal of protecting the weak is predominant, then to minimize the costs of war intervention should be strong enough to avoid going back and forth between states where one part in turn is considerably stronger than the other, and reduce the war to what we have called a "hot peace" - which can be thought of as "border skirmishes", and hopefully end in reaching an unarmed negotiation stage.

We may ask: why do we see prolonged war at all? Should not the participants knowing that fighting will simply rage back and forth between the intervention thresholds just skip the conflict? We refer the reader to section 7 of Levine and Modica (2018) for analysis of costs and benefits of intervention and the game being played when there are two symmetric intervenors in competition with one another, the equilibrium of which may result in a prolonged conflict between the two societies involved in the original conflict.

15.5.4 History of modern war

We shortly turn to details of different configurations and illustrate them with examples. In addition to discussing specific cases, we gather the substantial post World War II conflicts in the form of tables. Cases where one combatant did not occupy any land are excluded as the theory does not apply. For the rest we examined each postwar conflict in the Uppsala database. We excluded those marked as insignificant, those involving military coups, those involving invasions of minor powers by major powers (for example: 1956 invasion of Hungary) and guerrilla conflicts where the guerrillas did not control land and resources (for example: the Basque region). We examined each remaining conflict and believe that we have included the most significant. In some cases there were several intervention regimes: we discuss those separately. The data about individual conflicts is taken from Wikipedia. The tables show the region, the year in which the conflict began, and the number of years it lasted. Casualties (including civilian casualties) are reported in deaths per 100,000 per year which is the standard unit for reporting, for example, murder rates.[24] To put these numbers in context, note that the overall murder rate for Europe and Asia is about 3, for the entire world about 6, and for Africa about 12 and for the Americas about 16. So, for example, the death rate of 20 in the Sri Lankan civil war (a hot peace) is comparable to the murder rate in the Americas, while the death rate of 380 in the Syrian civil war (a prolonged war) is an order of magnitude higher. Following the casualty rates we list the parties and outside intervenors. In cases when war ended due to the withdrawal of intervention we report the "collapse" as the number of subsequent years until one side achieved victory. Entries in the table are arranged in chronological order.

Before examining the details, it is worth taking a broad overview of our findings. Intervention that either is designed to preserve the balance of power or which does so because of conflicting interests of

---

[24] Civilian casualties are the bulk of casualties and there are a wide range of estimates. We used the middle of the range of estimates.

the intervenors can lead either to a hot peace or a prolonged war. There is a large discontinuity in the amount of harm done in a hot peace and a prolonged war: in a hot peace death rates are on the order of relatively high murder rates, or in some cases lower, while in a transitional or prolonged war they are an order of magnitude larger than very high murder rates. Taking the Sri Lankan civil war as an example of hot peace we see that for 26 years the death rate was about 20, comparable to the highest murder rates in the world. Taking the breakup of India and Pakistan after the British withdrawal as an example of a transitional war it was vastly bloodier - the death rate was about 250. However, the Sri Lankan civil war lasted 26 years so the total is about 520, more than double that in India and Pakistan where the transitional war lasted only a year. Overall a hot peace does not seem to represent much of savings in terms of casualties over non-intervention and a transitional war - but it does protect the weak. From a policy point if we were to take the point of view that, say, Lebanon posed a threat, then keeping it a bloody mess for three decades would surely neutralize that threat - but from a humanitarian point of view it represents a catastrophe. If we are to take a very cynical view of the conflict between Shia and Sunni, especially the current war in Syria, as a Western effort to preserve a balance of power that neutralizes the Arab world as a threat - the wave of refugees descending on Europe with the consequent social and political problems shows that such an effort can have pretty heavy unintended consequences.

We compare prolonged war - brought about by medium intervention - to hot peace. As we have indicated, this seems the least justifiable form of intervention. Data are collected in Table 15.2. The only rationale for medium intervention we can think of is that a region poses a particular danger and hence the importance of keeping it weak offsets the bloody harm of prolonged war. Yet, if we look at the record, Vietnam, Sudan, Angola, Lebanon, and Syria do not appear to have ever presented any great danger to the intervening powers. It is interesting that while the US intervention in Vietnam is widely criticized outside the US, it seems to be so for mostly the wrong reasons. Surely there was nothing wrong with supporting the South, for, despite all the shortcomings of its government, there was no popular desire to be ruled by the equally bad or worse government in the North. Nor can there be much moral doubt about opposing the spread of communism: one need not look further than North

Table 15.2 Medium Interventions with Prolonged Wars.						
Region	**Start**	**Duration**	**Casualties**	**Parties**	**Intervenors**	**Collapse**
Vietnam	1955	20	170	North South	Soviets US	1
Sudan	1955	60	330	North Sudan Southern Sudan	Egypt Ethiopia/Uganda	
Angola	1975	27	86	MPLA UNITA	Soviets South Africa	1 [1]
Lebanon	1975	31	400	Shia Christian/Druze	Syria Israel	1
El Salvador	1979	12	138	Government FMLN	United States Soviet Union	
Syria	2011	5+	380	Government Insurgents	Russia, Iran West	
1. The date at which intervention on behalf of UNITA ceased is unclear. We dated it to May 2001 when DeBeers - the main source of funding and illicit weapons shipments to UNITA - ceased operation in Angola.						

Korea and Cuba - two of the most miserable places in the world - to see that. Nor is it clear why the direct involvement of the US is worse than indirect Russian involvement. From our point of view the US should be rather criticized for creating a prolonged and costly conflict by attempting to maintain a balance of power in the South.

Table 15.3 shows, by contrast, that hot peace has much lower cost.

Table 15.3 Significant Modern Hot Peace Episodes with Strong Intervention.

Region	Start	Duration	Casualties	Parties	Intervenors	Collapse
Iron Curtain	1945	46	0	Eastern Europe Western Europe	Soviets US	1
Sinai	1948	68+	1	Israel Egypt	West Soviets [1]	
Korea	1950	66	8	North South	China US	
Nagorno-Karabakh	1988	28	26 [2]	Armenia Azerbaijan	Turkey Russia	

1. It should be noted that originally the Soviets supported Israel.
2. It is unclear in which population the casualties occurred. Virtually all deaths occurred during the six years of active war beginning in 1988. It is estimated that 28,000–38,000 died in that conflict. The population of Nagorno-Karabakh is only 147,000, but it is highly unlikely the bulk of casualties occurred among that population. We used the average of the population of Azerbaijan and Armenia as our base population.

15.6 Prosperity[25]

We lastly build on the understanding of evolution of institutions we have gained in the previous sections to address the highly debated issue of why the industrial revolution took place in the West rather than, say, China. To do so we use a model where some of the basic conclusions reached above are taken for granted in order to go into more details about institutional arrangements and warfare technology. The specification of the model is motivated by the widely held belief that technological progress was favored by competition between relatively inclusive institutions such as those in Western Europe, and hindered by the relatively extractive hegemonies found in China (see, for example, Landes (2003), Lin (1995), and Liu and Liu (2007)). Accepting this basic conclusion we ask: why was there competition between relatively inclusive institutions in Europe while in China we find an extractive hegemony? Why did India - made up of competing societies not an extractive hegemony - generate relatively little innovation? To address the issue we have to somehow formalize the ideas of extractive and inclusive societies, and to be able to talk about "who may include whom" we will have two groups in a society. Assuming for simplicity that there are only two societies we take for granted that the long run possibilities are hegemony and balance of power - but which now may feature extractive and inclusive societies. The puzzle of the emergence of the inclusive balance of power in Europe is that since extractive institutions generally levy higher taxes and have larger armies, if evolution is driven by conflict

---

[25] Based on Levine and Modica (2019).

how come these "strong" extractive institutions do not predominate over "weaker" inclusive institutions? Outsiders - whose influence we have stressed in the previous sections - will still be an important part of the picture but we now want to open the model to the different possible institutional equilibrium arrangements, and to do this we have to be more specific about how wars develop. As we shall report in this section, we find that when outsiders are weak extractive hegemonies will predominate, while when outsiders are strong military technology matters: if war outcomes are insensitive to defensive strength - fortifications are well able to resist siege - an extractive balance of power will predominate, while good siege technology will result in the predominance of an inclusive balance of power. The last possibility may be thought of as "survival of the weakest". In brief, in Europe around 1500 CE we argue that outsiders were strong and military technology (think of the cannon) was already well developed; while in China the Mongolian diaspora greatly weakened the strength of outsiders, resulting in the extractive hegemony from the Yuan dynasty onward. We now turn to details.

15.6.1 Model basics

The basic elements are a stripped down version of the previous ones: there are two societies and two units of land, one for each society; and there are two possible configurations: a *balance* of power in which each society occupies its own unit of land and *hegemony* in which one society, the *occupier*, occupies both units of land and the other society is referred to as the *occupied*.

The novel element is that there are two groups in each society: the *commercial elites* and the *military elites*. There are two types of institutions, inclusive institutions w and extractive institutions s. Roughly speaking with inclusive institutions the commercial elites have the upper hand, while with extractive institutions the military elites have the upper hand. Depending on circumstances either society may have either type of institution. There are five possible states of the system: $z \in Z = \{w, s, ww, sw, ss\}$. The first two correspond to hegemony in which the occupier has inclusive and extractive institutions respectively and the remaining three correspond to a balance of power in which both have inclusive, one has extractive, the other inclusive, and in which both have extractive institutions.

Conflict between societies takes place over time $t = 1, 2, \ldots$. At the beginning of period t there is a status quo given by the state from the previous period z_{t-1}. A game between the two groups in the two societies is played and the outcome determines the state z_t in the current period. The particular game depends upon the status quo z_{t-1} and a iid random shock. It takes place in two stages. In the first stage only one of the four groups is *active* and may decide to initiate a conflict to achieve a particular *goal*. The decision is based on a stochastic utility shock. If the active group is part of an occupied society the conflict is a *rebellion* to liberate their land and the goal is to install particular institutions there; thus if the rebellion is successful the hegemonic state will transit to a balance of power. If the active group is part of a balance of power the conflict is to *attack* the other society and the goal is to occupy their land; in this case success will result in hegemony. If the active group chooses not to initiate a conflict the status quo remains unchanged and $z_t = z_{t-1}$. If the active group initiates a conflict a second stage simultaneous move game is played. The active group initiating the conflict is designated as the *aggressor* and one group from the opposing society is the *defender*. Each simultaneously decides the level of effort to devote to the conflict and these effort levels stochastically determine the new state. All of the groups are myopic in the sense that they care only about the consequences of their actions in the current period.

In addition to the four decision making groups of insiders there are a number of *outsiders* whose strength relative to the insiders is denoted as before by $y > 0$. Our basic hypothesis remains that outsiders are disruptive of hegemony but supportive of a balance of power.

15.6.2 The initiation of conflict

We now describe in greater detail the game and payoffs.[26] In a balance of power each society has an equal chance of being active. The goal is to occupy the land belonging to the other society and install the active group's institutions there. In a society with inclusive institutions the active group is the commercial elite; in a society with extractive institutions the active group is the military elite.

In an inclusive hegemony the active group is the occupied commercial elite. In an extractive hegemony the active group is the occupied military elite. There are two possible goals: either to revolt and install inclusive institutions, or to revolt and install extractive institutions. It is possible, for example, that the commercial elites would agree to extractive domestic institutions in return for liberation from foreign domination by inclusive institutions.

Once the active group and goal are determined an iid random utility shock $\tilde{u}$ occurs. The active group then decides whether or not to initiate conflict - to attack or revolt. If the active group decides not to initiate a conflict the game ends and the state remains unchanged. In this case $z_t = z_{t-1}$ and the utility of all groups is that in the status quo. If the active group decides to initiate conflict the utility of the active group is increased by $\tilde{u}$, the current state z_t is randomly determined through conflict resolution, and the utility of all groups is determined by the current state (as specified shortly) minus the costs of conflict plus the utility shock for the active group.

As conflict - at least in the sense of an all-out revolt or attempt to occupy a foreign nation - is rare, we assume that the utility shock is with high probability negative. If $\tilde{u}$ is very negative the active group will not choose to initiate a conflict, so it is only the upper tail of this random variable that matters. We assume this has an exponential form given by three parameters $U > 1$, $0 < P < 1$, and $\sigma > 0$ so that if $v \geq -U$ then $\Pr(\tilde{u} \geq v) = Pe^{-\sigma(v+U)}$. Observe in particular that $\Pr(\tilde{u} \geq -U) = P$. With probability $1 - P$ the shock is smaller than $-U$ and no conflict is initiated. The parameter σ is a scale parameter for the utility shock distribution. If it is large the probability of a shock much bigger than $-U$ is very small. We will be interested in the case in which σ is large.

15.6.3 Conflict resolution

The simultaneous move game following the decision of the active group to initiate a conflict is as follows. If conflict takes place the active group - now called the *aggressor* - determines the level of effort $1 \geq x_a \geq 0$ to devote to the conflict. In a balance of power the defender is the commercial elite if the society under attack has inclusive institutions and the military elite if the society under attack has extractive institutions. In an inclusive hegemony the defender is the occupier commercial elite; in an extractive hegemony the defender is the occupier military elite. The defender determines a level of effort $1 \geq x_d \geq 0$ to devote to the conflict. Each contestant group $i \in a, d$ faces a quadratic cost of effort provision $C(x_i) = (\gamma/2)x_i^2$ where $\gamma \geq 1$. The two groups who are neither aggressor nor defender do not bear any cost of conflict. Note also our base assumption that every society regardless of its type

---

[26] The model is simple and stylized; robustness to more general formulations is discussed in Levine and Modica (2019).

faces the same cost of raising resources: our explanation of social outcomes - in contrast to Hoffman (2013)'s theory of the great divergence after 1600 - does not rest on the idea that there are systematic differences in the cost of raising resources due to social organization.

Let $\zeta \in \{h, b\}$ be an indicator of whether the state is hegemonic or a balance of power. The probability the aggression succeeds depends on the resources committed by the contestant groups and is given by a conflict resolution function

$$\pi(x_a, x_d) = \Pi_\zeta(y) + \alpha \left(x_a - [(1-\varphi)x_d + \varphi] \right)$$

where $0 \le \varphi \le 1$, $\Pi_\zeta(y) > 0$ is continuous with $\Pi_h(y)$ strictly increasing in y, $\Pi_b(y)$ strictly decreasing in y and $\alpha > 0$, which is consistent with our view of that outsiders help rebels chances of success - $\Pi_h(y)$ increasing - but hurt those of an aggressor in a balance of power - $\Pi_b(y)$ decreasing. We also assume that there is a unique value y^* such that $\Pi_h(y^*) = \Pi_b(y^*)$. The parameter α measures the sensitivity of the outcome to the differential effort of the two combatants. We have assumed that this is not too large. The parameter φ measures the sensitivity of the outcome to defensive effort. The coefficient on x_d is $(1-\varphi)x_d + \varphi$ a weighted average of the defensive effort and 1. Our interpretation is that φ measures the value of fixed fortifications. The reason for this is that the benefit of fortifications is that they enable a small army to hold off a much larger force. In Masada in 66 CE, for example, a group of roughly 1,000 men women and children held off the Roman Empire for about seven years before being overcome by a military force of around 15,000. On the other hand, effective fortifications reduce the benefit of a larger defending force: it is unlikely that a Jewish force of 2,000 or 3,000 would have had much more success against the Romans than 1,000. Here the effectiveness of defense is measured by $(1-\varphi)x_d + \varphi$ where φ captures the basic idea that with effective fortifications the defense is strong but not particularly sensitive to defensive strength. Hence our interpretation of φ as the effectiveness of fortifications.

If the aggression fails the status quo remains unchanged, $z_t = z_{t-1}$ and the utility of all groups is that in the status quo less the effort and plus the utility shock. If the status quo is a balance of power and the aggression succeeds the new state is hegemony with the institutions of the aggressor. If the status quo is hegemony and the aggression succeeds the new state is a balance of power in which the defender institutions are unchanged and the aggressor institutions are those determined by its goal. In all success cases the utility of all groups is that of the new state less the effort and plus the utility shock.

15.6.4 Incentives: transfers and utility

In addition to the random utility shock and conflict costs the utility of groups is determined by the current state z_t. From the economic point of view the two groups in each society are characterized by a *transfer* of resources from the commercial elites to the military elites. Extractive societies are defined so that this transfer is larger than in inclusive ones. So there are two possible transfer levels representing a transfer from the commercial elites to the military elites on each unit of land; we normalize high transfers to 1, and low transfers are $0 < \tau < 1$. In a balance of power the military elites receive the transfers from their own land, so for example in a w-type society we can write the transfer vector as $(-\tau, \tau)$. In hegemony the occupier military elites receive the transfers from both units of land and high transfers are always taken from the occupied commercial elites; and the occupier commercial elites pay τ in an inclusive hegemony and 1 if the hegemony is extractive. The transfers are summarized in the following table (for example the $-\tau, 1 + \tau$ entry says that in an inclusive hegemony the occupier commercial elite pays τ and the occupier military elite gets τ from them plus 1 form the occupied commercial elite)

	s	w
balance	$-1, 1$	$-\tau, \tau$
occupier	$-1, 2$	$-\tau, 1+\tau$
occupied	$-1, 0$	$-1, 0$

The key features are that there is a preference against foreign rule by both commercial elites and military elites and that occupier military elites benefit from occupation at the expense of the occupied military elites.

15.6.5 Equilibrium

An equilibrium is the stochastic process in which a Nash equilibrium occurs within each period. It is shown in Levine and Modica (2019) that equilibrium is unique and it is an aperiodic and ergodic Markov process on the state space $Z = \{w, s, ww, sw, ss\}$. From what we have seen the possible transitions other than remaining at the status quo are the following:

$$w \to ww, sw \quad s \to ss, sw \quad ww \to w \quad sw \to s, w \quad ss \to s$$

We denote the unique ergodic probability distribution over the state space by μ_σ. As before as $\sigma \to \infty$ the ergodic distributions μ_σ have a unique limit μ and the stochastically stable states are those for which $\mu(z) > 0$. These are the states which are observed "most of the time" when σ is large - the case of interest given that serious conflict is infrequent.

15.6.6 Stochastic stability

The "typical" institutional configurations are characterized in the following result.[27]

Theorem 15.5 (Prosperity). *Only one of s, ss, ww can be stochastically stable (w and sw cannot). There exist τ^*, φ_τ such that:*
  1. if $\tau > \tau^*$ or $\varphi > \varphi_\tau$: for $y < y^*$ the stochastically stable state is s, for $y > y^*$ it is ss
  2. if $\tau < \tau^*$ and $\varphi < \varphi_\tau$ there is a function $y(\varphi) \leq y^*$ such that: for $y < y(\varphi)$ the stochastically stable state is s, for $y > y(\varphi)$ it is ww ("survival of the weakest").

Let us see what the result says. If $\tau > \tau^*$ - inclusive institutions do not differ much from extractive ones - the only stable institutions are extractive. Roughly: the commercial elites are unwilling to make much effort to defend inclusive institutions that are not all that inclusive. Its interesting implication is that we will not often see "somewhat inclusive" institutions, only extractive or "strongly inclusive" institutions. Turning to the case $\tau < \tau^*$, first observe that if $y < \min_\varphi y(\varphi)$ - sufficiently weak outsiders - then only extractive hegemony is stochastically stable, regardless of military technology. By contrast

---

[27] More complete statement and proof in Levine and Modica (2019).

with stronger outsiders, that is larger values of y, we will see a balance of power - but military technology determines which type: large φ - effective fortifications, large defensive armies not needed - favors extractive institutions, while small φ - good siege technology - favors inclusive technology.

As we mentioned, our reading of this result is that the invention of gunpowder led to a great reduction in the effectiveness of fortifications. Small φ and strong outsiders made stable inclusive balance of power possible in Europe; in China extractive hegemony was favored by weak outsiders; and in India an extractive balance of power emerged as a consequence of strong outsiders but primitive siege technology (the cannon arriving late). We look at history in the next section.

15.6.7 History

We report here historical data from Maddison (2007) Table 15.4 below covers the three major regions: India, China, and Europe up to the period of globalization beginning around 1500 CE and beginning - for reasons of data reliability - about 0 CE. For each region epochs reported by historians are given and the strength of outsiders and fortifications reported. The penultimate column reports the actual state and the final column the stochastically stable state predicted by the theory. Eyeballing the data, the theory does quite well, missing only one epoch, the Sui/Tang period in China where the theory says we should have seen an extractive balance of power, but in fact see an extractive hegemony. The states that the theory says are not stochastically stable are never seen in the data.

We can subject this data to a formal analysis. Recall that $z \in \{ss, s, ww\}$ are the possible observed states and let $\hat{z}(\eta, \varphi)$ the stochastically stable state determined by the exogenous variables. Our theoretical model says that the stochastically stable state should be observed with high probability over sufficiently long periods. We take "long periods" to mean 2.2 to 5.6 centuries. We model "high probability" empirically by assuming that with probability β the stochastically stable state $\hat{z}(\eta, \varphi)$ is observed and that with probability $1 - \beta$ the observed state is drawn randomly with probabilities $\alpha(z)/(1 - \beta)$ where $\sum_{z \in \{ss, s, ww\}} \alpha(z) = 1 - \beta$. This gives rise to the linear conditional probability model $\Pr(z|\eta, \varphi) = \alpha(z) + \beta \cdot 1(z = \hat{z}(\eta, \varphi))$.

Maximum likelihood estimation of this model gives estimates $\overline{\alpha}(ss) = \overline{\alpha}(ww) = 0$ and $\overline{\beta} = 0.91$ with a standard error 0.08.[28] This indicates that the model does well in both economic terms - $\overline{\beta}$ is close to 1 and far from 0 - and in statistical terms - $\overline{\beta}$ is estimated with a high degree of reliability.

To understand better the importance of sampling error we draw $\lambda(\beta)$ the log likelihood function as a function of β in the graph below. The solid vertical line in the graph is the left limit of the 95% confidence interval based on the estimated standard error of $\overline{\beta}$. Also, twice log of the likelihood ratio $-2(\lambda(\beta) - \lambda(\overline{\beta}))$ is approximately chi-squared with one degree of freedom. Above the horizontal line is the 5% acceptance region of the likelihood ratio test, which thus shows that the range $[0.60, 0.99]$ are those values of β that cannot be rejected at the 5% level.[29]

---

[28] From Table 15.4 we see that the log-likelihood is equal to $8 \ln(\alpha(ss) + \beta) + 4 \ln(\alpha(s) + \beta) + \ln \alpha(s) + 2 \ln(\alpha(ww) + \beta)$. The solution to the constrained maximization was computed using R (code available).

[29] The acceptance region is $-2(\lambda(\beta) - \lambda(\overline{\beta})) \leq \overline{\chi} = 3.841$ or $\lambda(\beta) \geq \lambda(\overline{\beta}) - \overline{\chi}/2$: the chi-squared line in the top graph above plots $\lambda(\overline{\beta}) - \overline{\chi}/2$ so the 5% acceptance region is above the line, and rejection region below it.

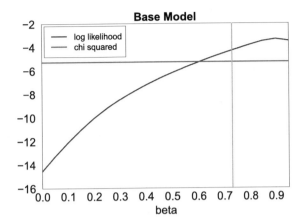

Base Model

Table 15.4 Data. The duration of most episodes is from 2.2 to 5.6 centuries.							
Region	**Description**	**Period**	**Duration**	**Outsiders** η	**Fortifications** φ	**Actual state**	**Stable state**
India	Classical/Medieval	200 BCE - 320	5.2	strong	strong	*ss*	*ss*
India	Classical	321 - 650	3.3	strong	strong	*ss*	*ss*
India	Early Medieval	651-1200	5.5	strong	strong	*ss*	*ss*
India	Late Medieval	1200 - 1525	3.3	strong	strong	*ss*	*ss*
India	Mogul	1526 - 1748	2.2	weak	weak	*s*	*s*
China*	Han	202 BCE - 220	4.2	weak	strong	*s*	*s*
China	Warring Kingdoms	221-588	3.7	strong	strong	*ss*	*ss*
China	Sui/Tang	589 - 906	3.2	strong	strong	*s*	*ss*
China*	Song	960 - 1279	3.2	strong	weak	*ww*	*ww*
China	Yuan/Ming/Qing	1280-1839	5.6	weak	weak	*s*	*s*
Europe	Roman	149 BCE - 329	4.8	weak	strong	*s*	*s*
Europe	Byzantine	330 - 628	3.0	strong	strong	*ss*	*ss*
Europe	Medieval	629 - 1054	4.3	strong	strong	*ss*	*ss*
Europe	Middle Ages	1054 - 1292	2.4	strong	strong	*ss*	*ss*
Europe*	Renaissance	1293-1607	3.1	strong	weak	*ww*	*ww*
Asterisks denote technological progress.							

References

Acemoglu, D., Robinson, J.A., 2000. Why did the West extend the franchise? The Quarterly Journal of Economics 115, 1167–1199.

Aoki, K., Lehmann, L., Feldman, M.W., 2011. Rates of cultural change and patterns of cultural accumulation in stochastic models of social transmission. Theoretical Population Biology 79, 192–202.

Bacci, M., 2006. A Concise History of World Population. Wiley Blackwell.

Bowles, S., Choi, J.-K., Hwang, S.-H., Naidu, S., 2021. How institutions and cultures change: an evolutionary perspective. In: Bisin, A., Federico, G. (Eds.), The Handbook of Historical Economics. Elsevier. Chapter 14 (in this book).

Clark, G., 2007. A Farewell to Alms. Princeton University Press.

Ellison, G., 2000. Basins of attraction, long run stochastic stability and the speed of step-by-step evolution. The Review of Economic Studies 67, 17–45.

Ely, J., 2002. Local conventions. The B.E. Journals in Theoretical Economics 2, 1–32.

Fenby, J., 2008. Modern China: The Fall and Rise of a Great Power, 1850 to the Present. Penguin Press.

Fudenberg, D., Maskin, E., 1986. The folk theorem in repeated games with discounting or with incomplete information. Econometrica 54, 533–554.

Gibbon, E., 1776. The History of the Decline and Fall of the Roman Empire.

Hansen, G., Prescott, E., 2002. Malthus to Solow. The American Economic Review 92, 1205–1217.

Hoffman, P.T., 2013. Why Did Europe Conquer the World? Princeton University Press.

Ladurie, L.R., 1974. The Peasants of Languedoc. University of Illinois Press.

Landes, D.S., 2003. The Unbound Prometheus: Technological Change and Industrial Development in Western Europe from 1750 to the Present. Cambridge University Press.

Levine, D., Modica, S., 2013. Anti-Malthus: conflict and the evolution of societies. Research in Economics 76, 289–306.

Levine, D.K., Modica, S., 2016. Dynamics in stochastic evolutionary models. Theoretical Economics 11, 89–131.

Levine, D., Modica, S., 2018. Intervention and peace. Economic Policy, 361–402.

Levine, D., Modica, S., 2019. Survival of the weakest: why the West rules. Working paper. www.dklevine.com.

Lin, J., 1995. The Needham puzzle: why the industrial revolution did not originate in China. Economic Development and Cultural Change 43 (2), 269–292.

Liu, Y., Liu, C., 2007. Diagnosing the cause of scientific standstill, unravelling the Needham puzzle. China Economist 10, 83–96.

Maddison, A., 2007. Contours of the World Economy 1-2030 AD. Oxford University Press.

Young, P., 1993. The evolution of conventions. Econometrica 61, 57–84.

Culture, institutions, and policy[☆]

Torsten Persson[a,b,c,d,e] **and Guido Tabellini**[f,b,c]

[a]*IIES, Stockholm University, Stockholm, Sweden*
[b]*CEPR, London, United Kingdom*
[c]*CESIfo, Munich, Germany*
[d]*LSE, London, United Kingdom*
[e]*NBER, Cambridge, MA, United States*
[f]*Department of Economics and IGIER, Università Bocconi, Milan, Italy*

16.1 Introduction

In this chapter, we highlight how culture, institutions, and policymaking relate to each other and how they coevolve over time. While our treatment draws on insights from several existing literatures, these typically deal with only one, or a couple, of the various links we consider.

An important big-picture question motivates much of the existing research. How is it that some societies are more successful than others, in terms of a number of economic and political outcomes? To put it differently, why do successes and failures tend to correlate across many domains? Societies that successfully fight corruption, are also successful in fighting tax evasion, in administering justice, in providing collective services, in growing the economy, in maintaining macroeconomic stability, and in avoiding that political conflicts spill into violence. In the same way as successes, policy failures too are correlated across seemingly unrelated dimensions. It is plausible that these correlations reflect a few fundamental national factors – specifically, country-specific institutions and culture – acting as common drivers of many outcomes.[1]

"Culture" and "institutions" are both vague concepts that different scholars employ to capture different notions. Thus, culture is alternatively used to label *values* that govern people's behavior, *social norms* that prescribe certain behaviors in certain groups, and *beliefs* that coordinate expectations about the strategic choices by others. Here, we mainly focus on culture in the sense of individually held values, which also map into policy preferences. Throughout, we assume that culture in this interpretation is persistent. It is not exogenous, however, but adapts to incentives and environments. As this adaptation takes place slowly, it is still meaningful to discuss the causal links from culture to other outcomes, at a given time.

When it comes to institutions, we reserve the concept for formalized rules of the game, such as the rules for political and judicial procedures. Institutions are thus different from policy outcomes. We do

---

[☆] We are grateful to Alberto Bisin for helpful comments and suggestions. Tabellini acknowledges financial support from ERC grant 741643.

[1] Evidence that policy outcomes are correlated across several policy domains is provided by Tabellini (2008a) and Besley and Persson (2011).

not adopt the wider definition advocated by some scholars (such as Acemoglu et al., 2005), namely to let institutions also encompass internalized norms that affect how rules of the game shape behavior. But we will treat formal institutions as endogenous and persistent.

These interpretations are reflected in the theoretical framework outlined in the chapter. Policy outcomes are determined in equilibrium, and within each period they are forged by given institutions and a given culture. We thus treat institutions as having more inertia than policy outcomes. When we consider explicit dynamic models, though, we take culture to be the slowest moving variable in the system. This simplifies the dynamic analysis, because culture becomes the single state variable.

Related to this distinction, we postulate different mechanisms for the alterations of cultures and institutions. To capture the idea that culture (interpreted as values) changes slowly, we speak about *cultural evolution*. A key aspect of such evolution is that each new generation of individuals tends to adopt a stable set of values – as a result of education and socialization – during their most impressionable years, for example when they have to make their first political decisions. Instead, we speak about *institutional change*. With this terminology, we intend to capture the fact that institutions often change suddenly and as a result of strategic decisions. Such decisions can reflect collective political choices, or bursts of collective action – for example, when polities change their governance from democratic to autocratic, or vice versa.

Our focus on how culture and institutions shape policy outcomes abstracts from the direct effects exerted by culture and institutions on private economic decisions, including investment, innovation, and market interactions. These direct effects obviously help determine economic development, and they have been extensively studied in the literature (see, in particular, Acemoglu et al., 2005; Tabellini, 2008a; Besley and Persson, 2020a). But the joint evolution of culture and institutions in these richer economic environments remains similar to the one described in this chapter.

Though our topics are strongly motivated by data, we center our attention on theoretical ideas and mechanisms. However, we do not want to overburden the reader with different models and different sets of notation. So we stick to one specific example throughout the chapter, in which we gradually allow for more complex interactions. This example is a simple model of political agency, where politicians can extract rents from the political process at the voters' expense. But, along the way, we discuss other applications of the same general ideas.

16.1.1 Referencing

When it comes to the existing literature, the running text comments directly on the initial research that introduced the key ideas that underlie our modeling. Without too much apology, we focus these comments on research that is most closely related to our own work and interests. Comments on subsequent research about the same topic, or similar research on related topics, are collected at the end of each section under the heading "Notes on the literature." Relative to the existing research on culture and institutions, our selection of references is probably biased towards formal theoretical work and direct evidence on the mechanisms emphasized in this work. Our selective coverage also reflects a division of labor, since traditional historical research is the focus of other chapters in the Handbook – in particular, those by Allen, Broadberry, Federico, Mokyr, and Voth. There also exist other excellent surveys of the topic, which focus more squarely on measurement and empirical work – see, in particular, Alesina and Giuliano (2015).

the candidate whose policy announcement entails lower rents. Because all voters evaluate rents r in the same way, a voter with higher weight λ^i is more likely to vote on the basis of public interest, as opposed to partisan or parochial interests. A higher value of λ^i thus indicates a more civic political culture and more universalistic values, in the sense that the individual cares more about social outcomes.

We consider two (given) types of values held by voters. They can hold "civic values", a high value of λ^i, which we set at $\bar{\lambda} > 1$, or "partisan values", with a lower λ^i, which we set at 1. Let $\lambda = \bar{\lambda} - 1 > 0$ denote the difference between civic and partisan values – i.e., the difference in political culture. The distribution of candidate preferences σ^i is the same for voters whichever their values. Finally, let $\gamma \in [0, 1]$, denote the fraction of civic types in the population at a given point in time. This will be our measure of culture throughout the chapter. In Sections 16.3 and 16.5, this cultural variable will evolve endogenously over time, as people actively chose which values to adopt – that is, whether to evaluate the policy effects on (common) welfare via parameter $\lambda^i = \bar{\lambda}$ or $\lambda^i = 1$.

16.2.3 Electoral competition

As in standard models of probabilistic voting, the candidates simultaneously announce their policies r_A and r_B. Readers who find it implausible that candidates would announce rents can think about them as announcing public consumption (valued by voters) and taxes, with political rents residually determined from the government budget constraint. As long as the utility from private consumption is linear, voter utility takes the form in (16.1).

Candidates announce r_C before knowing the realization of aggregate and idiosyncratic popularity shocks δ and σ^i, but with full knowledge about the distributions of these shocks. They also know the distribution of values – that is, they know political culture as captured by γ – but they do not know which individual voters hold which values. Finally, the popularity shocks are realized and citizens vote, based on their common preferences and alternative cultural values.

Using these assumptions – together with the voter and politician objectives in (16.1) and (16.2) – it is easy to show that the probability that candidate A wins the election satisfies:

$$p_A = \frac{1}{2} + (1 + \lambda\gamma)(r_B - r_A). \tag{16.4}$$

To summarize, our simple model contains many ingredients discussed in the literature on culture and institutions. Values and political culture are captured by parameters λ and γ, which determine the voters' willingness to punish politicians for their misbehavior. Institutions are captured by parameter β, which influences the incentives of politicians to misbehave. As should be clear – and as we show next – it is the interactions of these forces that shape policy outcomes.

16.2.4 Equilibrium policy

The two political candidates simultaneously announce their policies, so as to maximize their expected benefits from office in (16.2), while taking into account the probability of winning the election in (16.4). They face a simple tradeoff: extracting more rents makes them better off for a given election probability, but it also lowers this probability (and thus their benefit from inframarginal rents). Solving for candidate optimal choices along this tradeoff and exploiting the symmetry of the model, we find the same equilibrium policy announcements by both candidates. Assuming that the non-negativity constraint on r is not binding, we obtain equilibrium rents as:

$$r^*(\beta, \gamma) = \frac{1}{2(1 + \lambda\gamma)} - \beta R. \tag{16.5}$$

The comparative statics are straightforward. Not surprisingly, stronger institutions, higher β, map into lower equilibrium rents, because politicians have weaker incentives to exploit the voters when institutions make rent extraction less efficient. A larger share of the electorate with civic cultural traits, higher γ (or a higher degree of civicness, higher λ), has the same dampening effect on rent-extraction incentives, because a larger group of voters are more willing to punish candidates for bad policies.

This prediction is supported by the evidence in Nannicini et al. (2013). They compare Italian electoral districts with different levels of "civic values," measured by average blood donations (or other types of civic behavior). Members of Parliament elected from districts that score lower on this measure do engage in more misbehavior, as gauged by criminal investigations or absenteeism. More importantly, misbehaving political incumbents are punished more severely by voters in electoral districts with higher civic values, consistent with the idea that a good political culture discourages politician misbehavior through stricter accountability via voter punishments.

16.2.5 Substitutes or complements

In this static formulation, the policy effects of civic cultures and good institutions are additive rather than interactive. However this may be an artifact of our simple framework. In a dynamic model, where the same incumbent may stay on for multiple periods – like the accountability model of Persson et al. (1997) – the value of office R would capture the expected present value of future rents, which depend on both culture and (future expected) institutions. If the value of office R were a decreasing function of γ (that is, a more civic culture reduced the personal value of office), then strong institutions and civic culture would be substitutes. The same interaction would apply if R were a decreasing function of β (i.e., stronger institutions reduce the future value of office). In other words, strong institutions (high β) would be more effective with a partisan culture (associated with high R), while a civic culture would have a larger effect with weak institutions (because the dampening effect of a higher R would be smaller with β small).

The question whether institutions and culture are substitutes or complements in their consequences has been discussed in the literature on economic development. An argument for substitutability is that reputational mechanisms based on reciprocity are easier to sustain if formal institutions are weak, because the punishment of exclusion is harsher and thus the need for civic culture is strongest when institutions are weak (Kranton, 1996; McMillan and Woodruff, 2000; Dhillon and Rigolini, 2007). Some empirical results are also suggestive of substitutability: Guiso et al. (2004) find that social capital boosts financial development more in Italian provinces with less efficient courts. Following Nunn (2007) and Levchenko (2007), Tabellini (2008a) contrasts culture and institutions as sources of comparative advantages in international trade. He too finds evidence of substitutability: civic culture has a larger positive effect on exports of "contract-intensive" sectors in countries where law enforcement is weak.

But the observed long-run clustering of low corruption (and good development outcomes more generally) and strong institutions points in the other direction. As we shall see in the subsequent sections, the dynamic analysis builds a convincing case for (dynamic) complementarity.

16.2.6 **Notes on the literature**

The general notion that economic and political institutions are central for economic and political outcomes goes far back in time, at least to the 18th century treatises by Smith (1759, 1776), Montesquieu (1748), and Hamilton et al. (1788). The idea that institutions govern economic outcomes and economic change has also been emphasized by 20th century scholars, perhaps most convincingly by Douglas North (1990). Drawing on English history, North famously argued that the 1688 Glorious Revolution was central for establishing the protection of property rights and that these rights, in turn, played a key role in paving the way for the Industrial Revolution (see also North and Weingast, 1989). The survey by Acemoglu et al. (2005) provides more recent references.

To home in more closely on the specific issues modeled in this section, several papers have studied empirically whether specific institutional features do discourage corruption. The main findings are in line with the predictions of our simple model: politicians do respond to institution-based incentives. In particular, Ferraz and Finan (2008) and Avis et al. (2018) find evidence that (randomly imposed) government audits of municipal budgets in Brazil reduce the incidence of corruption. One channel is that these audits provide information to voters about government. Another, separate channel is that the audits raise the non-electoral expected cost of corruption. Khemani et al. (2016) obtain related findings.

Additional evidence suggests that the information *cum* electoral-accountability channel is important. Using the same Brazilian audit data, Ferraz and Finan (2011) show that elections discourage politicians from appropriating rents: mayors who do not face re-election because of term limits misappropriate about 25 percent more resources than mayors who do face re-election. Cruz et al. (2020a, 2020b) document the importance of institutions that allow voters to make more informed choices. In field experiments in the Philippines, they show that informing voters about campaign promises, or about what voters could do, increase the leverage they exercise over incumbents.

The notion that a civic culture is a central determinant of well-functioning institutions and of development is also an old one and appears already in de Tocqueville (1840). In more recent 20th century work, this idea has commonly appeared in social sciences outside of economics, including prominent research by anthropologists (Murdock, 1965), historians (Landes, 1998), and political scientists (Putnam, 1993, 2000). From the 1990s, the topic has also been increasingly picked up by economists. Guiso et al. (2006) and Fernández (2011) survey this first wave of work. Tabellini (2008a, 2010) provides evidence that a more civic culture favors economic development. Gorodnichenko and Roland (2011) argue that the individualism-collectivism cultural dimension – which had originally been suggested by Hofstede (1984) – is a robust predictor of long-run growth. Mokyr (2016) discusses how specific European cultural traits facilitated the onset of the industrial revolution.

Closer to the specific topic of this section, the influence of civic culture on corruption has been studied by Nannicini et al. (2013). They consider the accountability model in Persson and Tabellini (2000), and allow the incumbent to choose not only rents, but also targeted benefits to different voter groups. Voters can condition a retrospective vote for or against the incumbent on either an aggregate measure of welfare, or on group-specific welfare, depending on their cultural traits. That richer model has implications equivalent to those of the simple model in this section. In particular, a more universalistic and civic culture is one where voting is based on aggregate (rather than group-specific) welfare. The greater is the fraction of voters that hold such a culture, the larger is public-good provision and the lower are political rents. Their evidence is also consistent with these predictions.

Yet another channel for influence runs via the *selection* of politicians rather than the behavior of existing politicians. If an environment has high equilibrium rents (legally or illegally extracted), due to weak institutions and a partisan culture, it is likely to attract into politics individuals with poor values and with poor earning prospects in other careers. This is what Brollo et al. (2013) find using data on Brazil: larger federal transfers to municipalities raise local corruption and this in turn deteriorates the quality of local political candidates.

A large literature in comparative politics discusses how specific features of political institutions, such as the electoral rule and the form of government, shape economic policy and political outcomes in democracies. Some of these ideas are discussed in Persson and Tabellini (2003). The empirical links between corruption and different aspects of electoral systems are explored by Persson et al. (2003).

Another line of research has explored the effects of democratic transitions on economic growth and other policy outcomes, finding a positive – though small – effect of democracy on subsequent economic growth (Barro, 1996; Przeworski et al., 2000; Giavazzi and Tabellini, 2005; Persson and Tabellini, 2006, 2008, 2009; Acemoglu et al., 2019). Giavazzi and Tabellini (2005) specifically find that economic liberalizations, as well as democratizations, are associated with subsequent reductions of corruption.

16.3 Cultural evolution

Neither culture nor institutions are fixed, but change endogenously over time. In this section, we study cultural evolution under given institutions. In the next section, we do the opposite, modeling institutional change for a given culture.

The general question how various aspects of human behavior – in particular human cooperation – change over time has been treated in the field of evolutionary anthropology, which was started off by Cavalli-Sforza and Feldman (1981) and Boyd and Richerson (1985). Similar questions have been the subject of evolutionary game theory, surveyed by Weibull (1995) and Sandholm (2010). In economics, a growing literature has discussed the evolution of cultural traits, beginning with the seminal work of Bisin and Verdier (2000a, 2001) on cultural transmission across generations. Given that Bisin and Verdier (2011) already provides an excellent survey of that literature, we focus this section on illustrating how cultural values may evolve in our specific model framework, and how this evolution may depend on (for now) fixed institutions.

Different mechanisms of cultural evolution and transmission have been studied in the literature, but most of these share a "Darwinian" property: cultural traits change in the direction suggested by their *relative fitness*. Traits that prove more successful thus tend to spread, while those that do not fit the prevailing social environment tend to disappear.

16.3.1 Relative cultural fitness

The model in the previous section allows for two sets of values that correspond to different weights λ^i on general outcomes and partisan outcomes. Citizens who hold civic values ($\lambda^i = \bar{\lambda} > 1$) care more about common policies than those holding partisan values ($\lambda^i = 1$).

At any moment in time, the relative fitness of civic vs. partisan values can be captured by the difference in the expected welfare of holding them. We thus compute the expected welfare levels under equilibrium policies, taking into account both political and policy preferences. Specifically, using

(16.1), (16.3), and (16.5), the expected fitness of civic relative to partisan values can be written as:

$$\Delta(\gamma, \beta) = E[\delta + \sigma^i + (\bar{\lambda} - 1)W(r^*)] = \lambda[\varpi - r^*(\gamma, \beta)] \tag{16.6}$$

$$= \lambda[\varpi + \beta R - \frac{1}{2(1 + \lambda\gamma)}].$$

In writing (16.6), we have taken the expectation under a veil of ignorance about the popularity shocks δ and σ^i, that both have expected values of 0. Evidently, the relative fitness of holding civic vs. partisan values depends on the prevailing culture – the share γ – and institutions – the value of β. Since citizens with civic values attach a greater weight to rents in their welfare function, whatever reduces equilibrium rents increases the relative fitness of civicness. Thus, a greater share of civic citizens and stronger institutions, by reducing equilibrium rents, increase the expected fitness of being civic rather than partisan. Formally, Δ is globally increasing and continuous in β and γ in its full domain: we have $\Delta_\gamma > 0$ and $\Delta_\beta > 0$.[3]

16.3.2 A threshold culture

Note that $\Delta(\gamma, \beta)$ can be either positive or negative, depending on parameter values. To obtain a rich cultural dynamics, we assume that:

$$\frac{1}{2(1 + \lambda)} < \varpi + \beta R < \frac{1}{2}, \tag{16.7}$$

which in turn implies

$$\Delta(0, \beta) < 0 < \Delta(1, \beta). \tag{16.8}$$

That is, if all citizens are civic, then civic traits have higher fitness than partisan traits for all institutions (because equilibrium political rents are sufficiently low). Conversely, if all citizens are partisan, the relative fitness of partisan traits is higher.[4]

By continuity of $\Delta(\gamma, \beta)$ in γ, the inequalities in (16.8) imply that there exists an intermediate culture (share of values) $\hat{\gamma} \in (0, 1)$ – defined by $\Delta(\hat{\gamma}, \beta) = 0$ – such that the two values are equally fit. By (16.6), we can solve for this threshold critical culture as:

$$\hat{\gamma} = \frac{1}{2\lambda(\varpi + \beta R)} - \frac{1}{\lambda}. \tag{16.9}$$

Hence, threshold $\hat{\gamma}$ is a decreasing function of institutional quality, β. This is intuitive: as institutions improve, the relative fitness of civic values rises, and hence a lower share $\hat{\gamma}$ of civic values in the population is sufficient for the two cultural traits to be equally fit.

---

[3] Implicitly, we assume that equilibrium rents are non-negative for any $\gamma \in [0, 1]$ and for all feasible institutions β.

[4] Note that these conditions are consistent with non-negativity of rents, as long λ is sufficiently large and/or ϖ is sufficiently small.

16.3.3 Dynamics

We are now ready to discuss how culture evolves over time. Let t-subscripts stand for time periods, such that γ_t is the population share of civic-minded people at the beginning of period t. Elections are held at the end of each period, after a round of electoral competition over policy, in the same way as in Section 16.2. We assume that γ_t evolves over time as:

$$\gamma_{t+1} = \gamma_t + q(\gamma_t)(1 - q(\gamma_t))Q(\Delta(\gamma_t, \beta)), \tag{16.10}$$

where $q(\gamma_t) \in [0, 1]$ is an arbitrary, continuously increasing function with $q(1) = 1$ and $q(0) = 0$. Further, $Q(\cdot)$ is an arbitrary, continuously increasing function with $Q(0) = 0$, and $\Delta(\gamma, \beta)$ is the relative fitness of civic vs. partisan values defined in (16.6). The share of civic citizens is thus growing (shrinking), whenever the relative fitness of civic values is positive (negative).

A subtle – substantive and methodological – question is whether the cultural share γ that enters $\Delta(\gamma, \beta)$ should be dated by t or $t + 1$. The first, backward-looking case – with $Q(\Delta(\gamma_t, \beta))$ – turns Eq. (16.10) into a form of replicator dynamics, which is widely used in evolutionary game theory – see Weibull (1995) or Sandholm (2010). Besley (2017) and Besley and Persson (2019a) give explicit microfoundations for this kind of assumption in the recent economics literature on cultural evolution. The second, forward-looking case – with $Q(\Delta(\gamma_{t+1}, \beta))$ – turns Eq. (16.10) into a cultural-transmission mechanism that captures the consequences of purposeful socialization. Bisin and Verdier (2000a, 2001), Tabellini (2008b), and Besley and Persson (2019b) give explicit microfoundations for this formulation in the recent economics literature on cultural evolution. However, it turns out that the important lessons we want to draw here do not hinge on which of the two cases we adopt. As it is slightly simpler, we go with the backward-looking version.

16.3.4 Dynamic complementarity of culture

Eq. (16.10) says that the population share holding civic, rather than partisan, values rises over time if this trait gives a higher expected utility in the current social environment ($\Delta > 0$), and falls in the opposite case ($\Delta < 0$). This property together with the earlier result that $\Delta_\gamma > 0$ produces a dynamic complementarity. A rising share of citizens with civic values – a higher γ – makes it more attractive to espouse such values, which further raises γ in the case when $\Delta > 0$. Conversely, a lower share γ makes it less attractive to hold civic values, which further lowers γ in the case when $\Delta < 0$.

This dynamic complementarity implies that Eq. (16.10) generates unique, but divergent, dynamics with three possible steady states: two "monocultural" ones and one "multicultural" one. The results can be summarized as follows:

Proposition 16.1. *The model has two stable steady states: $\gamma = 1$ where everyone is civic, and $\gamma = 0$ where everyone is partisan. The interior steady state, $\gamma = \hat{\gamma}(\beta)$ depends negatively on the quality of institutions, but is unstable. Society converges to the civic steady state $\gamma = 1$ from any initial population share $\gamma_0 > \hat{\gamma}(\beta)$, and to the partisan steady state $\gamma = 0$ from any initial $\gamma_0 < \hat{\gamma}(\beta)$.*

The instability of the multicultural (internal) steady state and stability of the monocultural (corner) steady states both follow from the facts that $\Delta_\gamma > 0$, and that $\Delta \lesseqgtr 0$ and hence $\gamma_t \lesseqgtr \gamma_{t+1}$ as $\gamma \lesseqgtr \hat{\gamma}(\beta)$.

To put the proposition in words, if initially a civic culture is sufficiently (insufficiently) diffused, society eventually reaches a good (bad) state with a civic (partisan) monoculture. Intuitively, a civic culture is relatively more fit only with sufficiently many civic types around, so that the equilibrium entails low political rents. If this condition is not satisfied, civic types experience a form of cognitive dissonance. They are thus permanently disappointed, such that partisan types have higher expected welfare, and society gradually evolves towards the steady state with a partisan monoculture. The dynamics are illustrated in Fig. 16.1 for two values of β.

Importantly, the critical threshold (unstable steady state) $\hat{\gamma}(\beta)$ that governs the cultural dynamics depends on the institutional strength. As discussed above, stronger institutions (higher β) raise relative fitness $\Delta_\beta > 0$. This, in turn, lowers the critical threshold for culture $\hat{\gamma}(\beta)$, which makes it more likely that society reaches the civic steady state for any given initial values γ_0. This is illustrated in Fig. 16.1, where the upper and lower curves refer to strong institutions β^S and weak institutions $\beta^W < \beta^S$. In other words, strong institutions can breed a civic culture, because they increase the relative fitness of civic cultural traits by generating (rational) expectations of lower corruption.

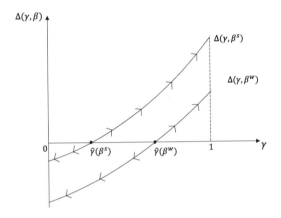

FIGURE 16.1

16.3.5 Discussion

Historical evidence is consistent with the prediction that strong institutions exert a positive long-run influence on culture. Environments that centuries ago had stronger checks and balances on the executive and more participatory institutions currently display a more civic and universalistic culture. This finding emerges from a variety of empirical studies carried out on different types of data. These include analyses of Italian and European municipalities and regions that vary by the quality of historical local political institutions (Banfield, 1958; Putnam, 1993, 2000; Guiso et al., 2008; Tabellini, 2008a, 2010), of the cultural traits among second-generation US immigrants whose parents arrived from countries with different degrees of democratic government (Tabellini, 2008a). Similar results show up in experiments run in Switzerland with individuals who were historically exposed to different political institutions (Rustagi, 2020), and in the attitudes of individuals whose ancestors were raided by slave traders (Nunn and Wantchekon, 2011). The survey by Nunn (2009) provides further references. These studies do not explore the precise mechanisms behind cultural evolution, but the reduced-form association from past institutions to current cultural traits is very robust and in line with the predictions of our simple model.

16.3.6 Notes on the literature

Tabellini (2008b) contrasts the evolution of universalistic vs. limited morality. He shows that cultural evolution reflects the spatial patterns of social interactions and of external enforcement. Universalistic values are discouraged if interactions and external enforcement of cooperation are mainly local. Conversely, well-functioning legal institutions breed universalistic values, since law enforcement facilitates transactions and cooperation between unrelated individuals. Thus, his model predicts that clan-based societies develop very different value systems compared to societies relying on the abstract rule of law. Greif and Tabellini (2010, 2017) apply this insight to the coevolution of culture and social organization, contrasting the historical bifurcation of China (where dynastic organizations prevailed) and Europe (where instead corporate organizations and legal institutions sustained cooperation between unrelated individuals). Hauk and Saez Marti (2002) is an early study of how the intergenerational transmission of values may affect corruption. See also the survey by Francois et al. (2019).

In this chapter, we think about culture mainly as manifested in a set of values. An important branch of the political-science literature considers socialization into political values, in the sense of which party to support, and shows that these are very persistent across an individual's life. This literature has recently been surveyed by Neundorf and Smets (2017). For an example of high-quality empirical work that focuses on identifying such persistence in cross-sectional and time-series data, see Ghitza and Gelman (2014).

16.4 Institutional choice

Ultimately, institutions are endogenous as well. To introduce new elements simply and gradually into the analysis, we postpone until the next section a full discussion of how (discrete) institutional change interacts with (gradual) cultural evolution. In this section, we take the necessary first step towards that discussion. Thus, we study how politicians choose institutions in a given time period, where culture (the share of people with civic values) is parametrically given (from the past).

We assume that the outgoing incumbent from the last period chooses institutions (checks and balances, β) at the beginning of each period before elections are held. Citizens also have a chance to protest against the incumbent, which may prevent her from running in the upcoming election. The chosen institutions then act as a constraint on subsequent policy choices (rents, r) announced by both candidates in the course of the electoral competition.

16.4.1 Within-period timing

Formally, the timing of events in period t, is as follows

1. The election winner from period $t - 1$ chooses institutions, β_t.
2. Civic (but not partisan) citizens may protest against the incumbent's choice of institutions, and a successful protest prevents the incumbent from running as a candidate at stage 3.
3. If the incumbent is not ousted, she runs against an opponent candidate with an identical objective. If the incumbent is ousted, two new candidates run against each other. The two candidates announce policy, r_t, taking institutions as given.
4. Elections are held and the winner's policy is enacted.

The same sequence is repeated in every period. In equilibrium, institutions have to be incentive-compatible, in the sense of maximizing the expected utility of the incumbent. The only difference between the incumbent and the opponent is that the former sets the institutions at stage 1, which will constrain the effects of the policy platforms announced by both candidates. The incumbent also faces prospective protests at stage 2. However, as all prospective candidates have the same objectives, they would pick the same institution if they had this opportunity.

At electoral stage 3, candidates act as described in Section 16.2. Below, we discuss the behavior at institutional stages 1 and protest stage 2, in reverse order.

Our timing not only endogenizes institutions, but assumes that they act as a constraint on subsequent policy choices. This is related to the recent political-economics literature. Starting with Acemoglu and Robinson (2000), endogenous political institutions are indeed viewed as a commitment device that impacts on subsequent equilibrium policies. The only difference is that in our model there is no commitment beyond the current period, whereas in the recent literature institutional commitments are typically made for one period into the future. This distinction will matter in the dynamic analysis of Section 16.5. Given our assumed timing, institutions are not a state variable, whereas they are a state variable in the theoretical literature on institutions.

To simplify the formal treatment, we adopt an analogous assumption to the treatment of the franchise by Acemoglu and Robinson (2000, 2006). That is, we assume that the institutions limiting political rents – like citizen values – come in only two forms, which we call strong and weak. Formally, $\beta_t \in \{\beta^S, \beta^W\}$, with $\beta^W = 1 < \beta^S \leq \frac{1}{2(1+\lambda)R}$, where the last equality guarantees that rents are non-negative even when everybody in population is civic ($\gamma = 1$). Castañeda Dower et al. (2020) provide a full-fledged treatment of the franchise-choice model, when the institutional variable is chosen on a continuous domain.

16.4.2 Civic protests (stage 2)

Picking the weaker institution at stage 1 of the within-period game will confer benefits on all incumbents, since it raises the equilibrium rents that can (probabilistically) be extracted. To have a meaningful tradeoff, the incumbent must also face a cost from choosing $\beta_t = \beta^W$. Such costs arise if elections are not the only mechanism for disciplining politicians. This is the rationale behind stage 2, whereby the incumbent can be ousted as a stage-3 election candidate, if her stage-1 institutional choice triggers citizen protests.

Specifically, we assume that: (i) civic citizens – but not partisan ones – may protest in the streets, (ii) a larger share of civic citizens turn out to protest if they expect higher rent extraction under the chosen institution, (iii) a successful protest prevents the incumbent from running as a candidate. A simple way to formalize assumptions (i)-(iii) is to postulate that the period-t incumbent is ousted at stage 2 with probability

$$z_t = z(\gamma_t, \beta_t) = \gamma_t F(r^*(\gamma_t, \beta_t)), \tag{16.11}$$

where F is an increasing protest function with $F(0) = 0$. Clearly, $z(\gamma_t, \beta^S) < z(\gamma_t, 1)$ as stronger institutions bring about lower rents.

16.4.3 The incumbent objective

Relying on these assumptions and normalizing an ousted incumbent's payoff to zero, we can write the incumbent's objective at stage 1 of period t as the expected value

$$\phi(\gamma_t, \beta_t) = (1 - z(\gamma_t, \beta_t))v_t = (1 - z(\gamma_t, \beta_t))p_t \left(\frac{r(\gamma_t, \beta_t)}{\beta_t} + R \right). \tag{16.12}$$

To study the decision problem, we define the expected payoff difference between strong and weak institutions $\Phi(\gamma_t) = \phi(\gamma_t, \beta^S) - \phi(\gamma_t, 1)$. Using this definition, (16.12), and our earlier result that in equilibrium $p_t = 1/2$, we can write

$$\Phi(\gamma_t) = \frac{1}{2} \left[\frac{1}{\beta^S} r^*(\gamma_t, \beta^S) - r^*(\gamma_t, 1) \right] \tag{16.13}$$

$$+ \frac{\gamma_t}{2} \left[F(r^*(\gamma_t, 1))(r^*(\gamma_t, 1) + R) - F(r(\gamma_t, \beta^S))(\frac{1}{\beta^S} r^*(\gamma_t, \beta^S) + R) \right]$$

What are the properties of $\Phi(\gamma_t)$? The first term on the right-hand side is negative (as $\beta^S > 1$ and $r^*(\gamma_t, \beta^S) < r^*(\gamma_t, 1)$), since rents are lower with strong institutions. But the second term is non-negative (for the same reasons, and as F is increasing), since protests are less vigorous and the incumbent's probability to be ousted lower when institutions are strong. Clearly, we have $\Phi(0) < 0$, as the second term is zero at $\gamma_t = 0$: no ousting takes place when no civic citizens can take to the streets. To cut down on the taxonomy of possible cases, we assume that $\Phi(1) > 0$. Finally, it is easy to show that Φ is monotonic in the share of citizens with a civic culture, with $\Phi_\gamma > 0$ (due to the direct effect as well as $r_\gamma < 0$).[5]

16.4.4 Equilibrium institutions (stage 1)

With these properties, we have the following result:

Proposition 16.2. *There exists a threshold value of culture* $\tilde{\gamma}$ *defined by* $\Phi(\tilde{\gamma}) = 0$, *such that the incumbent's optimal institutional choice satisfies:*

$$\beta_t = \begin{cases} \beta^W = 1 & \text{if } \gamma_t < \tilde{\gamma} \\ \beta^S & \text{if } \gamma_t \geq \tilde{\gamma}. \end{cases}$$

Given $\Phi(0) < 0$, $\Phi(1) > 0$ and monotonicity of Φ with $\Phi_\gamma > 0$, the existence of critical value $\tilde{\gamma}$ follows from the intermediate-value theorem. Because $\Phi(\gamma)$ is defined as the expected-payoff difference to the incumbent between strong and weak institutions, the institutional choices are immediate by monotonicity of Φ.

Let us summarize and give the intuition for the formal result in Proposition 16.2. The incumbent faces a tradeoff: stronger institutions cut expected rents conditional on survival, but they also raise the probability of survival. Moreover, the slope of that tradeoff varies with the prevailing culture, as

---

[5] Formally, $\Phi(\gamma_t)$ also depends on the level of β^S. That relation is ambiguous in sign, however, since the first term in $\Phi(\gamma_t)$ is decreasing in β^S while the second term is increasing in β^S.

measured by γ_t. When more people are civic, the probability of non-electoral ousting increases (as more people are prepared to take to the streets). Moreover, equilibrium rents fall as γ_t rises (as electoral punishments are stronger), and this makes weaker institutions less appealing to the incumbent (because institutions determine what fraction of rents is appropriated by politicians). Both forces thus push in the same direction: a more widespread civic culture (a higher γ_t) makes strong institutions more attractive to the incumbent.

16.4.5 Discussion

The analysis in this section is related to Acemoglu and Robinson (2000, 2001, 2006) and some of the research inspired by their work. Our framework focuses on agency conflicts within a democracy with an open franchise, rather than redistributive struggles and the choice of whether to install or repeal the franchise. However, as in their analysis, the threat of non-electoral removal from political privilege can make an incumbent forego the direct benefits from less constraining institutions. Moreover, even though institutions constrain policy only within the current period – rather than across periods – the reason for reform is analogous: changing institutions allows incumbents to influence future equilibrium policies. In other words, institutions allow the incumbent to make commitments that cannot be credibly made directly over policies.

In Acemoglu and Robinson (2006), institutional reforms have an additional feature: they are hard to reverse. Once the franchise has been introduced, it is difficult for an incumbent to repeal it, and vice versa once a coup has occurred. This irreversibility is particularly important in a stochastic setting – for example, when the protest function F is affected by exogenous shocks. Contingencies that make protests more effective – say, coordination of collective action becomes easier, or the incumbent is weakened by external events – create opportunities for institutional change. If institutions are irreversible, or can be reversed only at additional costs, then these critical junctures have long-lasting effects. Clearly, irreversibility is more natural for institutional reforms that drastically change the overall rules of the game, like fully extending the suffrage or devolving decision-making powers. This important aspect is missing in our model, since institutions are not a state variable (they are chosen at the end of each period, and existing institutions do not constraint institutional choice).

In some instances, irreversibility (or partial reversibility) of institutions reflects how power is allocated in society or across different offices. In this sense, it is a technological assumption about the consequences of institutions. But institutional inertia can also result from behavioral features. Protests do not take place in a vacuum, they also reflect emotions and feelings of entitlements. These behavioral features have been modeled in the literature with the idea that institutions and other state variables affect individual reference points. Then, people's sense of entitlements reflects expectations of what it is reasonable to obtain in a given environment. Institutional reforms change these expectations, making protests more or less likely. Once suffrage has been extended, the decision to remove this fundamental right is likely to trigger outrage and protests, in excess of what would have happened if the status quo of limited suffrage had been preserved. This may create institutional inertia.

Passarelli and Tabellini (2017) study a model of protests where citizens have reference-dependent preferences. They focus on the choice of state variables like public debt, and show that, by issuing public debt, governments can mitigate both current and future protests. A similar mechanism can be used to study institutional reforms. Besley and Persson (2019a) do so in their study of democratic values and democratic reforms. Specifically, they assume that citizens with democratic values who contemplate defending democracy against an autocratic threat (demanding a democracy in an autocracy) uses the outcome under autocracy (democracy) as a reference point, against which they evaluate the outcome with the existing institution.

16.4.6 Notes on the literature

Both economists and political scientists have done early theoretical research on endogenous democratic institutions, along similar lines as in this chapter and in Acemoglu and Robinson's research. Among the former, one may mention Lizzeri and Persico (2004), who argue that the introduction of the franchise may reflect benefits tied to general versus particularistic spending. Among the latter, one should mention Boix (2003), who also proposes a model of endogenous democratic reforms, where the latter not only resolve commitment problems but coordination problems.

Economists and political scientists have long debated which cultural and economic features are favorable to the emergence and stability of democracy. Lipset (1959) advocates the thesis of modernization (a positive link between democracy and economic development), while Almond and Verba (1963) emphasize that a well-functioning democracy requires a civic culture. More recently, Glaeser et al. (2007) stress that democratic institutions are endogenous and reflect the accumulation of human capital, while Acemoglu et al. (2008) argue that the time-series evidence is inconsistent with the idea of modernization.

The idea that institutions are chosen strategically to influence future policy choice is also at the heart of the important literature on state capacity. While the powers of the state have been discussed informally by political scientists and sociologists, the first formal modeling of state capacity can be found in Cukierman et al. (1992), Acemoglu (2005), and Besley and Persson (2009, 2010, 2011). The empirical and historical work on the topic includes Levy (1988) and more recently Dincecco (2017), and Dincecco and Onorato (2017). (See also the survey by Dincecco and Wang, 2018.)

Grillo and Prato (2020) study reference-dependent preferences in elections, in a model with endogenous institutions. They show that in some instances this mechanism can lead to democratic backsliding (that is, a process of gradual and progressive institutional weakening). As already mentioned, Castañeda Dower et al. (2020) consider a franchise model, when the institutional variable also can be chosen continuously. Alesina and Giuliano (2011) show a link from culture to politics more generally, in the sense that strong family ties relate negatively to political participation.

A literature in economic history studies the evolution of state institutions in Europe, and how they constrained the absolutist powers of the sovereign – see the survey by Johnson and Kom (2017).

16.5 Cultural evolution and institutional change

We are now ready to discuss the full-equilibrium dynamics as culture evolves over time (like in Section 16.3) and incumbents are free to pick whichever institution they see fit in each period (like in Section 16.4).

An early application of this approach can be found in Tabellini (2008b), who studies how endogenous culture dynamically interacts with endogenous law-enforcement institutions. The dynamic complementarities between culture and institutions give rise to hysteresis: depending on initial conditions, societies can remain trapped in bad steady states with weak institutions and particularistic values, or converge to a steady state with strong institutions and universalistic values. In his model, however, law-enforcement institutions are a policy outcome and not a constraint on subsequent policy choices.

The dynamic interaction of proper political institutions and culture features in Persson and Tabellini (2009). They study how the appreciation of democratic institutions (called democratic capital) is associated with transitions from autocracy to democracy and the stability of the latter (and vice versa). In their model, however, the endogenous accumulation of democratic capital is mechanical.

Besley and Persson (2019a) take a further step, by studying the interaction between democratic reforms and democratic values, when these values are not only endogenous but subject to choice. Similar ideas have also been applied to culture and social organizations in China and Europe (Greif and Tabellini, 2017) and organizational cultures and organizational design (Besley and Persson, 2020b).

Analyzing how culture and institutions jointly coevolve over time may appear as a difficult task, at least upon a first reflection. However, as will soon be apparent, clear-cut results come relatively easily. Formally, this is because we can carry out the analysis with culture as the single state variable. In the research tradition of Acemoglu and Robinson (2000), endogenous institutions (having the franchise or not) is the only state variable, on the argument that they are more inertial than policy (redistribution from elite to the masses). As per the model in Section 16.4, we maintain that assumption *within* each period. But when it comes to comparing culture and (formal) institutions, the most plausible assumption – at least to us – is that culture has more inertia than institutions. Thus we maintain the assumption from the cultural-evolution model in Section 16.3 that culture is predetermined *across* the adjacent period. The alternative, where both culture and institutions are predetermined across periods would make the analysis much more difficult, as we would have two state variables (see Ticchi et al., 2013; Bisin and Verdier, 2017 for such analyses).

16.5.1 Combining the building blocks

To pursue the full analysis, we first recall the results on cultural evolution in Proposition 16.1 and define the critical cultural value (unstable steady state) for each of the two institutions as $\hat{\gamma}(\beta^S)$ and $\hat{\gamma}(\beta^W) = \hat{\gamma}(1)$. It follows from the results in Section 16.3, that $\hat{\gamma}(\beta^S) < \hat{\gamma}(1)$. By Proposition 16.1, culture evolves monotonically towards the civic (partisan) steady state, whenever initial culture γ_0 is above (below) its relevant critical value.

Next, we recall the results on institutional choice in Proposition 16.2, which say that the incumbents pick strong (weak) institutions, whenever the current value of culture exceeds (falls below) the threshold $\tilde{\gamma}$. As explained in Section 16.4, the latter is defined by the indifference condition $\Phi(\tilde{\gamma}) = 0$.

Putting these pieces of analysis together, we can describe the equilibrium dynamics as follows:

Proposition 16.3. *There are three possible parameter configurations with different cultural and institutional dynamics:*

(a) $\tilde{\gamma} > \hat{\gamma}(1)$. *If $\gamma_0 > \tilde{\gamma}$, society starts out with strong institutions β^S and its culture converges to $\gamma = 1$ without any institutional reform. If $\gamma_0 < \hat{\gamma}(1)$, society starts out with weak institutions $\beta^W = 1$ and its culture converges to $\gamma^s = 0$ without any reform. If $\hat{\gamma}(1) < \gamma_0 < \tilde{\gamma}$, society starts out with weak institutions with culture converging towards $\gamma = 1$, then makes a reform towards strong institutions as γ_t reaches $\tilde{\gamma}$, which further boosts civic values until they have converged to a civic monoculture.*

(b) $\tilde{\gamma} < \hat{\gamma}(\beta^S)$. *If $\gamma_0 < \tilde{\gamma}$, society starts out with weak institutions $\beta^W = 1$ and its culture converges to $\gamma = 0$ without any institutional reform. If $\gamma_0 > \hat{\gamma}(\beta^S)$, society starts out with strong institutions β^S and its culture converges to $\gamma^s = 1$ without any reform. If $\hat{\gamma}(\beta^S) > \gamma_0 > \tilde{\gamma}$, society starts out with strong institutions with culture converging towards $\gamma = 0$, then makes a reform towards weak* *institutions as γ_t reaches $\tilde{\gamma}$, which further boosts partisan values until they have converged to a partisan monoculture.*

(c) $\hat{\gamma}(\beta^S) < \tilde{\gamma} < \hat{\gamma}(1)$. *If $\gamma_0 < \tilde{\gamma}$, society starts out with weak institutions $\beta^W = 1$ and its culture converges to $\gamma = 0$ without any institutional reform. If $\gamma_0 > \tilde{\gamma}$, society starts out with strong institutions β^S and its culture converges to $\gamma = 1$ without any reform.*

The proposition provides an exhaustive list of possibilities. Its taxonomy of cases could be reduced by specific assumptions regarding the general form of functions F, q, Q, and W, the distributions of shocks σ^i and δ, and parameters R, λ, and β^S. The three possible cases in Proposition 16.3 are illustrated in Figs. 16.2a, 16.2b, and 16.2c, respectively.

16.5.2 Mutual feedbacks

Proposition 16.3 conveys a basic dynamic complementarity between cultural evolution and institutional change. For certain configurations – essentially when initial cultural values are predominantly civic (partisan) – electoral accountability is high (low), so rents are low (high). In those cases, the gains from weak institutions are relatively small (large), so politicians tend to pick strong (weak) institutions. This, in turn, further raises the fitness of a civic (partisan) culture and society converges to a civic (partisan) monoculture without any institutional change. Such cases are illustrated in Fig. 16.2c, and would also occur in Fig. 16.2a when initial culture γ_0 satisfies $\gamma_0 > \tilde{\gamma}$ or $\gamma_0 < \hat{\gamma}(1)$, and in Fig. 16.2b if $\gamma_0 > \hat{\gamma}(\beta^S)$ or $\gamma_0 < \tilde{\gamma}$.

For more intermediate cultural values – the last possibility in cases (a) and (b) – culture starts developing either towards a partisan monoculture with weak institutions, or towards a civic monoculture with strong institutions. This starts changing equilibrium rents, which feeds back to cultural evolution via the expected payoffs of civic vs. partisan values. As culture reaches its critical juncture $\tilde{\gamma}$, however, incumbents undertake a reform towards strong or weak institutions, respectively, which further boost the relative fitness of civic or partisan values. These cases are illustrated by Fig. 16.2a when initial culture γ_0 fulfills $\hat{\gamma}(1) < \gamma_0 < \tilde{\gamma}$, and by Fig. 16.2b, when initial culture γ_0 fulfills $\hat{\gamma}(\beta^S) > \gamma_0 > \tilde{\gamma}$.

16.5.3 Discussion

Since the empirical work by Acemoglu et al. (2001), historical research has documented the surprisingly persistent effects of past institutions on economic and political development. Three good examples out of a large and growing literature are Dell (2010), Nunn and Wantchekon (2011), and Dell et al. (2018). The dynamic and two-way complementarities between culture and institutions we have illustrated in this section can shed light on the mechanisms behind the persistence documented in this kind of historical research. Weak institutions allow those in power to extract rents at the expense of citizens at large. Such a political environment breeds a culture of clientilism and discourages the emergence of strong civic values. Partisan cultural traits, in turn, may be counter-productive in several ways. They amplify political distortions and enable those in power to get away with even more rents. This in turn strengthens political incentives to keep institutions weak, because the advantages of weak institutions are enhanced by a partisan culture. Finally, if few citizens have civic values, few are willing to fight for institutional improvements, which further undermines institutional development. Hence society remains trapped in an environment of high rents, weak institutions and a clientelistic culture. We have not modeled economic development here, but it is easy to see how political rents and a partisan culture may also undermine economic growth. Dynamic complementarities operate in reverse in an environment with strong institutions and a strong civic culture.

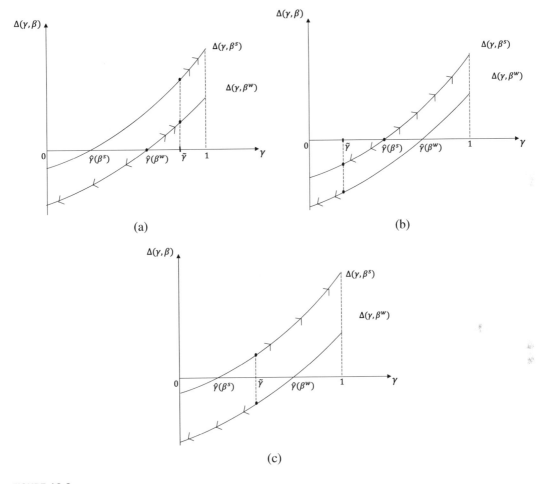

FIGURE 16.2

The different panels in the figure refer to the following parameter constellations: (a) $\hat{\gamma}(\beta^W) < \tilde{\gamma}$. (b) $\tilde{\gamma} < \hat{\gamma}(\beta^S) < \hat{\gamma}(\beta^W)$. (c) $\hat{\gamma}(\beta^S) < \tilde{\gamma} < \hat{\gamma}(\beta^W)$.

These arguments also reveal that a debate on whether culture or institutions are more important determinants of economic development is like a debate over chicken and eggs. In the grand scheme of things, both culture and institutions are endogenous and they are jointly determined. Both display inertia and persistence, although in some instances institutions can overcome inertia and change rapidly.

To see the implications of these features, suppose country-level panel data on institutions and culture were generated by a set of models all like the one in this chapter, but with different country-specific functions, parameters, and distributions. Then the simultaneity in these panel data of culture and institutions would make it a hazardous exercise to tease out a causal one-directional link from one of these variables to the other. If one swallows our assumption that culture is the slowest moving variable, however, the *initial conditions* for culture are the first chickens in the system. It is these that govern the joint coevolution of culture (the subsequent stream of chickens) and institutions (the subsequent stream of eggs) over time.

Some evidence do indeed support the causal chains captured by the model in this section. Persson and Tabellini (2009) theoretically postulate that the appreciation for democracy amongst citizens is enhanced by the history of past democracy and by the geographic proximity to other democracies, and that these values induce citizens to support democratic institutions. They then show that the evidence from democratic transitions (in both directions) is consistent with these predictions. Consistent with a channel of cultural transmission across countries, Magistretti and Tabellini (2018) show that trade integration with other democracies increases the quality of home democratic institutions, particularly for countries with lower initial level of economic and institutional development. Along similar lines, Giuliano and Nunn (2013) find that democracy spreads from the local to the national level.

Besley and Persson (2019a) study a setting where political culture in the sense of democratic values coevolves with strategically chosen (by political leaders) reforms between democratic and autocratic institutions. They show that such a setting with minimal persistence of democratic institutions, but persistence in democratic values, can reproduce the strong patterns observed in historical democracy data. That is, one set of countries make a single transition to democracy, another set stay autocratic (or transit once and for all to autocracy), and a third set of countries flip-flop between the two modes of political governance. Besley and Persson (2020b) study a related model at the level of the organization, where organizational cultures, designs, and performance interact over time, and where strong organizational cultures can be both a virtue and a vice.

The emphasis on hysteresis and path dependence has induced some scholars to pay attention to critical junctures, and to ask where the key initial conditions come from. Roland (2019) contrasts the broad features of political regimes in ancient history. He argues that where geographic conditions and factor endowments were more conducive to domestic and foreign trade, market-supporting institutions emerged together with an individualistic culture. Where instead initial conditions of production were more homogeneous, leading to specialization and division of labor, a system of state control emerged together with a collectivistic culture. Along similar lines, Talhelm et al. (2014) argue that geographic features led to specialization in rice production in certain areas of China, and that this specialization can explain psychological and cultural within-country differences.

Greif and Tabellini (2017) instead emphasize how religion may shape the initial conditions of culture. They contrast the historical coevolution of culture, social organizations, and institutions in China vs. Europe. Because of their different religions, these continents began the second millennium AC with very different cultural initial conditions, which led to starkly different development paths. China's dynastic value system facilitated the evolution of clan-based organizations, and the persistence of an unchallenged autocratic form of government. By contrast the European Church pushed to dismantle large extended families and spread a culture of universalistic values, which facilitated the emergence of corporate organizations, and legal institutions that enforced cooperation amongst strangers. These corporate-governance principles tilted the emerging organization of the state towards the rule of law and participatory institutions, as extensively discussed in Greif et al. (2020, ch. 7).

Consistent with this idea, Schulz (2016) finds that, within Europe, exposure to the Church's medieval prohibition of kin marriage is correlated with the emergence of participatory city institutions. Exploiting evidence from the Ethnographic Atlas, he also finds that weak kin networks in pre-industrial societies are associated with more democratic forms of government. Similar evidence is discussed at length in the monograph by Henrich (2020).

16.5.4 Notes on the literature

Bisin and Verdier (2000b) is one of the first papers to study the dynamic evolution of culture and public policies in a political equilibrium. Gorodnichenko and Roland (2013, 2017) as well study how culture influences political institutions and economic development, contrasting individualism vs. collectivism. They find that an individualistic, as opposed to a collectivist, culture facilitates earlier adoption of democracy and innovation-led economic development.

Stasavage (2020) discusses how early European state institutions evolved from principles of corporate governance. Acemoglu and Robinson (2018, 2019) stress the important interaction between civil society and inclusive political institutions in the unique path of European institutional development. The evolution of European state institutions, and their interaction with distinctive elements of European cultural traditions, has also been studied by historians like Hintze (1975), Tierney (1982), Mitterauer (2010) amongst others.

16.6 Taking stock

The research discussed in this chapter is motivated by two facts. Policy failures and successes – and associated economic and political outcomes – are highly correlated across countries. Moreover, these economic and political outcomes are remarkably persistent. Together, these facts mean that some countries are very resilient in their prosperity and well-functioning institutions, while others are conspicuously stable in their economic and political backwardness. The interaction of culture and institutions can account for these patterns in the data.

Both cultural traits and formal institutions are inertial and – at any given moment – they shape economic and political outcomes. In a static setting, their effects are similar, and possibly substitutable. Efficient market interactions can be sustained by effective law enforcement or, alternatively, by a cooperative and civic culture. Good political outcomes can reflect either well-designed constitutions or, alternatively, informed and well-meaning participation by citizens.

But both culture and institutions are endogenously changing over time, and their dynamics are likely to mirror different forces. While strategic expediency for the incumbent may drive institutional reforms, relative fitness may drive the evolution of alternative cultural traits. Surprisingly, these two drivers give rise to dynamic complementarities and rich two-way interactions. In our simple model of political agency, a culture of strong civic engagement is more fit – and thus more favored – if strong political institutions also discourage political abuse. Conversely, political incumbents are less tempted to weaken political institutions if they fear the reaction of vigilant and engaged citizens.

These dynamic interactions between culture and institutions can explain why economic and political development outcomes cluster together, why critical junctures could make a society change course, and why otherwise similar countries which start off with different initial conditions for culture or institutions can follow very different development paths. Rapidly growing lines of research rely on these general insights to explore a variety of problems at the frontier of economics, evolutionary anthropology, history, political science, and sociology. Some applications are summarized in other parts of this handbook.

Our specific analysis has singled out two particular aspects of institutions and culture. Strong institutions, like checks and balances on the executive, discourage political abuse and rent seeking. Civic cultural traits, like universalistic values, facilitate coordination and cooperation between unrelated individuals. In our simple model, both aspects are captured as parameters, but they can be given more complete microfounded representations in richer models (for example, Persson et al., 1997; Aghion et al., 2004; Tabellini, 2008b; Besley and Persson, 2019b).

These insights notwithstanding, our discussion has omitted other aspects of institutions and cultural traits that have received attention in the literature. In particular, culture can be seen as a system of beliefs about the behavior by others, rather than as a system of values. This is the approach taken by many papers on social norms (for example, Kotlikoff et al., 1988; Kreps, 1990; Greif, 1994; Acemoglu and Jackson, 2015). A problem with beliefs-driven models is that they have multiple equilibria and thus less sharp predictions. Another line of research instead views social norms as beliefs about the values of others (rather than about the behavior of others) – see, for instance, Bicchieri (2006), Benabou and Tirole (2011), and D'Adda et al. (2020). There is certainly room for more than one approach to these issues, and the direction of future research will have to be guided by solid empirical evidence.

Ongoing research on culture and institutions is mostly motivated by positive questions. The reason that normative issues have attracted less attention may be that institutions and culture are highly persistent and difficult to change. Yet, normative questions are absolutely vital. How is it possible to exit from a "corruption trap" where a clientelistic culture and weak institutions mutually reinforce each other? What role can education play in promoting values that would induce more (or less) civic behavior by citizens? Do citizens become politically more engaged if they are exposed to more information about the performance of politicians? Should institutional reforms begin with local governments, where democratic interactions may be easier, and only proceed to national government once citizens have learnt how to appreciate their new local institutions? Or – reversing the argument – should one avoid decentralized powers in countries where civic and partisan cultures cluster geographically, to avoid economic, institutional and cultural divergence?[6]

Other equally important questions concern democratic backsliding in well-functioning political systems. Adverse economic shocks can make radical or populist politicians more popular, and bring some of them to office, setting in motion a process of institutional and cultural deterioration.[7] What specific institutional safeguards, if any, can prevent democratic backsliding? How far can free media serve as a channel for alerting public opinion to the dangers of democratic backsliding? Can international pressure prevent the erosion of democratic institutions without further galvanizing domestic nationalistic forces? Addressing these and other normative questions is an important priority for future research on culture and institutions.

References

Acemoglu, D., 2005. Politics and economics in weak and strong states. Journal of Monetary Economics (Swiss National Bank Special Issue) 52, 1199–1226.

---

[6] Myerson (2020) argues in favor of letting policymakers be held accountable locally rather than centrally, Martinez-Bravo et al. (2017) find that the introduction of local elections in rural China increased public good provisions, Mansuri and Rao (2013) favorably discuss development strategies that are based on community empowerment. Mauro et al. (2020) take the opposite position, and argue that decentralization has been harmful to the Italian South, because it has enhanced the negative influence of local (less civic) political culture.

[7] As shown by Funke et al. (2016), this risk is particularly high after deep financial crises.

Acemoglu, D., Jackson, M., 2015. History, expectations, and leadership in the evolution of social norms. The Review of Economic Studies 82, 423–456.

Acemoglu, D., Johnson, S., Robinson, J.A., 2001. The colonial origins of comparative development: an empirical investigation. The American Economic Review 91, 1369–1401.

Acemoglu, D., Johnson, S., Robinson, J.A., 2005. Institutions as a fundamental cause of long run growth. In: Aghion, P., Durlauf, S.N. (Eds.), Handbook of Economic Growth, Volume IA. Elsevier B.V.

Acemoglu, D., Johnson, S., Robinson, J.A., Yared, P., 2008. Income and democracy. The American Economic Review 98, 808–842.

Acemoglu, D., Naidu, S., Restrepo, P., Robinson, J.A., 2019. Democracy does cause growth. Journal of Political Economy 127, 47–100.

Acemoglu, D., Robinson, J.A., 2000. Why did the West extend the franchise? Democracy, inequality and growth in historical perspective. The Quarterly Journal of Economics 115, 1167–1199.

Acemoglu, D., Robinson, J.A., 2001. A theory of political transitions. The American Economic Review 91, 267–293.

Acemoglu, D., Robinson, J.A., 2006. Economic Origins of Dictatorship and Democracy. Cambridge University Press.

Acemoglu, D., Robinson, J.A., 2018. The Emergence of Weak, Despotic and Inclusive States. Mimeo.

Acemoglu, D., Robinson, J.A., 2019. The Narrow Corridor. States, Societies and the Fate of Liberty. Penguin Random House.

Aghion, P., Alesina, A., Trebbi, F., 2004. Endogenous political institutions. The Quarterly Journal of Economics 119, 565–611.

Alesina, A., Giuliano, P., 2011. Family ties and political participation. Journal of the European Economic Association 9, 817–839.

Alesina, A., Giuliano, P., 2015. Culture and institutions. Journal of Economic Literature 53, 898–944.

Almond, G., Verba, S., 1963. The Civic Culture: Political Attitudes and Democracy in Five Nations. Sage Publications.

Avis, E., Ferraz, C., Finan, F., 2018. Do government audits reduce corruption? Estimating the impacts of exposing corrupt politicians. Journal of Political Economy 126, 1912–1964.

Banfield, C.E., 1958. The Moral Basis of a Backward Society. The Free Press.

Barro, R.J., 1996. Democracy and growth. Journal of Economic Growth 1, 1–27.

Benabou, R., Tirole, J., 2011. Laws and Norms. NBER Working Paper 17579.

Besley, T., 2017. Aspirations and the political economy of inequality. The 2016 Hicks Lecture in Economics. Oxford Economic Papers 69, 1–35.

Besley, T., Persson, T., 2009. The origins of state capacity: property rights, taxation and politics. The American Economic Review 99, 1218–1244.

Besley, T., Persson, T., 2010. State capacity, conflict, and development. Econometrica 78, 1–34.

Besley, T., Persson, T., 2011. Pillars of Prosperity. The Political Economics of Development Clusters. Princeton University Press.

Besley, T., Persson, T., 2019a. Democratic values and institutions. American Economic Review Insights 1, 59–76.

Besley, T., Persson, T., 2019b. The dynamics of environmental politics and values. Journal of the European Economic Association 17, 993–1024.

Besley, T., Persson, T., 2020a. Escaping the Climate Trap? Values, Technologies, and Politics. Mimeo.

Besley, T., Persson, T., 2020b. Organizational Dynamics: Culture, Design, and Performance. Mimeo.

Bicchieri, C., 2006. The Grammar of Society: The Nature and Dynamics of Social Norms. Cambridge University Press.

Bisin, A., Verdier, T., 2000a. Beyond the melting pot: cultural transmission, marriage, and the evolution of ethnic and religious traits. The Quarterly Journal of Economics 115, 955–988.

Bisin, A., Verdier, T., 2000b. A model of cultural transmission, voting, and political ideology. European Journal of Political Economy 16, 5–29.

Bisin, A., Verdier, T., 2001. The economics of cultural transmission and the dynamics of preferences. Journal of Economic Theory 97, 298–319.

Bisin, A., Verdier, T., 2011. The economics of cultural transmission and socialization. In: Benhabib, J., Bisin, A., Jackson, M.O. (Eds.), Handbook of Social Economics, vol. 1A. Elsevier B.V.

Bisin, A., Verdier, T., 2017. On the Joint Evolution of Culture and Institutions. NBER Working Paper 23375.

Boix, C., 2003. Democracy and Redistribution. Cambridge University Press.

Boyd, R., Richerson, P.J., 1985. Culture and the Evolutionary Process. University of Chicago Press.

Brollo, F., Nannicini, T., Perotti, R., Tabellini, G., 2013. The political resource curse. The American Economic Review 103, 1759–1796.

Castañeda Dower, P., Finkel, E., Gehlbach, S., Nofziger, S., 2020. Democratization as a continuous choice: a comment on Acemoglu and Robinson's correction to why did the West extend the franchise. The Journal of Politics 82, 776–780.

Cavalli-Sforza, L.L., Feldman, M.W., 1981. Cultural Transmission and Evolution: A Quantitative Approach. Princeton University Press.

Cruz, C., Labonne, J., Keefer, P., 2020a. Buying Informed Voters: New Effects of Information on Voters and Candidates. Mimeo.

Cruz, C., Labonne, J., Keefer, P., Trebbi, F., 2020b. Making Policies Matter: Voter Responses to Campaign Promises. Mimeo.

Cukierman, A., Edwards, S., Tabellini, G., 1992. Seigniorage and political instability. The American Economic Review 82, 537–555.

D'Adda, G., Dufwenberg, M. Passarelli, F., Tabellini, G., 2020. Social Norms with Private Values: Theory and Experiments. Bocconi University. Mimeo.

Dell, M., 2010. The persistent effects of Peru's mining mita. Econometrica 78, 1863–1903.

Dell, M., Lane, N., Querubin, P., 2018. The historical state, local collective action, and economic development in Vietnam. Econometrica 86, 2083–2121.

de Secondat, C.-L., known as Montesquieu, 1748. De l'esprit des Lois. Published anonymously.

Dhillon, A., Rigolini, J., 2007. Development and the interaction of enforcement institutions. Journal of Public Economics 95, 79–97.

Dincecco, M., 2017. State Capacity and Economic Development. Present and Past. Cambridge University Press.

Dincecco, M., Onorato, M., 2017. From Warfare to Wealth: The Military Origins of Urban Prosperity in Europe. Cambridge University Press.

Dincecco, M., Wang, Y., 2018. Violent conflict and political development over the long run: China versus Europe. Annual Review of Political Science 21, 341–358.

Enke, B., Rodriguez-Padilla, R., Zimmermann, F., 2020. Moral Universalism and the Structure of Ideology. Mimeo.

Feddersen, T., Sandroni, A., 2006. A theory of participation in elections. The American Economic Review 96, 1271–1282.

Fernández, R., 2011. Does culture matter? In: Benhabib, J., Bisin, A., Jackson, M.O. (Eds.), Handbook of Social Economics, Vol. 1A. Elsevier B.V.

Ferraz, C., Finan, F., 2008. Exposing corrupt politicians: the effects of Brazil's publicly released audits on electoral outcomes. The Quarterly Journal of Economics 123, 703–745.

Ferraz, C., Finan, F., 2011. Electoral accountability and corruption: evidence from the audits of local governments. The American Economic Review 101, 1274–1311.

Francois, P., Fujiwara, T., van Ypersele, T., 2019. The origins of human pro-sociality: cultural group selection in the workplace and laboratory. Science Advances 4. https://doi.org/10.1126/sciadv.aat2201.

Funke, M., Schularick, M., Trebesch, C., 2016. Going to extremes: politics after financial crises, 1870-2014. European Economic Review 88, 3–20.

Ghitza, Y., Gelman, A., 2014. The Great Society, Reagan's Revolution, and Generations of Presidential Voting. Mimeo.

Giavazzi, F., Tabellini, G., 2005. Economic and political liberalizations. Journal of Monetary Economics 52, 1297–1330.

Giuliano, P., Nunn, N., 2013. The transmission of democracy: from the village to the nation-state. The American Economic Review 103, 86–92.

Glaeser, E.L., Ponzetto, G.A.M., Shleifer, A., 2007. Why does democracy need education? Journal of Economic Growth 12, 77–99.

Gorodnichenko, Y., Roland, G., 2011. Which dimensions of culture matter for long run growth? The American Economic Review: Papers and Proceedings 101, 492–498.

Gorodnichenko, Y., Roland, G., 2013. Culture, Institutions, and Democratization. Mimeo.

Gorodnichenko, Y., Roland, G., 2017. Culture, institutions and the wealth of nations. Review of Economics and Statistics 99, 402–416.

Greif, A., 1994. Cultural beliefs and the organization of society: a historical and theoretical reflection on collectivist and individualist societies. Journal of Political Economy 102, 912–950.

Greif, A., Mokyr, J., Tabellini, G., 2020. Two Paths to Prosperity: Culture and Institutions in Europe and China, 1200-2000. Manuscript in preparation.

Greif, A., Tabellini, G., 2010. Cultural and institutional bifurcations: China and Europe compared. The American Economic Review: Papers and Proceedings 100, 135–140.

Greif, A., Tabellini, G., 2017. The clan and the corporation: sustaining cooperation in China and Europe. Journal of Comparative Economics 45, 1–35.

Grillo, E., Prato, C., 2020. Reference points and democratic backsliding. Available at SSRN https://ssrn.com/abstract=3475705.

Guiso, L., Sapienza, P., Zingales, L., 2004. The role of social capital in financial development. The American Economic Review 94, 526–556.

Guiso, L., Sapienza, P., Zingales, L., 2006. Does culture affect economic outcomes? The Journal of Economic Perspectives 20, 23–48.

Guiso, L., Sapienza, P., Zingales, L., 2008. Social capital as good culture. Journal of the European Economic Association 6, 295–320.

Hamilton, A., Madison, J., Jay, J., 1788. The Federalist Papers, J. and A. Mc Lean.

Hauk, E., Saez Marti, M., 2002. On the cultural transmission of corruption. Journal of Economic Theory 107, 311–335.

Henrich, J., 2020. The WEIRDest People in the World, How the West Became Psychologically Peculiar and Particularly Prosperous. Farrar, Straus and Giroux.

Hintze, O., 1975. The preconditions of representative government in the context of world history. In: Gilbert, F. (Ed.), The Historical Essays of Otto Hintze. Oxford University Press.

Hofstede, G., 1984. Culture's Consequences: International Differences in Work-Related Values. Sage Publications.

Johnson, N.D., Kom, M., 2017. States and economic growth: capacity and constraints. Explorations in Economic History 64, 1–20.

Khemani, S., Dal Bó, E., Ferraz, C., Finan, F., Stephenson, J., Corinne, L., Odugbemi, A.M., Thapa, D., Abrahams, D.S., 2016. Making Politics Work for Development: Harnessing Transparency and Citizen Engagement. Policy Research Reports. World Bank Group.

Kotlikoff, L.J., Persson, T., Svensson, L.E.O., 1988. Social contracts as assets: a possible solution to the time-consistency problem. The American Economic Review 78, 662–677.

Kranton, R., 1996. Reciprocal exchange: a self-sustaining system. The American Economic Review 86, 830–851.

Kreps, D.M., 1990. Corporate culture and economic theory. In: Alt, J.A. (Ed.), Perspectives on Positive Political Economy. Cambridge University Press.

Landes, D.S., 1998. The Wealth and Poverty of Nations: Why Some Are so Rich and Some so Poor? W.W. Norton.

Levchenko, A., 2007. Institutional quality and international trade. The Review of Economic Studies 74, 791–819.

Levy, M., 1988. On Rule and Revenue. University of California Press.

Lipset, S.M., 1959. Some social requisites of democracy: economic development and political legitimacy. American Political Science Review 53, 69–105.

Lizzeri, A., Persico, N., 2004. Why did the elites extend the suffrage? Democracy and the scope of government, with an application to Britain's 'Age of reform'. The Quarterly Journal of Economics 119, 707–765.

Magistretti, G., Tabellini, M., 2018. Economic Integration and Democracy: An Empirical Investigation. Mimeo.

Mansuri, G., Rao, V., 2013. Localizing Development: Does Participation Work? Report. International Bank for Reconstruction and Development.

Martinez-Bravo, M., Padro i Miquel, G., Qian, N., Yao, Y., 2017. The Rise and Fall of Local Elections in China: Theory and Empirical Evidence on the Autocrat's Tradeoff. NBER Working Paper 24032.

Mauro, L., Pigliaru, F., Carmeci, G., 2020. Further Lessons from the Dynamics of the Italian Divide: Social Capital and Decentralization. Università di Trieste. Mimeo.

McMillan, J., Woodruff, C., 2000. Private order under dysfunctional public order. Michigan Law Review 98, 2421–2458.

Mitterauer, M., 2010. Why Europe? The Medeival Origins of Its Special Path. University of Chicago Press.

Mokyr, J., 2016. A Culture of Growth. Princeton University Press.

Murdock, G.P., 1965. Social Structure. Free Press.

Myerson, R., 2020. Local Agency Costs of Political Centralization. University of Chicago. Mimeo.

Nannicini, T., Stella, A., Tabellini, G., Troiano, U., 2013. Social capital and political accountability. American Economic Journal: Economic Policy 5, 222–250.

Neundorf, A., Smets, K., 2017. Political Socialization and the Making of Citizens. Oxford Handbooks Online. Oxford University Press.

North, D.C., 1990. Institutions, Institutional Change and Economic Performance. Cambridge University Press.

North, D.C., Weingast, B.R., 1989. Constitutions and commitment: the evolution of institutions governing public choice in seventeenth-century England. The Journal of Economic History 49, 803–832.

Nunn, N., 2007. Relationship-specificity, incomplete contracts and the pattern of trade. The Quarterly Journal of Economics 122, 569–600.

Nunn, N., 2009. The importance of history for economic development. Annual Review of Economics 1, 65–92.

Nunn, N., Wantchekon, L., 2011. The slave trade and the origins of mistrust in Africa. The American Economic Review 101, 3221–3252.

Passarelli, F., Tabellini, G., 2017. Emotions and political unrest. Journal of Political Economy 125, 903–946.

Persson, T., Roland, G., Tabellini, G., 1997. Separation of powers and political accountability. The Quarterly Journal of Economics 112, 1163–1202.

Persson, T., Tabellini, G., 2000. Political Economics. Explaining Economic Policy. MIT Press.

Persson, T., Tabellini, G., 2003. The Economic Effects of Constitutions. MIT Press.

Persson, T., Tabellini, G., 2006. Democracy and development: the devil in the details. The American Economic Review: Papers and Proceedings 96, 319–324.

Persson, T., Tabellini, G., 2008. The growth effect of democracy: is it heterogenous and how can it be estimated? In: Helpman, E. (Ed.), Institutions and Economic Performance. Harvard University Press.

Persson, T., Tabellini, G., 2009. Democratic capital: the nexus of political and economic change. American Economic Journal: Macroeconomics 1, 88–126.

Persson, T., Tabellini, G., Trebbi, F., 2003. Electoral rules and corruption. Journal of the European Economic Association 1, 958–989.

Przeworski, A., Alvarez, M.E., Cheibub, J.A., Limongi, F., 2000. Democracy and Development. Political Institutions and Well-Being in the World, 1950–1990. Cambridge University Press.

Putnam, R.D., 1993. Making Democracy Work: Civic Traditions in Modern Italy. Princeton University Press.

Putnam, R.D., 2000. Bowling Alone. The Collapse and Revival of American Community. Simon & Schuster.

Roland, G., 2019. Comparative economics in historical perspective. In: Presidential Address at the 2018 Meeting of the Association of Comparative Economics.

Rustagi, D., 2020. Historical Self Governance and Norms of Cooperation. University of Nottingham. Mimeo.

Sandholm, W.H., 2010. Population Games and Evolutionary Dynamics. MIT Press.

Schulz, J., 2016. Kin-networks and institutional development. Available at SSRN https://ssrn.com/abstract.

Smith, A., 1759. The Theory of Moral Sentiments, A. Strahan and T. Cadell.

Smith, A., 1776. The Wealth of Nations, A. Strahan and T. Cadell.

Stasavage, D., 2020. The Decline and Rise of Democracy: A Global History from Antiquity to Today. Princeton University Press.

Tabellini, G., 2008a. Institutions and culture, presidential lecture. Journal of the European Economic Association 6, 255–294.

Tabellini, G., 2008b. The scope of cooperation: values and incentives. The Quarterly Journal of Economics 123, 205–250.

Tabellini, G., 2010. Culture and institutions: economic development in the regions of Europe. Journal of the European Economic Association 8, 677–716.

Talhelm, T., Zhang, X., Oishi, S., Shimin, C., Duan, D., Lan, X., Kitayama, S., 2014. Large-scale psychological differences within China explained by rice versus wheat agriculture. Science 344, 603–608.

Ticchi, D., Verdier, T., Vindigni, A., 2013. Democracy, Dictatorship and the Cultural Transmission of Political Values. IZA Discussion Paper 7441.

Tierney, B., 1982. Religion, Law, and the Growth of Constitutional Thought, 1150-1650. Cambridge University Press.

de Tocqueville, A., 1840. Democracy in America. George Dearborn & Co and Adlard and Saunders.

Weibull, J.W., 1995. Evolutionary Game Theory. MIT Press.

Phase diagrams in historical economics: culture and institutions[☆]

Alberto Bisin[a,b,c] **and Thierry Verdier**[d,e,f,c]

ᵃDepartment of Economics, New York University, New York, NY, United States
ᵇNBER, Cambridge, MA, United States
ᶜCEPR, London, United Kingdom
ᵈParis School of Economics, Paris, France
ᵉEcole des Ponts-Paris Tech, Champs-sur-Marne, France
ᶠPUC-Rio, Rio de Janeiro, Brazil

17.1 Introduction

Historical economics is mostly an empirical field, centered on the application of statistical and econometric methods to the identification of causal relationships and the persistence of interesting phenomena over historical times. The field however also relies in part on formal modeling of the historical dynamics of interest, to help frame the empirical questions. This is especially the case in the study of the dynamics of institutions, starting with the pathbreaking influential work of Daron Acemoglu and James Robinson (Acemoglu and Robinson, 2001, 2006a).[1]

In this chapter, we focus, like Persson and Tabellini (2021, in this book), on models of the interaction of institutions and culture. While providing a brief (and somewhat idiosyncratic) survey of this literature, we aim first of all at a methodological point; that is, illustrating the (metaphorical) power of explicit formal dynamic modeling, differential/difference equations and the like, for historical analysis. Deirdre McCloskey sets the methodological issue beautifully,

> The differential equation itself might be looked on as the model/metaphor. Alternatively, and I think better, the honor of the word "metaphor" might be reserved for the timeless physical or economic or historical idea behind the equation, such as [...] that people pursue profits in buying wheat or that the men of Athens were very fools in their imperial might. The actual numerical time paths from the solution of a differential equation is the narration in time, and the solution (which can also generate the numerical path) is the thematized narrative -transparent or muddy depending on how neat the solution is, when it exists. The

☆ In memory of Alberto Alesina, whose comments and enthusiasm about this line of research permeate this chapter. Thanks to Simone Meraglia for comments and references. This research has been undertaken in part under financial support from the ERC Advanced Grant TECTACOM °324004.

1 Several chapters of the Handbook survey in detail the different approaches developed to the theoretical study of the dynamics of institutions: Acemoglu et al. (2021, in this book); Bowles et al. (2021, in this book); Levine and Modica (2021, in this book); Persson and Tabellini (2021, in this book).

The Handbook of Historical Economics. https://doi.org/10.1016/B978-0-12-815874-6.00024-1
Copyright © 2021 Elsevier Inc. All rights reserved.

analytic solutions correspond to simply predictable histories, that is, histories that can be reexpressed as equations. The differential equations embody what we think we know about societies as theory, such as a Marxist theory.

McCloskey (1991), p. 24

McCloskey's discussion centers on the distinction between non-linear and linear (difference) equations. Non-linear (systems of) equations can generate chaotic dynamics, which in the historical narration corresponds to assigning "small causes" to "large events." But non-linear (systems of) equations can generate other interesting phenomena, e.g., non-ergodic solutions, that is, dynamics which converge to different stationary states depending on the initial conditions. The corresponding historical narration in this case is not necessarily the identification of the "small" cause, that "if Cleopatra had a different nose; unattractive to Roman generals, the battle of Actium might not have happened;" but rather that different initial conditions (be that small or large) might have "large" effects. The initial distribution of a society's cultural traits, civic culture for instance, might have very persistent effects over its history, affecting its whole institutional dynamics, fostering or damaging its economic development. Non-linear dynamics can even generate historical reversal, whereby for instance poverty contains the seeds of economic success, as in Acemoglu et al. (2002) or Ashraf et al. (2010); see Bisin and Moro (2021, in this book) for a discussion. Whatever the qualitative dynamics that is generated, it is still the case that, with McCloskey (1991), "life gets difficult for the [economist][2] and the historian when the differential equation does [...] when variables feed back into themselves, we have an exciting story to tell, but unless we know its metaphors already we have no way to tell it." More generally, phase diagrams are useful representations of interesting qualitative dynamics generated by non-linear dynamical systems. The analysis of the qualitative aspects of the dynamics of a system in the long-run are (methodologically) a first step to the construction of quantitative structural models to be estimated with historical data. Most importantly, qualitative dynamics are complementary to the causal analysis of historical phenomena, e.g., in persistence studies in that they substantiate the assumptions underlying instrumental variables, natural historical experiments, regression discontinuity techniques; see Voth (2021, in this book) and Bisin and Moro (2021, in this book).

In this chapter we will constrain our analysis to the study of systems of differential/difference equations representing the historical, that is, long-term, dynamics of the distribution of cultural traits, norms, conventions, and of institutions. Indeed, the recent literature in historical economics has identified various aspects of culture and institutions as the principal factors explaining economic development; the importance of the interaction of culture and institutions has also been stressed in various contributions to this literature; see Section 17.3 for a discussion and some references. Models of institutional change often have change implemented by "large players" in a game determining policies and outcomes in society; see Acemoglu et al. (2006) and Acemoglu et al. (2021, in this book) for surveys. These models are typically referred to as *top-down*. A different class of models, where agents are "small" and institutions, norms, and cultural traits are formed as the result of some form of a selection processes, are typically referred to as *bottom-up*; see Bowles et al. (2021, in this book). For simplicity we will think of top-down change as institutional change and of bottom-up change as cultural change, but the dynamics we shall obtain are relatively fungible (some institutional change can be bottom-up, e.g., norms and conventions; some cultural change can be top-down, e.g., prescribed by religious authorities).

---

[2] McCloskey says "engineer."

In the rest of the chapter we first construct abstract dynamic models of institutional and cultural change, mapping some prominent contribution to this literature into them. We then show how these models interact and illustrate graphically the qualitative properties of the dynamical paths representing the solution of systems of differential/difference equations by means of *phase diagrams*.

17.2 Institutional and cultural change

In the following sections we will briefly survey top-down and bottom-up models of the dynamics of institutions and culture. We will express them as dynamic differential/difference equations and discuss how can their dynamics be usefully represented qualitatively by means of *phase diagrams*.

17.2.1 (Top-down) models of institutional change

Top-down modeling has institutions as a representation of the relative power of different political groups. This is consistent with the traditional classic approach to political science: from the central role of city factions in Machiavelli's Istorie Fiorentine (1532), to the concept of classes in Marxist thought[3] and the concept of elites in sociology.[4] More distinctively, institutions are modeled as the mechanisms through which policy choices are delineated and implemented. Formal models along these lines have been pioneered by Acemoglu and Robinson (2001, 2006a) and taken up, along similar lines, e.g., by Acemoglu et al. (2010, 2012, 2015, 2018); Besley and Persson (2009a, 2009b, 2010, 2011); Bisin and Verdier (2017); Tabellini (2008). In this class of models, institutional change takes different forms, but it is generally the way the political system imperfectly and indirectly internalizes the externalities which plague social choice problems.

A simple abstract structure should help clarify the core elements of this class of models. Consider a society constituted by two groups $i \in \{1, 2\}$, characterized by distinct preferences (cultural traits) and technologies. Each period t, a societal policy game is played between private individuals and a hierarchical public policy authority (the state) controlling socio-economic policies. Individuals in each group $i \in \{1, 2\}$ are characterized by an objective function $V^i = U^i(a^i, p, A)$ that depends on private actions a^i, a policy vector p, and some measure of socio-economic outcomes A, capturing the aggregate (society-wide) outcomes of the interactions between private agents and public authorities. These aggregate outcomes naturally depend on the vector $a = [a^1, a^2]$ of actions by individuals of the two groups and on the public policy vector p: $A = A(a, p)$.

Policies are the outcome of a (collective) decision problem, in accordance with the distribution of political power between the two groups encoded and represented by institutions. Institutions can then be abstractly defined and represented by the (Pareto) weights $\beta^1 = \beta$ and $\beta^2 = 1 - \beta$ of the two groups 1 and 2 in the decision making problem regarding to the policy vector p.[5] Specifically, we could have

---

[3] See e.g., Balibar (1970) and Poulantzas (1973).

[4] See e.g., Pareto (1901, 1920) and Aron (1950a, 1950b).

[5] See Gradstein (2007, 2008) and Guimaraes and Sheedy (2017) who more explicitly ground the study of institutions in the theory of coalition formation.

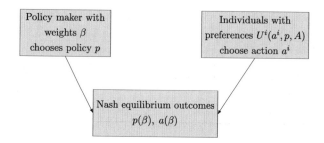

FIGURE 17.1

Societal policy game.

the objective of the public policy authority identified by a Social welfare function

$$\beta U^1(a^1, p, A) + (1 - \beta)U^2(a^2, p, A). \tag{17.1}$$

As illustrated in Fig. 17.1, given institutions β, a set of policies $p = p(\beta)$, and actions $a = a(\beta)$, characterize the equilibrium of the societal policy game between individuals and the public authority.

It should be noted that the policy game is in general characterized by several economic and political externalities that are not fully accounted for by private and public decisions. Externalities typically arise because of socio-economic or political imperfections associated with the existence of various frictions going from asymmetric/incomplete information, matching problems, limited rationality and cognitive biases, strategic behaviors associated with market power, private opportunism, and lack of political commitment. The equilibrium outcomes $a(\beta)$ $p(\beta)$ of the societal policy game do not fully internalize their impacts on aggregate social outcomes $A(a, p)$, and as a result inefficient policies and social allocations are implemented.[6]

The core element of this class of models, is the mechanism driving institutional change. A society characterized by a power structure β_t at any point in time t, might have an incentive to change the distribution of political power in the future, to internalize the externalities responsible for the inefficiencies at equilibrium. The direction of institutional change relates to the general principle that the political group most likely to internalize the externality is the group receiving more residual decision rights along the institutional dynamics. This mechanism for institutional change is consistent with several interesting large scale historical phenomena. For instance, McCloskey (2006, 2010, 2017) sees institutions evolving during the Industrial Revolution, alongside liberal ideas (Bourgeois Ideology), to allow the efficiency of the market economy to display its power to spread technology, innovation, and capital accumulation. Also, the process which controlled the transfer of power from the landed aristocracy in favor of the merchant class in Medieval Western Europe is generally interpreted to have resulted in a more efficient fiscal administration; see Bates and Lien (1985). Interestingly, however, it

---

[6] For instance, political groups can strategically exploit socio-economic or political frictions to their own advantage. Interesting examples of inefficient institutional changes induced by elites with oligarchic powers, which we do not discuss in this chapter, are Puga and Trefler (2014) and Carvalho and Dippel (2016).

is generally not the case that the stationary state of these processes is efficient; see Acemoglu (2003); Acemoglu et al. (2010); Acemoglu and Robinson (2008, 2012); Bisin and Verdier (2017).

We illustrate this class of models of institutional change by our own rendition of four examples, North et al. (2009); Acemoglu and Robinson (2000, 2006b); Besley and Persson (2011), and Bisin and Verdier (2017).[7] More specifically, consider the following environment: i) the two political groups represent elites and workers, $i = \{e, w\}$; ii) total resources are $A = A(a, p, q)$, where q is the fraction of elites in the population; iii) policy p controls the distribution of total resources A: $(1 - p)A$ to workers and pA to elites; iv) the social welfare function takes the simple form $\beta U^e(pA, a^e) + (1 - \beta)U^w((1 - p)A, a^w)$, where a^i is individual production effort, $i = \{e, w\}$.

In North et al. (2009) institutions are supported by monopoly of violence and are distinguished in terms of *Limited access* (autocracy) and *Open access* (democracy). Limited access institutions could be represented by $\beta = 1$ and Open access by $\beta = \frac{1}{2}$. The fundamental driver of institutional change is lack of commitment. It is then easy to construct an explicit formal structure such that, under no commitment on p, a Limited access $\beta = 1$ society might want to delegate power (control of violence) and allow for Open access, $\beta = 1/2$. In Acemoglu (2003) and in Acemoglu and Robinson (2006a) institutions coincide with the political pressure group exercising the power to control social choice; and institutional change takes the form of voluntary transfer of power across groups, typically under threat of social conflict.[8] In particular, institutions can be autocratic or democratic, $\beta = 1, 1/2$, as in North et al. (2009), but can also be controlled by workers, $\beta = 0$. Institutional change is driven by lack of commitment, but the mechanism is more specifically modeled as the outcome of conflict for political power between the elites and the workers. Consider for instance the case in which institutions are autocratic. Workers are endowed with a technology of revolution, $R = \{1, 0\}$, which they can switch on at some cost C^w, imposing a (large) cost C^e on elites but allowing them to access to all the resources produced. Policy p is chosen under limited commitment: with probability π, the choice of p is re-set after action a^w is taken. In this last case, elites take all resources for themselves and $p = 1$. The commitment distribution of resources p is chosen by the elites as a solution to the following problem:

$$\max_p \pi U^e(A, a^e) + (1 - \pi)U^e(pA, a^e)$$

$$s.t. \quad \begin{array}{c} \pi U^w(0, a^w) + (1 - \pi)U^w((1 - p)A, a^w) \geq U^w(1, a^r) - C^w \\ a^w \in \arg\max \pi U^w(0, a^w) + (1 - \pi)U^w((1 - p)A, a^w) \\ a^r \in \arg\max U^w(1, a) \\ a^e \in \arg\max \pi U^e(A, a^e) + (1 - \pi)U^e(pA, a^e) \end{array}$$

Assume (to avoid trivial cases) that workers prefer a revolution to being completely dispossessed,

$$U^w(0, a^w) < U^w(1, a^r) - C^w.$$

---

[7] We do not attempt an accurate rendering the interesting complexities of the modeling of institutional change in these papers. Indeed we might trivialize them, to illustrate (what appear to us as) the core aspects of their modeling of the dynamics and to be able to project them into a common abstract dynamical system.

[8] Historical examples of the role of revolutions, or of the threat of revolutions, in fostering institutional change are discussed by Acemoglu and Robinson (2000, 2001, 2005, 2006b, 2012). A prominent case in the literature is the extension of the franchise in early nineteenth century England, as an effect of threats to the established order; see Acemoglu and Robinson (2000, 2001, 2006b); Conley and Temimi (2001), and Lizzeri and Persico (2004) for an alternative explanation.

If π high enough, the constraint might never be satisfied and an autocratic society might want to delegate to a democratic society $\beta = \frac{1}{2}$ (or even to a workers' society, where $\beta = 0$).

In Bisin and Verdier (2017), the policy p is chosen under no commitment, as in Acemoglu (2003) and in Acemoglu and Robinson (2006b).[9] Lack of commitment is directly modeled by having the public policy authority choosing p simultaneously with respect to the choices of the (two groups of) agents, (a^w, a^e). An equilibrium is a Nash equilibrium of this game:

$$p \in \arg\max \beta U^e(pA, a) + (1 - \beta)U^w((1 - p)A, a)$$
$$a^e \in \arg\max U^e(pA, a)$$
$$a^w \in \arg\max U^w((1 - p)A, a)$$

The equilibrium is generally inefficient. The inefficiency is due to lack of commitment in the policy decision making as well as to the externalities in the determination of $A = A(p, a)$. Institutional change is a mechanism operating on the distribution of political power to internalize externalities due to some form of lack of commitment on the part of the public policy decision maker, without an explicit role of social conflict and the threat of revolution.[10] An important distinction of the analysis of Bisin and Verdier (2017) is that $\beta \in [0, 1]$ allows for smooth institutional change; that is, it allows for institutional change to be incremental. Their analysis therefore captures long-run historical dynamics of institutions rather than more extreme phenomena like democratization, revolutions, regime changes like political coups leading to autocratic regimes. A rich set of examples consistent with this view, whereby institutional change occurs through gradual and piecemeal changes that manifest themselves mostly in the long run, are discussed by Mahoney and Thelen (2010). With respect to the study of dynamical systems in history which motivate this chapter, allowing for $\beta \in [0, 1]$ (a continuous rather than a discrete change in political control) leads directly to the formulation of the dynamics of institutions as a differential/difference equation. Indeed, in Bisin and Verdier (2017) institutional change takes a relatively simple form:

$$\beta_{t+1} \in \arg\max \beta_t U^e(\beta_{t+1}) + (1 - \beta_t)U^w(\beta_{t+1})$$

where $U^w(\beta_{t+1}) = U^w((1 - p(\beta_{t+1})A(\beta_{t+1}), a(\beta_{t+1}))$ and $U^e(\beta_{t+1}) = (p(\beta_{t+1})A(\beta_{t+1}), a(\beta_{t+1}))$ are utilities evaluated at future equilibrium choices with institution β_{t+1}.[11]

---

[9] On the role of commitment on institutional change, see also Tim Besley's Econometric Society Presidential address, Besley (2020) and the comments by Bisin (2020).

[10] Besides Lizzeri and Persico (2004) work on the extension of the franchise in England, other historical examples along these lines include: the transition of Western European towns in the XV-XIX centuries to inclusive forms of political institutions, as a commitment on the part of the urban oligarchies to limit the inefficiently high indirect taxes on primary goods on trade and production they imposed to the lesser strata of the bourgeoisie (Chittolini, 1979; Tabacco, 1989; Nicholas, 1992; Peytavin, 1997; Sabatini, 2010); the evolution of inclusive institutions at the town level in England, from the Norman conquest until the 1800s, as a commitment on the part of the king to allow self-government to merchant towns to check and control the "widespread opportunistic and distortionary behavior" of fiscal bureaucracies (Angelucci et al., 2017); the formation of local merchant guilds in the Medieval Europe as a commitment on the part of the rulers of the polities in which they traded as a mechanism to raise fiscal revenues more efficiently (Dessi and Piccolo, 2016). Even in the context of explaining the emergence of democracy from autocratic rule, threat of revolutions explains about half the cases in Treisman (2017) classification of all historical democratization events since 1800 (see Table 1 in the paper).

[11] For convenience we denote $A(\beta_{t+1}) = A\left(p(\beta_{t+1}), a(\beta_{t+1})\right)$.

In fact, there is no reason why the institutional dynamics in Acemoglu and Robinson (2000, 2006b) be restricted to discrete changes between $\beta = 1, 0, 1/2$ or why these changes be induced by unanticipated shocks. In a dynamic environment, that is, where A_t changes over time, e.g., due to q_{t+1} changing, a smooth dynamics will be induced. As in Bisin and Verdier (2017) this dynamics takes the form of delegation of power on the part of the elites, but in this case delegation is not motivated to commit policies or to internalize externalities but to avoid social conflict. For instance, assuming complete lack of commitment, $\pi = 1$, for simplicity, under certain initial conditions, in our rendition of Acemoglu and Robinson (2000, 2006b), the fundamental dynamics of β_{t+1} is represented in indirect form by the condition:

$$U^w(\beta_{t+1}) = U^w\left((1 - p(\beta_{t+1}))A(\beta_{t+1}), a^w(\beta_{t+1})\right) \geq U^w(1, a^r(\beta_{t+1})) - C^w.$$

In Besley and Persson (2009a, 2009b, 2010) a society is faced with pressure groups alternating in the power to control economic institutions regarding taxation and contractual enforcement. Policy p represents a commitment component (the choice of state capacity in the future), at some cost. Institutional change is not driven by lack of commitment in this case. Indeed, institutional change is exogenous $\beta_{t+1} = g(\beta_t)$. But the dynamics of β_t imposes an inefficiency on the choice of p: elites and/or workers might under-invest in state capacity if β changes.[12] An ex-ante choice, under commitment, of a restriction on the dynamics of β, e.g., by controlling $g(\beta_t)$ would allow for the endogenous dynamics of β_t, to improve efficiency. Indeed, in Besley and Persson (2011), assuming σ is the institutional variable for the control of institutions, the differential equation for the dynamics of β_{t+1} takes the form:

$$\beta_{t+1} = g(\beta_t, \sigma_{t+1}), \text{ with } \sigma_{t+1} \in \arg\max \beta_t U^e(g(\beta_t, \sigma_{t+1})) + (1 - \beta_t)U^w(g(\beta_t, \sigma_{t+1})).$$

Our rendition of these models of institutional change is meant to show that they all induce a mapping from the institutional system at t, β_t, into the one at $t+1$, β_{t+1}, as schematically illustrated in Fig. 17.2. We obtain therefore a differential/difference equation whose solution describes the path of institutional dynamics[13]:

$$\beta_{t+1} = \Theta(\beta_t). \tag{17.2}$$

---

[12] More specifically, in Besley and Persson (2011), $\beta_{t+1} \in \{0, 1\}$, is random, with probability of $\beta = 1$ equal to γ. In this case both elites and workers under-invest in state capacity under the risk of a change in β. We do not explicit report here on this model, as we want to restrict the dynamic analysis to deterministic systems.

[13] Formally, these models often assume that institutional design is myopic, that is, institutions are designed for the future as if they would never be designed anew in the forward future. When the institutional design is less myopic, a power structure β_t at time t will internalize the fact that by moving to a different structure of decision rights β_{t+1}, this may in turn trigger subsequent institutional changes $\beta_{t+2}, \beta_{t+3}, \dots$ leading to suboptimal outcomes from the point of view of the initial power structure β_t. In order to prevent or mitigate the logic of this institutional "slippery slope", the current system β_t may then try to reduce the speed or even stop the process of institutional change, leading therefore to stronger institutional inertia than what myopic institutions would design; see Acemoglu et al. (2015) for such an analysis in a discrete institutional policy context, Bisin and Verdier (2017) for a simple discussion in the continuous institutional policy context outlined here, and Lagunoff (2009) who provides a general study of the theoretical properties of political economy equilibria with dynamic endogenous institutions. While this assumption simplifies the analytics, it is also factually motivated, e.g., in the historical process which underlies the emergence of democracy. Treisman (2017) argues that in the majority of the democratization events he classifies (in about 65% of them, in fact) democracy has not been primarily the outcome of deliberate institutional choice but rather of various forms of miscalculation and lack of anticipation of the effects of the process set in motion by institutional change. In particular, in almost in half of these instances,

17.2.2 (Bottom-up) models of cultural change

Bottom-up models of the dynamics of cultural traits, norms, and conventions in a society focus on evolutionary selection mechanism operating directing on agents' actions/strategies, or indirectly on preference traits, which in turn determine agents actions/strategies. Bottom-up cultural dynamics have been studied and documented in several contexts.[14] Of particular interest for the topic of this book, are *Persistence studies* in which culture is a channel of a long-lasting influence of historical events on present-day outcomes; see Cioni et al. (2021, in this book), Bisin and Moro (2021, in this book), and Voth (2021, in this book) for surveys. For instance, the importance of historical and cultural factors on inter-ethnic conflicts has been documented between Hindus and Muslims in India (Jha, 2013), and against Jews in Germany (Voigtlander and Voth, 2012).

The evolutionary dynamics induced by bottom-up selection mechanisms are typically represented by a (logistic) replicator dynamics. Formally, consider a society composed of agents identifying in one of two distinct cultural groups $i = \{1, 2\}$. Let q denote the fraction of group 1 in the population and $1 - q$ the fraction of group 2. At each time t, the (logistic) replicator dynamics of q_t is given by

$$q_{t+1} - q_t = q_t(1 - q_t)S(q_t), \tag{17.3}$$

where $S(q_t)$ is the *cultural relative fitness* of that trait in the population.

The replicator dynamics can be derived from several micro-founded cultural selection mechanisms. We illustrate these different evolutionary selection mechanisms through our rendition of several examples: from simple evolutionary models in large populations games as in Hofbauer (1998) and Weibull (2005), to the indirect evolutionary models in Güth and Yaari (1992) and Besley and Persson (2019, 2020); and to the cultural anthropology models developed by Cavalli Sforza and Feldman (1981) and Boyd and Richerson (1985).

Consider first evolutionary models based on payoff imitation protocols in large population games, as in Hofbauer (1998) and Weibull (2005). At each time t, each agent is randomly matched with another to play a simple simultaneous stage game. The strategic interaction is described in a stylized way by two possible actions/strategies, $A = \{1, 2\}$. The payoff of an agent playing $a \in A$ matched with an agent playing $a' \in A$ is $\pi(a, a')$. The fraction q_t of agents playing strategy $a = 1$ evolves then according to the replicator dynamics in Eq. (17.3), with

$$S(q_t) = E\pi(1, a') - E\pi(2, a')$$

where

$$E\pi(1, a') = q_t\pi(1, 1) + (1 - q_t)\pi(1, 2)$$
$$E\pi(2, a') = q_t\pi(2, 1) + (1 - q_t)\pi(2, 2)$$

---

the process inducing democratization is characterized by the fact that the "incumbent initiates a partial reform, [...] but cannot stop" (see Table 2 in the paper), a representation which closely maps our modeling of myopic institutional change.

[14] This large literature is too vast to be even cursorily discussed here; see Bisin and Verdier (2010) for a survey.

are the expected payoffs of agents adopting actions/strategies 1 and 2 respectively.[15] Stable stationary states of these dynamics describe specific cultural conventions on how the stage game is played in the long run, and they generally correspond to a Nash equilibrium of the stage game.[16]

The precise formulation of the strategic environment depends on the application. The pioneering studies by Greif (1989, 1994) on the Maghrebi and Genoese traders in the historical economics literature can be mapped into this formal structure. In this case, the strategic environment is one of cooperation with internal punishment and the actions/strategies on which cultural selection acts are bilateral vs. multi-lateral punishment of non-cooperators, respectively adopted by the Genoese and the Maghrebi. Greif (1989, 1994)'s analysis shows how networks (of merchants, in his environment) can enforce contracts in the absence of any formal institutions.[17] Relatedly, Young and Burke (2001) highlight how an evolutionary process along these lines helps explain the structure of customary crop-sharing contracts in the context of Illinois agriculture.[18]

A distinct class of bottom-up models of the dynamics of cultural traits, norms, and conventions has evolutionary selection processes applying on preferences rather than on action/strategies. In these models the agents' preferences determine their actions/strategies (typically as rational choices) which then are transmitted across and within generations through various imitation and socialization mechanisms; see e.g., Güth and Yaari (1992); Besley and Persson (2019, 2020). Consider a society with two cultural groups $i = \{1, 2\}$. Let a^i denote the action of an agent in group i and let the fraction of group $i = 1$ in the population be denoted q. Each group is characterized by a specific preference trait, $U^i(a^i, a^j, q)$, $i, j \in \{1, 2\}$. In this case, equilibrium actions are a Nash equilibrium of the game, given

---

[15] In several applications, society is composed of two distinct groups, $i \in \{1, 2\}$, each with action/strategy space $\{1, 2\}$. At each time t, individuals of one group are randomly matched with individuals from the other group to play the simultaneous stage game. Let $a^i \in \{1, 2\}$ denote the action of an agent of group i and $\left[\pi^i\left(a^i, a^j\right)\right]_{i=1,2}$ the payoff matrix. Let the fraction q_t^i of agents of type i playing strategy $a^i = 1$. In this case the dynamics of q_t^i, $i \in \{1, 2\}$, is represented by

$$q_{t+1}^i - q_t^i = q_t^i(1 - q_t^i)\left[E\pi^i(1, q_t^j) - E\pi^i(2, q_t^j)\right] \quad \text{for } i, j = 1, 2 \text{ and } i \neq j$$

where

$$E\pi^i(1, q_t^j) = q_t^j \cdot \pi^i(1, 1) + (1 - q_t^j)\pi^i(1, 2)$$
$$E\pi^i(1, q_t^j) = q_t^j \cdot \pi^i(2, 1) + (1 - q_t^j)\pi^i(2, 2)$$

are the expected payoffs of individuals of group i adopting actions/strategies 1 and 2.

[16] Because of strategic complementarities, the stage game often involves multiple equilibria (social conventions). Consequently an equilibrium selection mechanism needs to be included to explain where the social system converges and how a specific social convention may persist or eventually transit to another one. Introducing stochastic elements in the evolutionary selection process is instrumental to this end; see Young (1998). For instance, Bowles and Choi (2019) introduces idiosyncratic random (non-best-response) play in a modified Hawk-Dove-Bourgeois game (Maynard Smith, 1982) to analyze the transition from foraging to farming and the origins of private property; Hwang et al. (2018) add intentional idiosyncratic play to study unequal conventions in an environment in which disadvantaged groups may try to force institutional change by withdrawing their consent from current institutional arrangements; see Bowles et al. (2021, in this book) for a survey.

[17] In the context of development, Fafchamps (2003) has demonstrated the pervasive importance of social networks and customary enforcement mechanisms for trade in Africa.

[18] Hwang et al. (2018) discusses several other application of these mechanisms, from the move from seldom to land leasing contracts in agricultural England between 1350 and 1450, to the political transition from apartheid to democracy in South Africa, or racial desegregation of the U.S. South in the 1960s. See Bowles et al. (2021, in this book) for an exhaustive survey.

the preferences, and q_t evolves according to the replicator dynamics in Eq. (17.3), where the cultural relative fitness of trait 1 in the population, $S(q_t)$, depends on the societal equilibrium set of actions a that individuals undertake, as well as on the specific cultural transmission process through which cultural traits are learnt in society. Typically, $S(q)$ takes the form

$$S(q) = W^1(a, q) - W^2(a, q), \tag{17.4}$$

where $W^i(a, q)$ is an appropriate "cultural fitness" function of trait i in the population. More specifically, in *pairwise comparison random matching* models with imitation driven by dissatisfaction or success, the cultural fitness $W^i(a, q)$ of trait i is simply proportional to the payoff function of type i, $U^i(a^i, a^j, q)$; see Weibull (2005) and Sandholm (2010). In *indirect evolutionary* models, similar dynamics are obtained, though cultural evolution on preferences occurs indirectly through the consequences of their induced behaviors on some material reproduction or survival criterion $W^i(a, q)$, generally distinct from $U^i(a^i, a^j, q)$; see Güth and Yaari (1992); Güth (1995); Dekel et al. (2007); Heifetz et al. (2007).

Finally, evolutionary anthropology models also provide "cultural fitness" functions which are derived from the modeling of explicit processes of cultural transmission across and within generations; see Cavalli Sforza and Feldman (1981) and Boyd and Richerson (1985). These models emphasize the relative importance of different channels of socialization (parents, peers, or society at large), as well as forces of social influence (frequency-bias, prestige-bias). Expanding on this perspective, Bisin and Verdier (2000b; 2000a, 2001) considers intergenerational cultural transmission mechanisms resulting from the joint influence of paternalistic parents (who spend costly resources to bias the process of preference acquisition of their children) and other role models in society at large. In this case, the cultural fitness function of trait i, $W^i(a, q)$ is increasing in $\Delta V^i(a, q)$, the paternalistic utility gain a parent of cultural type i obtains when he/she successfully socializes his/her child to his/her own trait rather than the other trait. It also depends on pecuniary and non-pecuniary opportunities, as well as the technological environment in which socialization typically occurs.[19]

17.3 The interaction of culture and institutions

Along the course of history, over the long term at least, institutional and cultural change interact in interesting ways and with great significance.[20] A vibrant historical literature identifies (or can be interpreted to identify) the interaction of culture and institutions as a fundamental factor for long run

---

[19] See Bisin and Verdier (2010) for an extensive survey of this approach and of applications. More recently, models of the dynamics of cultural traits along these lines, in different institutional contexts have been studied in the literature: Ticchi et al. (2013) and Besley and Persson (2019) on the evolution of civil culture and its interaction with the structure of political systems; Bidner and Francois (2011) on the emergence of internalized norms of honesty, given incentives from top-down institutions; Bidner and Francois (2013) on political norms (specifically, the extent to which leaders abuse office for personal gain and citizens punish such transgressions); Grosjean (2014) on the culture of honor in the U.S.; Besley (2016) on the dynamics of aspirational preferences and their consequences for the political economy of redistribution; Grosjean and Khattar (2019) on gender bias; Besley and Persson (2020) on the diffusion of corporate culture and its implications for the internal organization of firms.

[20] A number of papers study the implications of the interaction of culture and institutions for economic activities. These papers typically focus each on a distinct context-specific case: e.g., Bisin and Verdier (2000b) and (2004) on work norms and the

prosperity.[21] In this section we show how, combining models of top-down institutional dynamics with models of bottom-up cultural dynamics, we obtain a useful representation of these interactions, as a system of differential/difference equations represented by a phase diagram.[22]

Specifically, consider for simplicity an environment in which the dynamics of aggregate social outcomes, A_t, are driven by the dynamics the distribution of the population by cultural trait, q; so that $A_t = A(a_t, p_t, q_t)$ and the equilibrium outcomes also depend on q_t: $a_t = a(\beta_t, q_t)$, $p_t = p(\beta_t, q_t)$, so that $\Theta(.)$ in Eq. (17.2) writes as $\Theta(\beta_t, q_t)$. Similarly, consider the case in which the relative cultural fitness of the two groups depends on the institutional set-up in which the policy game is played, β_t; so that $S(.)$ in Eq. (17.3) writes as $S(\beta_t, q_t)$. The institutional and cultural dynamics of the society are then characterized by $(\beta_t, q_t))$ as described in Fig. 17.2.

Joining together the top-down dynamics of institutional change in (17.2) and the bottom-up dynamics of the distribution of cultural traits in (17.3), the dynamics of institutions and culture are summarized by a dynamic non-linear system:

$$\beta_{t+1} - \beta_t = \Theta(\beta_t, q_t) - \beta_t \tag{17.5}$$

$$q_{t+1} - q_t = q_t(1 - q_t)S(\beta_t, q_t) \tag{17.6}$$

Bisin and Verdier (2017) provide conditions for this system to eventually reach a long run steady state (β^*, q^*) which, when *interior*, solves:

$$\Theta(\beta, q) - \beta = S(\beta, q) = 0. \tag{17.7}$$

At this level of generality, it is however difficult to get a precise analytical characterization of the trajectory of the system (17.5) and (17.6). Still, one may obtain interesting qualitative insights about how culture and institutions display interactions, analyzing the associated phase diagram in the space of the state variables (q_t, β_t).

To this end, denote $\beta = \beta(q)$ the steady state manifold associated with Eq. (17.5), that is, the set of points $(\beta, q) \in [0, 1]^2$ such that $\Theta(\beta(q), q) = \beta$. Intuitively, $\beta = \beta(q)$ represents the set of steady

welfare state; Dixit (2004) on informal (cultural) and formal (institutional) contract enforcement; Doepke and Zilibotti (2008) on preference for discounting and labor markets in the Industrial Revolution; Tabellini (2008) on norms of cooperation and legal systems; Aghion et al. (2010) on trust and regulation; Besley and Ghatak (2017) on organizational culture and incentives. See also Lindbeck (1995); Francois and Zabojnik (2005); Lindbeck and Nyberg (2006); Bidner and Francois (2011); Greif and Tabellini (2010); Hiller (2011); Benabou et al. (2015); Ticchi et al. (2013); Hori (2017); Jeong (2018); Besley and Persson (2019). See also Alesina and Giuliano (2015) for an empirical survey.

[21] Studies along these lines include: Ortiz (1963) on the authoritarian culture of the sugar plantation regions of Cuba operated with slave labor as opposed to the liberal culture of the tobacco farms; Miguel et al. (2006) on capital and industrialization in Indonesia; Guiso et al. (2008, 2016) on social capital and Italian independent city states in the Renaissance; Greif and Tabellini (2010, 2017) on the role of different moral systems and kinship organization in explaining China's and Europe's historical growth divergence over the last millennium; Alesina et al. (2013) on patriarchal institutions and gender attitudes; Grosjean (2014) on the traditional (Scottish-Irish) pastoral society honor code and the differential institutional environment in the North and the South of the U.S.; Gorodnichenko and Roland (2017) and Roland (2017) on the parallel development, since antiquity, of broad institutional and cultural systems (planning institutions associated to collectivist cultural traits and market institutions to individualistic traits); McCloskey (2006, 2010, 2017) on the relative role of *bourgeoise* culture as a complement to inclusive institutions in the understanding of the historical factors giving rise to the Industrial Revolution in England.

[22] We follow Bisin and Verdier (2017) in this exposition.

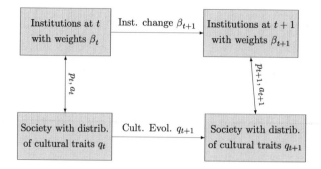

FIGURE 17.2

Joint dynamics of culture and institutions.

state institutional structures, for given time invariant distribution of cultural trait. Similarly denote $q = q(\beta)$ the steady state interior cultural manifold associated with Eq. (17.6); that is, the set of points $(\beta, q) \in [0, 1]^2$ such that $S(\beta, q(\beta)) = 0$. The manifold $q = q(\beta)$ represents the set of steady states distribution of cultural traits, for given time invariant institutional structure.

Consider then an interior long run steady state (β^*, q^*) towards which the joint dynamics of culture and institutions converge, located at the intersection of the two manifolds $\beta = \beta(q)$ and $q = q(\beta)$. The stability conditions of this steady state imply that around the steady state the local dynamics can be immediately inferred: i) β_t increases (resp. decreases) when the system is in the region below (resp. above) the curve $\beta = \beta(q)$; and similarly, ii) q_t increases (resp. decreases) when the system is in the region below (resp. above) the curve $q = q(\beta)$. This is qualitatively well illustrated by the phase diagram in Fig. 17.3. Suppose also, for the sake of exposition, that the diffusion of cultural trait of a given group is favored when that group gets more political power in the societal policy game, i.e., $q(\beta)$ is increasing in β. As illustrated in Fig. 17.3a) and 17.3b), two generic cases may occur depending on whether the slopes of the manifolds at (β^*, q^*) have the same signs or different signs. This feature matters for the comparative dynamics of culture and institutions and for the response of the system to exogenous shocks, e.g., natural historical experiments. Indeed when the manifolds' slopes share the same sign (resp. opposite signs) the joint dynamics reinforce (resp. hinder) each other in response those shocks, and culture and institutions are dynamic complements (resp. substitutes).

To get an intuition for the mechanism, consider for instance the case of dynamic complementarity. Take then an exogenous shock to the system that makes more salient the existence of an externality or a political commitment issue. Such a shock triggers an institutional response aimed at internalizing the externality and/or committing policy choices. This institutional response implies augmenting the political weight to the group who gains relatively more from a policy change that helps correct the externality and/or the commitment issue. When the strength of this institutional response is positively related to the frequency of the cultural traits carried by that group, and that such more empowered group has in turn a higher success at diffusing those specific traits, then complementarity between institutions and culture prevails. Over time, institutional and cultural dynamics re-inforce each other and therefore act as dynamic complements. This is illustrated in Fig. 17.3a) where the exogenous shock triggers an institutional response that translates upward the institutional manifold $\beta = \beta(q)$ at any given cultural state of the society q. As long as cultural evolution has not yet taken place and starting from the initial

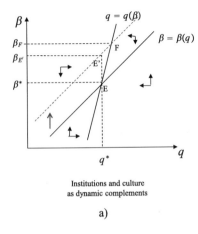

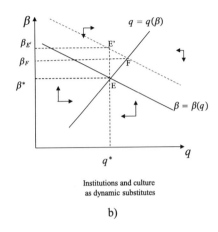

a)

Institutions and culture
as dynamic complements

b)

Institutions and culture
as dynamic substitutes

FIGURE 17.3

Joint evolution of institutions and culture phase diagram.

steady state at point E, the shock implies a new pattern of institutional change that moves the political weight β of group 1 eventually up to $\beta = \beta_{E'}$ at point E'.[23] In the joint dynamics and because of the dynamic complementarity, this in fact stimulates the successful diffusion of the cultural trait of that group. As its frequency q increases, the institutional and the cultural dynamics reinforce each other to end up at the new steady state F with corresponding higher steady state values β_F and q_F. The ratio $\frac{\beta_F - \beta_{E'}}{\beta_{E'} - \beta_E}$ corresponds to what Bisin and Verdier (2017) describes as a *cultural multiplier*, namely the ratio of the long run change in institutions relative to the counterfactual long run change that would have happened had the cultural composition of society remained fixed.[24] Conversely, Fig. 17.3b) illustrates the case of dynamic substitution between institutions and culture. The positive institutional response to a given shock at any fixed cultural state, triggers a cultural dynamic that in that case mitigates the initial impact of the shock on institutional change. Correspondingly, the new resulting steady state value β_F is such that the cultural multiplier $(\beta_F - \beta_{E'})/\beta_{E'}$ is now negative.

The cultural (and symmetrically institutional) multipliers are in principle important conceptual tools, useful alongside causation analysis, to identify and measure the relative contribution of different factors to economic development. While no empirical study has yet attempted to estimate the size of these multipliers in a relevant context, several papers provide explicit quantitative evidence about their sign; that is, they document whether culture and institutions acted as complements or substitutes, reinforcing or hindering economic activity after an exogenous shock. More specifically, recent studies of the interactions of culture and institutions in various specific historical processes, can generally be interpreted as qualitative evidence of either complementarity or substitutability. This is the case, for instance, of the study by Lowes et al. (2017) on the creation of the Kuba Kingdom in Central Africa

---

[23] With much faster institutional adjustment than cultural adjustment, the value of β will directly jump to $\beta_{E'}$, as the institutional dynamics are always located on the manifold $\beta = \beta(q)$.

[24] Obviously, symmetric arguments and conditions hold for the existence of an *institutional multiplier*.

in the 17th century as a natural historical experiment for the formation of a well-functioning institutional system. They find evidence for substitution between culture and institutions in the development process. A more centralized and effective administrative structure associated to the Kuba Kingdom gave rise to "weaker norms of rule following and a greater propensity to cheat for material gain," as measured in the field experiments run by the authors (see Table I in the paper). Even more directly, Lowes and Monteiro (2017) study the effects in terms of economic outcomes of the concession to extract rubber granted in the north of the Congo Free State during the colonial era, as a natural historical experiment for a negative institutional shock. They also find evidence for substitution, in that exposure to the concessions has led to worse economic outcomes but positive effects on various cultural traits like e.g., pro-social attitudes. Related, though less clearcut, results are also found in the study of the effects of the Cultivation System for producing sugar of the Dutch colonial enterprise in 19th century Java by Dell and Olken (2017). On the other hand, Dell (2010)'s study of the effects of the forced mining labor system in effect in Peru and Bolivia in the 16th century provides suggestive evidence of complementarity between culture and institution, inasmuch as extractive institutions have led to large negative effects on present day living standards as well as education and other measures of cognitive and psychological development of children.

The property of dynamic complementarity or substitutability between institutions and culture, also matters for the shape of the trajectories taken by society. Indeed as suggested by the direction of variation of the state variables in phase diagrams 17.3a) and 17.3b), the local joint dynamics between institution and culture tend to generate cyclical and non-monotonic trajectories under substitution, while on the contrary they tend to show some degree of joint monotonicity under complementarity. Specifically, Bisin and Verdier (2017) show that when institutions and culture are dynamic complements, the joint local dynamics do not exhibit any converging oscillatory dynamics, while on the contrary such spiraling trajectory may occur under dynamic substitution. Such feature is interesting as it provides a rationale for why societies need not follow linear and monotonic paths along their historical trajectories. Furthermore, it suggests that empirical studies that only consider the impact of far away historical conditions on current outcomes, obviate potentially important cyclical or oscillatory dynamics that in themselves could have socio-economic implications from an efficiency or welfare point of view.[25]

17.4 Property rights and conflict

In this section we illustrate the methods and the concepts outlined previously by means of a simple analytical example which we study and solve in some detail, showcasing the explanatory power of phase diagrams in the study of the dynamics of culture and institutions.[26] Specifically, we study a conflictual society and characterize conditions under which the cultural and institutional dynamics in

---

[25] Bidner and Francois (2013), in their study of the evolution of honesty norms, find a dynamic complementarity between norms and institutions, with two types of possible social outcomes. The first one is a functional institutions/high trust equilibrium with widely diffused honesty norms and efficient trade between individuals. The second one is a dysfunctional institutions/low trust equilibrium, where honesty norms are not followed and trade is limited.

[26] See Bisin and Verdier (2017) for two applications of similar methods and concepts. In the first example, we study conditions under which the cultural and institutional dynamics may maintain or reverse *extractive institutions*. The second example focuses on the dynamics of *civic culture* either complementing or substituting public governance institutions. See also Bisin et al.

this society, between groups with different propensities to act violently, favor or hinder the development of a legal system for the protection of *property rights.*[27]

A legal system for property right protection is the main policy variable in this society. Property rights reduce the incentives to engage in violent conflict at equilibrium and are therefore valuable in terms of efficiency. The dynamics of culture and institutions in this society display several complex features, including, notably, an interesting form of hysteresis. More specifically, societies where the more conflict-prone group is relatively small but powerful tend to rely on limited property rights protection. When however this group is relatively large, it develops enough incentives to devolve institutional power to the other group to build institutions for property right protection. The qualitative dynamics represented in the phase diagram display interesting patterns where a society with a powerful conflict-prone group in control of its institutional arrangement is up-rooted by cultural dynamics which, by leading to the expansion of the size of the conflict-prone group, trigger the formation of institutions favoring property rights protection.

More in detail, consider a society where couples of agents are matched randomly in contest. Each agent's endowment prior to the contest is $\omega > 0$. Property rights protection is represented by the fraction $p \in [0, 1]$ of each agent's endowment which is protected in the contest. After two agents match, their relative effort in the conflict determines the probability that each of them succeeds in the contest, hence winning the fraction of the endowment of the opponent which is not protected by property rights. More specifically, let a^{ij} denote the effort exerted by an agent of group i when matching with an agent of group j. The probability of agent i winning the contest is $\frac{a^{ij}}{a^{ij}+a^{ji}}$.[28] The winner of the contest appropriates of the fraction of the total endowment of the other agent which is not protected by property rights, $(1-p)\omega$.

We assume that there are two political groups $i \in \{1, 2\}$ which are fully identified to cultural groups. The two groups are culturally differentiated by their propensity to act into conflict: group 1 is more prone to violence. Formally, group 1 has cultural traits inducing, for a fixed initial cost $F > 0$, a higher propensity for violent action, i.e., a low marginal cost of effort in conflict, c^1.[29] Group 2 is instead composed of *conflict-averse,* agents, with a higher marginal cost of effort in conflict, $c^2 > c^1$. The size of "conflict-prone" agents is $q^1 = 1 - q^2 = q$.

Agents observe the opponent type before choosing their effort.[30] The Nash equilibrium effort of an agent of type i in his contest with an agent of type j, for given property rights p is

$$a^{ij}(p) = 2(1-p)\omega \frac{c^j}{\left(c^i + c^j\right)^2}.$$

(2020) for a model of religious legitimacy, where culture and institutions support either theocratic or secular states, providing an explanation the *Long Divergence* between Middle Eastern and Western European economies.

[27] See Nisbett (1993); Cohen and Nisbett (1994), and Grosjean (2014), for the study of societies where a *culture of honor* may breed violence in social interactions and is supported and transmitted because of weak institutions of property rights protection. The society we study has characteristics consistent also with various anthropological observations that suggest that cultures of violence are more likely to develop in pastoralist societies since property rights protection on cattle is more difficult to enforce than property rights on land in agrarian societies (see Campbell (1965); Edgerton (1971); Peristiany (1965)).

[28] Formally, this is the case if $a^{ij}, a^{ji} > 0$; while the probability of winning is $1/2$ if $a^{ij} = a^{ji} = 0$.

[29] Cost F could represent the cost of rituals and practices to develop a "culture of honor."

[30] That is, the contest is a complete information game. The expected payoff of an agent of cultural group i matching with an agent of group j is $W^i(a^{ij}, a^{ji}) = p\omega + 2(1-p)\omega \frac{a^{ij}}{a^{ji}+a^{ij}} - c^i a^{ij}$.

Matching is random, so that an agent in group i will match another agent in the same group with probability q^i and an agent in the other group with probability $1 - q^i$. Let the ex-ante expected payoff for agents of each of the groups at equilibrium be denoted $U^i(p, q)$. It is decreasing in q as a larger fraction of conflict-prone agents hurts both groups ex-ante. It induces a larger rent dissipation for the conflict-prone agents and a larger probability of extortion (loss of endowment) for the conflict averse agents. On the other hand, while $U^2(p, q)$ is always increasing in p, $U^1(p, q)$ is increasing in p only for a large enough fraction q. Indeed, conflict-averse agents always benefit from property rights protection, while conflict-prone agents gain as a consequence of better property rights protection only when their fraction in the population is large enough. Finally, assume that implementing a level p of property rights protection requires a resource cost $C(p)$ satisfying standard convexity properties.

Denote by $\beta^1 = 1 - \beta^2 = \beta$, the institutional weight of the conflict prone group. Consider first the equilibrium outcome of the societal policy game between the agents and a public authority that chooses the degree of property rights protection, taking as given the effort choices in conflict of the agents of the two groups, a^{ij}.[31] When $\beta \geq q$, *this societal equilibrium* involves no property right protection and therefore $p^*(\beta, q) = 0$. For $\beta < q$, instead, $p = p^*(\beta, q) > 0$. Moreover, $p^*(\beta, q)$ is decreasing in β and increasing in q. The larger the weight of the "conflict prone" group, the smaller the level of property rights protection, as such group benefits less from this protection. On the other hand, the larger the fraction of the conflict prone agents in society, the larger the social welfare from a reduction of conflict effort dissipated into contests.

Institutional dynamics. Modeling institutional change in this society along the lines of theoretical constructs in Section 17.2, we postulate that the dynamics of the political weight of the conflict-prone group β_t, for given q, $\beta_{t+1} = \Theta(\beta_t, q)$, is determined as the solution of the following program:

$$\beta_{t+1} = \arg \max_{\beta \in [0,1]} \beta_t V_1(\beta, q) + (1 - \beta_t) V_2(\beta, q) \tag{17.8}$$

where $V_i(\beta, q) = U^i(p^*(\beta, q), q)$ are the societal equilibrium expected payoffs of members of group i. The resulting dynamics can be formally and intuitively represented with the help of the function $p^{com}(\beta, q)$ defined as the solution of the optimal choice of property rights protection a public authority with weight β would want to implement if it could fully internalize the impact of such choice on the agents equilibrium actions $a^{ij}(p)$:

$$p^{com}(\beta, q) = \arg \max_{p \in [0,1]} \beta U_1^1(p, q) + (1 - \beta) U^2(p, q). \tag{17.9}$$

In fact, the dynamics of β_{t+1} induced by (17.8) can be written in terms of $p^{com}(\beta, q)$ and the equilibrium policy function $p^*(\beta, q)$ in the following way:

$$\beta_{t+1} = \begin{cases} \beta \text{ such that } p^{com}(\beta_t, q) = p^*(\beta, q) & \text{if it exists} \\ \begin{bmatrix} 1 & \text{if } p^{com}(\beta_t, q) > p^*(\beta, q), \ \forall 0 \leq \beta \leq 1 \\ 0 & \text{if } p^{com}(\beta_t, q) < p^*(\beta, q), \ \forall 0 \leq \beta \leq 1 \end{bmatrix} & \text{else} \end{cases} .$$

---

[31] See the Appendix for detailed calculations.

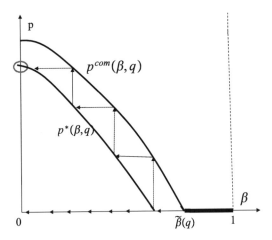

FIGURE 17.4

Property rights and conflicts. Institutional dynamics.

Intuitively, institutional change is driven by the difference between the equilibrium protection of property rights $p^*(\beta, q)$ and the normative protection level $p^{com}(\beta, q)$, which internalizes the inefficient dissipation of effort in conflict. Indeed, $p^*(\beta, q) \leq p^{com}(\beta, q)$ since at the societal equilibrium the public authority does not provide the efficient (higher) level of property rights protection: see Fig. 17.4, the phase diagram summarizing the dynamics of institutions.[32] For any given q, i) if $\beta_0 > \tilde{\beta}(q)$, then $\beta_{t+1} = \beta_t = \beta_0$ and there is no institutional change; ii) if instead $\beta_0 < \tilde{\beta}(q)$, then β_t converges towards $\beta = 0$, namely full power to the conflict-averse group.

Cultural dynamics. Following Bisin and Verdier (2001), the cultural fitness function of each trait $i = 1, 2$ is increasing in the paternalistic incentives $\Delta V^i(\beta, q)$ to transmit that trait. Conflict-prone agents have positive incentives $\Delta V^1(\beta, q)$ to transmit their trait, but such incentives decrease with their fraction q in society. The incentives for conflict-averse agents, $\Delta V^2(\beta, q)$, are also positive. They are increasing with the fraction q of conflict-prone agents in the population.[33] As a consequence, the cultural dynamics has a unique interior stationary state $q(\beta)$, which is increasing in the weight of the "conflict-prone" group β. Property rights protection affects negatively the socialization incentives of the conflict-prone and promotes on the opposite the socialization incentives of conflict-averse agents.

---

[32] See the Appendix for the characterization of the properties of $p^*(\beta, q)$ and $p^{com}(\beta, q)$. $p^{com}(\beta, q) = 0$ when $q < \tilde{q}(\alpha)$ and $\beta \geq \tilde{\beta}(q)$, with $\tilde{q}(\alpha) \in]0, 1[$ and $\tilde{\beta}(q) \in [0, 1]$ an increasing function of q. Furthermore, $\tilde{\beta}(q)$ is increasing in q and satisfies $\tilde{\beta}(0) < 1$ and $\tilde{\beta}(q) = 1$ for $q < 1$ large enough. Conversely $p^{com}(\beta, q) > 0$ when β, q do not satisfy such relations. In such a case, $p^{com}(\beta, q)$ is as well decreasing in β and is increasing in q.

[33] A larger value of q in fact has two opposing effects on the incentive to socialization of conflict-averse agents: it reduces their expected payoff when matched with conflict-prone agents, thereby reducing their incentives to transmit their own trait; but at the same time, a larger q also increases the cost of effort for conflict-averse agents whose children turn out to be conflict-prone and undertake effort a^{11} when facing other conflict-prone agents in a contest. It turns out that this last effect dominates.

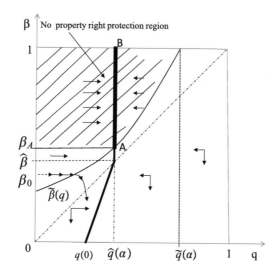

FIGURE 17.5

Property rights and conflicts. Joint dynamics ($\alpha = \frac{c_2}{c_1} - 1$ large enough).

Joint dynamics of culture and institutions. The joint dynamics of culture and institutions is summarized by the phase diagram in the space $(\beta, q) \in [0, 1]^2$ in Fig. 17.5.[34] When initial conditions (β_0, q_0) are in the highlighted region in the figure and the conflict-prone group is powerful but relatively small, there are no institutional dynamics, no protection of property rights and a diffusion of the cultural traits of the conflict-prone group towards a long run value $\widehat{q}(\alpha)$. On the other hand, outside of this region of initial conditions the institutional dynamics evolve towards increasing the political power of the conflict-averse group, inducing more protection of property rights. Indeed the system converges towards an institutional set-up giving no power to the conflict-prone group ($\beta = 0$). In this case, $p^*(\beta, q) > 0$ along the equilibrium path and the interaction of the dynamics of institutions and culture leads progressively towards a reduction of the size of the conflict-prone group and in turn a reduction of the resources spent in conflict.

Interestingly, when the conflict-prone is initially at some intermediate degree of political power, i.e., such that $\beta_0 \in [\widetilde{\beta}(q_0), \beta_A]$, even a small fraction of conflict-prone individuals in society can be ultimately self-defeating in terms of institutional dynamics. While the system does not exhibit any institutional change, in this case, the underlying cultural dynamics tend to favor the socialization of the conflict-prone agents towards $\widehat{q}(\alpha)$. As soon as q_t passes the threshold of $\widetilde{\beta}^{-1}(\beta_0)$, endogenous institutional dynamics are triggered which induce the implementation of more extensive property rights

---

[34] We consider for simplicity the case in which $\frac{c^2 - c^1}{c^1}$ is large enough, so that conflict-prone agents have a significant advantage in conflict. When instead the marginal effort costs c^i are similar across groups property rights are protected for any initial conditions. The joint dynamics of culture and institutions converge to a stationary state characterized by institutions giving all power to the conflict-averse group, supporting a maximal level of protection of property rights.

and institutions biased in favor of the conflict-averse group. As a consequence, q_t regresses towards the long run steady state $q(0)$ and the conflict-prone group ends-up with no power ($\beta = 0$).

Similar non-monotonic dynamics of culture and institutions in this society may manifest themselves also as interesting forms of hysteresis after an exogenous institutional shock. Indeed a temporary shock giving more political power to the conflict-averse group might irreversibly take the system into a new long run trajectory of the institutional and cultural dynamics. Suppose for instance that the society has settled to a point like point A in Fig. 17.5 with no property rights and $\widehat{q}(\alpha)$. A political power shock, e.g., reducing β below β_A, would induce an endogenous institutional response conceding further power to the conflict-averse group. This in turn would trigger a complementary reinforcing cultural dynamics favoring this group. A successive opposite institutional shock of similar amplitude would not bring back the system towards to region with no property right protection. Indeed even when/if the conflict-prone group regains some formal power, the cultural dynamics might have irreversibly driven the system into a region of the phase diagram where property rights are protected.

This example illustrates the importance of initial institutional and cultural conditions for the long run of society and the non-ergodicity properties of this system. It suggests that external interventions that change the balance of power domestically between groups may have long term effects in terms of institutional and cultural evolution.

17.5 **Conclusions**

Motivated by a rich rapidly expanding economic and historical literature studying institutional and cultural change, this chapter emphasized the role of explicit formal dynamic models in our understanding of socio-economic history. Coming back to the initial quote of Mc Closkey, systems of differential/difference equations are interesting frames useful to identify and organize historical narratives by means of simple phase diagrams between relevant historical state variables. In the context of the joint interactions of culture and institutions, this approach provides a simple and easily applicable analysis uncovering the nature and source of important feedback effects between these variables.

Indeed depending on whether culture and institutions are dynamic complements or substitutes, exogenous historical shocks propagating over the joint dynamics induced by institutions and culture may have magnified or mitigated effects on long-run socio-economic outcomes. Importantly, this type of analysis identifies the extent of the comparative dynamic bias that is generated by conditioning on one of the two dynamics, when the other one is affected by an exogenous shock (the *cultural and institutional multipliers*).

Again, consistently with Mc Closkey's view, this approach indicates that in general the joint evolution of culture and institutions has some highly non-linear components. This feature has a number of implications involving for instance the fact that the dynamics of culture and institutions are prone to display sensitivity of equilibrium trajectories to initial conditions, existence of irreversibility and thresholds effects, and non-monotonicity of cultural and institutional changes over transition paths. From an empirical point of view, these phenomena appear quite consistent with the great diversity of development trajectories encountered across the world and in time. They also suggest that beyond standard causal identification strategies based on the use of specific instrumental variables or restricted natural experiments, focusing more structurally on the positive or negative interactions between prominent state variables such as institutions and culture along the development process might result more fruitful in terms of historical understanding, as well as in terms of policy implications.

17.6 Appendix Property rights and conflict

In this Appendix we report the detailed characterization of the equilibrium dynamics in the example on Property Rights in Section 17.4.

Equilibrium expected payoffs. Given random matching in contests, the expected payoffs of conflict-prone and conflict-averse agents are:

$$U^1(p,q) = p\omega + 2(1-p)\omega \left[\frac{q}{4} + (1-q)\left(\frac{c^2}{c^1 + c^2} \right)^2 \right] - F$$

$$U^2(p,q) = p\omega + 2(1-p)\omega \left[q\left(\frac{c^1}{c^1 + c^2} \right)^2 + \frac{(1-q)}{4} \right]$$

Letting $c^1 = c$ and $c^2 = c(1+\alpha)$ with $\alpha > 0$:

$$U^1(p,q) = p\omega + 2(1-p)\omega \left[\frac{q}{4} + (1-q)\left(\frac{1+\alpha}{2+\alpha} \right)^2 \right] - F \qquad (17.10)$$

$$U^2(p,q) = p\omega + 2(1-p)\omega \left[q\left(\frac{1}{2+\alpha} \right)^2 + \frac{(1-q)}{4} \right]$$

It readily follows that:

$U^1(p,q)$ is decreasing in q and

$$\frac{\partial U^1(p,q)}{\partial p} \geq 0 \text{ iff } q \geq \tilde{q}(\alpha) = \frac{\left(\frac{1+\alpha}{2+\alpha} \right)^2 - \frac{1}{2}}{\left(\frac{1+\alpha}{2+\alpha} \right)^2 - \frac{1}{4}};$$

$U^2(p,q)$ is decreasing in q and that

$$\frac{\partial U^2(p,q)}{\partial p} \geq 0.$$

Societal equilibrium. The expected payoffs of conflict-prone and conflict-averse agents in a *societal equilibrium* are given by:

$$G_1(p,q,a^{11},a^{12},a^{21}) = p\omega + q\left(2(1-p)\omega \frac{a^{11}}{a^{11} + a^{11}} - c^1 a^{11} \right)$$

$$+ (1-q)\left(2(1-p)\omega\frac{a^{12}}{a^{12}+a^{21}} - c^1 a^{12}\right) - F$$

$$G_2(p,q,a^{21},a^{12},a^{22}) = p\omega + q\left(2(1-p)\omega\frac{a^{21}}{a^{21}+a^{12}} - c^2 a^{21}\right)$$

$$+ (1-q)\left(2(1-p)\omega\frac{a^{22}}{a^{22}+a^{22}} - c^2 a^{22}\right)$$

where a^{ij} is the Nash equilibrium effort level exercised in a contest by an agent of type i matched with one of type j, for any $i, j \in \{1, 2\}$. It can be readily shown that the Nash equilibrium effort levels are:

$$a^{11} = \frac{2(1-p)\omega}{4c}, \quad a^{22} = \frac{2(1-p)\omega}{4c(1+\alpha)}, \quad a^{12} = 2(1-p)\omega\frac{1+\alpha}{c(2+\alpha)^2}, \quad a^{21} = 2(1-p)\omega\frac{1}{c(2+\alpha)^2}.$$
$$(17.11)$$

The public authority in the policy game chooses the level of property right protection p to solve the following problem[35]:

$$\max_{p\in[0,1]} \beta G_1(p,q,a^{11},a^{12},a^{21}) + (1-\beta)G_2(p,q,a^{21},a^{12},a^{22}) - C(p)$$

taking as given the values a^{ij}, for any $i, j \in \{1, 2\}$. The First Order Condition of this problem is:

$$\beta\omega\left[1 - 2\left(q\frac{a^{11}}{a^{11}+a^{11}} + (1-q)\frac{a^{12}}{a^{12}+a^{21}}\right)\right]$$
$$+ (1-\beta)\omega\left[1 - 2\left(q\frac{a^{21}}{a^{21}+a^{12}} + (1-q)\frac{a^{22}}{a^{22}+a^{22}}\right)\right]$$
$$= C'(p)$$

At equilibrium, the level of property right protection p^* is then characterized by the following condition:

$$\beta\omega\left[1 - 2\left(\frac{q}{2} + (1-q)\frac{1+\alpha}{2+\alpha}\right)\right] + (1-\beta)\omega\left[1 - 2\left(q\frac{1}{2+\alpha} + \frac{(1-q)}{2}\right)\right] = C'(p). \quad (17.12)$$

As a consequence, we obtain the following characterization:

When $\beta < q$, the societal equilibrium policy outcome involves strictly positive protection of property right with $p^*(\beta,q) > 0$. Moreover $p^*(\beta,q)$ is decreasing in β and increasing in q. When $\beta \geq q$, there is no property right protection in the societal equilibrium (i.e., $p^*(\beta,q) = 0$).

---

[35] We assume for regularity that the property rights cost function $C(p)$ is increasing and convex, i.e., $C'(p) \geq 0$, $C''(p) > 0$; and that it satisfies $C(0) = C'(0) = 0$, and $C'(1) = +\infty$.

Institutional dynamics. The dynamics of the political weight of the conflict-prone group β_t, evolves according to the solution of the following program:

$$\beta_{t+1} = \arg\max_{\beta \in [0,1]} \beta_t V_1(\beta, q) + (1 - \beta_t)V_2(\beta, q) \tag{17.13}$$

where $V_i(\beta, q) = U^i(p^*(\beta, q), q)$ are the societal equilibrium expected payoffs of members of group i. As in the text, in Section 17.4, consider the following auxiliary policy problem:

$$\max_{p \in [0,1]} W(p, q, \beta) = \beta U^1(p, q) + (1 - \beta)U^2(p, q) \tag{17.14}$$

Under the convexity assumption in Footnote 35, problem (17.14) has a unique solution. Using the expressions of $U^i(p, q)$ from (17.10), the solution p^{com} of this problem satisfies the following First Order Condition[36]:

$$\beta\omega\left[1 - 2\left(\frac{q}{4} + (1-q)\left(\frac{1+\alpha}{2+\alpha}\right)^2\right)\right] + (1-\beta)\omega\left[1 - 2\left(q\left(\frac{1}{2+\alpha}\right)^2 + \frac{(1-q)}{4}\right)\right] = C'(p^{com}). \tag{17.15}$$

We obtain the following characterization, which we prove next:

If $1/\sqrt{2} < \phi(\alpha) = \phi(\alpha) = \frac{1+\alpha}{2+\alpha}$,

i) *there exist a threshold $\tilde{q}(\alpha) \in]0, 1[$ and an increasing function $\beta = \tilde{\beta}(q)$ with $\tilde{\beta}(0) < 1$ such that $p^{com}(\beta, q) = 0$ if and only if $(\beta, q) \in [0, 1]^2$ are such that $q < \tilde{q}(\alpha)$ and $\beta \geq \tilde{\beta}(q)$.*
ii) *When $p^{com}(\beta, q) > 0$, then it is decreasing in β and increasing in q.*
iii) *One has $p^*(\beta, q) \leq p^{com}(\beta, q)$.*

Proof. To prove i) note that the First Order Condition of problem (17.14) implies that

$$p^{com}(\beta, q) = 0 \quad \text{when} \quad \beta \geq \tilde{\beta}(q) = \frac{\frac{1}{4} + q\left[\frac{1}{4} - (1 - \phi(\alpha))^2\right]}{q\left[\frac{1}{4} - (1 - \phi(\alpha))^2\right] + (1-q)\left[\phi(\alpha)^2 - \frac{1}{4}\right]}$$

with $\tilde{\beta}(q) > q$ for all $q \in [0, 1]$ and $\phi(\alpha) = \frac{1+\alpha}{2+\alpha}$, an increasing function of α. Notice as well that for all $\alpha > 0$, one has

$$\frac{1}{4} - (1 - \phi(\alpha))^2 > 0 \text{ and } \phi(\alpha)^2 + (1 - \phi(\alpha))^2 > \frac{1}{2}.$$

Moreover $\tilde{\beta}(q) = 1$ at $\tilde{q}(\alpha) \in (0, 1)$ given by

$$\tilde{q}(\alpha) = \frac{\phi(\alpha)^2 - \frac{1}{2}}{\phi(\alpha)^2 - \frac{1}{4}}.$$

---

[36] We assume the solution is interior.

Hence it follows that a $p^{com}(\beta, q) = 0$ if and only if

$$\frac{1}{\sqrt{2}} < \phi(\alpha) \quad \text{and} \quad q < \tilde{q}(\alpha).$$

It is also immediate to see that $\tilde{\beta}(q)$ is increasing in q with

$$\tilde{\beta}(0) = \frac{\frac{1}{4}}{\left[\phi(\alpha)^2 - \frac{1}{4}\right]} \quad \text{and} \quad \tilde{\beta}(1) > 1.$$

To prove ii) note that, by differentiating the First Order Condition of problem (17.14), it follows that the (assumed interior) solution $p^{com}(\beta, q) > 0$ satisfies:

$$\frac{\partial p^{com}}{\partial \beta} < 0 \quad \text{and} \quad \frac{\partial p^{com}}{\partial q} > 0.$$

To show iii), i.e., that $p^*(\beta, q) \le p^{com}(\beta, q)$, consider the difference of the Left-Hand-Side of the two Eqs. (17.15) and (17.12):

$$\beta\omega\left[1 - 2\left(\frac{q}{4} + (1-q)\left(\frac{1+\alpha}{2+\alpha}\right)^2\right)\right] + (1-\beta)\omega\left[1 - 2\left(q\left(\frac{1}{2+\alpha}\right)^2 + \frac{(1-q)}{4}\right)\right]$$
$$- \beta\omega\left[1 - 2\left(\frac{q}{2} + (1-q)\frac{1+\alpha}{2+\alpha}\right)\right] - (1-\beta)\omega\left[1 - 2\left(q\frac{1}{2+\alpha} + \frac{(1-q)}{2}\right)\right].$$

This difference can be written as:

$$2\beta\omega\left[\frac{q}{2} + (1-q)\frac{1+\alpha}{2+\alpha} - \left(\frac{q}{4} + (1-q)\left(\frac{1+\alpha}{2+\alpha}\right)^2\right)\right]$$
$$+ 2(1-\beta)\omega\left[\left(q\frac{1}{2+\alpha} + \frac{(1-q)}{2}\right) - \left(q\left(\frac{1}{2+\alpha}\right)^2 + \frac{(1-q)}{4}\right)\right];$$

and finally, as:

$$2\beta\omega\left[\frac{q}{4} + (1-q)\frac{1+\alpha}{(2+\alpha)^2}\right] + 2(1-\beta)\omega\left[q\frac{1+\alpha}{(2+\alpha)^2} + \frac{(1-q)}{4}\right] > 0$$

Hence $C'(p^{com}) > C'(p^*)$ and the result $p^*(\beta, q) < p^{com}(\beta, q)$ follow. Obviously, for $\beta > \tilde{\beta}(q)$, $p^*(\beta, q) = p^{com}(\beta, q) = 0$. ∎

Consider β_t. The solution $p^{com}(\beta_t, q)$ of problem (17.14) reflects the optimal choice of property right protection p a public authority with weights $(\beta_t, 1 - \beta_t)$ wants to implement when it fully internalizes the impact of such choice on the agents equilibrium actions $a^{ij}(p)$. The resulting effort levels in conflict $[a^{ij}(p^{com}(\beta_t, q))]_{i,j\in\{1,2\}}$ are therefore associated to the maximal social outcome from the point of view of this public authority, using a policy of protection of property rights $p \in [0, 1]$. The public authority designs an institutional structure $\beta \in [0, 1]$ such that this preferred outcome is implemented (when reachable) as an equilibrium outcome $\left[a^{ij}\left(p^*(\beta, q)\right)\right]_{i,j \in \{1,2\}}$ of a feasible societal equilibrium with institutional weights $(\beta, 1 - \beta)$.

Three cases may happen:

- There exists $\beta \in [0, 1]$ is such that $p^*(\beta, q) = p^{com}(\beta_t, q)$. In such a case, the solution of problem (17.13) is to set $\beta_{t+1} = \beta$. Indeed, a societal policy game with a public authority with weights $(\beta, 1 - \beta)$ generates the best possible equilibrium allocation from the point of view of the public authority with weights $(\beta_t, 1 - \beta_t)$.
- For all $\beta \in [0, 1]$ $p^*(\beta, q) < p^{com}(\beta_t, q)$. In such a case, then the fact that $p^*(\beta, q)$ is decreasing in β and the concavity of $W(p, q, \beta_t)$ with respect to p, ensures that the best implementable policy that can be reached from the point of view of the public authority with weights $(\beta_t, 1 - \beta_t)$ is obtained when $p^*(\beta, q)$ is as close as possible to $p^{com}(\beta_t, q)$, namely when $\beta_{t+1} = 0$. This ensures that the equilibrium societal policy game with a public authority with weights $(0, 1)$ generates the best possible equilibrium allocation from the point of view of the public authority with weights $(\beta_t, 1 - \beta_t)$.
- For all $\beta \in [0, 1]$ $p^*(\beta, q) > p^{com}(\beta_t, q)$. This case is symmetric to case ii). By the same reasoning setting $\beta_{t+1} = 1$ ensures that the equilibrium societal policy game with a public authority with weights $(1, 0)$ generates the best possible equilibrium allocation from the point of view of the public authority with weights $(\beta_t, 1 - \beta_t)$.

As a conclusion, the solution of problem (17.13) is given by:

$$
\beta_{t+1} = \begin{cases} \beta \text{ such that } p^{com}(\beta_t, q) = p^*(\beta, q) & \text{if it exists} \\ \begin{bmatrix} 1 & \text{if } p^{com}(\beta_t, q) > p^*(\beta, q), \forall 0 \le \beta \le 1 \\ 0 & \text{if } p^{com}(\beta_t, q) < p^*(\beta, q), \forall 0 \le \beta \le 1 \end{bmatrix} & \text{else} \end{cases}.
$$

Cultural dynamics. We adopt the economic cultural transmission model of Bisin and Verdier (2000a, 2000b, 2001). Cultural transmission is modeled as the result of *direct vertical* (parental) socialization and *horizontal/oblique socialization* in society at large. Denote the cultural state of the population by $q^1 = 1 - q^2 = q$:

i) direct vertical socialization to the parent's trait $i \in I = \{1, 2\}$ occurs with probability d^i;

ii) if a child from a family with trait i is not directly socialized, which occurs with probability $1 - d^i$, he/she is horizontally/obliquely socialized by picking the trait of a role model chosen randomly in the population inside the political group (i.e., he/she picks trait i with probability q^i and trait $i' \neq i$ with probability $q^{i'}$.

Let $P^{ii'}$ denote the probability that a child, in (a family in) group $i \in I$, is socialized to trait i'. From i) and ii) above, we obtain:

$$
P^{ii'} = d^i + (1 - d^i)q^{i'}. \tag{17.16}
$$

Let $V^{ii'}(p,q)$ denote the utility to a cultural trait i parent of a type i' child when the policy p is implemented and the state of the cultural population is q. Let $C(d^i)$ denote socialization costs.[37] Direct socialization, for any $i \in I = \{1, 2\}$, is then the solution to the following parental socialization problem:

$$\max_{d^i \in [0,1]} -C(d^i) + \sum_{i' \in I} P^{ii'} V^{ii'}(p,q), \text{ s. t. (17.16).}$$

As usual in this literature, define $\Delta V^i(p,q) = V^{ii}(p,q) - V^{ii'}(p,q)$ as the paternalistic motive to transmit trait i. It follows that the direct socialization, with some notational abuse, has the form:

$$d^i(p,q) = (1 - q^i)\Delta V^i(p,q) \, i \in I = \{1, 2\}. \tag{17.17}$$

The dynamics of culture $q_t^1 = 1 - q_t^2 = q_t$ is then governed by the following difference equation:

$$q_{t+1} - q_t = q_t(1 - q_t)\left[d^1(p, q_t) - d^2(p, q_t) \right];$$

Evaluated at the societal equilibrium policy $p = p^*(\beta_t, q_t)$, the dynamic equation becomes:

$$q_{t+1} - q_t = q_t(1 - q_t)S(\beta_t, q_t); \tag{17.18}$$

where $S(\beta_t, q_t)$ is the relative cultural fitness of trait 1:

$$S(\beta, q) = d^1(p^*(\beta, q), q) - d^2(p^*(\beta, q), q)$$
$$= (1 - q)\Delta V^1(p^*(\beta, q), q) - q\Delta V^2(p^*(\beta, q), q).$$

In the specific case of our example, the socialization incentives $\Delta V^1(p, q)$ of conflict-prone agents are readily obtained:

$$\Delta V^1(p,q) = q\left(2(1 - p)\frac{\omega}{2} - c^1 a^{11}\right) + (1 - q)\left(2(1 - p)\omega\frac{1 + \alpha}{2 + \alpha} - c^1 a^{12}\right) - F$$
$$- \left[q\left(2(1 - p)\omega\frac{1}{2 + \alpha} - c^1 a^{21}\right) + (1 - q)\left(2(1 - p)\frac{\omega}{2} - c^1 a^{22}\right)\right].$$

After substitution of the Nash equilibrium a^{ij}, for all $i, j \in \{1, 2\}$ from Eq. (17.11), these socialization incentives become:

$$\Delta V^1 = 2(1 - p)\omega\left[q\left(\frac{1}{4}\right) + (1 - q)\left(\frac{1 + \alpha}{2 + \alpha}\right)^2\right] - F$$
$$- 2(1 - p)\omega\left[q\frac{1 + \alpha}{(2 + \alpha)^2} + (1 - q)\frac{1 + 2\alpha}{4(1 + \alpha)}\right]$$

---

[37] We assume for simplicity and convenience that socialization costs are quadratic, $C(d^i) = \frac{1}{2}\left(d^i\right)^2$.

$$= 2(1-p)\omega\left[q\left(\frac{1}{4}-\frac{1+\alpha}{(2+\alpha)^2}\right)+(1-q)\left(\left(\frac{1+\alpha}{2+\alpha}\right)^2-\frac{1+2\alpha}{4(1+\alpha)}\right)\right]-F$$

$$= \frac{2(1-p)\omega\alpha^2}{4(1+\alpha)(2+\alpha)^2}[(3+\alpha)-q(2+\alpha)]-F$$

Similar calculations for the conflict-averse agents produce the following expression for socialization incentives:

$$\Delta V^2 = 2(1-p)\omega\left[q\frac{1}{(2+\alpha)^2}+(1-q)\frac{1}{4}\right]$$

$$-2(1-p)\omega\left[q\left(\frac{1}{2}-(1+\alpha)\frac{1}{4}\right)+(1-q)\frac{1+\alpha}{(2+\alpha)^2}\right]+F$$

$$= 2(1-p)\omega\left[q\frac{\alpha^2}{4(2+\alpha)}+\frac{\alpha^2}{4(2+\alpha)^2}\right]+F>0$$

The locus $q_{t+1}=q_t$ of stationary culture is then obtained from (17.18), as the set of points $(\beta,q)\in[0,1]^2$ such that

$$\frac{\Delta V^1(p^*(\beta,q),q)}{\Delta V^2(p^*(\beta,q),q)}=\frac{q}{1-q}. \tag{17.19}$$

After straightforward computations, we obtain

$$\frac{\Delta V^1(p,q)}{\Delta V^2(p,q)}=\frac{\frac{1}{(1+\alpha)}[(2+\alpha)(1-q)+1]-\frac{2F(2+\alpha)^2}{(1-p)\omega\alpha^2}}{q(2+\alpha)+1+\frac{2F(2+\alpha)^2}{(1-p)\omega\alpha^2}}=\Phi(q,p,\alpha).$$

It follows that $\Phi(q,p,\alpha)$ is a decreasing function of p and q.[38] The characterization of the interior cultural steady state is obtained from (17.19):

$$\Phi(q,p^*(\beta,q),\alpha)=\frac{q}{1-q}. \tag{17.21}$$

The Left-Hand-Side of Eq. (17.21) is a decreasing function of q. In fact, $\Phi(q,p,\alpha)$ is decreasing in q; $p^*(\beta,q)$ is increasing in q; and $\Phi(q,p,\alpha)$ is decreasing in p. The Right-Hand-Side of (17.21) is increasing in q and goes from 0 to ∞ when q goes from 0 to 1. Hence, since $\Phi(0,p^*(\beta,0),\alpha)>0$ by (17.20), it follows that Eq. (17.21) has a unique solution $q=q(\beta)$ and $q(\beta)<1/2$. Moreover $q(\beta)$

---

[38] We assume that F/ω is small enough,

$$\frac{F}{\omega}<\frac{(1-p(0,0))}{2(1+\alpha)}\left(\frac{\alpha}{2+\alpha}\right)^2[3+\alpha], \tag{17.20}$$

to ensure that for all $(\beta,q)\in[0,1]^2$, one has $\Delta V^1/\Delta V^2$ to be strictly positive. Otherwise we could get a cultural steady state without conflict-prone individuals.

is an increasing function of β. Finally there is a unique value $\widehat{\beta}(\alpha)$ such that $q(\beta) = \beta$. Indeed such β is determined by

$$\Phi\left(\beta, p^*(\beta, \beta), \alpha\right) = \Phi(\beta, 0, \alpha) = \frac{\beta}{1 - \beta};$$

or after substitution

$$\frac{1 - \beta}{(1 + \alpha)}[(2 + \alpha)(1 - \beta) + 1] - \beta(\beta(2 + \alpha) + 1) = \frac{2F(2 + \alpha)^2}{\omega\alpha^2}. \tag{17.22}$$

Denote the Left-Hand-Side of (17.22) as a function $\Sigma(\beta, \alpha)$. Simple differentiation shows that $\Sigma(\beta, \alpha)$ is decreasing in β and takes value $\Sigma(0, \alpha) = \frac{4+\alpha}{1+\alpha} > 0$ and $\Sigma(1, \alpha) = -((2+\alpha)+1) < 0$. Therefore, (17.20) implies

$$\frac{2F(2 + \alpha)^2}{\omega\alpha^2} < \frac{(1 - p(0,0))}{(1 + \alpha)}[3 + \alpha] < \frac{4 + \alpha}{1 + \alpha} = \Sigma(0).$$

We conclude that there exists a unique value $\widehat{\beta}(\alpha) \in (0, 1)$ satisfying (17.22); and there exists a corresponding unique value $\widehat{q}(\alpha) = q(\widehat{\beta}(\alpha))$.

Joint dynamics of culture and institutions. We can show the following result, which we prove next,

The dynamics of culture and institutions represented in the phase diagram in Fig. 17.5 holds for $\alpha = \frac{c^2}{c^1} - 1$ large enough.

Proof. Recall that $\widetilde{\beta}(q) = 1$ at a value $\widetilde{q}(\alpha) \in (0, 1)$ given by

$$\widetilde{q}(\alpha) = \frac{\phi(\alpha)^2 - \frac{1}{2}}{\phi(\alpha)^2 - \frac{1}{4}},$$

with $\phi(\alpha) = \frac{1+\alpha}{2+\alpha}$. Consider then

$$\Sigma(\widetilde{q}(\alpha), \alpha) = \frac{1 - \widetilde{q}(\alpha)}{(1 + \alpha)}[(2 + \alpha)(1 - \widetilde{q}(\alpha)) + 1] - \widetilde{q}(\alpha)(\widetilde{q}(\alpha)(2 + \alpha) + 1).$$

Recall that $\widetilde{q}(\alpha_{\min}) = 0$ and $\lim_{\alpha \to \infty} \widetilde{q}(\alpha) = \frac{2}{3}$, for $\alpha_{\min} = \frac{2-\sqrt{2}}{(\sqrt{2}-1)}$. It then follows that

$$\Sigma(\widetilde{q}(\alpha_{\min}), \alpha_{\min})) = \frac{(3 + \alpha_{\min})}{(1 + \alpha_{\min})} > \frac{(1 - p^*(0,0))}{(1 + \alpha_{\min})}[3 + \alpha_{\min}] > \frac{2F(2 + \alpha_{\min})^2}{\omega\alpha_{\min}^2};$$

and therefore that $\widetilde{q}(\alpha_{\min}) < \widehat{\beta}(\alpha_{\min}) = \widehat{q}(\alpha_{\min})$. Clearly, this also holds for α close enough to $\alpha_{\min}$, by continuity. Similarly

$$\lim_{\alpha \to \infty}\left[\Sigma(\widetilde{q}(\alpha), \alpha) - \frac{2F(2 + \alpha)^2}{\omega\alpha^2}\right] = \lim_{\alpha \to \infty}\Sigma(\widetilde{q}(\alpha), \alpha) - \frac{2F}{\omega} = -\infty.$$

Thus, for α large enough,

$$\Sigma\left(\widetilde{q}(\alpha),\alpha\right) < 0 < \frac{2F(2+\alpha)^2}{\omega\alpha^2} = \Sigma\left(\widehat{q}(\alpha),\alpha\right);$$

and therefore $\widehat{q}(\alpha) < \widetilde{q}(\alpha)$. ∎

References

Acemoglu, D., 2003. Why not a political Coase theorem? Social conflict, commitment, and politics. Journal of Comparative Economics 31, 620–652.

Acemoglu, D., Egorov, G., Sonin, K., 2010. Political selection and persistence of bad governments. The Quarterly Journal of Economics 125 (4), 1511–1575.

Acemoglu, D., Egorov, G., Sonin, K., 2012. Dynamics and stability of constitutions, coalitions, and clubs. The American Economic Review 102 (4), 1446–1476.

Acemoglu, D., Egorov, G., Sonin, K., 2015. Political economy in a changing world. Journal of Political Economy 123 (5), 1038–1086.

Acemoglu, D., Egorov, G., Sonin, K., 2018. Social mobility and stability of democracy: reevaluating de Tocqueville. The Quarterly Journal of Economics 133 (2), 1041–1105.

Acemoglu, D., Egorov, G., Sonin, K., 2021. Institutional change and institutional persistence. In: Bisin, A., Federico, G. (Eds.), The Handbook of Historical Economics. Elsevier. Chapter 13 (in this book).

Acemoglu, D., Johnson, S., Robinson, J.A., 2002. Reversal of fortune: geography and institutions in the making of the modern world income distribution. The Quarterly Journal of Economics 118, 1231–1294.

Acemoglu, D., Johnson, S., Robinson, J.A., 2006. Institutions as the fundamental cause of long-run growth. In: Aghion, P., Durlauf, S. (Eds.), Handbook of Economic Growth. Elsevier, Amsterdam.

Acemoglu, D., Robinson, J.A., 2000. Why did the West extend the franchise? Democracy, inequality, and growth in historical perspective. The Quarterly Journal of Economics 115 (4), 1167–1199.

Acemoglu, D., Robinson, J.A., 2001. A theory of political transitions. The American Economic Review 91 (4), 938–963.

Acemoglu, D., Robinson, J.A., 2005. The rise of Europe: Atlantic trade, institutional change, and economic growth. The American Economic Review 95 (3), 546–579.

Acemoglu, D., Robinson, J.A., 2006a. Economic backwardness in political perspective. American Political Science Review 100 (1), 105.

Acemoglu, D., Robinson, J.A., 2006b. Economic Origins of Dictatorship and Democracy. Cambridge University Press, Cambridge.

Acemoglu, D., Robinson, J.A., 2008. Persistence of power, elites, and institutions. The American Economic Review 98 (1), 267–293.

Acemoglu, D., Robinson, J.A., 2012. Why Nations Fail. Crown Publishers, New York.

Aghion, P., Algan, Y., Cahuc, P., Shleifer, A., 2010. Regulation and distrust. The Quarterly Journal of Economics 125 (3), 1015–1049.

Alesina, A., Giuliano, P., 2015. Culture and institutions. Journal of Economic Literature 53 (4), 898–944.

Alesina, A., Giuliano, P., Nunn, N., 2013. On the origins of gender roles: women and the plough. The Quarterly Journal of Economics 128 (2), 469–530.

Angelucci, C., Meraglia, S., Voigtlander, N., 2017. The Medieval Roots of Inclusive Institutions: from the Norman Conquest of England to the Great Reform Act. NBER WP 23606.

Aron, R., 1950a. Social structure and the ruling class: part 1. The British Journal of Sociology 1 (1), 1–16.

Aron, R., 1950b. Social structure and the ruling class: part 2. The British Journal of Sociology 1 (2), 126–143.

Ashraf, Q., Ozak, O., Galor, O., 2010. Isolation and development. Journal of the European Economic Association 8 (2-3), 401–412.

Balibar, E., 1970. Fundamental concepts of historical materialism. In: Althusser, L., Balibar, E. (Eds.), Reading Capital. Pantheon Books, New York.

Bates, R., Lien, D.-H.D., 1985. A note on taxation, development and representative government. Politics & Society 14, 53–70.

Benabou, R., Ticchi, D., Vindigni, A., 2015. Religion and innovation. The American Economic Review 105 (5), 346–351.

Besley, T., 2016. Aspirations and the political economy of inequality. Oxford Economic Papers 69 (1), 1–35.

Besley, T., 2020. State capacity, reciprocity, and the social contract. Econometrica 88 (4), 1307–1335.

Besley, T. Ghatak, M., 2017. The Evolution of Motivation. London School of Economics. Mimeo.

Besley, T., Persson, T., 2009a. The origins of state capacity: property rights, taxation, and politics. The American Economic Review 99 (4), 1218–1244.

Besley, T., Persson, T., 2009b. Repression or civil war? The American Economic Review 99 (2), 292–297.

Besley, T., Persson, T., 2010. State capacity, conflict and development. Econometrica 78 (1), 1–34.

Besley, T., Persson, T., 2011. Pillars of Prosperity: The Political Economics of Development Clusters. Princeton University Press, Princeton.

Besley, T., Persson, T., 2019. Democratic values and institutions. American Economic Review: Insights 1 (1), 59–76.

Besley, T., Persson, T., 2020. The Joint Dynamics of Organizational Culture, Design, and Performance. LSE. Mimeo.

Bidner, C., Francois, P., 2011. Cultivating trust: norms, institutions and the implications of scale. Economic Journal 121 (555), 1097–1129, 09.

Bidner, C., Francois, P., 2013. The emergence of political accountability. The Quarterly Journal of Economics 128 (3), 1397–1448.

Bisin, A., 2020. A comment on: State capacity, reciprocity, and the social contract, by Timothy Besley. Econometrica 88 (4), 1345–1349.

Bisin, A., Rubin, J., Seror, A., Verdier, T., 2020. Culture, Institutions & the Long Divergence. PSE. Mimeo.

Bisin, A., Moro, A., 2021. LATE for history. In: Bisin, A., Federico, G. (Eds.), The Handbook of Historical Economics. Elsevier. Chapter 10 (in this book).

Bisin, A., Verdier, T., 2000a. Beyond the melting pot: cultural transmission, marriage and the evolution of ethnic and religious traits. The Quarterly Journal of Economics 115, 955–988.

Bisin, A., Verdier, T., 2000b. Models of cultural transmission, voting and political ideology. European Journal of Political Economy 16, 5–29.

Bisin, A., Verdier, T., 2001. The economics of cultural transmission and the dynamics of preferences. Journal of Economic Theory 97, 298–319.

Bisin, A., Verdier, T., 2004. Work Ethic and Redistribution: A Cultural Transmission Model of the Welfare State. NYU. Mimeo.

Bisin, A., Verdier, T., 2010. The economics of cultural transmission. In: Benhabib, J., Bisin, A., Jackson, M. (Eds.), Handbook of Social Economics. Elsevier, Amsterdam.

Bisin, A., Verdier, T., 2017. On the Joint Evolution of Culture and Institutions. NBER WP 23375.

Bowles, S., Choi, J.-K., 2019. The neolithic agricultural revolution and the origins of private property. Journal of Political Economy 127 (5), 2186–2228.

Bowles, S., Choi, J.-K., Hwang, S.-H., Naidu, S., 2021. How institutions and cultures change: an evolutionary perspective. In: Bisin, A., Federico, G. (Eds.), The Handbook of Historical Economics. Elsevier. Chapter 14 (in this book).

Boyd, R., Richerson, P., 1985. Culture and the Evolutionary Process. University of Chicago Press, Chicago, IL.

Campbell, J.K., 1965. Honour and the Devil. In: Peristiany, J.G. (Ed.), Honour and Shame: The Values of Mediterranean Society. Weidenfeld & Nicolson, London, pp. 112–175.

Carvalho, J.P., Dippel, C., 2016. Elite Identity and Political Accountability: A Tale of Ten Islands. NBER Working Paper 22777.

Cavalli Sforza, L.L., Feldman, M., 1981. Cultural Transmission and Evolution: A Quantitative Approach. Princeton University Press, Princeton, NJ.

Chittolini, G. (Ed.), 1979. La Crisi degli Ordinamenti Comunali e le Origini dello Stato del Rinascimento. Bologna, Il Mulino.

Cioni, M., Federico, G., Vasta, M., 2021. The two revolutions in economic history. In: Bisin, A., Federico, G. (Eds.), The Handbook of Historical Economics. Elsevier. Chapter 2 (in this book).

Cohen, D., Nisbett, R.E., 1994. Self-protection and the culture of honor: explaining southern violence. Personality & Social Psychology Bulletin 20 (5), 551–567.

Conley, J., Temimi, A., 2001. Endogenous enfranchisement when groups' preferences conflict. Journal of Political Economy 109 (1), 79–102.

Dekel, E., Ely, J.C., Yilankaya, O., 2007. Evolution of preferences. The Review of Economic Studies 74, 685–704.

Dell, M., 2010. The persistent effects of Peru's mining mita. Econometrica 78 (6), 1863–1903.

Dell, M., Olken, B.A., 2017. The Development Effects of the Extractive Colonial Economy: The Dutch Cultivation System in Java. NBER Working Paper 24009.

Dessi, R., Piccolo, S., 2016. Merchant guilds, taxation and social capital. European Economic Review 83, 90–110.

Dixit, A., 2004. Lawlessness and Economics, Alternative Modes of Governance. Princeton University Press, Princeton, New Jersey.

Doepke, M., Zilibotti, F., 2008. Occupational choice and the spirit of capitalism. The Quarterly Journal of Economics 123 (2), 747–793.

Edgerton, R., 1971. The Individual in Cultural Adaptation. Berkeley University of California.

Fafchamps, M., 2003. Market Institutions in Sub-Saharan Africa: Theory and Evidence. MIT Press, Cambridge.

Francois, P., Zabojnik, J., 2005. Trust, social capital, and economic development. Journal of the European Economic Association 3 (1), 51–94.

Gorodnichenko, Y., Roland, G., 2017. Culture, institutions, and the wealth of nations. Review of Economics and Statistics 99 (3), 402–416.

Gradstein, M., 2007. Inequality, democracy and the protection of property rights. Economic Journal 117, 252–269.

Gradstein, M., 2008. Institutional traps and economic growth. International Economic Review 49 (3), 1043–1066.

Greif, A., 1989. Reputation and coalitions in medieval trade: evidence on the Maghribi traders. The Journal of Economic History 49 (4), 857–882.

Greif, A., 1994. Cultural beliefs and the organization of society: a historical and theoretical reflection on collectivist and individualist societies. Journal of Political Economy 102 (5), 912–950.

Greif, A., Tabellini, G., 2010. Cultural and institutional bifurcation: China and Europe compared. The American Economic Review: Papers and Proceedings 100 (2), 1–10.

Greif, A., Tabellini, G., 2017. The clan and the corporation: sustaining cooperation in China and Europe. Journal of Comparative Economics 45 (1), 1–35.

Grosjean, P., 2014. A history of violence: the culture of honor and homicide in the US South. Journal of the European Economic Association 12 (5), 1285–1316.

Grosjean, P., Khattar, R., 2019. It's raining men! Hallelujah? The long-run consequences of male-biased sex ratios. The Review of Economic Studies 86 (2), 723–754.

Guimaraes, B., Sheedy, K.D., 2017. Guarding the guardians. The Economic Journal 127 (606), 2441–2477.

Guiso, L., Sapienza, P., Zingales, L., 2008. Social capital as good culture. Journal of the European Economic Association 6 (2–3), 295–320.

Guiso, L., Sapienza, P., Zingales, L., 2016. Long-term persistence. Journal of the European Economic Association 14 (6), 1401–1436.

Güth, W., 1995. An evolutionary approach to explaining cooperative behavior by reciprocal incentives. International Journal of Game Theory 24, 323–344.

Güth, W., Yaari, M., 1992. An evolutionary approach to explain reciprocal behavior in a simple strategic game. In: Witt, U. (Ed.), Explaining Process and Change—Approaches to Evolutionary Economics. University of Michigan Press, Ann Arbor.

Heifetz, A., Shannon, C., Spiegel, Y., 2007. The dynamic evolution of preferences. Economic Theory 32, 251–286.

Hiller, V., 2011. Work organization, preferences dynamics and the industrialization process. European Economic Review 55, 1007–1025.

Hofbauer, J., 1998. Evolutionary Games and Population Dynamics. Cambridge University Press, Cambridge.

Hori, N., 2017. Political regime change and cultural transmission of securarism. Asia-Pacific Journal of Regional Science 1, 431–450.

Hwang, S-H., Naidu, S., Bowles, S., 2018. Social Conflict and the Evolution of Unequal Conventions. KAIST. Mimeo.

Jeong, M., 2018. Culture, Institutions and Growth. Washington Un. St. Louis. Mimeo.

Jha, S., 2013. Trade, institutions, and ethnic tolerance: evidence from South Asia. American Political Science Review, 806–832.

Lagunoff, R., 2009. Dynamic stability and reform of political institutions. Games and Economic Behavior 67 (2), 569–583.

Levine, D.K., Modica, S., 2021. State power and conflict driven evolution. In: Bisin, A., Federico, G. (Eds.), The Handbook of Historical Economics. Elsevier. Chapter 15 (in this book).

Lindbeck, A., 1995. Hazardous welfare state dynamics. The American Economic Review 4, 9–15.

Lindbeck, A., Nyberg, S., 2006. Raising children to work hard: altruism, work norms, and social insurance. The Quarterly Journal of Economics 121 (4), 1473–1503.

Lizzeri, A., Persico, N., 2004. Why did the elite extend the suffrage? Democracy and the scope of government, with an application to Britain's age of reform. The Quarterly Journal of Economics, 707–765.

Lowes, S., Monteiro, E., 2017. Concessions, Violence, and Indirect Rule: Evidence from the Congo Free State. Harvard University. Mimeo.

Lowes, S., Nunn, N., Robinson, J.A., Weigel, J., 2017. The evolution of culture and institutions: evidence from the Kuba Kingdom. Econometrica 85 (4), 1065–1091.

Mahoney, J., Thelen, K. (Eds.), 2010. Explaining Institutional Change –Ambiguity, Agency, and Power. Cambridge University Press.

Maynard Smith, J., 1982. Evolution and the Theory of Games. Cambridge University Press, Cambridge.

McCloskey, D.N., 1991. History, differential equations, and the problem of narration. History and Theory 30 (1), 21–36.

McCloskey, D.N., 2006. The Bourgeois Virtues: Ethics for an Age of Commerce. University of Chicago Press, Chicago.

McCloskey, D.N., 2010. Bourgeois Dignity: Why Economics Can't Explain the Modern World. University of Chicago Press, Chicago.

McCloskey, D.N., 2017. Bourgeois Equality: How Ideas, Not Capital or Institutions, Enriched the World. University of Chicago Press, Chicago.

Miguel, E.A., Gertler, P., Levine, D.I., 2006. Does industrialization build or destroy social networks? Economic Development and Cultural Change 54 (2), 287–318.

Nicholas, D.M., 1992. Medieval Flanders. Longman Publishing, London.

Nisbett, R.E., 1993. Violence and U.S. regional culture. The American Psychologist 48, 441–449.

North, D.C., Wallis, J.J., Weingast, B.R., 2009. Violence and Social Orders: A Conceptual Framework for Interpreting Recorded Human History. Cambridge University Press.

Ortiz, F., 1963. Contrapunteo Cubano del Tabaco y el Azucar. Editorial Ariel, Barcelona.

Pareto, V., 1901. Un'applicazione di Teorie Sociologiche. Vivista Italiana di Sociologia, 402–456. English translation (1968).

Pareto, V., 1920. The Rise and Fall of Elites: An Application of Theoretical Sociology. The Bedminster Press, London.

Persson, T., Tabellini, G., 2021. Culture, institutions, and policy. In: Bisin, A., Federico, G. (Eds.), The Handbook of Historical Economics. Elsevier. Chapter 16 (in this book).

Peristiany, J.G. (Ed.), 1965. Honour and Shame: The Values of Mediterranean Society. Weidenfeld & Nicolson, London.

Peytavin, M., 1997. Naples, 1610: comment peut-on etre officier? Annales: Histoire, Sciences Sociales 52 (2), 265–291.

Poulantzas, N., 1973. Political Power and Social Classes. New Left Books, London.

Puga, D., Trefler, D., 2014. International trade and institutional change: Medieval Venice's response to globalization. The Quarterly Journal of Economics 129 (2), 753–821.

Roland, G., 2017. The deep historical roots of modern culture: a comparative perspective. In: 2nd World Congress in Comparative Economics. Mimeo.

Sabatini, G., 2010. La Fiscalita' Antico Regime tra Assolutismo Regio e Processi di Negoziazione: Il Caso della Napoli Spagnola (Secc. XVI-XVII). Illes Imperis.

Sandholm, W., 2010. Population Games and Evolutionary Dynamics. MIT Press, Cambridge, Mass.

Tabacco, G., 1989. The Struggle for Power in Medieval Italy: Structures of Political Rule. Cambridge University Press, Cambridge.

Tabellini, G., 2008. The scope of cooperation: normes and incentives. The Quarterly Journal of Economics 123 (3), 905–950.

Ticchi, D., Verdier, T., Vindigni, A., 2013. Democracy, Dictatorship and the Cultural Transmission of Political Values. IZA Discussion Papers 7441.

Treisman, D., 2017. Democracy by Mistake. NBER WP 23944.

Voigtlander, N., Voth, J., 2012. Persecution perpetuated: the medieval origins of anti-semitic violence in Nazi Germany. The Quarterly Journal of Economics 127 (3), 1339–1392.

Voth, J., 2021. Persistence – myth and mystery. In: Bisin, A., Federico, G. (Eds.), The Handbook of Historical Economics. Elsevier. Chapter 9 (in this book).

Weibull, J., 2005. Evolutionary Game Theory. The MIT Press, Cambridge MA.

Young, H.P., 1998. Individual Strategy and Social Structure. Princeton University Press, Princeton N.J.

Young, H.P., Burke, M.A., 2001. Competition and custom in economic contracts: a case study of Illinois agriculture. The American Economic Review 91 (3), 559–573.

PART

3

Topics

The economic history of commodity market development

Giovanni Federico[a,b]
[a]*Division of Social Sciences, NYUAD, Abu Dhabi, United Arab Emirates*
[b]*CEPR, London, United Kingdom*

18.1 Introduction

The study of trade is arguably one of the most traditional issues in economics, as trade policy has been one of the few tools that has been used to steer the economy since the mercantilist age. While interest in trade among historians is almost as keen as it is among economists, over the last thirty years, the field has undergone a deep data-driven transformation. Economic historians have systematically used the wealth of data available from trade statistics since the 19th century even if far from exploiting it in full. Furthermore, they have started to use price data to address issues and periods they had not previously been able to analyze for lack of data. They have been able to go back in time to the prestatistical age and to study domestic trade, which was at least as important as international trade, and much less documented. In theory, the price approach is complementary to the quantity approach (O'Rourke and Williamson, 2002a). In an ideal world with perfect data, the analysis of trade would provide the big picture, and market integration would address microlevel issues such as the efficiency of markets or the effects of specific institutions. In the harsh reality of historical research, the two literatures have evolved separately, focusing on different research questions and on different periods.

Last but not least economic historians have widened the scope of their work on institutions and largely due to growing interest among economists for the issue. In the early days, they focused almost exclusively on legislation and on the histories of specific commercial institutions from Medieval guilds to trading companies. More recently, they have started to look to evidence on the actual workings of markets and commercial institutions as opposed to formal rules, have studied the political economy of trade policy with quite a few forays into formal testing, and have reconsidered the role of the state in the development of markets.

This chapter will document these scholarly achievements but also remaining shortcomings. It addresses with both the trade and market integration literature(s), covering whenever possible domestic trade and integration, even if the historical literature is much less robust.[1] In brief, we will argue that we have made much progress in measuring the development of markets and some progress in exploring its causes while the analysis of effects of market development on welfare and economic growth is still in its infancy. There has been considerable work on a specific issue, the effects of protection, but even

---

[1] See Federico (2012a, 2019) for the literature on market integration, Donaldson (2015) and Lampe and Sharp (2019) for the literature on trade, and Meissner (2014) and Keller et al. (2019) for the literature on market integration, trade, and factor flows.

The Handbook of Historical Economics. https://doi.org/10.1016/B978-0-12-815874-6.00034-4

for this topic the results are on the whole disappointing. This reflects a deeper theoretical issue: in spite of recent remarkable progress made in estimating static gains from trade, we do not yet have a method estimate dynamic ones.

The literature on the development of markets is potentially boundless, forcing us to make some choices. First, we deal with commodity markets only. They are clearly related to the development of factor markets, even if it is still uncertain whether flows of goods and factors were complements or substitutes (Lampe and Sharp, 2019). However, we cannot cover literature(s) on capital flows and migrations, which are not only very large which but also address (partially) different issues with substantially different methods. Second, we cover only the period before World War Two, quoting postwar changes only when strictly necessary as a yardstick for historical analysis (e.g., in comparisons between the two waves of globalization). Consequently, we discuss recent developments in trade theory and methods only when used in historical works. Third, we focus on estimation issues and on the big picture without going into the detailed results of specific papers. Finally, we treat policies as exogenous without delving into the political economy of trade policies or into institutional change.

In contrast, we pay some attention to an often overlooked issue: the availability and reliability of data. The recent research has produced a wealth of new databases with great prospects for new research, but scholars must be warned of the price to be paid. The farther the data extend back in time and the less developed the countries they refer to are, the more likely they are to be qualitatively poor. To be sure, poor quality data would not yield biased results as long as errors are randomly distributed with zero mean. At worst, they would reduce the precision of estimates. Thus, we focus on the (alas, not so infrequent) cases for which there is reason to suspect systematic biases. The size and impact of these biases are difficult to estimate precisely, but they might affect results more than biases which are attracting the most attention in the literature such as evergreen endogeneity (see the introduction) and newly identified biases such as spatial autocorrelation (Kelly, 2019).

The next section surveys the evidence on long term changes in the integration of markets and in total trade (Section 18.2). Then, we deal with the causes of such development, distinguishing effects of changes in trade costs as determined by technical progress and political decisions on barriers to trade (Section 18.3) from a more general discussion of the role of institutions (Section 18.4). In Section 18.5, we survey the literature on the effects of market development on welfare and economic growth. Section 18.6 concludes with a potential research agenda.

18.2 What happened: the growth of markets over the very long run

1. On paper, measuring the development of commodity markets is fairly simple. Domestic trade can be estimated with data on transportation, and international trade can be estimated from exports at constant prices, which can be summed to obtain series of trade by any group of countries (advanced countries, African countries, etc.) or for the whole world.[2] The parallel measure using price data is the convergence of prices for a given commodity either between pairs of trading locations or, more

---

[2] Exports are a more precise measure of trade than imports because the latter, according to international conventions, include insurance and transportation costs (measured as c.i.f.). Thus, a decrease in trade causes the measured value of imports to decline even if the quantity remains constant.

generally, across several (σ-convergence), but prices can also be used to assess the growing efficiency of markets à la Fama (1970).[3] Thus, the only real limit to our knowledge is the availability of data and, for prices, the representativeness of commodities and/or locations.

Unfortunately, there are no comprehensive data on trade before the late 18th century, but its development can be inferred from the size of urban populations. They had to be fed by imports from neighboring areas, and the area of catchment had to be larger the larger the urban population was. In 1205, roughly 15 million Chinese, an eight of the whole population, lived in cities, and in the next half millennium, the number rose to over twenty even though the urbanization rate declined to 7% in 1776 (Yi et al., 2018). Thus, total trade in food must have grown, but it might have declined as share of GDP. The urbanization rate was comparable, if not higher, during the Roman Empire at its peak around 165 AD. The number of urban dwellers is uncertain with estimates ranging from 7-9 million (Scheidel, 2007, p. 79) to 14-15 (Hanson et al., 2017), but it is evident that their needs for food and other products could not be supplied by the nearby countryside. One million inhabitants of Rome needed at minimum 150,000 tons of wheat and 75 million liters of wine per year (Morley, 2007). The collapse of the Roman Empire caused a fall in urban population rates and thus also in long-range trade, with the exception of a very limited range of luxury goods for the elite. In 1300, after some centuries of recovery, centers with over 10,000 inhabitants accounted for 6.1% of the total population of Europe, including Russia, and for 21.3% of that of Centre-North Italy (Malanima, 2010). The urbanization rate fell sharply after the Black Death and took two centuries to recover, further rising to almost 10% by 1800 with 18 million people on the continent. In the Netherlands, the most advanced country, urban dwellers accounted for a fifth of the total population in 1500 and for roughly a third two centuries later. Local production could not feed this population even if Dutch agriculture was among the most advanced of Europe. Indeed, a substantial share of Dutch consumption of wheat and rye was imported from the Baltic region (i.e., present-day Poland) in exchange for manufactures and herring. In the province of Holland, the economic powerhouse of the country, the value added in international trade boomed until the early 17th century, with growth rates over 1.5% per year and fluctuated without any trend until the end of the 18th century while domestic trade and transportation grew steadily almost six-fold (Van Zanden and van Leeuwen, 2012). The growth of trade was even more impressive in England (Broadberry et al., 2015, Tab. 4.08): from the 1450s to 1700s, domestic trade grew over forty-fold and international trade grew eight-fold (with annual rates of 1.5% and 0.8%, respectively). The rate of growth of British international trade accelerated to 1.3% in the 18th century (Mitchell, 1988: 448-450). Pfister (2015) tentatively estimated a slightly lower rate for the German area from 1730s to the foundation of the Zollverein in 1834. There are no data for other major trading powers, but anecdotal evidence suggests that international trade grew less in Spain and Portugal and declined in Italy. According to the very tentative estimates by Van Zanden, the total tonnage of the European fleet tripled from 300,000 tons approximately 1500 to 1 million in 1670 and then tripled again to almost 3.5 million by the eve of the French Revolution, i.e., growing at annual rates of 0.7 and 1.1%, respectively (Lucassen and Unger, 2011). Intercontinental trade grew faster: in the same period, the number of ships increased thirty-fold (1-1.2% per year) and their tonnage rose as well (O'Rourke and Williamson, 2002b; Vries, 2010; Lucassen and Unger, 2011). Thus, trade grew faster than GDP. According to available, very tentative, estimates,

---

[3] Price convergence and increased efficiency, as measured by the speed of return of price gaps to their equilibrium value, are the two conditions for growing integration (Federico, 2012a). We deal with tests of efficiency in Section 18.5.

openness (imports and exports as a share of GDP) rose from 1720 to the eve of the French Revolution from 8% to 24% in England, from 5.5% to 20% in France and from 82% to 110% in the Netherlands (O'Rourke et al., 2010, Tab 4.5). Europe traded with its colonies and with Africa (Darlymple Smith and Woltjer, 2016) while its commerce with large independent Asian countries was either forbidden (Japan) or heavily restricted (China). Both countries were forcibly opened to trade in the 19th century respectively by the Americans in 1853 and by the British with the First Opium War in 1839-1842.

2. When compared to the dearth of data on trade in the early modern period, the evidence on prices, especially of cereals, is very abundant and the literature on market integration is correspondingly extensive. The earliest works on the integration of the European wheat market date back to the late 1950s, but there is not yet a consensus on what happened. Scholars would likely agree that price dispersion on the eve of the French Revolution was lower (but not much lower) than it was five hundred years before and that in the early modern period dispersion was lower in areas around the North Sea than in the rest of the continent. However, in the meanwhile, levels of integration fluctuated widely, causing scholars to reach different conclusions depending on the period and sample of locations considered. The most recent contribution (Federico et al., 2021) shows that in core area of Europe (extending from southern England to northern Italy and western Germany), price dispersion was fairly low in the 15th and 16th centuries, jumped in the early 17th century and declined again slowly but steadily from approximately 1650 to the French Revolution. Integration in Central Europe and in the Iberian Peninsula was slower, especially in the late 17th and 18th centuries.

Unfortunately, it is unclear to what extent the results for cereals can be extended to other commodities. Cereals were reasonably homogeneous commodities and the number and quality of series are unparalleled for any other good, reflecting rulers' obsessions for the food supply. On the other hand, for the same reason, the cereal markets were often strictly regulated, and thus arbitrage might have been hampered and prices might not reflect underlying supply and demand. The Qing China, set up a system of public granaries aimed at reducing the impact of local shocks and at dampening fluctuations, which ultimately reduced price dispersion (Will and Bin Wong, 1991; Shiue, 2002). On a more general level, arguably no commodity could be fully representative, as trade costs depended on the bulkiness of the product and on barriers to trade. Price gaps could be great for bulky products freely traded, such as timber but also for high-value goods subject to heavy barriers to trade, such as, sugar. This point is highlighted by the results of work on price gaps between Europe and its Asian colonies. O'Rourke and Williamson (2002a) argued that they were kept much above transportation costs by the monopoly power of trading companies. The comprehensive work of De Zwart (2016) shows that price gaps had already started to decline for some goods (e.g., sugar) in the 17th century and that convergence extended to the majority of commodities (with exceptions such as mace and nutmeg) in the 18th century. However, in the early 1810s, mark-ups on Asian products in Europe were still quite high from 70% to 220% and substantially greater than price gaps between Europe and the United States (Chilosi and Federico, 2015).

3. The development of markets accelerated in the 'long nineteenth century' from Waterloo to World War One. The start of modern economic growth in Europe and in the Western Offshoot increased the urbanization rate and the purchasing power of the population, technical progress reduced transportation costs and trade was liberalized. Wheat prices within Europe and across the Atlantic converged rapidly from the 1830s to the 1870s (Jacks, 2005; Federico, 2011; Federico et al., 2021; Chilosi and Federico,

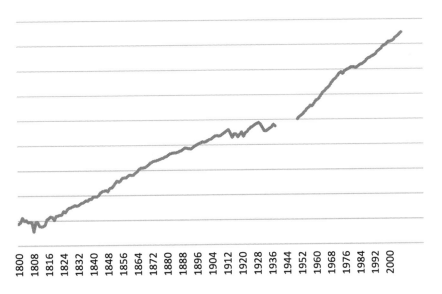

FIGURE 18.1

Growth of world trade, 1800-2007 (log scale). *Source*: 1800-1938: Federico and Tena-Junguito (2019) and the United Nations.

2015) and rebounded in the last decade of the century. The trend also extended, with some delay, to prices of coal, the quintessential bulky good (Murray and Silvestre, 2020). Price gaps between Europe and Asia for high value goods collapsed in the early 19th century (Chilosi and Federico, 2015) and in India, price dispersion fell very quickly in the second half of the century (Hurd, 1975; Andrabi and Kuehlwein, 2010; Studer, 2008). The main exception to this pattern of growing integration was northern China: price dispersion doubled at the turn of the 18th century and remained high until World War One (Li, 2000).

We know much more on the development of international market after 1800 because countries started to collect and publish trade statistics. The forerunner was Britain, since 1696, which was imitated by France and the United States in the late 18th century by many other countries and colonies followed in the 19th century. Federico and Tena-Junguito (2016) have estimated series of imports and exports at current and constant prices for a growing number of polities – from eleven in 1800 to over 100 (i.e., almost all the existing ones) from 1850 to 1938.[4] The initial sample includes most major trading countries, and thus the world trade series (Fig. 18.1) is representative across the whole period.

World trade rose rapidly in the 'long nineteenth century' (slightly faster from 1815 to 1870 than from 1870 to World War One), declined by a quarter during the war, recovered in the 1920s, collapsed

---

[4] The series at current prices can be linked to post-war series from the United Nations database for almost all countries with some exceptions for Africa where some were divided several independent states. In contrast, there are gaps in the series at constant prices for quite a few countries in the 1950s and 1960s, which made it impossible to link the pre-war series to the post 1980 ones.

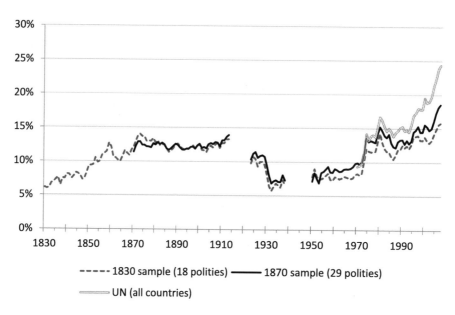

FIGURE 18.2

Export/GDP ratios, 1830-2007. *Source*: 1830-2007: Federico and Tena-Junguito (2017).

during the Great Depression and grew quickly from 1950 to the outbreak of the financial crisis in 2007 with a marked slow-down in the late 1970s and in the early 1980s.

Movements of total trade also depended on GDP and not just on trade costs. Thus, the ratio to GDP is an arguably more precise measure of globalization, and it tells a somewhat different story (Fig. 18.2) at least for the (mostly advanced) countries for which the computation is possible.[5]

From the 1870s to World War One and again in the 1950s and 1960s, the growth of GDP was fast enough to prevent or greatly dampen the effect of growth of trade, leaving the periods from 1830 to about 1870 and from the 1990s as the 'true' globalization eras. The latter was clearly stronger: the median export/GDP ratio (for a sample of 37 countries) was 18.4% in 1913 and 23.3% in 2007 (Federico and Tena-Junguito, 2017, Online Statistical Appendix Table S1). The difference in openness between the first and second rounds of globalization would be much larger if the denominator included only tradables, as their share of GDP was lower in 2007 than in 1913.

4. These aggregate data offer just a first coat of paint. What was traded and which countries were trading with which others are arguably as important as total trade. The conventional wisdom stresses the difference between the 'vertical' trade of the first globalization and the 'horizontal' one of the second.

---

[5] Federico and Tena-Junguito (2017) use data at current prices to minimize distortions and prefer export/GDP to the openness ratio with imports plus exports as a numerator, as imports include transport costs (footnote 2). Countries included in the 1830 sample are Argentina, Brazil, Chile, Colombia, Cuba, Peru, the United States, Venezuela, the Ottoman Empire, Belgium, Denmark, France, the Netherlands, Norway, Portugal, Sweden, the United Kingdom, and Australia. The 1870 sample also includes Canada, China, India, Finland, Germany, Greece, Italy, Japan, Spain, Switzerland, and New Zealand.

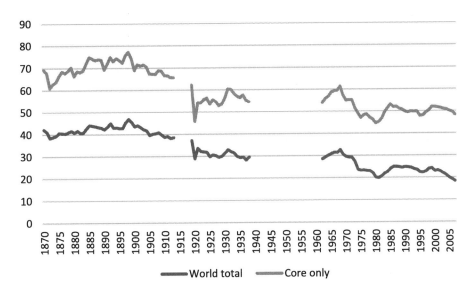

FIGURE 18.3

Share core-core exports of core country and total global exports, 1870-2007. *Source*: 1870-1938: RICARDO database and Federico and Tena-Junguito (2019); 1961-2007: Comtrade.

Since World War Two trade has consisted increasingly in exchange of manufactures first among advanced countries and, since the 1990s, also involving less developed countries both as consumers and producers. In contrast, pre-1913 globalization is said to have featured mostly the exchange of manufactures from core countries with primary products from the periphery (Findlay and O'Rourke, 2007, pp. 411-414). In spite of massive research efforts, the data on trade by product/country before 1938 (and indeed before 1960) are still incomplete. On the bright side, the RICARDO database (Dedinger and Girard, 2017) supplies data on bilateral trade for a large number of countries, greatly expanding the coverage (in terms of the number of dyads and years) of Barbieri et al.'s (2009) database, which has so far been as the main reference for empirical work. Fig. 18.3 shows that conventional wisdom on patterns of trade by country must be reconsidered.

The share of bilateral trade between core countries (core-core) in exports of core countries and in world trade was distinctly higher in the first globalization than it is today.[6] Bilateral flows between the United Kingdom and the United States alone accounted for a twelfth of world trade in the 1870s and still for roughly 4% at the eve of World War One. In contrast, work on the composition of trade by product is just beginning and data on the composition of trade according to modern comparable classifications (SITC or its evolution, the HS) are available only for few countries.[7] It is nevertheless

---

[6] The 'core' includes all countries that in 1870 had a per capita GDP higher than half the British one (Maddison project), i.e. Australia, Canada, Belgium, Denmark, France, Germany, the Netherlands, New Zealand, Switzerland, the United Kingdom, and the United States.

[7] As far as we know, yearly series of the composition of trade are only available for Italy for 1861-1939 (Federico et al., 2011). Data for benchmark years have been collected for Japan for 1870 to 1938 (Meissner and Tang, 2018; Ayuso Diaz and Tena

FIGURE 18.4

Share of manufactures of global trade, 1870-2007. *Source*: 1820-1938: Federico and Tena-Junguito (2019); 1948-1960: UN Historical; 1962-2007: COMTRADE.

possible to roughly estimate the share of manufactures and thus of primary products of global trade at current prices (Fig. 18.4).

The series by and large confirms the conventional wisdom: the share of manufactures grew slowly before World War Two, rose quickly up to the late 1990s with a sharp drop during the oil crises, and fluctuated thereafter, with another drop just after the turn of the century. However, a look at the country data shows a more complex pattern. Over the whole period 1850-1938, manufactures accounted for 11% of the exports of peripheral countries (the sample includes Italy, Japan, and Austria-Hungary and her successor states) while primary products accounted for 45% of their imports and for 40% of the exports of rich countries. It is well known that land-abundant western offshoots such as Canada, Australia, and New Zealand grew rich by exporting primary products, but also United States and Great Britain exported massively commodities. Wheat and cotton accounted for most American exports before its Civil War and for a third *s* late as 1913, when coal accounted for 20% of British exports.

Some studies show the potential of detailed data by product. Federico and Wolf (2013) trace long-term changes in the composition of Italian trade from the country's unification in 1861 to the present. Consistent with conventional wisdom, industrialization caused a long-run increase in the share of manufactures on exports, but the share on imports remained constant and fairly low as it did in other peripheral countries until the 1960s. Two other studies distinguish between intensive and extensive

Junguito, forthcoming), for Belgium (Huberman et al., 2017) and Canada (Beaulieu and Cherniwchan, 2014; Alexander and Keay, 2019) for before World War One and for Great Britain for the interwar years (De Bromhead et al., 2019). Work is ongoing at least for France (Becuwe et al., 2019) and Germany (personal communication Wolf).

margins in the growth of exports before World War One.[8] Belgium defended its share of world exports (slightly above 2%) by diversifying its exports, also thanks to quite effective trade promotion policies (Huberman et al., 2017). In contrast, three quarters of the spectacular growth of Japanese exports (a more than seven-fold rise from 0.35% to 1.7% of world trade) came from intensive margins with huge increases in market share for raw silk and cotton manufactures (Meissner and Tang, 2018).

18.3　Why it happened: trade costs

Modern trade theory assumes that (bilateral) trade depends on competitiveness relative to all suppliers, the type of consumer demand, the size of trading partners (the gravitational constant) and trade costs (Head and Mayer, 2014; Donaldson, 2015). Anderson and van Wincoop (2003, pp. 691ff) define the latter as "all costs incurred in getting a good to a final user other than the marginal cost of producing the good itself: transportation costs (both freight costs and time costs), policy barriers (tariffs and non-tariff barriers), information costs, contract enforcement costs, costs associated with the use of different currencies, legal and regulatory costs, and local distribution costs (wholesale and retail)." The market integration literature uses a similar framework to explain the price gap (or ratios) between two markets or, less frequently, the speed of return to equilibrium, which is a measure of efficiency (Section 18.5). Thus, one can write the most general specification of the estimating equation, known as the gravity model in the trade literature, as

$$M = f(S, Tc, B, I, \mathbf{E}, \mathbf{X}) \tag{18.1}$$

where S is the size of trading partners (for trade analysis only), Tc measures transport costs, B barriers to trade, I information costs, $\mathbf{X}$ all other trade costs and $\mathbf{E}$ is a set of dummies to capture specific large shocks (e.g., wars). These models are generally estimated with panel regressions using fixed effects and/or county and time dummies to take into account unobserved characteristics of countries or markets and their changes (structural gravity models). It is important to stress a major difference between different categories of trade costs. Transportation and information costs depend mostly on technology, and thus gains are likely to be permanent. After inventing and building railroads, it would be difficult to return back to the horse and cart, barring exceptional circumstances such as wars (and possibly decisions on freights). In contrast, barriers to trade depend mostly on political decisions. They seldom exist in modern polities and thus domestic trade costs are likely to decline or, at worst, remain stable. In contrast, barriers to trade (and thus integration) proliferate across borders, and thus international trade costs are equally likely to rise and fall.

　　Gravity-type models have been used for a wide range of case studies in the trade and market integration literatures, and it would be impossible to report all their results in detail. In the following, we give a flavor of the main conclusions by category of costs and then discuss possible biases resulting from the omission and/or imperfect measurement of variables.

---

[8]　The underlying trade theory refers to 'varieties,' which in modern empirical works are proxied with flows by country/product at a very high level of disaggregation (up to six-digit HS). This level of detail is difficult to achieve in historical studies, as the classification of products changed considerably. Thus, the two articles consider a small number of 'varieties' - 205 for Belgium and 116 for Japan.

1.1. Unsurprisingly, the (very few) scholars in the market integration literature who have pieced together series of transportation costs find that their decline was a powerful force for integration. It accounted for roughly a third of convergence in prices of commodities between Europe, Asia and the United States (Chilosi and Federico, 2015). Many authors, following a well-established tradition in gravity models, proxy transportation costs with distance, sometimes adding dummies for relevant geographical characteristics such as the access to seas or rivers. In most cases, these prox(ies) are significant and correctly signed, i.e., they are negative if the dependent variable is bilateral trade and positive if it is the gap in prices. Quite a few authors have tried to probe deeper by assessing the effect of the construction of transportation infrastructures (Bogart, 2019). Railways have attracted the most attention, as the symbol of 19th century modernity, but roads and canals also played an important and somewhat understated role. The Roman roads, while built mostly for military purposes, formed a key component of an integrated transport system that greatly fostered trade within the empire (Fluckiger et al., 2019). They were no longer maintained after the fall of the empire and paved roads of arguably comparable quality were built only in the 18th century. Uebele and Gallardo-Albarran (2015) show that the construction of (paved but free) roads reduced gaps in rye prices in Westphalia in middle decades of the 19th century while the effect of waterways was mixed, and railroads had little impact, possibly because the network was not yet fully developed.

This latter result hints to a sometimes overlooked fact: the impact of any means of transportation depended on competition with other means. For instance, the Rhine lost its traditional role as a major connector of western Germany to the North Sea in the 1850s and 1860s but recovered this role in the 1890s thanks to massive investments in navigability (Klemann and Schenk, 2013). Railways fostered the integration of the wheat market in the Po Valley, but not in the rest of Italy because of the competition of coastal trade (Federico, 2007), showing that the impact of railway building in Italy was limited for several decades. Likewise, Andrabi and Kuehlwein (2010) downplay the contribution of railways to a mere fifth of the impressive price convergence in Indian rice and wheat prices (Section 18.2). Donaldson (2018) is much more optimistic about the Indian railways. Altogether (i.e., including the positive effect on information and so on) reduced costs of trading a specific quality of salt from unique production sites to the whole country by 55-60% relative to road and river and, somewhat surprisingly, by over 80% relative to coastal trade. Jacks (2006a) summarizes different cases by finding that railways had a small positive effect on trade costs for wheat between European and American markets.[9]

1.2. The development of efficient systems for the transmission of relevant information to all agents (as opposed to official couriers that had existed in all major civilizations and to private communication networks) is essential for the development of markets. In Europe, the first public mail services were established in the 16th century and the first newspapers, with commercial information, started to be published at the turn of the following century. The system was quite efficient already at the beginning of the 19th century and speeds of transmission were declining in the first half of the century. A letter took 4-5 weeks to cross the Atlantic in the 1820s and only two in the 1860s, mostly thanks to steamships (Kaukianinen, 2001). The invention of the telegraph in the 1840s was groundbreaking, as it slashed the time of transmission to a few minutes. Unfortunately, historical data on the amount of

---

[9] This result is not strictly comparable with the other quoted estimates. These latter use as dependent variable yearly series of price gaps, while Jacks uses his own estimates of the commodity points (i.e. of the equilibrium level of price gaps) with a TAR (Threshold-Autoregressive) model for eleven year periods.

information and on its costs are not available and thus most works simply omit the relative variable. One notable exception is a recent article by Brunt and Cannon (2014) on England at the turn of the 19th century, who find that the number of local newspapers in each county was positively related to the efficiency of the wheat market. Data on the traffic of information levels of information traffic remain scarce even for the 19th century (Lampe and Ploeckl, 2014), but it is at least possible to capture the effect of the telegraph line with a dummy. This variable usually comes out highly significant and negative as expected with quite substantial effects: for instance, telegraph accounted for two fifths of the convergence in coal prices between Germany and the United Kingdom from 1850 to 1913 (Murray and Silvestre, 2020). Lew and Cater (2006) go a step further and use the number of total (domestic and international) telegrams as an explicative variable in a gravity model for trade from 1870 to 1913. The coefficient implies that had telegraph traffic remained constant at its 1870 level, trade in 1910 would have been half the actual level. The authors argue that this humongous effect reflects the increase in the efficiency of tramp shipping brought about by the telegraph. It made it possible to change routes during a trip, to call at different ports and to reduce idle time spent in each of them.

1.3. The effects of barriers to trade have understandably attracted attention in the literature on trade but they have been widely considered also in the literature on market integration. So far, the empirical research on trade has mostly focused on two key issues, the liberalization of trade in middle decades of the 19th century and the sharp increase in barriers during the Great Depression.[10] The abolition of the British corn laws in 1846 has become the symbol of the liberalization but actually it was only the last measure of a process started more than twenty years before, in the 1820s. Liberalization extended also to wheat, as the 1828 Corn Laws were much less protectionist than the 1815 ones. Furthermore, liberalization extended to most continental countries for wheat (Federico, 2012b) and industrial goods as well (Tena-Junguito et al., 2012). Global average duties on British exports of manufactures collapsed from 50% in 1846 to roughly 20% in 1863. Most cuts in wheat duties were unilateral decisions by each country, while the reductions of duties on manufactures were usually agreed upon in bilateral agreements. Some trade treaties had been stipulated since the 1820s, but the watershed was the Cobden-Chevalier treaty between France and the United Kingdom of 1861 (Pahre, 2008). It unleashed a wave of agreements, which greatly accelerated the liberalization via the MFN (most favored nation) clause. This latter extended the cuts to duties granted to one signatory to all trading partners, thus substantially increasing their exports, by up to a fifth for France (Lampe, 2009b).

There is no doubt that protectionism contributed substantially to the Great Depression (Irwin, 2012). It is often repeated that the protectionist backlash started with the Smoot-Hawley tariff (June 1930), which however was the outcome of a domestic political process rather than a reaction to the economic crisis (Irwin, 2017). However, once the genie was out of the bottle, duties became a key tool of economic policy in all countries. They were used to prop up domestic production but also to reduce trade deficits to defend the gold parity (Eichengreen and Irwin, 2010). Ultimately, all countries had to yield and shift to floating rates, but in the meanwhile the depreciation of floating currencies stimulated countries to still cling to gold to raise duties. Albers (2020) estimates that this effect alone accounted for a decline of up to 6% in world trade. This is only a component of the overall effect of protectionist

---

[10] We will deal with the effects of the 1880s protectionist backlash on trade and openness in Section 18.6. We can anticipate that they were small, if not altogether minimal, because the increases in duties were not large and were limited to certain products (wheat, sugar, and some manufactures) in Continental European countries.

backlash on world trade. Madsen (2000) estimated that protection caused world trade to fall by a 60% from 1929 to 1933, but this seems an overestimation, as world trade declined only by 29% and overall GDP was surely not growing. More recent work finds that protection in the early 1930s reduced total imports by about a tenth in the United Kingdom (De Bromhead et al., 2019) and India (Arthi et al., 2020). However, the 1931 British general tariff and the Indian one were quite mild for standards of the time, and it is likely that the effect of protection was greater in other countries.

2.1. This list of results, even if admittedly partial, shows very substantial advances in our knowledge on a wide range of issues. However, one should not rejoice prematurely, as quite a few theoretical and practical shortcomings remain. First, as argued by Anderson and van Wincoop (2003), trade flows depend not only on bilateral costs but also on costs of trade between any other pair of countries or markets (the resistance). Inwood and Keay (2015) include domestic transport costs for both finished products and raw materials in their analysis of the determinants of British exports of iron to the United States. This strategy is unfeasible in trade analysis, as one should take into account trade costs between all potential suppliers and consumers. Thus, authors assume that fixed effects and/or dummies could also capture the resistance effect as well as omitted costs and other country-specific features, including their relative size. This assumption is decidedly optimistic, and even if true, the results of the gravity models should be taken with a grain of salt.

First, not all dependent variables are unbiased. Price gaps are good measures of trade costs only if two markets trade regularly: otherwise, they may fluctuate randomly without any relation to trade costs as long as they remain within commodity points (Federico, 2012a). The allocation of trade by country is notoriously the weakest information in trade statistics (Federico and Tena-Junguito, 1991; Lampe, 2009a). Custom officials had few incentives to ascertain the exact provenance or destination of products unless goods were subject to differential duties, and thus the data were often biased towards nearby countries. The English statistics for before 1904 made this bias explicit by registering as the country of origin (destination) the country boarding (landing) of the products.

These issues, however, pale in comparison to the problems of explicative variables. Let us start with the simplest case: price convergence for a single product. One would need product-specific series of transportation costs, data on duties and information costs as well as evidence on other relevant causes, including exchange regimes, institutions and so on (see Section 18.5). The difficulties increase exponentially in a trade analysis, as in theory all of these product-specific data should be somehow weighted with the composition of bilateral trade. Thus, all works in the trade literature widely resort to proxies, introducing potentially serious biases (cf. Section 18.1).

2.2. As said, transportation costs are often proxied by distance with or without additional geographical dummies, but using time-invariant features to explore changes in time is clearly contradictory (and, indeed, gravity models often omit it, leaving pairwise fixed effects to also capture distance). Several authors deal with the contradiction with econometric fixes, such as interacting distance with time trends (Jacks, 2006a) or period-specific dummies (Standaert et al., 2016). Pascali (2017) adds a further distinction between distance under sail, which depends on winds, and under steam, which does not. It is unclear whether these strategies are sufficient. The historical evidence suggests that sea-borne freights, in contrast to the iceberg approximation, were seldom proportional to the value of products and that their changes were not linear. Long-run trends depended on technical progress and changes in organization, including harbor organization, with fluctuations as a function of economic activity and peaks occurring in wartime. The productivity of Dutch shipping increased in the 16th and early 17th centuries, causing freights to decline, but it stagnated thereafter (Van Zanden and van Tielhof, 2009). Further innovations of the late 18th-early 19th centuries greatly increased speeds (Solar, 2013; Solar and Hens, 2016; Kelly and O'Grada, 2019), but the effects on freights seem to have been modest (Harley, 1988; Klovland, 2009). In the second half of the 19th century, the introduction of steamships and innovations in organization caused a massive decline in freights (Shah Mohammed and Williamson, 2004; Kaukianinen, 2006; Jacks and Pendakur, 2010), possibly differentiated by product (Harley, 2008). The data on freights by route are fairly abundant in the 19th century and it is possible to estimate the costs of (steam) navigation per mile, and thus total costs between any other pair of ports, with information about distances, which are easy to retrieve from specialized websites.

The construction of series of costs for overland transport is more challenging, as they depended not only on unit costs per mile for each transportation mean (road, railway, and inland navigation) but also on competition from other means and on the shapes of networks. For instance, let us consider the case of transportation between Genoa, the main Italian port and Rome, some 400 km away by sea. The two cities were connected by rail for the first time in 1866, via Florence, Bologna, and Turin (905 km) and nine years later the opening of new line along the Tyrrhenian coast slashed the length of the by 40% (to 553 km) with a corresponding cut in fares. It is easy to compute distances by road or rail at any given moment in time, with historical maps and GIS technology, (Atack, 2019), but this is only the first step. Road transport technology changed little before the introduction of the internal combustion engine in the early 20th century, but the improvement of infrastructure reduced the costs of transportation: the construction of turnpikes (paved toll roads) in England in the second half of the 18th century cut them by 40% (Bogart, 2005). In contrast, the productivity of railways steadily improved, but gains did not necessarily accrue to consumers in the form of lower fares. In many countries, fares were set by the states either as the owners of railways (as in France) or as regulators of privately owned companies, as in the United States after the Interstate Commerce Act (1887). Before the war, the Interstate Commerce Commission had promoted competition among companies to keep rates low, but in the 1920s it changed its policy (Federico and Sharp, 2013). It kept rates stable to guarantee a fair return to the railways and it did not cut them until May 1934, while prices were collapsing, causing American consumers to lose the potential gains from productivity growth. Thus, dummies for a road or railway connection or even data on actual distances are very imperfect and possibly misleading proxies for overland transportation costs. On the other hand, building a series of cost of railway transportation is far from easy. The official fares were public, but they varied by distance, product, speed, and quantity, with rebates for large shipments.

Last but not least, one cannot rule out the possibility that transport costs were endogenous. Roads and railways might have been designed to meet existing traffic needs, and thus recent papers add placebo tests to their robustness checks (Jedwab et al., 2017; Donaldson, 2018). Jacks and Pendakur (2010) suggest that trends in maritime freights depended on trade. This is unlikely to be a major issue in product-specific analyses of convergence, but it might affect results of any trade analysis that uses actual freight indexes as opposed to distance as measure of transportation costs. On the other hand, it is not easy to find a suitable instrument that could meet the exclusion restriction.

2.3. Estimating barriers to trade is fairly easy for a single product. Before the Great Depression protective policies relied almost exclusively on duties, which can be retrieved from legislative sources or trade statistics. During the Depression, quotas, which previously had been imposed only in exceptional circumstances (e.g., during commercial wars), became quite popular, but their effects can be measured by computing the price gap between domestic and world prices, or nominal rate of assistance (NRA). Indeed the unweighted average of NRAs by product, increased by 2.5 times, up to 80-100%, in 'protectionist' countries such as France and Germany, by 7.5 times in Great Britain and by 9 times in Belgium, up to 'only' 33% (Swinnen, 2009). As far as we know, NRAs have not been used to compute economy-wide protection, in all likelihood because collecting domestic and international prices for a representative set of industrial products is very difficult. Almost all empirical works in the trade literature measure barriers to trade with nominal (or average) protection, i.e., the ratio of revenues from trade duties to imports, which is equivalent to a trade-weighted average of product-specific duties (e.g., Clemens and Williamson, 2004; Lampe and Sharp, 2013). This measure is extremely simple to compute but is unfortunately biased and not representative, even when protection is based on duties only. First, gravity models need barriers to bilateral trade, which would be equal to country-wide nominal protection only if the composition of the bilateral flow (e.g., British exports to Germany) matched the composition of total trade, which is implausible. Second, nominal protection is downward biased even as an aggregate measure. The more elastic imports of a good are, the lower its share of total imports for a specific level of protection. Indeed, low-elasticity exotic (mostly tropical) products accounted for a substantial share of custom revenues in the 19th century (Lehmann and O'Rourke, 2011; Beaulieu and Cherniwchan, 2014). This bias has been addressed two different ways. Lampe (2020) estimates protection with the unweighted average of product specific duties, which he computes for seventeen countries in eleven benchmark years. This approach addresses the endogeneity of the composition of trade, but the results are sensitive to the structure of tariffs and may be unduly affected by few outliers.[11] A more precise measure of protection is Anderson and Neary's Trade Restrictiveness Index (henceforth TRI), which is defined as 'the uniform tariff which, if applied to all goods, would yield the same welfare as the existing tariff structure.' The original version is computationally challenging from a historical perspective, as it requires a CGE model of the whole economy, but Feenstra (1995) has suggested an approximation that requires only tariffs by product, the share of products of trade and own-price elasticities. So far, his approximation has been used to compute series of TRI for the United States for 1869 to 1961 (Irwin, 2010), for Italy for 1861 to 1929 (Federico and Vasta, 2015) and for Canada for nine benchmark years between 1870 and 1910 (Beaulieu and Cherniwchan, 2014). The Feenstra approximation might undervalue protection relative to the original Anderson-Neary measure (Lloyd and MacLaren, 2010) and yet the computed TRI substantially exceeds the nominal protection in all three cases – on average by a third for Canada, by 75% for the United States and by 100% for Italy. Furthermore, patterns of TRI and of nominal protection may differ considerably. The series of nominal protection captures the impact of the first Canadian protectionist tariff (National Policy) of 1879, but misses the impact of subsequent tariffs of 1887 and 1894. Thus, there is reason to suspect that the coefficients of nominal protection in gravity equations systematically underestimate the historical impact of barriers to trade.

---

[11] As a rule, tariff schedules were more detailed for manufactures than for primary products: the Italian one before World War One featured more than 50 different types of cotton yarns. Thus, a simple unweighted average would over-weigh industrial products. Lampe (2020) deals with this bias with two-stage stratification. He first computes the average duty for 18 broad categories and then nominal protection as an average of these categories.

3. The discussion so far boils down to a somewhat disappointing conclusion: an accurate measure of key explicative variables in gravity models would require considerable research efforts to collect data. Not surprisingly, economists have explored alternative approaches to avoid this painstaking task. Federico and Tena-Junguito (2017) estimate the contribution of trade costs to changes in world export/GDP ratios (Fig. 18.2) as a residual in a simple decomposition exercise. Ceteris paribus, changes in trade costs would have increased the ratio by four points from 1870 to 1913 and reduced it by 3.4 points from 1913 to 1950 – accounting in both cases for roughly half the actual change in the ratio.[12] Building on earlier work by Head and Ries (2001) and Anderson and van Wincoop (2003), Jacks et al. (2011) show that it is possible to compute all-inclusive bilateral trade costs between countries i and j as

$$T_{ij} = [(X_{ii} * X_{jj})/(X_{ij} * X_{ji})]^{-1/2\sigma} - 1 \qquad (18.2)$$

where X_{ij} and X_{ji} are bilateral trade flows, X_{ii} and X_{jj} are domestic trade flows in the i-th and j-th country which are proxied by the difference between GDP and exports, and σ is the elasticity of substitution between domestic production and imports.[13] The decline in trade costs accounted for almost two thirds of the rise of trade before World War One while their increase from 1921 to 1938 fully compensated the growth in income, leaving trade constant.[14] This approach is very attractive but rather questionable. First, it assumes that all changes in trade patterns depend on trade costs, and thus it implicitly neglects all supply-side factors, including technical progress (Hilberry and Hummels, 2014). Second, the elasticity σ is assumed to have been equal across countries and constant in time, and this may not be the case. Imbs and Mejan (2017) show that import elasticities differ substantially across countries according to the composition of GDP, the openness of single sectors and above all elasticities by sector. De Bromhead et al. (2019) and Arthi et al. (2020) find quite different elasticities for the United Kingdom and India for the 1930s with a nearly identical model. By the same token, one cannot rule out that elasticity may change as result of structural change and/or of changes in the composition of trade changed as a result of modern economic growth. Fouquin and Hugot (2014) find that in 19th century France, elasticity was less than 5 (not significantly different from their 3.78 benchmark) and constant in time, but one would need more tests to be reassured. Last but not least, Eq. (18.2) yields series of bilateral trade costs, which must be somehow aggregated for historical interpretation. Jacks et al. (2011) experiment with different weighting schemes based on trade or total GDP and obtain substantially different results. Fouquin and Hugot (2014) extract a series from coefficients of a panel regression with (common) time dummies, which is ultimately an elegant version of an unweighted average.

---

[12] The sample features 16 countries whose total export/GDP ratio rose by 2 points before World War One and declined by 6 points from 1913 to 1950. The exercise split this change between the 'location effect' (changes in the distribution of global GDP by country), 'structural change' (the change in the share of non-tradables of GDP by country) and residual.

[13] The exact definition of this parameter differs slightly according to the underlying trade model (Jacks et al., 2009). In the estimation, Jacks et al. (2011) assume it to be 8, while Fouquin and Hugot (2014) assume it to be 3.78, which is the median of present-day estimates (Head and Mayer, 2014). Trade costs would be overvalued if the assumed elasticity exceeded the true one and vice-versa.

[14] These results are qualitatively similar to estimates made by Estevadeordal et al. (2003) with an early version of the gravity model. Trade accounted for 25% of the rise in trade from 1870 to 1913 and for all of its decline from 1913 to 1938.

18.4 Why it happened: institutions and efficient markets

1. Nowadays, no one would deny that the smooth functioning of markets depends on good institutions, and this is also true in historical perspective. Good institutions were not necessary public ones: in a series of articles and a book, A. Greif (Greif, 1989, 1993; Greif et al., 1994; Greif, 2006) argued that in the Middle Ages, informal networks or free associations (guilds) offered traders enough protection without the need for state support, even if the historical accuracy of his view is highly controversial (Ogilvie, 2011). Some centuries later, the commercial and colonial expansion of Europe into Asia was spearheaded by private trading companies such as the British East India Company and the Dutch VOC, which acted as quasi-independent powers with their own army and navy forces (Rei, 2019). They did open new markets, but they also exploited Asian producers and European consumers for the benefit of shareholders. The different trends of price gaps between Asia and Europe in the early modern period (cf. Section 18.2) depended on the extent of monopoly power that the VOC enjoyed over the trade of each commodity. The restrictions on trade with Asian colonies continued into the first half of the 19th century, and their eventual abolition was a major factor in price convergence between Europe and Asia (Chilosi and Federico, 2015). These bad practices continued in the colonial world: Tadei (2020) estimates that price management by French trading companies squeezed roughly one third of potential income for African farmers in the 1930s. In contrast, Murray and Silvestre (2020) find no impact of German cartels on the integration of the European coal market before World War One.

In spite of these historical examples, very few authors doubt that in the long run, the evolution of markets was mostly shaped by the visible hand of the state. Markets developed when smaller polities were unified into larger ones and/or when each polities adopted market friendly institutions. The two processes did not necessarily coincide: in quite a few cases, newly annexed territories maintained their traditional institutions and privileges, and restrictions on domestic trade (tolls, duties, monopolies, privileges and so on) were common in Ancient regime polities. These barriers were dismantled over a century-long process that was essential to the development of the modern state (Epstein, 2006). In many European countries, the liberalization of the domestic wheat market, the most sensitive to the political implications of a shortage, started in the 18th century and accelerated during the Enlightenment, but in some cases, including in France, lasted well into the 19th century (Persson, 1999; Miller, 1999). Testing the impact of institutions is notoriously difficult, but there is a substantial body of research on efficiency in the market integration literature, and numerous insights can be gleaned from gravity-type regressions provided in the trade literature.

2. As is well known, Fama (1970) defined a market as efficient if prices take into account all available information and there are thus no opportunities for profitable arbitrage in space or time. In this case, the price gap between two trading locations must be equal to transaction costs, and the difference between current and future (expected) prices must be equal to storage costs.[15] The standard framework

---

[15] Coleman (2009) points out that the standard model of spatial arbitrage neglects the intertemporal equilibrium. The equilibrium condition compares prices at the origin (Chicago) PC and at destination (New York) PNY at the same time t_0 – i.e., $PNY_{t0} = PC_{t0} + \tau$. However, the arbitrageurs must compare the price they can obtain at the arrival in New York (PNY_{t1}) with the value of grain in Chicago at the same time, which is equal to the original price in Chicago plus the storage costs s. Thus, the condition becomes $PC_{t0} + \tau = PC_{t0} + s$ and the equilibrium price gap $\tau - s$. The difference between the definitions of commodity points with and without adjustment for storage would be the larger the longer the time necessary for transportation and the higher the interest rates.

used in the market integration literature assumes that prices in each location are set according to available information about local supply and demand and about prices in other locations. An increase in local prices could push price differentials beyond costs of trading (or commodity points), triggering spatial arbitrage by profit-maximizing traders. The faster the gap returns to its equilibrium, the more efficient the market is. Testing efficiency has somewhat inadvertently gained prominence in the literature on market integration, largely because historians have been chasing state-of-the-art econometric techniques without bothering to consider their economic implications (Federico, 2012a, 2019).

An interesting example of this focus is found in the debate on market integration in 18th century China triggered by the publication of Pomeranz's book on the Great Divergence (2000). The author argues that the Heavenly Empire was as advanced as England and cites its highly integrated domestic market as one of the main evidence for his claim. In a very influential paper, Shiue and Keller (2007) confirmed that China was no less 'integrated' (or more precisely no less efficient) than Western Europe, while her most advanced area, the Lower Yangtze Valley, lagged behind England. Consistent with Pomeranz's thesis (2000), China and Europe diverged in the 19th century when massive integration in Europe was not matched by a parallel process in the Heavenly Empire. This interpretation is contested by Bernhofen et al. (2016) with a more sophisticated cointegration model. They show that adjustment to price shocks took more time in China than in the European 'national' markets (e.g., four times longer in the Yangtze Delta than in England), and, above all, that its speed was increasing (i.e., the market was becoming less efficient) already towards the end of the 18th century, well before the mid-19th century crisis. Their results tally well with the evidence for price divergence in northern China from the 1740s to the end of the 19th century (Li, 2000).

One might argue that market efficiency is not a big issue. Indeed, only extreme levels of inefficiency, up to the actual harassment of traders, would truly hamper trade and seriously damage welfare. In all other cases, the impact of differences in efficiency is small to negligible (cf. Section 18.5). However, this stand of research is relevant to the bigger picture because a comparison between timing of changes in efficiency and in price convergence (Section 18.2) can shed light on the process of market development itself. Price gaps and the speed of adjustment might respond differently to the same underlying forces. A decline in transport costs or the abolition of barriers to trade, in an efficient market, would cause the price gap to shrink, but would not necessarily increase the speed of adjustment after a shock.[16] On the other hand, an improvement in information flows (a decrease in costs or an increase in the speed of transmission) or an institutional change (e.g., the abolition of restrictions to arbitrage) may increase the speed of adjustment without affecting equilibrium price gaps.[17] In fact, Chilosi et al. (2013) and Federico et al. (2021) highlight some relevant differences between trends in price dispersion and in efficiency for the same set of European markets. The two series moved together over the long run but not in the medium term: efficiency started to rise in the 18th century and remained high during the French wars when price dispersion peaked.

---

[16] Note that a reduction in the commodity gap increases ceteris paribus the likelihood of co-movements, as it limits the scope for independent movements. However, this appears as an increase in efficiency only because co-movement measures are an imperfect measure of efficiency.

[17] They might affect the observed price gaps to the extent that price differentials are computed as averages of actual prices, inclusive of periods of disequilibrium. The average gap would shrink if the latter became shorter because arbitrage is more efficient and/or less risky, even if the underlying equilibrium gaps remain constant.

3. The gravity models offer many insights into the effects of specific institutions, even if the list is unavoidably limited by available sources. The Latin Monetary Union (an agreement between France, Italy, and other European countries) sizably increased bilateral trade before 1874 when all participants switched to the gold standard (Timini, 2018). The timing of changes in exchange rate regimes is well known and thus almost all studies on trade take into account their effect. The gold standard dummies come out positive and significant as expected (López-Córdova and Meissner, 2003; Estevadeordal et al., 2003; Mitchener and Weidenmier, 2008; Timini, 2018). The gold standard reduced aggregate trade costs according to Jacks et al. (2011) and reduced the speed of adjustment of wheat prices in 19th century Europe but, somewhat unexpectedly, increased, though only marginally, trade costs (Jacks, 2006a). Quite a few studies include a variable for common language or ethnicity across borders, which predictably fostered trade and integration (cf. e.g., Jacks, 2006a; Mitchener and Weidenmier, 2008). On the other hand, differences in the ethnic compositions of cities of the Habsburg Empire increased ceteris paribus gaps in wheat prices before World War One (Schulze and Wolf, 2009).

Of course, political events and institutions loom large in the literature. Wars did disrupt trade and caused price dispersion to rise, but the effects seem to have been smaller than hypothesized. The collapse in world trade during World War One, though very substantial, was dampened by massive trade diversion toward allied countries (Glick and Taylor, 2010; Gowa and Hicks, 2015). The fragmentation of the Ottoman and Austrian-Hungarian Empires after the war did increase international trade, transforming some domestic flows into cross-border ones, but the effect was not large and faded fairly quickly.[18] Indeed, railway traffic between successor states of the Habsburg Empire not fall much relative to its prewar level, possibly because the new borders followed pre-existing informal, ethnicity-determined, cleavages (Wolf et al., 2011). As expected, the unifications of Italy (1861) and Germany (1871) boosted integration, but the contribution of institutional change might not have been large. Keller and Shiue (2014) estimate that the entry of a polity into the German custom union (Zollverein), the harbinger of political unification, reduced = gaps in wheat prices with other Zollverein cities by 28% on average. The authors do not specify to what extent this fall reflects specific events such the final abolition of duties on the Rhine in 1868 (Klemann and Schenk, 2013) or a more general institutional convergence. Italian unification featured both the total liberalization of domestic trade and brutal institutional convergence with the widespread adoption of Piedmontese legislation by the stroke of a pen. Once the effect of the abolition of the wheat duty is accounted for, the dummy for unification comes out as not significant (Federico, 2007).

The 19th century colonial empires have also attracted much attention in the trade literature. They shared currency and a legal framework, but colonies and above all (British) dominions enjoyed some degree of autonomy in trade policy, possibly with some preferential treatment for imperial goods. Mitchener and Weidenmier (2008) find that before World War One, bilateral trade between polities of the same empire (treated pairs) was 2.5 times higher and that its rate of trade growth was higher by one percentage point relative to nontreated pairs. In those years, there were no imperial preferences in the British empire: their adoption in 1932 increased the share of British trade with the empire by roughly eight percentage points, i.e., three quarters of its total growth (De Bromhead et al., 2019). The role of the empire was much greater for 1930s Japan: colonies accounted for one third of the spectacular

---

[18] Federico and Tena-Junguito (2019) estimate series of trade at constant (1913) borders by deducting trade with former territories. The gap with trade at current borders peaked in 1924 at 3% of global trade (6.2% for Europe only) and declined to 1.4% (2.7% for Europe) on the eve of World War Two.

growth of total exports and for over two thirds of the growth of high tech ones (Ayuso Diaz and Tena Junguito, forthcoming).

While historically meaningful, all of these results are far from covering the full effect of institutions on the development of markets. By their nature, it is impossible to deal with informal institutions but also information on the formal ones is very often scattered and too anecdotal for quantitative analysis. A very interesting exception is the Sejim, the Polish parliament before the 18th century partition of the country, which is exceptionally well documented (Malinowski, 2019). It was a particularly dysfunctional institution, as its voting procedure with individual veto rights made it extremely difficult to reach a decision: Malinowski shows that this hampered market integration and reduced state revenue, ultimately causing the demise of the kingdom.

18.5 On the effects of the development of markets

1. Economists tend to assume that the development of markets brought about prosperity, and indeed there are impressive coincidences in time and space between periods of integration and the growth of trade and periods of prosperity. The large domestic market is regarded as key to the relative prosperity of China (Pomeranz, 2000; Rosenthal and Bin Wong, 2011) and of the Roman Empire (Temin, 2013; Erdkamp, 2016). After the disintegration of the latter, Europe underwent several centuries of political fragmentation and then a similarly long process of reaggregation. In preindustrial Europe, technical progress was slow and intermittent and thus economic historians regard the growing size of markets and their liberalization as essential sources of ('Smithian') growth (Epstein, 2006; Johnson and Koyama, 2017; Persson and Sharp, 2015). After the Industrial Revolution, periods of economic growth such as 19th century industrialization, the 'golden age' of the 1950s and 1960s in Western Europe and global economic growth in the decades before the Great Recession coincided with rapid increases in trade and growing market integration while the Great Depression featured a collapse of world trade (Section 18.2). However, coincidence in time not sufficient. Van Bavel (2016), in his recent book, argues that market freedom did help economic growth at first, but over the long run elites succeeded in exploiting market institutions for their exclusive advantage, ultimately stifling growth. Even without endorsing this extreme view, one can argue that the causal relation went the other way with economic growth causing the development of markets. Furthermore, one would need to measure the (static) welfare benefits and (dynamic) effects on rates of market development.

2. Very few works in the market integration literature bother to estimate welfare gains from integration. Two estimates strongly downplay efficiency gains from the establishment of telegraph lines between the United States and United Kingdom in 1866: it increased American wheat exports by 2% (Ejrnæs and Persson, 2010) and cotton exports by 8% (Steinwender, 2018), respectively corresponding to 0.0073% and 0.0015% of GDP. Gains from price convergence were undoubtedly greater. Chilosi and Federico (2021) estimate that intercontinental integration in the markets for wheat and cotton in the 'long nineteenth century' increased GDP by roughly a half a percentage point in large diversified countries such as the United States, the United Kingdom, Western Europe, and India and by up to 5% in a small specialized exporter such as Egypt. The partial equilibrium estimates for one or two products are bound to underestimate total gains of benefits from the integration of the international market, and gains from domestic integration are likely to be substantially greater. The regulatory policy of the ICC (Section 18.4) caused welfare losses during the Great Depression equivalent to at least 0.5% of GDP and possibly up to 3% (Federico and Sharp, 2013). Costinot and Donaldson (2016), with a linear programming approach, estimate that the convergence of local (county) prices to New York caused American agricultural production to increase by 62% from 1887 to 1920 and by 55% from 1954 to 1997, roughly as much as technical progress (respectively 30% and 70%). These figures imply that market integration accounted for about a tenth of total growth in American GDP before 1920.[19] The railways increased Indian agricultural output by 16% and about 85% of this increase can be explained by additional trade from railways rather than by the substitution of rail with other means of transportation (Donaldson, 2018). Furthermore, railways improved welfare by reducing the likelihood of famines (Burgess and Donaldson, 2010).

3. The issue of effects of the development of markets, and most notably of trade policies, is central in the literature on trade. Some authors have estimated static losses from protection with the well-known Haberger triangles, using the Feenstra approximation to TRI (cf. Section 18.3) as a measure of protection.[20] Not unexpectedly, the losses are found to have been small with peaks of approximately 1.2% of GDP in the United States (in the early 1870s), and 1.5% in Italy (in the mid-1890s) and Canada (in 1905). To be sure, the Feenstra approximation is likely to underestimate TRI and that the Haberger triangles ignore the general equilibrium effects of protection. Computable General Equilibrium models have been widely used to analyze the effect of 19th century protectionism following the pioneering work by Williamson (1990) on the welfare effect of the abolition of the British Corn Laws (O'Rourke and Williamson, 1994; O'Rourke, 2007; Bohlin, 2010; Federico and O'Rourke, 2000). Most estimates deal with its distributional effects with the ultimate goal of understanding the political economy of tariffs rather than economy-wide ones. Some studies do not even report figures for aggregate losses, and reported ones are small even if not negligible: the Corn Laws reduced British GDP by 1.5%. Indeed, a small impact of protection is consistent with evidence on the growth world trade with roughly constant compositions and levels of openness in the second half of the 19th century (Section 18.2). In other words, the protectionist backlash of the 1880s in Continental Europe seems to have been too hyped and it is absolutely not comparable to the Great Depression or, a fortiori, with the Napoleonic Continental System (1807-1814) and the parallel British blockade of French trade and American embargo (Davis and Engerman, 2006). In principle, they should have suppressed all trade, although smuggling was extensive. However, according to estimates by O'Rourke (2007), with a highly simplified CGE model, they reduced GDP by 1.5% in the United Kingdom, by 2.75% in France and by 4.5% in the United States.

Estimating losses from protection is not the same as measuring gains from trade, which imply a different counterfactual, i.e., autarky rather than free trade. Arkolakis et al. (2012) offer a simple

---

[19] Agriculture produced about 27% of GDP in 1890 so that, given a VA/output ratio around 0.9, the additional gross output corresponded to approximately 18% of GDP.

[20] The Haberger triangles estimate losses relative to free trade under the assumption that the country is a price taker. Hufbauer et al. (2002) put forward a modified formula for partial liberalization that has not been used in historical research as far as we know. The assumption of price taking is almost always accepted without much discussion with one major exception: the United States before its Civil War. The country dominated the global market for raw cotton, but, given the competitive nature of production, this position could have been exploited only with an export tax (Irwin, 2003). An optimal 50% tax would have increased GDP by 0.3 points.

formula to estimate total gains from trade G_i (or more precisely the increase in income that would compensate the representative consumer from a move to autarky) as

$$G_i = 1 - (\lambda_{ii})^{-1/\varepsilon} \tag{18.3}$$

where λ_{ii} is the share of domestic expenditures (usually proxied by the difference between GDP and imports at current prices) and ε is its elasticity to trade costs. Federico and Tena-Junguito (2017) use this formula to compute gains for a sample of 37 polities in 1913: they ranged from a minimum of 1.4% of GDP for the United States to a maximum of 12.1% for Switzerland with median of 5.4% and an average of 6.3% against respectively 7.9% and 11.5% for the same countries at the peak of the second globalization in 2007. The 'world' gains, as proxied by a GDP-weighted average of 18 polities for 1830 to 1870 and of 29 country series for 1870 to 1938, moved in time similarly to export/GDP (Fig. 18.3). They rose from about 2% in 1830 to 4% in 1870 and then to almost 5% on the eve of World War Two to collapse back to 2-2.5% during the Great Depression. These estimates assume, as those of bilateral aggregate costs (cf. Section 18.3), constant elasticity for all polities ($\varepsilon = 3.78$) and are subject to the same possible biases. If the elasticity were lower (higher), gains would have been higher (lower). Arkolakis et al.'s (2012) baseline formula assumes perfect competition, one sector and one product for each country. More complex models yield greater gains of up to nine times the baseline for a model with tradable inputs, monopolistic competition and heterogeneous firms (Costinot and Rodriguez-Clare, 2014). Some of these additional hypotheses, such as that of monopolistic competition, might not truly be suited to historical analysis, but some refinements of the Arkolakis' baseline formula would be necessary, subject to data availability. Thus, the estimates by Federico and Tena-Junguito (2017) are in all likelihood a lower bound of actual gains. This statement is confirmed by the results of a CGE model for Great Britain during the Industrial Revolution (Clark et al., 2014). Even in its basic version, with constant returns to scale and no learning by doing, autarky would have reduced English GDP in the 1760s by 3.3% and by one quarter in the 1850s.

4. An alternative narrative on the effects of trade policy can be traced to 19th protectionist century thinkers, from F. List onwards. Most of them did admit that protection caused short-term welfare losses, but deemed the latter a price worth paying for long-term industrialization. This view is now enjoying a revival among economic historians. The authoritative synthesis by Allen (2011) includes protection, jointly with the development of a modern banking system and publicly funded education, in his 'standard model,' i.e., the set of policies/features that fostered the industrialization of Europe and the United States in the 19th century. O'Rourke and Williamson (2017) argue that protection was indispensable to the industrialization of labor scarce countries, including of course the western offshoots. Consistently, the lack of protection of traditional industries is a key link in Williamson's (2011) interpretation of the causes of underdevelopment in the periphery. He argues that improvement in terms of trade in the early and mid-19th century pushed peripheral countries towards specialization in primary products, which increased volatility, and thus the likelihood of short term macroeconomic shocks, and caused causing deindustrialization with highly negative effects on their long term economic growth. Early protection could have prevented this, but only few countries, most notably Mexico (Dobado et al., 2008), adopted it. As said, protection among the successful industrializers was relatively low. Thus, it would appear to have been a bargain if instrumental to modern economic growth. However, was it truly instrumental?

We do not have a good answer. The results of sector-specific studies are mixed. Duties were extremely helpful for the development of iron and steel industries in the late 19th century in Canada

(Inwood and Keay, 2015) and the United States (Irwin, 2000a,b), but in both cases domestic production would have started and survived, though at a substantially smaller scale without protection. In a recent paper, Juhasz (2018) attributes the relocation of the French textile industries from the south to the north and thus ultimately the concentration of industry in the north to regional differences in the enforcement of the Continental Blockade. The prohibition of British goods imports was implemented much more strictly in the north and this offered additional protection to northern industries, which developed and later became internationally competitive. Some recent works measure the effect of protection by comparing performance by sector with a diff-in-diff approach. Lloyd and Solomou (2020) find that higher than average protection under the British general tariff of 1931 had positive effects on production and productivity but not on employment. Harris et al. (2015) go a step further by showing that different duties of 1879 Canadian national policy changed the relative performance of sectors in terms of production and TFP growth and then explaining the positive effect of protection on the latter with two (non-mutually exclusive) models. The 'industrial organization model' (i.e., increasing returns to scale) and 'learning by doing' respectively account for 15% and 25% of the measured increase from additional protection, leaving three fifths of the positive effect of protection on productivity unexplained.[21]

It is hardly surprising that protection fostered the growth of benefiting industries, even if some skeptics would not expect a substantial positive effect on productivity. But what was the effect of trade and market integration on economy-wide growth? For a while, after the pioneering work of Edwards (1998), the answer seemed to be the growth regressions approach. Thus, Hadass and Williamson (2003) find that improvement in terms of trade had a significantly positive effect in the core and a significantly negative effect in the periphery. Blattman et al. (2007) add that growth in the periphery was negatively affected by volatility in terms of trade, echoing much of the research on present-day developing countries. With a conceptually similar approach, Bateman (2012) has tried to measure the impact of market integration (as proxied by price gaps and price volatility) on development (as proxied by urbanization and real wages) in early modern Europe, but the results have been disappointing. In any case, most of the works deal again with the effects of protection. The debate was started by an article by O'Rourke (2000), who, in contrast to expectations, found positive effects of tariffs on growth for a sample of core countries before 1913. Clemens and Williamson (2004), with an extended sample, confirm this result, while they find no impact in the interwar years and a negative impact of protection on growth after 1950. In the most detailed work to date, with a rich set of controls (but a somewhat smaller sample of countries), Schularick and Solomou (2011) find no consistent positive effect of tariffs.

These mixed results might reflect specific shortcomings. First, the results depend on the measure of protection used. Most studies use nominal protection with all its biases (Section 18.3) and, intriguingly, Jacks (2006b) obtains conflicting results with different measures. GDP growth for eight European countries is positively related to overall openness when estimated with Frankel-Romer's (1999) method, but, contrary to expectations, also to nominal protection and to an econometric estimate of transaction costs in wheat trade. Second, the relation between protection and economic growth

---

[21] The role of learning by doing and increasing returns to scale is also highlighted in a somewhat different context in a recent article by Yoon (forthcoming). He finds that welfare effects of aggregate American industrial protection were negative with constant returns and no learning by doing and slightly positive with them. In the more favorable scenario protection, increased cumulated GDP by 8.2% from 1870 to 1913.

might differ among countries according to their levels of development, the factor endowments and details of trade policy as shown by the VAR exercise by Lampe and Sharp (2013). The authors hint to potential reverse causation: economic growth increased taxation potential and thus reduced the need for custom revenues, making liberalization easier (Cage and Gadenna, 2018). Lehmann and O'Rourke (2011) show that the protection of manufactures fostered growth in core countries before 1913, while duties on agricultural goods reduced it and revenue tariffs on exotic products had no effect whatsoever on growth. Tena-Junguito (2010) further restricts the positive effect on the products of skill-intensive industries. However, the failure to find a stable relation between protection and economic growth may also simply reflect shortcomings of the growth regression approach. Trade-related variables compete with many other causes of growth without a clear theory-inspired ranking of them.

18.6 **Conclusions**

One could end this survey on a fairly optimistic note, at least for the two first topics. We have a quite strong theoretical framework to measure the development of markets and to investigate its causes and we have many relevant results. We understand rather well the evolution of some markets through history, even if there are still major gaps in our knowledge in time and geographical coverage. We also have a broad understanding of the causes of market development, though one should not downplay the complementary shortcomings of the market integration and trade literatures. The former better measures explicative variables (freights, trade costs, etc.) and thus provides more accurate results, though these results are difficult to generalize because they are product- and location-specific. In contrast, the trade literature yields more general results, but they are often based on low-quality data.

In both cases, the simple solution is to collect more data. It is unlikely that it will ever be possible to obtain series of trade for before 1800, so our quantitative analysis of the development of markets could be improved by as much as possible extending the set of available prices both to commodities other than cereals and to areas other than Europe and to its Asian colonies. The trade data become fairly abundant from the second half of the 19th century: a growing number of polities, including colonies, started to publish trade statistics and/or improved the precision or the of their data. So far, these sources are underexploited, possibly due to their size (some European statistics registered thousands different products with completely different definitions and classifications), but they have great potential. It would be possible to build an accurate price index, to analyze changes in composition and, with all caveats on the reliability of the allocation of flows by country of origin and destination, to produce product/country series extending before 1961 the already available series from the databases of international organizations such as the United Nation's COMTRADE and the IMF's Direction of Trade Statistics.

The situation is broadly similar for trade costs. It should be possible to collect additional data for the preindustrial period and to imaginatively use proxies (e.g., wages and prices of oats for transport by cart), but building a full set of cost variables seems unlikely. In contrast, sources on trade costs in the statistical age are abundant. Data on duties by product can be extracted from legislative acts and trade statistics, freights can be collected from different sources and railway fares were in theory public, even if extracting series of costs by product/route is labor intensive. In both cases, the global research effort needed to attain the Holy Grail of precisely measured costs for bilateral trade extends well beyond the resources likely available now and in the foreseeable future. However, of all these tasks are scalable. Much work is currently being done, and thus, prospects are heartening.

The situation is less favorable for two other topics discussed here, the role of institutions and economic effects of the development of markets. Some relevant institutions can be neatly captured by variables (e.g., the exchange rate regime) while others are very difficult to measure (e.g., the business-friendliness of the legal system) and all might be endogenous. Thus, econometric analysis must be supplemented with and often substituted by historical narratives.

The most difficult task appears to be the analysis of effects of the development of markets. This is ultimately the key research question which motivates the whole field, but it needs a theoretically consistent and comprehensive framework. The growth regression approach has failed to live up to the expectations of the 1990s and has faded without being substituted. Arkolakis et al.'s (2012) work and further developments are a major step forward but measure only static gains, which, as stated repeatedly, are secondary to dynamic effects of market development. So far, we have ideas about some dynamic mechanisms, and most notably the natural selection of firms via entry and exit firms (cf. e.g., Sampson, 2016). Any forecast of the future development of economics is to some extent futile, but moving from modeling specific channels to whole dynamic impacts, including learning by doing, transfer of technology, etc., seems a daunting task. Even more daunting would be to find an identification strategy that could be applied to the data-scarce historical environment.

References

Albers, T., 2020. Currency devaluation and beggar-my-neighbour penalties: evidence from the 1930s. Economic History Review 73, 233–257.

Alexander, P., Keay, I., 2019. Responding to the first era of globalization: Canadian trade policy, 1870-1913. The Journal of Economic History 79, 826–861.

Allen, R., 2011. Global Economic History. A Very Short Introduction. Oxford University Press, Oxford.

Anderson, J., van Wincoop, E., 2003. Gravity without gravitas. The American Economic Review 93, 170–192.

Andrabi, T., Kuehlwein, M., 2010. Railways and price convergence in British India. The Journal of Economic History 70, 351–377.

Arkolakis, C., Costinot, A., Rodriguez-Clare, A., 2012. New trade models, same old gains? The American Economic Review 102, 94–130.

Arthi, V., Lampe, M., Nair, A., O'Rourke, K.H., 2020. The impact of interwar protection: evidence from India. CEPR Discussion Paper DP14775.

Atack, J., 2019. Railroads. In: Diebolt, C., Haupert, M. (Eds.), Handbook of Cliometrics, 2nd edition. Springer, Berlin-Heidelberg, pp. 1423–1451.

Ayuso Diaz, A., Tena Junguito, A., forthcoming. The imperial trade in the shadow of power: Japanese industrial exports in the interwar years.

Barbieri, K., Keshk, O., Pollins, B., 2009. TRADING DATA: evaluating our assumptions and coding rules. Conflict Management and Peace Science 26, 471–491.

Bateman, V., 2012. Markets and Growth in Early Modern Europe. Pickering and Chatto, London.

Beaulieu, E., Cherniwchan, J., 2014. Tariff structure, trade expansion and Canadian protectionism, 1870-1910. Canadian Journal of Economics 47, 144–172.

Becuwe, S., Blancheton, B., Onfroy, K., 2019. « Base Montesquieu » les données du commerce extérieur français de 1836 à 1938. Revue de L'OFCE 164, 87–109.

Bernhofen, D., Eberhard, M., Li, J., Morgan, S., 2016. Assessing market (dis)integration in early modern China and Europe. CEPR DP 11288.

Blattman, C., Hwang, J., Williamson, J.G., 2007. Winners and losers in the commodity lottery: the impact of terms of trade growth and volatility in the periphery 1870-1939. Journal of Development Economics 82, 156–179.

Bogart, D., 2005. Turnpike trusts and the transportation revolution in 18th century England. Explorations in Economic History 42, 479–508.

Bogart, D., 2019. Clio on speed. In: Diebolt, C., Haupert, M. (Eds.), Handbook of Cliometrics, 2nd edition. Springer, Berlin-Heidelberg, pp. 1453–1478.

Bohlin, J., 2010. The income distributional consequences of agrarian tariffs in Sweden on the eve of World War One. European Review of Economic History 14 (1), 1–45.

Broadberry, S., Campbell, B.M.S., Klein, A., Overton, M., van Leeuwen, B., 2015. British Economic Growth. Cambridge University Press, Cambridge.

Brunt, L., Cannon, E., 2014. Measuring integration in the English wheat market, 1770-1820: new methods, new answers. Explorations in Economic History 52, 111–130.

Burgess, R., Donaldson, D., 2010. Can openness mitigate the effect of weather shocks? Evidence from India's famine era. The American Economic Review 100, 449–453.

Cage, J., Gadenna, L., 2018. Tax revenues and the fiscal cost of trade liberalization. Explorations in Economic History 70, 1–24.

Chilosi, D., Federico, G., 2015. Early globalizations: the integration of Asia in the world economy, 1800-1938. Explorations in Economic History 57, 1–18.

Chilosi, D., Federico, G., 2021. The effects of market integration during the first globalization: a multi-market approach. European Review of Economic History 25 (1), 20–58.

Chilosi, D., Murphy, T., Studer, R., Tuncer, C., 2013. Europe's many integrations: geography and grain markets. Explorations in Economic History 50, 46–68.

Clark, G., O'Rourke, K., Taylor, A., 2014. The growing dependence of Britain on trade during the Industrial revolution. Scandinavian Economic History Review 62, 109–136.

Clemens, M., Williamson, J., 2004. Why did the tariff-growth correlation change after 1950? Journal of Economic Growth 9, 5–46.

Coleman, A., 2009. Storage, slow transport and the law of one price: theory with evidence from nineteenth century US corn markets. Review of Economics and Statistics 91, 332–350.

Costinot, A., Donaldson, D., 2016. How large are the gains from economic integration? Theory and evidence from US agriculture, 1880-1997. NBER WP 22496 Oct 2016.

Costinot, A., Rodriguez-Clare, A., 2014. Trade theory with numbers: quantifying the consequences of globalization. In: Gopinath, G., Helpman, E., Rogoff, K. (Eds.), Handbook of International Economics, Vol. 4. Elsevier-North Holland, pp. 197–261.

Darlymple Smith, A., Woltjer, P., 2016. Commodities, price and risk: the changing market for non slave products in pre-abolition in West Africa. African Economic History Network WP 31/2016.

Davis, L., Engerman, S., 2006. Naval Blockades in Peace and War. An Economic History Since 1750. Cambridge UP, Cambridge.

De Bromhead, A., Fernihough, A., Lampe, M., O'Rourke, K., 2019. When Britain turned inward: the impact of interwar British protection. The American Economic Review 109 (2), 325–352.

De Vries, J., 2010. The limits of globalization in the early modern world. Economic History Review 63, 710–733.

De Zwart, P., 2016. Globalization in the early modern era: new evidence from the Dutch-Asian trade, c 1600-1800. The Journal of Economic History 76, 520–558.

Dedinger, B., Girard, P., 2017. Exploring trade globalization in the long run: the RICardo project. Historical Methods 50, 30–48.

Dobado, R., Gomez Galvarriato, A., Williamson, J., 2008. Mexican exceptionalism: globalization and de-industrialization, 1750–1877. The Journal of Economic History 68, 758–811.

Donaldson, D., 2015. The gains from market integration. Annual Review of Economics 7, 619–647.

Donaldson, D., 2018. Railroads of the Raj: estimating the impact of transportation infrastructure. The American Economic Review 108, 899–934.

Edwards, S., 1998. Openness, productivity and growth: what do we really know? The Economic Journal 108, 383–398.

Eichengreen, B., Irwin, D., 2010. The slide to protectionism in the Great Depression: who succumbed and why? The Journal of Economic History 70, 871–897.

Ejrnæs, M., Persson, K.G., 2010. The gains from improved market efficiency: trade before and after the transatlantic telegraph. European Review of Economic History 14, 361–381.

Epstein, S.R., 2006. Freedom and Growth. The Rise of States and Markets in Europe 1300-1750. Routledge, London. 1st ed. 2000.

Erdkamp, P., 2016. Economic growth in the Roman Mediterranean world: an early good-bye to Malthus? Explorations in Economic History 60, 1–20.

Estevadeordal, A., Frantz, B., Taylor, A.M., 2003. The rise and fall of world trade, 1870-1939. The Quarterly Journal of Economics 118, 359–407.

Fama, E., 1970. Efficient capital markets: a review of theory and empirical work. Journal of Finance 25, 383–417.

Federico, G., 2007. Market integration and market efficiency. The case of 19th century Italy. Explorations in Economic History 44, 293–316.

Federico, G., 2011. When did the European market integrate? European Review of Economic History 15, 93–126.

Federico, G., 2012a. How much do we know about market integration in Europe? Economic History Review 65, 470–497.

Federico, G., 2012b. The Corn Laws in continental perspective. European Review of Economic History 16, 166–187.

Federico, G., 2019. Market integration. In: Diebolt, C., Haupert, M. (Eds.), Handbook of Cliometrics, 2nd edition. Springer, Berlin-Heidelberg.

Federico, G., Natoli, S., Tattara, G., Vasta, M., 2011. Il commercio estero italiano 1861-1939. Laterza, Bari.

Federico, G., O'Rourke, K., 2000. Much ado about nothing? The Italian trade policy in the 19th century. In: Williamson, J., Pamuk, S. (Eds.), The Mediterranean Response to Globalisation Before 1950. Routledge, London, pp. 269–296.

Federico, G., Schulze, M.-S., Volckart, O., 2021. European goods market integration in the very long run: from the black death to the First World War. The Journal of Economic History 81.

Federico, G., Sharp, P., 2013. The cost of railroad regulation: the disintegration of American agricultural markets in the interwar period [with Sharp, Paul]. Economic History Review 66, 1017–1038.

Federico, G., Tena-Junguito, A., 1991. On the accuracy of foreign trade statistics (1909-35): Morgestern revised. Explorations in Economic History 28, 259–273.

Federico, G., Tena-Junguito, A., 2016. World trade, 1800-1938: a new data-set. EHES Working paper n. 93.

Federico, G., Tena-Junguito, A., 2017. A tale of two globalizations: gains from trade and openness 1800-2010. Review of World Economics 153, 601–626.

Federico, G., Tena-Junguito, A., 2019. World trade, 1800-1938: a new synthesis. Revista de Historia Economica/Journal of Iberian and Latin Economic History 37, 1–33.

Federico, G., Vasta, M., 2015. What do we really know about protection before the Great Depression: evidence from Italy. The Journal of Economic History 75, 993–1029.

Federico, G., Wolf, N., 2013. Comparative advantage: a long-run perspective. In: Toniolo, G. (Ed.), Handbook of Italian Economic History Since the Unification. Oxford University Press, Oxford, pp. 327–350.

Feenstra, R.C., 1995. Estimating the effects of trade policy. In: Grossman, G., Rogoff, K.S. (Eds.), Handbook of International Economics, vol. 3. Elsevier, Amsterdam, pp. 1553–1595.

Findlay, R., O'Rourke, K., 2007. Power and Plenty Trade, War and the World Economy in the Second Millennium. Princeton University Press, Princeton.

Fluckiger, M., Hornung, E., Larch, M., Ludwig, M., Mees, A., 2019. Roman transport network connectivity and economic integration. Cesifo working papers 7740.

Fouquin, M., Hugot, J., 2014. Trade globalization 1827-2012. When did trade costs start to fall? CEPII Document de travail.

Frankel, J., Romer, D., 1999. Does trade cause growth? The American Economic Review 89, 379–399.

Glick, R., Taylor, A.M., 2010. Collateral damage: trade disruption and the economic impact of war. Review of Economics and Statistics 92, 102–127.

Gowa, J., Hicks, R., 2015. Commerce and conflict: new data about the Great War. British Journal of Political Science 47, 653–674.

Greif, A., 1989. Reputation and coalition in medieval trade: the Maghribi traders. The Journal of Economic History 49, 857–882.

Greif, A., 1993. Contract enforceability and economic institutions in early trade: the Maghribi traders' coalition. The American Economic Review 83, 525–548.

Greif, A., 2006. Institutions and the Path to Modern Economy. Lessons from Medieval Trade. Cambridge University Press, Cambridge.

Greif, A., Milgrom, R., Weingast, B., 1994. Coordination, commitment and enforcement; the case of merchant guilds. Journal of Political Economy 102, 745–776.

Hadass, Y.S., Williamson, J.G., 2003. Terms of trade shocks and economic performance 1870-1940: Prebisch and Singer revisited. Economic Development and Cultural Change 51, 629–658.

Hanson, G.W., Ortmann, S.G., Lobo, J., 2017. Urbanism and the division of labour in the Roman empire. Interface 14.

Harley, K., 1988. Ocean freight rates and productivity, 1740-1913: the primacy of mechanical invention reaffirmed. The Journal of Economic History 48, 851–876.

Harley, K., 2008. Steers afloat: the North Atlantic meat trade, liner predominance and freight rates, 1870-1913. The Journal of Economic History 68, 1028–1058.

Harris, R., Keay, I., Lewis, F., 2015. Protecting infant industries: Canadian manufacturing and the national policy. Explorations in Economic History 56, 15–31.

Head, K., Mayer, T., 2014. Gravity equations: workhorse, toolkit and cookbook. In: Gopinath, G., Helpman, E., Rogoff, K. (Eds.), Handbook of International Economics, Vol. 4, pp. 131–195.

Head, K., Ries, J., 2001. Increasing returns versus national product differentiation as an explanation for the pattern of U.S.-Canada trade. The American Economic Review 91, 858–876.

Hilberry, R., Hummels, D., 2014. Trade elasticity parameters for a computable general equilibrium model. In: Dixon, P.B., Jorgenson, D.W. (Eds.), Handbook of Computable General Equilibrium Modelling. Elsevier North Holland, Amsterdam, pp. 1213–1269.

Huberman, M., Meissner, C.M., Oosterlink, K., 2017. Technology and geography in the second industrial revolution: new evidence from the margins of trade. The Journal of Economic History 77, 39–89.

Hufbauer, G., Wada, E., Warren, T., 2002. The Benefits of Price Convergence: Speculative Computations. Institute for International Economics, Washington.

Hurd II, J., 1975. Railways and the expansion of markets in India, 1861-1921. Explorations in Economic History 12, 263–288.

Imbs, J., Mejan, I., 2017. Trade elasticities. Review of International Economics 25, 383–402.

Inwood, K., Keay, I., 2015. Transport costs and trade volumes: evidence from the trans-Atlantic iron trade 1870–1913. The Journal of Economic History 75, 95–124.

Irwin, D., 2000a. Could the United States iron industry have survived free trade after the civil war? Explorations in Economic History 37, 278–299.

Irwin, D., 2000b. Did late-nineteenth-century U.S. tariff promote infant industries? Evidence from the tinplate industry. The Journal of Economic History 60, 335–360.

Irwin, D., 2003. The optimal tax on antebellum US cotton exports. Journal of International Economics 60, 275–291.

Irwin, D., 2010. Trade restrictiveness and deadweight losses from U.S. tariffs, 1859-1961. American Economic Journal: Economic Policy 2, 111–133.

Irwin, D., 2012. Trade Policy Disaster. Lessons from the 1930s. MIT Press, Cambridge (Mass).

Irwin, D., 2017. Clashing over Commerce. A History of US Trade Policy. Chicago University Press, Chicago and London.

Jacks, D., 2005. Intra – and international commodity market integration in the Atlantic economy. Explorations in Economic History 42, 381–413.

Jacks, D., 2006a. What drove 19th century commodity market integration. Explorations in Economic History 43 (3), 383–412.

Jacks, D., 2006b. New results on the tariff-growth paradox. European Review of Economic History 10, 205–230.

Jacks, D., Meissner, C., Novy, D., 2009. Trade booms, trade busts and trade costs. NBER Working Paper 15267.

Jacks, D., Meissner, C., Novy, D., 2011. Trade booms, trade busts and trade costs. Journal of International Economics 83, 185–201.

Jacks, D.S., Pendakur, K., 2010. Global trade and the maritime transport revolution. Review of Economics and Statistics 92, 745–755.

Jedwab, R., Kerby, E., Moradi, A., 2017. History, path dependence and development: evidence from colonial railways, settlers and cities in Kenya. The Economic Journal 127, 1467–1494.

Johnson, N.D., Koyama, M., 2017. States and economic growth: capacity and constraints. Explorations in Economic History 64, 1–20.

Juhasz, R., 2018. Temporary protection and technology adoption: evidence from the Napoleonic blockade. The American Economic Review 108, 3339–3376.

Kaukianinen, Y., 2001. Shrinking the world. Improvements in the speed of information transmission, c 1820-1870. European Review of Economic History 5, 1–28.

Kaukianinen, Y., 2006. Journey costs, terminal costs and ocean tramp freights: how the price of distance declined from the 1870s to 2000. International Journal of Maritime History 18, 17–44.

Keller, W., Lampe, M., Shiue, C., 2019. International transactions: real trade and factor flows between 1700 and 1870. NBER Working paper 26865. Cambridge Economic History of the World, 2021, in press.

Keller, W., Shiue, C.H., 2014. Endogenous formation of free trade agreements: evidence from the Zollverein's impact on market integrations. The Journal of Economic History 2014 (74), 1168–1204.

Kelly, M., 2019. The standard errors of persistence. CEPR DP 13783.

Kelly, M., O'Grada, C., 2019. Speed under sail during the early industrial revolution (c. 1750-1850). Economic History Review 72, 459–480.

Klemann, H.A.M., Schenk, J., 2013. Competition in the Rhine delta: waterways, railways and ports, 1870-1913. Economic History Review 66, 826–847.

Klovland, J.T., 2009. New evidence on the fluctuations in ocean freight rates in the 1850s. Explorations in Economic History 46, 266–284.

Lampe, M., 2009a. Bilateral trade flows in Europe, 1857-1875: a new data-set. Research in Economic History 26, 81–155.

Lampe, M., 2009b. Effects of bilateralism and the MFN clause on international trade. Evidence for the Cobden-Chevalier network (1860-1875). The Journal of Economic History 69, 1012–1040.

Lampe, M., 2020. European Trade Policy in the Nineteenth Century. Oxford Research Encyclopedia.

Lampe, M., Ploeckl, F., 2014. Spanning the globe: the rise of global communication systems and the first globalization. Australian Economic Review 54, 242–261.

Lampe, M., Sharp, P., 2013. Tariffs and income: a time series analysis for 24 countries. Cliometrica 7, 207–235.

Lampe, M., Sharp, P., 2019. Cliometrics approaches to international trade. In: Diebolt, C., Haupert, M. (Eds.), 2nd edition. Handbook of Cliometrics. Springer, Berlin.

Lehmann, S., O'Rourke, K., 2011. The structure of protection and growth in the late 19th century. Review of Economics and Statistics 93, 606–616.

Lew, B., Cater, B., 2006. The telegraph, co-ordination of tramp shipping and growth in world trade 1870-1910. European Review of Economic History 10, 147–173.

Li, L., 2000. Integration and disintegration in North China's grain markets, 1738-1911. The Journal of Economic History 60, 665–699.

Lloyd, P., MacLaren, D., 2010. Partial and general-equilibrium measures of trade restrictiveness. Review of International Economics 18, 1044–1057.

Lloyd, S., Solomou, S., 2020. The impact of the 1932 general tariff: a difference-in-difference approach. Cliometrica 14, 41–60.

López-Córdova, E.J., Meissner, C., 2003. Exchange-rate regime and international trade: evidence from the classical gold standard era. The American Economic Review 93, 344–353.

Lucassen, J., Unger, R.W., 2011. Shipping, productivity and economic growth. In: Unger, R.W. (Ed.), Shipping and Economic Growth. Brill, Leiden-Boston, pp. 3–44.

Madsen, J., 2000. Trade barriers and the collapse of world trade during the Great Depression. Southern Economic Journal 67, 848–868.

Malanima, P., 2010. Urbanization. In: Broadberry, S., O'Rourke, K. (Eds.), The Cambridge Economic History of Modern Europe. Vol I: 1700-1870. Cambridge University Press, Cambridge, pp. 236–263.

Malinowski, M., 2019. Economic consequences of state failure – legal capacity, regulatory activity and market integration in Poland, 1505-1772. The Journal of Economic History 79, 862–896.

Meissner, C., 2014. Growth from globalization? A view from the very long run. In: Aghion, P., Durlauf, S. (Eds.), Handbook of Economic Growth Amsterdam Elsevier, Vol. 2B, pp. 1033–1069.

Meissner, C., Tang, J.P., 2018. Upstart industrialization and exports: evidence from Japan, 1880-1910. The Journal of Economic History 78, 1068–1102.

Miller, J.A., 1999. Mastering the Market the State and the Grain Trade in Northern France, 1700-1860. Cambridge University Press, Cambridge.

Mitchell, B., 1988. British Historical Statistics. Cambridge University Press, Cambridge.

Mitchener, K.J., Weidenmier, M., 2008. Trade and empire. The Economic Journal 228, 1805–1884.

Morley, N., 2007. The early Roman empire: distribution. In: Scheidel, W., Morris, I., Saller, R. (Eds.), The Cambridge Economic History of the Greco-Roman World. Cambridge University Press, Cambridge, pp. 570–591.

Murray, J., Silvestre, J., 2020. Integration in European coal markets, 1833-1913. Economic History Review 73, 668–702.

Ogilvie, S., 2011. Institutions and European Trade. Merchant Guilds 1000-1800. Cambridge University Press, Cambridge, p. 430.

O'Rourke, K., 2000. Tariffs and growth in the late 19th century. Economic Journal 110, 456–483.

O'Rourke, K., 2007. War and welfare: Britain, France and the United States 1807-1814. Oxford Economic Papers 59 (S1), i8–i30.

O'Rourke, K., de la Escosura, L.P., Daudin, G., 2010. Trade and empire. In: Broadberry, S., O'Rourke, K. (Eds.), The Cambridge Economic History of Modern Europe. Vol I: 1700-1870. Cambridge University Press, Cambridge, pp. 96–120.

O'Rourke, K., Williamson, J., 1994. Late 19th century Anglo-American factor price convergence: were Heckscher and Ohlin right? The Journal of Economic History 54, 892–916.

O'Rourke, K., Williamson, J.G., 2002a. When did globalization begin? European Review of Economic History 6, 23–50.

O'Rourke, K., Williamson, J.G., 2002b. After Columbus: explaining Europe's overseas trade boom, 1500-1800. The Journal of Economic History 62, 417–456.

O'Rourke, K., Williamson, J.G., 2017. Introduction. In: The Spread of Modern Industry to the Periphery Since 1871. Oxford University Press, Oxford, pp. 1–11.

Pahre, R., 2008. Politics and Trade Cooperation in the Nineteenth Century. Cambridge University Press, Cambridge.

Pascali, L., 2017. The wind of change: maritime technology, trade and economic development. The American Economic Review 107, 2821–2854.

Persson, K.G., 1999. Grain Markets in Europe 1500-1900. Cambridge University Press, Cambridge.

Persson, K.G., Sharp, P., 2015. An Economic History of Europe: Knowledge, Institutions and Growth, 600 to Present, 2nd edition. Cambridge University Press, Cambridge.

Pfister, U., 2015. The quantitative development of Germany's international trade during the eighteenth and early nineteenth centuries. Revue de L'OFCE 140, 175–221.

Pomeranz, K., 2000. The Great Divergence. Princeton University Press, Princeton.

Rei, C., 2019. Merchant empires. In: Diebolt, C., Haupert, M. (Eds.), Handbook of Cliometrics, 2nd edition. Springer Berlin-Heidelberg, pp. 761–783.

Rosenthal, J.L., Bin Wong, R., 2011. Before and Beyond Divergence. Harvard University Press, London and Cambridge, Mass.

Sampson, T., 2016. Dynamic selection: an idea flows theory of entry, trade, and growth. The Quarterly Journal of Economics 131, 315–380.

Scheidel, W., 2007. Demography. In: Scheidel, W., Morris, I., Saller, R. (Eds.), The Cambridge Economic History of the Greco-Roman World. Cambridge University Press, Cambridge.

Schularick, M., Solomou, S., 2011. Tariffs and economic growth in the first era of globalization. Journal of Economic Growth 16, 33–70.

Schulze, M.-S., Wolf, N., 2009. On the origins of border effects: insights from the Habsburg empire. Journal of Economic Geography 9, 117–136.

Shah Mohammed, S.I., Williamson, J.G., 2004. Freight rates and productivity gains in British tramp shipping 1869-1950. Explorations in Economic History 41, 174–203.

Shiue, C., 2002. Transport costs and the geography of arbitrage in 18th century China. The American Economic Review 92, 1406–1419.

Shiue, C.H., Keller, W., 2007. Markets in China and Europe on the eve of the Industrial revolution. The American Economic Review 97, 1189–1216.

Solar, P., 2013. Opening to the East: shipping between Europe and Asia, 1770-1830. The Journal of Economic History 73, 625–661.

Solar, P., Hens, L., 2016. Ship speeds during the Industrial revolution: East India company ships, 1770-1828. European Review of Economic History 20, 66–78.

Standaert, S., Ronnse, S., Vandermaliere, B., 2016. Historical trade integration: globalization and the distance puzzle in the long twentieth century. Cliometrica 10, 225–250.

Steinwender, C., 2018. Real effects of information frictions: when the States and the Kingdom became United. The American Economic Review 108, 657–696.

Studer, R., 2008. India and the great divergence. Assessing the efficiency of grain markets in 18th and 19th century India. The Journal of Economic History 68, 393–437.

Swinnen, J., 2009. The growth of agricultural protection in Europe in the 19th and 20th centuries. World Economy 32, 1499–1537.

Tadei, F., 2020. Measuring extractive institutions: colonial trade and price gaps in French Africa. European Review of Economic History 24, 1–24.

Temin, P., 2013. The Roman Market Economy. Princeton University Press, Princeton.

Tena-Junguito, A., 2010. Bairoch revisited: tariff structure and growth in the late nineteenth century. European Review of Economic History 14, 111–145.

Tena-Junguito, A., Lampe, M., Tamega-Fernandes, F., 2012. How much trade liberalization was there in the world before and after Cobden-Chevalier? The Journal of Economic History 72, 708–740.

Timini, J., 2018. Currency unions and heterogeneous trade effects: the case of the Latin Monetary Union. European Review of Economic History 22, 322–348.

Uebele, M., Gallardo-Albarran, D., 2015. Paving the way to modernity. Prussian roads and grain market integration in Westphalia, 1821-1855. Scandinavian Economic History Review 63, 69–92.

Van Bavel, B., 2016. The Invisible Hand? How Market Economies Have Emerged and Declined Since AD 500. Oxford University Press, Oxford. 316 pp.

Van Zanden, J.L., van Leeuwen, B., 2012. Persistent but not consistent: the growth of national income in Holland 1348-1807. Explorations in Economic History 49, 119–130.

Van Zanden, J.L., van Tielhof, M., 2009. Roots of growth and productivity change in Dutch shipping industry. Explorations in Economic History 46, 389–403.

Will, P.-E., Wong Roy, B., with Lee, J., 1991. Nourish the People. The State Civilian Granary System in China 1650-1850. Center for Chinese Studies Publications, University of Michigan.

Williamson, J., 1990. The impact of the corn laws just prior to repeal. Explorations in Economic History 27, 123–156.

Williamson, J., 2011. Trade and Poverty. When the Third World Fell Behind. MIT Press, Cambridge (Mass).

Wolf, N., Schulze, M.-S., Heinemeyer, H.-C., 2011. On the economic consequence of the peace: trade and borders after Versailles. The Journal of Economic History 71, 915–947.

Yi, X., van Leeuwen, B., van Zanden, J.L., 2018. Urbanization in China, ca 1100-1900. Frontiers of Economics in China 13, 322–368.

Yoon, Y.J., forthcoming. Tariffs and industrialization in late nineteenth century America: the role of scale economies. European Review of Economic History.

Why Africa is not *that* poor

Ewout Frankema

Wageningen University, Wageningen, The Netherlands

πάντα ῥεῖ ∼ *everything flows*
Heraclitus of Ephesus

19.1 Introduction

To the envy of many other fields of scholarship, economic history can boast with a strong academic identity grounded in a collective effort to unravel a highly complex and important puzzle held together by a single meta-question: why are some societies rich and others poor? As long as questions of wealth, poverty, and inequality resonate with public audiences there is a place for a community of economic historians. In times of methodological contestation, such as the Cliometric turn of the 1960s, this community may experience an identity crisis, but one that typically stimulates creativity and debate. It remains to be seen whether the second revolution in economic history, driven by so-called persistence studies, equally justifies the term 'revolution', but it is hard to deny that it has sparked new conversations (Cioni et al., 2021). Whether one identifies as an economic *historian* or as a historical *economist*, when we are able to stir debate, to rejuvenate, to excite, and to draw in new members from the outside, our community will thrive.[1]

This is no less true for *African* economic history. Since the late 1990s a rising flow of studies has constituted, in the words of Hopkins (2009), a 'new' economic history of Africa, a renaissance of a field that faced near existential threats in the early 1990s (see also Austin and Broadberry, 2014; Cogneau, 2016). Africa became especially popular among scholars working in the new branch of persistence studies. Since 2001, more persistence papers have appeared on Africa than on all OECD countries together, and these have also been cited much more (Cioni et al., 2021, Table 4, p. x).[2] In addition, a considerable number of persistence studies of global scope, including the now famous "AJR 2001", developed viewpoints on African comparative development that have gained considerable traction (Acemoglu et al., 2001).

Why did Africa attract the spotlight of the second revolution? And how has this new branch of research shifted the knowledge frontier on questions of long-term African development? This essay

---

[1] I deliberately refrain from backing up these claims with references to publications that have had far-reaching societal impact. I presume all readers can fill this in for themselves.

[2] Most of the studies discussed in this chapter focus on parts of Sub-Saharan Africa. For convenience sake I will mainly refer to Africa.

The Handbook of Historical Economics. https://doi.org/10.1016/B978-0-12-815874-6.00035-6

addresses both questions by surveying and classifying the various causal narratives that have been advanced in, what I for convenience-sake label as, African historical economics (AHE henceforth). The discussion will focus on the contribution of the persistence studies (PS). Persistence studies link historical phenomena – often referred to as 'events' or 'treatments' – to present-day societal conditions – often dubbed 'outcomes' – usually spanning one or more centuries in time. While the historical 'events' are wide-ranging, the 'outcomes' are mostly confined to indicators of current economic performance. I will highlight how many of these studies are inspired by, and rooted in, older strands of African economic history (AEH). I will also discuss some theoretical and empirical contributions that qualify as non-economic outcome studies (NEOS), or studies that engage with African economic history by focusing on processes of transition instead of continuity.[3]

Three interrelated arguments will tie this essay together. Firstly, I contend that the conception of Africa as an *exceptionally* poor region offers a highly attractive *explanandum* for empirical tests of historical persistence in which poverty is implicitly equated with economic and institutional stasis. Secondly, I argue that a pre-occupation with proving persistence has led to a *surplus of explanations* of structural poverty and an *underexposure* of both the realities as well as possibilities of social, political, economic, and cultural change: Africa is neither as poor nor as static as the collective body of persistence studies suggests. Thirdly, I posit that the overwhelming success of the persistence studies in unearthing correlations between historical and contemporary variables impels scholars working with the notion of *path dependence* to reflect more systematically on the relationship between forces of persistence and forces of mutability (see also Voth, 2021).[4]

Such systematic reflections include questions such as: how many paths from the deep past can run into the present without drifting apart or evaporating and petering out? How do paths from the deep past collide into other, younger paths without being overridden? How accurate is the term historical 'event' in reference to eight decades of colonial institutional development, four centuries of slave trading, or millennia of ethnic and genetic drift? Can such 'events' or 'treatments' be meaningfully cast into a single numerical variable, and if so, what are such variables exactly capturing, and what do they ignore – the baby, the bathwater? Has post-colonial history had any effect on the economic performance of African societies, or have the structural impediments of Africa's historical legacies chiseled the region's development trajectories in stone? And at the most fundamental level: how useful is it to conceptualize history in a classic Marxist fashion, as a chain of multiple equilibria, instead of a continuum of disequilibria? (Nunn, 2009, p. 75). Engaging with such fundamental questions of durability and change in human history requires a shift in focus from static comparative research designs, towards more dynamic conceptions of long-term development. In such conceptions, *history* cannot be treated as a bridge connecting two banks of a sleepy river. History, as Heraclitus famously pondered, is an ever-flowing river in which one cannot step twice.

I do not aim to provide a comprehensive survey of the AHE literature. Several reviews have appeared in the past decade, including a recent one by Michalopoulos and Papaioannou (2020) which is more extensive than mine, but adopts a different categorization (see also Nunn, 2009; Fenske, 2010; Fourie, 2016; Fourie and Obikili, 2019). I will also largely refrain from discussing the methodological boundaries between the *historical economics* and *economic history* of Africa, apart from noting that

---

[3] See Cioni et al. (2021) for the acronyms PS and NEOS, the acronyms AHE and AEH are mine.

[4] For a fine example of the concepts used by sociologists to analyze the tensions between institutional durability and institutional change, see Clemens and Cook (1999).

there is substantial overlap, cross-fertilization as well as some outspoken heuristic antagonism (Hopkins, 2009; Fenske, 2012; Akyeampong et al., 2014; Austin and Broadberry, 2014; Cogneau, 2016).[5]

The persistence studies as such have been criticized from many sides – and not just by professional historians. Comments have been made on the reliability, validity, and uncritical use of historical data (Albouy, 2012; Jerven, 2013; Meier zu Selhausen, 2019), on estimation methods and specifications (Cogneau and Dupraz, 2014; Bickenbach et al., 2016; Kelly, 2019), on conceptual issues related to the 'compression of history' (Austin, 2008a; Jerven, 2015), and euro-centric bias (Austin, 2007; Bayly, 2008; Frankema et al., 2018). Voices have also been raised against the historical determinism inherent to persistence studies and their neglect of fundamental patterns of change in Africa and beyond (Jerven, 2010; Frankema and van Waijenburg, 2012; Banerjee and Duflo, 2014; Arroyo Abad and Maurer, 2019). I will keep most of these cans of worms closed. It is clear that persistence studies are hitting a nerve. This essay touches upon the nerve of the narrative.

19.2 Africa in the spotlight

Why has Africa attracted the spotlight? I believe the most important reason is that in the past three decades the *global* poverty problem has become the *African* poverty problem. Whereas in 1990 ca. 80% of the world's extreme poor were of Asian descent, in 2020 ca. 85% of the world's extreme poor are concentrated in Africa, and especially south of the Sahara. Despite the steady decline in relative rates of poverty, Africa's total poverty headcount has continued to rise under pressure of population growth, and it may well continue to do so in the coming decades (World Bank, 2020; Frankema and van Waijenburg, 2018). Understanding why Africa is poor – or more precisely formulated, why the region faces greater barriers to overcoming poverty than other parts of the Global South – is not just a question of world historical significance, but also key for the design of effective development policies.

The conception of Africa as an *exceptionally poor* region offers a highly attractive explanandum for empirical research aiming to test forces of historical persistence. After all, poverty is associated with economic stagnation and institutional stasis. Right at the time that worldwide poverty eradication moved to the top of the international community's policy agenda with the development and implementation of the UN Millennium Development Goals, debates on the *geographic versus institutional* roots of (under)development caught on. The proposition that Africa's unique biogeographic endowments have placed constraints on long-term economic development was put forward in a series of papers (e.g. Sachs and Warner, 1997; Bloom et al., 1998; Gallup et al., 1999) and one very popular book (Diamond, 1997) appearing in the late 1990s. These studies provoked instant responses by proponents of the neo-institutional school (Acemoglu et al., 2001, 2002; Rodrik et al., 2004). Instead of infertile soils, endemic droughts, and endemic tropical disease, these studies pointed in the direction of ethnic heterogeneity, colonial institutions, and the African slave trades to explain persistent African underdevelopment (Easterly and Levine, 1997; Bertocchi and Canova, 2002; Nunn, 2008; Acemoglu and Robinson, 2010). This all happened at a time when a large number of African countries reached the trough of a prolonged post-colonial depression, a series of 'lost decades' that were also observed

---

[5] Not only are the boundaries with African Economic History diffuse, next to Historical Economics there is also something that could be called Historical Political Science.

in 19th century Latin America (Bates et al., 2007). At the time, influential media outlets such as *The Economist* characterized Africa as the 'hopeless continent'.[6] As we will see below, some of the early AHE studies used similar frames.

Although economists, as most social scientists, are ultimately driven to understand the challenges of the world today, and not primarily the problems of the past (Abramitzky, 2015), *African history* quickly began to capture the imagination. Earlier generations of historians, anthropologists, sociologists, and economists had formulated a range of thought-provoking theses on the deeper roots and nature of African development. Armed with state-of-the-art regression techniques, a new generation of economists, including some political scientists, ventured out to put these theses to the test. Add to the presence of testable theses the fact that the African continent – as well as many African countries – contain high degrees of demographic, genetic, ethno-linguistic, geographic, and ecological variation, and one can see the treasure trove for econometricians in search of large N-samples shining. Heterogeneity is the fuel that keeps the motor of multivariate regression models roaring, and is key for obtaining the statistically significant results that top journals in economics find worth publishing.

Africa not only held the key to the global question of poverty, it also turned out that the quantitative data that could shed light on its *exceptional* development path were not as scarce as long thought. Colonial governments and 'native' authorities, Christian churches and missionaries, European slave traders and railway companies, courts and custom houses, they had all kept records on historical phenomena that are relevant to the study of long-term African development. Anthropologists, geographers, and demographers had also compiled extensive qualitative and quantitative reports on topics as varied as the location of missionary stations, rates of urbanization, land use, agricultural output, marriages, polygamy, and ethno-linguistic profile. Data sources such as the British colonial Blue Books, Murdock's ethnographic atlas (1967) and the missionary maps of Beach (1903) and Roome (1925) have now been exploited for dozens of research projects. That these data were almost exclusively produced by non-Africans was of concern to hairsplitting historians who did (and do) not understand our models and techniques anyway, so I was told in the corridor. Meanwhile the data on contemporary societal conditions also expanded quickly, with micro-level data contained in censuses made accessible by IPUMS, public opinion data by the Afrobarometer, household survey and living standards data by, amongst others, the World Bank. Influenced by the burgeoning field of behavioral economics, historical economists have even started to generate new data in-the-field, through behavioral experiments wrapped up in pre-designed 'games' (e.g. Lowes et al., 2017).

Advancements in GIS-software further enabled researchers to map ecological, demographic, and geographical variation at fine-grained spatial resolutions, which have in turn allowed for the construction of new dependent variables as well as large batteries of control variables (e.g. colonial borders, ethnic borders, light density, ruggedness, crop suitability indices). While the first AHE papers were based on cross-country regressions, and mostly analyzed Africa's economic standing in a global comparative frame to maximize estimation power, in the 2010s the field moved on to exploit the promises of more fine-grained data at the sub-national level, shedding new light on Africa's highly diverse economic geography and its inherent spatial inequalities.

However, new data, methods, and techniques cannot explain the sudden popularity of Africa as a place for persistence studies. After all, these factors were not unique to Africa. The real attraction of

---

[6] Front cover of the issue of 13 May 2000. An apology followed in the 'Africa rising' issue of 3 December 2011.

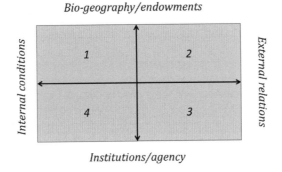

Bio-geography/endowments

Internal conditions

External relations

Institutions/agency

FIGURE 19.1

Diagram to classify explanations of long-term African development. *Source*: author's own.

the region appears to be in its image of the exception: the only world region that remains mired in a state of poverty that other world regions escaped, or are escaping. It is this image of stasis that has sparked a wave of scholarly creativity and associated rhetoric of tragedy and failure. We shall now look more deeply into the explanations of African poverty.

19.3 Historical causes of African underdevelopment

The simple 2 × 2 diagram provided in Fig. 19.1 helps us to classify the key explanations of long-term African development that have been advanced in both the AHE as well as the more 'traditional' AEH literature. The two axes divide the field into four areas. The vertical axis juxtaposes Africa's bio-geographic conditions – or endowments – with the role of institutions. The term endowment here refers to natural resources and ecological conditions as well as relative factor proportions (i.e. land, labor, and capital). Institutions are broadly understood as the "*humanly devised constraints that structure political, economic, and social interaction*", loosely put "the rules of the game", the fruit of human agency (North, 1991, p. 97). The horizontal axis then contrasts internal conditions with external relations, including foreign interventions. The conditions (and structures) that are endogenous to African environments and societies have obviously been of greater relative importance in times preceding globalization and imperial encroachment. The influence of external forces on the development of African economies have arguably grown with the rise of global trade and the onset of European imperialism. This temporal context is important to keep in the back of our minds.

In what follows I will trace the underlying logic of proposed causal mechanisms which are often cutting across two or more quadrants. Q1 refers to the various opportunities of, and constraints imposed on, long-term development by African endowments. Q2 refers to Africa's biogeography interacting with external forces, such as the comparative (dis)advantages underpinning Africa's trade relations with the rest of the world (e.g. slave exports, tropical cash-crop exports), as well as foreign (European) settlement patterns that have been determined by local biogeographic conditions (e.g. tropical disease incidence). Q3 refers to the institutions that have arisen in the context of external relations, especially those imposed by colonial powers. Q4 refers to historical institutions of African societies that have not, or only lightly, been affected by external forces.

19.3.1 Africa's biogeographic misfortunes

African bio-geographies, so it is argued by many, have severely constrained the region's opportunities of agricultural productivity growth, commodity transportation, and demographic expansion, more so than in other world regions (Sachs and Warner, 1997; Bloom et al., 1998; Gallup et al., 1999). These impediments include relatively poor soils that tend to be quickly exhausted, vast savannah and desert ecologies that are unsuitable for (intensive) crop cultivation, and highly erratic rainfall regimes which have kept African farmers mobile and risk averse. The relatively limited number of navigable waterways and natural harbors made human porterage the default mode of transportation in many places before the arrival of motorized transportation technology. Compared to the possibilities of water transportation in Europe and North Africa, with its inland Mediterranean Sea, dense web of navigable rivers and meandering coastlines dotted with navigable inlets, Sub-Saharan Africa indeed seems to have unfavorable geographic conditions for processes of agricultural commercialization and market integration.

A high incidence of tropical diseases has placed additional limits on the reproduction of human and animal populations. Farm animals were relatively hard to integrate into systems of crop cultivation and mixed husbandry was the exception, not the rule. Such diseases did not only check demographic expansion; the prevalence of lethal tropical diseases, malaria in particular, was also one of the main reasons why Europeans invaded the African interior later than they did in other world regions (Curtin, 1989). Studies by Weil (2014) and Alsan (2015) have offered quantitative estimates of the direct and indirect impact of respectively malaria and trypanosomiasis on African economic development. Weil has argued that the direct negative effects of malaria are not immediately evident, as the disease mainly raises child mortality and not so much morbidity later in life (Weil, 2014, 90-91). Alsan has argued that tsetse made a real difference, as the disease had a negative impact on population density and precolonial political centralization, which has in turn constrained economic development (captured by the nighttime luminosity). I will further discuss such indirect channels in Section 19.3.2.

Jared Diamond's (1997) *Guns, Germs and Steel* has pushed back the biogeographic explanation of current global inequality to the start of the Neolithic Revolution. Diamond argued that, in comparison to Eurasia, African agriculture has been held back by a relative paucity of wild grasses and animals suitable for domestication. The ecological heterogeneity associated with the many latitudes along the continent's vertical axis, as well as the presence of large inhospitable areas such as the Sahara Desert, have hampered the diffusion of the domesticated food crops and farm animals from the Fertile Crescent, many of which found their way into Europe, but much less so into Africa. This idea has been taken to the test by Olsson and Hibbs (2005) who confirm that initial biogeographic conditions correlate with the location and timing of transitions to sedentary agriculture and, in turn, with the development of social complexity and industrialization.

Taking all these adverse environmental conditions together it seems as if Africa has drawn virtually all the short straws. I agree with the view that Sub-Saharan African ecologies have constrained demographic expansion and agricultural intensification for a major part of the Holocene. However, there is no basis for geographic determinism. Environmental conditions may, on the whole, be slow to change, they are certainly not static. Biological globalization, technological change, and (global) market dynamics have radically shifted production possibility frontiers in rural societies out- and inwards, but mostly outwards, and this has happened in Africa on numerous occasions. For instance,

Diamond's vertical-axis argument ignores the fact that the desertification of the Sahara begun *long after* the Neolithic revolution (Diamond, 1997, Chapter 10). While tropical climates may have hindered the southward diffusion of food crops from the Eastern Mediterranean basin, there is no evidence that domesticated animals were stopped on their way to the South. In fact, there is recent evidence suggesting that the desertification of the Sahara may have been aggravated by *overgrazing*, as nomadic pastoralism spread widely into the Northern half of the continent before cattle entered into Europe. At that time the Sahara was richly endowed with water resources, plants, and forests (Wright, 2017).[7] Indeed, environments are not stable, and this is important to keep in mind when we seek to mold environmental conditions into time-invariant independent variables.

I do concur with Diamond that Sub-Saharan Africa was not well endowed with high-caloric food crops, that is, until 1492. The single biggest transition in African agriculture occurred with the introduction of a range of previously unknown crops from the New World. Earlier introductions from Asia were certainly important too, but the arrival of food crops such as maize, manioc, sweet potatoes, tomatoes, and several types of beans, as well as a large number of commercial export crops (e.g. cocoa, rubber, tobacco, vanilla, groundnuts), fundamentally altered African agriculture from the 16th through the 20th century (Crosby, 2003; McCann, 2005). Maize and manioc came to play a key role in the underpinning of African and Atlantic systems of slave raiding and trading (Wilks, 1993; Miller, 1988). The New World crops had a lasting effect on the ability of African farmers to feed expanding human populations. Modeling the demographic implications of the adoption of maize, Cherniwchan and Moreno-Cruz (2019) recently suggested that the resulting agricultural productivity gains may have stimulated both local population growth as well as the intensity of slave raiding, such that the *net* demographic effect of the Columbian exchange has been close to zero. This paper thus focuses on understanding a key transition in African history, without making a connection to the present. The modeling of transition scenarios can help to circumvent the obvious limitations of historical data, especially in periods before 1900. It wouldn't surprise me if this is one of the routes in which the AHE literature develops in the coming years along with the persistence studies wave.

The combination of tropical ecologies and the diffusion of New World crops gave African economies a specific edge in the development of commercial export crops during the so-called 'commercial revolution' of the late 18th and 19th centuries (Hopkins, 1973; Law, 1995; Austin, 2005; Dalrymple-Smith, 2020). The export of palm oil (an indigenous crop), groundnuts and gum overtook West African slave exports in total value in the 1830s, and the export crop portfolio expanded with amongst others rubber, cocoa, cotton, coffee, tea, and tobacco in the colonial era (Frankema et al., 2018). A recent study by Roessler et al. (2020) addresses the long-term effects of this 'cash-crop revolution'.[8] Using agroclimatic suitability scores and historical data on the production location of export crops they demonstrate that colonial cash crop production exhibited a large and positive long-run effect on the spatial distribution of cities, road infrastructure, nighttime luminosity, and household wealth. They also show that colonial infrastructural investments related to the cash-crop booms deepened spatial economic inequalities and that these effects rival or surpass other geographic and historical drivers of African development. This paper thus shows how new paths of persistence may override older paths

---

[7] Elsewhere I have questioned Diamond's idea that domesticated animals were crucial in the development of human diseases, as many of Africa's lethal diseases appear to stem from wild animals (Frankema, 2015).

[8] The term was popularized by John Tosh (1980).

of persistence. In a region where, in a very short window of time, modern infrastructure and urbanization has profoundly reconfigured the geographies of human settlement, including production and consumption patterns, the appearance of such effects makes good sense.

Indeed, the diffusion of new technology has been the key factor in overcoming many of Africa's biogeographic misfortunes. The great advances made in combatting tropical diseases reveal that poverty traps caused by hostile ecological conditions are not insurmountable (Deaton, 2013, Chapter 3). Medical technologies have contributed to rapid decreases in child mortality, increases in life expectancies and rapid demographic growth that is bound to continue far into the 21st century. Jedwab and Moradi (2016) have shown how railroad infrastructure has been key in the formation of cities and has decisively reconfigured the economic geography of Africa by lifting constraints on transportation and agglomeration (see also Jedwab et al., 2017). Green revolution technologies, revolving around the adoption of improved seed varieties, offer another example of the potential to overcome malnutrition in rural areas, to further lower child mortality and to raise agricultural productivity and income, even though part of the potential remains to be reaped (Larson and Otsuka, 2013; von der Goltz et al., 2020).

19.3.2 Indirect effects of African endowments

Let us return to the diagram (Fig. 19.1). In addition to the shifting palette of direct bio-geographic constraints on long-term African demographic and economic expansion, there are several indirect effects of the historical endowment structure that have received emphasis in the AEH and AHE literatures.[9] Such indirect effects involve more complex channels of influence. I will confine the discussion to two of these channels, which I label the *factor market* channel and the *state formation* channel.

The factor market channel is primarily associated with the Nieboer-Domar thesis.[10] This thesis holds that in a context of low population densities (labor scarcity) and open land frontiers (land abundance), which characterizes the majority of pre-20th century Africa, two possible institutional equilibria can arise: 1) an egalitarian social order with free farmers who add value to land by clearing and preparing it for agriculture. This equilibrium emerges where aspirant-elites fail to control the peasantry by limiting their access to land; or 2) an inegalitarian social order in which elites extract surpluses by controlling the peasantry. This situation emerges where elites succeed in limiting peasant's access to (virgin) land or in monopolizing critical agricultural inputs, skills, or capital. Only by limiting the mobility of peasants can elites have the power to coerce labor and avoid paying prohibitively high market-clearing wages. Historical institutions of serfdom and slavery are key examples of such forms of labor coercion (Domar, 1970, pp. 18-21).

The Nieboer-Domar thesis has been widely embraced in AEH to explain the prevalence of African slavery, as well as other labor market institutions such as human pawning, debt-bondage, and various forms of colonial labor coercion (Hopkins, 1973; Iliffe, 2007; Austin, 2008b; van Waijenburg, 2018). For a formal test of the thesis, Fenske compiled cross-sectional data on a global sample of societies from Murdock's (1967) *Ethnographic Atlas*, showing that the historical nature of land rights, slavery and population density are indeed co-determined. Modern survey data for Ghana suggests that histori-

---

[9] Acemoglu et al. (2001) have classified biogeographic explanations of development into 'simple' and 'sophisticated' geography hypotheses, where the latter refers to the effects of the natural environment on economic development via their influence on institutional development.

[10] Domar built his thesis on ideas originally posited by the Dutch ethnologist H.J. Nieboer.

cal institutions with regards to land tenure are related to the functioning of land markets today (Fenske, 2013). In a related case-study, Fenske used colonial court records showing that, up to the early 20th century, the Egba in Nigeria had imprecisely defined land rights, systems of forced labor and labor-secured lending practices. Subsequent changes in endowment structures and the introduction of tree crops led to the rise of markets for credit and the most valuable portions of land (Fenske, 2012). These two papers are not only interesting for their results but also because of their varying research design. The first is an example of a persistence study, but the second analyses a historical transition in factor market institutions, revealing an important driver of historical change: altering relative factor proportions and natural endowments (i.e. tree crops) provoke processes of fundamental institutional change. These rapid shifts in factor ratios are another reason, in addition to technological change, to treat claims of long-term persistence with caution (Austin, 2016; Frankema and van Waijenburg, 2018).

The *state formation* channel follows a comparable line of reasoning, starting from endowments. Carneiro (1970) formulated the 'environmental circumscription thesis' to account for the historical origins of the state as a centralized political body. His thesis holds that ancient states were more likely to emerge in areas where the available agricultural land was scarce and clearly circumscribed by non-agricultural land, such as river basins, highlands and islands, than in areas without such natural boundaries. The Egyptian Nile basin surrounded by extensive desert areas offers a clear example of such a circumscribed setting, the Amazonian rain forest its antithesis. Carneiro reasoned that in the circumscribed areas, where possibilities for people to escape and sustain their original livelihoods were limited, warfare would ultimately lead to one group being subjected to another. Following defeat, tribute systems (in kind, people (slaves) or cash) would arise and support the verticality of political relations. If such processes of economic and political integration are extended to other settlements in the area, the process of state centralization gains momentum. In the rain forest, in contrast, cross-community warfare would lead to a dispersal of human settlements at distances far enough to seek refuge in isolation. In such a context vertical power structures are less likely to emerge.

Jeffery Herbst (2000) did not cite Domar, nor Carneiro, when he set out his thesis of historical state formation in Africa, but his ideas are closely related. Herbst argues that in lowly populated parts of Africa state centralization has been challenging since the marginal costs of tax collection and border defense easily exceeded expected marginal revenues. These constraints gave rise to a scattered landscape of African states and acephalous societies with fluid territorial boundaries and extensive uncontrolled hinterlands. African states, Herbst argues, prioritized control over people in the centers of power, instead of controlling clearly delineated territories which had formed the basic principle of state formation and state competition in Europe (see Tilly, 1990). The high mobility of Africans, especially among pastoral or semi-pastoral peoples, further complicated processes of state formation.

Osafo-Kwaako and Robinson (2013) have countered Herbst by arguing that contrary to the rest of the world, *within* Africa, there exists a negative correlation between population density and state centralization. Building on anthropological work by McIntosh (1999), amongst others, they contend that the critical factors of Eurasian state formation, including trade and warfare, fail to explain the rise of vertical political hierarchies in Africa. Acephalous societies in Africa could be densely populated and have horizontal authority structures. According to the authors, the social logic underpinning ancient processes of African state formation require a deeper understanding of cultural evolution instead of plain demographics.

One of the reasons that a correlation between state centralization and population density may fail to show up within Africa – apart from the fact that claims to the use of accurate pre-colonial population data must be taken with a large grain of salt – is that the military and logistic technologies that supported the rise of savannah states were ineffective in the forest zones. Like the Mongol empire of the 13th century, the West African savannah states were able to bring vast lowly populated territories under control via horse and camel-back warriors that could cover large distances irrespective of seasonal weather patterns. These states could tap into the rents of long-distance trade and force major trade hubs (cities) to pay tribute with the credible threat of force in case of non-compliance. The internal cohesion of these centralized states remained fragile, and the risk of imperial overstretch was large. In the forest zones, states remained smaller, as they were mainly held together by foot soldiers whose mobility depended on the dry season. These conditions constrained the reach of armies, as well as possibilities of fiscal expansion based on elaborate systems of tax assessment (Goody, 1971; Coquery Vidrovitch, 1985; Frankema, 2015). But apart from the ecology-dependent mechanisms of state formation, the other question that looms large over this debate is how the anthropologist George Murdock managed, without any professional experience in Africa, to gather all the 'historical' data that underpins several claims of African exceptionalism.[11]

19.3.3 The African slave trades

Slave raiding and trading are another 'exceptional' aspect of African history not because slavery as such was unique to the region, but because of its pervasive and prolonged nature: the sea-bound trades carried on until the last decade of the 19th century, and the intra-continental trades continued several decades more into the 20th century (Manning, 1990; Lovejoy and Hogendorn, 1993). To what extent the slave trades may be classified as an internal (Q4) or external driver (Q2) of African development is difficult to judge. It was the interplay between the internal supply of, and external demand for, slaves – as well as external demand for slave-produced commodities within Africa – that shaped the systems of slave raiding and trading for several centuries. The slave trades are also problematic to understand from an endowments point of view: why would labor scarce economies engage in large-scale export of its most valuable production factor? What is clear though, is that volatile markets and local institutional changes generated continuous reconfigurations in practices of enslavement, in trade relations with Europeans, Americans, Arabs, as well as Africans, and that the integration of slaves within African societies was also affected by the forces of external demand (Miers and Kopytoff, 1977; Lovejoy, 2000). These tight connections between internal and external slave trade networks should deserve particular attention in studies trying to grapple with the long-term effects of the African slave trades, as Whatley (2020) rightly observes.

What do these effects look like? I will confine the discussion to three aspects: demography, state formation and (mis)trust. Thanks to the collective effort of a large group of historians, a vast database of the trans-Atlantic slave trades has been constructed that provides a much more accurate picture of many dimensions of these trades than existed a few decades ago (Eltis et al., 1999; Klein, 2010). Other parts of the external trade, such as the Indian Ocean and Red Sea trades, have not been nearly so precisely documented. The numbers of enslaved Africans shipped abroad remain guesstimates based mainly on the work by Austen (1988; 1992) and Manning (1990; 2010). Data on the volumes of internally traded and retained slaves are even harder to come by, although Austen (1979) provides estimates of the

---

[11] See for instance Murdock (1959, 1967).

trans-Saharan trade, the most important internal trade system. The large gap between the observed and un(der)observed parts of the trade complicates efforts to pin-down the long-term effects of the African slave trades, especially in terms of its effect on the distribution of population.

The negative demographic effects of the trades at the macro level are clear. Especially in the two centuries between 1650 and 1850, the large-scale export of young men and women in their reproductive ages as well as children prior to their reproductive ages seriously reduced Africa's population growth potential, while many Eurasian populations in those days doubled in size. Not only captives that were shipped abroad, but also people who were wounded or killed in raids and long-distance travels reduced demographic growth. Starting in the late 1970s, Manning has led the research on the demographic consequences of the slave trade, by developing and refining simulation methods. He extended his models of the trans-Atlantic slave trades to the Indian Ocean and intra-African slave trade systems, using census estimates of the 1950s–1960s to project population series back in time (Manning, 2010; 2014; see also Frankema and Jerven, 2014).

Of course, the demographic consequences of the slave trades have also had multiple indirect effects. One of these indirect effects was the undermining of local processes of state formation in areas being depopulated and the associated erosion of state institutions by endemic violence. The crumbling of the Kongo kingdom (present-day Northern Angola) and the disintegration of the Joloff empire in the Senegambia are oft-cited examples (Nunn, 2008, p. 143). Whatley and Gillezeau (2011) have argued that the slave trades have spurred ethnic fragmentation in Africa. They take a stance against the view that ethnic identity is something primordial, or even primitive, and link the roots of ethnicity as a defining feature of identity to the intensification of slave raiding in the wake of external demand. These processes of fragmentation and endemic violence were stimulated by the guns-for-slaves cycle (Whatley, 2018). Obikili (2016) has used anthropological data to show that villages and towns of ethnic groups affected by slave raiding for the export trade were politically more fragmented, and that this fragmentation continues to influence political institutions today. He finds that in Nigeria and Tanzania, areas with higher levels of precolonial political fragmentation have a higher incidence of bribery at present.

By focusing on export slavery the AHE scholarship on the topic has remained fairly one-sided, however. The internal slave trades, which almost certainly intensified along with the ocean-bound trades, have been largely neglected. Apart from the drain overseas, the intensification of slave trading *also* led to intra-African shifts in human resources. Female slaves were more often integrated into local societies than male slaves, partly for reproductive purposes, or for sale into the trade with North Africa, Arabia, and the Persian Gulf, where demand for female slaves was higher (Lovejoy, 2000, pp. 64-67). Various West African states such as Asante, Dahomey, and Oyo that specialized in slave raiding, or controlled considerable parts of the trade, did this by amassing and centralizing (fiscal) and human resources to extend their military capacity. Such processes underpinned state formation in the coastal rainforest. In the West African savannah the absorption of slaves was also a key feature in the rise of the 19th century Jihadist empires (Lovejoy, 2016). In East Africa, the majority of slaves were retained within Africa throughout the 19th century, causing notable spatial shifts in economic activity from the interior to the coast (Cooper, 1974; Sheriff, 1987). It is, therefore, not so clear what the net effects of the slave trades on state centralization have been and the historical counterfactual is absent.

Nunn's (2008) study of the long-term effects of the slave trades argues that present-day African countries that include heavily raided areas are poorer today than those that stayed outside the main arteries of raiding and trading (or were on the receiving end). While it has become one of the best

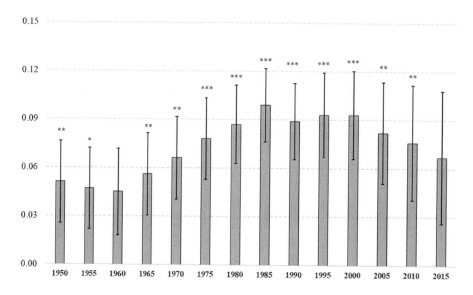

FIGURE 19.2

Regression coefficients, robust standard errors and p-values (in stars) of slave exports on GDP per capita, 1950-2015. *Source*: Replication of Nunn's regression model (2008, Table III, column 5, p. 155), using GDP per capita series 1950-2015 from the *Maddison Project Database, version 2020*. Missing values for Somalia imputed from Maddison (2010). *Note*: See Frankema and van Waijenburg (2011) for the original version of this argument.

cited works in AHE, this study is not a textbook example of robust evidence for long-term persistent effects of the African slave trades. The core regression model reveals a strong association between slave exports per area and per capita income levels in 2000. Fig. 19.2, shows a replication of the core model on a time-series of GDP per capita from 1950 and 2015 including all control variables. This replication exercise reveals how instable the main regression coefficient is in a dynamic framework: the leading regression variable, which is specified as the log of slave exports normalized by land area, rises from 1960 up to 1985, then reaches a plateau, to fall rapidly after 2000, while standard errors rise. The statistical significance of the regression coefficient is also highly volatile.

This replication underpins a crucial point of historical dynamics: how sure can we be of persistent long-term effects if we do not establish that such effects actually persist *over the course of time*? The slave trades have been an integral part of many African societies for centuries, generating a plethora of local experiences, leaving smaller and larger but in all cases highly varied imprints. That the slave trades have had long-term effects is beyond doubt, but it is rather implausible that these long-term effects are so straightforward that they show up in GDP per capita of countries that did not even exist at the time the slaves were exported.[12] It is far more likely, that the effects of the slave trades consisted of *multiple paths* that have interacted with multiple patterns of social change over time. The instability of the estimated regression points to the ever-present undercurrents of Heraclitus' river. Historical dynamics

---

[12] Note that the colonial borders of these countries may also have been affected by these trades.

were not only at work during the centuries-spanning era of the slave trades, they were also operating in the period of decolonization, post-colonial crisis and (partial) recovery since the 1950s. This begs the question to what extent the effects, as well as the outcomes, of these trades can be meaningfully cast into a single dependent and independent variable.

The follow-up study by Nunn and Wantchekon (2011) focuses on a potential mechanism and is based on sub-national data. The core finding is that levels of individual mistrust among people whose ancestors were heavily affected by the slave trade appear to be higher than among those whose ancestors have been less exposed. This result may be considered as one of the transmission channels via which export slavery has generated long-term economic underperformance. The idea is also potentially compatible with the dynamics shown in Fig. 19.2. The major slave exporting areas started to experience a set-back precisely in the period that the power vacuums of decolonization and early nation-state formation led to intensive political conflict, with severely negative economic consequences. In that case, the effects of the slave trades were *interacting* with historical processes that unfolded later in time and subsided accordingly. But the trend in Fig. 19.2 may also just reflect spurious correlation or alternative forms of historical interaction. Perhaps the major slave exporting regions have retained more open economies after abolition and were hit particularly severely by the depression in commodity prices in the 1970s to the 1990s?

The take-home message here is that forces of persistence never carve out their path through history in isolation. Instead of relegating relevant historical dynamics to the realm of control variables, it seems worthwhile to bring such dynamics to the fore. After all, *history also matters when the stars do not shine*.

19.3.4 Colonial institutions

The *Colonial Origins* paper by Acemoglu et al. (2001) became the best cited study in historical economics (Cioni et al., 2021, p. x). The idea that high rates of settler mortality due to tropical diseases incentivized European powers to impose 'extractive institutions' at arm's length, and that these colonial institutions, in turn, have led to persistently weak systems of property rights and rule of law today, gained enormous traction. Contrary to what new generations of economists seem to believe, "AJR" were certainly *not* the first to argue that areas with a high incidence of tropical diseases, such as malaria, yellow fever and tsetse, were less attractive to European settlers than areas with temperate climates where such diseases did not exist. Yet, the paper also caught attention because of its bold thesis, its sweeping global scope, as a critical intervention in the 'geography *versus* institutions' debate and because of its revolutionary identification strategy, in which settler mortality rates were used as an *instrumental variable* for the type of institutions established in European colonies. Indeed, this study put the second revolution in economic history on the radar once and for all.

Interestingly, the authors framed their paper as evidence of how institutions rule over geography in explaining present-day distribution of income across the globe, while the core narrative basically follows the 'sophisticated geography' argument they seek to reject: internal biogeographic conditions (Q1) shape colonial institutions (Q3), and colonial institutions shape present-day institutions (Q4). It is also interesting to note that the proposed global relationship, as Acemoglu and Robinson (2012) admitted in *Why Nations Fail*, fails to hold for Africa as such.[13] In Africa's *settler colonies* the degree of extraction, in the form of systematic labor repression, racial discrimination, regressive taxation, and land alienation, was (far) more intense than in colonies where Europeans hardly settled, especially those where African producers remained dominant in agricultural export sectors, many of which had originated in the era prior to colonization. In most of the *peasant export colonies* real wages were higher, taxes were less regressive and, in some cases, foreign land ownership was even prohibited (Bowden et al., 2008; Austin, 2008a; Frankema, 2011; Frankema and van Waijenburg, 2012). Nevertheless, AJR 2001 has been extremely influential in staging the debate on colonial legacies in Africa and have inspired a vast number of follow-up studies.

One of these wider debates concerns the question to what extent colonial institutions have been shaped by the identity of the colonizer and specific metropolitan policy goals, and to what extent these were dictated by local African conditions, including the agency of Africans to co-design (in)formal institutions.[14] Such questions have, amongst others, been explored with respect to legal origins (Lange, 2004), colonial investments (Huillery, 2009), and the supply of (missionary) education (Bolt and Bezemer, 2009; Gallego and Woodberry, 2010; Nunn, 2010; Cogneau and Moradi, 2014; Dupraz, 2019). Revisionist studies have highlighted how missionary movements have been misrepresented as a 'European' or 'colonial' legacy, as various scholars have ignored the momentous importance of the *Africanization* of the mission in terms of initiative, labor input, spatial diffusion and the maintenance of mission schools (Frankema, 2012; Meier zu Selhausen, 2019; Jedwab et al., 2019). Questions regarding the role and interaction of endogenous and exogenous forces also play a major role in studies on the development of colonial fiscal regimes: how extensive was the political control of colonial regimes, and what were the countervailing powers or conditions that limited the arm of the state? (Gardner, 2012; Frankema and van Waijenburg, 2014). Put differently, how does Cooper's conceptualization of the colonial state as a 'gatekeeper state' relate to Young's view of *Bula Matari*, the 'absolutist' state that crushes rocks? (Young, 2012; Cooper, 2002, see also Kirk-Greene, 1980).

Another strand of literature has engaged with the long-term effects of the artificial state borders established by colonial powers and the effects these borders had on the political amalgamation of different ethnic groups, as well as the splitting apart of ethnic homelands. The seminal study by Easterly and Levine (1997) in which ethnic diversity in a global sample is linked to a range of contemporary economic and political indicators, including schooling, political stability, financial development, foreign exchange markets, government deficits, and infrastructure, did not see Africa's ethnic heterogeneity as a result of the Scramble, but rather as a deeper social condition. In later studies these borders came to the fore (Englebert et al., 2002). Alesina et al. (2011) constructed new variables to measure the artificiality of borders and concluded that these were negatively related with GDP per capita in a global sample of countries. Michalopoulos and Papaioannou (2016) explored within-country variation in ethnic partitioning, conflict, and public goods, revealing that individuals who self-identify with partitioned ethnicities have fewer household assets, poorer access to utilities, and worse educational outcomes as

---

[13] In Why Nations Fail Acemoglu and Robinson modified their original account, arguing that the settler colonies of Africa, and especially South Africa, were characterized by dual institutional structures: inclusive institutions were exclusively reserved for European settlers, while exclusive institutions applied to indigenous peoples (Acemoglu and Robinson, 2012, pp. 258-271).

[14] This debate is also of central importance in the literature on the American economic divergence. See, for instance, North et al. (2000); Engermann and Sokoloff (2005); Mahoney (2010); see Elliott (2006) for a brilliant historical synthesis.

compared to respondents from ethnic groups that were not split by a border.[15] In a regression discontinuity analysis of the border regions Côte d'Ivoire is sharing with Mali, Ghana, and Guinee, Cogneau et al. (2015) have argued against the idea that predetermined geographical and historical conditions were decisive. Their study suggests that reversible post-colonial policies with respect to cash-crop farming (cocoa and coffee) explain a great deal of the discontinuities in consumption and nutrition observed in border regions, which points to an ongoing process of national integration. I will get back to the pressing question of how history overtakes history in Section 19.4.

19.3.5 Indigenous institutions and cultural roots

The final category of theories pertains to the role of indigenous institutions in long-term African development (Q4 in Fig. 19.1). The dominant research question focuses on the link between indigenous institutions, formal and informal, and African poverty, or related vices such as political conflict, violence, or entrepreneurial disincentives.

Africa's fragmented landscape of centralized polities and acephalous societies in pre-colonial times has been the main point of departure for a series of persistence studies that have emphasized how weak state centralization has led to present-day underdevelopment. On a global scale, 'state antiquity' has been shown to positively correlate with present-day income levels, and since Africa does not have a strong legacy of antique states it is now poor (Bockstette et al., 2002; Putterman and Weil, 2010). Gennaioli and Rainer (2007) have used the Murdock atlas to argue that state centralization is positively correlated with cross-country differences in school attainment, literacy, paved roads, and immunizations. Englebert (2000) has argued that modern states in Africa which inherited their legitimacy from a pre-colonial predecessor have fared better than those that emerged from a colonial blueprint. Michalopoulos and Papaioannou (2013) have shown that the complexity and hierarchical structure of pre-colonial ethnic institutions correlates with current nightlight density, which they use as a proxy for local (i.e. sub-national) economic development.[16] Huillery (2009) has pointed out that the parts of French West Africa that had more centralized states in pre-colonial times offered more resistance to French conquest and received less investments after the establishment of French control.

No doubt, processes of state formation are deeply intertwined with processes of long-term economic development and Africa is no exception in this regard. Yet, how exactly the remnants of pre-colonial states interacted with newly imposed institutions of the colonial state, and whether these interactions are sufficiently patterned to allow for generalizations, remains an unresolved question.

Changing the focus from political institutions to institutions governing social relations, Africa is also often portrayed as a world in itself. Polygamous households, for instance, are largely confined to a so-called 'polygamy belt' stretching from present-day Senegal through to Tanzania. Polygamy has, amongst others, been associated with the crowding out of productive investment (Tertilt, 2005) and underinvestment in girls' education (Edlund and Lagerlöf, 2006). Fenske (2015) has made an important point, one that is not very often made in the persistence literature, by showing how polygamy in Africa

---

[15] There is much more work done by political scientists on the nexus between ethnicity, conflict, and public goods provision, for which I refer to the survey by Michalopoulos and Papaioannou (2020).

[16] For critique on the use of nightlight as a proxy for regional income, see Cogneau and Dupraz (2014); Bickenbach et al. (2016). See also Chen and Nordhaus (2011, p. 8594) for the original warning that luminosity data have high measurement error and cannot be used in all settings.

is on the decline. In his words, the decline of polygamy in Africa reveals "an evolution of marriage markets *as dramatic as* [Italics are mine] the rise in divorce in the United States or the decline of arranged marriage in Japan over the same period." He argued that colonial and missionary education have contributed substantially to the erosion of the values underpinning the institution. But apart from the causes, it is worth stressing that we observe no persistence here, but rather rapid institutional change.

The insight that institutions are mutable has wider relevance for a booming literature at the intersection of anthropology, psychology, and economics that emphasizes cultural evolution as a key factor in long-term economic development. One of the leading ideas in this literature is that in tight kinship systems effective cooperation occurs within cohesive in-groups, while outsiders are treated a-priori with distrust (Enke, 2019). The emergence of the nuclear family – or the loosening of such tightly knit kinship structures – has come along with moral systems that value trust and cooperation beyond the interpersonal level. The priority given to impersonal pro-sociality over interpersonal relationships, has, in turn, been considered a key condition for the emergence of well-functioning (factor) markets. An important notion in this literature is that these interactions between kinship ties, economic needs, and moral systems are amplified over time because they are self-reinforcing. This underpins explanations for the widening of global income gaps (Enke, 2019).[17]

An important cluster of arguments for the African context revolves around the role of sharing norms and redistributive pressures. Platteau (2014) provides an overview of the causes and consequences of redistributive norms in lineage-based societies in Sub-Saharan Africa (see also Platteau, 2009). He explains how the pressure of sharing norms and gift giving practices undermines economic incentives and how specific sanctions, such as witchcraft accusations, reinforce beliefs in, and practices of, redistribution. In moral systems where witch beliefs play a role, economic fortune is generally considered as a result of luck, if not predatory behavior, rather than the result of personal effort, risk taking, or talent. The less fortunate channel their envy, anger, and hatred through accusations or physical attacks on the more socially mobile members in the community. Withstanding such social pressures is costly and thus impedes entrepreneurship and the unfolding of human talents. Gershman (2016) has empirically tested the connection between witchcraft beliefs and trust, revealing that the erosion of social capital as a result of 'witch beliefs' is not an exclusively 'African' phenomenon: Europeans whose parents were born in countries with widespread witchcraft beliefs also turn out to be less trusting.

Goldstein and Udry (2008) conducted a micro-economic study linking political institutions to productivity, showing that in Akwapim (Ghana) people's position in the local political hierarchy is positively related with the security of their land tenure rights. More secure tenure leads to more investment in land fertility and higher output, which in turn, reinforces the individual's position in the political hierarchy. Acemoglu et al. (2014) explore the effect of constraints on chiefs' power on economic outcomes in Sierra Leone. In the colonial era, chiefs were selected from a ruling family that was formally recognized by the British colonial government. Chiefs ruling in chiefdoms with fewer ruling families faced less political competition and display significantly worse development outcomes today. A possible mechanism is that in such chiefdoms the security of property rights over land is weaker, as the powerful chief is subjected to fewer checks and balances.

---

[17] Ideas about the role of kinship ties, trust, and impersonal institutions are far from new. The autonomous individual as the cornerstone of market-based societies is a classic Weberian/Marxian notion, and theories connecting tribalism, lineage-based or collectivist-oriented societies, marriage patterns, and gender roles to the functioning of economic systems have a long tradition in anthropology and heterodox economics (e.g. Evans-Pritchard, 1940; Polanyi, 1944; Boserup, 1970; Goody, 1971).

Such connections between historical state institutions and present-day informal norms are also made in the work by Lowes et al. (2017) on the former Kuba Kingdom (Central Africa). The 17th century Kuba Kingdom exhibited a range of centralized institutional arrangements including an unwritten constitution, a separation of political powers, an army, police force, and judiciary, and a tax system that allowed for public goods provision. The authors find that people living within the area of the former Kuba Kingdom display weaker norms of rule following and a greater propensity to cheat for material gain than persons living just outside that territory. Their interpretation is that socially desirable behavior enforced by formal institutions tends to lower parental propensity to teach children the values of rule-following behavior. This argument goes against a larger strand of literature, partly alluded to above, that associates historical state centralization with superior development outcomes.

19.3.6 Summing up

What started with a debate on the relative importance of geography *versus* institutions in long-term economic development underpinned by cross-country regressions, has evolved into an expanding research frontier using fine-grained micro-data to explore the historical drivers and mechanisms of comparative development trajectories. The juxtaposition of geography with institutions has now been largely substituted for deeper explorations into the linkages between natural endowments and institutional design. This switch from contrast to connection has been a major improvement. After all, questions of the type 'what is more important for a car to drive, the engine or the fuel?' are much less relevant than questions of the type 'how do engines and fuel work together to move a car?'.

What should receive more emphasis, however, is the basic historical logic that biogeographic conditions have a much greater bearing on long-term economic development in the context of pre-industrial technologies and high costs of long-distance trade and communication, while institutions may start to "rule" in societies that are increasingly exposed to industrial technology, science, urbanization, globalization, and digitization. This means that supposedly persistent causal mechanisms are in fact context and time-dependent: biogeographic conditions that have constrained African population growth in one era, may evaporate in the next. Indigenous institutions that have worked well in the context of pre-industrial societies, may hamper growth in the 20th century. Such aspects of time- and context-dependence are not taken into account in the literally *decontextualized* research designs of most persistence studies.

Taking stock of the other axis, the internal *versus* external forces, a different problem comes to the fore: the bias in historical sources produced by foreigners (i.e. non-Africans) underpins Eurocentric conceptions of long-term African development. The AHE literature on missionary schooling has come a long way to acknowledge that the spread of Christianity and associated public goods such as schooling and health care have been as much an 'African' as a 'colonial' undertaking. Studies on the long-term effects of the African slave trades have focused almost exclusively on export slavery in the context of European demand, but have largely ignored the effects of internal slave mobilization on long-term institutional development and shifts in human resources and political gravity. The problem of finding a good balance between internal and external forces entails another aspect that I will highlight in the next section: historical explanations of African poverty overlook the possible impact on African economies of the outside world in the post-colonial era, an era in which external forces may have actually started to matter even more, not less.

19.4 **Why Africa is not *that* poor**

Africa is poor because of erratic rainfall, infertile soils, and its vertical continental axis, because of tsetse, ethnic fragmentation, and the slave trades. Africa is poor because of indirect rule, weak pre-colonial state centralization, and artificial states, because of extractive (or exclusive?) colonial institutions, because of polygamy, witch beliefs, pervasive mistrust and persistent sharing norms. According to some, Africa was predestined to be poor even long before the Neolithic revolution, at the time our ancestors wandered out of Africa, leaving a region behind with exceptional genetic heterogeneity (Ashraf and Galor, 2013). If all of this is true then, for sure, the hydra of poverty will never be defeated. But can all of these historical legacies be active at the same time? Are we gaping into a trap of overdetermination, or unresolved contradiction? What is going on here?

If history is only thought to matter when it shows up in models of long-term persistence, and if such models are a gateway to publishing in the top-field economics journals, then the incentives are pretty clear, and economists more than any other scholarly tribe believe in incentives. The rewards to showing *significant* correlates are high. Why would one care much about the millions of estimated *insignificant* relationships ending up in the trash bin? Damned those instances of historical change that got in my way!! What happens to the conception of long-term African development if one systematically disregards the insignificant correlations, in order to selectively distill the significant ones?[18]

But it is not only a pre-occupation with persistence, it is also the framing of the narratives in which the results are shared with academic and public audiences. Easterly and Levine (1997) set the tone with their account of Africa's "growth tragedy". Bertocchi and Canova (2002, p. 1851) sought to explore "the disastrous economic performance of Africa", which in their view "represents one of the most challenging puzzles of growth theory". Bloom et al. (1998, p. 207) set themselves the task to explain why Sub-Saharan Africa "has been the world's poorest and also its most slowly growing region [...] since the Industrial Revolution".[19] Alesina et al. (2011, p. 246) investigated the roots of Africa's economic "tragedy" and refer to other studies accounting for the region's economic and political "failures". There are many problems with framing Africa as a basket case, but the most important is that it doesn't survive a simple reality check. Africa is not *that* poor.

Wealth and poverty are relative and subjective terms. They shift along with the norms, benchmarks, and mirrors that we adopt to assess trajectories of comparative development. What do these mirrors tell us? The *global economic mirror* tells us that Africa has clearly fallen behind the Western world, as did all other regions in the world at some point during the past millennium. However, *within* the Global South, Sub-Saharan Africa has certainly *not* been the poorest region since the Industrial Revolution. As Table 19.1 shows, until the 1970s, the three largest economies of Asia in terms of population size, China, India, and Indonesia, were at least as poor as Sub-Saharan Africa in terms of average income per head of the population. Long-run GDP per capita series reveal that the South-South divergence occurred in the past half century, when large parts of Africa plunged into a prolonged depression from the 1970s to 1990s, while many Asian economies joined the convergence club. This pattern of recurrent African growth is corroborated by empirical historical research on human stature, real

---

[18] See Sala-I-Martin (1997) for the original argument in relation to the empirical growth literature. See also Lamoreaux (2015), p. 1255.

[19] Allen even took it a step further by claiming, without any evidence, that Sub-Saharan Africa has been "the poorest region of the world in 1500" and has "remained so" until the present (Alesina et al., 2011, p. 91).

Table 19.1 GDP per capita in Sub-Saharan Africa, China, India, and Indonesia, 1870-2018 (2011 US$).

	1870	1900	1920	1950	1970	2000	2018
China	945	972		799	1398	4730	13,102
India	850	955	1012	987	1384	2753	6806
Indonesia	810	1151	1409	1280	1882	5384	11,852
Sub-Saharan Africa	800	850	950	1323	**1958**	**1981**	3532

Source: *Maddison Project Database 2020; see for alternative series for British Africa, displaying similar trends, Broadberry and Gardner (2019).*

wages, reconstructed social tables, and commodity trades (Jerven, 2010; Moradi, 2009; Cogneau and Rouanet, 2011; Frankema and van Waijenburg, 2012; Juif and Frankema, 2018; Bolt and Hillbom, 2016; Federico and Tena, 2017; Frankema et al., 2018).

Let us throw some blankets over the mirrors of other world regions in order to focus exclusively on Africa's *longitudinal mirror*. What do we see? Well, it is very hard to miss the reflections of profound social and economic change, including broad-based and unprecedented improvements in human welfare. These improvements, it must be noted, have come along with increasing personal and spatial income inequalities, but African societies are certainly not unique in this regard (Chancel et al., 2019; Roessler et al., 2020). Of course, these improvements are no reason to swap Afro-pessimism for Afro-euphoria, if only because there are so many different stories of progress and retrogression, growth and decline, joy and trauma. My point is not that Africa is rich, my point is that we are looking at societies *in flux*.

The total Sub-Saharan African population has expanded from ca. 110 million in 1900 to ca. 1100 million in 2020, which is a ten-fold increase in 120 years.[20] This demographic transition, the mother of all transitions, has turned a range of economic and institutional equilibria on its head. The labor scarce continent has become the labor abundant continent. The rural landscape of yesteryear is now dotted with vast urban sprawls. Social systems, including marriage, kinship ties, communal relations, are being reconfigured with dazzling speed. The demographic revolution itself has been driven by major improvements in human health, decreasing child mortality, increasing life-expectancies and successful strides against endemic tropical diseases, despite important setbacks such as the HIV/AIDS epidemic and the current COVID-19 pandemic.

To counter the deeply ingrained pessimism about African population growth, it is worth emphasizing that the ten-fold increase in population has come along with a quadrupling of per capita GDP from ca. $850 in 1900 to ca. $3500 today (Table 19.1). Of course, the error margins of both historical as well as contemporary GDP estimates are large, but they will have to be enormous to sustain the claim that African poverty today is the same as it was 120 years ago. How does the image of the 'stagnant' African economies that 'fail' to grow relate to a ten-fold population increase times a four-times rise in per capita income, that is, a 40-fold expansion of the Sub-Saharan African economy since 1900? Just try to visualize the swelling of Heraclitus' river! Again, this is not to say that all of the change is for the

---

[20] The 1900 estimate is from Frankema and Jerven (2014); the 2020 estimate from the UN (2020).

better, but to make a case for exploring dynamics instead of stasis if we want to understand long-term African development.

Add to this the ongoing revolutions in communication, transportation, electrification, and mass education. All of these keys to productivity growth have been expanding at a faster pace than African populations have. The percentage shares of people connected to the grid (or generating electricity with solar panels) have grown, cell phones and internet are everywhere, travel times have fallen, and the majority of African children now goes to school. Educated and skilled labor have become so abundant that it has allowed for a dramatic fall in skill premiums (Frankema and Waijenburg, 2019). A recent map drawn by Smits et al. (2020) compares the *subnational human development index data* for Africa of the year 2000 and 2018. During this period, the figures for nearly all of the 546 regions reveal a marked improvement in living conditions. The few exceptions are regions in Libya, Somalia, and South Sudan for understandable reasons.

This 40-fold expansion of the Sub-Saharan African economy in the past 120 years has generated major shifts in the geography of human settlement, as well as a partial ossification of centers of economic activity that have deepened the spatial economic inequalities in the sub-continent. It is not at all surprising that micro-data reveal correlations between railways and cities, cash-crop areas and night-light density, or colonial investments and household wealth. As Voth (2021) put it '*Overwhelmingly, both the cultural universe and the built environment we inhabit was created before our time*'. Yet, for Africa, perhaps more than for any other world region, much of these built environments, and the cultural universes that encapsulate these spaces, are of comparatively recent date. What is presented as persistence are often the settlings of recent revolutionary change.

To readers who remain sceptical of the long-term effects of Africa's demographic transition: this is not just a matter of many more poor people, or swelling younger generations without perspective. It is *also* a matter of ten times as many human brains interacting at much higher levels of intensity. It is *also* a matter of a vastly growing pool of human talents, creativity and ingenuity, which increasingly surface because of steady progress in health and education, as well as unrelenting personal efforts to seek betterment, day in, day out. Africa is poor, but it is not *that* poor.

How do we reconcile persistence with change in constructing narratives of long-term African development? The research designs of persistence studies are unsuitable to tackle this question as they are inherently imbalanced: they put all the weight on deep historical forces, but treat contemporary historical developments as weightless. As long as the black box of time-fixed effects remains closed, this imbalance will persist. To give one example, persistence studies have done much to bring the external world into accounts of *deep* history, as I have shown above. But why is the external world absent in the episodes of recurrent growth in post-independence Africa? The effects of on-going globalization, technology diffusion, the Cold War, the debt crisis, the SAPs, the Asian renaissance, the rise of China? Where are they? Well, the historical forces that have *co-determined* economic development in the post-independence era have been relegated to the realm of control variables, mostly left unspecified in time-fixed effects. As long as this box stays closed, we can forget about the possibility to seriously engage with questions of opportunity, or 'scope for action', as Banerjee and Duflo (2014) have put it.

To assess the opportunities of African economies, instead of staring blind on their constraints, we need to better understand how the river of Heraclitus bends and flows. The first-order question in this regard is a classic one, namely, what it means to be economically 'behind' in the context of a rapidly changing global economic order (Gerschenkron, 1962; Austin, 2016; Frankema and van Waijenburg, 2018). How does the Asian miracle, and in particular the rise of China, shift the parameters of African economic development? To what extent does the Asian renaissance close the windows of opportunity for labor-intensive industrialization in Africa? To what extent do foreign capital investments pouring into the region hamper or stimulate economic diversification in Africa? What type of policies, neo-liberal or neo-protectionist, would be best suited to stimulate diversification? What can be expected from the newly established African free trade area? Closely linked with these questions of external competition and investment, there are questions of internal capacity: industrial technologies are widely available, capital is cheap, domestic consumer markets are growing, what is it that impedes large-scale adoption? Are African labor forces sufficiently educated to kickstart industrialization? Historical perspectives are indispensable to formulate and sharpen the key questions of present-day economic opportunity in Africa. However, if history is reduced to a collection of legacies, economic historians cannot assume that role.

19.5 Epilogue

A few years ago I attended a conference where a paper was presented on corruption in Africa. Not a persistence study, but a time-invariant RCT. The trial was set up in such a way that it allowed 'us', the audience, to observe "stealing" by African chiefs from public resources provided by the researchers. During the presentation a colleague sitting next to me whispered in my ear: "Why, Ewout, do you think they are always playing such games in African villages?". I was taken aback by the question, shook my head and turned my face, curious to hear the answer, "....because if you play such games in Russia or the US they will cost you a fortune!". Smothered laughter. (S)he then added "...I bet they do not have the research budget for that!". A joke, of course, but a biting one. Our community is often led to believe that the historical narratives we construct are formed by evidence from regression analyses and academic exchanges about identification strategies, endogeneity issues and robustness checks. This is only partly the case. The narratives we construct are also the outcome of personal priors, conceptual stretching, data-driven problem development, and many other implicit selection processes that we leave unquestioned. Once you start thinking about these questions, many emerge. I wonder, for instance, why witchcraft in Africa is always portrayed as an aspect of 'traditional' belief systems, while the mass chanting of "lock her up!" is seen as an aberration of 'modern' democratic politics. Historical research is not value-free. We need to discuss these sensitive issues more frequently and it would be a step forward if the top-field economics journals create space for such conversations.

Acknowledgments

I am grateful for comments on earlier drafts by Leticia Arroyo Abad, Denis Cogneau, Michiel de Haas, Kate Frederick, and Marlous van Waijenburg. I deeply thank Giovanni Federico and Alberto Bisin for their patience and encouragement. The usual disclaimer applies.

References

Abramitzky, R., 2015. Economics and the modern economic historian. The Journal of Economic History 75 (4), 1240–1250.

Acemoglu, D., Johnson, S., Robinson, J.A., 2001. The colonial origins of comparative development: an empirical investigation. The American Economic Review 91 (5), 1369–1401.

Acemoglu, D., Johnson, S., Robinson, J.A., 2002. Reversal of fortune: geography and institutions in the making of the modern world income distribution. The Quarterly Journal of Economics 117 (4), 1231–1294.

Acemoglu, D., Reed, T., Robinson, J.A., 2014. Chiefs: economic development and elite control of civil society in Sierra Leone. Journal of Political Economy 122 (2), 319–368.

Acemoglu, D., Robinson, J.A., 2010. Why is Africa poor? Economic History of Developing Regions 25 (1), 21–50.

Acemoglu, D., Robinson, J.A., 2012. Why Nations Fail. The Origins of Power, Prosperity and Poverty. Crown Publishers, New York.

Akyeampong, E.K., Bates, R.H., Nunn, N., Robinson, J., 2014. Africa - the historical roots of its underdevelopment. In: Akyeampong, E.K., Bates, R.H., Nunn, N., Robinson, J. (Eds.), Africa's Development in Historical Perspective. Cambridge University Press, Cambridge.

Albouy, D., 2012. The colonial origins of comparative development: an empirical investigation: comment. The American Economic Review 102 (6), 3059–3076.

Alesina, A., Matuszeski, J., Easterly, W., 2011. Artificial states. Journal of the European Economic Association 9 (2), 246–277.

Alsan, M., 2015. The effect of the TseTse fly on African development. The American Economic Review 105 (1), 382–410.

Arroyo Abad, L., Maurer, N., 2019. The long shadow of history? The impact of colonial labor institutions on economic development in Peru. SSRN. https://ssrn.com/abstract=3559510.

Ashraf, Q., Galor, O., 2013. Genetic diversity and the origins of cultural fragmentation. The American Economic Review: Papers and Proceedings 103 (3), 528–533.

Austen, R.A., 1979. The trans-Saharan slave trade: a tentative census. In: Gemery, H.A., Hogendorn, J.S. (Eds.), The Uncommon Market: Essays in the Economic History of the Atlantic Slave Trade. Academic Press, New York.

Austen, R.A., 1988. The 19th century Islamic slave trade from East Africa (Swahili and Red Sea coasts): a tentative census. Slavery & Abolition 9, 21–44.

Austen, R.A., 1992. The Mediterranean Islamic slave trade out of Africa: a tentative census. Slavery & Abolition 13, 214–248.

Austin, G., 2005. Labour, Land and Capital in Ghana: From Slavery to Free Labour in Asante, 1807–1956. University of Rochester Press, New York.

Austin, G., 2007. Reciprocal comparison and African history: tackling conceptual eurocentrism in the study of Africa's economic past. African Studies Review 50 (3), 1–28.

Austin, G., 2008a. The 'reversal of fortune' thesis and the compression of history: perspectives from African and comparative economic history. Journal of International Development 20, 996–1027.

Austin, G., 2008b. Resources, techniques, and strategies South of the Sahara: revising the factor endowments perspective on African economic development history. Economic History Review 61 (3), 587–624.

Austin, G., 2016. Is Africa too late for 'late development'? Gerschenkron South of the Sahara. In: Andersson, M., Axelsson, T. (Eds.), Diverse Development Paths and Structural Transformation in the Escape from Poverty. Oxford University Press, Oxford.

Austin, G., Broadberry, S., 2014. Introduction: the renaissance of African economic history. The Economic History Review 67 (4), 893–906.

Banerjee, A.V., Duflo, E., 2014. Under the thumb of history? Political institutions and the scope for action. Annual Review of Economics 6 (1), 951–971.

Bates, R.H., Coatsworth, J.H., Williamson, J.G., 2007. Lost decades: postindependence performance in Latin America and Africa. The Journal of Economic History 67 (4), 917–943.

Bayly, C.A., 2008. Indigenous and Colonial Origins of Comparative Economic Development: the Case of Colonial India and Africa. World Bank Policy Research Working Papers, 4474.

Beach, H.P., 1903. A Geography and Atlas of Protestant Missions: their environment, forces, distribution, methods, problems, results and prospects at the opening of the twentieth century, vol. 2. Student Volunteer Movement for Foreign Missions, New York.

Bertocchi, G., Canova, F., 2002. Did colonization matter for growth? An empirical exploration into the historical causes of Africa's underdevelopment. European Economic Review 46 (10), 1851–1871.

Bickenbach, F., Bode, E., Nunnenkamp, P., Söder, M., 2016. Night lights and regional GDP. Review of World Economics 152, 425–447.

Bloom, D., Sachs, J., Collier, P., Udry, C., 1998. Geography, demography, and economic growth in Africa. Brookings Papers on Economic Activity 2, 207–295.

Bockstette, V., Chanda, A., Putterman, L., 2002. States and markets: the advantage of an early start. Journal of Economic Growth 7, 347–369.

Bolt, J., Bezemer, D., 2009. Understanding long-run African growth: colonial institutions or colonial education? Journal of Development Studies 45 (1), 24–54.

Bolt, J., Hillbom, E., 2016. Long-term trends in economic inequality: lessons from colonial Botswana, 1921-74. Economic History Review 69 (4), 1255–1284.

Boserup, E., 1970. Woman's Role in Economic Development. Allen & Unwin, London.

Bowden, S., Chiripanhura, B., Mosley, P., 2008. Measuring and explaining poverty in six African countries: a long-period approach. Journal of International Development 20 (8), 1049–1079.

Broadberry, S., Gardner, L., 2019. Economic growth in sub-Saharan Africa, 1885-2008. LSE Economic History Working Paper no. 296.

Carneiro, R.L., 1970. A theory of the origin of the state. Science 169 (3947), 733–738.

Chancel, L., Cogneau, D., Gethin, A., Myczkowski, A., 2019. How Large Are African Inequalities? Towards Distributional National Accounts in Africa, 1990-2017. WID.world Working Paper no. 2019/13.

Chen, X., Nordhaus, W.D., 2011. Using luminosity data as a proxy for economic statistics. Proceedings of the National Academy of Sciences 108 (21), 8589–8594.

Cherniwchan, J., Moreno-Cruz, J., 2019. Maize and precolonial Africa. Journal of Development Economics 136, 137–150.

Cioni, M., Federico, G., Vasta, M., 2021. The two revolutions in economic history. In: Bisin, A., Federico, G. (Eds.), The Handbook of Historical Economics. Elsevier. Chapter 2 (in this book).

Clemens, E.S., Cook, J.M., 1999. Politics and institutionalism: explaining durability and change. Annual Review of Sociology 25, 441–466.

Coquery Vidrovitch, C., 1985. Afrique noire: permanences et ruptures. Payot, Paris.

Cogneau, D., 2016. The economic history of Africa: renaissance or false dawn? Annales (English Edition) 71 (4), 539–556.

Cogneau, D., Dupraz, Y., 2014. Questionable Inference on the Power of Pre-Colonial Institutions in Africa. PSE Working Paper N° 2014–25.

Cogneau, D., Mesplé-Somps, S., Spielvogel, G., 2015. Development at the border: policies and national integration in Côte d'Ivoire and its neighbors. World Bank Economic Review 29 (1), 41–71.

Cogneau, D., Moradi, A., 2014. Borders that divide: education and religion in Ghana and Togo since colonial times. The Journal of Economic History 74 (3), 694–729.

Cogneau, D., Rouanet, L., 2011. Living conditions in Côte d'Ivoire and Ghana 1925-1985: what do survey data on height stature tell us. Economic History of Developing Regions 26 (2), 55–82.

Cooper, F., 1974. Plantation Slavery on the East Coast of Africa in the Nineteenth Century. Yale University.

Cooper, F., 2002. Africa Since 1940. The Past of the Present. Cambridge University Press, Cambridge MA.

Crosby, A.W., 2003. The Columbian Exchange: Biological and Cultural Consequences of 1492. Praeger, Westport, Conn (1972).

Curtin, P.D., 1989. Death by Migration. Europe's Encounter with the Tropical World in the Nineteenth Century. Cambridge University Press, Cambridge UK.

Dalrymple-Smith, A., 2020. Commercial Transitions and Abolition in West Africa: 1630-1860. Brill, Leiden, Boston.

Deaton, A., 2013. The Great Escape: Health, Wealth, and the Origins of Inequality. Princeton University Press, Princeton, New Jersey.

Diamond, J., 1997. Guns, Germs and Steel. The Fates of Human Societies. W.W. Norton & Company, New York.

Domar, E.D., 1970. The causes of slavery or serfdom: a hypothesis. The Journal of Economic History 30 (1), 18–32.

Dupraz, Y., 2019. French and British colonial legacies in education: evidence from the partition of Cameroon. The Journal of Economic History 79 (3), 628–668.

Easterly, W., Levine, R., 1997. Africa's growth tragedy: politics and ethnic divisions. The Quarterly Journal of Economics 112 (4), 1203–1250.

Edlund, L., Lagerlöf, N.-P., 2006. Individual versus parental consent in marriage: implications for intra-household resource allocation and growth. The American Economic Review 96 (2), 304–307.

Elliott, J.H., 2006. Empires of the Atlantic World. Britain and Spain in America 1492-1830. Yale University Press, New Haven.

Eltis, D., Behrendt, S.D., Richardson, D., Klein, H.S., 1999. The Trans-Atlantic Slave Trade: A Database on CD-Rom. Cambridge University Press, New York.

Englebert, P., 2000. Pre-colonial institutions, post-colonial states and economic development in tropical Africa. Political Research Quarterly 53 (1), 7–36.

Englebert, P., Tarango, S., Carter, M., 2002. Dismemberment and suffocation. A contribution to the debate on African boundaries. Comparative Political Studies 35 (10), 1093–1118.

Engermann, S.L., Sokoloff, K.L., 2005. The evolution of suffrage institutions in the New World. The Journal of Economic History 65 (4), 891–921.

Enke, B., 2019. Kinship, cooperation, and the evolution of moral systems. The Quarterly Journal of Economics 134 (2), 953–1019.

Evans-Pritchard, E., 1940. The Nuer a Description of the Modes of Livelihood and Political Institutions of a Nilotic People. Clarendon Press, Oxford.

Federico, G., Tena, A., 2017. Lewis revisited: tropical polities competing on the world market, 1830-1938. Economic History Review 70 (4), 1244–1267.

Fenske, J., 2012. Land abundance and economic institutions: Egba land and slavery, 1830-1914. The Economic History Review 65 (2), 527–555.

Fenske, J., 2010. The causal history of Africa: a response to Hopkins. Economic History of Developing Regions 25 (2), 177–212.

Fenske, J., 2013. Does land abundance explain African institutions? The Economic Journal 123 (573), 1363–1390.

Fenske, J., 2015. African polygamy: past and present. Journal of Development Economics 117, 58–73.

Fourie, J., 2016. The data revolution in African economic history. Journal of Interdisciplinary History 47 (2), 193–212.

Fourie, J., Obikili, N., 2019. Decolonizing with data: the cliometric turn in African economic history. Stellenbosch Working Paper Series No. WP02/2019.

Frankema, E., 2011. Colonial taxation and government spending in British Africa, 1880-1940: maximizing revenue or minimizing effort? Explorations in Economic History 48 (1), 136–149.

Frankema, E., 2012. The origins of formal education in sub-Saharan Africa: was British rule more benign? European Review of Economic History 16 (4), 335–355.

Frankema, E., 2015. The biogeographic roots of world inequality. Animals, disease, and human settlement patterns in Africa and the Americas before 1492. World Development 70, 274–285.

Frankema, E., Jerven, M., 2014. Writing history backwards or sideways: towards a consensus on African population, 1850-2010. Economic History Review 67 (4), 907–931.

Frankema, E., van Waijenburg, M., 2011. Structural Impediments to African Growth? New Evidence from Real Wages in British Africa, 1880-1960. CGEH Working Paper No. 24. Utrecht University, Utrecht.

Frankema, E., van Waijenburg, M., 2012. Structural impediments to African growth? New evidence from real wages in British Africa, 1880-1965. The Journal of Economic History 72 (4), 895–926.

Frankema, E., van Waijenburg, M., 2014. Metropolitan blueprints of colonial taxation? Lessons from fiscal capacity building in British and French Africa, c. 1880-1940. Journal of African History 55 (3), 371–400.

Frankema, E., van Waijenburg, M., 2018. Africa rising? A historical perspective. African Affairs 117 (469), 543–568.

Frankema, E., Williamson, J.G., Woltjer, P.J., 2018. An economic rationale for the West African scramble? The commercial transition and the commodity price boom of 1835-1885. The Journal of Economic History 78 (1), 231–267.

Frankema, E., Waijenburg, v.M., 2019. The Great Convergence. Skill Accumulation and Mass Education in Africa and Asia, 1870-2010. CEPR Discussion Paper No. 14150.

Gallego, F.A., Woodberry, R., 2010. Christian missionaries and education in former African colonies: how competition mattered. Journal of African Economies 19 (3), 294–329.

Gallup, J.L., Sachs, J.D., Mellinger, A.D., 1999. Geography and economic development. International Regional Science Review 22 (2), 179–232.

Gardner, L.A., 2012. Taxing Colonial Africa: The Political Economy of British Imperialism. Oxford University Press, Oxford.

Gennaioli, N., Rainer, I., 2007. The modern impact of precolonial centralization in Africa. Journal of Economic Growth 12, 185–234.

Gerschenkron, A., 1962. Economic Backwardness in Historical Perspective: A Book of Essays. Belknap Press of Harvard University Press, Cambridge, MA.

Gershman, B., 2016. Witchcraft beliefs and the erosion of social capital: evidence from Sub-Saharan Africa and beyond. Journal of Development Economics 120, 182–208.

Goldstein, M., Udry, C., 2008. The profits of power: land rights and agricultural investment in Ghana. Journal of Political Economy 116 (6), 981–1022.

Goody, J., 1971. Technology, Tradition, and the State in Africa. Oxford University Press, London.

Herbst, J., 2000. States and Power in Africa. Comparative Lessons in Authority and Control. Princeton University Press, Princeton, NJ.

Hopkins, A.G., 1973. An Economic History of West Africa. Longman, London.

Hopkins, A.G., 2009. The new economic history of Africa. Journal of African History 50 (2), 155–177.

Huillery, E., 2009. History matters: the long-term impact of colonial public investments in French West Africa. American Economic Journal: Applied Economics 1 (2), 176–215.

Iliffe, J., 2007. Africans: The History of a Continent, second edition. Cambridge University Press, New York.

Jedwab, R., Kerby, E., Moradi, A., 2017. History, path dependence and development: evidence from colonial railways, settlers and cities in Kenya. The Economic Journal 127 (603), 1467–1494.

Jedwab, R., Meier zu Selhausen, F., Moradi, A., 2019. The Economics of Missionary Expansion: Evidence from Africa and Implications for Development. African Economic History Network Working Paper No. 49/2019.

Jedwab, R., Moradi, A., 2016. The permanent effects of transportation revolutions in poor countries: evidence from Africa. Review of Economics and Statistics 98 (2), 268–284.

Jerven, M., 2010. African growth recurring: an economic history perspective on African growth episodes, 1690-2010. Economic History of Developing Regions 25 (2), 127–154.

Jerven, M., 2013. Poor Numbers: How We Are Misled by African Development Statistics and What to do About It. Cornell University Press, Ithaca.

Jerven, M., 2015. Africa: Why Economists Get It Wrong. Zed Books, London.

Juif, D., Frankema, E., 2018. From coercion to compensation: institutional responses to labour scarcity in the Central African Copperbelt. Journal of Institutional Economics 14 (2), 313–343.

Kelly, M., 2019. The Standard Errors of Persistence. CEPR Discussion Paper No. 13783.

Kirk-Greene, A.H.M., 1980. The thin white line: the size of the British colonial service in Africa. African Affairs 79 (314), 25–44.

Klein, H.S., 2010. The Atlantic Slave Trade, new edition. Cambridge University Press, Cambridge UK, New York.

Lamoreaux, N., 2015. The future of economic history must be interdisciplinary. The Journal of Economic History 75 (4), 1251–1257.

Lange, M.K., 2004. British colonial legacies and political development. World Development 32 (6), 905–922.

Larson, D.F., Otsuka, K., 2013. Towards a green revolution in Sub-Saharan Africa. In: Larson, D., Otsuka, K. (Eds.), An African Green Revolution. Finding Ways to Boost Productivity on Small Farms. Springer Verlag, Dordrecht.

Law, R. (Ed.), 1995. From Slave Trade to Legitimate Commerce: the Commercial Transition in Nineteenth-Century West Africa. Cambridge University Press, Cambridge.

Lovejoy, P.E., 2000. Transformations in Slavery: A History of Slavery in Africa Second. Cambridge University Press, Cambridge UK.

Lovejoy, P.E., 2016. Jihad in West Africa During the Age of Revolutions. Ohio University Press, Athens.

Lovejoy, P.E., Hogendorn, J.S., 1993. Slow Death for Slavery: The Course of Abolition in Northern Nigeria 1897-1936. Cambridge University Press, Cambridge.

Lowes, S., Nunn, N., Robinson, J.A., Weigel, J., 2017. The evolution of culture and institutions: evidence from the Kuba Kingdom. Econometrica 85 (4), 1065–1091.

Maddison, A., 2010. Historical statistics on world population, GDP and per capita GDP, 1-2008 AD. http://www.ggdc.net/maddison/. Version of February 2010.

Mahoney, J., 2010. Colonialism and Postcolonial Development. Spanish America in Comparative Perspective. Cambridge University Press, Cambridge MA.

Manning, P., 1990. Slavery and African Life. Occidental, Oriental and African Salve Trades. Cambridge University Press, Cambridge, UK.

Manning, P., 2010. African population: projections, 1851-1961. In: Ittmann, K., Cordell, D.D., Maddox, G.H. (Eds.), The Demographics of Empire. The Colonial Order and the Creation of Knowledge Athens. Ohio University Press, Ohio.

Manning, P., 2014. African population, 1650-2000: comparisons and implications of new estimates. In: Akyeampong, E.K., Bates, R.H., Nunn, N., Robinson, J.A. (Eds.), Africa's Development in Historical Perspective. Cambridge University Press, Cambridge, Mass.

McCann, J.C., 2005. Maize and Grace. Africa's Encounter with a New World Crop, 1500-2000. Harvard University Press, Cambridge MA.

McIntosh, S.K. (Ed.), 1999. Pathways to Complexity. Cambridge University Press, New York.

Meier zu Selhausen, F., 2019. Missions, Education and Conversion in Colonial Africa. AEHN Working Paper No. 48/2019.

Michalopoulos, S., Papaioannou, E., 2013. Pre-colonial ethnic institutions and contemporary African development. Econometrica 81 (1), 113–152.

Michalopoulos, S., Papaioannou, E., 2016. The long-run effects of the scramble for Africa. The American Economic Review 106 (7), 1802–1848.

Michalopoulos, S., Papaioannou, E., 2020. Historical legacies and African development. Journal of Economic Literature 58 (1), 53–128.

Miers, S., Kopytoff, I. (Eds.), 1977. Slavery in Africa: Historical and Anthropological Perspectives. University of Wisconsin Press, Madison.

Miller, J.C., 1988. Way of Death. Merchant Capitalism and the Angolan Slave Trade 1730-1830. University of Wisconsin Press, Madison, WI.

Moradi, A., 2009. Towards an objective account of nutrition and health in colonial Kenya: a study of stature in African army recruits and civilians, 1880-1980. The Journal of Economic History 96 (3), 720–755.

Murdock, G.P., 1959. Africa: Its Peoples and Their Culture History. McGraw Hill, New York.

Murdock, G.P., 1967. Ethnographic Atlas. University of Pittsburgh Press, Pittsburgh, PA.

North, D.C., 1991. Institutions. The Journal of Economic Perspectives 5 (1), 97–112.

North, D.C., Summerhill, W., Weingast, B.R., 2000. Order, disorder and economic change. In: Bueno de Mesquita, B., Root, H.L. (Eds.), Governing for Prosperity. Yale University Press, New York.

Nunn, N., 2008. The long-term effects of Africa's slave trades. The Quarterly Journal of Economics 123 (1), 139–176.

Nunn, N., 2009. The importance of history for economic development. Annual Review of Economics 1, 65–92.

Nunn, N., 2010. Religious conversion in colonial Africa. The American Economic Review: Papers and Proceedings 100, 147–152.

Nunn, N., Wantchekon, L., 2011. The slave trade and the origins of mistrust in Africa. The American Economic Review 101 (7), 3221–3252.

Obikili, N., 2016. The trans-Atlantic slave trade and local political fragmentation in Africa. The Economic History Review 69 (4), 1157–1177.

Olsson, O., Hibbs, D.A., 2005. Biogeography and long-run economic development. European Economic Review 49 (4), 909–938.

Osafo-Kwaako, P., Robinson, J.A., 2013. Political centralization in pre-colonial Africa. Journal of Comparative Economics 41 (1), 6–21.

Platteau, J.-P., 2009. Institutional obstacles to African economic development: state, ethnicity, and custom. Journal of Economic Behavior & Organization 71 (3), 669–689.

Platteau, J.-P., 2014. Redistributive pressures in Sub-Saharan Africa: causes, consequences, and coping strategies. In: Akyeampong, E., Bates, R.H., Nunn, N., Robinson, J.A. (Eds.), Africa's Development in Historical Perspective. Cambridge University Press, New York.

Polanyi, K., 1944. The Great Transformation: The Political and Economic Origins of Our Time. Amereon House, New York.

Putterman, L., Weil, D.N., 2010. Post-1500 population flows and the long run determinants of economic growth and inequality. The Quarterly Journal of Economics 125 (4), 1627–1682.

Rodrik, D., Subramanian, A., Trebbi, F., 2004. Institutions rule: the primacy of institutions over geography and integration in economic development. Journal of Economic Growth 9 (2), 131–165.

Roessler, P., Pnegl, Y.I., Marty, R., Titlow, K.S., van de Walle, N., 2020. The Cash Crop Revolution, Colonialism and Legacies of Spatial Inequality: Evidence from Africa. CSAE Working Paper WPS/2020-12.

Roome, W.R.M., 1925. Ethnographic Survey of Africa: Showing the Tribes and Languages; also the Stations of Missionary Societies. Edward Stanford Ltd., London.

Sachs, J.D., Warner, A.M., 1997. Sources of slow growth in African economies. Journal of African Economies 6 (3), 335–376.

Sala-I-Martin, X., 1997. I just ran two million regressions. Papers and Proceedings of the Annual Meeting of the American Economic Association 87 (2), 178–183.

Sheriff, A., 1987. Slaves, Spices and Ivory in Zanzibar: Integration of an East African Commercial Empire into the World Economy, 1770-1873. Currey, London.

Smits, J., Permanyer, I., Wildeman, J., Dietz, T., 2020. ASCL Thematic Map: Subnational Human Development Index (SHDI) of Africa. African Studies, Centre Leiden.

Tertilt, M., 2005. Polygyny, fertility, and savings. Journal of Political Economy 113 (6), 1341–1374.

Tilly, C., 1990. Coercion, Capital, and European States, A.D. 990-1992. Blackwell, Cambridge MA.

Tosh, J., 1980. The cash-crop revolution in tropical Africa: an agricultural reappraisal. African Affairs 79 (314), 79–94.

United Nations, 2020. World Population Prospects 2019. Department of Social and Economic Affairs. https://population.un.org/wpp/Download/Standard/Population/. (Accessed 24 November 2020).

van Waijenburg, M., 2018. Financing the African colonial state: the revenue imperative and forced labor. The Journal of Economic History 78 (1), 40–80.

von der Goltz, J., Dar, A., Fishman, R., Mueller, N.D., Barnwal, P., McCord, G.C., 2020. Health impacts of the green revolution: evidence from 600,000 births across the developing world. Journal of Health Economics 74.

Voth, H.-J., 2021. Persistence – myth and mystery. In: Bisin, A., Federico, G. (Eds.), The Handbook of Historical Economics. Elsevier. Chapter 9 (in this book).

Weil, D.N., 2014. The impact of Malaria on African development over the Longue Durée. In: Akyeampong, E., Bates, R.H., Nunn, N., Robinson, J.A. (Eds.), Africa's Development in Historical Perspective. Cambridge University Press, New York.

Whatley, W.C., 2018. The gun-slave hypothesis and the 18th century British slave trade. Explorations in Economic History 67, 80–104.

Whatley, W., 2020. Up the River: International Slave Trades and the Transformations of Slavery in Africa. African Economic. History Network Working Paper No. 51/2020.

Whatley, W., Gillezeau, R., 2011. The impact of the transatlantic slave trade on ethnic stratification in Africa. The American Economic Review 101 (3), 571–576.

Wilks, I., 1993. Forests of Gold. Essays on the Akan and the Kingdom of Asante. Ohio University Press, Athens.

Wright, D.K., 2017. Humans as agents in the termination of the African humid period. Frontiers in Earth Science 5 (4), 1–14.

World Bank, 2020. World development indicators 2020. https://databank.worldbank.org/source/world-development-indicators. (Accessed 10 November 2020).

Young, C., 2012. The Postcolonial State in Africa Fifty Years of Independence, 1960-2010. University of Wisconsin Press, Madison.

Religion in economic history: a survey[☆]

Sascha O. Becker[a,b,c,d,e,f,g,j], **Jared Rubin**[h], and **Ludger Woessmann**[i,j,e,f,c]

[a]Monash University, Melbourne, Victoria, Australia
[b]University of Warwick, Coventry, United Kingdom
[c]CAGE, Coventry, United Kingdom
[d]CEPR, London, United Kingdom
[e]CESifo, Munich, Germany
[f]IZA, Bonn, Germany
[g]ROA, Maastricht, Netherlands
[h]Chapman University, Orange, CA, United States
[i]University of Munich, Munich, Germany
[j]ifo Institute, Munich, Germany

20.1 Introduction

Historically, religion has played an important role in Western societies, affecting or even defining individual beliefs and traits, cultural norms and values, social groups and organizations, and political and military power. A rapidly growing literature works to advance our understanding of the role of religion in economic history. How did religion and religious beliefs in God and the afterlife affect economic history? And how did historical socioeconomic circumstances shape religious beliefs and activities? In line with the recent revival of interest in the role of culture in economics more generally (e.g., Guiso et al., 2006; Alesina and Giuliano, 2015), study of the relevance of religion has entered center stage in the study of economic history.

The past two decades have seen the emergence of the study of "religion in economic history" as a new field. Although a subfield of both economic history and the economics of religion, the overlap between these two fields is a relatively recent development. Certainly, the economic study of religion has a long history itself, with a chapter of Adam Smith's (1776) *Inquiry into the Nature and Causes of the Wealth of Nations* famously exploring the market for religion. But in Larry Iannaccone's 1998 survey on the economics of religion in the *Journal of Economic Literature*, only 18 of the 141 cited

☆ For constructive comments, inspiring discussions, and/or joint work over many years, we thank Ran Abramitzky, Jeanet Bentzen, Alberto Bisin, Jean-Paul Carvalho, Eric Chaney, Francesco Cinnirella, Giovanni Federico, Avner Greif, Erik Hornung, Larry Iannaccone, Sriya Iyer, Murat Iyigun, Saumitra Jha, Mark Koyama, Timur Kuran, Rachel McCleary, Felix Meier zu Selhausen, Alex Moradi, Markus Nagler, Luigi Pascali, Steve Pfaff, and Felipe Valencia. Participants at the October 2019 Handbook Conference at NYU and at Robert Barro and Rachel McCleary's course on The Political Economy of Religion at Harvard University gave insightful feedback. Woessmann gratefully acknowledges the hospitality of the Hoover Institution, Stanford University, while working on this paper.

The Handbook of Historical Economics. https://doi.org/10.1016/B978-0-12-815874-6.00029-0

articles (12.8%) could reasonably be construed to be historical, and many of those were directly related to Max Weber's (1904/05) thesis of a Protestant ethic. At the turn of the millennium, the nascent economics of religion field was, if anything, much more closely related to the sociology of religion than economic history. This has changed in the last two decades. In this period, there has been enough work in the field to warrant two recent surveys on *individual* religions and economic history: Becker et al. (2016) on the Protestant Reformation and Kuran (2018) on Islam (covering mostly historical, but also contemporary aspects). The broader economics of religion field has produced two handbooks in the last decade—McCleary (2011) and Carvalho et al. (2019)—both of which have numerous entries from economic history. The field is now sufficiently large that it warrants a survey that highlights unifying themes, overviews the big problems that the literature aims to address, and points to gaps that could be addressed by future research.

In line with the focus of the economics of religion in general, the study of religion in economic history covers two main areas of investigation. The first area is which (economic) factors cause religious adoption, religiosity, and religious change. The second area is which consequences religion exerts on economic development. While the new literature of the past two decades covers many different and sometimes disparate aspects within these two areas, we think that a few general insights have emerged that deserve highlighting.

First, the monotheistic character of the main Abrahamic religions facilitated a close historical interconnection of religion with political power and conflict. The doctrine that there is "one true God" that is the defining characteristic of monotheistic faiths was both a stabilizing factor for societies—because monopolized rule could curtail disagreements within religious groups—and a destabilizing factor because it spurred conflict between religions (Iyigun, 2015). Some of these aspects have been shown for Catholicism, where the institutionalized Church acted as a strong political player and religious doctrine influenced the development of communes, guilds, and lending markets. Similarly, different features of Islamic law affected conflict, finance, and many aspects of economic development in the Islamic world.

Second, human capital often played a leading role in the interconnection between religion and economic history. Religious norms spurred or prevented literacy and mass education in many societies. Religion-induced human capital has been a defining element both in Jewish economic history and in the Protestant-Catholic divide in Christian economic history, as well as in how Christian missionaries impacted the historical development in affected areas.

Third, it is possible to describe economic and wider factors that have facilitated the adoption and spread of religions and religious beliefs. While the specific causes studied in the literature are clearly diverse—ranging from practices of the incumbent religion and earthquake incidents to economic potential, trade routes, printing technology, competition, educational expansion, and personal ties—it is fair to conclude that the recent literature has produced ample evidence that socioeconomic factors matter in the historical development of religions.

We employ two criteria to define the coverage of our survey. We cover works that analyze one of the three main monotheisms—Judaism, Christianity, or Islam—and that primarily cover the period prior to 1945. While both of these criteria are somewhat arbitrary, there is a rationale for each. In line with the particular role of monotheistic faiths outlined above, the vast majority of the work in this field has concerned one of the three Abrahamic religions. This is not to say there has not been good work done on Hinduism (especially the caste system), Buddhism, Shintoism, or animistic religions. Yet, there has not been nearly enough written on non-Abrahamic religions by quantitative economic historians to begin to categorize or search for running themes in the literature. We will return to this in the conclusion when we discuss potentially fruitful areas of future research. After all, Abrahamic religions only account for a little more than half of the world's population. We chose the end of World War II as an end date not because there is a fundamental divide at the point in time, but in large part because we needed to pick *some* point in time as a cut-off for a survey on economic history, and at minimum we thought it was appropriate to include the growing set of papers on the Holocaust. Moreover, Sriya Iyer (2016) has recently updated Iannaccone's (1998) JEL survey, nicely covering many of the papers on religion in the latter half of the 20th century. Extending our date too far would therefore create many redundancies. In any case, the pre-WWII literature on the economic history of the Abrahamic faiths is more than large enough to fill a survey, as the reader shall see below.

The research we highlight in this survey is largely from the last two decades; indeed, most of it is from the last decade. This is for two reasons. For one, the field has advanced immensely in the last two decades, and a majority of the social scientific work at the intersection of economics of religion and economic history is recent. Second, advancements in methodological and data-gathering techniques have been so rapid that most empirical works of the last decade or so have a fundamentally different feel to them than their predecessors. For this reason, we largely focus on "large-N" studies. Historical case studies and smaller-scale studies are valuable—especially to derive broader hypotheses and to focus on local religious heterogeneity where it exists—but tend not to yield the type of causal claims or external validity that is possible with larger-scale studies. In covering topics of economic history (broadly defined), we also confine this survey (mostly) to work using an economics approach, i.e., applying economic concepts, methodology, and/or intuition. This includes some works of political science and sociology, but excludes many more that have limited economics focus. Of course, many of the covered topics—in particular, non-economic topics such as anti-Semitism or the sources of religious feelings—inevitably are much more complex than the literature on the economics of religion can cover. The contribution by economics offers a complementary perspective to the richer coverage of these topics by historians, theologians, ethnographers, and other disciplines. In fact, multidisciplinary approaches may prove particularly fruitful in furthering our understating of the role of religion in economic history in the future. Finally, the papers we review are somewhat idiosyncratic and reflect our own biases (conscious and unconscious). This is probably unavoidable, but we do our best to bring together papers that fit into general themes that have arisen in the literature.

We organize this survey by religion, in order of the religion's age: Judaism, then Christianity, then Islam. Work on Judaism mostly covers two themes: first, Jewish occupational specialization, human capital, and emancipation (section 20.2.1); second, Jewish persecution (section 20.2.2). We subdivide the coverage of Christianity in three sections. First, work on Catholicism has a strong focus on the role of the Catholic Church in historical development (section 20.3.1). Second, recent studies of Protestantism cover both the socioeconomic consequences of the Reformation and the socioeconomic causes of its spread (section 20.3.2). Third, while the work on Catholicism and Protestantism per se mostly focuses on European history, recent work also studies how Christian missionaries affected historical development in sub-Saharan Africa, Asia, and Latin America (section 20.3.3). We structure the work on Islam into three themes: politics and law (section 20.4.1); finance and trade (section 20.4.2); and human capital (section 20.4.3). We close our survey with a section on cross-country studies that investigate economic causes and consequences of religion (section 20.5). The final section concludes with ideas for directions in which future research in the area might tread.

20.2 Judaism

Judaism is the oldest of the three Abrahamic religions and our natural starting point. Study of the economic history of Jews has a long pedigree in the social sciences. Salient contributions by Kuznets (1960) and Baron and Kahan (1975) provide ample descriptive evidence on the economic structure and life of the Jews in the 20th century and before. Our focus is on more recent research, in this millennium, which has increased our understanding of Jewish economic history in two broad areas: first, economic specialization, and second, the causes and consequences of anti-Semitism. Naturally, the two are interlinked, as anti-Semitism may have affected occupational specialization, and vice versa.

20.2.1 Jewish occupational specialization, human capital, and emancipation

The recent literature on Jewish occupational specialization and human capital primarily takes its inspiration from Botticini and Eckstein (2005, 2007, 2012), whose work has advanced our understanding of Jewish economic life over the last two millennia. Table 20.1 overviews this literature.

The conventional wisdom was that Jews specialized in human-capital-intensive sectors as a result of two factors: first, Jews faced various restrictions on their economic activity (e.g., guilds did not permit them to enter certain sectors) and second, they were often not allowed to own land, and hence were less likely to permanently settle. Botticini and Eckstein challenge this view, based on novel evidence on the specialization of Jews starting at the beginning of the first millennium CE. The exogenous shock of the Roman destruction of the Jerusalem temple in 70 CE shifted Judaic focus away from the cult of sacrifice to investment in literacy. Between the 3rd and 5th centuries, the writing of the two Talmuds, the construction of synagogues, and the institution of the kallah (the teachers' convention) represented Judaism's considerable investment in education. Prior to the 8th century CE, most Jews, like the rest of the population, were farmers (Botticini and Eckstein, 2005). With the establishment of the Muslim Empire, literate Jews voluntarily migrated to urban areas seeking skilled employment despite no restrictions prohibiting them from remaining in agriculture. This occupational selection remained their distinctive mark thereafter.

But why did this happen? Botticini and Eckstein (2007) explain this transition into skilled urban occupations with an economic model that describes the choices regarding religious affiliation (remain Jewish or convert) and children's education in a world populated by Jewish and non-Jewish farmers. Education is costly not only for the individual and his family, but to the Jewish community that must raise funds to hire teachers and construct synagogues. Several options arose. The first option is that some farmers would not educate their children because they could not afford to do so, or did not see a return on their investment, or were marginally affiliated with Judaism. They converted to Hellenist paganism or Christianity with lower entry costs (no circumcision, no reading of the Torah, no required observance of the Sabbath). The second option is that farmers derived utility from Judaism, and from educating themselves and their sons. Belonging to Judaism raised their participation through education. These farmer Jews, however, had to abandon farming if they were going to get a return on their educational investment. Hence, Judaism transitioned from an illiterate agrarian religion to a literate urban one. Indeed, Jewish farmers who invested in education gained a comparative advantage and an incentive to enter skilled occupations during a period of increased urbanization in the Abbasid empire in the Near East (8th and 9th centuries). They likewise selected themselves into skilled occupations in Spain, France, England, and Germany. Both Jewish and non-Jewish merchants preferred to educate

Table 20.1 Jewish occupational specialization, human capital, and emancipation.

Study	Setting	Method	Summary
Jewish occupational specialization and human capital			
Botticini and Eckstein (2005, 2007, 2012)	Near East and Europe, 70CE-1492	Empirical, theory	Jews highly educated as result of religious norms from first century CE; farmers struggling with education norm converted, reinforcing norm of stayers
Becker and Cinnirella (2020)	Prussia 1871	Empirical	Positive association between share of Jews and literacy in rural, but not in urban areas
Abramitzky and Halaburda (2020)	Interwar Poland	Empirical	Jewish education advantage masks composition effect: Jews more likely to live in towns; Jews more educated in countryside, but less educated in cities
Botticini et al. (2019)	Central and Eastern Europe, 1500-1930	Empirical	Lower child mortality rates and faster population growth as result of breastfeeding norm
Pascali (2016)	Italy, 1470-2003	Empirical	Cities with history of Jewish lending in Middle Ages and later lending through Monti di Pietà supported by Catholic Church have better financial development
Jewish emancipation			
Carvalho and Koyama (2016)	Europe, 19th c	Theory	Reform Judaism in more developed German Empire as optimal response to increased economic opportunities; more traditional model in Eastern Europe
Carvalho et al. (2017)	Europe, 19th c	Theory	Less education to preserve cultural identity among Orthodox Jews
Johnson and Koyama (2017)	Europe, 1400-1850	Empirical	Cities with Jewish communities grew faster; emancipation as key mechanism

their children. However, Jewish merchants invested in their children's education comparatively more because they and their family derived direct utility from their religion.

Their earlier papers are summarized and extended in Botticini and Eckstein (2012), which covers Jewish economic history until 1492, the year in which mass expulsions of Jews from the Iberian Peninsula commenced. The key take-away from their work is that Jewish specialization in high-skilled jobs is not so much the result of external constraints set by non-Jews, but the result of an inner-Jewish battle in the first century CE which gave way to religious norms focusing on human capital acquisition.

The work by Botticini and Eckstein clearly shows the historic roots of the Jewish emphasis on education. At the same time, it is important to take into account the specific historical and institutional context when considering the Jewish relative education advantage. In fact, two recent papers highlight that the Jewish education advantage may not be universal in all geographic and temporal contexts. In 1871 Prussia, having more Jews was associated with higher literacy in rural villages and manors but not urban towns, where a majority of Jews lived (Becker and Cinnirella, 2020). A related and more nuanced finding arises in interwar Poland. Abramitzky and Halaburda (2020) document a Jewish literacy advantage in rural areas and a Jewish literacy *disadvantage* in urban areas. Both of these results suggest that in more recent European history, Christians in urban areas benefited from a good schooling infrastructure, leveling out any historical Jewish education advantage. Yet, in rural areas, Jews continued to stay ahead, consistent with Spitzer's (2019) finding that Jews tended to hold similar education regardless of whether they lived in cities or in rural areas. Spitzer (2019) focuses on Jews in the Pale of Settlement,[1] the region in the Russian Empire where Jews were allowed to settle, studying their occupational selection. He uses data from the 1897 Russian census to challenge the over-simplistic view that characterizes Jews as (always) an urban minority. Jewish population numbers in the Pale were substantially higher than elsewhere and Jews in this area should be seen rather as a *rural* service minority, with comparative advantage in countryside commerce, not in dense urban centers.

Education is only one dimension of human capital. Religious norms affect also another dimension of human capital: health. Focusing on Central and Eastern Europe after 1500, Botticini et al. (2019) show that breastfeeding played an important role in Judaism and was one key factor in the lower child mortality rates among Jews and the resulting faster population growth among Jews.[2]

Although over many centuries European Jews did not enjoy equal rights to the majority populations, the 19th century brought Jews closer to emancipation, a theme that is central to the work of Carvalho and Koyama (2016) and Carvalho et al. (2017). Both papers look into the response of the Jewish community in Germany and Eastern Europe to the opportunity afforded by increased citizen rights, in combination with differential degrees of economic development. Two polarized responses emerged. In Germany, a liberal Reform movement developed in response to emancipation, while Ultra-Orthodox Judaism emerged in Eastern Europe. Carvalho and Koyama (2016) develop a historical narrative and model of religious organization that accounts for the polarized responses by Jewish communities. Similar to Iannaccone (1992) and Berman (2000), strictness acts as a screening device for community membership. The Jewish population is composed of low attachment and high attachment types. Earned income can be spent on a consumption good or donated to the community. Furthermore, there is a tradeoff between effort and money contributions. When economic development is low

---

[1] The Pale of Settlement included all of modern-day Belarus, Lithuania, and Moldova, much of Ukraine, parts of eastern Latvia, eastern Poland, and some parts of western Russia.

[2] Lehrer (2008) shows how this pattern continues today when comparing educational attainment in Judaism to other religions.

(as was the case in Eastern Europe), a religious leader wants to maintain a cohesive community and does not screen out low attachment types. At higher levels of development (as in Germany), the group endogenously switches to screening, i.e., permits low attachment types to reduce effort in exchange for increased monetary contributions. In related work, Carvalho et al. (2017) show that, in Germany, non-religious and Reform Jews dramatically increased their rates of education. In the less developed parts of Eastern Europe, Orthodox and ultra-Orthodox communities imposed unprecedented restrictions on secular education and isolated themselves from society. They explain this bifurcation in a model where education not only confers economic benefits but also transmits values that undermine the cultural identity of minority groups. Johnson and Koyama (2017) consider the consequences of Jewish emancipation on economic development, proxied by city growth over the years 1400-1850. In their difference-in-differences setting, cities with Jewish communities grew about 30% faster than comparable cities without Jewish communities. Jewish emancipation is a key mechanism to explain these results: Cities that gave increased citizenship rights to Jews earlier saw stronger population increases.

Returning to the theme of occupational specialization, several papers have looked at Jewish specialization in financial services and its long-run effects. Pascali (2016) looks at Jewish communities in Italy, the heartland of the Catholic Church. The Lateran Council of 1215 extended the prohibition of Christians to lend to each other at interest (which had previously been limited to the Catholic clergy)[3] to the Catholic laity. Moreover, Jews were silently allowed to lend at normal interest rates, carving out a niche market for them. However, Franciscan propaganda against usury became ferocious during the 15th century and led to the creation of charitable loan banks sanctioned by the Catholic Church, called Monti di Pietà,[4] that were intended to drive the Jews out of the local financial market. Their role in Italian society during the Renaissance was not markedly different from that of modern microfinance in developing countries. Pascali shows that the combination of Jewish lending and its successor in the form of Monti di Pietà were able to foster financial development and, through this channel, economic development in modern-day Italy.

Pascali's use of modern-day outcomes in connection with historic treatments is a recurrent theme throughout this chapter which is worth highlighting (see also Cantoni and Yuchtman, 2021). Most of the papers discussed in this section are concerned with historic developments in their own historic context. However, other papers draw on history as laboratory for current outcomes. One such example is the work by D'Acunto et al. (2019) which links historic anti-Semitism with modern-day financial (under-)development. We will return to this in the next section.

A final fascinating agenda in recent years covers a key Jewish institution, the kibbutz, which arose from the Zionist Jewish movement in the early 20th century. While most of the empirical work focuses on the post-WWII period, Abramitzky (2018) highlights the role played by Jewish norms, historical circumstances, and persecution in creating these communities in the 1910s and 1920s. He also studies conceptually and empirically the (lack of) stability of communes, contrasting religious, and socialist communes. The former turn out to be more stable than the latter, likely because religious beliefs are more easily verifiable than socialist ones and because religious group cohesion is less reliant on equality than socialist beliefs.

---

[3] The First Council of Nice in Canon VII deposed clerics who took usury from the clergy and from all ecclesiastical rank.

[4] For instance, Banca Monte dei Paschi di Siena, Italy's second-largest bank as recently as 2017, was founded in 1472 as one such charitable bank.

Assessing the state of research on occupational specialization, human capital, and emancipation of Jews after the pathbreaking work by Botticini and Eckstein with its worldwide perspective, there is still relatively little work using individual-level, city-level, or regional data exploring Jewish life across time and space within countries.

20.2.2 Jewish persecution

The other primary literature on Judaism in economic history focuses on Jewish persecution. Table 20.2 overviews this literature.

Following up on the theme of persistence (see also Voth, 2021), Voigtländer and Voth (2012) document an exceptional geographic persistence in patterns of anti-Semitism, showing that German cities that experienced anti-Jewish pogroms in 1348 ('Black Death pogroms') also showed higher levels of anti-Semitism in the interwar period. Similarly drawing on historic anti-Semitism, D'Acunto et al. (2019) find that present-day financial development is lower in German counties where historical anti-Semitism was higher, compared to otherwise similar counties. Relatedly, Grosfeld et al. (2013) show that current-day residents of the former Pale of Settlement, which we touched on earlier, have lower support for the market compared to those outside the Pale. The mechanism they document is that anti-Semitism generated persistent anti-market culture and trust among non-Jews.

Going beyond the long-term effects of anti-Semitism, a large body of recent research has tried to understand the causes of anti-Semitism, referring to both direct effects of economic distress and more sophisticated political-economy mechanisms. Anderson et al. (2017) employ a long panel covering 936 European cities over the years 1100 to 1800. They show that persecutions were more likely following colder growing seasons. This effect is strongest in weak states and those with poor-quality soil. They also notice and try to explain the long-run decline in persecutions over their sample period and point to greater market integration and state capacity as one factor. Johnson and Koyama (2019) extend on these insights to provide a unifying theory of toleration and persecution. They argue that Jews and other religious minorities were "conditionally tolerated" in medieval Europe because states had low capacity and relied on religious legitimacy. This meant that although Jews were tolerated because they were useful to local rulers, this toleration could be revoked at any time, especially during periods of instability. It was only when state capacity increased and religious legitimacy became less important following the Reformation that more generalized toleration emerged.

In related work, Finley and Koyama (2018) explore the institutional determinants of persecution by studying the intensity of the Black Death pogroms in the Holy Roman Empire. Communities governed by archbishoprics, bishoprics, and imperial free cities experienced more intense and violent persecutions than did those governed by the emperor. The political fragmentation outside areas under the emperor's rule exacerbated competition for the rents generated by Jewish moneylending, which made Jews more vulnerable during periods of crisis. Jedwab et al. (2019a) analyze how the Black Death interacted with patterns of economic complementarity and substitutability. While negative shocks increased the likelihood that minorities were persecuted as shocks become more severe, the persecution probability decreased if there were economic complementarities between majority and minority groups.

The Pale of Settlement is a natural area to study questions of economic and political factors behind anti-Semitism. Grosfeld et al. (2020) look at pogroms between 1800 and 1927 and show that ethnic violence broke out when crop failures coincided with political turmoil. Crop failures without political

Table 20.2 Jewish persecution.

Study	Setting	Method	Summary
Persistence of anti-Semitism			
Voigtländer and Voth (2012)	Germany, 1348-WWII	Empirical	German cities that experienced anti-Jewish ('Black Death') pogroms in 1348 also showed higher levels of anti-Semitism in interwar period
D'Acunto et al. (2019)	Germany, 1348-today	Empirical	Places with historic anti-Semitism show lower modern-day financial development
Grosfeld et al. (2013)	Russian Empire, 19th c - today	Empirical	Current-day residents of former Pale of Settlement (where Jews were confined to live within Russian Empire) have lower support for market
Roots of anti-Semitism			
Andersen et al. (2017)	Europe, 1100-1800	Empirical	More persecutions following colder growing seasons; effect strongest in weak states and those with poor quality soil
Johnson and Koyama (2019)	Medieval and early modern Europe	Empirical, analytic narrative	Persecution of religious minorities more likely to happen when states have low capacity and rely on religious legitimacy; application to Jewish persecutions
Finley and Koyama (2018)	Holy Roman Empire, 1348/49	Empirical	Black Death pogroms were affected by institutional determinants
Jedwab et al. (2019a)	Europe, 1100-1850	Empirical	Black Death interacted with economic complementarity and substitutability
Grosfeld et al. (2020)	Russian Empire, 1800-1927	Empirical	When crop failures coincided with political turmoil, pogroms occurred in Pale of Settlement in places where Jews dominated moneylending and trade in grain
Becker and Pascali (2019)	Germany, 1300-1900	Empirical	Protestant Reformation led to increased competition between Christian majority and Jews who specialized in banking and led to increased anti-Semitism

continued on next page

Table 20.2 (*continued*)

Study	Setting	Method	Summary
The Holocaust			
Spenkuch and Tillmann (2018)	Germany, 1920s/30s	Empirical	Protestantism strongest predictor of Nazi vote shares
Buggle et al. (2020)	Germany, 1930s/40s	Empirical	Emigration of Jews from Nazi Germany hampered by immigration restrictions; network effects important in decision to emigrate
Becker et al. (2020b)	Germany, 1930s/40s	Empirical	Emigration of Jewish academics exploits academic networks; early dismissal a blessing in disguise
Blum and Rei (2018)	Portugal, 1940s	Empirical	Persecuted Jews fleeing Europe for the US positively selected on education
Hoffman (2011)	Europe, 1930s/40s	Empirical	More rescuers of Jews in richer countries; rescuers richer individuals
Braun (2016)	Netherlands, 1930s/40s	Empirical	Minorities help minorities: Jews more likely to be rescued by respective Christian minority in different parts of Netherlands
Finkel (2015)	Jewish ghettos, 1930s/40s	Analytic narrative	Jewish resistance increases with previous experience of selective repression
Consequences of the Holocaust			
Acemoglu et al. (2011)	Russia, WWII and today	Empirical	Cities with intense Holocaust have lower population today and more communist votes since collapse of Soviet Union
Voigtländer and Voth (2015)	Germany, 1930s/40s and today	Empirical	Germans who grew up under Nazi regime more anti-Semitic than those born before or after that period
Waldinger (2010)	Germany, 1933 and after WWII	Empirical	Negative effects of expulsion of Jewish math professors on PhD student outcomes
Waldinger (2012)	Germany, 1933 and after WWII	Empirical	No evidence of negative effects on productivity of colleagues after dismissal of Jewish scientists
Moser et al. (2014)	US, after 1933	Empirical	Patenting by US inventors increased in fields of émigré Jewish professors from Nazi Germany

turmoil did not cause pogroms. At the intersection of economic and political shocks, pogroms occurred in places where Jews dominated moneylending and trade in grain.

In recent work, Jha (2013, 2018) argued that an ethnic division of labor is sufficient to reduce ethnic tensions when the specific advantage of a certain ethnicity cannot be replicated or expropriated by the others. Following the same spirit, economic incentives are at the core of the work by Becker and Pascali (2019). Looking at the period 1300 to 1900, they argue that the Catholic usury ban and higher literacy rates gave Jews a specific advantage in the moneylending sector. Following the Protestant Reformation (1517), Jews lost these advantages in regions that became Protestant and were exposed to competition with the Christian majority, especially in moneylending, leading to an increase in anti-Semitism in Protestant areas. As a long-term consequence of this shift, the share of Jews in moneylending is lower in Protestant areas of 19th century Prussia than in Catholic areas. This latter finding is an example of the link between anti-Semitism and occupational specialization.

The fate of the Jews during fascism and World War II has attracted particular attention in the literature. Since the Holocaust was engineered by Nazi Germany, it is natural to ask how the Nazis rose to power in the first place. It has long been noted that the Nazis had more support in Protestant areas of Germany. Spenkuch and Tillmann (2018) go one step further and show that constituencies' religious composition is a key empirical predictor of Nazi vote shares—dwarfing the explanatory power of any other demographic or socioeconomic variable. Their evidence suggests that this disparity was, in large part, due to the sway of the Catholic Church and its dignitaries and was helped by the fact that the Catholic *Zentrumspartei* (center party) held Catholic voters back from the extremes of the political spectrum.

After the Nazis rose to power in 1933, Jews came under increased pressure by anti-Semitic acts as well as laws that increasingly restricted their rights. As a result, many Jews contemplated whether to stay or leave, before their emigration from Germany was banned in 1941. While immigration restrictions made escape to certain countries difficult if not impossible, staying in Germany implied, in most cases, death in the Holocaust. Two recent complementary papers highlight the role of networks in the decision to emigrate. Buggle et al. (2020) estimate a structural model of migration where individuals base their own migration decision on the observation of persecution and migration among their network of peers. The authors use individual-level data of a large fraction of German Jews in the so-called *Residentenliste*, the list of Jewish residents in the German Empire 1933-1945. Identification exploits both immigration restrictions in potential destination countries as well as the fact that Jews living in the same place of residence may learn from emigration decisions of their childhood peers at their place of origin. While covering a large fraction of Jewish citizens in Nazi Germany, the *Residentenliste* is short on characteristics of Jews other than basic demographics. Becker et al. (2020b) focus on Jewish academics—a group whose biographies are well documented—to study who left, when exactly, and which destinations and jobs Jewish academic émigrés chose. Emigration probabilities increase sharply with the number of colleagues who had migrated. Since networks of colleagues may be endogenously formed, for identification, the authors exploit the early dismissals of colleagues as instruments for (early) migration of colleagues. While the majority of professors were dismissed in 1933, some could stay until 1935 because they had WWI frontline experience or qualified for other exemptions. Early dismissals are a powerful predictor of early migration of colleagues and can be used to identify the causal effect of the network.

An interesting aspect of that work is that while the emigration rate of Jewish academics is well above 80%, the emigration rate of the overall German Jewish population is only about 50%. This positive selection by education also shows up in work by Blum and Rei (2018), who analyze passenger lists of ships leaving Lisbon for New York in the years 1940-1942. This last wave of Holocaust refugees was characterized by a large share of highly educated Jews, with selectivity by education even more pronounced than among the non-Jewish passengers.

Escaping persecution was by no means easy and often relied on the help of non-Jews. Recent studies look at the characteristics of rescuers of Jews. Hoffman (2011) looks at the "Righteous Among the Nations", gentiles who rescued Jews and who are honored with a tree or plaque in Israel. He shows that the rescue of Jews during World War II is positively correlated with rescuer income at the country and the individual levels (using occupational status and self-perceived economic status as proxies for income). Given Hoffman's interest in using rescuing efforts to test for altruism, he argues that richer people had more to lose by rescuing. The positive link between income and rescuing is consistent with the view that altruism increases with income.

Contextual factors and inter-group relations have also been shown to be important in the rescue of Jews. Braun (2016) shows that minority groups are more likely to protect persecuted groups during episodes of mass killing. Using individual-level geo-coded data on Dutch Jews who escaped the Holocaust, he shows that proximity to Catholic churches increased evasion in dominantly Protestant regions, but proximity to Protestant churches had the same effect in Catholic regions. This finding is in line with his minorities-help-minorities story and shows that context matters.

While the work described so far focuses on survival and escape given the circumstances, Finkel (2015) highlights factors behind success or failure of Jewish resistance against Nazi oppression in different ghettos in Eastern Europe (Minsk, Kraków, and Białystok). His hypothesis is that successful resistance to state repression requires experience with targeted (as opposed to untargeted) repression. He shows that if there were people in the targeted population who were subject to selective repression in the preceding period, large-scale repression had a higher chance of being met with sustained organized resistance in the subsequent period.

Finally, several studies look at the legacy of the Holocaust. Focusing on Russia, Acemoglu et al. (2011) show a link between the severity of the persecution, displacement, and mass murder of Jews by the Nazis during World War II and long-run economic and political outcomes. Cities where the Holocaust was more intense have relatively lower population today and have voted in greater numbers for communist candidates since the collapse of the Soviet Union. The authors argue that the mechanism behind these results is the shrinking of the pre-WWII middle class in which Jews were over-represented. An unfortunate repercussion of Nazi indoctrination is its long shadow, as Voigtländer and Voth (2015) have shown for a representative sample of Germans surveyed in 1996 and 2006. Germans who grew up under the Nazi regime are much more anti-Semitic than those born before or after that period. These effects are more pronounced in districts that supported anti-Semitic parties already before 1914, i.e., where Nazism could tap into pre-existing prejudices.

As highlighted earlier, the Nazi regime dismissed Jewish academics from their positions when Hitler came to power in 1933. This might have had consequences not only for Jewish academics themselves, but also for their non-Jewish colleagues and PhD students. Waldinger (2010) provides evidence of negative effects of the expulsion of Jewish mathematics professors on PhD student outcomes. However, peer interactions seem to become less important in this context once scientists established a career: Waldinger (2012) finds no evidence for peer effects when looking at researchers in physics, chemistry, and mathematics. Even very high-quality scientists did not affect the productivity of their local peers. Moser et al. (2014) study the impact of the arrival of expelled Jewish chemists from Germany on US innovation activity. They show that patenting by US inventors increased significantly in émigré fields. Émigrés encouraged innovation by attracting new researchers to their fields.

The recent work on anti-Semitism in the historic social sciences using large-scale data sets has covered not only deep roots of anti-Semitism, but also its contemporaneous and long-run effects on socioeconomic outcomes. Many country-specific contexts remain unexplored with detailed micro empirical analyses. Also, the political economy of anti-Semitism in cross-country perspective remains under-studied.

20.3 Christianity

By far the largest share of the economics of religion in history literature focuses on various aspects of Christianity. This is not surprising, given that much of this research is conducted in Europe and North America. Yet, despite the obvious importance of religion to European economic history—even schoolchildren know that the Church was one of the dominant institutions of the medieval period— only recently has Christianity been the subject of serious study by economic historians. In this section, we break these studies into three groups: Catholicism, Protestantism, and missionaries. The literature on Catholicism in economic history primarily covers the various avenues through which the Catholic Church affected economic and political life. The large literature on Protestantism largely seeks to understand the social, economic, and political causes and consequences of the Reformation. The literature on missionaries sheds light on the many long-run consequences of Catholic and Protestant missionary activity around the world, primarily in sub-Saharan Africa, Asia, and Latin America. Of these three, Protestantism has garnered most of the recent attention. The reasons for this renewed interest in Protestantism and the Reformation are numerous: a persisting fascination with Weber's "Protestant Ethic" hypothesis, the increasing data availability via digitization, and the fact that the many political units of the Holy Roman Empire and its relative religious heterogeneity offer the type of variation needed for econometric analysis. Below we survey these recent advancements.

20.3.1 Catholicism

The literature on Catholicism in economic history primarily focuses on the many consequences of actions and doctrines promulgated by the Catholic Church. Table 20.3 overviews this literature.

The Catholic Church was one of the monolithic institutions of medieval Europe. Yet, what this meant for economic outcomes is not obvious. On the one hand, the Church provided numerous goods commonly associated with economic success: poor relief, investment in (religious) infrastructure, literacy, and manuscript production. However, the most common association many have with the medieval Church is one of a greedy, anti-scientific enterprise. Much high-quality recent research has attempted to parse out the various channels through which the medieval Church affected economic activity.

One of the most important demographic-cum-economic doctrines put forth by the medieval Church affected kin marriage. Building off the pioneering study by Goody (1983), Greif (2006a, 2006b) and Greif and Tabellini (2017) argue that restrictions on cousin marriages imposed by the medieval Church facilitated the growth of institutions in which the immediate family was the focal unit. According to Goody (1983), the medieval Church sought to break kin ties in order to break up inheritances both among members of the Church (thus the medieval ban on priestly marriage) and among the laity (the

Table 20.3 Catholicism.

Study	Setting	Method	Summary
Family structure and rise of communes			
Greif (2006a, 2006b); Greif and Tabellini (2017)	Medieval Europe	Theory	Church restrictions on cousin marriage contributed to weaker "clan" relations and the rise of the corporate form
Schulz (2019); Schulz et al. (2019)	Medieval Europe	Empirical	Exposure to Church predicts formation of communes
Belloc et al. (2016)	1000–1300, Italy	Empirical	Earthquakes gave local political authority more power and delayed communes
State development, guilds, and human capital			
Blaydes and Paik (2016)	Medieval Europe	Empirical	Crusades played a role in medieval state formation
Richardson (2005)	Medieval Europe	Theory	Religion held guilds together by increasing cost of expulsion
Andersen et al. (2017)	England, 1377–1801	Empirical	Exposure to Cistercian monasteries increased city productivity growth
Akçomak et al. (2016)	14th c Netherlands	Empirical	Brethren of the Common Life responsible for early Dutch capitalism
Squicciarini (2020)	19th c France	Empirical	Negative effect of French Church on industrialization during second phase
Finley et al. (2019)	19th c France	Empirical	Regions where Church land was redistributed during French Revolution had greater subsequent productivity
Uribe-Castro (2019)	19th c Colombia	Empirical	Regions where Church land was expropriated had less subsequent political conflict
The Counter-Reformation			
Ekelund et al. (1996, 2004)	16th c Europe	Theory	Church as incumbent trying to fight off new entrants
Becker et al. (2019)	16th–18th c Europe	Empirical	Cities defying index of prohibited books grew faster and attracted famous people
Church doctrine			
Barro and McCleary (2016)	1590–present	Empirical	Beatification, canonization of saints respond to religious and political incentives
Rubin (2009)	Late Roman Empire	Theory	Christian usury ban enacted to discourage moral hazard in late Roman Empire
Koyama (2010)	Medieval Europe	Theory	Medieval usury ban allowed small number of merchants to make monopoly rents

Church tended to be bequeathed the land of those without heirs). Forbidding marriages between cousins (up to the sixth degree) was one way to do this, since cousin marriage was a way of keeping property in the family. As a consequence, the family unit tended to not extend much beyond the nuclear family. In contrast, places like China and the Middle East tended to have more "clan"-like arrangements, where cousins of many degrees were all part of the same social unit. While this may have limited gains from exchange within the family unit for Europeans, it also incentivized Europeans to create governance institutions that relied on cross-kin cooperation. In other words, because the immediate family was too small to take advantage of specialization or gains from trade, institutions emerged in late medieval Europe that facilitated *impersonal* exchange (i.e., exchange with previously unknown relations). Specifically, Greif (2006a, 2006b) and Greif and Tabellini (2017) argue that the more generalized morality of Christian doctrine favored (relative to China) the formation of organizations that brought together unrelated people in pursuit of a common goal. In Europe, this took the form of the corporation, which became the organizational form of choice for cities, guilds, communes, and (ultimately) business associations. Such institutions were unnecessary in the Middle East or China, where clans were the primary familial unit. Clans were large enough and tended to cover enough economic and geographic space that exchange within the clan was profitable, and social sanctions could be used to punish shirkers or those who reneged on their promises. Yet, while the clan facilitated small-scale exchange, it was inherently limited in size and scope. Thus, an unintended consequence of the Church's restriction on kin marriages was that it facilitated the growth of institutions responsible for impersonal exchange.

One such institution was the commune, i.e., the self-governed city with inclusive institutions. Schulz (2019) and Schulz et al. (2019) find that exposure to the Church (i.e., the longer that Christianity was the dominant religion) predicts the formation of self-governing communes. These communes were the types of institutions that facilitated impersonal exchange by providing an identity to those engaged in exchange that went beyond the family. Schulz (2019) shows that the Church-family association persisted for a long time: longer Church exposure still (negatively) predicts cousin marriage in the 20th century.

An alternative (although not mutually exclusive) explanation for the rise of communes is the presence of earthquakes. Belloc et al. (2016) argue that earthquakes were dramatic, unexplainable events that were justified as acts of a vengeful God. They thus represented a shock to religious beliefs, making it easier for religious leaders to restore social order. Indeed, they find that earthquakes delayed commune development only in places governed by bishops, presumably because bishops had a stronger hold of their subjects than did secular rulers whose lands experienced earthquakes.

Numerous other studies look at the role of the Catholic Church in various parts of medieval and early modern economic and political life. Blaydes and Paik (2016) study the role the Crusades played in medieval state development. Crusades were expensive to fund; the Crusade tithe used to fund these ventures set a precedent for larger-scale taxation that would eventually become the hallmark of the early modern European state. Moreover, the Crusades reintegrated Europe into global trade networks (which were much more connected to the Holy Land at the time). This enabled the rise of towns which produced, consumed, and traded those goods involved in long-distance trade.

Indeed, the Church played an important role in medieval urban economic life. Richardson (2005) studies the role that religion had in strengthening the economic role played by urban craft guilds. Craft guilds were the life blood of urban economic activity. Almost all manufactured goods produced for market were produced by members of guilds. Richardson argues that guilds overcame a free-rider problem by their association with the Church. The free-rider problem faced by craft guilds arose because they desired to act like a monopolist in a certain town and produce a standardized good of a certain quality. Given weak monitoring technology, guild members were incentivized to either produce too many goods (the standard cartel problem) or produce goods cheaply, which would hurt the guild's reputation in the long run. Richardson argues that guilds overcame this problem by providing all sorts of expensive religious services (e.g., burials, prayers for souls in purgatory, feasts on saints' days) which increased the cost of expulsion from the guild.

Religious orders were institutions within the Catholic Church itself. Andersen et al. (2017) argue that the Catholic order of Cistercians favored hard work and thrift, in a precedent of the Protestant ethic (see Section 20.3.2.1). They show that in England, counties with Cistercian monasteries had faster population growth over the period 1377-1801—even after the liquidation of the monasteries in the 1530s, which suggests cultural appreciation of hard work and thrift as a relevant mechanism. Across Europe, regions with historical Cistercian monasteries are more likely to exhibit work- and thrift-related values.

Another religious community, the Brethren of the Common Life, was founded in the late 14th century in the Netherlands. Akçomak et al. (2016) argue that this institutional innovation within the Catholic Church was responsible for early capitalist development in the region. Their empirical analysis suggests that the Brethren contributed not to cultural change in the Weberian sense, but rather to local human capital through providing schools, translations into vernacular, and book production. As a result, the Netherlands had much higher literacy than most parts of Europe by 1600, and was a central locus of humanist and Reformation thought.

Moving to the late 19th century, Squicciarini (2020) finds that the French Church had a negative effect on human capital accumulation during the second Industrial Revolution. She shows that places with significant Church penetration were more likely to have their school curricula influenced by the Church, which at that time promoted a relatively anti-scientific program. Such a curriculum would not have had a large effect on economic output in the period prior to the second Industrial Revolution, since high-human capital labor was not overly complementary to capital prior to this time. However, the types of technologies that emerged in this period increased the returns to technical knowledge, so that places with high Church influence—and thus a slower introduction of the technical curriculum—suffered economically.

These results are broadly consistent with the idea that the French Church was a hindrance to development, an issue also studied in Finley et al. (2019). They look at the effect of the massive redistribution of Church land that resulted from the French Revolution. They find that areas in which more Church land was redistributed had greater productivity in the first half of the 19th century, suggesting that these regions were underutilized when under Church control. Uribe-Castro (2019) also studies the effect of the redistribution of Church land, in this case in 19th-century Colombia. He finds that places in which Church land was expropriated had much less political violence in the ensuing decades. This was due to changing political alliances: where the Church was strong, it pitted liberals versus conservatives, the latter of whom aligned with the Church. Where the Church was weakened, differences in policy preferences were not as stark, and conflict was less common.

Although the Reformation has been subject to immense study in recent years by social scientists (see Section 20.3.2), the Counter-Reformation has seen relatively little study, even though its long-run impact on European history and economic history is immense. The Counter-Reformation was the Catholic Church's (delayed) response to the Reformation. It began with the Council of Trent (1545-

1563) and lasted through the Peace of Westphalia in 1648. In this period, the Church increasingly allied with secular authorities to put down (often violently) rising Protestant sentiment. The Counter-Reformation sparked massive religious conflict in this period, most notably the Thirty Years' War (1618-48), the most violent conflict on European soil until the 20th century. Ekelund et al. (2002) argue that the Church was a monopolist provider of spiritual goods that used its position to place its members on the margin of defection, thus opening the gates for the success of the Reformation (see Section 20.3.2.2). This insight reflects the broader point made in Ekelund et al. (1996) that various practices of the medieval Church make sense if one views the Church as a firm. They lay out the "industrial organization of the Church" to understand why the Church interfered in marriage markets, promoted doctrine limiting economic exchange (i.e., usury and price restrictions), instigated Crusades, and used monastic agents. Building on these insights, Ekelund et al. (2004) suggest that, following the initial success of the Reformation, the Church acted like an incumbent firm trying to fight new entrants: it rewrote its corporate charter (e.g., the Council of Trent) in response to the new market conditions. However, the Counter-Reformation largely failed because entrenched interests within the Church—the pope and the college of cardinals—had too much power that would have been relinquished with any type of major reform like those demanded by the Protestants. One of the ways in which the Church attempted to suppress the Reformation and "maintain its monopoly position" was to suppress books via the *Index Librorum Prohibitorum* (Index of Prohibited Books). Becker et al. (2019) find that the Index did indeed reduce the output of forbidden authors. They also find that cities which defied the Index grew faster and attracted more famous people.

The previously mentioned studies analyze the effect of the Church, its institutions, or its doctrine on economic outcomes. A smaller literature seeks to understand the reverse: the effect of economic conditions on Church doctrine. Barro and McCleary (2016) provide an analysis of the determinants of the beatification and canonization of Catholic saints. They find that beatification and canonization respond to numerous incentives, including religious (a pope's tenure, a region's Catholic population), political (Catholic-Protestant competition), and historical (the stock of already-canonized saints from a region) circumstances.

Among the most well-known of the economic doctrines of the Church are those related to usury, i.e., taking interest on loans. Rubin (2009) studies the origins of usury prohibitions in the late Roman Empire. Usury was not always banned by the Church; the first widespread denunciation of usury occurred at the Council of Nicaea in 325. Rubin argues that the usury ban can be seen in the light of a commitment problem faced by the Church, which became wealthy after the Emperor Constantine adopted Christianity in 312. The Church had previously provided social insurance to its entire flock, and because it was relatively poor could commit to only providing to the "deserving poor" (i.e., those who had not taken excessive risk). With a much larger budget, it could no longer commit to this policy, which encouraged moral hazard among Christians, such as taking excessive loans. The Church responded by banning interest, which prevented such individuals from obtaining risky loans in the first place. Koyama (2010) also studies the Church's medieval usury restrictions. He argues that the Church continued to enforce the usury ban long after its original intentions were relevant due to an equilibrium which emerged between merchants, rulers, and the Church. In this equilibrium, the usury ban was a barrier to entry that permitted a small number of merchants to make monopoly rents, which were partially siphoned by rulers and the Church. Although the usury ban placed some restrictions on merchants' activities, those with a first-mover advantage preferred these restrictions because they were even more onerous on their competitors. One silver lining of the usury ban, at least for Catholics, is that it may have reduced anti-Semitism. Since Catholics were discouraged from lending openly at interest, Jewish lenders filled this role, meaning there was little direct competition between Catholics and Jews. However, as Becker and Pascali (2019) show (see Section 20.2.2), Protestants did not abide by the usury ban, putting them in direct competition with Jews in the lending market, which contributed to persistent anti-Semitic attitudes amongst Protestants.

The recent work on Catholicism in history primarily focuses on the various ways in which the Catholic Church affected economic, demographic, and political outcomes. With the exception of a few papers, it is relatively silent on the role of the Church, Catholic doctrine, or other Catholic institutions in the post-Reformation era.

20.3.2 Protestantism

When Martin Luther composed his 95 Theses in 1517, he triggered the Protestant Reformation, which led to the persistent split of the Protestant denominations from Catholicism. A large body of recent research focuses on the socioeconomic consequences of the Protestant Reformation, as well as its socioeconomic causes. We highlight leading contributions here; a more extensive recent survey is provided by Becker et al. (2016).

20.3.2.1 Socioeconomic consequences of the reformation

Theories of the consequences of the Reformation date at least to Max Weber and his well-known "Protestant ethic" thesis. In the last two decades, this literature has seen a massive resurgence. Table 20.4 overviews this literature.

In his seminal contribution on the socioeconomic effects of Protestantism, *The Protestant Ethic and the Spirit of Capitalism*, Max Weber (1904/05) famously argued that there is a particular Protestant ethic that was instrumental in facilitating industrial capitalism.[5] In contrast to the Catholic ideal of surpassing worldly morality in monastic asceticism, Weber argued that the notion of the "calling" introduced by the Reformation sanctified labor as a task set by God, thereby creating a Protestant work ethic that valued the fulfillment of worldly duties as a moral achievement. By approving the accumulation of wealth, the Protestant ethic provided the moral foundation for capitalist industrialization, with economic success regarded as a sign of God's salvation. Important mechanisms by which the Protestant ethic is argued to further economic progress include hard work and thrift. While the Weber thesis has created a lot of controversy, not least about its correct interpretation, a commonly adopted simple interpretation of its economic bearing is that the Protestant ethic furthered economic development.

As an alternative to the Weber thesis, Becker and Woessmann (2009) propose a human capital theory of Protestant economic history. They argue that Martin Luther urged his followers, including the Protestant rulers, to advance education so that they could read the Bible. As a side effect, higher levels of education served as human capital in the economic sphere, increasing productivity and economic development. Using distance to Wittenberg as an instrument for Protestantism that exploits the initial concentric dispersion of the Reformation in Prussia, Becker and Woessmann find that Protestantism led to higher literacy across Prussian counties in the late 19th century: the average literacy rate in Protestant-majority counties was 90%, 8 percentage points higher than in Catholic-majority

---

[5] Weber traces back his central notion of a Protestant "calling" to Martin Luther but sees it more strongly developed in other Protestant denominations, such as Calvinism and Puritanism.

Table 20.4 Socioeconomic consequences of the reformation.

Study	Setting	Method	Summary
Protestantism, human capital, and socioeconomic outcomes			
Becker and Woessmann (2009)	Prussia, late 19th c	Empirical	Human capital theory of Protestant economic history: Protestantism increased literacy and economic outcomes
Becker and Woessmann (2010)	Prussia, 1816	Empirical	Effect of Protestantism on education already before industrialization
Becker and Woessmann (2008)	Prussia, 19th c	Empirical	Protestantism decreased gender gap in education
Boppart et al. (2013, 2014)	Switzerland, late 19th c	Empirical	Effect of Protestantism on educational spending and performance in Switzerland
Becker et al. (2010)	Prussia, 1849-1905	Empirical	Protestantism-induced education reduced fertility
Becker et al. (2011)	Prussia, 19th c	Empirical	Protestantism-induced education increased non-textile industrialization in both phases of Industrial Revolution
Hornung (2014)	Brandenburg, 1700, 1802	Empirical	Long-run effect of Huguenot immigrants on productivity of textile manufactories
Reformation, Protestant ethic, and socioeconomic outcomes			
Cantoni (2015)	Germany, 1300-1900	Empirical	No effect of Protestantism on German city growth
Dittmar and Meisenzahl (2020)	Germany, 1520-1819	Empirical	Adoption of church ordinances after plagues increased upper-tail human capital and city population growth
Spenkuch (2017)	Germany, 17th c, today	Empirical	Protestant areas in 1624 have longer working hours, but not hourly wages, today
Basten and Betz (2013)	Switzerland, 16th c, today	Empirical	Protestantism reduced political preferences for leisure time, redistribution, and government intervention
Beatton et al. (2019)	Germany, WWII	Empirical	Protestant soldiers expend more effort than Catholic soldiers in WWII
Blum and Strebel (2016)	Germany, WWI	Empirical	Height decrease of cohort born in WWI lower for Protestants than Catholics
Cantoni et al. (2018)	Germany, 1480-1600	Empirical	Reallocation of human and physical capital investment from religious to secular purposes in immediate aftermath of Reformation
Heldring et al. (2017)	England, 16th-18th c	Empirical	Dissolution of monasteries increased agricultural and industrial productivity
Negative socioeconomic consequences of Reformation			
Becker and Woessmann (2018)	Prussia, early and late 19th c	Empirical	Protestantism increased suicide; social cohesion as mechanism
Leeson and Russ (2018)	Europe, 1500-1700	Empirical	Catholic-Protestant battles increased witch trial incidence

counties. They also show that Protestant counties had higher income and higher non-agricultural employment. Both in a horse race and in a bounding analysis, their results suggest that the higher literacy of Protestants is able to account for most of the Protestant economic advantage over Catholic regions of Prussia. In supplementary analyses, Becker and Woessmann (2010) show that the effect of Protestantism on education is already visible in early 19th century data, ruling out a Weberian interpretation where better education just resulted from industrialization, and Becker and Woessmann (2008) show that the effect was particularly pronounced among girls, decreasing the gender gap in basic education. In a cross-country analysis, Becker and Woessmann (2009) show that a positive association between Protestantism and economic development mirrors a strong positive association between Protestantism and literacy across countries in 1900.

Using variation in the share of Catholics and Protestants across Swiss districts in the late 19th century, Boppart et al. (2013) also find a positive association of Protestantism with education in terms of educational spending per student and educational performance. This association is stronger in regions with conservative milieus, as measured by votes on different referenda. Using data on pedagogical examinations of military conscripts across Swiss districts, Boppart et al. (2014) show that the effect of Protestantism was particularly strong for reading, but also extended to essay writing, math, and history.

By affecting the population's education, Protestantism also led to changes in the historical development of other socioeconomic outcomes. Using Wittenberg-induced variation in education, Becker et al. (2010) show that education led to a reduction in fertility across Prussian counties in the mid-19th century. Education in 1849 also predicts the fertility transition at the turn to the 20th century. This link from education to fertility is a crucial factor for the transition from Malthusian stagnation to sustained growth in unified growth theory (Galor, 2011). The evidence suggests that the demographic transition may in part reflect an indirect effect of Protestantism.

Using factory employment data for Prussian counties from the early, mid, and late 19th century, Becker et al. (2011) focus on the adoption of the new industrial production technologies and the major transformation of the economic structure brought about by the Industrial Revolution. Both in cross-sectional models that exploit pre-industrial variation in education and in panel models with county fixed effects, they show that education increased industrialization in the metal sector and in other sectors outside metal and textiles (such as rubber, paper, and food), but not in the textile sector. The effect on the non-metal/non-textiles sectors is visible in both phases of the Industrial Revolution, whereas the effect on metalworking factories is strongest in the second phase (1849-1882). These results are confirmed in specifications that use distance to Wittenberg as an instrument for education, thereby exploiting variation in the education of the native population induced by Protestantism.

A different source of religiously induced variation in the skilled population stems from the religious persecution that led to the mass migration of French Protestants—the Huguenots—to Brandenburg-Prussia in 1685. Hornung (2014) argues that large parts of the Huguenot population were skilled in textile production and brought technological knowledge with them. Using plague losses during the preceding Thirty Years' War as an instrument for the settlement of the Huguenots, he shows substantial positive effects of Huguenot settlement in 1700 on the productivity (value of output per inputs) of textile manufactories one hundred years later. The immigration of skilled Protestants thus appears to have led to the long-term diffusion of better technology before the Industrial Revolution.

Apart from the work on Protestantism and education, the literature continuous to create controversy about Weber's thesis of a Protestant ethic. While the human capital results of Becker and Woessmann (2009) leave little room for alternative mechanisms in line with the Weber thesis (such as work effort and savings propensity), results in other settings cover the whole spectrum from questioning the economic advantage of Protestant regions in the first place to aspects consistent with the Weber thesis to ethical interpretations beyond the Weber thesis.

Using a panel of cities in Germany over the period 1300-1900, Cantoni (2015) does not find that cities that converted to Protestantism after the Reformation show a different path of the size of their city population compared to cities that did not. Compared with the results in Becker and Woessmann (2009), this may suggest that the effect of Protestantism on economic outcomes may have been restricted to areas outside the major cities, where literacy was relatively high independent of religious denomination.

Studying church ordinances introduced with the Reformation in German cities, Dittmar and Meisenzahl (2020) focus on the interaction between religious competition and local political economy. They argue that the introduction of church ordinances—which acted as public goods institutions that expanded welfare provision and public education—was facilitated by the interaction of the global shock of the Reformation, which introduced religious competition, with shocks to local politics that facilitated political action by citizens. Using plague incidents as an instrument for the adoption of church ordinances, their empirical analysis shows that cities that were induced to adopt church ordinances attracted and produced more upper-tail human capital over the period in 1520-1819 (as measured by the number of individuals documented in the *Deutsche Biographie*, a collection of biographies of famous Germans) and show a larger increase in city population from 1500-1800. They argue that the adoption of public goods institutions, rather than the adoption of Protestantism per se, accounts for the different population development.

Another approach to study long-run effects of the historical adoption of Protestantism is to use contemporary German data. Using territories' official religion as defined by their princes' religion around 1624—the "normal year" of the Peace of Westphalia—as an instrument for contemporary religious affiliation, Spenkuch (2017) draws on the historical variation in Protestantism in the aftermath of the Peace of Augsburg. Results suggest that historical Protestantism is associated with longer working hours, but not higher hourly wages, today. This is interpreted as evidence consistent with a value-based interpretation, as in the Weber thesis.

The use of contemporary data also allows researchers to focus on direct measures of preferences for work and political intervention. Using a spatial discontinuity in the Swiss cantons of Vaud and Fribourg created by a 16th century split between Catholicism and Reformed (Calvinist) Protestantism, Basten and Betz (2013) study votes in modern-day referenda and find that the historically induced split is associated with lower political preferences of Protestants for increased leisure time, redistribution, and government intervention. Beyond preferences, the Protestant regions show higher inequality and (weakly) higher income. The results are interpreted as being in line with the Weber thesis of a Protestant ethic.

Studying effort provision of German WWII soldiers as proxied by military decorations, promotions, injuries, and deaths, Beatton et al. (2019) find that Protestants outperform Catholics, and Calvinists outperform Lutherans, which they interpret as consistent with a Protestant work ethic. Blum and Strebel (2016) study body height in a sample of Germans born between 1910 and 1924. They find that while height was lower among those born during WWI for both Protestants and Catholics, the decrease of Protestants' height was smaller, which is interpreted as higher resilience of Protestants to war-related deprivation.

Another mechanism by which the Protestant Reformation may have spurred economic development is the reallocation of investments in human and physical capital from religious to secular purposes.

Cantoni et al. (2018) argue that the new religious competition shifted political power from religious to secular authorities, which gained wealth from the closure of monasteries especially in Protestant regions.[6] As a result, in the immediate aftermath of the Reformation, graduates of Protestant universities tended to choose secular (administrative) majors and occupations rather than religious ones, and construction shifted from religious buildings to secular palaces and administrative buildings, particularly in Protestant regions. The results suggest that the Protestant Reformation triggered secularization processes.

A related institutional consequence has been highlighted for the English Reformation. Heldring et al. (2017) show that the dissolution of English monasteries in 1535 created a more efficient allocation of agricultural resources and helped bring about the Agricultural Revolution. They also find a positive relationship between monastic land holdings and industrialization around the time of the Industrial Revolution.

Beyond its effects on different aspects of economic and educational development, several studies also point to potential negative socioeconomic consequences of the Reformation. Durkheim (1897) documented that Protestant countries and regions had higher suicide rates and suggested the religious individualism of Protestantism as a mechanism. While Catholics' unified community embedded them socially, the Protestant doctrine promoted independent thinking, making Protestants less reliant on their religious community. In addition to this social-cohesion channel, Becker and Woessmann (2018) also model a religious-beliefs channel in an economic theory of religion-specific suicide: Catholic doctrine emphasized more than the Protestant one that the deadly sin of suicide prevented access to paradise in afterlife. Again exploiting the concentric dispersion of Protestantism around Wittenberg, they show that suicide rates are significantly larger in Protestant compared to Catholic Prussians counties in the early and late 19th century. The effect is large: Protestantism increased the annual suicide rate by about 15-20 suicides per 100,000 inhabitants, compared to a mean of 13 suicides. Tests of the two suggested mechanisms by which Protestantism increases suicide propensity suggest that the sociological channel is more relevant than the theological channel: among others, using historical church attendance data the authors show that the suicidal tendency of Protestants is more pronounced in areas with low church attendance, indicating that the strongest effect is found in areas with little social integration rather than in areas with high devotion to the Protestant doctrine.

Recent studies also indicate that the Protestant Reformation may have led to an increase in anti-Semitism. As discussed in Section 20.2.2 above, Becker and Pascali (2019) indicate an increase in Jewish persecution in Protestant areas, and Spenkuch and Tillmann (2018) document Protestantism as a leading predictor of Nazi vote shares.

It has also been argued that Catholic-Protestant competition was a leading source of witch trials. Leeson and Russ (2018) show that witch-trial activity is positively associated with confessional battles in a panel of 21 European countries observed at the decadal level over the period 1500-1699. The association is robust to the inclusion of country and decade fixed effects.

In sum, the recent burst of work on how the Reformation affected historical economic developments highlights the role of human capital in Protestant economic history, which was interrelated with increasing income, productivity, industrialization, secular resource use, and reduced fertility. At the same time, the emergence of Protestantism also affected the incidence of suicides, anti-Semitism, and

---

[6] See Becker et al. (2016) for work on effects of the Reformation on political governance more generally.

witch trials. The empirical bearing of a particular Protestant ethic remains subject to continuing controversy.

20.3.2.2 Socioeconomic causes of the reformation, of its spread, and of Protestant religiosity

The combination of advances in digitization along with the variation in the adoption of the Reformation (especially in the Holy Roman Empire) has made it possible to econometrically study the causes of the spread of the Reformation. Table 20.5 overviews the emerging literature that addresses this topic.

Substantial recent work on the causes of the Protestant Reformation has highlighted factors both on the supply side and on the demand side of the market for religion. Luther's open deviation from the Roman Catholic Church in 1517 triggered extensive religious conflict. Wide-ranging choices of territorial rulers to adopt the new denomination or to remain Catholic were institutionalized by the rule "cuius regio, eius religio" (whose realm, his religion) in the Peace of Augsburg (1555). When the Peace of Westphalia finally terminated the savage Thirty Years' War (1618-1648), it guaranteed the religious status quo of the "normal year" 1624. Analyses of the causes of the spread of Protestantism range from its early adoption during Luther's time to the subsequent diffusion of the Protestant faith.[7] In addition, secularization analyses study causes of the later decline in Protestant religiosity.

The initial successes and failures of the Protestant Reformation have been studied in the framework of an industrial-organization model. Ekelund et al. (2002) argue that the monopolistic practices of the medieval Catholic Church encouraged the entry of Protestantism as a competitor. The Catholic Church placed many consumers of spiritual services on the margin of defection by manipulating doctrine to increase its revenues, excluding rivals, and performing price discrimination. Their key hypothesis is that entrepreneurial societies where feudalism was in decline and the distribution of wealth was unstable facilitated the entry of Protestantism. By contrast, homogeneous rent-seeking societies that dissipated rather than created wealth repressed Protestant entry, and the Catholic Church could continue to price discriminate. Consistent with this model, the authors descriptively show that societies with partible inheritance laws that likely catered to a wider wealth distribution embraced Protestantism, whereas societies ruled by primogeniture were more likely to remain Catholic.

Relational factors appear to have played a role in the diffusion of the Protestant Reformation. Kim and Pfaff (2012) argue that, depending on whether the universities that students attended mobilized them for the new denomination or were loyal to the Catholic Church, university students acted as facilitators or blockers of the religious reform movement in their home towns. The authors show that cities in the Holy Roman Empire that had more students enrolled in universities in Protestant strongholds (Wittenberg and Basel) and less in Catholic strongholds (Cologne and Louvain) in 1517-1522 were more likely to institute the Reformation (abolish or reform the Catholic Mass) in 1523-1545.

Another source of relational diffusion is the role of Martin Luther himself as a social entrepreneur. Becker et al. (2020a) study social proximity to the ideological leader in his personal network. They show that cities with personal ties to Luther—measured by having received a letter from Luther, having been visited by Luther by 1522, or being home to one of Luther's students—had a higher probability of being Protestant in 1530. Results of simulation models are consistent with the view that the early

---

[7] A more encompassing discussion of the causes of the Reformation, its spread, and the political economy of religion in Western Europe on the eve of the Reformation is given in Becker et al. (2016).

Table 20.5 Socioeconomic causes of the Reformation, of its spread, and of Protestant religiosity.

Study	Setting	Method	Summary
Causes of adoption and spread of Reformation			
Ekelund et al. (2002)	Reformation	Theory, narrative	Monopolistic practices of medieval Catholic Church encouraged Protestant entry in entrepreneurial societies with declining feudalism and unstable wealth distribution
Kim and Pfaff (2012)	Germany, 1517–1545	Empirical	Cities with students in Protestant rather than Catholic universities before 1523 more likely to enact Reformation
Becker et al. (2020a)	Germany before 1530	Empirical	Cities with personal ties (letters, visits, Wittenberg students) to Luther before 1523 more likely to enact Reformation; interacts with spatial diffusion along trade routes
Cantoni (2012)	Germany, 1600	Empirical	Distance to Wittenberg, ecclesiastical rule, and political and economic power reduce Protestantism
Curuk and Smulders (2019)	Germany, 1600	Empirical	Agricultural potential and smaller population 1500 increase Protestantism
Rubin (2014)	European cities, 1500–1600	Empirical	Having printing press by 1500 increases Protestant adoption by 1600
Boerner et al. (2019)	European cities, 1450–1600	Empirical	Indirect effect of mechanical clock on Reformation through printing press
Dittmar and Seabold (2020)	Germany, 1454–1600	Empirical	Printing competition increased Protestant book content and Reformation adoption
Iyigun (2008)	Europe, 1521–1650	Empirical	Ottoman incursions reduced Catholic-Protestant conflicts within Europe
Causes of Protestant secularization			
Becker and Woessmann (2013)	Prussia, 1886–1911	Empirical	No effect of income on church attendance in panel models
Becker et al. (2017)	Germany, 1890–1930	Empirical	Advanced-school expansion reduced church attendance in panel models

spread of the Reformation resulted from a combination of Luther's personal ties with spatial diffusion along contemporaneous trade routes.

Exploiting the high territorial fractionalization of the Holy Roman Empire, Cantoni (2012) studies which German territories and cities chose to adopt the Protestant Reformation by 1600. He finds that territories more distant from Wittenberg (as in Becker and Woessmann, 2009), under ecclesiastical rule, and with more political and economic power (measured by contributions to the federal budget of the Holy Roman Empire) were less likely to become Protestant. The findings of a spatial panel model are consistent with a theory of strategic neighborhood interactions where conversion was less risky if a strong neighbor had already done so.

Another argument is that conversion to Protestantism had a larger appeal to local authorities of territories that had more to gain from the institutional change, as it provided legitimacy for secular governance and allowed the use of resources for local and secular purposes. Using the same setting as Cantoni (2012) of German cities in 1600, Curuk and Smulders (2019) show that the adoption of Protestantism was positively associated with agricultural potential (based on climatic suitability and soil quality) and negatively with population size in 1500. The results are interpreted as consistent with a Malthusian model of untapped economic potential and thus the potential benefits of regime change.

Yet another theory is that the printing press facilitated the spread of the Protestant Reformation. The reformers used printed materials to propagate their cause. Because of high transportation cost, these materials spread through reprinting, so that the existence of a printing press increased access to Reformation ideology. Using distance from Mainz—where Gutenberg had invented the printing press—as an instrument, Rubin (2014) shows that having a printing press by 1500 increases a city's likelihood of adopting Protestantism by 1600 by at least 29 percentage points. Extending the analysis, Boerner et al. (2019) show that the adoption of the printing press had even deeper roots, as cities that had adopted mechanical clocks early on were also more likely to adopt presses early. But while the effect of the printing press on the adoption of the Reformation was direct, the effect of the clock was only indirect via the press.

It has also been argued that competition in the printing industry affected the content of the printed material and thereby the adoption of the Reformation. Dittmar and Seabold (2020) classify printed books in the period 1454-1600 by their denominational orientation. Arguing that recent printer deaths provide a source of exogenous variation in the competitive environment in the local printing market, they show that higher competition in printing before the Reformation increases the spread of religious media and of Protestant content during the Reformation in a sample of German-speaking cities. This diffusion of Protestant content increased the likelihood that a city adopted the Reformation.

Political economy factors have also been shown to be relevant for the spread of the Reformation. Iyigun (2008) argues that the survival of the Protestant Reformation was facilitated by Ottoman incursions. As described in greater detail in Section 20.4.1 below, he shows that the number of conflicts in which the Ottoman Empire confronted European powers is negatively associated with the number of violent conflicts within continental European countries over the period 1450-1700, and in particular with those of Catholic-vs-Protestant religious nature over the period 1521-1650.

Beyond the initial adoption of the Reformation, recent studies have also used Protestantism to test leading theories of determinants of religiosity. Classic secularization hypotheses suggest that different dimensions of modernization, including economic and educational development, affect religiosity. Marx (1844) famously portrayed religion as "opium of the people" that was needed only to alleviate the misery of poor economic circumstances.

In their study of the relation of income and secularization, Becker and Woessmann (2013) exploit a historically unique indicator of churchliness provided by the headcounts of participations in Holy Communion that are contained in the Sacrament Statistics of the statistical surveys of the Protestant Regional Churches of Germany on the Expressions of Churchly Life. In a panel of Prussian counties over the period 1886-1911, they show a marked decline in church attendance among the Protestant population that coincides with increasing income. However, the association between income and church attendance disappears in panel models with county and time fixed effects, as well as in long-term first-differenced models and in panel Granger-causality tests. The findings provide no indication that the reduction in religiosity at the turn to the 20th century was the result of improved material conditions.

Others have argued that education and science would lead to a decline in religion because increased critical thinking and advanced scientific knowledge may reduce belief in supernatural forces (e.g., Hume, 1757; Freud, 1927). Becker et al. (2017) combine religious attendance data from the same source with school enrollment data for a panel of German cities between 1890 and 1930. In panel models with fixed effects for cities and time, they find that the expansion of advanced-school enrollment was positively associated with subsequent reductions in church attendance. No such effects are found for income and urbanization. The relationship between educational expansion and declining church attendance is as strong for classical humanist grammar schools as for newly emerging upper secondary schools with a curricular focus on natural sciences, consistent with an important role for general critical thinking—which may have undermined belief in the institutionalized church—rather than specific scientific knowledge of facts of natural sciences. More broadly, similar to the effect of Protestantism on the secularization of occupational choice and resource investments in the immediate aftermath of the Reformation shown by Cantoni et al. (2018), these results indicate that the expansion of education brought about by Protestantism may have laid the foundation for an ultimate decline in the importance of the church in everyday social life.

In sum, many supply-side and demand-side factors of the market for religion appear to have contributed to the adoption and spread of the Protestant Reformation. Monopolistic practices of the medieval Catholic Church, relational factors, strategic neighborhood interactions, economic potential, technological factors like the printing press, and political-economy factors like Ottoman incursions all appear to have played a role. Tests of secularization hypotheses indicate a role for education, but not income, in reduced church attendance of Protestants during the secularization phase at the turn to the 20th century.

20.3.3 Missionaries

While most of the research on Christianity in economic history is concerned with European countries, another important strand of the literature considers the role of Christian missionaries outside Europe. Exploiting the recent data collection efforts on missions around the globe pioneered by Robert Woodberry (2004), researchers have looked at whether the presence of missionaries had long-term effects on modern-day outcomes.[8] Table 20.6 overviews this literature.

---

[8] See Woodberry (2011) for an early survey on the literature on missionaries. The literature on missionaries and education is more extensively covered in recent surveys for Africa by Meier zu Selhausen (2019) and for Latin America and Asia by Valencia Caicedo (2019b).

Table 20.6 Missionaries.

Study	Setting	Method	Summary
Missionaries, human capital, and health: Africa			
Gallego and Woodberry (2010)	Africa	Empirical	Regions where Protestant missionaries dominated have higher literacy; role of competition
Nunn (2014)	Africa	Empirical	In areas with Protestant missionaries, education effect more pronounced for women
Wantchekon et al. (2015)	Benin	Empirical	Village-level externalities: descendants of the uneducated in villages with schools do better than those in control villages
Doyle et al. (2020)	Uganda	Empirical	Christian African converts adopted healthier sexual behavior already during colonial period
Cagé and Rueda (2020)	Africa	Empirical	Christian missionaries influenced sexual beliefs and behaviors that affected risk of HIV contagion
Wietzke (2015)	Madagascar	Empirical	Colonial institutions had stronger effect on local economic outcomes than missionary schools
Missionaries, human capital, and health: Asia			
Ma (2020)	China	Empirical	Jesuits missionaries stimulated Confucian literati to study science
Bai and Kung (2015)	China	Empirical	Protestant missionaries associated with schools, hospitals, and better economic development
Calvi et al. (2020)	India	Empirical	Protestant missionaries associated with higher literacy
Calvi and Mantovanelli (2018)	India	Empirical	Current health outcomes better the closer a village to historical Protestant medical missions
Castelló-Climent et al. (2018)	India	Empirical	Catholic missions associated with higher secondary school completion
Missionaries, human capital, and health: Latin America			
Waldinger (2017)	Mexico	Empirical	Areas with historical presence of Catholic mendicant orders have higher literacy and education today
Valencia Caicedo (2019a)	S. America	Empirical	Jesuit missions in South America promoted education; effects persist 250 years later
Missionaries and other outcomes			
Nunn (2010)	Africa	Empirical	Christian missionaries had lasting impact on religious beliefs
Woodberry (2012)	Worldwide	Empirical	Protestant missionaries influenced rise and spread of stable democracy
Cagé and Rueda (2016)	Africa	Empirical	In regions close to Protestant missions, proximity to printing press associated with higher newspaper readership, trust, education, and political participation
Missionary expansion			
Meier zu Selhausen (2019)	Africa	Empirical	Africanization of missions relevant to understand reach of initially European missionaries
Jedwab et al. (2019a)	Africa	Empirical	Smaller effect size of missionaries when considering local determinants of missionary expansion

Most of this literature focuses on the effects of missionaries on human capital and health. Evidence comes from Africa, Asia, and Latin America, which we cover in turn. We close with studies looking at a broader range of outcomes and at the dynamics of missionary expansion.

Much of the evidence on positive effects of missions on education and health comes from sub-Saharan Africa. Gallego and Woodberry (2010) provide evidence that regions in former Colonial Africa in which Western Protestant missionaries dominated have higher literacy rates than those where Catholic missionaries dominated.[9] They also highlight the importance of competition: where missionaries competed, they provided more services like schools and health centers. Nunn (2014) finds that Protestant and Catholic missionary activity in Africa both had long-term positive impacts on education, although women profited more in Protestant areas. Studying colonial Benin, Wantchekon et al. (2015) show that missionaries increased the valuation of education in families close to historical mission stations. Their results indicate that missionaries even changed the values of non-Christians in the same village, suggesting human capital externalities. Studying long-term health effects in Uganda, Doyle et al. (2020) show that (mostly Protestant) Christian African converts adopted healthier sexual behavior during the colonial period. Cagé and Rueda (2020) qualify the overall positive image of missionaries: while they were the first to invest in modern African healthcare, Christianity influenced sexual beliefs and behaviors that affected the risk of HIV contagion.

In many cases, missionary activities took place alongside colonial conquest and the introduction of legal and economic institutions. This raises the question of what is the counterfactual to missionary activity: no missionary activity but still a presence of colonial institutions, or no foreign presence at all? While this question is often neglected, a rare exception is the work by Wietzke (2015), who exploits historical differences in the timing and organization of historical school investments and colonial legal-institutional reforms in Madagascar. Christian missionaries introduced formal schooling several decades before the imposition of French colonial rule and were thus unrelated to the economic or military objectives of the colonizers. Results indicate that colonial institutions had comparatively stronger effects on local economic outcomes than missionary school investments.

The question of missionary activity versus colonial activity does not arise in the case of China, where missionary activity initially happened outside any colonial context. After 1580, the Jesuits introduced European sciences to China, where the intelligentsia was dominated by Confucian literati who lived largely in autarky. Ma (2020) demonstrates that the Jesuits stimulated Confucian literati to study science. However, effects do not persist after the Jesuits were expelled by the emperor of China in 1723. Looking at a later period of missionary activity, Bai and Kung (2015) find that Chinese regions that had higher penetration of Protestant missionaries during the 19th century also had higher urbanization rates at the beginning of the 20th century. The mechanism identified by the authors is knowledge diffusion activities associated with schools and hospitals erected by the missionaries.

Additional evidence of positive effects of missionaries on education and health comes from India. Calvi et al. (2020) show that Protestant missionaries in India are associated with higher literacy. Similarly, current health outcomes are better the closer a village is to historical Protestant medical missions (Calvi and Mantovanelli, 2018). Using Catholic missions as an instrumental variable to look at the effect of completed secondary education in India today on night light intensity, Castelló-Climent et al.

---

[9] This is consistent with the finding of Becker and Woessmann (2009), who point to a Protestant advantage in literacy in 19th-century Prussia and in a cross-section of countries in 1900.

(2018) show a positive link between Catholic missions and completed secondary education. They explain the seeming contrast with Calvi et al. (2020) by showing that Protestant missions affect completed middle school, but have no effect on other education levels, such as completed secondary schooling.

The Latin American experience allows to study the effects of different kinds of Catholic missionaries. Waldinger (2017) examines the long-run effects of different Catholic missionary orders in colonial Mexico on educational outcomes. She shows that different monastic traditions pursued different aims and transported different values. Mendicant orders were committed to poverty and sought to reduce social inequality in colonial Mexico by educating the native population. The Jesuit order, by contrast, focused educational efforts on the colony's elite in the city centers, rather than on the native population in rural mission areas. Mendicant orders left a lasting mark in the Mexican countryside with higher educational attainment in areas where they held a stronger historic presence.

Jesuits were, in contrast, very influential among the Guarani people whose homelands straddle three South American countries—Argentina, Brazil, and Paraguay. Jesuit missions in South America instructed indigenous inhabitants in reading, writing, and various crafts. While the Jesuits were expelled from the Americas in 1767, Valencia Caicedo (2019a) shows that, in areas of former Jesuit presence, educational attainment was higher and remains so 250 years later, compared to areas outside the Jesuit reach.

Beyond effects on human capital and health, some work has looked at effects of missionaries on a broader range of outcomes. Nunn (2010) provides evidence that foreign missionaries altered the religious beliefs of Africans, and that these beliefs persist as they are passed on from parents to children. The results indicate that Christian missionaries had a lasting impact on culture. Woodberry (2012) highlights the role Western Protestant missionaries played in influencing the rise and spread of stable democracy around the world. Cagé and Rueda (2016) combine the direct influence of missionaries with the technology that some missionaries brought with them in the form of the printing press. They show that, within sub-Saharan African regions close to main European missions, proximity to a printing press is associated with higher newspaper readership, trust, education, and political participation.

While much of the literature links historical Christian missionary activities to various socioeconomic outcomes, only recently has focus shifted to better understanding the dynamics of missionary expansion per se. Meier zu Selhausen (2019) gives a comprehensive account of Christian missionary expansion in Africa during the colonial era. He emphasizes the Africanization of the mission, i.e., the fact that much of the effect of Christian missionary work should be attributed not to the first European missionaries, but to their local followers and supporters who expanded missionary activities into territories not reached before. This theme is also at the core of the work by Jedwab et al. (2019b), who study the drivers and long-term consequences of Christian missionary expansion across colonial Africa, with a particular emphasis on Ghana. Their paper reassesses the reliability of widely used data sets of missionary activity based on early missionary atlases[10] and concludes that they miss 90% of the missions in early colonial Africa. Investigating the local determinants of missionary expansion, the authors show that missions expanded initially within more developed, healthier, safer, and more accessible areas. Reassessing the long-term effects of Christian missions in Ghana by reconstructing the full set of missions for the period 1751-1932, the authors conclude that the effect of Christian missions on modern African economic development was much more moderate.

---

[10] Widely used sources for missionary activity are the 1900 Atlas of Protestant Missions (Beach, 1903) and the 1924 Ethnographic Survey of Africa (Roome, 1925).

While most of the numerous recent advances in research on Christian missionaries indicate positive long-term impacts of Christian missionaries worldwide, some caveats remain. Certain religious norms (such as Catholic opposition to family planning) may have negative consequences for economic development. Importantly, selection of missionaries into different locations gives rise to endogeneity concerns that have not always been fully addressed. Another understudied area is research on different streams within one religion, such as different Catholic missionary orders (Waldinger, 2017 being one exception) and different types of Protestantism.[11]

20.4 Islam

In the last two decades, economists have become increasingly interested in the economic history of the Islamic world. Indeed, the topic has now been studied enough to warrant a survey piece in the *Journal of Economic Literature* (Kuran, 2018). There are multiple reasons for this increased interest. For one, the Islamic world has played a central role in world politics and economics, with the aftermath of 9/11, the Arab Spring, and outflows of Muslim immigrants into Europe among the many important events. Understanding the role that history and Islam have played in these events is of clear importance. Moreover, new sources of data and econometric techniques have allowed social scientists to answer questions that were previously answerable only via qualitative methods.

The biggest question addressed in this literature is at the heart of the research program spear-headed by Timur Kuran (which culminated in his 2011 book, *The Long Divergence*): why did the Middle East fall behind the West economically after being ahead for so long? Works asking this question fall into the greater debate regarding the "great divergence" between the West and the rest of the world. These works tend to focus on three themes: i) politics and law; ii) finance and trade (and its impediments); and iii) the human capital deficit of the Islamic world. In this section, we overview recent works which address each of these topics.

20.4.1 Politics and law

Since its inception, Islam has been intertwined with politics and law. Much of the literature analyzing the economic consequences of Islam naturally focuses on this aspect of Islam and Islamic institutions. Table 20.7 overviews this literature.

Over much of the history of the Islamic world, religion has played an important role in politics. In the early Caliphates—the First Four Caliphs following Muhammad (632-661) and the Umayyad Empire (661-750)—the line between political and religious leader was blurred. Rulers claimed religious authority, and there was no independent religious establishment to speak of. This changed under the Abbasid Empire (750-1258), when the religious establishment asserted its independence and began to play a role in politics as a player separate from the ruling elite. This arrangement was common in many parts of the world ruled by Muslims, including North Africa, the Middle East, and Central Asia (and to a lesser extent, South Asia).

---

[11] McCleary (2013) has cautioned against equating all forms of Protestantism as equally beneficial for human capital acquisition. In Guatemala, Evangelical, Pentecostal, and neo-Pentecostal denominations and churches focused their efforts on evangelizing, emphasizing eschatological urgency of conversion with little investment in human capital.

Table 20.7 Islam: politics and law.

Study	Setting	Method	Summary
Religious legitimacy and political economy			
Rubin (2017)	Roman Empire–1600	Analytic narrative, theory	Legitimating role of Muslim clerics meant that economic elite had little say at political bargaining table, unlike in (post-Reformation) Europe
Coşgel et al. (2012)	Ottoman Empire, 1485–18th c	Theory, analytic narrative	Legitimating role of Ottoman clerics enabled prohibition of printing press for over two centuries
Blaydes et al. (2018)	Medieval Middle East and Europe	Empirical, text analysis	Increase in religious appeals in advice given to Muslim rulers in political texts beginning in 12th–14th centuries
Chaney (2013)	Medieval Egypt	Empirical	Religious authority gained power and security with flooding or drought of Nile River
Ticku et al. (2020)	Medieval India	Empirical	Muslim desecration of Hindu temples more likely following economic shocks
Blaydes and Chaney (2013); Chaney (2019)	Medieval Europe and Middle East	Empirical	Slave soldiers allowed Muslim rulers to not have to bargain with other elites; European rulers constrained by feudal lords
Auriol and Platteau (2017); Platteau (2017)	Early Islam to present	Theory, analytic narrative	Decentralized nature of Islam meant that rulers had to appease marginal cleric, leaving many on outside, increasing instability
Iyigun (2015)	Roman Empire to present	Theory, empirical	Monotheism, "one true God" doctrine mean that inter-faith conflict is existential in Western religions
Iyigun (2008, 2013)	16th c Europe, Ottoman Empire	Empirical	Intra-European conflict less likely when Ottomans threatened Habsburgs; Ottoman threat in Europe less likely when sultan's mother was Christian
Islamic law			
Kuran (2005, 2011)	Medieval, early modern Middle East	Theory, analytic narrative	Combination of Islamic inheritance and partnership law stifled emergence of large partnerships and corporate form
Kuran (2001, 2011)	Medieval, early modern Middle East	Theory, analytic narrative	Islamic *waqf* law used to evade inheritance law; inflexibility meant it could not turn into more advanced, long-lived institution
Kuran and Lustig (2012)	16th–19th c Ottoman Empire	Empirical	Ottoman Islamic courts biased in favor of men, Muslims, and elites
Kuran and Rubin (2018)	16th–19th c Ottoman Empire	Empirical	Ottoman Islamic court bias meant that men, Muslims, and elites paid higher interest rates
Saleh (2018); Saleh and Tirole (2019)	8th c to early modern Egypt	Empirical, theory	Islamic tax on religious minorities led to negative socioeconomic selection in converts; incentivized rulers to over-tax

Rubin (2017) hypothesizes that the legitimating relationship between rulers and the Muslim religious elite can account for numerous long-run economic outcomes. In his framework, religion is one of many tools rulers have to stay in power because of the legitimacy it provides. Muslim rulers have historically used religious authorities as a central source of legitimation because Islam is relatively effective at legitimating rule. Islam emerged conterminously with an expanding empire that was in need of legitimation, and there are consequently numerous Islamic doctrines consistent with the idea that a ruler should be followed as long as he acts like a "good Muslim." Blaydes et al. (2018) reveal the importance of religious legitimation in a study of political advice texts in the Muslim and Christian worlds. They analyze the texts from the medieval period and find a break around the 12th-14th centuries: after this point, Muslim rulers were advised to increase religious appeals while there was a decline in such advice to Christian rulers. According to Rubin (2017), this increased emphasis on religious legitimation gave religious authorities a stronger seat at the political bargaining table, which meant that their preferences were reflected in policy. Coşgel et al. (2009) present a similar framework based on the legitimating role of Islam in a political economy equilibrium. They focus on the relationship between religious legitimacy and tax collection and how this affected the ruler's relationship with the legal community. Kuru (2019) likewise argues that this "ulema-state" alliance kept the bourgeoisie and intelligentsia out of political decision-making in the Islamic world after the 11th century, to the detriment of the region's long-run economic development.

The confluence between religion and political legitimacy had numerous consequences. Rubin (2017, ch. 5) and Coşgel et al. (2012) employ these insights to answer one of the big puzzles of Middle Eastern history of technology: why did the Ottoman Empire ban the printing press for over two centuries, foregoing what was ostensibly a free lunch? A framework relying on the legitimating power of religious authorities makes sense of this puzzle. Religious authorities stood to lose their monopolies over intellectual output and the interpretation of religious works had the printing press spread (fears that were justified by events happening in Europe). Yet, it was rulers, not religious scholars, who had the coercive capacity to prohibit the printing press. The reason that Ottoman rulers agreed to do so—despite the numerous economic and propaganda benefits offered by the press—was that anything that would undermine the religious establishment would also undermine their capacity to rule.

Chaney (2013) presents evidence from medieval Egypt, consistent with the political economy framework described above, in which religious authorities play a central role in legitimating the state. Chaney provides evidence that religious authorities became more powerful in medieval Egypt when the Nile River was either too low (meaning drought) or too high (meaning flooding). He provides evidence that, under these conditions, the tenure of religious authorities was longer and they received more policy concessions. While Chaney argues that this is because religious authorities were able to coordinate rebellions, a related explanation has to do with their role in legitimating rule. Periods of drought or flooding are precisely when rulers were in the direst need of legitimacy, and thus the bargaining power of religious authorities was greatest. Ticku et al. (2020) find evidence of a similar mechanism in historical India, showing that historical economic shocks are associated with Muslim desecration of Hindu temples. Like Chaney's finding, a likely cause is that desecrations were an attempt to employ the legitimating power of religion in times of instability.

Blaydes and Chaney (2013) present a hypothesis for the divergence between the Christian West and the Islamic world that is related to the ones laid out above. They argue that the different types of groups that negotiated and constrained rulers played an important role in the long-run political and economic trajectories of the regions. Specifically, Muslim rulers' access to slave soldiers—a non-hereditary class which had little power to constrain rulers—meant that they did not have to negotiate with other segments of society. According to Chaney (2019), the relative lack of constraint on Muslim rulers was a residue of the Arab conquests and the tribal modes of governance that spread in its wake. This favored the rise of military slavery, the decay of secular bureaucracy, and, ultimately, the emergence of an influential class of religious scholars. Chaney (2019) reasons that in the first decades of Islam, tribal elites were able to use the fiscal systems of recently conquered populations to their own ends, developing a military system of slave soldiers that would be the predominant military form in the Muslim world for over a millennium. As Blaydes and Chaney (2013) argue, this reduced the power of other elites to bargain with and constrain rulers. Meanwhile, weaker European rulers had to cede much to their feudal elites in return for military service and revenue. The authors argue that this meant greater stability for European rulers, who faced a lower threat of revolt due to a larger set of interests having a seat at the political bargaining table. Indeed, they show that beginning with the feudal revolution of the Carolingian Empire (around the 9th century), the tenure of European rulers became increasingly longer than of those in the Islamic world, in large part due to the latter being subject to revolt. One consistent thread in all of the research cited above is that the relationship between rulers and those who keep them in power—religious or not—matters for long-run economic and political development.

Jean-Philippe Platteau has also proposed theories relating the legitimating rule of Islamic religious authorities to economic and political outcomes. His primary focus, however, is on the horizontal structure of Islamic institutions in relation to the more hierarchical, vertical institutional structure of the Catholic Church. Auriol and Platteau (2017) and Platteau (2017) propose a theory suggesting that when rulers have to negotiate with hierarchically-structured religious authorities (such as the Catholic Church), they only have to appease those at the head of the hierarchy, and the rest of the religious class will follow. In other words, rulers have to appease the *average* cleric. On the other hand, when rulers have to negotiate with decentralized religious elites (as in Islam), they will co-opt a fraction of them (depending on their desired policy choices). In other words, their choices are made to co-opt the *marginal* cleric. Auriol and Platteau argue that this means that hierarchical religions are associated with more stable political regimes, since there is a smaller set of clerics who will revolt against the ruler. Moreover, decentralized religions are more often associated with theocracy, as rulers attempt to gain the support of a large fraction of the religious establishment and thus propose policies to satisfy its most extreme elements. Platteau (2017) supports this theory with great detail from historical Muslim polities throughout the world.

Another key feature of Western religions is monotheism, and the "one true God" doctrine it entails. Iyigun (2015) argues that rulers who are legitimated by one of the monotheistic, Abrahamic religions face existential threats when confronted by enemies of opposite faiths. Unlike conflict between co-religionists, a goal of inter-faith conflict is to spread the message of the "one true God," which would undermine the prevailing religious-political equilibrium. This is why, as noted in Section 20.3.2.2, Iyigun (2008) argues that the Catholic Habsburg Empire felt the pressure to deal with the Ottoman threat rather than the looming Protestant Reformation: Ottoman conquest would have fundamentally undermined the existing social and political order, whereas the intra-Christianity threat posed by the Protestants, while dangerous, was not existential. Iyigun (2013) provides additional support for this hypothesis by studying the relationship between the religion of the Ottoman sultan's mother (who was generally a slave in the harem) and Ottoman conflict with Europe. When the sultan's mother was Christian—as was frequently the case—conflict with Europe was much less likely.

In a series of articles which culminated in his 2011 book *The Long Divergence*, Timur Kuran has spelled out one of the most important economic consequences of these dominant political arrangements in the Islamic world: religious authorities maintained purview over commercial law, i.e., commerce was subject to Islamic law. One unforeseeable consequence of this arrangement was that two aspects of Islamic law—regarding partnerships and inheritance—contributed to the persistent simplicity of Islamic business organization. Kuran (2005) argues that two features of these laws were salient. First, partnerships dissolved upon the death of any of the partners. Second, Islamic inheritance law entailed a pre-ordained split among numerous heirs. Hence, while one's heirs could re-form a partnership upon the death of their benefactor, this was subject to the heirs not needing the funds for other pursuits, which was not always assured. Combined, these laws provided disincentive to form large, long-lasting partnerships. As a result, the institutional evolution that occurred in Europe—which helped solve problems such as short-lived enterprises and unlimited liability—never emerged in the Islamic world.

Alternative institutions did exist, however. Kuran (2001) notes that the *waqf* (pious trust) served many of the same functions as the corporation: it was long-lived and relatively free from confiscation by the grabbing hands of rulers. *Waqf*s were trusts endowed by wealthy individuals that provided public goods such as water fountains, schools, or poor relief. They lived beyond their founder, while partnerships did not. They were also relatively free from confiscation because there was a pious element associated with their founding, which increased the cost to rulers from confiscating their funds. Yet, there were two problems with *waqf*s which prevented them from transforming into organizations akin to the corporation. First, *waqf*s became an attractive means of evading Islamic inheritance law. If one did not want their estate split among multiple heirs, one could endow a *waqf* and pay one of their heirs a handsome salary to run it. This ostensibly entailed funneling one's inheritance to one (or a few) desired heir(s). Second, *waqf* law placed severe restrictions on the extent to which one could change the mission of the *waqf*. For instance, a *waqf* that was established to fund a madrasa (educational institution) was only permitted to fund that madrasa in perpetuity, even if alternative uses of the funds became available over time. This restrictive nature of the *waqf* meant that it was unlikely to be used for business purposes, which required more flexibility.

Kuran and co-authors reveal another aspect of Islamic law that had a dampening effect on economic activity: it was partial in favor of men, elites, and Muslims. Kuran and Lustig (2012) show that Ottoman courts were biased in favor of these groups, and that inter-faith and inter-class commerce suffered as a result. If those who faced bias knew that they would have a difficult time winning restitution, they were unlikely to enter into transaction in the first place. Kuran and Rubin (2018) extend this logic to the credit market. They show that Muslims, men, and elites paid 1.9-3.4 percentage points higher interest rates on loans, presumably because they could renege with impunity and were thus greater credit risks.

Another important policy that was ubiquitous throughout early Muslim empires was the taxing of non-Muslims at higher rates. Saleh (2018) shows that in Egypt this policy had the effect of creating selection among converts to Islam. Poorer Coptic Christians converted to Islam to avoid paying the tax, while wealthier Copts could afford to pay the tax and tended not to convert. Over time, this led to Copts being a well-off minority with greater human capital and other characteristics of high socioeconomic standing. Saleh and Tirole (2019) build on this idea with a model of the tradeoffs faced by a ruler who desires both tax revenue and conversion to Islam. They show that it can be optimal for rulers to operate on the downward-sloping part of the Laffer curve, since extraordinarily high tax rates (which do not maximize total revenue) serve to induce conversion to Islam.

In sum, the literature suggests that Islam and Islamic institutions have played an important historical role in the political economy of the Middle East. A variety of consequences of this role are apparent, including relative economic backwardness, conflict with Christian Europe, and relatively slow adoption of new technology and economic institutions. This literature is mostly concerned with the Middle East and North Africa. Extending these insights to other parts of the Muslim world, including South, Central, and Southeast Asia, should be a fruitful area for future research.

20.4.2 Finance and trade

Given the role of Islamic law—especially commercial law—in political economy outcomes, it is not surprising that Islam affected finance and trade. The literature has sought to understand some of the mechanisms through which this connection arose (to the extent that it exists at all). Table 20.8 overviews this literature.

Beyond its role in politics, Islam has been shown to affect numerous aspects of finance and trade. Perhaps most famously, Islam prohibits the taking of interest. Rubin (2011) provides an institutional reason for why interest prohibitions remained in Islam—even if they were easy to evade—but not in Christianity, which prohibited interest for over a millennium but gradually relaxed the prohibition in the medieval period. Rubin argues that an equilibrium emerged in the Islamic world in which religious authorities permitted interest as long as a sufficiently costly ruse was undertaken,[12] political authorities allowed what was permitted by religious authorities, and merchants (and other economic elites) lent at interest while at least paying lip service to the ruse. There were multiple consequences of this equilibrium, which persisted until at least the 18th century in the Ottoman Empire. First, Rubin (2017) points out that it almost certainly inhibited the indigenous growth of banking in the Middle East, or any type of activity in which deposits were openly taken and interest paid on those deposits. Indeed, the first bank in the Middle East was not formed until the mid-19th century, and it was built using European capital.

There were other, unforeseeable, consequences of interest restrictions. Rubin (2010) shows that they affected how bills of exchange emerged in the Middle East and Western Europe and contributed to financial development. In Europe, bills of exchange were used as financial instruments to skirt the Church's usury restriction, and doing so required inter-regional trade (since profit was made by taking advantage of differences in exchange rates). This encouraged the growth of large-scale, inter-regional organizational forms that could take advantage of the opportunities provided by bills of exchange, such as the Medici enterprise of the 15th century. This encouraged the economic elite to engage in impersonal exchange—and to build organizations capable of carrying out impersonal exchange—since the benefits to long-distance exchange with unknown parties were much greater. In the Islamic world, however, the interest ban prevented bills of exchange (known as *suftaja*) from ever being used in such a manner, and thus the institutional evolution that occurred in Europe never did in the Middle East, and exchange largely remained personal (i.e., with known relations) until the modern period.

Another example of the long-run consequences of interest restrictions is provided by Grosjean (2011), who shows that historical interest restrictions still affect financial development today, even in

---

[12] A classic example of a ruse is the double sale, whereby one party would sell a good to another and then immediately buy it back for a higher price payable at a later date. This is ostensibly a loan with interest, but the ruse must be undertaken for it to be considered valid.

Table 20.8 Islam: finance and trade.

Study	Setting	Method	Summary
Usury restrictions			
Rubin (2011, 2017)	Medieval Middle East	Theory; analytic narrative	Middle Eastern reliance on religious legitimacy enabled equilibrium in which usury was banned but permitted if ruse performed
Rubin (2010)	Medieval Middle East	Theory; analytic narrative	Islamic usury ban prevented bills of exchange from being used as they were in Europe, which stifled commercial development
Grosjean (2011)	Southeastern Europe	Empirical	Formerly Ottoman territories in Southeastern Europe have lower financial development today, plausibly due to usury restrictions
Trade and conflict			
Jha (2013)	Medieval-20th c India	Empirical	Historical trade between Hindus and Muslims decreased 20th c inter-faith riots
Michalopoulos et al. (2016, 2018)	7th and 8th c Middle East	Theory; empirical	Role of trade in early spread of Islam; spread of early Islam and Islamic doctrine as means of reducing conflict between groups with different factor endowments
Chaney and Hornbeck (2016)	17th–19th c Spain	Empirical	Very slow economic catch-up in Spain after 1609 expulsion of Moriscos
Legal pluralism and merchants			
Kuran (2004)	17th–19th c Ottoman Empire	Analytic narrative	Ottoman legal pluralism became disadvantage to Muslim merchants in 18th and 19th c as European commercial law became more complex
Artunç (2015)	19th c Ottoman Empire	Empirical	Ottoman exemption licenses to Europeans harmed native, Muslim merchants

locations where they are no longer in place. Using within-country variation in the extent to which the Ottoman Empire ruled in Southeastern Europe, Grosjean finds that even though economic development in general is not associated with historical Ottoman rule, financial development is: former Ottoman rule is associated with a 10% lower bank penetration across countries and 4% lower penetration within countries. The Islamic ban on interest is provided as the most likely cause of these results.

Islam also affected trade through inter-religious conflict, or lack thereof. Jha (2013) provides evidence from South Asia, where Hindus and Muslims have lived together since the first century of Islam. He finds that a history of economic interdependence, which was especially stark in Indian port towns due to the dominance of Muslim traders in the medieval period, were much less prone to Hindu-Muslim riots between 1850 and 1995. Jha argues that the channel connecting old trade routes to modern-day outcomes is economic institutions that fostered positive interactions—and thus inter-ethnic trust—between members of the two religions. These institutions had a persistent effect on the occupational structure of South Asia, which may have affected conflict. It may have also had an effect on important health outcomes like polio vaccinations. After a rise in beliefs in the early 2000s that polio vaccinations are a vehicle for minority male sterilization, Muslims tended to vaccinate their children less throughout India. This inter-religious difference did not arise, however, in medieval port towns (i.e., those with a history of positive economic interactions), where there was no difference in Muslim and Hindu vaccination rates.

In fact, trade may have been important to the initial *spread* of Islam. Michalopoulos et al. (2018) find that the spread of Islam is associated with proximity to pre-Islamic trade routes. They argue that multiple mechanisms associated with Islamic religion and society may account for this phenomenon. First, the prevalence in Islam of direct trade, whereby traders would travel with their goods instead of trade through intermediaries, can account for the more personal ties that were made around the time of the initial spread of Islam. Moreover, this encouraged merchants to trade with co-religionists, who often shared a common language and were subject to similar institutional constraints, thus increasing trust among the parties.

Furthermore, Michalopoulos et al. (2016) show that the type of trade and the associated geography of early Islamic expansion had an effect on the type of religious doctrine formulated at this time. Specifically, since Islam spread along trade routes, this ultimately entailed the possibility of predatory behavior, as inequalities due to different factor endowments were exacerbated by trade, leaving the wealthy areas prone to attack from the poorer ones. In order to overcome this issue while maintaining the trade possibilities opened up by Islam, early Islamic doctrine sought redistributive mechanisms, such as *zakat* (charitable giving), to reduce the predatory incentive.

Another example of the long-run effects of conflict in the Muslim world is provided by Chaney and Hornbeck (2016), who analyze the long-run effects of the 1609 Morisco expulsion by the Spanish. Following the expulsion, Spain experienced sharp population declines in places where Moriscos were populous, and in the short run experienced decreased output and increased per capita output (as predicted by Malthusian models). Yet, the authors show that Malthusian convergence (to pre-expulsion conditions) was delayed for nearly *two centuries* in former Morisco districts. They propose that extractive institutions in Morisco areas persisted after the expulsions, which would have discouraged the level of in-migration necessary for Malthusian conditions to arise. They cannot rule out cultural differences, however; since Christians tended to have fewer children, married older, and lived more lavishly, Malthusian dynamics possibly took a longer time to arise than they would have had the Morisco population not be expelled.

Moving to the 18th and 19th centuries, a couple of studies indicate that special trade privileges given to European traders may have been responsible for exacerbating the economic differences between the two regions. Kuran (2004) argues that the long-standing tradition of Ottomans permitting religious minorities to adjudicate disputes in their own courts (unless one of the parties was Muslim) had little impact on economic development until the 18th century, when for the first time European organizational forms became vastly superior. Once Europe pulled ahead, legal pluralism gave Europeans a distinct advantage over Muslims, who were forced to adjudicate disputes in Islamic courts. Muslims could thus not employ the more advanced organizational forms created in Europe if they wanted to have access to the court system in case of dispute. Differential access to economic institutions *within* the Ottoman Empire thus likely contributed to the economic divergence. Artunç (2015) shows that this differential access to courts was part of a larger Ottoman policy of selling exemption licenses (called *berat*s) to Europeans. These tax exemptions were unavailable to Muslim Ottomans. Because foreign, non-Muslim merchants had these institutionalized advantages over domestic, Muslim merchants, by the early 19th century *berat* holders dominated Ottoman trade.

In sum, Islamic doctrine was both caused by and has since caused financial developments in the Muslim world. This includes usury restrictions, trade complementarities, and legal pluralism. Each of these developments may shed some light on the relative reversal of fortunes between Western Europe and the broader Muslim world. Importantly, these studies are distinct from "Islamic economics" or "Islamic finance," both of which are inventions of the 20th century and seek to understand economics and finance within an Islamic theological context.

20.4.3 Human capital

A final part of the economic sphere in which Islam has affected outcomes is human capital accumulation. The literature on this topic largely seeks to understand the role religion and religious institutions (*madrasas*) play in incentivizing human capital accumulation. Table 20.9 overviews this literature.

For the first four to five centuries after the spread of Islam, literature and science in the Islamic world were vastly superior to that of Western Europe. At some point in the late medieval period, however, Europe caught up with and eventually far surpassed the Middle East (and the rest of the world). Chaney (2016) provides a massive amount of data detailing this reversal of fortunes. He shows that the proportion of books dedicated to scientific topics declined dramatically in the Islamic world in the medieval period, mostly at the expense of religious texts. The reversal is starkest in the 11th and 12th centuries, just as madrasas begin to spread throughout the Islamic world. Chaney argues that this reflected the "Sunni revival" of the period, in which religious leaders gained significant political power. Since the payoff to religious production was much greater than that of scientific production, many of the great Middle Eastern minds of the period entered the religious establishment. Importantly, it is unlikely that religious leaders were directly responsible for the decline in scientific productivity. The reversal was more of a bottom-up process (i.e., fewer great minds going into science) rather than a top-down process directed from above.

Moving to the 19th and 20th centuries, Saleh (2015) provides evidence for the role that Egyptian industrialization played in attenuating human capital differences between Christians and Muslims. He finds that the first wave of industrialization (beginning in 1848) resulted in a "deskilling" of Muslims and an "upskilling" of Christians, likely because the pre-ordained spatial (urban/rural) composition of the various religious populations and the number of administrative jobs open to Christians in the

Table 20.9 Islam: human capital.

Study	Setting	Method	Summary
Scientific vs. religious human capital			
Chaney (2016)	Europe and Islamic world, 8th-19th c	Empirical	Rise of early Islamic science and decline, relative to religious texts, beginning in 11th-12th c
Human capital and industrialization			
Saleh (2015)	19th c Egypt	Empirical	Deskilling of Muslims and upskilling of Christians in first wave of industrialization; upskilling of both in second wave
Saleh (2016)	1950s Egypt	Empirical	Reform of secular education improved outcomes for Muslims but not Christians
Islam and literacy			
Chaudhary and Rubin (2011, 2016)	19th-20th c India	Empirical	Parts of British India with more recent collapse of Muslim rule had lower Muslim literacy; Princely States ruled by Muslims had lower Hindu literacy

government. However, there was an upskilling of both religious groups during the second wave of industrialization (beginning in 1868), in part because more Muslims became "medium skilled", while many Christians became high skilled. Saleh (2016) provides further insight into Christian-Muslim human capital differences in Egypt by examining a massive transformation of traditional (religious) schools into modern primary schools in the early 1950s. He finds that Muslims benefited significantly from the reforms, while Christians were unaffected. This is likely because of the religious curriculum in traditional (pre-reform) schools, which tended to leave Muslim students ill-equipped for the job market. Relatively few Christians attended these schools prior to the reforms, and hence the reforms had the effect of leveling the playing field between students of the two religions.

There is similar evidence for the role of religious schools in generating human capital differences between Hindus and Muslims in colonial India in the early 20th century. Chaudhary and Rubin (2011) find that the parts of British India that had a more recent collapse of Muslim rule had lower Muslim literacy, although Hindu literacy was not affected. They surmise that religious authorities had more power in places with more recent collapse of Muslim rule, and thus Muslim religious schools were more prevalent. Since Muslim religious schools were not as effective at providing literacy, those regions had fewer literate Muslims. Chaudhary and Rubin (2016) focus on the Indian Princely States (i.e., those not directly ruled by the British). They find that states with Muslim rulers had lower Hindu literacy, but there was no effect on Muslim literacy or other public good provision. They suggest that rulers provided fewer public goods when there were privately-provided substitutes that were excludable by religion. Numerous Muslim religious schools existed on the continent, and hence Muslim rulers would have provided less funding towards public education to the extent that they were motivated by supporting their co-religionists.

In sum, the historical legacy of Islam on human capital outcomes tends to be negative, although there is limited evidence of catch up in the 20th century. This statement comes with an important caveat: the relationship between Islam and human capital is *vastly* understudied. To the extent that human capital accumulation played any role in the rise of the modern economy or the long-run divergence between Western Europe and the Muslim world, this is a major shortcoming of the literature. Of the many mechanisms through which Islam may have played a role in economic development, human capital accumulation seems to be among the most ripe for researchers to study.

20.5 Cross-country studies

Beyond the study of specific religions in different country settings, some studies exploit the wider historical variation in religions and religiosity that exists across countries. These studies use either variation across different world religions or variation in religiosity that pools individuals from different religions. The cross-country studies have analyzed both economic causes and consequences of religion. Table 20.10 overviews this literature.

In terms of consequences of religion, Young (2009a) revisits the association between Protestantism and economic development at the country level. Looking at the GDP per capita of Protestant and Catholic countries in Europe over the period 1500-2000, he shows that Protestant countries—which had been behind Catholic countries before the Reformation—outperformed the Catholic countries by 1700, even before the Industrial Revolution. For more than 250 years, their income was substantially higher than that of the Catholic countries, with an increasing gap until about 1870, when it stabilized.

Table 20.10 Cross-country studies of religion in economic history.

Study	Setting	Method	Summary
Economic consequences of religion			
Young (2009a)	Europe, 1500-2000	Empirical	Protestant countries' GDP overtakes Catholic's by 1700
West and Woessmann (2010)	OECD countries, 1900, 2003	Empirical	Catholicism in 1900 related to larger private-school shares and better student achievement today
Economic causes of religion			
Franck and Iannaccone (2014)	Western countries, 1925-1990	Empirical	Church attendance negatively associated with government spending on education
Barro and McCleary (2005)	World, 1900, 1970, 2000	Empirical	Persistent element in having a state religion
Bentzen (2019)	World, 1981-2009	Empirical	Religiosity increases in districts hit by earthquake

Only since the 1960s did the Catholic countries start to converge. This research follows cross-country work on religion and economic growth by Barro and McCleary (2003) for the post-WWII period (1965-1994). Barro and McCleary find that economic growth is positively associated with religious beliefs in heaven and hell but negatively with church attendance across countries.[13]

In many Western countries, state school systems emerged during the 19th century that aimed to serve all children. West and Woessmann (2010) document that the Catholic Church strongly opposed this secular development, urging Catholics to educate their children in non-secular Catholic schools. They show that the historical resistance to state schooling persisted: countries that had higher Catholic shares in 1900 (but did not have Catholicism as a state religion) continued to have substantially higher private school shares in 2003. The authors exploit this historical source of variation in private schooling in a cross-country student-level analysis to show that private competition improves students' academic achievement (which, in turn, has been shown to improve economic prosperity across countries (Hanushek and Woessmann, 2015)). The positive effect of Catholic-induced school competition runs counter to any direct positive effect of Protestantism on educational achievement (a cross-country pattern described in Becker and Woessmann, 2009), which West and Woessmann account for with contemporary data on religious shares.

Turning to cross-country analyses of economic causes of religion, Franck and Iannaccone (2014) use retrospective questions posed in two waves of the International Social Survey Program (ISSP) in the 1990s to study religious decline in a panel of ten Western countries over the period 1925-1990.[14] Estimating panel models with country and time fixed effects, they find that church attendance is negatively associated with government spending on education, whereas other factors such as government spending on health and family, urbanization, income, and educational attainment do not enter the model significantly. The authors interpret the results as indicating lack of support for traditional theories of secularization or crowd-out by welfare states, but being consistent with a role for state indoctrination in schools. In their analysis of determinants of state religions, Barro and McCleary (2005) show a strong element of historical persistence in state religions in that having a state religion in 1900 predicts having a state religion in 1970 and 2000, in particular in countries that did not have a major regime change over the period.

To test whether religious coping—i.e., turning to religion in times of hardship—can account for global differences in religiosity, Bentzen (2019) combines individual-level data on religiosity from the World Values Survey and the European Values Study with data on earthquake incidences across 884 subnational districts in 85 countries. Her results indicate that individuals in districts closer to high-risk earthquake zones are more religious, and that different measures of religiosity increase after an earthquake hit a district (also when including country-by-year fixed effects).

In sum, cross-country studies of religion in economic history have highlighted the global relevance of religious affiliations and beliefs for economic and institutional development. Government educational spending and earthquake shocks have been highlighted as determining factors of religiosity in a cross-country perspective. While posing substantial challenges to convincing identification, steps for-

---

[13] Replicating these findings, Durlauf et al. (2012) find that the relationship of church attendance and economic growth is robust across a variety of statistical specifications, whereas the relationship of religious beliefs and economic growth is not (see also Young, 2009b).

[14] This work follows on prior cross-country work by McCleary and Barro (2006a, 2006b, 2019) studying determinants of religiosity in the post-WWII period (1981-1999).

ward in cross-country comparative work could help form a broader picture of the role of religion and religiosity in economic history.

20.6 **Conclusion**

The rise of the economics of religion has met the digitization revolution affecting the study of economic and social history (Abramitzky, 2015; Mitchener, 2015) to create a new but rapidly growing subfield: religion in economic history. Much of this recent research has focused on the three Abrahamic religions and how some of their salient religious norms have influenced socioeconomic outcomes.

Jewish economic history has been studied both in the Jewish homeland as well as in the diaspora. There are two primary aspects of Jewish history studied in the literature: the Jewish edge in human capital accumulation and Jewish persecutions. In the human capital literature, a key finding is that the Jewish focus on high-skilled occupations is not so much the result of their minority status and persecution in the diaspora, but the result of religious norms on reading the Torah. Similarly, Protestants have emphasized the need for every Christian to read God's word for themselves. These two religious groups have been shown in many contexts to be better educated than Catholics or Muslims. Studies of Christian missionaries confirm the Protestant education lead over Catholics when contrasting long-term effects of missionary presence on education outcomes in colonial countries. Jewish educational differences affected various outcomes like occupational specialization and income.

Jews have always constituted a minority outside their homeland, and discrimination and ethnic violence have been a recurrent theme in their history. Anti-Semitism has shaped Jewish life for centuries and has been shown to be persistent as a result of both cultural and economic factors. The period of Jewish emancipation in the 19th century in many European countries brought with it a bifurcation between Orthodox and Reform Judaism that has been widely studied. This period came to a tragic end with the fascist period and the Holocaust that eliminated Jewish life in vast parts of Europe. The research described has studied the causes and consequences of anti-Semitism in many different countries.

The literature on Catholicism focuses largely on the role the institutionalized Church played in various economic outcomes. This includes prohibitions on cousin marriage and usury, as well as human capital accumulation in monasteries and religious schools. The Church was also a major political player in the medieval and early modern periods. The literature addresses some aspects of Church involvement in politics, such as guild participation and the Counter-Reformation.

The largest literature in the field of religion in economic history is on Protestantism. This is in part due to continued fascination with Weber's Protestant ethic hypothesis. It also has much to do with the digitization revolution that has made available massive amounts of data from the Reformation period and beyond. It is likewise reflective of the enormous political and religious heterogeneity of the Holy Roman Empire—the birthplace of the Reformation and the setting for much of its study—which allows for the variation needed to test for effects empirically. The literature on Protestantism can broadly be placed into three categories: causes of the Reformation, consequences of the Reformation for human capital and industrialization, and the Protestant ethic. These studies almost all have an empirical emphasis. While some reveal limited support of Weber's Protestant ethic hypothesis in certain contexts, others suggest that there is a human capital channel connecting Protestantism with economic success. Several economic, social, political, and technological factors have been shown to have contributed to the adoption and spread of the Reformation.

The economics of Islam literature largely focuses on the ways that Islam has affected economic outcomes via law or politics. Islam is a legalist religion and Islamic law has been the law of the land in much of the "Islamic world" throughout history. Various works have shown how the presence of Islam in law and politics has affected economic outcomes such as corporate development, usury restrictions, conflict, finance, and human capital development. Much of this literature studies the Western Islamic world: Turkey, North Africa, and Muslim Spain.

When looking across these recent contributions to the study of religion in economic history, a few themes run through these works. First, the "empirical/credibility revolution" that has dominated much of the economics literature over the last two decades has greatly influenced work on the economics of religion in history. Most of the papers surveyed are empirical and use econometric or methodological techniques to address causality, such as instrumental variables, differences-in-differences, or natural experiments. This was clearly not the case when Iannaccone wrote his 1998 survey on the economics of religion. At that time, most papers in the field were either applications of rational-choice theory or analyses of survey data. In several cases, the use of new methodological approaches and fine-grained data reversed prior correlational findings based on coarser data. Second, many of the works seek the "deep roots" of larger economic differences between regions and religious communities. This is the case with respect to works on the prosperity of Jews, Jewish persecutions, Protestant-Catholic differences, Muslim-Christian differences, human capital development, cultural attitudes, doctrinal differences, legal development, and financial development. Third, a primary reason religion seems to matter so much in economic history (at least for places practicing Abrahamic religions) is that religion and politics are often intertwined. This connection manifests itself in legal systems, state capacity, religious persecution, investments in religious vs. secular education, and economic organization. Fourth, human capital has played a key role in the economic history of all three Abrahamic religions.

While these general themes provide some overarching structure, it has also become evident from the survey that parts of the recent literature are somewhat eclectic and fractionalized, focusing on specific aspects and scrutinizing individual relationships—as should be expected in a recently emerging field. It is fair to say that in several areas, a unifying picture of the socioeconomic causes and consequences of religion and religiosity in economic history still needs to be developed.

While the religion in economic history literature has blossomed over the last decade, there are still many low-hanging fruits for future generations of scholars to pick. Perhaps the most obvious are studies of non-Abrahamic faiths. Studies on non-Abrahamic, and in particular polytheistic, religions in economic history are relatively rare. This may be due to language barriers—most of the scholarly work in the field to date, with the exception of some work on Islam, studies parts of the world that speak European languages. But this is all the more reason for scholars to study the other religions. We know relatively little about the economic consequences of the roles that Hinduism and Confucianism, or other religions such as Buddhism and Shintoism, played in politics. We also know little about their effect on human capital accumulation. Given the importance of religion for politics and human capital accumulation in the Abrahamic faiths, these seem like natural questions to ask.

In particular, Hinduism seems ripe for study using modern methodological and data-collection techniques. Its importance in world history as well as the contemporary world is undeniable: there are currently around 1.1 billion Hindus worldwide, accounting for 15% of the world's population. Moreover, through the caste system Hinduism arguably has had as much of a direct impact on economic outcomes as any major world religion. However, unifying *economic* analyses of Hinduism are largely lacking. Although economists have long been interested in the caste system (e.g., Akerlof, 1976), and

Deepak Lal's 1988 book *The Hindu Equilibrium* placed Hinduism in a broader social, economic, and historical context, there is precious little work using cutting-edge data-collection and econometric techniques. This is a missed opportunity. Not only is Hinduism important in its own right, but the massive amount of variation on most socioeconomic and political dimensions on the Indian subcontinent makes rigorous analysis feasible (much as is the case with the Holy Roman Empire in the literature on the Reformation).

Even rarer is work on ancient, pre-historical religion. Anthropologists have long been fascinated with why societies worship different types of gods (moralizing, punishing, etc.) and what this means for cooperation, coordination, and markets (e.g., Shariff et al., 2010; Henrich et al., 2010; Norenzayan, 2013). Societies have always struggled to solve these key economic features. Bringing this line of work into economics and economic history should yield enormous insight into the role that religion and religious beliefs can play in historical and contemporary socioeconomic outcomes.

Even within the Abrahamic faiths, the literature has numerous blind spots. One vastly understudied religion is Shi'a Islam. We know little about its economic consequences in places like Iran, whether via politics, human capital accumulation, or any other economic outcome.[15] Within Sunni Islam, relatively little work has been done on the role that tribes and extended kin groups have played in affecting the evolution of Islam and Muslim economies. Given the recent importance placed on kin groups in the Christian world (e.g., Greif and Tabellini, 2017; Schulz et al., 2019), this seems like a fruitful topic for future research. Likewise, we know relatively little about the role of the Orthodox Christian Church in the economic history of Eastern Europe. Another under-researched topic are possible socioeconomic determinants of the emergence and spread of Christianity in the first place, and (beyond the work on the Protestant Reformation) how new religions more generally do or do not spread successfully.

Surprisingly, we also know relatively little about the role that religion played in the development of the US economy. This is surprising for multiple reasons. To the extent that the sociology of religion literature of the 1980s and 1990s focused at all on history, it tended to be US history (e.g., Finke and Stark, 2005). Moreover, US data tend to be richer and publicly available. While some recent studies have focused on the US—such as Ager and Ciccone (2018) on religious communities and agricultural risk, and Xiong and Zhao (2020) on the link between religious fragmentation and the establishment of colleges—there are no common themes in the recent literature.

We suspect that one reason so little research has been conducted on certain religious faiths is a lack of data availability. Consistent, clean, and insightful data are simply more easily available in some places than in others. For instance, so much work on Islamic economic history has been done on Sunni Islam in general and Turkey in particular because of the meticulous record-keeping done by the Ottomans.[16] As early as the 15th century, the Ottomans kept detailed court records from the major Istanbul courts. Many of these records still exist today and are available to researchers (who know Ottoman Turkish); Kuran (2010-13) has translated many of the 17th century records into English in a ten-volume set. Meanwhile, verdicts and contracts in Iran were not written down until the late 19th century. Contracting tended to be oral, with witnesses rather than documents called to reproduce facts. This is likely why there is very little quantitative economic history of Iran, the Persians, or the Shi'a Safavids.

---

[15] Shi'a Islam has not been ignored altogether. For example, Jha's (2013) study of trade complementarities between Muslims and Hindus in South Asia focuses in part on Gujarati Hindus who converted to Ismaili Shi'a Islam in the 11th century.

[16] We thank Timur Kuran for making this point to us.

The next generation of religion in economic history is also likely to take advantage of technological advancements to use methodologies and data that were unavailable to previous generations of scholars. Even in the case of the Istanbul court documents, these data were only very recently constructed in a manner that could be useful for the social scientists, and a large fraction of the archives remains undocumented in a systematic way. New and better technology provides promise to alleviate this issue. The digitization revolution and progress in computer linguistics have opened new opportunities to employ text as data (Gentzkow et al., 2019), which opens a big opportunity for historic research. Given the scarcity of historic censuses and the near absence of census-type data before 1800, researchers have often drawn on city-level data because, if anything, cities might have had the infrastructure to collect data earlier on. Of course, written records have been at the heart of research in economic history, including religion in economic history. But text as data may be the next big step to systematically explore written records. For instance, the Vatican archives hold vast amounts of documents that have only been accessed in a piecemeal approach, and using them in their entirety by employing natural language processing could shed light on the workings of the longest-running major religious institution in history.

A systematic exploration of alternative data sources may also provide new insights about religious and economic life outside of cities. Many historical studies use city-level data because they are the most widely available. Yet, in doing so they arguably miss insights into the role that churches, mosques, and clerics played in the life of the vast majority of the population living in the countryside. Moreover, even if technology provides us with the opportunity to digitize data that used to be more difficult to collect, there is still the issue of finding these data in the first place. This is no small task, especially for cross-country or cross-religion comparisons where data are not systematized or held in one place. Such data collection efforts would be of enormous use to the broader research community but are also expensive to conduct. Fortunately, funders like the National Science Foundation and John Templeton Foundation have shown a willingness to fund such data collection efforts in the past. It will take a diverse set of scholars in terms of background, languages, and institutional knowledge, but this is an area with enormous potential.

Future work can also take advantage of new technology to document the reach and power of institutionalized religion over time and space. There have been efforts to document the universe of church building activities in selected countries, e.g., Denmark (Paldam and Paldam, 2017). Buringh et al. (2020) study church building and economic development during Europe's 'Age of the Cathedrals,' 700-1500. This work partly draws on the data collection efforts of enthusiastic hobbyists (e.g., OpenStreetMap) who make geo-coded data of places of worship, past and present, available on the web. Similar efforts to document the reach of churches, synagogues, and mosques in other countries, as well as systematic evidence on the presence and features of places of worship in other religions, would be a fruitful avenue to document the influence of institutionalized religion over space and time.

Another method that may bring future advances in the field is network analysis, which has seen a recent surge of interest in economic history (Esteves and Mesevage, 2019). Little of this work has looked at religious networks, but it seems natural to try to understand the rise and fall of religions or specific denominations in light of network theories. Network analysis may also be used to gain deeper understanding of the spread of doctrine, religious dissent, and human capital.

Religious history can also serve as a useful testing ground for theories in various fields of economics. For instance, the industrial-organization approach which has been applied to the behavior of churches might prove fruitful for other dimensions as well, such as understanding the role of religious orders as "departments" of the Catholic Church or missionary "strategies" in religious markets outside the US (see, e.g., the recent work on contemporary Pentecostal churches as multinationals in Hanson and Xiang (2013)). Other areas of economics where religion may prove influential include health, gender norms, and family economics. Public economics is another field that could benefit from studies in religion and history. Religious institutions in numerous religions have provided social safety nets. Explorations into what this meant for economic activity and how it crowded out (or in) public and other private investments seem an interesting direction for future research.

Maybe the most challenging theme for future research on religion in economic history would be to dig deeper into the link between economics and religiosity rather than religious affiliation—what people think and feel and which specific beliefs they do and do not adhere to. Measuring religiosity and beliefs is demanding in contemporary work, and it is even harder in the historical context where the option of fielding a survey is no longer viable. While the work surveyed here has clearly shown that religion has played an important role in economic history, there remains ample room for advancements in our understanding of how religious thoughts and activities changed people's lives over the course of history.

References

Abramitzky, R., 2015. Economics and the modern economic historian. The Journal of Economic History 75 (4), 1240–1251.

Abramitzky, R., 2018. The Mystery of the Kibbutz: Egalitarian Principles in a Capitalist World. Princeton University Press, Princeton and Oxford.

Abramitzky, R., Halaburda, H., 2020. Were Jews in interwar Poland more educated? Journal of Demographic Economics 86, 29–304.

Acemoglu, D., Hassan, T.A., Robinson, J.A., 2011. Social structure and development: a legacy of the Holocaust in Russia. The Quarterly Journal of Economics 126 (2), 895–946.

Ager, P., Ciccone, A., 2018. Agricultural risk and the spread of religious communities. Journal of the European Economic Association 16 (4), 1021–1068.

Akçomak, İ.S., Webbink, D., ter Weel, B., 2016. Why did the Netherlands develop so early? The legacy of the Brethren of the common life. Economic Journal 126 (593), 821–860.

Akerlof, G., 1976. The economics of caste and of the rat race and other woeful tales. The Quarterly Journal of Economics 90 (4), 599–617.

Alesina, A., Giuliano, P., 2015. Culture and institutions. Journal of Economic Literature 53 (4), 898–944.

Andersen, T.B., Bentzen, J., Dalgaard, C.-J., Sharp, P., 2017. Pre-reformation roots of the Protestant ethic. Economic Journal 127 (604), 1756–1793.

Anderson, R.W., Johnson, N.D., Koyama, M., 2017. Jewish persecutions and weather shocks: 1100–1800. Economic Journal 127 (602), 924–958.

Artunç, C., 2015. The price of legal institutions: the Beratlı Merchants in the eighteenth-century Ottoman empire. The Journal of Economic History 75 (3), 720–748.

Auriol, E., Platteau, J.-P., 2017. Religious co-option under autocracy: a theory inspired by history. Journal of Development Economics 127, 395–412.

Bai, Y., Kung, J.K.-s., 2015. Diffusing knowledge while spreading God's message: Protestantism and economic prosperity in China, 1840–1920. Journal of the European Economic Association 13 (4), 669–698.

Baron, S.W., Kahan, A., 1975. Economic History of the Jews. Schocken Books, New York.

Barro, R.J., McCleary, R.M., 2003. Religion and economic growth across countries. American Sociological Review 68 (5), 760–781.

Barro, R.J., McCleary, R.M., 2005. Which countries have state religions? The Quarterly Journal of Economics 120 (4), 1331–1370.

Barro, R.J., McCleary, R.M., 2016. Saints marching in, 1590-2012. Economica 83 (331), 385–415.

Basten, C., Betz, F., 2013. Beyond work ethic: religion, individual, and political preferences. American Economic Journal: Economic Policy 5 (3), 67–91.

Beach, H.P., 1903. A Geography and Atlas of Protestant Missions: Their Environment, Forces, Distribution, Methods, Problems, Results and Prospects at the Opening of the Twentieth Century, vol. 2. Student Volunteer Movement for Foreign Missions, New York.

Beatton, T., Skali, A., Torgler, B., 2019. Protestantism and Effort Expenditure on the Battlefield: Soldier-Level Evidence from World War II. Working Paper.

Becker, S., Cinnirella, F., 2020. Prussia disaggregated: the demography of its universe of localities in 1871. Journal of Demographic Economics 86 (3), 259–290.

Becker, S.O., Cinnirella, F., Woessmann, L., 2010. The trade-off between fertility and education: evidence from before the demographic transition. Journal of Economic Growth 15 (3), 177–204.

Becker, S.O., Hornung, E., Woessmann, L., 2011. Education and catch-up in the industrial revolution. American Economic Journal: Macroeconomics 3 (3), 92–126.

Becker, S.O., Hsiao, Y., Pfaff, S., Rubin, J., 2020a. Multiplex network ties and the spatial diffusion of radical innovations: Martin Luther's leadership in the early Reformation. American Sociological Review 85 (5), 857–894.

Becker, S.O., Lindenthal, V., Mukand, S., Waldinger, F., 2020b. Persecution and Escape: The Fate of Skilled Jews in Nazi Germany. Mimeograph.

Becker, S.O., Nagler, M., Woessmann, L., 2017. Education and religious participation: city-level evidence from Germany's secularization period 1890–1930. Journal of Economic Growth 22 (3), 273–311.

Becker, S.O., Pascali, L., 2019. Religion, division of labor and conflict: anti-semitism in German regions over 600 years. The American Economic Review 109 (5), 1764–1804.

Becker, S.O., Pfaff, S., Rubin, J., 2016. Causes and consequences of the Protestant reformation. Explorations in Economic History 62, 1–25.

Becker, S.O., Pino, F.J., Vidal-Robert, J., 2019. Economic Effects of Catholic Censorship during the Counter-Reformation. Working Paper.

Becker, S.O., Woessmann, L., 2008. Luther and the girls: religious denomination and the female education gap in 19th century Prussia. Scandinavian Journal of Economics 110 (4), 777–805.

Becker, S.O., Woessmann, L., 2009. Was Weber wrong? A human capital theory of Protestant economic history. The Quarterly Journal of Economics 124 (2), 531–596.

Becker, S.O., Woessmann, L., 2010. The effect of Protestantism on education before the industrialization: evidence from 1816 Prussia. Economics Letters 107 (2), 224–228.

Becker, S.O., Woessmann, L., 2013. Not the opium of the people: income and secularization in a panel of Prussian countries. The American Economic Review 103 (3), 539–544.

Becker, S.O., Woessmann, L., 2018. Social cohesion, religious beliefs, and the effect of Protestantism on suicide. Review of Economics and Statistics 100 (3), 377–391.

Belloc, M., Drago, F., Galbiati, R., 2016. Earthquakes, religion, and transition to self-government in Italian cities. The Quarterly Journal of Economics 131 (4), 1875–1926.

Bentzen, J., 2019. Acts of God? Religiosity and natural disasters across subnational world districts. Economic Journal 129 (622), 2295–2321.

Berman, E., 2000. Sect, subsidy, and sacrifice: an economist's view of ultra-Orthodox Jews. The Quarterly Journal of Economics 115 (3), 905–953.

Blaydes, L., Chaney, E., 2013. The feudal revolution and Europe's rise: political divergence of the Christian West and the Muslim world before 1500 CE. American Political Science Review 107 (1), 16–34.

Blaydes, L., Grimmer, J., McQueen, A., 2018. Mirrors for princes and sultans: advice on the art of governance in the Medieval Christian and Islamic worlds. The Journal of Politics 80 (4), 1150–1167.

Blaydes, L., Paik, C., 2016. The impact of holy land crusades on state formation: war mobilization, trade integration, and political development in Medieval Europe. International Organization 70 (3), 551–586.

Blum, M., Rei, C., 2018. Escaping Europe: health and human capital of Holocaust refugees. European Review of Economic History 22 (1), 1–27.

Blum, M., Strebel, M., 2016. Max Weber and the First World War: Protestant and catholic living standards in Germany, 1915–1919. Journal of Institutional Economics 12 (3), 699–719.

Boerner, L., Rubin, J., Severgnini, B., 2019. A Time to Print, a Time to Reform. Working Paper.

Boppart, T., Falkinger, J., Grossmann, V., 2014. Protestantism and education: reading (the Bible) and other skills. Economic Inquiry 52 (2), 874–895.

Boppart, T., Falkinger, J., Grossmann, V., Woitek, U., Wüthrich, G., 2013. Under which conditions does religion affect educational outcomes? Explorations in Economic History 50 (2), 242–266.

Botticini, M., Eckstein, Z., 2005. Jewish occupational selection: education, restrictions, or minorities? The Journal of Economic History 65 (4), 922–948.

Botticini, M., Eckstein, Z., 2007. From farmers to merchants, conversions and diaspora: human capital and Jewish history. Journal of the European Economic Association 5 (5), 885–926.

Botticini, M., Eckstein, Z., 2012. The Chosen Few: How Education Shaped Jewish History, 70-1492. Princeton University Press, Princeton.

Botticini, M., Eckstein, Z., Vaturi, A., 2019. Child care and human development: insights from Jewish history in central and eastern Europe. Economic Journal 129 (10), 2637–2690.

Braun, R., 2016. Religious minorities and resistance to genocide: the collective rescue of Jews in the Netherlands during the Holocaust. American Political Science Review 110 (1), 127–147.

Buggle, J., Mayer, T., Orcan Sakalli, S., Thoenig, M., 2020. The Refugee's Dilemma: Evidence from Jewish Migration out of Nazi Germany. CEPR Discussion Paper No. DP15533.

Buringh, E., Campbell, B.M.S., Rijpma, A., Luiten van Zanden, J., 2020. Church building and the economy during Europe's 'Age of the cathedrals', 700–1500 CE. Explorations in Economic History 76, 101316.

Cagé, J., Rueda, V., 2016. The long-term effects of the printing press in sub-Saharan Africa. American Economic Journal: Applied Economics 8 (3), 69–99.

Cagé, J., Rueda, V., 2020. Sex and the mission: the conflicting effects of early Christian missions on HIV in sub-Saharan Africa. Journal of Demographic Economics 86 (3), 213–257.

Calvi, R., Mantovanelli, F.G., 2018. Long-term effects of access to health care: medical missions in colonial India. Journal of Development Economics 135, 285–303.

Calvi, R., Mantovanelli, F.G., Hoehn-Velasco, L., 2020. The Protestant legacy: missions and human capital in India. The Journal of Human Resources. forthcoming. http://jhr.uwpress.org/content/early/2020/11/12/jhr.58.2.0919-10437R2.abstract.

Cantoni, D., 2012. Adopting a new religion: the case of Protestantism in 16th century Germany. Economic Journal 122 (560), 502–531.

Cantoni, D., 2015. The economic effects of the Protestant reformation: testing the Weber hypothesis in the German lands. Journal of the European Economic Association 13 (4), 561–598.

Cantoni, D., Dittmar, J., Yuchtman, N., 2018. Religious competition and reallocation: the political economy of secularization in the Protestant reformation. The Quarterly Journal of Economics 133 (4), 2037–2096.

Cantoni, D., Yuchtman, N., 2021. Historical natural experiments: bridging economics and economic history. In: Bisin, A., Federico, G. (Eds.), The Handbook of Historical Economics. Elsevier. Chapter 8 (in this book).

Carvalho, J.P., Iyer, S., Rubin, J. (Eds.), 2019. Advances in the Economics of Religion. Palgrave Macmillan, New York.

Carvalho, J.P., Koyama, M., 2016. Jewish emancipation and schism: economic development and religious change. Journal of Comparative Economics 44 (3), 562–584.

Carvalho, J.P., Koyama, M., Sacks, M., 2017. Education, identity and community: lessons from Jewish emancipation. Public Choice 171 (1), 119–143.

Castelló-Climent, A., Chaudhary, L., Mukhopadhyay, A., 2018. Higher education and prosperity: from catholic missionaries to luminosity in India. Economic Journal 128 (616), 3039–3075.

Chaney, E., 2013. Revolt on the Nile: economic shocks, religion, and political power. Econometrica 81 (5), 2033–2053.

Chaney, E., 2016. Religion and the Rise and Fall of Islamic Science. Working Paper.

Chaney, E., 2019. Religion and Political Structure in Historical Perspective. Working Paper.

Chaney, E., Hornbeck, R., 2016. Economic dynamics in the Malthusian era: evidence from the 1609 Spanish expulsion of the Moriscos. Economic Journal 126 (594), 1404–1440.

Chaudhary, L., Rubin, J., 2011. Reading, writing, and religion: institutions and human capital formation. Journal of Comparative Economics 39 (1), 17–33.

Chaudhary, L., Rubin, J., 2016. Religious identity and the provision of public goods: evidence from the Indian princely states. Journal of Comparative Economics 44 (3), 461–483.

Coşgel, M.M., Miceli, T.J., Ahmed, R., 2009. Law, state power, and taxation in Islamic history. Journal of Economic Behavior & Organization 71 (3), 704–717.

Coşgel, M.M., Miceli, T.J., Rubin, J., 2012. The political economy of mass printing: legitimacy, revolt, and technology change in the Ottoman empire. Journal of Comparative Economics 40 (3), 357–371.

Curuk, M., Smulders, S., 2019. Malthus Meets Luther: The Economics behind the German Reformation. Mimeograph.

D'Acunto, F., Prokopczuk, M., Weber, M., 2019. Historical antisemitism, ethnic specialization, and financial development. The Review of Economic Studies 86 (3), 1170–1206.

Dittmar, J., Meisenzahl, R., 2020. Public goods institutions, human capital, and growth: evidence from German history. The Review of Economic Studies 87 (2), 959–996.

Dittmar, J., Seabold, S., 2020. New media and competition: printing and Europe's transformation after Gutenberg. Journal of Political Economy. forthcoming.

Doyle, S., Meier zu Selhausen, F., Weisdorf, J., 2020. The blessings of medicine? Patient characteristics and heath outcomes in a Ugandan mission hospital, 1908-1970. Social History of Medicine 33 (3), 946–980.

Durkheim, É., 1897. Le suicide: étude de sociologie. Félix Alcan, Paris. English translation: translated by J.A. Spaulding and G. Simpson. Suicide: A Study in Sociology. The Free Press, Glencoe, 1951.

Durlauf, S.N., Kourtellos, A., Ming Tan, C., 2012. Is God in the details? A reexamination of the role of religion in economic growth. Journal of Applied Econometrics 27 (7), 1059–1075.

Ekelund Jr., R.B., Hébert, R.F., Tollison, R.D., 2002. An economic analysis of the Protestant reformation. Journal of Political Economy 110 (3), 646–671.

Ekelund Jr., R.B., Hébert, R.F., Tollison, R.D., 2004. The economics of the counter-reformation: incumbent-firm reaction to market entry. Economic Inquiry 42 (4), 690–705.

Ekelund, R.B., Tollison, R.D., Anderson, G.M., Hébert, R.F., Davidson, A.B., 1996. Sacred Trust: The Medieval Church as an Economic Firm. Oxford University Press, Oxford.

Esteves, R., Mesevage, G.G., 2019. Social networks in economic history: opportunities and challenges. Explorations in Economic History 74, 101299.

Finke, R., Stark, R., 2005. The Churching of America, 1776-2005: Winners and Losers in Our Religious Economy, second edition. Rutgers University Press, New Brunswick, NJ.

Finkel, E., 2015. The Phoenix effect of state repression: Jewish resistance during the Holocaust. American Political Science Review 109 (2), 339–353.

Finley, T., Franck, R., Johnson, N.D., 2019. The Effects of Land Redistribution: Evidence from the French Revolution. Working Paper.

Finley, T., Koyama, M., 2018. Plague, politics, and pogroms: the black death, the rule of law, and the persecution of Jews in the Holy Roman Empire. The Journal of Law & Economics 61 (2), 253–277.

Franck, R., Iannaccone, L.R., 2014. Religious decline in the 20th century West: testing alternative explanations. Public Choice 159 (3–4), 385–414.

Freud, S., 1927. The Future of an Illusion. W. W. Norton, New York. Edited by J. Strachey (1961).

Gallego, F.A., Woodberry, R., 2010. Christian missionaries and education in former African colonies: how competition mattered. Journal of African Economics 19 (3), 294–329.

Galor, O., 2011. Unified Growth Theory. Princeton University Press, Princeton.

Gentzkow, M., Kelly, B., Taddy, M., 2019. Text as data. Journal of Economic Literature 57 (3), 535–574.

Goody, J., 1983. The Development of the Family and Marriage in Europe. Cambridge University Press, Cambridge.

Greif, A., 2006a. Family structures, institutions, and growth. The American Economic Review 96 (2), 308–312.

Greif, A., 2006b. Institutions and the Path to the Modern Economy: Lessons from Medieval Trade. Cambridge University Press, New York.

Greif, A., Tabellini, G., 2017. The clan and the corporation: sustaining cooperation in China and Europe. Journal of Comparative Economics 45 (1), 1–35.

Grosfeld, I., Rodnyansky, A., Zhuravskaya, E., 2013. Persistent antimarket culture: a legacy of the pale of settlement after the Holocaust. American Economic Journal: Economic Policy 5 (3), 189–226.

Grosfeld, I., Orcan Sakalli, S., Zhuravskaya, E., 2020. Middleman minorities and ethnic conflict: anti-Jewish pogroms in the Russian Empire. The Review of Economic Studies 87 (1), 289–342.

Grosjean, P., 2011. The institutional legacy of the Ottoman empire: Islamic rule and financial development in South Eastern Europe. Journal of Comparative Economics 39 (1), 1–16.

Guiso, L., Sapienza, P., Zingales, L., 2006. Does culture affect economic outcomes? The Journal of Economic Perspectives 20 (2), 23–48.

Hanson, G.H., Xiang, C., 2013. Exporting Christianity: governance and doctrine in the globalization of US denominations. Journal of International Economics 91 (2), 301–320.

Hanushek, E.A., Woessmann, L., 2015. The Knowledge Capital of Nations: Education and the Economics of Growth. MIT Press, Cambridge, MA.

Heldring, L., Robinson, J.A., Vollmer, S., 2017. The Long-Run Impact of the Dissolution of the English Monasteries. Working Paper.

Henrich, J., Ensminger, J., McElreath, R., Barr, A., Barrett, C., Bolyanatz, A., Cardenas, J.C., et al., 2010. Markets, religion, community size, and the evolution of fairness and punishment. Science 327 (5972), 1480–1484.

Hoffman, M., 2011. Does higher income make you more altruistic? Evidence from the Holocaust. Review of Economics and Statistics 93 (3), 876–887.

Hornung, E., 2014. Immigration and the diffusion of technology: the Huguenot diaspora in Prussia. The American Economic Review 104 (1), 84–122.

Hume, D., 1757. The Natural History of Religion. Oxford University Press, Oxford. Edited by J.C.A. Gaskin (1993).

Iannaccone, L.R., 1992. Sacrifice and stigma: reducing free-riding in cults, communes, and other collectives. Journal of Political Economy 100 (2), 271–291.

Iannaccone, L.R., 1998. Introduction to the economics of religion. Journal of Economic Literature 36 (3), 1465–1495.

Iyer, S., 2016. The new economics of religion. Journal of Economic Literature 54 (2), 395–441.

Iyigun, M., 2008. Luther and Suleyman. The Quarterly Journal of Economics 123 (4), 1465–1494.

Iyigun, M., 2013. Lessons from the Ottoman harem on culture, religion, and wars. Economic Development and Cultural Change 61 (4), 693–730.

Iyigun, M., 2015. War, Peace and Prosperity in the Name of God: The Ottoman Role in Europe's Socioeconomic Evolution. University of Chicago Press, Chicago.

Jedwab, R., Johnson, N., Koyama, M., 2019a. Negative shocks and mass persecutions: evidence from the black death. Journal of Economic Growth 24 (4), 345–395.

Jedwab, R., Meier zu Selhausen, F., Moradi, A., 2019b. The Economics of Missionary Expansion: Evidence from Africa and Implications for Development. AEHN-WP-49.

Jha, S., 2013. Trade, institutions, and ethnic tolerance: evidence from South Asia. American Political Science Review 107 (4), 806–832.

Jha, S., 2018. Trading for peace. Economic Policy 33 (95), 485–526.

Johnson, N.D., Koyama, M., 2017. Jewish communities and city growth in preindustrial Europe. Journal of Development Economics 127, 339–354.

Johnson, N.D., Koyama, M., 2019. Persecution and Toleration: The Long Road to Religious Freedom. Cambridge University Press, Cambridge.

Kim, H., Pfaff, S., 2012. Structure and dynamics of religious insurgency: students and the spread of the reformation. American Sociological Review 77 (2), 188–215.

Koyama, M., 2010. Evading the taint of usury: the usury prohibition as a barrier to entry. Explorations in Economic History 47 (4), 420–442.

Kuran, T., 2001. The provision of public goods under Islamic law: origins, impact, and limitations of the Waqf system. Law & Society Review 35 (4), 841–897.

Kuran, T., 2004. The economic ascent of the middle East's religious minorities: the role of Islamic legal pluralism. The Journal of Legal Studies 33, 475–515.

Kuran, T., 2005. The absence of the corporation in Islamic law: origins and persistence. American Journal of Comparative Law 53, 785–834.

Kuran, T. (Ed.), 2010-13. Mahkeme Kayıtları Işığında 17. Yüzyıl İstanbul'unda Sosyo-Ekonomik Yaşam (Social and Economic Life in Seventeenth-Century Istanbul: Glimpses from Court Records, 10 vols). İş Bank Cultural Publications, Istanbul.

Kuran, T., 2011. The Long Divergence: How Islamic Law Held Back the Middle East. Princeton University Press, Princeton.

Kuran, T., 2018. Islam and economic performance: historical and contemporary links. Journal of Economic Literature 56 (4), 1292–1359.

Kuran, T., Lustig, S., 2012. Judicial biases in Ottoman Istanbul: Islamic justice and its compatibility with modern economic life. The Journal of Law & Economics 55, 631–666.

Kuran, T., Rubin, J., 2018. The financial power of the powerless: socio-economic status and interest rates under partial rule of law. Economic Journal 128 (609), 758–796.

Kuru, A.T., 2019. Islam, Authoritarianism, and Underdevelopment: A Global and Historical Comparison. Cambridge University Press, New York.

Kuznets, S., 1960. Economic structure and life of the Jews. In: Finkelstein, L. (Ed.), The Jews: Their History, Culture, and Religion, vol. 2. Harper, New York, pp. 1597–1666.

Lal, D., 1988. The Hindu Equilibrium. Vol. I Cultural Stability and Economic Stagnation. India c. 1500 BC-AD 1980. Clarendon Press, Oxford.

Leeson, P.T., Russ, J.W., 2018. Witch trials. Economic Journal 128 (613), 2066–2105.

Lehrer, E., 2008. Religion, Economics, and Demography: The Effects of Religion on Education, Work, and the Family. Routledge, London.

Ma, C., 2020. Knowledge Diffusion and Intellectual Change: When Chinese Literati Met European Jesuits. Working Paper.

Marx, K., 1844. Zur Kritik der Hegel'schen Rechtsphilosophie: Einleitung. In: Ruge, A., Marx, K. (Eds.), Deutsch-Französische Jahrbücher. Bureau der Jahrbücher, Paris, pp. 71–85.

McCleary, R.M. (Ed.), 2011. Oxford Handbook of the Economics of Religion. Oxford University Press, Oxford.

McCleary, R.M., 2013. Protestantism and Human Capital in Guatemala and the Republic of Korea. Working Paper Series No. 332. Asian Development Bank Economics.

McCleary, R.M., Barro, R.J., 2006a. Religion and political economy in an international panel. Journal for the Scientific Study of Religion 45 (2), 149–175.

McCleary, R.M., Barro, R.J., 2006b. Religion and economy. The Journal of Economic Perspectives 20 (2), 49–72.

McCleary, R.M., Barro, R.J., 2019. The Wealth of Religions: The Political Economy of Believing and Belonging. Princeton University Press, Princeton.

Meier zu Selhausen, F., 2019. Missions, education and conversion in colonial Africa. In: Cappelli, G., Mitch, D. (Eds.), Globalization and Mass Education. Palgrave Macmillan, London. Chapter 2.

Michalopoulos, S., Naghavi, A., Prarolo, G., 2016. Islam, inequality, and pre-industrial comparative development. Journal of Development Economics 120, 86–98.

Michalopoulos, S., Naghavi, A., Prarolo, G., 2018. Trade and geography in the spread of Islam. Economic Journal 128 (616), 3210–3241.

Mitchener, K., 2015. The 4D future of economic history: digitally-driven data design. The Journal of Economic History 75 (4), 1234–1239.

Moser, P., Voena, A., Waldinger, F., 2014. German Jewish Émigrés and US Invention. The American Economic Review 104 (10), 3222–3255.

Norenzayan, A., 2013. Big Gods: How Religion Transformed Cooperation and Conflict. Princeton University Press, Princeton.

Nunn, N., 2010. Religious conversion in colonial Africa. The American Economic Review 100 (2), 147–152.

Nunn, N., 2014. Gender and missionary influence in colonial Africa. In: Akyeampong, E., Bates, R.H., Nunn, N., Robinson, J. (Eds.), Africa's Development in Historical Perspective. Cambridge University Press, New York, pp. 489–512.

Paldam, E., Paldam, M., 2017. The political economy of churches in Denmark, 1300–2015. Public Choice 172 (3–4), 443–463.

Pascali, L., 2016. Banks and development: Jewish communities in the Italian renaissance and current economic performance. Review of Economics and Statistics 98 (1), 140–158.

Platteau, J.-P., 2017. Islam Instrumentalised: Religion and Politics in Historical Perspective. Cambridge University Press, Cambridge.

Richardson, G., 2005. Craft guilds and Christianity in late-medieval England. Rationality and Society 17 (2), 139–189.

Roome, W.R.M., 1925. Ethnographic Survey of Africa: Showing the Tribes and Languages; also the Stations of Missionary Societies. Edward Stanford, London.

Rubin, J., 2009. Social insurance, commitment, and the origin of law: interest bans in early Christianity. The Journal of Law & Economics 52 (4), 761–777.

Rubin, J., 2010. Bills of exchange, interest bans, and impersonal exchange in Islam and Christianity. Explorations in Economic History 47 (2), 213–227.

Rubin, J., 2011. Institutions, the rise of commerce and the persistence of laws: interest restrictions in Islam and Christianity. Economic Journal 121 (557), 1310–1339.

Rubin, J., 2014. Printing and Protestants: an empirical test of the role of printing in the reformation. Review of Economics and Statistics 96 (2), 270–286.

Rubin, J., 2017. Rulers, Religion, and Riches: Why the West Got Rich and the Middle East Did Not. Cambridge University Press, Cambridge.

Saleh, M., 2015. The reluctant transformation: state industrialization, religion, and human capital in nineteenth-century Egypt. The Journal of Economic History 75 (1), 65–94.

Saleh, M., 2016. Public mass modern education, religion, and human capital in twentieth-century Egypt. The Journal of Economic History 76 (3), 697–735.

Saleh, M., 2018. On the road to heaven: taxation, conversions, and the Coptic-Muslim socioeconomic gap in medieval Egypt. The Journal of Economic History 78 (2), 394–434.

Saleh, M., Tirole, J., 2019. Taxing Identity: Theory and Evidence from Early Islam. CEPR Discussion Paper 13705.

Schulz, J.F., 2019. Kin Networks and Institutional Development. Working Paper.

Schulz, J.F., Bahrami-Rad, D., Beauchamp, J.P., Henrich, J., 2019. The church, intensive kinship, and global psychological variation. Science 366 (6466), eaau5141.

Shariff, A.F., Norenzayan, A., Henrich, J., 2010. The birth of high gods: how the cultural evolution of supernatural policing influenced the emergence of complex, cooperative human societies, paving the way for civilization. In: Schaller, M., Norenzayan, A., Heine, S.J., Yamagishi, T., Kameda, T. (Eds.), Evolution, Culture and the Human Mind. Psychology Press, New York, pp. 119–136.

Smith, A., 1776. An Inquiry into the Nature and Causes of the Wealth of Nations. Clarendon Press, Oxford. 1979.

Spenkuch, J.L., 2017. Religion and work: micro evidence from contemporary Germany. Journal of Economic Behavior & Organization 135, 193–214.

Spenkuch, J.L., Tillmann, P., 2018. Elite influence? Religion and the electoral success of the Nazis. American Journal of Political Science 62 (1), 19–36.

Spitzer, Y., 2019. Pale in Comparison: Jews as a Rural Service Minority. CEPR Discussion Paper 14262.

Squicciarini, M., 2020. Devotion and development: religiosity, education, and economic progress in 19th-century France. The American Economic Review 110 (11), 3454–3491.

Ticku, R., Shrivastava, A., Iyer, S., 2020. Economic Shocks and Temple Desecrations in Medieval India. Working Paper.

Uribe-Castro, M., 2019. Expropriation of church wealth and political conflict in 19th century Colombia. Explorations in Economic History 73, 101271.

Valencia Caicedo, F., 2019a. The mission: human capital transmission, economic persistence, and culture in South America. The Quarterly Journal of Economics 134 (1), 507–556.

Valencia Caicedo, F., 2019b. Missionaries in Latin America and Asia: a first global mass education wave. In: Cappelli, G., Mitch, D. (Eds.), Globalization and Mass Education. Palgrave Macmillan, London. Chapter 3.

Voigtländer, N., Voth, H.-J., 2012. Persecution perpetuated: the medieval origins of anti-semitic violence in Nazi Germany. The Quarterly Journal of Economics 127 (3), 1339–1392.

Voigtländer, N., Voth, H.-J., 2015. Nazi indoctrination and anti-semitic beliefs in Germany. Proceedings of the National Academy of Sciences 112 (26), 7931–7936.

Voth, H.-J., 2021. Persistence – myth and mystery. In: Bisin, A., Federico, G. (Eds.), The Handbook of Historical Economics. Elsevier. Chapter 9 (in this book).

Waldinger, F., 2010. Quality matters: the expulsion of professors and the consequences for PhD student outcomes in Nazi Germany. Journal of Political Economy 118 (4), 787–831.

Waldinger, F., 2012. Peer effects in science: evidence from the dismissal of scientists in Nazi Germany. The Review of Economic Studies 79 (2), 838–861.

Waldinger, M., 2017. The long-run effects of missionary orders in Mexico. Journal of Development Economics 127, 355–378.

Wantchekon, L., Novta, N., Klašnja, M., 2015. Education and human capital externalities: evidence from colonial Benin. The Quarterly Journal of Economics 130 (2), 703–757.

Weber, M., 1904/05. Die protestantische Ethik und der "Geist" des Kapitalismus. Archiv für Sozialwissenschaft und Sozialpolitik 20, 1–54 and 21, 1–110. Reprinted in: Aufsätze zur Religionssoziologie, 17–206 (1920). English translation: translated by T. Parsons. The Protestant Ethic and the Spirit of Capitalism. Routledge Classics, London, 1930/2001.

West, M.R., Woessmann, L., 2010. 'Every catholic child in a catholic school': historical resistance to state schooling, contemporary private competition and student achievement across countries. Economic Journal 120 (546), F229–F255.

Wietzke, F.-B., 2015. Long-term consequences of colonial institutions and human capital investments: subnational evidence from Madagascar. World Development 66, 293–307.

Woodberry, R.D., 2004. The Shadow of Empire: Christian Missions, Colonial Policy, and Democracy in Postcolonial Societies. Ph.D. dissertation. University of North Carolina at Chapel Hill.

Woodberry, R.D., 2011. Religion and the spread of human capital and political institutions: Christian missions as a quasi-natural experiment. In: McCleary, R. (Ed.), The Oxford Handbook of the Economics of Religion. Oxford University Press, Oxford, pp. 111–131.

Woodberry, R.D., 2012. The missionary roots of liberal democracy. American Political Science Review 106 (2), 244–274.

Xiong, H., Zhao, Y., 2020. Sectarian Competition and the Market Provision of Human Capital. Working Paper.

Young, C., 2009a. Religion and Economic Growth in Western Europe: 1500–2000, Stanford University, Mimeograph.

Young, C., 2009b. Model uncertainty in sociological research: an application to religion and economic growth. American Sociological Review 74 (3), 380–397.

Persistent failure? International interventions since World War II

Matt Malis, Pablo Querubin, and Shanker Satyanath
Wilf Family Department of Politics, New York University, New York, NY, United States

21.1 Introduction

In an early survey of the literature on international intervention, James Rosenau (1969) rendered a bleak assessment:

> The deeper one delves into the literature on intervention, the more incredulous one becomes. The discrepancy between the importance attached to the problem of intervention and the bases on which solutions to it are founded is so striking... The spirit of scientific explanation appears to have had no impact on it whatsoever.

Having just passed the fiftieth anniversary of Rosenau's initial survey, it is worth taking stock of how the accumulated scientific knowledge on the topic has developed in the last half century, and what are the prospects for its advancement going forward.

International intervention has been a pervasive feature of the post-World War II international order. From 1946-2005, twelve percent of country-years were the target of a foreign military intervention (Pearson and Baumann, 1993; Pickering and Kisangani, 2009). Three out of five civil wars from 1946-1999 experienced intervention by a third party (Regan, 2002). Twenty percent of country-years during the Cold War were led by governments that were installed or propped up by the CIA, with another ten percent similarly supported by the Soviet KGB (Berger et al., 2013b). Foreign actors sought to influence eight percent of post-war national elections through threats of withholding aid or other things of value (Hyde and Marinov, 2012); accounting for other forms of intervention, in competitive elections from 1946-1999, the rate increases to eleven percent (Levin, 2019a). The rigorous scientific examination of the causes and consequences of foreign intervention is no less important now than it was at the time of Rosenau's writing.

The objectives of the present review are threefold. We first aim to summarize the findings of the existing literature on international interventions. The study of foreign intervention has no clear disciplinary home, with important contributions spread across subfield journals in comparative politics, international relations, development economics, and political economy, among others; we hope to better integrate these various streams of literature which exhibit a surprising degree of isolation given their substantive overlap. Our survey reveals a striking pattern: extant research tells us that foreign interventions overwhelmingly fail to achieve their purported objectives. The second goal of our analysis is to explain this puzzling but recurrent finding in the literature. We suggest that the results may be explained by three general phenomena: econometric issues of measurement, sample selection, and endogeneity; theoretical issues regarding assumptions made of the interveners' objectives; or alterna-

The Handbook of Historical Economics. https://doi.org/10.1016/B978-0-12-815874-6.00038-1

tively, a persistent tendency of policy makers to pursue strategies that consistently fail to achieve their objectives. Finally, in light of these findings, we offer our assessment of some promising directions for the advancement of the study on foreign interventions. Future research faces both daunting challenges and exciting opportunities in the face of newly available data and empirical methods, as well as the changing nature of intervention itself.

Overall, our assessment is far more optimistic than Rosenau's. The present review highlights an active and exciting research program on foreign interventions which has developed rich theoretical insights, collected valuable data sources for empirical investigation, and progressed significantly in its methodological rigor and in the breadth of questions explored. The accumulated findings on the topic advance our understanding of the causes and consequences of interventions, while continually raising new questions of increasing intellectual interest and policy relevance.

Our contribution complements two other recent reviews of a similar body of literature. First, Krasner and Weinstein (2014) review a body of primarily political science research examining how foreign influence can shape domestic political institutions, with a particular interest in "whether, and under what conditions, tools of external pressure can promote improvements in governance, especially democratic governance". The present review is somewhat broader in scope, examining a wider range of intervention outcomes and incorporating more literature from economics as well as political science journals (in addition to the several years of new contributions that have followed Krasner and Weinstein's review). Second, Aidt et al. (2020) provide an extremely thorough review of literature from both economics and political science, covering a wide range of policy instruments and policy outcomes of interest. We differ from them in that our goal is to provide a critical assessment of the existing literature and illustrate the diversity of work in the field rather than place it within a single framework. Moreover, our review stands out from both of these other contributions in its focus on a central puzzle implied by the accumulated empirical findings in the literature— that there is limited empirical justification for interventions, yet they continue to be a persistent feature of international politics—and in its emphasis on analyzing the research design choices and theoretical assumptions that may account for this paradox. We hope that our approach will prove useful to future researchers in making sense of a diverse body of findings and in highlighting the pitfalls and promises of empirical research on this important topic.

21.2 Scope, definitions, and data sources

A general challenge to the study of foreign intervention is the diversity of definitions and operationalizations of the concept used throughout the literature. In this section we propose a working definition of intervention, discuss the most common data sources used in quantitative analysis of the topic, and provide an overview of the topics that will and will not fall within the scope of our review.

21.2.1 Defining intervention

We begin by discussing the definition of foreign intervention. An early attempt to pin down the concept in concrete terms comes from Rosenau (1968), who identifies two central characteristics of an action which classify it as an intervention: that it be "*convention-breaking*", and "*authority-oriented*". "[O]bservers from a wide variety of perspectives," Rosenau writes, "seem inclined to describe the behavior of one international actor toward another as interventionary whenever the form of behavior constitutes a sharp break with then-existing forms *and* whenever it is directed at changing or preserving the structure of political authority in the target society." Much of the social scientific literature on international intervention in the fifty years since Rosenau's contribution seems to have adopted this definition, sometimes explicitly though much more often implicitly.

Identifying these two defining features of an international intervention proves useful for both the behaviors it encapsulates and the behaviors it excludes. On the one hand, it suggests the potential for quite a broad range of interventionary behavior. An intervention may involve the use of force, the threat to use force, or neither; it may be conducted publicly or privately, overtly or covertly; it may employ economic, military, diplomatic, or various other policy instruments. Yet this definition also serves an important delimiting function. Not every public threat, economic sanction, mobilization of troops, or withholding of aid or other material benefit constitutes a form of intervention. These behaviors are often meant to induce the leadership within the target state to revise a policy position or proffer a concession; but unless they are targeted at the structure of political authority itself, they would not be considered interventionary. In addition (and perhaps more controversially), Rosenau's definition states that even behaviors explicitly seeking to alter or sustain the structure of political authority within a foreign polity are only interventionary insofar as they mark a break from convention. The provision of material assistance by the Cold War superpowers to their respective client states, for instance, was often intended to support the incumbent leadership in the face of domestic challengers; but such efforts were largely ongoing, conventional modes of international behavior—and thus not interventionary, according to Rosenau.

To be sure, this definition of intervention is not without ambiguity. All conventional behaviors began as non-conventional, and all breaks from convention, if they persist long enough, eventually become conventional in their own right; where the intervention ends and the convention begins (or vice-versa, for that matter) will rarely be an uncontroversial demarcation. Further, many international behaviors are (or claim to be) motivated by objectives other than the undermining or bolstering of the incumbent leader in the target state, but nonetheless carry major ramifications for that state's domestic politics; whether the impact on the authority structure was intended or incidental may likewise be difficult to discern.

An alternative approach to the topic would follow the framework developed in a seminal contribution by Gourevitch (1978), titled "The second image reversed: the international sources of domestic politics". As the title suggests, Gourevitch's innovation was to reverse the causal logic underlying Waltz (1959)'s "second image" of war—that international conflict may be explained by the "internal structure of states"—and instead examine the role played by the international system writ large in shaping domestic politics. Given the vast expansion of literature fitting this characterization over the past few decades, such a comprehensive definition of intervention would inevitably entail a body of research far beyond what could be contained within a single review essay: it would reasonably include, for instance, studies of how domestic politics are shaped by various foreign-originating economic shocks (Ramsay, 2011; Arias, 2017; Dube and Vargas, 2013), by interstate conflict (Chiozza and Goemans, 2004), or by diffusion of political institutions (Gleditsch and Ward, 2006; Abramson and Montero, Forthcoming), to name just a few forms of foreign influence.

Given these considerations, our approach tracks more closely to the definition proposed by Rosenau. We focus on actions and policies undertaken by one state with the goal of influencing structures of political authority within another state. Thus we emphasize the "authority-oriented" nature of intervention, while downplaying the "convention-breaking" aspect that Rosenau requires; and we focus primarily on actions for which the intended (rather than incidental) outcome is to influence politics (rather than just policy) within the target state.

21.2.2 Data sources

Demonstrating the diversity of activities that can be characterized as interventionary, Table 21.1 reports a list of common data sources used in the quantitative study of foreign interventions. Clearly none of these sources is (nor claims to be) all-encompassing, but rather each records a particular form of intervention. They also do not all comport precisely with the definition of intervention articulated above, nor with one another's operational definitions. Each has its own virtues and limitations, and care should always be taken to employ the dataset that best fits the particular question at hand.

21.2.2.1 Data on military interventions

The International Military Intervention (IMI) dataset (Pickering and Kisangani, 2009) catalogs all instances of military forces being deployed to the territory of another sovereign state. Not all instances are intended to alter or revise the structure of political authority within the target state, but the data are coded to identify the motives behind the force deployment, including some authority-oriented motives. Importantly, these data also indicate the direction of the intervention, i.e. whether it is in support of, in opposition to, or neutral toward the government or anti-government forces.

A more recently developed dataset is the Militarized Intervention by Powerful States (MIPS) dataset (Sullivan and Koch, 2009). MIPS documents a similar kind of event as those recorded in IMI; where the two differ is that the MIPS trades off cross-sectional breadth—covering only interventions by the five post-World War II major powers (US, UK, France, China, and Russia)—in favor of substantive depth. The main contribution of the MIPS dataset is its focus on the political objectives of military interventions. Included in the data are a categorical classification of the primary political objective (PPO),[1] a brief narrative of that objective, an indicator for whether that PPO was attained by the end of the intervention, and if so, for how many months was the PPO maintained.

Some studies of international intervention rely on the popular Militarized Interstate Dispute (MID) dataset (Palmer et al., 2019). MIDs are more inclusive than IMI and MIPS in that they do not require the actual deployment of troops onto foreign territory (unlike IMI) or a 500-troop deployment threshold (unlike MIPS); but they are more restrictive in that they only include instances of conflict between states. Cases of intervention that occur on foreign soil but are not directed against the host state (i.e. interventions against non-state actors) may appear in the IMI or MIPS data but cannot constitute MIDs.

Several data sources focus specifically on civil conflicts, with varying levels of specificity for different aspects of the conflicts and interventions. Patrick Regan (2002) has compiled a widely used dataset on third-party interventions into civil wars. While the data are restricted in scope to include only episodes of intrastate conflicts with at least 200 battle deaths, they are quite thorough in the information coded within that sample—recording, among other things, several different types of military and economic interventions and the amounts of each type. An extension of this dataset by Regan et

---

[1] Note that IMI codes nine possible motives for intervention, and a given intervention can be coded with more than one motive; whereas MIPS identifies a single primary objective among six categories of motives.

Table 21.1 Sources of data on foreign interventions.

Source	Citation	Coverage and Observations	Definitions and Notes
International Military Intervention (IMI)	Pickering and Kisangani (2009)	1,111 incidents of IMI from 1946-2005; observations at level of directed dyad-intervention. Motivations of interventions are coded, including: taking sides in a domestic dispute (n=255); changing target political regime or its core policies (n=529); and others.	The dataset "catalogs episodes when national military personnel are purposefully dispatched into other sovereign states". It is an extension of Pearson and Baumann (1993), which "documents all cases of military intervention across international boundaries by regular armed forces of independent states and by national armed forces operating under multinational command."[a]
Military Interventions by Powerful States (MIPS)	Sullivan and Koch (2009)	126 military interventions, 1945-2003; coded as pursuing one of six primary political objectives, including: "maintain foreign regime authority" (n=36), and "remove foreign regime" (n=12)	"The MIPS project defines military intervention as a use of armed force that involves the official deployment of at least 500 regular military personnel (ground, air, or naval) to attain immediate-term political objectives through action against a foreign adversary."
Militarized Interstate Disputes (MID)	Palmer et al. (2019)	2,315 unique MIDs, with 1,608 post-WWII; coding of "revision type" includes "government/regime" (n=124 total, 90 post-WWII)	"Militarized interstate disputes are united historical cases of conflict in which the threat, display, or use of military force short of war by one member state is explicitly directed towards the government, official representatives, official forces, property, or territory of another state." (Jones et al., 1996)
Regan's civil war data	Regan (2002)	150 episodes of intrastate conflicts from 1944-1999; observations at level of conflict-month (or intervener-conflict-month in the event of multiple interveners); variables denoting kind and degree of intervention (if any)	Intrastate conflict defined as "armed, sustained combat between groups within state boundaries in which there are at least 200 fatalities". Military interventions include: troops; naval forces; equipment/aid; intelligence/advisors; air support; military sanctions. Economic interventions include: grants; loans; equipment/expertise; credits; relieving past obligations; economic sanctions.
Uppsala Conflict Data Program (UCDP) External Support Dataset	Högbladh et al. (2011)	6,519 supporter-recipient-opponent-triad-year observations, for 168 conflicts, 1975-2009; data include indicators for ten types of external support (but not their levels/intensities)	Armed conflict defined as "a contested incompatibility that concerns government and/or territory where the use of armed force between two parties, of which at least one is the government of a state, results in at least 25 battle-related deaths in a calendar year." Support types include: provide troops; military or intelligence infrastructure; access to territory; weapons; logistics support; training; economic support; intelligence material.
Correlates of War (COW) civil war data	Sarkees and Wayman (2010)	334 intrastate wars from 1818-2007; generally one observation per war, with multiple observations when there more than one participant per side; intervention coded as indicator for whether war was "internationalized"	Intrastate war defined as "any armed conflict that involved a) military action internal to the metropole of the state system member, b) the active participation of the national government, and c) effective resistance by both sides (as measured by the ratio of fatalities of the weaker to the stronger forces), and (d) a total of at least 1,000 battle deaths during each year of the war" (Sarkees and Schafer, 2000).[b]

[a] Note: Data by Pearson and Baumann (1993) end in 1988; Pickering and Kisangani (2009) extend to 2005 using the same coding rules.
[b] Note: For reasons we have not been able to discern, the COW data includes several civil wars not included in the Regan data (for the period in which they overlap), despite the higher threshold of battle deaths that the COW dataset uses to define civil wars.

continued on next page

Table 21.1 (*continued*)

Source	Citation	Coverage and Observations	Definitions and Notes
CIA/KGB influence	Berger et al. (2013b)	60 episodes of CIA intervention, and 25 episodes of KGB intervention, from 1946-1989, with years of onset and offset	CIA interventions coded as either installing a foreign leader in power (and subsequently supporting that leader), or just supporting an existing leader
Foreign Imposed Regime Change (FIRC)	Downes and O'Rourke (2016)	95 successful overt FIRCs by any country from 1816-2000, and 25 successful and 32 failed covert FIRCs by the United States	Extension of Downes and Monten (2013), which defines FIRC as "the forcible or coerced removal of the effective leader of the state—which remains formally sovereign afterward—by the government of another state"[c]
Archigos	Goemans et al. (2009)	3,409 leadership spells for all sovereign states 1918-2015 (excluding microstates), with coding of leader means of entry and exit; 37 instances of foreign involvement in leader removal after 1946	Exit codes denoting foreign intervention include: "Removed by Military, with Foreign Support" (n=6); "Removed by Other Government Actors, with Foreign Support" (n=4); "Removed by Rebels, with Foreign Support" (n=8); "Removed through Threat of Foreign Force" (n=19)
Threat and Imposition of Economic Sanctions (TIES)	Morgan et al. (2014)	1,412 sanctions episodes from 1945-2005; observations are sanction-targets (each with one or more senders)	Economic sanctions defined as "actions that one or more countries take to limit or end their economic relations with a target country in an effort to persuade that country to change its policies." Each sanction episode is coded by the issues involved; 54 instances are coded as aiming to overthrow the regime in power
National Elections across Democracy and Autocracy (NELDA)	Hyde and Marinov (2012)	3,748 direct national elections from 1945-2015	Variables include: NELDA45: Were international monitors present? (yes: n=1,375). NELDA47: Were there allegations by Western monitors of significant vote-fraud? (n=246). NELDA49: Did any monitors refuse to go to an election because they believed that it would not be free and fair? (n=72). NELDA58: Did an outside actor attempt to influence the outcome of the election by making threats to withhold, or by withholding, something of value to the country? (n=213).
Partisan Electoral Interventions by the Great Powers (PEIG)	Levin (2019a)	937 competitive national-level executive elections, with 117 partisan interventions by the US (n=81) or the USSR (n=36)	Partisan electoral intervention defined as "a situation in which one or more sovereign countries intentionally undertakes specific actions to influence an upcoming election in another sovereign country in an overt or covert manner which they believe will favor or hurt one of the sides contesting that election and which incurs, or may incur, significant costs to the intervener(s) or the intervened country"

[c] *Note: Data by Downes and Monten (2013) include only successful instances of FIRC, and their data extend to 2008.*

al. (2009) also records various forms of diplomatic intervention, including mediation, arbitration, international forums, and recalling ambassadors, as well as whether a third party made an offer for a diplomatic intervention which was refused. The UCDP External Support data provide more detail on the identities of the combatants and recipients of external support, but less detail on the intensity of support and less temporal disaggregation. The Correlates of War project's civil war dataset preceded both the Regan and UCDP datasets, but is considerably less detailed than either of the above in the information that is included regarding interventions.

21.2.2.2 Data on non-military interventions

Other datasets record instances of intervention outside the context of active militarized hostilities.[2] Berger et al. (2013b) rely on archival evidence, in large part from declassified government documents, to code covert interventions by the US and USSR, whether those interventions involved removal of an incumbent leader or ongoing support to prop up a leader in office. Downes and O'Rourke (2016) expand on this data by adding failed US attempts to covertly remove a foreign leader; they also include all successful instances of overt foreign-imposed regime change (FIRC) by any country, not only the US. (To our knowledge, data on covert interventions by countries other than the US and USSR/Russia have not been collected systematically.) The Archigos dataset of national political leaders records leaders' means of exit from office, including whether there was any foreign involvement in a leader's removal. The Archigos data seems to impose a higher threshold for determining which leaders are removed by foreign intervention; for instance, while the US- and UK-backed ouster of Iranian Prime Minister Mohammad Mossadeg in 1953 is considered by Downes and O'Rourke to be a foreign-imposed covert regime change, Archigos codes Mossadeg's exit from office as "Removed by Other Government Actors, without Foreign Support".

Finally, another form of typically non-violent intervention which has been measured and analyzed systematically is intervention into foreign elections. The NELDA dataset by Hyde and Marinov (2012) was not collected specifically for the purpose of examining foreign intervention, but it does include variables that indicate foreign efforts to influence elections. These include indicators of whether an election was monitored and/or criticized by international monitors, as well as whether foreign actors issued threats or inducements in the hopes of shaping the electoral outcome.[3] More specifically tailored to present purposes is Levin (2019a)'s Partisan Electoral Intervention by the Great Powers (PEIG) dataset. Just recently released, the PEIG data include detailed information on various forms of electoral intervention, as well as whether the intervention was intended to support an incumbent or challenger.

---

[2] Note that both here and in the review of empirical findings, we separate the literature into "military" and "non-military" interventions. However, some of the interventions under consideration in the latter group, particularly in studies of foreign-imposed regime change, may involve the threat or use of force by the intervener.

[3] Another data source for election monitoring is Kelley (2012)'s Data on International Election Monitoring (DIEM). Kelley's DIEM dataset does not provide the same breadth of coverage as does NELDA, covering only monitored elections in 108 countries from 1980–2004. But NELDA provides somewhat coarser measures of monitoring activity, whereas DIEM provides the identity of each monitor that observed a given election and the assessments issued by each one. This is a non-trivial distinction, as over half of elections in the DIEM data were observed by multiple international monitors, and nearly half of those multiply-monitored elections received divergent assessments from the different monitoring organizations present.

21.2.2.3 Implications for empirical research

At first glance, this multiplicity of data sources presents some clear complications to the study of foreign intervention: a theoretical notion of intervention may be operationalized by a variety of different measures, using subtly divergent coding rules or case selection criteria. It would thus be unsurprising if empirical tests of nominally similar research questions reached starkly different conclusions, depending on the data set used in the analyses (even setting aside questions of model specification). Beyond the comparability across datasets, there are other issues of particular concern to the present subject matter. The data on various forms of covert intervention, for instance, rely largely on previously classified information which has either been declassified or leaked; this makes it difficult for researchers to cross-validate their coding across multiple primary sources, and further, calls into question whether the cases identified in any given dataset are truly the universe of cases of the phenomenon of interest. Relatedly, even declassified sources are often redacted, with sections of documents whitened out to protect confidentiality of participants. This requires the coder to sometimes make judgement calls on what exactly happened. Even for data on overt interventions, which are presumably easier to observe and verify, serious disagreements may arise over coding decisions: a recent exchange between Gibler et al. (2016) and Palmer et al. (2019), for instance, resulted in a re-coding of a substantial portion of disputes recorded in the widely used MID dataset. This was most certainly not a consequence of any particular weakness of the MID dataset, but rather of the inherent difficulty of systematically quantifying the subject matter under examination; were researchers to re-examine any of the other datasets mentioned above with the same attention and thoroughness exhibited by Gibler and colleagues, it seems quite likely that similar disagreements would arise. These coding difficulties make it all the more important to provide detailed codebooks where the exact source and judgement that justifies a particular coding decision is clearly listed, so that readers can conduct their own robustness checks.

The discussion in Section 21.4 provides a critical analysis of various aspects of the research designs employed in empirical studies of intervention, setting aside concerns over the quality of data; researchers should keep in mind, however, that all of the concerns discussed below are further complicated by the inherent limitations of the underlying data sources themselves.

21.2.3 Topics omitted from this review

While we aim to provide a broad overview of the academic literature on foreign interventions, the scope of our review is delimited in some important respects. Methodologically, our focus is on either game-theoretic or quantitative (statistical) approaches to the study of foreign intervention. These are certainly not the only approaches to the topic; for a range of constructivist and social-practice perspectives, for instance, readers may consider a recent special issue of the Review of International Studies titled "Intervention and the Ordering of the Modern World" (MacMillan, 2013). Given that the target audience of this review are economists and other social scientists interested in quantitative or formal work, qualitative and historical accounts of intervention are likewise omitted.

There are also a number of substantive topics omitted from consideration. Voluntary agreements between states to alter policies for mutual benefit—"contracting", in Krasner and Weinstein (2014)'s classification, or "agreement interventions" in Aidt et al. (2020)'s—will generally fall outside the scope of this review. Thus we will not be covering international trade and investment agreements, which may have considerable implications for the political survival of the contracting leaders (Arias et al., 2018; Hollyer and Rosendorff, 2012), nor international military alliances, which have been theorized as an exchange of sovereignty for security (Morrow, 1991; Lake, 2009). Foreign influence exerted primarily through normative or social pressure, for instance through "naming and shaming" mechanisms often cited in the human rights literature (Lebovic and Voeten, 2006; Kelley and Simmons, 2015), will also be omitted.[4] And as mentioned above, our review will exclude studies of various international forces or behaviors which may influence domestic politics but which are not primarily intended to do so.

Finally, we will note that while our review includes both military and non-military interventions, we will be giving relatively greater attention to those involving military force ("imposition", according to Krasner and Weinstein (2014), or "institution interventions", according to Aidt et al. (2020)). The reasoning for this choice is that military interventions are generally the most costly—in human and economic terms, for target and intervener alike—and thus pose the greatest need for policy-relevant scientific analysis.

21.3 Summary of findings

In this section, we provide an overview of the accumulated empirical findings on foreign intervention. The goal of this section is to summarize rather than analyze the literature under consideration; in Section 21.4 we turn to a critical analysis of the research reviewed here in Section 21.3.

The study of international interventions has largely been oriented around two central questions: what are the causes of international interventions, and what are their consequences. These two questions are of course intrinsically linked, as decisions to intervene are made by strategic actors anticipating the consequences of their actions. Most studies tend to assume that the specified outcome variable (e.g.: civil war duration, democracy promotion, etc) is the variable that was meant to be affected by the intervention, a point also made by Regan (2010). Our summary of the literature will thus focus primarily on consequences of interventions, rather than treating their causes as a separate object of inquiry.

The top-line finding that emerges from our survey of the intervention literature is that interventions generally fail to achieve their stated objective (or the one purported or assumed by the researchers). This finding is certainly not unanimous, and there are important exceptions which we review as well. The focus of our review, however, is on the failure of foreign interventions, as this is both the predominant pattern that we observe, and the more puzzling one which begs further explanation.

We first review the literature on the consequences of military interventions, assessed according to both conflict and non-conflict outcomes. We then turn to a review of various non-military interventions, organized by means of intervention: economic aid, election monitoring, sanctions, and covert intervention and electoral interference.

---

[4] We should note, however, that normative pressure is sometimes cited as an operative mechanism in the election monitoring literature, which we do review here.

21.3.1 Military interventions

In analyzing military interventions into ongoing conflicts, a natural starting point is to consider the impacts of interventions on conflict outcomes. We begin with studies of this variety, and then turn to studies examining other social, political, and economic consequences of military interventions.

21.3.1.1 Military interventions and conflict outcomes

According to Regan (2010), one of the (often implicit) assumptions "shap[ing] almost all of the systematic studies of interventions [into civil conflicts]... is that interventions reflect some form of conflict management... designed to make conflicts less likely, shorter, or less violent." By this metric, the accumulated record of foreign interventions is abysmal. A set of early cross-national studies of civil war duration and termination reach similarly pessimistic conclusions: Considering post-WWII civil wars from the COW data, Mason and Fett (1996) find no effect of foreign intervention on a binary outcome of settlement versus non-settlement as the mode of war termination; a subsequent analysis finds that interventions actually reduce the probability of a settlement (Mason et al., 1999). Using the full COW sample dating back to the early 19th century, Balch-Lindsay and Enterline (2000) and Balch-Lindsay et al. (2008), respectively, find that third-party interventions extend the duration of civil wars, and decrease the hazard of civil wars ending by way of negotiated settlement. Regan (2002) reaches the same general conclusion regarding conflict duration from analyzing his original dataset of post-WWII civil wars, with its more fine-grained coding of various features of interventions. The results are consistent for military and economic interventions alike, and for interventions in support of either the government or the opposition: "Overwhelmingly", Regan writes, "the conclusion is that regardless of the target or the type, an intervention tends to decrease the likelihood that a conflict will end in the next month."

Beyond the duration and outcome of civil wars, interventions may impact how combatants conduct themselves in the course of fighting. Wood et al. (2012) analyze the UCDP civil conflict data and find that foreign interventions in support of one side of a civil conflict increase the opposing side's propensity to perpetrate attacks against civilians. The authors explain this relationship as resulting from the disadvantaged group's decreased capacity to maintain control over the civilian population and obtain necessary resources through voluntary and non-violent means. In a similar vein, Choi and Piazza (2017) and Piazza and Choi (2018) document positive relationships between international military interventions and suicide terrorism conducted both in the target country and in the territory of the intervening state.

The cross-national evidence of the failure of civil war interventions to bring about an end of hostilities has been reinforced by more recent micro-level analyses. Separate studies by Kocher et al. (2011) and by Dell and Querubin (2018) restrict attention to the case of US intervention in the Vietnam War, and consider within-conflict variation in the intensity of intervention—specifically the intensity of US bombing, disaggregated at the hamlet-month level. The primary outcome in Kocher et al. is the relative degree of insurgent versus government control, while Dell and Querubin examine a broader range of outcomes, including measures of Viet Cong guerrilla presence, attacks, and extortion; local government capacity and public goods provision; and public opinion towards the United States and the South Vietnamese government. Kocher et al. theorize that the indiscriminate nature of the US bombing campaign led civilians to rationally participate in the insurgency as a strategic response. Dell and Querubin point to the accumulation of civilian grievances as a primary operative mechanism. In both cases the authors convincingly demonstrate that increased intensity of force in the US intervention in Vietnam undermined the US's objective of defeating the Viet Cong insurgency. A separate analysis of US intervention in the Colombian civil war Dube and Naidu (2015) finds similar evidence of the counter-productivity of US efforts: Colombian municipalities which housed a military base experienced a differential increase in paramilitary violence as a result of inflows of US military and counternarcotics assistance. The authors attribute this effect to the military's sharing resources with paramilitary groups, and interpret it as evidence of a weakening of state authority due to foreign intervention.

21.3.1.2 Military interventions and governance and development outcomes

A separate set of studies focuses on another common justification employed by policy makers in support of foreign intervention: the promotion of democracy and political liberalization in the target state. Again, the results paint a grim picture. Pickering and Peceny (2006) find that international military interventions by the US, UK, and France—the most common interveners among liberal democracies— fail to democratize target states. With a separate operationalization of intervention, which combines MIDs, Fortna (2004)'s data on UN peacekeeping, and Regan (2002)'s civil war intervention data, Bueno de Mesquita and Downs (2006) likewise conclude that military intervention does not systematically improve democratic governance in target countries. Similarly, Peksen (2012) finds that foreign military interventions harm human rights conditions within the target state—a finding that holds across interventions in support of, against, or neutral to the target government, and even when the intervention is conducted by a liberal democracy or intergovernmental organization.

Given the wide-ranging societal consequences of political violence, it is perhaps surprising that only a few studies have examined the relationship between foreign military intervention and various social and economic outcomes other than post-intervention governance (as well as direct conflict outcomes, as discussed above). One such study is by Kim (2017), who finds that unilateral interventions into civil wars are cross-nationally associated with a deterioration in civilians' post-war quality of life, as measured by life expectancy and infant mortality rates. Miguel and Roland (2011) also conduct a within-case analysis of the economic impact of military intervention, focusing on the US bombing of Vietnam. The authors show that the most heavily-bombed areas exhibited lower levels of economic consumption for up to two decades after the end of the US campaign, but saw faster growth rates from 1993-2002, likely as a result of increased state investment to spur recovery in those hardest-hit regions. Similar findings for the Vietnam War are documented by Dell and Querubin (2018) who show that more heavily bombed hamlets experience worse economic outcomes in the short run, but not in the long run. Davis and Weinstein (2002) find similar evidence of a long-term economic recovery following the US bombing of Japan in WWII. In contrast, Riano and Valcia Caicedo (2020) show that the US bombing campaign in Laos had a detrimental impact on economic development which persists to the present day. Examining a less conventional outcome, Beber et al. (2017) use individual-level geolocated survey data to show that the presence of international peacekeepers in Monrovia, Liberia dramatically increased female civilians' entry into the transactional sex market.

21.3.2 Non-military interventions

We now review a body of empirical findings regarding consequences of various other forms of foreign intervention. As noted above, while we group these studies under the classification of "non-military interventions", this is not a perfectly clean distinction: some of the contributions reviewed here (particularly those on foreign-imposed regime change) examine intervention tactics which may involve military force on the part of the intervener, depending on the particular data source and operationalization of intervention employed in each study.

21.3.2.1 Economic aid

Economic assistance is often viewed as a means of improving not only economic development within the recipient country, but also political development as well.[5] As Knack (2004) suggests, this may occur either through aid that directly supports democratic institution-building, through conditioning aid on political liberalization and other good-governance policies, or indirectly through aid's impact on economic development which may in turn spur democratization. Knack tests these propositions with cross-national data on government receipts of development assistance, and finds no support for them. Djankov et al. (2008) investigate a similar question, with some modifications to the research design (notably using a panel structure instead of a cross-sectional design, and using different outcome measures) and reach an even more damning conclusion: not only does aid fail to democratize recipient governments, but it has a significantly negative impact on democratization. The authors theorize that aid functions analogously to the "resource curse" for economic growth, in that it provides a sudden windfall of revenues which lessens incumbents' reliance on tax revenues—and in turn their accountability to the tax-paying citizenry—and they estimate that aid's negative impact on democracy is even greater in magnitude than that of oil revenues. A different take on the question comes from Wright (2009), who argues and demonstrates empirically that the potential for aid to democratize autocratic governments is conditional on the breadth of the incumbent regime's support base: only autocrats with sufficiently broad coalitions of support anticipate being able to survive in office after liberalization, and are thus willing to implement liberalizing reforms in return for aid; leaders in smaller-coalition systems, however, cannot survive liberalization, and if they do receive aid, will simply use it to maintain power within the current institutional structure.

In addition to its effect on political institutions, another concern for the study of foreign aid is its impact on conflict. On this score we find similarly dispiriting results. World Bank development aid in the Philippines (Crost et al., 2014) and US counterinsurgency aid in Afghanistan (Sexton, 2016) are both found to increase insurgent violence; in both cases, the authors argue, insurgents respond strategically to the opportunities presented to undermine the implementation of aid programs and thus weaken the legitimacy of the government in the eyes of the public. Nunn and Qian (2014) find that US food aid increases the incidence of civil conflict, a finding they attribute to combatants seizing the aid shipments and using them to subsidize the costs of fighting.

21.3.2.2 Election monitoring

An increasingly common form of foreign involvement in domestic politics is international election monitoring: three out of five post-Cold War national elections have been observed by international monitors, compared to less than one of ten during the Cold War (Hyde and Marinov, 2012). It may seem somewhat unintuitive to refer to nominally unbiased efforts to promote the transparency and credibility of elections as interventionary; non-governmental and intergovernmental organizations that conduct monitoring activities are even reluctant to use the term "monitoring" because of the heavy-handedness

---

[5] We focus on the impact of aid on political outcomes, since this most closely fits our definition of foreign intervention. We do not review here the literature on the impact of economic aid on economic outcomes such as GDP growth – see Easterly et al. (2004) and Easterly (2006) for an excellent overview and critical assessment of this literature.

it suggests, generally preferring the term "election observation". Yet the practice is explicitly directed toward altering the structure of political authority within the target country, in that it is intended (at least purportedly) to ensure that political authority is determined according to the results of free and fair elections.[6]

An early contribution to the topic by Hyde (2007) gave some cause for optimism. Examining polling station-level results from the 2003 Armenian presidential election, the author found that the presence of international monitors reduced vote shares for the incumbent (who was widely believed to have manipulated the overall vote count) by about six percent, relative to polling stations that were not monitored. Subsequent research has complicated this finding, pointing out that while monitoring may have the desirable effect of reducing election-day fraud at monitored polling locations, there are a number of pernicious second-order and spillover effects at play. Focusing on pre-election manipulation, Ichino and Schündeln (2012) leverage random assignment of observers to voter registration centers in the lead-up to the 2008 Ghanaian general election.[7] They show that while observation decreases (presumably fraudulent) registration at the observed locations, it also has the effect of displacing irregularities to nearby, unobserved locations. This logic of displacing rather than deterring electoral manipulation has also been supported in cross-national analyses. Simpser and Donno (2012) show that incumbents respond to election monitoring by shifting strategies away from election-day fraud and toward broader institutional manipulation, as measured by indices of administrative performance, rule of law, and freedom of the press. Beaulieu and Hyde (2009) show that opposition parties, cognizant of these strategic responses on the incumbents' part, become more likely to boycott monitored elections, wanting to deprive incumbents of the international stamp of approval they would receive for having substituted one form of manipulation for another.

Spillovers aside, there is also evidence that the presence of election monitors causes some domestic unrest which would not occur in their absence. The effectiveness of monitoring, as Hyde and Marinov (2014) argue, rests on a basic logic of deterrence: by providing credible information on election quality, monitors can facilitate coordination of opposition protests in the event of electoral fraud, thus raising the incumbent's cost of perpetrating fraud. Furthermore, recent research has called into question the basic mechanisms through which election monitoring is believed to help coordinate opposition efforts. In a survey experiment conducted following Tunisia's 2014 presidential election, neither positive nor negative aspects of monitor reports highlighted in separate experimental treatments significantly shifted respondents' views of the credibility of the election, relative to a no-information control group (Bush and Prather, 2017). Other survey experimental evidence indicates that voters and activists do not give more credence to reports issued by more objective or credible monitoring organizations, as intuition would suggest they might (Bush and Prather, 2018; Nielson et al., 2019).

21.3.2.3 Sanctions

Another frequently used tactic for bringing about political change in a target country is the imposition of economic sanctions. Sanctions are typically employed with the stated purpose of bringing about

---

[6] Though see recent work by Bubeck and Marinov (2017) that seeks to theoretically integrate strategies of election monitoring and biased electoral interference, examining the extent to which third-party interventions are intended to support the electoral process versus supporting a particular candidate.

[7] The observers in this study are operating under the auspices of domestic rather than international civil society organizations, but the findings and causal mechanisms should largely carry over to our understanding of international monitoring.

a change in policy in the target state, though in practice—and particularly in autocratic systems—it is often understood that the only way such policy change can actually occur is through a change in leadership (McGillivray and Stam, 2004).

On the specific question of whether sanctions spur leadership change, the record is mixed: Marinov (2005) finds that sanctions do destabilize target leaders, and that the effect is larger for democratic targets. Escribà-Folch and Wright (2010) focus specifically on sanctions imposed on autocratic targets and find substantial variation by regime type, with personalist regimes being the most destabilized by sanctions but single-party and militarist regimes being largely unaffected. Yet on the broader question of whether sanctions can achieve the more normatively appealing aims that justify their imposition, there is more consistent evidence of failure. Both Wood (2008) and Peksen (2009) find that sanctions lead to worsened human rights conditions in the target states, as target leaders turn to repression as a means of compensating for the destabilizing economic costs of sanctions. Escribà-Folch (2012) examines the same question and finds heterogeneous responses to sanctions across authoritarian regime types, as some increase repression and some instead increase spending that benefits groups whose support they rely on for political survival. Along similar lines, Peksen and Cooper Drury (2010) show that target leaders respond to sanctions by curtailing civil and political liberties. Considering sanctions in conflict settings in particular, Hultman and Peksen (2017) show that economic sanctions—either threatened or imposed—increase the intensity of violence in recent African civil conflicts; threats of arms embargoes are found to increase violence, while the actual imposition of arms embargoes decreases it.

21.3.2.4 FIRC, covert intervention, and electoral intervention

Finally, we can consider a set of studies that examine consequences of efforts by intervening states to directly remove or prop up an incumbent leader in a target state, through overt or covert means. One notable consequence of these efforts identified in the literature is the instigation of violent conflict. Peic and Reiter (2011) show that foreign imposed regime change (FIRC), as coded in the Archigos data, corresponds to an increased probability of subsequent civil war onset, when the FIRC follows an interstate war. Downes and O'Rourke (2016) consider international rather than civil conflict as an outcome of interest, relying on their original dataset which employs a more expansive definition of FIRC. Their findings overall indicate a positive relationship between FIRC and subsequent onset of militarized disputes (MIDs) between the target and the intervener. Levin (2018) also observes that non-violent but overt electoral interventions are followed by increased incidence of domestic terrorism within the target state.

In addition to the risk of conflict brought about by these intervention efforts, we also observe detrimental consequences for governance within the target states. Downes and Monten (2013) likewise find that the targets of overt regime changes imposed by foreign democracies do not become more democratic as a result. Considering covert interventions, either to install a leader or prop up an existing leader, Berger et al. (2013a) find that such interventions by both the US and the USSR tend to harm democratization in the target state in the short- to medium-term (though the effect dissipates over time). Using yet another measure of foreign electoral intervention, Levin (2019b) finds that covert interventions lead to an increased risk of subsequent democratic breakdown.[8]

---

[8] Levin (2019b) also provides some suggestive evidence that only Soviet/Russian interventions have a negative impact on the Polity IV democracy score. However, this differential impact of Soviet/Russian interventions (relative to those conducted by the U.S.) does not extend to other outcomes such as democratic breakdowns or transitions to democracy.

Overall, a fairly consistent pattern emerges from our survey of international interventions. These findings hold across various measures of intervention, various outcomes of interest, and a diversity of research designs and empirical specifications. For the more normatively appealing outcomes that we might hope to follow from foreign interventions, the historical record disappoints.

21.3.3 Some bright spots

The failure of foreign interventions is not a unanimous finding throughout the literature. For instance, Krain (2005) finds that interventions specifically to prevent genocide or politicide have generally succeeded in that goal; Regan and Aydin (2006) find that, unlike more conventionally studied military and economic interventions, diplomatic interventions are effective in shortening conflict duration. Some earlier studies, including Hermann and Kegley (1998) and Peceny (1999), find that US interventions do succeed in promoting democracy.

Here we briefly review two more general patterns of intervention success that emerge from the broader literature: first, that multilateral interventions tend to be more effective than unilateral interventions; and second, that interventions targeted at winning "hearts and minds" in the target country tend to be more successful than those operating through force and coercion.

21.3.3.1 *Multilateral intervention*

Some of the aforementioned studies with a top-line finding of intervention failure do find some evidence of multilateral success: while both Pickering and Peceny (2006) and Kim (2017), for instance, find negative consequences of unilateral military interventions on democracy and development respectively, those studies also find positive impacts on the same outcomes for interventions conducted by the United Nations. In fact, the tendency of multilateral interventions to succeed where unilateral interventions fail is a more general pattern throughout the literature. Gilligan and Sergenti (2008) find that while UN interventions into ongoing conflicts do not affect the hazard of termination, post-conflict peacekeeping operations (PKOs) do decrease the risk of war recurrence; the latter of these findings confirms earlier results by Fortna (2004). With UN peacekeeping data disaggregated to the level of government/rebel group-dyad-month, and with separate measures of peacekeeping troops, police, and observers deployed, Hultman et al. (2013, 2014) find that higher numbers of UN peacekeeping troops correspond to decreases in both battlefield deaths and civilian casualties. This finding is partly confirmed in more recent work by Carnegie and Mikulaschek (2017), which shows that peacekeeping deployments reduce the number of civilians killed by rebel forces, but not by government forces.

Beyond the deployment of peacekeeping troops, other aspects of interventions by multilateral institutions into post-conflict settings have shown a track record of some success. Avdeenko and Gilligan (2015) study the effectiveness of a World Bank-funded Community Driven Development (CDD) program—an increasingly popular policy instrument for supporting social and economic development, with approximately 1.3 billion USD of World Bank loans allocated to CDD programming per year—implemented in randomly-assigned villages in post-conflict Sudan from 2008 to 2011. The authors use household surveys and behavioral lab-in-the-field experiments to construct a novel measure of social capital. They find that while the CDD program failed to increase participants' social capital as intended, it did increase the inclusiveness of local governance and consequently citizens' civic participation. Considering a separate aspect of multilateral efforts in post-conflict reconstruction, Blair (2019a,b) examines the effects of UN peacekeeping operations on post-conflict rule of law. Using both micro-level survey evidence from Liberia, and macro-level rule-of-law indices for a cross-national panel of UN missions, the author finds that UN presence improves government performance along those measures.

While the aforementioned studies of foreign aid find overall detrimental effects on democratization, there is a notable exception in recent work by Carnegie and Marinov (2017) focusing specifically on development aid from the European Union.[9] The authors show that EU aid causes a significant but short-lived improvement in measures of both democracy and human rights protections, an effect the authors attribute to minor political reforms implemented by recipient governments in response to the conditionalities attached to the aid. Finally, we observe similar patterns in multilateral versus unilateral sanctions, though to opposite effect: in assessing the consequences of sanctions for human rights in the target states, both Peksen (2009) and Wood (2008) find multilaterally-imposed sanctions be more detrimental—precisely because those sanctions are more effective at destabilizing the target regimes, which in turn provokes even more aggressive compensatory responses by the incumbents.

21.3.3.2 Hearts and minds

A separate aspect of foreign interventions that has proven to be predictive of success is a focus on winning popular support among the citizens in the target state. Formalizing the logic underlying the U.S. Army's counterinsurgency doctrine, Berman et al. (2011) model an interaction among a (foreign-backed) government and a rebel group competing for control over territory, and a community that can strategically assist the government's counterinsurgency efforts by sharing information about rebel activities. They hypothesize that increased government service provision, the enjoyment of which is conditional on government control over territory, will incentivize citizens to support the government through information-sharing. Empirically the authors show that increased reconstruction spending by the US-led coalition in Iraq from 2004 to 2008, analyzed at the level of district-half year, led to a decrease in insurgent violence against coalition and government forces.

Lyall et al. (2013) conduct a survey experiment in the midst of the Taliban insurgency in Afghanistan in 2011, results of which are somewhat ambiguous but broadly consistent with the "hearts and minds" hypothesis. The study reveals that victimization by the US-led International Security Assistance Force (ISAF) reduced citizens' support for the ISAF and increased support for the Taliban; subsequent ISAF efforts at harm mitigation (in the form of a condolence payment to the victim or their family) did not improve support for the ISAF, but did substantially reduce support for the Taliban. In relative terms, at least, intervention tactics that avoid civilian victimization, and that provide compensation when victimization occurs, appear more conducive to achieving interveners' objectives. A similar conclusion is reached in an analysis by Dell and Querubin (2018) comparing counterinsurgency outcomes in neighboring regions of Vietnam under the respective commands of the U.S. Marine Corps and the U.S. Army. The Marine Corps' overall strategy emphasized winning popular support through development programs and minimal use of force, whereas the Army adopted an "overwhelming fire-power" approach; and again, comparatively speaking, the former approach proved more effective in undermining the insurgency and supporting the South Vietnamese government.

---

[9] Note that in the three studies of aid and democratization mentioned above, the main independent variables are total aid receipts (usually per capita, or as a share of national income or government revenues). These measures will thus include both unilateral and multilateral aid. Carnegie and Marinov (2017) isolate multilateral aid, specifically from the EU.

21.3.3.3 Bottom line

To summarize, we find some evidence in the accumulated empirical literature of foreign interventions achieving their purported or assumed objectives. The findings of intervention success, however, appear to be more the exception than the rule. Multilateral interventions appear to have a better record of success than unilateral interventions, yet unilateral interventions proliferate. It should also be noted that the successes of "hearts and minds" strategies documented above are all estimated relative to other intervention strategies, rather than relative to a non-intervention baseline.

From a social scientific perspective, it is the failures of intervention that warrant further investigation and explanation; the tendency of political actors to repeatedly pursue policies that fail to achieve their purported objectives is a far more puzzling phenomenon than the instances in which those policies succeed. For this reason, the remainder of our review focuses on the general pattern of intervention failure. In addition, the studies that find evidence of success are generally subject to the same theoretical and methodological concerns as those finding evidence of failure, as we discuss in depth below.

21.4 Explaining intervention failure

Given the predominant finding of failure of foreign interventions, our next task is to seek to explain this pattern of results. Our first two explanations are not mutually exclusive, and either would be a sufficient condition to generate a given study's finding of intervention failure. The first highlights a set of econometric issues which may give rise to misleading estimates of intervention effectiveness. The second relates to the outcomes under consideration, and whether interventions are being assessed as succeeding or failing according to the appropriate criteria.

21.4.1 Econometric issues

Here we consider three separate methodological concerns which may help explain the predominant finding of intervention failure: first, selection on unobservables or omitted variable bias; second, the challenges of drawing inferences from the cases of realized interventions; and third, issues surrounding the measurement of the independent variables of interest and the substitutability of intervention strategies.

21.4.1.1 Selection on unobservables

A fundamental challenge faced by the majority of studies reviewed thus far is bias due to selection on unobservables. The basic subject matter at hand makes this a difficult if not impossible problem to overcome: interventions are conducted by strategic actors who make intervention decisions in anticipation of the consequences of their actions. Most of the theoretical claims discussed above do not lend themselves to any sort of randomized controlled trial (RCT), and natural experiments are hard to come by. Thus the predominant identification strategy in the papers reviewed above is controlling for observable covariates. The papers discussed above vary in the exhaustiveness of the covariates they condition on, in the precision of those covariate measurements, and in the sophistication of their conditioning strategies (multivariate regression, more flexible controls, matching, etc.). But regardless of the particular approach to conditioning on observables, the threat of omitted variable bias and reverse causality looms large. Thus it remains possible that some of the above findings of intervention failure are the result of biased estimation due to non-random assignment.

Approaches to causal identification

There are some notable exceptions to this general pattern. As mentioned above, some specific research questions surrounding foreign intervention are amenable to randomization, which in practice often involves researchers collaborating with better-resourced IGOs or NGOs (as exemplified by Ichino and Schündeln (2012) and Avdeenko and Gilligan (2015)). Survey experiments have also been employed to study various aspects of foreign interventions (Bush and Prather, 2017, 2018; Nielson et al., 2019; Lyall et al., 2013), though these designs are naturally limited in the types of substantive questions they are able to address.

Other studies have found compelling natural experiments that support causal interpretations of the effects of interventions. The routinized procedures of decision-making and power-sharing within international organizations give rise to exogenous variation that can be exploited in observational studies, as demonstrated by Carnegie and Mikulaschek (2017) and Carnegie and Marinov (2017). The former leverages a natural experiment of UN peacekeeper allocations: the rotating presidency of the UN Security Council creates short-term exogenous shifts in UNSC members' influence over UN peacekeeping operations, which the temporarily empowered members use to increase peacekeeper deployments in their own geographic regions. The authors use this as-if random variation to show that peacekeeping reduces civilian victimization in civil wars. The latter study leverages the rotating presidency of the European Council as an exogenous source of variation in foreign aid allocation, as the country holding the presidency during the EU budgeting period will use its temporarily heightened influence to allocate more EU aid to its former colonies; with this design, the authors identify a causal effect of aid on democracy and human rights.

Incidentally, the functioning of a multilateral institution also gives rise to the exogenous variation used in Hyde (2007)'s study of election observation in Armenia, though through a different mechanism: OSCE observers were assigned sporadically to polling stations throughout the country, with a general objective of geographic diversity in coverage but lacking sufficiently detailed information about local political conditions to allow for strategic assignment to polling stations based on anticipated incumbent vote share (or anticipated vote manipulation). A similar mechanism of bureaucratic haphazardness generates the identifying variation in Sexton (2016)'s study of US counterinsurgency aid in Afghanistan. The author claims that weak oversight of program administration, along with bureaucratic incentives to spend down funds quickly and without concern for consequences, creates variation in aid expenditures which can be considered as-if random with respect to insurgent violence.

Another approach to causal identification in the intervention literature comes from shift-share instruments. With this approach, Dube and Naidu (2015) leverage heterogeneity in Colombian municipalities' exposure to supply shocks to US military and antinarcotics assistance: specifically, they interact out-of-region US aid (the "shift") with the presence of a US military base in a given municipality (the "share"), and use this difference-in-differences to isolate exogenous variation in the municipality-year receipt of US aid—which in turn is used to estimate the effect of aid on paramilitary and guerrilla violence. With a similar analysis of a country-year panel, Nunn and Qian (2014) identify exogenous variation in US food aid by interacting annual US wheat prices (translating to wheat surpluses which the US government donates abroad) with a country's total number of aid-receiving years over the period with (proxying for exposure to the wheat supply shock). This enables estimation of the causal impact of food aid on civil conflict. Simpser and Donno (2012) similarly instrument for monitoring of a given national election using the lagged regional incidence of monitoring.

Finally, two of the studies cited above use regression discontinuity designs to support their causal claims. Dell and Querubin (2018) leverage two separate discontinuities. First, a rounding discontinuity in an algorithm employed by the US Air Force, in which a continuous hamlet-level security rating was discretized to a five-point scale, proves predictive of hamlet-level bombing: that is, hamlets just below a rounding cutoff were more likely to be bombed, but are otherwise comparable to hamlets just above the cutoff. Second, the authors examine a geographic discontinuity along the border of areas within Vietnam controlled by different branches of the US military which followed different counterinsurgency doctrines. Crost et al. (2014) use a discontinuous threshold in Philippine municipalities' eligibility for receipt of World Bank assistance to estimate the effect of aid on insurgent violence—exploiting yet another source of exogenous variation that arises from the routinized procedures of multilateral institutions.

Implications

The studies reviewed in the preceding paragraphs demonstrate creative and compelling approaches to estimating the causal impacts of international interventions. What should be clear from this discussion, however, is just how difficult it is to develop research designs on this topic that overcome problems of non-random assignment of interventions. Further, as is the case for empirical research in other domains, there is a perennial tension between internal and external validity. The most credible causal estimates in this literature, in our view, rely on more narrow, within-case variation; but it is unclear the extent to which any one of these internally-valid studies of individual historical cases can be prudently generalized to policy implications for present-day purposes. Similarly, findings generated from idiosyncratic features of multilateral institutions may be limited in their applicability to our understanding of unilateral interventions. And research designs relying on shift-share instruments, while possibly enabling more systematic cross-national analyses, may be susceptible to confounding due to spurious trends (see, for instance, Christian and Barrett (2017)).

We should also be sure not to lose sight of the substantive results that emerge from this group of well-identified studies: generally speaking, these studies reach qualitatively similar conclusions to those reached by the larger set of studies that rely on controlling for observables. The distinction between findings of intervention success versus failure seems to map more closely to a distinction of multilateral versus unilateral interventions, as depicted above, rather than a distinction of well-identified versus inconsistent estimation techniques. (It may be merely incidental that multilateral institutions both execute more successful intervention strategies and lend themselves to better-identified causal estimation.) In short, as a first approximation, the possibility of bias due to non-random assignment of interventions does not seem to be the predominant explanation for the widely documented empirical pattern of failure of foreign interventions. We thus turn to consider other possible explanations.

21.4.1.2 Defining the sample of analysis and accounting for off-path interventions

Beyond non-random assignment, the study of international intervention is bedeviled by some more subtle econometric concerns. One issue arises from the selection of the sample of analysis, and the possibility that the sample of observed cases is shaped in important ways by considerations that arise off the equilibrium path of play. We explicate this concern with a focus on interventions into civil conflicts, for which the issue of off-path expectations seems especially pervasive and problematic, but the general concern applies to other forms of intervention as well.

Studies of the consequences of foreign intervention on civil conflicts typically define their sample by the existence of ongoing civil conflicts. However, it is entirely plausible that the anticipation of intervention affects whether a civil war emerges in the first place. The bias arising from these concerns is potentially large and of indeterminate direction. It could be that the expectation of an overwhelmingly effective foreign intervention motivates would-be combatants to settle their disagreements short of armed conflict, in which case the most successful cases of intervention are removed from the sample, and our estimates of effectiveness are biased toward zero. Or alternatively, the cases in which intervention would be ineffective may be the cases where the party relying on intervention opts out of conflict, thus inflating our estimates of intervention success when analyzing only the cases in which civil war actually occurs.

Some theoretical and empirical work has taken on the task of accounting explicitly for expectations of intervention. A common approach of these studies is to view a third-party intervention as a subsidy that partially offsets the fighting cost of one of the parties to the conflict, or alternatively, as a supplement to that party's fighting capabilities and thus its probability of victory. Cetinyan (2002) takes the latter approach, and argues that a commonly-shared expectation of third party intervention in support of a domestic group will simply be priced into that group's bargaining with the government, shifting the equilibrium bargaining outcome (i.e. the distribution of goods at issue) but not affecting the probability of bargaining failure (i.e. the outbreak of war).

Thyne (2006) approaches the question somewhat differently. He examines (informally) a bargaining context in which the domestic would-be combatants are incompletely informed as to the third party's probability of intervening, but rely on the signals sent by that actor regarding its intentions. By a similar reasoning to Cetinyan's, Thyne predicts that costly signals will be interpreted clearly and will not affect the probability of conflict onset. But cheap signals, he argues, can lead to divergent expectations, which can either increase or decrease the probability of war. The argument relies on an asymmetry in the government's and rebels' processing of signals sent by a potential intervener: in essence, the claim is that rebels are less diplomatically sophisticated and more likely to perceive cheap talk as credible. The rebels' overly-optimistic interpretation of a cheap foreign signal of support for their cause will in turn lead them to demand too much, resulting in a war which the government knows it will win (and so does not make concessions to avoid); while the rebels' misperception in the opposite direction—believing a third party to be more likely to support the government than it actually is—leads them to demand too little, decreasing the risk of conflict.

Yet another approach comes from Cunningham (2016), who focuses on one largely neglected aspect of the domestic conflict bargaining game: the corner solution. Standard bargaining models of conflict tend to focus on interior solutions, in which either peaceful settlement or bargaining failure could occur depending on the size of the offer or demand. But Cunningham argues that, in many contexts, a foreign intervention in support of the government would bring such overwhelming and decisive victory that it pushes the domestic players into a corner solution where the government offers nothing and the rebels prefer that to the costly lottery of war. The author uses Lake (2009)'s index of US security hierarchy as a proxy for intervention expectations, and shows that this index is related to both a decreased probability of civil conflict and an increase in state-perpetrated human rights abuses, where the latter serves to proxy for the state's excessive "demand" in the bargaining game.

Focusing on external support for anti-government forces, Kuperman (2008) argues that such an intervention constitutes a subsidy to the rebels' fighting costs, and that the expectation thereof thus encourages excessively risky behavior on the rebels' part which raises the risk of conflict. Kuperman describes this phenomenon as moral hazard, though Rauchhaus (2009) points out that it may be better understood as a commitment problem. Moral hazard would involve the agent (rebels) taking risky actions which the principal (third-party intervener) cannot observe but would refuse to "insure" were those actions observable. The more typical problem facing the intervener, Rauchhaus argues, is not that it is unaware of the rebels' provocative behavior; rather, the problem is that once the foreign actor has issued a security guarantee to the rebels, it becomes politically difficult or otherwise undesirable to renege on that guarantee, regardless of whether or not the rebels are to blame for the ensuing conflict. Knowing this, rebels will take advantage of the third-party commitment by making more excessive demands of their government than they would make absent the guarantee.

Theoretical work by Spaniel (2018) formalizes this cost-subsidy logic, and demonstrates conditions under which intervention expectations can either raise or lower the risk of conflict, depending on the particular nature of the intervention and the informational asymmetries at play. Considering one-sided incomplete information—side A knows only its own costs of conflict, while side B knows both—Spaniel shows that an intervention to mitigate the costs for A increases the risk of conflict: the expected payoff for fighting increases relative to the expected payoff for any given demand A makes in the bargaining stage, thus inducing A to demand more and increase the probability that B rejects the demand in favor of war. An intervention in support of B, however, can have the opposite effect: by mitigating B's costs, the intervener effectively reduces the variance (from A's perspective) of potential reservation values B might have. A marginal reduction of A's demand thus has a larger effect on reducing the probability of bargaining failure, making the "gamble" of a greedy demand relatively less attractive.

The above studies do not examine the effectiveness of interventions per se, but they all highlight the same general concern for the empirical assessment of interventions' effects: many interventions exist off the equilibrium path of play, because the civil wars in which a third party would intervene do not occur in equilibrium—due, in part or in whole, to the anticipation of the intervention itself. This problem has been examined the most thoroughly and directly with respect to militarized interventions into civil wars, but the general point applies more broadly. Extending beyond the civil war context, recent work has considered how the prospect of foreign intervention affects the day-to-day politics of autocratic regimes: Di Lonardo et al. (2019) model the interaction between an autocrat, a domestic opponent, and a foreign intervener, showing how the autocrat can exploit the prospect of foreign intervention to deter domestic threats (and vice versa); Boutton (2019) finds that the expectation of a supportive intervention (as proxied by defense agreements and security assistance) leads autocrats to engage in more aggressive coup-proofing behavior, even when facing substantial risk of retaliatory violence. Marinov (2005)'s study of the destabilizing effect of economic sanctions points out that the sanctions that are the most damaging to the target leader's survival prospects are also the most likely to occur off the path of play. The general takeaway is that in any situation in which an intervention is likely to occur, rational expectations will drive domestic actors to adjust their behavior in light of that fact, possibly preempting the intervention through their strategic anticipatory responses. An unbiased assessment of the consequences of foreign interventions must take account of these considerations.

To our knowledge, the study that most thoroughly integrates off-path expectations into the analysis of interventions is a recent paper by Gibilisco and Montero (2019). They conduct a structural analysis, with an integrated theoretical and statistical model of conflict onset and intervention, which yields some striking implications: were the five major powers (US, UK, France, Russia, and China) all able to commit to intervene in all civil conflicts, there would be little aggregate effect on the onset of civil conflicts; yet if they made a commitment to *never* intervene, the probability of conflict outbreak would increase substantially. Thus in the real world, the authors conclude, absent any such counterfactual commitments, the coordination that we observe among the major powers "has been maximally successful at deterring civil conflict"—a starkly different qualitative conclusion from that reached by previous empirical analyses which selected on cases of conflict. As an additional implication, the authors find that the US is unique among the major powers in its effect on conflict onset: the average direct effect of a US intervention on a rebel group's payoff for initiating a conflict is positive, and the US's counterfactual unilateral commitment to intervene in all conflicts increases the aggregate risk of conflict onset. This finding calls into question the generalizability of empirical studies focusing exclusively on US interventions, as the other major power interventions may differ not only in the magnitude but also in the direction of their impact.

21.4.1.3 *Measuring and substitutability of intervention strategies*

A separate but similarly pernicious concern for studying the consequences of foreign interventions pertains to the measurement of the independent variable. Recent work by Albornoz and Hauk (2014) outlines some of these concerns:

> Interventions in foreign conflicts are often secretive and indirect and therefore unlikely to be fully reflected in available data. As an additional difficulty, many are the ways for foreign governments to intervene in domestic civil wars. They can provide covert encouragement, allow for (and promote) arms transactions, supply war intelligence and resources, and give sanctuary to rebels or support a third state that is also involved in the civil war.

Rarely will an empirical analysis be able to capture all relevant forms of intervention; indeed, the multitude of means of foreign intervention (as alluded to in this quote and in Section 21.2 above) implies that any study focusing on a single one necessarily omits others from consideration.

Even in its most innocuous form, random measurement error of the independent variable of interest will bias estimated effects towards zero. In most applications, erroneous measurement of international interventions will rarely resemble this best-case scenario. For one, there is reason to suspect that certain kinds of intervention, particularly those of a covert or inconspicuous nature, will be more likely to be recorded systematically when they succeed, or alternatively, when they fail spectacularly and are subsequently discovered, publicized, and politicized. Further, existing studies have found evidence of substitution effects in the various means of intervention that a foreign actor can employ. Regan (2000) finds that a variety of both domestic and international factors predict the tendency of US administrations to switch from one intervention tactic to another in the foreign conflicts in which it involves itself. Similarly focusing on US intervention tactics, Joseph and Poznansky (2018) find that the decision to intervene covertly versus overtly (versus refraining from intervention entirely) is influenced by the quality of information and communication technologies in the target state which heighten the risk of exposure. Garcia-Alonso et al. (2016) demonstrate theoretically how direct intervention and military assistance to a target state are substitutable tactics for an intervening state in its counterterrorism efforts. The general implication of these analyses follows straightforwardly from the logic of omitted variable bias: if a state's use of one intervention tactic is negatively correlated with its use of a different tactic, then finding that one tactic fails to achieve its objectives could either mean that the tactic under examination is ineffecive or that it is simply less effective than the omitted tactic.

Beyond the finding of substitutability of intervention tactics, other work has examined the possibility of spillovers in different third-parties' decisions to intervene at all. Gent (2007) finds evidence of strategic substitution, or free-riding incentives, among potential third-party interveners in civil conflicts when their interests are closely aligned. Studies of interventions by one major power may therefore be biased by omission of interventions by other major powers, with the direction of the bias being a function of the particular issues at stake. In contrast, Gibilisco and Montero (2019) generally find evidence of strategic complementarities among interveners (with the notable of exception of substitution between US and French interventions), a discrepancy which may be due to the fact that Gent selects on cases of civil conflict whereas Gibilisco and Montero attempt to account for off-path interventions.

Given the multitude of concerns surrounding measurement of foreign interventions, a number of recent contributions have found ways to circumvent the problem. The aforementioned study by Albornoz and Hauk aims to identify the effect of foreign interventions on the incidence and onset of civil conflicts, and they do so while excluding measures of intervention from the analysis entirely. Instead they examine the reduced-form relationship between predictors of intervention and consequences of intervention: specifically, the independent variables in their analyses are US presidential approval and the party of the US presidential administration, following the theoretical expectations that both Republican presidents and presidents facing low prospects of reelection will find greater political advantage to intervening in foreign conflicts. They find that these factors indeed increase the global incidence of civil conflict, a result that comports with Gibilisco and Montero's finding that the US is unique among great powers in its propensity to encourage civil conflicts abroad through the prospect of its intervention.

Another reduced-form analysis comes from Lee (2018), who examines the effect of foreign intervention on state consolidation. Hostile neighbors, the author argues, have both a variety of incentives and a variety of means through which to undermine a neighboring state's authority over its entire geographic territory—but the means of interference are neither common across contexts nor systematically observable. The author thus uses as an independent variable a measure of susceptibility to foreign intervention, coded as one for province-years sharing a border with a rival state and zero otherwise. This measure of susceptibility to intervention proves to be a negative predictor of state capacity, which is itself proxied using a measure of accuracy of census data. The reduced-form approaches employed both by Lee and by Albornoz and Hauk entail a tradeoff between two competing methodological concerns: on the one hand, they rely on an untestable claim that the relationship they document is in fact mediated by the unmeasured and unobserved factor of foreign intervention; but the payoff, on the other hand, is that they are able to avoid the more common problem of erroneous or incomplete measures of intervention.

21.4.2 Interveners' objectives

The preceding discussion considered the possibility that econometric issues may account for the general finding that international interventions fail to achieve their objectives. A second class of explanation, independent of any econometric concerns, pertains to the objectives themselves: perhaps scholars have simply been looking at the wrong outcomes, but once we assess interventions according to their actual objectives—rather than their assumed or purported objectives—they prove to be a successful instrument of foreign policy. As Regan (2010) has previously pointed out (with specific reference to civil war interventions but with arguably broader applicability), "[a]s a result of all the research on interventions... we know next to nothing about the goals of the interveners." Here we review a collection of articles which do away with the standard assumptions that interventions are meant to manage or mitigate conflict or to improve governance and development, and examine a range of other outcomes instead.

One possibility is that interventions are not intended to bring about an end to hostilities per se, but rather to enhance the prospects of victory for one side of a domestic conflict, even at the cost of extending the conflict or worsening the pain and suffering borne by the target population. Balch-Lindsay et al. (2008), for instance, use a competing risks model to show that while third-party interventions decrease the hazard of a negotiated settlement to a conflict, they increase the hazard of victory for the beneficiary of the intervention. Examining interventions into elections rather than civil conflicts, Levin (2016) finds that partisan interventions do provide a substantial boost for the party or candidate receiving the external support; simply getting a preferred candidate in office may be the extent of the intervener's aims—even when the intervention carries the risk of inciting domestic terrorism or heightening the risk of democratic breakdown (as documented in Levin (2018, 2019b)).

Several studies reviewed above likewise reject the supposition that interventions aim to democratize or otherwise improve governance within the target states. According to Bueno de Mesquita and Downs (2006), predictions regarding objectives of foreign intervention should be derived from the utility functions of the leaders in the intervening state, and in particular from their incentives to retain office. From this perspective, it is not clear that an intervening power will generally stand to benefit from truly democratizing the target state. Instead, the more politically profitable strategy will often to be to install a less democratic, less domestically accountable regime which will be more accommodating of the intervener's demands—while maintaining a window dressing of democratic institutions to appease the intervener's domestic audiences. Taking a similar perspective on foreign aid, Bueno de Mesquita and Smith (2007); Bueno de Mesquita and Smith (2009) develop and test a model of an aid-for-policy exchange between donor and recipient, in which both participants' primary objective is to maximize their own political survival. Many policy concessions prove more politically beneficial for the donor than will the recipient's democratizing reforms, so it should be entirely unsurprising that aid from strategic donors fails to promote democracy.

Continuing in this spirit, other work has suggested that some interventions are conducted not to improve governance but rather explicitly to undermine it. This is the central claim of Lee (2018) (discussed above), and it comports with the conventional wisdom regarding Russian efforts to interfere in the 2016 US presidential election (Mueller, 2019). A set of experiments by Tomz and Weeks (2020), motivated by the latter example, demonstrate that "even modest forms of electoral intervention can divide and demoralize" the target society—a conclusion consistent with Corstange and Marinov (2012)'s finding of a broadly polarizing effect of foreign interventions in the very different context of the 2009 Lebanese parliamentary elections.

A separate strand of literature locates the impetus for interventions in the private interests that stand to benefit from them. Aidt and Albornoz (2011) develop a formal model in which a foreign government can intervene in a target state's politics so as to impose a set of policies more amendable to the interests of firms within the intervener state that wish to invest in the target state. A similar claim underlies the predictions in Albornoz and Hauk (2014): for an unpopular US president, a foreign intervention provides the opportunity to "gamble for resurrection" in part because US corporations will reward the president with campaign contributions in exchange for expanding business opportunities within the target state. If the primary goal of a foreign intervention is to improve business conditions for domestic firms operating abroad, then any detrimental impact on security, governance, or development in the target state is simply an inconvenient byproduct, rather than evidence of a policy failure.

Examining declassified records of US covert interventions in support of foreign coups d'etat, Dube et al. (2011) find that the US corporations standing to benefit from a given coup enjoy abnormal returns to their stock prices at the time of the coup authorization, but not at the time of the coup itself—indicating that those corporations and their shareholders were privy to the plans for covert operations in advance. This evidence does not necessarily imply that the coups were undertaken for the benefit of corporate interests, but it is certainly consistent with an account of US corporations wielding substantial influence over US intervention decisions. Berger et al. (2013b) systematically examine US covert interventions to install and/or support foreign leaders, and the effect of those interventions on US exports. They find that US interventions not only increase US exports to the target state, but that they do so largely through government purchases, and particularly in sectors in which US firms are comparatively disadvantaged; taken together, these findings provide compelling evidence of the US using covert interventions to exert political influence over the target governments for the benefit of US exporters. Finally, Maurer (2013) documents how interventions aimed at protecting the property or interests of U.S. investors in foreign countries have shifted from politicized military confrontations early in the 20th Century to legal disputes in international forums in recent decades.

To our knowledge, research interrogating the role of private interests in foreign intervention policy has been overwhelmingly US-centric. Future work may seek to extend these analyses beyond the US context, or alternatively, to consider whether these empirical patterns are uniquely resultant of the influence that US corporations wield in shaping US foreign policy.

21.4.3 Persistent failure

There remains another possible explanation for the overall pattern of intervention failure described above: that international interventions do systematically fail to achieve their intended objectives, and that policy makers continue to undertake foreign interventions despite this fact.

A number of formal models provide a theoretical basis for such pessimistic expectations. Luo and Rozenas (2018) identify an "election monitor's curse", whereby a monitor's overall effectiveness in deterring fraud and preventing violence requires that they cause greater violence in fraudulent elections. This gives rise to a sort of impossibility theorem in election observation, in that "election monitors who simultaneously aim to deter fraud and prevent post-election conflict while trying to remain impartial will neither deter election fraud nor prevent conflicts." Russell and Sambanis (2018) likewise identify a set of dilemmas that plague foreign actors' (even well-intended) efforts to promote post-conflict national-building: an "institutional dilemma" arises when the foreign power crowds out the legitimacy of indigenous leaders, while a "sovereignty dilemma" arises when the foreign power succeeds in fostering a national identity, thus inducing the population to reject the foreign presence. A model of economic sanctions by Smith (1995) yields a similar conclusion of the impossibility of effective sanctions: sanctions generally occur and persist only when they are politically beneficial for the sender, and when acquiescing to the policy demand is more costly for the target than abiding the sanctions.

As an empirical matter, a systematic failure of interventions does seem plausible. As discussed above, substantive findings from a handful of causally well-identified studies tend to comport with findings of the broader body of research designs which we might expect to be susceptible to bias due to non-random assignment. And even in cases where the intervener's true objective is essentially unambiguous—there is little doubt that the US genuinely sought to defeat the Viet Cong insurgency in South Vietnam, for instance—we still find compelling empirical evidence of counterproductive means being employed to that end.

If empirical investigation of foreign intervention continues to produce causally-identified findings of intervention failure, assessed according to the interveners' clearly defined objectives, that would be the most puzzling conclusion to emerge from this review. In this case, researchers may want to turn to examination of the bureaucratic, organizational, or group-psychological factors which lead to sub-optimal information aggregation and decision making in the foreign policy domain (Allison, 1971; Halperin and Clapp, 2007; Horowitz et al., 2019). Alternatively, we may wish to interrogate why it is the accumulated scientific knowledge on a policy-relevant subject has failed to translate from the academy into government and policy circles (Desch, 2019).

21.5 Future directions

We close by offering some suggestions for promising directions of future research on foreign interventions.

21.5.1 New research designs

The last several years have seen the emergence of some especially well-identified research designs estimating the causal impact of various international interventions. Almost all of these rely on natural experiments that exploit within-country variation and we believe this is the most promising avenue for the research agenda. Of course natural experiments are, by their nature, idiosyncratic and difficult to generalize to a broader research program. But the recent development of various micro-level datasets, as discussed above, presents promising opportunities for a wide range of novel empirical tests.

Another potentially fruitful avenue for new research designs would be the leveraging of exogenous "supply-side" determinants of interventions in macro-level analyses. For instance, Salehyan (2008) and Bove and Böhmelt (2019) respectively argue that the presence of refugees, and of emigrants more generally, increases the probability that one country intervenes militarily in another; Fordham (1998) and Albornoz and Hauk (2014) demonstrate how domestic political and macroeconomic concerns shape the US President's propensity to use foreign intervention as a tactic for improving his domestic popularity. Insofar as these various predictors of interventions are orthogonal to intervention outcomes in potential target states, they can be incorporated into empirical designs to estimate the consequences of interventions. Researchers may similarly seek to identify supply-side determinants of various non-military means of intervention, such as sanctions, foreign aid, and election monitoring.

21.5.2 New forms of intervention

While the data sources and methodological tools for studying historical interventions continue to expand, so too do the means of intervening. New military technologies, such as drones, alter the lethality, accuracy, and collateral consequences of military interventions, with potentially dramatic strategic and political implications (Fuhrmann and Horowitz, 2017; Horowitz, 2016, 2020; Jetter and Mahmood, 2020). Instruments of cyber warfare may be even more disruptive (Gartzke and Lindsay, 2015; Baliga et al., 2019). Propaganda and (dis-)information campaigns provide potentially powerful means of intervening in a target state's electoral processes and politics more broadly (Golovchenko et al., Forthcoming; Martin et al., 2019; Tomz and Weeks, 2020). All of these fast-moving changes in the contemporary practice of intervention will require the development of new theories and the adaptation of old ones, the collection of new datasets and the execution of new research designs.

Similarly, the release of classified information via leaks and whistle blowers allows for a better understanding of foreign intervention but also opens up concerns about the ethics of using data from these sources.

21.5.3 Changing balance of power

Most existing work on foreign intervention since World War II focuses on the United States, the Soviet Union, and other Western nations. This is partly explained by the distribution of power in the context of the Cold War.

However, the changing balance of power in recent decades, in particular the rise of China as a global leader, points to the importance of researching foreign intervention by new actors. For example, it is often claimed that aid by China is less likely to be conditional on the implementation of political or institutional reforms by recipient countries, which can in turn delay democratic transitions and crowd out aid from other countries (see Dreher et al. (2018) for work on this topic).

There is also limited quantitative research on intervention by other regional leaders such as Iran and Saudi Arabia in the Middle East (one notable exception is Corstange and Marinov (2012) that studies voter's attitudes towards Iranian intervention in the 2009 Lebanese elections).

Finally, future work should study the role of *regional* (as opposed to UN) peacekeeping forces that may have greater legitimacy in the eyes of local actors and may thus be more effective in preventing conflict (see for example, Bara and Hultman (2020)).

References

Abramson, S., Montero, S., Forthcoming. Learning about growth and democracy. American Political Science Review. https://doi.org/10.1017/S0003055420000325.

Aidt, T.S., Albornoz, F., 2011. Political regimes and foreign intervention. Journal of Development Economics 94 (2), 192–201.

Aidt, T.S., Albornoz, F., Hauk, E., 2020. Foreign influence and domestic policy.

Albornoz, F., Hauk, E., 2014. Civil war and US foreign influence. Journal of Development Economics 110, 64–78.

Allison, G.T., 1971. Essence of Decision: Explaining the Cuban Missile Crisis. Number 327.5 (729.1). Little, Brown and Company.

Arias, E., 2017. Patronage by credit: International sources of patronage politics.

Arias, E., Hollyer, J.R., Rosendorff, B.P., 2018. Cooperative autocracies: leader survival, creditworthiness, and bilateral investment treaties. American Journal of Political Science 62 (4), 905–921.

Avdeenko, A., Gilligan, M.J., 2015. International interventions to build social capital: evidence from a field experiment in Sudan. American Political Science Review 109 (3), 427–449.

Balch-Lindsay, D., Enterline, A.J., 2000. Killing time: the world politics of civil war duration, 1820–1992. International Studies Quarterly 44 (4), 615–642.

Balch-Lindsay, D., Enterline, A.J., Joyce, K.A., 2008. Third-party intervention and the civil war process. Journal of Peace Research 45 (3), 345–363.

Baliga, S., Bueno de Mesquita, E., Wolitzky, A., 2019. Deterrence with imperfect attribution.

Bara, C., Hultman, L., 2020. Just different hats? Comparing UN and non-UN peacekeeping. International Peacekeeping 27 (3), 341–368. https://doi.org/10.1080/13533312.2020.1737023.

Beaulieu, E., Hyde, S.D., 2009. In the shadow of democracy promotion: strategic manipulation, international observers, and election boycotts. Comparative Political Studies 42 (3), 392–415.

Beber, B., Gilligan, M.J., Guardado, J., Karim, S., 2017. Peacekeeping, compliance with international norms, and transactional sex in Monrovia, Liberia. International Organization 71 (1), 1–30.

Berger, D., Corvalan, A., Easterly, W., Satyanath, S., 2013a. Do superpower interventions have short and long term consequences for democracy? Journal of Comparative Economics 41 (1), 22–34.

Berger, D., Easterly, W., Nunn, N., Satyanath, S., 2013b. Commercial imperialism? Political influence and trade during the Cold War. The American Economic Review 103 (2), 863–896.

Berman, E., Shapiro, J.N., Felter, J.H., 2011. Can hearts and minds be bought? The economics of counterinsurgency in Iraq. Journal of Political Economy 119 (4), 766–819.

Blair, R.A., 2019a. International intervention and the rule of law after civil war: evidence from Liberia. International Organization 73 (2), 365–398.

Blair, R.A., 2019b. UN peacekeeping and the rule of law after civil war. Working paper. https://papers.ssrn.com/sol3/papers.cfm?abstract_id=3420115.

Boutton, A., 2019. Coup-proofing in the shadow of intervention: alliances, moral hazard, and violence in authoritarian regimes. International Studies Quarterly 63 (1), 43–57.

Bove, V., Böhmelt, T., 2019. International migration and military intervention in civil war. Political Science Research and Methods 7 (2), 271–287.

Bubeck, J., Marinov, N., 2017. Process or candidate: the international community and the demand for electoral integrity. American Political Science Review 111 (3), 535–554.

Bueno de Mesquita, B., Downs, G.W., 2006. Intervention and democracy. International Organization 60 (3), 627–649.

Bueno de Mesquita, B., Smith, A., 2007. Foreign aid and policy concessions. The Journal of Conflict Resolution 51 (2), 251–284.

Bueno de Mesquita, B., Smith, A., 2009. A political economy of aid. International Organization 63 (2), 309–340.

Bush, S.S., Prather, L., 2017. The promise and limits of election observers in building election credibility. The Journal of Politics 79 (3), 921–935.

Bush, S.S., Prather, L., 2018. Who's there? Election observer identity and the local credibility of elections. International Organization 72 (3), 659–692.

Carnegie, A., Marinov, N., 2017. Foreign aid, human rights, and democracy promotion: evidence from a natural experiment. American Journal of Political Science 61 (3), 671–683.

Carnegie, A., Mikulaschek, C., 2017. The promise of peacekeeping: Protecting civilians in civil wars. Available at SSRN 2909822.

Cetinyan, R., 2002. Ethnic bargaining in the shadow of third-party intervention. International Organization 56 (3), 645–677.

Chiozza, G., Goemans, H.E., 2004. International conflict and the tenure of leaders: is war still ex post inefficient? American Journal of Political Science 48 (3), 604–619.

Choi, S.-W., Piazza, J.A., 2017. Foreign military interventions and suicide attacks. The Journal of Conflict Resolution 61 (2), 271–297.

Christian, P., Barrett, C.B., 2017. Revisiting the effect of food aid on conflict: a methodological caution. https://elibrary.worldbank.org/doi/abs/10.1596/1813-9450-8171.

Corstange, D., Marinov, N., 2012. Taking sides in other people's elections: the polarizing effect of foreign intervention. American Journal of Political Science 56 (3), 655–670.

Crost, B., Felter, J., Johnston, P., 2014. Aid under fire: development projects and civil conflict. The American Economic Review 104 (6), 1833–1856.

Cunningham, D.E., 2016. Preventing civil war: how the potential for international intervention can deter conflict onset. World Politics 68 (2), 307–340.

Davis, D.R., Weinstein, D.E., 2002. Bones, bombs, and break points: the geography of economic activity. The American Economic Review 92 (5), 1269–1289.

Dell, M., Querubin, P., 2018. Nation building through foreign intervention: evidence from discontinuities in military strategies. The Quarterly Journal of Economics 133 (2), 701–764.

Desch, M., 2019. Cult of the Irrelevant: The Waning Influence of Social Science on National Security. Princeton University Press.

Di Lonardo, L., Sun, J., Tyson, S., 2019. Autocratic Stability in the Shadow of Foreign Threats. Available at SSRN 3437859.

Djankov, S., Montalvo, J.G., Reynal-Querol, M., 2008. The curse of aid. Journal of Economic Growth 13 (3), 169–194.

Downes, A.B., Monten, J., 2013. Forced to be free?: why foreign-imposed regime change rarely leads to democratization. International Security 37 (4), 90–131.

Downes, A.B., O'Rourke, L.A., 2016. You can't always get what you want: why foreign-imposed regime change seldom improves interstate relations. International Security 41 (2), 43–89.

Dreher, A., Fuchs, A., Parks, B., Strange, A.M., Tierney, M.J., 2018. Apples and dragon fruits: the determinants of aid and other forms of state financing from China to Africa. International Studies Quarterly 62 (1), 182–194. https://doi.org/10.1093/isq/sqx052.

Dube, A., Kaplan, E., Naidu, S., 2011. Coups, corporations, and classified information. The Quarterly Journal of Economics 126 (3), 1375–1409.

Dube, O., Naidu, S., 2015. Bases, bullets, and ballots: the effect of US military aid on political conflict in Colombia. The Journal of Politics 77 (1), 249–267.

Dube, O., Vargas, J.F., 2013. Commodity price shocks and civil conflict: evidence from Colombia. The Review of Economic Studies 80 (4), 1384–1421.

Easterly, W., 2006. The White Man's Burden: Why the West's Efforts to Aid the Rest Have Done so Much Ill and so Little Good. Penguin Press. https://books.google.com/books?id=5Iw5IZCTh-kC.

Easterly, W., Levine, R., Roodman, D., 2004. Aid, policies, and growth: comment. The American Economic Review 94 (3), 774–780. https://www.aeaweb.org/articles?id=10.1257/0002828041464560.

Escribà-Folch, A., 2012. Authoritarian responses to foreign pressure: spending, repression, and sanctions. Comparative Political Studies 45 (6), 683–713.

Escribà-Folch, A., Wright, J., 2010. Dealing with tyranny: international sanctions and the survival of authoritarian rulers. International Studies Quarterly 54 (2), 335–359.

Fordham, B., 1998. Partisanship, macroeconomic policy, and US uses of force, 1949-1994. The Journal of Conflict Resolution 42 (4), 418–439.

Fortna, V.P., 2004. Does peacekeeping keep peace? International intervention and the duration of peace after civil war. International Studies Quarterly 48 (2), 269–292.

Fuhrmann, M., Horowitz, M.C., 2017. Droning on: explaining the proliferation of unmanned aerial vehicles. International Organization 71 (2), 397–418.

Garcia-Alonso, M.D.C., Levine, P., Smith, R., 2016. Military aid, direct intervention and counterterrorism. European Journal of Political Economy 44, 112–135.

Gartzke, E., Lindsay, J.R., 2015. Weaving tangled webs: offense, defense, and deception in cyberspace. Security Studies 24 (2), 316–348.

Gent, S.E., 2007. Strange bedfellows: the strategic dynamics of major power military interventions. The Journal of Politics 69 (4), 1089–1102.

Gibilisco, M., Montero, S., 2019. Do major-power interventions encourage the onset of civil conflict? A structural analysis. http://michaelgibilisco.com/papers/intervention.pdf.

Gibler, D.M., Miller, S.V., Little, E.K., 2016. An analysis of the militarized interstate dispute (MID) dataset, 1816–2001. International Studies Quarterly 60 (4), 719–730.

Gilligan, M.J., Sergenti, E.J., 2008. Do UN interventions cause peace? Using matching to improve causal inference. Quarterly Journal of Political Science 3 (2), 89–122.

Gleditsch, K.S., Ward, M.D., 2006. Diffusion and the international context of democratization. International Organization 60 (4), 911–933.

Goemans, H.E., Gleditsch, K.S., Chiozza, G., 2009. Introducing Archigos: a dataset of political leaders. Journal of Peace Research 46 (2), 269–283.

Golovchenko, Y., Brown, M., Eady, G., Yin, L., Tucker, J.A., Forthcoming. Cross-platform state propaganda: Russian trolls on Twitter and YouTube during the 2016 US presidential election. The International Journal of Press/Politics. https://doi.org/10.1177/1940161220912682.

Gourevitch, P., 1978. The second image reversed: the international sources of domestic politics. International Organization 32 (4), 881–912.

Halperin, M.H., Clapp, P., 2007. Bureaucratic Politics and Foreign Policy. Brookings Institution Press.

Hermann, M.G., Kegley Jr., C.W., 1998. The US use of military intervention to promote democracy: evaluating the record. International Interactions 24 (2), 91–114.

Högbladh, S., Pettersson, T., Themnér, L., 2011. External support in armed conflict 1975–2009: presenting new data. In: 52nd Annual International Studies Association Convention. Montreal, Canada, pp. 16–19.

Hollyer, J.R., Rosendorff, B.P., 2012. Leadership survival, regime type, policy uncertainty and PTA accession. International Studies Quarterly 56 (4), 748–764.

Horowitz, M.C., 2016. Public opinion and the politics of the killer robots debate. Research & Politics 3 (1). https://doi.org/10.1177/2053168015627183.

Horowitz, M., 2020. Do emerging military technologies matter for international politics? Annual Review of Political Science 23, 385–400.

Horowitz, M., Stewart, B.M., Tingley, D., Bishop, M., Resnick Samotin, L., Roberts, M., Chang, W., Mellers, B., Tetlock, P., 2019. What makes foreign policy teams tick: explaining variation in group performance at geopolitical forecasting. The Journal of Politics 81 (4), 1388–1404.

Hultman, L., Peksen, D., 2017. Successful or counterproductive coercion? The effect of international sanctions on conflict intensity. The Journal of Conflict Resolution 61 (6), 1315–1339.

Hultman, L., Kathman, J., Shannon, M., 2013. United Nations peacekeeping and civilian protection in civil war. American Journal of Political Science 57 (4), 875–891.

Hultman, L., Kathman, J., Shannon, M., 2014. Beyond keeping peace: United Nations effectiveness in the midst of fighting. American Political Science Review 108 (4), 737–753.

Hyde, S.D., 2007. The observer effect in international politics: evidence from a natural experiment. World Politics 60 (1), 37–63.

Hyde, S.D., Marinov, N., 2012. Which elections can be lost? Political Analysis 20 (2), 191–210.

Hyde, S.D., Marinov, N., 2014. Information and self-enforcing democracy: the role of international election observation. International Organization 68 (2), 329–359.

Ichino, N., Schündeln, M., 2012. Deterring or displacing electoral irregularities? Spillover effects of observers in a randomized field experiment in Ghana. The Journal of Politics 74 (1), 292–307.

Jetter, M., Mahmood, R., 2020. Gone with the Wind: The Daunting Legacy of Drone Strikes. Working Paper.

Jones, D.M., Bremer, S.A., Singer, J.D., 1996. Militarized interstate disputes, 1816–1992: rationale, coding rules, and empirical patterns. Conflict Management and Peace Science 15 (2), 163–213.

Joseph, M.F., Poznansky, M., 2018. Media technology, covert action, and the politics of exposure. Journal of Peace Research 55 (3), 320–335.

Kelley, J.G., 2012. Monitoring Democracy: When International Election Observation Works, and Why It Often Fails. Princeton University Press.

Kelley, J.G., Simmons, B.A., 2015. Politics by number: indicators as social pressure in international relations. American Journal of Political Science 59 (1), 55–70.

Kim, S.Ki., 2017. Third-party intervention in civil wars and the prospects for postwar development. The Journal of Conflict Resolution 61 (3), 615–642.

Knack, S., 2004. Does foreign aid promote democracy? International Studies Quarterly 48 (1), 251–266.

Kocher, M.A., Pepinsky, T.B., Kalyvas, S.N., 2011. Aerial bombing and counterinsurgency in the Vietnam War. American Journal of Political Science 55 (2), 201–218.

Krain, M., 2005. International intervention and the severity of genocides and politicides. International Studies Quarterly 49 (3), 363–387.

Krasner, S.D., Weinstein, J.M., 2014. Improving governance from the outside in. Annual Review of Political Science 17, 123–145.

Kuperman, A.J., 2008. The moral hazard of humanitarian intervention: lessons from the Balkans. International Studies Quarterly 52 (1), 49–80.

Lake, D.A., 2009. Hierarchy in International Relations. Cornell University Press.

Lebovic, J.H., Voeten, E., 2006. The politics of shame: the condemnation of country human rights practices in the UNCHR. International Studies Quarterly 50 (4), 861–888.

Lee, M.M., 2018. The international politics of incomplete sovereignty: how hostile neighbors weaken the state. International Organization 72 (2), 283–315.

Levin, D.H., 2016. When the great power gets a vote: the effects of great power electoral interventions on election results. International Studies Quarterly 60 (2), 189–202.

Levin, D.H., 2018. Voting for trouble? Partisan electoral interventions and domestic terrorism. Terrorism and Political Violence, 1–17.

Levin, D.H., 2019a. Partisan electoral interventions by the great powers: introducing the PEIG dataset. Conflict Management and Peace Science 36 (1), 88–106.

Levin, D.H., 2019b. A vote for freedom? The effects of partisan electoral interventions on regime type. The Journal of Conflict Resolution 63 (4), 839–868.

Luo, Z., Rozenas, A., 2018. Strategies of election rigging: trade-offs, determinants, and consequences. Quarterly Journal of Political Science 13 (1), 1–28.

Lyall, J., Blair, G., Imai, K., 2013. Explaining support for combatants during wartime: a survey experiment in Afghanistan. American Political Science Review 107 (4), 679–705.

MacMillan, J., 2013. Intervention and the ordering of the modern world. Review of International Studies 39 (5), 1039–1056.

Marinov, N., 2005. Do economic sanctions destabilize country leaders? American Journal of Political Science 49 (3), 564–576.

Martin, D.A., Shaprio, J.N., Nedashkovskaya, M., 2019. Recent trends in online foreign influence efforts. Journal of Information Warfare 18 (3), 15–48.

Mason, T.D., Fett, P.J., 1996. How civil wars end: a rational choice approach. The Journal of Conflict Resolution 40 (4), 546–568.

Mason, T.D., Weingarten Jr, J.P., Fett, P.J., 1999. Win, lose, or draw: predicting the outcome of civil wars. Political Research Quarterly 52 (2), 239–268.

Maurer, N., 2013. The Empire Trap: The Rise and Fall of U.S. Intervention to Protect American Property Overseas, 1893-2013. Princeton University Press. https://books.google.com/books?id=dfx4oAm7pLgC.

McGillivray, F., Stam, A.C., 2004. Political institutions, coercive diplomacy, and the duration of economic sanctions. The Journal of Conflict Resolution 48 (2), 154–172.

Miguel, E., Roland, G., 2011. The long-run impact of bombing Vietnam. Journal of Development Economics 96 (1), 1–15.

Morgan, T.C., Bapat, N., Kobayashi, Y., 2014. Threat and imposition of economic sanctions 1945–2005: updating the TIES dataset. Conflict Management and Peace Science 31 (5), 541–558.

Morrow, J.D., 1991. Alliances and asymmetry: an alternative to the capability aggregation model of alliances. American Journal of Political Science, 904–933.

Mueller, R.S., 2019. Report on the investigation into Russian interference in the 2016 presidential election. https://www.justice.gov/storage/report.pdf.

Nielson, D.L., Hyde, S.D., Kelley, J., 2019. The elusive sources of legitimacy beliefs: civil society views of international election observers. The Review of International Organizations 14 (4), 685–715.

Nunn, N., Qian, N., 2014. US food aid and civil conflict. The American Economic Review 104 (6), 1630–1666.

Palmer, G., D'Orazio, V., Kenwick, M.R., McManus, R.W., 2019. Updating the militarized interstate dispute data: a response to Gibler, Miller, and Little. International Studies Quarterly.

Pearson, F.S., Baumann, R.A., 1993. International military intervention, 1946-1988. Inter-university Consortium for Political and Social Research, Ann Arbor, MI.

Peceny, M., 1999. Forcing them to be free. Political Research Quarterly 52 (3), 549–582.

Peic, G., Reiter, D., 2011. Foreign-imposed regime change, state power and civil war onset, 1920–2004. British Journal of Political Science 41 (3), 453–475.

Peksen, D., 2009. Better or worse? The effect of economic sanctions on human rights. Journal of Peace Research 46 (1), 59–77.

Peksen, D., 2012. Does foreign military intervention help human rights? Political Research Quarterly 65 (3), 558–571.

Peksen, D., Cooper Drury, A., 2010. Coercive or corrosive: the negative impact of economic sanctions on democracy. International Interactions 36 (3), 240–264.

Piazza, J.A., Choi, S.-W., 2018. International military interventions and transnational terrorist backlash. International Studies Quarterly 62 (3), 686–695.

Pickering, J., Kisangani, E.F., 2009. The international military intervention dataset: an updated resource for conflict scholars. Journal of Peace Research 46 (4), 589–599.

Pickering, J., Peceny, M., 2006. Forging democracy at gunpoint. International Studies Quarterly 50 (3), 539–559.

Ramsay, K.W., 2011. Revisiting the resource curse: natural disasters, the price of oil, and democracy. International Organization 65 (3), 507–529.

Rauchhaus, R.W., 2009. Principal-agent problems in humanitarian intervention: moral hazards, adverse selection, and the commitment dilemma. International Studies Quarterly 53 (4), 871–884.

Regan, P.M., 2000. Substituting policies during US interventions in internal conflicts: a little of this, a little of that. The Journal of Conflict Resolution 44 (1), 90–106.

Regan, P.M., 2002. Third-party interventions and the duration of intrastate conflicts. The Journal of Conflict Resolution 46 (1), 55–73.

Regan, P.M., 2010. Interventions into civil wars: a retrospective survey with prospective ideas. Civil Wars 12 (4), 456–476.

Regan, P.M., Aydin, A., 2006. Diplomacy and other forms of intervention in civil wars. The Journal of Conflict Resolution 50 (5), 736–756.

Regan, P.M., Frank, R.W., Aydin, A., 2009. Diplomatic interventions and civil war: a new dataset. Journal of Peace Research 46 (1), 135–146.

Riano, J.F., Valencia Caicedo, F., 2020. The Legacy of the Secret War in Laos. Working paper. https://papers.ssrn.com/sol3/papers.cfm?abstract_id=3723538.

Rosenau, J.N., 1968. The concept of intervention. Journal of International Affairs, 165–176.

Rosenau, J.N., 1969. Intervention as a scientific concept. The Journal of Conflict Resolution 13 (2), 149–171.

Russell, K., Sambanis, N., 2018. The occupier's dilemma: foreign-imposed nation-building after ethnic war. Working paper. http://web.sas.upenn.edu/sambanis/research/articles-on-civil-war/.

Salehyan, I., 2008. The externalities of civil strife: refugees as a source of international conflict. American Journal of Political Science 52 (4), 787–801.

Sarkees, M.R., Schafer, P., 2000. The correlates of war data on war: an update to 1997. Conflict Management and Peace Science 18 (1), 123–144.

Sarkees, M.R., Wayman, F.W., 2010. Resort to War: A Data Guide to Inter-State, Extra-State, Intra-State, and Non-state Wars, 1816-2007. Cq Pr.

Sexton, R., 2016. Aid as a tool against insurgency: evidence from contested and controlled territory in Afghanistan. American Political Science Review 110 (4), 731–749.

Simpser, A., Donno, D., 2012. Can international election monitoring harm governance? The Journal of Politics 74 (2), 501–513.

Smith, A., 1995. The success and use of economic sanctions. International Interactions 21 (3), 229–245.

Spaniel, W., 2018. Only here to help? Bargaining and the perverse incentives of international institutions. International Studies Quarterly 62 (1), 14–22.

Sullivan, P.L., Koch, M.T., 2009. Military intervention by powerful states, 1945—2003. Journal of Peace Research 46 (5), 707–718.

Thyne, C.L., 2006. Cheap signals with costly consequences: the effect of interstate relations on civil war. The Journal of Conflict Resolution 50 (6), 937–961.

Tomz, M., Weeks, J.L., 2020. Public opinion and foreign electoral intervention. American Political Science Review.

Waltz, K.N., 1959. Man, the State, and War: A Theoretical Analysis. Columbia University Press.

Wood, R.M., 2008. "A hand upon the throat of the nation": economic sanctions and state repression, 1976–2001. International Studies Quarterly 52 (3), 489–513.

Wood, R.M., Kathman, J.D., Gent, S.E., 2012. Armed intervention and civilian victimization in intrastate conflicts. Journal of Peace Research 49 (5), 647–660.

Wright, J., 2009. How foreign aid can foster democratization in authoritarian regimes. American Journal of Political Science 53 (3), 552–571.

The ancient origins of the wealth of nations

22

Quamrul H. Ashraf[a,b], Oded Galor[c], and Marc Klemp[d]

[a]*Department of Economics, Williams College, Williamstown, MA, United States*
[c]*Department of Economics, Brown University, Providence, RI, United States*
[d]*Department of Economics, University of Copenhagen, Copenhagen K, Denmark*

22.1 Introduction

The past two centuries have borne witness to an extraordinary transformation in living standards across the globe. After stagnating for millennia preceding the Industrial Revolution, income per capita in the world economy has since undergone a remarkable 17-fold increase, bringing dramatic improvements in education, health, and wealth around the world. Nonetheless, the fruits of these improvements have not been equally shared across nations. Variation across societies in the timing of their take-off from the epoch of stagnation to the modern era of sustained economic growth has generated a great divergence in income per capita.[1] While global inequality in living standards was rather moderate across societies and regions until the nineteenth century, it has since intensified considerably, as reflected by a 5-fold increase in the income gap between the richest and poorest regions of the world.

Over the last two decades, an influential body of research has uncovered the ancient origins of the astounding transformation in the pattern of economic development across regions, countries, and ethnic groups. While early research focused on the proximate forces that contributed to the divergence in living standards in the era following the Industrial Revolution, attention has shifted toward ultimate, deep-rooted, prehistoric factors that may have affected the course of comparative development since the emergence of *Homo sapiens*. A significant portion of research on the long shadow of prehistory has highlighted the roles played by evolutionary forces since the Neolithic Revolution and the prehistoric "out of Africa" migration of humans in shaping the composition of individual and cultural traits as well as the degree of diversity among populations across the globe.

The exploration of the interaction between evolutionary processes and the pattern of economic development has centered around two fundamental lines of inquiry. The first avenue examines the effect of the environment on the evolution of individual and cultural traits as well as the contribution of this evolutionary process to economic development in the long run. The central hypothesis in this research avenue suggests that in the era following the Neolithic Revolution, Malthusian pressures acted as a key determinant of the size of a population and conceivably shaped, via the forces of natural selection, its composition as well. Lineages of individuals whose traits were complementary to the economic

---

[b] Ashraf acknowledges research support from the Center for Development Economics at Williams College.
[1] See Galor (2011).

environment generated higher levels of income and, thus, a larger number of surviving offspring.[2] The gradual increase in the representation of these growth-enhancing traits in the population contributed to the process of development and the emergence of modern growth.

This body of research has identified several traits that may have proliferated during the Malthusian era due to their conduciveness to human-capital formation, technological progress, and economic development. In particular, these studies have examined the evolution of predisposition towards child quality, time preference, risk and loss aversion, and resistance to infectious diseases, highlighting the contribution of this evolutionary process to the transition from stagnation to growth.

The second research avenue on the interaction between human evolution and the process of economic development has explored the persistent effect of the prehistoric exodus of *Homo sapiens* from Africa on the diversity of human traits and, thus, on comparative economic development across societies from the dawn of civilization to the contemporary era. In particular, this line of research suggests that migratory distances from the cradle of humankind in East Africa to indigenous settlements across the globe diminished their levels of interpersonal diversity and, thereby, generated a persistent hump-shaped influence on development outcomes, reflecting a fundamental trade-off between beneficial and detrimental effects of diversity on productivity at the societal level. Although diversity can reduce interpersonal trust and social cohesiveness, and can hence adversely affect the productivity of society, diversity can also foster the cross-fertilization of ideas for innovations and stimulate gains from specialization, and it can thus contribute to society's productivity. Therefore, in the presence of diminishing marginal effects of diversity and homogeneity on productivity, the economic performance of ethnic groups, countries, or regions possessing intermediate levels of diversity would be expected to be higher than that associated with more homogeneous or heterogeneous societies.

Consistent with each of the fundamental building blocks of this hypothesis, interpersonal population diversity has been shown to have contributed to ethnocultural heterogeneity, diminished interpersonal trust, and the emergence of social conflicts. Moreover, evidence suggests that interpersonal diversity has fostered innovative activity, occupational heterogeneity, and gains from specialization. Further, interpersonal diversity appears to have shaped the nature of both precolonial and contemporary political institutions. In particular, although diversity may have triggered the development of institutions for mitigating the adverse influence of population diversity on social cohesion, the contribution of diversity to economic inequality and class stratification may have ultimately led to the formation and persistence of extractive and autocratic institutions.

This essay surveys the existing literature on the role of evolutionary processes in comparative economic development. Section 22.2 is devoted to explorations of the effect of the environment on the evolution of individual and cultural traits——predisposition towards child quality, time preference, loss aversion, and risk aversion, amongst others——and the contribution of these evolutionary process to economic development in the long run. Section 22.3 focuses on the examination of the persistent impact of the prehistoric exodus of *Homo sapiens* from Africa on the global distribution of interpersonal population diversity and, consequently, on comparative economic development across societies. Section 22.4 provides some brief concluding remarks.

---

[2] In contrast, due to the egalitarian nature of hunter-gatherer societies, the forces of evolutionary selection within a society were largely muted prior to the Neolithic Revolution and the emergence of the nuclear family.

22.2 Evolutionary processes and the transition from stagnation to growth

Geographical characteristics have shaped the evolution of individual and cultural traits, as well as their lasting effects on the transition from stagnation to growth. These evolutionary processes and their contribution to the variation in preferences and cultural traits across countries, regions, and ethnic groups are therefore critical for understanding inequality across societies.

The impact of the environment on the evolution of individual and cultural traits as well as the contribution of this evolutionary process to economic development in the long run have been the subject of an intensive research program over the past two decades. The fundamental hypothesis in this body of research, originating in Galor and Moav (2002), suggests that in the era following the Neolithic Revolution, Malthusian pressures, which acted as a key determinant of the size of a population, shaped via the forces of natural selection, the composition of traits in society. Lineages of individuals whose traits were complementary to the economic or geographical environment generated higher levels of income and, thus, in this Malthusian environment, a larger number of surviving offspring. This reproductive success gradually increased the prevalence of growth-enhancing traits in the population, contributing to the process of development, and amplifying the pace of the transition from stagnation to growth across the globe.

Consistent with evidence regarding significant human evolutionary adaptations since the onset of the Neolithic Revolution, Galor and Moav (2002) additionally argue that, due to the egalitarian nature of hunter-gatherer societies and the resultant neutrality of economically productive traits for reproductive success, these forces of evolutionary selection of individual and cultural traits had been largely muted prior to the adoption of farming and the emergence of the nuclear family. The transition to sedentary agriculture and the emergence of property rights, however, reinforced the association between parental traits and reproductive success and, thus, boosted the pace of these evolutionary processes.

This section surveys evolutionary growth theories that have explored the evolutionary forces that emerged during the Malthusian epoch and have generated testable predictions that have been confirmed to be central for the understanding of the process of development and the transition from stagnation to growth. In particular, these theories have explored the evolution of various societal traits, such as predisposition toward child quality, the ability to delay gratification, as well as risk and loss aversion, that may have been subjected to positive selection during the Malthusian era due to their conduciveness to human-capital formation, technological innovations, and economic development.[3] Their testable predictions link ancestral geographical and climatic characteristics, as well as the stages of economic development, to the prevalence of these traits in a contemporary population.

22.2.1 Evolution of preference for child quality

Predisposition towards investment in child quality has been instrumental for the process of human-capital formation, the onset of the demographic transition, and the take-off of the world economy from an epoch of Malthusian stagnation to an era of sustained economic growth.

---

[3] This interaction between human evolution and the process of development may capture cultural and, possibly, genetic propagation mechanisms for the intergenerational transmission of individual and societal traits (Bisin and Verdier, 2000, 2001, 2011; Weibull and Salomonsson, 2006; Bowles and Gintis, 2011; Robson and Samuelson, 2011; Sacerdote, 2011; Doepke and Zilibotti, 2014).

Galor and Moav (2002) have advanced the hypothesis that during the Malthusian epoch, natural selection brought about a gradual increase in the prevalence of traits associated with stronger preferences for the quality rather than the quantity of offspring. The positive influence of this evolutionary process on investment in human capital stimulated technological progress and contributed to the reinforcing interaction between human-capital investment and technological progress, ultimately triggering the demographic transition and accelerating the shift to a state of sustained economic growth. However, the onset of the demographic transition reversed this evolutionary process and generated an evolutionary advantage to individuals with a predisposition toward higher fertility and lower investment in human capital, thereby limiting the rates of human-capital accumulation and economic growth in the long run.[4]

22.2.1.1 Theory

Consider a society during the Malthusian epoch. It consists of two types of individuals: the Quantity type and the Quality type. Individuals of the Quantity type allocate their limited resources between consumption and child rearing, whereas those of the Quality type additionally allocate some resources to the quality (human capital) of their offspring.

Although a quantity-biased preference has a positive effect on fertility rates and may appear to generate a direct evolutionary advantage, it adversely affects the quality of offspring, their income, and their fitness, and it may therefore generate an evolutionary disadvantage. In contrast, the Quality type will generate higher income and, therefore, to the extent that their quality bias is moderate, enjoy higher reproductive success. Thus, the prevalence of this growth-enhancing trait will gradually increase in the population and will contribute to the formation of human capital, the onset of the demographic transition, and the transition to modern growth.

However, in the post-demographic-transition era, as higher income no longer translates to greater reproductive success, the Quantity type is favored by evolutionary forces. Namely, as technological progress brings about increases in income and relaxes Malthusian pressures, the importance of income in fertility decisions is diminished, and the inherent advantage of higher valuation of quantity in reproduction starts to dominate. As individuals whose preferences are biased toward child quantity gain the evolutionary advantage, human-capital formation subsides, diminishing the long-run growth potential of the economy.

22.2.1.2 Evidence

The selection of greater predisposition towards child quality in a Malthusian environment has been explored by Galor and Klemp (2019). Using an extensive data set of genealogical records for nearly half a million individuals in Quebec between the 16th and 18th centuries, the study establishes that while higher fecundity was associated with a larger number of children, perhaps paradoxically, moderate fecundity maximized the number of descendants after several generations, reflecting the beneficial effects of lower fecundity on various measures of child quality (e.g., marriageability and literacy) and, thus, on the reproductive success of each child (Fig. 22.1).[5] Moreover, the analysis further suggests that

---

[4] The quantitative analysis of Collins et al. (2014) corroborates this hypothesis.

[5] Evidence from England in the 1541–1851 time period reveals a similar pattern. Middle-class families that tended to invest in their children's human capital had the largest number of children surviving to adulthood (de la Croix et al., 2019). These data also indicate the negative impact of high fecundity on offspring quality (Klemp and Weisdorf, 2019).

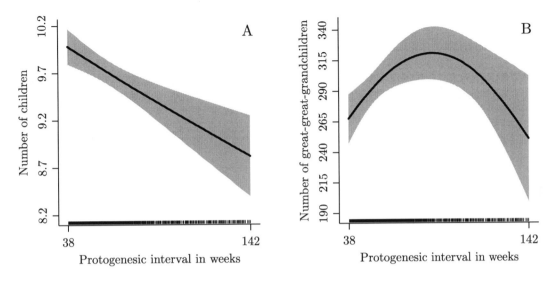

FIGURE 22.1

Fecundity and long-run reproductive success. *Notes*: This figure depicts the predicted number of children (panel A) and of great-great-grandchildren (panel B) as functions of the level of fecundity of 3,798 heads of lineages, where fecundity is inversely captured by the protogenesic interval (i.e., the time interval between the date of marriage and the first live birth). The shaded areas represent 95 percent confidence bands, and the rugs at the bottom of each panel represent the distribution of observations. *Source*: Galor and Klemp (2019).

over this period, evolutionary forces decreased the level of fecundity and, thus, increased the prevalence of predisposition towards child quality in the population.

Interestingly, the conditions that were faced by the founder population of Quebec during this time period of high fertility may have resembled the environment that anatomically modern humans confronted during their migration from Africa, as they settled new territories where the carrying capacity of the environment was an order of magnitude greater than the size of the founder population. Thus, the findings suggest that during the high-fertility regime of the Malthusian epoch, in which evolutionary forces could have had a significant impact on the composition of the population (e.g., during the Neolithic transition and the formation of sedentary agricultural communities), natural selection favored individuals with stronger predisposition towards child quality, contributing to the formation of human capital, the onset of the demographic transition, and the evolution of societies from an epoch of stagnation to sustained economic growth.

While Galor and Klemp (2019) uncover evidence in line with Galor and Moav's (2002) theoretical predictions for the pre-demographic-transition Malthusian epoch, the findings of Kong et al. (2017) are consistent with their predictions for the post-demographic-transition era. Specifically, based on data for Icelandic individuals born between 1910 and 1990, Kong et al. (2017) uncover evidence for an evolutionary disadvantage of parental genomic variants associated with children's educational attainment.

22.2.2 Evolution of time preference

Future-oriented behavior, as reflected by the ability to delay gratification and the rate of time preference, has been pivotal for the growth process and long-run prosperity. Long-term orientation has governed the pace of human- and physical-capital formation, technological advancement, and economic growth, and has been widely considered as a fundamental determinant of the wealth of nations.

Galor and Özak (2016) has advanced the hypothesis and established empirically that the trait of long-term orientation, reflecting individual characteristics as well as societal norms, has evolved over the course of human history in a process of adaptation to local geographical environments. Pre-industrial agroclimatic characteristics that were conducive to higher crop returns, triggered an evolutionary process of adaptation, as well as learning to delay gratification, that contributed to the prevalence of long-term orientation in the contemporary era. In line with this hypothesis, variation in the degree of long-term orientation across individuals, as well as across countries and regions, have been traced to variation in the natural return to agricultural investment across the ancestral environments of these individuals and societies.

22.2.2.1 Theory

Consider farmers during the Malthusian epoch who are contemplating between two strategies regarding the use of their land. The first strategy is to exploit the entire plot for gathering, fishing, and hunting, in order to guarantee a modest, yet stable, year-round food supply. The second strategy is to use only part of the land for ongoing consumption while planting crops on the remaining segment. This investment strategy would generate a larger food supply in the long run, but it would require a capacity for delayed gratification, since it would involve sacrificing short-term consumption for the sake of greater consumption in the future.

According to the theory, the investment strategy was more profitable in regions in which crops generated a higher rate of return (higher average daily yield) over the required period from planting to harvesting. In areas with relatively high returns on harvestable crops, farmers that chose to engage in crop cultivation, forgoing consumption units in the present for additional ones in the future, enjoyed higher income and, in the Malthusian era, higher reproductive success. Their rewarding experience reinforced their outlook about the virtues of delayed gratification, and this enhanced capacity was transmitted to their offspring and diffused to society at large. The capacity for delayed gratification, therefore, gradually spread in the population, and this essential trait for the growth process became more prevalent in those regions.

The ability to delay gratification might have spread through a process of biological or cultural evolution. Since this trait contributed to higher earnings and, thus, a larger number of children, if this ability is transmitted genetically from parent to child, the number of carriers of this trait would have increased over time, and it would inevitably become more prevalent in the population. In addition, the ability to delay gratification could have plausibly diffused through a process of cultural evolution. Parents could have taught their children about the virtues of delayed gratification, and society as a whole could have emulated farmers that amassed wealth due to their ability to delay gratification, increasing the representation of this trait in the population.

The theory generates several testable predictions regarding the effect of the natural rate of return to agricultural investment on the rate of time preference. First, in societies in which the ancestral population was exposed to a higher crop yield (for a given growth cycle), the rewarding experience of agricultural investment triggered selection, adaptation, and learning processes that gradually increased

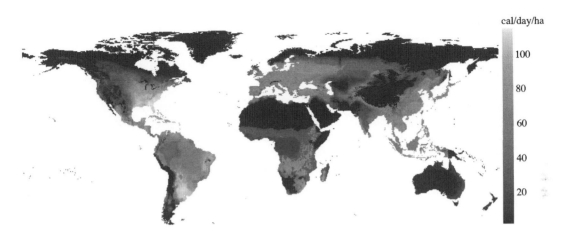

FIGURE 22.2

The global distribution of the potential caloric return of native crops before AD 1500. *Notes*: This figure depicts the worldwide distribution of daily crop yields, as measured by the ratio of total crop yields to crop growth cycles, for crops that were native to a location before AD 1500. Lighter (darker) shaded areas of the map correspond to regions possessing higher (lower) daily crop yields. *Source*: Based on data from Galor and Özak (2016).

the representation of the trait of stronger long-term orientation in the population. Thus, individuals, countries, and regions whose ancestral populations resided in environments with higher natural return to agricultural investment would be expected to possess stronger long-term orientation. Second, societies that benefited from an expansion in the spectrum of suitable crops in the post-1500 period, and could therefore have adopted crops with higher rates of return, would be expected to experience further gains in the degree of long-term orientation.

22.2.2.2 Evidence

Potential crop returns, as measured by the maximal average daily calories that can be generated by an acre of land, over the period from planting to harvesting, are distributed rather unevenly across the globe and even within continents and modern national borders (Fig. 22.2). Consistent with the proposed theory, individuals, countries, and regions whose ancestral populations originated in areas with higher potential caloric returns tend to be more forward-looking.

Clearly, the positive relationship between caloric return and the ability to delay gratification is not necessarily indicative of an evolutionary process. It might instead reflect the choice of farmers, with a greater ability to delay gratification, to adopt crops with higher caloric returns that require longer-term investment. However, *potential* caloric return, as predicted by agroclimatic characteristics that are orthogonal to human cultivation, is shown by Galor and Özak (2016) to impart a positive impact on the ability to delay gratification, reaffirming the influence of these geographical attributes on the evolution of the ability to delay gratification.

Nevertheless, the association across regions between potential caloric return and the ability to delay gratification could have reflected the selective migration of individuals that were able to delay gratification into regions better-suited for high-yield crops that required long-term investment. However, the findings show that the potential for adoption of high-yield New World crops (such as maize and the potato) following the Columbian Exchange had a significant impact on the capacity for delayed gratification among the already settled populations of Europe and Asia, mitigating the potential role of selective migration in this relationship and lending further credence to the evolutionary mechanism.

Exploiting a natural experiment associated with the expansion of suitable crops for cultivation in the course of the Columbian Exchange (i.e., the pervasive exchange of crops between the New and Old World), Galor and Özak (2016) establish that pre-industrial agroclimatic characteristics that were conducive to generating higher returns to agricultural investments, indeed triggered selection, adaptation, and learning processes that have had a persistent positive influence on the prevalence of long-term orientation in the contemporary era. This suggests that the evolutionary process has taken place in both the pre- and the post-1500 time periods. Furthermore, these agroclimatic characteristics have had a culturally-embodied impact on economic behavior such as technological adoption, human-capital formation, the propensity to save, and the inclination to smoke.

The empirical analysis is robust to the use of distinct samples and to examining patterns at different units of analysis, exploiting variation in preferences and behavior across individuals, countries, and ethnic groups, based on data from the European Social Survey (ESS), the General Social Survey (GSS), a cross-country sample, the World Values Survey (WVS), the Ethnographic Atlas (EA), and the Standard Cross-Cultural Sample (SCCS).

This evidence therefore suggests that crop yields have shaped humans' capacity for delayed gratification through a process of adaptation. The evidence further suggests that the capacity for delayed gratification among second-generation immigrants that currently reside in Europe and the United States is linked to potential crop yields in their parental homelands rather than in the adopted countries where they were born and raised. In other words, the capacity for delayed gratification was determined by cultural attributes that had evolved in the distant past and were passed down intergenerationally.

22.2.3 Evolution of loss aversion

Entrepreneurship is a significant determinant of economic prosperity in the modern world. One of its main determinants—the degree of loss aversion—has evolved over the course of human history in a process of adaptation to the climatic environment. Thus, the evolutionary origins of this intriguing phenomenon of loss aversion—the tendency of people to attach disproportionate weight to losses than to comparable gains (Tversky and Kahneman, 1991)—has critical implications for the understanding of human behavior and the growth process.

In light of existing evidence that resources per capita during the Malthusian era were near the subsistence-consumption level, lineages of individuals that were subjected to significant adverse transitory productivity shocks during this period became extinct, while lineages of individuals that experienced favorable climatic realizations enjoyed higher reproductive success only temporarily. In other words, unfavorable climatic conditions could have driven entire populations to extinction, while transitory favorable conditions bestowed only temporary gains in productivity and modest and temporary gains in reproductive success.

The potential for catastrophes arising from adverse climatic fluctuations made it advantageous from an evolutionary viewpoint to minimize losses even on the account of forgoing expected potential gains. Thus, in the present day, the tendency of humans to attribute greater importance to losses than comparable gains may reflect the formation of natural instincts shaped in an evolutionary process that unfolded during an epoch when losses often drove populations to extinction.

Galor and Savitskiy (2020) explore the origins of loss aversion and the variation in its prevalence across regions, nations, and ethnic groups. They advance the hypothesis and establish empirically that the evolution of loss aversion in the course of human history can be traced to the adaptation of humans to the asymmetric effects of climatic shocks on reproductive success during the epoch in which subsistence consumption was a binding constraint. Regions with greater climatic volatility and lower spatial correlation in climatic shocks experienced an evolutionary process that contributed to the prevalence of lower degrees of loss aversion in the contemporary era.

22.2.3.1 Theory

Consider a continuum of loss-averse individuals on the edge of the subsistence consumption constraint during the Malthusian epoch. They deliberate between two agricultural modes of production: a safe one and a risky one. The safe mode of production is climatically insensitive, assuring a subsistence level of consumption as well as one surviving offspring. The risky mode, in contrast, is vulnerable to climatic volatility, but it generates an expected consumption above subsistence, and, thus, expected reproductive success above replacement in this Malthusian environment, although it may lead to extinction following unfavorable climatic realizations.

Ex ante, individuals who are loss averse may favor the safe agricultural practices that would assure their subsistence consumption and reproductive success, minimizing the risk for catastrophic realizations that would inevitably make their dynasties extinct. In contrast, individuals who are loss neutral may favor the riskier agricultural practices that are associated with a higher expected return, higher reproductive success, but a higher risk of extinction.

In a Malthusian environment characterized by aggregate productivity shocks, loss-neutral individuals who were engaged in risky agricultural practices would have eventually been affected by a catastrophic climatic realization and would have become extinct. Hence, in an environment characterized by aggregate productivity shocks, the trait of loss aversion, and the associated choice of the safer production mode, would have been favored by the forces of natural selection and would have dominated in the population in the long run.

However, in a Malthusian environment characterized by idiosyncratic shocks, although the trait of loss aversion would have still maximized the survival probability of each individual, some loss-neutral dynasties would have experienced a long realization of favorable climatic conditions and, thus, significantly higher reproductive success, and would have ultimately dominated in the population in the long run.

The theory generates two fundamental testable predictions about the climatic origins of the observed variation in predisposition toward loss-aversion. It suggests that individuals, as well as societies, that originate from regions of the world in which climatic shocks tended to be spatially correlated, and thus aggregate in nature, should be characterized by a greater intensity of loss aversion. In contrast, descendants of populations indigenous to regions of the world that had been characterized by greater climatic volatility should tend to exhibit a higher degree of loss neutrality.

22.2.3.2 Evidence

Empirical evidence based on historical climate data and contemporary survey and experimental data on loss aversion are in line with the theory. Exploiting regional variations in vulnerability to climatic shocks, as well as their exogenous changes over the course of the Columbian Exchange, the analysis of Galor and Savitskiy (2020) suggests that individuals and ethnic groups that originate from regions marked by greater climatic volatility have a higher predisposition toward loss neutrality, while descendants of populations native to regions where climatic conditions tended to be spatially correlated, and where shocks were, thus, aggregate in nature, are characterized by a greater intensity of loss aversion. These findings are robust to the use of distinct samples and to exploiting variations at different units of analysis (i.e., individuals, ethnic groups, and countries).

Remarkably, populations retain their predisposition to loss aversion even when they depart from their native homelands. Among European-born and American-born children of immigrants, the degree of loss aversion reflects the climatic conditions of their *parental* countries of origin, rather than the climate, institutions, or economic incentives in the location where they were born and raised. That is, the critical determinants of individuals' loss aversion are the climatic conditions in their ancestral homelands and the contribution of these historical factors to the evolution and intergenerational transmission of cultural traits over centuries or millennia.

22.2.4 Causes and consequences of other evolutionary processes
22.2.4.1 Evolution of entrepreneurial spirit

Galor and Michalopoulos (2012) have explored the coevolution of entrepreneurial spirit and the process of long-run economic development. Their analysis suggests that Darwinian selection of entrepreneurial traits may have played a significant role in the process of economic development and influenced the dynamics of inequality both within and across societies. Specifically, they argue that entrepreneurial spirit evolved nonmonotonically over the course of human history. In early stages of development, risk-tolerant growth-promoting traits possessed an evolutionary advantage, and their increased representation in the population over time accelerated the pace of technological progress and, thereby, the process of economic development. In mature stages of development, however, risk-averse traits gained an evolutionary advantage, diminishing the growth potential of advanced economies and contributing to convergence in economic growth across countries.

The predictions of the theory are in line with the recent findings of Bouchouicha and Vieider (2019). In particular, their findings indicate the existence of a positive association between risk tolerance and the number of children in early stages of development, and a negative association in later stages of development, as reflected by a negative impact of the interaction between income per capita and risk tolerance on the fertility rate across countries. Moreover, consistent with the theory, the analysis suggests that risk tolerance is less prevalent in richer societies.

22.2.4.2 Evolution of physical and biological traits

The evolutionary origins of worldwide variations in resistance to infectious diseases have been examined by Galor and Moav (2007). This research hypothesizes and provides empirical evidence that the socioeconomic transformations associated with the Neolithic Revolution triggered an evolutionary process that imparted positive selective pressures on disease resistance. Consequently, heterogeneity across societies in their length of exposure to this evolutionary process, as captured by their differential timing of the transition to sedentary agriculture, may have significantly shaped the contemporary global distribution of human longevity. Cook (2015) further links this evolutionary process to the degree of intrapopulation genetic diversity in the human leukocyte antigen (HLA) system.

In related research, Lagerlöf (2007) has argued that resource depletion associated with technological progress and rising population density during the Malthusian epoch may have triggered a shift in reproductive advantage from large to small body sizes, thereby generating an endogenous reversal of the long-run time trend in human body mass.[6]

22.2.4.3 Barrier effects

Differential evolutionary processes across societies and regions may have contributed to their cultural and biological divergence, creating biocultural and institutional barriers to the diffusion of development across countries and regions.

In line with such "barrier effects" associated with cultural and biological divergence, this research program, pioneered by Spolaore and Wacziarg (2009), has established a reduced-form contribution of pairwise F_{ST} genetic distance between societies to dyadic differences in income per capita, technology adoption, and institutional quality, amongst other outcomes. The exploited measure predominantly captures the time elapsed since two societies diverged from a common ancestral population and, therefore, the time over which intersocietal cultural and biological differences could have accumulated due to the forces of cultural and genetic drift, differential selection, and divergent gene-culture coevolution (Spolaore and Wacziarg, 2014).[7]

22.2.5 Evolutionary processes in genetic traits since the Neolithic Revolution

Existing scientific evidence suggests that the composition of genetic traits within a population has evolved rather swiftly in the course of human history and that differential evolutionary processes have transpired in human populations since the onset of the Neolithic Revolution, lending credence to the nature and intensity of the evolutionary forces highlighted by evolutionary growth theories.[8] The transition from hunting and gathering to sedentary agriculture apparently triggered selection at genetic loci associated with skin pigmentation, resistance to infectious diseases, height, and diet. The differential onset of the Neolithic transition across regions has therefore contributed to the emergence of variations across populations in their composition of genetic traits.

Lactase persistence emerged among European and Near Eastern populations due to their early domestication of dairy-producing animals during the Neolithic Revolution, whereas in regions that experienced a delayed exposure to these domesticates, a larger fraction of the contemporary adult population continues to experience lactose intolerance (Bersaglieri et al., 2004; Burger et al., 2007; Tishkoff et al., 2007). Similarly, genetic immunity to malaria provided by the sickle cell trait is highly prevalent among the descendants of African populations whose early engagement in agriculture provided fertile breeding grounds for mosquitoes and, thus, elevated the incidence of malaria, whereas

---

[6] The long-run codetermination of human physiology and economic development is explored further by Dalgaard and Strulik (2015, 2016).

[7] The study by Becker et al. (2020) is another example of the application of pairwise F_{ST} genetic distance as a measure of the temporal divergence between societies. Specifically, the authors uncover evidence linking this measure with dyadic intersocietal differences in economic preferences, particularly risk aversion and the prosocial traits of altruism, positive reciprocity, and trust.

[8] Voight et al. (2006) detected about 700 regions of the human genome in which genetic loci appear to have been reshaped by natural selection within the past 5,000 to 15,000 years. Moreover, Mekel-Bobrov et al. (2005) reports that a variant of the *ASPM* gene (a specific regulator of brain size in the lineage leading to *Homo sapiens*) arose in humans merely about 5,800 years ago and has since swept into high frequency under strong positive selection. Additional evidence on recent human adaptive evolution is provided by Sabeti et al. (2006), Hawks et al. (2007), and Nielsen et al. (2007).

this trait is largely absent among descendants of populations that did not practice early agriculture (Livingstone, 1958; Wiesenfeld, 1967; Tishkoff et al., 2001).

Moreover, evidence based on comparing the genomes of ancient West Eurasians, dated to have lived between 6500 BCE and 300 BCE, with the genomes of present-day Europeans indicates that adaptive immunity was apparently favored by natural selection due to the rise in population density and the associated increase in the prevalence of infectious diseases over the course of the Neolithic Revolution. In addition, lactase persistence, reduced blood plasma triglyceride levels, and regulators of vitamin D levels were selected to provide protection against the ergothioneine deficiency associated with the shift from hunter-gatherer to agricultural diets. Furthermore, early Neolithic migrants to southern Europe were under selection pressures that favored decreased height, while the selection of increased height operated on the steppe populations that ultimately migrated to northern Europe (Mathieson et al., 2015).[9]

22.3 The "out of Africa" hypothesis of comparative development
22.3.1 The main hypothesis

An emergent body of research on the deep roots of comparative development has advanced the hypothesis that migratory distances from the cradle of humankind in East Africa to the ancestral populations of contemporary societies affected the worldwide distribution of interpersonal diversity and generated a persistent hump-shaped effect on development outcomes, reflecting the trade-off between the beneficial and detrimental effects of diversity on productivity at the societal level.[10]

This research program, originating in Ashraf and Galor (2013a), suggests that interpersonal diversity may have opposing effects on aggregate productivity. It can enhance economic development by widening the spectrum of individual traits (e.g., skills, abilities, and approaches to problem-solving), thus fostering specialization, stimulating the cross-fertilization of ideas in innovative activities, and facilitating more rapid adaptation to changing technological environments. Conversely, by widening the spectrum of individual values, beliefs, preferences, and predispositions in social interactions, diversity can reduce trust and social cohesion, generate social conflicts, and introduce inefficiencies in the provision of public goods, thus adversely affecting economic performance.

Therefore, so long as the beneficial effects of diversity and homogeneity on productivity are diminishing, the degree of interpersonal diversity would be expected to confer a hump-shaped effect on economic development. In particular, the economic performance of ethnic groups, countries, or regions that are characterized by intermediate levels of diversity would be expected to be higher than that associated with largely homogeneous or heterogeneous societies.

---

[9] Independently of the Neolithic Revolution, natural selection led to the emergence of hemoglobin-regulating high-altitude adaptations among Tibetans, allowing carriers to survive in low-oxygen conditions (Simonson et al., 2010).

[10] The discussion in these sections partly draws on Ashraf and Galor (2018) and Arbatlı et al. (2020).

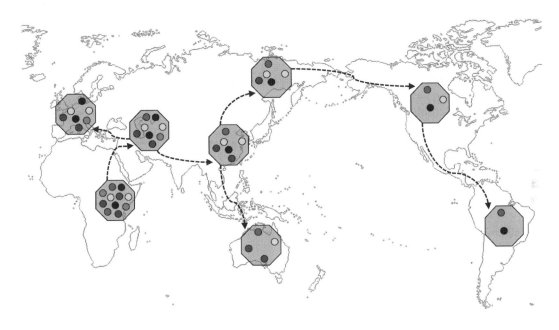

FIGURE 22.3

The "out of Africa" migration and the associated serial founder effect. *Notes*: This figure depicts the "out of Africa" migration pattern of *Homo sapiens*, while illustrating its impact on the worldwide distribution of interpersonal population diversity. With each outward migration event, the departing (founder) population carries with it only a subset of the diversity of its parental colony, as reflected by the decline in the representation of the different variants of a hypothetical trait in the founder population, relative to its source population. The dashed arrows represent approximate migration paths, and the small colored circles (depicted in grayscale in the print version) represent the variants of the hypothetical trait. *Source*: Ashraf and Galor (2018).

22.3.2 The origins of worldwide variations in human population diversity

The expansion of anatomically modern humans from the cradle of humankind in Africa has imparted a deep and indelible mark on the worldwide variation in the degree of interpersonal diversity across populations. According to the widely accepted "out of Africa" hypothesis of human origins, the human species, having evolved to its anatomically modern form in East Africa nearly 300,000 years ago, embarked on populating the entire globe in a stepwise migration process commencing 90,000–70,000 BP. The world map in Fig. 22.3 depicts the approximate migration routes that characterized this prehistoric process of human expansion from Africa.

The "out of Africa" migration was inherently associated with a reduction in the extent of diversity in populations that settled at greater migratory distances from Africa. In particular, as follows from a *serial founder effect* akin to that illustrated in Fig. 22.3, since the spatial diffusion of humans to the rest of the world occurred in a series of discrete steps, where in each step a subgroup of individuals left their parental colony to establish a new settlement farther away, carrying with them only a subset of the traits of their parental colony, the extent of diversity observed *within* a geographically indigenous contemporary ethnic group decreases with distance along ancient migratory paths from East Africa

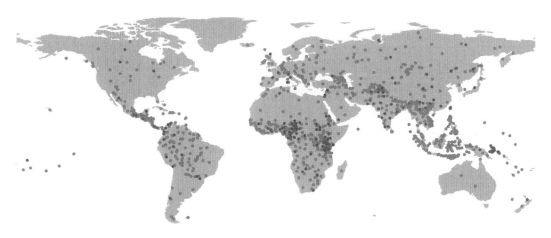

FIGURE 22.4

The global distribution of ethnic groups with observed or predicted population diversity. *Notes*: This figure depicts the worldwide distribution of ethnic groups for which interpersonal population diversity is either observed or predicted based on migratory distance from East Africa. Each point represents the centroid of the historical homeland of an ethnic group. Red points (depicted in dark gray in the print version) represent homelands for which population diversity is observed, whereas blue points (depicted in medium gray in the print version) represent homelands for which it is predicted. *Source*: Arbatlı et al. (2020).

(e.g., Harpending and Rogers, 2000; Ramachandran et al., 2005; Prugnolle et al., 2005; Ashraf and Galor, 2013a).

Reflecting this chain of ancient population bottlenecks originating in East Africa, the scatter plot in Fig. 22.4 depicts the negative influence of migratory distance from the cradle of humankind on intrapopulation genetic diversity in a sample comprising 207 globally representative ethnic groups examined in the literature on human population genetics (Pemberton et al., 2013; Arbatlı et al., 2020).[11] According to population geneticists, these groups are both indigenous to their current geographical locations and have been largely isolated from genetic flows from other ethnic groups. The spatial distribution of these ethnic groups is depicted on the world map in Fig. 22.5.

In order to measure the extent of diversity in genetic material across individuals in a given population (e.g., an ethnic group), population geneticists employ an index known as expected heterozygosity, which captures the probability that two individuals, selected at random from the relevant population, are genetically different from one another with respect to a given spectrum of genetic traits. In particular, a gene-specific expected heterozygosity index (i.e., the probability that two randomly selected individuals differ with respect to a given genetic trait) is first constructed, based on the proportional representations of different alleles or variants of this trait in the population, and upon measuring heterozygosity for a large number of genes or DNA loci, this information is averaged across loci to yield

---

[11] This sample of 207 ethnic groups consists of all observations from the data set of Pemberton et al. (2013) that can be mapped to distinct ethnic homelands, excluding the Surui of South America, who are viewed by population geneticists as an extreme outlier in terms their measured level of expected heterozygosity (Ramachandran et al., 2005). Including this outlier observation in the sample does not qualitatively affect the results.

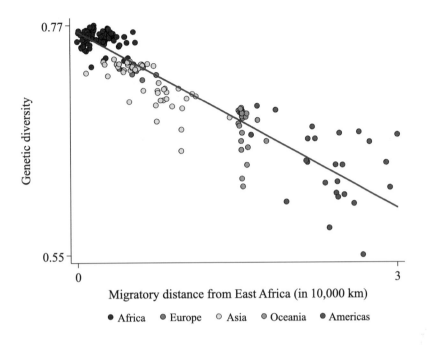

FIGURE 22.5

Expected heterozygosity and migratory distance from East Africa. *Notes*: This figure depicts the negative impact of migratory distance from East Africa on expected heterozygosity in a sample of 207 ethnic groups, drawn from the data set of Pemberton et al. (2013). *Source*: Arbatlı et al. (2020).

the overall expected heterozygosity for the relevant population. Thus, expected heterozygosity for a population, H_{exp}, takes the form:

$$H_{exp} = 1 - \frac{1}{m} \sum_{l=1}^{m} \sum_{i=1}^{k_l} (p_i)^2,$$

where m is the number of genes or DNA loci being considered, k_l is the number of naturally occurring variants or alleles of gene l, and p_i is the proportional representation (or frequency of occurrence) of allele i of gene l in the population.

The measure of expected heterozygosity for geographically indigenous ethnic groups is constructed by population geneticists using data on allelic frequencies for a particular class of DNA loci known as microsatellites. These DNA loci reside in non-protein-coding regions of the human genome (i.e., regions that do not directly result in phenotypic expression) and are therefore viewed as selectively neutral. For the purposes of examining the influence of interpersonal diversity on socioeconomic outcomes across populations, this measure possesses a key advantage of not being tainted by any unobserved heterogeneity in the forces of natural selection that may have operated on these populations since their exodus from Africa; forces that could have obscured the relationship predicted by an ancient serial founder effect. In addition, differential selection and its underlying forces could have also influenced socioeconomic outcomes, thus making it difficult to identify the causal socioeconomic influence of interpersonal diversity.

Nevertheless, to be conceptually meaningful for socioeconomic outcomes, the measure of neutral genetic diversity ought to serve as a valid proxy for diversity in phenotypically and behaviorally expressed traits. Indeed, mounting evidence from the fields of physical and cognitive anthropology suggests the existence of an ancient serial founder effect originating in East Africa on the observed worldwide patterns in various forms of intragroup morphological and cognitive diversity (Henn et al., 2012), including interpersonal diversity in skeletal features pertaining to cranial characteristics (Manica et al., 2007; von Cramon-Taubadel and Lycett, 2008; Betti et al., 2009), dental attributes (Hanihara, 2008), pelvic traits (Betti et al., 2013), and birth canal morphology (Betti and Manica, 2018), as well as intralingual phonemic diversity (Atkinson, 2011).[12] Thus, as argued by Ashraf and Galor (2013a, 2018) and discussed in the next section, a proxy measure of population diversity *predicted* by the migratory distance of the ancestral populations of a society from East Africa would indeed capture the latent impact of interpersonal diversity in phenotypically and behaviorally expressed traits on societal outcomes. Importantly, in light of gene-culture coevolution and transgenerational epigenetic inheritance, the socioeconomic influence of population diversity may be interpreted as reflecting the impact of interpersonal diversity in traits rooted in both "nature" and "nurture" as well as the interaction between the two.[13]

In addition to giving rise to the worldwide variation in interpersonal diversity *within* human societies, the prehistoric "out of Africa" dispersal also imparted a deep and long-lasting influence on the extent of genetic differentiation *between* societies, as measured by population geneticists using an index called F_{ST} genetic distance. For any two populations, this index captures the extent of their combined genetic diversity that is *unexplained* by the population-weighted average of their respective expected heterozygosities. Thus, the F_{ST} genetic distance between populations i and j is given by:

$$F_{ST}^{ij} = 1 - \frac{\theta_i H_{exp}^i + \theta_j H_{exp}^j}{H_{exp}^{ij}},$$

where H_{exp}^i and H_{exp}^j are the individual expected heterozygosity indices of i and j, θ_i and θ_j are the population shares of i and j in the combined population, and H_{exp}^{ij} is the expected heterozygosity of the combined population comprising i and j.

Following the splitting up of populations from one another during the "out of Africa" migration process, the residual genetic variation between populations, as captured by F_{ST} genetic distance, arose

---

[12] Moreover, a serial founder effect associated with the initial expansion of humans across Polynesian islands has been shown to exist in the context of intrapopulation diversity in functional markers pertaining to material culture (Rogers et al., 2009).

[13] For instance, introducing the concept of "genetic nurture," Kong et al. (2018) find that parental genotype associated with the educational attainment of parents in turn affects the educational attainment of children even when the latter do not carry the relevant allelic variants, thus suggesting the intergenerational propagation of traits that may initially be rooted in "nature" through the transmission mechanism of "nurture."

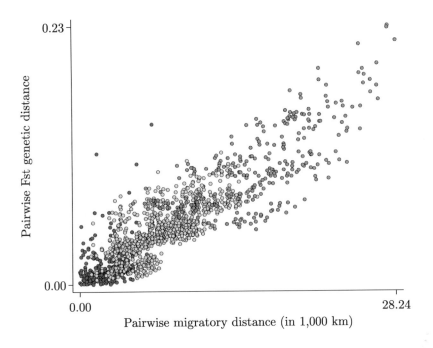

FIGURE 22.6

Pairwise F_{ST} genetic distance and pairwise migratory distance. *Notes*: This figure depicts the positive impact of pairwise migratory distance on pairwise F_{ST} genetic distance across all 1,378 ethnic group pairs from the set of 53 ethnic groups that constitute the HGDP–CEPH Human Genome Diversity Cell Line Panel. Orange points (depicted in dark gray in the print version) represent observations in which the two ethnic groups in the pair belong to the same world region (i.e., both come from either Africa, the Middle East, Europe, Central and South Asia, East Asia, Oceania, or the Americas). Yellow points (depicted in light gray in the print version) represent pairs in which the two groups belong to different world regions, involving neither Oceania nor the Americas. Blue points (depicted in medium gray in the print version) represent pairs in which the two groups belong to different world regions, with at least one group representing Oceania or the Americas. *Source*: Ashraf and Galor (2013a, 2018).

from (i) random mutations that caused genetic drift within each population over time; and (ii) heterogeneity in environmentally driven selective pressures across their different eventual habitations. In particular, since migratory distance between a pair of populations partly reflects the length of time elapsed since they diverged from their common ancestral population, and because it also reduces the likelihood that they would have subsequently come into contact with one another, a direct implication of the "out of Africa" hypothesis is that pairwise F_{ST} genetic distance increases with the pairwise migratory distance between populations. Using a measure of F_{ST} genetic distance based on selectively neutral genetic markers (i.e., distance that only captures genetic drift due to random mutations), the scatter plot in Fig. 22.6 depicts the aforementioned relationship arising from "isolation by distance" across all pairs of populations in a sample of 53 ethnic groups from the HGDP-CEPH Human Genome Diversity Cell Line Panel (Cann et al., 2002; Ramachandran et al., 2005; Ashraf and Galor, 2013a).

22.3.3 Predicted population diversity
22.3.3.1 Measurement and identification at the country level

In light of the absence of measures of interpersonal diversity for national populations, as well as the scarcity of such measures for ethnic groups, one can exploit the strong negative impact of migratory distance from East Africa on interpersonal diversity in observable traits to generate an index of population diversity levels for every country, region, or ethnic group, based on the migratory distances of their respective *ancestral* populations from East Africa. In particular, following the association depicted in Fig. 22.4, the interpersonal diversity of an indigenous population can be *predicted* based on the distance that its ancestors had traveled over the course of their migration from East Africa. The discussion to follow provides an elaboration of this insight.

A naïve approach to measuring interpersonal diversity at the country level would be to simply aggregate the *observed* expected heterozygosity measure, as calculated by population geneticists, across the ethnic groups belonging to a given country. However, such an approach faces several major shortcomings. First, although the ethnic groups for which observed population diversity is available are globally representative in terms of their spatial distribution across continents and world regions, they span only a modest fraction of nations. As such, the naïve approach would yield observed population diversity for a limited sample of countries. Second, a simple (or even population-weighted) averaging of the expected heterozygosity index across ethnic groups in a national population would fail to account for the additional diversity that results from the pairwise biocultural distances among the constituent groups. This issue would be particularly salient for the New World, where contemporary national populations are comprised of groups that can trace their ancestries to world regions that were once geographically rather isolated from one another. Third, the potential endogeneity of observed population diversity with socioeconomic outcomes at the ethnic-group level would imply that, under the naïve approach to measurement, the country-level diversity measure would also be tainted by concerns regarding reverse causality and omitted variables.

To overcome sample limitations, dependence on neutral genetic markers, and potential concerns about endogeneity in the use of an *observed* population diversity measure under the naïve approach, the research program originated by Ashraf and Galor (2013a) adopts the strategy of exploiting the strong explanatory power of migratory distance from East Africa for the worldwide variation in observed expected heterozygosity across ethnic groups, similar to that depicted in Fig. 22.4. Specifically, in a first step, the coefficients from a regression of expected heterozygosity on migratory distance from East Africa across 53 ethnic groups in the HGDP-CEPH sample are employed to generate a measure of *predicted* interpersonal diversity for all precolonial societies spanning the globe, based on their respective geographical locations in AD 1500.[14] Importantly, prior to the discovery of the New World and the great intercontinental migrations of the colonial era, the geographical locations of historical societies largely reflected the locations to which their ancestral populations had arrived at the end of their prehistoric "out of Africa" migration, and as such, the diversity of a precolonial society was presumably determined overwhelmingly by the ancient serial founder effect originating in East Africa. As corroborated by the discussion in the next section, the plausible exogeneity of distance along the ancient "out of Africa" migratory paths implies that the measure of predicted population diversity

---

[14] Exploiting the more recent and larger data set of Pemberton et al. (2013), rather than the HGDP-CEPH sample, would generate nearly identical results.

generated in this step is appropriate for identifying the impact of interpersonal diversity on comparative economic and institutional development across societies in the precolonial era.

Nevertheless, to identify the impact of diversity on comparative economic development and comparative sociopolitical institutions across countries in the modern world, it is necessary to construct a measure of predicted population diversity that incorporates the additional diversity arising from the multiethnic ancestries of modern national populations, reflecting the great intercontinental and interregional migrations over the past half millennium. Thus, the measure of predicted diversity for a contemporary national population as developed by Ashraf and Galor (2013a) is based on (i) the proportional representation of each ethnic group in the national population[15]; (ii) the population diversity of each of these groups, as *predicted* by its ancestral migratory distance from East Africa; and (iii) the pairwise biocultural distances among these ethnic groups, as *predicted* by the migratory distance between the ancestral populations of each pair.

In particular, following the definition of F_{ST} genetic distance presented earlier, and considering the hypothetical case of a contemporary national population comprised of two ethnic groups, whose ancestors originate from different locations, A and B, the overall diversity of this national population is calculated as:

$$\widehat{H}_{exp}^{AB} = \frac{\theta_A \widehat{H}_{exp}^A (d_A) + \theta_B \widehat{H}_{exp}^B (d_B)}{1 - \widehat{F}_{ST}^{AB} (d_{AB})},$$

where, for $i \in \{A, B\}$, $\widehat{H}_{exp}^i (d_i)$ denotes the expected heterozygosity predicted by migratory distance, d_i, of ancestral location i from East Africa (i.e., the predicted population diversity of the precolonial population native to location i), and θ_i is the proportional representation (in the national population being considered) of the ethnic group whose ancestors immigrated from location i since the onset of the colonial era in AD 1500. Moreover, $\widehat{F}_{ST}^{AB} (d_{AB})$ is the biocultural distance predicted by the migratory distance between ancestral locations A and B, obtained by applying the coefficients associated with a regression line similar to that depicted in Fig. 22.6. In practice, since contemporary national populations are typically composed of more than two ethnic groups, the procedure above is applied recursively for national populations with a larger number of constituent groups.

The fact that the measure of population diversity for contemporary national populations incorporates both within-group diversity and between-group distances makes it particularly valuable for identifying the impact of population diversity on cross-country comparative economic development and comparative sociopolitical institutions in the modern era. In contrast, other commonly used measures of diversity that aim to capture variation in the degree of ethnic fragmentation across national populations typically do not exploit information beyond the proportional representations of ethnolinguistically differentiated groups in the national population—namely, they implicitly assume that these groups are internally homogeneous and bioculturally equidistant from one another.[16] Aside from accounting for

---

[15] The data on the population shares of these subnational groups are obtained from the *World Migration Matrix, 1500–2000* of Putterman and Weil (2010), who compiled, for each country in their data set, the share of a country's population in 2000 that is descended from the population of every other country in 1500.

[16] More sophisticated measures of ethnic fragmentation—such as (i) the Greenberg index of "cultural diversity," as measured by Fearon (2003) and Desmet et al. (2009), or (ii) the ethnolinguistic polarization index, as measured by Desmet et al. (2009) and by Esteban et al. (2012)—do incorporate information on pairwise linguistic distances, wherein pairwise linguistic proximity monotonically increases in the number of shared branches between any two languages in a hierarchical linguistic tree. This

both intragroup diversity and intergroup distances, the use of plausibly exogenous migratory distances (of a nation's ancestral populations from East Africa and from one another) to predict within-group diversity and between-group distances makes it possible for the measure to identify the impact of national population diversity on contemporary outcomes, even for countries for which observed expected heterozygosity and F_{ST} genetic distance data are unavailable for their constituent ethnic groups.

Further, insofar as interregional migrations since AD 1500 and, thus, the proportional representation of ethnic groups within each national population may have been affected by historically persistent spatial patterns of comparative development and conflict, contemporary national population diversity may be endogenous to these societal outcomes. To confront this issue, two alternative empirical strategies have been implemented by previous works in this research program. The first strategy confines the empirical analysis to variations in a sample of countries that only belong to the Old World (i.e., Africa, Europe, and Asia), where the diversity of contemporary national populations predominantly reflects the diversity of indigenous populations that became native to their current locations well before the colonial era. This strategy rests on the observation that population movements since AD 1500 within the Old World did not result in the significant admixture of populations that were very distant from one another. The second strategy exploits variations in a globally representative sample of countries using a two-stage estimator, in which the migratory distance of a country's prehistorically native population from East Africa is employed as an instrumental variable for the diversity of its contemporary national population. It rests on the identifying assumption that the migratory distance of a country's prehistorically native population from East Africa is plausibly exogenous to economic and sociopolitical outcomes of the country's overall population in the contemporary era.

22.3.3.2 Measurement and identification at the ethnic-group level

The research program on the role of population diversity in comparative economic development and comparative sociopolitical institutions employs several strategies to mitigate concerns about reverse causality, omitted cultural, geographical, and human characteristics, as well as selection bias from sorting, in the observed association between population diversity and economic, political, and social outcomes at the ethnic-group level. Over the course of human history, differential patterns across ethnic groups in their levels of economic development and in the incidence of internal conflicts may have altered the degree of *observed* interpersonal diversity within these groups. Thus, the association between the observed population diversity of an ethnic group and outcomes such as group productivity or internal conflicts may partly reflect reverse causality. Furthermore, these associations at the ethnic-group level could be partly governed by omitted cultural, geographical, and human characteristics. To mitigate these concerns, empirical analyses in this research program have exploited the strong negative association between the observed population diversity of an indigenous contemporary ethnic group and its migratory distance from East Africa—arising from the previously highlighted ancient serial founder effect (e.g., Harpending and Rogers, 2000; Ramachandran et al., 2005; Prugnolle et al., 2005; Ashraf and Galor, 2013a)—to generate a measure of *predicted* population diversity for a globally representative sample of over 900 ethnic groups.

Nevertheless, several scenarios could a priori weaken the credibility of this methodology. First, selective migration out of Africa, or natural selection along the ancient migratory paths, could have

---

information, however, is constrained by the nature of a hierarchical linguistic tree, where languages residing at the same level of branching of the tree are necessarily equidistant from one another.

affected human traits and, therefore, group-level outcomes independently of the impact of migratory distance from East Africa on the degree of *diversity* in human traits. However, while migratory distance from East Africa has a significant negative association with the degree of diversity in human traits, it appears uncorrelated with the *mean* levels of different traits in a population, such as height, weight, and skin reflectance, conditional on distance from the equator (Ashraf and Galor, 2013a). Second, migratory distance from East Africa could be correlated with distances from important historical locations (e.g., technological frontiers) and could, therefore, capture the effect of these other distances on the process of development and the incidence of conflicts, rather than its impact that operates through population diversity. Nevertheless, conditional on migratory distance from East Africa, distances from historical technological frontiers in AD 1, AD 1000, and AD 1500 do not qualitatively alter the impact of predicted diversity on either group productivity or internal conflicts (Ashraf and Galor, 2013a; Arbatlı et al., 2020), further justifying the reliance on the serial founder effect associated with the "out of Africa" migration of humans for identifying the influence of population diversity on various group-level outcomes.

Moreover, a threat to identification would emerge if the actual migratory paths from Africa would have been correlated with geographical characteristics (e.g., soil quality, ruggedness, climatic conditions, and propensity to trade) that can directly influence both innovative activities and internal conflicts. This would have involved, however, that the favorability of these geographical factors for these outcomes would be aligned along the main root of the migratory path from Africa as well as along each of the main forks that emerge from this primary path. Specifically, in several important forks of this migration process (e.g., the Fertile Crescent and the associated eastward migration into Asia versus the westward migration into Europe), geographical factors that are conducive to these outcomes would have to diminish symmetrically along these divergent secondary migratory paths, a requirement that appears implausible in reality. Nevertheless, analyses in this research program show that the influence of predicted population diversity on group-level outcomes remains qualitatively unaffected when accounting for a host of potentially confounding geographical characteristics of ethnic homelands, spatial dependence, as well as time-invariant unobserved heterogeneity across regions, identifying the association between interpersonal diversity and outcomes across ethnic societies in the same world region.

The observed associations between population diversity and outcomes at the ethnic-group level may further reflect the sorting of less diverse populations into geographical niches that carry lower conflict risk but are also less conducive to innovative activities. While sorting would not affect the existence of a positive association between population diversity and either conflicts or innovative activities, it would weaken the proposed interpretation of these associations. However, such sorting would require that the spatial distribution of ex ante conflict risk and innovation potential would have to be negatively correlated with migratory distance from East Africa, and the conduciveness of geographical characteristics to conflicts and innovations would have to be negatively aligned with the primary migratory path out of Africa as well as with each of the main subsequent forks and their associated secondary paths. Despite the implausibility of these requirements in nature, concerns pertaining to sorting are further mitigated by accounting for heterogeneity in a wide range of geographical characteristics across ethnic homelands, spatial autocorrelation, and world region fixed effects.

22.3.4 Empirical findings

22.3.4.1 Population diversity and comparative development across countries

Exploiting the country-level measures of interpersonal diversity discussed in Section 22.3.3.1, Ashraf and Galor (2013a) empirically examine their prediction regarding the trade-off between the beneficial and detrimental effects of the degree of diversity on productivity at the societal level. Consistent with their hypothesis, they find that interpersonal diversity, as determined predominantly by a serial founder effect associated with the prehistoric "out of Africa" migration process, does indeed confer a significant hump-shaped influence on income per capita, explaining 16 percent of the worldwide cross-country variation in the standard of living in the year 2000.

Although Ashraf and Galor's main focus is on *contemporary* comparative development, they confirm the hump-shaped influence of diversity on economic development in both historical and contemporary time periods, demonstrating that diversity within societies has shaped their comparative development since well before the advent of the Industrial Revolution. In the preindustrial era, comparative development was characterized by Malthusian forces—namely, gains in productivity at the societal level were channeled primarily towards population growth rather than growth in income per capita. During this era, more developed societies were therefore characterized by higher population density, rather than a higher standard of living (Ashraf and Galor, 2011). Thus, Ashraf and Galor's historical analysis focuses on explaining variation across societies in their population density in AD 1500.

Employing the measure of predicted diversity for precolonial societies, the authors document a hump-shaped influence of interpersonal diversity on productivity in AD 1500, as captured by population density, in a sample of observations spanning the entire globe. Notably, the relationship accounts for potentially confounding effects due to heterogeneity across societies in the timing of the Neolithic Revolution and in various geographical factors relevant for their historical development, as well as confounding effects arising from unobserved time-invariant cross-continental differences. This finding is robust to a large number of sensitivity checks, including "placebo tests" showing that a similar hump-shaped pattern does not exist when employing either aerial distance from East Africa or migratory distances from other geographical locations.

Columns 1 and 2 of Table 22.1 reproduce this finding using updated specifications that account for variations in a sizable vector of geographical, climatic, and historical institutional characteristics, the timing of the Neolithic Revolution and of initial human settlement, and world region fixed effects. The full specification for examining population density in column 2 reveals a significant hump-shaped relationship, which predicts population density at the diversity level associated with the inflection point to be 3.3 and 0.9 log points higher than at the minimum and maximum levels of diversity, respectively. This relationship is depicted on the scatter plot in panel A of Fig. 22.7. In addition, using a similar pair of specifications, columns 3 and 4 of Table 22.1 demonstrate that the hump-shaped influence of interpersonal diversity on preindustrial productivity holds when the rate of urbanization in AD 1500 is employed as an alternative measure of comparative development across preindustrial societies. The scatter plot in panel B of Fig. 22.7 shows the hump-shaped relationship estimated by the regression in column 4.

Applying the measure of diversity for contemporary national populations, Ashraf and Galor (2013a) find a significant hump-shaped influence of diversity on income per capita in the year 2000. This finding accounts for cross-country heterogeneity in the timing of the Neolithic Revolution, various geographical, cultural, and institutional correlates of contemporary economic development, and un-

Table 22.1 Population diversity and comparative development across countries.

	Log population density in AD 1500		Log urbanization rate in AD 1500		Log income per capita, 2010–18		Log luminosity per capita, 1992–2013	
	(1)	(2)	(3)	(4)	(5)	(6)	(7)	(8)
Population diversity	277.7***	288.9***	408.0***	364.8***	328.8**	416.1***	467.8***	431.5***
	(86.7)	(90.7)	(73.2)	(57.1)	(128.0)	(124.2)	(170.9)	(163.5)
Population diversity (squared)	-190.2***	-207.0***	-298.4***	-271.1***	-231.9**	-292.5***	-336.4***	-308.8***
	(63.5)	(67.1)	(57.6)	(44.2)	(92.9)	(88.5)	(123.2)	(116.2)
Baseline controls	Yes	Yes	Yes	Yes	Yes	Yes	Yes	Yes
World region FE	Yes	Yes	Yes	Yes	Yes	Yes	Yes	Yes
Additional controls (past)	No	Yes	No	Yes	No	No	No	No
Additional controls (present)	No	No	No	No	No	Yes	No	Yes
Number of observations	140	140	80	80	132	132	134	134
Adjusted R^2	0.64	0.68	0.58	0.67	0.65	0.86	0.71	0.84

*Notes: This table presents OLS regressions demonstrating the hump-shaped impact of interpersonal population diversity on historical and contemporary economic development across countries, conditional on relevant covariates noted below. Columns 1–4 examine the impact of predicted diversity (based on migratory distance from East Africa) on economic development in AD 1500, as reflected by either log population density (columns 1–2) or log urbanization rate (columns 3–4). Columns 5–8 examine the impact of predicted ancestry-adjusted diversity (i.e., population diversity predicted by the migratory distances of a country's ancestral populations from East Africa, as well as the pairwise migratory distances among them) on economic development in the contemporary era, as reflected by either log income per capita during the 2010–18 time period (columns 5–6) or log nighttime luminosity per capita during the 1992–2013 time period (columns 7–8). The baseline controls in all columns include time since the Neolithic Revolution, time since initial human settlement, absolute latitude, the mean and standard deviation of caloric suitability, the percentage of land in tropical climate zones, a measure of disease richness, distance to coasts or rivers, and an island nation dummy. The world region fixed effects in all columns are captured by dummies for Sub-Saharan Africa, Middle East and North Africa, Europe and Central Asia, South Asia, East Asia and the Pacific, North America, and Latin America and the Caribbean. Columns 2 and 4 additionally control for an index of state antiquity. Columns 6 and 8 add even further controls for the percentage of the population at risk of contracting malaria, the percentages of the population that fall into four religious categories (Protestant, Catholic, Muslim, and other denominations), ethnic fractionalization, an index of the degree of democracy, measures of dependence on oil and gas exports, an ex-colony dummy, and dummies for different legal origins (British, French, Socialist, German, and Scandinavian). Heteroskedasticity-robust standard errors are reported in parentheses. *** denotes statistical significance at the 1 percent level, ** at the 5 percent level, and * at the 10 percent level, all for two-sided hypothesis tests.*

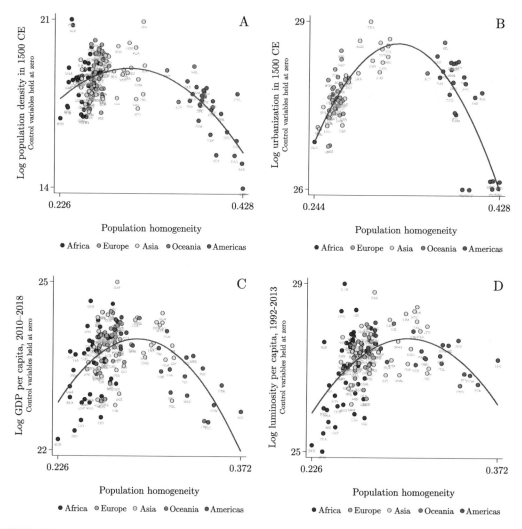

FIGURE 22.7

Population diversity and comparative development across countries. *Notes*: This figure depicts the hump-shaped impact of interpersonal population diversity on historical and contemporary economic development across countries, conditional on geographical, climatic, cultural, and institutional characteristics, the timing of the Neolithic Revolution and of initial human settlement, and world region fixed effects. The top panels depict the impact of predicted population homogeneity (i.e., 1 minus population diversity predicted by migratory distance from East Africa) on economic development in AD 1500, as reflected by either log population density (panel A) or log urbanization rate (panel B). The bottom panels depict the impact of predicted ancestry-adjusted homogeneity (i.e., 1 minus population diversity predicted by the migratory distances of a country's ancestral populations from East Africa, as well as the pairwise migratory distances among them) on economic development in the contemporary era, as reflected by either log income per capita during the 2010–18 time period (panel C) or log luminosity per capita during the 1992–2013 time period (panel D). Each panel presents an augmented-component-plus-residual plot with a quadratic fit, corresponding to the relevant even-numbered column of Table 22.1.

observed time-invariant continent-specific characteristics. The relationship is additionally robust to controlling for population density in AD 1500, indicating that the hump-shaped influence of diversity does not merely reflect long-run persistence in economic development. Moreover, it continues to hold when limiting the sample to countries in which the overwhelming majority of the population has remained geographically native since the precolonial era, thus alleviating concerns regarding the endogeneity of interregional population flows over the past half millennium.

The significant hump-shaped impact of interpersonal diversity at the country level on contemporary comparative development is reproduced in columns 5 and 6 of Table 22.1, using updated specifications that augment those from earlier columns of the table with contemporary malaria risk and a considerable set of cultural and institutional covariates relevant for modern-day outcomes, while exploiting average income per capita during the 2010–18 time period as the dependent variable. As depicted on the scatter plot in panel C of Fig. 22.7, the full specification for examining income per capita in column 6 predicts income per capita at the diversity level associated with the inflection point to be 2.1 and 1.2 log points higher than at the minimum and maximum levels of diversity, respectively.

Confronting the possibility that income per capita in the modern world could be noisily measured, especially for less-developed economies, Ashraf et al. (2014) find that the hump-shaped influence of diversity on contemporary comparative development additionally holds when relative prosperity is measured by the cross-country variation in per-capita adjusted nighttime luminosity, as observed by satellites from outer space, averaged over the 1992–2013 time period. Their analysis of nighttime luminosity is reproduced in columns 7 and 8 of Table 22.1, using the updated specifications employed for examining income per capita in the preceding two columns. The significant hump-shaped relationship estimated by the full specification in column 8 is depicted on the scatter plot in panel D of Fig. 22.7. These findings mitigate the potential concern that the estimated costs of high diversity on aggregate productivity could be biased upward when productivity is measured using income per capita, because the shadow economy may well be larger in more diverse societies in light of the adverse influence of diversity on social cohesion.

The relative importance of population diversity and other fundamental determinants

This section provides an assessment of the relative contribution of interpersonal population diversity and of six other fundamental channels—geoclimatic factors, political institutions, ethnocultural composition, historical determinants, disease ecology, and legal environment—to the contemporary disparity in economic prosperity across nations, as reflected by the cross-country variation in average income per capita during the 2010–18 time period. Specifically, as presented in Table 22.2, the analysis explores the *added* explanatory power (partial R^2 statistic) associated with distinct groups of covariates that correspond to these various channels.

The analysis commences with a baseline specification in column 1 in which each of the six alternative fundamental channel is represented by a core set of covariates. However, in order to assure a balanced assessment of all channels, the analysis then proceeds in subsequent specifications (columns 2–7) with a one-at-a-time expansion of the set of covariates representing each alternative channel, relative to the set employed in the baseline specification. The analysis concludes with examining a

Table 22.2 Explanatory power of population diversity and other determinants for contemporary comparative development across countries.

	Baseline	Expanded geoclimatic controls	Expanded historical controls	Expanded disease controls	Expanded ethnocultural controls	Expanded legal envi. controls	Expanded institutional controls	Full specification
	(1)	(2)	(3)	(4)	(5)	(6)	(7)	(8)
Population diversity	360.0***	403.8***	430.1***	356.8***	362.4***	364.0***	356.3***	492.1***
	(91.9)	(93.5)	(95.5)	(91.8)	(92.0)	(92.3)	(90.2)	(92.3)
Population diversity (squared)	-251.7***	-284.8***	-301.2***	-249.0***	-253.2***	-254.7***	-249.6***	-347.0***
	(65.7)	(67.1)	(68.2)	(65.6)	(65.8)	(66.0)	(64.5)	(66.1)
Number of Observations	129	129	129	129	129	129	129	129
Adjusted R^2	0.86	0.87	0.86	0.86	0.86	0.86	0.86	0.88
Partial R^2 (in percent) by channel								
Population diversity	16.5	18.1	20.4	17.1	17.1	16.7	16.3	26.3
Geoclimatic factors	27.2	34.2	27.3	25.8	27.6	27.4	27.9	38.9
Historical determinants	3.4	7.4	8.3	2.3	3.5	3.5	3.3	12.8
Disease ecology	15.6	9.5	17.7	16.7	16.2	15.1	15.6	14.6
Ethnocultural composition	20.5	20.0	22.5	20.7	21.1	20.6	19.1	21.9
Legal environment	24.6	27.0	17.3	24.7	25.1	25.0	16.1	13.0
Political institutions	2.8	1.6	3.4	2.4	2.3	2.3	7.2	8.1

Notes: This table employs OLS regressions to explore the added explanatory power of the hump-shaped impact of interpersonal population diversity for log income per capita across countries during the 2010–18 time period, along with the added explanatory power of each of six covariate groups that represent other determinants of comparative development. The six covariate groups, along with the baseline set of variables in each group (as employed in column 1), include: (a) geoclimatic factors: absolute latitude, caloric suitability; distance to coasts or rivers, the percentage of land in tropical climate zones, and terrain ruggedness; (b) historical determinants: time since the Neolithic Revolution and time since initial human settlement; (c) disease ecology: the percentage of the population at risk of contracting malaria; (d) ethnocultural composition: the percentages of the population that belong to each of four religious denominations, including Protestant, Catholic, Muslim, and "other"; (e) legal environment: dummies for each of three legal origins, including British, French, and Socialist; and (f) political institutions: an index of the degree of executive constraints during the 1960–2000 time period. Relative to the baseline specification, (a) column 2 additionally controls for the arable percentage of land, average monthly temperature and average monthly precipitation during the 1961–1990 time period, and an island nation dummy; (b) column 3 additionally controls for an index of state antiquity and an ex-colony dummy; (c) column 4 additionally controls for a measure of disease richness; (d) column 5 additionally controls for the degree of ethnic fractionalization; (e) column 6 additionally controls for dummies for each of two legal origins, including German and Scandinavian; and (f) column 7 additionally controls for an index of the degree of democracy during the 1960–2000 time period. The set of covariates in the full specification of column 8 represents the union of the sets from all preceding columns. The added explanatory power of a given covariate group in a specification is represented by the partial R^2 of the set of independent variables representing that group in the specification. The specifications in all columns control for the full set of world region fixed effects, as captured by dummies for Sub-Saharan Africa, Middle East and North Africa, Europe and Central Asia, South Asia, East Asia and the Pacific, North America, and Latin America and the Caribbean. Heteroskedasticity-robust standard errors are reported in parentheses. *** denotes statistical significance at the 1 percent level, ** at the 5 percent level, and * at the 10 percent level, all for two-sided hypothesis tests.

full specification in which all channels are represented by their respective augmented set of covariates considered in earlier columns.[17]

Turning to the results, the partial R^2 statistic associated with the reported hump-shaped impact of interpersonal population diversity suggests that, across specifications, this channel explains between 16% and 26% of the residual variation in contemporary income per capita, conditional on the other fundamental channels. Amongst the other fundamental channels, the geoclimatic one possesses partial R^2 values in the range of 26%–39%, whereas the channels capturing the legal environment, ethnocultural composition, and disease ecology respectively possess partial R^2 values in the range of 13%–27%, 19%–23%, and 10%–18%. On the other hand, the channels capturing historical determinants (i.e., time since the Neolithic Revolution, time since initial human settlement, state antiquity, and colonial history) and the extent to which political institutions can minimize expropriation risk (i.e., executive constraints and the degree of democracy) appear to possess partial R^2 values in the range of 2%–13% and 2%–8% respectively. Finally, focusing on the full specification in column 8 that includes all the covariates for each channel, population diversity enters with an added explanatory power of 26%, geoclimatic factors with 39%, ethnocultural composition with 22%, disease ecology with 15%, legal environment and historical determinants with 13% each, and political institutions with 8%.

22.3.4.2 Population diversity and comparative development across ethnic homelands

Ashraf et al. (2020a) have empirically examined the influence of population diversity on productivity at the ethnic group level, while accounting for potentially confounding effects arising from observed heterogeneity in various ethnicity-specific geographical, cultural, and institutional factors, as well as unobserved heterogeneity in time-invariant region-specific characteristics. This research finds that observed diversity in a worldwide sample of 207 ethnic groups (Pemberton et al., 2013), as well as predicted diversity (based on migratory distance from East Africa) in a global sample of over 900 ethnic groups, has imparted a significant hump-shaped influence on economic prosperity throughout the course of human history since the onset of the Neolithic Revolution in the Fertile Crescent. The results demonstrate that the variation in interpersonal diversity across ethnic homelands has contributed to variations in their economic development in the very long run, as captured by their historical population densities at various points in time, corresponding to the initial year of every thousand-year time interval between 10,000 BC and AD 1500, as well as by their per-capita adjusted nighttime luminosities in the contemporary era.

Table 22.3 highlights a modest subset of the findings of Ashraf et al. (2020a). Exploiting variations across ethnic homelands, the regressions reveal the significant hump-shaped influence of interpersonal diversity on population density in 5000 BC (columns 1–2), 3000 BC (columns 3–4), 1000 BC (columns 5–6), and AD 100 (columns 7–8), as well as a qualitatively similar impact on per-capita adjusted nighttime luminosity during the 1992–2013 time period (columns 9–10), using either observed diversity (odd-numbered columns) or predicted diversity (even-numbered columns). The regressions examining historical population densities account for the timing of initial human settlement and a host of geographical and climatic factors, along with world region fixed effects, whereas those examining contemporary nighttime luminosity additionally control for contemporary malaria risk and contemporary cultural and institutional covariates.

---

[17] See the notes section of Table 22.2 for the list of variables employed in the baseline and expanded representations of each channel examined by the analysis.

Table 22.3 Population diversity and comparative development across ethnic homelands.

	Log population density in 5000 BC		Log population density in 3000 BC		Log population density in 1000 BC		Log population density in AD 100		Log luminosity per capita, 1992–2013	
	(1)	(2)	(3)	(4)	(5)	(6)	(7)	(8)	(9)	(10)
Population diversity	470.5***	294.9***	490.0***	274.9***	411.1***	378.8***	404.8***	676.2**	203.1***	199.0***
	(70.0)	(110.6)	(71.5)	(104.2)	(74.8)	(93.0)	(76.0)	(306.5)	(74.5)	(71.7)
Population diversity (squared)	-341.0***	-193.8**	-357.9***	-179.8**	-298.4***	-263.0***	-294.2***	-471.8**	-158.3***	-134.2***
	(53.0)	(78.0)	(53.3)	(73.6)	(55.6)	(65.8)	(56.1)	(215.5)	(57.0)	(50.6)
World region FE	Yes	Yes	Yes	Yes	Yes	Yes	Yes	Yes	Yes	Yes
Baseline controls	Yes	Yes	Yes	Yes	Yes	Yes	Yes	Yes	Yes	Yes
Additional controls	Yes	Yes	Yes	Yes	Yes	Yes	Yes	Yes	Yes	Yes
Sample	Observed	Predicted	Observed	Predicted	Observed	Predicted	Observed	Predicted	Observed	Predicted
Number of observations	173	838	184	849	196	873	199	877	207	909
Adjusted R^2	0.50	0.39	0.53	0.41	0.55	0.42	0.57	0.42	0.65	0.69

*Notes: This table presents OLS regressions demonstrating the hump-shaped impact of interpersonal population diversity on historical and contemporary economic development across ethnic homelands, conditional on relevant covariates noted below. The odd-numbered columns examine the impact of observed population diversity, whereas the even-numbered ones explore the impact of diversity predicted by migratory distance from East Africa. Columns 1–8 examine the impact of population diversity on long-run historical economic development, as reflected by log population density in 5000 BC (columns 1–2), 3000 BC (columns 3–4), 1000 BC (columns 5–6), and AD 100 (columns 7–8), whereas columns 9–10 examine its impact on contemporary economic development, as reflected by a per-capita adjusted measure of log nighttime luminosity during the 1992–2013 time period. The baseline controls in all columns include time since initial human settlement, absolute latitude, the mean and standard deviation of caloric suitability, distance to coasts or rivers, mean elevation, and ruggedness. Columns 1–8 additionally control for the means and standard deviations of temperature and precipitation, the range of temperature, and the percentage of land in tropical climate zones. Columns 9–10 add even further controls for contemporary malaria risk and ethnic fractionalization. In columns 1–8, the world region fixed effects are captured by dummies for the "New World" (i.e., the Americas and Oceania) and for Sub-Saharan Africa, whereas in columns 9–10 they are captured by separate dummies for each continent. Heteroskedasticity-robust standard errors are reported in parentheses. *** denotes statistical significance at the 1 percent level, ** at the 5 percent level, and * at the 10 percent level, all for two-sided hypothesis tests.*

To interpret a subset of the significant hump-shaped patterns revealed in Table 22.3, the regression in column 5 predicts historical population density at the diversity level associated with the inflection point to be 5.4 and 1.9 log points higher than at the minimum and maximum levels of diversity, respectively. Moreover, the regression in column 9 predicts contemporary nighttime luminosity at the diversity level associated with the inflection point to be 1.2 and 2.5 log points higher than at the minimum and maximum levels of diversity, respectively. The hump-shaped relationships between observed diversity and comparative development across ethnic homelands in the different time periods, as revealed by the regressions in odd-numbered columns of Table 22.3, are depicted sequentially on the scatter plots in the different panels of Fig. 22.8.

The ethnic-group-level analysis of Ashraf et al. (2020a) provides the first-best setting for confirming the robustness of the main prediction of Ashraf and Galor's hypothesis to using Pemberton et al.'s (2013) data on observed diversity in the extended sample of 200+ ethnic groups (relative to the HGDP-CEPH sample of 53 groups employed by Ashraf and Galor's original analysis). Nevertheless, the results for the influence of interpersonal diversity on comparative development in both precolonial and modern periods are robust in a second-best country-level setting. In particular, following Ashraf and Galor's (2013a) methodology, one can generate measures of *predicted* population diversity for a *globally representative* sample of countries, based on their respective migratory distances from East Africa. Since the coefficients of the estimated relationship between migratory distance and observed diversity are virtually identical in the HGDP-CEPH sample versus the extended sample of ethnic groups, the hump-shaped influence of predicted diversity on both historical and contemporary cross-country comparative development remains unaffected.[18]

22.3.4.3 Mechanisms of the influence of population diversity

The reduced-form hump-shaped influence of interpersonal diversity on productivity suggests several mechanisms through which diversity can influence economic performance, reflecting various elements of the trade-off between the costs and benefits of diversity. This section reviews the evidence on these mechanisms, as uncovered by various works in this research program.

---

[18] A third-best approach would be to conduct a preliminary (non-inferential) exploration of the association between observed diversity and economic prosperity at the country level. This is the approach of Rosenberg and Kang (2015), who argue that the hump-shaped pattern between observed diversity and historical population density is statistically insignificant in a thirty-nine-country sample, constructed by averaging expected heterozygosity across the subset of ethnic groups that are observed within each country. However, their attempt to use this approach to test for the hump-shaped influence of interpersonal diversity on economic prosperity is fundamentally flawed for two major reasons. First, because the subset of only observed ethnic groups in a country is not necessarily representative of the country's entire population, and since the ethnic groups from their extended sample span only thirty-nine (globally nonrepresentative) countries, their study is severely marred by sample selection bias *at the country level.* Specifically, the actual presence of a hump-shaped cross-country association between observed diversity and economic prosperity cannot be confirmed or rejected based on a nonrepresentative sample of countries. Second, observed diversity may reflect past socioeconomic outcomes such as intra-regional social conflicts and migrations that are themselves driven by past economic prosperity. Thus, Rosenberg and Kang's explorative analysis is afflicted by issues of reverse causality and omitted variables that serve to mask the existence of a hump-shaped relationship between diversity and economic prosperity. Indeed, even in the context of their nonrepresentative sample of country populations, Ashraf et al. (2020b) find that a significant hump-shaped association emerges between observed diversity and historical population density once a sufficient set of potential geographical confounders is accounted for. Moreover, as shown by Ashraf et al. (2020a), conditional on employing a *valid* statistical methodology, the main prediction of Ashraf and Galor's hypothesis is fully robust to exploiting genetic data from the extended sample of ethnic groups.

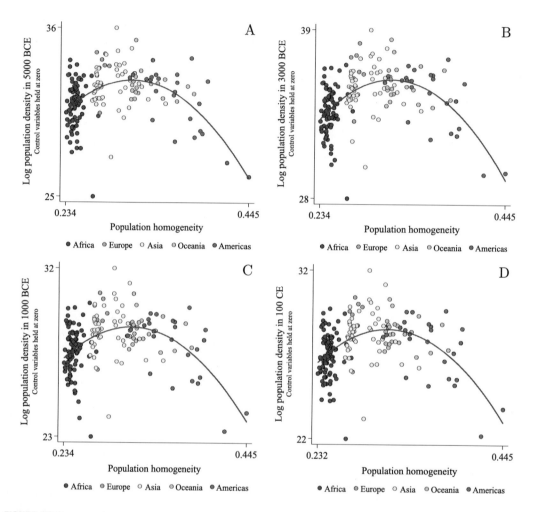

FIGURE 22.8

Population diversity and comparative development across ethnic homelands. *Notes*: This figure depicts the hump-shaped impact of interpersonal population diversity on historical and contemporary economic development across ethnic homelands, conditional on geographical, climatic, cultural, and institutional characteristics, the timing of initial human settlement, and world region fixed effects. The first four panels depict the impact of observed population homogeneity (i.e., 1 minus observed population diversity) on long-run historical economic development, as reflected by log population density in 5000 BC (panel A), 3000 BC (panel B), 1000 BC (panel C), and AD 100 (panel D), whereas the last panel depicts its impact on contemporary economic development, as reflected by a per-capita adjusted measure of log luminosity during the 1992–2013 time period. Each panel presents an augmented-component-plus-residual plot with a quadratic fit, corresponding to the relevant odd-numbered column of Table 22.2.

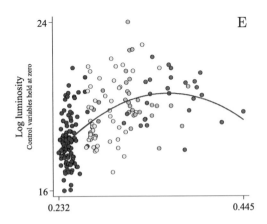

FIGURE 22.8

(*continued*)

Mechanisms capturing the adverse impact of diversity on social cohesiveness

Impact on internal conflicts

Intra-societal conflicts capture a fundamental mechanism though which the interpersonal diversity of a population can lead to its economic underperformance.[19] Exploiting variations across countries and ethnic groups, Arbatlı et al. (2020) demonstrate that population diversity, as determined primarily by the ancient migration of humans from East Africa, has been a pivotal contributor to the risk and intensity of both historical and contemporary internal conflicts, conditional on various geographical, cultural, and institutional correlates of conflict, outcomes of economic development, and unobserved time-invariant continent- or region-specific characteristics. Importantly, unlike commonly used measures of ethnic fractionalization and polarization, because interpersonal diversity captures both intergroup and *intragroup* differences in individual traits, the latter possesses explanatory power for not only intergroup conflicts but *intragroup* conflicts as well. This research additionally finds that interpersonal diversity may have contributed to internal conflicts in society through the channels of greater ethnic fragmentation at the country level, reduced interpersonal trust, and sharper divergence in preferences for public goods and redistributive policies. As established by Arbatlı et al. (2020), the scatter plots in Fig. 22.9 depict (i) the positive influence of observed population diversity on the prevalence of civil conflicts across ethnic homelands over the 1989–2008 time period (panel A); and (ii) the positive influence of contemporary national population diversity on the annual frequency of civil conflict onsets across countries during the 1960–2017 time period (panel B).

Impact on ethnocultural fragmentation

A previous literature (e.g., Easterly and Levine, 1997; Alesina et al., 2003; Alesina and La Ferrara, 2005) has shown that ethnic diversity at the national level, as measured by the degree of fraction-

---

[19] For a comprehensive review of the multifaceted links between conflict and economic underdevelopment, see Ray and Esteban (2017).

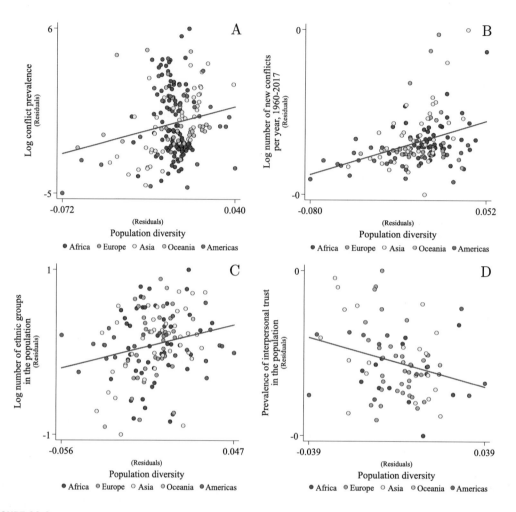

FIGURE 22.9

Mechanisms of the impact of population diversity on aggregate productivity. *Notes*: This figure depicts the impact of interpersonal population diversity across either ethnic homelands or countries on various outcomes that capture the mechanisms through which diversity can influence aggregate productivity. Panel A depicts the impact of observed population diversity across ethnic homelands on the prevalence of civil conflicts over the 1989–2008 time period. The remaining panels depict the impact of predicted ancestry-adjusted diversity across countries on (i) the annual frequency of civil conflict onsets across countries during the 1960–2017 time period (panel B); (ii) the number of ethnic groups (panel C); (iii) the prevalence of interpersonal trust in data covering the 1981–2008 period from the World Values Survey (panel D); (iv) the intra-country dispersion in individual political attitudes (expressed on a politically "left"–"right" categorical scale) in data covering the 1981–2008 period from the World Values Survey (panel E); and (v) the number of scientific articles per real GDP dollar over the 2010–18 time period (panel F). Each panel presents an added-variable plot, capturing a relationship that is conditioned on a sizeable vector of control variables relevant for explaining the outcome of interest. *Source*: Ashraf and Galor (2013a, 2013b, 2018), Arbatlı et al. (2020).

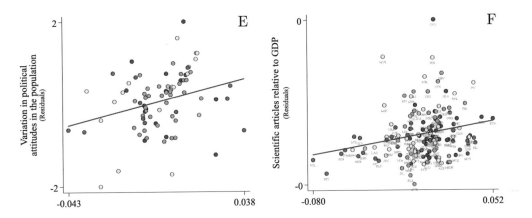

FIGURE 22.9

(*continued*)

alization and polarization across ethnic groups, is associated with various dimensions of economic underperformance. Examining the deeper roots of this causal chain, the evidence uncovered by Ashraf and Galor (2013b) suggests that prehistorically determined interpersonal diversity could be an underlying cause of different manifestations of the ethnolinguistic fragmentation of national populations. Specifically, their hypothesis suggests that following the ancient "out of Africa" migration, the initial endowment of population diversity in a given location may have catalyzed the formation of distinct groups at that location through a process of endogenous group selection, reflecting the trade-off associated with the scale and internal cohesion of each group. Although a larger group can benefit from economies of scale, it is more likely to be less cohesive due to costly coordination. Thus, in light of the added contribution of interpersonal diversity to the lack of cohesiveness of a group, a larger initial endowment of population diversity in a given location may have given rise to a larger number of groups. Over time, due to the forces of "cultural drift" and "biased transmission" of cultural markers that serve to distinguish "insiders" from "outsiders" of a group (e.g., language dialects, customs and traditions, norms of social conduct), intergroup divergence in such markers became more pronounced, leading to the formation of distinct collective identities along ethnic lines.

In line with this hypothesis, interpersonal diversity at the national level is found to impart a strong positive influence on various alternative measures of ethnolinguistic diversity, while accounting for the potentially confounding influence of the timing of the Neolithic Revolution, the time elapsed since initial human settlement, colonial history, the geographical determinants of ethnic diversity, and unobserved time-invariant continent-specific factors. Further, to address the issue of causality, the findings are shown to hold in a sample restricted to only countries from the Old World, which were largely immune from the potentially endogenous intercontinental migrations of the colonial era. In the same vein, the findings are also shown to be robust to employing the prehistoric migratory distance of the indigenous (precolonial) population of a country from East Africa as a plausibly exogenous source of variation of contemporary population diversity in a global sample of countries. The positive influence of interpersonal diversity on the number of ethnic groups at the national level, as uncovered by Ashraf and Galor (2013b) and further examined by Arbatlı et al. (2020), is depicted by the scatter plot in panel C of Fig. 22.9.

Impact on reduced interpersonal trust

Consistent with the hypothesis that interpersonal diversity can reduce social capital, and thus economic development, by widening the spectrum of individual values, beliefs, preferences, and predispositions, Ashraf and Galor (2013a) and Arbatlı et al. (2020) demonstrate that contemporary population diversity imparts a significant negative influence across countries on the prevalence of generalized interpersonal trust, based on data covering the 1981–2008 time period from the World Values Survey.[20] As depicted on the scatter plot in panel D of Fig. 22.9, the relationship accounts for cross-country heterogeneity in various geographical correlates of economic development and of ethnic diversity, as well as unobserved world region fixed effects.

Further, Arbatlı et al. (2020) employ two distinct analyses that exploit variations across individuals to show that the prevalence of mistrust at the individual level is significantly linked to the degree of interpersonal diversity in the individual's ancestral population.

- The first analysis connects the level of mistrust across individuals from the Afrobarometer surveys with the observed population diversity of their respective ancestral ethnic homelands in Africa, regardless of whether the surveyed individuals currently reside in their respective ancestral homelands or have migrated to a different location. The relationship is robust to accounting for a sizable vector of potential confounders, including (i) country-of-residence fixed effects, (ii) individual-level characteristics (age, gender, education, occupation, living condition, and religion), (iii) the degree of exposure of the ancestral homeland to slave exports, (iv) district-of-residence characteristics (i.e., presence of school, electricity, piped water, sewage, health clinic, and urban status), (v) ancestral-country fixed effects, and (vi) the current levels of ethnolinguistic diversity in both the district of residence and the ancestral homeland.
- The second analysis links the level of mistrust across second-generation U.S. immigrants from the General Social Survey with the contemporary national population diversity of their respective parental countries of origin. The focus on immigrants to a single country permits the analysis to implicitly account for unobserved time-invariant host-country characteristics (in geographical, cultural, and institutional dimensions). Moreover, the analysis explicitly accounts for a considerable set of potential individual-level confounders, as well as geographical characteristics, world region fixed effects, and the degree of ethnolinguistic fractionalization and polarization, all with respect to the individual's parental country of origin.

Impact on divergence in political preferences

Interpersonal diversity in values, beliefs, and preferences in general can capture heterogeneity in preferences over types of public goods in particular, as well as divergence in individual dispositions towards economic inequality and redistributive government policies, thereby leading to social conflicts and economic underperformance by contributing to political polarization and related institutional distortions.

---

[20] See Algan and Cahuc (2014) for a review of the empirical literature that has established the causal impact of generalized trust on economic performance and examined the various mechanisms through which this impact is manifested in the data.

In line with this mechanism, Ashraf and Galor (2018) and Arbatlı et al. (2020) document that contemporary population diversity imparts a significant positive influence across countries on the degree of heterogeneity in political preferences, as captured by the intra-country dispersion in self-reported individual positions on a politically "left"–"right" categorical scale, based on data covering the 1981–2008 time period from the World Values Survey. The scatter plot in panel E of Fig. 22.9 depicts this relationship, conditional on various geographical correlates of development and political economy, as well as unobserved world region fixed effects.

Impact on extractive institutions

The emergence and persistence of autocratic forms of societal governance is another crucial mechanism through which interpersonal diversity may have given rise to contemporary economic underperformance. Specifically, Galor and Klemp (2017) advance the hypothesis that although prehistorically determined interpersonal diversity may have raised society's demand for formal institutions that mitigated the adverse influence of diversity on social cohesion, the contribution of diversity to economic inequality and class stratification within societies may have also shaped institutional development toward more extractive and autocratic forms of governance. Exploiting variations across precolonial ethnic homelands, the authors find that conditional on the potentially confounding effects of a host of geographical factors and unobserved time-invariant continent-specific characteristics, interpersonal diversity imparts a positive influence on the prevalence of precolonial autocratic institutions, plausibly reflecting the dual impact of diversity on the demand for formal institutions and the emergence of social stratification. Furthermore, the research documents that the spatial variation in interpersonal diversity across the globe may have contributed to the cross-country variation in contemporary autocracy, partly reflecting the persistence of institutional, cultural, and compositional characteristics of populations over time.

Mechanisms capturing the beneficial impact of diversity on productivity

Impact on innovative activities

Consistent with their hypothesis that interpersonal diversity can foster innovative activity by expanding the domain of distinct varieties of complementary cognitive approaches to problem-solving and knowledge production, Ashraf and Galor (2013a) demonstrate that contemporary population diversity bears a significant positive association across countries with the average annual number of scientific articles per capita in the 1981–2000 time period. Their finding accounts for potentially confounding variation across countries in the timing of the Neolithic Revolution, various geographical, cultural, and institutional correlates of contemporary economic development, and unobserved time-invariant continent-specific factors. The scatter plot in panel F of Fig. 22.9 depicts a similar positive influence of contemporary population diversity across countries on the total number of scientific articles per real GDP dollar over the 2010–18 time period, conditional on geographical and climatic factors as well as unobserved time-invariant regional characteristics.[21]

---

[21] The beneficial effects of interpersonal diversity on economic development are also documented empirically by Ager and Brueckner (2018). Exploiting variations across counties in the United States in the late nineteenth century, these authors find that county-level populations that experienced a larger initial increase in their diversity due to the arrival of European immigrants also subsequently experienced higher rates of growth in both income and scientific patents per capita during the 1870–1920 time

Impact on the division of labor and gains from trade

In a recent paper, Depetris-Chauvin and Özak (2020) empirically examine Ashraf and Galor's (2013a) hypothesis that interpersonal diversity could have fostered the division of labor in society by widening the spectrum of individual skills, abilities, and cognitive approaches. Exploiting variations observed across precolonial ethnic homelands, they document that, consistently with Ashraf and Galor's original hypothesis, prehistorically determined interpersonal diversity may have conferred a positive influence on the degree of economic specialization in different production activities in a society, thereby fostering its proclivity to engage in and reap the economic benefits of market-based exchange.[22] The authors additionally show that ethnic homelands that were characterized by a higher degree of precolonial economic specialization, partly due to their higher levels of interpersonal population diversity, tend to exhibit significantly higher levels of both precolonial and contemporary economic development.

Impact via cross-fertilization of ideas in cognitive and human capital development

Interestingly, the beneficial impact of interpersonal diversity on productivity has also been documented at a much lower level of aggregation than countries or ethnic groups. Specifically, exploiting variations across ethnically homogeneous high schools in the state of Wisconsin, Cook and Fletcher (2018) find that the expected heterozygosity of the student body of a high school in 1957 may have conferred a significant positive influence on the economic performance of the school's graduates later in life, as captured by completed years of schooling, measures of occupational prestige of the graduate's first job, and family income in 1974 and 1992. The authors additionally provide evidence in line with a novel behavioral mechanism—namely, that exposure to more diverse schooling environments may have shaped individual personality traits towards greater creativity and openness to new ideas and, thus, behaviorally conditioned the individual for greater socioeconomic success later in life. Importantly, because the high-school student bodies in the authors' data set were entirely composed of individuals of European ancestry, the cultural homogeneity and social cohesiveness within these groups assure that the analysis overwhelmingly captures the benefits of diversity, rather than its costs. Further, because the findings are established by exploiting variations within a single state, they are immune to cross-country (and even within-country, cross-state) confounders.

22.3.5 Policy implications

Ashraf and Galor (2013a) and Ashraf et al. (2020a) document a fundamental trade-off associated with the influence of interpersonal diversity, as reflected by predicted population diversity, on economic performance. Nevertheless, the finding that predicted diversity, based on migratory distance from East

---

horizon. In another interesting study by Delis et al. (2017), the authors exploit panel variations across firms listed in the stock markets of North America and the United Kingdom to show that adding members to a firm's board of directors from countries of origin with differing levels of genetic diversity increases its corporate performance. The authors hypothesize that their finding reflects the productivity-enhancing benefits of interpersonal differences in cultural, psychological, physiological, and other traits that cannot be captured by alternative measured indices of diversity.

[22] Interestingly, as one would expect from preindustrial production activities, in which characteristics of the physical environment and individual abilities behave as complementary inputs, the research also documents that the degree of agro-ecological and agro-climatic heterogeneity reinforces the positive influence of interpersonal diversity on the emergence of economic specialization in precolonial societies.

Africa, has been a deep *determinant* of economic development does not imply that the composition of heritable traits in a population governs its economic *destiny*. Migratory distance from East Africa affected interpersonal diversity via the interaction of geographical, biological, and cultural attributes, and policies could thus be aimed at conditioning the intervening channels.

In particular, the influence of diversity on productivity implies that a society can shape the context in which the *existing* diversity of its population influences socioeconomic outcomes, by enacting policies to harness the beneficial effects of the existing level of diversity and mitigate its potentially detrimental consequences. Overly diverse societies could focus on fostering interpersonal trust and mediating the potential for social conflict, by encouraging civic participation, improving the quality of political institutions, and mitigating inefficiencies and distortions in the provision of public goods. Overly homogeneous societies, on the other hand, could aim to increase diversity in skills, occupations, and training programs in order to foster specialization and innovative activity. In both cases, the orientation of the educational system appears to be the most promising avenue: education can help instill the values of tolerance needed in overly diverse societies, and it can promote cultural receptiveness to different types of productivity-enhancing knowledge in overly homogeneous societies.

22.3.6 Common misconceptions

The literature on the influence of interpersonal diversity on comparative development across societies has attracted the attention of the scholarly community beyond the discipline of economics and, given methodological divisions, perhaps unsurprisingly generated unfounded criticisms. Three main criticisms have been raised by scholars from other disciplines, predominantly, cultural anthropologists. As discussed below, they reflect a basic misunderstanding of the conceptual framework, the statistical methodology, the scope of the analysis, and its policy implications.

22.3.6.1 Potential underestimation of population density in pre-Columbian Americas

Some have argued that the hump-shaped relationship between population diversity and aggregate productivity is an artifact of imperfections in the measure of population sizes during the precolonial era. In particular, they contend that the underestimation of population sizes for precolonial Amerindian societies contributed to the documented relationship.

In fact, the historical analysis of Ashraf and Galor (2013a) accounts for the possibility that the data on population density from the precolonial era could indeed be afflicted by measurement errors, establishing through various methods that this issue has no bearing on the validity of their empirical findings:

- Since population density is the *dependent* variable, classical measurement error in this variable does not generate bias in the estimates of the hump-shaped influence of diversity on historical development. In fact, in the absence of such measurement error, the statistical significance of the estimates would be even higher.
- If there are *systematic* differences across continents in the measurement of historical population density (e.g., if historical population density in the Americas is indeed consistently underestimated), then the estimated effects could have been biased. However, the use of continent fixed effects in the statistical analysis of Ashraf and Galor (2013a), assures that the influence of diversity on historical development is identified based on intersocietal variations within continents, rather than across

continents, and hence systematic under-estimation of population levels in the Americas would have no bearing on the results.

- Employing an alternative measure of historical development based on the extent of urbanization in AD 1500, rather than population density, does not qualitatively alter the hump-shaped influence of interpersonal diversity on historical development, as shown by the regressions in columns 3 and 4 of Table 22.1 and by the scatter plot in panel B of Fig. 22.7.[23]
- The significant hump-shaped impact of interpersonal population diversity on historical population density at various points in time between 10,000 BC and AD 1500 is established across ethnic homelands (derived from the extended sample of ethnic groups in Pemberton et al. (2013) by Ashraf et al. (2020a). A subset of their findings are highlighted in columns 1–8 of Table 22.3 and illustrated in panels A–D of Fig. 22.8.
- The main analysis of Ashraf and Galor (2013a) focuses on *contemporary* comparative development, in which the dependent variable is income per capita in the year 2000 (rather than historical population density). Further, the significant hump-shaped impact of interpersonal population diversity on an updated measure of contemporary comparative development, captured by average income per capita during the 2010–18 time period, is apparent in the regression results presented in columns 5–6 of Table 22.1 and in the scatter plot in panel C of Fig. 22.7.
- As shown by regressions in columns 7–8 of Table 22.1 and columns 9–10 of Table 22.3, and depicted in the scatter plots presented in panel D of Fig. 22.7 and panel E of Fig. 22.8, the hump-shaped impact of interpersonal population diversity is robust to the use of an alternative measure of contemporary economic development, captured by per-capita adjusted nighttime luminosity, either across countries or across the ethnic homelands based on the extended sample of groups in Pemberton et al. (2013).

Thus, concerns about the potential underestimation of populations in the Americas in the pre-Columbian era and its impact on the analysis are based on a misunderstanding of the statistical methodology employed by this research program. Moreover, the presence of a hump-shaped impact of interpersonal population diversity on: (i) the rate of urbanization in AD 1500, (ii) the population density of ethnic groups at various points in the considerable expanse of time between 10,000 BC and AD 1500, and (iii) contemporary measures of income per capita (for which potential mismeasurements of population density in the pre-Columbian period are entirely irrelevant), further highlight the uninformed nature of this criticism.

22.3.6.2 The mapping from diversity in neutral genetic markers to social outcomes

Some have questioned the research program by arguing that expected heterozygosity in neutral genetic markers, employed to proxy for the degree of interpersonal diversity within individual ethnic groups, does not reflect diversity in functional (phenotypic) markers and, therefore, cannot influence behavioral and social interactions.

The measure of observed genetic diversity for the 53 ethnic groups in the HGDP-CEPH sample, as well as for the 200+ groups in the extended data set of Pemberton et al. (2013) are indeed based neutral genetic markers and, thus, do not *directly* reflect diversity in functional (phenotypic) markers.

---

[23] It may be noted that the data source for urbanization rates in AD 1500 is independent of the source for historical population density.

However, the core analysis of Ashraf and Galor (2013a) is based not on *observed* genetic diversity but rather on *predicted* diversity, implied predominantly by the migratory distances from East Africa of the ancestral populations of contemporary nations. In particular, as discussed in Section 22.3.3.1, in order to overcome sample limitations and potential concerns about reverse causality associated with the use of *observed* genetic diversity, Ashraf and Galor (2013a) exploit the pronounced impact of migratory distance from East Africa on observed genetic diversity across ethnic groups in the HGDP-CEPH sample in order *predict* interpersonal diversity for all societies, based on the geographical locations of their precolonial ancestral populations, relative to East Africa and to one another.

Importantly, since migratory distance from East Africa has a negative influence on various forms of intragroup phenotypic diversity, *predicted* interpersonal diversity is a valid proxy for diversity in phenotypically and behaviorally expressed traits. As noted earlier in Section 22.3.2, evidence from the fields of physical and cognitive anthropology suggests that an ancient serial founder effect originating in East Africa has influenced observed worldwide patterns in various forms of intragroup morphological and cognitive diversity, including interpersonal diversity in skeletal features pertaining to cranial characteristics (Manica et al., 2007; von Cramon-Taubadel and Lycett, 2008; Betti et al., 2009), dental attributes (Hanihara, 2008), pelvic traits (Betti et al., 2013), and birth canal morphology (Betti and Manica, 2018), as well as intralingual phonemic diversity (Atkinson, 2011).

Hence, the assertion that inferences cannot be made regarding the impact of interpersonal diversity on socioeconomic outcomes, because the measure of diversity in the HGDP-CEPH sample is based on neutral genetic markers reflects a misunderstanding of the empirical strategy of Ashraf and Galor (2013a). Since migratory distance from Africa affects diversity in neutral genetic markers as well as diversity in phenotypically expressed morphological and cognitive traits, the empirical strategy of exploiting *predicted* population diversity is well positioned to capture the effect of interpersonal diversity on socioeconomic outcomes.

22.3.6.3 Potential misuse

Some critics have raised concerns that the finding that productivity tends to be maximized at intermediate levels of diversity could be used to justify disturbing policies, such as the forcible movement or "engineering" of populations, designed to achieve the desirable diversity level in a population.

This view, however, reflects a misunderstanding of the most fundamental insight of this research agenda and its main policy implications. The influence of diversity on productivity operates through various mechanisms, and policies can thus be targeted on these mediating forces, allowing societies to shape the context in which their *existing* levels of diversity can further promote productivity. For instance, as noted in Section 22.3.5, education policies geared towards pluralism can advance cultural receptiveness to different types of productivity-enhancing knowledge (in overly homogeneous societies) while instilling cultural values of trust and tolerance (in overly diverse societies).

22.4 Concluding remarks

The past two decades have witnessed the emergence of an influential body of research that has focused on uncovering the ancient roots of economic development across countries, regions, and ethnic groups. This line of inquiry has been exploring the influence of evolutionary processes in the transition from stagnation to growth, as well as the impact of the diversity of human traits on comparative economic development across societies, highlighting the role of the prehistoric "out of Africa" migration of anatomically modern humans in shaping variations in the composition of human traits among populations across the globe.

This exploration of the interaction between evolutionary processes and long-run economic development has centered around two major lines of inquiry. The first suggests that in the era following the Neolithic Revolution, Malthusian pressures not only acted as a key determinant of the size of a population but conceivably shaped, via the forces of natural selection, its composition as well. Lineages of individuals whose traits were complementary to the economic environment generated higher levels of income and, thus, a larger number of surviving offspring. Consequently, the gradual increase in the representation of these growth-enhancing traits in the population over time contributed to the process of development and the emergence of modern growth.

The second line of research advances the hypothesis that migratory distances from the cradle of humankind in East Africa to indigenous settlements across the globe diminished their levels of interpersonal diversity and, thereby, generated a persistent hump-shaped influence on development outcomes, reflecting a fundamental trade-off between beneficial and detrimental effects of diversity on productivity at the societal level. Although diversity can reduce interpersonal trust and social cohesiveness, and can hence adversely affect the productivity of society, diversity can also foster the cross-fertilization of ideas for innovations and stimulate gains from specialization, and it can thus contribute to society's productivity. Therefore, in light of diminishing marginal effects of diversity and homogeneity on productivity, intermediate levels of diversity have contributed to economic prosperity across countries, regions, and ethnic groups.

References

Ager, P., Brueckner, M., 2018. Immigrants' genes: genetic diversity and economic development in the United States. Economic Inquiry 56 (2), 1149–1164.

Alesina, A., Devleeschauwer, A., Easterly, W., Kurlat, S., Wacziarg, R., 2003. Fractionalization. Journal of Economic Growth 8 (2), 155–194.

Alesina, A., La Ferrara, E., 2005. Ethnic diversity and economic performance. Journal of Economic Literature 43 (3), 762–800.

Algan, Y., Cahuc, P., 2014. Trust, growth, and well-being: new evidence and policy implications. In: Aghion, P., Durlauf, S.N. (Eds.), Handbook of Economic Growth, vol. 2A. Elsevier, North-Holland, Amsterdam and Boston, pp. 49–120.

Arbatlı, C.E., Ashraf, Q.H., Galor, O., Klemp, M., 2020. Diversity and conflict. Econometrica 88 (2), 727–797.

Ashraf, Q., Galor, O., 2011. Dynamics and stagnation in the Malthusian epoch. The American Economic Review 101 (5), 2003–2041.

Ashraf, Q., Galor, O., 2013a. The 'out of Africa' hypothesis, human genetic diversity, and comparative economic development. The American Economic Review 103 (1), 1–46.

Ashraf, Q., Galor, O., 2013b. Genetic diversity and the origins of cultural fragmentation. The American Economic Review 103 (3), 528–533.

Ashraf, Q.H., Galor, O., 2018. The macrogenoeconomics of comparative development. Journal of Economic Literature 56 (3), 1119–1155.

Ashraf, Q., Galor, O., Klemp, M., 2014. The 'Out of Africa' Hypothesis of Comparative Development Reflected by Nighttime Light Intensity. Working Paper 2014-4. Brown University, Department of Economics.

Ashraf, Q.H., Galor, O., Klemp, M., 2020a. Population Diversity and Differential Paths of Long-Run Development since the Neolithic Revolution. Unpublished.

Ashraf, Q.H., Galor, O., Klemp, M., 2020b. Interpersonal Diversity and Societally Important Disparities across Populations: A Reply to Rosenberg and Kang. Unpublished.

Atkinson, Q.D., 2011. Phonemic diversity supports a serial founder effect model of language expansion from Africa. Science 332 (6027), 346–349.

Becker, A., Enke, B., Falk, A., 2020. Ancient origins of the global variation in economic preferences. AEA Papers and Proceedings 110, 319–323.

Bersaglieri, T., et al., 2004. Genetic signatures of strong recent positive selection at the lactase gene. American Journal of Human Genetics 74 (6), 1111–1120.

Betti, L., Manica, A., 2018. Human variation in the shape of the birth canal is significant and geographically structured. Proceedings of the Royal Society B: Biological Sciences 285 (1889), 20181807.

Betti, L., Balloux, F., Amos, W., Hanihara, T., Manica, A., 2009. Distance from Africa, not climate, explains within-population phenotypic diversity in humans. Proceedings of the Royal Society B: Biological Sciences 276 (1658), 809–814.

Betti, L., von Cramon-Taubadel, N., Manica, A., Lycett, S.J., 2013. Global geometric morphometric analyses of the human pelvis reveal substantial neutral population history effects, even across sexes. PLoS ONE 8 (2), e55909.

Bisin, A., Verdier, T., 2000. 'Beyond the melting pot': cultural transmission, marriage, and the evolution of ethnic and religious traits. The Quarterly Journal of Economics 115 (3), 955–988.

Bisin, A., Verdier, T., 2001. The economics of cultural transmission and the dynamics of preferences. Journal of Economic Theory 97 (2), 298–319.

Bisin, A., Verdier, T., 2011. The economics of cultural transmission and socialization. In: Benhabib, J., Bisin, A., Jackson, M.O. (Eds.), Handbook of Social Economics, vol. 1A. Elsevier, North-Holland, Amsterdam and Boston, pp. 339–416.

Bouchouicha, R., Vieider, F.M., 2019. Growth, entrepreneurship, and risk-tolerance: a risk-income paradox. Journal of Economic Growth 24 (3), 257–282.

Bowles, S., Gintis, H., 2011. A Cooperative Species: Human Reciprocity and Its Evolution. Princeton University Press, Princeton and Oxford.

Burger, J., Kirchner, M., Bramanti, B., Haak, W., Thomas, M.G., 2007. Absence of the lactase-persistence-associated allele in early Neolithic Europeans. Proceedings of the National Academy of Sciences 104 (10), 3736–3741.

Cann, H.M., et al., 2002. A human genome diversity cell line panel. Science 296 (5566), 261–262.

Collins, J., Baer, B., Weber, E.J., 2014. Economic growth and evolution: parental preference for quality and quantity of offspring. Macroeconomic Dynamics 18 (8), 1773–1796.

Cook, C.J., 2015. The natural selection of infectious disease resistance and its effect on contemporary health. Review of Economics and Statistics 97 (4), 742–757.

Cook, C.J., Fletcher, J.M., 2018. High school genetic diversity and later-life student outcomes: micro-level evidence from the Wisconsin longitudinal study. Journal of Economic Growth 23 (3), 307–339.

Dalgaard, C.-J., Strulik, H., 2015. The physiological foundations of the wealth of nations. Journal of Economic Growth 20 (1), 37–73.

Dalgaard, C.-J., Strulik, H., 2016. Physiology and development: why the West is taller than the rest. Economic Journal 126 (598), 2292–2323.

de la Croix, D., Schneider, E.B., Weisdorf, J., 2019. Childlessness, celibacy and net fertility in pre-industrial England: the middle-class evolutionary advantage. Journal of Economic Growth 24 (3), 223–256.

Delis, M.D., Gaganis, C., Hasan, I., Pasiouras, F., 2017. The effect of board directors from countries with different genetic diversity levels on corporate performance. Management Science 63 (1), 231–249.

Depetris-Chauvin, E., Özak, Ö., 2020. The origins of the division of labor in pre-industrial times. Journal of Economic Growth 25 (3), 297–340.

Desmet, K., Weber, S., Ortuño-Ortín, I., 2009. Linguistic diversity and redistribution. Journal of the European Economic Association 7 (6), 1291–1318.

Doepke, M., Zilibotti, F., 2014. Culture, entrepreneurship, and growth. In: Aghion, P., Durlauf, S.N. (Eds.), Handbook of Economic Growth, vol. 2A. Elsevier, North-Holland, Amsterdam and Boston, pp. 1–48.

Easterly, W., Levine, R., 1997. Africa's growth tragedy: policies and ethnic divisions. The Quarterly Journal of Economics 112 (4), 1203–1250.

Esteban, J., Mayoral, L., Ray, D., 2012. Ethnicity and conflict: an empirical study. The American Economic Review 102 (4), 1310–1342.

Fearon, J.D., 2003. Ethnic and cultural diversity by country. Journal of Economic Growth 8 (2), 195–222.

Galor, O., 2011. Unified Growth Theory. Princeton University Press, Princeton and Oxford.

Galor, O., Klemp, M., 2017. The Roots of Autocracy. Working Paper 23301. National Bureau of Economic Research.

Galor, O., Klemp, M., 2019. Human genealogy reveals a selective advantage to moderate fecundity. Nature Ecology & Evolution 3 (4), 853–857.

Galor, O., Michalopoulos, S., 2012. Evolution and the growth process: natural selection of entrepreneurial traits. Journal of Economic Theory 147 (2), 759–780.

Galor, O., Moav, O., 2002. Natural selection and the origin of economic growth. The Quarterly Journal of Economics 117 (4), 1133–1191.

Galor, O., Moav, O., 2007. The Neolithic Revolution and Contemporary Variations in Life Expectancy. Working Paper 2007-14. Brown University, Department of Economics.

Galor, O., Özak, Ö., 2016. The agricultural origins of time preference. The American Economic Review 106 (10), 3064–3103.

Galor, O., Savitskiy, V., 2020. Climatic Roots of Loss Aversion. Working Paper 25273. National Bureau of Economic Research.

Hanihara, T., 2008. Morphological variation of major human populations based on nonmetric dental traits. American Journal of Physical Anthropology 136 (2), 169–182.

Harpending, H., Rogers, A., 2000. Genetic perspectives on human origins and differentiation. Annual Review of Genomics and Human Genetics 1, 361–385.

Hawks, J., Wang, E.T., Cochran, G.M., Harpending, H.C., Moyzis, R.K., 2007. Recent acceleration of human adaptive evolution. Proceedings of the National Academy of Sciences 104 (52), 20753–20758.

Henn, B.M., Cavalli-Sforza, L.L., Feldman, M.W., 2012. The great human expansion. Proceedings of the National Academy of Sciences 109 (44), 17758–17764.

Klemp, M., Weisdorf, J., 2019. Fecundity, fertility and the formation of human capital. Economic Journal 129 (618), 925–960.

Kong, A., et al., 2017. Selection against variants in the genome associated with educational attainment. Proceedings of the National Academy of Sciences 114 (5), E727–E732.

Kong, A., et al., 2018. The nature of nurture: effects of parental genotypes. Science 359 (6374), 424–428.

Lagerlöf, N.-P., 2007. Long-run trends in human body mass. Macroeconomic Dynamics 11 (3), 367–387.

Livingstone, F.B., 1958. Anthropological implications of sickle cell gene distribution in West Africa. American Anthropologist 60 (3), 533–562.

Manica, A., Amos, W., Balloux, F., Hanihara, T., 2007. The effect of ancient population bottlenecks on human phenotypic variation. Nature 448 (7151), 346–348.

Mathieson, I., et al., 2015. Genome-wide patterns of selection in 230 ancient Eurasians. Nature 528 (7583), 499–503.

Mekel-Bobrov, N., et al., 2005. Ongoing adaptive evolution of *ASPM*, a brain size determinant in *Homo sapiens*. Science 309 (5741), 1720–1722.

Nielsen, R., Hellmann, I., Hubisz, M., Bustamante, C., Clark, A.G., 2007. Recent and ongoing selection in the human genome. Nature Reviews Genetics 8 (11), 857–868.

Pemberton, T.J., DeGiorgio, M., Rosenberg, N.A., 2013. Population structure in a comprehensive genomic data set on human microsatellite variation. G3: Genes, Genomes, Genetics 3 (5), 891–907.

Prugnolle, F., Manica, A., Balloux, F., 2005. Geography predicts neutral genetic diversity of human populations. Current Biology 15 (5), R159–R160.

Putterman, L., Weil, D.N., 2010. Post-1500 population flows and the long-run determinants of economic growth and inequality. The Quarterly Journal of Economics 125 (4), 1627–1682.

Ramachandran, S., Deshpande, O., Roseman, C.C., Rosenberg, N.A., Feldman, M.W., Luca Cavalli-Sforza, L., 2005. Support from the relationship of genetic and geographic distance in human populations for a serial founder effect originating in Africa. Proceedings of the National Academy of Sciences 102 (44), 15942–15947.

Ray, D., Esteban, J., 2017. Conflict and development. Annual Review of Economics 9, 263–293.

Robson, A.J., Samuelson, L., 2011. The evolutionary foundations of preferences. In: Benhabib, J., Bisin, A., Jackson, M.O. (Eds.), Handbook of Social Economics, vol. 1A. Elsevier, North-Holland, Amsterdam and Boston, pp. 221–310.

Rogers, D.S., Feldman, M.W., Ehrlich, P.R., 2009. Inferring population histories using cultural data. Proceedings of the Royal Society B: Biological Sciences 276 (1674), 3835–3843.

Rosenberg, N.A., Kang, J.T.L., 2015. Genetic diversity and societally important disparities. Genetics 201 (1), 1–12.

Sabeti, P.C., et al., 2006. Positive natural selection in the human lineage. Science 312 (5780), 1614–1620.

Sacerdote, B., 2011. Nature and nurture effects on children's outcomes: what have we learned from studies of twins and adoptees? In: Benhabib, J., Bisin, A., Jackson, M.O. (Eds.), Handbook of Social Economics, vol. 1A. Elsevier, North-Holland, Amsterdam and Boston, pp. 1–30.

Simonson, T.S., et al., 2010. Genetic evidence for high-altitude adaptation in Tibet. Science 329 (5987), 72–75.

Spolaore, E., Wacziarg, R., 2009. The diffusion of development. The Quarterly Journal of Economics 124 (2), 469–529.

Spolaore, E., Wacziarg, R., 2014. Long-term barriers to economic development. In: Aghion, P., Durlauf, S.N. (Eds.), Handbook of Economic Growth, vol. 2A. Elsevier, North-Holland, Amsterdam and Boston, pp. 121–176.

Tishkoff, S.A., et al., 2001. Haplotype diversity and linkage disequilibrium at human G6PD: recent origin of alleles that confer malarial resistance. Science 293 (5529), 455–462.

Tishkoff, S.A., et al., 2007. Convergent adaptation of human lactase persistence in Africa and Europe. Nature Genetics 39 (1), 31–40.

Tversky, A., Kahneman, D., 1991. Loss aversion in riskless choice: a reference-dependent model. The Quarterly Journal of Economics 106 (4), 1039–1061.

Voight, B.F., Kudaravalli, S., Wen, X., Pritchard, J.K., 2006. A map of recent positive selection in the human genome. PLoS Biology 4 (3), e72.

von Cramon-Taubadel, N., Lycett, S.J., 2008. Brief communication: human cranial variation fits iterative founder effect model with African origin. American Journal of Physical Anthropology 136 (1), 108–113.

Weibull, J.W., Salomonsson, M., 2006. Natural selection and social preferences. Journal of Theoretical Biology 239 (1), 79–92.

Wiesenfeld, S.L., 1967. Sickle-cell trait in human biological and cultural evolution: development of agriculture causing increased malaria is bound to gene-pool changes causing malaria reduction. Science 157 (3793), 1134–1140.

Social mobility in historical economics

Gregory Clark[a,b,c]
[a]*Department of Economics, University of California, Davis, CA, United States*
[b]*Department of Economic History, LSE, London, United Kingdom*
[c]*CEPR, London, United Kingdom*

23.1 Introduction

Social mobility is a vital component of any well-functioning society and economy. Talent and ability pass imperfectly from parents to children. Thus over generations, in a society with barriers to social mobility, there will be a misallocation of talents to occupations. That creates both a static loss of economic output, as well as a dynamic loss of future output from reductions in the rate of technological advance.

The literate in medieval Europe, for example, were less than 1 percent of the population. Likely the division between the literate landed upper classes, and the peasants, artisans, and laborers who constituted the overwhelming bulk of the population, was based on arbitrary acts of earlier conquest. Without social mobility between the landed and peasant classes, potentially 99 percent of the talented of the population would be locked out of education in medieval Europe.

But even at the level of the artisanal skills that Joel Mokyr emphasizes in his chapter were a vital part of the Industrial Revolution, if the artisans in each generation were drawn only from a closed artisan class, there would be the same problem of mismatch of talents and occupations (Mokyr, 2021). So this raises the issue of whether increases in social mobility rates were one component of the social changes that led to European societies experiencing an Industrial Revolution in the late eighteenth century.

Yet despite its importance, the topic of social mobility is little discussed in the historical literature for societies before the late nineteenth century. And even for the nineteenth century conventional measures have serious problems of comparability with modern measures. This is because measuring mobility is impossible because of data limitations for most pre-industrial societies. In this chapter it is shown how alternative measures of social mobility, which focus on surname distributions rather than individual family links, can extend the study of social mobility in some societies to much earlier times.

Intergenerational social mobility rates seem an easy thing to measure, since they represent just the correlation in social status between parents and children. However if b is the true underlying correlation in intergenerational status, in practice we typically derive only an attenuated estimate of that, θb, where $\theta < 1$, caused by errors in measurement of actual status, and errors in linkage of parents to children. And this degree of attenuation can vary substantially across societies and time periods.

The Handbook of Historical Economics. https://doi.org/10.1016/B978-0-12-815874-6.00033-2

Measuring social mobility rates using conventional techniques also requires considerable amounts of data. We must identify for children who their parents were, and measure for both parents and children status on a comparable social or economic status scale.

Linking parents and children is easy in areas such as modern Nordic countries where every individual is assigned by the government a unique ID at birth, and this ID is used to track individuals in education, employment, medical care and taxation. But even in such status measures such as years of education, or occupational rank, can differ significantly in their meaning about true underlying status across even a single generation. But if we want to measure social mobility rates in any society before the last 50 years, we immediately run into significant data problems.

Consider, for example, attempts to measure social mobility rates in the USA or UK in the era where large scale census data is available, 1850-1940. A recent paper (Song et al., 2020) reports that sons born 1830 is the US had only a 0.17 correlation in occupational rank with their fathers, compared to 0.27 for sons born 1880, and 0.30 for sons born 1980.[1] US mobility rates have seemingly substantially declined. This decline in occupational mobility was significantly associated with a decline in the share of the population in agriculture. In other work nineteenth century US occupational mobility rates have been found to be much higher than those in England.[2]

However markers of social status can vary significantly across societies and time periods in how well they indicate underlying social status. In the nineteenth century in the USA, for example, vast numbers of men were described as "farmers." Thus in a sample of 2005 fathers in the US in the 1850 census, 1370, 68% were "farmers".[3] But farmers varied enormously in social status from smallholders with a few rented acres, to large scale operators with many hired laborers. In contrast in the English census sample of 1851 only 279 out of 2076 fathers, 9%, were "farmers."[4] Was the nineteenth century US really the land of opportunity, or did it instead just have a very uninformative vocabulary for occupations in the censuses? Was nineteenth century England was a much less mobile society than the USA, or was England just a much more urbanized and industrialized society where occupational titles were much more revealing of true social status?

A second problem has been in matching parents to children across censuses. Here there has been debate about the accuracy of matching algorithms, with claims that many early parent-child matches are mistaken, and also that matches are more likely when both parent and child are of higher social status, overestimating persistence in status across generations.[5]

What is discussed in this chapter is another way of measuring social mobility in early or less institutionally developed societies, which uses the status of surnames. This measure has several advantages for measuring mobility in such societies. First it can be done without having to link individuals across generations, so it is informationally less demanding. We can get estimates for societies long before the

---

[1] Song et al. (2020), Fig. 2. Note that this paper limits itself to measuring the occupational mobility of white males.

[2] Long and Ferrie (2013).

[3] Long and Ferrie (2013), Table 3, p. 1121.

[4] Long and Ferrie (2013), Table 3, p. 1121. To deal with this issue Long and Ferrie use a much less intuitive measure of mobility than the intergeneration correlation of status, instead using a metric the Altham Statistic which gives a summary measure of the strength of the association between rows and columns in a two-dimensional table, as well as a measure of how the strength of that association differs between two tables.

[5] The criticism is by Bailey et al. (2017). A defense of the accuracy of nineteenth century matching across censuses is Abramitzky et al. (2019). See also Price et al. (2019) and Ruggles et al. (2018).

census era, or where censuses do not identify individuals. Second it can also be done where we have just three pieces of information:

1. the general population distribution of surnames or surname types,
2. the distribution of these surname types among some elite or underclass: university students, doctors, or property holders, as elites, for example, or convicts or paupers as an underclass,
3. a measure of how elite or underclass the relevant status group is.

Third it measures mobility rates independently of how much randomness there is in the measure of social status in terms of capturing "true" underlying status. Thus this method can produce estimates which are truly comparable across societies and time periods.

Finally these surname estimates reveal important things about the dynamics of the mobility process across multiple generations, as will be discussed below, that show that it is impossible to correctly describe the process of social mobility using just the intergenerational correlation of status between parents and children.

23.2 Conventional measures of social mobility

Assume social status can be measured by a cardinal number y which measures some aspect of social status such as income, wealth, or occupational status. Conventionally social mobility rates have been estimated by economists from the estimated value of β in the equation

$$y_t = \beta y_{t-1} + u_t \tag{23.1}$$

where y is the measure of social status (normalized to mean 0), t indexes the generation, and u_t is a random shock. β will typically lie between 0 and 1, with lower values of β implying more social mobility. β is thus the persistence rate for status, and $1 - \beta$ the social mobility rate. Also if the variance of status on this measure is constant across generations then β is also the intergenerational correlation of status. And in this case β also estimates the share of the variance of status in each generation that is explicable from inheritance. This share then will be β^2. The reason for this is that if σ^2 measures the variance of the status measure y, and σ_u^2 measures the variance of the random component in status, then, from Eq. (23.1)

$$var\,(y_t) = \beta^2 var\,(y_{t-1}) + var(u_t)$$
$$\sigma^2 = \beta^2\sigma^2 + \sigma_u^2$$

If Eq. (23.1) is the correct description of the inheritance of social status in any society, then in steady state any measure of status such as the logarithm of income or wealth will show a normal distribution.

Eq. (23.1) involves a number of strong simplifying assumptions. It assumes, for example, that social mobility rates are the same across the whole of the status distribution, from top to bottom. But we shall see that the empirical evidence is that this assumption is not too far from reality.

For example, a recent study of intergenerational wealth mobility in Sweden assembled data from Danish tax records that allows a comparison of the wealth of 1.2 million children with that of their parents (Boserup et al., 2013) The huge size of the Danish wealth data set means that the authors can

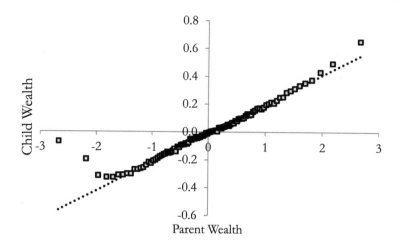

FIGURE 23.1

Inheritance of wealth in Denmark, 1997-2012. *Source*: Boserup et al. (2013).

divide the parents into percentiles and look at the average wealth of children for each parent percentile, measured again as a percentile of the child wealth distribution. Other than the top and bottom 3 or 4 percent of parental wealth, the picture has the linear character equation (23.1) assumes. One persistence rate, 0.20, describes inheritance across the middle 92 percent of the distribution (Fig. 23.1). The greatest deviation appears in the bottom 4 percent of parental wealth, where the children are much richer than we would expect. But the parents at the bottom of the distribution have negative wealth. This suggests not chronic, grinding poverty (the truly poor do not get to borrow much), but more likely indebtedness to finance a business venture or training. The fact that this is not truly the bottom of the wealth distribution explains the breakdown of the stable relationship. Children in the top 3 percent of the parental-wealth distribution also show slightly greater wealth inheritance. But though this effect is statistically significant, it represents only modest deviations from the single persistence rate in real terms: the persistence rates implied by the top three percentiles are 0.24, 0.23, and 0.22 respectively.

Eq. (23.1) also assumes implicitly that social mobility is a first-order Markov process, if it is to be a complete description of the mobility process. Child outcomes must depend only on those of the parents. In that case social mobility over n generations will be

$$y_{t+n} = \beta^n y_t + u_{t+n} \tag{23.2}$$

With the intergenerational occupational correlations of 0.17-0.30 measured for the USA 1820-1980 in the Song et al. (2020) paper this would imply that the correlation in occupational status between grandfathers and grandsons in the USA would be between 0.03 and 0.09. There are no persistent upper and lower classes. However, there is good evidence that after the first generation, persistence of status increases greatly, and is indeed strong. For a high status individual the typical path of their descendants towards mean status levels will look as in Fig. 23.2. After initial substantial mobility between parent and child, the decline of the correlation across generations becomes much slower, and is also constant across generations. This process can be well described by Eqs. (23.3) and (23.4). The manifest status

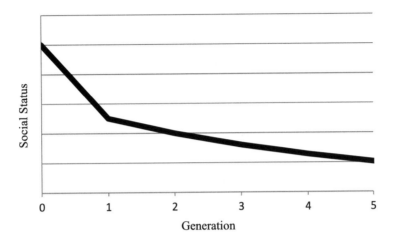

FIGURE 23.2

Paths of regression to the mean for an individual family.

in each generation is composed of an underlying component, x, which is strongly transmitted across generations, and a transitory component, u, which is not transmitted.

$$y_t = x_t + u_t \qquad (23.3)$$

The underlying status is inherited strongly, so that

$$x_t = bx_{t-1} + e_t \qquad (23.4)$$

where b is in the order of 0.7-0.8. In this case if we regress, as is conventionally done

$$y_t = \beta_1 y_{t-1} + v_t \qquad (23.5)$$

so that we are looking at the parent-child correlation, then $E\left(\hat{\beta}_1\right) = \frac{\sigma_x^2}{\sigma_y^2}b = \theta b$. But if we look over n generations, where β_n is the correlation across n generations, $E(\hat{\beta}_n) = \theta b^n$.

Fig. 23.3 gives a diagrammatic picture of the structure that underlies observed social status transmission. The transitory component in social status exists for two reasons. First all measures of status are made with substantial amounts of error. That creates an appearance just of enhanced mobility across single generations. Second there is an element of luck in the actual status attained by individuals.

This means social mobility has two components, both of which are needed to describe the full process. There is the short-run parent-child mobility, the rate of which can vary substantially across aspects of status such as wealth, education, income, occupational status and longevity. Then there is the underlying long run persistence, which may be the same across all aspects of status.

With a social mobility process of this form we will observe that any group within the population – including those identified with particular surnames or surname types – regresses to mean status at the rate of underlying mobility in Fig. 23.3 $(1 - b)$. Since b seems to be of the order of 0.75, this implies that at the group level social status is very persistent.

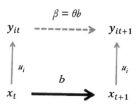

FIGURE 23.3

Underlying structure of intergenerational status transmission.

23.3 Measuring social mobility rates from surnames

For the reasons given in the introduction we have until recently had no idea of what social mobility rates were in pre-industrial societies. In particular we did not know whether pre-industrial Europe or China was indeed, for example, a static society where the peasant class continued unchanged from generation to generation. There has been debate for China about whether the Imperial exam system promoted social mobility, or entrenched a fossilized elite (Ho (1964); Elman (1992)). We also had no idea whether, for example, the Industrial Revolution in England was associated with a period of enhanced social mobility compared to what came before and what came after.[6]

However, in many societies people have surnames, and these surnames are inherited unchanged through the patriline. In England, for example, most people had inherited surnames by 1300. Men bearing the surname *Pepys* born in England 1900-1930, for example, are descended from someone in the group of men bearing the surname *Pepys* in 1870-1900. And indeed this same surname *Pepys* was already visible in records by the 15th century. Thus using surnames to group people we can identify groups of sons who collectively descended from a group of fathers, without knowing the exact descent relationships. The fact that surnames can proxy for the transmission of the y chromosome between generations has long been of interest to geneticists.[7] However only recently have there been attempts to utilize surnames to estimate social mobility rates. Here we describe two methods of estimating intergenerational social mobility from surnames.

Instead of estimating β from

$$y_t = \beta y_{t-1} + u_t \tag{24.1}$$

we can use

$$\overline{y}_{kt} = \beta \overline{y}_{kt-1} + \overline{u}_{kt} \tag{23.6}$$

where k indexes surname groups and $^-$ indicates averages. We can, for example, compare the average status of everyone born with the surname *Pepys* in 1800-1829 to those born with this surname 1830-1859, the 30 year interval between the time periods here representing the assumed average length of a generation.

---

[6] See Clark and Cummins (2014), for a review of the evidence on this.
[7] See, for example, King and Jobling (2009).

Table 23.1 Convention intergenerational mobility estimates, England, births 1840-1929.			
Birth period of sons	**Ln wealth at death**	**Higher education**	**Occupational rank**
1840-69	0.403	0.458	0.529
	(0.020)	(0.015)	(0.015)
1870-99	0.311	0.353	0.446
	(0.018)	(0.014)	(0.013)
1900-29	0.247	0.246	0.415
	(0.022)	(0.020)	(0.019)
All	0.352	0.358	0.465
	(0.012)	(0.009)	(0.009)

Note: *Standard Errors in Parentheses. Wealth at death is normalized relative to that of the population dying in each decade. Higher education is 1 for those attaining a university education or equivalent. Occupational rank is an index ranging 0-1.*

If we have identified the surnames used here as elite or underclass from some other source, or an earlier period, then in Eq. (23.6) the value of $\overline{u}_{kt}$ will tend towards 0. This implies we are effectively observing as $\overline{y}_{kt}$, and $\overline{y}_{kt-1}$ the underlying social status of this group of people as in the x in Eq. (23.4). Thus the surname estimate will approximate not the conventional estimate of social mobility $\beta = \theta b$, but the underlying long run status persistence b. But this underlying persistence parameter is very important for a lot of social issues. It tells how long it will be before elite or underclass groups in a society become average. It tells how long, at a minimum, ethnic and racial group status differences will persist.

One advantage of estimating the underlying mobility rate is that this estimate will not be affected by differences over time in how well occupational status is measured by conventional occupational descriptors. The estimate will similarly be independent of differences in the way educational status is measured over time, and the measurement error that introduces. Thus the estimates here will be fully comparable across societies and across time periods in a way that conventional estimates are not.

Note that by averaging in the way described in Eq. (23.6) we will actually get an attenuated estimate of the underlying parameter b for the parent-child connection. By averaging across 30 year time intervals we will sometime be including in adjacent periods grandfathers and grandchildren. Further we will include in the initial period with the same weight those who have no children, those with one child, and those with many children. Also there will potentially be some adopted children among the younger generation, as well as those who changed surnames from their birth surname. For all these reasons the surnames can only provide an imperfect estimate of the average of the actual parent child status linkages. This imperfection should, however, bias the surname estimates towards zero.

To illustrate the difference between the two types of estimate of social mobility rates let us make the two types of estimate for a large genealogical database for families in England for individuals born 1750-2019, based around families with rarer surnames. Such rare surnames make it much easier to link individuals across generations. For these families we have multiple measures of social status. Looking just at men these include wealth at death, attainment of higher education (university or equivalent), and occupational rank at age 40. Table 23.1 shows the intergenerational correlation of status on these measures for the generations born in 1840-69, 1870-99, and 1900-29 compared with their fathers,

Table 23.2 Difference in status between elite and average surnames, men.

Birth period	Ln wealth at death	Higher education	Occupational rank
1810-39	3.628	0.328	0.318
	(0.102)	(0.011)	(0.007)
1840-69	2.625	0.250	0.264
	(0.079)	(0.008)	(0.005)
1870-99	1.604	0.166	0.179
	(0.064)	(0.007)	(0.005)
1900-29	1.125	0.146	0.147
	(0.069)	(0.009)	(0.006)

Note: *Standard Errors in Parentheses.*

Table 23.3 Intergenerational correlations of status revealed by surnames.

Birth period of sons	Ln wealth at death	Higher education	Occupational rank
1840-69	0.724	0.762	0.831
	(0.038)	(0.037)	(0.025)
1870-99	0.611	0.664	0.677
	(0.038)	(0.044)	(0.027)
1900-29	0.701	0.877	0.819
	(0.053)	(0.061)	(0.036)
All	0.677	0.763	0.772
	(0.021)	(0.032)	(0.021)

Note: *Standard errors in parentheses.*

where the lineages included are those surnames which had average status in the nineteenth century. These correlations average around 0.4, which would be typical for modern mobility estimates. The picture conveyed is of a relatively mobile society even back in the nineteenth century, with inheritance determining a small share of the variance in status.

We can implement with the same database an estimate of social mobility through surnames by instead looking at the average social status of all men with high status surnames (measured by average wealth at death by surname 1858-1887) relative to men with average status surnames. Table 23.2 shows the different between average status for the initially elite surnames and for average surnames by period. Note how slowly the status of the elite surnames, on all dimensions, are regressing towards 0. Taking just the ratio of status from one period to the next we can derive an implied correlation of status across generations, as shown in Table 23.3. These estimates show much greater persistence of status than the estimates for the individual father-son combinations, with correlations in the range 0.7-0.75 as opposed to 0.4. It implies that the holders of the wealthy surnames identified in Table 23.2 will only converge to within 10% of average wealth at death after another 7 generation from those born 1900-29. Average status will only come for those born 2110-2149 (assuming a persistence parameter of 0.7).

The difference in these estimates shows that there is much more persistence of status in England, and indeed in all societies, across multiple generations than conventional estimates portray. Note that the *b* estimated above for richer surnames in England is estimated in a society where most of the surname holders were white, and had similar religious affiliations, in a society without explicit barriers to intermarriage between social groups. Potentially the underlying persistence of status could be much greater in societies with more obvious ethnic or racial divisions.

23.4 Estimating long run mobility rates from surnames, Australia 1903-1980

As a second example of estimating social mobility rates from surnames let us consider a case where we have occupations by surname.[8] This will be a common result where there is a census of a population such as for England 1841-1939, USA 1850-1940. But it can also result where there is voter roll which gives the occupations of voters as in Australia 1903-1983, New Zealand 1853-1980, and Canada 1935-1980.

Here we use the Australian electoral rolls to make an estimate of long-run mobility rates in Australia, 1903-1980. In 1902 the first Commonwealth Parliament granted universal adult suffrage to most men and women over 21 in Commonwealth Elections.[9] In 1911 compulsory enrollment was introduced. The voting rolls 1903-1983 include occupations. Thus we have from the rolls a census of the occupations of all the non-indigenous Australian population 1912-1983,[10] and for 1903-1911 equivalent data for most of the adult population.

We define a set of elite rare surnames in 1900 as those surnames where 29 or fewer people held the name in Australia in 2014, and where someone holding that name graduated from Melbourne or Sydney universities 1870-1899.[11] Since less than 0.5% of men attended university before 1900 in Australia, those rare surnames with such a distinction were typically those whose social status in general was high. This defines a set of 159 surnames. Most of these surnames were British in origin, though a significant minority were from other European countries.

For the benchmark years 1903-1907, 1926-1930, 1954, 1980 we calculate the average status of these surnames, for men, in each period t as

$$Z_t = \frac{\sum y_{ijt} - \overline{y}}{\sigma_x} \tag{23.7}$$

where y is an index of occupational status for each occupation, derived below, j indexes the rare elite surnames, i indexes the individual men with that surname, $\overline{y}$ is the mean of occupational status in the population as a whole, σ_y is the standard deviation of occupational status in the male population.

The intergenerational correlation of status across each period was calculated as

$$\rho = \left(\frac{Z_{t+n}}{Z_t}\right)^{\frac{30}{n}} \tag{23.8}$$

---

[8] See Clark et al. (2020).

[9] Indigenous Australians were excluded.

[10] Indigenous Australians were not permitted to vote in Commonwealth Elections until 1962. They are thus only included on the rolls after 1962, and for them enrollment was not compulsory until 1984.

[11] 29 was chosen just as the number which gave a reasonable sample size.

Table 23.4 Status index mean and standard deviations, Australia, 1904-1980.

Year	Social status scale	Elite N	Elite mean	Elite standard deviation	Smith N	Smith mean	Smith standard deviation
1904	English	358	40.95	26.30	1037	22.29	12.11[*]
1929	English	559	38.70	24.06			
1954	English	547	36.23	21.36	380	23.84	13.22
1954	ANU2	556	592.7	156.3	389	496.8	111.6
1980	ANU2	570	608.8	146.6	412	527.8	127.0
1980	ANU3	570	46.76	24.76	406	33.08	20.72

Notes: * average of 1903 and 1928. Males only.

This assumes that a generation is 30 years. Thus the intergenerational correlation between 1954 and 1980 is

$$\rho = \left(\frac{Z_{1980}}{Z_{1954}} \right)^{1.15} \tag{23.9}$$

Can we be sure that this correlation ρ will correspond to the underlying correlation of status at the family level as posited in Eqs. (23.3) and (23.4)? In many cases, for example, the same person will appear in the 1903 electoral roll and in the 1928 electoral roll. Will that not drive up the measured correlation? However, intuitively, what we are doing is comparing people observed in 1904, born 1839-1883, with people born on average 25 years later, 1864-1908. Thus while there will be some people who are observed in both samples, there will also be an equivalent sized group where the relationship is across three generations, grandfather to grandson. As long as there is a constant underlying intergenerational correlation, on average we will be observing a correlation close to that for one generation.

To derive mean population occupation status for the relevant social group in Australia we used a sample of occupations for the common surname *Smith* (and variants such as *Smyth*) for each benchmark period. Smith was chosen since the majority of the rare surnames were British and Irish in origin, so this would be the relevant comparison group.

For 1980 social status was assigned to occupations using the index of occupational status for Australia derived by Broom et al. (1977) (ANU2). For 1954 we also applied the ANU2 scale.

In addition for 1903, 1928, and 1954 we applied a scale derived from English occupation data 1841-1929, where that scale was based for each occupation on reported wealth at death, higher educational attainment, and probability of being at work aged 11-20. This is the occupational scale used in Tables 23.1–23.3 on English mobility rates.

Table 23.4 shows the estimated average status of the sample of the elite Australian surname in each period, as well as the estimated average status of the equivalent population as a whole derived from the *Smith* sample. The table also shows the standard deviation of status in the elite surname group and in the *Smith* sample. Also shown are the sample sizes which were modest, though the results actually have relatively high precision. As can be seen the elite surnames deviate very significantly, in quantitative and statistical terms, from mean surname status, even in 1980. These surnames, remember, were identified as high status based on someone with the surname graduating from Melbourne or Sydney Universities before 1900. This shows the slowness of social mobility in twentieth century Australia.

Table 23.5 Estimated pre 1900 elite surname status, Australia, 1904-1980.

Period	Social status scale	Elite status (SD units)	Elite standard deviation (SD units)
1904	English	1.541	0.121
1929	English	1.355	0.091
1954	English	0.937	0.089
1954	ANU2	0.859	0.078
1980	ANU2	0.638	0.069
1980	ANU3	0.660	0.071

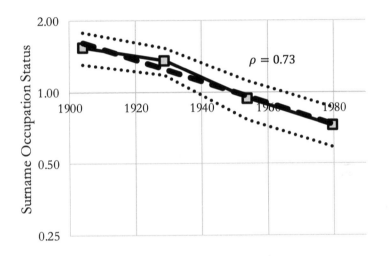

FIGURE 23.4

Rare elite surname occupation status, Australia, 1904, 1929, 1954, 1980. *Note*: the light dotted lines show the 95% confidence interval on mean status for the elite surnames.

Table 23.5 shows the implied deviation of the elite surnames from average status in standard deviation units (measured for the population from the *Smiths*) for each benchmark year and each status measure (corresponding to (23.7)). Table 23.5 shows that it makes little difference to estimated status of the elite surname group in standard deviation units whether we use the English occupational status rank, or that of ANU2 or ANU3. From the numbers in Table 23.5 we can calculate the implied intergenerational correlation of status as described in Eq. (23.8).

Fig. 23.4 shows the estimated status of the elite surnames at each benchmark, measured in standard deviation units above mean social status, as well as the 5% confidence interval around these estimates. Also shown is the best fitting estimate with a constant rate of intergenerational mobility from 1904 to 1980. The best fitting correlation of status across generations for the whole period is $\rho = 0.73$.

The fit across all four generations is very tight, with the intergenerational correlation very similar across all periods. If we just compare 1903 and 1980 then the estimated correlation of status across generations, assumed 30 years, is 0.732 with a standard deviation of 0.037. The 95% confidence for this correlation is thus 0.68-0.82, well above conventional estimates for social mobility for Australia in recent years.

Three things stand out about this estimate. The first is that underlying social mobility rates are again very low, despite Australians priding themselves on the openness and meritocracy of Australian society. The descendants of the Colonial elite pre-1900 are becoming more average with each passing generation, and will eventually be completely average in status. However, this process is taking a very long time. The holders of rare elite surnames in Table 23.5 had an average occupational status 1.54 standard deviations above the social mean in 1904. With an intergenerational correlation of 0.73 in occupational status their average status will lie within 0.1 standard deviations of the social mean by the generation of 2174. It takes about 9 generations, 270 years, for such an elite set of families to become effectively average.

In particular note that the social mobility rates estimated for Australia 1903-1980 (0.73) are very similar to those estimated for England for occupational status for those born 1840-1929 in Table 23.3 (0.77). A second feature that should be emphasized is that the data do suggest there will be complete social mobility in Australia, if we wait enough generations. At least in England and Australia there are no signs of any persistent elites or underclasses. The third feature to note is that the rise of the modern social democratic state with expanded access to education has no apparent effect on long run social mobility rates in places like Australia.

How does 20th century Australian occupational status mobility compare to pre-industrial populations? One place we have occupational data from 1500-1860 is Barcelona. The marriage license records of the Barcelona Diocese, which record all marriages 1500-1860, give measures of status by surname in the form of the social positions and/or occupations of grooms. For any 30 year period we can identify a set of surnames that have unusually high or low status in that period, then track the average status of these surnames over the entire 360 years. Table 23.6 shows the overall data availability.

We employ just data for the years 1500-1859 because for 1481-1499 the number of observations is too small, and for the years 1860-1905 ever increasing numbers of grooms are described just as "worker", as can be seen in Table 23.6.

Using standard pre-industrial occupational status classifications we can assign to each surname in each 30 year period an average status, measured in standard deviation units from the mean. We can then see what happens to these surname statuses across later and earlier generations. Fig. 23.5 shows the typical status of a high status surname identified in one period in each subsequent and earlier period. As can be seen, status in the generations after the base period follows exactly the pattern predicted in Fig. 23.3. In the first generation after observation there is rapid convergence on the mean. But thereafter further social mobility is very slow. Even 10 generations after the initial observation these surnames remain above average status.

Fig. 23.5 also shows is that in the generations before the surnames are observed as high status there is a near symmetrical upwards path from average status to elite status, such that 10 generations before they are observed, these names already have elite status. This is just a consequence of what Eqs. (23.3) and (23.4) imply would be the dynamics of status for any elite group of families observed at generation t. They would typically arrive at upper status by a path where they showed steady but slow upwards deviation from the mean over many generations.

Figs. 23.6 and 23.7 show the estimates for each generation in Barcelona, for both high and low status surnames, identified across 11 generations of 30 years 1500-1829, of the short run implied correlation in status, and then the long run underlying correlation. As can be seen for both the elites and the

Table 23.6 Numbers of grooms in Barcelona Cathedral Marriage Registers, 1481-1905.

Generation	Grooms	"Worker"	Fraction "worker"
1481-1499	3650	0	0.00
1500-1529	12,402	50	0.00
1530-1559	10,224	193	0.02
1560-1589	18,339	108	0.01
1590-1619	23,948	300	0.01
1620-1649	27,251	453	0.02
1650-1679	21,850	508	0.02
1680-1709	26,354	498	0.02
1710-1739	36,145	1914	0.05
1740-1769	58,644	4020	0.07
1770-1799	33,650	5125	0.15
1800-1829	48,411	4737	0.10
1830-1859	74,957	10,116	0.13
1860-1889	114,986	48,873	0.43
1890-1905	37,056	30,304	0.82

Source: *Barcelona Historical Marriage Database (BHMD). See Jordà et al. (2018).*

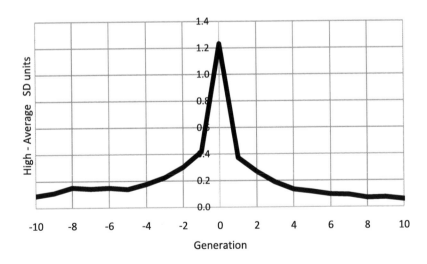

FIGURE 23.5

High status surnames observed over 21 synthetic generations, Barcelona, 1500-1859. *Note*: Generation 0 is the base generation, in which the surnames are classified as high status. The status of the surnames identified as high status in the base period can then be estimated for up to ten generations later and earlier.

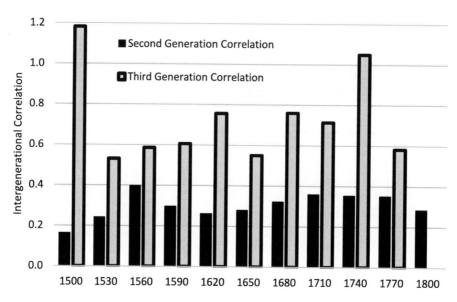

FIGURE 23.6

Intergenerational correlation, second and third generations, Barcelona, high status. *Note*: For the base generation 1800-29 there is no third generation correlation since useful data on status ends in 1859.

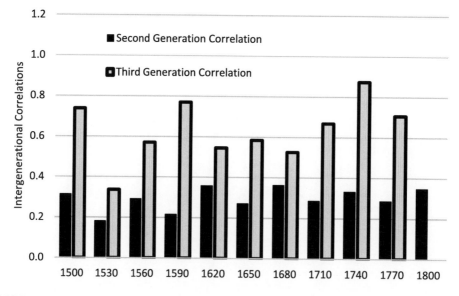

FIGURE 23.7

Intergenerational correlation, second and third generations, Barcelona, low status. *Note*: For the base generation 1800-29 there is no third generation correlation since useful data on status ends in 1859. Barcelona as in the modern world. Note also that mobility rates are very similar for high and low status surnames.

underclass surnames the short run correlation is only around 0.3, and is essentially trendless 1500-1859. Despite significant social and political changes across these years there is no sign of any trend in underlying mobility, and mobility is as fast in pre-industrial.

The underlying correlation in occupational status across multiple generations is in the order of 0.7 for the high status surnames and 0.65 for the low status surnames, with again no trend over time. This is very similar to what we find for Australia 1903-1980, and England for births 1800-1930. Note again that the process is very similar for high and low status surnames, with long run mobility just being slightly faster for the low status surnames. Thus between early modern Barcelona, nineteenth century England, and modern Australia we see little sign of any change in underlying social mobility rates. Other surname studies have similarly found low rates of long run social mobility (Barone and Mocetti (2016); Collado et al. (2008)).

23.5 Estimating social mobility rates from surnames with less information

A nice feature of using surnames to estimate social mobility rates is that we can derive the long run underlying correlation of status with even less information than is used in the examples above. In particular suppose all we know about a society is the general distribution of surnames in the population, the distribution of surnames among an elite, and what percent of the population that elite represents. Then we can still get a good estimate of social mobility rates. See Clark et al. (2015).

In England, for example, we know the general distribution of surnames 1538 and later.[12] We also know the distribution of surnames at Oxford and Cambridge universities, the only universities in England until 1836, and always the most prestigious universities, from 1200 onwards. And we also know what share of males in each cohort attended these two elite universities from at least 1500 onwards. This allows an estimate of the persistence of educational status in England from 1500-2015.

Suppose, for example, the variance of status in an elite or underclass set of surnames can be assumed to be the same as that for the population as a whole. Then the situation is as in Fig. 23.8. For names in general we will find that about 1% are at Oxford or Cambridge. But for more elite surnames a high fraction will be present at the university. Thus for each period after 1500 we can estimate for each surname its relative status, the measure being

$$Relative\ Representation = \frac{Share\ of\ surname\ z\ at\ Oxbridge}{Share\ of\ surbame\ z\ in\ Oxbridge\ age\ cohort} = RR_z$$

By definition for the average surname in England in any period this number will be 1. But for high status surnames the number will exceed 1, and for low status surnames it will fall below 1.

If the variance in educational status is the same for the elite surname group as for the population as a whole, then from that overrepresentation of elite surnames at Oxford or Cambridge we can in each period estimate the mean status, in standard deviation units of deviation from the population mean.[13]

---

[12] There are extensive records of baptisms and marriages from parish records in England 1538-1837, and then national registers of births, deaths and marriages 1837-2019.

[13] We consider how reasonable this assumption is below.

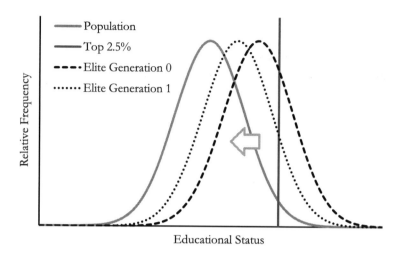

FIGURE 23.8

Regression to the mean of elite surnames.

Then the implied intergeneration correlation of status for these surnames across a generation will just me the estimated mean status in generation $t + 1$ divided by that in generation t.

To see how this works in practice, let us construct a set of surnames that was elite in England in terms of educational status in 1800-29. To do this we simply include all English surnames where less than 500 people held the surname in the census of 1881, but someone with that surname attended Oxford or Cambridge 1800-1829.[14] This generates 2354 individual surnames held by Oxbridge students in these years. These surnames were held by 277,247 people in 1881, and by 473,595 people in 2002. To estimate the population share with these rare surnames in each student cohort we use records of marriages in England 1837-1915, and records of births 1916-1995. The share of the population with this sample of rare surnames in each generation of students is shown in the second column of Table 23.6. This share was 1.16% of the population in 1800-29, but had fallen to 0.85% by 2010-13. This reflects the substantial migration of people into England 1800-2013.

Table 23.6 shows the numbers of students with these surnames in each 30 year period starting 1800-29 at Oxbridge, as well as the total numbers of students observed in each period.[15] Column five shows the share of these surnames as a share of all Oxbridge students with English surnames. In 1800-29 these surnames represent more than 21 percent of students despite being held by an estimated 1.2 percent of the population. The last column shows the relative representation of these surnames at Oxbridge 1800-2013. This declines steadily across generations, though it is still around 1.5 in 2010-13.[16]

---

[14] We use the 1881 census to find the rarer surnames because this is one of the most carefully digitized 19th century censuses.

[15] If a surname occurred multiple times that was counted.

[16] To calculate the relative representation in the periods after 1829 an allowance has to be made for the increasing share of foreign students at Oxbridge. The England and Wales surname share of students is calculated from 1830 on by period as 0.99, 0.97, 0.95, 0.92, 0.90, 0.82, and 0.69.

Table 23.7 Rare surnames at Oxbridge, 1800-29.

Generation	Share population rare Oxbridge surnames (%)	Rare surnames 1800-29 at Oxbridge	All Oxbridge attendees	Share rare 1800-29 surnames Oxbridge (%)	Relative representation
1800-29	1.16	3991	18,650	21.57	18.57
1830-59	1.16	2856	24,415	11.82	10.17
1860-89	1.13	2951	38,678	7.84	6.93
1890-1919	1.09	1477	30,961	5.02	4.61
1920-49	1.04	1917	67,927	3.08	2.96
1950-79	0.99	2628	156,645	1.86	1.87
1980-2009	0.85	2383	222,063	1.32	1.55
2010-3	0.85	437	49,243	1.28	1.51

What is the intergenerational correlation of educational status implied by Table 23.6? To calculate that we translate the relative representation of the rare surnames into an implied deviation of mean educational status for this group from the social mean as in Fig. 23.8. To do this we must estimate for each generation the percentage of the population attending Oxford or Cambridge, to establish how elite this social group is. Column three of Table 23.7 shows this estimate. In 1830-59, for example, only 0.6% of each generation attended Oxford or Cambridge. By 2010-3 the estimated share of the population aged 20 attending Oxford or Cambridge had risen to 1.24%. This yields the estimate in column four of the average educational status of the elite surnames for each generation, measured as standard deviation units above the social mean. For 1830-59 the estimated mean is at +0.97 SD units, while by 2010-3 that had fallen to +0.16 SD units. Note that in Table 23.7 we use only 1830-59 and later because in the generation where the elite rare surnames were established, 1800-29, the estimate of surname status will be contaminated with random shocks to status, and will show the faster short term mobility illustrated in Fig. 23.2. In later generations the numbers of surname holders at Oxford and Cambridge will give an unbiased estimate of the average educational status of the target surnames. The estimated mean statuses by generation are graphed in Fig. 23.9, where the vertical axis is graphed as a log scale.

Once we know the implied mean of status for the 1800-29 elite rare surname group 1830-2013, we then calculate for each period the implied correlation of status b with the previous generation. From Eqs. (23.3) and (23.4), and assuming with averaging that $\overline{y}_t = \overline{x}_t$, that is that the average measured educational status of the surnames is the average actual status,

$$\overline{y}_{t+1} = b\overline{y}_t + \epsilon_{t+1} \tag{23.10}$$

where ϵ_{t+1} is an error term corresponding to various mis-measurements. The unbiased estimated value of b for each period is then just

$$\frac{\overline{y}_{t+1}}{\overline{y}_t} \tag{23.11}$$

These estimates are shown in the final column of Table 23.7. The average is 0.74, though the individual b estimates range from 0.60 to 0.99.

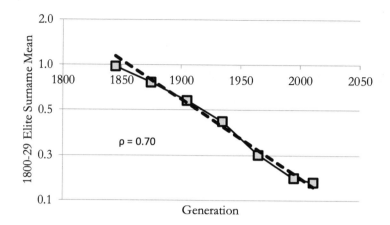

FIGURE 23.9

Mean status, rare elite surnames, Oxbridge, 1830-2013.

Suppose we assume, however, that this variation is just the product of the aforementioned measurement errors, and fit one b value to the whole of the data. To do this note that Eq. (23.10) implies

$$\ln \overline{y}_{t+n} = \ln \overline{y}_t + \ln (b) .n + \ln \epsilon^*_{t+n} \qquad (23.12)$$

So just by estimating the coefficient h in the OLS best fitting relationship

$$\ln \overline{y}_{t+n} = g + h.n \qquad (23.13)$$

we can estimate the best fitting b for the whole set of observations, assuming this has a constant value. The b estimated in this way is 0.70, with 5 percent confidence bounds of $(0.67, 0.72)$. As Fig. 23.9 shows the R^2 of this fit is good, being 0.99.

Three things stand out in this estimate. First the high degree of persistence of status implied in the estimates. Second the estimated persistence here is very similar to that found for wealth, education and occupation in the high status surnames in the lineage dataset discussed above (Table 23.3). But third is the seeming constancy of this strong persistence over generations.

Over the course of the generations entering college 1830-2013 the social and institutional circumstances of England have changed considerably. England came late to the idea of state support for education. Until late in the nineteenth century education was largely organized through an ad doc system of charity schools, religious schools, and local private provision. Thus only with the *Forster Act of 1870* was there any requirement of school attendance. And this requirement was only for ages 5-10, with exemptions for children who were sick, working, or living too far from a school. Also before 1870 central government support for education was minimal. Not until 1833 did the Central Government direct any monies in support of constructing or maintaining schools.

Over the years 1880 to 1918 there were a series of Parliamentary Acts that expanded significantly both educational requirements and state support for education. Through these Acts, required school attendance was extended eventually to ages 5-14 by 1922. School fees were also abolished for all children in publicly supported schools.

Table 23.8 Implied persistence rates for 1800-29 elite rare surnames.

Generation	Relative representation	Oxbridge elite share (%)	Implied sean status (standard deviation units)	Implied *b*
1830-59	10.17	0.62	0.97	–
1860-89	6.93	0.53	0.76	0.79
1890-1919	4.61	0.48	0.58	0.76
1920-49	2.96	0.70	0.42	0.72
1950-79	1.87	1.16	0.25	0.60
1980-2009	1.55	1.27	0.18	0.70
2010-3	1.51	1.24	0.16	0.89
All				0.73

Table 23.9 Social status as measured by MPs, 1800-2019.

Generation	All MPs	Rare surname MPs	Share rare surnames MPs (%)	Relative representation among MPs
1800-29	2064	396	19.2	16.51
1830-59	2473	417	16.9	14.51
1860-89	1848	225	12.2	10.76
1890-1919	1779	122	6.9	6.30
1920-49	1914	75	3.9	3.77
1950-79	1421	47	3.3	3.33
1980-2009	1107	32	2.9	3.41
2010-3	488	9	1.8	2.18

The *Education Act of 1944* extended compulsory schooling to age 15 in 1946 and eventually to age 16 in 1972. It also codified a tripartite system of education. At age 11 students were assigned, based on an exam, either to elite grammar schools, or to more vocational secondary modern or technical schools.

Thus we see families experience substantially different social and institutional regimes with respect to education across the course of their histories. Those cohorts born 1780-1869, and entering college 1800-1890, mostly existed in the laissez faire era, where there were no schooling requirements, and only private and religious support for education for the poor. The cohort born 1870-1899, and entering college 1890-1920, experienced the modest beginnings of the modern welfare state in education. Compulsory education was imposed for the first time, and state support to parents extended. Finally the cohort born 1900-1929, and entering college 1920-1950, experienced for the first time substantial state imposed educational requirements, with most children born in this cohort required to attend school to age 14, and with public funding of the costs of schooling. But remarkably the extension of state support for schooling seemingly had no impact on long run mobility rates. See Table 23.8.

If we take the 2354 rarer surnames which appear in the rolls of students at Oxford and Cambridge 1800-29 then we can also look at how this group did on other measures of social status in England 1830-2019. One of these is the political elite. We know the names of all of the 460-533 members of Parliament (MPs) from England and Wales for every year in this interval. Table 23.9 shows the total numbers of MPs entering Parliament by 30 year period from 1800 on, where we count each member just once, by their year of first entry to Parliament. This is a much smaller group than students enrolling at Oxford and Cambridge so the results are noisier. But as columns three and four show the rare surnames enrolling at Oxford and Cambridge 1800-29 were also heavily overrepresented among MPs, and continued to be overrepresented even in the period 2010-19.

Table 23.9 shows the calculated persistence rates of these surnames among the political elite under alternative assumptions about how elite class MPs were and are. We start with the generation of politicians entering Parliament 1830-59, since the typical age of entry to Parliament would be 20-30 years later than entry to college. The first assumption is that since the number of MPs increased little between 1800 and 2019, yet the population of England increased by nearly 8 fold, MPs represented an increasingly elite segment of society. Thus MPs are assumed to now represent the top 0.1% in terms of social status, but the top 0.4% in 1830. Column three shows the implied average status of the rare Oxbridge surnames in terms of the political elite by generation, and column four the implied persistence rate of that status. Fig. 23.5 shows the average status by generation, and the fitted overall mobility rate which is 0.78.

How sensitive is the estimated persistence rate b to assumptions about the eliteness of MPs in England? To test this Table 23.9 also shows the calculation of b if we just assumed that MPs represented a constant elite of the top 0.1% of the population throughout the period. As can be seen in Fig. 23.6 the results change very little with this change in assumptions. The estimated b changes from 0.78 to 0.80.

The estimation of b above using just surnames identified as initially elite because of their presence at Oxford and Cambridge 1800-29 attendance relies on three assumptions. Specifically

(a) Oxford and Cambridge attendance represent the top x% of the educational status distribution, where x is measured in each cohort by the share of eligible persons in England and Wales who attend these universities.[17]

(b) Educational status is normally distributed with constant variance.

(c) The elite surname group from 1800-29 has the same variance of educational status as the population as a whole among its members 1830-2013.

How reasonable are these assumptions, and how sensitive are the estimates to them?

Let us consider first assumption (c) that elite groups have the same variance of status as the population as a whole. If Eqs. (23.3) and (23.4) are indeed descriptive of the mobility process, then any elite group, no matter its initial variance of status, would soon converge close to the social variance of status over a modest number of generations. Based on Eqs. (23.3) and (23.4) the long run variance of observed status will be

$$\sigma^2 = \sigma_y^2 = \frac{\sigma_e^2}{1-b^2} + \sigma_u^2 \tag{23.14}$$

If in the initial period there is no variance in y, then the variance in the subsequent periods will be

$$\sigma_1^2 = \sigma_e^2 + \sigma_u^2$$
$$\sigma_2^2 = \left(1+b^2\right)\sigma_e^2 + \sigma_u^2$$

---

[17] Until 1920 Oxford and Cambridge admitted only men.

$$\sigma_3^2 = \left(1 + b^2 + b^4\right)\sigma_e^2 + \sigma_u^2 \cdots$$

For the estimates for England discussed above, $b^2 \approx 0.5$, and $\sigma_u^2 \approx 2\sigma_e^2$. In this case an elite that started all at the same social level with no variance would have a variance three quarters of the social variance after one period, seven eighths after the second period, fifteen sixteenths after the third period and so on. Thus any elite that has been in existence for more than a couple of generations should have a variance nearly as great as that of the whole population.

Similarly if the elite were to start with greater variance than the general population, then even if all that extra variance comes from a greater dispersion of underlying status, which is the persistent element, there will be quick convergence on the variance of the general population. Thus if the initial variance is

$$\sigma_0^2 = \sigma^2 + \sigma_A^2$$

where σ^2 is the variance of the population, and σ_A^2 the additional variance of underlying social status, then in generation n the variance of status of the elite will be

$$\sigma_n^2 = \sigma^2 + b^{2n}\sigma_A^2$$

which, given that $b^2 \approx 0.5$, implies that within four generations less than ten percent of the excess variance in status will remain.

All this suggests that if we identify some elite or underclass population through surnames, then no matter how that group was initially formed, within 2-3 generations its variance in status will be similar to that of the general population. Thus if we want to estimate social mobility rates using the method above for the generation entering college 1830-1859 then the most reliable set of elite surnames to use would be those identified as having high status in the period 1740-1769 or earlier.

We can simulate, using the Oxford and Cambridge data displayed in Fig. 23.4, what the effects would be on estimated social mobility rates if we allowed that in the first generation, 1800-29, the elite surnames had a variance of educational status that was twice that of the general population.[18] This actually increases the measured persistence of the data since it reduces the estimated status of the elite group in the first few generations (until the variance of the elite group converges on that of the general population).

Assumption (a) above assumes that we know the status cutoff for Oxbridge, which is estimated through the share of each the male population cohort attending Oxbridge. This implies in Table 23.4 that Oxbridge has become a less elite club over time, now encompassing about twice as many of each cohort. But in reality there were other avenues available to ambitious young men (and later women) aside from Oxbridge in the nineteenth century: the armed forces, the legal profession, banking and finance, commerce. The Oxbridge elite of 1800-29 might thus be a much less exclusive club than the 0.64% of the cohort estimated from the share of each cohort of males attending. Similarly now there are other excellent universities that people can attend that offer alternatives to Oxford and Cambridge, so while only 1.2% of the current generation attends Oxbridge, it may represent a much less exclusive elite than this. See Figs. 23.10 and 23.11.

---

[18] The Australian data in Table 23.4 shows the elite group having a much higher variance of occupational status earlier, though the occupational status measures all show a non-normal distribution with a skewness in the higher status occupation.

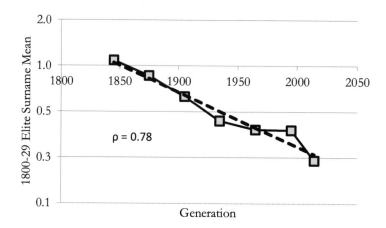

FIGURE 23.10

Social mobility rates, political elite, 1830-2019.

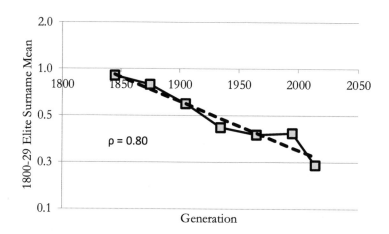

FIGURE 23.11

Social mobility rates, political elite, 1830-2019, alternative assumptions.

Fig. 23.12 shows the implied mean status of the restricted group of rare Oxbridge surnames of 1800-29 under the assumption that the Oxbridge share did not increase over time, and always represented the top 1.27%, or that it did not increase over time, but was always a more encompassing 3% of each cohort. These alternative assumptions do not significantly change the conclusions above that mobility rates revealed by surnames are slow, and that they show no sign of increase in the modern era. Thus if we assume that Oxbridge represented the upper 1.27% of the educational status distribution throughout, then the implied persistence parameter declines from 0.70 to 0.69. If we assume further that Oxbridge always actually represented the top 3% of the educational status distribution throughout, this implies

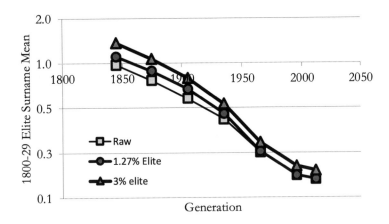

FIGURE 23.12

Paths of implied mean status, different sizes of Oxbridge elite.

an even lower persistence parameter of 0.68. These are marginal changes, and the same pattern with no increase in mobility rates over time persists.

23.6 Are there immobile societies?

Clark et al. (2014) applies the methods above to a variety of societies: the USA, England, Sweden, Chile, China, Japan, and India. In all cases and all periods the rate of long-run social mobility is low, with the implied intergenerational correlation mostly in the range 0.7-0.8. While these mobility rates are low, however, they will ensure that common surnames and classes of surnames gradually lose the status information they conveyed at the time of their formation. After around 300 years all classes or types of surnames in a society will have average status.[19] Surnames of Norman origin, for example, had high status in England still in 1200-1400, but now are just slightly above average social status. Similarly surnames of native English origin that refer to places (Berkeley, Sussex, Rockingham, etc.), which again were high status in medieval times, are now average in status in England. The processes of social mobility may be slow, but given enough time it will do its work. In most of these societies there are no persistence social classes in the very long run.

However, there are societies where we can observe in surnames even slower rates of social mobility, at least at the group level, and where there seem to be near permanent social classes. Egypt is one such society. After the Muslim conquest of Egypt in 646 CE conversion to Islam was not obligatory. The economic and social elites in pre-conquest Egypt were Greek Christians and Jews, with Coptic Christians forming the bulk of the population. However, conversion to Islam was most economically

---

[19] Rare surnames will, however, show on average high or low status just by random processes of social mobility, and so can be used still to estimate social mobility rates as is done in Tables 23.2–23.3.

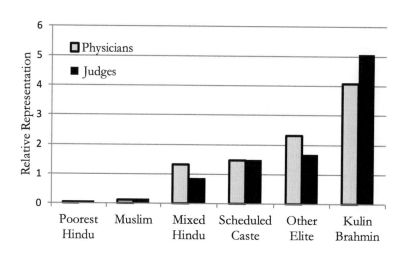

FIGURE 23.13

Representation of different surname types in Bengal elites, 2010-13.

attractive to the lowest status Copts.[20] As a result from 646 CE to the present about 10% of Egyptian population remained Coptic. But this Coptic residue was and remains a social and economic elite within Muslim Egypt, even though they had little political power. This implies that in Egypt, b, the intergenerational correlation of status at the surname level for Coptic surnames must be very close to 1. Interestingly the absolute persistence of status at the group level is associated with a near complete absence of intermarriage between Muslims and Copts.

Another society with unusually low rates of social mobility, at least at the level of social groups, is India. As in many societies the Indian upper classes were the first to adopt surnames. In Bengal, where the East India Company established its rule in 1757, upper class Hindus seem to have been already using surnames by the time of the British conquest. Petitioners to the East India Company courts in Bengal, for example, in the late eighteenth century typically have surnames, and these names are still common in Bengal: *Banarji, Basu, Chattarji, Datta, Ghosh, Haldar, Khan, Mandal, Mitra, Sen.*[21] Similarly when the Hindoo College was established in Calcutta in 1817, its initial Directors, Governors, and Secretary, upper class Hindus, were all men with surnames: *Roy, Bahadur, Thakoor, Deb, Sinha, Banerjee, Doss, Mukherjee.*

Within Bengali surnames the most elite now are those belonging to the Kulin Brahmin group: Mukherjee, Banerjee, Chatterjee, Ganguly, Bhattacharjee, and Chakrabarti.[22] Among judges and registered doctors in West Bengal 2011 these names are 4-5 times overrepresented compared to their population shares, as can be seen in Fig. 23.13. This implies extremely slow rates of social mobility at the group level over the years 1757-2011.

[20] Saleh (2018).

[21] Government of Bengal, Political Department (1930).

[22] Kulin just designates a superior Brahmin group.

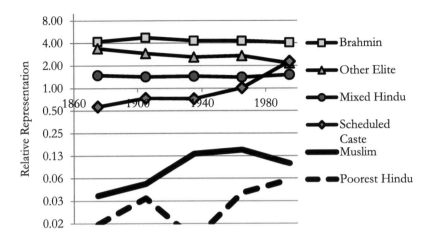

FIGURE 23.14

Relative representation of surname types among Doctors in Bengal, 1860-2011.

The same figure shows the dramatic underrepresentation of two other sets of surnames. The first are surnames associated with the Muslim community. These surnames have a relative representation among judges and doctors that is 0.12. The second set of surnames are those associated with lower caste Hindu groups that had little or no representation among physicians before Independence. The main one is *Shaw/Show*, held by 3.7 percent of men on the Kolkata voting rolls. Others are *Rauth/Routh, Paswan, Dhanuk, Balmiki*, and *Mahata/Mahato*. Together these surnames are held by 7 percent of the population of West Bengal: These surnames again show a relative representation among elites in 2010-13 that is 0.05-0.08.

Since there are records of who were the doctors in the Province of Bengal under British Rule 1860-1947, and who were registered doctors in West Bengal after Indian independence we can thus estimate social mobility rates by surname types in Bengal as long as we can estimate what the population frequencies of the surname types were over the period 1860-2013. Fig. 23.14 shows the relative representation of surname groups in Bengal amongst doctors 1860-2011.

For the Muslim population, their relative representation is shown relative to the entire population and is always very low. Muslims were always a tiny share of doctors compared to their population share.[23] The partition of Bengal in 1947 into largely Hindu West Bengal and mainly Muslim East Pakistan significantly reduced the Muslim population share in West Bengal relative to colonial Bengal. The removal of a large fraction of the population containing very few doctors has the effect of decreasing the relative representation of all the Hindu surname groups among physicians post 1947. Their share of doctors increased little as their population share increased. Since this partition created decline gives a spurious impression of social mobility, for these other groups, relative representation is shown always with respect to the non-Muslim population only.

---

[23] Because Muslim and Hindu first names are also distinctive, the fraction of Muslim physicians in Bengal in the years 1860-2011 is easily estimated.

Census reports exist giving the Muslim share of the population in Bengal and West Bengal for each decade from 1871 on. Thus there are good measures of the relative representation among physicians in Bengal from 1860 on. The striking feature is the very low representation of Muslims among physicians in all periods. Under British rule, Muslims experienced limited upward mobility. The implied persistence of status was high, with a calculated intergenerational correlation of 0.91.

However, from the 1970s until very recently, the Muslim community in West Bengal saw a further decline in representation among physicians, with no implied regression to the mean. Indeed, starting with the generation entering practice since Independence in 1947, the implied persistence coefficient is 1.2, indicating that the Muslim community has been diverging further from the mean.

Bengal's system of reserving educational places and employment opportunities for disadvantaged castes and tribes explicitly excluded Muslims and Christians before 2014: only Hindus, Sikhs, and Buddhists were eligible.[24] Thus Muslims have been disadvantaged in admission to medical practice in West Bengal, compared to the Hindu, Sikh, and Buddhist populations, since Independence. They could compete on equal terms for the unreserved positions in medical schools, but the advantages offered by the reservation system to other disadvantaged groups effectively penalized Muslims. This situation helps explain the surprising negative social mobility implied for the Muslim community in recent generations. However, even absent the disadvantages imposed by the reservation system, there would be no group level social mobility by Muslims 1947-2011.[25]

Even within the Hindu population, there has been very little social mobility among surname groups in Bengal from 1860 on. The Brahmin group of surnames is almost as heavily overrepresented among the non-Muslim population in the period 1980-2011 as it was in the period 1860-89. Other elite Hindu surnames show a slow rate of decline in status. But the relative representation of mixed Hindu surnames, which are modestly elite, does not change. And the relative representation of poor Hindu surnames of the nineteenth century, those with the highest potential for regression to the mean, also changes little. The only group showing a marked change in status is the group of surnames associated with scheduled caste lists for positions in universities and the police. This group went from being modestly disadvantaged among non-Muslim groups in 1860 to being one of the most elite surname groups, as measured by their relative representation among physicians now.

India here seems very distinct from England, Barcelona, or Australia over the last 150 years. Note that India may well have similar rates of social mobility within such collections of families as the Kulin Brahmin surname group. The methods here are simply comparing these surnames as a group to those of, for example, the Muslim population.

Why is social mobility, at the group level, so low within India? One interesting difference between India and societies such as England, Barcelona, or Australia is the high degree of group marital endogamy still found in India. As late as the 1960s, caste endogamy still seemed to be the rule for most marriages in Bengal, as seen in a detailed study of a modest-sized town in Bengal in the late 1960s.[26] Another study, looking at marriages in rural villages in Karnataka and Uttar Pradesh 1982-1995, found that of 905 marriages in the study, none involved couples who differed in their caste status.[27] In a

---

[24] In 2013 a law was passed reserving 17 percent of places in state run universities for "other backward classes."

[25] Examination of the recent records of applicants to university in Bengal shows that a switch to a pure merit entry system would increase the numbers of people with Muslim surnames by very small amounts.

[26] Corwin (1977).

[27] Dalmia and Lawrence (2001).

Table 23.10 Social mobility as measured by MPs, 1830-2019.

Generation	Assumed eliteness MPs (%)	Rare mean status	Implied b	Assumed eliteness MPs (%)	Rare mean status	Implied b
1830-59	0.4	1.09	–	0.1	0.96	–
1860-89	0.2	0.86	0.79	0.1	0.91	0.87
1890-1919	0.2	0.63	0.73	0.1	0.79	0.75
1920-49	0.1	0.43	0.69	0.1	0.60	0.70
1950-79	0.1	0.38	0.88	0.1	0.42	0.90
1980-2009	0.1	0.38	0.99	0.1	0.38	1.02
2010-3	0.1	0.24	0.48	0.1	0.39	0.47
Average			0.76			0.79

Table 23.11 Relative representation of surname types among Doctors in Bengal, 1860-2011.

Period	Muslim	Brahmin	Other elite	Poor Hindu	Scheduled caste	Mixed Hindu
1860-1889	0.04	4.19	3.39	0.02	0.57	1.49
1890-1919	0.05	4.73	2.92	0.03	0.73	1.42
1920-1946	0.13	4.30	2.60	0.01	0.72	1.45
1947-1979	0.15	4.27	2.71	0.04	1.01	1.40
1980-2011	0.10	4.05	2.15	0.06	2.26	1.51

high-caste group in Hyderabad, Kayasthas, only 5 percent of marriages were outside the caste even by 1951-1975.[28] Information, however, on the degree of endogamy for marriages in Bengal in the 1970s and 1980s, which produced the most recent crop of physicians, is not readily available.

One source of information on the likely endogamy rate is the 2010 Kolkata voter roll, which gives surnames, first names, and ages of all voters. Many first names are highly specific to the Hindu, Muslim, and Christian/Jewish communities. Women who marry into one of these groups from another group will almost always have different first names from women born in within the group. Also, if families with surnames associated with one group are assimilated into another group, then, as a result of intermarriage and adoption of at least some elements of the culture of the wives, the children will again have different first names. See Table 23.10.

As Table 23.11 shows, the percentage of women in the Kulin Brahmin surname group with non-Hindu first names is extremely small. Because Muslims constitute nearly a quarter of the Kolkata population, this implies that intermarriage rates between Kulin Brahmin men, and women of Muslim origin are extremely low, on the order of 0.1 percent. A similar result holds for other high-caste Hindu surnames. More women with Muslim surnames have Hindu first names: 0.9 percent. But given the near-total absence of any sign of Muslim women's marriage into high-caste Hindu groups, if these findings are indicative of marriage alliances, they are likely with lower-caste Hindus. See Table 23.12.

Intermarriage between Christians and high-caste Hindus appears to be substantially more common. Christian surnames account for a very small share of the surname stock in Kolkata, about 0.3 percent, and are mainly Portuguese in origin. Given this small Christian population, the small share of women

---

[28] Leonard and Weller (1980), Tables 23.1–23.3.

Table 23.12 Female first-name origins by surname group, Kolkata.

First-name type	Incidence in surname group (%)			
	Kulin Brahmin	*Other high-caste Hindu*	*Muslim*	*Christian*
Hindu	99.6	99.3	0.9	30.2
Muslim	0.1	0.1	98.9	0.4
Christian	0.3	0.6	0.2	57.4
Hindu and Christian	0.0	0.0	0.0	11.9

with high-caste surnames who have Christian surnames is nevertheless suggestive of significant inter-marriage.

An alternative explanation for these female Christian first names may be that high-caste Hindu girls are given Christian first names at birth. The possibility of significant intermarriage between Christians and Hindus is, however, supported by the fact that just over 30 percent of women with Christian surnames have first names that are Hindu. Also, almost 12 percent of women with Christian surnames have a combination of Christian and Hindu first names.

The first-name and surname evidence suggests almost no intermarriage between the largely poor Muslim community and either Hindus or Christians. Within the Hindu community, first-name evidence does not allow us to determine the degree of marital endogamy within castes because many female first names are common to high- and low-caste groups.

If the marital endogamy of castes and religions in India explains low average social mobility for surname groups, we should find higher rates of social mobility for individual families within these groups. Families sharing the surname *Banerjee*, for example, will have the same rates of mobility as in any other society. It is just that the average status of the *Banerjee*s will not converge toward that of the *Shaw*s. We should also find that over time, all the major Kulin Brahmin surnames have the same average social status. This hypothesis is borne out by the incidence of these surnames among physicians.

23.7 Conclusion

This chapter outlines how we can use information on surname status to estimate social mobility rates in pre-industrial societies. Surname methods allow us to extend the study of social mobility before the census era that began with the nineteenth century back as far as 1300 in a society such as England. The surname estimates show first that social mobility is a more complex process than is typically assumed in conventional estimates. It is a combination of relatively rapid mobility in the first generation, followed by much slower mobility in all subsequent generations. The surname estimates can be used to capture both types of mobility as in the case of Barcelona 1500-1859. But the surname method is best suited to capturing the multi-generation component of mobility. This is the component that describes the behavior of social classes, and racial and ethnic groups. The case studies discussed above show that such social mobility rates show little sign of any increase with the onset of the Industrial Revolution, mass education, and the welfare state.

We also see that even though social mobility is slow, at least in some societies – England, Catalonia, Sweden, China, Australia – it is complete over time, even in the preindustrial era. There are no permanent social classes. We can find some societies where at least some groups are completely immobile. Examples include Copts and Muslims in Egypt 646-2020, and Hindus and Muslims in India 1860-2020. Notably societies where social and ethnic classes show a complete lack of convergence to the mean are those characterized by marital endogamy within social groups.

References

Abramitzky, R., Boustan, L., Eriksson, K., Feigenbaum, J., Pérez, S., 2019. Automated Linking of Historical Data. NBER Working Paper.

Bailey, M., Cole, C., Henderson, M., Massey, C., 2017. How Well do Automated Methods Perform in Historical Samples? Evidence from New Ground Truth. National Bureau of Economic Research Working Paper No. 24019.

Barone, G., Mocetti, S., 2016. Intergenerational Mobility in the Very Long Run: Florence 1427-2011. Bank of Italy Temi di Discussione (Working Paper) No. 1060. SSRN. https://ssrn.com/abstract=2856359. or https://doi.org/10.2139/ssrn.2856359.

Boserup, S.H., Kopczuk, W., Kreiner, C.T., 2013. Intergenerational Wealth Mobility: Evidence from Danish Wealth Records of Three Generations. Working Paper. University of Copenhagen.

Broom, L., Jones, F.L., Duncan-Jones, P., McDonnell, P., 1977. Status scores for all Australian occupations. In: Broom, et al. (Eds.), Investigating Social Mobility, Department of Sociology RSSS, Monograph No. 1. ANUTECH, Australian National University, Canberra, pp. 58–111.

Clark, G., et al., 2014. The Son also Rises: 1,000 Years of Social Mobility. Princeton University Press. Book Manuscript in preparation.

Clark, G., Cummins, N., 2014. Inequality and social mobility in the industrial revolution era. In: Floud, R., Humphries, J., Johnson, P. (Eds.), The Cambridge Economic History of Modern Britain. Cambridge University Press, Cambridge.

Clark, G., Cummins, N., Hao, Y., Vidal, D.D., 2015. Surnames: a new source for the history of social mobility. Explorations in Economic History 55 (1), 3–24.

Clark, G., Leigh, A., Pottenger, M., 2020. Frontiers of mobility: was Australia 1870-2017 a more socially mobile society than England? Explorations in Economic History 76.

Collado, M.D., Ortín, I.O., Romeu, A., 2008. Surnames and social status in Spain. Investigaciones Económicas 32 (3), 259–287.

Corwin, L.A., 1977. Caste, class and the love-marriage: social change in India. Journal of Marriage and the Family 39 (4), 823–831.

Dalmia, S., Lawrence, P.G., 2001. An empirical analysis of assortative mating in India and the U.S. International Advances in Economic Research 7 (4), 443–458.

Elman, B.A., 1992. Political, social, and cultural reproduction via civil service examination in late imperial China. Journal of Asian Studies 50 (1), 7–28.

Government of Bengal, Political Department, 1930. Press List of Ancient Documents Relating to the Provincial Council of Revenue at Calcutta. Preserved in the Secretariat Room of the Government of Bengal. Series 2: Intermediate Revenue Authorities, vol. 3, part 1. pp. 1773–1775.

Ho, P.-t., 1964. The Ladder of Success in Imperial China: Aspects of Social Mobility (1368-1911). Wiley, New York.

Jordà, J.-P., Pujadas-Mora, J.-M., Clark, G., 2018. Social Mobility through Surnames: Barcelona, 1500-1859. Working Paper.

King, T.E., Jobling, M.A., 2009. What's in a name? Y chromosomes, surnames and the genetic genealogy revolution. Trends in Genetics 25 (8), 351–360.

Leonard, K., Weller, S., 1980. Declining subcaste endogamy in India: the Hyderabad Kayasths, 1900-75. American Ethnologist 1 (3), 504–517.

Long, J., Ferrie, J., 2013. Intergenerational occupational mobility in Great Britain and the United States since 1850. The American Economic Review 103 (4), 1109–1137.

Mokyr, J., 2021. Attitudes, aptitudes, and the roots of the great enrichment. In: Bisin, A., Federico, G. (Eds.), The Handbook of Historical Economics. Elsevier. Chapter 25 (in this book).

Price, J., Buckles, K., Riley, I., Van Leeuwen, J., 2019. Combining Family History and Machine Learning to Link Historical Records. NBER Working Paper #26227.

Ruggles, S., Fitch, C.A., Roberts, E., 2018. Historical census record linkage. Annual Review of Sociology 44, 19–37.

Saleh, M., 2018. On the road to heaven: taxation, conversions, and the coptic-Muslim socioeconomic gap in medieval Egypt. The Journal of Economic History 78 (2), 394–434.

Song, X., Massey, C.G., Rolf, K.A., Ferrie, J.P., Rothbaum, J.L., Xie, Y., 2020. Long-term decline in intergenerational mobility in the United States since the 1850s. Proceedings of the National Academy of Sciences 117 (1), 251–258. https://doi.org/10.1073/pnas.1905094116.

The Industrial Revolution and the Great Divergence: recent findings from historical national accounting

Stephen Broadberry

Nuffield College, Oxford, United Kingdom

24.1 Introduction

This chapter provides a survey of recent findings in historical national accounting since the publication in 2001 of Angus Maddison's major work, *The World Economy: A Millennial Perspective.* Although Maddison's (2001) dataset represented a major breakthrough for the quantification of long run economic growth, it contained a large amount of "guesstimation" or "controlled conjectures" for the pre-1870 period. Furthermore, Maddison provided his conjectural estimates only for a small number of benchmark years before the nineteenth century.

Stimulated by Maddison's work, economic historians began to produce estimates of per capita national income for the pre-nineteenth century period that were based on contemporary data rather than guesstimation, and a firmer picture has begun to emerge of the contours of long run growth and development in both Europe and Asia. This is possible because medieval and early modern Europe and Asia were much more literate and numerate than is often thought, and left behind a wealth of data in documents such as government accounts, customs accounts, poll tax returns, parish registers, city records, trading company records, hospital and educational establishment records, manorial accounts, probate inventories, farm accounts, tithe files, and other records of religious institutions. With a national accounting framework and careful cross-checking, it is possible to reconstruct population and GDP back to the medieval period, often at decadal or even annual frequency.

I will focus on the implications of this work for understanding the world's first Industrial Revolution in Britain and the dating of the Great Divergence in living standards between Europe and Asia. Broadberry et al.'s (2015a) new estimates of British GDP per capita show episodes of pre-industrial growth, interspersed with stagnation rather than decline. This implies that the Industrial Revolution built on prior developments. The British economy was substantially richer on the eve of the Industrial Revolution than it had been on the eve of the Black Death, having already developed the ability to maintain living standards during periods of positive population growth. In this way, the British economy was already breaking free from Malthusian constraints long before the Industrial Revolution.

New work in historical national accounting also casts fresh light on the Great Divergence debate. The traditional view, embodied in the work of Maddison (2001) saw a gap in productivity and living standards between Europe and Asia beginning to emerge perhaps as early as 1300 and certainly by 1500. Kenneth Pomeranz (2000) and other members of the California School argued strongly that this view represented a Eurocentric bias, and that no such gap had emerged until after 1800. This radical disagreement owes much to controversy over the appropriate territories to be compared, and quantification can be helpful here in narrowing the difference between the two sides. Comparing similar sized regions within both Europe and Asia, the view that emerges from recent work in historical national accounting is that the Great Divergence dates from around 1700. However, this was also the culmination of a dynamic process that began in northwest Europe after the Black Death of the mid-fourteenth century, whereby Britain and the Netherlands avoided the sustained periods of negative growth that continued to follow periods of positive growth in the rest of Eurasia. Understanding how to avoid sustained shrinking was the key to economic development in the past as well as for today's developing countries (Easterly et al., 1993).

24.2 Data and methods

24.2.1 Data for the pre-1870 period

The Maddison Project, which seeks to extend the work of Maddison (2010), distinguishes four types of GDP data: (1) official estimates by national statistical offices (2) historical estimates based on the same methods and broad range of data (3) historical estimates based on indirect or proxy variables (4) "guesstimates" (Bolt and van Zanden, 2014, 629). It will be helpful to keep these distinctions in mind when assessing the quality and reliability of the per capita GDP estimates considered in this paper.

The historical estimates based on the same methods as those used by national statistical offices were often carried out by teams of researchers shortly after the introduction of official national accounts on a regular basis, and they were typically produced back to the first regular appearance of time series in statistical yearbooks. Although the precise dates varied across nations, official national accounts began to appear in western Europe and North America during or shortly after World War II, while official statistical yearbooks began to appear during the nineteenth century. Such data provide a natural source for the construction of historical national accounts from around 1870, and this material formed the basis of Maddison's (1964, 1985, 1991) early work on economic growth in OECD countries. However, the effects of these changes were not limited to western countries, as a result of the wide reach of European imperialism, with the imperial powers also collecting large amounts of data on their colonies.

In some nations, the state already collected large amounts of data before 1870 in connection with taxation and regulation, while other institutions such as the church, charities, and corporations kept accounts so that the transition to the modern statistical age after 1870 was gradual rather than a dramatic break. In these nations, it has been possible to reconstruct historical national accounts for the period 1870-1950 that are relatively similar to the early official national accounts of the postwar period in terms of coverage of the different parts of the economy and the quality of the underlying data. Feinstein (1972) for the United Kingdom, Kuznets (1946) for the United States, and Hoffmann (1965) for Germany provide early examples of this.

In these data-abundant countries, it is also possible to reconstruct historical national accounts for the pre-1870 period, at least on the output side, that have a similar coverage to the 1870-1950 accounts. Even here, however, there is typically more use of proxy variables, and the number of series declines the further back in time that the series are pushed. This reduction in the number of series is partly inevitable, as poorer, less developed economies are typically dominated by agriculture and experience limited structural change, so that this reduction in the number of series does not necessarily indicate larger error margins. For nations with less abundant data, a short-cut method has been developed, which is described below. This method economises on the number of data series required to reconstruct GDP per capita.

24.2.2 Methods for data-abundant nations

GDP can be estimated from the income, expenditure, and output sides of the economy. In theory, all three approaches should give the same answer, although in practice there is often a residual due to measurement error. The most common method used to estimate GDP for the pre-1870 period is the output approach, which has been adopted by van Zanden and van Leeuwen (2012) for the Netherlands and by a series of authors working on Britain, from the pioneering work of Deane and Cole (1962) through the revised estimates of Crafts and Harley (1992) for the period since 1700, to the more recent estimates of Broadberry et al. (2015a), which reach back to 1270.

The richness of the British sources offers an opportunity to illustrate the methods used for the estimation of pre-1870 annual GDP in data-abundant nations. Since Broadberry et al. (2015a) incorporate data from the earlier works, I will focus here on their study. For the period after 1700, the data cover the territory of Great Britain, including Scotland and Wales as well as England, but for the period 1270-1700 only England is covered. Output is estimated separately for the agricultural, industrial, and service sectors. For medieval agriculture, three main data sources are available, covering different periods. First, the Medieval Accounts Database of Campbell (2000, 2007) is based mainly on a large sample of manorial accounts drawn up using a common template by the reeve who managed the demesne under close supervision of the lord's bailiff or steward. These accounts provide detailed information on land use, crops, animals, and livestock products. Second, the Early Modern Probate Inventories Database assembled by Overton (1991, 2000) and Overton et al. (2004), pulls together similar information for the period between the mid-sixteenth and the mid-eighteenth centuries, extracted from inventories drawn up by the Church Commissioners for the estates of farmers. Third, the Modern Farm Accounts Database of Turner et al. (2001), which runs from 1720 until 1913, is based on a large sample of accounts produced by farmers and kept in local record offices. For all three datasets, agricultural outputs were calculated by multiplying the acreage for each crop by the yield per acre. The trends in yields were estimated for each of the three main time periods, based on microdata obtained from the three databases, and applied to the total acreage for the country as a whole. For output of the livestock sector, a similar procedure was undertaken, multiplying the number of animals by the shares producing and their yields. Prices for individual arable and livestock products are used to convert the output into current prices and create weights for the agricultural real output index.

Production estimates or indicators existed for the key English industries up to 1700, based on careful reconstruction from archival records by generations of scholars. Crucial sources included Carus-Wilson and Coleman (1963) for wool and woolen cloth, drawing on detailed records of exports of wool and woolen cloth; King (2005) for iron, based on a reconstruction of all blast furnaces, their capacity and knowledge of when they were in blast; and Hatcher (1973) for tin, based on receipts of coinage dues. Outputs related to leather and food processing were estimated by Broadberry et al. (2015a) on the basis of key inputs obtained from the reconstruction of the agricultural sector. Construction combines detailed information on cathedral building with an index of housebuilding based on population and urbanization, while the growth of book production is based on titles listed by the British Library. These series are combined to generate an index of industrial production from 1264 to 1700. Crafts and Harley (1992) offer an index from 1700 until 1870, to which Broadberry et al. (2015a) add some new series.

The service sector followed the approach developed by Deane and Cole (1962), with some adjustments. The sector is broken down into commerce, housing, domestic services, and government. The commerce indicator is based on combining estimates of domestic trade (the volume of agricultural and industrial output adjusted for the growing share that was marketed) and international trade (derived from the detailed records of trade that were kept for taxation purposes), freight transport (based on merchant shipping tonnage, distances traveled on the main trade routes and volumes shipped) and financial services (using the velocity of money, derived by comparing estimates of the stock of money with existing estimates of nominal, as opposed to real, national income). Housing and domestic services were assumed to grow at the same rate as population. Government activity was based on its revenue, which exists in detailed annual exchequer accounts back to the early twelfth century (O'Brien and Hunt, 1999).

The three real output series for the agricultural, industrial, and service sectors were combined using a set of sectoral weights which capture the changing structure of the economy. The starting point is an input-output table for 1841 from Horrell et al. (1994). The nominal value added shares for 1841 are projected back using the sectoral real output series reflated to convert them into nominal series. The principal sources for the price series used include Clark (2004, 2005, 2006), Beveridge (1939), and Thorold Rogers (1866–1902). Value-added shares for each sector are derived in this way at roughly 50-year intervals, and used to create a chained index of GDP, following Feinstein (1972). To estimate GDP per capita, this aggregate GDP series is divided by population, taken from Wrigley and Schofield (1989) and Wrigley et al. (1997) for the period since 1541, and derived from information on the number of tenants in a regionally representative sample of manors using the method of Hallam (1988) for the pre-1541 period.

There have also been attempts to estimate British national income from the income side. The approach here is to estimate labor income from data on employment and real wages and combine it with income from capital and rental income from land. In the absence of readily available data on the returns to capital and land, the real wage has been the most popular alternative to GDP per capita since the pioneering work of Phelps Brown and Hopkins (1955, 1956), who provided an annual series for England back to the mid-thirteenth century. However, this approach requires care because the nominal wage data are most readily available as daily wage rates, which do not come with information on the number of days worked per year. As Angeles (2008) points out, there can be substantial divergence between the trends in real wages and GDP per capita as a result of a change in the number of days worked per year, a shift in labor's share of income or a change in the relative price of consumption goods. He shows that there was considerable divergence in English GDP per capita and real wages between 1700 and 1820 due primarily to an "industrious revolution" (or increase in days worked per year), with a distributional shift against labor and an increase in the relative price of food also having significant effects. Broadberry et al. (2015a) use the same framework to explain the divergence between the daily real wage rate and GDP per capita between 1270 and 1870. The key factor explaining the divergence between the trend growth of GDP per capita and the stationarity of the real wage was the long drawn-out increase in days worked per year between the post-Black Death period and the Industrial Revolution. Subsequent research by Humphries and Weisdorf (2019) has confirmed this, with their estimates of days worked per year derived from a comparison of daily wages with annual wages from long-term contracts. Clark's (2007, 2010) British GDP per capita series, which adds income from capital and land rents to wage income derived on the assumption of constant days worked per year, follows a very similar path to daily real wages, and is therefore not a reliable guide to long-term growth between 1250 and 1850.

In the case of the Netherlands, the data for the period since 1806 are constructed using similar methods to Feinstein (1972), providing detailed estimates for all sectors of the economy encompassing the income, expenditure, and output sides (Smits et al., 2000). For the period 1510-1806, the approach is similar to that of Broadberry et al. (2015a), concentrating on the output side with fairly comprehensive coverage of the main sectors, but only for the province of Holland (van Zanden and van Leeuwen, 2012). For the period 1347-1510, the number of series is relatively small and the coverage less complete, leading van Zanden and van Leeuwen (2012, 120-121) to describe this series as "a likely 'scenario' for the pace and character of economic growth during the late Medieval period".

24.2.3 Methods for data-scarce nations

Where data are less abundant, economic historians have developed an indirect or short-cut approach to estimating GDP per capita, which relies more heavily on modeling or using proxies to generate indicators of economic output. Rather than measuring agricultural output directly, it is derived from the demand for food. This demand-based approach builds on the work of Crafts (1976), who criticized Deane and Cole's (1962) early work on eighteenth century Britain, which assumed constant per capita corn consumption while real incomes were rising and the relative price of corn was changing. Crafts (1985) recalculated the path of agricultural output in Britain with income and price elasticities derived from the experience of later developing countries. The approach was developed further by Allen (2000) using consumer theory. Allen (2000, 13-14) starts with the identity:

$$Q^A = rcN \tag{24.1}$$

where Q^A is real agricultural output, r is the ratio of production to consumption, c is per capita consumption and N is population. Real agricultural consumption per capita is assumed to be a function of its own price in real terms (P^A/P), the price of non-agricultural goods and services in real terms (P^{NA}/P), and real income per capita (y). Assuming a log-linear specification yields:

$$\ln c = \alpha_0 + \alpha_1 \ln(P^A/P) + \alpha_2 \ln(P^{NA}/P) + \beta \ln y \tag{24.2}$$

where α_1 and α_2 are the own-price and cross-price elasticities of demand, β is the income elasticity of demand and α_0 is a constant. The adding-up property in linear models of consumer behavior requires that the own-price, cross-price, and income elasticities should sum to zero, which sets tight constraints on the plausible values, particularly given the accumulated evidence on elasticities in developing countries (Deaton and Muellbauer, 1980, 15-16, 60-82). For early modern Europe, Allen (2000, 14) works with an own-price elasticity of -0.6 and a cross-price elasticity of 0.1, which constrains the income elasticity to be 0.5. Allen also assumes that agricultural consumption is equal to agricultural production.

In the indirect approach, the growth of the non-agricultural sector is proxied by the share of the population living in towns. This approach began with Wrigley (1985), and has recently been combined with the demand approach to agriculture to provide indirect estimates of GDP in a number of European countries during the early modern period (Malanima, 2011; Álvarez-Nogal and Prados de la Escosura, 2013; Schön and Krantz, 2012). With the path of agricultural output (Q^A) derived using equations (1) and (2), overall output (Q) is derived as:

$$Q = \frac{Q^A}{1 - \left(Q^{NA}/Q\right)} \tag{24.3}$$

where the share of non-agricultural output in total output (Q^{NA}/Q) is proxied by the urbanization rate. The approach can be made less crude by making an allowance for higher productivity in the non-agricultural sector, so that (Q^{NA}/Q) increases more than proportionally with the urbanization rate. The empirical implementation of the indirect approach relies on the availability of data on long run trends in urbanization rates. Here, Bairoch's (1988) data set of European towns greater than 5,000 inhabitants going back 1,000 years provides an important historical resource, but data are also available for individual Asian countries, including China, India, and Japan (Rozman, 1973; Habib, 1982; Saito and Takashima, 2015, 2017).

24.2.4 Dealing with data reliability

Maddison (2001) was transparent about the element of guesstimation in his database, taking the view that setting out a number focuses the mind and stimulates others to provide a better alternative. However, the appearance of Maddison's database has undoubtedly allowed some economists to use the pre-1870 data in ways for which the data were never designed, without paying any attention to their fragility. Clark (2009, 1160) cites a number of papers published in leading journals, including the *American Economic Review*, *Quarterly Journal of Economics*, *Journal of Monetary Economics*, *Journal of Economic Growth*, and *Journal of Economic History*, where the Maddison data are used inappropriately to test various theories. An attempt has been made above to offer a guide to the accuracy of the data by distinguishing between the direct approach used for data-rich countries such as Britain and the Netherlands and the indirect approach for data-poor countries such as Italy and Spain. Yet the distinction is not always clear-cut. First, as pointed out above, the method used can sometimes vary within the same series. The per capita GDP series for Holland produced by van Zanden and van Leeuwen (2012) is an example of this: the data for Holland before 1510 are far less reliable than the data between 1510 and 1807, because the former are based on modeling agricultural demand and proxies for industry and services, whereas the latter are based on direct output measures. But second, some studies based on the indirect method go on to incorporate cross-checks based on the direct method. Thus, Álvarez-Nogal and Prados de la Escosura (2016) use tithe data to directly estimate agricultural output, which was previously estimated indirectly via a demand function in Álvarez-Nogal and Prados de la Escosura (2013). Similarly Broadberry et al. (2015b) cross-check their demand-side estimates of the growth of Indian agricultural output between 1600 and 1870 using reconstructions of the acreage and yields of all the main crops in two benchmark years.

There have also been attempts to add a quantitative dimension to guidance on the accuracy of historical national accounts using subjective error margins. Bowley (1911–12) pioneered this approach which was subsequently taken up in the construction of historical national accounts by Chapman (1953) and Feinstein (1972) for the case of Britain. Feinstein and Thomas (2002) provide a more recent statement of the case for the use of subjective error margins. In this approach, series are assigned reliability

Table 24.1 Data reliability assessments.

A. Data reliability grades

Reliability grade	Margin of error	Average margin of error
A. Firm figures	± less than 5%	± 2.5%
B. Good figures	± 5% to 15%	± 10%
C. Rough estimates	± 15% to 25%	± 20%
D. Conjectures	± more than 25%	± 40%

B. Reliability assessments for GDP in the Netherlands, China, and Japan

	Grade
Netherlands	
1347-1510	C
1510-1650	B
1650-1750	A
1750-1807	B
China	
Northern Song (980-1120)	B
Ming (1400-1620)	B
Qing (1690-1840)	A
Japan	
Ancient (730-1150)	D
Medieval (1250-1450)	C
Tokugawa (1600-1846)	B

Sources: NL: van Zanden and van Leeuwen (2012); China: Broadberry et al. (2018); Japan: Bassino et al. (2019).

grades corresponding to error bands. Feinstein (1972, 21) suggested that for firm figures (grade A), the margin of error around the reported series should be judged to be ± less than 5%. For good estimates (grade B), the margin of error is ± 5% to 15%, while for rough estimates (grade C) the margin of error is ± 15% to 25% and for conjectures (grade D) it is ± more than 25%.

These subjective margins of error, set out in Table 24.1A, are then assumed to be held with 95 percent confidence, so that the average margin of error can be interpreted as two standard errors. Perkins (1969, 216) suggested an 80 percent confidence interval would be more appropriate for the less well documented Chinese case, although the statistical basis for either of these assumptions is somewhat tenuous. Bowley (1911–12) goes on to suggest that when constructing a composite series such as GDP, it is likely that some errors will be offsetting, with an upward bias in one series countered by a downward bias in another series.

The subjective error margins approach has been adopted explicitly in a number of the recent studies in historical national accounting that have been used in the Great Divergence debate. The study of the Netherlands by van Zanden and van Leeuwen (2012) was the first long run study to make use of this approach, which has also been applied to the cases of China and Japan (Broadberry et al., 2018; Bassino et al., 2019). The latter two studies also conduct sensitivity analysis, reporting the percentage increase (decrease) in GDP in response to an increase (decrease) of one average margin of error in each component series.

These exercises help to highlight where the strengths and weaknesses of the estimates lie. First, and perhaps unsurprisingly, for all three countries, the GDP series listed in Table 24.1B become more reliable as they move nearer the present, due to the greater quantity of available data. Second, since it is likely that some series are biased upwards and others downwards, some offsetting errors may be expected in the aggregates derived as the sum of individual series, so long as those series are derived independently (Feinstein and Thomas, 2002; Bowley, 1911–12). This explains the higher grades for GDP than for some of the component series in all three countries. Third, error margins for ratios may also be lower than suggested by the accumulation of error margins for the component series where the errors are positively correlated (Feinstein and Thomas, 2002; Bowley, 1911–12). In the case of China, this applies to GDP per capita, which is heavily influenced by the ratio of cultivated land to population. Since the population and cultivated land data were collected by the imperial authorities, it is likely that an under-estimate of one was accompanied by an under-estimate rather than an over-estimate of the other (Broadberry et al., 2018, 981).

24.3 The Industrial Revolution
24.3.1 British economic growth in long run perspective

Although there has been broad agreement about the quantitative dimensions of British economic growth during the period 1700-1870 since the work of Crafts and Harley (1992), Broadberry et al. (2015b) shed new light on this work by providing historical national accounts for Britain reaching back to the late thirteenth century. An important result of the Crafts-Harley work was that economic growth during the Industrial Revolution was much slower than had originally been suggested by Deane and Cole (1962). This meant that Britain must have entered the Industrial Revolution already richer and more developed than earlier economic historians had assumed. To understand Britain's transition to modern economic growth, it is therefore necessary to examine what happened further back in time.

Fig. 24.1 shows the long run evolution of real GDP, population, and real GDP per capita over the long period 1270-1870. GDP per capita stagnated during 1270-1348, before increasing sharply between 1348 and 1400, as population declined more sharply than GDP following the shock of the Black Death. GDP per capita then remained on a plateau between c.1400 and 1650 as population at first continued to fall and then began to recover from the late fifteenth century. A new GDP per capita growth phase started around 1650, as population stagnated and then declined slightly. Although GDP per capita growth slowed down after 1700 as population growth resumed, it remained positive and became increasingly stable, with fewer and milder years of negative GDP per capita growth. It seems, then, that the Industrial Revolution was less about growing faster and more about avoiding periods of negative growth or shrinking, than has previously been realized (Broadberry and Wallis, 2017).

Table 24.2 presents the average annual growth rates for the same three series: GDP, population, and GDP per capita. Notice how the growth rate of GDP per capita after 1800 was actually slightly slower than after the Black Death (1350s-1400s) and after the Civil War (1650s-1700), despite the fact that GDP growth was much faster. The reason for this was the very different paths of population in these three periods. Whereas population declined very sharply after the Black Death, and still declined slightly after the Civil War, it grew very rapidly during the first two-thirds of the nineteenth century.

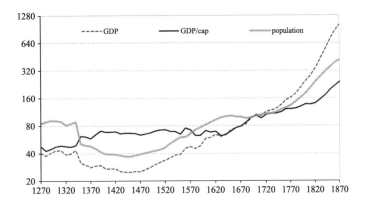

FIGURE 24.1

Real GDP, population, and real GDP per capita, England 1270-1700 and Great Britain 1700-1870 (averages per decade, log scale, 1700 = 100). *Source*: Broadberry et al. (2015a, 204).

This points to a major difference between modern economic growth and pre-industrial growth, as highlighted by Kuznets (1966). Pre-industrial growth required falling population, and this led to an increase in land per capita and capital per capita, which in turn led to higher output per capita. However, this was clearly not a route to sustained growth. For Kuznets, sustained or modern economic growth required rising output per capita together with a growing population.

24.3.2 Structural change in Britain

Another important aspect of modern economic growth is structural change. It has long been noted that economic development is associated with a shift in the structure of the economy away from dependence on agriculture. This has traditionally been seen as a process of industrialization, although recent research suggests that this understates the role of services. Broadberry et al. (2015a) note that the British economy diversified away from agriculture over a longer time span than was once believed by economic historians. Agriculture was less important and services more important earlier than widely perceived, with important consequences for sectoral productivity performance. Labor productivity growth was faster in industry than in agriculture during the Industrial Revolution rather than the reverse, as early quantification of the Industrial Revolution had appeared to suggest.

The quantitative dimensions of the structural shift away from agriculture in the British economy are set out in Table 24.3. The first point to note is that agriculture's share of output and employment declined in importance over time, while the shares of industry and services increased, as would be expected for a developing nation. Second, however, note that even as early as 1381, agriculture accounted for less than 60 per cent of employment and less than 50 per cent of nominal GDP, so that even in the fourteenth century, industry and services accounted for a substantial share of economic activity. Third, although agriculture accounted for a smaller share of output than employment for most of the period under consideration here, thus making agriculture a low productivity sector, this had ceased to be the case by 1801, a point first noted by Crafts (1985). Fourth, although industry increased its share of nominal GDP more rapidly than services until 1700, this ceased to be the case during the Industrial

Table 24.2 Annual growth rates of real GDP, population, and real GDP per capita, England 1270-1700 and Great Britain 1700-1870 (%).

	Real GDP	Population	Real GDP per capita
A. England			
1270s-1300s	-0.02	0.27	-0.29
1300s-1350s	-0.64	-0.52	-0.12
1350s-1400s	-0.30	-1.06	0.76
1400s-1450s	-0.06	-0.21	0.15
1450s-1500s	0.40	0.25	0.15
1500s-1550s	0.51	0.65	-0.14
1550s-1600s	0.81	0.62	0.19
1600s-1650s	0.41	0.51	-0.10
1650s-1700	0.78	-0.04	0.82
1270s-1700	0.22	0.04	0.18
B. Great Britain			
1700-1750s	0.49	0.30	0.19
1750s-1800s	1.21	0.77	0.44
1800s-1850s	2.08	1.34	0.74
1850s-1870	0.12	1.54	0.58
1700-1870	1.31	0.84	0.48

Source: Broadberry et al. (2015a, 208).

Revolution period. This may at first sight seem surprising, but can be explained by a decline in the relative price of industrial goods, as technological progress increased productivity and drove down prices. By contrast, the more modest productivity improvement in services led to an increase in their relative price, so that the share of services in nominal GDP increased more rapidly than the share of industry after 1700.

A fifth striking feature of Table 24.3 is that much of the shift of labor from agriculture to industry occurred before 1759, which has important implications for the pattern of labor productivity growth before and during the Industrial Revolution. If, as was once believed, the shift of labor from agriculture to industry had taken place at the same time as the Industrial Revolution, then much of the growth of industrial output could be explained by increased labor input rather than by productivity growth. This counter-intuitive result was implicit in the work of Deane and Cole (1962), and also confronted more explicitly by Crafts and Harley (1992). With much of the shift of labor from agriculture to industry occurring between 1522 and 1759, there was a period of labor-intensive industrialization (or proto-industrialization) without dramatic industrial productivity growth, which can be tracked in Table 24.4. This was then followed by an Industrial Revolution, where capital deepening and technological progress raised industrial labor productivity rapidly after 1759.

Table 24.3 Sectoral shares in nominal GDP and the labor force, England 1381-1700 and Great Britain 1700-1870 (%).

A. Nominal GDP shares

Year	Region	Agriculture	Industry	Services	Total
1381	England	45.5	28.8	25.7	100.0
1522	England	39.7	38.7	21.6	100.0
1700	England and Britain	26.7	41.3	32.0	100.0
1759	Britain	29.7	35.2	35.1	100.0
1801	Britain	31.3	32.7	36.0	100.0
1841	Britain	22.1	36.4	41.5	100.0

B. Labor force shares

Year	Region	Agriculture	Industry	Services	Total
1381	England	57.2	19.2	23.6	100.0
1522	England	58.1	22.7	19.2	100.0
1700	England and Britain	38.9	34.0	27.2	100.0
1759	Britain	36.8	33.9	29.3	100.0
1801	Britain	31.7	36.4	31.9	100.0
1841	Britain	23.5	45.6	30.9	100.0

Source: Broadberry et al. (2015a, 344).

Table 24.4 Sectoral annual growth rates of output, labor-force, and labor productivity, England 1381-1700 and Great Britain 1700-1851.

Period	Annual % growth:					
	Agriculture			Industry		
	Output	Labor-force	Labor productivity	Output	Labor-force	Labor productivity
1381-1522	0.01	-0.01	0.02	0.27	0.10	0.17
1522-1700	0.38	0.25	0.13	0.73	0.66	0.07
1700-1759	0.79	0.22	0.57	0.63	0.31	0.32
1759-1801	0.85	0.44	0.41	1.54	0.97	0.57
1801-1851	0.74	0.64	0.10	3.00	1.74	1.23
	Services			GDP		
	Output	Labor-force	Labor productivity	Output	Labor-force	Labor productivity
1381-1522	0.06	-0.16	0.23	0.11	-0.02	0.14
1522-1700	0.74	0.60	0.14	0.60	0.45	0.16
1700-1759	0.70	0.44	0.26	0.69	0.32	0.38
1759-1801	1.36	1.00	0.36	1.23	0.79	0.44
1801-1851	2.16	1.45	0.71	2.10	1.35	0.74

Source: Broadberry et al. (2015a, 367).

24.4 The Great Divergence

New estimates of GDP per capita during the period 1000-1870 have recently been produced in a number of European and Asian economies, making use of historical data collected at the time. These estimates show reversals of fortune within as well as between the two continents. First, they show a much clearer Little Divergence within Europe between the northwest and the rest of the continent than had been suggested by Maddison (2001), with Britain and the Netherlands overtaking Italy and Spain. Second, these estimates also show a much clearer Asian Little Divergence, with Japan overtaking China and India. And third, they show a later Great Divergence between Europe and Asia than suggested by Maddison, taking account of regional variation within the two continents. Although individual European nations or small regions were ahead of the whole of China as early as 1300, the leading Chinese region did not fall decisively behind the leading European nation until the eighteenth century. This is a lot later than suggested by earlier western economic historians such as Weber (1930), Landes (1969), or North and Thomas (1971), although not quite as late as suggested by Pomeranz (2000), who argued for parity until the early nineteenth century. However, Pomeranz (2011, 2017) has more recently accepted that his earlier claims were exaggerated and now sees the Great Divergence as dating from the eighteenth century.

The data are displayed in 1990 international dollars for comparability with each other and with the estimates of Maddison (2010). GDP per capita in national currencies cannot simply be compared at the nominal exchange rates which may move to clear international asset markets rather than reflect the price of goods and services that people living in the different countries purchase. The purchasing power parity (PPP) between two currencies is obtained by comparing the prices of individual products and services, weighted by their importance in the expenditure of households. In a two-country comparison, say between Britain and Italy, a different PPP would be obtained using British weights rather than Italian weights, so a compromise estimate can be obtained by taking the geometric mean of British and Italian weighted PPPs. However, a series of bilateral comparisons made this way may not be transitive, so in multi-country comparisons, it is necessary to choose a set of international weights. Most international comparisons are now carried out in 1990 Geary-Khamis international dollars, named after the economic statisticians who derived the weighting scheme.

Using PPPs for 1990, GDP per capita for all countries can be converted to 1990 international dollars, which provides a convenient standard for comparing per capita incomes over space and time. The World Bank poverty standard in 1990 suggested "bare bones subsistence" income was $1 per day, or $365 per year. Since any society has a rich elite living well above this level, Maddison adopted $400 as a guide to the minimum level of GDP per capita that should be expected. This is a useful figure to bear in mind when assessing the plausibility of the GDP per capita estimates.

24.4.1 Europe's Little Divergence

Europe's Little Divergence can be captured graphically in Fig. 24.2, which presents data for Britain and the Netherlands in northwest Europe and Italy and Spain in Mediterranean Europe (Broadberry et al., 2015a; van Zanden and van Leeuwen, 2012; Malanima, 2011; Álvarez-Nogal and Prados de la Escosura, 2013). Although the new estimates in panel A are available on an annual basis from the late thirteenth century, they are plotted here on a decade-average basis for comparison with Maddison's data in panel B. A number of differences between the two data sets are immediately apparent. First, the new estimates revise upwards the level of per capita GDP in the middle ages. Medieval western Europe was

A. New estimates

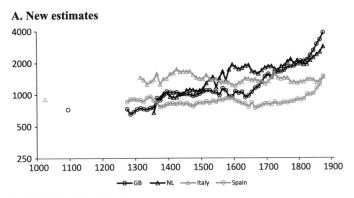

B. Maddison's estimates

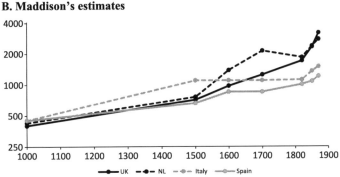

FIGURE 24.2

New estimates of GDP per capita in western Europe compared with Maddison's estimates, 1000-1870 (1990 international dollars). *Sources*: Panel A: GB: Broadberry et al. (2015a); NL: van Zanden and van Leeuwen (2012); Italy: Malanima (2002, 2011); Spain: Álvarez-Nogal and Prados de la Escosura (2013). Panel B: Maddison (2010).

substantially richer than Maddison thought, and subsequent growth therefore more gradual. Second, the new estimates suggest a different pattern of Europe's Little Divergence. Maddison saw more or less continuous growth in the whole of western Europe, with slightly faster growth in Britain and the Netherlands. The new estimates, by contrast, show little or no trend growth in Mediterranean Europe, where GDP per capita stagnated between 1300 and 1800, combined with relatively short bursts of episodic growth interspersed with long periods of stagnation in northwest Europe.

The reversal of fortunes between northwest Europe and Mediterranean Europe occurred in two phases. The first turning point came with the Black Death in 1348. Before then, per capita incomes were substantially higher in Italy and Spain than in Britain and the Netherlands. Although Italy, Britain, and the Netherlands all received a positive boost to per capita incomes following the collapse of population beginning in the mid-fourteenth century, only Britain and the Netherlands remained permanently richer as population recovered. A second turning point occurred around 1500, as new trade opportunities opened up between Europe and Asia via trade routes around the south of Africa, and between Europe and the Americas via the Atlantic Ocean. This led to a shift in the focus of economic activity in Europe

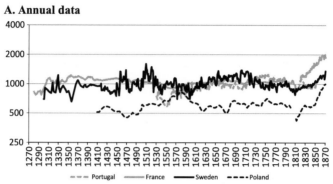

A. Annual data

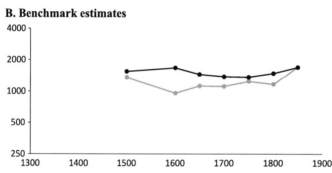

B. Benchmark estimates

FIGURE 24.3

Real GDP per capita in other parts of Europe, 1270-1850 (1990 international dollars, log scale). *Sources*: Panel A: Portugal: Palma and Reis (2019); France: Ridolfi (2016); Sweden: Krantz (2017), Schön and Krantz (2012); Poland: Malinowski and van Zanden (2017); Panel B: Germany: Pfister (2011); Belgium: Buyst (2011).

away from the Mediterranean towards the Atlantic. The Netherlands first caught up with Italy then forged ahead during its Golden Age, while Britain experienced a further growth episode from the mid-seventeenth century.

Annual data are also available now for other European countries, including France, Sweden, Portugal, and Poland (Ridolfi, 2016; Schön and Krantz, 2012; Krantz, 2017; Palma and Reis, 2019; Malinowski and van Zanden, 2017). In addition, some linked benchmarks are available for Belgium and Germany (Buyst, 2011; Pfister, 2011). These estimates are shown in Fig. 24.3 and confirm the picture of no trend growth outside northwest Europe, which forged ahead of the rest of the European continent from around 1500, led initially by the Netherlands, then by Britain.

24.4.2 Asia's Little Divergence

Data are available in abundance for some Asian economies for some time periods, but there has been relatively little work so far processing this material. Much work remains to be done on the Chinese data, but it is now possible to produce decadal estimates of GDP from the output side, apart from during dynastic changes (Broadberry et al., 2018). Indian data are less abundant, and it has so far only been possible to produce decadal estimates back to 1800 and benchmarks every half century between 1600 and 1800 (Broadberry et al., 2015b). Most of the information about India comes from the records of the European East India Companies and the British Raj, apart from Abū'l-Fazl's (1595) remarkable document, The Ā' īn–i-Akbarī, which provides a wealth of information for the Mughal Empire in a single year at the end of the fifteenth century. Japan also has a wealth of data, but at this stage the estimates are available only for a handful of benchmark years (Bassino et al., 2019).

The results for Asia in Fig. 24.4, like those for Europe in Fig. 24.2, suggest a general upward revision of early GDP per capita compared with Maddison's estimates. China was substantially richer than Maddison thought during the Northern Song and Ming dynasties and India was richer than Maddison believed at the height of the Mughal Empire. Interestingly, however, the upwards revision of Maddison's conjectural estimates of GDP per capita in Japan is for the late nineteenth century, as Fukao et al. (2015) argue that Maddison overstated Japanese growth during the late nineteenth century and first half of the twentieth. This means that projecting back from 1990, by the time of the Meiji Restoration in 1868, Japan was more developed than has been widely appreciated.

As a result of these changes, the new estimates show a much more significant reversal of fortunes within Asia than suggested by Maddison. This is consistent with a number of important strands in Asian economic history. First, there are writers such as Needham (1954), Wittfogel (1957) and Elvin (1973) who stress China's early economic leadership in science, irrigation and agricultural productivity. Second, the decline in Chinese per capita incomes during the Qing dynasty is consistent with the work of Huang (1985, 2002) on agricultural involution. Third, the progress of Japan before the Meiji restoration, particularly during the Tokugawa shogunate, fits well with the influential work of Smith (1959) and Hayami (1967, 2015) on agricultural development and the industrious revolution.

24.4.3 Dating the Great Divergence

Fig. 24.5 puts together the new GDP per capita estimates for Europe and Asia from Figs. 24.2 and 24.4 to provide a focus on the Great Divergence. China was surely one of the richest countries in the world at the beginning of the second millennium, with per capita GDP of around $1,000 in 1990 international prices. The most reliable estimate that we have for Europe around this time is the figure of $723 for Britain in 1086, based on the Domesday Survey (Broadberry et al., 2015a, 375; Walker, 2014). For Italy, Malanima (2011) suggests a per capita GDP of close to $1,500 by 1300, but this had grown substantially since the eleventh century as long distance trade recovered following its collapse during the Dark Ages, and using Malanima's (2002, 450) growth rate between 1000 and 1300 yields an estimate of $911 for the early eleventh century. China was going through its Mongol interlude in the fourteenth century, so that estimates of GDP per capita are not available, but it is unlikely that Chinese per capita incomes were any higher than during the preceding Northern Song dynasty or the following Ming dynasty. It is therefore tempting to use the Italian and Chinese data to conclude that the Great Divergence was already underway by the fourteenth century, while in the fifteenth and sixteenth centuries the temptation becomes even stronger with both Italy and the Netherlands clearly ahead of China in terms of GDP per capita.

However, we must be careful here before concluding that the Great Divergence began in the early modern period or even during the late medieval period, since China was dramatically larger than any individual European country. Chinese population in 1600 was 160 million, compared with just 13.1

A. New estimates

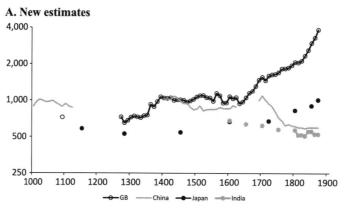

B. Maddison's estimates

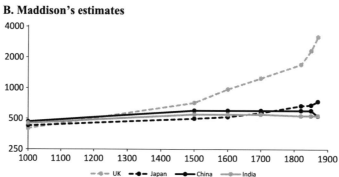

FIGURE 24.4

New estimates of GDP per capita in Asia compared with Maddison's estimates, 1000-1870 (1990 international dollars). *Sources*: Panel A: GB: Broadberry et al. (2015a): China: Broadberry et al. (2018); Japan: Bassino et al. (2019); India: Broadberry et al. (2015b); Panel B: Maddison (2010).

million in Italy, 4.2 million in Great Britain and 1.5 million in the Netherlands (Maddison, 2010). Even France, which was western Europe's largest nation, had a population of only 18.5 million in 1600. While the GDP per capita gap between the leading west European nations and China remained small, as it did until the eighteenth century, smaller Chinese regions of comparable size, such as the Yangzi delta, may still have been on a par with the richest parts of Europe.

Li and van Zanden (2012) have produced a comparison of GDP per capita in the Yangzi delta and the Netherlands in the early nineteenth century, finding per capita incomes in the Yangzi delta to be around half of the level in the Netherlands in the 1820s. This suggests a per capita GDP figure of around $1,050 for the Yangzi delta, in 1990 international dollars, or about 75 percent higher than in China as a whole. Applying the ratio between the Yangzi delta and China as a whole in the 1820s to Chinese GDP per capita for earlier years produces a quantification of the leading Chinese region

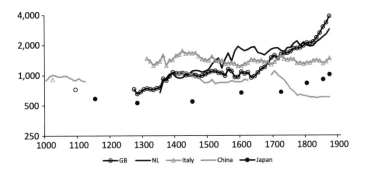

FIGURE 24.5

GDP per capita in Europe and Asia, 1000-1870 (1990 international dollars). *Sources*: GB: Broadberry et al. (2015a); NL: van Zanden and van Leeuwen (2012); Italy: Malanima (2002, 2011); China: Broadberry et al. (2018); Japan: Bassino et al. (2019).

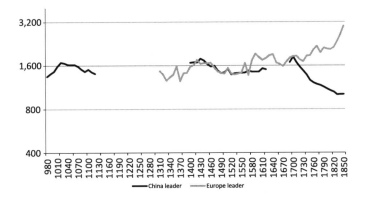

FIGURE 24.6

Real GDP per capita in the leading regions of China and Europe, 980-1850 (1990 international dollars, log scale). *Source*: Broadberry et al. (2018).

for comparison with the European leader in Fig. 24.6.[1] The "European leader" series is based on Italy until the 1540s, followed by the Netherlands until the 1800s and then Great Britain. On this basis, it is only after 1700 that a significant gap opened up between the leading regions of Europe and Asia.

It is reassuring that the historical national accounting evidence suggests the first half of the eighteenth century as the point in time when the leading regions of Europe and Asia first diverged, since this seems to be the new consensus that is emerging from both California School authors such as Pomeranz

---

[1] This does not have to mean that the Yangzi delta was always the leading region, but rather that there was always a region that was proportionally as far above the Chinese average as the Yangzi region in the 1820s.

(2011, 2017) and from economic historians using other quantitative indicators such as real wages and urbanization rates (Broadberry and Gupta, 2006; Allen et al., 2011). The California School authors were right to point to the importance of regional variation within both Asia and Europe, but a bit too optimistic about the performance of the richest parts of Asia during the eighteenth century.

24.4.4 The dynamics of the Great Divergence

Settling the dating of the Great Divergence does not mean that what happened earlier can be disregarded in seeking to understand its origins. It is important to also examine the dynamics of the income process. One of the most interesting developments of the recent wave of research in historical national accounting has been the construction of annual estimates of GDP per capita reaching back to the thirteenth or fourteenth century for a number of countries. Using these data, a radically new picture of the Little and Great Divergences has appeared. Northwestern Europe forged ahead of the rest of Europe and also diverged from Asia not by growing faster during periods of positive growth, but rather by reducing the frequency and rate of shrinking during periods of negative growth (Broadberry and Wallis, 2017). Indeed, a key feature of British economic growth during the transition to modern economic growth was its relatively slow rate. This has been noted since the work of Crafts (1985), but it is given added emphasis by Broadberry et al.'s (2015a) finding that the growth rate was actually slower during the eighteenth century than during the second half of the seventeenth century. What mattered was that as population growth returned, the British economy did not experience negative per capita income growth. This process of avoiding growth reversals in northwestern Europe can be traced back to the growth episode following the Black Death of the mid-fourteenth century. In this sense, the origins of the Great Divergence are still to be found in the late medieval period, as earlier generations of economic historians argued, even though at this stage northwestern Europe had not forged ahead of the rest of Europe or Asia.

Explaining the Industrial Revolution has more in common with solving the problem of development today than is usually acknowledged. Getting growth going in the first place, the traditional focus of analysis, is only part of the story. Just as important is ensuring that periods of positive growth are not followed by periods of negative growth, or shrinking. This has been highlighted in the case of developing economies today by Easterly et al. (1993) and Pritchett (2000). For the transition to modern economic growth in Britain during the Industrial Revolution, it means paying as much attention to the absence of negative trend growth after the gains of the post-Black Death growth episode as to the innovations that started episodes of positive growth during the eighteenth century.

Fig. 24.7 plots the new estimates of GDP per capita in northwest and Mediterranean Europe between 1270 and 1870. This shows the alternation of periods of positive growth and negative growth or "shrinking" in Italy and Spain, leaving little or no progress in the level of per capita incomes over the long run. For Britain and the Netherlands, by contrast, although there were alternating periods of positive and negative growth until the eighteenth century, there was also a clear upward trend, with the gains following the Black Death being retained, and the periods of shrinking eventually disappearing with the transition to modern economic growth. One way to think about Europe's Little Divergence, and also the Great Divergence, is therefore not so much the beginning of growth, but rather the weakening and ending of periods of shrinking.

In one way, the Asian Little Divergence resembles its European counterpart, with Japan achieving trend growth over the long run, like Britain and the Netherlands. However, there were also important

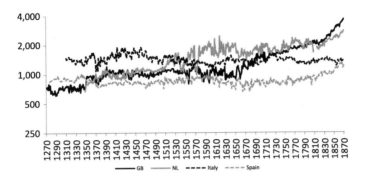

FIGURE 24.7

New estimates of GDP per capita in western Europe, 1270-1870 (1990 international dollars). *Sources*: GB: Broadberry et al. (2015a), NL: van Zanden and van Leeuwen (2012), Italy: Malanima (2011), Spain: Álvarez-Nogal and Prados de la Escosura (2013).

differences. First, economic growth was slower in Japan than in northwest Europe, and second, the divergence was as much the result of an increase in negative growth or shrinking in China and India. Note further that, given the wide acceptance by researchers of the low levels of per capita income in Asia in the nineteenth century and the relatively high levels of per capita income in medieval Europe, China can only have been a relatively rich country in the Northern Song and Ming dynasties if there was significant shrinking of per capita incomes during the population expansion of the Qing dynasty.

24.5 Conclusions

This chapter surveys recent research on historical national accounting since Angus Maddison's (2001) *The World Economy: A Millennial Perspective*, focusing on the implications for the Industrial Revolution and the Great Divergence. Maddison's data are best seen as "guesstimates" which were intended to spark further research using the existence of historical data for pre-industrial Europe and Asia. Utilizing these data within a national accounting framework has produced a number of findings concerning the development process over the long period 1000-1870.

The first set of findings concerns the Industrial Revolution. Eighteenth century Britain was the first economy to make the transition to modern economic growth, but this breakthrough built upon earlier episodes of growth after the Black Death in the fourteenth century and the Civil War in the seventeenth century. Between these two episodes, the economy remained on a plateau rather than sinking back to Malthusian subsistence as population recovered. As a result, Britain improved its position relative to the rest of Europe (the Little Divergence) and relative to Asia (the Great Divergence).

The second set of findings concerns the Great Divergence, where the old idea of a uniformly modernizing Europe forging ahead of a uniformly stagnating Asia needs to be modified to take account of regional variation within both continents. There were reversals of fortune in the form of a European Little Divergence as Britain and the Netherlands overtook Italy and Spain, and an Asian Little Divergence as Japan overtook China and India, at the same time as the Great Divergence as the leading

European region (the North Sea area) forged ahead of the leading Chinese region (the Yangzi delta). In terms of dating, the Great Divergence occurred in the first half of the eighteenth century at around the same time as the first transition to modern economic growth in Britain and the start of a period of shrinking in Qing dynasty China. However, this can also be seen as the culmination of a dynamic process beginning in northwest Europe in the fourteenth century, with a reduction in the frequency and rate of shrinking during periods of negative growth.

References

Abū 'l-Fazl, 1595. The Ā' īn–i-Akbarī. Translated into English by H. Blochman. Low Price Publications, Delhi.

Allen, R.C., 2000. Economic structure and agricultural productivity in Europe, 1300-1800. European Review of Economic History 3, 1–25.

Allen, R.C., Bassino, J.P., Ma, D., Moll-Murata, C., van Zanden, J.L., 2011. Wages, prices, and living standards in China, 1738-1925: in comparison with Europe, Japan, and India. Economic History Review 64 (S1), 8–38.

Álvarez-Nogal, C., Prados de la Escosura, L., 2013. The rise and fall of Spain (1270-1850). Economic History Review 66, 1–37.

Álvarez-Nogal, C., Prados de la Escosura, L., 2016. Spanish agriculture in the little divergence. European Review of Economic History 20, 452–477.

Angeles, L., 2008. GDP per capita or real wages? Making sense of conflicting views on pre-industrial Europe. Explorations in Economic History 45, 147–163.

Bairoch, P., 1988. Cities and Economic Development: From the Dawn of History to the Present. University of Chicago Press, Chicago.

Bassino, J.-P., Broadberry, S., Fukao, K., Gupta, B., Takashima, M., 2019. Japan and the Great Divergence, 730-1874. Explorations in Economic History 72, 1–22.

Beveridge, W., 1939. Prices and Wages in England from the Twelfth to the Nineteenth Century, vol. I, Price Tables: Mercantile Era. Longmans, Green, London.

Bolt, J., van Zanden, J.L., 2014. The Madison project: collaborative research on historical national accounts. Economic History Review 63, 627–651.

Bowley, A.L., 1911–12. The measurement of the accuracy of an average. Journal of the Royal Statistical Society 75, 77–88.

Broadberry, S.N., Campbell, B., Klein, A., Overton, M., van Leeuwen, B., 2015a. British Economic Growth, 1270-1870. Cambridge University Press, Cambridge.

Broadberry, S., Custodis, J., Gupta, B., 2015b. India and the Great Divergence: an Anglo-Indian comparison of GDP per capita, 1600-1871. Explorations in Economic History 55, 58–75.

Broadberry, S., Guan, H., Li, D., 2018. China, Europe and the Great Divergence: a study in historical national accounting, 980-1850. The Journal of Economic History 78, 955–1000.

Broadberry, S., Gupta, B., 2006. The early modern Great Divergence: wages, prices and economic development in Europe and Asia, 1500-1800. Economic History Review 59, 2–31.

Broadberry, S., Wallis, J., 2017. Growing, Shrinking and Long Run Economic Performance: Historical Perspectives on Economic Development. Working Paper No. 23343. National Bureau of Economic Research, Cambridge, MA. http://www.nber.org/papers/w23343, 2017.

Buyst, E., 2011. Towards estimates of long term growth in the southern low countries, ca.1500–1846. In: Quantifying Long Run Economic Development. University of Warwick in Venice, March 22–24. http://www2.warwick.ac.uk/fac/soc/economics/events/seminars-workshops-conferences/conferences/venice3/programme/buyst.pdf.

Campbell, B.M.S., 2000. English Seigniorial Agriculture, 1250-1450. Cambridge University Press, Cambridge.

Campbell, B.M.S., 2007. Three centuries of English crop yields, 1211-1491. http://www.cropyields.ac.uk.

Carus-Wilson, E.M., Coleman, O., 1963. England's Export Trade, 1275-1547. Clarendon, Oxford.

Chapman, A.L., 1953. Wages and Salaries in the United Kingdom 1920-1938. Cambridge University Press, Cambridge.

Clark, G., 2004. The price history of English agriculture, 1209-1914. Research in Economic History 22, 41–125.

Clark, G., 2005. The condition of the working-class in England, 1209-2004. Journal of Political Economy 113, 1307–1340.

Clark, G., 2006. England, Prices and Wages Since 13th Century. Global Price and Income History Group. University of California, Davis. http://gpih.ucdavis.edu/Datafilelist.htm.

Clark, G., 2007. A Farewell to Alms: A Brief Economic History of the World. Princeton University Press, Princeton.

Clark, G., 2009. Review of "Contours of the world economy, 1-2030 AD: essays in macro-economic history, by Angus Maddison". The Journal of Economic History 69, 1156–1161.

Clark, G., 2010. The macroeconomic aggregates for England, 1209-1869. Research in Economic History 27, 51–140.

Crafts, N.F.R., 1976. English economic growth in the eighteenth century: a re-examination of Deane and Cole's estimates. Economic History Review 29, 226–235.

Crafts, N.F.R., 1985. British Economic Growth During the Industrial Revolution. Oxford University Press, Oxford.

Crafts, N.F.R., Harley, C.K., 1992. Output growth and the Industrial Revolution: a restatement of the Crafts-Harley view. Economic History Review 45, 703–730.

Deane, P., Cole, W.A., 1962. British Economic Growth, 1688-1959: Trends and Structure. Cambridge University Press, Cambridge.

Deaton, A., Muellbauer, J., 1980. Economics and Consumer Behaviour. Cambridge University Press, Cambridge.

Easterly, W., Kremer, M., Pritchett, L., Summers, L.H., 1993. Good policy or good luck? Journal of Monetary Economics 32, 459–483.

Elvin, M., 1973. The Pattern of the Chinese Past. Stanford University Press, Stanford.

Feinstein, C.H., 1972. National Income, Expenditure and Output of the United Kingdom, 1855-1965. Cambridge University Press, Cambridge.

Feinstein, C.H., Thomas, M., 2002. A plea for errors. Historical Methods 35, 155–165.

Fukao, K., Bassino, J.-P., Makino, T., Paprzycki, R., Settsu, T., Takashima, M., Tokui, J., 2015. Regional Inequality and Industrial Structure in Japan: 1874-2008. Maruzen Publishing, Tokyo.

Habib, I., 1982. Population. In: Raychaudhuri, T., Habib, I. (Eds.), The Cambridge Economic History of India, vol. 1: c.1200-c.1750. Cambridge University Press, Cambridge, pp. 163–171.

Hallam, H.E., 1988. Population movements in England, 1086-1350. In: Hallam, H.E. (Ed.), The Agrarian History of England and Wales, vol. II, 1042-1350. Cambridge University Press, Cambridge, pp. 508–593.

Hatcher, J., 1973. English Tin Production and Trade Before 1550. Clarendon Press, Oxford.

Hayami, A., 1967. Keizai shakai no seiritsu to sono tokushitsu (The emergence of economic society and its characteristics). In: Gakkai, S.-K. (Ed.), Atarashii Edo Jidaizo wo Motomete. Tōyō Keizai Shinpōsha, Tokyo.

Hayami, A., 2015. Japan's Industrious Revolution: Economic and Social Transformations in the Early Modern Period. Springer, Tokyo.

Hoffmann, W.G., 1965. Das Wachstum der deutschen Wirtschaft seit ser Mitte des 19. Springer, Jahrhunderts, Berlin.

Horrell, S., Humphries, J., Weale, M., 1994. An input-output table for 1841. Economic History Review 47, 545–566.

Huang, P., 1985. The Peasant Economy and Social Change in North China. Stanford University Press, Stanford, CA.

Huang, P., 2002. Development or involution in eighteenth-century Britain and China? A review of Kenneth Pomeranz's the Great Divergence: China, Europe and the making of the modern world economy. Journal of Asian Studies 61, 501–538.

Humphries, J., Weisdorf, J., 2019. Unreal wages? Real income and economic growth in England, 1260-1850. Economic Journal 129, 2867–2887.

King, P., 2005. The production and consumption of bar iron in early modern England and Wales. Economic History Review 58, 1–33.

Krantz, O., 2017. Swedish GDP 1300-1560: A Tentative Estimate. Lund Papers in Economic History, vol. 152. Department of Economic History, Lund University. http://portal.research.lu.se/portal/files/21081639/LUP_152.pdf.

Kuznets, S., 1946. National Product Since 1869. National Bureau of Economic Research, New York.

Kuznets, S., 1966. Modern Economic Growth: Rate, Structure and Spread. Yale University Press, New Haven.

Landes, D.S., 1969. The Unbound Prometheus: Technological Change and Industrial Development in Western Europe from 1750 to the Present. Cambridge University Press, New York.

Li, B., van Zanden, J.L., 2012. Before the Great Divergence? Comparing the Yangzi Delta and the Netherlands at the beginning of the nineteenth century. The Journal of Economic History 72, 956–989.

Maddison, A., 1964. Economic Growth in the West. Twentieth Century Fund, New York.

Maddison, A., 1985. Phases of Capitalist Development: A Long-Run Comparative View. Oxford University Press, Oxford.

Maddison, A., 1991. Dynamic Forces in Capitalist Development. Oxford University Press, Oxford.

Maddison, A., 2001. The World Economy: A Millennial Perspective. Organisation for Economic Co-operation and Development, Paris.

Maddison, A., 2010. Statistics on World Population, GDP and Per Capita GDP, 1-2008 AD. Groningen Growth and Development Centre. http://www.ggdc.net/MADDISON/oriindex.htm.

Malanima, P., 2002. L'economia italiana: dalla crescita medieval all crescita contemporanea. Il Mulino, Bologna.

Malanima, P., 2011. The long decline of a leading economy: GDP in central and northern Italy, 1300-1913. European Review of Economic History 15, 169–219.

Malinowski, M., van Zanden, J.L., 2017. Income and its distribution in preindustrial Poland. Cliometrica 11, 375–404.

Needham, J., 1954. Science and Civilization in China, vol. 1. Cambridge University Press, Cambridge.

North, D.C., Thomas, R.P., 1971. The Rise of the Western World: A New Economic History. Cambridge University Press, New York.

O'Brien, P.K., Hunt, P.A., 1999. England, 1485-1815. In: Bonney, R. (Ed.), The Rise of the Fiscal State in Europe, c.1200-1850. Oxford University Press, Oxford, pp. 53–100.

Overton, M., 1991. The determinants of crop yields in early modern England. In: Campbell, B.M.S., Overton, M. (Eds.), Land, Labor and Livestock: Historical Studies in European Agricultural Productivity. Manchester University Press, Manchester, pp. 284–322.

Overton, M., 2000. Prices from probate inventories. In: Arkell, T., Evans, N., Goose, N. (Eds.), When Death Do Us Part: Understanding and Interpreting the Probate Records of Early Modern England. Leopard's Head Press, Oxford, pp. 120–143.

Overton, M., Whittle, J., Dean, D., Hann, A., 2004. Production and Consumption in English Households, 1600-1750. Routledge, London.

Palma, N., Reis, J., 2019. From convergence to divergence: Portuguese economic growth, 1527-1850. The Journal of Economic History 79, 477–506.

Perkins, D.H., 1969. Agricultural Development in China, 1368-1968. Aldine, Chicago.

Pfister, U., 2011. Economic growth in Germany, 1500–1850. In: Quantifying Long Run Economic Development. University of Warwick in Venice, March, 22–24. https://warwick.ac.uk/fac/soc/economics/seminars/seminars/conferences/venice3/programme/pfister_growth_venice_2011.pdf.

Phelps Brown, H., Hopkins, S.V., 1955. Seven centuries of building wages. Economica 22, 195–206.

Phelps Brown, H., Hopkins, S.V., 1956. Seven centuries of the prices of consumables, compared with builders' wage-rates. Economica 23, 296–314.

Pomeranz, K., 2000. The Great Divergence: China, Europe, and the Making of the Modern World Economy. Princeton University Press, Princeton.

Pomeranz, K., 2011. Ten years after: responses and reconsiderations. Historically Speaking 12 (4), 20–25. Project Muse. https://muse.jhu.edu/login?auth=0&type=summary&url=/journals/historically_speaking/v012/12.4.coclanis.html.

Pomeranz, K., 2017. The data we have vs. the data we need: a comment on the state of the "divergence" debate (part I). The NEP-HIS Blog https://nephist.wordpress.com/2017/06/06/the-data-we-have-vs-the-data-we-need-a-comment-on-the-state-of-the-divergence-debate-part-i/#comments.

Pritchett, L., 2000. Understanding patterns of economic growth: searching for hills among plateaus, mountains and plains. World Bank Economic Review 14, 221–250.

Ridolfi, L., 2016. The French economy in the longue durée. A study on real wages, working days and economic performance from Louis IX to the Revolution (1250-1789). PhD thesis. IMT School for Advanced Studies, Lucca.

Rozman, G., 1973. Urban Networks in Ch'ing China and Tokugawa Japan. Princeton University Press, Princeton.

Saito, O., Takashima, M., 2015. Population, urbanisation and farm output in early modern Japan, 1600-1874: a review of data and benchmark estimates. RCESR Discussion Paper Series, No. DP15-3 https://hermes-ir.lib.hit-u.ac.jp/rs/handle/10086/27295.

Saito, O., Takashima, M., 2017. Jinkō to toshika, idō to shūgyō (Population and urbanisation, migration and employee structure). In: Fukao, K., Nakamura, T., Nakabayashi, M. (Eds.), Kinsei, Iwanami Kōza Nihon Keizai no Rekishi 2 (Iwanami Lecture Series on the History of the Japanese Economy, vol. 2, The Pre-modern Period). Iwanami Shoten, Tokyo, pp. 61–104.

Schön, L., Krantz, O., 2012. The Swedish economy in the early modern period: constructing historical national accounts. European Review of Economic History 16, 529–549.

Smith, T.C., 1959. The Agrarian Origins of Modern Japan. Stanford University Press, Stanford CA.

Smits, J.P., Horlings, E., van Zanden, J.L., 2000. Dutch GNP and Its Components, 1800-1913. Groningen Growth and Development Centre, Groningen. https://www.rug.nl/ggdc/docs/mono5.pdf.

Thorold Rogers, J.E., 1866–1902. A History of Agriculture and Prices in England, vols. 1-6. Clarendon Press, Oxford.

Turner, M.E., Beckett, J.V., Afton, B., 2001. Farm Production in England 1700-1914. Oxford University Press, Oxford.

Walker, J.T., 2014. National income in domesday England. In: Allen, M., Coffman, D. (Eds.), Money, Prices and Wages: Essays in Honour of Professor Nicholas Mayhew. Palgrave Macmillan, Basingstoke, pp. 24–50.

Weber, M., 1930. The Protestant Ethic and the Spirit of Capitalism. Allen and Unwin, London.

Wittfogel, K.A., 1957. Oriental Despotism: A Comparative Study of Total Power. Yale University Press, New Haven.

Wrigley, E.A., 1985. Urban growth and agricultural change: England and the continent in the early modern period. Journal of Interdisciplinary History 15, 683–728.

Wrigley, E.A., Davies, R.S., Oeppen, J.E., Schofield, R.S., 1997. English Population History from Family Reconstitution, 1580-1837. Cambridge University Press, Cambridge.

Wrigley, E.A., Schofield, R.S., 1989. The Population History of England, 1541-1871: A Reconstruction. Cambridge University Press, Cambridge.

van Zanden, J.L., van Leeuwen, B., 2012. Persistent but not consistent: the growth of national income in Holland, 1347-1807. Explorations in Economic History 49, 119–130.

Attitudes, aptitudes, and the roots of the great enrichment

Joel Mokyr[a,b,c]

[a]Departments of Economics and History, Northwestern University, Evanston, IL, United States
[b]Berglas School of Economics, Tel Aviv University, Tel Aviv, Israel

25.1 Introduction

The term "Great Enrichment" proposed by McCloskey (2016, p. 5) should be regarded as a better term to describe the hockeystick-like time series of income and living standards after 1800 than the "Great Divergence" proposed by Pomeranz (2000). The latter is a statement about *relative* income between the West and the Rest, whereas "enrichment" points to the world-wide increase in almost every measure of living standards than one can think of. But what drove that divergence were the unprecedented events that started in western Europe in the eighteenth century and that started the ball rolling — and rolling it still is. The economies that fell behind the West in the nineteenth century have experienced dramatic improvements in absolute terms as well, even if the income per capita gaps are still profound. If poverty is now declining world-wide, the "deep" reason is the growth of what Europeans called "the useful arts" or "useful knowledge."

   The dynamic process leading to the Great Enrichment and its timing matter a great deal. Scholars of the fundamentalist Malthusian school such as Clark (2007) and Galor (2011) have argued that prior to the Industrial Revolution there was little or no growth in income per capita and that all improvements in productivity were, in H.G. Wells's (1923, p. 68) famous formulation, wasted "as rapidly as it got them in a mere insensate multiplication of the common life." But recent work has raised effective criticism against these interpretations. Voigtländer and Voth have noted the possibility of multiple equilibria in a Malthusian system due to urbanization and changes in agricultural practices, whereas Dutta et al. (2018) show that in a Malthusian world with luxury products, living standards can rise without being undone by relentless population growth. The new data summarized by Broadberry et al. (2018) show remarkable long term growth in many pre-modern economies. To be sure, many of these economies eventually reached some kind of plateau (but at very different levels) but the reasons for stagnation include other factors as well (Mokyr, 2018).

---

[c] Note: Some of the below is adapted from my *A Culture of Growth: Origins of the Modern Economy*. Princeton: Princeton University Press, 2016. I am grateful to Michael Giordano for research assistance and to Morgan Kelly and Deirdre McCloskey for comments on an earlier version.

25.2 Europe and the world

Trained economists will find it surprising that there is a school of historians who still regard modern economic growth primarily as a case of successful predation, according to which the West enriched itself at the expense of other civilizations that were less committed to capitalist practices and less aggressive. While they rarely use the term, these scholars see the Great Enrichment fundamentally as a zero-sum game, in which colonial plunder and enslavement enriched a few nations in Europe at the expense of the rest of humanity (e.g., Inikori, 2002). State actions, often driven by mercantile political influence led to the forceful seizure of Atlantic markets by British and French agencies, and the technological progress that occurred was the outcome of an "explicit rejection of market outcomes" (Parthasarathi, 2011, pp. 143, 62). Others see the European expansion after 1500 as creating a web of commercial and financial relationships engendered by the Atlantic slave trade, which prove a critical factor in Britain's capitalist industrialization, further assisting its global supremacy.[1] Equally explicit is Sven Beckert's much-praised volume on the history of cotton (Beckert, 2014), who explains Europe's economic successes by a "coercive European mercantile presence in many of the regions of the world" (p. 37) and asserts the existence of something he calls "war capitalism," by which he means the combination of imperial expansion, slavery, and land expropriation (p. 52) as the engines that drove dynamic markets, capital formation, and eventually innovation and economic growth in the West.

The "history of capitalism" notion of capitalism red in tooth and claw as the dynamic force behind the Great Enrichment, in its haste to distance itself from any interpretation that could be accused of "Eurocentric" or "triumphalist," essentially abstracts from the deep changes in Europe that made it possible. Nobody will deny the salient facts of colonialism, slavery, and the ruthless domination and exploitation of non-European populations. But the exact causal chain behind the Great Enrichment is simply too important to be glossed over in a wave of ideological zeal by those who see a malevolent force named "capitalism" as the primary force behind global imperialism and inequality. This literature seems to assume that given of the devastating effects that European domination often had on the colonized, there must have been proportional gains to the perpetrators. But as McCloskey (2010, pp. 229–48) and many others have pointed out, this interpretation is still based on an implicit zero-sum image of the world. In economic history, zero sum games are exceedingly rare. Violence, trade wars, conquests, and exploitation are negative sum, trade and technological progress are positive sum.

Much more plausible is the causal chain suggested by Daniel Headrick (1981, 2012), who shows in detail how western technology made colonialism possible (as opposed to the other way around). European military technology remained ahead of that of the rest of the world, in large part, because Europe was fragmented into large and small units that fought each other almost incessantly. These wars led to growing investment in weapons and through learning by doing and competitive pressures, Europe developed military hardware and organizational capabilities that gave it an edge in its battles with non-western adversaries (Hoffman, 2015). Superior technology made it possible for Europeans to enslave Africans, ship them across the Atlantic, and make them work in plantations in the new world. Slavery was an essential part of a global act of ecological and economic arbitrage, in which European ships sent new world crops to Asia and Africa as well as to Europe itself (Nunn and Qian, 2010).

---

[1] Anievas and Nisancioglu (2015, pp. 121–122) argue that the "limits of 17th-century English agrarian capitalism" could be overcome because England's "ruling class was able to exploit the widened sphere of economic activity offered by the Atlantic."

Yet a simple causal chain that runs from technology to arbitrage and colonialism leaves us dissatisfied, because the *primum movens* remains mysterious. Why did Europeans, at least for many years, outperform other civilizations technologically and what allowed them to subjugate, rob, and exploit non-Europeans, from Peru to the Gold Coast to Java? It just cannot stand up to scrutiny to assert, as does Parthasarathi (2011), that as late as 1750 Europe and India were at comparable levels of development. One might well ask the unanswered question that "Had Britain and India been at the same level of economic and institutional development in 1750, why was there no 'Western Europe Company' set up in Delhi that would have exploited the political divisions within Europe, established an Indian "Raj" based in London that forced Europe to accept Indian calicoes without tariffs?" (Mokyr, 2012).

The same question was already asked at the time. In an interesting (and widely cited) passage, Dr. Samuel Johnson's fictional Abyssinian prince Rasselas asked his philosopher friend "by what means are the Europeans thus powerful; or why, since they can so easily visit Asia and Africa for trade or conquest, cannot the Asiatics and Africans invade their coasts, plant colonies in their ports... the same winds that carry them back would bring us thither." The answer that was provided would horrify ideologically pure historians of capitalism: "they are more powerful than we, sir, because they are wiser; knowledge will always predominate over ignorance. But why their knowledge is more than ours I know not" (Johnson, 1759, Vol. 1, p. 74). Yet question "why" is not unanswerable; by 1750, surely, Europeans knew more than non-Europeans about subjects that affected or would soon affect economic performance and material living standards. The summary answer to Johnson's question is differences not in "wisdom," as the philosopher surmised, but in *attitudes* and *aptitudes*, that is cultural beliefs and technical competence. Both of these were the result, and in turn causal of, differences in institutions.

25.3 Attitudes

Since Greif's pathbreaking paper (1994) it has been recognized that cultural beliefs matter a great deal to the formation and operation of markets and the expansion of commerce. The importance of such concepts as general vs. local morality and trust as a means of saving on transaction costs and supporting markets have been widely recognized. But what about useful knowledge, that is, the understanding of natural phenomena and regularities that lent themselves to being harnessed for productive purposes? Past societies have differed in their willingness and ability to introduce technological innovations that led to creative destruction and possibly social instability as the price of higher productivity and living standards. It stands to reason that *institutions* mattered a great deal here, providing incentives and support for entrepreneurs and inventors and a safety net for workers whose earnings were disrupted by technological progress. But what about attitudes? Religion and a vision of nature surely mattered. An anthropocentric view of the world, in which nature was regarded as an exploitable resource and where its manipulation and disruption by humans were regarded as inherently virtuous and an expression of God's will were surely at the base of a technologically aggressive society. A famous example of such an interpretation is the work of Lynn White (1978), who saw the roots of technological progress in the doctrines and institutions of the medieval Latin Church.[2]

---

[2] If metaphysical beliefs are such that manipulating and controlling nature invoke a sense of fear or guilt, technological creativity will inevitably be limited in scope and extent. The legends of the ill-fated innovators Prometheus and Daedalus illustrate the deeply ambiguous relationship between the ancient Greeks' religious beliefs and their attitudes toward technology.

One of the most striking examples of how cultural beliefs affect scientific and technological progress is the inferiority complex with respect to ancient wisdom. Intellectual ancestor worship was one of the most underrated obstacles to technological progress. A famous dictum from the Jewish *Chazal* (earlier sages) has it that "if those who were before us (*rishonim*) were like angels, we are but men; and if those who were before us were like men, we are but asses" (Sabbath, 112b, see for instance https://en.wikipedia.org/wiki/Yeridat_ha-dorot).[3] This was not, in its basic outlook, inherently different from the attitudes in China toward the founding intellectuals of Chinese philosophy Confucius, Mencius, and Xunzi, and that of Moslems for the Quran and the *Hadith* (sayings attributed to the prophet Muhammad compiled in the 8th and 9th centuries). The veneration for ancient knowledge had a distinct dampening effect on the ability of society to experience knowledge progress, since it imposed constraints on what new knowledge was and was not permissible. It created a rigid box, and thinking outside that box could entail accusations of heresy.[4] Within the box, there still could be lively debates and discussions, but they were seriously constrained.

One of the most dramatic developments in Europe's cultural life after 1500 was the slow but inexorable melting away of this inferiority complex and the rise of heterodox ideas in a host of areas. Medieval science was not nearly as stagnant and as homogeneous as it is often portrayed.[5] But it was hamstrung by primitive instruments and inaccurate measurement, the fear of being accused of apostasy, and the legacy of classical science, above all Aristotle, Pliny, and Galen. In the later Middle Ages a powerful syncretic orthodoxy had been established that merged Christianity with Aristotelian philosophy and classical science, the monumental life's work of Thomas Aquinas. Renaissance scholars discovered more and ancient scientific writings and made them part of their world-view. A few early doubts cast on the orthodoxy can be seen already in the early Renaissance.[6] Yet only after 1450 did deep cracks in this structure start to emerge, and in the next centuries it showed serious signs of weakening. An early example was the devastating attack on Pliny's scientific work launched by the Ferrara Professor Niccolò Leoniceno in 1492. In the middle of the sixteenth century, the French philosopher Pierre de la Ramée (1515–1572) already wrote freely "on the errors of Aristotle" and by the early seventeenth century Francis Bacon insolently wrote that "[the Greek writers of science] certainly do have a characteristic of the child: the readiness to talk with the inability to produce anything; for their wisdom seems wordy and barren of works" (Bacon [1620] 2000, aphorism 121, p. 59). Without skepticism, there could be no progress.

By the late seventeenth century, at the dawn of the Enlightenment, European intellectual respect for the science of the ancients was largely gone. The slogan of the Royal Society, *nullius in verba*

---

[3] The Hebrew expression *yeridat hadorot* means literally the decline of generations, that is, a sense of inferiority compared to earlier sages and an unwillingness to challenge them. It is quite widespread in the rabbinical literature.

[4] As Carl Becker noted in a classic work written in the early 1930s, "a Philosopher could not grasp the modern idea of progress ... until he was willing to abandon ancestor worship, until he analyzed away his inferiority complex toward the past, and realized that his own generation was superior to any yet known" (Becker, 1932, p. 131).

[5] One fierce debate between the natural philosophers and the theologians concerned the questions of the eternity of the world and whether there were any limitations were imposed on God's powers by the laws of nature.

[6] One of them concerned Aristotle's laws of motion. The 12th-century Andalusian philosopher Ibn Bajja (known as Avempace in the Christian world) already saw the flaws in Aristotle's theory and his ideas found their way to the writings of Aquinas himself. Other medieval scientists such as Nicolas of Oresme and John Buridan also criticized some details of Aristotelian physics. That said, the consensus remains that "only in the sixteenth and seventeenth centuries was Aristotelianism seriously challenged" (Grant, 1996, p. 88, citation on p. 162).

(on nobody's word) could well have been applied to the dominant parts of European intellectual life. True, in the late seventeenth century both France and England witnessed a *querelle des anciens en des modernes* — a battle between the ancients and the moderns (Levine, 1981, 1991; Lecoq, 2001). But any notion that this battle ended in a draw, as Swift implied in his priceless parody of the debate (Swift, [1704] 1753, p. 170), is mistaken: by the late seventeenth century Newton and his contemporaries had hammered the last nail in the coffin of ancient physical science.[7] It was more than physics. The Florentine physician Francesco Redi (1626–1697) showed convincingly that the Aristotelian belief in spontaneous generation of plants and insects was false and William Harvey (1578–1657) showed the same for the Galenic model of blood circulation.

To what can we attribute this rather unique cultural turn? One of them is rather obvious: from the late fifteenth century on Europeans were repeatedly confronted with discoveries that contradicted the received wisdom of the ancients, making classical science continuously lose credibility. In part this was due to the great voyages, which showed that the earth was not what Aristotle and Ptolemy had described. Whereas Copernicus was still basing his revolutionary view of the universe on known facts and theory, Galileo was able to prove him right through his ability to discern the phases of Venus.[8] From Paracelsus to Andreas Vesalius to Galileo and William Gilbert, early-modern European scientists felt free to criticize classical medicine and science, and suggested new theories incompatible with the ancients. New scientific instruments and tools, unavailable to classical philosophers, underlined the superiority of the moderns who rightfully argued that they could observe phenomena and see things that the ancients could not. By the mid seventeenth century, even the holy bible itself did not escape dispassionate textual analysis despite fierce indignation by devout clerics of various stripes.

The change in attitudes was driven in part by institutional change. The new discoveries would not have been effective in overthrowing the classical orthodoxy had it not been for an environment in which intellectual innovation was rewarded and incentivized and moreover could not be effectively suppressed by conservatives and vested interests. A new set of institutions (above all the Reformation), improved technology (above all the advent of the printing press and the decline in transportation costs), and the rather sudden appearance of new information with the great voyages encouraged out-of-the-box thinking that led to the rapid proliferation of intellectual innovations. The market for ideas became more active and more competitive, especially when the monopoly of the Catholic Church collapsed after 1517. Like every market, the market for ideas needed an institutional foundation that defined the basic rules of the game and allowed it to function effectively.

The sixteenth- and seventeenth-century market for ideas in early modern Europe consisted of a demand side based primarily on patronage by princely courts and wealthy individuals, and by other institutions such as universities and academies. Success was correlated with reputation — mostly created by peers who were in the best position to evaluate scientific work (Dasgupta and David, 1994). Reputation in turn correlated with financial security and social standing. University appointments, then as now, were an important component of patronage for intellectuals, and the desire for a secure and comfortable income (if not riches) was a main driver of scholarly efforts. Some of the court patronage appointments are well-known, such as the Grand Duke of Florence, who employed Galileo as the court scientist, and that of the Habsburg Emperor Rudolf II in Prague, who employed not only the

---

[7] Swift concluded that "we cannot learn to which side Victory fell" (Swift, [1704] 1753, p. 170).

[8] Tycho Brahe's well-known observation of a nova (refuting Aristotle's belief of an fixed and unchanging sky) and the demonstration that nature, after all, does not abhor a vacuum cast further doubt on the infallibility of ancient wisdom.

great astronomers Brahe and Kepler, but also botanists like Carolus Clusius, (né Charles de l'Écluse 1526–1609).[9] Louis XIV, always keen on bolstering his international image, attracted to the French Royal Academy some of the great superstars of the age such as the Dutch mathematician Christiaan Huygens and the Italian astronomer Giovanni-Domenico Cassini, as well as French scientists such as the architect and anatomist Claude Perrault (1613–1688) and the Abbé Jean Picard (1620–1682), the first person to measure the size of the Earth with a reasonable degree of accuracy. Many lesser rulers and wealthy nobles similarly extended patronage to leading scholars.

The demand for scholars had a practical side. Many of the most successful practical intellectuals in early modern Europe had been trained as physicians and were employed in that capacity by their patrons. Mathematicians and physicists could help with military matters.[10] Others were employed as tutors, most famously René Descartes at the court of Queen Christina of Sweden.[11] Still others were political counselors, even if their mathematical and philosophical skills did not always match their political insights, as was the case with Leibniz, an advisor to the Duke of Brunswick. Equally in demand were physicians.[12] In all of those cases, reputations — as established through publication and correspondence with peers — were decisive to ensure an appointment. The demand side was thus highly competitive.[13]

On the supply side competition was equally fierce. Intellectuals shamelessly pandered to wealthy patrons, dedicating their books to them and writing fawning prefaces thanking their benefactors. Being a member of a court provided security and protection, but also involved a rise in social standing. It mattered for scientists and artists to be recognized by figures of high social standing and power, because such recognition conveyed respectability in an age in which outside the scholarly community "whom you knew" conveyed as much social prestige as "how much you owned" (Hahn, 1990, p. 7). Biagioli (1990) has made this a central argument in his "new view" of patronage, in which he explicitly tried to minimize the economic motives that drove scientists. Instead he argued that the incentive that drove them was being associated with the mighty and rich elite that provided scientists with "social and intellectual legitimacy." Patronage in this view was a means to an end. While such legitimization may have been important in some cases, it would be rash to dismiss material motives in an age in which many talented scholars found it difficult to earn a living. All the same, the patronage transaction was clearly a multidimensional exchange.

What made this market work, and what ultimately drove the market for ideas, was an underlying institution that set the rules of the scholarly game that were accepted by the vast majority of participants.

---

[9] Clusius, one of the founders of modern botany, was learned, cosmopolitan, widely traveled, and well-connected. He worked for both Rudolf II and Rudolf's father Maximilian II (Evans, 1973, pp. 119–20).

[10] Galileo, while still working in Padua, freelanced for the Venetian arsenal and in the late 1500s invented a geometric and military compass (used for gunnery), as well as other militarily useful devices.

[11] Thomas Hobbes was originally hired by the Cavendish family to teach their children, as was the mathematician William Oughtred, who was a member of the household of the earl of Arundel.

[12] The astronomer and physician Jean Fernel (1497–1558) served as the king's personal physician at the court of Henry II and the physician and polymath Pierre Michon Bourdelot (1610–1685) served as the personal physician of Queen Christina of Sweden. Both William Gilbert and Francesco Redi were well-known physicians even if their contributions to knowledge were elsewhere.

[13] An example is the distinguished Florentine mathematician Vincenzo Viviani (1622–1703), a student and protegé of Galileo in his later years. In 1666 his reputation was such that he was offered lucrative positions by both Louis XIV and John II Casimir of Poland, whereupon Grand Duke Ferdinand de Medici made him a counteroffer and appointed him court mathematician.

It was not a formal, state-run institution but a virtual international network of scholars sharing interests and scholarly ambitions.[14] Known to its members as the "Republic of Letters," it served simultaneously as a clearinghouse and sounding board for scholarly work written in Europe. It served as a mechanism to evaluate intellectual innovations and indirectly the reputation of scholars and intellectuals. The vast bulk of the intellectual innovators recognized by posterity as having made major contributions to science were already world-famous superstars in their own time, no one more so than Newton himself. The Republic of Letters ensured the emergence of open science, since keeping discoveries a secret would do little for a scholar's reputation.[15] It surely is true that scientific knowledge that is kept secret can hardly contribute to economic progress, and that the emergence of open science was the critical development of the age (David, 2008). By reducing the secretiveness of knowledge and turning useful knowledge into what today would be called an open-source system, European intellectuals created an institution that reduced access costs. But it is only in a community that is both competitive and collaborative — such as was the case in a comparatively free market for ideas — that genuine progress was achieved and that the knowledge-foundation of the techniques that drove the Great Enrichment was laid.[16]

In this competitive environment, paralyzing intellectual ancestor worship had little chance of surviving despite stubborn rear-guard actions by conservative writers defending the "ancients." The most desirable sign of success was *influence*, that is, success in persuading others of the merits of a new idea or theory. Such influence depended on the rhetorical rules of science determined (if informally) by the Republic of Letters. Persuasion increasingly turned from finding textual support in the traditional books in the "canon" to observations, experiments, and logic (including mathematics). Transitions were slow and gradual, and even when ancient truths were overturned, it was often hard to abandon Aristotelian and other antiquated concepts such as astrology and numerology altogether. William Harvey, whose discovery of the circulation of the blood challenged age-old fundamental physiological doctrines still adhered as much as he could to Aristotelian methods (Cook, 2006, pp. 425–426). Yet even Aristotle's immense prestige in the end was not sufficient to save the ancients. By Galileo's time, Gillispie has observed, the science and authority of Aristotle had "led the western mind to a dead end" (Gillispie, 1960, p. 11).[17] Innovative natural philosophers, in their eagerness to impress one another (and hence

---

[14] Some of the following is adapted from Mokyr (2016), chapter 12.

[15] Science was seen as a "hunt," a metaphor that appealed to the upper class patrons of philosophers in search of employment (Eamon, 1991, p. 27; 1994, pp. 269–300).

[16] To be sure, intrinsic motivation — curiosity and a desire to make the world a better place — continued to play a role in motivating intellectual innovators. The human need to be respected by peers played a role beyond the competition for patronage positions. Robert Boyle was one of the richest men in England, but this did not stop him from getting annoyed by people using his work without attribution (Shapin, 1994, p. 183; Hunter, 2009, p. 190). In the Netherlands, Spinoza diligently made his living grinding lenses (supplemented by funds from a few admirers), while gradually establishing a continent-wide reputation as a radical (and highly controversial) philosophical innovator. His contemporary, the microscopist Anthonie van Leeuwenhoek, a well-to-do draper and official, communicated his scientific findings (written originally in Dutch) to the Royal Society in London, which published many of his letters. In 1680 he was elected a Fellow, and clearly this was a source of pride for him, as he had it engraved on his tombstone and a painting of him by Jan Verkolje shows him proudly displaying his Royal Society diploma of membership.

[17] Modern scholarship may take issue with Gillispie's judgment that while Aristotelian physics "made sense of the world" it suffered from one major defect: it was wrong (1960, p. 13). It seems more plausible that it eroded because new and indisputable evidence inconsistent with its propositions was discovered.

indirectly those who would extend patronage to them), increasingly dared to criticize the conventional wisdom, and if they only could, shot it to pieces.

Intellectual property rights assumed the form of priority rights: the first person to enunciate a new idea theoretically received the credit for the new idea and the concomitant reputation effects. The system, of course, worked far from perfectly, but it worked well enough to establish the reputation of dozens of intellectual superstars active in Europe in the years between Erasmus and Newton. Priority fights were the natural consequence of the competition for priority in the market for ideas. As Wootton (2015, p. 96) summarized, "priority disputes are an infallible indicator that knowledge has become public, progressive and discovery-oriented"[18]

Progress occurred, but the new interpretations did not invariably offer what posterity would judge to be improvements on existing knowledge: the iconoclastic Swiss physician Paracelsus and his seventeenth century follower Jan-Baptist van Helmont dismissed Galenian medicine, but in retrospect it is hard to conclude that the iatrochemical school they established constituted a dramatic improvement in terms of its clinical outcomes. Similarly, there was the influence of phlogiston theory, proposed by German scientists in the late seventeenth century replacing the four elements of the Greek classics by a new set of elements, one of which was phlogiston that flowed out of a material when it burned. Yet the eventual transformation of chemistry in the age of the Industrial Revolution is emblematic of how the competitive market for ideas worked. When the experimental work of Lavoisier and his students in the late eighteenth century showed unequivocally that phlogiston theory was erroneous and inadequate, it was discarded.

Europe's intellectual progress between 1500 and 1700 paved the road for the subsequent prosperity it was to enjoy, as well as for its ability to dominate, colonize, and exploit other civilizations. The success of its market for ideas, however, in generating this progress was the result of neither design nor intent, but a classic "emergent property," the macro-level system-wide unintended consequences of lower-level interactions. What made Europe the birthplace of the Great Enrichment was a unique set of circumstances, many of them quite accidental. Europe was highly politically fragmented, with city states, and small duchies and bishoprics interspersing larger nation states. Fragmentation has often been credited as a key to Europe's success (see Jones, 1981, pp. 104–126 for a canonical statement and Scheidel, 2019 for a more recent analysis). Between 1500 and 1700 European polities were constantly at war with one another. The customary dynastic squabbles were compounded by the Reformation, which created another casus belli in Europe, and aggravated dynastic and colonial conflicts.

And yet the political fragmentation of Europe was indispensable for its intellectual development. The reactionary forces and entrenched incumbents in Europe defending the ancients against "heretics" faced an almost impossible coordination problem. Much as the Jesuits, for instance, would have loved to suppress Copernican astronomy and infinitesimal mathematics (Alexander, 2014), they could not impose their will north of the Alps. Above all, iconoclastic intellectuals moved on the seams between polities and religions and expertly played the great powers against one another. Suppressing non-conformists became almost impossible, as scholars found it easy to circumvent censors by publishing their work abroad, and when necessary could themselves move across the border, where their

---

[18] Most famous, of course, was the fight between Newton and Leibniz on the development of infinitesimal calculus. Equally nasty, if more obscure, was the fight between two Dutch scientists, Jan Swammerdam and Reinier de Graaf, over the discovery of a technique to study female reproductive organs around 1665. According to an unsubstantiated account, De Graaf died as a result of the exhaustion caused by the priority dispute (Cobb, 2006, pp. 184–85).

international reputations often meant a warm welcome and a nice pension. Once the knowledge of the futility of suppression sank in, the suppression of unconventional thought dwindled down to window dressing. As a result, despite some local defeats, at the end of the day the moderns decisively won the *querelle* with the ancients.

The Republic of Letters created an intellectual institution that was truly transnational and that ensured that every scholar catered to a continent-wide constituency.[19] European intellectual life thus enjoyed the benefits of both a polycentric political system and the economies of scale of a continent-wide community of scholars. The long-run benefits to the growth of knowledge were substantial. The centuries-old monopoly of Christianity on the European market for ideas, protected by the effective use of the concept of heresy, slowly receded. The Republic of Letters is an illustration of Cipolla's (1972, p. 52) insightful remark that the same qualities that make people tolerant also make them receptive to new ideas.[20]

One of the great winners in the increasingly effective and active market for ideas was a belief in progress. Not just progress in knowledge as argued by the *modernes* but also economic progress and even social and political progress toward more harmonious institutions and a better society, as enunciated by the more ebullient Enlightenment writers.[21] Much of the latter eventually turned out to be illusory. The only areas in which there can be little doubt that the improvement was real and demonstrable were technological progress and economic growth. The attitudes and beliefs that prevailed in the early modern market for ideas created the historical phenomena that eventually led to the Great Enrichment: the Scientific Revolution, the Enlightenment, and the Industrial Revolution.

How crucial was the knowledge produced by natural philosophers in the European Republic of Letters to the Industrial Revolution? The debate on that matter is still far from settled. Early modern Europe made many advances that are now recognized as milestones in our understanding of nature, but relatively few of them found an application in the early inventions in the Industrial Revolution, especially in the cotton industry. Yet before dismissing the role of science in the Great Enrichment as done by McCloskey (2010, ch. 38), three matters should be considered. First, even in the early stages of the Industrial Revolution there were some notable triumphs attributable to what we would regard today as scientific knowledge, especially if we include practical mathematics: hydraulic and steam power, chlorine bleaching, gas lighting, longitude determination, surveying instruments, slide rules, and smallpox inoculation should all be placed in that category (Kelly and Ó Gráda, 2020). To be sure, in many of those cases the epistemic base on which the techniques rested were incomplete and

---

[19] Edward Gibbon observed that the philosopher, unlike the patriot, was permitted to consider Europe as a single "great republic" in which the balance of power may continue to fluctuate and the prosperity of some nations "may be alternately exalted or depressed." But this concept of a single "great republic" (intellectually speaking) coupled to political fragmentation guaranteed a "general state of happiness, system of arts and laws and manners." It "advantageously distinguished" Europe from other civilizations (Gibbon, 1789, vol. 3, pp. 633–34).

[20] Even scholars of fundamentalist religious beliefs, such as the great Swiss Huguenot polymath Louis Bourguet (1678–1742), were able to develop what Barnett (2015, p. 149) has felicitously called a "strategy of toleration" in which deeply felt religious differences were papered over in scientific exchanges and a scholarly civility was maintained despite private outrage at the heretical opinions of "unbelievers."

[21] The term used in early modern Britain was "improvement" rather than progress. Slack (2015) traces the term "improvement" through seventeenth-century English culture and correctly observes that while economies and cultures move together, in this case cultural beliefs came first, because the "improving frame of mind" fostered the economic behavior that led to its realization (Slack, 2015, p. 4). See also Friedel (2007).

at times even misleading, yet without the formal knowledge they would not have emerged.[22] Second, notwithstanding the many disappointments and dead ends to which the application of science led, the most innovative and progressive entrepreneurs and industrialists of the age fervently held on to the cultural attitudes central to the Industrial Enlightenment.[23] The key to economic growth was useful knowledge, and its expansion and diffusion was therefore at the heart of institutions and policies that would bring about social progress.[24]

Third and most importantly, science mattered because it made the difference between an Industrial Revolution that was a minor and ephemeral blip in technological progress that eventually petered out into a new stationary state, and one that led to the continuous and cumulative growth we see after 1815, when formal knowledge increasingly found new ways to affect technology. After elementary modern chemistry emerged in the closing decades of the eighteenth century, thermodynamics, organic chemistry, and electricity followed in the first half of the nineteenth century, and metallurgy a few decades later — to name just a few.

25.4 Aptitudes

To make a difference in economic performance, the insights of natural philosophers and practical mathematicians had to be implemented. Ingenious devices should not only work, but be within range of the workmanship and materials of the age, so they could be scaled up and used widely. The brilliant sketches made by Leonardo Da Vinci in the late fifteenth century were never turned into working models, in large part because the workmanship and materials needed to produce them in quantities at reasonable cost were not available. The famous submarine built by the Dutch engineer Cornelis Drebbel in the 1620s and the calculating machine designed by Blaise Pascal in 1642 did not take off for similar reasons. Yet if breakthroughs in useful knowledge were to result in economic progress, they had to be transformed from blueprints into models, be tolerably free from breakdowns, and capable of being repaired by local mechanics. In the process of being implemented, the newly-invented techniques normally had to be tweaked, debugged, and adapted. To do so required, above all, technical competence, that is, highly skilled artisans working with good tools (made by other skilled artisans). What

---

[22] Formal knowledge contains not just abstract and theoretical science but also experimental work, applied mathematics, and systematic data-collection. Progress in useful knowledge depended on insights generated by experimental scientists and well-educated engineer-savants such as John Theophile Desaguliers, René Réaumur, Joseph Black, Joseph Priestley, Charles Augustin Coulomb, Claude Berthollet, and Humphry Davy. Such people moved seemingly effortlessly between what McKendrick (1973, p. 313) has called the various "gradations of scientific knowledge and expertise" and the spread and adoption of experimental methods, mathematical practice, and the culture of open science.

[23] James Watt wrote in 1790 (of himself in the third person) "These Gentlemen [Boulton & Watt] owe much of their success to the accurate philosophy of the last age, to the enterprising spirit of the present age, to the opulence of this country & to the decline of prejudice & attachment to ancient [candour?]. Had they lived in another age or in some other country, they might have been mere theorists or have rubbed through life unknowing & unknown unless they had happened to turn their abilities to the contrivance of instruments for the destruction of the human species?" Cited by Miller, 2009, p. 41.

[24] The belief in the ability of science to aid production is supported by the many scientists who were hired as consultants by progressive farmers and manufacturers, foremost among them the Scottish physician and chemist William Cullen, the physicist and philosopher Joseph Priestley, and the practical mathematician and politician Davies Gilbert. For more details see Mokyr (2009), p. 58.

made the difference whether new technological ideas could actually have economic effects, more than most economists would assess, was the human capital and dexterity of the shopfloor workers using the devices.

In 1500 it would have been hard to observe that Europe's artisans were in any sense more skilled than those of India or China. Europeans sent their ships across the oceans to buy goods made by skilled Asian artisans, such as Indian cottons, Persian rugs, and Chinese porcelain. In many areas, European technology was still backward, though not quite as backward as it had been in 1000 AD. After 1500 things started to change. Two centuries later European had seen and described objects too small or too remote to be ever observed by human eyes, proved the shape and dynamics of the solar system beyond any reasonable doubt, manufactured objects that measured the time accurately and built musical instruments that played perfectly. By 1750, moreover, European artisans had acquired the capabilities that within a century would flood the Indian market with cheap cotton goods and defeat the Chinese navy in the first Opium War. These same capabilities allowed them within the next decades to design the devices that allowed them to determine longitude at sea, to defeat gravity, to conquer smallpox, to refine wrought iron from pig iron, to utilize binary coding to weave patterns into fabrics, and to convert heat into work using ever-more efficient engines. No other civilization had managed to solve so many difficult practical problems in such a short time. The Great Enrichment and the Great Divergence evolved cheek-by-jowl.

For such a history-changing phenomenon to occur, artisanal skills mattered. Scholars such as Epstein (2013) or Berg (2007) have indeed argued for the pre-eminence of the role of tacit skills that artisans possessed and transmitted through instruction and imitation. Relying on scattered evidence, Epstein (2008, p. 71) has suggested considerable productivity growth due to the anonymous improvements and experimentation carried out by Europe's craftsmen, from the woolen industry to printing and clockmaking. Whether technological progress occurred thanks to the benevolent actions of the guilds (as Epstein insists) or in spite of them, as Sheilagh Ogilvie (2014, 2019) has argued, is immaterial here. What matters is that such technological progress did occur in early modern Europe and that its artisans without any question were getting better. A perfect example of this continuous improvement is provided by Kelly and Ó Gráda (2017). In the seventeenth century, the English watch industry experienced a major technological shock by the invention of the spiral-spring balance in watches. No such discrete macro-invention occurred over the subsequent century, yet the real price of watches fell by an average of 1.3 percent a year between 1685 and 1810 (Kelly and Ó Gráda, 2017), the result of an increasingly finer division of labor and learning by doing. Another example is in the small arms industry. Hoffman (2015) shows the secular decline in the prices of firearms due to the growth in total factor productivity. He estimates a rise in total factor productivity of pistols at 1.1 percent a year (1556–1706) relative to a low-tech product such as spades. This, as he points out, is an underestimate since it does not account for quality improvements in muskets and pistols.

Epstein and his followers have argued that such cumulative incremental tweaks and improvements introduced by artisans alone might have been enough to sustain technological progress for a long time. Epstein dismissed the economic significance of codified formal knowledge that was generated and distributed by the Republic of Letters as inconsequential. By stressing the role of artisans, these scholars highlight a crucial component of the Great Enrichment but may have missed the profound complementarity between tacit skills and natural philosophy. Adam Smith expressed this when he noted that "to think or to reason comes to be, like every other employment, a particular business, which is carried on by very few people who furnish the public with all the thought and reason possessed by the vast multitudes that labour." The benefits of the "speculations of the philosopher ... may evidently descend to the meanest of people" if they led to improvements in the mechanical arts (Smith, [1776] 1976, pp. 569–72). Smith's "speculations" were strongly complementary to the kind of practical skills that could actually produce the goods in the workshops in which Europe's skilled artisans worked.

When this process of improvement in artisanal competence actually started is not easy to pin down precisely, and the timing surely differed from industry to industry and location to location. Many years ago Edgar Zilsel (1942) pointed out that artisans and craftsmen before 1600 were the "real pioneers of empirical observations, experimentation and causal research" (Zilsel, 1942, p. 551). Skilled craftsmen thrived in Elizabethan London and a few of them actually committed their practical knowledge to writing, such as Sir Hugh Plat (1552–1608), the author of many practical books full of recipes and prescriptions on a range of topics, from meat preservation and pest control to gardening (Harkness, 2007). In Germany, Augsburg and Nuremberg were renowned for their extremely skilled blacksmiths, with expertise in lock-making, sheet metalworking, etching, hammered inlay, steel-plate engraving, painting, and rustproofing. While German artisanal leadership experienced a major set-back during the thirty-years war, skills continued to advance elsewhere in Europe.

In Meisenzahl and Mokyr (2012), we distinguish between three levels of technological activity that drove innovation in this period. One entails the major breakthroughs (macroinventions) that solved a bottleneck or opened a new door. These were, by and large, the ones that made it into high school history books, making top of the line inventors engineers such as James Watt, John Harrison, and Samuel Crompton famous. Others in the top level contributed major improvements, and their names still appear in standard economic history texts, such as Richard Trevithick, Matthew Murray, and Henry Maudslay. However, the second level was what made their breakthroughs practical and economically significant. These were the myriad of small and medium-sized cumulative microinventions that improved and debugged existing inventions, scaled them up, adapted them to new uses, and combined them in new applications. The people behind these advances, the "tweakers," are harder to find in the historical record, because they improved and debugged *existing* inventions and thus appear in the shadow of the great inventors. Examples of those whose work has survived for posterity are Josias C. Gamble (1775–1848), an Irishman trained in Glasgow, who was essential to James Muspratt's introduction of the Leblanc process in Britain (Musson and Robinson, 1969, p. 187); William Horrocks of Stockport whose 1803 patent improved upon Cartwright's powerloom (Marsden, 1895, pp. 70–72); and William Woollat, who was Jedediah Strutt's brother in law and helped him develop a mechanized stocking frame that could make ribbed hosiery (Fitton and Wadsworth, 1958, p. 24).

The third level of activity, and perhaps the least recognized of Britain's advantages, were brought about by the thousands of skilled workmen capable of building, installing, operating, and maintaining new and complex equipment. The skills needed for these pure implementers were substantial, but they did not have to be creative themselves. It goes without saying that the line between tweakers and implementers is blurry, but at the very least a patent or some prize for innovation would be a clear signal of original creativity.

The high quality of craftsmanship in the eighteenth century was particularly notable in Britain, and it is thus not surprising that it was in that country that the inventions that created the Industrial Revolution, whether local inventions or ideas imported from the Continent, were first carried out on a massive scale (Kelly et al., 2014; 2020), even though Britain never accounted for even half of all the major inventions in that period. Contemporaries on both sides of the channel knew this all too well.[25] But the evidence is more than just contemporary opinion. As Henderson (1954) has shown in great detail, British engineers and mechanics swarmed all over the Continent, installing, operating, and maintaining equipment. Much of this knowledge was what we could call "tacit knowledge."[26]

One good example of a person embodying the kind of aptitude that made the British Industrial Revolution possible was John Whitehurst, a Derbyshire clockmaker and hydraulic engineer who also made important contributions to geology. A member of the Birmingham Lunar Society as well as the Royal Society, his consultant services were widely sought. While a contemporary wrote of him condescendingly as "an ingenious mechanic and worthy man but possessed of very little science" (cited by Vaughan, 2004), he was clearly the kind of top-of-the-line engineer that in Britain, perhaps more than anywhere else, was widely respected. Patronage was the result. Whitehurst was appointed in 1775 to the newly established office of stamper of money weights to the mint. The careers of men like Whitehurst, Smeaton, Watt, Rennie, Telford, and many others show the high social prestige associated with engineering skills and mechanical aptitude during the Industrial Revolution. Recent research (Hanlon, 2020) has stressed the key role that people who called themselves "engineers" played in the British Industrial Revolution.

Such people were not unique to Britain, even if Britain had a far larger that proportional share of them. The French instrument and clockmaker Jacques de Vaucanson was appointed inspector of the French silk industry and a member of the French *académie des sciences*. A striking example of the kind of high quality craftsmen in France who personified the cooperation between artisans and scientists is provided by Hilaire-Pérez (2007). She sees artisans not just as skilled but as incorporating a great deal of knowledge even if it was not, strictu sensu, scientific "in order to contrive new products and processes."[27] Paola Bertucci (2017) speaks of a French "Artisanal Enlightenment" driven by a group she calls *artistes*, somewhat vaguely defined as artisans with *esprit*. A small elite of skilled, creative, and well-trained workmen, the *crème de la crème* of French workmen, they included watchmakers, enamelers, instrument makers, high-end furniture makers and other high-skill artisans. *Artistes* were thus a middle category, wedged between uneducated artisans and intellectuals. More than most of the top echelons of Britain's mechanics, these people were literate who read Bacon and Descartes and some wrote books and articles on their crafts.

The class of elite artisans in France was different from Britain's. France was missing something that Britain had in large quantities, namely the very skilled but unpretentious down-to-earth practical mechanics slaving away in the grimy workshops of Leeds and Keighley (Cookson, 2018). French mechanics catered to the fashions and whims of the rich and glamorous rather than the needs of the masses. The French Enlightenment — including the Industrial Enlightenment — was first and foremost a social elite project, and its top artisans reflected this, worrying about elegance and taste more than

---

[25] One French writer in the mid 1780s feared much of the short-lived free trade between Britain and France and sighed that "We have set the French workmen to grips with the English workman. It is the combat of a naked man against an armed man and it has the outcome we may expect and the victory cannot be disputed. Is no resource left to us?" Cited by Harris (1998, p. 412). For other examples of contemporaries pointing to British superiority in technical competence, see Mokyr (2009, pp. 108–110).

[26] Harris (1992), p. 33 referred to these skills as "unanalyzable pieces of expertise" and "the knacks of the trade."

[27] Hilaire-Pérez (2007) cites the example of the French artisan Edmé Régnier (1751–1825), apprenticed as a gunmaker, whose talents as a craftsman allowed him to enter the circles of intellectuals, where he met such scientific celebrities as the Comte de Buffon and the physicist Charles-Augustin de Coulomb. His dynamometer designed to measure muscular strength was in Hilaire-Pérez's words, "an essential mechanism as quantification of labour became the cornerstone of engineering sciences" (p. 139).

price and cost. In France, the politics of class and status got often in the way of progress. British engineers (unlike their French colleagues) had few political ambitions or intellectual pretensions, rarely wrote books and chose to solve practical problems that would make money rather than earn them the approval of their social superiors.[28]

25.5 Apprenticeship and human capital

It is no secret where technical aptitude came from before and during the Industrial Revolution. As formal structured training in technical schools was practically non-existent, skilled artisans were trained in formal or informal apprenticeship relations with existing masters. Europe's master artisans thus produced two different outputs: material goods and technical training for the next generation. The process of intergenerational transmission of such tacit knowledge can become highly rigid and conservative, so that each generation reproduces accurately the knowledge of the previous one, or it can be flexible and open so that innovations are introduced, passed on, and become widely used, increasing average skill level and thus productivity.

How and why was the apprenticeship system in Europe different from the rest of the world? The key to the preservation and transmission of these tacit skills and there was the institutions that regulated apprenticeship. The need for such institutions is obvious once it is realized that the contract between master and apprentice is a highly asymmetrical one, riven with opportunities (for both sides) to cheat, shirk, or engage in other forms of opportunistic behavior (De la Croix et al., 2018; Mokyr, 2019). Without some institutional arrangement that would supervise and enforce the contract and resolve disputes, the system could well unravel. The nature of these institutions varied, but they helped determine the quality of the craftsmen.

How and why was the apprenticeship system in Europe different from the rest of the world? The key to the preservation and transmission of these tacit skills and their evolution depended on the institutions that regulated apprenticeship. The need for such institutions is obvious once it is realized that the contract between master and apprentice is a highly asymmetrical one, riven with opportunities (for both sides) to cheat, shirk, or engage in other forms of opportunistic behavior (De la Croix et al., 2018; Mokyr, 2019). Without some institutional arrangement that would supervise and enforce the contract and resolve disputes, the system could well unravel. The nature of these institutions varied, but they helped determine the quality of the craftsmen.

Two basic characteristics of the apprenticeship in Europe made the difference. One was that European apprentices could choose over a wider range of masters as they were not confined to members of their extended family. Family connections still mattered, but they did matter far less than elsewhere. European society was organized since medieval times by nuclear families, and every young lad looking to learn a trade from a master could pick a high quality one (if he could afford the fee) — hence minor innovations that improved the craftsman's skills and raised the quality and efficiency of production spread faster (De la Croix et al., 2018). It stands to reason that the most productive and sophisticated

---

[28] Bertucci rightly points out the differences between the French and British Societies of Arts: the British one (founded in 1754) encouraged artisanal creativity and did not seek state support (Howes, 2020). The difference was symbolic and underlines the different national styles of Enlightenment.

masters would attract the most apprentices, unless guild regulations prohibited them. The second feature of apprenticeship in much of Europe was mobility. Apprentices upon completion of their training moved about and learned from craftsmen other than their main master (or these learned from them) through the institution of journeymen (Lis et al., 1994; Belfanti, 2004). In that way, best-practice artisanal knowledge circulated in early modern Europe and led to the adoption of more efficient techniques and the slow but relentless improvement of skills.

As noted above, there is no reason to think that by the time Europeans reached Asia the European artisans were on average more skilled than their colleagues in India, China, or Japan. Yet by 1600 there are signs of an opening gap in some areas: Europe was pulling ahead in basic mechanical technology: screws, levers, pulleys, as well as optical instruments, printing, hydraulic technology, and precision mechanisms such as clocks, watches, toys, musical instruments, and guns. They were still behind in high-end textiles and ceramics, but by the eighteenth century those gaps were closed as Europeans built large mechanical silk-throwing plants and learned to spin high quality fine cotton yard, and print the fabrics in vivid colors. The aptitude of a highly skilled artisan such as Thomas Newcomen, who built the first working steam engine in 1712, was enhanced by the highly skilled workmen in the midlands.[29] The kind of continuous labor productivity growth mentioned earlier in firearms and watches also led to hard-to-observe but equally important improvements in quality, both of consumer goods and the tools available to artisans.

The separation I proposed between "propositional knowledge" and "prescriptive knowledge" (Mokyr, 2002) is an epistemic one — not a strictly social one. In early modern Europe, as well as during the period of the Industrial Revolution, the distinction between "knowers" (*savants*) and "producers" (*fabricants*) was hazier than sharp categories will allow for. Many artisans such as the sixteenth-century French potter Bernard Palissy were learned and sophisticated.[30] Leading natural philosophers were also skilled tool- and clockmakers, none more so than the great Robert Hooke and his contemporary, the Dutch mathematician Christiaan Huygens. As Edward Zilsel (1942) was one of the first to insist, early modern natural philosophers realized that the practical world of artisans was crucially important if material progress was to be achieved. The French philosopher Pierre de la Ramée wrote proudly that he had visited every mechanical workshop in Paris more than once and advised other philosophers to do the same (Hooykaas, 1972, pp. 99–100).[31] Paracelsus regarded artisans as the kind of practitioners who were in direct contact with nature, and who could be trusted more than natural philosophers because they relied on experience rather than on reasoning (Smith, 2006, pp. 298–299). Newcomen was

---

[29] When Newcomen came to the Midlands to install his steam-powered engine, he and his assistant were "at a loss about pumps, but being near Birmingham and having the assistance of so many ingenious and admirable workmen, they soon came to methods of making the pump-valves, clacks, and buckets" (Desaguliers, 1734–44, Vol. 2, p. 533).

[30] Palissy proudly conceded that he was a modest potter ignorant of classical languages, but would openly challenge the theories of the ancient and modern physicians, alchemists, and philosophers (Deming, 2005, p. 971).

[31] Indeed, some scholars (e.g. Roberts and Schaffer, 2007) have gone so far as to deny altogether a meaningful separation between science and technology at this time, and have proposed new concepts such as the "mindful hand"— educated and informed craftsmen. The notion that there was no meaningful between theory and practice seems far-fetched, but there were many skilled and trained people who were in the gray area that straddled both. Among those we should think of "practical mathematicians" — surveyors, map makers, optical instrument makers, and such. As Kelly and Ó Gráda (2020) note, "these practitioners spanned a continuous spectrum from anonymous artisans and schoolmasters to figures now usually thought of as scientists and mathematicians but whom their contemporaries saw equally as teachers, instrument makers, and engineers: Jost Burgi, Johannes Regiomontanus, Peter Apian, Gemma Frisius, Gerard Mercator and, most notably, Simon Stevin and Galileo."

described in the phrase of a recent author as "the first (or very nearly) and clearly the most important member of a tribe of a very particular, and historically original, type: the English artisan-engineer-entrepreneur" (Rosen, 2010, p. 40). We now know for certain that Newcomen, though by all signs lacking in formal education, had access to the kind of basic knowledge he needed in order to recognize why his engine would work (Wootton, 2015, pp. 499–508).

In the age of Enlightenment, the Baconian notion of building communication channels between natural philosophers and artisans became a dominant theme, a perfect example of an idea gaining acceptance in the market for ideas. Many of the institutions of public science such as scientific societies and academies were aimed at the demonstrations of the miracles that science could accomplish (Stewart, 1992). In private gatherings, in coffeehouses, inns, and domestic residences, scientists and artisans met one another and exchanged ideas. Many of the leading inventors of the eighteenth century had close connections with scientists. Some of them, of course, were able to straddle theory and practice, none perhaps more so than John T. Desaguliers (1683–1744), one of Newton's protégés and a devoted acolyte of the master. Desaguliers, who in many ways embodied the Industrial Enlightenment, was a tireless experimenter and practical instrument maker. In collaboration with the instrument and pump maker William Vream, he worked on the ventilation and heating issues, and redesigned chimneys and air heaters. He designed new types of water wheels and steam engines and constructed improved versions of various instruments, including a pyrometer, a barometer, a crane, and various pumps (Fara, 2004; Carpenter, 2011).

There were many dexterous and competent mechanics and engineers during the British Industrial Revolution with little formal knowledge, none more so than the prodigiously gifted craftsman Richard Roberts, most famous for the automatic or "self-acting" mule in 1825. Many others were ingenious craftsmen without much former education, such as Henry Cort, the inventor of the pathbreaking puddling and rolling process.[32] The great engineers John Rennie, James Watt, and John Smeaton straddled the worlds we would regard as science and those that we would see as technology. Relatively poorly educated but ingenious artisans such as George Stephenson, Roberts, and Cort found it necessary and were able to consult people more formally educated than themselves. There were institutions, mostly of the informal and private-order type, that supported these connections.[33]

To implement radical new designs, make them work and scale them up required skilled mechanics and technicians, especially ironmasters, woodworkers, engineers, and instrument makers. Without these skilled workers, the great inventions would have remained unfulfilled promises. Perhaps the most famous of these mechanics and ironmasters was John Wilkinson, whose Bradley works pioneered new boring machines that were able to produce the cylinders Boulton and Watt needed for their engines with unrivaled accuracy. But many others could be mentioned: Charles Gascoigne, who took over the failing Carron ironworks in Falkirk (Scotland) in the 1760s and rescued it through relentless improvement and the design of new and effective naval artillery, and Bryan Donkin, famous for his improvements to the mechanized papermaking machine, who was also the inventor of the tachometer, a steel nib pen, and the metal tin for canned food. Millwrights played a special role (Mokyr et al., 2020). Writing retro-

---

[32] Cort was "a plain Englishman, without Science" whose discovery was due to "a dint of natural ingenuity and a turn for experiment" as the scientist Joseph Black wrote to James Watt (cited by Coleman and MacLeod, 1986, p. 603).

[33] Richard Roberts, who had a very poor education, joined the Manchester Literary and Philosophical Society in 1823, contributed to their proceedings, and in 1861 was made an honorary member. This connection allowed him to rub shoulders with such scientific luminaries as Robert Owen, John Dalton, and James Prescott Joule.

spectively in the 1860s, the Scottish engineer William Fairbairn wrote that "The millwright of former days was to a great extent the sole representative of mechanical art ... a kind of jack of all trades who could with equal facility work at a lathe, the anvil, or the carpenter's bench... a fair arithmetician who could calculate the velocities, strength and power of machines..." (Fairbairn, 1871, p. ix–x).

Because of the importance of ingenuity and dexterity, the mechanical engineering and machine tool industry was an unheralded hero of the Industrial Revolution (Musson, 1975, 1980). It was led by some of the most gifted craftsmen of the Industrial Revolution such as Joseph Bramah and Henry Maudslay (MacLeod and Nuvolari, 2009). The role of the machine tool industry was emphasized by Nathan Rosenberg (1976, p. 19) who pointed out that "the machine tool industry may be looked upon as constituting a pool or reservoir of skills and technical knowledge which are employed throughout the entire machine-using sectors of the economy." Between 1780/89 and 1840/49 the percentage of patents in the English mechanical engineering sector increased from 17.8 to 28.6 (MacLeod and Nuvolari, 2009, p. 224). A substantial number of those were taken out by engineers (Hanlon, 2020).

James Watt, of course, personifies everything that one could mean by "aptitude," and justly became a national hero (MacLeod, 2007). An instrument-maker, not formally trained in the sciences, he relied on the advice of some of Scotland's best scientists, Glasgow University's Joseph Black and Edinburgh's John Robison. The specialists concluded that "one can only say that Black gave, Robison gave, and Watt received" (Dickinson and Jenkins, [1927] 1969, p. 16). Next to Watt himself stood the greatest civil engineer of the period, John Smeaton. Unlike Watt, Smeaton never made a spectacular breakthrough that would enshrine his name in high school textbooks, yet his career contained all the ingredients of what made the British Industrial Revolution work. Originally trained as a lawyer and an empiricist par excellence, he made sure to inform himself of pertinent scientific developments of his age.[34] In every way the embodiment of the Industrial Enlightenment, Smeaton recognized the importance of networks in creating and diffusing new useful knowledge and founded a society of engineers in 1771, eventually named after him.

Technical skills of the third level were especially useful in the constructing and maintenance of modern equipment. They could be found over Britain, but were concentrated especially in areas close to coal mines and textiles (Kelly et al., 2020). Cookson (2018, 154–155) points out that "there was a limit to how many James Watts could be accommodated in a business" and that the real need was for "skilled workers with shopfloor duties." Her book on the Yorkshire machinery industry contains a detailed survey of the competence and creativity of Yorkshire's ingenious mechanics. Trained in such skilled occupations as clockmakers, millwrights, or whitesmiths, many of these Yorkshire artisans worked in small workshops, often family affairs, aided by apprentices, journeymen and a few skilled assistants. It is striking how agile they were. As Cookson notes repeatedly, not only were they dexterous and well-trained, but their skills were sufficiently flexible to help them adapt to a changing economic and technological environment and continuous changes in the demand for skilled labor.

These workers were a crucial component of upper-tail human capital in an age when mechanical skills were what counted for technological progress. It was not formal education or literacy that were the engine of progress during the Industrial Revolution, but mechanical aptitude and competence. These

---

[34] Smeaton's contributions ranged across many fields: harbor engineering, bridge construction, water mills, the chemistry of cement, steam engines, canals, and lighthouses. Yet Smeaton was very much a loyal citizen of the Republic of Letters. He traveled to the Low Countries to study their canal and harbor systems, and taught himself French to be able to read the theoretical papers of French hydraulic theorists despite his conviction that all theoretical predictions had to be tested empirically.

skills helped Britain construct and improve the machinery and equipment that we associate with the Industrial Revolution. For Britain, and to a lesser degree for the rest of Europe, artisanal aptitude was an indispensable factor in the Great Enrichment.

25.6 Conclusion

Attitudes (that is, cultural beliefs) and aptitudes (that is, technical competence) thus played central roles in the British Industrial Revolution and the origins of modern growth. One might ask if we could see these as necessary or sufficient conditions. The answer depends a bit on whether we try to explain a few isolated macroinventions in the cotton and iron industry that some scholars see as the essence of the Industrial Revolution, or whether we are trying to explain the sustained advance on an ever-broader technological front in the nineteenth century as well It is hard to see how a few inspired inventions by skilled artisans in the mid eighteenth century could have converted the economic trajectory of much of the western world into one of sustained progress without the ever-growing infusion of formal codified knowledge created by natural philosophers, physicians, mathematicians, and chemists, among others into the body of useful knowledge. At the same time, however, formal theoretical knowledge, no matter how sophisticated, depended on dexterous practical artisans to become economically significant. Both of these depended in turn on underlying institutions, often designed for very different purposes.

Modern economic growth, then, needed *both* attitude and aptitude as necessary conditions. Yet even together, a belief in progress-through-knowledge and the technical skills to turn them into a reality would not have been sufficient without the proper institutions in place. There was a deep complementarity and synergy between technological and institutional change (Mokyr, 2006, 2008; Hoffman, 2020). Advances in useful knowledge that were unaccompanied by institutional change could fizzle out. If institutions were not aligned to support an economically productive research agenda, the growth in useful knowledge might have continued apace, but be diverted into welfare-neutral or welfare-reducing directions, such as numerology, astrology, or more destructive weaponry.[35] More likely, however, technological progress would have slowed down and eventually ceased altogether much as happened in Ming-Qing China. Institutions needed to be in place to encourage, incentivize, and protect successful intellectual innovators. Intellectual and technological innovation might eventually end up being increasingly resisted by intellectual ancestor worship, an entrenched incumbent scientific paradigm, or by workers who felt that their livelihood was threatened by new techniques. If that resistance had not been overcome, technological progress might have been extinguished. It is thanks to the European Enlightenment that institutional change after 1750 became more or less aligned with the needs of a dynamic economy. Yet the institutional transformation was incomplete, and neither economic nationalism nor pervasive rent-seeking were extinguished. Unless institutional changes can be continuously aligned with technological progress, the road to sustained prosperity will remain hazardous. In our time, despite ever-accelerating technological progress and with the decline in civil society and the weakening of open and free economies, this seems less promising than in 1850.

---

[35] For more detailed surveys of the role of institutions in the Industrial Revolution see Mokyr (2008), Kapás (2012), and Hoffman (2020). For a critical view, see McCloskey (2010), pp. 296–346.

References

Alexander, A., 2014. Infinitesimal: How a Dangerous Mathematical Theory Shaped the Modern World. Farrar, Straus and Giroux, New York.

Anievas, A., Nisancioglu, K., 2015. How the West Came to Rule: The Geopolitical Origins of Capitalism. Pluto Press, London.

Bacon, F., [1620] 2000. The New Organon. Jardine, L., Silverthorne, M. (Eds.). Cambridge University Press, Cambridge.

Barnett, L., 2015. Strategies of toleration: talking across confessions in the Alpine Republic of letters. Eighteenth-Century Studies 48, 141–157.

Becker, C.L., 1932. The Heavenly City of the Eighteenth-Century Philosophers. Yale University Press, New Haven, CT and London.

Beckert, S., 2014. Empire of Cotton: A Global History. Vintage Books, New York.

Belfanti, C.M., 2004. Guilds, patents, and the circulation of technical knowledge. Technology and Culture 45 (3), 569–589.

Berg, M., 2007. The Genesis of Useful Knowledge. History of Science 45 (2), 123–134. No. 148.

Bertucci, P., 2017. Artisanal Enlightenment: Science and the Mechanical Arts in Old Regime France. Yale University Press, New Haven and London.

Biagioli, M., 1990. Galileo's system of patronage. History of Science 28 (1), 1–62.

Broadberry, S., Guan, H., Li Daokui, D., 2018. China, Europe, and the Great Divergence: a study in historical national accounting, 980–1850. The Journal of Economic History 78 (4), 955–1000.

Carpenter, A.T., 2011. John Theophilus Desaguliers. Continuum, London.

Cipolla, C.M., 1972. The diffusion of innovations in early modern Europe. Comparative Studies in Society and History 14 (1), 46–52.

Clark, G., 2007. A Farewell to Alms. Princeton University Press, Princeton, NJ.

Cobb, M., 2006. Generation: Seventeenth-Century Scientists Who Unravelled the Secrets of Sex, Life, and Growth. Bloomsbury, New York and London.

Coleman, D.C., MacLeod, C., 1986. Attitudes to new techniques: British businessmen, 1800–1950. Economic History Review, New Series 39 (4 (Nov.)), 588–611.

Cook, H.J., 2006. Medicine. In: Park, K., Daston, L. (Eds.), The Cambridge History of Science Vol. 3: Early Modern Science. Cambridge University Press, Cambridge, pp. 407–434.

Cookson, G., 2018. The Age of Machinery: Engineering in the Industrial Revolution, 1770-1850. Boydell and Brewer, London.

Dasgupta, P., David, P.A., 1994. Toward a new Economics of Science. Research Policy 23 (5), 487–521.

David, P.A., 2008. The Historical Origins of 'Open Science': an essay on patronage, reputation and common agency contracting in the Scientific Revolution. Capitalism and Society 3 (2), 1–103.

De la Croix, D., Doepke, M., Mokyr, J., 2018. Clans, guilds, and markets: apprenticeship institutions and growth in the pre-industrial economy. The Quarterly Journal of Economics 133 (1), 1–70.

Deming, D., 2005. Born to trouble: Bernard palissy and the hydrologic cycle. Ground Water 43 (6), 969–972.

Desaguliers, J.T., 1734–44. A Course of Experimental Philosophy, 2 vols. Printed for John Senex, London.

Dickinson, H.W., Jenkins, R., [1927] 1969. James Watt and the Steam Engine. Encore Editions, London. Repr. edn.

Dutta, R., Levine, D.K., Papageorge, N.W., Wu, L., 2018. Entertaining Malthus: bread, circuses, and economic growth. Economic Inquiry 56 (1), 358–380.

Eamon, W., 1991. Court, academy and printing house: patronage and scientific careers in late renaissance Italy. In: Moran, B.T. (Ed.), Patronage and Institutions: Science, Technology and Medicine at the European Court, 1500–1750. Boydell Press, Rochester, NY, pp. 25–50.

Eamon, W., 1994. Science and the Secrets of Nature. Princeton University Press, Princeton, NJ.

Epstein, S.R., 2008. Craft guilds, the theory of the firm, and the European economy, 1400-1800. In: Epstein, S.R., Prak, M. (Eds.), Guilds, Innovation and the European Economy, 1400-1800. Cambridge University Press, Cambridge, pp. 52–80.

Epstein, S.R., 2013. Transferring technical knowledge and innovating in Europe, c. 1200-c. 1800. In: Prak, M., van Zanden, J.L. (Eds.), Technology, Skills and the Pre-Modern Economy. Brill, Leiden, pp. 25–67.

Evans, R.J.W., 1973. Rudolf II and His World. Oxford University Press, Oxford. Rep. ed. 1997.

Fairbairn, W., 1871. Treatise on Mills and Millwork, vol. 1, 3rd edition. Longmans, Green and Co., London.

Fara, P., 2004. Desaguliers, John Theophilus (1683–1744). In: Oxford Dictionary of National Biography. Oxford University Press, Oxford.

Fitton, R.S., Wadsworth, A.P., 1958. The Strutts and the Arkwrights. Manchester University Press, Manchester.

Friedel, R., 2007. A Culture of Improvement: Technology and the Western Millennium. MIT Press, Cambridge, MA.

Galor, O., 2011. Unified Growth Theory. Princeton University Press, Princeton, NJ.

Gibbon, E., 1789. The History of the Decline and Fall of the Roman Empire, 3 vols, new ed. Printed for A. Strahan and T. Cadell, London.

Gillispie, C.C., 1960. The Edge of Objectivity. Princeton University Press, Princeton, N.J.

Grant, E., 1996. The Foundations of Modern Science in the Middle Ages. Cambridge University Press, Cambridge.

Greif, A., 1994. Cultural beliefs and the organization of society: a historical and theoretical reflection on collectivist and individualist societies. Journal of Political Economy 102 (5), 912–950.

Hahn, R., 1990. The Age of Academies. In: Frängsmyr, T. (Ed.), Solomon's House Revisited. Science History Publications, Canton, MA, pp. 3–12.

Hanlon, W., 2020. The Rise of the Engineer: Inventing the Professional Inventor During the Industrial Revolution. Unpublished working paper.

Harkness, D., 2007. The Jewel House: Elizabethan London and the Scientific Revolution. Yale University Press, New Haven, CT and London.

Harris, J.R., 1992. Skills, coal and British industry in the eighteenth century. In: Harris, J.R. (Ed.), Essays in Industry and Technology in the Eighteenth Century. Ashgate/Variorum, Aldershot.

Harris, J.R., 1998. Industrial Espionage and Technology Transfer: Britain and France in the Eighteenth Century. Ashgate, Aldershot.

Headrick, D.R., 1981. The Tools of Empire. Oxford University Press, New York.

Headrick, D.R., 2012. Power over Peoples: Technology, Environments, and Western Imperialism, 1400 to the Present. Princeton University Press, Princeton.

Henderson, W.O., 1954. Britain and Industrial Europe, 1750–1870; Studies in British Influence on the Industrial Revolution in Western Europe. Liverpool University Press, Liverpool.

Hilaire-Pérez, L., 2007. Technology as public culture. History of Science 45 (2), 135–153. No. 148.

Hoffman, P.T., 2015. Why Did Europe Conquer the World? Princeton University Press, Princeton, NJ.

Hoffman, P.T., 2020. The Great Divergence; why Britain industrialzed first. Australian Economic History Review 60 (2), 126–147.

Hooykaas, R., 1972. Religion and the Rise of Modern Science. Scottish Academic Press, Edinburgh.

Howes, A., 2020. Arts and Minds: How the Royal Society of Arts Changed a Nation. Princeton University Press, Princeton and Oxford.

Hunter, M., 2009. Boyle: Between God and Science. Yale University Press, New Haven, CT.

Inikori, J., 2002. Africans and the Industrial Revolution in England: A Study in International Trade and Economic Development. Cambridge University Press, New York.

Johnson, S., 1759. The Prince of Abisinnia. Printed for R. and J. Dodsley; and W. Johnston, London.

Jones, E.L., 1981. The European Miracle. Cambridge University Press, Cambridge.

Kapás, J., 2012. Which institutions caused the British Industrial Revolution? In: Kapás, J., Czeglédi, P. (Eds.), Institutions and the Industrial Revolution. In: Competitio Books, vol. 12. University of Debrecen, pp. 35–59.

Kelly, M., Mokyr, J., Ó Gráda, C., 2014. Precocious Albion: a new interpretation of the British Industrial Revolution. Annual Review of Economics 6, 363–391.

Kelly, M., Mokyr, J., Ó Gráda, C., 2020. The Mechanics of the Industrial Revolution. Unpublished working paper.

Kelly, M., Ó Gráda, C., 2017. Adam Smith, watch prices, and the Industrial Revolution. The Quarterly Journal of Economics 131 (4), 1727–1752.

Kelly, M., Ó Gráda, C., 2020. Connecting the Scientific and Industrial Revolutions: The Role of Practical Mathematics. University College Dublin. Unpublished ms.

Lecoq, A.-M. (Ed.), 2001. La Querelle des Anciens et des Modernes. Éditions Gallimard, Paris.

Levine, J.M., 1981. Ancients and moderns reconsidered. Eighteenth-Century Studies 15 (1), 72–89.

Levine, J.M., 1991. The Battle of the Books: History and Literature in the Augustan Age. Cornell University Press, Ithaca, NY.

Lis, C., Soly, H., Mitzman, L., 1994. 'An irresistible phalanx:' Journeymen Associations in Western Europe, 1300-1800. International Review of Social History 39, 11–52.

MacLeod, C., 2007. Heroes of Invention: Technology, Liberalism and British Identity. Cambridge University Press, Cambridge.

MacLeod, C., Nuvolari, A., 2009. Glorious Times: the emergence of mechanical engineering in early industrial Britain, c. 1700–1850. Brussels Economic Review 52 (3/4), 215–237.

Marsden, R., 1895. Cotton Weaving: Its Development, Principles, and Practice. George Bell, London.

McCloskey, D., 2010. Bourgeois Dignity: Why Economics Can't Explain the Modern World. University of Chicago Press, Chicago.

McCloskey, D., 2016. Bourgeois Equality: How Ideas, Not Capital or Institutions, Enriched the World. University of Chicago Press, Chicago.

McKendrick, N., 1973. The role of science in the Industrial Revolution. In: Teich, M., Young, R. (Eds.), Changing Perspectives in the History of Science. Heinemann, London, pp. 274–319.

Meisenzahl, R.R., Mokyr, J., 2012. The rate and direction of invention in the British Industrial Revolution: incentives and institutions. In: Stern, S., Lerner, J. (Eds.), The Rate and Direction of Innovation. University of Chicago Press, Chicago, pp. 443–479.

Miller, D.P., 2009. James Watt, Chemist: Understanding the Origins of the Steam Age. Taylor and Francis, London.

Mokyr, J., 2002. The Gifts of Athena. Princeton University Press, Princeton, NJ.

Mokyr, J., 2006. The Great Synergy: the European Enlightenment as a factor in modern economic growth. In: Dolfsma, W., Soete, L. (Eds.), Understanding the Dynamics of a Knowledge Economy. Edward Elgar, Cheltenham, pp. 7–41.

Mokyr, J., 2008. The Institutional Origins of the Industrial Revolution. In: Helpman, E. (Ed.), Institutions and Economic Performance. Harvard University Press, Cambridge MA, pp. 64–119.

Mokyr, J., 2009. The Enlightened Economy. Yale University Press, New York and London.

Mokyr, J., 2012. Review of Parthasarathi, 2011. https://eh.net/book_reviews/why-europe-grew-rich-and-asia-did-not-global-economic-divergence-1600-1850/.

Mokyr, J., 2016. A Culture of Growth. Princeton University Press, Princeton.

Mokyr, J., 2018. The Past and the Future of Innovation: some lessons from economic history. Explorations in Economic History 69, 13–26.

Mokyr, J., 2019. The Economics of Apprenticeship. In: Prak, M., Wallis, P. (Eds.), Apprenticeship in Early Modern Europe. Cambridge University Press, pp. 20–43.

Mokyr, J., Sarid, A., Van der Beek, K., 2020. The Wheels of Change: Technology Adoption, Millwrights, and the Persistence in Britain's Industrialization. Unpublished.

Musson, A.E., 1975. Joseph Whitworth and the growth of mass-production engineering. Business History 17 (2), 109–149.

Musson, A.E., 1980. The engineering industry. In: Church, R. (Ed.), The Dynamics of Victorian Business: Problems and Perspectives. George Allen and Unwin, London, pp. 87–106.

Musson, A.E., Robinson, E., 1969. Science and Technology in the Industrial Revolution. Manchester University Press, Manchester.

Nunn, N., Qian, N., 2010. The Columbian exchange: a history of disease, food, and ideas. The Journal of Economic Perspectives 24 (2 (Spring)), 163–188.

Ogilvie, S., 2014. The economics of guilds. The Journal of Economic Perspectives 28 (4), 169–192.

Ogilvie, S., 2019. The European Guilds: an Economic Analysis. Princeton University Press, Princeton.

Parthasarathi, P., 2011. Why Europe Grew Rich and Asia Did Not: Global Economic Divergence, 1600-1850. Cambridge University Press, Cambridge.

Pomeranz, K., 2000. The Great Divergence: China, Europe, and the Making of the Modern World Economy. Princeton University Press, Princeton, NJ.

Roberts, L., Schaffer, S., 2007. Preface. In: Roberts, L., Schaffer, S., Dear, P. (Eds.), The Mindful Hand: Inquiry and Invention from the Late Renaissance to Early Industrialization. Royal Netherlands Academy of Arts and Sciences, Amsterdam. pp. xiii–xxvii.

Rosen, W., 2010. The Most Powerful Idea in the World. Random House, New York.

Rosenberg, N., 1976. Perspectives on Technology. Cambridge University Press, Cambridge.

Scheidel, W., 2019. Escape from Rome: The Failure of Empire and the Road to Prosperity. Princeton University Press, Princeton.

Shapin, S., 1994. A Social History of Truth. University of Chicago Press, Chicago.

Slack, P., 2015. The Invention of Improvement: Information and Material Progress in Seventeenth-Century England. Oxford University Press, Oxford.

Smith, A., [1776] 1976. The Wealth of Nations. In: Cannan, E. (Ed.). University of Chicago Press, Chicago.

Smith, P.O., 2006. Laboratories. In: Park, K., Daston, L. (Eds.), The Cambridge History of Science Vol. 3: Early Modern Science. Cambridge University Press, Cambridge, pp. 290–305.

Stewart, L., 1992. The Rise of Public Science. Cambridge University Press, Cambridge.

Swift, J., [1704] 1753. A Tale of a Tub. Written for the Universal Improvement of Mankind. To Which Is Added, an Account of a Battle Between the Antient and Modern Books in St. James's Library. Printed by R. Urie, Glasgow.

Vaughan, D., 2004. Whitehurst, John (1713–1788). Oxford Dictionary of National Biography. Oxford University Press. online edn, Sept 2013.

Wells, H.G., 1923. Men Like Gods. Cassell, London.

White, L., 1978. Medieval Religion and Technology. University of California Press, Berkeley.

Wootton, D., 2015. The Invention of Science: A New History of the Scientific Revolution. Allen Lane, London.

Zilsel, E., 1942. The sociological roots of science. American Journal of Sociology 47 (4), 544–560.

The interplay among wages, technology, and globalization: the labor market and inequality, 1620-2020[☆]

Robert C. Allen

Faculty of Social Science, New York University Abu Dhabi, Abu Dhabi, United Arab Emirates

For the last four centuries, technology and wage rates have evolved together. Over the long term, productivity has risen, and wages have increased. The interplay between technology and wages has not been smooth, however: Periods when growth was 'successful' with wages and productivity rising together have alternated with periods in which that synchronization has broken down, the average wage has fallen behind productivity, and the dispersion of wages among workers has increased. The first aim of this chapter is to block out these phase over the past four centuries. A second aim is then to explore how technology has affected the labor market, and how the labor market, in turn, has affected the evolution of technology.

Other factors, of course, have been involved in the evolution of technology and wages. The development of science has contributed to the development of technology both by discovering new knowledge of the natural world as well as by promoting the idea that the collection of facts and the development of theories can help us understand the world around us (Mokyr, 1990, 2002, 2009, 2017). Globalization has also affected labor markets, although it needs to be recognized that globalization, in part, is the creation of technology. Finally, political and social institutions have influenced both technology and the labor market.

The history of the labor market bears on another issue of great importance–inequality. Piketty (2014), who has done much to advance our knowledge of the subject, has argued that inequality increases when the return on capital exceeds the growth in national income since the former (if re-invested) governs the growth in total capital and the income from it, while the latter equals the growth in incomes overall. But what determines the return on capital? When output per worker grows faster than the average wage, the share of profits in the economy rises and with it the return on capital. What is happening in the labor market, therefore, affects the overall degree of inequality. Technological change

---

[☆] I thank the following people for helpful comments and discussions: Alberto Bisin, Jonathan Chapman, Angus Deaton, Giovanni Federico, David Green, Jeff Jensen, Paul Johnson, Suresh Naidu, Patrick O'Brien, Jón Steinsson, and Peter Temin as well as the participants in seminars and workshops at New York University Abu Dhabi and New York, the Institute for Fiscal Studies, and the Centre for Economic Policy Research.

and globalization are important determinants of the critical balance between productivity and wages and, hence, of overall inequality.[1]

Historically, the feed back between wages and technology has been a slow process, so it is best grasped by surveying a long time frame. I consider the last four centuries, and I divide them into four periods. The focus is always on the leading economy of the period. In the first two periods that is Britain, and in the last two it is the USA. In all periods, output per worker has risen, but they differ greatly in their distributional stories. The periods are as follows (although all dates are approximate):

1. The pre-industrial revolution, 1620-1770.

   Agricultural employment declined as a fraction of the British work force, and employment in urban and rural handicraft manufacturing expanded as exports of these goods surged to supply European and then imperial markets in the future USA, the Caribbean, and other possessions. Manufacturing still meant 'working by hand,' and the typical worker was a man or woman working in the family's cottage rather than in a centralized factory. By the end of the eighteenth century, labor markets were tight, and English wages were amongst the highest in the world.

2. The Industrial Revolution, 1770-1867.

   High wages in Britain made it profitable to invent machines to save labor, and the result was the factory mode of production. Competition between the new factories and the established handicraft producers meant that some workers lost while others gained with the result that average wages were flat while output per worker expanded and inequality increased.

3. The Age of Manufacturing, 1867-1973.

   Except for cyclical fluctuations, manufacturing output and employment expanded continuously, and real wages as well as output per worker increased. Rising real wages induced the invention of capital-intensive, high output technologies. Product innovation sustained the growth of manufacturing but creating new goods that kept consumers buying more and more manufactures.

4. The Service Revolution, 1973-2020.

   Demand shifted away from manufactures towards services as technical change created more products dispensed through the service sector and more demand for its products. Output growth in manufacturing slackened. Imports and domestic outsourcing also made a contribution but of secondary importance. High wages in the immediate post-war period created an incentive to substitute capital for labor, and the more recent fall in computer IT prices created further incentives in that direction. As a result, manufacturing employment has collapsed, and the service sector has expanded. Services offer many low wage jobs (as well as high salary jobs), so wage dispersion and overall inequality have increased.

Capitalism worked well in the first and third periods in the sense that the incomes of the majority rose in step with overall labor productivity. In the second and fourth periods that synchronization came unstuck. Why? The common feature of periods two and four is that a new economic system has replaced the pre-existing one. In 1800 the factory replaced the cottage; in 2000 the hospital or restaurant replaced the factory. Schumpeter (1994, pp. 84, 87, 88) told us that capitalism progresses through a 'perennial gale of creative destruction.' Sometimes, that gale was exceptionally strong and

---

[1] Critiques of Piketty and the endogeneity of his explanatory variables include Acemoglu and Robinson (2015) and Ray (2015).

blew away the existing structures destroying many livelihoods in the process. At other times, it was more like a gentle breeze, and most people prospered.

26.1 The framework of analysis

I approach these issues from a perspective on the dynamics of economic growth that emphasizes the same themes as endogenous growth theories. Two generations ago, Solow (1956) formulated his growth model that was hegemonic in economics and economic history for many years. In important respects, however, it is not consistent with the facts of the last four centuries, and it fails to address key features of capitalist development so a different approach is needed. Anything less than an endogenous growth model is useless. In this chapter I follow a path blazed by Romer (1986, 1990), Lucas (1988), Grossman and Helpman (1991), and Aghion and Howitt (1992). My approach to technical change, which is a key part of the story, follows Acemoglu (2002) and Acemoglu and Restrepo (2018, 2019) recent. The following are some key features:

1. **Production function.**
   The Solow model posits a neoclassical production function in which GDP depends on the labor force and capital stock. Instead, we think of the available technology as a set of discrete input-output coefficients. These describe the actual ways in which production can take place. This approach is akin to Acemoglu and Restrepo's use of a task based model of production.

2. **Technical change.**
   The Solow model assumes labor augmenting technical change, in which case, output per worker and the real wage increase at the same rate. This is meant to model the 'stylized fact' that the two increase in tandem in historical data (Kaldor, 1957). However, this 'fact' is a generalization of what happened between the middle of the nineteenth century and the 1970s. It does not describe the industrial revolution or the past fifty years. Something is wrong.
   There are other difficulties. A prediction of the Solow model with labor augmenting technical change is that output per worker rises at the same rate at all capital-labor ratios. This has not occurred. Long run macro data show that output per worker has, indeed, risen at the high capital-labor ratios in rich countries. However, at low capital-labor ratios such as those found in poor countries today and in today's rich countries at the beginning of the nineteenth century, there has been no increase in output per worker for two centuries. In addition, the output-capital ratio has been declining over time, although the Solow model implies it should remain constant (Allen, 2012).
   Finally, on the theoretical plane, a neoclassical production function and any kind of factor augmenting technical change has the implication that the production function shifts inward at every capital-labor ratio, that is, at every value of the ratio of the wage to the price of capital. This set-up precludes finding that the factor price ratio guides the invention of new technology (Acemoglu and Restrepo, 2018, 2019). Indeed, Solow treated the evolution of technology as exogenous.
   Instead, of this representation of technical change, it is more useful to think of it as the invention of a technique with a new set of input-output coefficients. With this approach it is easy to see that factor prices affect the evolution of technology.

3. Wage evolution.

Since the Solow model assumes a neoclassical production function, the relation between wages and output per worker can be analyzed with standard marginal productivity theory in an aggregate framework. Instead, we take a disaggregated and historically specific approach to wage determination. In the Industrial Revolution, for instance, there is competition between new factories and old fashioned handy craft producers. The late nineteenth century looks much more like Solow-in-action, but even then the impact of immigration of the labor market must be analyzed to understand the evolution of the American labor market.

26.2 Phase 1: pre-industrial economic growth: 1620-1770

The pre-industrial revolution ran from roughly 1620 to 1770, when the industrial revolution began. This is the period when sustained economic development began in Britain, and it was marked by a 50% rise in output per worker (Broadberry et al., 2015). During this period, England achieved the most rapid rate of economic transformation of any country in Europe (Allen, 2000). The 'agricultural' share of the population dropped from 74% in 1500 to 35% in 1800, which was the lowest on the continent. The urban population and the rural handicraft sector that produced textiles and other goods for export expanded commensurately. London grew from 50 thousand people in 1500 to one million in 1800 when it became the largest city in Europe. The reallocation of labor out of agriculture underlay the rise in output per worker.

Pre-industrial economies were Malthusian: Wages were normally at subsistence. Demographic shocks like plagues caused wages to rise, but they then gravitated back to subsistence. Across Europe real wages rose after the Black Death in the mid-fourteenth century, and in most places fell back to subsistence as populations rebounded. The major exceptions were the maritime cities on the North Sea like Antwerp, Amsterdam, and London. Real wages in London dropped slightly in the fifteenth century, but they quickly reverted to a high level and stayed there through the Industrial Revolution. In the rest of Britain, wages fell to subsistence, as they did elsewhere in Europe. By the seventeenth century, however, wages in Southern England began rising to the London level and by the eighteenth century this dynamism had spread to northern England (Fig. 26.1) (Gilboy, 1934; Allen, 2001; Clark, 2005; Humphries and Weisdorf, 2019). Women's earnings rose relative to men's (Humphries and Weisdorf, 2015). These trends meant that British real wages were amongst the highest in the world in the mid eighteenth century (Allen et al., 2011). The Malthusian pattern was broken.

The cause of these high wage levels was the growth in British international trade and exports of handicraft manufactures like woolen cloth and iron products to Britain's colonies in north America, the Caribbean, and India (Allen, 2003). These markets were large–by 1770, the colonies of the future USA had a population of 2.4 million, about one third of England's. Incomes were as high or higher than in Britain (Allen et al., 2012; Lindert and Williamson, 2016), and most manufactures were imported. Additional demand came from the Caribbean colonies and elsewhere, so the export markets were substantial. Results included urbanization, the growth of rural manufacturing, rising agricultural productivity, and the development of the British coal mining industry (Allen, 2009a). Cheap coal was an important reason that the metal working industries could compete internationally even though they paid higher wages than their competitors. High wages may have induced some labor saving technical change before 1770, but the big impact was after 1770 when the textile industry was mechanized.

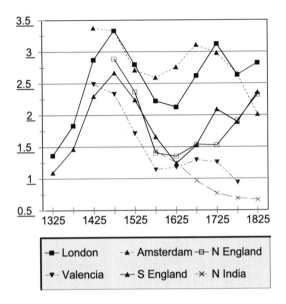

FIGURE 26.1

Real wages in England, Europe, and Asia. Sources are detailed in Allen et al. (2011) and Allen (2015, p. 8).

26.3 Phase 2: Industrial Revolution, 1770-1867: wages affected technology

This period is the classic Industrial Revolution. It was driven by technological change. The Industrial Revolution saw momentous technological inventions like factory spinning, power loom weaving, a coal based iron industry, steamships, and railways. Invention in this period was focused mainly on cutting the cost of manufacturing existing products rather than creating new products. The textile inventions are emblematic, and they lowered the cost of producing yarn and cloth that were already being made by hand or that were very close substitutes for them. For a century, the steam engine's sole contribution to progress was to reduce the cost of pumping water out of mines.

Invention in this period was not conducted in research laboratories but was rather the work of individuals following their own ideas. They did not always operate alone, however. At the highest level, the Royal Society heard papers on atmospheric pressure and was alive to possibilities of using that force for power generation. More prosaically inventors met in local groups, shared ideas, and learned from each other (Mokyr, 2009). It was not uncommon for inventors to share information so that they could learn from each others' experiences and push new design ideas forward. A good example of this sort of 'collective invention' was the perfection of Cornish pump engines in the first half of the nineteenth century (Allen, 1983; Nuvolari, 2004). The aim of inventors was generally to find a device they could exploit themselves or sell or license to someone else who would do so.

The search for better devices was a sensible response to Britain's economic expansion between 1600 and 1770, for it created a unique wage and price environment that made the new machines of the Industrial Revolution profitable. British wages were high relative to the price of consumer goods,

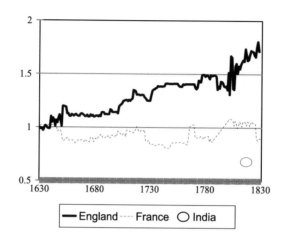

FIGURE 26.2

Wages relative to the user cost of capital. *Source*: Allen (2017, p. 72).

and, more to the point, relative to the price of capital services. Fig. 26.2 plots this ratio for England, France,[2] and India.

The impact of the high wage on invention is clearer if we think about technical change as the invention of new techniques represented by single points in capital-labor space rather than as shifts in a standard production function. Fig. 26.3 illustrates this point using spinning as an example. Two techniques are shown for spinning cotton yarn. The spinning wheel had a low capital-labor ratio, while the spinning jenny had a higher ratio. England in 1770 was characterized by the 'high wage cost line,' while the rest of the world (and England in 1600) had the 'low wage cost line.' Before 1770, the spinning wheel was the only technology available for making coarse cotton yarn, and it was used world wide, whatever the relative factor prices. In 1770, the spinning jenny was only profitable in England, so that was the only place it was used, and, indeed, the only place where it was worth inventing it (Allen, 2009b).

Mechanical spinning was continuously improved from the 1760s into the nineteenth century. Hargreave's first machine was followed by Arkwright's water frame (plus associated machines to make the first cotton mill), Crompton's mule, Robert's self-acting mule, and so forth. This trajectory of improvements is indicated on the diagram. Point C represents Hargreaves' first attempt at making a jenny. It was too inefficient to be used commercially. The thick dotted line represents the improvements Hargreaves made during the R&D phase of the project that turned it into a commercially successful technology. The double dotted line to the 'tipping point' represents improvements to mechanical spinning after the jenny entered commercial service. At the 'tipping point,' machine spinning became profitable in low wage economies. That is when the industrial revolution jumped to the continent, and it did so through

---

[2] Geloso (2018) has raised some concerns regarding the French wage series used in Fig. 26.2 for the years 1651-1764. Those issues, however, do not lead to appreciable changes in the figure since the wage enters the ratio both in the numerator as the cost of labor and in the denominator where it is a determinant of the cost of machinery.

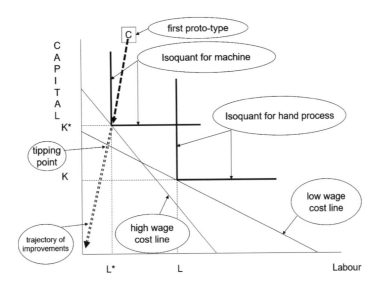

FIGURE 26.3

Production model of mechanization. *Note*: Both isoquants assume the same output level.

the adoption of the most advanced technology since that was the only technology that paid where labor was cheap. The double dotted line continues towards the origin indicating subsequent improvements.

The mechanization of spinning was followed by the invention of power loom weaving and similar incentives were in play (Allen, 2018). In the 1780s thousands of spinning jennies were installed in cottages and workshops and hundreds of Arkwright mills were constructed. Output of cheap cotton yarn surged. This yarn had to be woven into cloth, and the result was a large expansion in the handloom weaving sector. The weavers were mainly men, and at its peak employment in handloom weaving amounted to about 10% of the male labor force. As the sector expanded, wages, which had been similar to those of building laborers and farm workers in the 1770s, rose sharply (Fig. 26.4). The late eighteenth and early nineteenth century has come to be known as the 'golden age of the handloom worker' (Hammond and Hammond, 1919). Their high wages, however, became a target of inventors who sought to perfect the power loom to cut labor costs. This story was repeated in other handicraft trades.

26.4 Phase 2: Industrial Revolution: technology affected wages

The technological innovations of the Industrial Revolution had a dramatic impact on the labor market. The 'standard of living debate' dominates much discussion of the first half of the nineteenth century.[3]

---

[3] The matter has always been contentious. An intense debate on the question with many contributions raged between the exchanges between Hobsbawm (1957) and Hartwell (1961) through Feinstein (1998a, 1998b), which brought that controversy to a close.

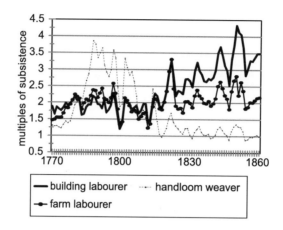

FIGURE 26.4

Lancashire male labor market real earnings, pence per week. *Source*: Allen (2017, p. 72).

How could the high wage economy of the eighteenth century have given rise to apparently wide spread poverty in the nineteenth? Fig. 26.4 shows the explosion in wage inequality in the Lancashire labor market. The 'golden age of the handloom weaver' around 1800 was followed by a collapse in their earnings as the power loom slashed the margin between yarn and cloth prices. Farm wages remained steady. The real wages of building workers rose consistently as did the wages of men employed in cotton mills after an initial dip during the French Wars. Eventually, handloom weavers were forced to give up the trade, and many redeployed to the remaining hand trades putting further down ward pressure on wages.

The combination of rising real wages in expanding trades with the falling wages in the hand trades meant that the average wage level remained unchanged even as output per worker rose (Fig. 26.5). The first half of the nineteenth century when this was occurring was the time when all social commentators–Malthus, Ricardo, Marx–thought that real wages would remain at subsistence no matter how much economic growth took place, and this period has been dubbed Engel's pause in view of Friedrich Engels' (1845) description of Manchester at this time (Allen, 2009c, 2019; Lindert, 2000).

26.5 Phase 3: the age of manufactures, 1867-1973: wages affected technology

The end of the Industrial Revolution ushered in a new phase when the economy did well–output per worker rose dramatically in today's developed countries, as did real wages. What determined the evolution of technology in this period, and how did it affect the labor market? I begin with technology and its determinants including the evolution of factor prices.

At the beginning of the period, innovation was much like it had been during the Industrial Revolution. New technology was developed by inventors working on their own who aimed to profit from it by exploiting it in their own businesses or selling the right to use it to other entrepreneurs. However,

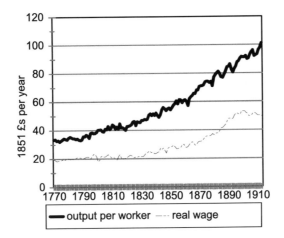

FIGURE 26.5

Output per worker and the real wage in Britain. *Source*: Allen (2017, p. 8).

as the period progressed, invention became more institutionalized. In 1876, Thomas Edison expanded his inventive capacity by founding the first industrial laboratory with about 60-80 employees. Many of the large American manufacturing firms produced by the mergers of the late nineteenth and early twentieth centuries quickly established industrial research laboratories (Chandler, 1977, p. 375). These firms had more resources than many of the individuals who proceeded them. They also had commercial objectives that conditioned the course of R&D.

Much of this private R&D was aimed at product innovation. Inventions like the railway that transformed the lives of ordinary people made their first appearance towards the end of the Industrial Revolution. Even the poor were affected. The Duke of Wellington, for instance, objected to Brunel's Great Western Railway because 'it will only encourage the lower classes to move about.'[4] The same thing happened in India. When railways were built, third class ticket sales boomed, and the 'poor moved about.' By the late nineteenth century, developments like electric power, automobiles, petroleum, modern chemicals, and air craft began transforming life on a greater scale. Modern living quarters with their modern conveniences were invented (Gordon, 2016). Product innovation was crucial in the growth process, for it sustained the continuous rise in demand for manufactures throughout this period: Had the consumption choices remained as they were in 1850, for instance, demand for manufactures would have been sated early on, and the economy would have evolved in a very different direction from that actually followed.

Government funded research also became important for the first time. In 1862, the Morrill Act provided for federally assisted land grant colleges in each state whose objectives included developing agriculture and engineering. In the same year the US Department of Agriculture was established. In 1887 the federal government began funding agricultural experiment stations in every state and in 1914 extension services to teach modern agriculture. In 1879 the US Geological Survey was established

---

[4] http://www.bbc.co.uk/history/british/victorians/brunel_isambard_01.shtml.

to survey and map the mineral resources of the country and promote their exploitation. These were scientific research organizations established to promote the settlement and economic development of the West. Their aim was not so much to promote the substitution of capital for labor as in Fig. 26.3, but rather to raise the value of land and natural resources. The USDA and USGS are early examples of 'mission oriented R&D.' This type of organization has played an increasingly important role in guiding invention in the twentieth century and broadening the range of objectives it serves.

Nevertheless, although product innovation and land value augmentation were important, much of the thrust of technological change in the period was aimed at cost reduction. In general, new technology was created with ever higher capital-labor ratios that produced ever more output per worker. We can study the evolution of this technology at both the industry and the macro level, and the same patterns emerge.

In his history of American management, Chandler (1977, pp. 240-283) wrote an overview of the development of manufacturing technology between 1870 and the First World War. He explains that the main objective in designing new plants was to increase 'throughput,' that is, output per factory. This was not done by increasing employment per factory, rather by increasing the capital in the plant, so that the work force could produce more per day. The iron smelting industry is a classic example. A key new technology was 'fast driving,' which meant blowing much higher volumes of air into the base of the blast furnace to increase production (Temin, 1964). The results show up in the statistics for the industry: The number of workers per blast furnace establishment only increased from 122 to 183 between 1879 and 1914. Over the same period, horsepower per establishment increased ten fold from about 793 to 7639, while output per establishment jumped fifteen fold from 5552 tons per year to 81363 tons per year. Technology evolved similarly in industries as diverse as flour milling, cigarette rolling, petroleum refining, and distilling.

This pattern described by Chandler corresponds to the same pattern as technical change in the British textile industry during the Industrial Revolution: New technology raised capital per worker and pushed up output per worker by an even greater amount.

Macro data for the nineteenth and twentieth centuries show the same pattern. Capital per worker and output per worker changed little over this period in countries that are still less developed. Development has taken place in a small number of pioneer countries. They have invented new technology that has created more capital per worker and even higher output per worker. Once the rich countries had abandoned a low capital labor ratio for a higher one, there has been no increase in productivity at the low capital labor ratio: At low capital labor ratios, output per worker in poor countries in 1990 was no higher than it had been in 1820 in the USA, UK, or Germany when they had similarly low capital labor ratios (Allen, 2012). The behavior of the macro ratios is the micro story writ large.[5]

Why did technology develop in this way? The answer is that economic development led to higher wages in rich countries, and the higher wages in turn made it profitable to develop technology with

---

[5] Kumar and Russell (2002) have fit frontier production functions to two cross sections of national data for 1965 and 1990 and show that the only movement in the function occurs at high capital labor ratios where the rich countries move high to even higher capital labor-ratios over the period. Allen (2012) extends these data back to 1820 for many countries and shows that it was always so. Jones (2005) develops a theory in which technologies are only a little more complicated than the Leontief isoquants in Fig. 26.3 and proves that the aggregate production function is Cobb-Douglas so long as the distribution of new ideas is Pareto. Allen (2012) fits a CES function to the aggregate data from 1820 to 1990 and cannot reject the hypothesis that the function is Cobb-Douglas, although there are discrepancies at low capital-labor ratios, as noted.

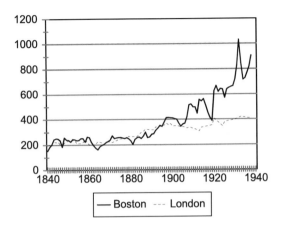

FIGURE 26.6

Unskilled real wages in 1905 British pence. *Sources*: Nominal weekly earnings divided by a consumer price index that (in the case of Boston) was converted to sterling using a PPP exchange rate. Nominal weekly earnings:
Boston: 1840-60: Margo (2000, Table 3A.5, Northeast). 1861-98: BLS 604, pp. 253-60. 1900-28: BLS 604, p.
185 (wage per hour multiplied by hours per week). London: 1840-1860 Schwartz (1985, pp. 36-8). 1861-1938
Bowley (1937, pp. 10, 15) and U.K. Department of Employment and Productivity (1971, p. 30, 32). Missing
values interpolated. Consumer prices indices: USA: Officer and Williamson (2020). UK: Allen (2007), Feinstein (1998a, pp. 652-3), Feinstein (1972, p. T140), 'A Millenium of Macroeconomic Data for the UK,' https://
www.bankofengland.co.uk/statistics/research-datasets, page A. 47. Wages and Prices, Column by: PPP exchange
rate for 1905. This was constructed using the retail prices of fifteen fuels, coal, kerosene, and house rent in the two
countries. Prices and expenditure patterns from U.K. Board of Trade (1911, pp. xxii, xxix-xlvii). Although the USA
data were collected in 1909, the Board of Trade concluded that they could be compared to the UK data collected in
1905 without impairing the comparison (p. iii).

even higher capital labor and capital output ratios. It is important in this regard to distinguish between
skilled and unskilled wages. Industries differed greatly in their mix of workers. In 1910, for instance,
48% of the work force in the iron and steel industry were unskilled workers as opposed to 14% in the
automobile industry. Skilled and unskilled workers presented different challenges, but in the USA, at
least, the movement of factor prices induced the substitution of capital for labor in both cases.

Fig. 26.6 shows unskilled wages expressed in 1905 British pence in the USA and UK. They were
strikingly similarly until the First World War. In contrast, skilled wages between the Civil War and the
First World War were very much higher in the USA than in Britain (Fig. 26.7). The high skill premium
had important implications for the evolution of technology (Habakkuk, 1962).

The incentives to mechanize depended on wages relative to capital prices rather than the cost of
living, and Fig. 26.8 shows this ratio for unskilled laborers. It was rising everywhere. There were two
responses.

One was the invention and application of scientific management with its time and motion studies.
In the classic account, Frederick Winslow Taylor (1911, pp. 39-44) explains how he pioneered the
approach in the 1890s. The most common job of a laborer in manufacturing was to carry materials or
product from one location to another. "Handling pig iron ... is chosen [as an example] because it is

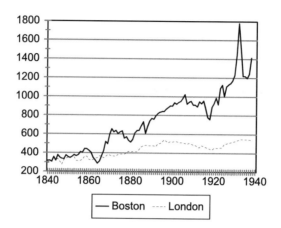

FIGURE 26.7

Skilled real wages in 1905 British pence. *Source*: same as Fig. 26.6.

typical of perhaps the crudest and most elementary form of labor which is performed by man. This work is done by men with no other implements than their hands. The pig-iron handler stoops down, picks up a pig weighing about 92 pounds, walks for a few feet or yards and then drops it onto the ground or upon a pile." At the Bethlehem Steel Company in 1898 a gang of pig-handlers "were loading on the average about 12-1/2 long tons per man per day. We were surprised to find, after studying the matter, that a first-class pig handler ought to handle between 47 and 48 long-tons per day." Taylor selected a German immigrant named Schmidt and offered him $1.85 per day instead of the usual $1.15 if he would load 48 tons per day. "You will do exactly as this man tells you tomorrow from morning till night. When he tells you to pick up a pig and walk, you pick it up and you walk, and when he tells you to sit down and rest, you sit down ... And what's more, no back talk." Taylor allowed that "this seems to be rather tough talk. And indeed it would be if applied to an educated mechanic, or even an intelligent laborer. With a man of the mentally sluggish type of Schmidt it is appropriate and not unkind, since it is effective in fixing his attention on the high wages which he wants and away from what, if it were called to his attention, he probably would consider impossibly hard work." If this approach worked, the wage increase would raise Bethlehem Steel's profits and also the measured real wage of Schmidt and the other laborers.

Time and motion studies had limits as a cost cutting strategy, so businesses also employed the classic response to high wages–namely, mechanization. In the mid-nineteenth century, the ore, coke, and limestone to be charged into a blast furnace were first raised to the top of the furnace stack with a lift. The materials were transferred to wheel barrows, and laborers pushed them across a gantry to the top of the stack where they were dumped into the furnace. American iron firms replaced this system in the early twentieth century with 'skip chargers'. These were containers that were filled at the base of the furnace with raw materials and then hoisted up a track to the top of the furnace where they were automatically tipped and their contents dumped into the furnace stack. The labor of the top loaders was dispensed with and the savings in their wages paid for the skip charger (Allen, 1977; Temin, 1964, pp. 162-3).

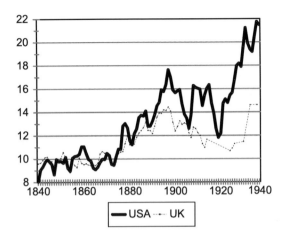

FIGURE 26.8

Unskilled wages relative to user cost of capital. *Source*: nominal wages as described in Figs. 26.6 and 26.7. User cost of capital: index equals (interest rate + depreciation rate) * index of cost of capital goods. Interest rate: USA new England municipal bonds, Homer and Sylla (1996, pp. 287-8, 342, 350). UK yield on long term government bonds, Homer and Sylla (1996, pp. 196-7, 444-5). Depreciation rate: assumed to be 5%. Index of cost of capital goods = geometric average of building labor wage rate and arithmetic average of prices of bar iron, copper, soft wood building lumber, and bricks. Sources of prices of bar iron, copper, and lumber have already been given (with the addition that the US bar iron price was extrapolated to 1937 using the price of steel rails). Bricks: USA: New York, 1849-1933: U.S. Census Bureau, *Historical Statistics of the United States*, online, Table Cc264. UK: Glasgow, 1863-1902, United Kingdom, Board of Trade, *Report on Wholesale and Retail Prices in the United Kingdom in 1902, with comparative statistical tables for a series of years*, House of Commons Parliamentary Papers, 1903, Vol. 68, p. 199. Softwood construction lumber: New York Hemlock: 1890-1920: United States, Department of Labor, Bureau of Labor Statistics (1922, p. 184, Table 9), 'New York Market, average price per M feet'. 1840-1890: extrapolated with Aldrich (1893, Vol. I, p. 46), 'one inch first quality hemlock boards not planed'. 1921-39: extrapolated with Potter and Christy (1962, p. 244, series L). UK Baltic: 1840-60: extrapolated with *Economist* series of price of Canadian yellow pine from Aldrich (1893, Vol. I, pp. 213-4). 1861-1937: United Kingdom, Board of Trade, *Statistical Abstract for the United Kingdom*, London, HMSO, various years and Sauerbeck (1886; 1907), unit value of imported timber, sawn or split, shillings per load of 50 cubic feet. Copper: USA: 1840-1891: Aldrich (1893, Vol. I, p. 40) copper ingots. 1892-1939: U.S. Census Bureau, *Historical Statistics of the United States*, online, Table Cc255-Cc257. Britain: 1846-91: Aldrich (1893, Vol. I, p. 234), Saurbeck's prices of copper bars from Chile. 1892-1937: Sauerbeck (1886; 1907), Editor of The Statist (1918, 1938) Iron: US bar iron: Philadelphia, best refined bar iron, United States of America, Department of Commerce, Bureau of the Census, *Statistical Abstract of the United States*, Washington, Government Printing Office, various years. Series extended forward with price of open hearth steel rails in U.S. Census Bureau, *Historical Statistics of the United States*, online, Table Cc245. UK bar iron: common bars, Mitchell and Deane (1971, pp. 493-4).

With unskilled wages rising with respect to capital costs on both sides of the Atlantic, there was an incentive to mechanize that work in Europe and the USA. With respect to skilled labor, the incentives were greater in New World, for skilled wages rose much more there with respect to the cost of capital

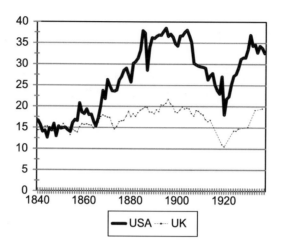

FIGURE 26.9

Skilled wages relative to user cost of capital. *Source*: same as Fig. 26.8.

(Fig. 26.9). This played out in industries like automobile manufacture that employed a high proportion of skilled labor. Henry Ford's Highland Park plant is the preeminent example. It was opened in 1910 to produce model T Fords, and it is most famous for installing the first moving assembly line in 1913. This invention accelerated throughput and displaced laborers. The bigger challenge, however, was to reduce the employment of high wage skilled machinists. This was accomplished through jigs, fixtures, and stops. General purpose machine tools that could perform many different tasks–and thus required the machinist to set the guides that controlled cutting and the depths to which drills would bore–were replaced with custom design machines in which pre-set jigs, fixtures, and stops controlled operation without the operator having to set them. Custom machines cost more than general purpose machines since a different design was required at every work station. This increase in capital intensity, however, allowed skilled machinists to be replaced by new immigrants from central European who had no machining experience (Meyer, 1981, pp. 24-26, 44-53).

> *The old time tool hardener was an expert. He had to judge the heating temperatures ... The wonder is that he hit it so often ... We introduced a system by which the man at the furnace has nothing at all to do with the heat. He does not see the pyrometer–the instrument which registers the temperature. Colored electric lights give him his signals (Ford, 1922, Chapter 6).*

Conceptualization, for instance the ability to lay out the work and locate the jigs and set the stops, was separated from execution–merely pushing the metal through the machine (Braverman, 1974). The 'semi-skilled' worker was born.

The Highland Park plant was a trend setter and not an isolated case. It epitomized mass production. The manufacturing sector as a whole shows the same patterns. The share of skilled workers dropped from about 40% in 1850 to about 15% in 2010 with most of that drop happening before 1940. There was at first a small rise and then a fall in the share of laborers/operatives–a category which requires further subdivision for understanding. What is also striking, however, is the rise in white collar jobs.

They amounted to only a few percent of employment in the mid-nineteenth century but over 40% in 2010. Most of the increased has occurred since the First World War (Katz and Margo, 2014, pp. 37, 45-6).

Census questions about occupations provide a finer classification of jobs and cover the entire economy.[6] Not surprisingly, between 1860 and 2000 there was a big fall in the share of farmers and farm laborers. In contrast to the manufacturing figures just reviewed, the economy-wide data show little change in the share of skilled workers in the labor force. This difference from manufacturing is down to the construction industry, which is large and where skilled workers still predominate. The share of non-farm laborers declined significantly, which one would expect given the incentives to mechanize material handling and transporting. The great expansion in white collar work–professional, managerial, clerical, and sales–stands out.

There are several reasons for the rise in white collar jobs. With respect to the manufacturing sector, the decline in skill work required a compensating increase in managerial and clerical activity as management assumed the conceptualization function that skilled workers had performed. Also skilled workers had often hired their assistants and subordinates, and these tasks were assumed by expanded personnel departments. Managers were also required to monitor and supervise the work of the semi-skilled workforce. In addition, the scale of business became larger to take advantage of the high throughput of advanced technology as well as to take advantage of the large national market created by the national rail system. The control of large organizations led to planning and cost accounting which entailed many office jobs.

Structural shifts in the economy also contributed to the growth in white collar employment. The rise of government with its tax systems and social welfare programs has entailed many clerical, managerial, and professional jobs. Higher incomes have led to shifts in consumer spending away from manufactured goods towards services like education and medical care, both of which required many professional employees.

Large numbers of clerical workers who were paid more than factory workers created an incentive to invent machines to save office labor. Type writers and dictating machines were early examples. A particularly interesting case is Herman Hollerith's invention of the electrical tabulating machine. It was first used to compile vital statistics in Baltimore in 1887 but its great breakthrough came when it was selected to compile the 1890 US census (Truesdell, 1965; Austrian, 1982). It is portentous in many ways including the fact that Hollerith's company became the core of IBM. Some European statistical agencies quickly took up the electrical tabulator as well as some American railway companies. An interesting case of non-adoption, however, is the Indian census. J.A. Baines (1900, pp. 50-51), the director, remarked to the Royal Statistical Society that there was no point using the electrical tabulator when Indian labor was so cheap. The economics of Hollerith's tabulator were much the same as Hargreave's jenny.

---

[6] U.S. Census Bureau, *Historical Statistics of the United States*, online, Table Ba1033-1046 - Major occupational groups–all persons: 1860-1990, extended.

26.6 Phase 3: the age of manufactures, 1867-1973: technology and globalization influenced wages

Despite–indeed, in part because of– the efforts of inventors to save money by inventing machines to substitute capital for labor, real wages rose rather than fell between the mid-nineteenth century and 1973. The First World War marked an important turning point in that process. Before the War, skilled workers in Britain earned higher wages than unskilled workers and factory production workers in the USA. All of that changed after the war: British wages stagnated, while American wages lept ahead. By 1940, American factory operatives and unskilled workers were making 50-100% more than British skilled workers (cf. Figs. 26.6 and 26.7). This marked the birth of the so-called 'American middle class.' Their wage gains continued after World War II and only ceased in 1973. Henry Ford summarized the impact of the new technology as follows: "I have heard it said, in fact I believe that it's quite a current thought, that we have taken skill out of work. We have not. We have put a higher skill into planning, management, and tool building, and the results of that skill are enjoyed by the man who is not skilled" (Ford, 1922, Chapter 5).

Ford was right that technical change played an important role in explaining the course of American wages, but other factors were also at play. Some affected the demand for labor and some the supply.

On the demand side, an important factor that sustained rising wages was the expansion of the American population as the continent was settled. Between 1850 and 1950, the population grew from 23 million to 152 million. Globalization played a role in this expansion. The international (read: British) demand for American grain and beef was buoyant throughout the century. For it to have been profitable to have settled the West, the price of wheat or cattle at the point of production on the frontier had to be high enough to induce labor to give up the chance of earning high wages in the east of the country and move west. The construction of ever more railways meant that more and more homesteads met this condition. Even after the frontier was closed, the West was not fully settled, and the population and economy continued to drift westwards well into the twentieth century. The Second World War gave a further boost to the great American boom, and the country enjoyed several decades of economic ascendancy in the post-war era.

The effect of the continual rise in population at high and rising wages combined with waves of product innovation was the fastest growing consumer demand in the world. Manufacturing expanded to meet it, and employment of production workers grew almost continuously from 1850 to 1979. The depression of the 1930s, of course, disrupted this expansion, and there was small cyclical fluctuation around the trend, but, in general, the trajectory was ever upward.

Technical progress also contributed to rising wages throughout the period 1867-1973. The replacement of skilled jobs by semi-skilled jobs might appear to be a counterexample, but the rapid expansion of the manufacturing sector meant that the demand for skilled labor was rising in the twentieth century, albeit at a lower rate than manufacturing employment as a whole. In addition, the elimination of laboring jobs as material transport was mechanized in conjunction with the creation of new semi-skilled jobs meant that skill level over all was rising (Goldin and Katz, 1998). As factory labor became more productive, competition among firms for workers led to rises in real wages.

The supply of labor also affected the evolution of wages. Supply changed after the first World War because immigration policy changed. Before World War I, there was no restriction on immigration from Europe. As the West was settled and the manufacturing sector expanded, the demand for both skilled and unskilled labor increased. It is hard to escape the conclusion that the supply of unskilled labor from the farms of eastern and southern Europe was much more elastic than the supply of skilled labor from the USA itself–with some assistance from the UK and northwestern Europe (Goldin, 1994; O'Rourke, 2019).[7] As a result, the rising demand for labor caused the wages of skilled workers to rise, while the immigration of farm laborers dampened any corresponding increase among the unskilled. This 'open door' immigration policy changed after 1921. Immigration no longer put a lid on the wages of unskilled and semi-skilled wages, and they rose closing the gap with skilled wages.[8] Thus began the 'great compression' of the 1930s and 1940s (Goldin and Margo, 1992).

Labor unions also contributed to the great compression. Unskilled workers in the manufacturing sector were unionized during the 1930s. Previously, unions had often been weak and generally involved only skilled craftsmen. New Deal labor legislation created a favorable environment for organization, and the CIO succeeded in unionizing most manufacturing workers. Wage negotiations tended to reduce wage inequality within the sector.

A final factor to consider is education. In their influential analysis of *The Race between Education and Technology*, Goldin and Katz (2008) maintain that technical change throughout the twentieth century has increased the demand for educated labor. Their evidence for this claim is that production workers with more schooling earned higher wages than those with less schooling early in the twentieth century. They contend that wage inequality decreases when the supply of educated workers increases. The spread of high schools in the USA during the early twentieth century was rapid enough to explain the fall in the skill premium. For emphasis, they dubbed the twentieth century the 'human capital century.'

It is difficult on the face of it to reconcile the Goldin-Katz view of the twentieth century with the de-skilling view of mass production advanced here. It is true that the educational level of the American work force has risen substantially, and conventional growth accounting attributes a lot of productivity growth to the rising educational level of the work force (Denison, 1962; Jorgenson and Griliches, 1967). However, most accounts of factory work emphasize that increases in mechanization made work more boring (Chinoy, 1955; Bright, 1958a,b; Meyer, 1981). One of the complex aspects of a craftsman's job was laying out the work. Knowledge of geometry and mathematics helped do that quickly and well. A craftsman could have made use on the job of the Euclidean geometry he had learned in high school. When the layout, however, was built into a machine, the need for that knowledge evaporated. Perhaps Bowles and Gintis (1976) got it right when they argued that what high school really taught students was how to follow instructions and fit into a routine.

26.7 Phase 4: the shift to services, 1973-present: wages affect technology

If the popular media and blogosphere are to be believed, we are now living through a period of unprecedented technological change. Terms like the 'fourth industrial revolution' encapsulate the view that IT and advanced digital technology are remaking the economy. In addition, the outsourcing of production

---

[7] This view has been contested, e.g. by Goldin and Katz (2008).

[8] The end of the mass immigration of European farmers created the opportunity for African-Americans to leave their farms in the South and move to factory work in the North (Collins, 1997).

to China and other developing countries highlights the (possibly growing) importance of globalization. We begin first with the character and causes of technological change and then consider its effects on labor incomes.

Product innovation was a critical feature of technical change in this period. The almost continuous expansion of output and employment in the manufacturing sector for a century was contingent on the creation of new products to the avoid the satiation of demand. Without automobiles, electrical appliances, air planes, and modern housewares demand growth would have stalled. Advances in medicines and pharmaceuticals were also made, although they contributed even more to the growth in services, which dispensed them. Laptops and smart phones are in the same tradition but have not had the decisive importance of the earlier inventions.

Many new products have their roots in mission oriented research (Nelson and Wright, 1992, pp. 1950-1954). Many of the electronics innovations are spin offs of technology developed for military purposes. All of the major features of the iphone–touch screens, for instance, and GPS–are commercial applications of technology developed under US defense contracts (Mazzucato, 2013). The original purpose was the solution of a military problem and not cost reduction or commercial advantage. Likewise, medical advances are the solutions to health problems and not cost minimization. It is significant that mission oriented research is paid for by the state or, in the case of medicine, by charities as well.

While much product innovation is the (long run) result of mission oriented research, how the products are produced requires decisions about plant design and production methods, and factor prices play an important role in directing those decisions–as they did in previous centuries. Businesses still found it in their interest to raise the capital labor ratio when labor was becoming relatively more expensive–as it was in the post-war period. Between 1950 and 2014, the wage of a US production worker relative to the Penn World Table cost of capital more than doubled, and the corresponding ratio in Britain increased almost four fold. The capital labor ratio increased almost seven fold between 1965 and 2014 in the UK, while it tripled in the USA. Capital per worker and output per worker both increased.

This period has been marked by the proliferation of computer and IT systems and their integration into business practice. These represent the substitution of capital for labor at an accelerated rate. The substitution was driven by rapidly falling prices: Computers and related equipment dropped in price (adjusted for quality) by about 20% per year between 1973 and 2010. Semiconductor and software prices also fell although not as rapidly. Between 1947 and 1973, computers made little contribution to the growth in aggregate US total factor productivity growth. Since 1973 TFP growth in the American economy has been driven mainly by productivity growth in the IT sector itself and in the industries that use IT extensively, which are mainly services. Labor productivity has risen in manufacturing outside of IT mainly because of increases in capital intensity (Jorgenson et al., 2016).

Since around 1990, the installation of industrial robots has proceeded very rapidly in east Asia, north America, and Germany. This trend was driven by a steep fall in the quality adjusted cost of robots. With constant or rising wages earned by the displaced workers, the rate of return to installing robots has risen dramatically. Robots are promoted on the grounds that they are a cost effective way of substituting capital for labor in manufacturing, so factor prices are integral to their diffusion and invention. Robots are an accelerated iteration of the technical change that has characterized the past two centuries.

FIGURE 26.10

Real output per worker and average labor income per employed person in the USA. *Note*: 'wage all workers' includes the self employed. In this graph, their income is set equal to the average wage and salary of all employed workers. Various alternatives were explored and gave similar results. *Sources*: GDP: GDP in billions of chained 2009 dollars from https://www.bea.gov.national/index.htm#gdp. Total workers: 1929-90: total employed civilian labor force, U.S. Census Bureau, *Historical Statistics of the United States*, online, Table Ba471. 1991-2016: Current Population Survey, Labor Force Statistics, series LNS 12000000. Total wage and salary income of all employed workers from U.S. Bureau of Economic Analysis, Table 2.1 Personal Income and Its Disposition, 1929-2019, online at https://apps.bea.gov/iTable/iTable.cfm?reqid=19&step=2#reqid=19&step=2&isuri=1&1921=survey. For 'production and non-supervisory workers,' total earnings, total number, and earnings per worker' were computed as: 1909-65: U.S. Census Bureau, *Historical Statistics of the United States*, online, Table Ba4361 and Ba4362. Hourly and Weekly Earnings of Production Workers in Manufacturing, 1909-1965. Hours worked per week calculated as the ratio. 1964-2016: Federal Reserve Bank of St. Louis, FRED economic data, average hourly earnings of production and non-supervisory employees, total private from https://fred.stlouisfed.org/series/CEU0500000008 and total number from Federal Reserve Bank of St. Louis, FRED economic data, production and non-supervisory employees, total private https://fred.stlouisfed.org/series/CES0500000006. Total earnings computed as hourly earnings multiplied by 40 hours per week multiplied by number of workers. 40 hours per week is consistent with corresponding data for 1909-65. For 'non-production and supervisory' total earnings, number of workers, and earnings per worker were computed as the totals of all employed workers minus the totals for 'production and non-supervisory workers.'

26.8 Phase 4: the shift to services, 1973-present: technology affects the labor market

The period since 1973 has much in common with the Industrial Revolution. In the USA, for instance, where the trends are most intense, the average real income of the labor force has risen slowly and fallen much behind the growth in output per worker (Fig. 26.10). This is the labor market manifestation of the rise in overall income inequality that has defined the period. Wage inequality has also increased dramatically. Since 1973 the real wages of production and non-supervisory workers have fallen slightly,

FIGURE 26.11

The wages of production and non-supervisory workers stagnate in USA while the salaries of professional and managerial workers rise. *Source*: See Fig. 26.10.

while the incomes of managerial and profession workers have skyrocketed (Fig. 26.11). These trends are similar to those in Britain during the Industrial Revolution.

There are also parallel causal explanations of these trends, although there are also important differences. What the two periods have in common is the emergence of a new production structure and the eclipsing of the old. In the Industrial Revolution it was the rise of the factory that drove handicraft cottage producers out of business. Post 1973, it is the rise of the service sector and the decline of manufacturing.[9] There is an important difference here, however; the factories of the industrial revolution produced the same or similar products to those of the handicraft sector, and the factories won by producing these goods at lower cost. This was creative destruction with a vengeance. Today, however, the service sector produces a different kind of output from manufacturing (cataract operations, for instance, versus paper towel dispensers), and the shift to services represents a shift of demand in that direction–creative destruction by subterfuge.

The first half of the twentieth century really was the age of industry. From 1900 to 1920, manufacturing accounted for almost 40% of the non-farm jobs. Together with its near relatives–mining, construction, and transportation (read: railways)–modern industry accounted for over 60% of the non-farm economy.[10] These sectors were closely linked and shared many of the same industrial relations practices and generated similar wages. The government also tended to match these wages. "Modern

---

[9] Temin (2017) offers another two sector model with a different division but many of the same themes.

[10] U.S. Census Bureau, *Historical Statistics of the United States*, online, Table Ba840-848, Employees on nonagricultural payrolls, by Industry: 1919-1999 [Bureau of Labor Statistics], extended to 2010.

industry" was a big enough share of the economy to sustain the American middle class, which is why it is important.

All this has change. The share of employment in manufacturing and related sectors declined modestly between 1920 and the 1960s, but was still large enough to provide widespread prosperity. Since the 1960s, the decline has been precipitous. By 2010, manufacturing employed only 9% of the non-farm workforce. Including mining, construction, and transportation only brings the share up to 19%. Government employs only 17%. All of the rest is private services. These range from doctors, teachers, and business consultants to waitresses, check out clerks, hospital orderlies, and parking lot attendants. Many of these jobs are managerial and professional and require university degrees, while others require little education and are found among the sales and service workers. The former populate the group with rapidly rising real incomes, while the latter fall into the category of production and non-supervisory workers with static and low incomes. The important point, however, is that the standard of living of the bulk of the American population is no longer determined by the wage level in manufacturing, transport, or construction, but rather in services. And wage inequality is very great in that sector.

What factors account for this enormous structural change? I begin with manufacturing. The Great Depression aside, we saw earlier that employment in manufacturing increased steadily after 1850. It peaked in 1979 at 20 million and has since fallen by half for a loss of almost 9 million jobs. Declines have been uneven across industries. Apparel, footwear, and textile mill products peaked earlier and have suffered declines on the order of 90% in employment. Primary metals have lost 70% of their peak number of jobs. On the other hand, chemicals, fabricated metals, and transportation equipment have seen only small falls, and employment in food and beverage production is at an all time high. Computers showed explosive growth for several decades, but in recent years employment in that industry has been falling as well.

Two factors that have played roles–but surprisingly small ones–are globalization and domestic outsourcing. Globalization is an obvious suspect, for the spread of industrialization to poor, low wage countries has made them competitive in cloth, apparel, and footwear, and imports of these products explain much of the decline in employment in these industries. Imports now account for almost 90% of the American market in footwear and apparel. Imports have also made inroads in cloth (41%), furniture (30%), computers (36%), and electrical machinery (58%). In other industries, however, import penetration is generally less than 10% and often negligible. Overall imports of manufactures equaled 12% of shipments of manufactures in 2016. If American factories had expanded to replace those imports and employment increased proportionally, manufacturing jobs would have been greater by 1.4 million workers. This figure is less than the 2 million workers suggested by the more complicated models of Autor et al. (2013, p. 2140) and Acemoglu et al. (2016, s145). These take account of re-allocation, inter-industry linkages, and general equilibrium effects. None of these estimates is large enough to explain the decline in manufacturing employment.[11] In addition, declines in manufacturing employment started in 1970 or earlier–when imports of manufactures were either non existent or inconsequentially small. Furthermore, as Feenstra et al. (2018) point out, the US is a major exporter of manufactures and increases in exports raised manufacturing employment by about as much as imports reduced. If the issue is the impact of greater globalization on US manufacturing employment, as it is, then the export side must be included, and that offsets the import side.

---

[11] Pierce and Shott (2016) argue that the US's granting Permanent Normal Trade Relations to China in 2000 explains the 18% decline in American manufacturing employment between 2000 and 2007.

Likewise for domestic outsourcing. It is not unusual now for employers to replace directly employed workers with workers provided by service firms or on other irregular contracts, in which case the worker is tallied in the service sector rather than in manufacturing. This practice is most common in education, health, construction, and business and personal services. Katz and Krueger (2019) estimated about 11% of workers in manufacturing were employed on these contracts.[12] Some of these would have been tallied (misleadingly) as service sector workers. If they all were so tallied, they would have totaled about one million in 2016. This is only a small fraction of the decline of production employees, let alone all employees, that the US manufacturing sector has experienced.

The factors that explain most of the decline in manufacturing employment were changes in the structure of demand and technological change. The structure of consumer demand has shifted from manufactures to services, and that has depressed the growth rate of manufacturing output. From 1929 until 1970, goods rather than services comprised at least half of what consumers bought. By the late 1980s the share had dropped to 40% and today it is 31%.[13] The price of services was rising with respect to the price of goods, which indicates that the shift to services reflected a demand increase in their favor. In part this is down to Engel's law–the observation that as people become richer their consumption of food levels out while their consumption of manufactures increases until it, too, decelerates and the consumption of services rises. Technical change (product innovation) made a contribution. In particular, the share of consumer spending on health care has risen from 2% in 1929 to 16% today, and that would not have happened without the advances in medical technology that prompted the expenditures. The growth of income in the health sector was also due to its organization, which has led to very high prices and the promotion of high cost interventions (Case and Deaton, 2020). The IT revolution has created many new jobs managing or exploiting information technology (Acemoglu and Restrepo, 2018, 2019). Many of these jobs are in the service sector, and schools and universities–components of the service sector–have expanded to train people in the new technology wherever it is used. In addition, globalization played a role as people's taste in cuisine was broadened to include eating dishes from around the world. A rising demand for travel was a counter part. These changes in spending shares mattered. Had the share spent on goods stayed at 50%, the consumption of manufactures by consumers would have been two-thirds greater than it is now, and that would have translated into a commensurately greater manufacturing sector and a higher level of employment had import penetration remained as it is. Under these circumstances, there would not have been much of an employment decline in manufacturing employment.

While product innovation is one channel through which technological advance led to a decline in manufacturing employment, a second was the traditional channel of inventing more capital intensive methods of production. Between 1970 and 2016, output per worker in manufacturing increased almost five fold.[14] If all else other than productivity had stayed the same, then today employment in manufacturing would be almost five times its present level. Half of this productivity growth occurred in the 1970s and 1980s before IT or robots had much impact. The change in manufacturing technology was the usual prosaic response to the rise in wages relative to the cost of capital.

---

[12] The surveys analyzed by Dorn et al. (2018) point to a similar conclusion.

[13] U.S. Bureau of Economic Analysis, Table 2.4.5 Personal Consumption Expenditures by Type of Product, 1929-2019. https://apps.bea.gov/iTable/iTable.cfm?reqid=19&step=2#reqid=19&step=2&isuri=1&1921=survey.

[14] In this calculation real gross output is divided by employment. A smaller increase is obtained by dividing real value added by employment.

Table 26.1   Earnings of low skill workers in manufacturing and services.

	Semi skilled manufacturing	Low skilled services
MEN		
1972		
FYFT	$49302	$41470
part time	10622	7141
all	41261	22624
2017		
FYFT	51075	39364
part time	20340	10215
all	45983	27914
WOMEN		
1972		
FYFT	28904	24342
part time	7904	7215
all	19942	11662
2017		
FYFT	40359	29745
part time	23458	10945
all	34927	20311

Notes: *FYFT = full year, full time. Full time, part year workers are included in 'all' but not separately tabulated.*
Source: *Current Population Survey, Annual Social and Economic Supplements for 1972 and 2017 (Flood et al., 2020).*

The problem with the decline in manufacturing and the rise of the service sector is that it depresses wage growth for less skilled workers. Table 26.1 summarizes annual earnings data for 1972, near the peak of real wages of production and non-supervisory workers, with 2017, the most recent year available. The focus is on semi-skilled operators in manufacturing given their significance in labor history and low skilled service employees like retail clerks, cashiers, waitresses, bartenders, cleaners, nursing aides, and hairdressers. Semi-skilled manufacturing workers who lost their jobs often moved into these service jobs, as did young people entering their labor force who might in an earlier generation have aspired to semi-skilled factory work. Comparisons are clearest for full-time, full-year employees (FTFY), but figures for part time workers and all workers are included since part-time work is prevalent, especially in the service sector, and many workers end up with part-time jobs who would prefer full time work. In both years, the manufacturing jobs paid more than the service jobs. This is not due to differences in human capital like education attainment, which was, in fact, slightly higher among the service workers and which does not explain the wage differentials when entered in standard wage regressions. Nor did other variables like race, ethnicity, or nativity play important roles. Probably unions played a role in raising manufacturing wages in 1972. Their importance was substantially lower in 2017, and yet their decline did not result in a real wage collapse in that sector. Why semi-skilled manufacturing wages still earn a premium is a puzzle.

Whatever the solution of that puzzle, the employment situation in 2017 is remarkably different from 1972. Like the Industrial Revolution, a new economic structure has displaced an old one–in this case the service sector has replaced manufacturing. The service sector provides many high salary professional jobs but also employment for a vast army of low skilled workers at pay lower than the factories offered. (This is a difference with the Industrial Revolution when the factory jobs paid at least as much as the handicraft jobs they replaced.) These service jobs are also often part-time work, which further depresses annual income. The ascendance of the service economy increases low wage work rather than eliminating it. The rise of the service economy has also resulted in a shift in the source of aggregate profits from manufacturing to services. Thus, the production structure of today and the immediate future is one that generates a high level of inequality both by producing high profits and by creating an non-egalitarian wage and salary distribution. What is to be done?

There are several possibilities and policy stances. Whether any are sufficient or feasible is unclear.

1. Keep calm and carry on.

   While the shift from manufacturing to services has lowered the incomes of less skilled workers, the idea is that eventually wages will rise in the service sector and all will be well. This idea receives some support from the polarization analysis of Acemoglu and Autor (2011, 2012), and Autor and Dorn (2013). This view begins with the well founded generalization that highly paid managerial and professional jobs have been increasing and their incomes rising and adds to this the observation that the personal service jobs at the bottom of the wage distribution have also been increasing both relatively and absolutely and have also experienced rising wages. Both wages and numbers could both be increasing only if demand for these jobs was rising, and the authors locate the cause of that increase in the rising incomes of the upper classes who demand more of the personalized services provided by these service jobs. Table 26.1 offers little support for this view in the case of men (where the earnings of full time men in services have fall between 1972 and 2017) but more so in the case of women where the income of full time workers has increased by 22% over the same period. How much 'personalized service' is offered by a Walmart check-out clerk or food court waitress is not so obvious, however. And, although the low skilled women in full time service work in 2017 have just realized the income that their predecessors received in manufacturing in 1972, there has been no overall advance for this broad category of workers in line with the aggregate productivity growth in the period.[15]

2. More education.

   The Goldin/Katz approach is to increase the educational level of the service workers. Something that gives us pause is that the educational attainment of this group has already increased substantially. In 1972, most had not completed high school, while today most of them have high school diplomas, and some have further education, which brings higher earnings, but not enough to reach factory standards. Higher educational and professional qualifications would presumably require a large scale transfer of waiters and clerks to professional jobs. Is this really feasible?

---

[15] The substantial real wage increase for full time full year women in manufacturing is of little moment since there are very few such jobs left anymore.

3. Non-competitive solutions.

If the above proposals are ineffective, is some combination of collective bargaining, higher minimum wages, a state provided minimum income (perhaps funded by a Piketty-style tax on capital) indicated?

Recent research supports the feasibility of higher minimum wages for raising the incomes of low wage service workers. The argument against such increases is that firms expand employment to the point where the wage equals the value of the marginal product of labor, in which case, a higher wage causes firms to reduce employment to maintain that equality. Attempts to measure the predicted reductions have yielded mixed results. However, a recent comprehensive study indicates no negative employment effect among service workers; rather, increases in the minimum wage cause firms to raise low wages to that minimum and, indeed, to raise the wages of some workers earning above it (Cengiz et al., 2019). There is scope for raising minimum wages without adverse employment effects.

The absence of an adverse employment effect highlights an important feature of the labor markets concerned, namely, that low wage workers were paid less than their marginal product (Case and Deaton, 2020, p. 237). This situation arises when firms have monopsony power manifest in the proliferation of noncompete agreements (even among fast food worker!), the rise of domestic outsourcing, the decline of trade unions, and outright collusion (Krueger, 2018).

If there is scope for legislation to raise wages, then there is also scope for trade unions to do the same thing. Changing labor law like abolishing certification elections could also contribute to raising wages in service industries.

26.9 Conclusion

The last four centuries have seen alterations in the relationship between growth in output per worker and the real wage. In the run up to the Industrial Revolution (1620-1770), both increased, and wages tended to converge upwards. High wages relative to capital prices precipitated the invention of capital-intensive factory production. Competition between the new factories and the remaining handicraft producers during the Industrial Revolution (1770-1867) led to rising inequality in wages, flat average real wages overall, and rising inequality as profits per worker rose. Once the handicraft sector was competed out of existence by the factories, a long period of fairly steady growth in output per worker ensued from 1867 to 1973. The endless invention of new manufactured goods was essential in maintaining buoyant demand for so long. Real wages rose in pace with overall labor productivity. By the end of the nineteenth century, the real wages of skilled workers in the USA, in particular, were leaping ahead, and the chance to eliminate their expensive jobs led to the invention of mass production and the routinization of work–a process that continued through the 1960s. By the 1930s, the spread of collective bargaining throughout manufacturing created an industrial relations system through which the manufacturing worker force could secure increases that matched productivity growth. This favorable situation lasted until about 1973, when the growth in manufacturing output slacked markedly as consumers shifted spending towards services. Slowly growing manufacturing output in conjunction with the continual substitution of capital for labor via new production technology meant that the number of manufacturing workers went into long term contraction. More and more of the new work force was absorbed in the new ascendant sector–services. While it provided many high wage technical and professional jobs, it also recruited large numbers of workers (who would have become factory workers in previous generations) into low paid jobs, many of which were part time. Weakness in the labor market contributed to a rise in profits, which now originate mainly in services. Responding to this new economy is the challenge of the future.

References

Acemoglu, D., 2002. Directed technical change. The Review of Economic Studies 69 (4), 781–810.

Acemoglu, D., Autor, D., 2011. Skills, tasks and technologies: implications for employment and earnings. Handbook of Labor Economics 4b, 1043–1069.

Acemoglu, D., Autor, D., 2012. What does human capital do? A review of Goldin and Katz's the race between education and technology. Journal of Economic Literature 50, 426–463.

Acemoglu, D., Autor, D., Dorn, D., Hanson, G.H., Price, B., 2016. Journal of Labor Economics 34 (S1 (Part 2)), S141–S198.

Acemoglu, D., Restrepo, P., 2018. The race between man and machine: implications of technology for growth, factor shares and employment. The American Economic Review 108 (6), 1488–1542.

Acemoglu, D., Restrepo, P., 2019. Automation and new tasks: how technology displaces and reinstates labor. The Journal of Economic Perspectives 33 (2), 3–30.

Acemoglu, D., Robinson, J.A., 2015. The rise and decline of general laws of capitalism. The Journal of Economic Perspectives 29 (1), 3–28.

Aghion, P., Howitt, P., 1992. A model of growth through creative destruction. Econometrica 60 (2), 323–351.

Aldrich, N.W., 1893. Wholesale prices, wages, and transportation. In: United States Senate. Senate Committee on Finance, 52nd Congress. Government Printing Office, Washington.

Allen, R.C., 1977. The peculiar productivity history of American blast furnaces, 1840-1913. The Journal of Economic History 37 (3), 605–633.

Allen, R.C., 1983. Collective invention. Journal of Economic Behavior & Organization 4, 1–24.

Allen, R.C., 2000. Economic structure and agricultural productivity in Europe, 1300-1800. European Review of Economic History 3, 1–25.

Allen, R.C., 2001. The great divergence in European wages and prices from the middle ages to the First World War. Explorations in Economic History 38, 411–447.

Allen, R.C., 2003. Poverty and progress in early modern Europe. Economic History Review LVI, 403–443.

Allen, R.C., 2007. Pessimism Preserved: Real Wages in the British Industrial Revolution. Working Paper 314. Oxford University, Department of Economics. https://www.nuffield.ox.ac.uk/media/2166/allen-pessimism-6.pdf.

Allen, R.C., 2009a. The British Industrial Revolution in Global Perspective. Cambridge University Press, Cambridge.

Allen, R.C., 2009b. The industrial revolution in miniature: the spinning jenny in Britain, France, and India. The Journal of Economic History 69 (4), 901–927.

Allen, R.C., 2009c. Engel's pause: technical change, capital accumulation, and inequality in the British industrial revolution. Explorations in Economic History 46 (4), 418–435.

Allen, R.C., 2012. Technology and the great divergence: global economic inequality since 1820. European Review of Economic History 40, 1–16.

Allen, R.C., 2015. The high wage economy and the industrial revolution: a restatement. Economic History Review 68 (1), 1–22.

Allen, R.C., 2017. The Industrial Revolution: A Very Short Introduction. Oxford University Press, Oxford.

Allen, R.C., 2018. The hand-loom weaver and the power loom: a Schumpeterian perspective. European Review of Economic History 22 (4), 381–402.

Allen, R.C., 2019. Class structure and inequality during the industrial revolution: lessons from England's social tables, 1688-1867. Economic History Review 72, 88–125.

Allen, R.C., Bassino, J.-P., Ma, D., Moll-Murata, C., van Zanden, J.L., 2011. Wages, prices, and living standards in China, 1739-1925: in comparison with Europe, Japan, and India. Economic History Review 64, 8–38.

Allen, R.C., Murphy, T., Schneider, E., 2012. The colonial origins of divergence in the Americas: a labour market approach. The Journal of Economic History 72 (4), 863–894.

Austrian, G., 1982. Herman Hollerith, Forgotten Giant of Information Processing. Columbia University Press, New York.

Autor, D., Dorn, D., 2013. The growth of low-skill service jobs and the polarisation of the US labor market. The American Economic Review 103, 1553–1597.

Autor, D., Dorn, D., Hanson, G.H., 2013. The China syndrome: local labor market effects of import competition in the United States. The American Economic Review 103, 2121–2168.

Baines, J.A., 1900. On census-taking and its limitations. Journal of the Royal Statistical Society 63 (1), 41–71.

Bowles, S., Gintis, H., 1976. Schooling in Capitalist America: Educational Reform and the Contradictions of Economic Life. Basic Books, New York.

Bowley, A.L., 1937. Wages and Income in the United Kingdom Since 1860. Cambridge University Press, Cambridge.

Braverman, H., 1974. Labor and Monopoly Capital. Monthly Review Press, New York.

Bright, J.R., 1958a. Does automation raise skill requirements? Harvard Business Review, 85–98.

Bright, J.R., 1958b. Automation and Management. Harvard University, Boston.

Broadberry, S., Campbell, B.M.S., Klein, A., Overton, M., van Leeuwen, B., 2015. British Economic Growth: 1270-1870. Cambridge University Press, Cambridge.

Case, A., Deaton, A., 2020. Deaths of Despair and the Future of Capitalism. Princeton University Press, Princeton.

Cengiz, D., Dube, A., Lindner, A., Zipperer, B., 2019. The effect of minimum wages on low-wage jobs. The Quarterly Journal of Economics 134 (3), 1405–1454.

Chandler, A.D., 1977. The Visible Hand: The Managerial Revolution in American Business. Belknap Press of Harvard University Press, Cambridge, MA.

Chinoy, E., 1955. Automobile Workers and the American Dream. Beacon Press, Boston.

Clark, G., 2005. The condition of the working class in England, 1209-2004. Journal of Political Economy 113, 1307–1340.

Collins, W.J., 1997. When the tide turned: immigration and the delay of the great black migration. The Journal of Economic History 57, 607–632.

Denison, E.F., 1962. The Sources of Economic Growth in the United States and the Alternatives Before Us. Committee for Economic Development, New York. Supplementary Paper No. 13.

Dorn, D., Schmidler, J.F., Spletzer, J.R., 2018. Domestic Outsourcing in the United States.

Editor of "The Statist", 1918. Wholesale prices of commodities in 1917. Journal of the Royal Statistical Society 81, 334–349.

Editor of "The Statist", 1938. Wholesale prices in 1937. Journal of the Royal Statistical Society 101, 376–393.

Engels, F., 1845. The Condition of the Working Class in England. Trans. and ed. by W.O. Henderson and W.H. Chaloner. Basil Blackwell, Oxford. 1958.

Feenstra, R., Ma, H., Sasahara, A., Xu, Y., 2018. Reconsidering the 'China shock' in trade. VoxEU. https://voxeu.org/article/reconsidering-china-shock-trade.

Feinstein, C.H., 1972. National Income, Expenditure and Output of the United Kingdom, 1855-1965. Cambridge University Press, Cambridge.

Feinstein, C.H., 1998a. Pessimism perpetuated: real wages and the standard of living in Britain during and after the industrial revolution. The Journal of Economic History 58, 625–658.

Feinstein, C.H., 1998b. Wage-earnings in Great Britain during the industrial revolution. In: Begg, I., Henry, S.G.B. (Eds.), Applied Economics and Public Policy. Cambridge University Press, Cambridge, pp. 181–208.

Flood, S., King, M., Rodgers, R., Ruggles, S., Warren, J.R., 2020. Integrated Public Use Microdata Series, Current Population Survey: Version 7.0 [ASEC for 1972 and 2017]. IPUMS, Minneapolis, MN.

Ford, H., 1922. My Life and Work. William Heinemann, London.

Geloso, V., 2018. Were wages that low? Real wages in the Strasbourg region before 1775. Journal of Interdisciplinary History 48, 511–522.

Gilboy, E.W., 1934. Wages in Eighteenth Century England. Harvard University Press, Cambridge.

Goldin, C., 1994. The political economy of immigration restriction in the United States, 1890 to 1921. In: Goldin, C., Libecap, G.D. (Eds.), The Regulated Economy: a Historical Approach to Political Economy. University of Chicago Press, Chicago, pp. 223–258.

Goldin, C., Katz, L., 1998. The origins of technology-skill complementarity. The Quarterly Journal of Economics 113, 693–732.

Goldin, C., Katz, L., 2008. The Race Between Education and Technology. Belknap, Cambridge, MA.

Goldin, C., Margo, R.A., 1992. The great compression: the wage structure of the United States at mid-century. The Quarterly Journal of Economics 107, 1–34.

Gordon, R.J., 2016. The Rise and Fall of American Growth. Princeton University Press, Princeton.

Grossman, G.M., Helpman, E., 1991. Innovation and Growth in the Global Economy. MIT Press, Cambridge, MA.

Habakkuk, H.J., 1962. American and British Technology in the Nineteenth Century. Cambridge University Press, Cambridge.

Hammond, J.L., Hammond, B., 1919. The Town Labourer: 1760-1832. 4th Impression, London.

Hartwell, R.M., 1961. The rising standard of living in England, 1800-1850. Economic History Review 13 (3), 397–416.

Hobsbawm, E.J., 1957. The British standard of living, 1790-1850. Economic History Review, 2nd Series 10 (1), 46–68.

Homer, S., Sylla, R., 1996. A History of Interest Rates, 3rd ed. rev. Rutgers University Press, New Brunswick, N.J.

Humphries, J., Weisdorf, J., 2015. The wages of women in England, 1260–1850. The Journal of Economic History 75, 405–447.

Humphries, J., Weisdorf, J., 2019. Unreal wages? Real income and economic growth in England, 1260–1850. The Economic Journal 129 (623), 2867–2887.

Jones, C.I., 2005. The shape of production functions and the direction of technical change. The Quarterly Journal of Economics 120 (2), 517–549.

Jorgenson, D., Griliches, Z., 1967. The explanation of productivity change. The Review of Economic Studies 34 (99), 249–280.

Jorgenson, D.W., Ho, M.S., Samuels, J.D., 2016. The impact of information technology on postwar US economic growth. Telecommunications Policy 40, 398–411.

Kaldor, N., 1957. A model of economic growth. The Economic Journal 67 (268), 591–624.

Katz, L.F., Krueger, A.B., 2019. The rise and nature of alternative work arrangements in the United States. Industrial & Labor Relations Review 72 (2), 382–416 (Internet).

Katz, L.F., Margo, R.A., 2014. Technical change and the relative demand for skilled labor: the United States in historical perspective. In: Boustan, L.P., Frydman, C., Margo, R.A. (Eds.), Human Capital in History: the American Record. University of Chicago Press, Chicago, pp. 15–57.

Krueger, A.B., 2018. Reflections on dwindling worker bargaining power and monetary policy. In: Jackson Hole Economic Symposium. https://www.kansascityfed.org/~/media/files/publicat/sympos/2018/papersandhandouts/824180824kruegerremarks.ped?la=en.

Kumar, S., Russell, R.R., 2002. Technological change, technological catch-up, and capital deepening: relative contributions to growth and convergence. The American Economic Review 92 (3), 527–548.

Lindert, P.H., 2000. Three centuries of inequality in Britain and America. In: Atkinson, A.B., Bourguignon, F. (Eds.), Handbook of Income Distribution. Elsevier, pp. 167–216.

Lindert, P.H., Williamson, J.G., 2016. Unequal Gains: American Growth and Inequality Since 1700. Princeton University Press, Princeton.

Lucas, R.E., 1988. On the mechanics of economic development. Journal of Monetary Economics 22 (1), 3–42.

Margo, R.A., 2000. New estimates for nominal and real wages in the antebellum period. In: Margo, R.A. (Ed.), Wages and Labor Markets in the United States 1820–1860. University of Chicago Press, Chicago, pp. 36–75.

Marx, K., 1867. Capital: A Critique of Political Economy. Progress Publishers, Moscow. First English edition of 1887. Marx/Engels Internet Archive (marxists.org) 1995, 1999, Volume I.

Mazzucato, M., 2013. The Entrepreneurial State. Anthem Press, London.

Meyer, S., 1981. The Five Dollar Day: Labor Management and Social Control in the Ford Motor Company, 1908-1921. State University of New York Press, Albany.

Mitchell, B.R., Deane, P., 1971. Abstract of British Historical Statistics. Cambridge University Press, Cambridge.

Mokyr, J., 1990. The Lever of Riches: Technological Creativity and Economic Progress. Oxford University Press, New York.

Mokyr, J., 2002. The Gifts of Athena: Historical Origins of the Knowledge Economy. Princeton University Press, Princeton.

Mokyr, J., 2009. The Enlightened Economy: The Economic History of Britain, 1700-1850. Penguin Press.

Mokyr, J., 2017. The Culture of Growth. Princeton University Press, Princeton.

Nelson, R.R., Wright, G., 1992. The rise and fall of American technological leadership: the postwar era in historical perspective. The Journal of Economic Perspectives 30, 1931–1964.

Nuvolari, A., 2004. Collective invention during the British industrial revolution: the cast of the Cornish pumping engine. Cambridge Journal of Economics 28, 347–363.

Officer, L.H., Williamson, S.H., 2020. The annual consumer price index for the United States, 1774-present. MeasuringWorth. http://www.measuringworth.com/uscpi/.

O'Rourke, K.H., 2019. Economic history and contemporary challenges to globalization. The Journal of Economic History 79, 356–382.

Pierce, J.R., Shott, P.K., 2016. The surprisingly Swift decline of US manufacturing employment. The American Economic Review 106 (7), 1632–1662.

Piketty, T., 2014. Capital in the Twenty-First Century. Harvard University Press, Cambridge, MA.

Potter, N., Christy Jr., F.T., 1962. Trends in natural resource commodities: statistics of prices, output, consumption, foreign trade, and employment in the United States, 1870-1957. In: Resources for the Future. The Johns Hopkins Press, Baltimore.

Ray, D., 2015. Nit-Piketty: a comment on Thomas Piketty's capital in the twenty first century. In: CESifo Forum, Ifo Institute - Leibniz Institute for Economic Research at the University of Munich, Vol. 16(01), pp. 19–25.

Romer, P.M., 1986. Increasing returns and long-run growth. Journal of Political Economy 94 (October), 1002–1037.

Romer, P.M., 1990. Endogenous technological change. Journal of Political Economy 98 (5), S71–S102.

Sauerbeck, A., 1886. Prices of commodities and the precious metals. Journal of the Statistical Society of London 49 (3), 581–648.

Sauerbeck, A., 1907. Prices of commodities in 1906. Journal of the Royal Statistical Society 70, 107–121.

Schumpeter, J.A., 1994. Capitalism, Socialism, and Democracy. Routledge, London (ebook).

Schwartz, L.D., 1985. The standard of living in the long run: London: 1700-1860. Economic History Review 38, 24–41.

Solow, R.M., 1956. A contribution to the theory of economic growth. The Quarterly Journal of Economics 70 (1), 65–94.

Taylor, F.W., 1911. The Principles of Scientific Management. Harper & Brothers, New York.

Temin, P., 1964. Iron and Steel in Nineteenth-Century America: An Economic Enquiry. The MIT Press, Cambridge, MA.

Temin, P., 2017. The Vanishing Middle Class: Prejudice and Power in a Dual Economy. The MIT Press, Cambridge, MA.

Truesdell, L.E., 1965. The Development of Punch Card Tabulation in the Bureau of the Census, 1890-1940. Bureau of the Census, Washington.

U.K. Department of Employment and Productivity, 1971. British Labour Statistics: Historical Abstract, 1886-1968. Her Majesty's Stationery Office, London.

Debt and taxes in eight U.S. wars and two insurrections[☆]

27

George J. Hall[a] and Thomas J. Sargent[b]

[a]*Brandeis University, Waltham, MA, United States*
[b]*New York University, New York, NY, United States*

A war can ravage half a continent and raise no new issues in economic theory.
George Stigler

A fellow may do many a crazy thing and as long as he has no theory about it, we forgive him. But if there happens to be a theory behind his actions, everybody is down on him.
Gene Henderson in *Henderson the Rain King* by Saul Bellow

. . . the study of the past with one eye, so to speak, upon the present is the source of all sins and sophistries in history.
Herbert Butterfield, *The Whig Interpretation of History (1931)*

27.1 Introduction

This paper describes an extended exercise in pattern recognition; or is it pattern imposition? We construct and interpret accounts that measure fiscal choices and some of their consequences during and after 10 surges of government spending that were associated with eight major U.S. wars and two insurrections, seeking to spot similarities and differences across these surges. We don't pretend to "let the data speak for themselves"[1] and admit that our interpretations are shaped by the economic theories described in section 27.2 and an accounting scheme that we describe in section 27.3. The section 27.3 decompositions of government budgets are designed to make contact with the section 27.2 theories.

Wartime surges in government expenditures have always provoked debates about how to pay for them. Those debates inspired classic theoretical contributions about the optimal mix of debt and taxes and whether the mix matters at all. The origin of theories of optimal tax-borrowing policies in those debates is an element of our defense against a Butterfieldian charge of inappropriate presentism (interpreting the past from a perspective and with information not available to those who acted in history). Statesmen who made the tax and borrowing decisions studied here had purposes and theories in mind, intellectual forces that will be important parts of our story. Therefore, we are naturally ambivalent

---

[☆] We thank William Berkley for supporting our research. Hall thanks the Theodore and Jane Norman Fund for financial support.
[1] If asked to do so they would have been silent.

The Handbook of Historical Economics. https://doi.org/10.1016/B978-0-12-815874-6.00036-8

about whether our section 27.2 theories are to be viewed as normative (how things should be) or positive (how things are). We use the theories both ways because key historical actors sometimes used them as rationalizations of their proposals. A poster child for this point of view is the coincidence of recommendations of the Barro (1979) model with Secretary of Treasury Albert Gallatin's 1807 Report as well as subsequent actions of Gallatin and his successors.

We appreciate Gary Becker's 1962 view that constraints alone go a long way in explaining patterns in outcomes, regardless of decision makers' purposes or their rationality. When we spot differences across our 8 + 2 wartime expenditures, our theories naturally direct us to ask how much of these are to be explained by decision makers' purposes or their constraints or their understandings, i.e., their theories. We describe the expenditure surges sequentially and note decision maker's evolving understandings. Memories of how the Continental currency that had financed the War of Independence from Great Britain had eventually depreciated to one penny on the dollar prompted War of 1812 decision makers to take steps to avoid that outcome. Non-callable Federal bonds issued to pay for the Mexican War appreciated in value after the war when interest rates fell, creating *ex post* regrets that the bonds had not been bundled with call options, something that the Union would do early in the Civil War. Rising nominal interest rates after World War I delivered nominal capital losses to owners of the Liberty Bonds that had been used to finance the war, teaching Captain Harry Truman a lesson that he would remember when as President he insisted that the Treasury and Federal Reserve manage interest rates after World War II to prevent that from happening again. We recount many other instances of later statesmen learning from what came to be recognized as mistakes during past wars. Prevailing understandings evolved about how government securities should be designed and marketed; about types of taxes to be imposed; and about the roles of the legal restrictions such as price controls and portfolio restrictions recommended by Keynes (1940) and formalized by a theory of Bryant and Wallace (1984). Statisticians tell us that the *only* things we can learn about are parameters of a necessarily restricted *model*, so perhaps it is excusable that we see successive government authorities processing information about past government expenditure surges in order to modify and refine their theories. (See the words written by Secretary McAdoo in the first paragraph of section 27.6.5.)

This brings us to a difficulty that we want to acknowledge. As we watch policy makers over two centuries confronting their predicaments by combining their recollections of histories with their theories, we'll see them struggle over and over again with the same forces. These include roll-over risks associated with unanticipated changes in market conditions and interest rates that bedevil decisions about the maturity structure of debt to sell; issues about units of account in which to denominate coupon and principal payments; interactions between banking and fiscal policies; temptations to default; and issues forced on them by prospective government creditors' incentives to delay supplying credit in anticipation of better terms later.[2] We admit that the section 27.2 benchmark models that frame this paper omit or oversimplify almost all of these forces, something that we'll try to keep in mind as we describe and interpret our 8 + 2 wartime expenditure surges in sections 27.4, 27.5, 27.6, and 27.7.

---

[2] But notice how our Lucas-Stokey (1983) benchmark model refines our Barro (1979) model by allowing returns on government debt to be state-contingent, a feature that we'll use to interpret evidence on postwar returns to government creditors. There have been many subsequent refinements of this type of model. For example, Pouzo and Presno (2016) studies defaults to government creditors as a way to provide some state-contingency with interesting incentive effects.

27.1.1 Reader's guide

Section 27.2 describes the two classic models of wartime finance that frame our analysis, one that we attribute to Gallatin (1837) and Barro (1979), the other to Lucas and Stokey (1983). We compare the composition of financing across wars extending from the American Revolution to Vietnam. Our analysis differs from previous studies in some important ways. Consistent with our benchmark theories, we measure government debt at its market value rather than its par value and we measure returns to bondholders in terms of *ex post* holding period returns instead of with the government's accounting measure of interest payments on its debt. In addition, we use GDP growth and inflation to help account the real debt burden relative to GDP.

In most wars, we see evidence of Gallatin-Barro tax smoothing (i.e., tax responding much less than one-for-one with spending), but only during the Civil War do we see a close approximation to the split between taxes and debt that the model recommends for a purely *temporary* expenditure surge. We also see negative wartime bond returns followed by positive postwar returns in the War of 1812, the Civil War, World War I, and the Korean War as prescribed by the Lucas-Stokey model. But we note this model directs that bondholders should receive an immediate capital loss at the *outbreak* of a war. We observe that only in the Korean War. To implement that Lucas-Stokey recommendation there had to be a sufficiently large outstanding stock of debt at the time of the wartime surge in government spending. At the starts of several wars (e.g., the Mexican War, Civil War, World War I), the U.S. had little debt. So for these wars, the Lucas-Stokey action would not help the government's financial situation.[3] In section 27.6 we discuss how Congress and Treasury secretaries experimented and innovated with various debt designs and management policies to induce potential investors to purchase bonds early in wars despite fears of wartime capital losses.

We detect some notable patterns. Over time, from the War of 1812 to the Vietnam War, the U.S. has financed larger shares of wartime spending with taxes and smaller shares with debt. Seignorage contributed a significant share of revenue in the Civil War, World War I, World War II, and the Korean War. Over time, post-war real returns paid to bondholders have declined. After four majors wars, the War of 1812, the Civil War, World War I, and World War II, average annual returns to bondholders were 12.0%, 8.5%, 5.5%, and -1.4%, respectively. We decompose changes in the debt/GDP ratio. We find that the U.S. didn't just grow out of its World War II debt. While GDP growth certainly played an important role, other forces also contributed. Inflation eroded between one-third and one-half of the debt, and primary budget surpluses also contributed. From the War of 1812 to World War II, there was a democratization of U.S. Treasury debt holding. We emphasize two forces that drove this extension of the Treasury market from the nation's elite to a wide range of investors: (i) as wars became more expensive, the Treasury wanted to raise more funds than banks and investment houses, particularly in the northeast, seemed willing to supply at prices acceptable to the Congress and Treasury; and (ii) Treasury secretaries and others viewed widespread purchases of debt as an indicator of patriotic support

---

[3] It is ironic that we only see these Lucas-Stokey start-of-war losses during the Korean War. President Harry Truman, was determined to ensure that returns on government debt was risk free – not state-contingent. For example, during the war he tried to make sure the Fed and Treasury kept the nominal yield curve fixed. However, he had limited control over the price level. Prices rose at the start of the Korean War generating the negative real returns.

for a war.[4] While this expansion of Treasury ownership might have resulted in increased political support to service the debt, we find that as federal debt became more widely held, postwar returns fell.

After studying eight wars, we compare fundings of two insurrections: the American colonists' successful war of secession from the British Empire from 1775 to 1873 and the Confederate States of America's (CSA) failed attempt to secede from the United States in the early 1860s. Both rebel governments had limited access to taxation and therefore funded their armed forces largely through debt and seignorage, but the timing of their issues of debt and money differed. The Continental Congress funded the first half of the American Revolution, from 1775 to 1780, almost exclusively through seignorage while it financed the second half by borrowing in the form of commissary and quartermaster certificates and other *ad hoc* I.O.U.s. Initially, the CSA financed much of their efforts with debt issues; as the war progressed the CSA relied more heavily on seignorage.

In section 27.8, we conclude this paper by offering qualifications involving the draft and other issues of fairness. We also note that while Treasury secretaries have viewed widespread purchases of debt as a sign of patriotic support for a war effort, contemporary op-ed writers and political scientists viewed higher taxes as a better way to signal broad-based support. Appendix A describes our accounting system while Appendix B tells data sources.

27.2 Two theories of war finance

As benchmarks, we use two classic models of about how a government optimally finances wartime surges of government expenditures, one due to Barro (1979), the other to Lucas and Stokey (1983). Both models are about how a government ought to adjust tax collections and government borrowing in response to random government expenditure shocks. The models differ in how much fiscal shock absorbing is done by adjusting tax collections and how much is done by adjusting *ex post* returns to government creditors and quantities of government debt. In our Barro model, fiscal shocks permanently affect both tax collections and government debt but leave *ex post* returns on government debt unaffected. Whether tax collections or government debt adjusts more depends on how permanent are the shocks to government expenditures, with tax collections adjusting relatively more the more permanent are the shocks. So in the Barro model, a war that is expected to be short should be financed more by borrowing while a war expected to be long should be financed more by raising taxes. In our Lucas-Stokey model, regardless of how persistent they are, fiscal shocks leave government tax collections completely unaffected but affect *ex post* returns to government creditors.

Our Barro (1979) model assumes that a government can trade only risk-free one-period bonds each period, while our stripped down Lucas and Stokey (1983) model allows a government to trade a complete set of one-period Arrow securities. Interest rates are exogenous in both models.[5] We make

---

[4] There were bumps along this road. For example, falling bond prices immediately after World War I soured many new investors on U.S. Treasuries. In response, in World War II the Treasury created non-marketable savings bonds and fixed the yield curve.

[5] Barro assumed an exogenous interest rate just as we do, but Lucas and Stokey did not. They analyzed a closed economy in which government tax and debt management policies influenced equilibrium state-contingent prices. An important part of their theorizing was how a benevolent government optimally uses its knowledge of equilibrium private sector decision rules to manipulate state-contingent prices and associated *ex post* returns on its state-contingent debt. Our simplified Lucas-Stokey

the models be as close as possible to each other by setting state-contingent prices in our Lucas-Stokey model so that the return on risk-free one-period debt is the same as it is in the Barro model.

In both models, a government seeks to minimize the intertemporal loss functional

$$L(\{T_t\}_{t=0}^{\infty}) = E\left[\sum_{t=0}^{\infty} \beta^t \ell(T_t)\right] |z_0 \tag{27.1}$$

where T_t is total tax collections at time t, $\ell(T_t) = T_t^2$, $\beta \in (0, 1)$ is a discount factor, and $E[\cdot|z_0]$, is a mathematical expectation conditional on a vector z_0 of information about future government expenditures that is available at time 0. Government expenditures $\{G_t\}_{t=0}^{\infty}$ are a scalar stochastic process that is a function of a Markov state z_t so that

$$G_t = G(z_t) \tag{27.2}$$

$$z_{t+1} \sim \phi(z_{t+1}|z_t) \tag{27.3}$$

where $\phi(z_{t+1}|z_t)$ is a Markov transition probability distribution defined on the time invariant state-space Z. In both models, an important role is played by the conditional expectation of the present value of future government expenditures PVG_t defined as

$$PVG_t = E\left[\sum_{j=0}^{\infty} \beta^t G_{t+j}\right] |z_t \tag{27.4}$$

$$= H(z_t) \tag{27.5}$$

where the function $H(z_t)$ satisfies the functional equation

$$H(z_t) = G(z_t) + \beta \int H(z_{t+1})\phi(z_{t+1}|z_t)dz_{t+1}$$

$$= G(z_t) + \beta E[H(z_{t+1})|z_t]. \tag{27.6}$$

Our two models share the loss function (27.1) and are distinguished only by the budget constraints that confront the government at times $t \geq 0$. In our version of the Barro (1979) model, the government faces

$$T_t + a_t = R^{-1}a_{t+1} + G_t \tag{27.7}$$

where R is a gross rate of interest on one-period risk-free loans that following Barro we assume is constant over time and equal to β^{-1}. Here a_t is a risk free claim on time t goods that the government purchased at time $t - 1$ for $t \geq 1$ or was endowed with at time $t = 0$. At time t, the government purchases risk-free claims a_{t+1} of time $t + 1$ goods. Thus, government risk-free *debt* coming into period t is $-a_t$.

---

model completely shuts down that interest-rate manipulation motive and instead focuses on how the government takes advantage of the opportunity to trade securities whose payoffs are contingent on realizations of the government expenditure process.

In our simplified Lucas and Stokey (1983) model, at time $t \geq 1$ the government faces the budget constraint

$$T_t + a_{t-1}(z_t) = G_t + \int q_t(z_{t+1}|z_t)a_t(z_{t+1})dz_{t+1} \tag{27.8}$$

where the density $a_{t-1}(z_t)$ represents a claim on time t goods contingent on the time t Markov state z_t that the government purchased at $t-1$ and $q_t(z_{t+1}|z_t)$ is a pricing kernel that encodes a complete list of time t prices of one-period ahead Arrow securities. We assume that the pricing kernel is time-invariant and given by

$$q_t(z_{t+1}|z_t) = \beta\phi(z_{t+1}|z_t) \tag{27.9}$$

so that for $t \geq 1$ budget constraint (27.8) becomes

$$T_t + a_{t-1}(z_t) = G_t + \beta E[a_{t+1}|z_t] \tag{27.10}$$

and at time 0 is

$$T_0 + a_0 = G_0 + \beta E[a_1|z_0], \tag{27.11}$$

where a_0 is an exogenous endowment of claims on time 0 goods owned by the government. Expression (27.9) for the pricing kernel tells how state-contingent prices discount the future through β and discount unlikely events through the conditional probability density $\phi(z_{t+1}|z_t)$.

The *ex post* gross return on the government's asset portfolio $a_t(z_{t+1})$, $z_{t+1} \in Z$ as a function of the realized time $t+1$ Markov state z_{t+1} is

$$R_t(z_{t+1}|z_t) = \frac{a_t(z_{t+1})}{\beta E(a_t(z_{t+1})|z_t)}. \tag{27.12}$$

The conditional expectation of the return on the government portfolio is then

$$E R_t(z_{t+1}|z_t)|z_t = \beta^{-1}, \tag{27.13}$$

which equals the one-period return on a risk-free claim on time $t+1$ output in the Barro model.

27.2.1 Optimal tax-borrowing plan: Barro's model

For Barro's model, a decision rule for collecting taxes that minimizes loss criterion (27.1) subject to the sequence of government budget constraints (27.7) is the following function of z_t and a_t

$$T_t = (1-\beta)[PVG_t + a_t]$$
$$= (1-\beta)[H(z_t) + a_t] \tag{27.14}$$

that has the implication that tax collections follow a random walk

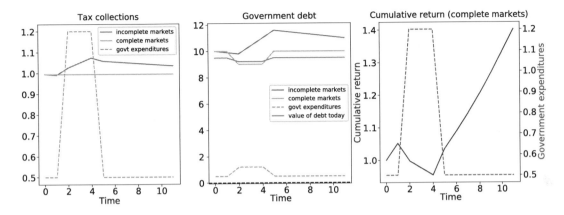

FIGURE 27.1

Tax smoothing in complete and incomplete markets economies.

$$ET_{t+1}|z_t = T_t \tag{27.15}$$

and that government assets a_t are a unit root process that is cointegrated with government assets.[6]

27.2.2 Optimal tax-borrowing plan: Lucas and Stokey's model

For our version of the Lucas-Stokey model, a decision rule for tax collections that minimizes criterion (27.1) subject to the sequence of budget constraints (27.8) completely smooths tax collections across time and states so that

$$T_t = T_0 \tag{27.16}$$

where a state-contingent asset-purchasing strategy supports this tax collection policy, namely,

$$a_{t-1}(z_t) = a(z_t, T_0) \equiv H(z_t) - \frac{1}{1-\beta}T_0. \tag{27.17}$$

27.2.2.1 Two state Markov example

Let's do an example in which z follows a two-state Markov chain in which state 1 denotes peace and state 2 denotes war. Let $G(1) = .5$, $G(2) = 1.2$, $P = \begin{bmatrix} .9 & .1 \\ .6 & .4 \end{bmatrix}$, and $\beta = .96$. *Ex post* returns on the government portfolio are described by a matrix $R = \begin{bmatrix} 1.052 & .949 \\ 1.084 & .977 \end{bmatrix}$ in which $R_{i,j}$ denotes the return when $s_{t+1} = j$ and $s_t = i$. Fig. 27.1 shows outcomes for a realization of Markov states of two peace

---

[6] See Ljungqvist and Sargent (2018, ch. 2) for analogous properties of a consumption-smoothing model that is isomorphic to the tax smoothing model.

times followed by a three year war that commences in period 2 and ends after period 5 and is not followed by a subsequent war during the following periods in the sample. The orange (light gray in print version) line in the middle panel depicts $a_{t-1}(z_t)$ realized along the sample path, while the red (mid gray in print version) line depicts $\beta E[a_t(z_{t+1})|z_t]$, today's value of the government's portfolio of Arrow securities that will pay off tomorrow. The panel on the right shows cumulative *ex post* gross returns on the government's portfolio of debts in our Lucas-Stokey model along a sample path. It displays negative gross returns during the war and positive gross returns during peace time.

27.2.2.2 Continuous state Markov example

Here we let the Markov state z_t be continuous and consist of $z_t = \begin{bmatrix} g_{1t} & g_{2t} \end{bmatrix}'$ where g_{1t} follows a random walk and g_{2t} is white noise:

$$G_t = g_{1t} + g_{2t} \tag{27.18}$$

where

$$
\begin{aligned}
g_{1,t+1} &= g_{1t} + \sigma_1 w_{1,t+1} \\
g_{2,t+1} &= \sigma_2 w_{2,t+1}
\end{aligned}
\tag{27.19}
$$

where $w_{t+1} = \begin{bmatrix} w_{1,t+1} & w_{2,t+1} \end{bmatrix}' \sim \mathcal{N}(0, I)$. Thus, the shock $\sigma_1 w_{1,t+1}$ has permanent effects on government expenditures while the shock $\sigma_2 w_{2,t+1}$ has purely transitory effects. What do these government expenditure shocks do to tax collections and government debt according to our two benchmark models? For our Barro model, the optimal decision rules imply

$$
\begin{aligned}
T_{t+1} - T_t &= \sigma_1 w_{1,t+1} + (1 - \beta)\sigma_2 w_{2,t+1} \\
a_{t+1} - a_t &= -\sigma_2 w_{2,t+1}
\end{aligned}
\tag{27.20}
$$

so that a permanent expenditure shock $\sigma_1 w_{1,t+1}$ leads to a permanent increase in tax collections by the amount of the shock and no increase in government debt, while a purely temporary shock $\sigma_2 w_{t+1}$ leads to a permanent increase in government debt in the amount of the shock and a permanent increase in tax collections of $(1 - \beta)$ times the amount of the shock, an increase that is just sufficient permanently to service the increase in interest payments on the government debt.

These outcomes indicate how the Barro model confirms Treasury Secretary Albert Gallatin's 1807 prescription that in the event of a war, tax rates should be set to ...

> provide a revenue at least equal to the annual expenses on a peace establishment, the interest on the existing debt, and the interest on the loans which may be raised ... losses and privations caused by war should not be aggravated by taxes beyond what is strictly necessary.[7]

In the "pure Gallatin" case that the surge in government expenditures is thought to be temporary (a war is forecast to be short), the increase in government spending is nearly all financed by borrowing with taxes increasing by just enough to cover the interest expenses on new debt. In Fig. 27.2, we plot paths of taxes and debt in response to one-time purely transitory 50% increase in government spending. Most of the increase in government spending is absorbed through a permanent increase in debt, while the remaining part of the increase is absorbed through a permanent increase in taxes.

---

[7] See page 360 of Gallatin (1837).

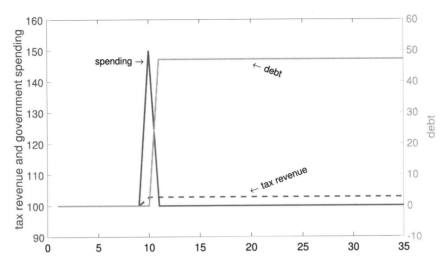

FIGURE 27.2

The response of taxes and debt to a temporary increase in government spending in the Gallatin-Barro model.

For our Lucas-Stokey model, tax collections are completely smoothed across time and Markov states, so $T_t = T_0$ for all $t \geq 0$. Calculating the fixed point of functional equation (27.6) yields the linear function

$$H(z_t) = (1 - \beta)^{-1} g_{1t} + g_{2t}$$

so that the government's optimal portfolio of state-contingent assets is

$$a_{t-1}(z_t) = (1 - \beta)^{-1} g_{1t} + g_{2t} - \frac{1}{1 - \beta} T_0$$

$$= (1 - \beta)^{-1} (g_{1,t-1} + \sigma w_{1,t}) + \sigma_2 w_{2t} \qquad (27.21)$$

The right side of the second line is a compact description of the shock-contingent date $t + 1$ payoffs that at time t the government purchases to insure itself against the two fiscal shocks.

27.2.3 U.S. government debt: risk-free or state-contingent?

In sections 27.4 and 27.5 below, we will use patterns presented in our benchmark models as guides for organizing and interpreting observed spending, taxes, debt, and *ex post* returns during and after eight wars. Most debt issued by the U.S. Treasury was not explicitly state-contingent debt.[8] But by accepting or engineering changes in price levels, capital tax rates, and interest rates, a government can deliver *ex post* state-contingent returns on its debt. Until World War II, the U.S. government encouraged

---

[8] Call and exchange options are notable explicit state-contingencies. Sections 27.6.3 and 27.6.5 describe call options in Civil War era 5-20 bonds and exchange options in the early Liberty Loans issued during World War I.

money- and bond-holding in the face of wartime inflations by promising postwar deflations. Bordo and Kydland (1995) argued that, as administered between 1880 and 1914, the gold standard facilitated making returns on a government's debt state-contingent. During calm periods, governments on the gold standard pegged their currencies to gold. But during a wartime fiscal emergency, gold convertibility could be suspended with the understanding that after the war convertibility at the original par would be resumed. During a war, a government could issue paper money and sell bonds to meet temporary spending demands, generating wartime inflation. But to do that, a government had to sustain prospects that it would preside over a postwar deflation that would allow it eventually to redeem those wartime debts in gold.

27.3 Government budget constraint

In the section 27.2 benchmark models, a government issues only one-period interest bearing debt. To connect those models with the full range of maturities of U.S. Treasury securities and the monetary base, let $B_{t-1} = \sum_{j=1}^{n} B_{t-1}^{j}$ be the total nominal value of interest bearing government debt at $t-1$, where B_{t-1}^{j} is the nominal value of zero coupon bonds of maturity j at $t-1$. The government budget constraint at time t is

$$B_t = B_{t-1} + r_{t-1,t} B_{t-1} + G_t - T_t - (M_t - M_{t-1}) \qquad (27.22)$$

where G_t is the dollar value of government purchases, T_t is the dollar value of taxes net of transfers, and M_t is the stock of non-interest bearing government debt called base money. Let $r_{t-1,t}^{j}$ be the net *nominal* return between $t-1$ and t on nominal zero-coupon bonds of maturity j, so the equality

$$\sum_{j=1}^{n} r_{t-1,t}^{j} B_{t-1}^{j} = r_{t-1,t} \sum_{j=1}^{n} B_{t-1}^{j} \qquad (27.23)$$

implicitly defines the value-weighted net nominal return $r_{t-1,t}$ on interest-bearing nominal government bonds from $t-1$ to t. As we explain in Appendix A, the U.S. Treasury's series *Interest Expense on the Debt Outstanding* is an accounting measure, not a value-weighted holding period return on the debt. Consistent with our theory, in our calculations we use the value-weighted holding period return on the portfolio of the Treasury debt to record the returns to bondholders.

To align our measurement of debt to theory, we make two adjustments to the U.S. Treasury's record of total public debt outstanding. First, we net out holdings by the Federal Reserve and Government Agencies and Trust Funds. Thus, we include only government debt held by private investors. In Fig. 27.3, we decompose the par value of the total public debt outstanding as a share of GDP from 1776 to 2018 into these three ownership classes. Prior to World War I, nearly all debt was held by private investors. At the end of 2018, of the nearly $22 trillion (measured at its par value) in total debt outstanding, 26% was held in government accounts and trust funds and 10% was held by the Federal Reserve. Second, we measure Treasury debt by its market value rather than its par value. In Appendix A we explain how the market value of the government debt is related to its par value. The market value takes into account differences between interest rates and coupon rates at the time the debt

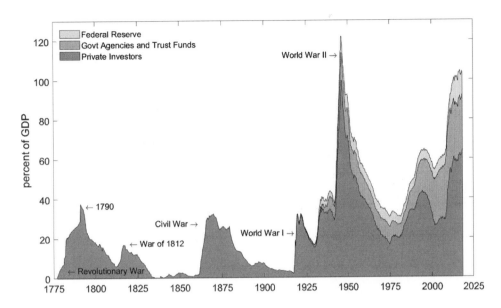

FIGURE 27.3

Par value of U.S. treasury debt by ownership as a percent of GDP: 1776 to 2018.

is issued as well as changes in interest rates and repayment probabilities since the debt was issued; it answers the question: how much would the government pay if it were to repurchase the entire portfolio of privately-held debt at current market prices? In Fig. 27.4, we plot the par value of the debt in red (mid gray in print version) and market value of the debt in blue (dark gray in print version) from 1776 to 2018. While the two series track each other closely over time, each series has exceeded the other at various times.

27.3.1 Decomposing wartime changes in revenue

Dividing each term in Eq. (27.22) by nominal GDP, Y_t, and rearranging terms yields

$$\frac{G_t}{Y_t} + r_{t-1,t}\frac{B_{t-1}}{Y_{t-1}} = \frac{T_t}{Y_t} + \left(\frac{B_t}{Y_t} - \frac{B_{t-1}}{Y_{t-1}}\right) + \frac{M_t - M_{t-1}}{Y_t} + g_{t-1,t}\frac{B_{t-1}}{Y_{t-1}}$$
$$+ \pi_{t-1,t}\frac{B_{t-1}}{Y_{t-1}} + r_{t-1,t}(\pi_{t-1,t} + g_{t-1,t})\frac{B_{t-1}}{Y_{t-1}} \quad (27.24)$$

where $g_{t-1,t}$ denotes the growth rate of real GDP, and $\pi_{t-1,t}$ denotes the inflation rate. The two terms on the left side are government purchases and transfers as a share of GDP and interest payments on government debt as a share of GDP, respectively. The first three terms on the right side record sources of government revenue as shares of GDP: taxes, new borrowing, and money creation. The next two terms record the diminution of the debt/GDP ratio due to real GDP growth and inflation. The final term is a cross-term.

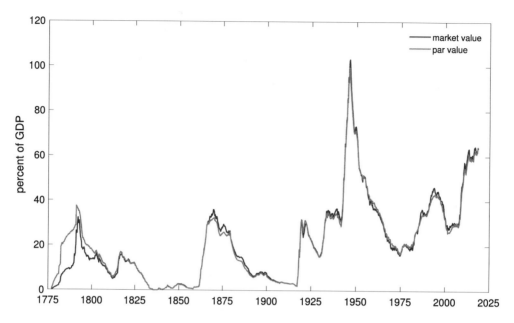

FIGURE 27.4

Par value and market value of U.S. treasury debt held by private investors as a percent of GDP: 1776 to 2018.

Consider a "peacetime baseline" version of Eq. (27.24):

$$
\left(\frac{G}{Y}\right)^{base} + \left(r_{-1,0}\frac{B_{-1}}{Y_{-1}}\right)^{base} = \left(\frac{T}{Y}\right)^{base} + \left(\frac{B}{Y} - \frac{B_{-1}}{Y_{-1}}\right)^{base} + \left(\frac{M - M_{-1}}{Y_{-1}}\right)^{base}
$$

$$
+ \left(g_{-1,0}\frac{B_{-1}}{Y_{-1}}\right)^{base} + \left(\pi_{-1,0}\frac{B_{-1}}{Y_{-1}}\right)^{base}
$$

$$
+ \left(r_{-1,0}(\pi_{-1,0} + g_{-1,0})\frac{B_{-1}}{Y_{-1}}\right)^{base}. \tag{27.25}
$$

Subtracting Eq. (27.25) from Eq. (27.24):

$$
\frac{G_t}{Y_t} - \left(\frac{G}{Y}\right)^{base} + \left[r_{t-1,t}\frac{B_{t-1}}{Y_{t-1}} - \left(r_{-1,0}\frac{B_{-1}}{Y_{-1}}\right)^{base}\right] = \left[\frac{T_t}{Y_t} - \left(\frac{T}{Y}\right)^{base}\right]
$$

$$
+ \left[\left(\frac{B_t}{Y_t} - \frac{B_{t-1}}{Y_{t-1}}\right) - \left(\frac{B}{Y} - \frac{B_{-1}}{Y_{-1}}\right)^{base}\right]
$$

$$
+ \left[\frac{M_t - M_{t-1}}{Y_t} - \left(\frac{M - M_{-1}}{Y_{-1}}\right)^{base}\right]
$$

$$+ \left[g_{t-1,t} \frac{B_{t-1}}{Y_{t-1}} - \left(g_{-1,0} \frac{B_{-1}}{Y_{-1}} \right)^{base} \right] + \left[\pi_{t-1,t} \frac{B_{t-1}}{Y_{t-1}} - \left(\pi_{-1,0} \frac{B_{-1}}{Y_{-1}} \right)^{base} \right]$$

$$+ \left[r_{t-1,t}(\pi_{t-1,t} + g_{t-1,t}) \frac{B_{t-1}}{Y_{t-1}} - \left(r_{-1,0}(\pi_{-1,0} + g_{-1,0}) \frac{B_{-1}}{Y_{-1}} \right)^{base} \right]. \quad (27.26)$$

For each war, we sum Eq. (27.26) from the beginning to the end of a war.

$$\underbrace{\sum_{t=T_1}^{T_2} \left[\frac{G_t}{Y_t} - \left(\frac{G}{Y} \right)^{base} \right]}_{\text{government spending}} + \underbrace{\sum_{t=T_1}^{T_2} \left[r_{t-1,t} \frac{B_{t-1}}{Y_{t-1}} - \left(r_{-1,0} \frac{B_{-1}}{Y_{-1}} \right)^{base} \right]}_{\text{nominal return on debt}} = \underbrace{\sum_{t=T_1}^{T_2} \left[\frac{T_t}{Y_t} - \left(\frac{T}{Y} \right)^{base} \right]}_{\text{explicit tax revenue}}$$

$$+ \underbrace{\sum_{t=T_1}^{T_2} \left[\left(\frac{B_t}{Y_t} - \frac{B_{t-1}}{Y_{t-1}} \right) - \left(\frac{B}{Y} - \frac{B_{-1}}{Y_{-1}} \right)^{base} \right]}_{\text{interest-bearing debt growth}}$$

$$+ \underbrace{\sum_{t=T_1}^{T_2} \left[\frac{M_t - M_{t-1}}{Y_t} - \left(\frac{M - M_{-1}}{Y_{-1}} \right)^{base} \right]}_{\text{money growth}}$$

$$+ \underbrace{\sum_{t=T_1}^{T_2} \left[g_{t-1,t} \frac{B_{t-1}}{Y_{t-1}} - \left(g_{-1,0} \frac{B_{-1}}{Y_{-1}} \right)^{base} \right]}_{\text{debt dilution via real GDP growth}}$$

$$+ \underbrace{\sum_{t=T_1}^{T_2} \left[\pi_{t-1,t} \frac{B_{t-1}}{Y_{t-1}} - \left(\pi_{-1,0} \frac{B_{-1}}{Y_{-1}} \right)^{base} \right]}_{\text{debt default via inflation}}$$

$$+ \underbrace{\sum_{t=T_1}^{T_2} \left[r_{t-1,t}(\pi_{t-1,t} + g_{t-1,t}) \frac{B_{t-1}}{Y_{t-1}} - \left(r_{-1,0}(\pi_{-1,0} + g_{-1,0}) \frac{B_{-1}}{Y_{-1}} \right)^{base} \right]}_{\text{cross-term}}$$

$$(27.27)$$

where T_1 is the first year of the war or the first year of U.S. involvement, and T_2 is the final year of the war.

Table 27.1 reports the decomposition. In columns (1) and (2) of Table 27.1, we report spending on the left side of Eq. (27.27). In columns (4) and (5), we report the wartime change in tax revenue and debt relative to the prewar baseline. In columns (6)-(8), we report wartime changes in money growth, real GDP growth, and inflation.[9] The final two columns report changes in the cross term and a sum of residuals. For each war, entries in the first row are percents of GDP, and values in columns (4)-(10) sum to column (3). The units are percents of GDP and we sum over years; so, for example, the total cost of the Civil War over four years was 33% of a single year's GDP. The numbers in the second row are percentages of the sum of war-related government spending and returns to bondholders (column (3)) accounted for by each term on the right hand side of Eq. (27.27).

Consider columns (4) and (5). If the net real interest rate r is 6% (so $\beta = 1/1.06$ in the section 27.2 benchmark models), and wartime spending shocks are purely temporary, then the policies in Eqs. (27.20) imply that a government that engages in Gallatin-Barro tax smoothing will finance 94% of its war costs with debt and the remaining 6% with taxes. The Barro model also implies that the share of a government spending shock that is absorbed by taxes increases with the persistence of the shock. For each war, in the second row of columns (4), (5), and (6) we report percentages of total war costs (column (3)) funded by taxes, debt, and money creation. These percentages are shaded light blue (light gray in print version). Only the decomposition for the Civil War is in line with Gallatin-Barro tax smoothing of a purely temporary expenditure shock: 6.8% from increased taxation, and 91% altogether from increased debt, money growth, and inflation.

The table reveals the striking pattern that the share of the war costs financed with taxes increased from -32.9% in the War of 1812 to 40.8% in the Vietnam War.[10] Accordingly, the share financed with debt decreased from 148.5% in the War of 1812 to 12.9% in the Vietnam War. The exception to these patterns was the Spanish-American War, the shortest (fighting lasted only three months) and least costly of the eight wars.

If a government uses Lucas and Stokey tax smoothing, then all unexpected increases in government spending should be absorbed by wartime decreases in returns to government creditors. Column (2) reports the increase in nominal payments to bondholders. Column (8) reports the increase in inflation. With the exception of the Mexican War and the Korean War, the contribution of inflation is greater than the contribution of the nominal return on the debt, consistent with bond holders earning negative wartime real returns.

During World War II, the Treasury and the Federal Reserve pegged the yield curve. While government creditors received positive nominal returns during the war, those returns were set so that wartime real returns were *below* those that government creditors received during the five years prior to the war.

Clark (1931), Goldin (1980), Edelstein (2000), Rockoff (2012), and Zielinski (2016) present alternative decompositions of U.S. war finances. Our accounts differ from theirs in two ways. First, these previous authors attributed increases in specific items in the federal government's budget to the war; we instead attribute to the war all deviations from a prior trend of components of the government budget constraint. During wars, expenditures on non-military items also increased. Second, we take into

---

[9] During the War of 1812 and the Mexican War we assume that the federal government issued no fiat currency. For the War of 1812, we treat U.S. Treasury Notes as interest bearing debt rather than currency. Though these notes were never declared legal tender, they had several money-like attributes such as small denominations and a small-rectangular shape. In January 1812, Albert Gallatin wrote to Congress, "Treasury notes, bearing interest, might to a certain extent be issued, and to that extent diminish the amount to be directly borrowed. The advantage they would have would result from their becoming a part of the circulating medium, and taking, to a certain degree, the place of bank-notes."

[10] During the 19th century, the main source of tax revenue was tariffs. See Fig. 27.7. During both of these wars, tariff revenue as a share of GDP fell. During the War of 1812, the U.S. went to war against its primary trading partner. During the Mexican War, the "Walker tariff" of 1846 lowered import duties across a wide range of goods.

Table 27.1 Decomposition of wartime revenue from Eq. (27.27).

War / Start - End (U.S. entry -)	(1) government spending	(2) return on debt	(3) (1)+(2)	(4) tax revenue	(5) debt growth	(6) money growth	(7) GDP growth	(8) inflation	(9) cross term	(10) residual
War of 1812										
1812:6 - 1815:2	7.34	-0.20	7.14	-2.35	10.60	0.00	-0.16	0.06	-0.39	-0.62
				-32.9	148.5	0.0	-2.2	0.8	-5.5	-8.7
Mexican War										
1846:5 - 1848:2	2.26	0.20	2.47	-0.06	2.72	0.00	-0.06	-0.01	-0.00	-0.12
				-2.4	110.4	0.0	-2.5	-0.5	-0.1	-4.8
Civil War (Union)										
1861:4 - 1865:4	31.04	2.10	33.14	2.26	19.74	6.49	1.08	3.95	0.40	-0.77
				6.8	59.6	19.6	3.2	11.9	1.2	-2.3
Spanish-American War										
1898:4 - 1898:8	0.78	0.11	0.90	0.45	-0.26	0.07	0.67	0.13	0.03	-0.18
				50.0	-28.9	7.3	74.3	14.6	3.2	-20.4
World War I										
1914:7 - 1918:11	36.11	0.43	36.54	6.83	26.76	3.41	0.52	1.22	0.03	-2.24
				18.7	73.2	9.3	1.4	3.4	0.1	-6.1
(1917:4 -)	36.93	0.30	37.23	7.76	27.79	2.59	0.05	0.76	0.00	-1.73
				20.8	74.6	7.0	0.1	2.1	0.0	-4.6
World War II										
1939:9 - 1945:8	129.50	0.10	129.60	49.91	54.78	11.32	15.42	9.62	0.26	-11.71
				38.5	42.3	8.7	11.9	7.4	0.2	-9.0
(1941:12 -)	116.48	2.00	118.48	35.80	54.53	11.96	8.99	6.05	0.43	0.71
				30.2	46.0	10.1	7.6	5.1	0.4	0.6
Korean War										
1950:6 - 1953:6	15.43	-0.71	14.73	5.42	4.17	2.53	10.99	-10.12	0.05	1.70
				36.8	28.3	17.2	74.6	-68.7	0.3	11.5
Vietnam War										
1964:8 - 1973:6	5.53	-2.13	3.41	1.39	0.44	-0.60	-5.55	3.91	0.19	3.63
				40.8	12.9	-17.8	-163.0	114.9	5.7	106.5

account GDP growth and inflation. For some wars, our results align with the calculations in those previous studies. For example, for World War I, Goldin (1980, Table 1, p. 938) finds that the total cost of the war was 41% of one year of GNP, and that taxes financed 24% of the cost while debt and money creation financed the remaining 76%; we estimate that the cost was 37% of one year of GDP, and that taxes financed 21% and debt and money growth financed 82% of the cost.

For four other wars, the differences highlight the distinction between the two methodologies.

- For the War of 1812, Goldin (1980) finds that 21% of the war was financed by taxes while we find that since tax revenue fell relative the peacetime baseline, making our estimate of the contribution from taxes negative.
- For World War II, we find that 11.5% of the war was "paid for" through real GDP growth and devaluation of the debt through inflation.
- For the Korean War, Goldin (1980), Ohanian (1997), Edelstein (2000), and Rockoff (2012) estimate that, consistent with President Truman's stated policy, the war was 100% tax financed. Indeed, the quantity of debt outstanding did remain virtually unchanged during that war. Further President Truman ran a balanced budget during the Korean War, with taxes rising sufficiently to cover the increase in spending. But prior to the war, the government ran a primary *surplus* and was paying down the debt incurred during World War II. The budget constraint decomposition reported in Table 27.1 and the spending and revenue prewar averages in Table 27.3 records that Truman's financing of the Korean War eliminated the primary surplus and deferred the post-World War II paydown of the debt. We compute that debt and money growth financed 45.5% of the costs because the Korean War halted this debt paydown. That is, although the debt/GDP ratio fell during the war, this ratio was higher in 1954 than it would have been had the war not occurred.
- Edelstein (2000) argues that the Vietnam War was paid in part by a decrease in non-defense spending. Our decomposition is not designed to capture this.

27.3.2 Decomposing postwar changes in the debt/GDP ratio

By rearranging Eq. (27.24), we decompose the evolution of the interest-bearing debt/GDP ratio into contributions made by nominal returns paid on Treasury securities, GDP growth, inflation, a cross-term, the primary deficit, and seignorage.

$$
\begin{aligned}
\frac{B_t}{Y_t} - \frac{B_{t-1}}{Y_{t-1}} = {} & r_{t-1,t}\frac{B_{t-1}}{Y_{t-1}} - g_{t-1,t}\frac{B_{t-1}}{Y_{t-1}} - \pi_{t-1,t}\frac{B_{t-1}}{Y_{t-1}} \\
& - r_{t-1,t}(\pi_{t-1,t} + g_{t-1,t})\frac{B_{t-1}}{Y_{t-1}} + \frac{G_t - T_t}{Y_t} - \frac{M_t - M_{t-1}}{Y_t}
\end{aligned}
\tag{27.28}
$$

In columns (1) - (3) of Table 27.2 we report the change in the debt-GDP ratio over the fifteen year period following the end of the each war.[11] For each war, in columns (4) - (10) of the first row, we report components attributable to (i) nominal interest payments, (ii) GDP growth, (iii) inflation, (iv) the primary deficit, (v) the cross-term, (vi) money growth, and (vii) a residual. Hence the elements

---

[11] Because our data begin in 1790, in the first row of Table 27.2 we include the 15-year period after Treasury Secretary Hamilton's refunding of the Revolutionary War debt.

Table 27.2 Decomposition of post-war changes to the debt/GDP ratio from Eq. (27.28).

War postwar period	100 × Debt/GDP			Contributions						
	(1) end of war	(2) 15 years postwar	(3) change	(4) nominal returns	(5) real GDP growth	(6) inflation	(7) primary deficit	(8) cross term	(9) seigniorage	(10) residual
War for Independence										
1791-1806	33.3	9.6	-23.8	11.3 / 47	-15.4 / -65	-7.6 / -32	-17.3 / -73	-1.0 / -4	— / —	6.3 / 26
War of 1812										
1815-1830	11.6	3.4	-8.2	10.5 / 128	-5.6 / -68	4.9 / 60	-19.4 / -237	0.1 / 1	— / —	1.3 / 16
Mexican War										
1848-1860†	2.7	1.2	-1.5	0.8 / 53	-0.9 / -60	-0.1 / -7	-1.5 / -100	-0.1 / -7	— / —	0.3 / 20
Civil War (Union)										
1865-1880	22.1	15.6	-6.5	21.4 / 329	-14.5 / -223	13.5 / 208	-29.5 / -454	0.1 / 2	1.2 / 18	1.3 / 20
Spanish-American War										
1898-1913	4.6	2.2	-2.4	0.9 / 38	-1.2 / -50	-1.1 / -46	-1.9 / -79	-0.1 / -4	0.8 / 33	0.1 / 4
World War I										
1919-1929‡	28.6	20.2	-8.4	12.5 / 149	-6.4 / -76	2.4 / 29	-20.3 / -242	0.3 / 4	2.0 / 24	1.0 / 12
World War II										
1945-1960	90.1	35.7	-54.4	14.3 / 26	-15.8 / -29	-38.9 / -71	-13.0 / -24	-0.6 / -1	-0.3 / -1	-0.2 / 0
Korean War										
1953-1968	49.9	21.8	-28.1	14.0 / 50	-20.3 / -72	-10.8 / -38	4.0 / 14	-0.8 / -3	-5.8 / -21	-8.5 / -30
Vietnam War										
1973-1988	16.4	34.7	+18.3	32.3 / 177	-12.2 / -67	-19.2 / -105	19.7 / 108	-2.7 / -15	-6.0 / -33	6.3 / 35

in columns (4) - (10) sum to column (3). Entries in the second row are percentages changes in the debt/GDP ratio accounted for by each component.

Except for Vietnam, the federal government reduced the debt/GDP ratio during the 12-15 year postwar period after every war, contrary to recommendations of the Gallatin-Barro and Lucas-Stokey models.

For each war, we highlight in light blue (light gray in print version) the largest contribution, in absolute value. For the first six wars, from the War for Independence to World War I, the value of the U.S. dollar was set by a bimetallic or gold standard. We see that after each of these wars, the largest forces *reducing* the debt/GDP ratio were primary surpluses followed by real GDP growth. Positive nominal returns to bondholders dampened these reductions, while changes in the price level went both ways. After the 1790 refunding of the War for Independence debt, the Mexican War, and the Spanish-American War, inflation helped diminish the value of the debt relative to GDP. But after the War of 1812, the Civil War, and World War I – three wars that brought large inflations, postwar deflations increased values of debt relative to GDP and delivered high real returns to government creditors.[12]

Relative contributions changed during the three most recent wars.[13] In contrast to the pre-World War II period, for World War II, the Korean War and the Vietnam War, primary surpluses were not the largest force pushing down the debt/GDP ratio postbellum, inflation, and real GDP growth having been more important. In particular, in the 24 months after the lifting of the World War II price controls in June 1846, the price level rose 46%, effectively inflating away nearly half the value of the debt.[14]

In the years following the Korean and Vietnam Wars, the government ran primary deficits that helped increase the debt/GDP ratio. After the Korean War, these modest deficits were more than offset by inflation and GDP growth so that the debt/GDP ratio declined. In the early 1980s Fed Chairman Paul Volker's conquest of the persistent 1970s inflation generated high returns to government bondholders that helped propel the debt/GDP ratio higher in the post-Vietnam period.

27.4 Expenditures and tax revenue

In the section 27.2 benchmark models, responses of tax collections and government debt to an unanticipated increase in government spending depend on the persistence of the government spending process. In the Barro model, a permanent shock is fully tax financed while a purely temporary shock is largely debt financed. See Eqs. (27.20). In our version of a Lucas and Stokey model, permanent shocks to government spending generate much larger (i.e., by a factor of $(1 - \beta)^{-1}$) capital gains and losses to government bondholders than do purely transitory shocks. See Eqs. (27.21).

In Fig. 27.5, we plot U.S. federal government receipts and expenditures from 1775 to 2018. For the Civil War, World War I, and World War II, we see that during the war, government spending rose while taxes increased much less. After the wars, government spending fell while tax revenues remained elevated, so that the government ran a primary surplus for many years. These patterns are consistent

---

[12] See Fig. 27.10 later in this paper for evidence of the sharp price level increases during these three wars and Hall and Sargent (2019, pp. 34-38) for an analysis of the post-World War I debt paydown.

[13] Hall and Sargent (2011) provides a more complete accounting of the contributions to the evolution of the debt/GDP ratio made by inflation, growth, and nominal returns paid on debts of different maturities for the post-World War II period.

[14] See Fig. 27.10f below.

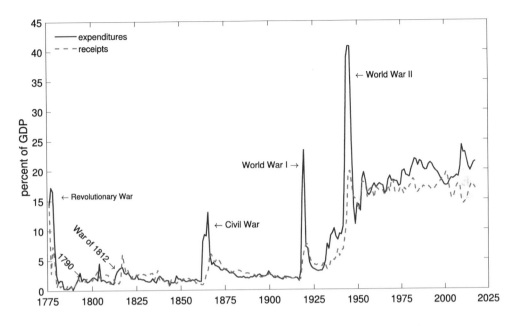

FIGURE 27.5

U.S. federal government expenditures and receipts: 1775 to 2018.

with the optimal tax-smoothing response to a *temporary* government spending shock illustrated in Fig. 27.2. However, large U.S. wars have been followed by enduring changes in the size and composition of government spending and taxation. These three wars were followed by permanent rises in federal expenditures as fractions of GDP.[15]

To view the long-run impact of wars on spending in more detail, Figs. 27.6 and 27.8 plot expenditure categories defined by the federal government. In Fig. 27.6, federal spending from 1791 to 1940 is the sum of the categories Civil, Pensions, and War+Navy.[16] Fig. 27.8 splits spending into four categories: national defense, human resources, physical resources, and other.[17] Fig. 27.6 reveals that spending stayed higher after the War of 1812, the Civil War, and World War I, but the categories that increased differed. As a share of GDP, spending on the military remained permanently higher after the War of 1812. After the Civil War, there was a persistent increase in pension payments to Union veterans and their families, while after World War I, it was the Civil category, which included non-transfer domestic

---

[15] Rothbard (2017, chs. 12-13) describes what he thinks were forces contributing to this outcome after World War I.

[16] The category Civil includes spending on the Treasury-defined category, Indians.

[17] As defined by the OMB, Human Resources include Education, Training, Employment, and Social Services, Health Medicare, Income Security, Social Security, and Veterans Benefits; Physical Resources include Energy, Natural Resources and Environment, Commerce and Housing Credit, Transportation and Community and Regional Development; Other includes International Affairs General Science, Space, and Technology, Agriculture, Administration of Justice, and General Government.

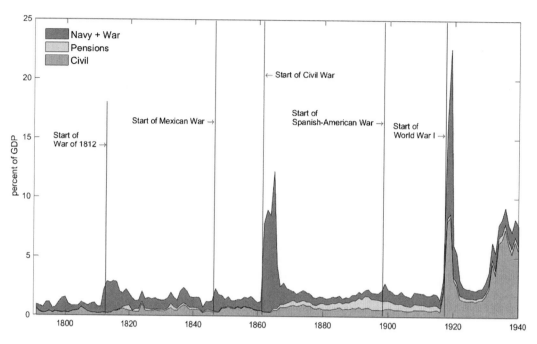

FIGURE 27.6

Composition of federal expenditures: 1791 to 1940.

spending, that stayed permanently higher.[18] Comparing Figs. 27.6 and 27.8 illustrates the enormous and permanent increase in government spending that occurred during World War II as government spending rose from under 10% of GDP before the war to 20% of GDP after the war.

In Figs. 27.7 and 27.9, we decompose federal tax revenue into various government defined categories. Prior to the Civil War, despite periodic attempts to diversify its revenue stream, the Treasury's primary revenue source was customs (i.e., tariff) revenue. During the Civil War, the federal government introduced a new set of internal taxes, including a personal income tax. Although many internal taxes (including the income tax) were removed shortly after the war, during the 50 years between the Civil War and World War I, Treasury revenue was roughly evenly split between customs and internal revenue. Principal sources of these internal revenue were taxes on liquor and tobacco. Internal revenue, especially from the income tax, surged during the Civil War, World War I, and World War II. Since the re-introduction of the income tax in 1914 and rises in income tax rates during World War I, internal revenues have been the primary sources of revenue for the Treasury. The Revenue Act of 1942, enacted shortly after the U.S. entered World War II, created today's system of personal and corporate income taxes.

---

[18] Between 1917 and 1922, the federal government advanced $9.5 billion to 11 Allied countries. Although at the time the Treasury viewed these advances as loans, they were recorded as Civil expenditures. As Hall and Sargent (2019) report, by the early 1930s most of these foreign loans became gifts.

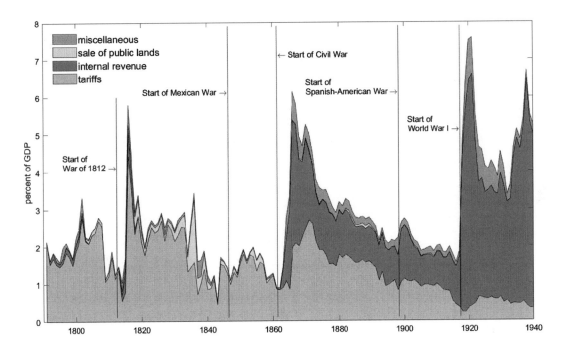

FIGURE 27.7

Composition of federal receipts: 1791 to 1940.

Debts incurred during the War for Independence, the War of 1812, and Mexican War were serviced with customs revenue. Debts incurred during the Civil War and Spanish-American War were serviced with a combination of customs revenue and taxes on liquor and tobacco. Debts incurred during World War I, World War II, the Korean War, and the Vietnam War were serviced largely with corporate and personal income tax revenue.

To supplement these figures with numbers, in Table 27.3 we report average spending and revenue as shares of GDP for the prewar, war and postwar periods for each of the eight wars. With the exception of the Civil War and World War II (both of which were preceded by an aggregate economic downturn), tax revenue exceeded government spending prior to the start of the war so that the government was running primary surpluses. During the War of 1812 and the Mexican War, T/Y fell relative to their prewar ratios as tariff revenues dropped. For the other six wars, consistent with tax smoothing, T/Y rose by less than the increase in G/Y. During the Korean War and the Vietnam War, wartime tax revenue exceeded government expenditures, but surpluses fell relative to their prewar averages. Finally note that, except for the Spanish-American War, government spending (net of interest payments) and tax revenue as shares of GDP were higher on average for the ten years after the war than they were for the five years prior to the start of the war.

For the 11 major wars in U.S. history, Edwards (2014) estimates that for every $1 increase in spending during the war, the U.S. federal government spent another $0.50 (in present value) over the following 80 years on transfer payments and in-kind benefits given to veterans and their spouses

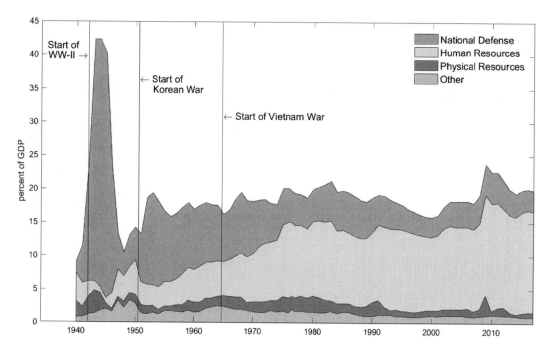

FIGURE 27.8

Composition of federal expenditures: 1940 to 2018.

and other survivors. We can match Edward's ratio of wartime/postwar spending in the Barro model by setting $\beta = .95$ and specifying that $\{G_t\}$ is a first-order autogressive process $G_{t+1} - \bar{G} = \rho(G_t - \bar{G}) + \sigma w_{t+1}$ with $\rho = 0.35$; in this case, Eq. (27.14) prescribes that 93% of wartime expenditures should be debt financed with the remaining 7% tax financed. Allowing for a realistic degree of persistence in the government spending process qualifies Albert Gallatin's rule only modestly.[19]

27.5 Returns to bondholders

Changes in the price level and interest rates are ways a government can deliver state-contingent returns. A black line in each panel of Fig. 27.10 reports the natural log of the price level for the 20 years following the start of each war. For each war, we normalize the price level by the transformation $100 \times (log P_t - log P_{\text{start of war}})$, so the series records cumulative percentage changes in the price level after the war's outbreak. The figures present faded lines that facilitate quick cross-war comparisons within a single panel. In each panel, faded lines are normalized price level series for the War of 1812 (orange

---

[19] The reader can experiment with other specifications for the $\{G_t\}$ process by using the Python code in the quantecon lecture https://python.quantecon.org/smoothing_tax.html together with the accompanying Jupyter notebook.

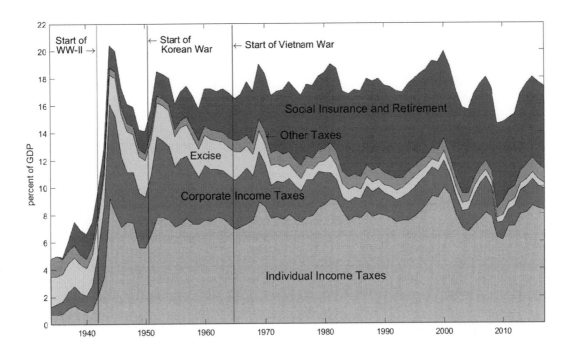

FIGURE 27.9

Composition of federal receipts: 1934 to 2018.

- mid gray in print version), the Civil War (purple - darker gray in print version), World War I (blue - light gray in print version), and World War II (red - dark gray in print version).

A black line in each panel of Fig. 27.11 reports cumulative real values coming from continually reinvesting in a value-weighted re-balanced portfolio of all outstanding U.S. Treasury securities, starting with an initial investment of \$100.[20] These cumulative returns are data analogs of simulated portfolio values from the Lucas-Stokey model plotted in the right panel of Fig. 27.1. In each panel, the faded lines are cumulative values of the portfolios for the War of 1812 (orange - mid gray in print version), the Civil War (purple - darker gray in print version), World War I (blue - light gray in print version), and World War II (red - dark gray in print version).

Notice three patterns. For the War of 1812, the Mexican War, the Civil War, and World War I, the price level rises during the war and falls after the war. (You have to squint to detect this for the Mexican War.) See panels 27.10a, 27.10b, 27.10c, and 27.10e. This pattern is consistent with the Bordo and Kydland (1995) view of the gold standard as helping to deliver Lucas and Stokey state-contingent returns on debt. These price level paths transmitted into wartime real capital losses for bondholders and postwar real capital gains for bondholders. Note that the cumulative real return series displayed

---

[20] The real value at time t is $100 \times \prod_{s=\text{start of war}}^{t} \frac{1+r_{s,s+1}}{1+\pi_{s,s+1}}$, where $r_{s,s+1}$ is the nominal net return on the portfolio between month s and $s+1$ and $\pi_{s,s+1}$ is the inflation rate between month s and $s+1$. Thus, the units are start-of-war dollars.

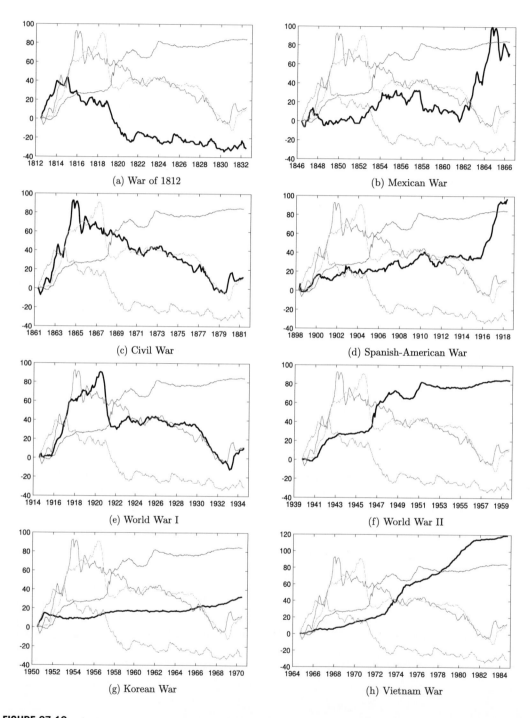

FIGURE 27.10

The natural log of the price level.

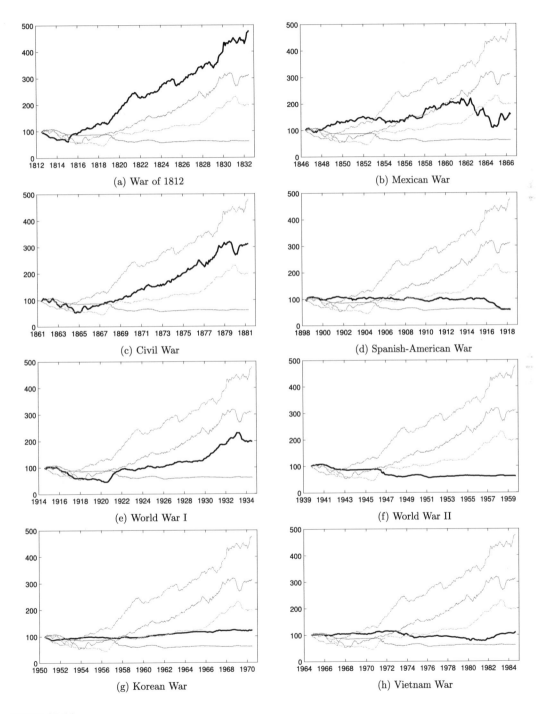

FIGURE 27.11

Real value of a $100 portfolio of treasury securities invested at the start of each war.

Table 27.3 Average government spending net of interest payments and tax receipts as a percent of GDP for the five years prior to each war, for the war period, and for the ten years following the war.

War Start - End (U.S. entry -)	Fiscal Years[†]	G/Y			T/Y		
		prewar	*war*	*postwar*	*prewar*	*war*	*postwar*
War of 1812							
1812:6 - 1815:2	1812-1815	0.88	2.72	1.82	1.95	1.37	3.14
Mexican War							
1846:5 - 1848:2	1847-1849	1.18	1.94	1.51	1.31	1.29	1.66
Civil War (Union)							
1861:4 - 1865:4	1861-1865	1.58	7.79	2.50	1.42	1.87	4.72
Spanish-American War							
1898:4 - 1898:8	1898-1899	2.15	2.55	1.98	2.20	2.42	2.14
World War I							
1914:7 - 1918:11	1915-1919	1.88	9.10	3.17	1.94	3.30	5.03
(1917:4 -)	1917-1919	1.76	14.07	3.17	1.80	4.39	5.03
World War II							
1939:9 - 1945:8	1940-1946	8.21	25.43	14.00	5.52	12.89	15.86
(1941:12 -)	1942-1946	8.31	31.97	14.00	6.15	15.43	15.86
Korean War							
1950:6 - 1953:6	1951-1953	13.79	15.70	15.84	15.07	16.91	16.52
Vietnam War							
1964:8 - 1973:6	1965-1973	16.13	16.45	18.29	16.67	16.65	17.35

panels 27.11a, 27.11b, 27.11c and 27.11e bear the "ladle" shape observed in right-hand side panel of Fig. 27.1. (Again, you have to squint at the Mexican War panel 27.11b.)

Table 27.4 summarizes numbers behind the graphs. The price level rose 14.70, 14.65, and 11.05 percent at annual rates during the War of 1812, the Civil War and World War I respectively, bringing wartime real returns on Treasury debt of -10.58, -5.69, and -8.60 percent at annual rates. During the 15 years after the war, deflations brought postwar real returns of 12.01, 8.47, and 5.52 percent at annual rates. For the Korean War, there was no postwar deflation, but we see wartime negative and postwar positive real returns.[21] We find this pattern of returns broadly consistent with the prescription of the Lucas-Stokey model.

A second pattern revealed by Fig. 27.11 is that postwar returns to government bondholders have declined steadily from the War of 1812 to the Vietnam War. After the three wars fought since the U.S. left the gold standard in 1933, postwar real returns were essentially flat. As reported in Table 27.4, the postwar real holding period returns fall from 12.01 percent after the War of 1812 to 8.47 percent after the Civil War to 5.52 percent after the World War I to -1.42 percent after World War II.

---

[21] See section 27.6.7 for further discussion of returns during the Korean War.

Table 27.4 Average annual returns and inflation rates during each war and for the subsequent 15 years.

War	War time			Postwar		
Start - End (U.S. entry -)	nominal holding period return	inflation rate	real holding period return	nominal holding period return	inflation rate	real holding period return
War of 1812						
1812:6 - 1815:2	4.20	14.70	-10.58	7.05	-4.73	12.01
Mexican War						
1846:5 - 1848:2	3.55	1.36	3.95	5.57	2.59	3.21
Civil War (Union)						
1861:4 - 1865:4	7.64	14.65	-5.69	5.66	-2.68	8.47
Spanish-American War						
1898:4 - 1898:8	8.09	0.00	8.14	1.86	2.10	-0.21
World War I						
1914:7 - 1918:11	2.00	11.13	-8.79	4.12	-1.31	5.52
(1917:4 -)	3.55	11.05	-8.60			
World War II						
1939:9 - 1945:8	2.16	2.62	-0.63	1.82	3.28	-1.42
(1941:12 -)	1.78	4.23	-2.50			
Korean War						
1950:6 - 1953:6	0.73	3.96	-3.24	2.85	1.72	1.13
Vietnam War						
1964:8 - 1973:6	4.40	4.02	0.46	8.57	6.55	2.02
Mean	4.10	6.56	-2.05	4.69	0.94	3.84
Mean (U.S. involvement)	4.24	6.75	-2.26			

Table 27.5 Price level increases in three wars.

	World War II	World War I	Civil War
start of war	Sept 1939	July 1914	April 1861
price peak (Friedman)	Aug 1948	May 1920	Jan 1865
price peak (this paper)	Aug 1948	May 1920	Aug 1864
Rate of Rise, Per Cent Per Year			
wholesale prices (Friedman)	8.7	15.3	24.5
wholesale prices (this paper)	8.2	15.6	27.8

Finally, we verify two important findings by earlier authors. Panels 27.10c, 27.10e, and 27.10f and numbers in Table 27.5 confirm the finding of Friedman (1952) that prices rose more slowly during World War II than in World War I or the Civil War. Our calculation of the nominal holding period returns during World War II, reported in Table 27.4, are consistent with Samuelson's (1945) characterization of World War II as a "2-per-cent war."

27.6 Debt design, marketing, and management

Since Albert Gallatin's 1807 Report, successive Secretaries of the Treasury have sought to finance wars at minimum cost to taxpayers, a motive captured by the loss function (27.1) for the section 27.2 benchmark models. However, during the four most expensive wars as measured by their government spending/GDP ratios, namely, the War of 1812, Civil War, and both World Wars, the Treasury faced an additional challenge ignored by our benchmark models. At the start of those big wars, possible government creditors anticipated the rapid expansion of Treasury debt required to finance prospective sharp increases in military and civilian expenditures. That made them reluctant to purchase long-term Treasury securities early in a war because they anticipated increased rises in the price level and nominal interest rates, so postponing bond purchases offered higher real returns.[22] To respond to such behavior by prospective government creditors, members of Congress, Treasury officials, and (after 1914) Federal Reserve officials experimented with new debt designs, methods for selling new issues to the public, and debt management policies that could attract early investors.

Article 1, Section 8 of the U.S. Constitution grants Congress exclusive authority to manage Federal debt. Between 1776 and 1920 Congress authorized and designed each individual Treasury security. For each security, Congress set the coupon rate, the principal or par value, the redemption and maturity dates, a unit of account, tax exemptions, and call and conversion features. Congress gradually abandoned these ways of doing things during the two decades after World War I. Acceding to requests from successive Secretaries of the Treasury, Congress delegated more and more authority to design securities and manage the composition of the debt to the Treasury.[23] By 1939, Congress had delegated nearly all decisions about security design and debt management to the Treasury.

Security design and debt management policies alter the allocation of interest rate risk between the Treasury and its creditors. Over time, innovations along both lines helped the Treasury to expand the market for Treasury securities from just the nation's elite to a broad spectrum of investors.

27.6.1 The war of 1812

Between 1801 and 1809, President Thomas Jefferson's administration dismantled the Federalists' administrative machinery for collecting internal revenue. Ignoring Albert Gallatin's warnings, the Jefferson administration's embargo of trade with Britain caused customs revenues to plunge from $16.4 million in 1808 to $7.3 and $8.5 million in 1809 and 1810, respectively. Partly as a consequence of these and other monetary, fiscal, and military preparedness policies of the two Jefferson and first Madison administrations, when Congress declared war on Britain on June of 1812, the U.S. was poorly prepared.

---

[22] In the Barro model, the interest rate is fixed. In the Lucas-Stokey model, at the outbreak of the war, the Ramsey equilibrium outcome awards a capital loss to existing government bondholders. Bondholders understood this possibility when they purchased the bonds and chose to bear this risk. In return, bondholders anticipate high returns when war ends. However, such a state-contingent policy would have been difficult to implement in practice. With the exception of the Korean War, at the start of each U.S. war the outstanding stock of Treasury debt was low, so imposing a one-time capital loss would not have generated much revenue. If a long spell of peace had preceded the war, a Ramsey plan for the Lucas model would have had the government acquiring claims on the public that it would redeem at the outset of the war.

[23] See Garbade (2012, ch.21) and Hall and Sargent (2015).

Between March 1812 and February 1815 the Congress authorized the Treasury to issue five long-term loans with a total face value of $66 million. Those bonds received a cautious reception from the relatively small group of wealthy men who comprised the main pool of prospective buyers. Opposition to the war from merchants and financiers in the Northeast and Congress's inability to put together a sustainable prospective revenue stream sufficient to service them limited what prospective buyers were willing to pay for these bonds. To respond to this situation, beginning in 1813 Albert Gallatin included in invitations for bond subscriptions a promise that if later subscribers were offered better terms, earlier subscribers would be "placed on the same footing."[24] Events in 1814 forced Gallatin to honor this promise.

Although loans issued in the previous year had sold for only $88.25 per $100 of face value, on March 24, 1814 Congress authorized the largest increase in new Treasury debt in the nation's short history, a $25 million loan promising a 6% coupon. In an attempt to obtain the most favorable terms for the government, the Treasury divided the sale of this loan into three installments. In the first installment of $10 million, a portion of the bonds were sold at $88 per $100 of face value; but the Treasury was soon forced to sell the remainder of the installment at $80 per $100 of face value, prompting the Treasury to issue additional shares to compensate earlier buyers. The Treasury canceled the second and third installments. The "Ten Million Loan of 1814" raised only $7,935,581 at the cost of increasing the face value of Federal debt by $9,919,476.25.[25] Further, this official $7.9 million figure overstates the true revenue raised because the Treasury accepted at face as payment private bank notes whose market values were much less than par.

Despite having issued debt at sharp discounts during the war, after the war Congress and the Treasury honored their financial commitments. This full repayment in conjunction with a falling price level resulted in high postwar real returns. As we report in Table 27.4, in the 15 years after the war, bond-holders earned on average 12% annual real returns. Also see Figs. 27.10a and 27.11a.

27.6.2 The Mexican War

When the Mexican War broke out in 1846, the U.S. government stood on much stronger financial footing than it had three and a half decades earlier. Three decades of strong economic growth and the credibility the U.S. Treasury earned from repaying its debts refinanced and assumed in 1790 and incurred during the War of 1812 meant that the federal government could borrow from domestic investors on better terms than it ever had.[26] To finance the war, along with two sales of short-term notes, the Treasury issued three long-term bonds. In contrast to the War of 1812, when the Treasury accepted depreciated private bank notes at face value, subscribers of these Treasury bonds and notes were required to pay in specie. Even so, there was ample demand for these bonds.

---

[24] See document B2 on page 562 and the letters from David Parish, Stephen Girard, and John Jacob Astor marked C and D on page 565 of Elliot (1845).

[25] See page 127 of Bayley (1882).

[26] The federal government did not possess the same credibility with international investors. Eight states and one U.S. territory defaulted on their debts in the early 1840s. Many European investors felt that the precedent set by the federal assumption of state debts in 1790 implied federal backing of state debts. Thus, despite the fact that the federal government had a 50 year record of full repayment on its own debts, Joshua Bates of Barings Bank wrote in October 1841, "At a distance people do not see the local differences and argue that as Mississippi may repudiate her debt, so may Massachusetts, and so the credit of all the States and that of the United States is involved in one common ruin."

Interest rates *fell* during the late 1840s. As Dewey (1912, p.256) notes

An error in judgement was made in compelling so high a rate of interest as 6 per cent with long terms of ten and twenty years before maturity, for on account of business prosperity the bonds quickly went to a premium, and their redemption when the government wished to pay its debt from the surpluses enjoyed in 1850-1856 was a costly operation.

Memories of this "error in judgement" motivated the Treasury to sell callable bonds during the Civil War.

27.6.3 The Civil War: 7-30s and 5-20s

During the U.S. Civil War, Treasury Secretary Salmon Chase made two significant innovations in wartime finance. First, in response to the Treasury's inability after the Mexican War to repurchase at par the non-callable debt it had issued to finance the war, Chase introduced long-term bonds with embedded calls. Second, he extended Treasury subscriptions beyond the financial institutions in Baltimore, Philadelphia, New York, and Boston, so that for the first time, the federal government actively marketed government securities to middle class households throughout the country.[27] When war came in Spring 1861, the federal government was under considerable financial stress. Tax revenues had not recovered from the drop in 1857 that coincided with a banking panic. Further reducing revenue, fears of secession had led to a failed loan offering in 1860 and by early 1861 southern ports diverted federal customs receipts to the CSA Treasury.

To meet war expenses, Congress authorized the Treasury to sell $250 million short-term, long-term, and non-interest bearing securities under the "Loan of July and August, 1861." Much of the short-term debt was in the form of three-year "7-30s" – Treasury notes paying an interest rate of 7.3% with a minimum denomination of $500.[28] To sell 20-year bonds, Chase continued the long-standing practice of soliciting subscriptions from banks in northeastern financial centers that would then resell these notes and bonds to a small circle of wealthy investors in a limited secondary market.

Union military defeats at Ball's Bluff and the failure of General George B. McClellan's peninsular campaign in the fall of 1861 followed by Treasury Secretary Chase's December request for an additional $200 million in borrowing led to a collapse in confidence in the Union military and Treasury. Northern banks were reluctant to purchase more Treasury securities at par, while the Treasury was unwilling to repeat its War of 1812 policy of selling bonds below their par values. By December 30, banks in New York, Boston and Philadelphia suspended specie payments and the federal government quickly followed.

There followed a strange episode involving what Simon Newcomb (1865) and other observers regarded as a serious case of "money illusion" on the part of Federal decision makers. To enable the Treasury to sell long term bonds at par, the Union issued a paper dollar not linked to the gold dollar but in terms of which Treasury bonds *would* sell at par.[29] In February 1862, Congress passed the Legal Tender Act. The Act authorized the Treasury to issue $150 million in United States notes

---

[27] McPherson (1988, pp. 428-453) and Thomson (2019) provide more complete descriptions of Union financing during the Civil War era. See Brands (2006, ch. 3) for a fascinating account of Jay Cooke and "The Bonds of Union".

[28] The 7.3 percent interest rate was chosen since it made it easy to compute the nominal return: 2 cents per day for every $100 in face value.

[29] Newcomb (1865) roundly criticized the reasoning that led to this and other aspects of how the Union financed the war.

("greenbacks") that were to be legal tender for all public and private debts, except customs receipts and coupon payments on federal bonds.[30] Official concerns about selling Union bonds below par were quickly assuaged when the market soon discounted a greenback relative to a gold dollar enough that federal bonds could be sold at par for greenback dollars, as the Act had authorized.[31] The Act also authorized the Treasury to sell $500 million of "5-20s," a bond bearing a 6 percent coupon, maturing in twenty years, and callable at par at the U.S. Treasury's discretion after five years. Over the next six years, the Congress authorized 7 tranches of these loans. The 5-20's were the first U.S. Treasury bonds to include a call option. Over the following two decades, the Treasury issued a sequence of partial calls. Calls were for bonds bearing particular serial numbers.

To sell bonds, Chase innovated by contracting with his friend Jay Cooke to purchase bonds as a monopolist wholesaler to distribute bonds retail.[32] Cooke owned a Philadelphia investment banking firm and was well-connected with Ohio Republican leaders. Cooke administered the first large-scale war-bond drive by hiring a network of sales agents and placing informative and patriotic advertisements in newspapers to sell bonds denominations as small as ten dollars to ordinary middle- and working-class northerners. Payments in greenbacks could be made in monthly installments. He dispatched sales agents throughout the states. Cooke's advertisements highlighted the high returns promised by the 5-20 bonds. For example, the poster in panel 27.12a proclaims "At the present PREMIUM ON GOLD these bonds yield about EIGHT per cent per annum."

Congress bedeviled the 5-20s with an ambiguity that it passed on to subsequent Congresses. The authorizing legislation provided that coupons would be paid in coin (i.e., gold), but it was silent about whether principal would be paid in coin or "lawful money" (i.e., greenbacks). Ambiguity about 5-20 principal payments would be resolved only with the election of U.S. Grant as President in 1868 and the March 1869 passage of 'An Act to Strengthen the Public Credit' that promised repayment in gold or its equivalent.[33] From 1866 to 1881, real returns to federal government creditors averaged 8.5% per year. See Table 27.4 and Fig. 27.11c.

The U.S. Treasury designed and sold other new securities, so that by the war's end, it had issued 19 unique interest-bearing securities and five different forms of currency. Panel 27.16c plots the Treasury's debt service profile at the end of 1865. The figure shows repayment of $676 million in principal for the 7-30s owed in 1868 and of $515 million in principal for the 5-20s of 1862 owed in 1882. Total federal tax revenues averaged a little over $350 million per year during the two decades after the war, so repaying all debt as it came due was out of the question. Instead, it was rescheduled, other securities being issued to raise funds to repay wartime loans.

---

[30] In 1870, the Chief Justice Chase wrote the 5-3 majority Supreme Court decision in Hepburn v. Griswold declaring the legal tender clause unconstitutional for violating the due process clause of the 5th amendment. Subsequent Courts soon reversed that decision in Knox v. Lee and Parker v. Davis. The great hard money Jacksonian Democratic historian George Bancroft (1886) passionately argued that it was Hepburn v. Griswold that had been decided correctly.

[31] Treasury notes issued during the War of 1812 could also be used to buy Federal bonds at par.

[32] Chase's actions were first steps on a process extending over succeeding wars in which Treasury Secretaries and Congresses struggled to strike a balance between "client private placement" vs "retail" vs "wholesale" vs "auction" vs "forced loan" financing. See the proposal of Friedman (1959, pp. 64-65) to reform the way the Treasury sold its bonds.

[33] Bondholders were also voters, and, evidently, Grant's electoral success benefitted from Jay Cooke's campaign to create widespread ownership of the 5-20s.

(a) Civil War

(b) World War I

(c) World War I

(d) World War II

FIGURE 27.12

Posters from the Civil War, World War I, and World War II.

Posters (b), (c) and (d) are courtesy of the Robert D. Farber University Archives & Special Collections Department, Brandeis University.

27.6.4 The Spanish-American War: 10-20s of 1908-1918

The Spanish-American War lasted for only three months in 1898. One bond was sold to finance the war: a 3 percent, 20 year bond, redeemable after 10 years. Congress designed the "10-20s of 1908-1918" to be sold widely to small investors rather than banks. It was sold by subscription at par in denominations between $20 to $300 with individual investors being given first priority. Two considerations motivated this design and marketing policy. First, there remained popular resentment over the government's relying on a J.P. Morgan and August Belmont syndicate to underwrite 4% bonds issued three years earlier than part of the Cleveland administration's efforts to defend the gold standard. Second, Congress intended that subscriptions should express popular support for the war. The bond issue was oversubscribed. Garbade (2012, pp. 41-44) tells how contemporary commentators argued that, had the 10-20s been auctioned, they would have sold above par. Hence, the government sacrificed revenue from those bond sales to gain what it interpreted as a popular expression of support for the war.

27.6.5 World War I: options and federal reserve "Borrow and buy"

To finance World War I, Secretary of the Treasury William Gibbs McAdoo studied how the Union had during the Civil War. McAdoo (1931, p. 373) said that he "did not get much in the way of inspiration or suggestion from a study of the Civil War, except a pretty clear idea of what not to do." Rather than issuing 19 separate securities that had been improvised as the Civil War had unfolded, McAdoo convinced Congress to authorize the Treasury to issue and market five securities sequentially.

McAdoo personally took an active role in marketing the new debt. He named the bonds "Liberty Loans" rather than giving them hyphenated natural number nicknames indicating coupon rates, maturities, and call dates. He sought to bypass middlemen, like Jay Cooke. Instead he established national fund drives that held mass rallies to sell Liberty bonds directly and widely. He enlisted celebrities such as Charlie Chaplin to act in short films and employed commercially successful artists, such as Howard Chandler Christy, to illustrate posters advertising Liberty Loans. Some of these posters now strike us as pretty heavy-handed, for example the posters in panels 27.12b and 27.12c. McAdoo (1931, pp. 378-9) described how

> We went direct to the people; and that means to everybody – to business men, workmen, farmers, bankers, millionaires, school-teachers, laborers. We capitalized on the profound impulse called patriotism.

The Federal Reserve actively helped market Liberty Loans. In particular, the Fed's "borrow and buy" program encouraged individual investors to finance purchases of Liberty Loans by borrowing from their local banks. The banks could discount those loans at the Fed's discount window.[34] Thus, the Fed lent to member banks at a preferred discount rate so long as proceeds were used to purchase Liberty and Victory bonds that the Fed then accepted as collateral. To finance this program, the Fed dramatically increased the monetary base, contributing what amounted to seignorage revenue.[35] See panels 27.13a and 27.13b.

Partially to protect its creditors from later rises in interest rates, the First and Second Liberty Loans granted the investor the right to convert their bonds into new ones bearing higher coupon rates if

---

[34] See the various advertisements and articles in the *New York Times* on October 24, 1917.

[35] For further discussion of the expansion of the Fed's balance sheet during World War I, see Friedman and Schwartz (1963), Meltzer (2010), and Hall and Sargent (2019).

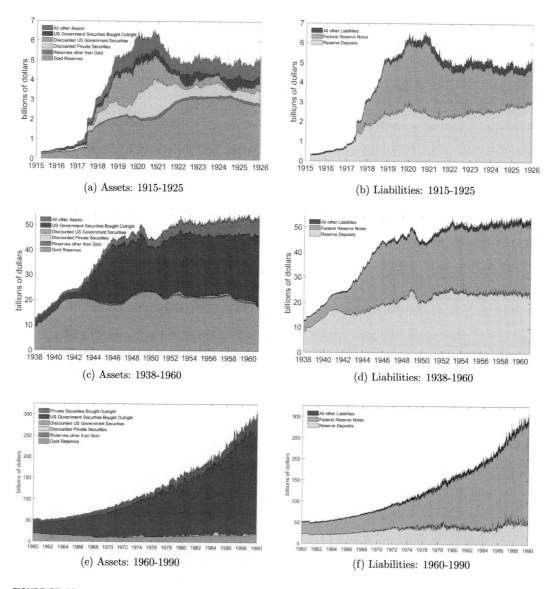

(a) Assets: 1915-1925

(b) Liabilities: 1915-1925

(c) Assets: 1938-1960

(d) Liabilities: 1938-1960

(e) Assets: 1960-1990

(f) Liabilities: 1960-1990

FIGURE 27.13

Federal reserve balance sheet.

subsequent issues paid higher coupon rates; these new bonds had the same maturity dates and call provisions as the original loans but bore the coupon rates and tax provisions of subsequent issues. Interest rates and coupon rates on the Liberty Loans indeed increased as the war went on, inducing many owners of First and Second Liberty Loan bonds to exercise their conversion options. Of the nearly

$2 billion First Liberty Bonds sold, about $560 million were converted into higher coupon-paying bonds. Of the nearly $4 billion Second Liberty Bonds sold, nearly all were ultimately converted.[36]

Despite these conversion provisions, interest rates, and consumer prices rose enough that by June 30, 1920 prices of the Liberty Loans had fallen to between $84.64 to $90.80 per $100 of face value. Furthermore, to take advantage of the Fed' "borrow and buy" program, many small investors bought Liberty Loans on credit, using the bonds themselves as collateral. Thus, the Federal Reserve had encouraged individual investors to borrow short from their bank and lend long to the government. This leveraged position meant that when bond prices fell after the War, many investors realized capital losses. For these losses, some blamed " ... the wicked devices of bond sharps and swindlers who took advantage of the inexperience of many small investors in Liberty bonds whom the Treasury was ... powerless to protect."[37] But Secretary McAdoo was less sympathetic to these new investors; before the Committee on Ways and Means of the House of Representatives in connection with the third Liberty bond bill, on March 27, 1918, he argued[38]:

> There is a curious feeling in the breast of the average man that if he buys a Government bond, even though he contracts to lend his money to the Government, nevertheless if he gets tired of his investment and wants to get his money back, that he ought to be able to sell the bond at par regardless of the fact that the Government is not under any obligation to redeem that bond before maturity. It is extraordinary the extent to which that feeling exists. ... It is a perfectly unreasonable feeling, but one of the things we have got to reckon with.

Ultimately, real returns to owners of Liberty Loans during the fifteen years after the war were far below those paid out during fifteen periods after the War of 1812 or the Civil War.[39] See panel 27.11e. This pattern opens up comparisons and interpretations taken up in detail in Hall and Sargent (2019).

27.6.6 World War II: non-marketable debt, fixed yield curve, fed support

Secretary of Treasury Henry Morgenthau Jr. sought to avoid a recurrence of the deep post-World War I losses incurred by savers who had participated in Secretary McAdoo's "borrow and buy" program. This inspired three key innovations in markets for Treasury securities:

1. Establishment of a non-marketable savings bond program,
2. A Federal Reserve and Treasury joint operation to peg and flatten the term structure of nominal yields on federal bonds, and
3. The Federal Reserve's policy of purchasing marketable securities rather than lending money to banks to finance loans to individuals who had purchased Treasury securities.

---

[36] The conversion rate was lower for the First Liberty Bonds because conversion to a higher coupon bond also meant a less favorable tax treatment.

[37] Treasury Secretary Carter Glass letter to Senator William Caldor, March 31, 1919, *Annual Report of the Secretary of the Treasury*, 1919, page 48.

[38] *Annual Report of the Secretary of the Treasury*, 1920, page 110.

[39] Again, bondholders were also voters, and these low returns came back to haunt the Democrats in the 1920 and 1924 elections. Hilt and Rahn (2018) document that relative to voting patterns prior to World War I, counties in which citizens purchased Liberty Loans at higher rates turned away from the Democratic Party after war.

By the late 1930s, Congress had delegated the design and management of the debt almost completely to the Treasury. In contrast to earlier wars, federal securities that financed World War II were designed by the Treasury and not by a Congressional committee. Secretary Morgenthau wanted "the securities offered should be those best suited to the needs of the investors to whom they are sold." To do that, the Treasury issued a wide range of marketable and non-marketable securities.

Relative to previous wars, the Treasury issued many more types of securities. Spacings of maturity dates were designed partly to smooth out prospective refinancings and rollovers. While there were only four different classes of marketable securities, the Treasury's designed securities with to meet "needs of the investors" by varying maturities, call features, and tax exemptions. That might have promoted initial sales, but it did so by limiting liquidity in secondary markets.

Like earlier Treasury secretaries, Morgenthau viewed successful bond sales as meaningful expressions of public support for the war. In his radio address of May 6, 1943 he said[40]

> When the people really become aflame with the war spirit, all other problems seem to solve themselves. Labor and management get together; production rises to an all time high; and bond sales go up automatically .... The sales of war bonds ... is actually a barometer of the spirit and enthusiasm of the Home Front.

Consequently, Secretary Morgenthau wanted to sell federal securities to small investors. To make that happen, he thought that he had to protect these investors against prospective declines in prices of their bonds. In his history of Treasury financing of World War II, Morse (1971, p. 22) recalled that

> Thousands of people with modest income still remember that they had purchased Liberty Bonds during World War I, only to find, when forced by circumstances to sell their bonds before maturity, that the market price had sharply declined. Bonds purchased for $100 often sold for as little as $82. Thousands of frugal and patriotic people felt that they had somehow been "swindled," and were likely to be "gun-shy" when again asked to buy Government bonds.

In response to those attitudes, the Treasury created a non-negotiable pure discount security, the U.S. Savings Bond. While the investor could not transfer ownership of the bond to someone else, he or she could redeem it on demand according to a fixed price schedule, assuring liquidity, and eliminating prospects of negative nominal returns. The Treasury promoted savings bonds through payroll savings plans and sold them at Post Offices in denominations starting at $25. Between May 1941 and January 1946, the Treasury sold $54.7 billion of such savings bonds to over 85 million individuals.[41] In December 1945, savings bonds accounted for over 17% of the par value of total Treasury debt.[42]

Investors of marketable securities also wanted protection from rising interest rates and declining bond prices. To satisfy that preference, in 1942 the Treasury and the Federal Reserve agreed to cap interest rates on long term Treasury debt at $2\frac{1}{2}$ percent and 3-month Treasury bills at 3/8 percent.[43]

---

[40] Morse (1971, p. 106).

[41] See Morse (1971, p. 285). Note that the U.S. population in 1945 was 140 million.

[42] Marketable securities are negotiable and transferable and thus may be sold on the secondary market. Today, marketable securities consist of bills, notes, bonds, and TIPS. During World War II, the Treasury did not issue TIPS but did issue marketable certificates of indebtedness, a short-term coupon-bearing security. Non-marketable securities such as U.S. savings bonds, special issues, debt series issued to government trust funds (e.g., OASDI, unemployment insurance, and civil service retirement funds), are not sold on a secondary market. Total gross debt is the sum of all marketable and non-marketable securities, matured debt and non-interest bearing securities, regardless of ownership. By the end of 1945, non-marketable debt comprised 28 percent of the total gross debt outstanding. See Fig. 27.14.

[43] See Garbade (2020) and Meltzer (2010, pp. 580-585).

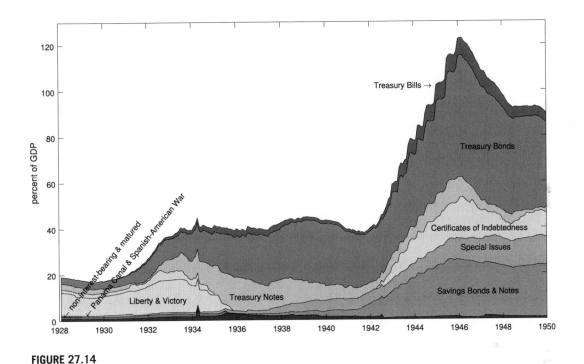

FIGURE 27.14

Face value of treasury gross debt outstanding decomposed by class.

Other rate caps were interpolated to give a smooth upward sloping yield curve; for example, the rate on 1 year bills was set at $\frac{7}{8}$ percent and the rate on 7 to 9 year bonds was set at 2 percent. In an attempt to limit inflation, from early 1942 until late 1946 the federal government instituted price controls on most consumer goods. These controls worked imperfectly, but they did slow the rate of price increases, at least according to official price indices.[44]

An unintended consequence of sharply reducing interest rate risk through the interest rate and price controls in combination with the Treasury's decision to issue a wide range of securities was that private buyers favored long-term bonds and shunned Treasury bills. This left the Federal Reserve to become the primary buyer of short-term Treasury securities. As in World War I, the Fed expanded its balance sheet to support the Treasury market, but unlike the World War I "borrow and buy" program, in World War II the Federal Reserve directly purchased these securities rather than holding them books as collateral. See panels 27.13c and 27.13d. As Fig. 27.15a illustrates, from 1944 to 1948, the Federal Reserve held between 40 and 89 percent of outstanding Treasury bills. Other government agencies held roughly 30 percent of the Treasury bills issued from 1944 to 1947.

Because the Treasury fixed the rate of return below a market clearing level, the Treasury again resorted to bond drives. The Treasury again induced celebrities to sell bonds. Posters and films were created. See the poster in Fig. 27.12d. Unlike Jay Cooke's Civil War advertisements, these posters did

---

[44] See Friedman and Schwartz (1963, p. 557).

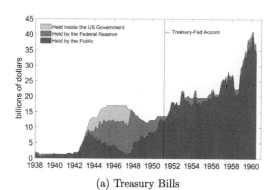

(a) Treasury Bills

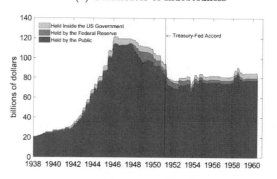

(b) Certificates of Indebtedness

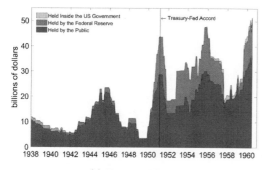

(c) Treasury Notes

(d) Treasury Bonds

FIGURE 27.15

Ownership of marketable U.S. treasury debt.

not promise high rates of return. The sales campaign was more positive and subtle than the ones that marketed World War I Liberty Loans.

Inflation surged when the government removed price controls after the war. Because private investors holdings were concentrated in long-term bonds, they were hit particularly hard by the real capital losses brought by inflation. Five years later, President Harry Truman would argue[45]

> *During World War II, taxes were not high enough, and the Government was forced to borrow too much. As a result, when controls were taken off after the war, prices skyrocketed and we paid in inflation for our failure to tax enough. The value of people's savings was cut down by the higher prices they had to pay.*

27.6.7 Korean War and treasury-federal reserve accord

At the start of the Korean War, federal debt held by the private investors stood at 66.5% of GDP. President Harry Truman opposed delivering the state-contingent capital loss to government creditors prescribed by a Lucas-Stokey model. Historian Robert Donovan (1996, p. 329) noted that

---

[45] Special Message to the Congress Recommending a "Pay as We Go" Tax Program, February 2, 1951.

Truman was dead set against the thought of tampering with government bonds, especially because some that he had bought while in the army plunged in value in the depression of 1920-21. It became an article of faith with him that if a person bought a government bond for $100, that person should be able to redeem it for $100.

Evidently, Truman was one of the inexperienced small investors who had felt "swindled" by the post-Armistice drop in Liberty bond prices. Nevertheless, as can be seen in panels 27.10g and 27.11g, when the war broke out, with fresh memories of World War II rationing, consumers rushed to purchase consumer goods, driving up the price level and delivering a small real capital loss to bondholders. Thus, under President Truman, real returns to bondholders fell with the arrival of *news of war* for the first time in American history.

In a continuation of its World War II policy, the Fed supported the Treasury market in the early months of the Korean by purchasing Treasury debt in order to fix the nominal yield curve and place a floor on bond prices. But the Treasury's goal of low interest rates conflicted with Fed's goal of using monetary policy to control inflation. That created pressure to revise coordination arrangements between Treasury and the Federal Reserve, a tension resolved when on March 4, 1951, the Treasury and Federal Reserve issued a joint statement ending the Fed's commitment to purchasing Treasury securities in order to maintain a floor on bond prices.[46]

While little new federal debt was issued during the Korean War, postwar real returns were low relative to earlier postwar experiences. As witnessed in Table 27.4 and panel 27.11g, in the 15 years after the war, the average annual real return on the Treasury's portfolio was a mere 1.13% – a sharp contrast to the more generous returns to bondholders after the War of 1812, the Civil War, and World War I.

27.6.8 Vietnam

After 1950, the Treasury standardized securities, shortened maturities on average, and space bonds in more orderly ways. As an example of increased standardization, the share of long term bonds with embedded call options declined sharply.[47] By the end of the Vietnam War in December 1974, there were 120 unique securities outstanding across three classes of marketable securities: bills, notes, and bonds. As can be seen in panel 27.16h, sales of securities were managed to avoid a lumpy debt service schedule.

27.7 Insurrections

In addition to the eight wars studied above, residents of the present-day United States participated in two insurrections: from 1775 to 1783, the War for Independence from England, which succeeded, and from 1861 to 1865 the attempt to secede from the United States and establish a Confederate States of America (CSA), which failed. We study the funding of these two conflicts in a manner that is not fully integrated with our treatment of the other eight conflicts for three reasons. First, at the start of a

---

[46] For a history of the Treasury-Fed Accord, see Meltzer (2010, pp. 684-724).

[47] See figure 14 of Faraglia et al. (2014).

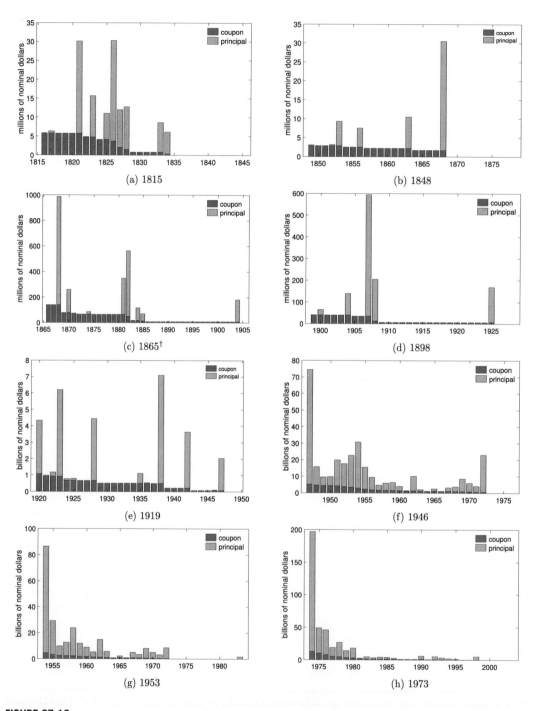

FIGURE 27.16

U.S. treasury debt service profiles on December 31.

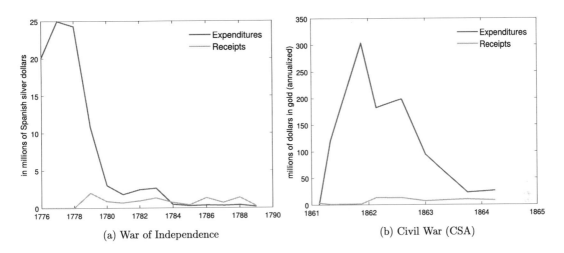

FIGURE 27.17

Government expenditures (net of interest payments) and revenues.

revolution, no tax and debt policies exist. A new government must create laws and administration to gather resources to fight. Second, unlike the other eight conflicts, these two revolutions were existential fights; failure to prevail meant that a government would cease to exist. Third, data shortcomings make it infeasible to construct our full accounting prior to 1790 or for the CSA.[48]

The Continental (1774-1781) and Confederation (1781-1789) governments and the Confederate States of America were organized under a strong state, weak federal government model. Power to tax stayed exclusively with state governments. In both insurrections, states' reluctance to remit revenue to the central government compelled the Continental and Confederation governments and the CSA government, respectively, to run large wartime deficits. In Fig. 27.17a and 27.17b, we plot expenditures (net of interest payments) and receipts for the Continental government during the American Revolution and the CSA during the U.S. Civil War. Both governments acquired substantial flows of resources during the first three years of their conflicts despite collecting little tax revenue.

The Continental and Confederate governments implemented different strategies for financing these large deficits. Ultimately, both governments issued large quantities of interest-bearing and non-interest bearing certificates, but with different intertemporal patterns. From 1775 to 1780, the Continental government relied almost entirely on seignorage from non-interest bearing notes; only after the value of these notes collapsed did the government begin issuing interest-bearing securities in substantial quantities. In contrast, the Confederate States of America issued a variety of interest and non-interest bearing securities from the start of the war. As the war progressed, the CSA gradually increased the relative issuance of non-interest bearing securities even as the value of Confederate money fell. Both funding strategies generated hyperinflations, with wartime price level increasing five times more than in the U.S. during the Civil War and World War I. In the end, both governments defaulted on their non-interest

---

[48] In particular, we have no consistent price data on Continental securities prior to mid-1786, and between 1787 and 1790 price quotes are spotty. We have no GDP data prior to 1790 and no GDP data for the CSA.

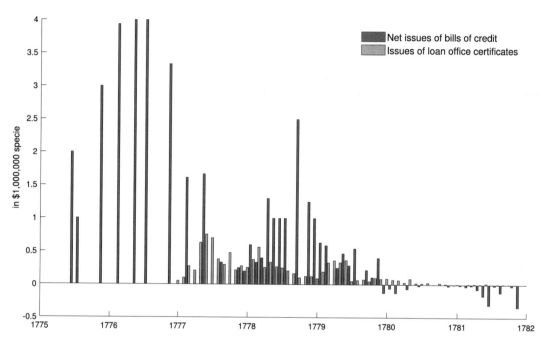

FIGURE 27.18

Monthly net issuance of continental bills of credit and loan office certificates by the continental government from June 1775 to December 1781.

bearing notes. Holders of Continental interest-bearing securities collected partial payment eventually; holders of Confederate securities received nothing.

In June 1775, the Continental Congress issued the first *bills of credit* that came to be known as Continental dollars, small denomination, non-interest bearing promises to pay Spanish dollars. As Fig. 27.18 illustrates, between 1775 and 1780 the Continental Congress issued many of these bills. At their peak in 1780 nearly $200 million in face value were outstanding. Over the following decade, roughly $120 million were accepted by the states for tax payments and currency swaps, remitted to the national government and burned.[49] Spanish dollars and British pounds, not Continental dollars served as units of account for both government and private transactions during and after the war.

By late 1776, markets valued Continental dollars far less than they did the Spanish dollars for which the Continental Congress had promised to redeem them. On June 28, 1780, the Continental Congress rescinded its earlier promise to repay one Continental dollar with one Spanish dollar and made a new promise to repay 40 Continental dollars with one Spanish dollar, never mind what was still written on faces of outstanding Continental dollars. That revised promise continued between 1780 and 1790, when the U.S. Congress reset the ratio to the 100 Continental dollars for 1 Spanish dollar that Alexander Hamilton (1790) had recommended in his *First Report on Public Credit*.

---

[49] See Grubb (2012).

Only after the 1780 "revaluation of" (i.e., reputation of most of) the Continental dollar did the Continental government issue large quantities of interest-bearing securities.[50] The two primary interest-bearing securities issued to finance the war were loan office certificates and certificates of indebtedness. Loan office certificates were bonds (most promised a 6 percent coupon) sold chiefly to domestic investors, but sometimes issued to pay suppliers. We plot the issuance of the loan office certificates in Fig. 27.18. As can be seen in this figure, the Continental government issued 4 times the number of bills of credit than it issued of loan office certificates. Issuance of the loan office certificates increased as the emission of bills of credit began to diminish.[51]

Certificates of indebtedness were interest-bearing, most promising a 6 percent coupon. They were issued by quartermasters, commissaries, and other officers to civilians in exchange for supplies impressed for the army. Ferguson (1961, ch. 4) asserts that after the collapse in value of the Continental dollar in 1778 and 1779, certificates issued by the Quartermaster and Commissary departments were the primary means of payments for supplies. Poor recording keeping and the destruction of many records prevent us from knowing how many of these certificates were actually issued.

In contrast, from the start of the war, the CSA financed its deficits with a more balanced mix of non-interest bearing and interest bearing debt than did the Continental government. In Fig. 27.19, we plot issues of non-interest bearing Confederate dollars and interest bearing Confederate bonds along with tax and miscellaneous revenue, from 1861 to 1864.[52] Note that in the second year of the war, from February 1862 to December 1862, the Confederate government issued over twice as much interest-bearing debt as non-interest bearing debt. Near the end of the war, issuance of Confederate dollars exceeded issuance of Confederate bonds.

Unlike the Continental period, during which a foreign coin was the domestic unit of account, the CSA Treasury succeeded in promoting the Confederate dollar as the unit of account throughout the Confederacy early in the Civil War.[53] When Confederate banks suspended specie payments in 1861, CSA Treasury Secretary Christopher Memminger convinced bankers at their July 24, 1861 Bankers' Convention to accept CSA dollars as the "standard value." In his March 14, 1862 *Report*, Memminger stated that

> *Throughout the Confederacy the banks and people promptly responded to these measures of the Government, and everywhere the Treasury Notes were accepted as currency. These notes thus became part of the regular circulating medium and furnished the Government with a large and available loan, free of interest.*

---

[50] Baack (2001) argues that, given the small outstanding quantity of interest-bearing debt issued by the Continental government in the fall of 1777, had the war ended after the Battle of Saratoga with a negotiated settlement, the U.S. would have avoided the debt crisis of the 1780s that led to the new constitution in 1787. In that case, the U.S. would have emerged as a loose confederation of 13 independent states.

[51] Scholars including Wright (2008, p. 53) have praised those who purchased these loan office certificates, naming some for special recognition as especially generous patriots. In on-going work with the original state loan office ledgers, we have reconfirmed and refined findings of Ferguson (1961, ch. 4) that many of these patriots recorded in these ledgers (including two of the three major purchasers mentioned by Wright) were actually members of the quartermaster, commissary, and hospital corps who used these loan office certificates to purchase supplies. Others on these lists were government contractors who accepted loan office certificates as payment of goods and services.

[52] Data in this figure are computed from eight CSA Treasury Reports. Note that the time periods are not equal, and the records end prior to the end of the war.

[53] See Ball (1991, p. 164) and Morgan (1985, ch. 9) for further discussion of the acceptance of the Confederate dollar.

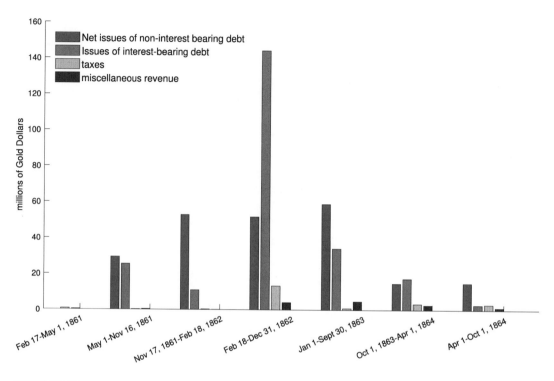

FIGURE 27.19

Issuance of interest-bearing and non-interest bearing debt, and tax and miscellaneous revenue for the confederate states of America from February 1861 to October 1864.

Despite governments' attempts to control prices, both wartime economies experienced big inflations with price levels increasing nearly 500 percent. In Fig. 27.20, we plot natural logs of price levels during the two wars, a counterpart to Fig. 27.10. In both conflicts, inflation was markedly higher than in the eight wars studied earlier in this paper.

Differences in returns to bondholders across the two wars were direct consequences of the wars' military outcomes. Creditors of the victorious Continental government were repaid something. Creditors of the lost cause CSA government received nothing. Data limitations render us unable to compute a time series of returns for the portfolio of debt for the Continental and CSA governments; so in Fig. 27.21, we plot the price in Spanish silver dollars of the Continental Loan Office Certificates, the main domestic bonds issued during the Revolution, and the price in gold of the CSA 100 Million Dollar Loan.

During the American War for Independence, the price of Continental Loan Office certificates fell steadily. During the Confederation period that followed peace but preceded the U.S. Constitution, prices of these certificates stabilized in a range between 20 and 40 percent of their face values. Via a sequence of refunding transactions that discriminated across different classes of Continental and state creditors, in 1790, the U.S. Treasury, led by Secretary Alexander Hamilton, issued new securities to holders of Revolutionary-era certificates. Continental creditors exchanged their claims for new se-

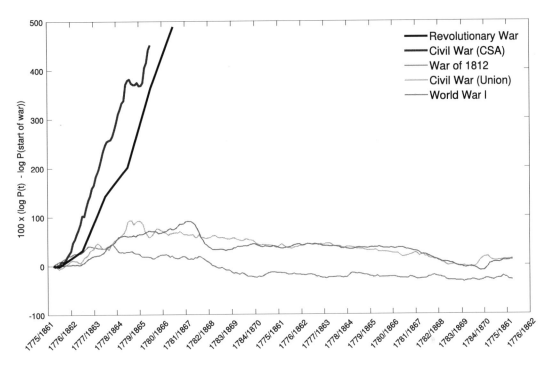

FIGURE 27.20

Natural log of the price level.

curities that had market values of about 75% of the original promises.[54] The new federal government did not pay as much as the Continental-era creditors had been promised, but it still paid substantial amounts to creditors other than holders of Continental dollars.

Confederate bondholders were less fortunate. As was the case with Continental-era certificates, the price of CSA securities fell steadily during the war. See Fig. 27.21. The U.S. Congress made sure that the Confederate government had no say in the postwar resolution of debts. In 1868, the 14th Amendment to the U.S. Constitution was adopted. Section 4 states that "neither the United States nor any state shall assume or pay any debt or obligation incurred in aid of insurrection or rebellion against the United States, ...; but all such debts, obligations and claims shall be held illegal and void."

27.8 Qualifications

In the government budget constraint, Eq. (27.22), we consider three explicit sources of revenue: taxes, debt, and money creation. However governments can also raise resources by nationalizing private as-

---

[54] Hall and Sargent (2014) document this refunding in detail.

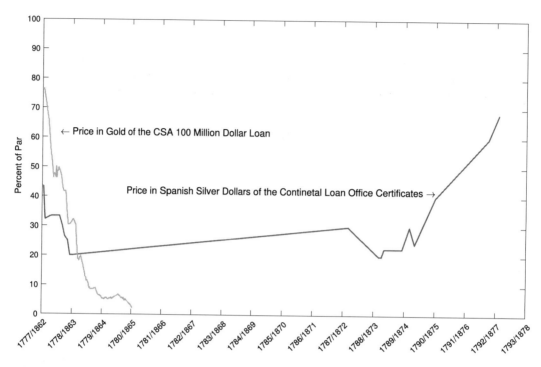

FIGURE 27.21

Bond prices.

sets, confiscating goods from enemies and its own people, and drafting its citizens into the military. At times, the U.S. government used each of these measures, with the most important of these measures having been the draft.[55]

In order to raise large fighting forces without paying market wages, during the Civil War, World War I, World War II, the Korean War, and the Vietnam War, the federal government drafted men into the military.[56] By requiring young men to join the military at below market wages, a reluctant soldier or sailor paid in kind a tax equal to the difference between what he could have earned elsewhere and his actual military pay. Previous authors have estimated revenues from this tax for various wars, but due to an absence of consistent data across wars on market wages and numbers of men drafted, we ignore this implicit tax in the revenue decomposition reported in Table 27.1.[57]

---

[55] See Ferguson (1961, ch. 4) for a description of the impressment of goods by Continental quartermasters and commissaries during the American Revolution and McAdoo (1931, ch. 29-30) for a first-hand account of the federal assumption of the railroads during World War I.

[56] As noted by Marmion (1969), during the American Revolution, Massachusetts and Virginia conscripted men into their militias. In February 1778, George Washington recommended to the Continental Congress that all colonies begin conscription, but no universal conscription was implemented.

[57] For World War I, Clark (1931, p. 110) estimates that average annual pay for soldiers and sailors for the three years 1917-19 was $1,015. Average rate of civilian pay for those three years was $1,055 per year – thus a $40 gap between civilian and military

In both the Barro (1979) and Lucas and Stokey (1983) models, wars are well-understood, purely exogenous shocks to government spending, and taxpayers and bondholders are the same people. In both models, the government wishes to minimize dead-weight losses from distorting taxes. These models provide sharp statements about optimal time paths of taxes, borrowing, and returns on debt for financing a large temporary government expenditure. In their elegance and simplicity, these models necessarily ignore three concerns that frequently arise in political discussions of war finance.

1. While some wars are thrust upon a government, in many cases, a government choses to go to war.
2. Soldiers and sailors risk their lives, while those who stay home risk less, bringing issues of fairness to the fore.
3. Taxpayers and bondholders are distinct people whose interests are not aligned.

In sections 27.4 and 27.6 we described how these three concerns influenced Congress' choices of debts and taxes and Congress' and Treasury's decisions on how to design and market the debt. We'll say a little more about this now.

While the U.S. arguably had no alternative to entering World War II after the bombing of Pearl Harbor, the U.S. government chose to enter the other wars studied here.[58] In the U.S. and elsewhere, contemporary observers have argued that by lowering deadweight losses from raising resources for making war, tax smoothing policies make it politically feasible for democratic governments to join and prolong wars. Adam Smith (1776, ch. 11) wrote:

> The ordinary expense of the greater part of modern governments in time of peace being equal or nearly equal to their ordinary revenue, when war comes they are both unwilling and unable to increase their revenue in proportion to the increase of their expense. They are unwilling for fear of offending the people, who, by so great and so sudden an increase of taxes, would soon be disgusted with the war; and they are unable from not well knowing what taxes would be sufficient to produce the revenue wanted. The facility of borrowing delivers them from the embarrassment which this fear and inability would otherwise occasion. By means of borrowing they are enabled, with a very moderate increase of taxes, to raise, from year to year, money sufficient for carrying on the war, and by the practice of perpetually funding they are enabled, with the smallest possible increase of taxes, to raise annually the largest possible sum of money.

More recently, Zielinski (2016) and Kreps (2018) argued that the use of debt-financing is inversely related to the public's support for the war. Kreps (2018, p. 8) stated

> leaders, seeking to minimize constraints in war, pursue strategies that both anticipate and deflect opposition that would arise from the public's sensitivity [to war costs]. That means they turn to less visible or onerous approaches such as borrowing rather than imposing war taxes when individuals express little appetite for fiscal sacrifice in wartime.

If taxes are a more visible means of finance relative to borrowing, then it is noteworthy that over the last 200 years the U.S. government has chosen to finance an increasing share of war costs with

---

pay. He put the "national dividend" from underpaying the soldiers and sailors at $230 million. For an analysis of the Vietnam War era draft, see Oi (1967) and Gates (1970).

[58] For a discussion of the choices that led to the U.S. entering World War I, see the introduction of Hall and Sargent (2019). For a statement of doubts about whether the U.S. should have entered World War II so controversial that his family and other defenders blocked its publication for decades, see Hoover (2011).

taxes.[59] Maybe it is that the public wants to demonstrate their support for a war by agreeing to incur the deadweight loss of taxation.[60] Newspaper op-ed writers often make this argument.[61] Rumbaugh (2013) recommended state-contingent wartime taxes so that all calls for military action must explicitly include a call for increased taxes, forcing the question of whether the stakes in the military situation are worth the cost. He stated "If the American people agree [that higher taxes] are worth it, the president will get both the political support and financing he needs. By tying military action to additional revenue, the president would actually have a freer hand in deciding when to use force." That policy involves tax-bunching – not tax smoothing.

Wars inspire calls for "shared sacrifices".[62] Some argued that tax-financing wartime expenditures would be fairer than debt-financing, particularly to those being drafted or volunteering to serve in the military. Before World War I Sprague (1917) argued that taxation placed the burden of paying for the war on those who could best afford it. With loans, a draftee or volunteer pays twice: first while serving in the army, and then again with higher taxes to service the bonds when he returned. During the Korean War, the same argument was made by House Speaker Sam Rayburn who stated, "I think the boys in Korea would appreciate it more if we in this country were to pay our own way instead of leaving it for them to pay when they get back." President Truman's Treasury Secretary James Synder agreed when he testified before the Senate Finance Committee, "You passed a bill up here to draft boys of 18, to send them to war. I think it is just as important we draft some of the profits to help pay for the expenditures."

Not all have agreed that tax financing a war is fairer than debt financing. As Treasury Secretary Andrew Mellon (1924, pp. 26-27) wrote regarding the financing of World War I:

> The view sometimes advanced that the present generation can avoid in part the burden of the cost of the war by passing the war debt on to future generations is fallacious when the debt is entirely domestic, as in the case of the present debt of the United States. A domestic debt is simply a liability of the people to pay themselves, or rather to pay the group holding Government securities; and while this liability may be handed down to the next generation, equivalent assets in the form of Government securities would also be handed down, and that generation, viewed as a whole, would be neither richer nor poorer. From the viewpoint of the country as a whole, the war was paid for when it was fought. ... If the war had been financed entirely through taxation, as some suggested at the time, or if the supplies needed by the Government had simply been commandeered and not paid for, it can readily be seen that the whole burden of the war would have been borne at that time. The financing of the conflict in part by loans was simply an arrangement under Government supervision whereby those who were in position could pay more than their proper proportion of the cost and be reimbursed later with interest by those who were not in position at the time to meet their proper proportion under the tax system without too great sacrifices and hardships.

Barro (1974) described conditions under which debt financing and tax financing are equivalent.

Finally, in both of our benchmark models, taxpayers, bondholders, and a government commit to streams of payments and returns conditional on realizations of a well understood shock process; promises are kept. Implementation depends on future governments' choosing to confirm promises

---

[59] See Table 27.1. The fact the Treasury advertised the bonds sold to finance various wars (e.g., the posters in Fig. 27.12) challenges the view that debt financing is necessarily less visible than tax financing.

[60] This argument contrasts with the view discussed in section 27.6 that popular support for a war can be expressed through robust bond sales.

[61] See Post (1898) and Dionne (2007) for examples.

[62] See Fisher (1918), Truman (1951), Bank et al. (2008), and Rockoff (2012).

made today. In democracies, commitments are sustainable only when future majorities want to honor promises made by earlier majorities. To purchase bonds when immediate returns are low during a war, selfish creditors must believe that future governments will want to deliver high rates of return. Experiences of USA and CSA creditors after the Civil War provide contrasting instances of such anticipations being fulfilled or disappointed. After the Civil War, the Union government confirmed creditors' wartime anticipations of high postwar real returns. Section 4 of the 14th Amendment to the US Constitution forbade payments to Confederate creditors.[63]

27.9 Appendix A Accounting

To understand how the par value of the government debt is related to the market value of debt, we bring in information about bonds' coupons and prices of (presumably risk-free) promises to future dollars. Let the market price q^t_{t+j} be the number of dollars at time t that it takes to buy a risk-free claim to a dollar at time $t + j$. Thus, the superscript t denotes the date at which the price is quoted, while the subscript $t + j$ refers to which the date at which a promise is to be fulfilled. At any date t, let there be a list of prices $\{q^t_{t+j}\}^{n_t}_{j=1}$, where n_t is the maximum horizon over which the government has promised payments.[64] The price q^t_{t+j} is linked to the yield to maturity ρ_{jt} for j-period risk-free zero-coupon bonds by

$$q^t_{t+j} = \frac{1}{(1 + \rho_{jt})^j}.$$

At time t the government promises to pay s^t_{t+j} dollars at times $t + j, j = 1, 2, \ldots, n_t$. Promised payments consist of coupons c^t_{t+j} and principal repayments (also known as par values) b^t_{t+j}:

$$s^t_{t+j} \equiv c^t_{t+j} + b^t_{t+j}. \tag{27.29}$$

These are sums of the corresponding components associated with each bond.

The market value of government debt at time t is

$$\sum_{j=1}^{n_t} q^t_{t+j} s^t_{t+j}, \tag{27.30}$$

which states that the total value of government debt is the sum of a collection of prices times quantities. The time t outstanding total par value is

$$\sum_{j=1}^{n_t} b^t_{t+j}, \tag{27.31}$$

---

[63] Nevertheless, states in the former Confederacy paid pensions to CSA veterans.

[64] When the government has issued perpetual *consols*, $n_t = \infty$.

which differs from the market value of government debt

$$\sum_{j=1}^{n_t} q_{t+j}^t s_{t+j}^t = \sum_{j=1}^{n_t} q_{t+j}^t (c_{t+j}^t + b_{t+j}^t)$$

for two reasons:

- It neglects the government's outstanding promises to pay coupons that are economically indistinguishable from promises to pay principal

$$\sum_{j=1}^{n_t} c_{t+j}^t; \tag{27.32}$$

  and
- The par value given by Eq. (27.31) fails to discount future payments of principal b_{t+j}^t by multiplying them by the market prices, or "discount factors," q_{t+j}^t.

The first omission causes the par value to understate the market value of debt, while the second omission tends to make it overstate it. This means that it is possible for the par value, $\sum_{j=1}^{n_t} b_{t+j}^t$, either to exceed or to fall short of the market value of government debt $\sum_{j=1}^{n_t} q_{t+j}^t s_{t+j}^t$. In Fig. 27.4, we plot the par value of the debt in red (mid gray in print version) and market value of the debt in blue (dark gray in print version) from 1776 to 2018.

In the analysis in this paper we report the value-weighted holding period return on the portfolio of U.S. Treasury debt as defined in expression (27.23). This measure differs from the U.S. Treasury's series of *Interest Expense on the Debt Outstanding*. The Treasury's series is an accounting measure of the interest on the government debt, namely:

1. Before 1929:

$$c_t^{t-1}$$

2. After 1929:

$$c_t^{t-1} + r_{t-1,t}^1 b_{1,t}^{t-1}$$

where $b_{1,t}^{t-1}$ is the par value of pure discount one-period treasury bills issued at $t-1$, and $r_{t-1,t}^1$ is the net nominal rate of return on one-period debt. This official measure reports the sum of coupon payments on longer maturity bonds and the net yield on one-period zero-coupon Treasury bills (these have existed only since 1929).

27.10 **Appendix B Data sources**

We use the prices and quantities of individual U.S. Treasury securities from Hall et al. (2018) and the CRSP Treasury bond files and the zero-coupon yield curves from Gurkaynak et al. (2007) to compute the par and market values, holding period returns, and decompositions of the U.S. Treasury's debt portfolio.

Nominal GDP and the GDP deflator come from www.measuringworth.com. We linearly extrapolate pre-1790 GDP in Figs. 27.3, 27.4, and 27.5. In Tables 27.1 and 27.2 we use the annual GDP deflator as our measure of the price index. For all other calculations we use the monthly price level index from Craighead (2010).

Federal expenditures and revenues from 1790 to 1940 are from the *Annual Report of the Secretary of the Treasury on the State of the Finances*.[65] The numbers we use are summarized on pages 642 - 650 of the 1940 Annual Report.[66] Federal expenditures and revenues from 1934 to 2018 are from the Office of Management and Budget (OMB).[67] The U.S. Treasury and OMB reports federal receipts and expenditure data annually by fiscal year. The first fiscal year after the establishment of the U.S. Treasury started January 1, 1789. In 1842, Congress changed the beginning of the fiscal year from January 1 to July 1. In 1977, it was changed again from July 1 to October 1 where it remains today. We interpolated the calendar-year GDP data to conform it with the fiscal data.

The money supply is the sum of the non-interest bearing Treasury debt and Federal Reserve credit outstanding. Federal Reserve credit outstanding represents the loans and investments of the twelve Federal Reserve Banks. It is the sum of bills discounted, bills bought, United States Government securities bought outright and discounted, deposits in foreign banks, industrial and commercial loans, municipal warrants, and Federal Reserve bank float.

27.10.1 Pre-1790

Continental expenditures from 1776 to 1781 were recorded by Joseph Nourse (1791) in Section E of his *Statements of Receipts and Expenditures of Public Monies*. This section is a report submitted by Henry Knox, the first Secretary of War. Most of the expenditures listed are clearly military in nature, but there are entries for expenditures on Indian Affairs, the Post Office, the Secret Committee, and Advances to the States.

The expenditures from 1781 to 1789 are reported by Robert Morris (1790) *Statement of the Financial Affairs of the United States*.[68] Total expenditures from 1775 through November 1, 1784 are also reported in *General Hamilton's estimate of revolutionary war expenditures, cut down to specie*. See Elliot (1845, p. 10).

The pre-1790 receipts data are from Robert Morris (1790).

In Fig. 27.18, we compute the emission of the loan office certificates using records from Record Group 53 of the National Archives and Records Administration. The sources for the net emissions of the bills of credit are Grubb (2008) and Grubb (2012). We deflate these emissions using the depreciation schedule of Bullock (1895, p. 135).

---

[65] See http://fraser.stlouisfed.org/publication/?pid=194.

[66] See http://fraser.stlouisfed.org/docs/publications/treasar/AR_TREASURY_1940.pdf.

[67] See http://www.whitehouse.gov/omb/budget/Historicals.

[68] There is one year of overlap between the two reports: 1781. The title of the table in Nourse's report states that the expenditures listed are exclusive of the money paid by the Superintendent of Finance and listed in Morris (1790) report.

27.10.2 Confederate States of America

Revenue and expenditures for the Confederate States of America (CSA) are from eight *Reports of the Secretary of the Treasury* issued by Christopher Memminger. The unit of account is Confederate dollars. To convert these numbers into gold dollars we use the gold-grayback exchange rates reported on page 375 of Schwab (1901). Since the eight Treasury reports cover periods of varying length, we annualize the revenue and expenditure flows.

These data are not complete. While the war ended in April 1865, the final Report was issued in October 1864. These Reports combine coupon and principal payments into "payments on the debt." Burdekin and Langdana (1993) provide an excellent discussion and analysis of the CSA Reports.

The source for CSA revenue and debt issuance debt in Fig. 27.19 is the CSA Treasury Reports. We convert nominal CSA dollars into gold dollars using the schedule from Todd (1954, Appendix C, p. 198).

In Fig. 27.21, the gold price of the 100 million dollar loan is from Burdekin and Weidenmier (2003).

27.10.3 Federal reserve balance sheets

The source of the weekly data displayed in Fig. 27.13 are the tables of assets and liabilities of the twelve Federal Reserve Banks reported in each issue of the Board of Governors of the Federal Reserve System (1915-2018).

The sharp increase in gold reserves on the assets side and Federal Reserve Notes in circulation on the liabilities side of the balance sheet that occurred on June 22, 1917 is due to an amendment of the Federal Reserve Act which permitted Federal Reserve Banks to count gold held by its Federal Reserve Agent as part of its required note reserve. Prior to this amendment, the liability of Federal Reserve Banks on outstanding Federal Reserve notes was reduced by the amount of gold held by the Federal Reserve Agent instead of the gold being considered as a collateral reserve.

For the Federal Reserve's assets, before the passage of the June 1917 amendment, *Gold reserves* are the sum of Gold coin and certificates in vault, Gold Settlement fund, and Gold redemption fund. After this amendment, Gold with Federal Agents and Gold with foreign agencies are included in the Gold Reserves. Gold reserves include Gold held against Federal Reserve Notes starting in November 1919, and Gold and Certificates held by banks starting in December 1923. *Reserves Other than Gold* are Legal tender notes, silver, etc. *Discounted U.S. Government Securities* are Bills discounted: Secured by U.S. Government obligations, and *Discounted Private Securities* are Bills discounted: All other. *U.S. Government Securities Bought Outright* include Bills bought in open market, U.S. government bonds, U.S. victory notes, Treasury notes, and U.S. certificates of indebtedness. *All Other Assets* are the sum of Non-Reserve Cash, All other earning assets/other securities, Bank Premises, Gold in transit or in custody in foreign countries, Due from other Fed Banks (in transit), Due from Foreign banks, Uncollected items, Federal Reserve Notes, net assets, Five per cent redemption fund against Federal Reserve Bank notes, All other assets, and Federal Deposit Insurance Corporation stock.

For the Federal Reserve's liabilities, *Reserve Deposits* are the sum of Government Deposits/U.S. Treasurer general account, Due to Members - reserve account/Member bank reserve account, Due to non-member banks clearing account, Deferred availability items, Reserved for Government franchise tax, Foreign bank, and Other deposits. Prior to the June 1917 amendment, *Federal Reserve Notes* are all notes and banknotes in circulation, net gold held by Federal Reserve Agents. After June 1917, *Federal Reserve Notes* records all Federal Reserve notes and banknotes in circulation. *All Other Lia-*

bilities are the sum of Capital paid in/Capital accounts, Surplus Funds, Special deposits, Reserve for contingencies, and All other liabilities.

We entered the balance sheet data by hand. We later learned that these data are available from Bao et al. (2018).

References

Baack, B., 2001. Forging a nation state: the continental congress and the financing of the War of American independence. Economic History Review 54 (4), 639–656.

Ball, D., 1991. Financial Failure and Confederate Defeat. University of Illinois Press.

Bancroft, G., 1886. A Plea for the Constitution of the United States: Wounded in the House of Its Guardians. Harper and Brothers, Publishers, New York.

Bank, S.A., Stark, K.J., Thorndike, J.J., 2008. War and Taxes. G - Reference, Information and Interdisciplinary Subjects Series. Urban Institute Press.

Bao, C., Chen, J., Fries, N., Gibson, A., Paine, E., Schuler, K., 2018. The Federal Reserve System's Weekly Balance Sheet Since 1914. Studies in Applied Economics, vol. 115. Johns Hopkins Center for Financial Stability.

Barro, R.J., 1974. Are government bonds net wealth? Journal of Political Economy 82 (6), 1095–1117.

Barro, R.J., 1979. On the determination of the public debt. Journal of Political Economy 87 (5), 940–971.

Bayley, R., 1882. The National Loans of the United States from July 4, 1776 to June 30, 1880, second edition. Government Printing Office, Washington DC.

Becker, G.S., 1962. Irrational behavior and economic theory. Journal of Political Economy 70 (1), 1–13.

Board of Governors of the Federal Reserve System, 1915-2018. Federal Reserve Bulletin. U.S. Government Printing Office.

Bordo, M., Kydland, F., 1995. The gold standard as a rule: an essay in exploration. Explorations in Economic History 32 (4), 423–464.

Brands, W.C., 2006. The Money Men: Capitalism, Democracy, and the Hundred Years' War over the American Dollar. W. W. Norton, New York.

Bryant, J., Wallace, N., 1984. A price discrimination analysis of monetary policy. The Review of Economic Studies 51 (2), 279–288.

Bullock, C., 1895. The Finances of the United States from 1775 to 1789, with Especial Reference to the Budget. University of Wisconsin Press, Madison, WI.

Burdekin, R.C.K., Langdana, F., 1993. War finance in the southern confederacy, 1861-1865. Explorations in Economic History 30 (3), 352–376.

Burdekin, R.C.K., Weidenmier, M.D., 2003. Suppressing asset price inflation: the confederate experience, 1861–1865. Economic Inquiry 41 (3), 420–432.

Clark, J., 1931. The Costs of the World War to the American People. Economic and Social History of the World War: American Series, Carnegie Endowment for International Peace. Division of Economics and History. Yale University Press.

Craighead, W.D., 2010. Across time and regimes: 212 years of the US-UK real exchange rate. Economic Inquiry 48 (4), 951–964.

Dewey, D.R., 1912. Financial History of the United States, 4th edition. Longmans, Green, and Company, New York.

Dionne, E., 2007. A tax test for the war. The Washington Post October 5, A21.

Donovan, R.J., 1996. Tumultuous Years: The Presidency of Harry S. Truman, 1949-1953. University of Missouri Press.

Edelstein, M., 2000. War and the American economy in the twentieth century. In: Engerman, S.L., Gallman, R.E. (Eds.), The Cambridge Economic History of the United States. In: Cambridge Economic History of the United States, vol. 3. Cambridge University Press, pp. 329–406.

Edwards, R.D., 2014. U.S. war costs: two parts temporary, one part permanent. Journal of Public Economics 113, 54–66.

Elliot, J., 1845. The Funding System of the United States and of Great Britain with Some Tabular Facts of Other Nations Touching the Same Subject. United States House of Representatives (28th 1st session), Washington DC.

Faraglia, E., Marcet, A., Oikonomou, R., Scott, A., 2014. Government Debt Management: The Long and the Short of It. Working Papers 799. Barcelona Graduate School of Economics.

Ferguson, E.J., 1961. The Power of the Purse: A History of American Public Finance, 1776-1790. The University of North Carolina Press, Chapel Hill, NC.

Fisher, I., 1918. How the public should pay for the war. The Annals of the American Academy of Political and Social Science 78, 112–117.

Friedman, M., 1952. Price, income, and monetary changes in three wartime periods. The American Economic Review 42 (2), 612–625.

Friedman, M., 1959. A Program for Monetary Stability. Fordham University Press, New York.

Friedman, M., Schwartz, A.J., 1963. A Monetary History of the United States, 1867-1960. Princeton University Press, Princeton, New Jersey.

Gallatin, A., 1837. Report on the Finances November, 1807. Reports of the Secretary of the Treasury of the United States, vol. 1.

Garbade, K., 2012. Birth of a Market: The U.S. Treasury Securities Market from the Great War to the Great Depression. MIT Press, Cambridge, MA.

Garbade, K., 2020. Managing the Treasury Yield Curve in the 1940s. Staff Reports 913. Federal Reserve Bank of New York.

Gates, T.S., 1970. The Report of the President's Commission on an All-Volunteer Armed Force. U.S. Government Printing Office.

Goldin, C.D., 1980. War. In: Porter, G. (Ed.), Encyclopedia of American Economic History: Studies of the Principal Movements and Ideas, v. 1. C. Scribner's Sons, pp. 935–957.

Grubb, F., 2008. The continental dollar: how much was really issued? The Journal of Economic History 68 (1), 283–291.

Grubb, F., 2012. State redemption of the continental dollar, 1779 - 90. The William and Mary Quarterly 69 (1), 147–180.

Gurkaynak, R.S., Sack, B., Wright, J.H., 2007. The U.S. treasury yield curve: 1961 to the present. Journal of Monetary Economics 54 (8), 2291–2304.

Hall, G.J., Sargent, T.J., 2011. Interest rate risk and other determinants of post-WWII US government debt/GDP dynamics. American Economic Journal: Macroeconomics 3 (3), 192–214.

Hall, G.J., Sargent, T.J., 2014. Fiscal discriminations in three wars. Journal of Monetary Economics 61 (C), 148–166.

Hall, G.J., Sargent, T.J., 2015. A History of U.S. Debt Limits. NBER Working Papers 21799. National Bureau of Economic Research, Inc.

Hall, G.J., Sargent, T.J., 2019. Complications for the United States from international credits: 1913-1940. In: Dabla-Norris, E. (Ed.), Debt and Entanglements Between the Wars. International Monetary Fund, pp. 1–58. Chapter 1.

Hall, G.J., Payne, J., Sargent, T.J., 2018. US federal debt 1776-1940: prices and quantities. https://github.com/jepayne/US-Federal-Debt-Public.

Hamilton, A., 1790. Report on public credit. Presented to Congress on January 9, 1790.

Hilt, E., Rahn, W.M., 2018. Financial Asset Ownership and Political Partisanship: Liberty Bonds and Republican Electoral Success in the 1920s. NBER Working Papers 24719. National Bureau of Economic Research, Inc.

Hoover, H., 2011. Freedom Betrayed: Herbert Hoover's Secret History of the Second World War and Its Aftermath. Hoover Institution Press, Stanford, California.

Keynes, J.M., 1940. How to Pay for the War: A Radical Plan for the Chancellor of the Exchequer. Macmillan and Co., London.

Kreps, S.E., 2018. Taxing Wars: The American Way of War Finance and the Decline of Democracy. Oxford University Press.

Ljungqvist, L., Sargent, T.J., 2018. Recursive Macroeconomic Theory, fourth edition. MIT Press, Cambridge, Massachusetts.

Lucas, R.J., Stokey, N.L., 1983. Optimal fiscal and monetary policy in an economy without capital. Journal of Monetary Economics 12 (1), 55–93.

Marmion, H.A., 1969. Historical background of selective service in the United States. In: Little, R.W. (Ed.), Selective Service and American Society. Russell Sage Foundation, New York, pp. 35–52.

McAdoo, W.G., 1931. Crowded Years: The Reminiscences of William G. McAdoo. Houghton Mifflin Company, New York.

McPherson, J.M., 1988. Battle Cry of Freedom: The Civil War Era. Oxford History of the United States. Oxford University Press.

Mellon, A., 1924. Annual Report of the Secretary of the Treasury on the State of the Finances. United States Department of the Treasury, Washington DC.

Meltzer, A.H., 2010. A History of the Federal Reserve, vol. 1: 1913–1951. University of Chicago Press.

Morgan, J.F., 1985. Graybacks and Gold: Confederate Monetary Policy. Southern History and Genealogy Series. Perdido Bay Press.

Morris, R., 1790. Statement of the Financial Affairs of the United States. Reprinted in The Bankers Magazine and Statistical Register IX (8) (February 1860).

Morse, J.M., 1971. Paying for a World War: The United States Financing of World War II. U.S. Department of Treasury.

Newcomb, S., 1865. A Critical Examination of Our Financial Policy During the Southern Rebellion. D. Appleton and Company, New York.

Nourse, J., 1791. Statements of the receipts and expenditures of public monies, during the administration of the finances by Robert Morris, esquire, late superintendant. Reprinted in In: Nuxoll, E.M., Gallagher, M.A. (Eds.), The Papers of Robert Morris, 1781-1784, vol. 9. University of Pittsburgh Press, 1999.

Ohanian, L.E., 1997. The macroeconomic effects of war finance in the United States: World War II and the Korean War. The American Economic Review 87 (1), 23–40.

Oi, W.Y., 1967. The economic cost of the draft. The American Economic Review 57 (2), 39–62.

Pouzo, D., Presno, I., 2016. Optimal taxation with endogenous default under incomplete markets. University of California, Berkeley. Unpublished manuscript.

Rockoff, H., 2012. America's Economic Way of War: War and the US Economy from the Spanish-American War to the Persian Gulf War. New Approaches to Economic and Social History. Cambridge University Press.

Rothbard, M.N., 2017. The Progressive Era. Mises Institute, Auburn, Alabama.

Rumbaugh, R.R., 2013. A tax to pay for war. The New York Times February 11, A19.

Samuelson, P.A., 1945. The effect of interest rate increases on the banking system. The American Economic Review 35 (1), 16–27.

Schwab, J.C., 1901. The Confederate States of America, 1861-1865: A Financial and Industrial History of the South During the Civil War. PCMI Collection. C. Scribner's Sons.

Smith, A., 1776. An Inquiry into the Nature and Causes of the Wealth of Nations. McMaster University Archive for the History of Economic Thought.

Sprague, O.M.W., 1917. Loans and taxes in war finance. The American Economic Review 7 (1), 199–213.

Thomson, D.K., 2019. Financing the war. In: Sheehan-Dean, A. (Ed.), The Cambridge History of the American Civil War, vol. 2. Cambridge University Press, pp. 174–192.

Todd, R.C., 1954. Confederate Finance. University of Georgia Press.

Truman, H., 1951. Text of Truman's message to congress asking 10 billion in new taxes. The New York Times February 3, 8.

Washington Post, 1898. The people will cheerfully pay the cost. The Washington Post April 7, 6.

Wright, R.E., 2008. One Nation Under Debt: Hamilton, Jefferson, and the History of What We Owe. McGraw-Hill, New York.

Zielinski, R.C., 2016. How States Pay for Wars, 1 edition. Cornell University Press.

Biogeography, writing, and the origins of the state

28

David Stasavage[a]

New York University, New York, NY, United States

In recent years historical economics has shed important new light on the question of when and why states form. Researchers have done this by using new data sources, by recovering forgotten data, and also by applying economic theory to sharpen existing ideas found in other disciplines. Much of this work has focused on deep determinants involving climate, geography, and natural habitats—features that I will refer to here as biogeography. Apart from intrinsic interest, one good reason for focusing on biogeography is that it can be described as exogenous as long as groups with specific societal characteristics do not move to particular biogeographic zones. This approach has generated a host of important new results.[1]

One of the most important conclusions has been to provide support for an argument laid out almost a century ago by the archaeologist, Gordon Childe ([2018] 1936). He believed that areas with biogeography favorable to developing an agricultural surplus were the first to see the development of early states. The modification to this argument offered recently by Mayshar et al. (2020), says that what actually mattered most was whether any eventual agricultural surplus generated could be stored. There is a fundamental distinction here between root and tuber crops on one hand and grains on the other. Roots and tubers such as yams, cassava, and plantains cannot be easily stored, unlike early grains such as wheat, barley, and millet. As perennial crops they can instead be left in the ground and harvested at consumption time. This likely makes it harder for a state to tax them. With cereals the nature of crop production requires storability because the time window for harvesting them is inevitably very short. Storability implies that cereals are easier to tax by a state. This then allows for the creation of an agricultural surplus in equilibrium. The most convincing evidence for this relationship has been provided by Mayshar et al. (2020), and this follows earlier arguments by Testart (1982).[2]

If biogeography has had an important place in recent historical economics work, the role of technology in state formation has received less attention of late.[3] In his original 1936 contribution, Gordon

---

[a] I would like to thank the editors, Alberto Bisin and Giovanni Federico, as well as Ali Ahmed, Omer Moav, and Luigi Pascali for comments on a previous draft.

[1] For work using biogeography to investigate both early state development and economic development see Fenske (2013, 2014), Heldring et al. (2020), Litina (2014), Matranga (2019), Mayshar et al. (2020), Michalopoulos and Papaioannou (2013), Schonholzer (2020), Ahmed and Stasavage (2020), and Boix (2015).

[2] See also Scott (2017). Another recent argument for state origins has to do with the need for collective action to deal with issues such as environmental change (Heldring et al., 2020) or to regulate potential gains from trade (Litina, 2014). See Matranga and Pascali (2021) for a review of further theories of state origins and how archaeological evidence can be used to test them.

[3] For a notable exception to this see Dal Bò et al. (2019). See also Levine and Modica (2021) in this book.

Childe emphasized not only geographic factors, but also how technological innovation allowed states to form.[4] Writing from a Marxist orientation, Childe himself did not distinguish between factors that led to economic development and those that allowed for a state to function: for him these were part of the same parcel.[5] There have been recent papers in historical economics that have considered the interplay between technology and state formation, but these have often been restricted to theory, something that may point to the difficulty in estimating technological effects.[6]

The main issue with empirically estimating a causal effect of technology on state origins is that technology is an endogenous development that depends on human ideas, implementation, and preferences. As soon as one wants to disentangle technology and state formation, then we have a big problem for inference. In a dataset like the Standard Cross Cultural Sample (Murdock and White, 1969) there are multiple measures of the technologies that societies disposed of, but to untangle the causal relationships we need a plausibly exogenous determinant of technology.

In order to estimate the effect of technology on the origins of the state, I will make use of the following fact: almost all societies adopted writing systems from others rather than inventing writing on their own. Writing is now believed to have originated independently only in three locations: Ancient Sumeria, Shang Dynasty China, and with the Olmecs of Mesoamerica.[7] This is unlike other technological developments, such as the all important technology of domesticating crops, which we now know emerged independently in thirteen locations or more.[8] This gives us the opportunity to use the geographic distances from Sumeria, Shang China, and Olmec Mesoamerica as instrumental variables for the presence of writing. Recognizing that distance from each of these three points of origin could be correlated with many different things that might affect state development, in order to provide a justification for the necessary exclusion restriction, I propose a further step in the analysis. Some time ago, Jack Goody, the well-known anthropologist, offered an explanation for why some societies that had the opportunity to adopt a system of writing from the outside chose not to do so.[9] He argued that if writing was useful to be able to record things over time, then some societies had less of a need for this than others. Societies that grew roots and tubers that could not be stored had less of a need for writing than did societies that grew cereals. This is obviously related to the argument made by Mayshar et al. (2020) about cereals leading to states and roots and tubers not doing so. The Goody argument is nonetheless distinct, as he did not imply that this effect would apply only in societies with states. Goody's argument helps provide a demand side explanation for the adoption of writing to complement the supply side explanation based on the ability to adopt writing from neighboring societies.

---

[4] See Service (1975) and Cohen and Service (1978) for more recent classic statements by anthropologists on the origins of the state.

[5] The same can be said of Engels ([1972] 1884, pp. 89-92) who wrote of the importance of technology but without distinguishing between economic and political development.

[6] See Baker (2008) and Baker et al. (2010) for exceptions that combine theory and empirics to investigate technology and state formation. See Boix (2015) for a broader discussion of technology and state formation.

[7] See Schmandt-Besserat, 2014; Senner, 1989, p. 2. This idea runs counter to earlier, largely unjustified, theories that writing emerged independently in only one place at one time. See Gelb (1963) for an example of this view with Ancient Mesopotamia as the point of origin. It is clear that Gordon Childe also believed that China, Mesoamerica, and Sumeria were the three locations in which writing was independently developed (see Childe, 1950).

[8] See Purugganan and Fuller (2009) as well as Fuller (2010) and Purugganan (2019).

[9] See Goody, 1986, pp. 103-104.

For my estimates of state origins I will rely on a measure of state presence in a cross section of 186 societies of the Standard Cross Cultural Sample (Murdock and White, 1969). This is a subset of societies from the well known *Ethnographic Atlas* (Murdock, 1967) for which anthropologists coded a large number of covariates. This measure of state presence, which is called "political integration" in the original dataset has been used in an extensive number of recent papers.[10] The measure of state presence adopted here is a very general one that refers to how many levels of governance exist above the level of the individual family, from community, to entities grouping together a small number of communities, to larger states. This measure does not describe how a state functions, whether it is hierarchical, whether governance is collective or autocratic, or other related features.

Using this variable from the Standard Cross Cultural Sample, I will operationalize state presence in two ways. The first will be to use the raw version of this variable where there are five different values ranging from one, where there is no governance beyond the individual family to those cases where there are three or more levels of governance above the level of the individual community. In other specifications I will employ a binary classification of state presence. With this binary measure a society is counted as having a state if it has governance extending at least two levels above that of the individual community.

I will investigate the partial correlation between both measures of state presence, the availability of writing as a tool for governance, and measures of suitability for cereal versus root and tuber crops that are plausibly exogenous to human intervention. These measures derive from Galor and Özak (2016, 2015). Since writing is endogenous, I will present 2SLS estimates where I instrument for its presence using geodetic (great circle) distances from the three origin points (Sumeria, Shang China, Olmec Mesoamerica). In some specifications I will use only the distance to the nearest of these three points of origin, and in others I will use the distances from all three of these points. In addition, in some specifications I will interact these distances with the relative suitability of land for root and tuber versus cereal crop production. This increases confidence that the instrument (or instruments) is not capturing the effect of just any type of diffusion of technological and cultural practices; it is instead capturing the effect of distance for societies located in areas suitable for cereal correlation.

As I say all the above, I should emphasize that the results I will present for writing should be seen as exploratory. Even after interacting distances from the three points of origin with cereal versus root and tuber suitability, it is possible that my estimates for the effect of writing are also capturing the diffusion of other technologies or practices from society to society. If so, this would not change the overall conclusion I want to make in this paper, which is that the origins of state lay in human know-how and not just favorable biogeography. It would, however, mean that I am estimating the impact of a bundled treatment, and not just that of writing. If there is a bundled treatment, one thing I will be able to rule out using available data is that I am capturing the effect of the initial diffusion of agriculture from one society to another.

In concrete terms, my results suggest a one standard deviation increase in suitability for cereals, as opposed to roots and tubers, is associated with a twelve percentage point increase in the probability of a state being present. A one standard deviation decrease in the value of the excluded instrument—distance from the closest of the three points of origin (2150 kilometers)—is associated with a twelve

---

[10] In the Ethnographic Atlas the analogous measure is referred to as "jurisdictional hierarchy." For examples see Fenske (2014, 2013), Osafo-Kwaako and Robinson (2013), Michalopoulos and Papaioannou (2013), Mayshar et al. (2020), and Ahmed and Stasavage (2020).

percentage point increase in the probability that a state is present (taking into account the effect of the excluded instrument on the endogenous variable for writing). It would appear then that the effects of biogeography and of technology were of very similar magnitude.

As a final step, I show also that the presence of writing is highly correlated with aspects of state governance that it facilitated: the presence of bureaucrats and of formal tax collection. This reinforces the idea that writing played an important point in increasing state capacity.

In the remainder of the paper, I first review classic and recent arguments about biogeography, technology, and state origins. I then take a closer look at historical evidence on the origins of writing. This is followed by the presentation of my estimation strategy and then my empirical results.

28.1 Biogeography and state origins

The argument linking biogeography and state origins can be said to have two main variants that each focus on two different features: population density and the existence of a surplus.

In the first, the presence of biogeography suitable for agriculture allowed for sustaining a high level of population density, and this concentration of people is then said to lead to the development of a state and to hierarchy along with that. One reason for this might be if natural barriers—deserts, mountains, etc.—around an area of high density led to a process that Carneiro (1970) called "circumscription."[11] According to Carneiro, when people were unable to expand into new territory because of this then it made it easier for rulers of a state to control them. Recently (Schonholzer, 2020) has provided important empirical evidence for Carneiro's original argument.

In the second variant, state origins depended on the presence of an agricultural surplus. An agricultural surplus could allow a state elite to prosper without itself having to directly engage in agricultural production, and so in this case a state served the purpose of upward redistribution.[12] The happier version of this argument is to suggest that by freeing a fraction of the population from the immediate needs to engage in agricultural production, then it was possible to have a greater division of labor that would eventually result in a higher level of overall social welfare.[13]

Recently, Mayshar et al. (2020) have emphasized that the surplus argument depends fundamentally not just on the ability produce a surplus but also on the ability to store it. Among domesticated plants, cereals can almost always be stored for long periods while root and tuber crops most generally cannot. The inference then is that it is above all favorability for cereal production that led to the development of a state. The three authors have provided convincing empirical evidence on this issue using data from the *Ethnographic Atlas* combined with data from the UN Food and Agriculture Organization's GAEZ (Global Agro-Economic Zones) database.

---

[11] See Allen (1997) for evidence on the Ancient Egypt, the prototypical case of environmental circumscription being said to have led to state development.

[12] See Flannery and Marcus (2012).

[13] See Blanton and Fargher (2008) for the view that early societies with an agricultural surplus varied considerably in the degree to which they were hierarchical.

28.2 **Technology and state origins**

If Gordon Childe's work provided the initial inspiration for thinking of state origins in terms of bio-geography, that was only half of what he said. A read through Childe ([2018] 1936) shows that he also believed technological developments to be fundamental in this process. I am going to refer to Childe here not because he is the most up to date authority on the subject—his work is after all nearly a hundred years old—but because he set the tone for the debate in a very lasting way. We can think of two variants of technology here; the first involves technologies for agricultural production that allow for an (appropriable) surplus. The second involves technologies for managing the state itself.

According to Gordon Childe ([2018] 1936, p. 105) between 6000 and 3000 BCE, humans in specific locations learned to harness the force of oxen and of the winds via the plough, the wheeled cart, and the sailing boat. They discovered how to smelt copper ores as well as to work other metals, and to develop a solar calendar. In Childe's words "he" (meaning humans) "has therefore equipped himself for urban life, and prepares the way for a civilization which shall require writing, processes of reckoning, and standards of measurement—instruments of a new way of transmitting knowledge of exact sciences."

The secondary inventions that Childe referred to, associated with "civilization," were not necessary to produce an agricultural surplus, but they were to prove critical in the origins of the state. Standards of measurement would prove critical in assessing the taxes that should be paid by farmers. In Ancient Egypt, particularly elaborate methods were developed to deal with the fact that farmers often had irregularly shaped plots and the Nile floods regularly washed away a portion of these.[14]

In later work Gordon Childe placed a tremendous emphasis on writing technology for the appearance of the state.[15] If one was to have a storable surplus, then it would certainly help to have ways of recording this. The use of simple tokens and marks could help with this, but they would not go nearly as far as having a full blown system of writing. Writing would also be critical for recording tax information and all other transactions involving the state.

28.3 **The origins of writing**

As I noted above, writing is thought to have emerged as a result of independent creation in only three places: Ancient Sumeria, Ancient China, and among the Olmecs in Mesoamerica.[16] There were other societies that had systems of tokens, mnemonic devices, and other ways of recording information, but that did not resemble true writing in the way that the systems developed by these three societies are thought to have done. There have been some claims that writing may also have emerged independently in the Indus Valley Civilization that flourished from the end of the fourth millennium BCE or in Ancient Egypt, instead of being derived from Sumera, but even if these claims were to prove true they would not dramatically change the picture: writing emerged independently in only a very few places. The clear implication here is that if a great many societies ended up eventually adopting writing, yet very

---

[14] See Stasavage, 2020, p. 86. Herodotus mistakenly believed that the Egyptians had invented geometry to deal with this problem.

[15] See Childe, 1950 as well as Senner (1989) and Wang (2014).

[16] See Schmandt-Besserat, 2014 and Senner, 1989, p. 2.

FIGURE 28.1

Cuneiform Sumerian tablet, 4th to 3rd millennium BCE. Metropolitan Museum of Art / Science Photo Library.

few invented it on their own, then a writing system must have been a very difficult thing to invent from scratch.

It is very common with technology for one society to borrow from another, but the rarity of cases where a system of writing was invented *de novo* seems like an extreme case of this. As mentioned earlier, when we think of the most critical development of the "neolithic revolution," the domestication of plants, we now have genetic evidence that this occurred in at least thirteen "primary" sites.[17] The word "primary" here refers to domestication as an independent development rather than something that was borrowed elsewhere.

28.3.1 Three points of origin

The manner in which writing first evolved appears to have been quite different in each of these three points of origin. Therefore it makes sense to consider each in turn.

Sumeria appears to be the one of the three locations where the earliest use of writing was most fundamentally driven by economic transactions with the substantial majority of individual cuneiform tablets that have been discovered being devoted to this use.[18] Evidence suggests that this form of writing emerged from an earlier system of using tokens to represent and record certain objects.[19] One might then imagine that writing evolved because it was needed, but we should remember that many other societies in the area had economic transactions at this point, yet they did not invent a system of writing on their own. See Fig. 28.1.

In China the first examples of writing were used for a very different purpose: inscriptions on oracles bones and tortoise shells.[20] The kings of the Shang dynasty (second millennium BCE) used these

---

[17] See Purugganan and Fuller (2009) as well as Fuller (2010).
[18] See Nissen (1986).
[19] See Schmandt-Besserat, 1997.
[20] See Figure 2 from https://syncedreview.com/2020/03/11/chinese-researchers-use-cnns-to-classify-3000-year-old-oracle-bone-scripts/.

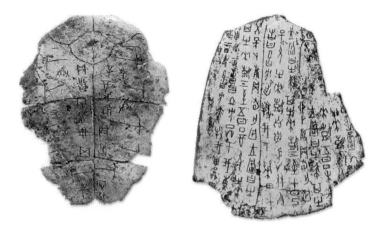

FIGURE 28.2

Chinese oracle bones from the Shang dynasty.

inscriptions as parts of divination rituals to connect with the ancestors, and it was believed that this could help predict things such as when it would rain, a critical factor in an agricultural economy. These early oracle bone inscriptions would form the basis for the development of the Chinese system of characters.[21] See Fig. 28.2.

The Olmecs of Mesoamerica are the third society that is thought to have independently invented a system of writing. The earliest potential evidence of Olmec writing comes from an archaeological find known as the Cascajal Block that has been dated to around 900 BCE. Some have claimed that the inscriptions on this block represent a form of writing, but others have disputed this notion.[22] Whatever interpretation one draws of the Cascajal Block, there is considerable evidence from later in the Olmec period that points to the development of writing and which also suggests how the Olmec legacy led to the spread of writing in neighboring and subsequent Mesoamerican societies.[23] See Fig. 28.3.

Neither the Sumerian, Chinese, nor Olmec systems of writing had the alphabetic form that is used in the majority of the world's writing systems today. One of the curious features here is that all alphabetic systems of writing today are believed to derive from a single point of origin: the Old Canaanite alphabet and its successor, the Phoenician alphabet.[24] This further underlines that fact that when it comes to writing technology, almost all societies have borrowed from others rather than creating a system on their own.

While each of the three societies that developed writing independently had a sophisticated state apparatus, we should acknowledge that writing as we think of it today was not strictly necessary in order to have a state, and some societies also developed sophisticated substitutes for writing. The prime

---

[21] See Keightley (1989) and Wang (2014), as well as Dematté (2010), who discusses potential pre-Shang origins.

[22] See Martínez et al. (2006) for evidence on the block and the argument that it represents writing and Bruhns and Kelker (2007) for a more skeptical view. See Mora-Marín (2009) for further discussion on interpretation of the Cascajal Block.

[23] See Pool (2007) for the discussion of this.

[24] See Cross (1989).

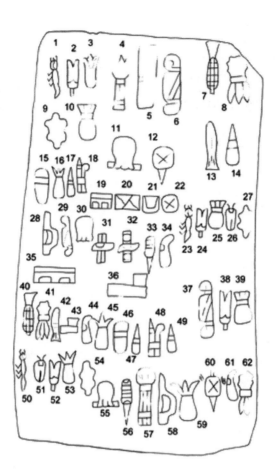

FIGURE 28.3

The Cascajal block: the earliest known writing in the Americas. From Martínez et al. (2006).

example of this was the *khipu* system used within the Inka state. The *khipu* was an object composed of multiple strings of varying lengths and colors with different knots. Each of these features conveyed information, and an individual who could interpret a *khipu* was known as a *khipucamayoc* or "keeper of the knots."[25] For a society with a sophisticated state that dispensed both with writing and with near substitutes, consider the case of the Asante kingdom in West Africa.[26] Perhaps not coincidentally the Asante had a food economy based on yams: a perishable tuber.

---

[25] See Given-Wilson (2016).
[26] See Wilks (1975).

28.3.2 The process of diffusion

There were two ways in which writing diffused from the three points of origin to other societies: conquest and imitation.

East Asia provides us with an example of both the conquest and imitation variants. In Vietnam, the Chinese system of writing was adopted as the area fell under Chinese control during the early part of the Han dynasty. Before that date the Vietnamese had no writing. Later Chinese control in Vietnam led to the adoption of other features of Chinese governance.[27] Japan presented the second variant; the country never fell under direct Chinese control, but it adopted the Chinese system of writing along with a host of other aspects of Chinese culture.

The fact that writing emerged independently in a very select set of societies gives us a possible strategy for identifying the causal effect of technology on the origins of states. Many scholars in historical economics have used distance from a point of origin as an instrumental variable for the adoption of a technology or other practices across societies. For example, distance from Wittenberg has been used as an instrument for the adoption of Protestantism (Becker and Woessman, 2009). In what follows I will suggest that we can use the same strategy to estimate the effect of the adoption of writing. As we use distance from one of the points of origin of writing as an instrumental variable, we need to also consider the possibility that other technologies and cultural practices spread as well. This was certainly the case in East Asia.

28.4 Data and empirical strategy

This section describes the data I will use and my estimation strategy. I will use two alternative dependent variables for state presence which each derive from a measure found in both the Standard Cross Cultural Sample and the *Ethnographic Atlas* that has been used in a number of recent papers.[28] I will combine the two alternative measures of state presence with measures of caloric potential for different types of crops that derive from Galor and Özak (2016, 2015). The data they use derive from the FAO GAEZ database and are combined with data on caloric content of specific crops from the US FDA. I will also make use of information from the Standard Cross Cultural Sample on the presence of writing in a society, which will be instrumented for using the distances from the three points of origin. In some specifications I will interact these distances with the relative suitability of an area for cultivating roots and tubers versus cereals.

28.4.1 State origins

In order to measure state presence I will make use of the Standard Cross Cultural Sample (Murdock and White, 1969). This is a dataset in which many characteristics and practices in 186 societies across the globe are covered. The SCCS is drawn from the larger *Ethnographic Atlas*, and it is designed to include one society from each micro-region in the EA so as to hopefully minimize problems of spatial correlation (or "Galton's problem" as the anthropologists who constructed the SCCS referred to it).

---

[27] See Dell and Querubin (2018) for econometric evidence.
[28] See Lowes (2021) in this book for an extensive review of these datasets and related sources.

Though the sample size of the SCCS is considerably smaller than the *Ethnographic Atlas*, in addition to being designed to minimize spatial correlation, it has the added advantage of coding not only whether a state is present, but also whether the society in question had writing. The *Ethnographic Atlas* has a measure of the former but not the latter. The Standard Cross Cultural Sample and *Ethnographic Atlas* each include measures of state presence, and a number of recent papers employ one of these two measures.[29] The measure of "political integration" as it is called in the Standard Cross Cultural Sample was first coded by Murdock and Provost (1973).

I will use two alternative measures of state presence. The first measure *State1* is simply the raw measure of "political integration" from the SCCS. It indicates the number of levels of governance above that of the individual family household ranging from no governance above the household, to governance only at the level of the community, and then to governance existing one, two, and three levels above the community. When using this first measure I will be taking an agnostic approach to defining the state, suggesting simply that larger entities with more layers of governance can be better characterized as states. The second measure I will use *State2* is a dichotomous indicator that takes a value of one if there is governance at two levels or more above the individual community. This would describe a polity that has a central level of governance and subsidiary districts each of which are composed of multiple communities. For many, anything smaller than this might be better described as a small chiefdom rather than a state.[30]

We should note that neither *State1* nor *State2* capture how exactly a society was governed. Within early societies—both with and without states—some were governed in an autocratic manner while others were more characteristic of early democracy.[31]

One caveat to mention about the data from both the Standard Cross Cultural Sample and the *Ethnographic Atlas* is that while the societies therein are sometimes referred to as "early" or "precolonial," this is inexact. The coding for each society was based on the earliest available thorough ethnographic record. In some cases this was indeed quite early, but in others, and in fact the majority of cases, the ethnographic accounts date from the late nineteenth or early twentieth centuries.

28.4.2 Writing

In order to measure writing, the Standard Cross Cultural Sample has a five fold classification distinguishing between true writing with substantial records, true writing without substantial records, the use of pictorial or related devices as substitutes for writing, use only of simple mnemonic devices, and finally the absence of any of these. In what follows I will make use of a dichotomous indicator that takes a value of one if a society has true writing and zero otherwise. Theories of the diffusion of writing apply principally to this category. The potential risk with this strategy is that some societies had quite advanced means for communicating information across space and time, even if they did not have what we would judge to be true writing. This was most notably the case with the Inkas and their *khipu* system. It would appear though that societies in this category were fairly small in number.

---

[29] See Mayshar et al. (2020), Ahmed and Stasavage (2020), Osafo-Kwaako and Robinson (2013), Fenske (2013, 2014), and Gennaioli and Rainer (2007) for examples.
[30] See Lowie (1927) for a discussion on what could be considered to be a state in early societies.
[31] See Stasavage, 2020, Chapter 2.

28.4.3 Basic cross tabulations

Table 28.1 shows a series of cross tabulations, reporting relative frequencies, between three variables: the presence of a state, of writing, and of cereals as the principal crop.[32] Societies that did not practice agriculture are coded as zero for this indicator. As can be seen, there is a very tight relationship between these three variables. As has previously been shown by Mayshar et al. (2020), societies without cereal crops were much less likely to have a state. However, the mere presence of cereals as the principal crop did not guarantee that a state would exist. Table 28.1 shows the same relationship between the presence of writing and the presence of a state; very few societies without writing had a state, but simply having writing did not guarantee that a state would exist. Finally, Table 28.1 shows the relationship between writing and the presence of cereals as the principal crop. Here the evidence shows that societies with writing were much more likely to have this characteristic.

Table 28.1 Relative frequencies of societies having a state, writing, and cereals. The "State" measure is based on the *State2* variable.

		Cereal Crop	
		no	yes
State	no	44.6%	24.7%
	yes	6.5%	24.2%
		Writing	
		no	yes
State	no	33.9%	35.5%
	yes	5.4%	25.3%
		Cereal Crop	
		no	yes
Writing	no	25.8%	13.4%
	yes	25.3%	35.5%

28.4.4 Estimation strategy

I will investigate the effect of both biogeography and writing technology on state origins. More specifically, I will try to take steps toward disentangling the relationships seen in Table 28.1. My estimation strategy will rely on two assumptions.

The first assumption is that the biogeographic features that allow for accumulation of a storable agricultural surplus were exogenous to state development and other human interventions. This is about as far as the existing literature goes, though we might want to also consider whether human groups with different technologies or cultural practices might choose to locate in habitats where they could best make use of those. In other words, we would want to consider whether a society like Sumeria—located in an area favorable for the production of cereals—was founded by people who chose to locate

---

[32] The *cereal crop* variable is based on v233 in the Standard Cross Cultural Sample.

there because they already had the technologies necessary to manage a state. There is no evidence that things actually worked this way in the Sumerian case.

The second assumption is that the geodetic ("great circle") distance from the original areas where writing was developed (Sumeria, China, and Olmec Mesoamerica) is a valid instrument for the presence of writing in other societies. While distance instruments are common in the historical economics literature, they do present potential problems. A first question one might ask is because the three points of origin for writing also constitute what were once thought to be three of the four original "cradles of civilization," perhaps societies closer to these points adopted not only writing but also the idea of a state itself. This seems unlikely given the definition of a state that I adopt in this article. We now know that many human societies independently invented the idea of expanding political control over a substantial territory. The big question was what technologies were available to further this goal.

The more likely issue for the IV strategy in my case is that distance from an original center where writing was developed might measure not only how easy it was to borrow a system of writing, but also how easy it was to borrow other technologies or cultural practices that would have facilitated state governance. It is not hard to see how this would happen. In East Asia, a number of societies adopted systems of writing based on the Chinese system of characters, but they also adopted many other features of state and cultural organization.[33]

To aid in further isolating the effect of writing technology on state formation, in some specifications I will consider the possibility that writing was adopted not only because it could be adopted from other societies, but also because the biogeography of an area made it particularly useful. This would have the effect of separating out the diffusion of technologies and cultural practices that did not depend on biogeography. To do this, I will make use of a further proposition first made by the anthropologist, Jack Goody (1986, pp. 103-104). He suggested that if writing is necessary to record things, then societies would be less likely to adopt this technology if they had little need to track things over time, especially because they had crops that were perishable. The inspiration for Goody's argument was that while all the societies of West Africa had been exposed to writing by the beginning of the colonial period, some of them adopted it and others did not. Take the case of two societies that can each be described as having states: the Hausa in present-day Nigeria, and the Asante in present-day Ghana. For the Asante the principal crop was yams, a non-storable tuber. For the Hausa cereals constituted the principal food crop. It turns out that the Asante did not adopt writing while the Hausa did. This argument is distinct from that made by Mayshar et al. (2020) because Goody did not suggest that it would only operate in societies with a state.

It remains possible that even when interacted with the suitability for cereals as opposed to roots and tubers, my distance instrument(s) will still be picking up not only the effect of writing, but also other technologies that facilitated governance of a state based on cereals. If that is the case, then my coefficient estimates for the effect of writing on its own would be inflated, but the underlying point of this article would remain; the emergence of states depended on technologies for governance as much as on favorable biogeography.

One final question one might ask about my IV strategy is given the long time lag between the invention of writing in the three points of origin and the observed presence of absence of writing in each of the SCCS societies, should we not assume that all societies had been exposed to writing? In

---

[33] See Keightley (1989).

fact, this was clearly not the case. If we imagine a world in which there were three societies, one of which was a point of origin for writing, a second that was located near to the first, and a third that was located somewhat further, then if the second society was exposed to writing but failed to adopt it, then the third may well have never been exposed to this. To see this consider the example of societies in Mesoamerica and Eastern North America. We know that the Mississippian societies that flourished in the Southeastern United States around the turn of the first millennium CE adopted a number of technological and organizational practices from Mesoamerican societies that had preceded them.[34] But the Mississippian societies never adopted a system of writing in spite of very likely being exposed to it. The consequence of this is that Native American societies in the Northeastern Woodlands, who might otherwise have been exposed to writing from the Mississippians, never had the opportunity.

The first estimation strategy is presented in Eqs. (28.1) and (28.2) below. In the first stage the presence of writing w in society i is regressed on a set of distances $\mathbf{D}$ from the three points of origin. In some specifications I will use distance only from the closest of the three points of origin. In other instances I will include distance from each of the three points of origin individually. All distances are measured in thousands of kilometers.[35] These distances will be the excluded instruments. The variable t is a measure of relative suitability for roots and tubers versus cereals. Measuring the difference in potential caloric output for each of these two classes of crops, it takes a positive value in areas where root and tuber suitability is higher than cereal suitability.[36] As shown by Mayshar et al. (2020) this is a predictor of state development.[37] While t measures relative suitability for roots and tubers versus cereal crops, one might also ask whether overall caloric suitability—combining all types of crops— should be added to the estimates. In separate tests including both t and a measure of overall caloric suitability I found that the latter was generally not statistically significant, and so I have not included the latter in the estimates that I will present here.[38] Finally, $\mathbf{X}$ is for a set of pretreatment controls involving environmental features that might be likely to have an effect agriculture but also a potential

---

[34] This was first argued by Kroeber (1928, pp. 392-396).

[35] There is no clear reason for using the log of the distance (or distances) here. Standard tests indicated that we cannot reject the null that the distance to the closest point of origin is normally distributed. Distances to individual points of origin do not appear to normally distributed, but nor are they heavily skewed. In terms of theory, there is no clear reason to think that the likelihood of diffusion of writing should be better predicted by a log as opposed to a linear specification. In fact, the latter makes more intuitive sense.

[36] These data derive from Galor and Özak (2016, 2015). The cereal crops considered are barley, buckwheat, foxtail millet, oats, rice, maize, pearl millet, rye, sorghum, wet rice, and wheat. The root and tuber crops are cassava, sweet potato, white potato, and yams.

[37] I directly include relative suitability for roots and tubers versus cereals rather than using this to instrument for cereals being the principal crop. Attempts to do the latter while simultaneously instrumenting for the presence of writing resulted in a weak instruments problem. In these specifications results regarding the impact of writing on state development were qualitatively similar. Also, including an additional variable measuring the absolute level of agricultural suitability, irrespective of whether this was with cereals or roots and tubers, did not fundamentally change any of the conclusions I report below. I will therefore leave those results unreported.

[38] It should be emphasized that this does not necessarily indicate that the Childe ([2018] 1936) agricultural surplus theory is wrong. The variable t is itself correlated with overall caloric suitability because places with very high caloric suitability tend to be areas where that results from cereal crops and not roots and tubers. For further discussion and evidence that attempts to disentangle the surplus and storability theories see Mayshar et al. (2020).

direct effect on the likelihood that a state would form.[39]

$$w_i = \alpha + \beta \mathbf{D}_i + \gamma t_i + \delta \mathbf{X}_i + \epsilon_i \tag{28.1}$$

In the second stage the presence of a state s (standing for *State1* or *State2*) is regressed on $\hat{w}$, the estimated probability of having writing and t, the relative suitability to roots and tubers versus cereals.

$$s_i = \alpha + \zeta \hat{w}_i + \eta t_i + \theta \mathbf{X}_i + \epsilon_i \tag{28.2}$$

The second estimation strategy—where distances from the three points of origin are interacted with relative suitability for cereals versus roots and tubers— are shown in a further set of specifications, in Eqs. (28.3) and (28.4). The distances from the three points of origin will be interacted with t. The interaction term (or terms) $t \times \mathbf{D}$ is (are) then the excluded instrument(s).

$$w_i = \alpha + \beta \mathbf{D}_i + \gamma t_i + \delta t_i \times \mathbf{D}_i + \zeta \mathbf{X}_i + \epsilon_i \tag{28.3}$$

$$s_i = \alpha + \eta \hat{w}_i + \theta \mathbf{D}_i + \mu t_i + \nu \mathbf{X}_i + \epsilon_i \tag{28.4}$$

The above systems of equations give us a way of plausibly estimating the effect of both the potential for root and tuber versus cereal production and the effect of writing technology on state formation.

28.5 First stage estimates

The first two columns in Table 28.2 show two different specifications of equation one; the first specification uses only the distance from the closest point or origin, and the second includes the distance from each of the three points of origin separately. In column one we see that distance from the closest of the three points of origins is negatively associated with the presence of writing, and the coefficient is very precisely estimated. All estimates reported in this paper report Conley (1999) standard errors that are adjusted for the potential presence of spatial correlation.[40] In substantive terms an increase of this distance by a thousand kilometers implies a ten percent reduction in the likelihood of a society having writing. In column two I include the distances from each of the three points of origin separately. The estimated coefficients for the distances from Sumeria, China, and Olmec Mesoamerica are very similar. This suggests that the diffusion process from each of these three centers was extremely similar in terms of rate of decay, possibly reinforcing the interpretation of these three centers being important for the diffusion of writing in particular.

---

[39] These are ruggedness, average annual rainfall, altitude, mean temperature, and the square of mean temperature. Several of these variables, not surprisingly, are highly correlated with the absolute value of latitude. After inclusion of these controls, inclusion of the absolute value of latitude rendered essentially unaltered results, and so it was excluded. The absolute value of latitude could also help in part capture the overall remoteness of a society. However, in practice the absolute value of latitude explains only four percent of the observed variance in distance to the closest of the three points of origin.

[40] These were implemented using the acreg package in Stata using a Bartlett kernel to allow the correlation to decay with distance and a distance cutoff of 6000 km. It makes sense to use a large distance cutoff in this instance given the wide range over which societal practices are thought to have spread. I also re-ran all estimates using standard heterokedastic-consistent standard errors. These were generally similar to the Conley standard errors though in a few cases they were substantially smaller.

Table 28.2 First Stage Estimates of the relationship between writing, root, and tuber versus cereal suitability, and distances from the three points of origin (Sumer, China, Olmec). All specifications included the following covariates for which coefficients are not reported: ruggedness, mean yearly rainfall, altitude, mean annual temperature, and mean annual temperature squared. Conley standard errors in parentheses.

	(1) Writing	(2) Writing	(3) Writing	(4) Writing	(5) Writing	(6) Writing
Tuber vs. cereal	-0.017	-0.016	-0.049	-0.062	-0.290	-0.239
	(0.009)	(0.009)	(0.015)	(0.012)	(0.097)	(0.098)
Distance closest	-0.101		-0.078		-0.084	
	(0.021)		(0.022)		(0.020)	
Sumer distance		-0.058		-0.049		-0.032
		(0.020)		(0.016)		(0.018)
China distance		-0.054		-0.048		-0.022
		(0.029)		(0.023)		(0.026)
Olmec distance		-0.049		-0.046		-0.012
		(0.034)		(0.029)		(0.034)
Distance closest*Tuber vs. cereal			0.008	0.012		
			(0.002)	(0.002)		
Sumer distance*Tuber vs. cereal					0.009	0.007
					(0.003)	(0.003)
Olmec distance*Tuber vs. cereal					0.011	0.009
					(0.005)	(0.005)
China distance*Tuber vs. cereal					0.009	0.008
					(0.003)	(0.004)
Constant	0.847	1.651	0.747	1.552	0.723	0.788
	(0.206)	(0.734)	(0.224)	(0.604)	(0.205)	(0.699)
N	165	165	165	165	165	165
adj. R^2	0.354	0.332	0.378	0.396	0.402	0.364

Columns three through six in Table 28.2 provide alternative estimates of equation three, a first stage relationship where distances from the points of origin are interacted with relative suitability of an area for root and tuber versus cereal cultivation. Following the arguments made by Goody (1986) we should expect the coefficients on these interaction terms to be positive. It should make less difference how closely a root and tuber-based society is from the three points of origin because of weaker demand for a system of writing. It should also be the case that the coefficient on the linear term for root and tuber versus cereal suitability should be negative. This is indeed what we see in all four specifications presented here. In column three the coefficient on the interaction term is positive and is estimated precisely. Recall that t, the measure for the relative suitability of roots and tubers versus cereals, takes a value of zero if an area is equally suitable for the two types of crops. Therefore in a society where $t = 0$, based on column 3 an increase in the distance from the closest point of origin would reduce the probability of a society having writing by a little less than eight percent. In a society in which t was one standard deviation above zero, the estimated effect of an increase in distance by one thousand kilometers would be 4.8 percent. Columns 4 through 6 then consider further specifications: (4) inclusion of each of the three point of origin distances along with an interaction term that multiplies the distance from the nearest point of origin with t, (5) inclusion of the distance from the nearest point of origin while separately interacting each of the three point of origin distances with t, and (6) the most flexible specification including each of the three point of origin distances separately interacted with t. I include this many alternative explanations to show the regularity of the relationship whereby distance from the three points of origin is correlated with the presence of writing but less so for societies situated in areas that were more suitable for tubers.

28.6 Second stage estimates

Table 28.3 shows the results of my second stage estimates (of Eqs. (28.2) and (28.4)) using *State1*, the "agnostic" measure of state presence. Recall from above that this variable is an index that breaks societies down into five categories: those where there is no governance beyond the individual family unit (1), those where there is no governance above the level of the individual community (2), and then those with one, two, or three levels of governance above the individual community, (3, 4, and 5). The relevant first stage estimates for column 2 in Table 28.2 can be found in column 1 in Table 28.1, and so on.

The first column in Table 28.3 shows the OLS estimates for reference purposes, and the remaining six columns then show 2SLS estimates using each of the six alternative instrument strategies shown in Table 28.4. As in Mayshar et al. (2020) we see consistent evidence that states were more likely to emerge in areas suitable to cereals as opposed to roots and tubers. However, as this result has already been established before, in what follows I will focus on the results regarding writing. In column two distance from the closest point of origin is the excluded instrument, and in column three all three distances from the point of origin are used as excluded instruments. In columns 4 and 5 the excluded instrument is the interaction between distance from the closest point of origin and relative suitability for roots and tubers versus cereals. Finally, in columns 6 and 7 the excluded instruments are the interactions between each of the three distances from a point of origin and relative suitability for roots and tubers versus cereals. In columns two through five the F statistic on the excluded instruments suggests that the estimates do not suffer from a weak instruments problem, though it is possible that this could be the case in columns 3 and 7.

Across all seven specifications in Table 28.3 we see fairly consistent results suggesting that the availability of writing had a strong effect on the development of a state. The estimated coefficients on the writing variable range from 1.17 to 2.06, recalling that *State1* takes a value ranging from one to five. The coefficients are also in most cases precisely estimated. The partial exceptions to this are in columns four and seven. The results point to a causal effect of writing when only the distances from the three points of origin are the excluded instruments (columns 2 and 3). They point similarly

Table 28.3 Second Stage Estimates of the relationship between State presence, Writing, and Agricultural Suitability. The excluded instruments by column are as follows: (1) None (2) Distance closest (3) Sumer distance, China distance, Olmec distance (4) Distance closest*Tuber vs. cereal (5) Distance closest*Tuber vs. cereal (6) Sumer distance*Tuber vs. cereal, China distance*Tuber cereal, Olmec distance*Tuber cereal (7) Sumer distance*Tuber vs. cereal, China distance*Tuber cereal, Olmec distance*Tuber cereal. All specifications included the following covariates for which coefficients are not reported: ruggedness, mean yearly rainfall, altitude, mean annual temperature, and mean annual temperature squared. Conley standard errors in parentheses. "Kleibergen-Paap statistic" refers to the Kleibergen-Paap rk Wald F statistic.

	(1)	(2)	(3)	(4)	(5)	(6)	(7)
	OLS	*2SLS*	*2SLS*	*2SLS*	*2SLS*	*2SLS*	*2SLS*
	State1	*State1*	*State1*	*State1*	*State1*	*State1*	*State1*
Writing	1.591	1.420	2.059	1.803	1.200	1.790	1.166
	(0.126)	(0.412)	(0.306)	(0.818)	(0.430)	(0.582)	(0.767)
Tuber vs. cereal	-0.073	-0.077	-0.061	-0.071	-0.074	-0.071	-0.075
	(0.018)	(0.020)	(0.020)	(0.023)	(0.020)	(0.020)	(0.023)
Distance closest				0.039		0.037	
				(0.101)		(0.076)	
Sumer distance					-0.039		-0.041
					(0.042)		(0.058)
China distance					0.022		0.021
					(0.065)		(0.073)
Olmec distance					0.027		0.026
					(0.066)		(0.074)
Constant	1.954	1.992	1.850	1.668	1.951	1.679	2.006
	(0.202)	(0.204)	(0.195)	(0.892)	(1.503)	(0.684)	(1.869)
N	165	165	165	165	165	165	165
adj. R^2	0.411	0.408	0.387	0.410	0.419	0.410	0.418
Kleibergen-Paap statistic		21.4	5.20	15.6	31.9	7.01	3.27

to a causal effect of writing on state development when the excluded instruments are the interaction terms $t \times D$ (columns 4 through 7). It is also worth noting that in these latter specifications when the distances from the three origin points are entered in the second stage, their coefficients are generally not statistically significant. This is further evidence that it was not distance from these three societies alone that mattered for the development of a state; distance mattered most for societies located in areas favorable to the production of crops that could be stored and which therefore created a demand for writing.

In Table 28.4 I repeat Table 28.3 specifications while using as dependent variable *State2* which takes a value of one if there are at least two levels of governance above the individual community and zero otherwise. As before, the relevant first stage estimates for column 2 in Table 28.4 can be found in

Table 28.4 Second Stage Estimates of the relationship between State presence, Writing, and Agricultural Suitability. The excluded instruments by column are as follows: (1) None (2) Distance closest (3) Sumer distance, China distance, Olmec distance (4) Distance closest*Tuber vs. cereal (5) Distance closest*Tuber vs. cereal (6) Sumer distance*Tuber vs. cereal, China distance*Tuber cereal, Olmec distance*Tuber cereal (7) Sumer distance*Tuber vs. cereal, China distance*Tuber cereal, Olmec distance*Tuber cereal. All specifications included the following covariates for which coefficients are not reported: ruggedness, mean yearly rainfall, altitude, mean annual temperature, and mean annual temperature squared. Conley standard errors in parentheses. "Kleibergen-Paap statistic" refers to the Kleibergen-Paap rk Wald F statistic.

	(1)	(2)	(3)	(4)	(5)	(6)	(7)
	OLS	*2SLS*	*2SLS*	*2SLS*	*2SLS*	*2SLS*	*2SLS*
	State2	*State2*	*State2*	*State2*	*State2*	*State2*	*State2*
Writing	0.610	0.575	0.836	0.604	0.420	0.925	0.647
	(0.058)	(0.141)	(0.128)	(0.409)	(0.232)	(0.214)	(0.297)
Tuber vs. cereal	-0.027	-0.028	-0.021	-0.028	-0.028	-0.022	-0.024
	(0.008)	(0.008)	(0.009)	(0.009)	(0.008)	(0.009)	(0.009)
Distance closest				0.003		0.035	
				(0.042)		(0.024)	
Sumer distance					-0.022		-0.009
					(0.020)		(0.024)
China distance					0.003		0.015
					(0.024)		(0.027)
Olmec distance					0.004		0.015
					(0.027)		(0.030)
Constant	-0.043	-0.035	-0.093	-0.059	0.140	-0.331	-0.234
	(0.075)	(0.073)	(0.073)	(0.380)	(0.653)	(0.225)	(0.755)
N	165	165	165	165	165	165	165
adj. R^2	0.393	0.392	0.355	0.393	0.400	0.341	0.405
Kleibergen-Paap statistic		21.4	5.2	15.6	31.9	7.00	3.27

column 1 in Table 28.2, and so on. In Table 28.4 we see that the coefficient on writing is positive and precisely estimated in most specifications, the exceptions being columns 4 and 5.

The estimates in Table 28.4 also allow us to compare the substantive effects of factors that led to the production of cereal crops and factors that led to the presence of writing. The coefficients on t are very consistent across the six 2SLS specifications, ranging from -.021 to -.028. If we use the column 2 estimate as a reference, a one standard deviation decrease in the value of t would be estimated to result in a twelve percent increase in the likelihood that a state is present. In this same specification (using both the first and second stage estimates), a one standard deviation decrease in the distance to the closest point of origin for writing would be estimated to result in a twenty one percentage point increase in the likelihood that writing is present, and therefore a twelve percentage point increase in

Table 28.5 Estimates of the presence of bureaucrats and taxation. In the 2SLS specification the excluded instrument is the distance from the nearest of the three points of origin for writing. All specifications included the following covariates for which coefficients are not reported: ruggedness, mean yearly rainfall, altitude, mean annual temperature, and mean annual temperature squared. Conley standard errors in parentheses. "Kleibergen-Paap statistic" refers to the Kleibergen-Paap rk Wald F statistic.

	(1)	(2)	(3)	(4)
	OLS	*2SLS*	*OLS*	*2SLS*
	Bureaucrats	*Bureaucrats*	*Taxes*	*Taxes*
Writing	0.631	0.654	0.361	0.555
	(0.100)	(0.148)	(0.085)	(0.198)
Tuber vs. cereal	-0.017	-0.017	-0.020	-0.015
	(0.012)	(0.013)	(0.008)	(0.011)
Constant	-0.096	-0.099	0.351	0.311
	(0.087)	(0.085)	(0.160)	(0.144)
N	81	81	108	108
adj. R^2	0.394	0.394	0.191	0.164
Kleibergen-Paap statistic		33.9		18.1

the likelihood that a state is present. It would seem then that the effects of biogeography and writing technology on state development were very similar in magnitude.

28.7 Writing and specific state characteristics

If we want to show that the availability of writing helped make the state possible, then it would be useful to be able to show that the presence of writing was correlated not only with the existence of a state, but also with those state functions that writing is most likely to have aided. I will do this by showing estimates which suggest that the presence of writing allowed for both the construction of a bureaucracy and for the development of a system of taxation. Each of these features of governance logically could operate much more easily and effectively with a system of writing in place.

The Standard Cross Cultural Sample contains a measure for the presence of bureaucrats that was coded by Whyte (1978). He only coded this for half of the SSCS societies (hence the smaller sample size in the regressions to follow), but sample selection was done randomly, and so we do not need to account for bias introduced by this procedure. Whyte found that bureaucrats, defined here as full-time officials unrelated to the head of government or ruler, were present in slightly less than a third of the societies in his sample. The SCCS also contains several measures that can assess whether some form of taxation—in either labor, goods, or money—was present.[41] This was the case about half of the time.

---

[41] The measure I constructed was based on variables 784 and 1736 in the SCCS.

It should be noted that for some societies data on the presence or absence of taxes was not recorded, and this process of sample selection may not have been random.

Table 28.5 presents OLS and 2SLS estimates where the endogenous variable is either the presence of bureaucrats or the presence of taxation. Given the reduced sample size, I only present 2SLS estimates using the baseline instrumentation strategy where distance from the closest of the three points of origin is the excluded instrument. The results suggest that the presence of writing made it more likely that a society would have a state that had bureaucrats, and the same can be said with respect to taxation.

28.8 Conclusion

Research in historical economics has provided compelling evidence that biogeography had a fundamental impact on the origins of the state. This advances greatly on the argument first laid out by Childe ([2018] 1936) and on all subsequent work. But none of the authors in this new literature claim that biogeography alone was all that mattered—it's simply the case that the effect of biogeography can be estimated because one can assume that it is exogenous. It seems logical that one new direction to pursue with this work is to consider the role of technology in the development of the state. In order to govern, state authorities found themselves in a stronger position if they had technologies for recording, measuring, and communicating over both distances and time. Writing was a crucial part of this.

References

Ahmed, A., Stasavage, D., 2020. Origins of early democracy. American Political Science Review 114, 502–518.

Allen, R., 1997. Agriculture and the origins of the state in Egypt. Explorations in Economic History 34, 135–154.

Baker, M.J., 2008. A structural model of the transition to agriculture. Journal of Economic Growth 13, 257–292.

Baker, M., Bulte, E., Weisdorf, J., 2010. The origins of governments: from anarchy to hierarchy. Journal of Institutional Economics 6, 215–242.

Becker, S., Woessmann, L., 2009. Was Weber wrong? A human capital theory of Protestant economic history. The Quarterly Journal of Economics 124, 531–596.

Blanton, R., Fargher, L., 2008. Collective Action in the Formation of Pre-Modern States. Springer, New York.

Boix, C., 2015. Political Order and Inequality: Their Foundations and Their Consequences for Human Welfare. Cambridge University Press, New York.

Bruhns, K.O., Kelker, N.L., 2007. Did the Olmec know how to write? Science 315, 1365.

Carneiro, R.L., 1970. A theory of the origin of the state. Science 169, 733–738.

Childe, G., [2018] 1936. Man Makes Himself. Aakar Books, Delhi.

Childe, G., 1950. The urban revolution. Town Planning Review 21, 3–17.

Cohen, R., Service, E., 1978. Origins of the State. Institute for the Study of Human Issues, Philadelphia.

Conley, T.G., 1999. GMM estimation with cross sectional dependence. Journal of Econometrics 92, 1–45.

Cross, F.M., 1989. The invention and development of the alphabet. In: Senner, W. (Ed.), The Origins of Writing. University of Nebraska Press, Lincoln.

Dal Bò, E., Lagos, P.H., Mazzuca, S., 2019. The Paradox of Civilization: Pre-Institutional Sources of Security and Prosperity.

Dell, M., Querubin, P., 2018. The historical state: local collective action and economic development in Vietnam. Econometrica 86, 2083–2121.

Demattè, P., 2010. The origins of Chinese writing: the neolithic evidence. Cambridge Archaeological Journal 20, 211–228.

Engels, F., [1972] 1884. The Origin of the Family: Private Property and the State. International Publishers, New York.

Fenske, J., 2013. Does land abundance explain African institutions? Economic Journal 123, 1363–1390.

Fenske, J., 2014. Ecology, trade, and states in pre-colonial Africa. Journal of the European Economic Association 12, 612–640.

Flannery, K., Marcus, J., 2012. The Creation of Inequality: How Our Prehistoric Ancestors Set the Stage for Monarch, Slavery, and Empire. Harvard University Press, Cambridge.

Fuller, D., 2010. An emerging paradigm shift in the origins of agriculture. General Anthropology 17, 1–12.

Galor, O., Özak, Ö., 2016. The agricultural origins of time preference. The American Economic Review 106, 3064–3103.

Galor, O., Özak, Ö., 2015. Land Productivity and Economic Development: Caloric Suitability vs. Agricultural Suitability. Brown Univ., Providence, RI. Unpublished manuscript.

Gelb, I., 1963. A Study of Writing. University of Chicago Press, Chicago.

Gennaioli, N., Rainer, I., 2007. The modern impact of precolonial centralization in Africa. Journal of Economic Growth 12, 185–234.

Given Wilson, C., 2016. Bureaucracy without alphabetic writing: governing the Inca Empire. In: Crooks, P., Parsons, T. (Eds.), Empires and Bureaucracy in World History: From Late Antiquity to the Twentieth Century. Cambridge University Press, Cambridge, pp. 81–101.

Goody, J., 1986. The Logic of Writing and the Organization of Society. Cambridge University Press, New York.

Heldring, L., Allen, R., Bertazzini, M.C., 2020. Institutional Adaptation to Environmental Change.

Keightley, D., 1989. The origins of writing in China: scripts and cultural contexts. In: Senner, W. (Ed.), The Origins of Writing. University of Nebraska Press, Lincoln.

Kroeber, A., 1928. Native Culture of the Southwest. University of California Publications in Archaeology and Ethnology, vol. 33, pp. 379–398.

Levine, D.K., Modica, S., 2021. State power and conflict driven evolution. In: Bisin, A., Federico, G. (Eds.), The Handbook of Historical Economics. Elsevier. Chapter 15 (in this book).

Litina, A., 2014. The Geographical Origins of Early State Formation.

Lowes, S., 2021. Ethnographic and field data in historical economics. In: Bisin, A., Federico, G. (Eds.), The Handbook of Historical Economics. Elsevier. Chapter 6 (in this book).

Lowie, R.H., 1927. The Origin of the State. Harcourt, Brace, and Company, New York.

Martínez, M.C.R., Ortíz Ceballos, P., Coe, M., Diehl, R., Houston, S., Taube, K., Calderon, A.D., 2006. Oldest writing in the New World. Science 313, 1610–1614.

Matranga, A., 2019. The Ant and the Grasshopper: Seasonality and the Invention of Agriculture.

Matranga, A., Pascali, L., 2021. The use of archaeological data in economics. In: Bisin, A., Federico, G. (Eds.), The Handbook of Historical Economics. Elsevier. Chapter 5 (in this book).

Mayshar, J., Moav, O., Pascali, L., 2020. Cereals, Appropriability, and Hierarchy.

Michalopoulos, S., Papaioannou, E., 2013. Pre-colonial ethnic institutions and contemporary African development. Econometrica 81, 113–152.

Mora-Marín, D., 2009. Early Olmec writing: reading format and reading order. Latin American Antiquity 20, 395–412.

Murdock, G.P., 1967. Ethnographic Atlas Pittsburgh. University of Pittsburgh Press.

Murdock, G.P., Provost, C., 1973. Measurement of cultural complexity. Ethnology 12, 379–392.

Murdock, G.P., White, D.R., 1969. Standard cross-cultural sample. Ethnology 8, 329–369.

Nissen, H., 1986. The archaic texts from Uruk. World Archaeology 17, 317–334.

Osafo-Kwaako, P., Robinson, J., 2013. Political centralization in pre-colonial Africa. Journal of Comparative Economics 41, 6–21.

Pool, C.A., 2007. The Olmecs and their legacy. In: Pool, C. (Ed.), Olmec Archaeology and Early Mesoamerica. Cambridge University Press, Cambridge, pp. 282–302.

Purugganan, M., 2019. Evolutionary insights into the nature of plant domestication. Current Biology 29, R705–R714.

Purugganan, M., Fuller, D., 2009. The nature of selection during plant domestication. Nature 457, 843–848.

Schmandt-Besserat, D., 1997. How Writing Came About. University of Texas Press, Austin.

Schmandt-Besserat, D., 2014. The Evolution of Writing.

Schonholzer, D., 2020. The Origins of the Incentive Compatible State: Environmental Circumscripton.

Scott, J., 2017. Against the Grain. Yale University Press, New Haven.

Senner, W., 1989. The Origins of Writing. University of Nebraska Press, Lincoln.

Service, E., 1975. Origins of the State and Civilization. W.W. Norton, New York.

Stasavage, D., 2020. The Decline and Rise of Democracy: A Global History from Antiquity to Today. Princeton University Press, Princeton.

Testart, A., 1982. Les tubercules sont-Ils aux céreales comme la sauvagerie est à la civilisation? Journal d'Agriculture Traditionnelle et de Botanique Appliquée 29, 349–354.

Wang, H., 2014. Writing and the Ancient State. Cambridge University Press, Cambridge.

Whyte, M., 1978. The Status of Women in Preindustrial Societies. Princeton University Press, Princeton.

Wilks, I., 1975. Asante in the Nineteenth Century. Cambridge University Press, New York.

The wife's protector: a quantitative theory linking contraceptive technology with the decline in marriage[☆]

29

Jeremy Greenwood[a], Nezih Guner[b], and Karen A. Kopecky[c]

[a]*University of Pennsylvania, Philadelphia, PA, United States*
[b]*CEMFI, Madrid, Spain*
[c]*Federal Reserve Bank of Atlanta, Atlanta, GA, United States*

29.1 Introduction

The forward motion of technology is unrelenting. It's hard to think of anything else that has affected the economy and society in such a fundamental way. The Second Industrial Revolution occurred as the clock chimed in the 20th century. It ushered in electricity, the petrochemical industry, and the internal combustion engine. Its ramifications were enormous. Electricity and the internal combustion engine changed the workplace since many manual tasks could now be mechanized. This combined with chemical fertilizers reduced the need for farm labor. Along with the automobile the reduction in the demand for farm labor encouraged the rise of cities and suburbs. Electricity also meant that the home could be mechanized. The mechanization of the home and industry allowed women to enter the labor force. This provided a catalyst for bestowing women's rights in the workplace.[1]

The Information Age (or the Third Industrial Revolution) is also transforming the economy and society. The ENIAC, the first general purpose computer, was set to work at the University of Pennsylvania in 1945. Machines like this were first used in academic and industrial research to perform calculations that were impractical or impossible to do manually. By the 1960s it was apparent that computers could be used to sort, store, process, and retrieve large volumes of data. Networking and the personal computers came online in the 1970s and the 1980s. All of this reduced the need for labor on factory floors, by using numerically controlled machines and flexible manufacturing, and eliminated the need for battalions of clerks, pools of secretaries, scores of purchasing and sales agents, and layers of supervisors and administrators. The recent rise of artificial intelligence is reducing the need for routine mental labor. The information age has also changed the household. Think about the hours saved

---

[☆] Dedicated to Stanley L. Engerman, one of the great economic historians. The authors thank Jordan Herring and Yueyuan Ma for research assistance. The title refers to John B. Beers's 1846 Wife's Protector contraceptive device.

[1] The impact of technology on family life is the subject of the prescient book by Ogburn and Nimkoff (1955) and more recently by Greenwood (2019).

The Handbook of Historical Economics. https://doi.org/10.1016/B978-0-12-815874-6.00037-X

from online shopping. Telecommuting allows parents to stay home with their children. People can now keep in touch easier with family and friends via social media and telecommuting, so distance matters less. Online dating has made it easier for singles to find mates.[2]

Seemingly small inventions can also have a huge impact on the economy and society. Take, for instance, the discovery of penicillin in 1928 by Sir Alexander Fleming, which was the dawning of the antibiotic era. The leading causes of death in the United States changed from infectious illnesses (cholera, diphtheria, pneumonia, smallpox, typhoid fever, plague, syphilis, tuberculosis, typhus) to noninfectious ones (cardiovascular disease, cancer, and stroke). At the beginning of the 20th century life expectancy was 47 years compared with 79 years today. Better health and longer lives have affected educational attainment, labor-force participation, retirement, and savings. Contraception is another small invention with profound implications.

Technological innovations such as these can be analyzed using quantitative theory. Quantitative-theoretic history aims to develop economic models of historical issues. The models generally start at the level of profit maximization by firms and/or utility maximization by individuals and then aggregate up to get a description of the economy as a whole. There are several key ingredients in this approach. First, is posing an interesting historical question. Second, is providing an historical narrative for the question's background. Third, is the development of an economic model to address the question. Fourth, is analyzing the model to glean intuition about its mechanics and establish any theoretical propositions. Fifth, is simulating the model to see if it can deliver a viable explanation of the historical data surrounding the question of interest. The analysis may end there but often counterfactual experiments are entertained. Hence, quantitative theory can take data and ideas from economic history and address them using the tool kit of modern macroeconomics. The question to be addressed here is: How did technological progress in contraception influence the decline in marriage over the course of the 20th century? The analysis will follow the above five steps.

29.1.1 Quantitative-theoretic history: some examples

Early examples using quantitative theory to address historical questions are Cooley and Ohanian (1997), Greenwood and Yorukoglu (1997), and Ohanian (1997). Cooley and Ohanian (1997) and Ohanian (1997) study whether it would have been better to finance World War II by debt or taxation. Their finding is that raising taxation in war times, as Keynes suggested, is a bad idea. Greenwood and Yorukoglu (1997) study three industrial revolutions and find that they are characterized by plunging prices for new technologies, productivity slowdowns, and rising income inequality. They model these phenomena.

Some more recent examples are Cole and Ohanian (2004), Greenwood et al. (2005a), Hansen and Prescott (2002), Kopecky (2011), Kopecky and Suen (2010), and Vandenbroucke (2008). Cole and Ohanian (2004) argue that Roosevelt's New Deal policies, by strengthening the power of monopolies and unions, prolonged the Great Depression. This is in stark contrast with the conventional fawning view of the New Deal. The secular decline in U.S. fertility from 1800, which was briefly interrupted by the baby boom, is addressed in Greenwood et al. (2005a). The transition from the preindustrial to the industrial era is modeled by Hansen and Prescott (2002), who emphasize the switch from land-intensive

---

[2] Billari (2019) reports that in 2017 nearly 40 percent of heterosexual couples met online.

to capital-intensive production technologies. Caucutt et al. (2013) built on Hansen and Prescott (2002) to study the emergence of the social security system along this transition. Kopecky (2011) analyzes the rise in retirement over the course of the 20th century. In 1880 more than 75 percent of 65-year-old males were still working, compared with only 20 percent in 2000. Kopecky and Suen (2010) develop a model of a city with two modes of transportation, namely buses and cars, and address the impact of the automobile on suburbanization between 1910 and 1970. The expansion of the American West is addressed in Vandenbroucke (2008), using a model that incorporates endogenous fertility and migration. Last, some of the literature reviewed in Section 29.10 also falls within the category of quantitative-theoretic history; viz., Albanesi and Olivetti (2016), Fernandez-Villaverde et al. (2014), Greenwood and Guner (2009, 2010), Greenwood et al. (2005b), Knowles and Vandenbroucke (2019), and Vandenbroucke (2014).

29.2 The decline in marriage

Since the best way to learn about someone else is by being together, intensive search is more effective when unwed couples spend considerable time together, perhaps including trial marriages. Yet when contraceptives are crude and unreliable, trial marriages and other premarital contact greatly raise the risk of pregnancy. The significant increase during this century in the frequency of trial marriages and other premarital contact has been in part a rational response to major improvements in contraceptive techniques, and is not decisive evidence that young people now value sexual experiences more than they did in the past. Gary S. Becker (1991, p. 326)

Since World War II there has been a dramatic increase in the fraction of young women who have never been married and the contemporaneous rise in the age of first marriage. These two trends are shown in Fig. 29.1. (All data sources are provided in Appendix C Data sources.) In 1900 only 40 percent of women in the 18-to-29 age range had never been married. By 2015 this had jumped to 77 percent. The median age of a first marriage rose from 22 to 28 years. The hypothesis entertained here is this: the decline in marriage is due, at least in part, to technological improvements in contraception. As the failure rate for contraception fell, the cost of a sexual relationship for a single woman also declined. This altered the cost/benefit calculation for marrying a partner at hand, favoring the option of postponing marriage until a more suitable partner is found.

Somewhat paradoxically as contraception improved, the number of non-marital births rose. Over the course of the 20th century non-marital births rose continuously, as is displayed by the right panel of Fig. 29.2. This occurred for two reasons: the fraction of never-married women has increased (Fig. 29.1) and never-married women are more sexually active today than in the past (which is discussed below). The left panel shows that non-marital births have increased throughout the postwar period for every age group of adult women. Additionally, non-marital births for women in the adult age groups now exceed those for teenagers.

Never-married women are much more sexually active today than in yesteryear. The percentage of 20-year-old women experiencing premarital sex rose precipitously over the course of the 20th century. Only 8 percent of women born around 1900 had premarital sex before age 20, compared with 76 percent born between 1978 and 88–see Fig. 29.3. Furthermore, the circa 1900 cohort of women had around 2.8 sexual partners before marriage, including their husbands, while the 1959-68 cohort had 7.0 partners.

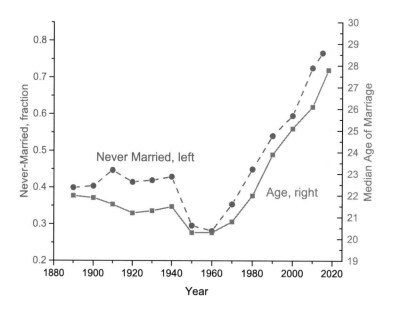

FIGURE 29.1

Marriage in the United States, 1880 to 2015-18. The figure plots the fraction of the female population, ages 18-29, that are never married and the median age of first marriage for women. See Appendix C Data sources for all data sources.

A marital search model is developed to examine, both theoretically and quantitatively, the impact on marriage of technological innovation in contraception. The model is set up in Section 29.4. In particular, each period a single searches for a partner on a marriage market. If the person is matched, they can choose either to have a casual relationship with the partner or enter into marriage. There are two types of casual relationships; viz., sexual and nonsexual ones. A non-marital sexual love affair involves the risk of pregnancy, which depends on the effectiveness of contraception.

When choosing between a casual relationship and marriage a person examines the marriageability of their partner versus the momentary utility from a non-marital romance and then continuing the search for a more marriageable mate. This choice is presented in Section 29.5. To keep things simple, the analysis abstracts from divorce. Likewise, when deciding between either a premarital abstinent or a sexual relationship the individual weighs off the extra utility from having sex against the expected cost of an out-of-wedlock birth. This decision is formalized in Section 29.6. It is established theoretically that an improvement in contraceptive technology leads to: a decline in the rate of marriage (Section 29.5); an increase in the fraction of the population that are never-married (Section 29.7.1); a postponement in the age of marriage (Section 29.7.1); and a rise in the fraction of singles that are sexually active (Section 29.7.2). Out-of-wedlock births may rise or fall with an advance in contraceptive technology (Section 29.7.4).

The theoretical model is subjected to some quantitative analysis in Section 29.8. To begin with, a series measuring the failure rate of contraception is constructed. The odds of a pregnancy for a sexually active woman dropped precipitously between 1900 and 2015-18. The analysis focuses on two periods

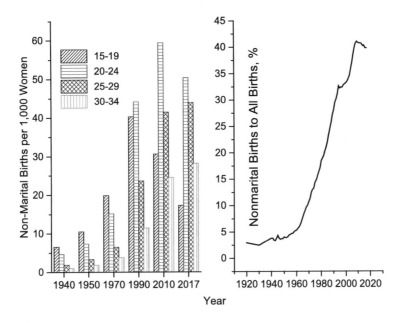

FIGURE 29.2

Non-Marital Births in the United States. The right panel shows non-marital births as a percentage of all births, 1920-2017. The left panel displays non-marital births by age group per 1,000 women at various times in the postwar period.

in U.S. history, 1900 and 2000. The model is calibrated to see if it can match facts from the U.S. data, such as the waning in the fraction of women who have ever been married, and the waxing in the fraction of single women who had premarital sex, out-of-wedlock births, and the number of sexual partners before marriage. The developed framework matches these facts well. The mapping between data targets and parameter values is unpacked by computing the Jacobian for the model.

Last, a review of the relevant economics literature on the decline in marriage is presented in Section 29.10. The discussion now turns to a brief history of contraception.

29.3 Contraception in the 19th and 20th centuries

Birth control advanced along two fronts in the 19th and 20th centuries. First, knowledge about contraception began to disseminate. Second, there was improvement in contraceptive technologies. Historically, fertility for married women was controlled in the United States, albeit very imperfectly, using primitive contraception. These technologies would have been too risky to use for unmarried women.

Using a reproductive period of 25 years and an interval between births of 1.5 years, Livi-Bacci (2012) estimates that a reasonable upper bound on the number of children that a woman can have is 16.7. No society has approached this theoretical maximal rate of reproduction. The closest examples are the 17th century Québécois and the interwar Canadian Hutterites with total fertility rates of 11.4

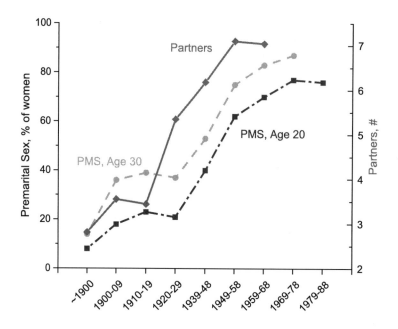

FIGURE 29.3

Premarital Sex in 20th-Century America. The graph plots the percentage of women, by various cohorts, who had premarital sex by ages 20 and 30, left axis. It also charts the number of partners these women had before marriage, right axis.

and 9, respectively.[3] The total fertility rate for white women in the United States fell from 7.1 children in 1800 to just 1.9 kids in 2015, as can be seen from the right panel of Fig. 29.4. The figure also plots the complementary cumulative distribution functions over births for four cohorts of married women in the United States before the baby boom–see the left panel. First, as can be seen, the distribution of births is well within the biological maximum. Second, the distribution functions are stochastically decreasing with the year of the cohort. That is, as time progresses a woman was less likely to have a large number of births. For example, the first group of bars shows that 15 percent of women born between 1835 and 1839 had 10 or more births. This had dropped to just 1.7 percent for the 1905-09 cohort. At the other end of the spectrum, it can be deduced from the difference in the heights between the fifth and sixth groups of bars that just 7.7 percent of women in the 1835-39 had no children, while 21 percent did for those born between 1905 and 1909. The mean number of births declines with the women's birth years. The mean of 2.5 for the 1905-09 cohort compares with a total fertility rate of 1.9 in 2015. The 1905-09 cohort would have been in their fifties by the time the pill was invented. So, the graph clearly illustrates that somehow family size was limited well before the advent of modern contraception. Historically, family size was limited by abortion, abstinence enforced by the prohibition and

---

[3] Galor and Klemp (2019), in their study of the fecundity of early French Canadian women, relay that one woman had 22 offspring.

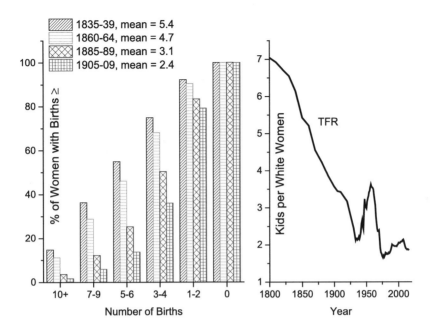

FIGURE 29.4

Fertility in the United States. The right panel shows the drop in the total fertility rate for white women from 1800 to 2015. Complementary cumulative distribution functions over children ever born for four cohorts of ever-married women are plotted in the left panel. As such, the vertical axis presents the percentage of women who had a number of births greater than or equal to that indicated on the horizontal axis.

stigmatization of premarital sex, crude contraception, child abandonment and infanticide, and delaying the age of marriage (which was important in light of short lifespans).

29.3.1 Dissemination of information

In 1823 Francis Place, an English social reformer, circulated a pamphlet in London titled *To the Married of Both Sexes of the Working People*. In it he wrote [Himes (1936, pp. 216-217)]

> *"What is done by other people is this. A piece of soft sponge is tied by a bobbin or penny ribbon, and inserted just before the sexual intercourse takes place, and is withdrawn again as soon as it has taken place. Many tie a piece of sponge to each end of the ribbon, and they take care not to use the same sponge again until it has been washed."*

An early 19th century sponge is shown in the right panel of Fig. 29.5.

In America, Dr. Charles Knowlton (1832) recommended douching in a pamphlet titled *The Fruits of Philosophy* (Chapter III on "Promoting and Checking Conception"), writing

> *"It consists in syringing the vagina immediately after connection with a solution of sulphate of zinc, of alum, pearl-ash, or any salt that acts chemically on the semen, and at the same time produces no unfavorable effect on the female."*

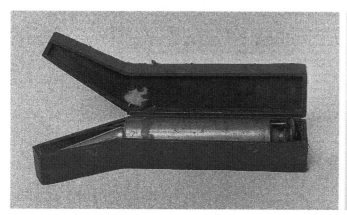 

FIGURE 29.5

A 19th century pewter vaginal syringe with its case is displayed in the left panel. The right panel shows a rubber sponge, in its original box (circa 1901-1930). Sponges were widely used as contraception in the early 1900s. Sponges were often soaked in spermicidal agents, of varying effectiveness. In a 1914 pamphlet *Family Limitation*, Margaret Sanger relayed that absorbing boric acid into the sponge yielded "satisfactory results." *Sources*: wellcomecollection.org and Science Museum, London.

The first edition was published anonymously, given the puritanical beliefs of the time. For trying to distribute his book, Knowlton was imprisoned for three months. Fig. 29.5, left panel, shows an early vaginal syringe used for douching. Last in *Moral Physiology; or, A Brief and Plain Treatise on the Population Question* (Chapter VI) Robert Dale Owen (1842) advocated withdrawal, stating

> "Among the modes of preventing conception which may have prevailed in various countries, that which has been adopted, and is now practised by the cultivated classes on the continent of Europe, by the French, the Italians, and, I believe, by the Germans and Spaniards, consists of complete withdrawal, on the part of the man, immediately previous to emission. This is, in all cases, effectual."

The dissemination of knowledge about birth control picked up dramatically at the start of the 20th century. In 1916 Margaret Sanger opened the first birth control clinic in America. Some 400 women received instruction about contraception before the clinic was closed by the police nine days later. Sanger served a thirty day jail sentence in 1917 for opening the clinic. Following a 1918 ruling by the New York State Court of Appeals in *The People of the State of New York v. Margaret H. Sanger*, which allowed contraception to be distributed by physicians, she opened the first continuously operational birth control clinic in 1923. The clinic was staffed by female physicians and counselors. In London, England, Mary Stopes did much the same thing, opening in 1921 the first birth control clinic in the British Empire. The first medical book in America aimed at providing physicians with up-to-date scientific information about contraception was the *Technique of Contraception: The Principle and Practice of Anti-Conceptional Methods*, written by Dr. James F. Cooper in 1928. A table in the book (p. 221) gave failures rates for condoms, douching, cervical stems, spermicides, withdrawal, etc. The book was dedicated to Margaret Sanger.

FIGURE 29.6

The left panel shows a European condom, made from animal gut, in a waxed paper envelope (circa 1801-1850). The right panel pictures a re-usable English rubber condom in its original box, complete with instructions (circa 1948). *Source*: Science Museum, London.

29.3.2 Technological advance

There also was considerable technological advance in contraception over this period. Start with the condom. Fig. 29.6 shows two early versions. In 1844 *The United States Practical Receipt Book* (p. 87) provided instructions on how to make a condom:

> *"Take the caecum of the sheep; soak it first in water, turn it on both sides, then repeat the operation in a weak ley of soda, which must be changed every four or five hours for five or six successive times; then remove the mucus membrane with the nail; sulphur, wash in clean water, and then in soap and water; rinse, inflate, and dry. Next cut it to the required length and attach a piece of ribbon to the open end. Used to prevent infection or pregnancy. The different qualities consist of extra pains being taken in the above process, and in polishing, scenting, &c."*

Packages of a dozen rubber condoms were selling in 1890 for 50 cents. At the time a tradesman would have earned an hourly wage of 20 cents, so this translates into a time price of 2.5 hours of work. Quality control was an issue; however, giving condoms a bad name. According to Tietze (1963), a study conducted in 1934-1935 found the following distribution over defects: burst, 29.4 percent; holes, 15.2 percent; flaws, 14.5 percent; total, 59.1 percent. This led to the U.S. Food and Drug Administration controlling quality standards. Also, Dr. Cooper in his 1928 medical book noted another disadvantage: "Blunting of sensation. Frequent refusal by male." The quality of condoms had increased dramatically by the 1960s, making them one of the most effective forms of contraception.

In 1846 the United States Patent Office granted patent number 4,729. The introduction to the patent specification read:

> *"Be it known that I, John B. Beers, of the city of Rochester, in the county of Monroe and State of New York, have invented a new Instrument called the 'wife's protector,' the design of which is to Prevent conception."*

The drawing that was submitted with his patent application is shown in Fig. 29.7. The specification of Beers's letters patent is provided in Appendix A Beers. His Wife's Protector instrument, a simple diaphragm-like device, inserted a hoop covered by an oil-silk membrane that prevented semen from entering the uterus. An interesting feature of the patent specification is that it explicitly stated that it was intended to prevent pregnancy, a risky venture at the time. Cervical caps and diaphragms also were

FIGURE 29.7

The drawing that was submitted with John B. Beers's 1846 patent application for his Wife's Protector contraceptive device. *Source*: United States Patent and Trademark Office.

introduced in the 1800s. The left panel of Fig. 29.8 shows a late 19th century German pessary. The pessary was an intracervical device (IUC). It worked after conception by provoking a foreign inflammatory reaction that stops a newly fertilized embryo from implanting and growing in the lining of the uterus.

There was also technological improvement in spermicides, used with or without other contraceptives such as condoms, diaphragms, sponges, etc. An English pharmacist introduced in 1885 a suppository made out of cocoa butter and quinine sulfate. Others at the time combined cocoa butter, which melted at a low temperature, with boric acid, tannic acid, or bichloride of mercury. In 1937 phenylmercuric acetate was introduced in a product called Volper. This was a highly effective spermicide, but was subsequently banned in the United States because of concerns about mercury. In the 1950s surface active agents (surfactants) were introduced. These are non-irritating. On this, in the past many products were used as spermicides. For example, Sanger (1914) mentions Lysol in *Family Limitation* and Belsky (1975) relays that Coca-Cola was used in India.

In the 1920s German gynecologist Ernst Grafenberg developed the intrauterine device (IUD), displayed in the right panel of Fig. 29.8. Both the pessary and this early IUD were infection prone. And it should be noted that pelvic infections could only be dealt with easily after the introduction of antibiotics in the 1940s. Fast forwarding to 1967, Howard Tatum and Jamie Zipper developed the first copper-bearing IUD. It was T shaped and made of inert plastics, which made it fit better and less vulnerable to infection. Zipper had shown that copper reduced the risk of pregnancy in rabbits. Interestingly, Grafenberg's IUD also contained copper, but its effect on preventing pregnancy went unnoticed.

Also in the 1920s and 1930s two gynecologists, Kyusaku Ogino and Hermann Knaus, provided an accurate tracking of the ovulation cycle. This provided a scientific basis for the rhythm method. As a result inexpensive devices were marketed, such as the Rythmeter, which calculated the time of ovulation and the periods of fertility and infertility. The rhythm method evolved into more modern

FIGURE 29.8

A gold wishbone stem pessary is pictured in the left panel. It was developed around 1880 in Germany. The right side panel shows a Grafenberg IUD, circa 1920s. *Source*: Science Museum, London.

ones, such as Sympto-Thermal Method of the late 1970s, which combines the rhythm calendar with changes in body temperature and cervical mucus.

The pill symbolizes technological improvement in contraception. It synthesizes two hormones, estrogen and progestin, in order to prevent ovulation. Scientists discovered and isolated hormones in the 1930s. Manufacturing them was expensive and slow, though. Russell Marker developed an efficient method for doing so in the 1950s. Around that time Carl Djerassi synthesized a progestin that could be taken orally. Capitalizing on these earlier breakthroughs, biologists Min Chueh Chang and Gregory Pincus teamed together with obstetrician John Rock to develop the pill, which was approved by the FDA in 1960. Today transdermal patches, implants, and injections can be used to deliver estrogen and progestin.

29.4 **Setup**

Each period a new cohort of adult singles enters the economy. The initial size of a cohort is one, with a per-period survival rate for a person of σ. The analysis focuses on steady states. Given this, the time-invariant size of the population is $1/(1 - \sigma)$.

Imagine the problem facing a single. This single will meet a partner in the current period with probability μ. If a meeting occurs, the person can decide to have either a marital or non-marital relationship with their partner. There are two types of non-marital love affairs: sexual and nonsexual ones. An abstinent romantic entanglement yields a momentary utility level of $a \geq 0$. A sexual liaison results in a current utility level of $l > a$. Libido, l, for the current love affair is drawn from the cumulative distribution function $L(l)$, with associated density function $L_1(l)$. The value of l is known at the time of deciding between either an abstinent or sexual relationship. A non-marital sexual relationship may

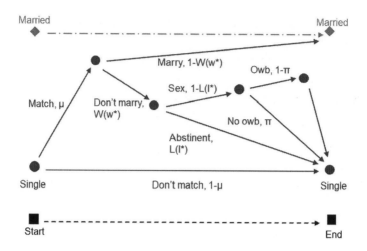

FIGURE 29.9

Timing of Events. The diagram shows the timing of events within a period. The circles denote nodes when an individual is single, whereas the diamonds represent nodes when they are married. A single matches with probability μ. If matched, they remain single with probability $W(w^*)$, have sex with odds $1 - L(l^*)$, and have an out-of-wedlock birth (owb) with probability, $1 - \pi$. The determination of w^* and l^* is discussed in the next two sections.

result in an out-of-wedlock birth. With probability π the person avoids a pregnancy, while with probability $1 - \pi$ they do not. Let an out-of-wedlock birth have a utility cost of O. Finally, if the person marries, then they get the random lifetime utility w. The value of being wed, $w \geq 0$, is drawn from the cumulative distribution function $W(w)$, with associated density function $W_1(w)$. The value of w is known at the time of the marriage decision, but the level of joy, l, from a casual sexual endeavour is not. Marriage is an absorbing state. People discount the future at rate β, which incorporates the survival rate of σ. Fig. 29.9 illustrates the timing of events in the model.

29.5 Married or single life?

The key step in the analysis is formulating the recursion that defines the expected lifetime utility of being single in the current period, S. Suppose that the person is single in the current period. With probability $1 - \mu$ the person remains unmatched. In this case, they realize no current utility. Since they enter next period as unmarried, the discounted expected utility for an unmatched single is βS. With probability μ they meet someone. If so, the single can choose either to marry or remain single. On the one hand, married life yields the lifetime utility w. On the other hand, let the expected momentary utility for a matched single be $N(\pi)$, which is increasing in the odds of safe sex π. The function $N(\pi)$ is unpacked in the next section. The matched single will enter next period still single, which has the discounted continuation value of βS. Hence, the expected lifetime utility for a matched single is $N(\pi) + \beta S$. Clearly, a matched single will choose the option that yields the highest level of expected lifetime utility. The decision to marry in the current period can be cast as

$$\text{MARRY,} \qquad \text{if} \quad w \geq N(\pi) + \beta S;$$
$$\text{REMAIN SINGLE,} \quad \text{if} \quad w < N(\pi) + \beta S,$$

where recall that the marriage decision is made after the value for w is realized. There will exist a threshold rule for w, denoted by w^*, such that

$$\text{MARRY,} \qquad \text{if} \quad w \geq w^*;$$
$$\text{REMAIN SINGLE,} \quad \text{if} \quad w < w^*,$$

where w^* is given by

$$w^* = N(\pi) + \beta S. \tag{29.1}$$

It is now easy to see that S satisfies the recursion

$$S = \underbrace{(1 - \mu)\beta S}_{\text{unmatched}} + \underbrace{\mu E[\max\{N(\pi) + \beta S, w\}]}_{\text{matched}}.$$

The above recursion can be rewritten as

$$S = (1 - \mu)\beta S + \mu\{W(w^*)\underbrace{[N(\pi) + \beta S]}_{w^*} + \int_{w^*} w dW(w)\},$$

which implies

$$S = \frac{\mu W(w^*)w^* + \mu \int_{w^*} w dW(w)}{1 - (1 - \mu)\beta}. \tag{29.2}$$

Therefore, by substituting (29.2) into (29.1), it follows that at the threshold

$$w^* = N(\pi) + \beta\mu[\frac{W(w^*)w^* + \int_{w^*} w dW(w)}{1 - (1 - \mu)\beta}].$$

So how does contraception affect marriage? To see this, totally differentiate the above equation with respect to π and w^* to get

$$\frac{dw^*}{d\pi} = \frac{N_1(\pi)}{1 - \beta\mu W(w^*)/[1 - (1 - \mu)\beta]} > 0.$$

In obtaining and signing this expression three facts are worth noting. First, the expected momentary utility for a matched single is increasing in the odds of safe sex, π, implying $N_1(\pi) > 0$–Proposition 29.3 in the next section establishes this. Second, at the threshold $d\beta[\mu W(w^*)w^* + \mu \int_{w^*} w dW(w)]/dw^* = \beta\mu W(w^*)$. Third,

$$1 - \beta\mu W(w^*)/[1 - (1 - \mu)\beta] = \left(1 - \beta\{1 - \mu[1 - W(w^*)]\}\right)/[1 - (1 - \mu)\beta] > 0.$$

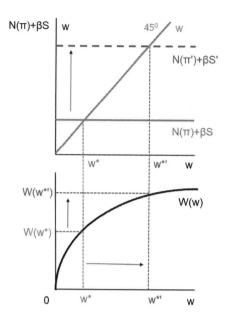

FIGURE 29.10

The determination of w^* and $W(w^*)$. The threshold for marriage, w^*, is determined where the $N(\pi) + \beta S$ and w lines intersect, as the top panel illustrates. To the left of w^* a person will choose single life, because the $N(\pi) + \beta S$ curve lies above the w one. To the right the opposite happens. An increase in the effectiveness of contraception, π, results in the $N(\pi) + \beta S$ curve shifting up to $N(\pi') + \beta S'$. As a consequence the threshold for marriage moves higher or rightward from w^* to $w^{*\prime}$. The fraction of matched singles choosing not to marry then rises from $W(w^*)$ to $W(w^{*\prime})$, as the bottom panel shows.

Intuitively speaking, when contraception becomes more effective there is a hike in the expected momentary utility for a matched single, $N(\pi)$. As a result, matched singles become choosier about who they will marry and the threshold value of love that has to be met for a marriage, w^*, moves up. The situation is portrayed in Fig. 29.10. For a matched individual the value of marriage is just w. This is shown by the 45^0 degree line marked w. The expected lifetime utility for a person who is currently single is shown by the line labeled $N(\pi) + \beta S$. This line is not a function of the realized value for w, as can be seen by inspecting Eq. (29.2). The threshold value for w, or w^*, at which the individual is indifferent between marriage and single life occurs where the w and $N(\pi) + \beta S$ lines intersect. Suppose that contraception improves; in other words, let π rise. The expected value of single life moves up, as shown by the shift in the curve from $N(\pi) + \beta S$ to $N(\pi') + \beta S'$. The fact that $S' > S$ is shown below. The w curve does not shift, since the random draw for married life is not a function of π. As a result, the threshold value for marriage, w^*, increases from w^* to $w^{*\prime}$. This causes the fraction of matched singles who choose not to marry to rise from $W(w^*)$ to $W(w^{*\prime})$. The above analysis is summarized by the proposition below.

Proposition 29.1 (Marriage Rate). *An improvement in contraception, or an increase in π, leads to a decline in the marriage rate, $1 - W(w^*)$, propelled by an increase in w^*.*

Interestingly, the expected lifetime utilities for both married and single lives, $\{1/[1-W(w^*)]\} \times \int_{w^*} w\,dW(w)$ and S, increase. For married life, it is straightforward to calculate that

$$\frac{d\big(\{1/[1-W(w^*)]\}\int_{w^*} w\,dW(w)\big)}{d\pi} = \frac{1}{1-W(w^*)}\Big[\frac{1}{1-W(w^*)}\int_{w^*} w\,dW(w) - w^*\Big]W_1(w^*)\frac{dw^*}{d\pi} > 0,$$

where the term in brackets on the righthand side is greater than 0. The expected lifetime value of married life rises because the expected value of single life has improved. This allows singles to be pickier about their marriage partner. For single life, it follows from Eq. (29.2) that

$$\frac{dS}{d\pi} = \frac{\mu W(w^*)}{1-(1-\mu)\beta}\frac{dw^*}{d\pi} > 0.$$

This justifies the upward shift of the $N(\pi)+S$ curve, following an increase in π, that is shown in Fig. 29.10–by assumption $N(\pi)$ is increasing in π. Single life improves because there is a boost in the expected momentary utility for a matched single, $N(\pi)$, due to the fact that premarital sex is now safer.

29.6 An abstinent or sexual non-marital relationship?

Consider the decision facing a matched single who has decided not to marry. An abstinent relationship yields a momentary utility value of a, while for a sexual one it depends on libido, l. At the time of making this decision the person knows the value of l. On the one hand, a sexual endeavour leads to the thrill l. On the other hand, the person may become pregnant with probability $1-\pi$ and suffer the cost of an out-of-wedlock birth, O. Therefore, the expected momentary utility from a sexual relationship is $l-(1-\pi)O$.

The momentary utility for a matched single who has decided not to marry and subsequently drawn a value for l is given by

$$\max\{a, l-(1-\pi)O\}.$$

Hence, the decision to have a non-marital sexual relationship is described by

$$
\begin{array}{ll}
\text{ABSTINENT,} & l \le a+(1-\pi)O; \\
\text{SEXUAL RELATIONSHIP,} & l > a+(1-\pi)O.
\end{array}
$$

There will exist a threshold rule for l, denoted by l^*, such that

$$
\begin{array}{lll}
\text{ABSTINENT,} & \text{if} & l \le l^*; \\
\text{SEXUAL RELATIONSHIP,} & \text{if} & l > l^*,
\end{array}
$$

where l^* is given by

$$l^* = a+(1-\pi)O. \tag{29.3}$$

Therefore, the odds of abstinent and sexual relationships, contingent on being matched, are $L(l^*)$ and $1-L(l^*)$. The fraction of singles having premarital sex is then $\mu[1-L(l^*)]$. As the efficacy

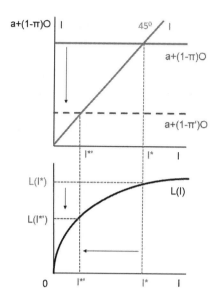

FIGURE 29.11

The determination of l^* and $L(l^*)$. The threshold level of libido, l^*, occurs where the l and $a + (1 - \pi)O$ lines in the upper panel intersect. An increase in π lowers the cost of premarital sex, so that $a + (1 - \pi)O$ shifts down to $a + (1 - \pi')O$. As a result, l^* drops to $l^{*\prime}$. The odds of abstinence for a matched single fall, consequently, from $L(l^*)$ to $L(l^{*\prime})$, as shown by the lower panel.

of contraception, π, improves, the probability of an out-of-wedlock birth for a sexually active single drops. So, the expected cost, $(1 - \pi)O$, of being sexually active declines. As a result, there will be more sexually active singles. Fig. 29.11 illustrates the situation. The 45^0 line marked l in the upper panel is the benefit from premarital sex. The horizontal line labeled $a + (1 - \pi)O$ represents its cost. This has two components; namely, the forgone value of abstinence, a, and the expected cost of an out-of-wedlock birth, $(1 - \pi)O$. The threshold level of libido, l^*, is determined in the upper panel where the l and $a + (1 - \pi)O$ lines intersect or where the cost and benefit of premarital sex are equalized. The lower panel plots the cumulative distribution function $L(l)$. As such, it gives the odds of abstinence, $L(l^*)$, conditional on a match. When contraception improves, the cost of premarital sex falls so that the $a + (1 - \pi)O$ line moves down to $a + (1 - \pi')O$, which results in l^* dropping to $l^{*\prime}$. The fraction of matched singles that pick abstinence declines from $L(l^*)$ to $L(l^{*\prime})$.

Proposition 29.2 (Sexually Active Singles). *The fraction of singles in a sexual relationship, $\mu[1 - L(l^*)]$, is increasing in the odds of safe sex, π.*

Proof. It's easy to see that

$$\mu \frac{1 - dL(l^*)}{d\pi} = \mu L_1(l^*)O > 0 \text{ [using (29.3)].} \qquad \blacksquare$$

The expected momentary utility of not marrying for a matched single is

$$N(\pi) = L(l^*)a + \int_{l^*} l\, dL(l) - [1 - L(l^*)](1 - \pi)O. \tag{29.4}$$

The level of expected utility for a matched single improves with technological progress in contraception for two reasons. First, for a sexually active single the odds of an out-of-wedlock birth have declined. Second, a single is more likely to be sexually active, since $1 - L(l^*)$ rises, and having sex yields a higher level of expected utility than abstinence because $\int_{l^*} l\, dL(l) - (1 - \pi)O > a$.

Proposition 29.3 (Current Utility for a Matched Single). *The level of current expected utility for a matched single, $N(\pi)$, is increasing in the odds of safe sex, π; i.e., $N_1(\pi) > 0$.*

Proof. Differentiating (29.4) with respect to π yields

$$N_1(\pi) = L_1(l^*)O[-a + l^* - (1 - \pi)O] + [1 - L(l^*)]O$$

$$= [1 - L(l^*)]O > 0,$$

where use is made of the facts that $dL(l^*)/d\pi = -L_1(l^*)O$ and $l^* = a + (1 - \pi)O$. Therefore, the momentary expected utility value for a matched single rises with the odds of safe sex, π. ∎

29.7 Statistical mechanics

29.7.1 Marriage by age

How many people will be married by a given age in the population? Recall that each period a cohort of new adult singles enters the economy. This cohort initially has unit mass but its size atrophies over time according to the survival rate σ. Follow this cohort as it ages period by period. Suppose that at the end of period $j - 1$ there are s_{j-1} singles around from the cohort. Then, there will be σs_{j-1} singles around at the beginning of period j. Out of this, $\mu\sigma s_{j-1}$ people match implying that the number of new marriages is

$$n_j \equiv \mu[1 - W(w^*)]\sigma s_{j-1}, \text{ where } s_0 \equiv 1/\sigma.$$

The number of singles in the cohort then evolves according to

$$s_j = \sigma s_{j-1} - n_j = [1 - \mu + \mu W(w^*)]^j \sigma^{j-1}.$$

The term on the right is easy to explain. If a person enters a period single, then the odds of them exiting the period single are given by $1 - \mu + \mu W(w^*)$. On this, the probability of not matching is $1 - \mu$, while the probability of matching and not marrying is $\mu W(w^*)$. So, the odds of not marrying at the end of j periods are $[1 - \mu + \mu W(w^*)]^j$ while the chance of surviving this long is σ^{j-1}. To summarize, the cohort evolves in the manner displayed in Table 29.1.

The impact of contraception on the married and never-married populations can now be analyzed. The fraction of the age-j population that is never married is

$$\frac{s_j}{\sigma^{j-1}},$$

Table 29.1 The evolution of a cohort by age. Each period a new cohort of unit mass enters the economy. The table gives the fractions by age of the original cohort that are newly married, single, married, and surviving. In a steady state the total size of the population is $1/(1-\sigma)$. An entry in a cell also represents number of people in the population in the designated situation. To get the fraction of the population in this case just divide by $1/(1-\sigma)$.

Marriage Statistics for a Cohort by Age				
Age	Newly Married, n	Remaining Single, s	Total Married, m	Surviving
1	$n_1 = \mu[1 - W(w^*)]$	$s_1 = 1 - \mu + \mu W(w^*)$	$m_1 = n_1$	1
2	$n_2 = \mu[1 - W(w^*)]\sigma s_1$	$s_2 = [1 - \mu + \mu W(w^*)]^2\sigma$	$m_2 = \sigma m_1 + n_2$	σ
$\vdots$	$\vdots$	$\vdots$	$\vdots$	$\vdots$
j	$n_j = \mu[1 - W(w^*)]\sigma s_{j-1}$	$s_j = [1 - \mu + \mu W(w^*)]^j\sigma^{j-1}$	$m_j = \sigma m_{j-1} + n_j$	σ^{j-1}

while the portion of the population up to and including age j that is never married is

$$\frac{\sum_{i=1}^{j} s_i}{\sum_{i=1}^{j} \sigma^{i-1}}. \tag{29.5}$$

Now suppose that the odds of safe sex, π, improve due to technological progress in contraception. From Proposition 29.3 single life becomes more enjoyable. Therefore, a matched single will become pickier about who they marry; that is, w^* rises from Proposition 29.1. The fraction of never-married individuals in the population at large moves up, as a consequence.

Proposition 29.4 (Never-Married Population). *The fraction of the population that is never married, as defined by (29.5), is increasing in the efficacy of contraception, π.*

Proof. Using the fact that $s_j = [1 - \mu + \mu W(w^*)]^j\sigma^{j-1}$, it is immediate that

$$\frac{ds_j}{d\pi} = j[1 - \mu + \mu W(w^*)]^{j-1}\sigma^{j-1}\mu W_1(w^*)\frac{dw^*}{d\pi} > 0,$$

where the sign follows from Proposition 29.1. ∎

The average age of marriage for the age-j population is

$$\frac{\sum_{i=1}^{j} i n_i}{\sum_{i=1}^{j} n_i}. \tag{29.6}$$

One may conjecture that an increase in the efficacy of contraception will postpone the mean age of marriage because the rate of marriage at any age drops by Proposition 29.1. This is true, but the reasoning is not straightforward because the number of the age-i newly married in the population, n_i, decreases in both the numerator and denominator of (29.6).

Proposition 29.5 (Mean and Median Ages of Marriage). *The mean and median ages of marriage are increasing in the efficacy of contraception, π.*

Proof. See Appendix B Theory. ∎

29.7.2 Premarital sex

Let v_{j-1} represent the size of the age-$(j-1)$ population that has never had sex. The size of the age-j populace that hasn't had sex is given by $v_j = [1 - \mu + \mu W(w^*)L(l^*)]\sigma v_{j-1}$, where $v_0 \equiv 1/\sigma$. To understand this expression, first note that only σv_{j-1} of the original age-$(j-1)$ virgin population will survive until age j. Second, out of this the fraction $1 - \mu$ will remain unmatched. The proportion μ will match, but from this segment the fraction $W(w^*)L(l^*)$ will choose both not to marry and not to have sex with their partner. Therefore, the fraction of the age-j population that has never had sex is

$$\frac{v_j}{\sigma^{j-1}} = [1 - \mu + \mu W(w^*)L(l^*)]^j.$$

Now,

$$\frac{d(v_j/\sigma^{j-1})}{d\pi} = j[1 - \mu + \mu W(w^*)L(l^*)]^{j-1}\mu\{\underbrace{W_1(w^*)L(l^*)\frac{dw^*}{d\pi}}_{+} + \underbrace{W(w^*)L_1(l^*)\frac{dl^*}{d\pi}}_{-}\} \gtrless 0.$$

This expression is ambiguous because while safer sex leads to a decrease in the number of age-j singles who are abstinent, via a drop in the threshold level of libido, l^*, it also increases the pool of age-j singles, through a rise in the threshold value for marriage, w^*.

Additionally, there are age-j marrieds who didn't have premarital sex. For example, at age j there will be $\mu[1 - W(w^*)]\sigma v_{j-1}$ individuals who marry but didn't have premarital sex. So, the fraction of the age-j population that didn't have premarital sex is

$$\frac{v_j + \mu[1 - W(w^*)]\sum_{i=1}^{j}\sigma^{j+1-i}v_{i-1}}{\sigma^{j-1}}.$$

The fraction of the age-j single population that has never had sex is

$$\frac{v_j}{s_j} = \frac{[1 - \mu + \mu W(w^*)L(l^*)]^j\sigma^{j-1}}{[1 - \mu + \mu W(w^*)]^j\sigma^{j-1}} = [\frac{1 - \mu + \mu W(w^*)L(l^*)}{1 - \mu + \mu W(w^*)}]^j.$$

Proposition 29.6 (Premarital Sex). *The fraction of the age-j single population that has had premarital sex, $1 - v_j/s_j$, is increasing in the odds of safe sex, π.*

Proof. The proposition holds because

$$\frac{d(v_j/s_j)}{d\pi} = j[\frac{1 - \mu + \mu W(w^*)L(l^*)}{1 - \mu + \mu W(w^*)}]^{j-1}\mu$$
$$\times \frac{[1 - \mu + \mu W(w^*)]W(w^*)L_1(l^*)dl^*/d\pi - (1 - \mu)W_1(w^*)[1 - L(l^*)]dw^*/d\pi}{[1 - \mu + \mu W(w^*)]^2} < 0.$$

∎

Table 29.2 The distribution over the number of premarital sexual partners that singles have at each age.

	Statistics on the Number of Singles with i Sexual Partners by Age j				
	Sexual Partners				
	0	**1**	**2**	**...**	**j**
Age 1	$p_1^0 = 1 - \mu + \mu W(w^*)L(l^*)$	$p_1^1 = \mu W(w^*)[1 - L(l^*)]$	$p_1^2 = 0$	$\cdots$	$p_1^j = 0$
Age 2	$p_2^0 = \sigma p_1^0 [1 - \mu$ $+ \mu W(w^*)L(l^*)]$	$p_2^1 = \sigma\{\mu W(w^*)[1 - L(l^*)]p_1^0$ $+ [(1 - \mu) + \mu W(w^*)L(l^*)]p_1^1\}$	$p_2^2 = \sigma\mu W(w^*)[1 - L(l^*)]p_1^1$	$\cdots$	$p_2^j = 0$
$\vdots$	$\vdots$	$\vdots$	$\vdots$		$\vdots$
Age j	$p_j^0 = \sigma p_{j-1}^0[1 - \mu$ $+ \mu W(w^*)L(l^*)]$	$p_j^1 = \sigma\{\mu W(w^*)[1 - L(l^*)]p_{j-1}^0$ $+ [(1 - \mu) + \mu W(w^*)L(l^*)]p_{j-1}^1\}$	$p_j^2 = \sigma\{\mu W(w^*)[1 - L(l^*)]p_{j-1}^1$ $+ [(1 - \mu) + \mu W(w^*)L(l^*)]p_{j-1}^2\}$	$\cdots$	$p_j^j = \sigma\mu W(w^*)$ $\times[1 - L(l^*)]p_{j-1}^{j-1}$

29.7.3 Number of sexual partners

A variable of interest is the average number of premarital sexual partners that an age-j person has. Let p_j^i be the number of singles that have had i sexual partners by age j. First, given the model's timing structure, $p_j^i = 0$ for $i > j$. Second, for an age-j single to have 0 sexual partners they must have had 0 sexual partners at age-$(j - 1)$, survive into period j with chance σ, and then either remain unmatched with probability $1 - \mu$ or match with odds μ, decide not to marry with likelihood $W(w^*)$, and not to have premarital sex with chance $L(l^*)$. Therefore, $p_j^0 = \sigma p_{j-1}^0[1 - \mu + \mu W(w^*)L(l^*)]$, with $p_0^0 \equiv 1/\sigma$. Likewise, for an age-j single to have j sexual partners they must have had $j - 1$ sexual partners at age-$(j - 1)$ which happens with probability p_{j-1}^{j-1}, survive with chance σ, then match and remain single in period j with odds $\mu W(w^*)$, and finally decide to have sex with probability $1 - L(l^*)$. This implies $p_j^j = \sigma\mu W(w^*)[1 - L(l^*)]p_{j-1}^{j-1}$.

Finally, there are exactly three ways for an age-j single to have i sexual partners, where $i < j$. First, they could have had $i - 1$ partners at age $j - 1$, survive, match, remain single, and then have decided to have sex. There will be $\sigma\mu W(w^*)[1 - L(l^*)]p_{j-1}^{i-1}$ people in this category. Second, they could have had i sexual partners in period $j - 1$, survive, but not match. There will be $\sigma(1 - \mu)p_{j-1}^i$ such singles. Third, they could have had i sexual partners in period $j - 1$, survive, match, remain single, and decide not to have sex. The number of singles here is $\sigma\mu W(w^*)L(l^*)p_{j-1}^i$. Hence, $p_j^i = \sigma\{\mu W(w^*)[1 - L(l^*)]p_{j-1}^{i-1} + [(1 - \mu) + \mu W(w^*)L(l^*)]p_{j-1}^i\}$.

The number of sexual partners that a person has before marriage can be computed using the statistics in Table 29.2. Let q_j^i be the number of age-j married people that have had i partners before marriage. First, to have had $j - 1$ partners by age j you must have had $j - 1$ partners while single up to age $j - 1$, survived to age j, and then gotten married. So, the number of age-j married people who have had $j - 1$ partners is $q_j^{j-1} = \sigma\mu[1 - W(w^*)]p_{j-1}^{j-1}$.

Second,

$$q_j^i = \sigma\mu[1 - W(w^*)]p_{j-1}^i + \sigma^2\mu[1 - W(w^*)]p_{j-2}^i + \cdots + \sigma^{j-i}\mu[1 - W(w^*)]p_i^i,$$

for $0 < i \leq j - 1$. On this, note that the earliest you can have i partners is at age i. At age i there will be p_i^i such singles. Out of this group, $\sigma\mu[1 - W(w^*)]p_i^i$ will marry at age $i + 1$ and then survive to period j with probability σ^{j-i-1}. Likewise, p_h^i singles of age h, for $i \le h \le j-1$, will have had i partners at age h, then gotten married at age $h+1$ with probability $\sigma \mu[1 - W(w^*)]$, and subsequently survived to age j with probability σ^{j-h-1}.

Last, for an age-j married person to have 0 sexual partners they must have survived until age j and gotten married without having premarital sex. They could marry at any age up to and including j. Thus, to summarize the cases,

$$q_j^i = \mu[1 - W(w^*)] \sum_{h=i}^{j-1} \sigma^{j-h} p_h^i, \quad \text{for } 0 \le i \le j-1. \tag{29.7}$$

Empirically, it may be desirable to include the person that you marry as a partner.

Now, the average number of sexual partners that an age-j married person has is

$$\frac{\sum_{i=0}^{j} i q_j^i}{\sum_{i=0}^{j} q_j^i} = \frac{\sum_{i=0}^{j} i q_j^i}{m_j}, \tag{29.8}$$

where m_j is the total number of people who are married at age j as defined in Table 29.1. A reasonable conjecture might be that the average number of premarital partners that an age-j married person has is increasing in the efficacy of contraception, π. While this can't be established theoretically speaking, it still can be true quantitatively.

29.7.4 Out-of-wedlock births

The fraction of matched singles that have an out-of-wedlock birth, o, is given by $o = (1 - \pi)[1 - L(l^*)]$. This can rise or fall with π, depending on whether

$$\frac{do}{d\pi} = \underbrace{-[1 - L(l^*)]}_{\text{IMPROVED CONTRACEPTION}} + \underbrace{(1 - \pi)\frac{1 - dL(l^*)}{d\pi}}_{\text{INCREASE IN SEXUAL ACTIVITY}} \gtrless 0.$$

This is an elasticity question that can be rephrased as

$$\frac{do}{d\pi} \gtrless 0 \text{ as } \frac{(1 - \pi)}{[1 - L(l^*)]} \frac{1 - dL(l^*)}{d\pi} \gtrless 1.$$

The shape of the distribution function $L(l)$ will determine whether out-of-wedlock births for matched singles rise or fall with the odds of safe sex, π.

For the population at large, Eq. (29.5) gives the fraction who have not married by age j. Out of this group, the portion μ will be matched in the current period. The fraction $1 - W(w^*)$ will marry, while the slice $W(w^*)$ won't. Therefore the fraction of the nonmarried population that will be matched and remain single is given by $\mu W(w^*)/\{1 - \mu[1 - W(w^*)]\}$. Out of this, the cut $1 - L(l^*)$ will be sexually active. Consequently, given the failure rate, $1 - \pi$, the fraction of the population up to and including age j that has an out-of-wedlock birth in the current period is

$$(1 - \pi)[1 - L(l^*)]\frac{\mu W(w^*)}{1 - \mu[1 - W(w^*)]}\frac{\sum_{i=1}^{j} s_i}{\sum_{i=1}^{j} \sigma^{i-1}}. \tag{29.9}$$

Clearly, this can rise or fall with π, because, as was just shown, $(1 - \pi)[1 - L(l^*)]$ can rise or fall in π.

29.8 Calibration

29.8.1 The procedure

The quantitative analysis focuses on two periods, namely 1900 and 2000. A steady state for the model is computed for each of these periods. The model period is taken to be four months (or a tertile). Functional forms for the distribution functions governing libido, l, and marriageability, w, need to be chosen. Let libido be governed by a Weibull distribution. Specifically,

$$L(l) = 1 - \exp[-(l/\lambda)^\eta], \text{ for } \lambda, \eta > 0,$$

where λ and η are the scale and shape parameters, respectively. Assume that marriageability has an exponential distribution. In particular,

$$W(w) = 1 - \exp[-(w/\xi)], \text{ for } \xi > 0.$$

Here ξ is the mean of the marriageability distribution.

Two criteria are used for selecting parameter values. First, the values for some parameters can be assigned from a priori information. Second, the remaining parameter values are chosen so that the model matches, as well as possible, a set of data targets. Start with the parameters chosen on the basis of a priori information. Denote the discount factor, sans the survival rate, by δ. Given this, $\beta = \sigma\delta$. The discount factor, δ, is given the standard value of $0.96^{1/3}$. People are assumed to have a life span relevant for marriage decisions of 30 years. The four month survival rate, σ, is set at $0.9925^{1/3}$ for 1900 and $0.9991^{1/3}$ for 2001.[4] The failure rates for contraception are taken directly from the data, as discussed below. Last, the mean for the marriageability distribution, or ξ, is just a normalization. On this, suppose that a solution to the model has been found for some value of ξ. The same solution obtains for $\phi \times \xi$, for $\phi > 1$, if a, O, and λ are also multiplied by ϕ. What matters for an individual's choices are the relative values of abstinence, premarital sex, and marriage. So, set $\xi = 1.0$.

The values for the rest of the parameters are selected to hit a set of stylized facts. Let D_j represent the j-th data target. Likewise, $P_j(\rho)$ is the model's prediction for the j-th target, as a function of the parameters, $\rho \equiv (a, \mu, O, \lambda, \eta)$, to be selected. These parameters are picked to minimize the relative

---

[4] The yearly survival probabilities are calculated for females ages 15 to 45, based on Table 10 in Arias (2004).

Table 29.3 Parameter Values. The parameters set on the basis of ex ante information are discussed in the text. The remaining parameters are selected in line with the minimization routine (29.10).

Parameter Values			
Parameter	Value, 1900	Value, 2000	Description
Set using ex ante information			
J	90	90	# of periods
δ	$0.96^{1/3}$	$0.96^{1/3}$	discount factor
σ	$0.9925^{1/3}$	$0.9991^{1/3}$	survival rate
π	$(1-0.72)^{1/3}$	$(1-0.28)^{1/3}$	Pr (safe sex)
ξ	1.0	1.0	exponential, mean–w
Set via calibration routine			
λ	0.085	0.085	Weibull, scale–l
η	22.723	22.723	Weibull, shape–l
a	0.027	0.027	abstinence
O	0.1806	0.1806	out-of-wedlock birth
μ	0.3359	0.3359	matching rate

prediction errors of the model. Therefore, ρ solves the minimization problem

$$\min_{\rho} \sum_{j=1}^{18} \omega_j [\frac{D_j - P_j(\rho)}{D_j}]^2, \tag{29.10}$$

where ω_j is the weight placed on target j. The set of targeted stylized facts is (where $\omega_j = 1$ unless indicated otherwise):

1. The median age of marriage in 1900 and 2000.
2. The fraction of women by the three age groups 15-24, 25-34, and 35-44 who had ever been married in 1900 and 2000. Each of the three age groups for a year has a weight of $1/3$.
3. The fraction of women by the three age groups 15-24, 25-34, and 35-44 who had premarital sex in 1900 and 2004. Again, each of the three age groups for a year is weighted by $1/3$.
4. The number of out-of-wedlock births per 1,000 unmarried women in 1920 and 1998.
5. The number of partners (including future husband) before marriage in 1900 and 2000.

The parameters values that result from the calibration procedure are listed in Table 29.3. All parameters values are kept constant across the two steady states, except for the failure rate of contraception, which is discussed now.

29.8.2 The failure rate for contraception, 1900 to 2015-2018

An important ingredient in the quantitative analysis is the failure rate for contraception. Fig. 29.12 shows the dramatic decline in the failure rate for contraception starting in 1900 and moving forward to 2015-18. The failure rate gives the odds of a woman becoming pregnant if she has sex at the normal

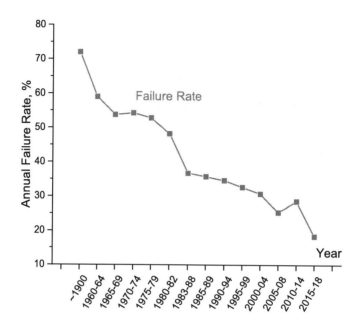

FIGURE 29.12

The annual failure rate for contraception, 1900 to 2015-18. The failure rate series is predicated upon the effectiveness of the contraceptive technologies available at each point in time as well as the usage distribution by women.

frequency for a period of one year. For each year the series harnesses the frequency distribution over the contraceptive practices used by women. This will depend on both the contraception technologies that are available at the time and their diffusion among sexually active women. The latter hinges upon the dissemination of information about, and the dispensation of, contraception. It also takes into account that some women won't use any method, including just withdrawal. Then, to compute the overall failure rate, the failure rate for each contraception is averaged across the different practices using the observed frequency distribution for usage. As can be seen, engaging in premarital sex in 1900 would have been very risky given the 72 percent odds of pregnancy. By 2015-18, the odds had dropped to 18 percent. The failure rate for the year 2000 steady state is set to 28 percent, the average failure rate over the 2000-14 period. Further detail on the construction of the failure rates is provided in Appendix C Data sources.

29.8.3 Findings

The upshot of the calibration procedure is presented in Table 29.4. First, between 1900 and 2000 the median age of marriage in the United States rose from 21.9 to 25.1 years. The model does a good job replicating this fact, with the median age of marriage moving up from 21.15 to 25.44 years. In the United States there was a big drop between 1900 and 2000 in the percentage of 15- to 24-year-old women that were ever married; an 11 percentage point drop from 29.62 to 18.17 percent. The model also displays an 11 percentage point drop, but too many women are married in this age group for both

Table 29.4 Data Targets. All statistics are for women. Data sources are detailed in Appendix C Data sources.

Data Targets				
Description	~1900		~2000	
	U.S. Data	Model	U.S. Data	Model
Marriage				
Median Age	21.9	21.15	25.1	25.44
Ever Married, %				
Age 15-24	29.62	34.93	18.17	23.95
Age 25-34	77.42	73.77	70.25	56.36
Age 35-44	88.90	89.43	86.60	74.96
Premarital Sex, %				
By Age 20	8	12	76	94
By Age 25	14	18	87	95
By Age 30	26	21	87	95
O.w.b.'s per 1,000 Singles	8.7	3.40	44.3	33.6
Partners before Marriage	2.8	1.18	7.0	8.2

periods. Additionally, in the model for the year 2000 too few women have been married in the 25-to-34 and 35-to-44 age groups.

Second, single women became much more sexually active between 1900 and 2000. In the U.S. data for 1900, only 8 percent of women had experienced premarital sex by age 20, 14 percent by age 25, and still only 26 percent by age 30. The model mimics this low level of sexual activity well, with the corresponding numbers being 12, 18, and 21 percent. It over predicts the rise in premarital sexual activity. In the 2000 data 76 percent of women had engaged in premarital sex by age 20, a rise of 68 percentage points, while in the model 94 percent did, which represents an increase of 82 percentage points.

Third, over the period in question out-of-wedlock births in the United States shot up from 8.7 per 1,000 single women to 44.3. There is also a large increase in the model from 3.4 to 33.6. This represents an increase in the data of 35.6 pregnancies per 1,000 single women and an increase of 30.2 for the model. Additionally, single women now have sex with more partners than in the past. In 1900 a woman had on average 2.8 partners before marriage, including her future husband. The corresponding figure in the model is 1.2, when the future husband is also counted. This rose to 7.0 partners in the 2000 data and to 8.2 for the model. Overall, the model does a good job explaining the targeted set of facts.

29.8.4 Opening the black box

The impact that parameter values have on the data targets can be analyzed by computing the model's Jacobian. The response of the j-th data target to a displacement in the value of the i-th parameter is calculated in elasticity form; i.e., $[\rho_i / P_j(\rho)] \times dP_j(\rho)/d\rho_i$. This is computed for all i and j involved in (29.10). It turns out that (locally) a, μ, O, λ, and η have a larger effect on sexual behavior in 1900 than in 2000. By contrast, the marriage statistics for 2000 display a bigger response to shifts in the parameters than do the ones for 1900.

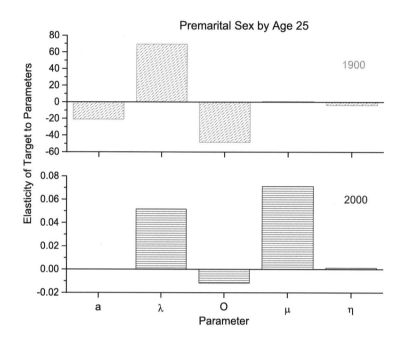

FIGURE 29.13

The part of the Jacobian showing the response of the percentage of women who had premarital sex before age 25 to a displacement in the parameters. The Jacobian is presented in elasticity form. Note that the units on the vertical scale for 1900 are much larger than the ones for 2000.

Fig. 29.13 shows how the percentage of women who had premarital sex by age 25 responds in the two steady states to a change in parameter values. The percentage impact of a percentage movement in parameter values is much larger for the 1900 steady state than for the 2000 one, as can be seen by the units on the vertical axes. In 2000 almost all matched singles in the model are having premarital sex so the percentage reaction is muted, while in 1900 a small minority are so the percentage response is much bigger. The reactions make sense too. For example, increasing the utility from abstinence, a, or the cost of an out-of-wedlock birth, O, reduce the amount of premarital sex in 1900. Raising the libido scale parameter, λ, which increases the flow of women into premarital sex given the threshold, results in a higher level of premarital sex. The utility level for abstinence, a, has a negligible impact on premarital sex in 2000, because almost no matched singles are abstinent.

Fig. 29.14 does the same thing for the median age of marriage. Now a given percentage displacement in the parameter values has a much larger percentage impact on the 2000 steady state than for the 1900 one, as can be seen by the units on the vertical axes. This is understandable. In the 2000 steady state the vast majority of matched singles choose to have a sexual relationship. So, for example, they respond to an increase in the cost of out-of-wedlock births, O, by moving into marriage (or marrying earlier). A rise in the matching rate, μ, leads to a delay in marriage for the 2000 steady state, but entices people to marry just slightly earlier in the 1900 one. This transpires because in the 2000 steady state the cost of waiting is lower because people can engage in non-marital sexual relationship. This

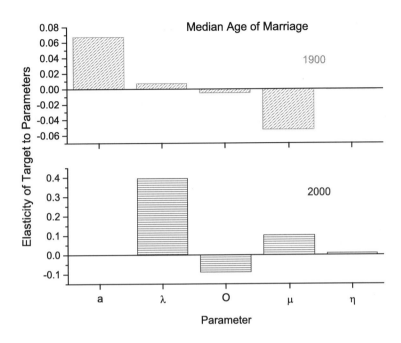

FIGURE 29.14

The part of the Jacobian showing the response of the median age of marriage to a displacement in the parameters. The Jacobian is presented in elasticity form. Note that the units on the vertical scale for 2000 are much larger than the ones for 1900, the opposite of Figure 29.13.

opportunity is more costly in the 1900 steady state, so people are less picky about their mate, and hence marry earlier.

29.9 Conclusions

While fertility has been controlled for eons, premarital sex would have been too risky for women historically. This began to change in the 19th century when contraceptive technology improved and information about contraception disseminated (Section 29.3). The 19th and 20th centuries saw improvements in condoms and spermicides, and the introduction of diaphragms, IUDs, and the pill. Just as important was the dissemination of information about contraception, often at personal risk for the providers. In America this started and ended with the crusaders Dr. Charles Knowlton and Margaret Sanger. The hypothesis here is that advancement in contraception led to a rise in premarital sex, an increase in out-of-wedlock births, and a fall in the fraction of the population that is married.

To address this hypothesis a marital search model is constructed. Each period a single may meet a partner. A person can choose to marry their partner or not (Section 29.5). If not, they can decide whether to have a premarital sexual relationship with the person (Section 29.6). The risk of a premarital sexual relationship is an out-of-wedlock birth. As contraception improves this risk is mitigated. It is shown theoretically that a drop in the failure rate for contraception leads to a decline in the rate of marriage (Section 29.5), an increase the fraction of singles who are sexually active (Section 29.6), a rise in the proportion of the population that is never married (Section 29.7), and a delay in the average age of marriage (Section 29.7).

The theoretical model is then confronted with the U.S. data (in Section 29.8). The quantitative analysis focuses on two periods in U.S. history; viz, 1900 and 2000. To start with, a time series is constructed measuring the efficacy of contraception. It is shown that the odds of a pregnancy for a sexually active woman dropped dramatically between 1900 and 2015-18. This made sex much safer for singles. The question then asked is whether the model can explain, as a function of technological progress in contraception, the following set of facts: the observed decline in marriage between 1900 and 2015-18, the rise in premarital sex, the increase in out-of-wedlock births, and the uptick in the number of sexual partners before marriage. The answer is yes.

A review of the relevant economics literature on marriage is presented now.

29.10 Literature review
29.10.1 Contraception and the age of marriage

An increasing use of birth control may be a cause of earlier marriage. For if a young couple can contemplate a marriage without a baby within a year, and hence with only two to provide for, and perhaps with the bride working at a paying job, we think there would be more marriage than if a baby is pretty sure to come within a year and the mother unable to earn any money.

Against this argument is the idea held by some that a young woman practicing birth control could have sexual intercourse without marrying and without becoming a mother, hence she can have a man without marrying; and similarly a man can have a woman without marriage. Thus marriage might be discouraged by the spread of birth control. Ogburn and Nimkoff (1955, pp. 89-90)

As a theoretical proposition, Ogburn and Nimkoff (1955) thought that the impact of contraception on the age of marriage could go either way. While they note that "(i)t is very difficult to test these ideas with data," they felt that the first hypothesis had more currency given that the age of marriage was decreasing at the time–note the dip in the median age of marriage between 1940 and 1960 shown in Fig. 29.1. Goldin and Katz (2002) advance a more modern version of this idea. They highlight two ways in which better contraception, the pill, changed the lives of college-educated women in the United States. First, the pill made the returns to investment in professional careers, such as law and medicine, less uncertain by allowing women to better time their fertility decisions. Second, the pill had a thicker marriage market effect: as more women delayed their entry into marriage, each individual woman became less concerned about being left out in the marriage market due to her career choice. In their empirical analysis, Goldin and Katz (2002) exploit variations across U.S. states in the access of young unmarried women to the pill. Their "most persuasive evidence for a role of the pill is that its initial diffusion among single women coincided with, and is analytically related to, the increase in the age at first marriage and the increase in women in professional degree programs" (p. 767).

Now, it is clear that fertility was under control well before the 1960s, as Fig. 29.4 showed. This is not to say that family planning policies, especially for developing countries, are not important.[5] Also, the number of sexually-active single women had risen dramatically before this time–Fig. 29.3. Furthermore, you can go to professional school while married. This is more common outside of the United States. The take off in women going to professional schools started after 1972. The flow of women into higher education had started well before this though. By 1972, 42 percent of bachelors degrees, 41 percent of masters degrees, and 18 percent of doctorates went to women, which amounted to 42 percent of all non-professional degrees. The respective numbers in 1900 were 19 percent, 19 percent, 8 percent, and 19 percent. The year 1972 was also when Title IX of the Education Amendments was signed into law. The law prohibited discrimination against women in any federally-funded education program. Goldin and Katz's (2002) defense is that its guidelines were not complete until 1975. While Title IX's statutory language was brief, it still would have been law upon enactment in 1972. It's likely that colleges and universities changed their admission policies before 1975, especially since there was uncertainty about what they would be legally liable for. In fact, one could argue that the passage of Title IX was itself a reaction to the changing place of women in education and the workplace. On this, see Greenwood et al. (2017) for a model where the passage of women's rights is an endogenous function of the state of the economy. Last, Meyers (2017), who revisits the empirical analysis by Goldin and Katz (2002), finds that the pill itself had little effect on the age of first marriages and births, while liberalized access to abortion had a much larger effect. So, the power of the pill, while important, may be overstated.

Before the pill was available to unmarried women, between its approval by the FDA in 1960 and the late 1960s or early 1970s, only married women could access it. Indeed, many U.S. states reduced the legal age of marriage from 21 to 18 during this period. According to Edlund and Machado (2015), these changes allowed women to marry early, which would be in line with Ogburn and Nimkoff's (1955) first idea. Combined with the pill, however, this also allowed them to widen the window between marriage and first birth and improve educational and professional outcomes. Gershoni and Low (2018a) document how the availability of in vitro fertilization in Israel has led to an increase in the average age at first marriage. In related work, Gershoni and Low (2018b) discuss how this increased education levels for women and resulted in higher paying careers. (Interestingly, Ogburn and Nimkoff (1955) discuss the transplantation of ova in their book, but speculated that its effect on the family would be negligible.)

29.10.2 Premarital sex and out-of-wedlock births

Technological advance in contraception allowed women to separate sex from marriage. This led to a dramatic increase in the fraction of women who engaged in premarital sex during the 20th century; again see Fig. 29.3. Yet, despite the improvements in contraceptive technology, out-of-wedlock births increased as well. Greenwood and Guner (2010) study premarital sex among teenagers within the context of an equilibrium matching model. In the model individuals rationally weigh the costs and benefits from this risky activity. Better contraceptives lower the expected cost of premarital sex. In

---

[5] Cavalcanti et al. (2020) introduce unwanted births into a model of fertility decisions and growth, and show that family planning programs, which reduce the number of unwanted pregnancies, can generate significant gains in the educational attainments of children and hence GDP.

their quantitative analysis better contraceptives result in both an increase in the fraction of teenagers having sex and the fraction of them becoming pregnant.

Akerlof et al. (1996) also focus on this puzzle. They suggest that better contraceptives, coupled with the availability of abortion, led to the disappearance of shotgun marriages, and as a result there was an increase in out-of-wedlock first births. In their framework prior to a sexual relationship single women may or may not ask for an implicit promise of marriage in the event of pregnancy. With the advance of contraception and the legalization of abortion, men can choose among many sexually active single women. Some single women who become pregnant may be willing to have an abortion, others won't. Competition on the marriage market may lead to women who are opposed to abortion being reluctant to ask for a promise of marriage should a pregnancy occur. But, why would men abide by such an *implicit* promise? (I.e., their equilibrium is not subgame perfect.) This is left unanswered in Akerlof et al. (1996).

On the basis of the observed decline of shotgun weddings, Kennes and Knowles (2019) argue that an important ingredient in the rise of out-of-wedlock births is an increase in the value of single life with children relative to marriage. Their vehicle for analysis is a repeated-matching model where women are heterogeneous in the number of previous children and where singles make decisions each period regarding their sexual activity, birth control, abortion, and whether to marry if pregnant. Low take-up rates of the pill and the availability of abortion are critical features in their analysis. Kennes and Knowles (2019) consider a number of candidates, such as the advent of legal abortion, lower divorce costs, and increased frictions in shotgun weddings, that might be responsible for the decline in shotgun marriages. Other things might also have reduced the value of marriage relative to single life with children: more generous welfare benefits, rising living standards together with the advent of labor-saving household technologies, and a lessening of the stigma associated with an out-of-wedlock birth.

Premarital sex and out-of-wedlock births were stigmatized in yesteryear in order to dissuade premarital sexual activity. Since societies then were much poorer than ones today, out-of-wedlock births placed an enormous financial burden on families, churches, and states. Fernandez-Villaverde et al. (2014) model the formation and evolution of such social norms. As premarital sexual activity became safer, parents, churches, and governments had less incentive to stigmatize premarital sex, given that socialization is a costly activity. The relaxation of sexual norms operated to reinforce the effect that technological advancement in contraception had on the rise in premarital sex and out-of-wedlock births. Fernandez-Villaverde et al. (2014) formalize this intuition in a model of intergenerational preference transmission. For models of preference transmission in other contexts, see Becker (1993), Bisin and Verdier (2001), and Doepke and Zilibotti (2008).

29.10.3 Other factors affecting the timing of marriage

Clearly factors other than contraceptives affect the timing of marriage. Browning et al. (2014), Greenwood et al. (2017), and Stevenson and Wolfers (2007) provide reviews of the literature.

29.10.3.1 Rising wages

In his classic treatment of the topic, Becker (1991, p. 350) states that "the family in the United States changed more rapidly (since 1950) than during any equivalent period since the founding of the colonies. I believe that a major cause of these changes is the growth in the earning power of women as the

American economy developed." Higher relative earnings reduce the gains from marriage for women and allow them to be more choosy between married and single life. Regalia and Rios-Rull (2001) formalize this idea in a quantitative model and show that increases in the relative earnings of women can potentially account for almost ninety percent of the observed rise in the share of single women since the mid-1970s. Shephard (2019) also focuses on the effects of a narrowing gender wage gap on marital outcomes. He builds a life-cycle equilibrium model with endogenous human capital accumulation, fertility, and home production to study time allocation and marriage decisions. His simulations show that the decline in the gender wage gap since the 1980s is able to generate an increase in female employment, a decline in male employment, an increase in the age-of-first marriage for women, and a reduction in the marital age gap between men and women.

Other aspects of the wage structure can also affect the incentive to marry. Olivetti (2006) documents that the returns to labor market experience increased for women since the 1970s and this was an important factor in generating rising female labor-force participation. Caucutt et al. (2002) show that, within a matching model of marriage, this will also increase the incentives of women to delay both fertility and marriage. Santos and Weiss (2016), instead, focus on the rising labor income volatility since the 1970s, and show that if marriage involves consumption commitments, such as children or housing, then a heightening in income volatility will delay entry into marriage.

29.10.3.2 Household technologies

Another key force that shaped families in the United States and elsewhere was the dramatic improvements in households technologies. Improvements in household durables freed women from housework and allowed them to enter the labor force–see Greenwood et al. (2005a, 2005b). (Relatedly, Albanesi and Olivetti, 2016, argue that advances in maternal medicine facilitated the entry of young women into the workplace.) These forces reduced the benefit from a traditional marriage; to wit, a breadwinner husband and a housekeeper wife. Greenwood and Guner (2009) integrate home production into a search model of marriage, and show that better household technologies can account for a significant part of the rise in divorce, the fall in marriage, and the increase in married female labor-force participation that occurred during the later half of the 20th century. According to Greenwood and Guner (2009, p. 233), "the reduction of the economic benefits of marriage allowed the modern criteria of mutual attraction between mates to come to the fore, a trend 'from economics to romance' in the words of Ogburn and Nimkoff (1955)." They also show how improvements in household technology and increases in income can explain the increase in marriage between 1940 and 1960–for one more time, recall Fig. 29.1.[6]

---

[6] The idea is that technological progress in the household sector, together with rising living standards, at first made it easier for young couples to leave their parents' homes and establish married households and then later on in time for singles to leave their parents' homes and establish single households before marriage. That is, there is a trend over time toward smaller and smaller households.

As marriage declined in the United States, there has also been an upswing in assortative mating, the tendency of people with similar educational attainments to marry each other (Chiappori et al., 2017, and Greenwood et al., 2014). Greenwood et al. (2016) develop a model, with heterogeneous agents, of marriage, divorce, educational attainment, and married female labor-force participation. They show how a hike in the college premium together with labor-saving technological progress in the household sector, led to a decline marriage, an increase married female labor-force participation, and widening inequality in the United States. The induced changes in married female labor-force participation and marriage play an important role in amplifying the impact of shifts in the wage structure on inequality.

29.10.3.3 The welfare state

The expansion of welfare state, in particular social assistance to single mothers with children, has often been pointed to as another important force that has shaped U.S. families. There are mixed views about this idea. The empirical evidence in favor of the idea, which relies on cross-time and cross-state variations in welfare policies, has been weak–see Moffitt (1992) for an early review and Moffitt et al. (2020) for a more recent analysis. Structural models such as Aiyagari et al. (2000) and Greenwood et al. (2000) predict that less generous welfare payments should reduce the number of single women. In line with this prediction, Low et al. (2018) show that the 1996 welfare reform did result in more married women.

29.10.3.4 Lack of marriageable men

A large literature in sociology and demography, emphasizes the lack of marriageable men as a potential factor for the decline of marriage in the United States. The basic idea, following Wilson and Neckerman (1986), is that low wage growth, declining manufacturing, and rising incarceration in recent decades made marriageable men scarce. Schneider et al. (2018) document, for example, that reduced economic prospects and increased risk of incarceration contributed significantly to the decline of marriage in the United States over the last 45 years. Incarceration has also been proposed as a factor that can explain why blacks marry at a much lower rate than whites in the United States. Exploiting cross-state U.S. data, Charles and Luoh (2010) find a strong negative effect of male incarceration rates on the likelihood of women ever getting married. Building on this intuition, Caucutt et al. (2018) develop an equilibrium search model of marriage, divorce, and labor supply that takes into account the transitions between employment, unemployment, and prison for individuals by education, gender, and race. They show that if black men had the same employment and prison transitions as whites, then about half of the racial marriage gap would be eliminated.

29.10.3.5 Changes in the sex ratio

Since historically it took two sexes, a man and a woman, to form a marriage, the sex ratio (defined as the number of single men to single women) can affect marriage decisions. If there is an imbalance in the sex ratio, whoever is on the short side of the market will have a harder time to find a partner. When a marriage is formed, the sex in short supply will have a higher bargaining power. These features emerge in standard search and matching models (e.g., Greenwood et al., 2000).

What can generate an imbalanced sex ratio? Some candidates are changes in population growth rates (say a baby boom or baby bust), male incarceration, sex-biased migration, and wars. Angrist (2002) exploits, as a natural experiment, variations in migration flows during the early 20th century in the United States. He finds that migration, which increased the size of the male population more for some ethnic groups than others, improved marriage prospects for women. In particular, it increased the likelihood of marriage for women and reduced female labor-force participation. The latter is a reflection of a tilt in household bargaining power toward women. Angrist (2002, p. 997) provides a quote from a Moroccan female immigrant saying "Every day I meet someone better. I am waiting for the best." Bronson and Mazzocco (2017) document, by analyzing nearly century of U.S. data, that higher cohort sizes are associated with lower marriage rates for *both* men and women. They find that variations in cohort sizes can explain a large variation in marriage rates since the 1930s.

Recent research suggests that the theoretical link between sex ratios and marriage can be complex. An excellent example is Knowles and Vandenbroucke (2019) who analyze the aftermath in France of World War I. They show that after World War I marriage rates increased for both men and women in France, despite a large drop in the sex ratio. They build a directed search model of marriage in which young and old men and women have different preferences for marriage. In particular, young men are less inclined to marry than either old men or young and old women. Due to bleak economic prospects, World War I was not a good time to marry and raise a family–see Vandenbroucke (2014) for an analysis of this. This impacted the marriage rates for older men more than younger ones, because the latter weren't as likely to marry. As a result the stock of single older men was affected more than the stock of younger ones. Consequently, following the war the stock of marriageable men was high despite large casualties; furthermore, casualties were higher for younger men which compounded the situation.

Bronson and Mazzocco (2018) note that standard models of marriage would have a difficult time explaining how an increase in cohort size leads to a fall in the marriage rates for both men and women. Since women usually marry older men an increase in a cohort would reduce the ratio of marriageable men to women. A standard model would predict a fall in the marriage rate for women and a rise in the one for men. To overcome this prediction, they adapt the standard model so that men can undertake a pre-marital investment that increases their probability of meeting a potential spouse (as in Chiappori et al., 2009). When the population is growing and men are in a relatively better position in the marriage market, they have lower incentives for pre-marital investment, which can result in lower marriage rates for them as well as women. Last, as discussed earlier, Caucutt et al. (2018) analyze how the high incarceration (and unemployment) rates for black males have reduced the stock of marriageable men and has led to low marriage rates for blacks.

29.11 Appendix A Beers's specification of letters patent

UNITED STATES PATENT OFFICE.

J. B. BEERS, OF ROCHESTER, NEW YORK.

PREVENTING CONCEPTION.

Specification of Letters Patent No. 4,729, dated August 28, 1846.

To all whom it may concern:

Be it known that I, JOHN B. BEERS, of the city of Rochester, in the county of Monroe and State of New York, have invented a
5 new Instrument, called the "wife's protector," the design of which is to Prevent conception; and I do hereby declare that the following is a full and exact description.

It consists of six separate pieces, viz,
10 hoop, band, joint, joint-pin, membranous covering, and handle.

It is constructed in the following manner: The hoop (A) is made of a piece of oval wire, formed into a ring about an inch and
15 a half in diameter, and to this, is soldered the point (B), formed from a piece of hollow wire about ½ an inch in length, which has two slots cut in it (C, C,) about ¼ of an inch apart, to receive the end of the
20 handle (D, D,) which forms the other half of the hinge or joint. The center of this joint, from one slot to the other, is flattened at right angles with the hoop (A) to which it is attached.
25 The handle consists of one piece of metal, (gold alloyed with platina is to be preferred on account of its great elasticity, and not being liable to change color.) It should be about eight inches in length, and about $\frac{1}{10}$
30 of an inch in width, except the end that is crooked, which is left larger merely for ornament. The other end is about ⅜ of an inch in width, and has two longitudinal slits extending ¼ of an inch from the end, and
35 about $\frac{1}{16}$ of an inch from either edge, running parallel with the handle. The two outside planes are then formed into knuckles, to work like a hinge in the slots (C, C,) cut in the joint (B,). The center F is cut off
40 even with the knuckles (D, D,) and is intended to rest upon the flat surface between the slots, and act as a spring, keeping the hoop while in use at right angles. The two are then united, and kept in their place
45 by a joint-pin. The hoop is then covered with oil-silk, or some other thin membranous substance (E,) and held in its place by a metallic band, made to slip snugly over the hoop and thus securing the edges of the covering between them. The edges of the
50 band are then to be burnished down smoothly; and lastly, the handle should be formed into shape, resembling the sectional view in the annexed drawing No. 2.

To use this instrument, the hoop is to be
55 pressed down upon the handle by the thumb of the right hand, turning it up edgewise, and then introduced into the vagina, when, immediately after, having passed the sphincter, and the bones of the pelvis, it
60 extends itself to its natural position, nearly at right angles with the rod or stem, and as it is farther introduced, the handle is to be turned downward ¼ of a circle. In this position the membrane on the hoop is made to
65 completely cover the os uteri, thus entirely preventing the semen from entering the uterus, without which, (it is assumed) conception can not take place.

While the rod aforesaid lies along the
70 lower side of the vagina, with a slight curve, to accommodate itself to the sphincter, and terminates in the angles above described, lying near the anus, and if properly adjusted, can not be felt by either party.
75 After coition, when the instrument is being withdrawn the spring joint permits the extension of the hoop to nearly a parallel line with the rod accommodating itself to the shape and size of the vagina, and bringing
80 the semen away with it.

What I claim as my invention, is—the particular combination of a covered hoop attached to a handle by a spring-joint as described and for the purposes above speci-
85 fied.

J. B. BEERS.

Witnesses:
DANIEL WOOD,
O. MORRIS.

Source: United States Patent and Trademark Office.

29.12 Appendix B Theory

Proof of Proposition 29.5 (Mean and Median Ages of Marriage). Focus on the mean age of marriage, as given by Eq. (29.6). As can be deduced from Table 29.1, the average age of marriage can be rewritten as

$$\frac{\sum_{i=1}^{j} i n_i}{\sum_{i=1}^{j} n_i} = \frac{\sum_{i=1}^{j} i s_{i-1}}{\sum_{i=1}^{j} s_{i-1}}, \text{ with } s_0 \equiv 1/\sigma.$$

Consider the distribution function given by $(\sum_{i=1}^{l} s_{i-1})/(\sum_{i=1}^{j} s_{i-1})$, for $0 \le l \le j$. Now, the odds of being around and single after $i-1$ periods are $s_{i-1} = [1 - \mu + \mu W(w^*)]^{i-1}\sigma^{i-2}$. Therefore,

$$\frac{\sum_{i=1}^{l} s_{i-1}}{\sum_{i=1}^{j} s_{i-1}} = \frac{1 - \phi^l}{1 - \phi^j}, \text{ with } \phi \equiv [1 - \mu + \mu W(w^*)]\sigma.$$

It is easy to check the righthand side is decreasing in w^*. This implies that the distribution function is stochastically increasing in w^* in the sense of first-order stochastic dominance; i.e., the odds of marrying by age l have decreased, while the odds of marrying after age l have increased. Trivially, the integer i is increasing in i. Consequently, by the theorem of first-order stochastic dominance [see Hadar and Russell (1971)] the average age of marriage must be increasing in w^* and hence π by Proposition 29.1.

The median age of marriage lies between l and $l+1$, where

$$\frac{\sum_{i=1}^{l} n_i}{\sum_{i=1}^{j} n_i} = \frac{\sum_{i=1}^{l} s_{i-1}}{\sum_{i=1}^{j} s_{i-1}} \le 0.5 \le \frac{\sum_{i=1}^{l+1} n_i}{\sum_{i=1}^{j} n_i} = \frac{\sum_{i=1}^{l+1} s_{i-1}}{\sum_{i=1}^{j} s_{i-1}}.$$

There are two cases to consider. The first case is where the median age of marriage moves out of the interval $[l, l+1]$. From the above analysis, the far righthand side is decreasing in w^*. This implies that the median age of marriage will increase in this situation. The second case is where the median age of marriage remains within the interval $[l, l+1]$. Here the median age of marriage is fixed at $(l + l + 1)/2 = l.5$. So in the second case the median age of marriage is nondecreasing in the efficacy of contraception. ∎

29.13 Appendix C Data sources
29.13.1 Figures and tables

- Fig. 29.1 (fraction of the female population, 18-29, never married, 1880-2015): The data for 1880-1990 is from the *Historical Statistics of the United States*: *Millennial Edition* (Table Aa614-683)–Carter et al. (2006). The data for 2000-2015 is based on the authors' calculations from the U.S. Census Bureau's American Community Survey.
- Fig. 29.1 (median age at first marriage, 1880-2018): United States Census Bureau, Historical Marital Status Tables, Table MS-2.

- Fig. 29.2 (percentage of births to unmarried women, 1920-2017): For 1920 and 1930, see Cutright (1972, Table 1, p. 383); for the data between 1940 and 1999, see Ventura and Bachrach (2000, Table 1, p. 17); for 1999-2013, see Curtin et al. (2014); for 2014, 2015, 2016, and 2017, see the National Vital Statistics Reports-Births: Final Data for the corresponding years.
- Fig. 29.2 (non-marital births by age group per 1,000 women): Computed for the years 1940 to 1990 from *Historical Statistics of the United States* (Tables Aa614-683 and Ab264-305). For the years 2000 and 2007, the numbers are calculated using the birth rates for unmarried women, as reported in the National Vital Statistics Reports, and the fraction of unmarried women, calculated using IPUMS USA.
- Fig. 29.3 (premarital sex): For birth cohorts pre-1900 to 1910-1919, the data is taken from Kinsey et al. (1953, Table 83, p. 339). The data for the later cohorts is from Wu et al. (2018, Table 3, p. 733).
- Fig. 29.3 (number of partners before marriage): The data for the birth cohorts from pre-1900 to 1910-1919 are from Kinsey et al. (1953, Table 78, p. 336). The numbers for the later cohorts are based on the authors' calculations from the National Health and Social Life Survey (NHSLS). The numbers presume that the woman had premarital sex with her future husband.
- Fig. 29.4 (total fertility rate for white women): The numbers for 1800 to 1990 are from the *Historical Statistics of the United States* (Table Ab52-117). For the years 1991 to 2015, the data comes from Martin et al. (2017, Table 4, p. 21).
- Fig. 29.4 (complementary cumulative distribution functions over children ever born): *Historical Statistics of the United States* (Table Ab498-535).
- Fig. 29.12 (annual failure rate for contraception, 1900 to 2015-18): The annual failure rate data is provided in the last column of Table 29.6. The series is constructed from the data presented in Tables 29.5 and 29.6 on the uses and effectiveness of contraception.
- Table 29.4 (data targets): The fraction of women ever married by age for 1900 comes from the *Historical Statistics of the United States: Millennial Edition* (Table Aa614-683). For the year 2000 the data is from the U.S. Census Bureau's brief "Marital Status: 2000." The number of out-of-wedlock births per 1,000 unmarried women in 1920 derives from Cutright (1972, Table 1, p. 383). The corresponding number for 1998 is taken from the *Historical Statistics of the United States: Millennial Edition* (Table Ab264-305). The fractions of women who had premarital sex in 1900 are taken from Kinsey et al. (1953, Table 83, p. 339). For 2004 the numbers are in line with Wu et al. (2018, Table 3, p. 733). In particular, the fraction for age 25 is set equal to the fraction found for age 30, which is what the Wu et al. (2018) data strongly suggests. For 1900 the number of partners before marriage is for the before-1900 cohort listed in Kinsey et al. (1953, Table 78, p. 336). The number for 2000 is based on the authors' calculations from the 1992 National Health and Social Life Survey (NHSLS) and pertains to women born between 1963 and 1972.
- Tables 29.5 and 29.6 (use and effectiveness of contraception): See the detailed discussion below.

29.13.2 Contraceptive use

Table 29.5 presents data on the use of contraception. For construction of the data before 1985, see Greenwood and Guner (2010). For 1985-2008, the numbers are taken from Mosher and Jones (2010, Table 3, p. 20). The data for 2010-18 are based on the authors' calculations from the National Survey of Family Growth (waves from 2006-10 to 2015-17). The usage of multiple contraceptives by users was

Table 29.5 The table shows contraception use at first premarital intercourse at various points in time. All numbers are expressed as percentages.

Contraceptive Use at First Premarital Intercourse, %					
Period	None	Pill	Condom	Withdrawal	Other
1900-59	61.4	-	9.42	11.19	17.99
1960-64	61.4	4.2	21.9	7.3	5.3
1965-69	54.2	8.6	24.0	9.5	3.7
1970-74	55.6	12.1	21.0	7.3	4.0
1975-79	53.5	12.8	22.0	7.5	4.2
1980-82	46.9	14.2	26.7	8.4	3.8
1983-88	34.6	12.1	41.8	8.9	2.6
1985-89	34.0	13.7	43.2	6.8	2.3
1990-94	30.3	15.4	47.3	4.5	2.5
1995-99	27.5	17.0	48.7	5.0	1.8
2000-04	24.2	17.0	53.4	2.5	2.9
2005-08	15.9	15.1	56.4	7.1	5.4
2010-14	19.4	21.9	51.3	3.3	4.2
2015-17	10.0	19.9	56.2	3.4	10.5

not reported until the 1995 NSFG. After that year, the sum across different methods is more than the total fraction who use any method. In Table 29.5 the percentage distribution across different methods is normalized to sum up to the total fraction who use any method. The "Other" methods category includes the use of diaphragms, cervical caps, IUDs, vaginal spermicides (such as foams, jellies, creams, and sponges), the rhythm method, and injections and implants which were introduced in the 1990s.

29.13.3 Contraceptive effectiveness

Table 29.6 gives the annual failure rates for condoms, the pill, withdrawal, and other methods. For construction of the failure rates before 2000, see Greenwood and Guner (2010). For 2000-2008, the failure rates for no method, the pill, condoms, and withdrawal are taken from Hatcher et al. (2004, Table 9-2, p. 226). For 2010-2014, the failure rates come from Hatcher et al. (2011, Table 3-2, p. 50). For 2015-2018, they derive from Hatcher et al. (2018, Table 3-2, p. 100).

Given the small number of people using other methods the results are not very sensitive to the assumption made regarding their effectiveness. In Greenwood and Guner (2010), the effectiveness of other methods is assumed to be 20 percent until the end of 1980s and 10 percent afterwards, until around 2000. Given the continuous improvements in many contraceptions, such as the IUD, diaphragms, and introduction of new ones, for example the patch, a failure rate of 5 percent is assumed for other methods since 2000.

The last column in Table 29.6 gives annual failure rate across all contraceptive technologies. This series is plotted in Fig. 29.12. To do this, an average is computed over the effectiveness of each method of birth control listed in Table 29.6. When doing this each practice is weighted by its yearly frequency of use, as shown in Table 29.5.

Table 29.6 The table shows the annual failure rates for contraception. All numbers are expressed as percentages.

	Effectiveness of Contraception (annual failure rates), %					
Period	*None*	*Pill*	*Condom*	*Withdrawal*	*Other*	*All (technology)*
1900-59	85.0	-	45.0	59.2	50.0	72.05
1960-64	85.0	7.5	17.5	22.5	20.0	59.04
1965-69	85.0	7.5	17.5	22.5	20.0	53.79
1970-74	85.0	7.5	17.5	22.5	20.0	54.29
1975-79	85.0	7.5	17.5	22.5	20.0	52.81
1980-82	85.0	7.5	17.5	22.5	20.0	48.25
1983-88	85.0	3.4	11.0	20.5	20.0	36.76
1985-89	85.0	3.4	11.0	20.5	10.0	35.73
1990-94	85.0	5.5	14.5	20.5	10.0	34.63
1995-99	85.0	5.5	14.5	23.0	10.0	32.69
2000-04	85.0	8.0	15.0	27.0	5.0	30.76
2005-08	85.0	8.0	15.0	27.0	5.0	25.38
2010-14	85.0	9.0	9.0	22.0	5.0	28.63
2015-17	85.0	7.0	7.0	20.0	5.0	18.39

References

Aiyagari, S.R., Greenwood, J., Guner, N., 2000. On the state of the union. Journal of Political Economy 108 (2), 213–244.

Akerlof, G., Yellen, J.L., Katz, M.L., 1996. An analysis of out-of-wedlock childbearing in the United States. The Quarterly Journal of Economics 111 (2), 277–317.

Albanesi, S., Olivetti, C., 2016. Gender roles and medical progress. Journal of Political Economy 124 (3), 650–695.

Angrist, J., 2002. How do sex ratios affect marriage and labor markets? Evidence from America's second generation. The Quarterly Journal of Economics 117 (3), 997–1038.

Arias, E., 2004. United States Life Tables, 2001. National Vital Statistics Reports, vol. 52 (14). National Center for Health Statistics, Hyattsville, MD.

Becker, G.S., 1991. A Treatise on the Family, enlarged edition. Harvard University Press, Cambridge, MA.

Becker, G.S., 1993. Nobel lecture: the economic way of looking at behavior. Journal of Political Economy 101 (3), 385–409.

Belsky, R., 1975. Vaginal Contraceptives: A Time for Reappraisal? Population Reports, Series H, vol. 3. George Washington University Medical Center.

Billari, F.C., 2019. Technology and Family: The Digital Revolution. Department of Social and Political Sciences, Bocconi University.

Bisin, A., Verdier, T., 2001. The economics of cultural transmission and the dynamics of preferences. Journal of Economic Theory 97 (2), 298–319.

Bronson, M.A., Mazzocco, M., 2017. Cohort Size and the Marriage Market: Explaining Nearly a Century of Changes in U.S. Marriage Rates. Georgetown University. Unpublished Paper.

Bronson, M.A., Mazzocco, M., 2018. Cohort Size and the Marriage Market: What Explains the Negative Relationship? Georgetown University. Unpublished Paper.

Browning, M., Chiappori, P.-A., Weiss, Y., 2014. Economics of the Family. Cambridge University Press, New York.

Carter, S.B., et al. (Eds.), 2006. Historical Statistics of the United States: Millennial Edition. Cambridge University Press, New York.

Caucutt, E.M., Cooley, T.F., Guner, N., 2013. The farm, the city, and the emergence of social security. Journal of Economic Growth 18 (1), 1–32.

Caucutt, E.M., Guner, N., Knowles, J.A., 2002. Why do women wait? Matching, wage inequality, and the incentives for fertility delay. Review of Economic Dynamics 5 (4), 815–855.

Caucutt, E.M., Guner, N., Rauh, C., 2018. Is Marriage for White People? Incarceration, Unemployment, and the Racial Marriage Divide. Western University. Unpublished paper.

Cavalcanti, T., Kocharkov, G., Santos, C., 2020. Family planning and development: aggregate effects of contraceptive use. Economic Journal. https://doi.org/10.1093/ej/ueaa070.

Charles, K.K., Luoh, M.C., 2010. Male incarceration, the marriage market, and female outcomes. The Review of Economics and Statistics 92 (3), 614–627.

Chiappori, P.-A., Iyigun, M., Weiss, Y., 2009. Investment in schooling and the marriage market. The American Economic Review 99 (5), 1689–1713.

Chiappori, P.-A., Salanié, B., Weiss, Y., 2017. Partner choice, investment in children, and the marital college premium. The American Economic Review 107 (8), 2109–2167.

Cole, H.L., Ohanian, L.E., 2004. New deal policies and the persistence of the Great Depression: a general equilibrium analysis. Journal of Political Economy 112 (4), 779–816.

Cooley, T.F., Ohanian, L.E., 1997. Postwar British economic growth and the legacy of Keynes. Journal of Political Economy 105 (3), 439–472.

Curtin, S.C., Ventura, S.J., Martinez, G.M., 2014. Recent Declines in Nonmarital Childbearing in the United States. NCHS Data Brief, vol. 162. National Center for Health Statistics, Hyattsville, MD.

Cutright, P., 1972. Illegitimacy in the United States: 1920-1968. In: Robert, C.F., Parke Jr., R. (Eds.), Demographic and Social Aspects of Population Growth, Vol. 1, U.S. Commission on Population Growth and the American Future. Government Printing Office, Washington, D.C., pp. 376–438.

Doepke, M., Zilibotti, F., 2008. Occupational choice and the spirit of capitalism. The Quarterly Journal of Economics 123 (2), 747–793.

Edlund, L., Machado, C., 2015. How the other half lived: marriage and emancipation in the age of the Pill. European Economic Review 80 (C), 295–309.

Fernandez-Villaverde, J., Greenwood, J., Guner, N., 2014. From shame to game in one hundred years: an economic model of the rise in premarital sex and its de-stigmatization. Journal of the European Economic Association 12 (1), 25–61.

Galor, O., Klemp, M., 2019. Human genealogy reveals a selective advantage to moderate fecundity. Nature Ecology & Evolution 3 (5), 853–857.

Gershoni, N., Low, C., 2018a. Older Yet Fairer: How Extended Reproductive Time Horizons Reshaped Marriage Patterns in Israel. The Wharton School, University of Pennsylvania. Unpublished paper.

Gershoni, N., Low, C., 2018b. The Impact of Extended Reproductive Time Horizons on Women's Human Capital Investments: Evidence from Israel's Expansion of Access to IVF. The Wharton School, University of Pennsylvania. Unpublished paper.

Goldin, C., Katz, L., 2002. The power of the Pill: oral contraceptives and women's career and marriage decisions. Journal of Political Economy 110 (4), 730–770.

Greenwood, J., 2019. Evolving Households: The Imprint of Technology on Life. The MIT Press, Cambridge, MA.

Greenwood, J., Guner, N., 2009. Marriage and divorce since World War II: analyzing the role of technological progress on the formation of households. In: Acemoglu, D., Rogoff, K., Woodford, M. (Eds.), NBER Macroeconomics Annual 2008. University of Chicago Press, Chicago, pp. 231–276.

Greenwood, J., Guner, N., 2010. Social change: the sexual revolution. International Economic Review 51 (4), 893–923.

Greenwood, J., Guner, N., Knowles, J.A., 2000. Women on welfare: a macroeconomic analysis. The American Economic Review 90 (2), 383–388.

Greenwood, J., Guner, N., Kocharkov, G., Santos, C., 2014. Marry your like: assortative mating and income inequality. The American Economic Review: Papers and Proceedings 104 (5), 348–353.

Greenwood, J., Guner, N., Kocharkov, G., Santos, C., 2016. Technology and the changing family: a unified model of marriage, divorce, educational attainment, and married female labor-force participation. American Economic Journal: Macroeconomics 8 (1), 1–41.

Greenwood, J., Guner, N., Vandenbroucke, V., 2017. Family economics writ large. Journal of Economic Literature 55 (4), 1346–1434.

Greenwood, J., Seshadri, A., Vandenbroucke, G., 2005a. The baby boom and baby bust. The American Economic Review 95 (1), 183–207.

Greenwood, J., Seshadri, A., Yorukoglu, M., 2005b. Engines of liberation. The Review of Economic Studies 72 (1), 109–133.

Greenwood, J., Yorukoglu, M., 1997. 1974. Carnegie-Rochester Conference Series on Public Policy 46 (1), 49–95.

Hadar, J., Russell, W.R., 1971. Stochastic dominance and diversification. Journal of Economic Theory 3 (3), 288–305.

Hansen, G.D., Prescott, E.C., 2002. Malthus to Solow. The American Economic Review 92 (4), 1205–1217.

Hatcher, R.A., et al., 2018. Contraceptive Technology. Ardent Media, Inc. and Ayer Company Publishers, New York.

Himes, N.E., 1936. Medical History of Contraception. Williams and Wilkins Company, Baltimore.

Kennes, J., Knowles, J.A., 2019. Single Mothers and Shotgun Weddings. University of Aarhus. Unpublished paper.

Kinsey, A.C., Pomeroy, W.B., Martin, C.E., Gebhard, P.H., 1953. Sexual Behavior in the Human Female. W.B. Saunders Company, Philadelphia, PA.

Knowles, J.A., Vandenbroucke, G., 2019. Fertility shocks and equilibrium marriage-rate dynamics. International Economic Review 60 (4), 1505–1537.

Kopecky, K.A., 2011. The trend in retirement. International Economic Review 52 (2), 287–316.

Kopecky, K.A., Suen, R.M.H., 2010. A quantitative analysis of suburbanization and the diffusion of the automobile. International Economic Review 51 (4), 1003–1037.

Livi-Bacci, M., 2012. A Concise History of World Population. John Wiley & Sons, Ltd., Chichester, U.K.

Low, H., Meghir, C., Pistaferri, L., Voena, A., 2018. Marriage, Labor Supply and the Dynamics of the Social Safety Net. National Bureau of Economic Research Working Paper 24356.

Martin, J.A., Hamilton, B.E., Osterman, M.J.K., Driscoll, A.K., Mathews, T.J., 2017. Births: Final Data for 2015. National Vital Statistics Reports, vol. 66 (1). National Center for Health Statistics, Hyattsville, MD.

Meyers, C.K., 2017. The power of abortion policy: reexamining the effects of young women's access to reproductive control. Journal of Political Economy 125 (6), 2178–2224.

Moffitt, R.A., 1992. Incentive effects of the U.S. welfare system: a review. Journal of Economic Literature 30 (1), 1–61.

Moffitt, R.A., Phelan, B.J., Winkler, A.E., 2020. Welfare rules, incentives, and family structure. The Journal of Human Resources 55 (1), 1–42.

Mosher, W.D., Jones, J., 2010. Use of Contraception in the United States: 1982–2008. Vital Health Stat, vol. 23 (29). National Center for Health Statistics, Hyattsville, MD.

Ogburn, W.F., Nimkoff, M.F., 1955. Technology and the Changing Family. Houghton Mifflin, Boston, MA.

Ohanian, L.E., 1997. The macroeconomic effects of war finance in the United States: World War II and the Korean War. The American Economic Review 87 (1), 23–40.

Olivetti, C., 2006. Changes in women's hours of market work: the role of returns to experience. Review of Economic Dynamics 9 (4), 557–587.

Regalia, F., Rios-Rull, J.-V., 2001. What Accounts for the Increase in the Number of Single Households? University of Minnesota. Unpublished paper.

Sanger, M., 1914. Family Limitations. Publisher not identified. Pamphlet.

Santos, C., Weiss, D., 2016. Why not settle down already? A quantitative analysis of the delay in marriage. International Economic Review 57 (2), 425–452.

Schneider, D., Harknett, K., Stimpson, M., 2018. Job Quality and the Educational Gradient in Entry into Marriage and Cohabitation. Washington Center for Equitable Growth. Unpublished paper.

Shephard, A., 2019. Marriage Market Dynamics, Gender, and the Age Gap. University of Pennsylvania. Unpublished paper.

Stevenson, B., Wolfers, J., 2007. Marriage and divorce: changes and their driving forces. The Journal of Economic Perspectives 21 (2), 27–52.

Tietze, C., 1963. The condom as a contraceptive. Advances in Sex Research 1, 88–102.

Vandenbroucke, G., 2008. The American Frontier: technology versus immigration. Review of Economic Dynamics 11 (2), 283–301.

Vandenbroucke, G., 2014. Fertility and wars: the case of World War I in France. American Economic Journal: Macroeconomics 6 (2), 108–136.

Ventura, S.J., Bachrach, C.A., 2000. Nonmarital Childbearing in the United States, 1940–99. National Vital Statistics Reports, vol. 48 (16). National Center for Health Statistics, Hyattsville, MD.

Wilson, W.J., Neckerman, K.M., 1986. Poverty and family structure: the widening gap between evidence and public policy issues. In: Danziger, S.H., Weinberg, D.H. (Eds.), Fighting Poverty: What Works and What Doesn't. Harvard University Press, Cambridge, MA, pp. 232–259.

Wu, L.L., Martin, S.P., England, P., 2018. Reexamining trends in premarital sex in the United States. Demographic Research 38, 727–736.

Index

Printed and bound by CPI Group (UK) Ltd, Croydon, CR0 4YY

13/05/2025

01869545-0001